The Republic of China Yearbook 2000

Since the first edition in 1912, *the Republic of China Yearbook* has been the most authoritative source of information on the Republic of China. Updated and revised each year, the *Yearbook* chronicles the tremendous changes that are reshaping the ROC. The 2000 edition of *the Republic of China Yearbook* assembles a wide array of new facts, figures and developments, concisely capturing the highlights of 1999-2000 and clearly presenting the diverse issues facing the ROC today.

In 25 comprehensive chapters, *the Republic of China Yearbook* provides detailed coverage of politics, culture, education, society and many other aspects of life in the ROC, focusing on recent developments in the Taiwan area. Each chapter is a fascinating collage of in-depth essays, color photos, graphs, charts, and statistical tables, creating a complete picture that is both balanced and easy to grasp.

Eight appendices put indispensable information at your fingertips, including a directory of governmental organizations, a list of important dates and holidays, and a table of weights and measures.

The rapid pace of change and development in the ROC today makes the updated "Who's Who" collection even more valuable. This section serves as a personal connection to today's leaders across the political spectrum and from all walks of life. To help readers keep abreast of the composition of ROC parliamentary body, all members of the Legislature are included in a special section.

Extensive Chinese annotation throughout the text and in the superbly organized index offers quick and accurate reference for bilingual readers.

The Republic of China Yearbook—the sine qua non of reference works on Asia's most dynamic democracy.

The Republic of China Yearbook

2000

The Republic of China **Yearbook**

Corrections

On page 693, the correct name of the chairman of the National Science Council, Executive Yuan, is Weng Cheng-i (翁政義). Chen Tan-sun (陳唐山) is still the magistrate of Tainan County. These corrections also apply to the section "Who's Who in the ROC."

2000

Published by the Government Information Office
2 Tientsin Street, Taipei 100, Taiwan, ROC

Printed by China Color Printing Co., Inc.
229 Pao Chiao Rd., Hsintien, Taipei County 231, Taiwan, ROC

1st edition, C74 May 2000
Catalog Card No.:GIO-EN-BO-89-070-I-1

ISBN 957-02-5921-3
ISSN 1013-0942

Hardcover: NT$1,200 US$45.00
Paperback: NT$800   US$30.00
CD-ROM: NT$600   US$20.00

For information on ordering the
Republic of China Yearbook 2000, please contact
SINORAMA MAGAZINE
5F, 54 Chung Hsiao East Rd., Sec. 1,
Taipei 100, Taiwan, ROC
Phone: (+886-2) 2392-2256 Fax: (+886-2) 2397-0655
or
KWANG HWA PUBLISHING (USA), Inc.
6300 Wilshire Blvd., Suite 1510A
Los Angeles, California 90048, USA
Phone: (213) 782-8770 Fax: (213) 782-8761~2

Cover: Over 60 percent of Taiwan's area consists of hills and rugged mountains, which
are often shrouded in mist, like a scene from an ancient Chinese landscape painting.
(Photo by Wei-chang Wang 王煒昶)
Cover design: HU Ru-yu 胡如瑜

Contents

Foreword from the Publisher

The last year of the 20th century has tested the resilience of the citizens of the Republic of China. Continued economic growth, diplomatic endurance, and fortitude in the face of national disaster, have bolstered the nation's ability and resolve to march into the next century.

The ROC was the focus of world attention in September, when central Taiwan was devastated by a major earthquake measuring 7.3 on the Richter scale, causing over 2,300 deaths, injuring thousands more, and leaving tens of thousands homeless. The combined efforts of the military, rescue teams, private organizations, individual citizens, and the government quickly restored public services and began the long and painful work of rebuilding. In retrospect, the talented individuals and variety of resources brought into play by this disaster are testimony to the progress the ROC has made in becoming an advanced and developed nation.

Each year, the ROC is faced with formidable challenges in its complex relationship with the Chinese mainland. In 1999, President Lee Teng-hui clarified these relations as "a special state-to-state relationship." Although meant to emphasize the equal status of the two sides in negotiation, the president's words caused a strong and impassioned barrage of words from Peking. The ROC maintains its eventual goal of peaceful reunification, but believes China must be unified under the principles of freedom, democracy, and equitable prosperity. It has been a challenge to clear the air and explain the political reality to the world. The *ROC Yearbook 2000* objectively presents the historical facts of the ROC's history and diplomatic relations with the Chinese mainland.

The "Taiwan experience" in economic and political development is not ony the envy of much of the world, but also a role model for developing nations. Good economic fundamentals and flexible management allowed the ROC to weather the Asian financial crisis of the past years, with economic growth increasing from 4.57% in 1998 to an expected 5.7% in 1999. Enormous changes in the global economy, the unpredictable forces of free-trade, and the continued role of high-technology in transforming our lives, have presented great challenges to the ROC. Taiwan's highly-educated and well-informed workforce, combined with farsighted government policy, will continue to carry the nation forward and write a new chapter in Chinese history.

The *Republic of China Yearbook 2000* records the remarkable story of this nation and provides a comprehensive and invaluable overview of the ROC. Throughout the text, an exchange rate of NT$32 to US$1 has been used to give meaning to financial statistics for non-Taiwan readers. Up-to-date developments in the ROC can also be found on the GIO web page (www.gio.gov.tw). This edition marks the beginning of a new century and new prospects for the citizens of the Republic of China. I hope you find this volume to be both informative and useful.

Editorial Staff and Major Contributors

National Symbols

National Designation

The Founding Father of the ROC, Dr. Sun Yat-sen, first proposed naming what was to ultimately become our country the "Republic of China" 中華民國 at the first official meeting of the Tung-meng Hui 同盟會 (Revolutionary Alliance) in Tokyo in 1905. Dr. Sun said: "It was not until the day in autumn of 1905 when outstanding individuals of the entire country gathered to found the Tung-meng Hui in Tokyo that I came to believe the great revolutionary task could indeed be achieved. Only at this point did I dare to propose the national designation of 'Republic of China' and announce it to the members of our party, so that each could return to his respective province and proclaim the message of the revolution and disseminate the ideas behind the founding of the Republic of China."

Dr. Sun's suggestion was officially adopted when the Provisional Assembly 臨時國民大會 was established in 1912.

ROC Year Designations

In official and most ordinary usages, years in the Republic of China are calculated from the year of the Republic's founding, 1912. Thus, 1912 was referred to as "the first year of the Republic of China," and 2000 is "the 89th year of the Republic of China," and so on. This is a continuation of the millennia-old system in China of beginning new year designations with the ascension of a new emperor.

National Anthem

The words of the ROC national anthem were first delivered as an exhortation at the opening ceremony of the Whampoa Military Academy 黃埔軍校 on June 16, 1924, by Dr. Sun Yat-sen. This exhortation was designated as the Kuomintang's (KMT) party song in 1928, after which the KMT then publicly solicited contributions for a tune to fit the words. The melody submitted by Cheng Mao-yun 程懋筠 was the undisputed winner out of 139 contenders.

In the late 1920s and early 1930s, the Ministry of Education held two separate competitions for lyrics for a national anthem, using the KMT party song in the meantime as a temporary national anthem. None of the entries reviewed by the Ministry of Education were deemed appropriate, so Dr. Sun's composition was finally adopted as the official national anthem of the Republic of China in 1937.

The anthem first declares the Three Principles of the People to be the foundation of the nation and guides to a world commonwealth of peace and harmony; and then calls upon the people to be brave, earnest and constant in striving to fulfill the nation's goals.

The piece was honored as the world's best national anthem at the 1936 Berlin Olympics.

National Flag

The "white sun in a blue sky" portion of the Republic of China's national flag was originally designed by Lu Hao-tung 陸皓東, a martyr of the Chinese revolution. Lu presented his design upon the founding of the Hsing-chung Hui 興中會 (Society for Regenerating China) in Hong Kong on February 21, 1895. It was redesigned to include a crimson background during the years just prior to the revolution. This design is still used today as the national emblem.

Before the Wuchang Uprising 武昌起義 in 1911, the revolutionary armies in different provinces had different flags: the one used in the Wuhan area had 18 yellow stars, representing the 18 administrative divisions of China at the time; the Shanghai army adopted a five-color flag of red, yellow, blue, white, and black, representing the five main ethnic groups of China; and Guangdong, Guangxi, Yunnan, and Guizhou provinces used the "white sun in a blue sky."

When the Provisional Government 臨時政府 was first established, the five-color flag was adopted as the national flag, the 18-star flag was used by the army, and the "white sun in a blue sky" by the navy. The five-color national flag was replaced by the current ROC national flag on May 5, 1921; however, it was only used in the south. It was officially adopted by the new national government on December 17, 1928, following the successful completion of the Northern Expedition and the unification of China. Thereafter, it was used nationwide.

The 12 points of the white sun in the emblem represent the 12 two-hour periods of the day, symbolizing unceasing progress. At one level, the three colors of blue, white, and crimson stand for the Three Principles of the People: nationalism 民族, democracy 民權, and social well-being 民生. At another level, the colors embody qualities that evoke other concepts enumerated in the Three Principles: the blue signifies brightness, purity, freedom, and thus a government that is of the people 民有; the white—honesty, selflessness, equality, and thus a government that is by the people 民治; and the crimson—sacrifice, bloodshed, brotherly love, thus a government that is for the people 民享.

National Flower

The plum blossom, *prunus mei*, was officially designated by the Executive Yuan of the Central Government to be the national flower on July 21, 1964. The plum blossom, which produces shades of pink and white and gives off a delicate fragrance, has great symbolic value for the Chinese people because of its resilience in harsh winter weather. The triple grouping of stamens (one long and two short) represents Dr. Sun Yat-sen's Three Principles of the People, while the five petals symbolize the five branches of the ROC government.

NATIONAL ANTHEM OF THE REPUBLIC OF CHINA

Dr. Sun Yat-sen
Translated by Tu Ting-hsiu
Maestoso

Music by Cheng Mao-yun
Accompaniment by Huang Tzu

Sun Yat-sen 孫中山

Founding Father, Republic of China

Dr. Sun Yat-sen, also known as Sun Chung-shan and Sun Wen, was born in 1866 in a coastal village of Hsiangshan County 香山縣, Guangdong Province. After receiving his early education in both Chinese and Western schools, he moved to Hawaii in 1879, where he attended Iolani and Oahu Colleges. In 1883, he returned to China to continue his studies, concentrating on the Chinese classics and history. He later moved to Hong Kong to attend Queen's College and in 1892 graduated from Hong Kong Medical College.

Seeing the weakness of the imperial Manchu court and the encroachment on China by foreign powers, Sun gave up his medical career to pursue political reform. In 1894, together with a group of overseas Chinese youths, Sun established his first revolutionary organization, the Hsing-chung Hui 興中會 (Society for Regenerating China), in Honolulu, Hawaii. His political ideals are summarized in a set of doctrines called the Three Principles of the People—nationalism, democracy, and the people's well-being—which were designed to build an independent, democratic, and prosperous China.

Over the next 16 years, Sun and his followers launched ten futile attempts to topple the corrupt imperial Manchu court. Finally, on October 10, 1911, forces loyal to Sun took over Wuchang, the capital of Hubei Province. Thereafter, other provinces and important cities joined the revolutionary camp and declared independence from the Manchu government. On December 29, 1911, Sun was elected provisional president of the new republic by delegates from 16 of the 17 provinces gathered in Nanjing. He was inaugurated on January 1, 1912, the founding day of the ROC.

To preserve national unity, Sun relinquished the presidency on April 1, 1912, to military strongman Yuan Shih-kai 袁世凱, who declared himself emperor in 1915. Sun and other leaders moved the revolutionary effort to Japan until Yuan Shih-kai's death in 1916. In 1917, the Provisional Assembly elected Sun to lead the Chinese Military Government 軍政府 based in Guangzhou, and in 1921 Sun assumed office as president of the newly formed government in Guangzhou. He devoted the rest of his life to uniting China's feuding factions.

Dr. Sun denied the inevitability of communism in China. He believed that class struggle, an intrinsic element of communism, was not a requirement of human progress. He reiterated this point in a joint declaration issued with Soviet envoy Adolf Joffe in 1923, which stated that the communist system was not suitable for China. He also believed that cooperation rather than class struggle was the motive force for social development.

Sun died of illness on March 12, 1925, at the age of 59 in Beijing. In 1940, he was posthumously declared the Founding Father of the Republic of China for his life-long contributions to the revolution.

Chen Shui-bian 陳水扁

Tenth-term President, Republic of China

Chen Shui-bian was born on February 18, 1951, in Hsi-chuang, a small village located in Tainan County's 臺南縣 Kuan-tien Township 官田鄉. Raised in a poor farming family, Chen excelled at academics and was first in his class from primary school through university. After graduating from high school in June 1969, Chen attained the highest score possible on the Joint College and University Entrance Examination and entered National Taiwan University 國立臺灣大學 (NTU), where he majored in commercial law.

Chen received his LL.B. from NTU in 1974, graduating with the Outstanding Performance Award in academic achievements. He was a highly successful attorney at the Formosan International Marine and Commercial Law Office, becoming the firm's chief lawyer in 1976 and remaining with the firm until 1989. In 1980, despite a lack of experience as a trial lawyer, Chen took on his first political case defending the staff and supporters of *Formosa* magazine, who had been charged with sedition and riot following the 1979 "Kaohsiung Incident" 美麗島事件. Although Chen lost the case, it marked the beginning of his career in politics.

Chen first ran for public office in 1981, winning a seat on the Taipei City Council as an independent. He became the council's youngest member ever elected. After serving as a city councilor for five years, Chen joined the Democratic Progressive Party 民主進步黨 (DPP), which became the first major opposition party following the lifting of martial law in 1987.

Chen enjoyed enormous popularity in the DPP and quickly advanced in rank within the party. He served as a member of the DPP Central Standing Committee 中央常務執行委員會 from 1987 to 1989; was elected to the Legislative Yuan 立法院 in 1989 and served until 1994; was executive director of the DPP caucus of legislators from 1990 to 1993; and served on the DPP Central Executive Committee 中央執行委員會 from 1991 to 1996. While a legislator, Chen also concurrently served as co-convener on both the National Defense Committee and the Rules Committee in the Legislative Yuan.

In 1994, Chen was recognized by *Time* magazine as one of the upcoming young leaders for the new millennium in its list, "The Global 100." Chen left the legislature that year to run in the Taipei mayoral election. Garnering some 44 percent of the votes, Chen earned a great victory for both himself and the DPP.

Chen's four-year tenure as Taipei mayor was quite successful, with his administration maintaining an almost constant approval rating of over 70 percent. Chen cracked down on the sex industry, attacked corruption, lowered the crime rate, alleviated the city's traffic problems, and demolished squatter settlements to construct public parks and recreational facilities. Chen also established ties with 14 foreign sister cities and helped to raise the international profile of Taipei. The improvements to the city's transportation, environment, and social services made by Chen earned Taipei a place in *Asiaweek*'s top five best cities in Asia.

In 1999, Chen was nominated by the DPP to represent the party in the second-ever direct popular presidential election held on March 18, 2000. With Taoyuan County Magistrate Annette Lu 呂秀蓮 as his running mate, the Chen-Lu ticket campaigned on a platform of eliminating government corruption, winning the election with close to 40 percent of the votes. Chen was sworn in as the tenth-term president of the Republic of China on May 20, 2000.

Hsiu-lien Annette Lu 呂秀蓮

Tenth-term Vice President, Republic of China

Hsiu-lien Annette Lu was born in Taoyuan 桃園, in northern Taiwan, on June 7, 1944. As the youngest child and the third girl in a family of modest means, on two occasions she was almost given away to other families, a common practice in Taiwan at the time. Nonetheless, as she grew older her parents encouraged her to study and excel academically. She attended Taiwan's top girls' high school, and then studied law at the country's top university, National Taiwan University 國立臺灣大學, graduating first in her class in 1967. She went on to earn a master's degree in Comparative Law from the University of Illinois at Urbana-Champaign in 1971, and an LL.M. from Harvard in 1978.

Lu first rose to prominence in the 1970's. In a series of groundbreaking newspaper articles and books, Lu introduced feminist ideas to Taiwan and became the country's leading women's rights activist. She established a feminist publishing house, founded a women's coffee shop/resource center, and set up hotlines for women during this period. It was at this time, also, while working in the executive branch of the government and witnessing its operations first hand, that she developed her deep distaste for the widespread corruption of the regime. Because of government harassment of her feminist activities, Lu left Taiwan in 1977 to study at Harvard.

In 1978, perceiving that the United States was likely soon to sever diplomatic relations with the ROC, she gave up her studies at Harvard and returned to Taiwan. She ran for a seat in the National Assembly that autumn, but when the US announced its derecognition only two weeks before the scheduled ballot, the KMT regime cancelled the elections.

Lu then became increasingly active in the *tang-wai* 黨外, the opposition movement calling for democracy and an end to authoritarian rule. In 1979 she delivered a 20-minute speech criticizing the government at an International Human Rights Day rally that later became known as the "Kaohsiung Incident." Following this rally, virtually the entire leadership of Taiwan's democracy movement was imprisoned, including Lu. She was tried and found guilty of violent sedition by a military court, and was sentenced to twelve years in prison. She was named by Amnesty International as a prisoner of conscience, and partly due to international pressure was released in 1985, after approximately 5½ years in jail.

Lu then recommenced her work for women's rights, democracy, and international recognition for Taiwan. In 1993 she founded the Taiwan International Alliance to press for Taiwan's entrance into the UN. In that year also, as a member of the opposition Democratic Progressive Party 民主進步黨 (DPP), Lu was elected to Taiwan's national legislature, where she served on the Foreign Relations Committee. In 1995 Lu chaired the Global Summit of Women, and in 1996 she chaired the Feminist Summit for Global Peace, held in Taipei. In 1996 President Lee Teng-hui 李登輝 asked her to serve as National Policy Advisor, breaking with the usual practice of appointing only members of the ruling party. Lu was elected Taoyuan County governor in a March 1997 by-election on a platform calling for reform and an end to government corruption. Nine months later she was reelected in the regular election by a large vote margin.

In December 1999, Democratic Progressive Party presidential candidate Chen Shui-bian 陳水扁 chose Lu to be his running mate, and on March 18th, 2000, Chen and Lu were elected. Their inauguration on May 20th, 2000, will be the first time the ruling party hands over power to an opposition party in Taiwan, and the first ever democratic and peaceful transition of power in an ethnically Chinese society.

Tang Fei (Frank) 唐飛

Premier, Republic of China

Tang Fei was born on March 15, 1932, in Taitsang County 太倉縣, Jiangsu Province 江蘇省, on the Chinese mainland. He enrolled in the Chinese Air Force Preparatory School at the age of 12 and graduated in 1950. He later studied at the ROC Air Force Academy 空軍軍官學校 from which he graduated in 1952. He completed advanced military education at the Air Force Squadron Officers' Course in 1963, Air Force Command and General Staff College of the Armed Forces University in 1971, and the War College in 1979.

He served in a wide range of combat, staff, and overseas positions during his military career, starting as a pilot from 1953 to 1960, then moving to operations officer from 1960 to 1961, flight leader from 1961 to 1965, and squadron commander from 1968 to 1970.

As his first overseas assignment, Mr. Tang was posted to the ROC Embassy in Washington as Assistant Air Attaché from 1972 to 1975.

Upon returning to Taiwan, he served as chief of the operations section of the Third Wing from 1975 to 1976, and later was Group Commander from 1976 to 1978.

From 1979 to 1982, he was again posted abroad, this time as Armed Forces Attaché in the ROC Embassy in South Africa.

Back in Taiwan, he served as Wing Commander from 1983 to 1984 and Air Force Deputy Chief of Staff for Planning from 1984 to 1985. In 1985, Mr. Tang was appointed Superintendent of the Chinese Air Force Academy, and was later promoted to Director of the Air Force's Department of Political Warfare, the position which he held from 1986 to 1989.

In 1989, he first served as Commanding General of the Combat Air Command and then Vice Commander-in-Chief of the ROC Air Force from 1989 to 1991. He was then appointed Director of the Department of Inspection of the Ministry of National Defense 國防部 (MND) from 1991 to 1992, Commander-in-Chief of the ROC Air Force from 1992 to 1995, and Vice Chief of the General Staff (Executive) from 1995 to 1998.

In 1998, he was promoted to four-star general and Chief of the General Staff. He became the first military officer to answer questions during interpellations at the Legislative Yuan. In 1999, he retired from the military, upon his appointment as Minister of National Defense, a civilian position.

Mr. Tang was not only responsible for essential military equipment and personnel modernization programs, but he was also instrumental in formulating the new *National Defense Law* 國防法 and the *Organization Law of the Ministry of National Defense* 國防部組織法, which reorganized and streamlined the military command structure, giving the MND more authority over the General Staff Headquarters 國防部參謀本部.

On March 29, 2000, President-elect Chen announced that Mr. Tang had been chosen as premier to head the new cabinet. With his wide-ranging military and overseas assignments, Mr. Tang has extensive administrative experience and an international outlook, which have promoted relations with other countries and will be necessary for the new cabinet.

As a KMT member, Mr. Tang confirms the ideal that the new government will not be restricted to persons of any particular political party or ethnic group. Rather, the new government will include the best qualified individuals, who will be able to formulate effective domestic policies, enhance prospects for peace and stability in the Taiwan Strait, and promote the ROC in the international community.

1
Geography

Located off the
southeast coast
of Taiwan,
Orchid Island is
known for its
rocky beaches
and rugged
mountains.

C hina is the second largest country in the world, with a total territorial area of 11.4 million sq. km (including Mongolia). Surpassed in size only by Russia, China is larger than the whole of Europe or Oceania. It occupies one-fourth of the land area of Asia and about one-thirteenth the area of the entire world.

The easternmost boundary of the Republic of China, at longitude 135° 4' E, is the junction of the Amur and Ussuri rivers while its westernmost boundary, at longitude 71° E, falls along the Panja River of the Pamir Plateau. The southernmost point of China crosses latitude 4° N at James Shoal 曾母暗沙 in the Nansha (Spratly) Islands 南沙群島 (see section on Nansha Islands at the end of this chapter) while the northernmost point is at 53° 57' N on the Sayan Ridge 薩彥嶺 in Tannu Tuva 唐努烏梁海.

However, since the Chinese mainland is not presently being administered by the ROC government, this chapter will focus on the Taiwan area, which includes Taiwan proper, Penghu (the Pescadores) 澎湖, Kinmen (Quemoy) 金門, and Matsu 馬祖, the major territories currently under the control of the Republic of China.

Taiwan

Off the eastern coast of Asia lie the mountainous island arcs of the Western Pacific. The island chain closest to the continent marks the edge of the Asiatic Continental Shelf. Taiwan, one of the islands of this chain, is the largest body of land between Japan and the Philippines.

The island of Taiwan is roughly shaped like a tobacco leaf. It is located between 21°53'50" and 25°18'20" N latitude and between 120°01'00" and 121°59'15" E longitude, straddling the Tropic of Cancer. It is 394 km long and 144 km broad at its widest point.

With a total area of nearly 36,000 sq. km, Taiwan is the smallest province of the Republic of China. (According to the current administrative divisions propounded by the communist authorities on the Chinese mainland, which the ROC does not recognize, Hainan Island became the smallest province in April 1988.) Taiwan is separated from the Chinese mainland by the Taiwan Strait, which is about 220 km at its widest point and 130 km at its narrowest. The island is almost equidistant from Shanghai and Hong Kong.

The surface geology of the island varies in age from very recent alluvial deposits to early sedimentary and crystalline rocks. The structure, relatively simple for the most part, is formed by a tilted fault block running roughly northeast to southwest along the entire length. The steep slope of this tilted block faces east and the rock mass slopes more gently to the west. This block is composed primarily of old rocks, some of which have been subjected to heat and pressure. Because of the terrain, scarcely more than one-third of the land area is arable. The mountains are mostly forested, with some minerals—chiefly coal—at the northern end.

On the east coast, the mountains fall away steeply to the Pacific. To the west, the level sediments lie just below the surface of the sea. As a result, river deposits have filled the shallow waters and extended the land 15 to 30 km westward from the foothills, giving Taiwan a larger proportion of useful level land than either Japan or the Philippines. Natural resources and agricultural potential make this coastal plain of great importance.

The shoreline of Taiwan is relatively smooth and unbroken with a total length of 1,566 km (including the Pescadore Islands). Off the southern end of the island lie a number of coral reefs built up along the island's shores during the Pleistocene Period. However, the area covered by these reefs is small.

The fundamental topographic feature of Taiwan is the central range of high mountains running from the northeast corner to the southern

Area of Taiwan			
Locality	Number of Islands	Area (sq. km)	Coastline (km)
Taiwan Area	86	35,961.17	1,566.34
Taiwan Proper & 21 offshore islands	22	35,834.30	1,239.58
Penghu Islands	64	126.86	326.76

Source: Department of Land Administration, Ministry of the Interior

tip of the island. Steep mountain terrain over 1,000 meters high constitutes about 32 percent of the island's land area; hills and terraces between 100 and 1,000 meters above sea level make up 31 percent; and alluvial plains below 100 meters in elevation, where most communities, farming activities, and industries are concentrated, account for the remaining 37 percent. Based on differences in elevation, relative relief character of rock formation, and structural pattern, the island can be divided physiographically into five major divisions: the Central Range, volcanic mountains, foothills, tablelands, and coastal plains and basins.

Mountain Ranges

Taiwan's five longitudinal mountain ranges occupy almost half of the island. As a group, they extend 330 km from north to south and an average of about 80 km from east to west. They include more than two hundred peaks with elevations of over 3,000 meters.

Central Range

The Central Range 中央山脈 extends from Suao 蘇澳 in the north to Oluanpi 鵝鑾鼻 in the south, forming a ridge of high mountains and serving as a major watershed for the island's rivers and streams. The range is composed predominantly of hard rock formations resistant to weathering and erosion, although heavy rainfall has deeply scarred its sides with gorges and sharp valleys. The relative relief of the terrain is usually great, and the forest-clad mountains with their extreme ruggedness are almost impenetrable. The east side of the Central Range is the

steepest mountain slope in Taiwan, with fault scarps ranging in height from 120 to 1,200 meters.

Mount Snow Range

The Mount Snow Range 雪山山脈 lies northwest of the Central Range, beginning at Santiao Chiao 三貂角 in the northeast and gaining elevation as it extends toward the southwest. Mount Snow 雪山, the main peak, is 3,884 meters tall.

Mount Jade Range

The Mount Jade Range 玉山山脈 runs along the southwestern flank of the Central Range. It includes the island's tallest peak—3,952-meter Mount Jade 玉山.

Mount Ali Range

The Mount Ali Range 阿里山山脈 lies west of the Mount Jade Range, with major elevations between 1,000 and 2,000 meters. The main peak, Mount Tata 大塔山, towers 2,676 meters.

East Coastal Range

The East Coastal Range 東部海岸山脈 extends from the mouth of the Hualien River 花蓮溪 in the north to Taitung County 臺東縣 in the south, and consists chiefly of Miocene and Pliocene sandstones and shales. Although Mount Hsinkang 新港山, the highest peak, reaches an elevation of 1,682 meters, most of the range is composed of large hills. Small streams have developed on the flanks, but only one large river cuts across the range. Badlands have developed locally on the western foot of the range, where the ground water level is the lowest and rock formations the least resistant to weathering. Evidence of raised coral reefs along the east coast and the frequent occurrences of earthquakes in the rift valley indicate that the fault block is still rising.

Volcanic Mountains

Although igneous rocks are not commonly found in Taiwan, smaller outcroppings of extrusive bodies are scattered over the island, representing at least five periods of igneous activity: a pre-Tertiary intrusion of acid igneous rocks, a pre-Oligocene intrusion of basic igneous rocks, Oligocene-Miocene volcanism, a pre-Pliocene intrusion of ultrabasic rocks, and Pleistocene volcanism.

The Tatun mountain area 大屯山 is a prominent group of volcanic peaks. It lies at the promontory between Keelung Port 基隆港 and the Tamsui River 淡水河 overlooking the Taipei metropolitan area. The entire area is covered by lava that poured out of the volcanic craters which now stand as conical notches of over 1,000 meters. The area is unique for its hot springs and fumaroles.

Earthquakes

Taiwan has a high degree of seismic activity due to its location at the junction of the Manila and Ryukyu Trench in the Philippine Sea. Two tectonic plates—the Philippine plate and the Eurasia plate—which created the uplift of land that became Taiwan's four major mountain ranges, continue to push against each other. In addition, the Philippine plate has been forced beneath the South China Sea plate to the south. The majority of earthquakes occur off the coast of eastern Taiwan and are deep beneath the sea floor causing little damage. The pushing together of plates has created numerous fault lines that crisscross the island.

The largest earthquakes in recent history include a 7.4 magnitude temblor that killed more than 3,250 people in 1935, and a 7.8 magnitude quake on November 14, 1986, which killed 15 and injured 44.

A powerful and devastating earthquake struck at 1:47 A.M. on September 21, 1999, toppling high-rise buildings, damaging roads and bridges, and severing power across the island.

According to statistics from the National Fire Administration of the Ministry of the Interior 內政部消防署, as of October 13, 1999, the massive "921 Earthquake" caused the deaths of 2,333 residents, injured 10,002, and left 39 still unaccounted for. The largest death toll was in Taichung County with 1,135 deaths and 4,886 injured, followed by Nantou County with 857 deaths and 2,421 injured; Taichung City with 113 deaths and 1,112 injured; Yunlin County with 80 deaths and 423 injured; and Taipei City with 71 deaths and 316 injured. More than 4,950 people were rescued from collapsed buildings.

The quake registered a magnitude of 7.3 on the Richter scale with the epicenter at Chi Chi township in Nantou County. More than 1,300 aftershocks were reported by the morning of September 22, with the strongest registering a magnitude of 6.8 in central Taiwan.

Position of Taiwan				
Locality	*Longitude*		*Latitude*	
	Aspect	Apex	Aspect	Apex
Total Taiwan Area	Eastern Point	124°34'09"	Southern Point	21°45'18"
	Western Point	119°18'03"	Northern Point	25°56'21"
Taiwan Proper	Eastern Point	121°59'15"	Southern Point	21°53'50"
	Western Point	120°01'00"	Northern Point	25°18'20"
Penghu Islands	Eastern Point	119°42'54"	Southern Point	23°09'40"
	Western Point	119°18'03"	Northern Point	23°45'41"

Source: Ministry of the Interior   Note: Reclaimed land is not included.

Major Rivers in Taiwan

River	Drainage (sq. km)	Length (km)	Passes Through
Lanyang River 蘭陽溪	979	73	Ilan County
Tamsui River 淡水河	2,726	159	Taipei City, and Taipei and Taoyuan counties
Touchien River 頭前溪	566	63	Hsinchu City and County
Houlung River 後龍溪	537	58	Miaoli County
Taan River 大安溪	759	96	Miaoli and Taichung counties
Tachia River 大甲溪	1,236	124	Taichung County
Wu River 烏溪	2,026	119	Taichung, Changhua, and Nantou counties
Choshui River 濁水溪	3,155	186	Nantou, Changhua, and Yunlin counties
Peikang River 北港溪	645	82	Yunlin and Chiayi counties
Putzu River 朴子溪	400	76	Chiayi City and County
Pachang River 八掌溪	475	81	Chiayi and Tainan counties
Chishui River 急水溪	410	30	Tainan County
Tsengwen River 曾文溪	1,177	139	Tainan City, and Chiayi and Tainan counties
Yenshui River 鹽水溪	222	87	Tainan City and County
Erhjen River 二仁溪	350	65	Tainan City, Tainan and Kaohsiung counties
Kaoping River 高屏溪	3,257	171	Kaohsiung and Pingtung counties
Tungkang River 東港溪	472	44	Pingtung County
Linpien River 林邊溪	344	42	Pingtung County
Peinan River 卑南溪	1,603	84	Taitung County
Hsiukuluan River 秀姑巒溪	1,790	81	Hualien County
Hualien River 花蓮溪	1,507	57	Hualien County

Source: Ministry of the Interior

On October 22, 1999, another major earthquake took place 2.5 km northwest of Chiayi City at 10:19 A.M. registering a magnitude of 6.4 on the Richter scale. The havoc wreaked was considerably less severe; although there were no deaths, 122 were injured, ten buildings severely damaged or collapsed, 37 cases of gas leaks, and 4 cases of fire.

Foothills

The physiographic division of the foothills is found in a narrow zone surrounding the Central Range. This zone, with an elevation of from 100 to 500 meters, is connected with the Central Range and linked with the tablelands in continuous slopes. It contains continuous mountain ranges and an unbroken series of ridges. Low hills with gentle slopes and longitudinal valleys woven with transverse gullies are characteristic topographic features of this zone, as are broad escarpments and short hogbacks formed on fault scarps or along rock formations.

Along the Central Range, the Keelung-Miaoli foothills and those extending from Chiayi 嘉義縣 to Pingtung 屏東 are the broadest. The Keelung-Miaoli foothills start from the coast at Keelung 基隆 and end south of Miaoli 苗栗. The Chiayi foothills rise in front of Mount Ali, with their northern border on the Choshui River 濁水溪 and the southern border between Kaohsiung 高雄 and

High Peaks in Taiwan (meters)	
Mount Jade (Mt. Morrison) 玉山:	
Main Peak 主峰	3,952
Eastern Peak 東峰	3,940
Northern Peak 北峰	3,920
Southern Peak 南峰	3,900
Mount Snow 雪山	3,884
Mount Hsiukuluan 秀姑巒山	3,860
Mount Wulameng 烏拉孟山	3,805
Mount Nanhu 南湖大山	3,740
Central Range Point 中央尖山	3,703
Mount Kuan 關山	3,666
Mount Chilai 奇萊山:	
Northern Peak 北峰	3,605
Main Peak 主峰	3,559
Mount Hsiangyang 向陽山	3,600
Mount Tachien 大劍山	3,593
Cloud Peak 雲峰	3,562
Mount Pintien 品田山	3,529
Mount Tahsueh 大雪山	3,529
Mount Tapachien 大霸尖山	3,505
Mount Tungchun 東郡大山	3,500
Mount Wuming 無明山	3,449
Mount Nengkao 能高山:	
Southern Peak 南峰	3,349
Main Peak 主峰	3,261
Mount Choshe 卓社大山	3,343
Mount Hsinkang 新康山	3,335
Mount Tao 桃山	3,324
Mount Paiku 白姑大山	3,341
Mount Taroko 太魯閣大山	3,282
Mount Tan 丹大山	3,240
Mount Hohuan 合歡山	3,146

Source: Ministry of the Interior

Pingtung. There is a shallow-faulted region between these foothills and the Fengyuan foothills, extending from Fengyuan 豐原, just north of Taichung 臺中, to Nantou 南投, some distance to the south. This is the widest section of western foothills in Taiwan. It is intersected by three rivers: the Tachia 大甲溪, Tatu 大肚溪, and Choshui. Included in this region is the Sun Moon Lake Basin 日月潭盆地, which lies about 765 meters above sea level and forms a graben basin. At the southern flank of the Central Range are the

Hengchun foothills that occupy most of the Hengchun Peninsula 恆春半島. The topography is down-graded on the eastern and western sides.

Terrace Tablelands

From the foothills, the terrain is gradually reduced to tableland of 100 to 500 meters in height. These thick deposits of well-rounded sandstone gravel are accumulations of eroded material washed down from higher areas. The gravel beds may have been deposited near the sea and then raised into flat-topped tablelands by recent tilting. The broadest tableland is the one between Taoyuan 桃園 and Hsinchu 新竹 in northern Taiwan. Next in size are the Houli Terrace 后里臺地 in Taichung, the Tatu Terrace 大度臺地 and the Pakua Terrace 八卦臺地 in Changhua 彰化, and the Hengchun Terrace 恆春臺地 in southern Taiwan.

Coastal Plains, Basins, and Valleys

To the west, the physical character of Taiwan changes through the foothill zone to the alluvial plain. Topographically, the coastal plains and basins are monotonously flat, except near the foothills. All of the larger rivers running through the plains have their sources in the high mountains. Flowing out of the western foothills, these rivers diverge into a number of channels and meander sluggishly to the ocean, forming large alluvial deltas. Many of these have been linked by irrigation and drainage canals.

The coastal plains are generally covered with gravel, sand, and clay, with an average slope of between 0.5 meters and one km. Slopes are gentle enough to eliminate the need for major terracing and are rarely subject to serious soil erosion. The western edge of the plain, where it meets the Taiwan Strait, is marked by wide tidal flats and the coast is swampy. Shore currents have built up a series of spits and offshore bars, and many lagoons have been formed through the shoreward shifting of the sandbars.

The Chianan Plain 嘉南平原 is the broadest in southwestern Taiwan, extending from Changhua to Kaohsiung. It is about 180 km long and 43 km wide at its broadest point, and makes up more

Although human beings sometimes despoil a green landscape over a period of years, the September 21, 1999 earthquake took just thirty seconds to strip Mount Chiuchiu bare.

than 12 percent of the total land area of Taiwan. Next largest are the Pingtung Plain 屏東平原 and the Ilan Plain 宜蘭平原. Finally, there are two major basins, the Taipei Basin 臺北盆地 and the Taichung Basin 臺中盆地.

The East Longitudinal Valley 臺東縱谷 is an extremely narrow fault valley in proportion to its length. It has a general elevation of about 120 meters above sea level and dips slightly toward the east. Coalescing alluvial fans have developed at the foot of both sides, and the river beds are filled with gravel. Due to repeated movements along the fault line and frequent shocks, subordinate watersheds have developed in the valley.

Rivers

The Central Mountain Range is the major watershed for Taiwan's rivers and streams. For this reason, most rivers in Taiwan flow in either an easterly or westerly direction. They are short and steep, especially on the eastern side of the island, and become torrential during heavy rainstorms,

City	Period	Average Temperature (°C)			Average Annual Rainfall (mm)	Average Rainy Days Per Year
		Annual	January	July		
Taipei	(1897-1998)	22.4	15.7	28.5	2,122.6	172
Keelung	(1903-1998)	22.0	15.5	28.5	3,358.5	210
Taichung	(1897-1998)	22.6	15.8	28.1	1,714.5	122
Hualien	(1911-1998)	22.8	17.4	27.8	2,096.1	183
Kaohsiung	(1932-1998)	24.5	18.7	28.5	1,748.6	96
Hengchun	(1897-1998)	24.7	20.4	27.9	2,163.9	141

Climatic Statistics for Selected Locations in Taiwan

Source: Central Weather Bureau

carrying heavy loads of mud and silt. The riverbeds tend to be wide and shallow, making it difficult to manage and develop as water resources.

Taiwan has 151 rivers and streams. The Choshui River 濁水溪 is the longest (186 km), while the Kaoping River 高屏溪 has the largest drainage basin (3,257 sq. km).

Natural Vegetation and Soils

Because of Taiwan's subtropical location, plant types are diverse and abundant. The high altitude of the island's mountains provides climatic and vegetation zones ranging from tropical to alpine. Except for the western coastal plain and the Pescadore Islands, Taiwan was once entirely covered by forests. The forested area today is estimated at 1.9 million hectares.

Acacia trees are ubiquitous on lower hills. Bamboo groves and forests are found naturally in central and northern Taiwan, whereas in the south, most stands of bamboo are cultivated on farms. Outside of forests, bamboo is normally confined to relatively moist areas; thus, it can be cultivated almost anywhere in the Taiwan area.

The flora of Taiwan resembles that of the Chinese mainland. A wide range of Asian tropical elements are found in the lowlands, and low altitude flora is closely related to that of the southern Chinese provinces. Mountain flora is related to that of western China, and high alpine flora to that of the Himalayan region.

Soils vary in fertility. Many have been drained of their inherent fertility through centuries of irrigation and heavy rainfall. In the north, the soils of arable land are primarily acid alluvials and latosols of diluvial, some of which are residuals. In the southwest, where agricultural production is concentrated, most of the arable soils are alluvials of neutral to weak alkalinity and planosol-like alluvials. Upland soils of mountainous areas are mostly lithosols, which are usually thin, immature, and infertile.

Climate

Situated off the east coast of Asia and in the path of warm ocean currents, Taiwan enjoys an oceanic and subtropical monsoon climate conspicuously influenced by its topography. Summers are long and accompanied by high humidity, while winters are short and usually mild. In the coldest months, a thin layer of snow is visible on the peaks of high mountains. Frost is rare in the lowlands, where most of the population live and work. The mean monthly temperature in the lowlands is about 16°C in the winter, and ranges between 24°C and 30°C the rest of the year. The relative humidity averages about 80 percent.

Taiwan is in the trade wind belt of the planetary wind system, and is greatly affected by the seasonal exchange of air masses between the continent and the ocean. Besides location and topography, the winter (northeast) and summer (southwest) monsoons are the main factors controlling the climate of Taiwan.

Due to the different directions of the winter and summer monsoons, seasonal distribution of rainfall in northern Taiwan is different from that in the south. The northeast monsoon 東北季風 in the winter lasts about six months from October to late March and brings steady rain to the windward (northeast) side of the island. The central and southern parts of the island, however, are on the leeward side of the northeast monsoon; thus, they enjoy crisp and sunny winters during this season, with less than 30 percent of their annual precipitation falling at this time.

In the summer, the southwest monsoon 西南季風 prevails for about five months, beginning in early May and ending in late September. During this period, southern Taiwan usually has wet weather, while northern Taiwan is relatively dry. The moisture, carried by the southwest monsoon and local terrestrial winds, falls largely in convectional form. Thundershowers and typhoons often bring Taiwan heavy rainfall during the summer months.

Taiwan lies in the track of severe tropical cyclones known in East Asia as typhoons. With their violent winds and tremendous rainfall, these storms often cause heavy damage, especially to crops. However, they are the greatest source of water in the Taiwan area. An average of three to

The "Three Immortal Reef" near Taitung is a unique geologic feature of Taiwan's east coast.
(Courtesy of Ming-chen Hsu)

four typhoons hit Taiwan every year, usually coming in July, August, or September. During a typhoon, windward mountain slopes may receive as much as 300 mm of rainfall in 24 hours.

According to a statistical analysis by the Water Resources Bureau (WRB) of the Ministry of Economic Affairs 經濟部水資源局 based on data collected from 1949 to 1990 at 440 rainfall gauging stations, the mean annual rainfall in the Taiwan area is 2,515 mm, with the hills receiving more than 5,600 mm, and lowland areas at least 1,200 mm. Rainfall is most abundant in the north with mean annual rainfall at 2,934 mm, followed by the eastern region at 2,715 mm, the southern region at 2,501 mm, and the central region at 2,081 mm. The southern area of Taiwan receives 90 percent of its rainfall between May and October. In the north, the seasonal distribution of precipitation is more even, with 60 percent falling between May and October. Throughout the entire Taiwan area, the driest months occur between November and February.

The year 1998 was noted worldwide for its unusual climatic conditions: First, the least number of typhoons occurred compared to the past eighty-some years. In general, the western part of the North Pacific experiences an average of 27.3 typhoons annually. In 1998, however, only 17 occurred, five of which swept across Taiwan. Compared with the average, this is a significant decline of 37.7 percent. Second, Taiwan experienced a record number of hailstorms in 1998. On average, a total of three to five hailstorms strike the Taiwan area annually; however, a total of ten hailstorms were reported in 1998. Compared to the average, this is a 285 percent increase. Third, torrential rains caused great havoc in 1998. The annual Plum Rain season in June, and Typhoon Zeb and Babs caused a number of deaths, and financial losses were estimated at US$10 billion. Fourth, highly unusual for Taiwan, a total of 14 tornadoes were reported in 1998, an increase of 560 percent over the average. Fifth, statistics from the US National Weather Data Center showed that 1998 was the warmest year on record worldwide. In the Taiwan area, the 1998 annual average temperature was much higher than the mean annual temperature, with all meterological stations, except those

17

Typhoons in 1998

Month	Name of Typhoon	Strength	Warning Issued	Warning Lifted	Damages
July	Nichole	Light	Sea: 9th, 05:55 Land: as above	Sea:10th, 09.45 Land: as above	Agricultural loss NT$20,070 million.
August	Otto	Light	Sea: 3rd, 09:45 Land: 3rd,14:55	Sea:5th, 09:00 Land: as above	1 death, 1 missing, 4 houses collapsed, 7 half-collapsed. Agricultural loss: NT$30,030 million.
September	Yanni	Light	Sea: 27th, 23:30 Land: as above	Sea: 29th, 14:45 Land: 29th, 08:55	1 death, over 60 landslides in roads & railroads. Agricultural loss: NT$1,171 million.
October	Zeb	Strong	Sea: 13th,14:20 Land: 13th, 20:20	Sea: 17th, 06:45 Land: 17th, 02:45	28 deaths, 10 missing, 27 injured, 4 houses collapsed, 16 half-collapsed. Agricultural loss: NT$ 5.16 billion.
October	Babs	Medium	Sea: 25th, 20:40 Land: 26th, 08:50	Sea: 27th, 23:05 Land: as above	3 deaths, 3 missing, 5 houses collapsed, 9 half-collapsed. Agricultural loss: NT$400 million.

Source: Central Weather Bureau

at Tamsui and Hengchun, registering record high. Record rainfall was also reported at Ilan, Suao, Taipei, and Hualien.

These fluctuations and unusual weather phenomena made 1998 a remarkable year as well as a cause for concern.

Penghu Islands

Lying between 119°18'03" and 119°42'54" E, 23°09'40" and 23°45'41" N, the Penghu Islands (the Pescadores) 澎湖群島 consist of 64 islets situated in the Taiwan Strait, midway between the Chinese mainland and Taiwan proper. They form a natural demarcation between the East China Sea and the South China Sea. In the past they were a key stop for ships sailing throughout the Far East and crossing the Pacific. Penghu is Taiwan's only county that is an archipelago.

Only 20 of the islands of Penghu are inhabited. Two of the three main islands, Yuweng 漁翁島 and Paisha 白沙島 are connected by two causeways, and the Cross-sea Bridge 跨海大橋, with its 76 spans, is the longest inter-island bridge in the Far East.

The total area of the islands is 126.86 sq. km. Penghu, the largest island of the archipelago, accounts for half of the total area, and is home to 70 percent of the population.

The islands were formed by a mass of basalt rising from the sea through volcanic action. Due to long-term underwater erosion, the islands have a relatively flat terrain. Their highest elevation, located on Tamao Yu 大貓嶼 (Greater Cat Islet), is only 79 meters above sea level. There is some arable land on the three main islands, with altitudes varying from three to five meters above sea level.

The islands have no rivers and are marked by winding coastlines forming numerous natural harbors. The shallow, warm water around the Pescadores favors the growth of coral. Numerous reefs shelter the coral from sea waves.

Climate

The Penghu Archipelago's climate is characterized by hot summers, cold winters, and strong winds. From October to March, the northeasterly wind (known as the northeast monsoon) blows at a high velocity of nine meters per second. This often brings sea water to the islands in the form of "salt rain." From June to October, the southwesterly wind is mild. Typhoons frequently hit the islands during the summer.

Annual rainfall in Penghu County is about 1,000 mm, only half the rainfall of the plains of Taiwan. Moreover, the strong monsoon winds result in a high rate of evaporation. Over 1,800 mm of water, or 1.8 times the annual rainfall, evaporate every year. Therefore, maintaining water supplies is a high priority. At present, there are five reservoirs in the Penghu area: Chengkung 成功, Hsingjen 興仁, Tungwei 東衛, Paisha Chihkan 白沙赤崁 (an underground reservoir with a capacity of 1,761,774 cubic meters) and Hsian 西安. Virtually every household has its own well.

Kinmen (Quemoy)

The 12 islands of Kinmen 金門 are located off the southeastern coast of Fujian Province, covering an area of 150.45 sq. km. They lie at approximately 118°24' E longitude and 24°27' N latitude, a key position in the Taiwan Strait that blocks the mouth of the Xiamen (Amoy) Bay and protects Taiwan and Penghu Islands.

The Kinmen Islands are 82 nautical miles west of the Penghu Islands and 150 nautical miles from Kaohsiung in southern Taiwan. The shortest distance from the main island, Kinmen, to communist-held territory is only 2,310 meters.

Although the satellite islets are low and flat, Kinmen itself is a hilly island. Mount Taiwu 太武山 marks the highest point of the island, rising to 253 meters in the eastern part of the island. Mount Shuhao 菽薆山 stretches into the sea where precipitous cliffs have formed as a result of sea wave erosion. Most rivers in Kinmen are short and narrow with unsteady flows, so it is necessary to construct reservoirs for water supply and irrigation.

Due to the hilly terrain, there are quite a few harbors around Kinmen. Liaolo Bay 料羅灣 on the south of the island is the most famous. Tzukan Harbor 子感港 of Liaolo Bay is deep enough to accommodate ships of several thousand tons.

Rain showers in the Kinmen area usually occur from April to August, and typhoons often strike the islands in July and August. East winds last for about eight months a year. The average temperature varies from 19°C to 25°C. The average relative humidity is 79 percent.

Matsu

Situated outside the mouth of the Min River 閩江, the Matsu Islands form the northern anchor of the offshore defense line commanding the Min River. The main island of the complex is Nankan 南竿, more commonly known as Matsu 馬祖, from the name of the major port of the island. It is 114 nautical miles northwest of Keelung, the port city on the northern tip of Taiwan, and is the same distance north of the Kinmen Islands. There are two harbors in Nankan: Fuwo 福沃 and Matsu. Other major islands of the group are Peikan 北竿, Kaoteng 高登, Tungyin 東引, Hsiyin 西引, Tungchu 東莒, and Hsichu 西莒. Nankan is the largest, with an area of 10.4 sq. km. Kaoteng is located only 5.5 nautical miles (9,250 meters) from the Chinese mainland.

The islands are composed of an uplift of igneous rock. Granite is the Matsu area's major natural resource. The climate is characterized by monsoon rains from August to December and typhoons during the summer.

Although the hilly terrain is not well suited for agriculture, 26 reservoirs, nine sea dikes, and 113 ponds have been constructed and 480 irrigation wells drilled to facilitate farming. Vegetable production has reached the point of self-sufficiency.

South China Sea

The South China Sea, with a surface area of nearly 3.5 million sq. km, is under the jurisdiction of the Republic of China. The ROC has all rights and privileges in this sea area, and any type of activity conducted in the South China Sea requires the approval of the ROC government. Four groups of coral reef archipelagoes are scattered over this immense area. They are Tungsha (the Pratas) Islands 東沙群島, Nansha (the Spratly) Islands 南沙群島, Hsisha (the Paracel) Islands 西沙群島, and Chungsha (the Macclesfield Bank) 中沙群島. All are part of the territory of the Republic of China.

In April 1993, the ROC Executive Yuan Council 行政院院會 approved the *Policy Guidelines for the South China Sea* 南海政策綱領, which affirm the ROC's sovereignty over the islands and other islets in the South China Sea. The guidelines also express the ROC's desire to step up the exploration and management of resources in the South China Sea, to promote cooperation with littoral states, to peacefully resolve disputes arising over the South China Sea, and to protect the ecology of this vast ocean expanse. Furthermore, these guidelines mandate a comprehensive survey of the South China Sea and an increase in naval patrols to protect the legal rights of ROC fishermen operating in the region.

Tungsha (Pratas) Islands

Tungsha Islands comprise Tungsha Island 東沙島 and two coral reefs, the North Vereker Bank 北衛灘 and the South Vereker Bank 南衛灘. The archipelago is located in a strategically important position along the major sea route connecting the Pacific and Indian oceans, between 116°40' and 116°55' E longitude, and 20°35' and 20°47' N latitude. The group is 140 nautical miles south of Swatow 汕頭 in Guangdong Province, 430 nautical miles northwest of Manila, 170 miles southeast of Hong Kong, and 240 nautical miles southwest of Kaohsiung. Tungsha Island is a coral atoll with a land area of 2.4 sq. km. Shaped like a horseshoe, it extends 0.9 km from east to west, and 2.7 km from north to south. Among

these islands, only Tungsha is always above water. North and South Vereker Banks are completely submerged at high tide. On Tungsha Island, the ROC government set up a national monument and a corridor on June 30, 1989, and May 18, 1992, respectively, to assert its sovereitnty over the archipelago.

Tungsha Islands enjoy a subtropical climate, which is influenced by northeast winds during the winter. They experience their warmest weather in June, with an average temperature of 29.5°C. Temperatures are lowest in December, when the average is 22.2°C.

The areas around Tungsha provide excellent fishing grounds, and ROC fishermen visit the region during March and April. In addition to being a source of salt, fish, and minerals, the islands are an outpost for the ROC navy in the South China Sea. A hospital, power station, and runway have been set up on Tungsha Island. A fishermen's service center also provides fishermen operating in the South China Sea with emergency shelter. There are three jetties and an onshore service center which gives directions to fishing boats.

Nansha (Spratly) Islands

Nansha Islands comprise 104 islands, reefs, cays, and banks. The area containing the islands stretches 810 km from north to south and 900 km from east to west. Taiping Island 太平島, the major island of the group, is located in the center of the island group. Six hundred and eighty miles to its north lies Hong Kong; 700 miles to its northeast is Kaohsiung; and Singapore is located 880 miles southwest of the island. James Shoal at the south of the island complex is the southernmost territory of China.

Taiping Island is located at 114°22' E longitude and 10°23' N latitude. The island has a land area of only 489,600 sq. meters, and stretches 1,360 meters from east to west and 350 meters from north to south. Its average altitude is 3.8 meters above sea level. A cross-island highway runs about one km long and a trip round the island can be completed in 30 minutes. The area has abundant fishing, mineral, and petroleum resources.

Nansha Islands have a strategic importance, and ROC coast guards are currently stationed on Taiping Island. Facilities on the island include a radar station, meteorological center, power plant, library, and activities center.

Pacific Coast Islands

The two major islands located off the Pacific coast of Taiwan are Green Island 綠島 and Orchid Island 蘭嶼. (For further information on these islands, see Chapter 22, Tourism.)

To the northeast of Taiwan are the Tiaoyutai Islets 釣魚臺列嶼, a tiny archipelago comprising Tiaoyu Tai 釣魚臺, Huangwei Yu Islet 黃尾嶼, Chihwei Yu Islet 赤尾嶼, Nan Hsiao-tao 南小島,

Pei Hsiao-tao 北小島, and three neighboring reefs. The group have a total area of 6.3 square kilometers, and lie just 75 nautical miles northeast of Pengjia Yu Islet (彭佳嶼), Keelung. These islets were officially included in China's territory as early as the Ming and Ching dynasties.

Further Reading (in Chinese):

Nei-cheng Tung-chi Ti-yao 內政統計提要 (Statistical Abstract of the Interior of the Republic of China). Taipei: Ministry of the Interior, annual. The Ministry of the Interior also publishes numerous maps, atlases, and local gazetteers of the Republic of China and Taiwan Province.

Wang Lu 王魯. *Chung-kuo Ti-li Tung-lun* 中國地理通論 (General Introduction to the Geography of China). Taipei: New Learning Publishing Center, 1988.

2

People

With a population density of 609 persons per square kilometer, Taiwan was home to more than 22 million people at the end of 1999.
(Courtesy of the Department of Information, Taipei City Government)

What's New

1. Figures updated
2. Population growth in metropolitan areas
3. Elderly population in the Taiwan area

C hina's total population is estimated at just over 1.2 billion, about one-fifth of the human race. In this chapter, we present a comprehensive view of the nation's population distribution and ethnic composition, as well as a summary of the emergence of the majority Han group, which forms the cultural core of the Chinese nation.

Taiwan's Population Distribution

According to statistics released by the Ministry of the Interior 內政部, the population of the ROC on Taiwan stood at 22.03 million as of August 1999. At 609 persons per square kilometer, the population density of the Taiwan area was the second highest in the world after Bangladesh. Taipei City, which covers 272 sq. km, is Taiwan's most crowded urban area with 9,710 persons per square kilometer. Kaohsiung City (154 sq. km) is next, with 9,577 persons per square kilometer, and Taichung City (163 sq. km), the third most populated area, has 5,715 persons per square kilometer.

Highly populated urban areas have grown around the official limits of major cities, forming large metropolitan areas, defined as urban centers with populations of over 1 million people. In 1998, they continued to grow and are now home to 68.09 percent of Taiwan's total population. Among the island's metropolitan areas, the Chungli-Taoyuan Greater Metropolitan Area grew most rapidly in 1998, as its population increased by 2.31 percent. The Taichung-Changhua Greater Metropolitan Area had the second fastest growth with 1.76 percent. The metropolitan area with the highest population remains the Taipei-Keelung Greater Metropoli-

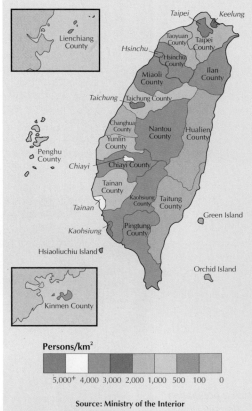

Population Density of the Taiwan Area, December 1999

Taipei · Keelung · Lienchiang County · Hsinchu · Taoyuan County · Taipei County · Hsinchu County · Miaoli County · Ilan County · Taichung · Taichung County · Changhua County · Nantou County · Hualien County · Yunlin County · Penghu County · Chiayi · Chiayi County · Tainan County · Tainan · Kaohsiung County · Taitung County · Green Island · Kaohsiung · Pingtung County · Hsiaoliuchiu Island · Orchid Island · Kinmen County

Persons/km²

5,000+ 4,000 3,000 2,000 1,000 500 100 0

Source: Ministry of the Interior

tan Area, with 6.4 million residents and almost 42.86 percent of the Taiwan's urban population. The Kaohsiung Greater Metropolitan Area comes next with 2.69 million residents, and the Taichung-Changhua Greater Metropolitan Area is third most populous, with 2.02 million people.

The earliest census taken in Taiwan put the island's population at 3.12 million in 1905. After 40 years, the figure had doubled to 6.02 million. The population further increased to 7.39 million in 1949 due to the influx of migrants from the Chinese mainland. The next year, the natural rate of increase peaked at 3.84 percent.

A baby boom in the postwar years put excessive population pressure on Taiwan's economy, and the ROC government began implementing family planning and other counter measures. By 1998, the population growth rate had dropped to 0.85 percent.

The birth rate was 1.27, rose to 1.68 percent and the death rate was 0.53 percent, fell to 3.09 percent in August 1999. Clearly, the population structure has undergone great changes over the last few decades. As those born during the baby boom and after have grown to maturity, the economically productive 15-to-64 age group increased to account for 69.79 percent of the total population in 1998. Meanwhile, the ratio of dependents dropped from 64 percent in 1975 to 43.3 percent in 1998.

Longer education, delayed marriages, the rise of nuclear families, and comparatively fewer potential mothers between the ages of 20 and 34 have reduced the birth rate. Since 1984, the population replacement rate has remained just below one, and it dropped to 0.8 in 1998.

Population Policy

As the Republic of China advances toward industrial nation status, the population of the Taiwan area is aging. According to 1997 figures from the Ministry of the Interior, the average life expectancy in the Taiwan area was 74.58 years, with men living an average of 71.93 years and women, 77.81 years. In 1998, 8.25 percent of the population was over 65 years of age, up from 8.06 in 1997. This puts Taiwan midway between "older" countries like Great Britain (16 percent), France (15 percent), Japan (13 percent), and the United States (13 percent) and "younger neighbors" like the Chinese mainland and Korea (6 percent each) and Thailand and Philippines (4 percent each).

The index of aging, which is calculated by dividing the number of people over 65 years of age by the number under the age of 15, stood at 37.59 percent in Taiwan. A national population policy and policy guidelines to cope with Taiwan's aging population were revised by the Ministry of the Interior and approved by the Executive Yuan in November 1992. Contrary to past family planning programs aimed at curtailing population growth, the ministry now proposes a moderate increase. "Two are just right" 兩個恰恰好 is the new family planning slogan, in contrast to the former slogan, "One is not too few; two are just right" 一個不嫌少, 兩個恰恰好. The ROC government's promotion of its population policy and national family planning program twice

Many of the young couples in this group wedding will likely choose to have small families, contributing to the graying of Taiwan's population.
(Courtesy of Cheng-hui Ko)

received top marks among developing countries from the US Population Crisis Committee in 1987 and 1992.

Gender Imbalance

Among the 271,450 births registered in the Taiwan area in 1998, there were 108.83 boys for every 100 baby girls. The global ratio of males to females at birth is about 105:100.

The ratio in Taiwan reflects the traditional preference among Asian parents for boys over girls. This preference has led to an imbalance between the numbers of boys and girls. Many young Taiwan newlyweds plan to have only one child for economic and lifestyle reasons. In 1965, 72 percent of parents wanted two children, but the percentage had decreased to 24 percent by 1991. Tradition dictates a male descendant, thus, parents who only want one child usually prefer a boy. In 1965, only 6 percent of potential mothers preferred their first child to be a baby boy; but by 1991, some 52 percent preferred boys.

According to 1997 figures, among families having more than one child, the male-to-female ratio was 108:100 for the first born, 107:100 for the second child, 112:100 for the third; and 121:100 for the fourth. These figures reveal the use of artificial manipulation to affect the gender of the children being born. Private hospitals and small clinics in Taiwan ignore the ban on using chorionic villus sampling as a means of determining fetus gender and still perform abortions for parents who do not want a girl.

Some medical professionals have even suggested that the situation is a result of the 1985 promulgation of the *Genetic Health Law* 優生保健法, which allows abortion 24 weeks into pregnancy if the fetus is found to have a congenital defect. The law may have been used by some doctors as a pretext for performing otherwise illegal abortions. However, according to a survey by the Family Planning Institute, the abortion rate in Taiwan increased only slightly after the *Genetic Health Law* was enacted.

China's Ethnic Composition

The Han 漢, the largest ethnic group in China, comprises more than 95 percent of the Chinese people. In addition to the Han, present-day China is home to a wide array of minority groups that display varying degrees of divergence from mainstream Han culture. There are about 60 such minority groups, including the Manchu 滿, Mongolian 蒙, Uighur 維吾爾, Tibetan 藏, Miao 苗, Yi 夷, Gerbao (Yao) 傜, and Chuang 羌 peoples, as well as the nine major indigenous tribes of Taiwan Province. The term "Chinese" includes all these peoples and is mainly a cultural designation. Throughout China's long history, numerous ethnic groups from diverse areas came to be united by a set of complex and generally consistent national characteristics; however, the origins of some of these groups remain unidentified. What is today called the majority Han people has been, from the outset, an aggregate ethnic group named after the Han dynasty. The ancient predecessors of the Han people were the Hua-Hsia 華夏 people. Similarly, *Cina* was an Indian transliteration of the name of the influential state of Chin 秦 during the Warring States Period 戰國時代. *Cina* was later transformed into the word "China," which still serves as a general western name for the nation.

The Emergence of the Han Culture

Members of the ethnic majority group in China have, for most of the Christian era, traditionally referred to themselves as the Han race, probably because of the relatively long period of social, political, economic, and military consolidation and stability enjoyed by the Chinese nation during the Han dynasty, its first sustained centralized imperial state with a coherent culture. The name "Han" recalls the glory of the dynasty, which spanned the latter part of the second century B.C. through the second century A.D., and roughly paralleled the ancient Roman empire in stature and cultural legacy throughout Asia.

The term "Han," however, does not fully account for the cultural and ethnic origins of the Chinese people. It is, instead, an inclusive name for the various peoples that lived together on the central plains of China at least two millennia prior to the time of Christ. Chinese today refer to themselves as the descendants of Emperor Yen

炎帝 and Emperor Huang 黃帝, the legendary founders of the Hua-Hsia nation. The imperial Huang clan was later divided into ten tribes that became the main components of the Hua-Hsia people. The people who first settled in the region of the sacred Mt. Hua 華山 in China's western mountain range, together with the Hsia people, who established themselves near the Hsia River 夏水 (the upper course of the Han River 漢水, a tributary of the Yangtze River), were referred to as the Hua-Hsia people. Both areas were located in the central southern region of Shaanxi Province.

The Hsia tribe formed the most important group of the Han people. In those days, the Hsia tribe lived in an area that comprises modern-day northern Shaanxi Province, northwestern Gansu Province, parts of Qinghai Province, all of Sichuan Province, and southwestern Shanxi Province. Gradually, the Hsia migrated eastwards into the border areas of what is presently Henan Province.

The Hsia were not the only tribe living in the central plains. Living adjacent to them were other ethnic groups with distinct tribes and territories, such as the Eastern Yi 東夷 group, who lived along the Huai and Yangtze rivers and contiguous areas; the Chu-Wu 楚吳 group, who lived along the middle and lower reaches of the Yangtze; and the Pai-Yueh 百越 group, who made their homes along the southeastern coast and southwestern mountains. Eventually, however, these groups were all assimilated into the Hua-Hsia people. Over the ages, various ethnic groups throughout the region had extensive contact in one form or another with neighboring areas: the Eastern Hu 東胡 tribes with the Eastern Yi tribes, the Miao-Yao 苗瑤 tribes with the Chu-Wu tribes, and the Miao-Yao and Po-Shan 僰撣 tribes with the Pai-Yueh tribes.

Recent archaeological findings throughout the Chinese mainland have spawned conflicting theories about the ultimate origin of Han Chinese culture. The concept expounded above of a nascent culture in the Central Plains that spread outward has been challenged by discoveries of cultural development taking place simultaneously all over the mainland area. Remnants of Paleolithic civilizations can be found in both northern and southern China, while Neolithic implements have been unearthed in various areas beyond the Central Plains, such as the lower reaches of the Yangtze River, Lake Tai, the Han River delta, Manchuria, Gansu and Qinghai provinces, the coastal region of southeastern China, and Taiwan. The picture of early Han culture, which will next emerge from anthropological research and debate, is still unclear.

Cultural Amalgamation and Assimilation

Over the ages, many ethnic groups living adjacent to the Hua-Hsia people were gradually assimilated in varying degrees into what ultimately became known as Han culture. The original ethnic stock for this amalgam seems to have primarily included the Hua-Hsia, the Eastern Yi, the Chu-Wu, and the Pai-Yueh groups mentioned above.

Other non-Han peoples were assimilated into the evolving culture of the Han group at different points in China's history: the Huns 匈奴 and the Hsienpei 鮮卑 of Tungusic origin between the second and third centuries A.D.; the Eastern Hu (a northern tribe) and the Jurchen (女眞, ancestors of the Manchus) from the tenth through the early 13th centuries; the Mongolians toward the end of the 13th century; and the Manchus through their conquest of the Chinese central plains in the 17th century. While the two latter groups retain a separate ethnic identity to a certain extent, all have fused with and become key elements of Han culture, which most Chinese regard as the cultural mainstream of the Chinese nation. Thus, the Chinese today are a pluralistic people: the land area they occupy encompasses a wide variety of geographical features; many diverse ethnic groups combine to form one people; languages belonging to distinct families and branches coexist side by side; and the national culture incorporates elements from a wide range of differing ethnic traditions.

Mainland Minorities

The Chinese nation boasts a large array of ethnic minorities that are distinct from China's mainstream Han culture, both in terms of cultural practice and historical tradition. They include the Manchus of the nine provinces of northeastern China (Manchuria); the Mongolians north of the Great Wall; the Uighurs and other Islamic peoples in Xinjiang Province; the Tibetans living in Tibet, Xikang, and Qinghai provinces and surrounding areas; and the Miao, Yi, Gerbao (Yao), Chuang, Kelao 仡佬, Li 黎, and others in the southern provinces of Sichuan, Xikang, Yunnan, Guizhou, Hunan, Guangxi, Guangdong, and the mountain areas of Hainan Island. In fact, many of these "minorities" outnumber the Han Chinese in a given province. A total of 57 different ethnic groups on the Chinese mainland have been identified.

The ethnic diversity of the Chinese people is demonstrated in the differences in economic lifestyle and religious practices. For instance, since the dawning of China's neolithic period, agriculture has been the economic mainstay of the Han people. In the early stages of their ethnic development, the Han group lived primarily along the banks of China's three main rivers: the Yellow River; the Yangtze River (along with its major tributaries the Huai River and the Han River); and the Pearl River. The first area, the Yellow River region, was characterized by a semiarid climate with loose, fertile soil and was well suited for growing millet. The subtropical climate of the Yangtze and Pearl rivers, however, was rather mild, and the rainfall plentiful year-round. Rice was an appropriate crop for these river valleys and could be planted every season in the southernmost part of the country. Thus, millet and rice could be said to be the staple crops that delineated early Han culture.

As Han culture continued to develop, the use of hydraulics, canal-fed irrigation, and waterborne transportation facilitated agriculture and commerce. Thus, while agriculture was the mainstay of the vast majority of the Han people, commerce, industry, education, and government service were also viable occupations. Today, agriculture remains the dominant economic activity of the Chinese people, although the demands of modern nationhood are drawing larger and larger numbers of the populace from the countryside to nonagricultural activities in urban areas.

The Tibetans and other peoples of western China, on the other hand, have traditionally had a mixed economy of agriculture and nomadism. The Uighurs of Xinjiang, or Chinese Turkestan, have historically engaged in either agriculture or nomadism, supplemented by commerce. The minority peoples of Jilin and Heilongjiang provinces rely on either fishing and hunting or nomadism, while the Mongolians have been mainly nomads.

A large proportion of Han Chinese engage in folk religious practices, often mixed with elements of Taoism and Buddhism (see Chapter 25, Religion). Moslems constitute a significant minority, scattered across the entire country. With the exceptions of the worshipping conventions of Islam, Christianity, and Judaism, there are no set patterns of worship for most Han Chinese. It is not unusual for each member of a given Han family to have individual religious beliefs. The father might believe in Buddha, while the son believes in Christ. The husband might go to mass, while the wife recites the Goddess of Mercy Mantra 觀世音. Each family member has freedom of worship, and many choose not to take part in any religious worship at all.

Such religious pluralism has not hindered the development of a unified and consistent set of ethics in Han society over the ages. Ethical conventions have consistently remained within the bounds of a set of orthodox principles: loyalty, filial piety, benevolence, righteousness, love, faith, harmony, and peace. These principles have applied to all strata of society, since the founding of the Han dynasty in 206 B.C.

Tibetans and Mongolians mostly follow the sect of Buddhism known as Tantric Buddhism; whereas minority peoples of southwestern China, such as the Tai 傣, tend to be adherents of the Hinayana school of Buddhism prevalent in Thailand and Burma. Some minority peoples of Jilin and Heilongjiang provinces subscribe to sha-

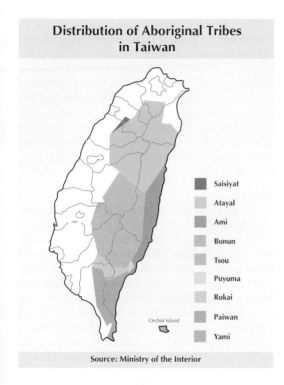

Distribution of Aboriginal Tribes in Taiwan

- Saisiyat
- Atayal
- Ami
- Bunun
- Tsou
- Puyuma
- Rukai
- Paiwan
- Yami

Orchid Island

Source: Ministry of the Interior

manism, and other ethnic groups living in the valleys of the southwestern mountain ranges embrace animism. There are also a number of Protestants and Roman Catholics, as a result of Western missionary efforts.

Taiwan's Indigenous Peoples

An excellent place to get a comprehensive firsthand introduction to Taiwan's nine major tribes is the Formosan Aboriginal Culture Village 九族文化村, located near Sun Moon Lake 日月潭 in Taiwan's Nantou County 南投縣. Designated areas of the village are devoted to displaying and explaining the common traditional dwellings, utensils, clothing, activities, and customs of the nine major peoples. Performances of tribal music and dance are also held daily.

In historical records, Taiwan's indigenous peoples were unflatteringly called the Eastern Ti 東鯷 or Eastern Fan 東番, terms which translate as "savages." During the Ching dynasty, the indig-

enous peoples all underwent Sinification, or Han assimilation, to varying degrees (for details see Chapter 4, History).

Archaeologists have found evidence of prehistoric human habitation in Taiwan that dates back 12,000 to 15,000 years and proves that Taiwan's tribes came from at least two different places: southern China and Austronesia. In general, early settlers from southern China settled in northern and central Taiwan, while Australoid settlements were mainly in southern Taiwan and along the eastern coast.

There are currently nine major indigenous peoples in Taiwan Province: the Atayal 泰雅族, Saisiyat 賽夏族, Bunun 布農族, Tsou 鄒族, Paiwan 排灣族, Rukai 魯凱族, Puyuma 卑南族, Ami 阿美族, and Yami 雅美族. Plain-dwelling tribes, or the Pingpu 平埔 people (including the Ketagalan, Luilang, Favorlang, Kavalan, Taokas, Pazeh, Papora, Babuza, Hoanya, Siraya, and Sao), have ceased to exist as distinct groups due to assimilation with Han Chinese over the last three centuries. The mountain peoples have maintained their cultural identities by resisting intermarriage with the Han. In 1998, the number of indigenous people in the Taiwan area was just over 396,000. The largest group, the Ami, accounts for over one third of the indigenous population, followed by the Atayal and Paiwan. The Yami, with less than 4,500 members, is the smallest group. Many indigenous people live in mountainous regions zoned as reservations, which cannot be sold to non-aborigines.

Each indigenous group has its own family of tribal languages. These languages are called "Formosan" to avoid confusion with "Taiwanese," which is the Southern Fukienese dialect of Chinese spoken widely in Taiwan. These languages belong to the Proto-Austronesian linguistic family, an agglutinative language type to which both Malaysian and Hawaiian also belong. The Austronesian language that is spoken in Taiwan can be subdivided into three branches: Atayalic, Tsouic, and Paiwanic. There is, however, a greater diversity among the Formosan languages than, for example, among those Philippine languages and dialects that are related to the Formosan languages. For this reason, some scholars believe that Taiwan may have been the original homeland of the vast Austronesian speech community.

Characteristics formerly common to all or most of the groups include a belief in animism; a lack of shrines or sanctuaries of any kind within tribal settlements (except for the *kuba* of the Paiwan people); a lack of written language; horizontal back-strap loom weaving and in-woven designs; bark cloth making *(tapa)*; ironsmithing to make knives, spearpoints, and other implements; slash-and-burn cultivation; cultivation of millet and tuber crops, such as sweet potatoes and taro; production of fermented-grain wine (except among the Yami); treatment of disease by trained female shamans; the hunting of deer, wild boar, and other animals with bow and arrow, harpoon-like spears, snares, and traps; and head-hunting (except among the Yami). Below are some of the distinctive historical traits of the nine main tribes in Taiwan.

Atayal

The Atayal are distributed over a large area in the northern part of Taiwan's central mountain regions: northern Nantou and Hualien 花蓮, Ilan 宜蘭, and Taipei counties. They can also be found in Taoyuan, Hsinchu 新竹, Miaoli 苗栗, and Taichung counties. Their language is divided into the Atayal and Sedeg branches and is apparently not closely related to any other aboriginal language. In the past their staple foods were corn, rice, sweet potatoes, and taro. The typical Atayal house was semi-subterranean and made of stacked branches and cordwood of varying lengths placed between upright roof supports, with gable roofs made of thatch, bark shingles, or slate. Clothing design was typified by rectilinear woven and beaded motifs. Facial tattooing among both men and women for personal adornment and to ward off harm was a special feature of this people. Their traditions of tattooing, head-hunting, and burial of the dead under dwelling structures vanished almost a century ago.

The Atayal kinship system is ambilineal, with a tendency for nuclear families preferring patrilocal residence. All three Atayal branches, the Segoleg, Tseole, and Sedeg, have patriarchal social systems. Several leaders from community ritual groups, or *gaga*, usually controlled the political authority and economy. Atayal society was relatively closed and did not readily accept outsiders. The Atayal believe in spirits and unnamed supernatural powers, which they call *utux*, as well as spirits of the dead.

Saisiyat

In terms of population, the Saisiyat are the second smallest of the island's aboriginal peoples. Their language is divided into northern and southern dialect groups. The Saisiyat of the northern branch live in the mountainous region of Hsinchu County. Most of the Saisiyat of the southern branch in Miaoli's highlands. The gentle Saisiyat were long threatened by their aggressive Atayal neighbors, and their culture has been strongly influenced by the Atayal. The early Saisiyat practiced crop rotation, slash-and-burn mountain cultivation, hunting, and river fishing. As the amount of available land diminished, they turned to settled agriculture and forestry.

The Saisiyat were among the first to be acculturated by the Han Chinese and adopted Chinese surnames that were transliterations of the Saisiyat totemic surnames such as bee, spider, and crab. The basic structural unit of Saisiyat society is the totemic clan linked by geographical and family ties. Three or four households of the same clan name or totem constitute a settlement and clan worship group. Several neighboring settlements might unite to form a village with shared farmland, fishing zones, and mutual assistance units.

As in the Atayal tribe, the Saisiyat habit of tattooing disappeared long ago. However, the Saisiyat continue to observe a unique rite, the Ceremony of the Dwarfs, or *Pastáai,* once every two years in November in Miaoli County. According to legend, a group of three-foot tall, dark-skinned dwarfs once taught the Saisiyat to farm, sing, and dance, but also harassed and threatened the Saisiyat women. The Saisiyat retaliated by inviting the dwarfs to a ceremony and then pushing them into a ravine as they crossed a narrow footbridge. The original purpose of the ceremony was to appease the souls of these dwarfs.

Bunun

The Bunun live in mountainous regions of central Taiwan, including Hualien, Taitung 臺東, and parts of Nantou, Kaohsiung, and Pingtung 屏東 counties. Six cognate groups are included under the designation "Bunun": the Taketodo, Takebaka, Takevatan, Takbanuath, Isibukun, and Takopulan. Alternating cultivation of corn and beans by slash-and-burn agriculture was typical of the Bunun. Corn was their staple food, and beans were an economic crop. Making liquor from corn was also typical of the Bunun. Hunting was a key occupation, and it figures importantly in the Bunun oral literary tradition. Traditional houses were made by digging into the slope of a hillside and constructing an earth and stone terrace in front to provide a level or split-level foundation for the house and a large courtyard.

The Bunun are patrilineal, with extended family households grouped in small villages. Usually, these extended families have more than 20 members living in the same house. Patriarchal rule is absolute regarding familial division of labor, but every member has fair access to the settlement's resources, such as arable land and hunting grounds. Their production-consumption mode of living and the group sharing norm made accumulation of wealth quite impossible, and thus social stratification did not emerge in Bunun society. Close family ties im-

Population of Indigenous Peoples in Taiwan, 1998		
	Individuals	Households
Plain Dwellers	185,652	49,174
Mountain Dwellers	210,442	53,814
Total	396,094	102,988
Source: Ministry of the Interior		

Minority Studies in Taiwan

Scholarly research on China's minority peoples and cultures is conducted by the Institute of Ethnology at the Academia Sinica 中央研究院民族學研究所.

Courses on the languages, histories, and cultures of the Mongolian, Tibetan, Manchu, Uighur, and Taiwan indigenous peoples are offered in both the Department and the Graduate School of Ethnology at National Chengchi University 政治大學民族學系暨研究所. The Tibetan language is offered at National Taiwan Normal University 臺灣師範大學. Some courses on China's minorities are offered through the Department of Archaeology and Anthropology at National Taiwan University 臺灣大學人類學系 and the Institute of Sociology and Anthropology at National Tsinghua University 清華大學社會人類學研究所.

Missionaries and others serving in the United Bible Societies in Taiwan have compiled numerous materials on indigenous languages and continue their work of translating the Bible into these languages.

bue Bunun communities with greater cohesion than exists in some of the other aboriginal groups. They have been relatively accepting of outsiders and have incorporated cultural traits such as clothing styles and facial tattooing from other peoples, including the Atayal, Tsou, Rukai, and Paiwan. The Bunun practiced the extraction of certain teeth as a sign of social identity and adulthood.

Bunun pottery features impressed geometric designs. The Bunun have a strong musical tradition, which was developed partly through the use of song to communicate over long distances. Early Bunun religious beliefs mentioned in oral literature include periodic offerings to the moon. The Bunun also believe in the existence of *hanido,* or guardian spirit, which determines the inborn ability of a person. The Bunun had male and female shamans, who were responsible for treating illnesses through sorcery.

Tsou

The Tsou depend mainly on mountain agriculture for their livelihood, but supplement it by hunting, fishing, and raising animals. Traditional Tsou houses had rounded corners and dome-shaped roofs of thatch, which extended nearly to the ground-level packed-mud floor. The men's meeting hut, or *kuba,* serves as a religious and political center. The activities carried out in the *kuba* enhance clan social solidarity. The coming-of-age ceremony takes place in these meeting huts, which also once housed the cage for enemy heads and the box of fire-striking implements. The *hosa* was the basic political unit and was composed of several small tribes or clans, which established the hierarchy of power and distributed wealth.

The Tsou are patrilineal, with high positions, such as chiefs, war leaders, and elders, are differentiated. The former prominence of hunting among the Tsou is demonstrated by the extensive use of leather in their clothing. Their pottery, like that of the Bunun, is also adorned with impressed geometric designs.

The Tsou speak one of three languages: Tsou, Kanakanabu, or Saaroa. Spirits are called *hicu, ucu,* and *i'icu* in the three language groups, but unlike the Atayal and Bunun, the Tsou also have many particularized names for gods and spirits. Of all aboriginal tongues, the Tsou language has the least common with the other Formosan languages, suggesting that it was separated from the common ancestral language in the very distant past. Tsou people are found in Chiayi 嘉義 (Mt. Ali 阿里山), Nantou (Sun Moon Lake), and Kaohsiung counties.

Paiwan and Rukai

The Paiwan, closely related in material culture to the Rukai, are divided into the Raval and Butaul peoples. The Butaul can be further subdivided into the Paumaumaq, Chaoboobol, Parilarilao, and Pagarogaro groups. The main occupation of the Paiwan and Rukai is agriculture. The traditional houses of the Paiwan and Rukai are similar to those of the Bunun. A site was leveled by digging into a slope, and then an earth and stone terrace was extended outward to provide a slightly lower than ground level floor and a slightly higher courtyard. Houses of the southern and eastern Paiwan, however, were frequently constructed at ground level. Paiwan and Rukai are noted for their outstanding wood and stone sculpture. Ancestral figures were often carved in shallow relief into house posts, slate, or plank panels.

Paiwan kinship was originally matrilineal but is now ambilineal. The custom is, however, not consistent among all branches. Most marriages are matrilocal. The hereditary chieftainship plays an important role in their oral literature. In the past, the Paiwan observed class distinctions between nobility and commoners, and interclass marriage was formerly forbidden.

Puyuma

Traditionally, the Puyuma depended on growing millet, taro, sweet potatoes, and beans on hillside plots cleared by burning. They supplemented farming with fishing and hunting. The Puyuma live in a flatland area of Taitung County, and they have been greatly influenced by Paiwan and Rukai culture. The Puyuma have a multilineal kinship system with ritual groups. The extended family inheritance goes to the eldest daughter, but the kinship system is ambilineal. The positions of chieftains and shamans are patrilineal. Like the closely-related Paiwan, Puyuma society is stratified into "chiefly" (noble) families and commoners. Marriage between the two classes is, however, not prohibited. The more prominent ritual groups in each village cluster around the various "chiefly" families.

The clergy come from the leading clans' ancestral worshipping groups, which are called *karumangan.* Since 1964, there have been only three groups, which are responsible for performing ceremonies during harvests twice a year. The largest basic unit of a Puyuma settlement is called a *samawan.* Each *samawan* has a *karumahan,* or center of ancestor worship, and a *parakoang,* or men's meeting house. *Karumahan* of the same name belong to the same ancestor. Men's meeting houses accept members at age 15.

Samawan are divided into *saja munan.* The latter are composed of groups of families, which share the same ancestor and bear the collective

Aboriginal women from the Ami tribe pose with their traditional festival finery during the tribe's harvest festival.

name of their leading clan. A chief's power is symbolized by his role in ancestor worship and the transfer of tribal knowledge, not from monopolization of land, as in the Paiwan and Rukai.

Ami

The Ami, the largest indigenous group in terms of population, are mainly plain dwellers, living in the valleys of the Hualien-Taitung area. The Ami can be divided into five groups based on geography, customs, and language: the northern Ami are also known as the Nanshih 南勢 group; the central Ami belong to the coastal and Hsiukuluan 秀姑巒 groups; and the southern Ami can be classified into the Peinan 卑南 and Hengchun 恆春 groups. The Ami began to use oxen to cultivate paddy fields relatively early. They continue to fish, but now hunt only for recreation.

Ami houses are traditionally built flat on the ground, with the main beams and posts made of hard wood, and subsidiary beams usually of bamboo or betel palm. Walls were made of double layers of plaited dwarf bamboo, with grass thatch in between to keep out the cold wind. Due to a comparatively advanced level of agriculture ca-

pable of supporting a considerable number of people, traditional Ami villages were relatively large, with populations of between 200 and 1,000 people each.

The Ami are the only indigenous group on the island of Taiwan (thus excluding the Yami) to preserve the art of pottery making. Pottery in the form of food vessels, water ewers, rice pots, and earthenware steamers is made by women. Sacrificial vessels in varying sizes are also made, and these are buried with their owner at death.

Ami society is matrilineal, and the oldest woman in the extended family is generally the household head. Men, however, exercise authority when village councils of leading men from each village ward are held in the men's meeting houses. A rigid system of authority based on age is enforced. The Ami have elaborate cosmogonic myths, which may be recited only by trained male "lineage priests" and are subject to strict recitation-related taboos.

Yami

The Yami live almost exclusively on Orchid Island, (Lanyu 蘭嶼 in Chinese), 44 nautical miles off the eastern coast of Taitung County. Culturally, the Yami are closely related to the inhabitants of the Batan Islands of the Philippines, and the Yami language and Ivatan dialect of the Batanes are mutually intelligible. The Yami language also seems to be quite closely related to the Paiwanic languages on Taiwan.

Fishing is central to the Yami economy, and many of the fish caught are preserved by drying. The basic cooperative and distributive units of the Yami are fishing groups formed by kinsmen in villages from the same region. Ceremonies related to fishing have become part of the Yami culture. The Yami grow taro extensively, as well as sweet potatoes, yams, and millet. Men are responsible for laying out fields, building boats, fishing, constructing homes, and making baskets, pottery, and metalwork. Women tend the fields, gather taro, cook, and weave cloth.

Yami dwellings are somewhat similar to those of the Paiwan, Rukai, and Bunun: a rectangular pit is first dug, then low stone walls line the top of the house pit as protection against frequent and fierce typhoons. Elevated "rest houses" called *tagakal* are used for sleeping or working when it is too hot to work in the house. The Yami live in nuclear families and tend towards patrilocality. Inheritance is patrilineal.

The Yami are constantly haunted by a fear and hatred of ghosts. They think ghosts exercising evil influence are the cause of all mischief. The Yami do not have regular shamans, but they do believe magical amulets to be an effective tool in protecting one from mischief.

The Yami are known for their unique and beautifully decorated dugout canoes, which can carry eight to ten people at a time. The Yami are the only indigenous group of Taiwan known to practice silversmithing, and the only people that have never practiced headhunting or made alcohol. There is no chieftainship. One of the more notable of the many colorful Yami celebrations is an elaborate ceremony held upon the launching of a newly-completed boat.

The Life of Taiwan's Indigenous Peoples Today

Changes are taking place in tribal culture and lifestyles as the descendants of Taiwan's earliest inhabitants struggle to adjust to rapid modernization. Young people are leaving traditional occupations, such as farming, hunting, and fishing and are taking up factory and construction in the cities.

The vigor of Formosan languages varies according to area. On Orchid Island, for example, Yami is still widely spoken; however, throughout Taiwan, native speakers are dwindling in number, and young people are usually not as fluent in their ancestral language as they are in Mandarin or Taiwanese. Bilingual education is being promoted and the publication of stories and legends is being undertaken as oral literary traditions attenuate (see Chapter 3, Language). A six-year research program covering a comprehensive history of Taiwan's indigenous peoples, was started in 1993 by the Historical Research Commission of Taiwan Province 臺灣省文獻會.

Some native traditions, such as periodic tribal harvest festivals that celebrate a rich crop with singing and dancing, are still maintained and, although most tribes have switched to Western attire, loincloths are still common attire on Orchid Island. By adopting Han Chinese dietary habits, most indigenous people now eat a much more varied diet than did their forefathers. Animistic and shamanistic beliefs have largely given way to Christianity, due to intensive missionary efforts.

Education is increasingly providing a way for the young to participate in mainstream Han Chinese culture. During the Japanese occupation, only 19 tribe members graduated from Taiwan's middle school. The figure for 1997 was over 56,900. More than 3,100 graduated from a university or technical college, and a significant number participated in master's and doctoral programs in foreign countries.

Members of Taiwan's indigenous peoples are increasingly active in local and national politics. More than 6,000 work in various government agencies, and the number is growing. As of June 1998, seven held seats in the National Assembly and seven in the Legislative Yuan. Four serve in the Taiwan Provincial Assembly, two as councilors in special municipalities, and 55 as provincial city and county council members. Thirty serve as magistrates of rural townships with predominately indigenous constituents. Similarly, Taitung County, where indigenous peoples comprise a large proportion of the electorate, has a county magistrate of indigenous descent.

The overall educational and income levels of Taiwan's indigenous people, however, still lag behind those of Han Chinese, and many face acute social problems such as alcoholism, unemployment, and adolescent prostitution. Therefore, in 1992 the Ministry of the Interior began implementing a six-year Living Guidance Plan for Aborigines Residing in Cities 都市原住民生活輔導計畫. The plan calls for spending approximately US$8 million to promote indigenous culture and to provide urban-based indigenous people with subsidized medical care, legal advice, educational guidance for adolescents, employment counseling, and loans for setting up businesses. By the end of June 1996, some 8,500 cases had been handled. Additionally, a construction plan drawn up by the Taiwan Provincial Government 臺灣省政府 to improve the roads which link tribal villages with nearby metropolitan communities was begun in 1992, further shortening the gap in living standards with the general citizenry of Taiwan.

The cabinet-level Council of Aboriginal Affairs under the Executive Yuan 行政院原住民委員會 is the agency responsible for indigenous affairs at the central government level. Corresponding organizations at the provincial and municipal levels of government are the Taiwan Provincial Government's Council of Aboriginal Affairs 臺灣省政府原住民事務委員會, the Taipei City Government's Commission for Native Taiwanese Affairs 臺北市政府原住民事務委員會, and the Kaohsiung City Government's Aboriginal Affairs Council 高雄市政府原住民事務委員會. Finally, in addition to government agencies, over 40 private organizations are devoted to tribal welfare, such as World Vision of Taiwan 臺灣世界展望會 and the ROC Aborigine Tribal Welfare Promotion Association 中華民國山胞福利策進會.

Search for an Appropriate Name

Heated controversy flared in Taiwan during the constitutional amendment process in the Second National Assembly session of 1992 regarding the official name to be used when referring to the island's indigenous peoples. For years, the various indigenous peoples had been collectively called *shan-pao* 山胞 "mountain compatriots," and the term is incorporated into the *Constitution of the Republic of China*. Many indigenous people proposed that this be amended, claiming that the term conveyed a certain degree of discrimination. They asserted that the term *yuan-chu-min* 原住民 (aborigines or indigenous peoples) is more suitable.

Parliamentarians representing indigenous people said that they wanted appropriate wording in the *Constitution* as a step toward giving these citizens the "dignity and justice" they seldom experienced in society. Indigenous people were looking forward to gaining greater social status via a constitutional amendment, which they felt would enhance their legal protection and lead to an increase in assistance from the government. Such benefits would in turn improve the overall standard of living among the indigenous population.

During the fourth extraordinary session of the Second National Assembly at its 32nd plenary meeting in July 1994, National Assembly members adopted the term *yuan-chu-min* to replace the expression *shan-pao* when they passed a series of *Additional Articles of the ROC Constitution* 中華民國憲法增修條文. According to the articles, "The state shall accord to the aborigines in the free area [the Taiwan area] legal protection of their status and the right to political participation. It shall also provide assistance and encouragement for their education, cultural preservation, social welfare, and business undertakings. The same protection and assistance shall be given to the people of the Kinmen and Matsu areas."

Mongolian and Tibetan Affairs

The ROC government agency which serves Mongolians and Tibetans worldwide, is the Mongolian and Tibetan Affairs Commission 蒙藏

委員會 of the Executive Yuan. The commission has organizations in many foreign countries, including the United States, Canada, Germany, Switzerland, India, and Nepal, to serve local Mongolian and Tibetan communities. The commission's goals are to build up and maintain a worldwide liaison network for Mongolians and Tibetans, offering programs to improve their living conditions, raise the level of education, and elevate vocational training. These training programs receive assistance from the Chinese Refugees Relief Association 中國災胞救助總會, which helps exiled Tibetans and Mongolians come to Taiwan to participate in such programs.

The commission puts out a colorful monthly pictorial, *Mongolian Tibetan Friendship* 蒙藏之友, with articles in Chinese, English, Mongolian, and Tibetan. Articles discuss current political affairs, as well as features on Mongolian and Tibetan culture, history, and art. The commission also provides regular Mongolian and Tibetan language broadcasts.

The Tibetan Children's Home in Taiwan 西藏兒童之家 provides a supportive home environment to Tibetan children, mainly from Nepal, who have been sent to Taiwan to receive an education. The home, established in 1980, has helped more than 100 children over the years. The children attend regular Chinese schools in Taipei, but receive special instruction in the Tibetan language, culture, and religion at the home. In 1991, the home was moved from Taipei City to the suburban town of Sanhsia 三峽.

Further Reading

(in Chinese unless otherwise noted):

Chen, Chi-lu 陳奇祿. *Material Culture of the Formosan Aborigines* (in English). Taipei: Taiwan Provincial Museum, 1968.

Chen, Chien-wu 陳千武. *Tai-wan yuan-chu-min te mu-yu chuan-shuo* 臺灣原住民的母語傳說 (Native Tongue Legends of Taiwan's Aborigines). Taipei: Taiyuan Publishing Co., 1991.

Ferrel, Raleigh. *Taiwan Aboriginal Groups: Problems in Cultural and Linguistic Classification* (in English). Taipei: Institute of Ethnology, Academia Sinica, 1969.

Tai-wan kao-shan-tsu yu tsu-kuo chih yuan-yuan 臺灣高山族與祖國之淵源 (The Historical Origins of Taiwan's Aborigines). Taipei County: Taiwan Aborigines' Association for Cultural and Economic Development, 1992.

Huang, Ying-kuei 黃應貴 (ed.). *Bibliography of Anthropological Works Published in Taiwan, 1945-82* (Chinese and English entries). Taipei: Ethnological Society of China and Resource Center for Chinese Studies, 1983.

Huang, Ying-kuei (ed.). *Tai-wan tu-chu she-hui wen-hua yen-chiu wen-chi* 臺灣土著社會文化研究文集 (Studies on Aboriginal Society and Culture in Taiwan). Taipei: Linking Publishing Co., 1986.

Kano, Tadao, and Segawa, Kokichi. *An Illustrated Ethnography of Formosan Aborigines: The Yami* (in English). Tokyo: Maruzen Company, Ltd., 1956.

Li, I-yuan 李亦園. *Tai-wan tu-chu min-tsu te she-hui yu wen-hua* 臺灣土著民族的社會與文化 (Society and Culture of Taiwan's Aboriginal Peoples). Taipei: Linking Publishing Co., 1982.

Tu-shih shan-pao sheng-huo fu-tao chi-hua 都市山胞生活輔導計畫 (Living Guidance Plan for Aborigines Residing in Cities). Taipei: Ministry of the Interior, 1992.

Ming, Li-kuo 明立國. *Tai-wan yuan-chu-min te chi-li* 臺灣原住民的祭禮 (Rituals of Taiwan's Aborigines). Taipei: Taiyuan Publishing Co., 1989.

Shepherd, John R. "Plains Aborigines and Chinese Settlers on the Taiwan Frontier in the Seventeenth and Eighteenth Centuries." (in English) Ph.D dissertation, Stanford University, 1991.

Shi, Wan-shou 石萬壽. *Tai-wan te pai-hu min-tsu* 臺灣的拜壺民族 (Worshipers of the Urn: the Pingpu Aborigines of Taiwan). Taipei: Taiyuan Publishing Co., 1990.

Starosta, Stanley. "A Grammatical Typology of Formosan Languages," *Bulletin of the Institute of History and Philology* (in English), Vol. 59, Part 2. pp. 541-576, Taipei: Academia Sinica. 1988.

Studies on Taiwan Plains Aborigines: a Classified Bibliography, 1988 (Chinese and English entries). Taipei: Institute of Ethnology, Academia Sinica.

Yao, Te-hsiung 姚德雄. *Formosan Aboriginal Culture Village* (九族文化村; 2nd English ed.). Taichung: Yin-shua Publishing Co., 1988.

Cheng-fu wei shan-pao tso shen-ma 政府為山胞做什麼 (What is the Government Doing for the Aboriginal People). Taipei: Ministry of the Interior, 1992.

3

Language

Calligraphy, far more than a method of writing, has been considered one of the highest Chinese art forms for centuries. In this letter, calligraphy master Tsai Hsiang 蔡襄 (1012-1067 A.D.) demonstrates his rich and graceful control of the brush.

(Courtesy of the National Palace Museum)

澄心堂紙一幅闊狹厚薄
堅實皆類此乃佳工者不
願為又恐不能為之試與
厚直莫得之見其楷細似
可作也便人只求百幅蔡卯重

What's New

1. A new Romanization system—Tongyong Pinyin
2. ROC's new bilingual education policy
3. Foreign Language Education

More people speak a Chinese language natively than any other tongue in the world. Phonetic diversity within the Chinese language family is manifested in its extreme by a large number of mutually unintelligible dialects, creating a historical need for a common language through which speakers from the various dialectical regions might readily communicate. In the Chinese-speaking world of today, most educated people share a *lingua franca*, usually referred to as the National Language 國語 in Taiwan, the "Common Language" 普通話 on the Chinese mainland, and Mandarin in English.

The Chinese language group 漢語 is regarded as a major branch of the Sino-Tibetan family of languages, which includes Tibetan, Burmese, and numerous minority languages. Some of the outstanding characteristics of this group are its monosyllabicity, relatively simple phonological system, use of tones to distinguish different meanings, and a word order dependent syntax that lacks inflection, grammatical gender, and pluralization.

Written Chinese, which has historically provided a link amongst the various Chinese dialects, is unique in that it is the only major modern writing system that uses thousands of semantically meaningful characters 漢字 rather than a phonetic alphabet or syllabary of a few dozen symbols. The traditional Chinese writing system has inspired and profoundly influenced other writing systems of East Asia, and Chinese characters are still used extensively in modern Japanese and, to a much lesser extent, in modern Korean. In terms of its origin and underlying linguistic characteristics, however, Chinese is totally unrelated to Japanese, Korean, Vietnamese, and Thai; any apparent similarities are due to extensive borrowing.

A Chinese language is spoken by most of China's minority peoples, as well as nearly all Han Chinese. Many minority peoples, though not all (for example, the Hui and Manchu), also speak languages outside the Chinese language group. Much work remains to be done in classifying and describing the many minority languages of China.

Linguistic Features of the Chinese Language Family

The Chinese languages and their dialects are characterized linguistically as isolating, or analytic, in that word units do not change due to inflection. Each Chinese character generally corresponds to exactly one syllable and one morpheme. The phonological structure of Chinese syllables is subject to strict limitations. In Mandarin, for example, it may have anywhere from a single vowel to up to five phonemes (the smallest unit of sound), and end in either a vowel, *-n*, *-ng*, or *-r*. With all these restrictions, the number of possible syllables in Chinese has a clear maximum limit. In practice, there are a total of only 1,277 different syllables in Mandarin, including the tonal variances, and 261 of these possible pronunciations correspond to only one word each. The number goes down to around 400 different syllables if tone distinctions are omitted. Since each of the Chinese languages has as rich a vocabulary as any other living language, this results in a tremendous number of homophones, with Mandarin demonstrating the greatest number.

There has been a strong tendency in the Chinese language family over the last 2,000 years for single morpheme words to develop into compounds of two or more morphemes. This has reduced ambiguity and enriched the language. The flexibility of Chinese compound formation patterns also makes it easy to invent new vocabulary items as needed. Thus, *airplane* in Mandarin is 飛機 or "flying machine," *shampoo* is 洗髮精 "wash-hair essence," and *automobile clutch* is 離合器 or "separate/combine device."

Tones (i.e., variations in vocal pitch while pronouncing each morpheme) go a long way to reducing the number of homophones. Homophonous words pronounced in different tones are as dissimilar to the ear of a native Chinese speaker as *bat*, *bet*, *bit*, and *but* are to a native English speaker, and thus are easily distinguished. Mandarin has four tones: The first is a high, level tone; the second starts mid-range and rises; the third starts mid-low, falls, then rises; and the fourth starts high and falls sharply. Some functional particles and unstressed syllables are pronounced in a fifth, or "neutral" tone.

Except for certain tone sandhi (predetermined tonal changes in the environment of adjacent tones), the tone of a word is invariable. In Mandarin, for instance, a third tone is changed to a second when it occurs before another third tone word; and some tones become "neutralized" in certain environments. The dynamic effect of these tonal variations in the voice pitch of Chinese language speakers is a distinctly different phenomenon from the emotion-colored intonation patterns of any language, including Chinese itself. For example, a question asked in Chinese is not necessarily indicated by a rise of the voice at the end of a phrase or sentence. Instead, a final interrogative particle or other grammatical means may be used. A word given particular stress in English by a vocal pitch rise could be emphasized in most Chinese languages by stretching out the length of utterance.

Grammatically, the Chinese languages display a basic subject-verb-object word order, as does English. Some linguists have proposed the topic-comment syntactic model as a more appropriate one for Chinese, where a topic is introduced, and then some comment is made on it. There is some logic to champion this model, since a common Chinese sentence pattern is "As for . . ., it . . . ." exemplified by the Chinese sentence 衣服我已經洗好了, "As for the clothes, I have already washed them." Many Chinese subscribe to the popular notion that Chinese languages have no grammar, partly because grammar is not taught as a subject in schools, and also because of the lack of inflection in Chinese. It would be more accurate to say that the Chinese languages have an uninflected, highly word order dependent grammar.

Rather than adding, for example, an ending (such as *-ed* in English) to indicate a past tense, Chinese speakers use particles (such as *le* 了, which indicates completion or a new situation) and context (words like *yesterday* or *next year*) to place ideas in time. The same applies to plurals.

Classifiers, or measure words, are a notable feature of modern Chinese and most Sino-Tibetan and Southeast Asian languages. Measure words, comparable to *piece* in *a piece of cake* and *sheet* in *a sheet of paper* in English, are required for almost all nouns in Mandarin when preceded by a number or demonstrative pronoun. Thus "a table" is 一張桌子 "one sheet of table;" "Two cats" are 兩隻貓 "two one-of-a-pair cats;" and, "this person" is 這個人 "this unit of person." Classifiers often describe the shape of the noun they modify: strip, piece, drop, and so forth. One classifier, 位, conveys respect, as in 一位教授 "one respected professor."

Traditional Chinese grammarians only divided the words of their language into two categories: substantial or "meaningful" words 實詞, and functional or "empty" grammatical particles 虛詞. This sparse distinction may reflect the fact that, even today, many words in the Chinese language family cannot be definitively classified as nouns, verbs, adjectives, adverbs, and so forth except as they are used in specific contexts. They can serve as one part of speech or another with no external change in form or pronunciation, although not every word occurs as every part of speech. For example, in Mandarin, the word 書 can be a noun meaning "book" or a verb meaning "write." Depending on context, 分 can be a verb, "to divide," an adjective, "branch" (as in *branch office*), or a measure word, "minute" or "cent."

The Regions of Chinese Dialects

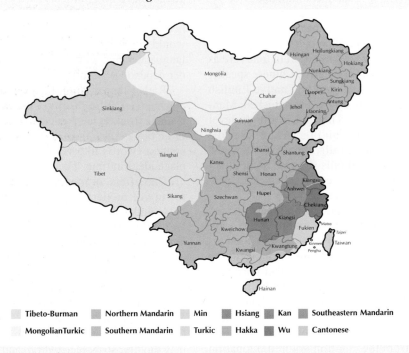

Tibeto-Burman	Northern Mandarin	Min	Hsiang	Kan	Southeastern Mandarin	
MongolianTurkic	Southern Mandarin	Turkic	Hakka	Wu	Cantonese	

The Dialects

Terminology Defined

Dialect distinctions are common in any language extending over a relatively large area, or even a relatively small one where geographic features traditionally have precluded easy communication. A geographically large nation such as China is no exception to this rule. However, in addition to a large number of dialect differences throughout the nation, certain regional groups of some dialects, mostly concentrated in the southeastern part of China, are for the most part so mutually unintelligible that they could be considered different languages of the same family. Phonetically, Fukienese, for example, is about as distinct from Mandarin as Dutch is from German, or French is from Italian. The reader therefore has to be prepared for a certain

amount of confusion caused by the various descriptions of differences between such dialects stemming from the fact that such English terms as "language" or "dialect" seem to imply either too much or too little of a linguistic difference than actually is felt to exist. The customary translation of the Chinese term for these regional languages 方言 is often rendered into English as "dialect" from its literal meaning of "regional speech." It is common to regard the term "language" as a marker of political boundaries or ethnic identity, even when historical linguistic evidence might suggest otherwise. At times, this connotation of the term "language" may even run counter to common sense: a particular dialect of the English language is spoken natively by inhabitants of India, the Philippines, and certain Caribbean island nations, as is a dialect of Spanish by non-European inhabitants of various

North, Central, and Latin American nations; furthermore, there are dialects of French in Haiti and Francophone Africa, and yet the speakers of these areas today share no common political or ethnic identity with England, Spain, or France, respectively. The language shared by such geographically disparate regions may primarily reflect a historical link of long-term cultural cross contact dating from earlier periods of colonial rule. Hence, our concept of language surpasses the traditional connotation of the term.

From a historical perspective, these disparate dialects of English, Spanish, or French share common roots with other dialects of the language in question and are more or less mutually intelligible, despite pronunciation, word usage and occasionally, minor syntactical differences. Thus, in this sense of common historical (and cultural) roots, use of the traditional term "dialect" to describe the regional tongues of China has a certain persuasive logic. In general, their syntactical differences are usually minor, and even in their purely spoken form, they share a very large base of common word usages inherited from Middle Chinese (or earlier). This is reinforced by the semantic word-root representation of Chinese characters in the literary language as it appeared in semi-literary and colloquial usages. Following this logic, however, creates the opposite problem, namely, how to readily express the long-standing fundamental lack of mutual intelligibility between such regional "dialects" and to account for the very palpable and at times extensive pronunciation, traditional tone class distinction, and word usage differences that exist within each regional tongue (i.e., the Chaozhou and Amoy dialects, or Cantonese and Taishan dialects). Thus, reserving the traditional term "dialect" for the regional tongues themselves forces us to express these more traditional dialect differences within each tongue through an arcane term like "sub-dialect," a term distinction generally lost on the nonspecialist. Accordingly, we refer to these regional tongues here as dialect groups which can be generally classified into the Mandarin, Hsiang 湘, Kan 贛, Hakka 客家,

Wu 吳, Min 閩, and Yue 粵 groups. Since each group preserves different features of Middle Chinese (dating back to early or even pre-Tang times), they have proven to be valuable research tools in the phonological reconstruction of Middle and even to some extent its ancestor, Old Chinese.

Dialect Group Characteristics

The Mandarin group is subdivided into Northern, Northwestern, Eastern, and Southwestern Mandarin. Dialects of the Mandarin group are spoken in three-quarters of the country by two-thirds of the population—one important reason why Mandarin was chosen for the national language (see section on the National Language in this chapter)—and are for the most part mutually intelligible. They are characterized by relatively simple phonological and tone systems.

Both the Hsiang group as spoken in Changsha and the Kan group as spoken in Nanchang have six tones, including the 入聲 "entering tone." The Changsha and Nanchang dialects of these groups do not distinguish between the sounds *l*- and *n*-. The Hakka group, whose speakers are mostly concentrated in Guangdong, Taiwan, and Southeast Asia, also has six tones. There are two main dialect divisions of Hakka: Sixian, represented by the speech of Meixian, considered the standard Hakka dialect; and Hailu, which has been strongly influenced by the Southern Fukienese group.

There is a great deal of variation among the dialects of the Wu group, spoken mostly in Zhejiang and Jiangsu provinces. The Suzhou dialect, representative of northern Wu, has seven tones, with complex tone sandhi; the Wenzhou dialect, representing southern Wu, has eight tones; and Shanghainese has five tones. In general, the group demonstrates a rich variety of nasality and voicing in its vowels.

The main dialect of the Yue group, Cantonese, is extensively spoken throughout Guangdong Province, Hong Kong, and many overseas Chinese communities. Some Yue dialects display perhaps more tones than any other dialect, a total of nine. The Yue group has been the most faithful of all the regional groups in preserving the full range of Middle Chinese final consonants into modern times, and special Chinese characters have been devised over the centuries for Cantonese to a greater extent than the dialects of other groups to record spoken forms not shared by standard written Chinese. Extensive contact with Western culture has also led to the coinage, especially in Hong Kong, of new words based on foreign loan words to a far greater extent than by any other regional group.

The Min group traditionally includes the Southern Fukienese group (one dialect of which is often called Taiwanese) spoken natively by perhaps 70 percent of the people of Taiwan. Min dialects are also spoken on Hainan Island, and many areas of Southeast Asia, including Singapore, southern Thailand and the Philippines. Most Southern Fukienese dialects have seven tones, each of which (with some exceptions) assumes the contour of a different tone when it is not the final word of a phrase or sentence. Distinctions between nasalized and non-nasalized vowel finals, as well as voiced and unvoiced initial consonants are another notable feature of dialects in this group. The Northern Fukienese group of dialects, found in the Fuzhou region, and the Southern Fukienese group are for the most part mutually unintelligible.

The National Language

Mandarin, the national language of the Republic of China and of the Chinese mainland, is based on the Peking dialect. Formerly referred to as Official Speech 官話, the Beijing dialect has had approximately 1,000 years of history as the koine of politics and commerce in China, particularly in the north.

The Choice of Mandarin

The need to establish an official national language was felt as early as the 17th century when the Qing dynasty established a number of "correct pronunciation institutes" to teach standard Beijing pronunciation, particularly in the Cantonese and Fukienese-speaking southern provinces. The success of these schools, however, was extremely limited.

The concept of a national language coalesced around 1910. In 1913, the Ministry of Education 教育部 convened a Commission on the Unification of Pronunciation 讀音統一會 to establish a standard national tongue. Delegates with linguistic backgrounds from all of China's provinces voted to decide on official pronunciations for each individual Chinese character. Wu Ching-heng 吳敬恆 (also known as Wu Chih-hui 吳稚暉), a philosopher and one of the founders of the ROC, was chosen to direct the task of creating a truly national language that would transcend locality and dialect. The Beijing dialect was the general foundation of the new national language, but features of various local dialects were also incorporated. This hybrid is now known to English speakers as Mandarin.

Phonetic Symbols

There was a great deal of disagreement as to the best way to notate the sounds of Mandarin. The three main options were modified Chinese characters, a new set of phonetic symbols, and Romanization. The system that was eventually adopted and developed was the predecessor of today's Mandarin phonetic symbols 注音符號. This collection of 39 symbols (later 40) plus four tone marks and a voicing symbol was designed by Chang Ping-lin 章炳麟 (also known as Chang Tai-yen 章太炎).

Once the phonetic alphabet was approved and promulgated by the Ministry of Education in November 1918, primary school textbooks were required to use it alongside Chinese characters. In April 1919, the Ministry of Education formally established the Preparatory Committee for the Unification of the National Language. Mandarin became the required language of instruction in elementary and middle schools. Gramophone records recorded by Wang Pu 王璞 in Shanghai and Y.R. Chao 趙元任 in the US in 1920 and 1921 were used as a standard reference for correct pronunciation. The tonal system used was basically that of the Beijing dialect, but originally a fifth tone marker for words pronounced in the "entering" tone of Middle Chinese (i.e., syllables ending in a -p, -t, or -k stop) was added, based on the Nanking dialect. Since the Beijing dialect had not preserved this distinction for over 500 years, this feature was latter eliminated in 1924. In 1932, a new system was devised for indicating the tone of a word, and three initials which were not used in standard Beijing dialect were dropped, bringing the total number of Mandarin phonetic symbols to today's 37.

Romanization

In 1928, the Ministry of Education (MOE) promulgated a system of Romanization for Mandarin, the *Gwoyeu Romatzyh*, dubbed the National Phonetic Alphabet II 國音字母第二式. This intricate system incorporated the tone of each character into its Romanized spelling. In spite of the system's official status, however, it has never been widely studied or used for two reasons: complexity and the dominance of the Wade-Giles Romanization system, which predates it. In 1984, the MOE announced the adoption of a modified form of the *Gwoyeu Romatzyh*, in which tone spellings were replaced by tone marks. This, however, did not succeed in improving public acceptance of the system. Wade-Giles is currently the de facto standard in Taiwan, despite official use of the Postal Standard by the Directorate General of Posts under the Ministry of Transportation and Communications 交通部郵政總局, and occasional utilization in the public and private sectors of spellings based on other Romanization standards. The simultaneous use of different Romanization systems to represent the same Chinese pronunciation often confuses non-Chinese speakers attempting to identify street or place names in Taiwan. Concerns were voiced that this might add to the woes of Taiwan's already weak incoming foreign tourism industry and slow the globalization of the ROC. Consequently, in April 1996, the Council for Economic Planning and Development under

the Executive Yuan 行政院經濟建設委員會 met with pertinent government agencies and decided that the Phonetic Symbols II adopted by the Ministry of Education in 1984 will be the official Romanization system for location names in the Taiwan area except for those widely known and used worldwide such as Taipei, Taiwan and Kaohsiung. This decision, however, aroused controversy. In December 1996, the Educational Reform Council 教改會, led by Dr. Lee Yuan-tseh 李遠哲, recommended that the government adopt a new Romanization system—Tongyong Pinyin 通用拼音, chiefly devised by Dr. Yu B.C. 余伯泉 of Academia Sinica 中央研究院. According to Dr. Yu, Tongyong Pinyin has a double advantage—it can be used to Romanize not only Mandarin Chinese but also local languages in Taiwan, including Southern Fukienese and Hakka; and it is compatible with the Hanyu Pinyin system 漢語拼言 promoted by the Chinese mainland, while at the same time overcomes its faults. The first version of this new system was officially adopted by the Taipei City Government in April 1997. At a time when Hanyu Pinyin has become internationally accepted, Tongyong Pinyin represents a conscious effort to promote a Romanization system suited to Taiwan's culture and society. [See Appendix VIII to find a comparison table of the most common Romanization systems and Mandarin phonetic symbols.]

However, in 1999, in its effort to internationalize Taipei city, the city government took the initiative to adopt the Hanyu Pinyin system as the official representation of the Chinese pronunciation of street and place names. About one month later, with the same concern in mind, and upon the recommendation of the MOE, the Executive Yuan decided to replace the Tongyong Pinyin system with the Hanyu Pinyin system. Adoption of this widely accepted Romanization system is also expected to enhance exchanges between the two sides of the Taiwan Strait.

The Ministry of Education (MOE) also saw a need to solve the existing phonetic system. In January 1998, the MOE promulgated the Taiwan language phonetic system 臺灣語言音標系統, which was proposed by an MOE task force aimed at compiling guidelines for teaching dialects and aboriginal languages in March 1995. This system includes phonetic systems for Southern Fukienese and Hakka as well as phonetic symbols for aboriginal languages. Except for part of the phonetic symbols for aboriginal languages, the MOE's system has been registered with the International Standard Organization (ISO). By doing so, the MOE hopes to facilitate the use of information worldwide. However, the Taiwan language phonetic system and the MOE's actions have aroused criticism from academic groups. Some academicians have been developing their own system and are declining the use of this system. (See section on Bilingual Education, below.)

The Written Language

The main unifying force of China's many diverse dialect groups and the link with the Classical Chinese 文言 language of the ancients has always been the written system comprising tens of thousands of ideographic characters. While speakers of different Chinese dialects may assign differing pronunciations to a given character, the meaningful content of the character is, for the most part, the same for all. This explains why a speaker of one dialect may not be able to understand what a speaker of another dialect says, but can still understand what that person writes. In theory, a well-educated Cantonese speaker and a well-educated Southern Fukienese speaker could both understand an article written by a Shanghainese speaker using Chinese characters in the virtually obsolete literary language; however, if the three people took turns reading the same article aloud, listeners would hear three completely different pronunciations. If our putative Shanghainese speaker wrote in the manner of contemporary speech, word usage differences among these three dialect groups might still preclude complete communication. In order to overcome this, modern written Chinese has evolved a standard modern vernacular 白話

This Mao tripod inscription (ca. 827 B.C.) is a representation of the writing style prevalent during the Chou dynasty. It tells of the appointment of Mao Yin to prime minister by King Hsuan and shows a small part of the long evolution of the Chinese writing system.
(Courtesy of the National Palace Museum)

(see section on the Written/Venacular Split in this chapter). Thus, literate Chinese, no matter which dialect they speak natively, share the same writing system.

Evolution of Chinese Writing

The evolution and gradual institutionalization of the Chinese writing system can be traced back to the fifth and fourth millennium B.C. when the earliest extant ancestors of modern Chinese characters were painted or engraved on ancient clay potsherds. In comparison, the earliest Egyptian hieroglyphics and the earliest Sumerian cuneiform writings have been dated to the sixth millennium B.C. and 3100 or 3200 B.C., respectively. The potsherds were first unearthed in Banpo 半坡, Shaanxi Province, in the 1950s, and have already been partially deciphered. The numerals one through eight have been conclusively identified, and scholars believe that symbols identifying the artisan or owner of the pot were also inscribed on the pieces.

Although most of the potsherd markings were only symbols and not true writing, they were significant in the development of Chinese writing. The later the period of the potsherds, the more the markings on them resembled the tortoise and oracle bone inscriptions soon to follow. The inscribed clay pots were almost certainly not the only materials of their time used for writing. In fact, writing on the clay pots was very limited in scope and somewhat incidental to the pots. It is extremely possible that wood, bamboo, and silk were already widely used as writing materials by this time; however, since these materials decompose relatively quickly, none have been found yet dating back to this early time period.

Oracle Bone and Tortoise Shell Inscriptions

Ox bones and tortoise shells inscribed with primitive Chinese characters were first discovered in 1899 in Xiaotun 小屯, Henan Province, at the site of a capital of the Shang dynasty (1766-1122 B.C.). Of the 2,000 or so different characters found on bones and tortoise shells, about 1,300 have been definitively deciphered. The bones and tortoise shells were used in making divinations for the king. For simplicity's sake, these inscribed bones and tortoise shells are now known collectively as oracle bones.

Judging by the ancient inscriptions, an oracle would be consulted, for example, to predict whether or not it would rain on a certain day. The oracle would then inscribe on the bone or tortoise shell questions and possible answers, one set affirmative and the other negative. The inscribed bone or tortoise shell was then heated in a fire. The oracle would make his predictions based on the pattern of the cracks in the bone produced by the heat. The oracle inscriptions were extremely limited in content, and many of the characters used were simplified since the materials used did not allow for elaborate flourishes. Characters often had several alternate forms, and could be written in reverse.

Despite a certain lack of consistency, the oracle inscriptions reveal that a Chinese grammar and writing system strikingly close to the modern one had already taken shape. Furthermore, a number of trends in the development of Chinese characters had emerged by the conclusion of the oracle inscription period: colored-in solids were replaced by lines; straight lines supplanted rounded ones; characters were gradually simplified, squared off, and standardized; and a set of stylized radicals (meaningful graphical classifying elements) was developed to be added to characters in order to distinguish among homophones.

Bronze Inscriptions

The next stage in the development of Chinese writing is represented by the inscriptions on bronzes which date back to at least the 15th century B.C. In the bronze inscriptions, meaningful pictures (radicals) began to be added onto characters borrowed purely for their sound. The addition of a radical to distinguish between two homophonous characters with different meanings is somewhat similar to having different spellings for homophones in English, such as *two*, *to*, and *too*. In Chinese, the addition of a radical suggested exactly which one of a series of homophones was being referred to. For example, if the intended object was a plant, the radical for "grass" or "wood" could be added. Since such characters give clues both to the meaning and pronunciation of a character, and reduced ambiguity to a minimum, they gradually came to comprise the largest category of Chinese characters. In modern Chinese, between 80 and 90 percent of all characters are phonetic ideographs.

By the end of the Bronze Age, Chinese writing began its trend from monosyllabicity to polysyllabic compounds. Another notable feature of writings at the end of the Bronze Age is the increasing use of functional grammatical particles. Few such particles had been used or needed in the elliptical oracle inscription style.

Types of Chinese Characters

Writing almost a thousand years after the end of the Bronze Age, China's first lexicographer, Hsu Shen 許慎, completed his compilation of the *Shuo-wen Etymological Dictionary* 說文解字 in 121 A.D. In the work, Hsu Shen noted six types of Chinese characters: (1) pictographs such as 日 "sun" and 月 "moon"; (2) ideographs such as 上 "above" and 下 "below" (indicating points above and below a line); (3) compound ideographs such as 信 "believe" (made up of character components for "person" plus "speech"); (4) characters with both a phonetic and pictographic or ideographic element such as 江 and 河 both meaning "river" (a phonetic element is added in each case to the radical indicating water); (5) characters borrowed to represent other homophones unrelated in meaning such as 而 "furthermore" or "however" (a borrowed character originally meaning "hair"); and (6) *chuan-chu* 轉注 which modern scholars have yet to exactly define.

The pictograph category was the earliest to appear; Chinese writing, like the Egyptian hieroglyphics, originated with increasingly stylized drawings of concrete objects. It is natural that many of the characters used in this early form of Chinese writing were pictographs, along with some ideographs of more abstract notions, a more advanced phase of character development. Phonetic borrowings and phonetic ideographs were also used, to a lesser extent. The pictographic category reached a point of maturity and saturation with the oracle inscriptions; very few new pictographs appeared after this point, though simplifications and modifications in established pictographs were later made.

Calligraphic Styles

Before the tyrannical first emperor of the Chin dynasty 秦始皇 seized power in 221 B.C., various nation-states in China had begun to develop their own individual—and sometimes outlandish—calligraphic styles. This ended with the unification of the written language during the Chin dynasty.

The standard script of the Chin dynasty is referred to as the large seal script 大篆, suggesting its use in name chops. The Chin dynasty Prime Minister Li Szu 李斯 later developed the small seal script 小篆, based on a combination of the ancient and large seal script styles. The small seal style is characterized by thin, meticulously-rendered lines. The invention of the official script style 隸書 is attributed to the Chin dynasty prison warden Cheng Miao 程邈, but it would be more accurate to say that he simply organized and standardized a script that had already developed over a period of time.

Although the official script was easier and faster to write, thereby speeding up the processing of official documents, the cursive script 草書 emerged as an even faster alternative some time later. The regular script 楷書 was developed in the second century A.D., based on the official script style. The regular script shed the wavy, thickened brush strokes of the earlier style and established a standard in the face of increasingly fanciful cursive scripts. It is the standard script used today.

The invention of the running script 行書 is attributed to Liu Te-sheng 劉德昇 of the second century A.D. The name of the script is self-explanatory: It is a flowing style that falls somewhere between the regular and cursive scripts.

Simplified Versus Standard Characters

The Chinese communists have promoted the use of a simplified form of Chinese characters, based on a list of 515 characters issued in 1956 and 2,236 characters published in 1964, in an effort to help alleviate widespread illiteracy in China. It is difficult to assess the pedagogical efficacy of the simplified characters 簡體字 in teaching, reading, and writing. However, the simplified characters themselves produced a new kind of cultural illiteracy: the inability to read materials written in standard characters 繁體字. This has resulted in the alienation of a people from their own literary tradition. An additional list of 200 simplified characters released in 1977 was later removed from use. People had begun inventing new simplified characters as they pleased, to the point where there was no longer a commonly observed standard. The traditional, standard forms of Chinese characters are the only ones in general use in the Taiwan area, thus providing everybody with full access to China's classics and other writings in standard script.

The Written/Vernacular Split

Into the second decade of the 20th century, most literate Chinese wrote in classical Chinese 文言, which was far removed from their vernacular tongue. In 1917, Hu Shih 胡適, a professor of philosophy at National Beijing University, led a group in launching a movement to promote a

Primary school children participate in a competition of traditional brush calligraphy, a skill that used to be an absolute necessity for all imperial officials during the Tang dynasty. Chinese intellectuals over the centuries have believed that the diligent practice of calligraphy helped to cultivate one's moral character.
(Photo by the Central News Agency)

written vernacular 白話. The attempts to encourage a new vernacular literature became an important focus of the May Fourth Movement 五四 運動 of 1919 and went on to spark a revolution in Chinese writing. This has not meant the complete end of the classical Chinese language. Today, classical Chinese is still used for certain kinds of formal writing and survives in the spoken language in the form of proverbs, idioms, and occasional sentence patterns in much the way Latin graced learned English prior to World War II.

Language in Taiwan Today

Although Mandarin is standardized nationwide, each region speaks its own local version of it, usually reflecting influence from the native dialects of the area. These regional variations of Mandarin are perhaps not even as great as the differences between British and American English, but are definable. Typical Taiwan Mandarin, for example, exhibits four major differences from the Mandarin spoken in Beijing:

- The retroflex series of initials *tʂ-, tʂ'-, ʂ-* has generally merged with the dental sibilants *ts-, ts'-, s-* .
- The retroflex - ɹ suffix common in Peking is rarely used in Taiwan.
- The neutral tone is used much less often than in Beijing.
- The third tone, which in Beijing falls sharply and then rises back up, tends in Taiwan to conclude as a "creaky" tone, i.e., at a speaker's lowest voice pitch, without rising.

These characteristics are likely attributable, at least in part, to influence from the Southern Fukienese 閩南 dialect widely spoken throughout the Taiwan area. Apart from these four major differences, there are also some relatively minor vocabulary and grammatical differences between the Mandarin spoken in Taiwan and on the Chinese mainland.

For many years, Chinese dialects like Southern Fukienese and Hakka 客家, as well as the aborigine languages, were not given much official attention in Taiwan. In the process of making sure everyone mastered the common national language,

the importance of other dialects and languages was played down. The benefit of this policy was the dismantling of language barriers between different linguistic and cultural groups; the drawback was the neglect of rich lingual traditions.

While Southern Fukienese is still widely spoken in Taiwan, especially outside of the Taipei area, there is little understanding of its structure, history, and folk traditions among the general population. Hakka is also being spoken less and less by younger generations who favor Mandarin and Southern Fukienese, and many aboriginal tongues now face extinction.

However, Taiwan society is a rich mixture of diverse cultures, and more and more people on the island are becoming aware of the importance of preserving various languages and dialects. This awareness has become the propelling force behind government efforts to promote "nativist" education 鄉土教育 in elementary, junior high, and senior high schools. The goal of nativist education is to teach students about the natural history, geography, environment, dialects, arts, and culture of Taiwan, and thus cultivate an affection for Taiwan and respect for the island's different cultures and ethnic groups. Under initial plans adopted by the Ministry of Education in 1997 for promoting nativist education, bilingual education is a primary focus.

Bilingual Education

Bilingual education has been introduced in the Taiwan area as a way of reversing the previous neglect of Chinese dialects other than Mandarin. The central government has been lagging behind several steps in its proponents for bilingual education; thus, the magistrates of three counties, making good on campaign promises, chose to "jump the gun" and institute programs in the areas under their jurisdiction prior to any decision by the central authorities.

Ilan County 宜蘭縣 was the first to initiate Southern Fukienese courses in elementary and junior high schools. The program was heralded by a county order in June 1990 that students should no longer be discouraged from or punished for speaking dialects at school. Pingtung County 屏東縣 followed suit in September 1991, and elective courses in Southern Fukienese, Hakka, and the Paiwan 排灣 and Rukai 魯凱 aboriginal languages are now taught in selected county schools. Additional activities, such as speech and singing contests, have also been held to further motivate students. These events led to the production of a full multicultural program of music and dance which was performed islandwide.

Extracurricular Atayal language lessons made their debut in 1990 at Taipei County's Wulai elementary and junior high schools 烏來國民小學和烏來國民中學, where the majority of students are Atayal 泰雅 aborigines. In the absence of ready-made teaching materials, teachers depended almost solely on a blackboard and their own ingenuity. Some were not very fluent in their ancestral language, and had to learn it themselves as they went along. Materials were compiled as courses were developed, the Taipei County Government 臺北縣政府 in 1992 commissioned its Bureau of Education 臺北縣政府教育局 and the Taipei County Cultural Center 臺北縣立文化中心 to compile teaching materials for the two most prevalent Chinese dialects in Taiwan, Southern Fukienese and Hakka, and two aboriginal languages, Ami 阿美 and Atayal. The center was also asked to publish a county periodical on bilingual education; sponsor community and campus activities; establish a teacher consultation center; and conduct teacher training programs, teaching workshops and Romanization contests. Textbooks compiled by linguistic specialists include content concerning the geography, history, famous people, religion, and arts of Taiwan.

However, the promotion of bilingual education by local governments has faced many obstacles. One of the obstacles comes from parents. Not all parents support bilingual instruction programs. Some, for example, worry that instruction time spent gaining competence in a chosen Chinese dialect or aboriginal language might negatively affect a student's ability to compose in standard written Chinese (see section on the Written Language, above), and possibly result in lower scores on senior high school or college entrance exams. Other parents feel that the usefulness of their native language is limited. "Wouldn't it be better to teach English or Japanese instead?" they reason. For aborigines who are less well off, economic and social advancement is a much more urgent concern; bilingual education may be a luxury that they feel they can't afford.

Another obstacle is caused by the absence of generally agreed-upon standard written forms for each of the Chinese dialects and aboriginal languages. Different phonetic systems have been proposed and tried out. The choices for representing aboriginal languages in the written content of textbooks range from a number of Romanization schemes to a phonetic symbol-based system similar to that for Mandarin. For Southern Fukienese and Hakka, the use of Chinese characters with no phonetic alphabet is a third option. However, simply using standard Chinese characters is problematic, since they may only indirectly indicate pronunciation, and some dialects lack widely known, written characters for some of their words.

Mandarin phonetic symbols have sometimes been adapted to represent Chinese dialects and aboriginal languages. But because Mandarin phonetic symbols are a part-alphabet, part-syllabary system created primarily for the language's relatively simple phonological and tonal structure, they are not particularly well-adapted for use with other dialects. This is especially true with multisyllabic Austronesian languages like Taiwan's aboriginal tongues.

Romanization systems are perhaps the most flexible and precise and are well suited to serve as the primary writing system for aboriginal languages. In addition, they can serve as an auxiliary system for teaching Chinese dialects. For example, the Romanization system developed by missionaries for Southern Fukienese has a long history and is currently in widespread use, so it would seem a natural candidate as a standard phonetic alphabet. As things stand, each method tends to start from scratch and contribute yet another idiosyncratic system to the existing jumble. Thus, progress is often held back simply due to indecision about which system to adopt in education.

To remedy the situation, the MOE revised guidelines and amended curriculum standards for elementary, junior high, and senior high schools. These amendments grant schools more leeway to work out curricula that allow students to receive bilingual instruction as extracurricular or elective courses. Participation by students is voluntary. Furthermore, the revised guidelines clearly stipulate that schools may teach in dialects. The government supports such courses with various levels of funding for compiling teaching materials, publishing teacher handbooks, holding teacher workshops, producing audio and video cassettes, and collecting teaching materials.

In August 1994, the MOE established a task force, composed of experts from the Institute of History and Philology of Academia Sinica, to research dialects and aboriginal languages and compile guidelines for teaching them. A guidebook of auxiliary teaching materials for dialects in junior and senior high schools which proposed a Taiwan language phonetic system was published by the task force in March 1995. Accordingly, the MOE commissioned the Taiwan Provincial Government's Department of Education 臺灣省政府教育廳 and seven counties to review and compile teaching materials for the Southern Fukienese and Hakka dialects. The project also involves developing materials for aboriginal languages, including Atayal 泰雅, Ami 阿美, Yami 雅美, Paiwan 排灣, Rukai 魯凱, Puyuma 卑南, Tsou 鄒, Bunun 布農, Saisiyat 賽夏, Kavalan 噶瑪蘭, and Sedeka 賽德克. Moreover, the Legislative Yuan passed the *Aboriginal Education Act* 原住民教育法 in 1998, which stipulates that the government should provide aborigines with opportunities to learn their native languages, history and culture at preschools and elementary schools in their hometowns.

In January 1998, the MOE promulgated the Taiwan language phonetic system after some moderate changes were made in line with the Romanization system developed by missionaries. Since then, official phonetic systems for Southern Fukienese and Hakka as well as phonetic symbols for aboriginal languages in Taiwan have been established. However, the adoption of this system is not compulsory. Academic groups or private sectors are free to develop their own phonetic systems for dialect materials.

Southern Fukienese has in the meantime very obviously entered the mainstream of popular culture. Taiwanese dialect pop songs tended in the past to be stereotyped and relegated to a subordinate position in the market. Now singers are often expected to produce at least a few songs or an album in Southern Fukienese. Use of Southern Fukienese in advertising and business—from TV commercials to restaurant names—is considered fashionable. Bookstores now offer entire sections of literature written in a style reflecting spoken Southern Fukienese. To encourage research on Southern Fukienese, Hakka, other Chinese dialects and non-Han languages of China, the MOE offers various levels of financial support in the form of awards for scholarly publications in these areas.

Foreign Language Education

In order to promote the globalization program of the ROC, the MOE has planned to extend the teaching of foreign languages to the elementary-school level. The MOE has focused on English as its first target in foreign language education. After assessment by scholars, educators, and school representatives, the MOE has scheduled the teaching of English to fifth and sixth grade students, beginning in the academic year 2001. The MOE has compiled textbooks and begun recruitment of teachers for this new curriculum. In 1999, a total of 3,536 individuals passed the qualification test, becoming the first group of English teacher candidates for elementary schools. These candidates will still be demanded to attend special courses for professional training to complete the requirements of the MOE.

Further Reading

(in Chinese unless otherwise noted):

Chao, Yuen Ren 趙元任. *A Grammar of Spoken Chinese*. Berkeley (in English). University of California Press, 1970.

Cheng, Robert L. 鄭良偉. *Yen-pien-chung ti Tai-wan she-hui yu-wen: to-yu she-hui chi shuang-yu chiao-yu* 演變中的臺灣社會語文：多語社會及雙語教育 (Taiwan's Society and Language in Transition: A Multilingual Society and Bilingual Education). Taipei: Independence Evening News 自立晚報出版社, 1990.

Forrest, R. A. D. *The Chinese Language* (in English). London: Faber and Faber, 1973.

Huang Tung-chiu 黃東秋, ed. *Tai-wan yuan-chu-min yu-yen min-su yen-chiu* 臺灣原住民語言民俗研究 (A Study of Taiwan Aborigine Customs and Languages). Taipei: Crane Publishing 文鶴出版社, 1993.

Hung Wei-jen 洪惟仁. *Tai-wan fang-yen chih lu* 臺灣方言之旅 (An Excursion into the Dialects of Taiwan). Taipei: Chien Wei 前衛出版社, 1992.

Kuo-wen tien-ti 國文天地 (The World of Chinese Language and Literature). Taipei: monthly.

Kuo-yin hsueh 國音學 (A Study of Mandarin Phonology). National Taiwan Normal University, Committee for the Compilation of Mandarin Phonology Teaching Materials, ed. Taipei: Cheng Chung 正中 Bookstore, 1982; 1993.

Li, Charles N. and Sandra A. Thompson. 'Chinese.' in Bernard Comrie (ed.), *The World's Major Languages* (in English). New York and Oxford: Oxford University Press, 1990: pp. 811-833.

Lo Chao-chin 羅肇錦. *Ke-yu yu-fa* 客語語法 (A Grammar of the Hakka Dialect).Taipei: Student Book Store 學生書局, 1985.

Lo Chao-chin 羅肇錦. *Kuo-yu hsueh* 國語學 (A Study of the National Chinese Language).Taipei: Wunan Publishers 五南出版社, 1990.

Norman, Jerry. *Chinese* (in English). Cambridge: Cambridge University Press, 1988.

Ramsey, S. Robert. *The Languages of China* (in English). Princeton: Princeton University Press, 1989.

Tai-yu wen-chai 臺語文摘 (Taiwanese Digest). Taipei, monthly.

Yang Hsiu-fang 楊秀芳. *Tai-wan Min-nan-yu yu-fa kao* 臺灣閩南語語法稿 (A Grammar of the Southern Min Dialect in Taiwan). Taipei: Tah-an Publishers 大安出版社, 1991.

4

History

This map of
Taiwan drawn
during the
Ching dynasty
is in the
collection of the
National Palace
Museum.
(Courtesy of the
National Palace
Museum)

What's New

More comprehensive information on the history of Taiwan

Since the appearance of writing in China some 6,000 to 7,000 years ago, Chinese people have been recording the history of their families, clans, and dynasties. As time passed, many Chinese rulers and the large bureaucracies under them collated these various historical materials to create macro histories that highlighted the ruler's place in Chinese history. Despite the fact that many Chinese rulers have challenged each other's legitimacy, that many times China was not being ruled by any central authority at all, and that non-Chinese peoples occasionally conquered Chinese states, Chinese historians filled in any blanks and thus linked China's present firmly together with her past. The resulting histories showed a cycle that began with the fall of a corrupt ruler and a weak dynasty followed by the rise of a new moral ruler and a strong dynasty. This historical pattern is called a "dynastic cycle," and all traditional Chinese histories were written in accordance with this formula. Many of these traditional histories are still extant and intelligible to readers of Chinese today. The Chinese people are thus the proud inheritors of the world's longest unbroken historical tradition.

The historical focus on political legitimacy and continuity was a powerfully conservative force in China. Traditional histories provided successive dynasties and governments with a set of precedents by which to rule. Thus, even though ruling power passed hands quite often in China, the way the country was ruled remained roughly the same. This lent a degree of stability (some would say inertia) to Chinese culture that was absent in the cultures bordering China.

One common explanation of the phenomenal endurance of Chinese civilization is that China was actually governed by an aristocracy of intelligentsia which had been continuously revitalized by the introduction of new personnel. A civil service examination system, first implemented in the Sui dynasty over 1,400 years ago, allowed young men who were well schooled in China's historical and literary traditions to enter the government bureaucracy, regardless of their family's social, political, or economic status. Theoretically, even the son of a farmer, butcher, or blacksmith could become prime minister one day as long as he could pass a series of imperial examinations. When an emperor was deposed, it mattered little who took his place, since the Chinese bureaucratic system continued to function.

Equally insulated from political infighting was the village economy, upon which China's agricultural civilization was based. Peasants seldom troubled themselves with national affairs unless war or imperial mismanagement threatened the livelihood of the village and its ability to raise grain, produce goods, and render the services of labor.

China's modern history began when the three pillars of Chinese stability—rule by historical precedent, bureaucratic conservatism, and village-based economics—were shaken by contact with the West. This chapter seeks to shed light on China's modern history, show Taiwan's place in this history, and then provide background information on the history of the Republic of China so that materials mentioned in other chapters of this book can be viewed in perspective.

East Meets West

For thousands of years, China has maintained close relations with the nation states on its periphery. These border states often served as intermediaries between China and other major civilizations in India and the Middle East. As far back as the Han dynasty (206 B.C.-A.D. 221), China was exporting silk, porcelain, and other trade goods to the Roman Empire. During the Yuan dynasty (1279-1368), China's Mongolian rulers, especially Kublai Khan 忽必烈, brought a significant number of Persians, Turks, and

Chinese Dynastic Chronology

Dynasty	Divisions	Dates	Capital
Hsia 夏		2205–1766 B.C.	Anyi
Shang 商 (or **Yin** 殷)		1766–1122 B.C.	Anyang
Chou 周	Western Chou	1122–770 B.C.	Hao (Sian)
	Eastern Chou	770–221 B.C.	Loyi (Loyang)
	(Spring and Autumn Period)	770–476 B.C.	
	(Warring States Period)	475–221 B.C.	
Chin 秦		221–206 B.C.	Hsienyang
Han 漢	Western Han	206 B.C.–A.D. 8	Changan (Sian)
	Hsin	8–25	Changan
	Eastern Han	25–220	Loyang
Three	Wei	220–265	Loyang
Kingdoms 三國	Shu	222–263	Chengtu
	Wu	222–280	Nanking
Chin 晉	Western Chin	265–316	Loyang
	Eastern Chin	317–420	Nanking
Southern	Sung	420–479	Nanking
Dynasties 南朝	Chi	479–502	Nanking
	Liang	502–557	Nanking
	Chen	557–589	Nanking
Northern	Northern Wei	386–534	Pincheng
Dynasties 北朝	Eastern Wei	534–550	Yeh (Honan)
	Western Wei	535–557	Changan
	Northern Chi	550–557	Yeh
	Northern Chou	557–581	Changan
Sui 隋		581–618	Changan
			Loyang
			Yangchow
Tang 唐		618–907	Changan
			Loyang
Five	Later Liang	907–923	Kaifeng
Dynasties 五代	Later Tang	923–936	Loyang
	Later Chin	936–946	Kaifeng
	Later Han	947–950	Kaifeng
	Later Chou	951–959	Kaifeng
Sung 宋	Northern Sung	960–1127	Kaifeng
	Southern Sung	1127–1279	Hangchow
Yuan 元		1279–1368	Beijing
Ming 明		1368–1644	Nanking
			Beijing
Ching 清		1644–1911	Beijing

other peoples from Central Asia to work in the Mongolian administration. The great Italian traveler, Marco Polo, visited China during this time and actually worked for the Mongolians as the Superintendent of Trade in Lanzhou 蘭州.

Early in the 15th century, an ambitious Ming monarch, Cheng Tsu 成祖 (commonly referred to as the Yung Lo Emperor 永樂大帝), showed an intense interest in overseas exploration. He equipped scores of seafaring ships, manned by tens of thousands of sailors, and placed them under the command of one of his closest advisors, the eunuch Cheng He 鄭和. In the years between 1406 and 1433, Cheng He made seven voyages through the South China Sea, past the Malaysian Peninsula, into the Indian Ocean, and on to the east coast of Africa. His travels to more than 50 countries constituted the greatest overseas venture in Chinese history.

Two main sea routes linking the East and West were discovered during the Ming dynasty, and by the early 16th century, Portugal, Spain, Holland, and England were sending powerful fleets to Asian waters. The Portuguese were the first Europeans to reach China by sea. With the permission of Ming officials, the Portuguese set up an entrepôt in Macau in 1535. In the years that followed, many Christian missionaries came to China on Portuguese ships. In 1601, the Italian Jesuit Matteo Ricci was granted an imperial stipend to reside in Beijing 北京 (Peking). Other missionaries soon followed in his footsteps. Julius Aleni, Johannes Terrens, Didacus de Pentoja, Johannes Adam Schall von Bell, and Ferdiandus Verbiest brought not only their religion, but also new concepts and ideas with respect to the arts, medical science, water conservancy, mathematics, geography, and astronomy, including the Gregorian calendar. As in the Yuan dynasty, some of these intrepid Christians even served as officials in the imperial bureaucracy.

China's Closed-door Policy

The Manchus established the Ching dynasty in 1644. During their rule over China, the Manchus subdued the remnants of Mongol resistance in the northwest, and conquered the Khalkhas, the Kalmuks, and the Turks. They also formally annexed Outer and Inner Mongolia, Sinkiang, Tsinghai, and Tibet, thereby fixing the modern boundaries of China. In 1683, Ching forces took over Taiwan.

At the height of Ching power, the Manchus utilized the best minds and richest human resources of the country, regardless of race, to carry out many scholarly projects. However, Western missionaries—active in China since the end of the Ming—lost the trust of the Yung Cheng Emperor 雍正 because of their role in a power struggle for the throne. Christianity was thus banned in 1724, and the flow of Western technology into China soon slowed to a trickle. During the entire 18th century and the early 19th century, while Europe was being transformed and invigorated by the rise of rationalism, nationalism, colonialism, and the industrial revolution, the Ching court was adopting a virtual closed-door policy toward the Western world.

Breaking Down the Door

The Western powers, however, were not content to leave China isolated, as they coveted Chinese markets and resources. They were dissatisfied with perennial trade deficits with China; unhappy with being treated unequally by the royal court of China, which viewed trade as bestowing a favor; and chafed at being restricted to doing business in only a few small ports. High productivity in both light and heavy industries drove European countries (especially England) outward in search of new markets and resources. By the early 18th century, England dominated overseas trade, having gained dominance of the seas over Spain and Holland. During the next century, colonialism and resource exploitation backed by military force went hand in hand with the push by major European nations to develop overseas markets.

The seeds of the Opium War of 1839-42 were sown in a worsening trade relationship between Great Britain and the Ching court. The

Ching government was gravely concerned about the loss of 1.8 million silver taels its populace was spending on 30,000 chests (each containing more than 100 catties) of opium each year. In January 1839, Ching Commissioner Lin Tse-hsu 林則徐 was made responsible for stamping out the opium trade. He closed down 13 guilds in Canton 廣州 after foreign merchants, such as Lancelot Dent, refused to yield all the opium stored on Lingding Island 伶仃島 (Lingting). The foreign merchants finally gave in and handed more than 20,000 chests of opium to Lin who, to the great dismay of the drug dealers, promptly burnt them all. In July 1840, British warships occupied Dinghai 定海 (Tinghai) and in August attacked Dagu 大沽 (Taku) near the northern port city of Tianjin 天津 (Tientsin). A Ching official, Chi Shan 琦善, gave in to English demands for indemnity and ceded Hong Kong 香港 to England. However, the British government was not satisfied with the agreement and sent a new plenipotentiary, Henry Pottinger, who attacked Amoy 廈門 (Xiamen) in 1841, and Shanghai 上海 in 1842. The Treaty of Nanking 南京條約 was consequently signed on August 29, 1842, and has proven to be one of the most influential treaties in China's modern history. Not only was it the first in a series of unequal treaties signed with Western powers, but it also marked the beginning of a long period of internal turmoil and external concessions for China over the next 150 years. The 13 articles in the treaty stipulated that five ports were to be opened for British trade and consulates were to be established there; Hong Kong was to be ceded to England; and 21 million silver taels were to be paid in four installments. Supplementary clauses that were signed later further stipulated consulate jurisdiction over Englishmen residing in China.

After the Treaty of Nanking, Belgium, Holland, Prussia, Spain, Portugal, the United States, and France also asked to establish consulates in China. In 1844, the Treaty of Wanghsia 望廈條約 was concluded with the United States, which stated that the US would enjoy whatever privileges China granted to other nations. Later that

year, a similar agreement, the Treaty of Whampoa 黃埔條約, was signed with France.

By signing the Treaty of Nanking, China agreed to open five ports, including Canton, to foreign trade. However, the residents of Canton at first refused to allow Englishmen to enter the city and then attacked those already there. In early 1856, a French missionary was killed in Guangxi Province 廣西省. Later that year the Arrow Incident 亞羅號事件 occurred, in which the Arrow—a Hong Kong-registered ship under the protection of the English government—was searched in Canton by Ching soldiers and 12 of its sailors were arrested. These incidents eventually led to an Anglo-French expedition against Beijing in 1858 and the burning of the imperial summer palace by invading troops. The Ching court was thus compelled to make further concessions in the 1860 Treaty of Peking 北京條約.

The signing of these treaties led to a flood of Western merchants selling foreign goods: textiles, kerosene, lamps, cigarettes, and opium. Consequently, the old Chinese system collapsed, and the village economy that had served as the backbone of China's agricultural society and sustained Chinese civilization for several millennia was seriously disrupted.

The proud imperial bureaucracy and the mandarin elite were woefully ill-equipped to deal with this onslaught. They were ignorant of the new forces to which China was being subjected. Their training had been in the old Chinese classics, and their experience had not prepared them to meet these new challenges. The scholarly elite were no more capable of dealing with the situation than the eunuchs who served the imperial family in the Forbidden City.

Reformers in the Ching court, however, were aware of the superiority of Western armaments. In 1861, Generals Tzeng Kuo-fan 曾國藩, Li Hung-chang 李鴻章, and Tso Tsung-tang 左宗棠 were able to convince the Ching court to initiate a 30-year "self-strengthening" program. Under this new program, the Ching dynasty began to train translators, import Western military technology, and set up armories. The Tsungli Yamen 總理衙門 was established to manage foreign affairs. The self-strengthening program, however, came too late. Further controversies with Russia in the northwest and with England and France in the southwest jeopardized the stability of the Ching dynasty. A war with France ended with the signing of the Treaty of Tientsin 天津條約 in 1885. In the latter half of the 19th century, China lost its suzerain rights and sovereignty over the Indo-China Peninsula and large areas of the northwest.

During this period, Chinese and Japanese spheres of influence overlapped in Korea, and Japan was showing interest in taking over Taiwan. The Ching court sent Liu Yung-fu 劉永福 and his armies to safeguard the island. The military modernization undertaken during the self-strengthening program proved to be a complete failure when war between China and Japan finally broke out in 1894. Japan quickly breached the Chinese defenses and sank most of her northern navy. The Treaty of Shimonoseki 馬關條約 was signed the next year, compelling the Ching government to pay a huge indemnity, open its seaports, recognize the independence of Korea, and cede the Liaodong Peninsula 遼東半島 (Liaotung), Taiwan, and the Pescadores to Japan.

The repeated defeats suffered by China at the hands of foreign powers, the weakness and incompetence of the Ching court, and the success of the Meiji Reformation in Japan prompted many Chinese to take action. Under the leadership of Kang Yu-wei 康有爲 and Liang Chi-chao 梁啓超, a reform movement was initiated in 1898. The Kuang Hsu Emperor 光緒 sympathized with this movement, but met with strong opposition from his aunt, the Empress Dowager Tzu-hsi 慈禧太后, as well as from other conservative elements in the Ching court. The movement came to an inglorious end after only 100 days and was followed by a coup d'état in which the Kuang Hsu Emperor was imprisoned by the Empress Dowager and those who had played a leading part in the movement were executed or exiled.

Popular discontent with internal misgovernment and anti-foreign sentiment aroused by the unequal treaties combined to spark the Boxer Uprising 義和拳之亂 in 1900. The Boxers laid siege to the foreign legation in Beijing, where a combined force of Japanese, French, British, Russian, and American troops held out for over a month. The siege was broken when the forces of eight foreign powers marched from Tianjin and scaled the walls of Beijing. The foreign powers then took the opportunity to loot Beijing in one of the most disgraceful episodes of modern diplomatic history. In the signing of the Treaty of Peking the following year, China was disarmed and forced to pay large indemnities. This treaty was regarded as the most humiliating of all the unequal treaties.

One of the foreign powers which sacked Beijing, Russia, also took this opportunity to occupy Manchuria. When the troops of the other foreign powers withdrew from Chinese territory, Russia refused to leave Manchuria, leading to conflicts with Japan and the outbreak of the Russo-Japanese War in 1904. Through the Treaty of Portsmouth signed in 1905, a victorious Japan obtained complete control over Korea and rights and interests in southern Manchuria, leaving the north to Russia. Thereafter, Manchuria and Mongolia became flash points of further conflict between Japan and Russia, with China the biggest loser of the three.

The Birth of a New China

After decades of pain and frustration brought about largely by the weakness of the imperial government, the Chinese people were disillusioned with the Ching dynasty and began to take a keen interest in the revolutionary movement launched by Dr. Sun Yat-sen 孫中山 in the late 19th century. Dr. Sun set up a series of secret societies that operated in inland Chinese cities and overseas. In 1887, Dr. Sun even set up a secret society in Japanese-controlled Taiwan, from where he directed an uprising in Huizhou 惠州 (Huichou).

In 1905, Dr. Sun Yat-sen, who had been exiled from China for his involvement in the anti-Ching movement, organized the Revolutionary Alliance 同盟會 (Tung-meng Hui) in Tokyo. This organization sponsored a network of revolutionaries inside China. On October 10, 1911, Dr. Sun's supporters in Wuchang 武昌, fearing their cover was blown by the recent arrest of one of their agents, seized the initiative and raised the standard of revolt in Hubei Province 湖北省 (Hupei). Drawing on a wellspring of popular support and the defection of numerous officers in the local garrison, the revolutionaries soon captured Wuhan 武漢. Two months later, revolutionaries fought and won a pitched battle in Nanjing 南京 (Nanking). On January 1, 1912, the Revolutionary Alliance, which by that time controlled 16 of the Ching dynasty's 22 provinces, established a provisional parliament in Nanjing and elected Dr. Sun Yat-sen to the provisional presidency of Asia's first democratic republic—the Republic of China.

Northern China, however, was effectively controlled by Yuan Shi-kai 袁世凱, who had served the Ching dynasty in a variety of high posts. To break the deadlock and unify China, a three-way settlement was reached between revolutionaries in the south and the military strongman Yuan in the north. On February 12, 1912, the last Ching ruler, Emperor Hsuan Tung 宣統, gave up his throne. The rule of the Manchus had lasted 268 years and spanned the rule of ten emperors. Dr. Sun Yat-sen agreed to relinquish the provisional presidency of the Republic of China to Yuan Shi-kai, and Yuan promised to establish a republican government.

Shaky Beginnings

The first half of the 20th century in China saw the gradual disintegration of the old imperial order. Foreign political philosophies had halted the traditional dynastic cycle, and nationalism became the dominant force in China. Externally, China was still confronted by strong foreign powers and subject to the terms of unequal treaties. Domestically, the new democracy was severely tested by its nominal leader, Yuan Shi-kai.

As the former governor-general of Zhili 直隸 (Chihli), Yuan had trained the elite, Western-style Beiyang Army 北洋軍 (Peiyang). He coerced the newly established parliament into formally electing him to the presidency, and was inaugurated on October 10, 1913. Upon his ascension to China's highest political office, Yuan Shi-kai sought to disband Dr. Sun Yat-sen's Revolutionary Alliance, which had been reorganized into the Kuomintang 國民黨. Yuan also dissolved the parliament and then assumed dictatorial powers. In an effort to appease China's rapacious neighbor in the northeast, Yuan Shi-kai agreed to Japanese demands—known as the Twenty-one Demands 二十一條款—for special rights and privileges in Shandong Province 山東省 (Shantung) in May 1915. As time passed, it became obvious that Yuan was planning to restore the imperial system with himself on the throne. Unmoved by the advice of foreign governments and opposition by the Kuomintang, Yuan Shi-kai declared himself emperor on December 12, 1915.

That same month, Chen Chi-mei 陳其美 led a revolt against the incipient restoration of monarchy in China. More significant was a military revolt in Yunnan Province 雲南 led by Governor Tang Chi-yao 唐繼堯 and General Tsai O 蔡鍔. Joined by Lee Lieh-chun 李烈鈞 and other revolutionary generals, these men established the National Protection Army 護國軍 and demanded that Yuan cancel his plan to reestablish monarchal rule in China. During the spring and early summer of 1916, one after another, provinces and districts declared independence from the Yuan regime. As fate would have it, however, Yuan Shi-kai fell gravely ill and died on July 6, 1916. General Li Yuan-hung 黎元洪, vice president of the democracy that Yuan Shi-kai had sought to dismantle, succeeded the presidency, and General Tuan Chi-jui 段祺瑞 retained his post as premier.

Highly ambitious and supported by many senior commanders from the old Beiyang Army clique, Tuan Chi-jui quickly began to strengthen his grip on power. In February 1917 when the American government severed diplomatic relations with Germany and pressed China to do the same, President Li Yuan-hung strongly opposed the move, but Premier Tuan and his supporters were able to push through China's declaration of war on Germany on August 14, 1917. Despite sending over 100,000 men to France during World War I, China reaped little benefit from its entry into the war. It was assured a seat at the Versailles Peace Conference, but the Chinese delegation was stunned to discover that Germany's holdings in China would not be returned to the Chinese people. Rather, the Western powers had agreed to Japanese claims to the German concession in Shandong Province. Major portions of Shandong were to be held by another foreign colonial power, Japan.

On May 4, 1919, students in Beijing protested the decision at the Versailles Peace Conference. A riot ensued and many students were arrested. Waves of protest spread throughout the major cities of China, merchants closed their shops, banks suspended business, and workers went on strike to pressure the government. The government was finally forced to release arrested students and discharge some of the Chinese officials who had collaborated with Japan. Ultimately, the Chinese government refused to sign the Treaty of Versailles.

An intellectual revolution sparked by the events of May 4, 1919, referred to as the May Fourth Movement 五四運動, gained momentum during the first decade of the Republic of China. The movement was led by a new generation of intellectuals who scrutinized nearly all aspects of Chinese culture and traditional ethics. This new intelligentsia emerged in China after the traditional civil service examination system was suspended in 1905. New educational reforms enabled thousands of young people to study science, engineering, medicine, law, economics, education, and military science in Japan, Europe, and the United States. The "overseas students" returned to modernize China and, through their writings and lectures, exercised a powerful influence on the next generation of students. Guided by concepts of individual liberty and equality, a scientific spirit of inquiry, and a pragmatic approach to the nation's problems, the new intel-

lectuals sought a more profound reform of China's institutions than what was accomplished by the self-strengthening movement of the late Ching dynasty or the republican revolution. National Beijing University 北京大學, China's most prestigious institution of higher education, was transformed by its chancellor, Tsai Yuan-pei 蔡元培, who had spent many years in advanced study in Germany. Tsai made the university a center for scholarly research and inspired educators all over China. A proposal by Professor Hu Shih 胡適 that literature be written in the vernacular language rather than the classical style also won quick acceptance.

Important economic and social changes occurred during the first years of the Republic. With the outbreak of World War I, foreign economic competition against native industries abated, and state-run light industries experienced brisk development. By 1918, the industrial labor force numbered 1.8 million workers. A large portion of capital flowed from the agricultural sector to new industries in China's coastal provinces, and modern Chinese banks with growing capital resources were able to meet expanding financial needs.

In the 1920s the United States, Great Britain, and Japan seemed to be moving toward a new postwar relationship with China. At the Washington Conference (1921-22), the major powers agreed to respect the sovereignty, independence, and territorial and administrative integrity of China; to give China the opportunity to develop a stable government; to maintain the principle of equal opportunity in China for the commerce and industry of all nations; and to refrain from taking advantage of conditions in China to seek exclusive privileges. The powers also agreed to take steps leading toward China's tariff autonomy and the abolition of extraterritoriality.

The Warlord Era

For a few years after the Washington Conference, foreign powers refrained from aiding particular Chinese factions in the recurrent power struggles. China was in turmoil, however, and regional militarism was in full swell. During the first two decades of the Republic, China had been fractured by rival military regimes to the extent that no one authority was able to subordinate all rivals and create a unified and centralized political structure. The powerful Beiyang Army had split into two major factions: the Zhili faction led by Feng Kuo-chang 馮國璋 and the Anhui faction under Tuan Chi-jui. These two factions controlled provinces in the Yellow River and Yangtze River valleys, and competed for control of Beijing. In Manchuria, Chang Tso-lin 張作霖 headed a separate army. Shanxi Province 陝西省 (Shansi) was controlled by Yen Hsi-shan 閻錫山.

Having witnessed the collapse of the fledgling central government he had worked so hard to create, Dr. Sun Yat-sen turned south to his home province of Guangdong 廣東 (Kwangtung), where he established a military government in August 1917. In 1919, Dr. Sun reorganized his party into the present-day Chinese Kuomintang (KMT, also known as the Nationalist Party), and in 1921, Dr. Sun Yat-sen assumed the presidency of the newly formed southern government in Guangdong. When war between the northern warlords erupted the following year, Dr. Sun issued a manifesto urging the reunification of China by peaceful means. A political idealist, Dr. Sun Yat-sen was to be disappointed by more years of sporadic fighting between warlords. Finally, in 1924, Dr. Sun Yat-sen and his southern government moved to set up a military academy that would train an officer corps loyal to the Kuomintang and dedicated to the unification of China. Dr. Sun appointed Chiang Kai-shek 蔣中正 as commandant of the Whampoa Military Academy 黃埔軍校.

On November 10, 1924, Dr. Sun Yat-sen called for the early convocation of a National People's Convention to bring each of China's regional leaders to the conference table. Two weeks later, Tuan Chi-jui became the provisional chief executive of the Beijing-based government and Dr. Sun Yat-sen, as head of the southern government, traveled north to hold talks with Tuan. While in Beijing, Dr. Sun succumbed to liver cancer and died on March 12, 1925, at the age of 59. His dream of a unified and democratic China freed of foreign constraint had yet to be realized.

Dr. Sun's untimely demise left the southern government in the hands of a steering committee. This 16-member committee established a national government in July 1925 and some 11 months later appointed Chiang Kai-shek commander-in-chief of the National Revolutionary Army 國民革命軍. In this capacity, Chiang Kai-shek launched a military expedition northward to eradicate various feuding warlords in central and northern China. This military campaign lasted three years and came to be known as the Northern Expedition 北伐. On March 22, 1927, the first troops of the National Revolutionary Army entered Shanghai and two days later, captured Nanjing. Despite a split between the right and left wings of the Kuomintang, Chiang Kai-shek was able to establish a new National Government in Nanjing on April 18, 1927, and the Northern Expedition continued without interruption.

Japanese Provocations

By the spring of 1928, the National Revolutionary Army was approaching Jinan 濟南 (Chinan), the provincial capital of Shandong Province. Japan dispatched 3,000 soldiers to the city under the pretext of protecting Japanese residents. On May 3, two days after the National Revolutionary Army moved into Chinan, Japanese soldiers killed the Chinese negotiator Tsai Kung-shi 蔡公時. Thousands of Chinese soldiers and civilians were slaughtered by Japanese regulars in the ensuing massacre. Less than a month later, the Japanese followed this atrocity with the assassination of the Chinese warlord in northeast China, Marshal Chang Tso-lin, after he had expressed his intention to surrender Manchuria to the National Government. Manchuria was a huge and rich area of China in which Japan had extensive economic privileges. Japan dominated much of the southern Manchurian economy through a monopoly of the Southern Manchuria Railway 南滿鐵路. Manchuria's impending unification with the rest of China threatened Japan's economic privileges in central China and its domination in Manchuria.

The Chinese government realized the Jinan massacre and the assassination of Chang Tso-lin were premeditated actions designed by the Japanese militarists to provoke war while China was still divided. Chiang Kai-shek thus ordered the National Revolutionary Army to continue its northward march but to avoid Japanese controlled areas in northern China. This strategy frustrated the Japanese schemes and effectively unified China under the National Government based in Nanjing.

Japanese militarists remained undaunted. Believing Manchuria to be strategically and economically vital to their plans for the conquest of all Asia, Japanese officers in Shenyang 瀋陽 (Mukden) sabotaged the Southern Manchuria Railroad on September 18, 1931, and ambushed the Northeastern Chinese Armies. On January 28, 1932, following a wave of murders and arson by their agents in Shanghai, Japanese armies attacked that city. Chinese defenders resisted heroically, thereby drawing international attention. To deflect world opinion, which had condemned their actions, the Japanese installed a puppet regime known as Manchukuo 滿洲國 in 1932. The "land of the Manchu" proved to be no more than another stepping stone for the extension of Japanese aggression. In 1933, the humiliating Tangku Truce 塘沽協議 was signed, which in effect yielded eastern Hebei Province 河北省 (Hepei) to the Japanese-controlled Manchukuo.

After long negotiations, Japan acquired the Soviet interests in the Chinese Eastern Railway 中東鐵路, the last legal trace of Russian influence in Manchuria. In 1935, Japanese armies attempted to detach Hebei and Chahar 熱河 provinces from Chinese control and threatened Shanxi, Suiyuan 綏遠, and Shandong provinces. The Japanese then set up the so-called East Hebei Anti-Communist and Self-Government Council 冀東反共自治會, another move after the Tangku Truce to extend Japanese control over northern China.

The Rise of the Chinese Communists

The Japanese were not the only threat to the integrity of Chinese democracy. The Chinese communists, who had rebelled against the government of the Republic of China (ROC), established a provisional Soviet "government" in Jiangxi Province 江西省 (Chianghsi) on November 7, 1931, and created 15 rural bases in central China. The ROC launched five successive military campaigns to eradicate the communist threat to central authority. The communist armies were, in the end, forced to abandon their bases and retreat. Communist troops led by Mao Zedong 毛澤東, Zhu De 朱德, Zhou Enlai 周恩來, and Lin Biao 林彪 marched and fought their way across western China on the 6,000-mile Long March. By mid-1936, Nationalist forces had cornered the remnants of several communist armies in the impoverished area of Yanan 延安 (Yenan) in northern Shanxi Province.

At this point, the Chinese communists opted for a new "united front" strategy against Japan. The ROC government, however, believed that the communists must capitulate to central authority before China could effectively repel Japanese encroachment. This policy, therefore, was one of "unity before resistance against foreign aggression." While further Japanese transgressions made this policy a costly one, Generalissimo Chiang Kai-shek was determined to carry on the anti-communist campaign. He ordered the Northeastern and Northwestern Armies to attack the communist forces in northern Shanxi Province. When the Northeastern Army, commanded by Chang Hsueh-liang 張學良, disobeyed the order to pursue the war against the communists, Chiang Kai-shek flew to Xian 西安省 (Sian) on December 12, 1936, to confront Chang Hsueh-liang. Chang's army subordinates, however, shot Chiang Kai-shek's bodyguards and arrested the generalissimo. After a series of behind-the-scenes negotiations, Chang Hsueh-liang freed the generalissimo and escorted him back to Nanjing on Christmas day of 1936. The Sian Incident 西安事件 was a severe setback to Generalissimo Chiang's efforts to subjugate the communists

The War Against Japan

On the eve of China's all-out war against Japan, the Japanese nation had a total of over 4.5 million soldiers. The total tonnage of its navy came to nearly two million, while its air force had 2,700 planes of various models. In comparison, the Chinese army had 1.7 million men, its navy had a total tonnage of 110,000, and its air force had 600 aircraft, only 305 of which were fighters.

On July 7, 1937, a minor clash between Japanese and Chinese troops near Beijing finally led China into war against Japan. (In Chinese, this conflict is called the Eight-year War of Resistance Against Japan 八年抗日戰爭.) From this point on, Chinese resentment of over half a century of Japanese barbarism was expressed in the form of overt, concerted, and armed resistance. The war against Japan unfolded in three stages: a first stage of undeclared war beginning with the Marco Polo Bridge Incident 七七事變 (or 蘆溝橋事變) on July 7, 1937; an intermediate stage beginning in late 1938; and a third stage that began with China joining the Allied Forces after the Japanese bombing of Pearl Harbor. The war ended with Japan's surrender in 1945.

During the first stage of the war, Japan won successive victories. Tianjin was occupied in July 1937 and Beijing in August. After three months of fierce fighting, Shanghai was captured by the Japanese on November 11, 1937. The ROC capital, Nanjing, fell in December. The fall of the capital is now known as the Rape of Nanking (Nanjing) because Japanese forces occupying the city killed some 300,000 people (defenseless civilians and Chinese troops that had already laid down their arms) in seven weeks of unrelenting carnage. The loss of Nanjing forced the ROC government to move its capital up the Yangtze River to the city of Chongqing 重慶 (Chungking), which was shielded by a protective mountain screen. By the end of this initial phase of the war, the ROC government had lost the best of its modern armies, its air force and arsenals, most of China's modern industries and railways, its major tax resources, and all the Chinese ports through which military equipment and civilian supplies might be imported. However, China had won a major battle at Taierzhuang 臺兒莊 (Taierchuang) on April 6, 1938.

In 1940, Japan set up a puppet government in Nanjing under Wang Ching-wei 汪精衛, but the Chinese people would not submit. Hundreds of thousands of patriotic Chinese continued to attempt the difficult trek to Chongqing. Students and faculties from most colleges in eastern China traveled by foot to makeshift quarters in distant inland towns. Factories and a skilled workforce were reestablished in the west.

The government rebuilt its scattered armies and tried to purchase supplies from abroad; however, the supply lines were long and precarious. When war broke out in Europe, shipments became even more scarce. After Germany's conquest of France in the spring of 1940, Britain bowed to Japanese demands and temporarily closed Rangoon, Burma to military supplies for China. In September 1940, Japan seized control of northern Indo-China and closed the supply line to Kunming 昆明. While Japan had more than 1,000 planes, China had only 37 fighter planes and 31 old Russian bombers that were not equipped for night flying. The United States, however, had by then sold the Republic of China 100 fighter planes—the beginning of an American effort to provide air protection to the ROC.

By the summer of 1941, the United States knew that Japan hoped to end the undeclared war in China and was preparing for a southward advance toward British Malaya and the Dutch Indies, planning first to occupy southern Indo-China and Thailand, even at the risk of war with Britain and the United States. On July 23, 1941, President Roosevelt of the United States approved a recommendation that the US send large quantities of arms and equipment to China, along with a military mission to advise on their use. The military mission arrived in October 1941. By December 1941, the United States had implicitly agreed to help create a modern Chinese air force, to maintain an efficient line of communication into China, and to arm 30 divisions of soldiers. The underlying goal was to revitalize China's war effort as a deterrent to Japanese military and naval operations in the south. The logistics line for all foreign aid depended on the 715-mile Burma Road, which extended from Chongqing to Lashio, the Burmese terminus of the railway and highway leading to Rangoon.

The third phase of the war against Japan began on December 7, 1941, when the Japanese bombed Pearl Harbor, and shortly afterwards the United States and Britain declared war on Japan. China, which also formally declared war against Japan after four years of staunch resistance, joined the Allies in waging the Pacific War. On January 2, 1942, Generalissimo Chiang assumed the office of Supreme Commander of the China Theater of War. This escalation of the Sino-Japanese conflict raised Chinese morale, but also damaged China's strategic position. With the Japanese conquest of Hong Kong on December 25, 1941, China lost its only air link to the outside world and one of its principal routes for shipping supplies. By the end of May 1942, the Japanese held most of Burma, and China was almost completely blockaded.

Following an initial grant of US$630 million in lend-lease supplies, the United States granted China a loan of US$500 million in February 1942, and Great Britain stated its willingness to lend £50 million. This helped to stabilize the Chinese currency and provided China with better terms of trade. A solution to the supply problem was found in an air route from Assam, India, to Kunming in southwest China—the dangerous "Hump" route along the southern edge of the Himalayas. In March 1942, the China National Aviation Corporation 中國航空公司 (CNAC) began freight service over the Hump, and the United States began a transport program the following month. It was not until December 1943 that cargo planes were able to equal the tonnage carried over the Burma Road by trucks two years before, but China's needs for gasoline, arms, munitions, and other military equipment were still not adequately met.

Both air force development and army modernization were pushed in early 1943. A training center was created near Kunming and a network of airfields was built in southern China. By the end of 1943, the China-based American Fifteenth Air Force had achieved tactical parity with the Japanese over central China, and began to bomb Yangtze River shipping. The Fifteenth Air Force even successfully raided Japanese airfields on Taiwan. China's determination was beginning to pay off. During November and December of 1943, the leaders of the Allied countries met in Cairo, Egypt. In the December 1st Cairo Declaration, the return of Manchuria, Taiwan, and the Pescadores was promised to China. The prewar system of extraterritoriality—whereby Chinese courts had no jurisdiction over any foreigner residing in China—was abolished. In addition, the Allies pledged themselves to "persevere in the prolonged operations necessary to procure the unconditional surrender of Japan."

On August 6, 1945, the United States dropped the first atomic bomb on Hiroshima. Three days later, a second atomic bomb was dropped on Nagasaki. The subsequent Japanese decision to surrender was delivered to the Allies through Switzerland the next day. On August 14, Japan announced its formal surrender in accordance with the terms of the Potsdam Declaration of July 1945 and declared that "the terms of the Cairo Declaration shall be carried out." The Japanese government accepted this in the instrument of surrender concluded on September 3, 1945, between Japan and the Allies. The Japanese armies on the Chinese mainland surrendered to the ROC government on September 9, 1945, in Nanjing.

Communist Rebellion

Even before Emperor Hirohito's announcement of Japan's surrender was known, the commander of the Chinese communist armies, Zhu De, ordered his troops to move into Japanese-held territory and seize Japanese arms. The American general, Douglas MacArthur, then ordered all Japanese forces in China to surrender their arms only to forces of the ROC government. Despite MacArthur's request, the Chinese communists sent

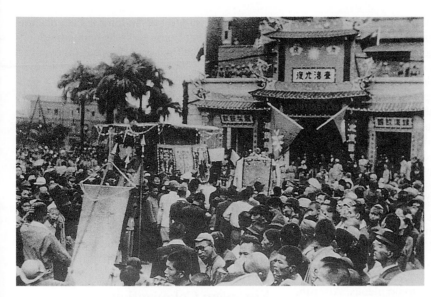

A crowd gathers in Taipei on October 25, 1945, to celebrate the retrocession of Taiwan after 50 years of Japanese colonial rule.
(Courtesy of the Historical Research Commission of Taiwan Province)

tens of thousands of political cadres and soldiers into Manchuria. The Chinese communists got most of the arms of the 600,000-strong Japanese army in Manchuria that had previously been confiscated by the Russians. The Soviet army dismantled most of the industrial machinery in Manchuria. The valuable equipment, so crucial to China's postwar revival, was shipped to the Soviet Union while immovable objects were mostly destroyed. The situation in northeastern China was clearly alarming.

The government and the Chinese communists held peace talks that culminated in an agreement on October 10, 1945. The agreement called for the convening of a multiparty Political Consultative Council 政治協商會議 to plan for a liberalized postwar government and to draft a constitution for submission to a National Assembly 全國代表大會. When the Chinese communists continued to accept the surrender of Japanese garrisons, occupy cities, and confiscate property, Chiang Kai-shek ordered an offensive against them in November. Hostilities lasted throughout December and the early part of January 1946. Hoping to help end the fighting, US President Harry S. Truman dispatched George Marshall to China in December 1945. Marshall was able to

negotiate several cease-fires during 1947, but a pattern of noncooperation between the government and the communists soon escalated into open conflict.

While ROC troops were busily suppressing the incipient communist rebellion, many citizens were working to implement true democracy. On January 1, 1947, the *Constitution of the Republic of China* was promulgated. Within the year, members of the National Assembly, Legislature (Legislative Yuan) 立法院, and Control Yuan 監察院 had been democratically elected. In April 1948, the new National Assembly elected Chiang Kai-shek to the presidency of the Republic of China. These moves toward democratic government, however, were overshadowed by a communist offensive that cut Manchuria off from the rest of China.

The military setback in Manchuria was compounded by serious economic problems. Inflation continued unabated, caused principally by government financing of military and other operations, particularly for maintaining large garrison forces. Apart from the loss of millions of Chinese lives, the war against Japan had generated huge war debts, not to mention serious financial distress in the private sector. The gov-

65

ernment had run a budget deficit every year since 1928. Alarmingly, the money supply in China increased by 500 times between 1937 and 1945. Retail prices of daily necessities were so inflated that even middle-class families tottered on the brink of abject poverty. This unrestrained inflation triggered a national recession and alienated the public from its elected representatives.

By 1948, communist forces had cut lines of communication and destroyed vital outposts along the Longhai 隴海 and Pinghan 平漢 railways, isolating many cities. In December, the pivotal battle for Xuzhou 徐州 (Hsuchou) was lost. This defeat was followed by the fall of Tianjin and Beijing on January 19, 1949. Other cities in northeastern China were lost by March. In early 1949, Chiang Kai-shek began deploying a force of 300,000 troops in Taiwan backed by a few gunboats and some planes. After the Chinese communists had successfully crossed the Yangtze River, the government of the Republic of China began relocating its offices to Taiwan. As the mainland was falling to the communist forces, some two million people (both soldiers and civilians) accompanied the ROC government to the island of Taiwan.

The History of Taiwan

Earliest Inhabitants

Taiwan's first inhabitants left no written records of their origins. Anthropological evidence suggests that Taiwan's indigenous peoples are from proto-Malayan ancestry. Their vocabulary and grammar belong to the Malayan-Polynesian family of modern day Indonesia, and they once shared many Indonesian customs such as tattooing, using identical names for father and son, gerontocracy, head-hunting, spirit worship, and indoor burials. Over 500 prehistoric sites in Taiwan, including many dwelling areas, tombs, and shell mounds, have provided more and seemingly contradictory clues to the origins of Taiwan's aborigines. The majority of prehistoric artifacts discovered so far, such as flat axes, red unpolished pottery, decorated bronze implements, and glass beads, suggest an Indonesian connection. However, other items, such as painted red pottery, red polished pottery, chipped stone knives, black pottery, stone halberds, pottery tripods, and bone arrowheads, suggest that Taiwan's earliest settlers might have come from the Chinese mainland. Many other questions remain unanswered. Were these prehistoric remains left by the ancestors of today's indigenous peoples? The question is a complex one, but many anthropologists have suggested that the remains discovered so far have no proven connection to the present indigenous cultures in Taiwan.

What is known for certain is that large tribes of indigenous peoples, plus many Han people from the Chinese mainland, were already living in Taiwan when Europeans first visited the island in 1590.

European Colonization

When Portuguese navigators first came upon Taiwan, they were struck by the tremendous beauty of its green mountains rising steeply of the blue-green waters of the Pacific. They named the island *Ilha Formosa*, or "beautiful island," a name by which the island has been known in the West for centuries after. Portuguese interest in the island was limited, for they left soon after establishing a settlement in the north.

The next group of Europeans to come to Taiwan were the Spanish and the Dutch. In 1622, the Dutch East India Company established a military base on the Pescadores Islands (Penghu 澎湖). In the following year, they were forced out by the Chinese and moved to the much larger island of Taiwan where they established a colonial capital and ruled for the next 30 years. The Dutch strengthened their foothold by forcing a small Spanish settlement in northern Taiwan to leave the island.

Dutch rule increased the amount of land under cultivation by reorganizing Chinese villages and indigenous territories. Taiwan became a trading and transshipment center for goods between a number of areas, such as Japan, China, Batavia (now Jakarta), and Holland. Taiwan's exports to

China included rice, sugar, rattan, deer hides, deer horns, and medicine. The island's imports from China included raw silk and silk textiles, porcelain, and medicine. Some products from China were again shipped either to Japan, Batavia, or Europe. Imports to Taiwan from Batavia included spices, amber, tin, lead, cotton, and opium, some of which was later traded to China. Before the Dutch arrived, the Chinese on Taiwan had enjoyed free trade with the Japanese without taxation. The Dutch subsequently established a tax on exports, which consisted mainly of deer hides and sugar. Taiwan proved to be one of the most profitable branches of the Dutch East India Company in the Far East, accounting for 26 percent of the company's world profits in 1649.

In addition to trade, Dutch missionaries were also active in converting Taiwan's population to Christianity. Protestant missionaries established schools where religion and the Dutch language were taught. By 1650, the Dutch had converted 5,900 of the island's inhabitants to Christianity.

Settlement by Han people in Taiwan dates back to the 12th century A.D., but large-scale immigration did not begin until the 17th century, during the period of Dutch administration. While the Dutch were colonizing Taiwan, China was going through a period of strife. In 1644, the Manchus invaded China and established the Ching dynasty. The struggle for control continued for several years in the south, affecting many people. At the same time, Japanese pirates repeatedly ravaged Chinese coastal towns. Consequently, thousands of people, especially from the coastal provinces of Fujian福建 (Fukien) and Guangdong, migrated across the Taiwan Strait to Taiwan. In the 20 years from 1624 to 1644, more than 25,000 Chinese households—some 100,000 people—immigrated to Taiwan.

This mass migration to Taiwan changed the character of the island. Recognizing the urgent need for industrious farmers, the Dutch employed the new immigrants, providing them with oxen, seeds, and implements. Every new settler was promised an annual subsidy of cash and an ox. Because all land in these areas belonged to the Dutch East India Company, the Dutch were able to profit enormously from collecting heavy rents from the Chinese tenants. Although settlers petitioned to be allowed to buy and own the land they were tilling, so that they could pay taxes instead of rent, the Dutch rulers refused. Mistreatment by the colonial rulers and collection of a new poll tax increased tensions. In September 1652, frustrated Chinese farmers revolted against the Dutch. The rebellions were violently suppressed by the Dutch, who slaughtered nearly 6,000 poorly armed peasants. The days of Dutch rule were numbered.

Cheng Cheng-kung and Defeat of the Dutch

As Manchu troops poured into northern China, many Ming loyalists escaped southwards, where they resisted the foreign invasion for over 20 years. One of the most celebrated resistance fighters was Cheng Cheng-kung 鄭成功, also known as Koxinga 國姓爺. Son of the pirate Cheng Chi-lung 鄭芝龍 and his Japanese mistress, Cheng made Taiwan his base to restore the Ming dynasty. Forcing the Dutch out in 1662, he established a capital at Anping 安平 (present-day Tainan). Dutch control over parts of Taiwan had lasted for 38 years.

Cheng Cheng-kung set up schools for the young, introduced Chinese laws and customs, and built the first Confucian temple in Taiwan. During his rule, a steady stream of Chinese continued to arrive in Taiwan and settlements sprang up in increasing numbers along the west coast. Agriculture developed primarily on the southern portion of the island. Industry consisted of refining sugar, tile manufacturing, and salt production. Trade, which had begun under the Dutch, continued with neighboring areas, such as the Philippines, Japan, and Okinawa.

Ching Rule Over the Island

Cheng's son and grandson ruled Taiwan for 20 years before surrendering control of the island to the Manchus in 1683, following military defeat. Taiwan was then ruled by the Manchus for the next 200 years.

Under Ching rule, agriculture expanded northward and increasing numbers of Chinese left the mainland to settle on the island, despite laws forbidding emigration. Camphor, a major cash crop, became a cause of conflict between the new arrivals and the indigenous peoples. Bamboo, rice, and tea were cultivated for the first time.

Four ports in Taiwan were forcibly opened to foreign trade following the Treaty of Tientsin in 1858. Foreign interest in the island made the Ching court realize Taiwan's importance as a gateway to the seven provinces along China's southeastern coast. Consequently, through the 1870s and 1880s, a number of progressive and ambitious Ching officials sent to Taiwan succeeded in strengthening defenses, exploiting coal, and constructing telegraph lines between central and southern Taiwan, as well as with Fujian Province across the Taiwan Strait. In 1885, the Ching dynasty made Taiwan its 22nd province.

Japanese Colonization

Achievements by the Ching administration were disrupted when Taiwan was ceded to Japan in 1895, under the terms of the Treaty of Shimonoseki. When Japanese troops formally entered Taipei on June 6 of that year, armed resistance broke out. By the time resistance was broken in October, over 7,000 Chinese soldiers had been killed and civilian casualties numbered in the thousands.

Unlike the Dutch, who in the 17th century colonized Taiwan more for immediate commercial gains, the Japanese at the start of the 20th century gave priority to establishing effective political control over the island. Thus, the Japanese policeman, rather than the Protestant missionary of Dutch times, became the most important tool in the exercise of colonial aims.

During its 50-year rule of Taiwan, Japan developed programs designed to supply the Japanese empire with agricultural products, create demand for Japanese industrial products, and provide living space for emigrants from an increasingly overpopulated home country. In short, Japan was intent on building an industrial homeland and an agricultural Taiwan.

The period of Japanese colonization can be roughly divided into three periods. The first, from 1895 to 1918, involved establishing administrative mechanisms and militarily suppressing armed resistance by local Chinese and indigenous peoples. During this period, the Japanese introduced strict police controls, carried out a thorough land survey, standardized measurements and currencies, monopolized the manufacture and sale of important products (such as salt, sugar, and pineapple), began collecting census data, and made an ethnological study of the island's indigenous peoples.

During the second period from 1918 to 1937, Japan consolidated its hold over Taiwan. Compulsory Japanese education and cultural assimilation were emphasized, while economic development was promoted to transform the island into a secure stepping stone from which Japan could launch its southward aggression.

The third period, which started in 1937 and lasted until 1945, entailed the naturalization of Taiwan residents as Japanese. The Chinese on Taiwan were forced to adopt Japanese names, wear Japanese-style clothing, eat Japanese food, and observe Japanese religious rites. Chinese dialects and customs were effectively discouraged. Heavy industry and foreign trade was strongly emphasized during this period, coinciding with the Second World War.

Japanese development of its Taiwan colony was extensive in areas such as railroads, agricultural research and development, public health, banking, education and literacy, cooperatives, and business.

–Transportation Infrastructure Recognizing the importance of transportation to Taiwan's economy, the colonial rulers constructed 2,857 miles of railroad lines, modernized harbors, and built 2,500 miles of highways.

–Irrigation and Agriculture Irrigation was considered the key to further developing Taiwan's agriculture, which was plagued by uneven rainfall. Concrete dams, reservoirs, and large aqueducts formed an extensive irrigation project that brought thousands of acres of poor

The first human rights memorial in Asia is erected on Green Island off the Pacific coast of Taiwan. The inscription reads: "In that age, many mothers cried endless nights for their children imprisoned on the island." (Photo by the Central News Agency)

farmland into production. Arable land for rice production increased by more than 74 percent and sugar cane, by 30 percent. The enormous increase in sugar cane production is considered to be one of the most spectacular achievements of Japanese colonization. Over a period of 30 years (1905-1935) the area planted in sugar cane increased 500 percent and output skyrocketed. By 1939, Taiwan was the world's seventh largest sugar producer.

–Industry   The Japanese policy of an agricultural Taiwan and industrial Japan did not call for significant development of Taiwan's indus-

try. Factories during the period were small—95 percent had fewer than 30 workers. Finally, during World War II, military necessity led the Japanese to develop aluminum, chemical, oil refining, metal, shipbuilding, and other strategic industries on the island. Around 90 percent of Taiwan's foreign trade was with Japan, mostly agricultural.

–Hydroelectric Power   Heavy rainfall and swift mountain streams on the island made hydroelectric power attractive to colonial administrators. In the 1930s, a large-scale project utilizing Sun Moon Lake 日月潭 and the Choshui River 濁水溪, greatly increased electric power, thus boosting aluminum, chemical, and steel alloy production.

Despite the Japanese success in transforming Taiwan into a society that, economically, was rather modern in comparison with its neighbors, resistance against alien rule never ceased on the island. One of the largest revolts, the Tapani Incident 礁吧哖事件 of 1915, resulted in the deaths of more than 10,000 Taiwanese. Liberation from colonial rule would only come with the total defeat of Japan in 1945.

The ROC on Taiwan

The history of Taiwan after 1949 is one of rapid and sweeping change over a short period. Following 50 years of Japanese colonization, an influx of around two million soldiers and civilians from the Chinese mainland turned the island into a frontline of the Cold War. Over the last five decades, intensive economic development made the island one of the world's largest economies, and rapid industrialization, urbanization, and modernization over a few decades has dramatically transformed the lives of the island's residents. The scale of this transformation has seldom been witnessed anywhere in world history.

Following Japan's defeat and surrender in 1945 at the end of World War II, Taiwan was retroceded to the Republic of China on October 25 of the same year. After having been occupied by the Portuguese, Dutch, Spanish, Manchus, and Japanese, Taiwan was finally under Chinese rule again.

The first years after the Japanese surrender were not smooth and resulted in one of Taiwan's greatest tragedies, the February 28 Incident 二二八事件. The first troops sent to take over Taiwan were poorly trained and undisciplined, while the major fighting component of Nationalist troops remained on the Chinese mainland battling the communist rebellion. Unjust appropriation of personal property, shortages of daily necessities, high inflation, and unchecked profiteering angered both long-time natives and new arrivals from the mainland.

The tense situation finally exploded on February 28, 1947, following an incident in Taipei where an elderly woman was beaten while resisting arrest for selling untaxed cigarettes in Taipei, and a bystander was shot in the commotion. Crowds rioted across the island, seizing police stations, arms, and radio stations and killing some 300 mainlanders. In the succeeding months, after the arrival of troop reinforcements from the mainland, the governor, Chen Yi 陳儀, proceeded to arrest and kill thousands of people who demanded government reform. Although Chen Yi was later tried and executed while serving as governor of Zhejiang Province 浙江省 (Chechiang) for conspiring with the communists to overthrow the ROC government, the incident remained a taboo topic for discussion and a source of tension between Taiwanese and mainlanders until the post-martial law period of the 1990s.

With the outbreak of the Korean War in late June 1950, US President Harry S. Truman ordered the US Seventh Fleet to protect Taiwan against attack by the Chinese communists, and the US began to provide Taiwan with considerable economic and military assistance. The international community sided with Taiwan and the internal situation began to stabilize. Taiwan became the focus of world attention again in August 1958, when the communists began shelling the island of Kinmen (Quemoy) in the Battle of the Taiwan Strait 八二三戰役. The attack was wound down, and on October 23, 1958, the US and ROC governments issued a joint communiqué reaffirming solidarity between the two countries. This invaluable military support continued through the 1960s and 70s.

Economic Transformation

When the ROC government moved to Taipei in 1949, the economy of Taiwan was still trying to recover from the heavy Allied bombing that had occurred during the war. The few industries remaining included sugar refining and some textile manufacturing. In the initial years, two factors stabilized the situation and laid the foundations for a future economic takeoff: aid from the US and the land reform program. From 1951 to 1965, large amounts of economic aid came from the US as part of its Cold War efforts to preserve this valuable ally in Asia. Much of the aid was used in the agricultural sector. Advisors and programs that sent Taiwanese abroad for education were directed at rebuilding the economy. The highly successful land reform program, which was completed in 1953, reduced land rents, distributed public land, and purchased and resold land from large landlords. Farmers were supplied with fertilizer, seeds, pesticides, expert advice, and credit. By 1959, 90 percent of exports were agriculture or food related. Increased production and higher income resulted in low inflation and capital accumulation, as importing food was unnecessary.

After land reform policies and economic assistance had laid a solid foundation for the economy, two policies of the 1950s and 60s led to the remarkable takeoff of the 1970s. The first was an "import substitution policy" aimed at making Taiwan self-sufficient by producing inexpensive consumer goods, processing imported raw materials, and restricting other imports. When far-sighted government planners realized the economic bottleneck poised by the narrow base of Taiwan's domestic economy, a second policy of "export promotion" was adopted in the late 1950s and continued throughout the 1960s. Using Japan as a model and employing US advice, the resource-poor, labor-rich island began to expand light manufacturing. Export processing zones, free of bureaucratic red-tape and with special tax incentives, were set up to attract overseas investment. Soon, Taiwan secured an international reputation as an exporter to the world.

Between 1962 and 1985, Taiwan's economy witnessed the most rapid growth in its history: an average annual rate of nearly 10 percent, over twice the average economic growth rate of industrialized countries during this period. Equitable distribution of income was a major objective in the government's economic planning. In 1953, the average income of the top one-fifth of families was estimated at 20 times that of the lowest one-fifth. In the 1980s this 1:20 ratio was reduced to a range of between 1:5 and 1:4, indicating a highly equitable distribution of income.

The economic structure of the nation shifted from reliance on agricultural exports in the 1950s to light manufacturing in the 1960s and 70s; and on to high technology and chemical product exports in the 1980s and 90s. By 1995, technology-intensive products constituted 46.7 percent of exports.

A new and highly-significant economic trend beginning in the 1980s was the rise of investments by the ROC business community on the Chinese mainland. After the Emergency Decree 戒嚴令 was lifted in 1987, non-government civilian contacts between Taiwan and the Chinese mainland were allowed, and, by 1998, Taiwan's business sector had invested over US$13 billion on the mainland, according to official ROC statistics. (Beijing's statistics indicated a much higher figure of US$21 billion.) The sharp increase of Taiwan exports to the Chinese mainland beginning in 1990 decreased Taiwan's dependence on the US market, but raised new concerns of growing economic reliance on the ROC's long-time foe. Although politically divided, investment and trade by the business community have begun a process of bringing the two sides closer together.

Education

Much of the credit for Taiwan's steady economic growth must go to the spread of universal education throughout the island. After 1949, the government expanded education and raised literacy rates. From 1950 to 1990 the number of university students, including those at private colleges and universities, increased by more than 90 times. Although there were only five M.A. candidates in 1950, and Taiwan had its first Ph.D. student in 1956, by 1997 there were 48,619 students in 766 graduate programs, with 10,013 students studying for doctorates. Thousands of others were enrolled in graduate programs abroad in the US, Canada, Australia, and Europe. The number of high school students also increased from around 34,000 in the 1950s to more than 400,000 in the 1990s. Most noticeable has been the change in the rate of illiteracy. In 1951, 34.6 percent of the population six years and older were illiterate. This figure had dropped to 15.3 percent by 1969. At present, less than six percent of the population is illiterate, mostly the elderly.

Politics and Foreign Relations

Despite restrictions under martial law, the ROC government has long promoted local self-government. Beginning in 1950, all the chief executive and representative bodies under the provincial level were directly elected by the people, and in 1951, 16 county and 5 city governments and councils were established. In June 1959, the first Taiwan Provincial Assembly was established, extending political participation from the county to the provincial level.

Following the death of Chiang Kai-shek in 1975, Yen Chia-kan 嚴家淦 briefly served as president until Chiang's son, Chiang Ching-kuo 蔣經國, was elected in 1978. It was under his rule that full democratization began, starting with the lifting of martial law in 1987 shortly before his death in 1988. In fact, the first major opposition party, the Democratic Progressive Party 民主進步黨 (DPP), was formally established on September 28, 1986, marking the beginning of multi-party democracy in the ROC. Chiang Ching-kuo's successor, President Lee Teng-hui 李登輝, continued to reform the rigid political system that had been developed after decades of civil war and martial law. Under his administration, press freedoms were guaranteed, opposition political parties developed, visits to the mainland continued, and revisions of the constitution encouraged.

Representatives of the National Assembly, the Legislative Yuan and the Control Yuan, who had been frozen in office since 1947, were also asked to step down during Lee's administration. Elections for total seats in the National Assembly and the Legislature were first held in 1991 and 1992. The Control Yuan was transformed into a semi-judicial institution following the 1992 constitutional amendment. On March 23, 1996, the democratization process peaked with the election of the ROC president, the first direct election of the head-of-state in the history of China. Provoking considerable debate and controversy, the provincial government was largely dissolved in 1998 in a government-downsizing move.

Economic policies, encouraging self-sufficiency and internal political reform, reflect changes the ROC experienced in the international arena during the 1970s and 80s. In 1971, the ROC suffered the first of a series of setbacks, beginning with the loss of its United Nations membership on October 25, 1971. Next, US President Richard Nixon visited the Chinese mainland from February 21 to 28, 1972, which culminated in the signing of the Shanghai Communiqué 上海公報 on the 27th. On September 29, 1972, Japan established diplomatic relations with the Chinese mainland. When the United States severed ties with the ROC on January 1, 1979, US military units were withdrawn in March 1979, and the Mutual Defense Treaty was terminated at the end of the year. Despite Washington's recognition of Beijing, ROC-US relations have remained relatively close, as the US has continued economic ties and sold military equipment to Taiwan in accordance with the *Taiwan Relations Act* 臺灣關係法.

Until 1987, the ROC remained under a weak version of martial law. At that time, opposition political parties were banned, publishing and the media were restricted, and relations with the mainland were forbidden. Religious and business activities were essentially free, and citizens

regularly traveled around the island and the world. This policy was adopted despite the continued military threat from the Chinese mainland; however, as Taiwan prospered economically and the mainland undertook radical reforms and began to open up to the outside world, reasons for martial law were no longer seen as valid. On November 2, 1987, the ROC officially permitted its citizens to visit relatives on the Chinese mainland. Since then, cross-strait ties have grown, and, by the late 1990s, Taiwan residents have made over 13 million trips, involving visits to relatives, tourism, and scholarly, cultural, and sports exchanges. The number of trips made by mainland Chinese to Taiwan for cultural and educational activities has totaled more than 34,000.

In February 1991, the semi-private Straits Exchange Foundation 海峽交流基金會 (SEF) was set up to deal with matters arising from contact between people from both sides of the Strait. Its mainland counterpart, the Association for Relations Across the Taiwan Straits 海峽兩岸關係協會 (ARATS), was established ten months later. These organizations have met intermittently to discuss matters of a technical or business nature across the Strait, such as the repatriation of hijackers and illegal entrants and solutions for fishing disputes.

Present and Future

Although the greatest change in post-1949 Taiwan has been the island's economic revolution and spectacular rise in income and living standards, the social transformation brought about following the lifting of martial law in 1987 cannot be overlooked. The legalization of labor strikes, demonstrations, and the formation of new political parties all gave greater power to the people. The lifting of restrictions on newspapers and publishing has produced an explosion in media growth and broadened the perspectives of an increasingly sophisticated audience.

Economic development over the past five decades has also taken a heavy toll on the living environment. Increased prosperity and greater democratic participation have brought about demands for a better quality of life. Anti-pollution protests have been common since the late 1980s. The Republic of China has continued to pursue a balance among democracy, prosperity, equality, a high quality of life, and environmental protection. As the ROC enters the 21st century, boisterous debates and energetic discussions in the media have become a daily part of life in Taiwan.

Historians have viewed the 19th and 20th centuries as a search by Chinese for modernity and inclusion with the outside world. Often, however, modernity and the opening of China have been forced on the nation at great cost. The world forces of imperialism, communism, and the Cold War have dragged China through turmoil and change. Centuries of imperial rule and a Confucian state disappeared at the dawn of the 20th century, and civil war and communism are disappearing at the dawn of the 21st century. Today, the forces of global capitalism, democracy, and the information age are carrying China into a new era, one in which the future of China and that of the world are undivided.

Further Reading

(in Chinese unless otherwise noted):

Erh-erh-pa shi-chien wen-hsien chi-lu 二二八事件文獻集錄 (The Historiographical Records of the February 28, 1947 Event). 2 vols. Taichung: The Historical Research Commission of Taiwan Province, 1991.

Fairbank, J.K. *China: A New History* (in English). Cambridge, Mass.: Belknap Press of Harvard University Press, 1992.

Hsieh Chiao-min. *Taiwan—Ilha Formosa* (in English). Washington: Butterworths, 1964.

Huang Ta-shou 黃大受. *Chung-kuo chin-tai shi-kang* 中國近代史綱 (Essentials of Modern Chinese History). Taipei: Wu Nan Publishing Company, 1991 edition.

———. *Tai-wan shi-kang* 臺灣史綱 (Essentials of Taiwan History). Taipei: San Min Bookstore, 1990 edition.

Lai Tse-han 賴澤涵, Ramon H. Myers, and Wei Wou 魏萼. *The Taiwan Uprising of February 28, 1947* (in English). Stanford: Stanford University Press, 1991.

Linda Chao, and Ramon H. Myers. *The First Chinese Democracy: The Republic of China on Taiwan* (in English). The Johns Hopkins University Press, 1998.

Liu Ning-yen 劉寧顏, ed. *Tai-wan shi-chi yuan-liu* 臺灣史蹟源流 (The Roots of Taiwan's History). Taichung: The Historical Commission of Taiwan Province, 1981.

Ronning, Chester. *A Memoir of China in Revolution—From the Boxer Rebellion to the People's Republic* (in English). New York: Pantheon Books, 1974.

Sheng Ching-yi 盛清沂, Wang Shi-lang 王詩琅, Kao Shu-fan 高樹藩, and Lin Heng-tao 林衡道. *Tai-wan-shi* 臺灣史 (A History of Taiwan). Taichung: The Historical Research Commission of Taiwan Province, 1977.

Spence, Jonathan D. *The Search for Modern China* (in English). New York: W.W. Norton & Company, 1990.

Tai Kuo-hui 戴國輝. *Tai-wan-shi yen-chiu* 臺灣史研究 (Studies in Taiwan History). Taipei: Yuan Liu Publishing Company, 1985.

Twitchett, Denis. *The Cambridge History of China* (in English). London: Cambridge University Press, 1980.

Weiss, H., & B.J. Weiss. *Hsien-min te tsu-chi* 先民的足跡 (The Authentic Story of Taiwan; Chinese-English bilingual). Taipei: Mappamundi Co., Ltd. Taiwan, 1991.

Yeh Chen-hui 葉振輝. *Ching-chi tai-wan kai-fu chi yen-chiu* 清季臺灣開埠之研究 (The Opening of Formosa to Foreign Commerce). Taipei, 1985.

5

Government

As one of the branches of the central government established by the ROC Constitution, the Executive Yuan is headed by the premier and consists of cabinet ministers, commission chairpersons, and five to seven ministers-without-portfolio.

Freedom and democracy are more than just slogans in the Republic of China. They are the tangible results of creatively applying constitutional government through the rule of law. In this chapter, we set forth a general outline of the ROC Constitution and the government which embodies its spirit. First, the essential concepts of the Constitution are explained, followed by a description of various parts of the highest level of government, the central government. This chapter concludes with a brief sketch of the workings of government at the municipal and local levels. Readers may locate information on a specific government agency most quickly by first referring to the index at the back of this book.

The Constitution

The Republic of China, founded on the Three Principles of the People, shall be a democratic republic of the people, to be governed by the people and for the people. (Article 1, *Constitution of the Republic of China*)

The ROC Constitution is based on the Principles of Nationalism, Democracy, and Social Well-being formulated by Dr. Sun Yat-sen, the Founding Father of the Republic of China. His political doctrine is known as the Three Principles of the People 三民主義.

The first Principle of Nationalism 民族主義 advocates not only equal treatment and sovereign status for the Republic of China in the interdependent commonwealth of nations but also equality for all ethnic groups within the nation. The Principle of Democracy 民權主義 as-

sures each citizen the right to exercise the political and civil liberties due to him or her. The Principle of Democracy is the guiding doctrine behind the organization and structure of the ROC government. The Principle of Social Well-being 民生主義 states that the powers granted to the government must ultimately serve the welfare of the people by building a prosperous economy and a just society. The three principles have extensively shaped current policies and legislation in areas ranging from education to land reforms, from social welfare to relations with mainland China, and, more recently, in increasingly extensive political and economic liberalization.

The Constitution spells out the rights, duties, and freedoms of the people, the overall direction for political, economic, and social policies, and the organization and structure of the government. (The full text of the Constitution and its eleven *Additional Articles* can be found in Appendix II.)

Constitutional Rights and Freedoms

The ROC Constitution guarantees various rights and freedoms to all citizens. Modeled after American constitutional concepts, the rights include equality, work, livelihood, and property, as well as the four political powers of suffrage, recall, initiative, and referendum. In return, the people have the duty to pay taxes and perform military service as prescribed by law. Obtaining an education is considered both a right and a duty of the people.

The people are also endowed with the basic freedoms of speech, residence, travel, assembly, confidential communication, religion, and association. Personal freedom is also guaranteed. Rights and freedoms not specified in the Constitution are also protected if they do not violate social order and public interest.

The law may not restrict freedoms stipulated in the Constitution unless the freedoms are abused, the freedoms of others are infringed upon, or public order is threatened. Even in these situations, the Constitution permits restrictions on constitutional rights and freedoms only under certain circumstances. This is designed to prevent legislative bodies from making

ROC Constitutional Amendment

On May 1, 1991, the ROC president promulgated ten *Additional Articles of the Constitution of the Republic of China* 中華民國憲法增修條文 that had just been passed by the First National Assembly. The articles were designed to reflect the fact that Taiwan and the Chinese mainland are administered by two separate political entities. The *Additional Articles* also provided the legal basis for the election of the Second National Assembly and the Second Legislative Yuan, which would be representative of Taiwan, a nationwide constituency covering the mainland, and overseas Chinese.

After the Second National Assembly assumed office on January 1, 1992, its delegates adopted *Additional Articles* 11 through 18. These articles were promulgated on May 28, laying the groundwork for the popular election of the president and vice president of the Republic, the transformation of the Control Yuan from a parliamentary body to a quasi-judicial organ, and the implementation of provincial and local self-governance.

Then, on July 28, 1994, the Second National Assembly revised the 18 *Additional Articles*, reducing the number to ten. Under this revised *Additional Articles of the Constitution:*

- The president (beginning with the ninth-term president since the Constitution went into effect in 1947) shall be directly elected by the entire voting population in the Taiwan area.
- The presidential and vice presidential candidates shall run on a single ticket.
- Overseas nationals may vote in the election for the president and vice president.
- The president can appoint and dismiss those officials who were appointed with the consent of the National Assembly or the Legislature without the countersignature of the president of the Executive Yuan.
- The National Assembly may have a Speaker and a Deputy Speaker.
- The dismissal of the president of the Executive Yuan may take effect only after the new nominee to this office has been confirmed by the Legislature.

From May 5 to July 23, 1997, the *Additional Articles* underwent yet another amendment. The roles of the provincial government and the Control Yuan have taken on drastic changes. Under this revision :

- The provincial government is to be streamlined and the popular elections of the governor and members of the provincial council are suspended.
- A resolution on the impeachment of the president or vice president is no longer to be instituted by the Control Yuan, but rather by the Legislative Yuan.
- The Legislative Yuan has the power to pass a no-confidence vote against the president of the Executive Yuan, while the president of the Republic has the power to dissolve the Legislative Yuan.
- The president of the Executive Yuan is to be directly appointed by the president of the Republic, thus, the consent of the Legislative Yuan is no longer needed.
- Educational, scientific, and cultural budgets, especially the compulsory education budget, will be given priority, but no longer restricted by Article 164 of the Constitution to remain at least fifteen percent of the total national budget.

On September 4, 1999, the ROC Third National Assembly passed another round of constitutional amendments which extend the current terms of deputies from May 2000 to June 2002. Under the newest revision:

- The Fourth Assembly shall have 300 delegates, who shall be elected by proportional representation based on the election of the Legislative Yuan. The seats shall be distributed among the participating parties in accordance with the proportion of votes won by the candidates nominated by each party and those members of each party running as independent candidates.
- Beginning with the Fifth National Assembly, the National Assembly shall have 150 delegates, who shall be elected by proportional representation based on the election of the Legislative Yuan.
- The delegates to the National Assembly shall serve a term of four years.
- The term of office of the Third National Assembly shall be extended to the day when the term of office of the Fourth Legislative Yuan expires.
- The terms of legislators are to be extended from the current three years to four years in the next Legislature.

Organization of the Central Government

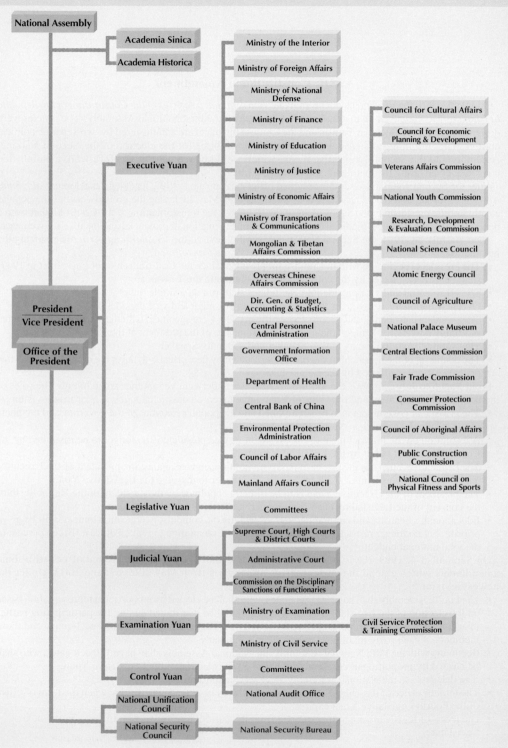

National Assembly

President
Vice President

Office of the President

Academia Sinica

Academia Historica

Executive Yuan

Ministry of the Interior

Ministry of Foreign Affairs

Ministry of National Defense

Ministry of Finance

Ministry of Education

Ministry of Justice

Ministry of Economic Affairs

Ministry of Transportation & Communications

Mongolian & Tibetan Affairs Commission

Overseas Chinese Affairs Commission

Dir. Gen. of Budget, Accounting & Statistics

Central Personnel Administration

Government Information Office

Department of Health

Central Bank of China

Environmental Protection Administration

Council of Labor Affairs

Mainland Affairs Council

Council for Cultural Affairs

Council for Economic Planning & Development

Veterans Affairs Commission

National Youth Commission

Research, Development & Evaluation Commission

National Science Council

Atomic Energy Council

Council of Agriculture

National Palace Museum

Central Elections Commission

Fair Trade Commission

Consumer Protection Commission

Council of Aboriginal Affairs

Public Construction Commission

National Council on Physical Fitness and Sports

Legislative Yuan

Committees

Judicial Yuan

Supreme Court, High Courts & District Courts

Administrative Court

Commission on the Disciplinary Sanctions of Functionaries

Examination Yuan

Ministry of Examination

Ministry of Civil Service

Civil Service Protection & Training Commission

Control Yuan

Committees

National Audit Office

National Unification Council

National Security Council

National Security Bureau

laws that overstep the limits set down in the Constitution. Restrictions on constitutional freedoms are valid only if contained in legislation necessary to prevent restrictions against the freedom of others, to respond to emergencies, to maintain social order, or to enhance social interest. In any case, arrest, trial, and punishment must be implemented in strict accordance with proper legal procedures. If human rights are violated by the government, the victims are entitled to compensation by the state.

Government, Economic, and Social Policies

The ROC Constitution contains directives for formulating legislation and procedures addressing important government, economic, and social issues. Chapter XIII of the Constitution, titled "Fundamental National Policies" 基本國策, contains articles on national defense, foreign policy, national economy, social security, education and culture, and frontier regions. The policies outline the government's responsibility to provide necessary support for the welfare and well-being of the people and also to foster an environment that will enable them to engage in various business and professional activities. Article 9 of the *Additional Articles of the Constitution* prescribes specific policy orientations on several modern issues including scientific development, industrial upgrading, environmental and ecological protection, national health insurance, and the elimination of sexual discrimination.

Governmental Structure

The ROC government is divided into three main levels: central, provincial/municipal, and county/city, each of which has well-defined powers. The central government consists of the Office of the President 總統府, the National Assembly 國民大會, and five governing branches (called "yuan" 院), namely the Executive Yuan 行政院, the Legislative Yuan 立法院, the Judicial Yuan 司法院, the Examination Yuan 考試院, and the Control Yuan 監察院.

At the provincial level, the provincial governments exercise administrative responsibility. Since the ROC government administers only Taiwan Province and two counties in Fukien Province, only two provincial governments are currently operational—the Taiwan Provincial Government 臺灣省政府 and the Fukien Provincial Government 福建省政府. The Fukien Provincial Government oversees the regional affairs of Kinmen County 金門縣 and Lienchiang County 連江縣. Likewise, the Taiwan Provincial Government exercises full jurisdiction over Taiwan's 16 counties and all the cities except for Taipei and Kaohsiung, which are special municipalities directly under the jurisdiction of the central government instead of the Taiwan Provincial Government.

At the local level and under the Taiwan Provincial Government, there are five cities— Keelung, Hsinchu, Taichung, Chiayi, and Tainan—and 16 counties, and under each county there are county municipalities 縣轄市.

The Presidency

The president of the Republic of China is the highest representative of the nation and is granted specific constitutional powers to conduct national affairs. Scores of agencies and advisors assist the president in reaching decisions on state affairs. They include senior advisors, national policy advisors, military advisors, and organizations and institutions such as the Academia Sinica, Academia Historica, National Security Council, and National Unification Council.

The May 20, 1996 inauguration of President Lee Teng-hui 李登輝 as the ninth-term president of the ROC ushered in a new period of development for the then 84-year-old republic. Lee served in the presidency as the first popularly elected head-of-state in Chinese history. Taiwan has undergone dramatic changes since Lee became the head-of-state in 1988 upon the death of President Chiang Ching-kuo. After accomplishing astounding economic development over the decades, the ROC achieved an equivalent political miracle—the much acclaimed "quiet revolutions."

The tenth term presidential election was held in March 2000. Nominees for president were Lien Chan for KMT, Chen Shui-bian for DPP, and Li Ao for the New Party, and two independents—James Soong and Hsu Hsin-liang. Chen Shui-bian 陳水扁 was the winner with 39.3 percent of the votes, followed closely by James Soong 宋楚瑜 with 36.84 percent. Lien Chan 連戰, the KMT candidate was a distant third with 23.1 percent. (For biographical information on President Chen Shui-bian, see Biographies.)

Functions

As chief of state, the president represents the country in its foreign relations and at state functions. All acts of state are conducted in his name, including command of the land, sea, and air forces; promulgation of laws and decrees; declaration of martial law with the approval of the Legislature; conclusion of treaties; declaration of war and cease-fire; convening of the National Assembly; granting of amnesty and commutations; appointment and removal of civil service officials and military officers; and conferring of honors and decorations. All these powers are exercised in accordance with the provisions of the Constitution and the law.

Special Powers
Nominating Officials

The President is entitled to appoint the president of the Executive Yuan. With the consent of the Legislature, he also appoints the auditor-general 審計長 of the Control Yuan, the president 院長, vice president 副院長, and the grand justices 大法官 of the Judicial Yuan (Judiciary); the president, vice president, and members of the Examination Yuan; and the president, vice president, and members of the Control Yuan.

Resolving Inter-Branch Disputes

In the event of a dispute among the various branches, such as a controversy between the Executive Yuan and the Legislature, the president may intervene to seek a solution. Article 44 of the Constitution states: "In case of disputes between two or more branches other than those for which there are relevant provisions in the Constitution, the president may call a meeting of the presidents of the branches concerned for consultation with a view to reaching a solution."

Exercising Emergency Powers

According to Article 2 of the *Additional Articles of the Constitution of the Republic of China* revised in July 1997, the president may, by resolution of the Executive Yuan council, issue emergency orders and take all necessary measures to avert an imminent threat to the security of the state or the people, or to cope with any serious financial or economic crisis, without being subject to the restrictions prescribed in Article 43 of the Constitution. However, such orders must, within 10 days of issuance, be presented to the Legislature for confirmation. Should the Legislature withhold confirmation, the said emergency orders immediately cease to be valid.

Dissolving the Legislative Yuan

The president may, within ten days following passage by the Legislative Yuan of a no-confidence vote against the president of the Executive Yuan, declare the dissolution of the Legislative Yuan after consulting with its president. However, the president may not dissolve the Legislative Yuan while martial law or an emergency order is in effect. Following the dissolution of the Legislative Yuan, an election for legislators will be held within 60 days. The new Legislative Yuan is to convene of its own accord within ten days after the results of the said election have been confirmed, and the term of the said Legislative Yuan will be figured from that date.

Following the dissolution of the Legislative Yuan by the president and prior to the inauguration of its newly elected members, the Legislative Yuan will be regarded as in recess.

The Office of the President
Administration

The secretary-general to the president takes general charge of the affairs of the Office of the President and directs and supervises staff members. The president is assisted by two deputy secretaries-general.

The bureaus and offices under the Office of the President perform the following functions: The First Bureau 第一局 is in charge of promulgation of laws and decrees, drafting and safekeeping of confidential documents, and other general political affairs, while the bureau director also serves as chancellor of the national seal; the Second Bureau 第二局 is in charge of information systems and transmission of documents; the Third Bureau 第三局 is in charge of protocol and awarding honors, making and distributing official seals, publications, and other administrative and technical affairs; the Code Office 機要室 is in charge of telegraphic correspondence and national archives; the Office of the Guards 侍衛室 is in charge of security. The Department of Public Affairs 公共事務室, set up in January 1996, is in charge of public relations.

Subordinate Offices

There are four institutions under the direct administrative supervision of the Office of the President: Academia Sinica, Academia Historica, the National Unification Council, and the National Security Council.

The Academia Sinica 中央研究院, the leading research institution in the ROC, was established in Nanking on June 9, 1928. Its two basic missions are to conduct scientific research and to direct, coordinate, and promote scientific research throughout the ROC. Although it is a unit of the government, the Academia Sinica enjoys virtually independent status. The most important body within the Academia Sinica is the Assembly of Members 院士會議. The members, commonly known as "academicians" 院士, are elected for life from among Chinese scholars of distinction. On July 9, 1998, 23 new members—ten from outside the ROC and 13 based in Taiwan— were elected, marking the first time that Taiwan-based scholars outnumbered those from overseas. The 23 new members brought the total number of academicians to 197. Their duties include formulating national research policy and pursuing specific research at the request of the government. As of mid-1998, the Academia Sinica had 24 institutes, six of them still preparatory offices, including the two newly established Institute of Bioagriculture and Institute of Linguistics. The Academia Sinica is staffed by approximately 800 full-time research fellows.

The Academia Historica 國史館 is responsible for preserving documents and conducting research in modern Chinese history, particularly that of the republican period. The academy has a collection of 7.5 million publications and national records, mainly from the Office of the President, the Executive Yuan, provincial and local governments, plus some personal and other archives. Most of the records are open to the staff of Academia Historica and researchers.

Founded in 1990, the National Unification Council 國家統一委員會 now consists of 32 leaders in various fields, from both the government and the private sector, organized into task groups. The NUC recommends national unification policies to the president, helps the government to devise a national unification framework, and builds consensus at all levels of society and in all political parties concerning the issue of national unification. The NUC has already approved the *Guidelines for National Unification* 國家統一綱領, which are the highest directives governing ROC mainland policy.

The National Security Council 國家安全會議, established in 1967 and chaired by the president, is an advisory body to the president. The main functions of the National Security Council and its subsidiary organ, the National Security Bureau 國家安全局, are to determine the ROC's national security policies and to assist in planning the ROC's security strategy.

The National Assembly

The National Assembly 國民大會 is more limited in scope than the parliament or congress of a Western democracy. In the Republic of China, the role of "parliament" is jointly filled by the National Assembly and the Legislative Yuan.

Six functions of the National Assembly were as follows: (1) to elect the vice president when the said office becomes vacant; (2) to recall the president and the vice president; (3) to pass a resolution on the impeachment of the president or vice president instituted by the Legislative Yuan; (4) to amend the Constitution; (5) to vote in the exercise of its rights of referendum on proposed constitutional amendments submitted by the Legislative Yuan; (6) to exercise the power of consent to confirm the appointment of personnel nominated by the president of the ROC.

The president may issue a notice of convocation when the National Assembly is to exercise its powers prescribed in items (4) and (5), or when requested by no less than two-fifths of its members. The Speaker of the National Assembly may convoke a session to institute the recall or impeachment of the president or vice-president. The National Assembly is required to implement initiatives and referendums decided by the people of the Republic of China in accordance with Article 17 of the Constitution.

Another unique power of the National Assembly is spelled out in Article 4 of the Constitution: "The territory of the Republic of China within its existing national boundaries shall not be altered except by resolution of the National Assembly."

The assembly is led by a Speaker and Deputy Speaker, both of whom are chosen by the Assembly from among its delegates.

Delegates

Delegates to the National Assembly are elected according to Article 1 of the *Additional Articles of the Constitution* without being subject to the restrictions in Articles 26, 28 and 135 of the Constitution. In 1996, an election for the Third National Assembly was held in accordance with the old version of the *Additional Articles of the Constitution of the Republic of China*. Of the 334 members elected, 234 delegates were from the Taiwan area, with an additional 80 members representing a nationwide constituency and 20 representing overseas Chinese.

The four-year tenure for the Third National Assembly began on May 20, 1996. Former Assembly Speaker Fredrick Chien 錢復 was nominated by President Lee Teng-hui on December 3, 1998, as the new president of the Control Yuan, and Shieh Lung-sheng 謝隆盛, former Deputy Speaker of the Assembly, was called upon to accept a new post. Su Nan-cheng 蘇南成 was elected Speaker of the National Assembly in a by-election on January 13, 1999 and Chen Ching-jang 陳金讓 was elected Deputy Speaker. On September 4, 1999, the Third National Assembly passed constitutional amendments which significantly changed the election and composition of the Fourth and Fifth National Assemblies. As a result of the controversy surrounding the tenure extension for members of the ROC's Third National Assembly, Su resigned in late September and Chen became the acting speaker.

The amendments on election procedures and composition were intended to make the National Assembly further reflect popular opinion. However, the Council of Grand Justices ruled the amendments invalid, because the deputies cast secret ballots. Claiming that the grand justices have no right to make this decision, the DPP wanted to dissolve the National Assembly immediately and establish a unicameral legislative system. With the support of the KMT and the New Party, the deputies passed yet another series of Constitution amendments on April 24, 2000. The Third National Assembly will be terminated on May 19, 2000, and a 300-member non-standing body will be elected on a proportional-representation system, according to laws to be passed by the Legislative Yuan. The National Assemblys functions will be limited to vote on Constitution amendments, presidential impeachment, or alternation of the national boundaries, as proposed by the Legislative Yuan. Other powers, such as hearing the presidents State of Nation Report and approving presidential appointments to the Judicial, Examination, and Control Yuans, will be transferred to the Legislative Yuan.

Five Government Branches

The ROC Constitution provides for a central government with five "yuan" (branches)—the Executive Yuan, the Legislative Yuan (Legislature), the Judicial Yuan (Judiciary), the Examination Yuan, and the Control Yuan.

Executive Yuan

The Executive Yuan 行政院 has a president, usually referred to as the premier of the ROC; a vice president; a number of ministers and chairmen of commissions; and five to seven ministers-without-portfolio. The president of the Executive Yuan is appointed by the president of the Republic. If the president of the Executive Yuan resigns or if his office becomes vacant, his functions are temporarily exercised by the vice president of the Executive Yuan. The vice president of the Executive Yuan, ministers, and chairmen are appointed by the president of the Republic on the recommendation of the president of the Executive Yuan. In addition to supervising the operations of the various subordinate agencies of the Executive Yuan, the president of the Executive Yuan is also responsible for the following: performing the duties of the president of the Republic in the event of vacancies in both the presidency and the vice presidency (this caretaker duty is limited to three months); presenting administrative policies and reports to the Legislature and responding, either orally or in writing, to the interpellations of legislators; countersigning laws and decrees proclaimed by the president of the Republic; and requesting, with the approval of the president, the Legislative Yuan to reconsider its resolutions.

Tang Fei 唐飛 was appointed to serve as the president of the ROC's Executive Yuan beginning May 20, 2000.

There are three levels of subordinate organizations under the Executive Yuan: the Executive Yuan Council 行政院院會; executive organizations, i.e., the eight ministries, the Mongolian and Tibetan Affairs Commission 蒙藏委員會 and the Overseas Chinese Affairs Commission 僑務委員會; and subordinate departments, including the Directorate General of Budget, Accounting, and Statistics 主計處, the Government Information Office 新聞局, and other special commissions and ad hoc committees.

Executive Yuan Council

The Executive Yuan Council is a policy-making organization that comprises the president of the Executive Yuan, who presides over its meetings, the vice president of the Executive Yuan, ministers-without-portfolio, the heads of the ROC's eight ministries, and the heads of the Mongolian and Tibetan Affairs Commission as well as the Overseas Chinese Affairs Commission. According to Article 58 of the Constitution, the Council discusses and decides on statutory and budgetary bills and bills concerning martial law, amnesty, declarations of war, conclusion of peace or treaties, and other important affairs, which are to be submitted to the Legislature, as well as matters of common concern to the various ministries and commissions. The Council may invite heads of other organizations under the Executive Yuan to attend council meetings and answer any questions that may arise pertaining to affairs under their jurisdiction. The secretary-general and the deputy secretary-general also attend the meetings; however, they have no vote.

Ministries and Other Organizations

There are eight ministries under the Executive Yuan. They are the ministries of the Interior 內政, Foreign Affairs 外交, National Defense 國防, Finance 財政, Education 教育, Justice 法務, Economic Affairs 經濟, and Transportation and Communications 交通.

In addition to the Mongolian and Tibetan Affairs Commission and the Overseas Chinese Affairs Commission, a number of commissions and subordinate organizations have been formed with the resolution of the Executive Yuan Council and the Legislature to meet new demands and handle new affairs. Examples include the Environmental Protection Administration 環境保護署, which was set up in 1987 as public awareness of pollution control rose; the Mainland Affairs Council 大陸委員會, which was established in 1990 to handle the thawing of relations between Taiwan and the Chinese mainland; the Fair Trade Commission 公平交易委員會, which was established in 1992 to promote a fair trade system; and the Consumer Protection Commission 消費者保護委員會, which was set up in July 1994 to study and review basic policies on consumer protection.

Since 1995, even more commissions have been set up to provide a wider scope of services: the Public Construction Commission 公共工程委員會 was set up in July 1995, the Council of Aboriginal Affairs 原住民委員會 in December 1996, and the National Council on Physical Fitness and Sports 體育委員會 in July 1997.

Relationship with the Legislative Yuan

The Executive Yuan has to present the Legislative Yuan with an annual policy statement and a report on administration. When the Legislative Yuan is in session, its members have the right to interpellate the premier, ministers, and chairmen of commissions of the Executive Yuan.

If the Legislative Yuan disagrees with an important policy of the Executive Yuan, it may, by resolution, request the Executive Yuan to alter it. Confronted with the Legislative Yuan's resolution, the Executive Yuan may, with the approval of the president of the Republic, request the Legislature's reconsideration. If after reconsideration one-half of the attending members of the Legislature uphold the original resolution, the premier must either abide by the same or tender his resignation. Similar procedures apply, if the Executive Yuan deems a resolution on a statutory, budgetary, or treaty bill passed by the Legislative Yuan difficult to execute. The Executive Yuan shall, three months prior to the end of each fiscal year, present to the Legislative Yuan the budgetary bill for the following fiscal year.

With the signatures of more than one-third of the total number of Legislative Yuan members, the Legislative Yuan may propose a no-confidence vote against the president of the Executive Yuan. Seventy-two hours after the no-confidence motion is made, an open-ballot vote is to be taken within 48 hours. Should more than one-half of the total number of Legislative Yuan members approve the motion, the president of the Executive Yuan must tender his resignation within ten days and at the same time may request that the president dissolve the Legislative Yuan. Should the no-confidence motion fail, the Legislative Yuan may not initiate another no-confidence motion against the same president of the Executive Yuan for one year.

Relationship with the Judicial Yuan

If problems arise in the enforcement of provincial self-governance regulations, the president of the Executive Yuan organizes a committee with the presidents of the Legislative Yuan, Judicial Yuan, Examination Yuan, and Control Yuan in a joint effort to solve them.

Meanwhile, after the constitutional amendment completed in July 1997, the proposed budget submitted by the Judicial Yuan may not be eliminated or reduced by the Executive Yuan,

which is noteworthy and significant. The Executive Yuan may instead indicate its opinions on the budget and include it in the central government's proposed budgetary bill for submission to the Legislative Yuan for deliberation.

Relationship with the Examination Yuan

Public functionaries to be appointed by the Executive Yuan must be qualified by examinations held by the Examination Yuan.

Relationship with the Control Yuan

The Control Yuan has the authority to request the Executive Yuan and its ministries and subordinate organizations to submit original orders issued for perusal.

The Control Yuan may set up a number of committees to investigate the activities of the Executive Yuan and its ministries and subordinate organizations to determine whether they are guilty of violation of the law or dereliction of duty. It may propose corrective measures and forward them to the Executive Yuan and the agencies concerned.

The Executive Yuan shall, within four months after the end of each fiscal year, present final accounts of revenues and expenditures to the Control Yuan for auditing.

Prosecutorial Arm

The Ministry of Justice 法務部 handles legal affairs for the Executive Yuan, including prosecution procedures, investigation of crimes, and management of prisons and rehabilitation programs. It consists of departments of Prosecutorial Affairs 檢察司, Corrections 矯正司, Rehabilitation and Social Protection 保護司, and Legal Affairs 法律事務司. The Investigation Bureau 調查局 is also under its jurisdiction.

Legislative Yuan

The Legislative Yuan 立法院 (Legislature) is the highest legislative organ of the state, comprising popularly elected representatives who serve for three years and are eligible for reelection. Elections for the Fourth Legislative Yuan were held in December 1998. Amendments made in 1999 will extend terms to four years beginning with the Fifth Legislative Yuan.

Functions and Powers

In accordance with the Constitution, the Legislature has the following functions and powers:

- General legislative power: The Legislature exercises legislative power on behalf of the people. The term "law" as used in the Constitution denotes any legislative bill passed by the Legislature and promulgated by the president of the Republic.

- Confirmation of emergency orders: Emergency orders and measures proclaimed by the president in the case of an imminent threat to national security or a serious financial or economic crisis during the recess of the Legislature are presented to the Legislature for confirmation within ten days of issuance. Should the president issue an emergency order after dissolving the Legislative Yuan, the Legislative Yuan is to convene of its own accord within three days and has seven days to decide whether to ratify the order.

- Hearing reports on administration and revision of government policy: The Executive Yuan presents to the Legislative Yuan a statement of its administrative policies and a report on its administration. If the Legislative Yuan does not concur in any important policy of the Executive Yuan, it may, by resolution, request the Executive Yuan to alter such a policy.

- Examination of budgetary bills and audit reports: The Legislative Yuan has the power to decide by resolution upon budgetary bills, which the Executive Yuan is required to present to the Legislative Yuan three months before the beginning of each fiscal year. The auditor-general, within three months after presentation by the Executive Yuan of the final accounts of revenues and expenditures, completes the auditing thereof in accordance with the law and submits an auditing report to the Legislative Yuan.

- Right of consent: The presidents of the Control, Examination and Judical Yuan are nominated and, with the consent of the Legislative Yuan, appointed by the president of the Republic.

- Amendment of the Constitution: Upon the proposal of one-fourth of the members of the Legislative Yuan, and also by a resolution of three-fourths of the members present at a meeting having a quorum of three-fourths of the members of the Yuan, a bill to amend the Constitution may be drawn up and submitted to the National Assembly for deliberation.

- Settlement of disputes concerning self-governance: The Legislature settles any disputes over items and matters of self-governance in provinces, special municipalities, counties/cities, or other administrative units.

DPP legislators discuss the proposed central government budget at the Legislative Yuan in May 1999.
(Photo by the Central News Agency)

Meanwhile, in accordance with the *Additional Articles of the Constitution of the Republic of China*, the Legislature has been given the additional power to institute impeachment proceedings against the president or vice president of the Republic. Impeachment of the president or vice president for treason or rebellion will be initiated upon the agreement of more than two-thirds of all members of the Legislative Yuan after being proposed by more than one-half of the legislators, whereupon the resolution will be submitted to the National Assembly. Should such a motion of impeachment be passed by a two-thirds majority of all delegates to the National Assembly, the party impeached will forthwith be dismissed from office.

Election and Tenure of Office

According to Article 4 of the *Additional Articles of the Constitution of the Republic of China*, beginning with the Fourth Legislative Yuan, the Legislative Yuan is to have 225 members, who are elected in accordance with the following provisions, the restrictions in Article 64 of the Constitution notwithstanding. First, one hundred and sixty-eight members are to be elected from the Special Municipalities, counties, and cities in the free area. At least one member is to be elected in each county and city. Second, four members each are to be elected from among the lowland and highland aborigines in the free area. Third, eight members are to be elected from among the Chinese citizens who reside abroad. Fourth, forty-one members are to be elected from the nationwide constituency.

Members for the seats set forth in the third and fourth items of the preceding paragraph are to be elected according to a formula for proportional representation among political parties. Where the number of seats for each Special Municipality, county, and city as set forth in the first item, and for each political party as set forth in the third and fourth items, is not less than five and not more than ten, one seat will be reserved for a female candidate. Where the number exceeds ten, one seat out of each additional ten is to be reserved for a female candidate.

Procedures pertaining to the election of members are conducted openly by universal, equal, and direct suffrage, which is also by single and secret ballot. The election is completed three months prior to the expiration of the current term. If the voters of a member's precinct feel that their elected representative has not duly performed his or her function, they may, after the member has been in office for six months, file a petition for recall (Article 133 of the Constitution and Article 40 of the *Public Officials Election and Recall Law* 公職人員選舉罷免法).

The Council of the Grand Justices overruled the 1999 amendment, which extended the members' tenure until June 30, 2002. Although there were debates on the validity of this ruling, an election of the Legislative will be held at the end of 2001.

Immunity and Restrictions

According to Article 73 of the Constitution, "No member of the Legislature shall be held responsible outside the Yuan for opinions expressed or votes cast in the Yuan." This is to protect members from outside threats or disturbances, so that they can express their views and cast ballots freely.

According to Article 4 of the *Additional Articles of the Constitution of the Republic of China*, no member of the Legislative Yuan may, except in case of *flagrante delicto*, be arrested or detained without the permission of the Legislative Yuan when that body is in session. The provisions of Article 74 of the Constitution shall cease to apply.

Article 75 of the Constitution reads:"No member of the Legislature shall concurrently hold a government post." This provision is quite different from that which functions in other cabinet systems. Its purpose is the complete separation of legislative from executive powers to avoid a monopolization of power by members of the Legislature.

Organization and Functions

The Legislature operates through sessions of the Yuan, committees, and the secretariat. The

Yuan holds two sessions each year and convenes of its own accord. The first session lasts from February to the end of May, and the second from September to the end of December. Whenever necessary, a session may be prolonged. An extraordinary session may be held at the request of no less than one-fourth of its members. Regular sittings of the Legislature require a quorum of one-third of the total membership. Unless otherwise stipulated in the Constitution, resolutions at sittings of the Legislature are adopted by a simple majority vote. In case of a tie, the chairman casts the deciding vote.

In exercising the power of consent in accordance with Article 104 of the Constitution, the Legislative Yuan, after hearing the report of the committee of the whole Yuan, may put the matter to vote. The chairman is elected by and from among the members present at a meeting of the committee of the whole Yuan.

The Legislative Yuan has the following ten standing committees: Home and Border Affairs 內政及邊政委員會, Foreign and Overseas Chinese Affairs 外交及僑政委員會, National Defense 國防委員會, Economics 經濟委員會, Finance 財政委員會, Budget 預算委員會, Education 教育委員會, Transportation and Communications 交通委員會, Judiciary 司法委員會, and Organic Laws 法制委員會. Each of the committees is composed of not more than 18 members, and no member may serve on more than one committee. Registration for committee membership may not be withdrawn. The Legislature has also set up the following five special committees: Discipline 紀律委員會, Rules 程序委員會, Accounts 經費稽核委員會, Publications 公報指導委員會, and Constitutional Amendment 修憲委員會.

Judicial Yuan

The Judicial Yuan 司法院 (Judiciary) is the highest judicial organ of the state. According to Article 5 of the *Additional Articles,* the Judicial Yuan is to have 15 grand justices. The 15 grand justices, including the president and the vice president of the Judicial Yuan to be selected from among them, will be nominated and, with the consent of the Legislative Yuan. appointed

by the president of the Republic. This will take effect from the year 2003 and the provisions of Article 79 of the Constitution will no longer apply. The subordinate organs of the Judicial Yuan are the Supreme Court, the high courts, the district courts, the Administrative Court, and the Commission on the Disciplinary Sanctions of Public Functionaries. The Judiciary exercises administrative supervision of the ROC court system while enforcing compliance by ROC court personnel with constitutionally mandated structures for juridical independence from the other branches of government.

The Council of Grand Justices

The sixth Council of Grand Justices 大法官會議, comprising 16 members, assumed office on October 3, 1994, following confirmation by the National Assembly. The grand justices will serve nine-year terms. However, according to Article 5 of the *Additional Articles* promulgated in July 1997, each grand justice of the Judicial Yuan is to serve a term of eight years, regardless of the order of appointment to office, and cannot serve a consecutive term. The grand justices serving as president and vice president of the Judicial Yuan do not enjoy the guarantee of an eight-year term.

Among the grand justices to be nominated by the president in the year 2003, eight members, including the president and the vice president of the Judicial Yuan, will serve for four years. The remaining grand justices will serve for eight years. The provisions of the preceding paragraph regarding term of office will not apply.

The Council of Grand Justices interprets the Constitution and unifies the interpretation of laws and ordinances. The Council meets thrice a week and holds additional meetings as necessary. Oral proceedings may be held whenever the need arises. After an interpretation of the Constitution or unified interpretation of a law is made, the Judiciary publishes the text of the interpretation, the reasons supporting it, and dissenting opinions, if any. The petitioner and persons concerned are also notified.

Interpretation of the Constitution

From 1948 to October 15, 1999, the Council of Grand Justices rendered 491 interpretations of

the Constitution at the request of government agencies, individuals, juridical persons and political parties. Constitutional interpretations are made when there are doubts or disputes concerning:
• the application of the Constitution;
• the constitutionality of laws, regulations or decrees; and
• the constitutionality of laws governing provincial or county self-governance, and laws and regulations promulgated by provincial or county governments.

Unified Interpretation of Laws and Ordinances

A petition for a unified interpretation of a law or ordinance may be filed with the Council of Grand Justices if:
• a government agency, when applying a law or ordinance, has an interpretation that is different from that already expressed by itself or another government organ, unless it is legally bound to obey the expressed opinion or has the authority to revise it;
• an individual, a juridical person, or a political party whose rights have been infringed upon and who or which believes that the final decision of the court of last resort was based on an interpretation of the applicable law or regulation that is different from that previously adopted in precedents by other courts, but such requests will not be accepted if the petitioner has not yet exhausted all judicial remedies or the opinion adopted in an earlier decision has been altered by a later one.

The Constitutional Court

In December 1993, the Judiciary formally established a Constitutional Court 憲法法庭 in accordance with Article 13 of the old version of the *Additional Articles of the Constitution* and the revised *Organic Law of the Judicial Yuan* 司法院組織法 to adjudicate cases concerning the dissolution of political parties that have violated the Constitution. The Constitutional Court is composed of the grand justices and presided over by its most senior member.

The Ministry of the Interior may, as the agency overseeing political parties, petition the Constitutional Court for the dissolution of a political party whose objectives and activities are found to endanger the existence of the ROC or its free and democratic constitutional order.

Commission on the Disciplinary Sanctions of Functionaries

The Control Yuan may impeach a public functionary for malfeasance, dereliction of duty, or any other neglect of duty, or if the head of any of the various branches, ministries or commissions or the highest local administrative head requests a disciplinary measure against a public functionary for the same reasons. The Commission on the Disciplinary Sanctions of Functionaries 公務員懲戒委員會, under the Judicial Yuan, exercises jurisdiction over such cases.

The committee comprises 9 to 15 senior members, one of whom serves as the chairman. Cases are decided without any outside interference. The committee orders the impeached functionary to submit a written reply within a prescribed period of time and, when it deems necessary, may summon him to appear before the committee to defend himself. Such a conference is not open to the public and its proceedings are kept strictly confidential.

There are six disciplinary measures which the committee may order: dismissal, suspension from office, demotion, reduction of salary, demerit, and reprimand. Only dismissal and reprimand are applicable to political appointees.

The ROC Court System

The judicial hierarchy in the Republic of China comprises three levels: district courts and their branches at the lowest level that hear civil and criminal cases in the first instance; high courts and their branches at the intermediate level that hear appeals, as the court of second instance, against judgments of district courts or their branches; and the Supreme Court at the highest appellate level which reviews judgments by lower courts as to their compliance with or violation of pertinent laws or regulations. Thus, issues of fact are decided in the first and second instances, while only issues of law are considered in the third instance. However, there are exceptions to this "three-level and three-instance" system. Criminal cases relating to rebellion, treason, and offenses against friendly relations with foreign states are handled by high courts as the court of first instance; and appeals may be filed with the Supreme Court.

District Courts

There are 19 district courts 地方法院 in the Taiwan area. Each has a president, appointed from among the judges, who takes charge of the administrative work of the court. Each court is divided into civil 民事庭, criminal 刑事庭, and summary divisions 民刑事簡易庭. Currently there are 44 summary divisions in the Taiwan area to adjudicate cases that may be disposed of in a prompt and simple manner in comparison to regular proceedings. Summary proceedings are conducted by a single judge in the first instance. Appeals may be filed with the civil or criminal division of the district court for review by a three-judge panel in the second instance.

Specialized divisions may also be set up by district courts to deal with juvenile, family, traffic, financial, and labor cases as well as motions to set aside rulings on the violations of the *Statute of the Maintenance of Social Order* 社會秩序維護法. Cases to be tried and decided by a district court are heard before a single judge, though more important cases may be heard before three judges sitting in council.

High Courts

At present there is one high court 高等法院 in Taipei serving all of Taiwan including the Pescadores, with four branch courts in Taichung, Tainan, Kaohsiung, and Hualien. In the part of Fukien Province under the control of the ROC there is the Kinmen Branch Court of the Fujian High Court 福建高等法院金門分院, which exercises jurisdiction over cases of appeal against judgments or rulings in Kinmen County and Lienchiang County.

A senior judge of the High Court is appointed to serve concurrently as president of the court to take charge of the administrative work of the court and to supervise the administrative work of its subordinate organs.

The High Court is divided into civil, criminal, as well as specialized divisions dealing with juvenile, traffic and labor cases. Each division is composed of a presiding judge and associates. Cases to be tried and decided by the High Court are heard before three judges sitting in council. However, one of the judges may conduct the preliminary proceedings alone.

The High Court and its branches exercise jurisdiction over the following cases:

- civil, criminal, and election cases of appeal against judgments of district courts or their branches as a court of the first instance;
- motions to set aside rulings of district courts or their branches;
- criminal cases relating to rebellion, treason, and offenses against friendly relations with foreign states, acting as a court of the first instance; and
- other lawsuits prescribed by law.

The Supreme Court

Although it lies under the administrative supervision of the Judiciary, the entire ROC court system has juridical independence in criminal and civil matters of law. The Supreme Court 最高法院 is the final level of appeal in the ROC court system.

The Supreme Court has a president, who is responsible for the administrative work of the Court and acts concurrently as a judge. The Supreme Court is divided into seven civil divisions and ten criminal divisions. An appeal may be made to the Supreme Court only on grounds that the decision made is in violation of a law or ordinance. Since the Supreme Court does not decide questions of fact, documentary proceedings are the rule, while oral proceedings are the exception. Cases before the Supreme Court are tried and decided by five judges sitting in council.

The Supreme Court exercises jurisdiction over the following kinds of cases:

- appeals against judgments in civil and criminal cases rendered by high courts or their branches as court of second instance;
- appeals against judgments of high courts or their branches in criminal cases as court of first instance;

- motions to set aside rulings of high courts or their branches in civil and criminal cases;
- appeals against or motions to set aside rulings of district courts or their branches as court of second instance in civil summary proceedings; and
- cases of extraordinary appeal.

The Administrative Court

The Administrative Court 行政法院 has a decidedly different sphere of juridical authority from that of the other courts in the system. Any person who deems that his rights are violated by an administrative action rendered by a government agency may institute administrative proceedings before the Administrative Court. He is entitled to this right if he objects to the decision on an administrative appeal submitted by him in accordance with the *Law of Administrative Appeal* 行政訴訟法, or if no decision is rendered over three months after the submission of his administrative appeal, or over two months of extension after the prescribed period for decision has expired. An administrative action which exceeds the legal authority of the government agency that rendered it or which results from an abuse of power is considered unlawful.

In administrative proceedings, the plaintiff is a private person and the defendant is a governmental agency, both being equally bound by the adjudication of the Administrative Court. Cases before the Administrative Court are tried and decided by five judges sitting in council. The Administrative Court decides questions of both fact and law; it may make investigations and hold oral proceedings. Since the cases have gone through appeal proceedings before the institution of administrative proceedings, adjudication by the Administrative Court is final. However, where there are legitimate grounds, retrial proceedings are permissible. Should a decision by the Administrative Court set aside or alter the original administrative action or decision, under no circumstances will such a decision be less favorable to the plaintiff than the original action or decision.

Judicial Reform

Significant reforms will be carried out to revamp the ROC judicial system and ensure fair trials. A consensus on the reform measures was reached in the National Conference on Judicial Reform held in July 1999.

One of the most significant reforms to emerge from this meeting is that experts can be brought into Taiwan's courts to assist in the trying of cases which involve family affairs, juvenile crimes, labor and medical disputes, and intellectual property rights.

Also, assessors may be called into court on major criminal and administrative cases. Assessors can assist presiding judges who may not necessarily be equipped with a technical expertise in areas outside the legal domain.

A framework for transforming the role of the judicial branch was reached. The Judiciary will adopt a short-term reform plan, under which it will have civil, criminal, constitutional and administrative courts. A long-term reform plan will eventually be implemented to seat 13 to 15 grand justices in the Judiciary. They will be responsible for conducting civil, criminal, and administrative litigations, as well as for handling cases on disciplining public functionaries, dissolving political parties, and interpreting the Constitution. This overhauling of the Judiciary is expected to boost public confidence in the independence of the judicial system.

Examination Yuan

The Examination Yuan 考試院 is responsible for the examination, employment, and management of all civil service personnel in the Republic of China. Specifically, the Examination Yuan oversees all examination-related matters; all matters relating to qualification screening, security of tenure, pecuniary aid in case of death, and the retirement of civil servants; and all legal matters relating to the employment, discharge, performance evaluation, scale of salaries, promotion, transfer, commendation, and award of civil servants.

The examination system is applicable to all Chinese civil servants, high- or low-ranking, appointed or elected. The system is also applicable to Chinese and foreign specialized professionals and technicians. The examination function, being exercised solely by the Examination Yuan at the level of the central government, is separated from the executive power and thereby free from partisan influence.

Organization and Functions

The Examination Yuan has a president, a vice president, and 17 members, all of whom are appointed for six-year terms by the president of the ROC with the approval of the Legislative Yuan. The Examination Yuan consists of a council, a secretariat, the Ministry of Examination 考選部, the Ministry of Civil Service 銓敘部, the Civil Service Protection and Training Commission 公務員保障暨培訓委員會, and the Supervisory Board for the Civil Servant Pension Fund 公職人員退休撫卹基金監理委員會. It also supervises the operations of the Central Personnel Administration 人事行政局 established under the Executive Yuan in 1967.

The Council of the Examination Yuan 考試委員會 is a policymaking organ that decides on all significant matters within the jurisdiction of the Examination Yuan. It is composed of the president, vice president, and 17 members of the Yuan, the minister of examination, and the minister of civil service.

Various examination boards are formed each year under the chairmanship of either the president, the vice president, or a member of the Examination Yuan. Members of examination boards formulate questions for and grade the examinations. They also determine the number of successful candidates in each examination. In addition, committees may be set up to facilitate the administration of examination and personnel projects.

The Ministry of Examination oversees all civil service, professional, and technological examinations. The Ministry of Civil Service is in charge of the government personnel system throughout the nation.

Examinations

The two main types of government examinations in the ROC are Civil Service Examinations 公務人員考試 and Examinations for Professionals and Technologists 專門職業及技術人員考試. Civil Service Examinations are divided into the following types:

• Senior-grade Civil Service Examinations 高等考試: Divided into Level I, for holders of Ph.D.; Level II, for holders of M.A. and M.S. degrees; and Level III, for holders of B.A. and B.S. degrees and for people who have passed the Senior Qualifying Examinations or those who passed the Junior-grade Civil Service Examinations at least three years prior to taking the exam;

• Junior-grade Civil Service Examinations 普通考試: Primarily for graduates of senior high schools or senior vocational schools and secondarily for those who passed the Junior Qualifying Examinations or those who passed Special Examination D at least three years prior to taking the exam;

• Special Examination A 特種考試（一等）: Corresponding to the Senior-grade Civil Service Examination Level I;

• Special Examination B 特種考試（二等）: Corresponding to the Senior-grade Civil Service Examination Level II;

• Special Examination C 特種考試（三等）: Corresponding to the Senior-grade Civil Service Examination Level III;

• Special Examination D 特種考試（四等）: Corresponding to the Junior-grade Civil Service Examination;

• Special Examination E 特種考試（五等）: Primarily for ROC citizens 18 years of age or older;

• Promotion Examinations 升等考試; and

• Qualifying Examinations 檢定考試.

Examinations for Professionals and Technologists are divided into the following types:

• Junior Examinations 普通考試;

• Senior Examinations 高等考試; and

• Special Examinations 特種考試: including tests for seafarers, harbor pilots, ship surveyors, crew of fishing boats, ship radiogram operators, doctors of Chinese medicine, and nutritionists.

The Ministry of Examination also screens qualifications for candidates running for elected posts, military personnel transferring to the civil service, and Chinese nationals and non-nationals for their technical skills.

Examinations for senior and junior civil servants are conducted every year, every other year, or whenever necessary. Categories of personnel needed, subjects to be tested, and dates are announced by the Ministry of Examination two months before the examination.

Civil Service

There were 602,396 civil servants in the ROC at the end of 1998. As a group, ROC civil servants are well-educated, with 65.8 percent holding college degrees or higher. As for gender, the majority—59.84 percent—were male, a 0.24 percent growth over the previous year. However, the ratio of males to females passing the civil service examinations over the last six years is 35:65.

Unlike the political appointees under whom they serve, civil servants are classified into senior (grades 10-14), intermediate (grades 6-9), or junior (grades 1-5) levels. The 14-grade scheme for administrative officials is designed to reflect an employee's abilities, experience, and seniority. One's salary increases with grade and civil servants at grade 14 can earn up to five times that of those at grade 1. Every year civil servants are reviewed by their superiors. In general, those servants who receive good reviews increase in grade annually. However, one must either pass a difficult civil service exam or be specially recommended by one's superior to enter grades six and ten.

Pay and Benefits

Civil servants receive a salary on a monthly basis, and also receive annual merit pay and allowances for special duties. The government offers subsidies for the education of its employees and their dependents, and for special and emergency financial needs, such as maternity, marriage, funerals, sickness, hospitalization, and injury while on official duty. Health insurance is also available to all government workers under the National Health Insurance program (see Chapter 15, Public Health).

Retirement from public service may be either voluntary or mandatory. Voluntary retirement is approved if one has reached the age of 60 and served in a government agency for at least five years or, for those under the age of 60, if one has served for 25 full years. Mandatory retirement applies to a civil servant who has served in a government agency for more than five years and has reached the age of 65 or is mentally or physically unable to continue to fulfill his or her duties.

Pensions are calculated on the basis of base pay and years of service. A pension payment may be disbursed either in one lump sum, for those who have reached the age of 60 and served between five to 15 years, or on a monthly basis, for those who have served more than 15 years and reached the age of 60, or who have served 25 years and reached the age of 50. In recent years, about 10,000 civil servants have applied for retirement annually, most of whom have opted to receive a monthly pension payment (61 percent in 1998). In 1998 alone, the government spent approximately US$4.7 billion, or a hefty 13.6 percent of its total annual expenditures, on civil service pensions. This heavy burden on public finances has been significantly alleviated, however, with the implementation of a new pension policy which requires each civil servant to contribute part of his or her salary to a pension fund. As of December 1998, the pension fund has accumulated nearly US$3.4 billion.

Compensation for the families of civil servants is provided in the case of death due to disease or accident, or while on official duty.

Control Yuan

The Control Yuan 監察院 is the highest control body of the state, exercising the powers of impeachment, censure, and audit. The Control Yuan was formerly a parliamentary body, with its members elected by provincial and municipal councils. However, constitutional amendments in May 1992 transformed it into a quasi-judicial organization. The new Control Yuan started operations on February 1, 1993. From July 1997 onwards, its power to institute the impeachment against the president and vice president of the

Republic expired after the constitutional amendment, and the Legislative Yuan has been empowered to take over the duty. It now has 29 members, including a president and a vice president, all of whom were nominated and, with the consent of the National Assembly, appointed by the president of the ROC, as stipulated in the *Additional Articles of the Constitution.* The term of office for all members is six years. The president of the Yuan takes overall charge of its affairs and serves as chairman at meetings.

Organization

The Control Yuan Council, which is composed of the president, vice president and 27 other members, is the policymaking body of all the Yuan's significant matters. Meetings are held monthly with the president acting as chairman. The Control Yuan has ten committees that handle cases on domestic affairs, foreign affairs, national defense, finance, economic affairs, education, transportation and communications, judicial affairs, frontier affairs and overseas Chinese affairs. Each Control Yuan member may join three of the ten committees and participate in other committees as a non-voting member. Each committee elects a convener from among its members to handle day-to-day affairs.

Members

Control Yuan members are responsible for correcting government officials at all levels and generally monitoring the government. Members of the Control Yuan must be beyond party affiliation and exercise their powers independently and discharge their responsibilities in accordance with the law. Article 103 of the Constitution also stipulates that "no member of the Control Yuan shall concurrently hold any other public office or engage in any other profession."

Functions

The Constitution defines the Control Yuan as the highest control organ of the Republic. It is empowered to institute impeachment proceedings against a public functionary of the central or local government, except for the president and the vice president of the Republic, if it deems that individual to be guilty of dereliction of duty or violation of law. A decision concerning a motion for impeachment requires the concurrence of nine Control Yuan members other than those who initiated the motion. If the case is passed in the Control Yuan it goes to the appropriate authority for action—the Committee on the Discipline of Public Functionaries in the case of a civil servant, or the Ministry of National Defense for military personnel.

A Control Yuan member may, with the support of three other members, file a written censure against a functionary whose offense he or she feels requires immediate suspension of duty or penalty. Pending legal proceedings, the superior of a censured functionary must deal with the matter in accordance with the *Law on Discipline of Public Functionaries* 公務員懲戒法 within one month of receiving the written censure.

The Control Yuan may investigate the operations of the Executive Yuan and its subordinate organizations and propose corrective measures, which are examined by relevant committees and referred to the ministry or commission concerned. This body must take appropriate action and report to the Control Yuan in writing.

By provision of the *Control Law* 監察法, the people are empowered to initiate proceedings against public functionaries by filing a written complaint with the Control Yuan. The complaint and any supporting evidence is taken into consideration by the member on duty, who will decide on investigation or other appropriate action.

The members of the Control Yuan or their designated personnel may conduct field investigations of public or private organizations based on people's complaints or press reports regarding dereliction of duty or violation of law. They may also initiate investigations.

The Control Yuan exercises its power of audit through its National Audit Office 審計部, which establishes audit departments in provinces and special municipalities, and sets up county and city audit offices. Audit departments or offices may be established in special government agencies, state-run enterprises, or public institutions.

According to the Constitution, the auditor-general is nominated by the president of the Republic and appointed with the consent of the Legislature. He or she is responsible for auditing central government expenditures.

The National Audit Office monitors public affairs, properties, institutions, as well as enterprises in which the state owns at least a 50-percent share. Auditing duties and functions include supervision over the execution of all government organization budgets, approval of receipts and disbursements, investigation of cases concerning irregularities and abuse of power in property and financial administration, evaluation of the efficiency of financial administration, decisions on financial responsibilities, and other auditing functions prescribed by law. The audit agencies also monitor the opening of bids, the awarding of contracts, and proceedings concerning the redemption of bonds, and conduct random inspections of ongoing construction projects.

The Control Yuan also established the Department of Assets Disclosure for Public Functionaries 公職人員財產申報處 in August 1993. In accordance with Article 4 of the *Public Functionary Assets Disclosure Law* 公職人員財產申報法, the Control Yuan receives assets disclosure reports from the president and vice president of the Republic, the presidents and vice presidents of the five Yuan, political appointees, paid advisors to the president of the Republic, elected officials at the level of township magistrates or above, and elected representatives of counties and cities under provincial jurisdiction and higher administrative units.

Provincial Government

A provincial government is the highest administrative organ of local self-governance prescribed by the *Constitution of the Republic of China*. Altogether, the ROC Constitution designates 35 provinces (see map on the inside of the front cover), but there is only one complete province, Taiwan, under the effective control of the ROC. The Fukien Provincial Government, head-

quartered in Kinmen County, enjoys fewer powers than its Taiwan counterpart as some of its powers have been relegated to the Kinmen and Lienchiang county governments.

The Future Role of the Provincial Government

Projects Drawn in the National Development Conference

At the end of 1996, the National Development Conference was convened to achieve consensus within society and draw up a blueprint for development into the next century. In this conference, projects to streamline the provincial government were laid down as the following:

• The functions, operations, and organization of the provincial government should be reorganized and streamlined; a committee to plan and implement these projects should be established; and elections for provincial offices should be suspended starting from the next term.

• Elections for rural township, urban township, and county municipality offices should be suspended, and the heads of these townships and municipalities should be appointed in accordance with the law.

• The offices of deputy magistrate (for counties) and deputy mayor (for provincial municipalities) should be created, and greater power delegated to the county and provincial municipality governments.

• The legislation governing local taxes and the revision of the *Law Governing the Allocation of Government Revenues and Expenditures* 財政收支劃分法 should be completed with all possible speed in order to provide a sound financial base for local governments.

The foregoing projects were made concrete provisions in the constitutional amendment of July 1997, setting the legal foundation for streamlining the Taiwan Provincial Goverment.

The first phase of the plan involved the appointment of a new provincial governor, Chao Shou-po 趙守博, to succeed popularly elected Taiwan Governor James Soong 宋楚瑜, whose

Budget Allocation

All governments from the central down to the county/city levels are required to submit their budgetary bills for review by the legislative body at their respective levels three months before the beginning of each fiscal year. Cities under county jurisdiction and urban and rural townships are required to submit their proposed budgets to their respective representative offices two months in advance.

Funding for these budgets comes mainly from national and local taxes, which are proportionally allocated to each government level in accordance with the *Law Governing the Allocation of Government Revenues and Expenditures* 財政收支劃分法. Each year, the Executive Yuan reviews the financial conditions of each government level and may revise the law to adjust the percentage of tax revenues to be appropriated to the different levels of government. The tax revenues shall, however, account for an appropriate proportion of the fiscal expenditures at each government level, which is also required to maintain a certain proportion of local financial resources. The figures for these two proportions, which are proposed by the Executive Yuan, require the approval of the Legislature.

Under the *Self-governance Law for Provinces and Counties* and the *Municipal Self-governance Law*, the local governments from the provincial level down may increase their revenues by levying taxes or charging fees for specific purposes in the areas under their jurisdiction. The fees may be charged in accordance with pertinent regulations or with the approval of the legislative body or representative conference at that government level.

As the supervisory organ of provincial and municipal self-governance, the Executive Yuan may provide subsidies or financial aid to the said governments with the approval of the Legislature. Such subsidies or financial aid may be cut if the government concerned does not levy taxes or fees which are permitted under the law.

This is also true for governments of counties, provincial municipalities, county municipalities, and urban and rural townships. Such subsidies or aid are provided with the approval of the respective county/city council or representative conference. The provincial government may demand funding for such purposes from counties/cities that are in better financial conditions.

term in office expired in December 1998. As mandated in the 1997 constitutional revisions, gubernatorial elections were indefinitely suspended on December 21 to pave the way for the streamlining of the provincial administration.

Second Phase Streamlining of the Taiwan Provincial Goverment

The streamlining plan entered a second phase on July 1, 1999 with a structural adjustment. The TPG has been downsized and divided into six sections, five offices, two committees and 13 affiliated organizations. The 148 administrative units, 36 health-care organizations and 70 provincial high schools originally listed under the provincial administration have been recategorized as units of the central government. Also, 59 organizations were either eliminated or merged. Altogether, 16 former TPG departments were transformed into the regional offices of the ministries and agencies under the Executive Yuan and 3 into similar offices of bodies under the Examination Yuan. The next year and a half will see positive efforts to restructure the government in Taiwan via such steps as merging departments and reassigning administrative affairs. After January 1, 2001, the organization, functions and administrative affairs of local-level governments will return to normal in accordance with regulations in the *Law on the System of Local Government*, which was passed by the Legislature on January 25, 1999.

The newly revised constitution details the streamlining of the Taiwan Provincial Government. Article 9 of the *Additional Articles* stipulates:

The system of self-government in the provinces and counties will include the following provisions: (1) A province shall have a provincial government of nine members, one of whom shall be the provincial governor. All members

shall be nominated by the president of the Executive Yuan and appointed by the president of the ROC. (2) A province is to have a provincial advisory council made up of a number of members who shall be nominated by the president of the Executive Yuan and appointed by the president of the Republic. (3) A county shall have a county council; members of which shall be elected by the people of the said county. (4) The legislative powers vested in a county are to be exercised by the county council of the said county. (5) A county should have a county government headed by a county magistrate who shall be elected by the people of the said county. (6) The relationship between the central government and the provincial and county governments. (7) A province shall execute the orders of the Executive Yuan and supervise matters governed by the counties.

The modifications of the functions, operations and organization of the Taiwan Provincial Goverment may be specified by law.

The Provisional Statute on the Adjustment of the Function, Business and Organization of the Taiwan Provincial Government

The Provisional Statute on the Adjustment of the Function, Business and Organization of the Taiwan Provincial Government 臺灣省政府功能業務及組織調整暫行條例 was passed in October 1998. The statute calls for suspension on December 21, 1998, of all stipulations pertaining to provincial autonomy in the existing *Self-Governance Law for Provinces and Counties* 省縣自治法. According to the statute, after the provincial government is streamlined, the central government will assume all of its assets and liabilities. The statute stipulates a two-year deadline for the completion of the streamlining process. The downsized provincial administration is to become a branch under the central government. In other words, it will turn into a non-autonomous body. The statute also states that regulations governing the makeup of the streamlined provincial administration should be made by the Executive Yuan and acknowledged by the Legislature. In addition to the statute, two other bills

were passed in 1999 to lay a complete legal framework for the downsizing project. They are a new *Law on Local Government Systems* 地方制度法 and a revised version of the *Law on the Allocation of Government Revenues and Expenditures* 財政收支劃分法.

The Fukien Provincial Government

The ROC government administers only two counties in Fukien Province: Kinmen County, which encompasses Kinmen, and Lienchiang County, which encompasses Matsu. In July 1956, the ROC military assumed full administrative responsibility for these two counties. Military administration lasted until August 7, 1992, when President Lee Teng-hui promulgated the *Statute for the Security and Guidance of Kinmen, Matsu, and the Pratas and Spratlys Areas* 金門、馬祖、東沙、南沙地區安全及輔導條例. The return of local autonomy to Kinmen County and Lienchiang County is part of the ROC's recent constitutional reforms. The residents of these counties now have the same rights and freedoms as all people in Taiwan. However, the *Self-governance Law for Provinces and Counties,* passed in July 1994, does not apply to the Fukien Provincial Government because of the small area under its jurisdiction.

Like its Taiwan counterpart, the Fukien Provincial Government has a council consisting of 11 members who are nominated by the premier and appointed by the president. Fukien Governor Yen Chung-cheng 顏忠誠, who is also a council member, presides over the council when it convenes once in June and once again in December.

The Kinmen County Government is responsible for the administration of six rural and urban townships, which are subdivided into 37 villages and boroughs. There is also a consultation delegation, composed of urban/rural township magistrates and village mayors and local leaders, which holds regular meetings and functions as a county council. Elections for township magistrates and village mayors as well as for representatives of the local and central governments have been held regularly since 1971.

The first popular election for county magistrate took place in November 1993, followed by an election for county council in January 1994.

Lienchiang County contains four urban and rural townships, subdivided into 22 villages and boroughs. Like Kinmen County, Lienchiang County held its first popular election for county magistrate in November 1993, followed by an election for county council in January 1994. This newly elected council took office on February 1, replacing the Provisional Lienchiang County Council set up on November 7, 1992.

The incumbent magistrates of Kinmen and Lienchiang counties are Mr. Chen Shui-tsai 陳水在, and Mr. Liu Li-chun 劉立群 respectively; and the council speakers of these two counties are Mr. Chen Shui-mu 陳水木 and Chen Chen-Ch'ing 陳振清. The election for both county magistrate and county council will be held in December 2001 and January 2002, when their four-year terms will have been completed.

Special Municipality Government

The passage of the *Municipal Self-governance Law* 直轄市自治法 in 1994 provides a clear demarcation of the powers to be exercised by the central and local governments. One distinct move towards local autonomy has been the popular election of Taipei and Kaohsiung city mayors, who, prior to 1994, were nominated by the premier and appointed by the president of the Republic. The mayors serve a four-year term and may be re-elected to a second term in office. They may appoint two deputies, one in charge of political affairs and the other in charge of administrative affairs. The political deputy mayor must resign if the mayor who appointed him is no longer in office.

Taipei City Government

The Taipei City Government 臺北市政府 is headed by Ma Ying-jeou 馬英九, a member of the Kuomintang. It has 21 departments, a secretariat, nine subordinate agencies, the Bank of Taipei, and an administrative office for each district (see Appendix III, ROC Government Directory).

In March 1990, the 16 districts of Taipei City were reorganized into 12 districts: Chungcheng 中正, Nankang 南港, Neihu 內湖, Shihlin 士林, Peitou 北投, Hsinyi 信義, Taan 大安, Sungshan 松山, Chungshan 中山, Wenshan 文山, Tatung 大同, and Wanhua 萬華. These districts encompass a total of 435 boroughs.

Kaohsiung City Government

The mayor of Kaohsiung City, Frank Hsieh 謝長廷, won the December 1998 election. He is a member of the Democratic Progressive Party. The Kaohsiung City Government 高雄市政府 comprises 18 departments, a secretariat, four subordinate agencies, the Bank of Kaohsiung, and an administrative office for each of its 11 districts (see Appendix III, ROC Government Directory).

The 11 districts in Kaohsiung City are Yencheng 鹽埕, Kushan 鼓山, Tsoying 左營, Nantzu 楠梓, Sanmin 三民, Hsinhsing 新興, Chienchin 前金, Lingya 苓雅, Chienchen 前鎮, Chichin 旗津, and Hsiaokang 小港. The districts comprise 466 boroughs.

City Councils

According to Article 15 of the *Municipal Self-governance Law*, the main functions of the Taipei and Kaohsiung city councils are:
• to adopt municipal statutes and regulations;
• to approve the municipal budget;
• to approve the levying of special taxes, temporary taxes and surtaxes in the special municipality;
• to approve the disposal of municipal properties;
• to approve the organic laws of the municipal government and municipally owned businesses;
• to approve proposals made by the city government;
• to screen the auditor's reports on municipal accounts;
• to approve proposals made by the council members;
• to hear petitions from citizens; and
• to carry out other functions as prescribed by law or endowed by laws promulgated by the central government.

The Taipei City Government's on-line service exposition demonstrated the speed and convenience of the new communication system down to the district level.
(Courtesy of the *Taipei Pictorial*)

The term of office for a city councilor is four years. Councils meet for 60 days every six months. A session may be extended by ten days at the request of the mayor, council speaker, or one-third of the council members. In each session, various committees are formed to scrutinize proposals. A councilor may join only one committee.

City Government and Council Relationship

The municipal council sends its resolutions to the city government for implementation. In case of delay or otherwise unsatisfactory performance on the part of the city government, the municipal council may ask for an explanation and, if necessary, request that the Executive Yuan invite pertinent agencies to a consultation for a resolution to be reached.

If a municipal council resolution is considered impracticable, the municipal government may send it back for reconsideration. If two-thirds of the council members present uphold the previous resolution, the municipal government is obliged to abide by their decision.

When the municipal council is in session, the mayor must periodically submit an oral or written report on the city government's administrative

policies, on how the resolutions of the previous session of the municipal council have been carried out, and on other major activities of the municipal government. Directors of departments in the municipal government must also submit reports on matters under their jurisdiction. The members of the council may interpellate the mayor and his or her subordinates. The mayor or officials concerned may be asked by the municipal council to submit special reports on matters of vital concern to the special municipality.

Every year the municipal government submits an administrative budget for the next fiscal year to the municipal council. Details of expected revenues and projected expenditures must be listed, but the council cannot propose spending increases.

County and Provincial Municipality Governments

Taiwan Province has 16 counties 縣: Taipei, Taoyuan, Hsinchu, Miaoli, Taichung, Changhua, Yunlin, Chiayi, Tainan, Kaohsiung, Pingtung, Taitung, Hualien, Nantou, Ilan, and Penghu; and five provincial municipalities 省轄市: Keelung, Hsinchu, Taichung, Chiayi, and Tainan. Each county/city has a county/city government and a county/city council, which is an important check and balance against the county/city government. County governments are headed by magistrates and city governments are headed by mayors popularly elected for up to two four-year terms. County and city councilors are elected by popular vote for four-year terms of office. The number of county or city councilors is determined by the population of each given county; several county and city council seats are reserved for women and aborigines.

City Rankings

There are three levels of cities in the Taiwan area: special municipalities 直轄市, which, like provinces, fall under the direct jurisdiction of the central government; provincial municipalities 省轄市, which are under direct provincial jurisdiction; and county municipalities 縣轄市, which are under direct county jurisdiction.

The Taiwan area presently has two special municipalities: Taipei City, which was elevated to this status in 1967, and Kaohsiung City, which gained similar status in 1979 when its population exceeded one million. The *Municipal Self-governance Law* passed in July 1994 raised this population requirement to 1.5 million.

Under the *Self-governance Law for Provinces and Counties*, an area with a population of over 600,000 and which is politically, economically, and culturally important shall be considered a provincial municipality. There are five such cities directly under Taiwan Province: Keelung City 基隆市, Hsinchu City 新竹市, Taichung City 臺中市, Chiayi City 嘉義市, and Tainan City 臺南市. These cities are equivalent to counties in status.

There are 28 county municipalities in the Taiwan area. According to the *Self-governance Law for Provinces and Counties*, an area with a population of over 150,000 may become a county municipality if it is industrially and commercially developed, and has ample financial resources, convenient transportation links, and complete public facilities. These population requirements are, however, not retroactive.

Special and provincial municipalities are subdivided into districts 區. Each district has an office headed by a chief administrator, who is appointed by the mayor. Districts and county municipalities are subdivided into boroughs 里. Each borough has a borough office headed by a warden who is elected by popular vote for a four-year term. The warden is assisted by an executive officers. Boroughs are subdivided into neighborhoods 鄰, which are the most basic unit of urban governance. Each neighborhood is represented by a chief who is nominated by the borough warden and contracted to a four-year term by the district office.

Cities and Townships under County Governments

Counties are subdivided into county municipalities 縣轄市, rural townships 鄉, or urban townships 鎮, depending on population density. Each city, rural township and urban township has a magistrate who is popularly elected for up to two four-year terms of office. Taiwan currently has 28 county municipalities, 221 rural townships, and 60 urban townships under county jurisdiction.

Villages and Boroughs

Rural townships are subdivided into villages 村, and urban townships are subdivided into boroughs 里. The residents of each village or borough elect their own wardens for four-year terms of office. The wardens work with executive officers to handle the administrative affairs of their village or borough. Villages and boroughs are subdivided into neighborhoods 鄰. Heads of neighborhoods are routinely recommended by wardens for appointment to the rural township or urban township office.

Reinvention of Government

The ROC has placed the reinvention of government at the top of its administrative agenda. The goal is the transformation of the entire government into a streamlined, flexible, innovative, and resilient organization that functions like a well-managed private enterprise. To achieve this goal, efforts will be taken in a number of areas: specifically, government agencies will be streamlined and the organization and functions of the central government will be modified to suit present needs. The government also plans to promote a more flexible hierarchy and personnel structure within government organizations as well as overhaul the government budgetary system. By computerizing operations and using information technology and networked systems, the ROC is seeking to establish "electronic" government, including an information service network to increase administrative efficiency and enhance public services. Finally, government ethics are being heavily emphasized.

Harmony and cooperation between the central and local governments are vital to the smooth implementation of any government policy. As part of streamlining efforts, the administrative and financial responsibilities of the Taiwan Provincial Government will be delegated to other local and central government offices.

In January 1998, the Executive Yuan passed the *Government Reinvention Guidelines* as well as established a committee to formulate policy and draw up plans for the reinvention of government and review implementation. The committee is convened by the premier, while other members are drawn equally from three groups: heads of government agencies, mid-level civil servants, and grassroots-level civil servants. In addition, a government reinvention advisory committee with the premier as convenor was established to provide advice and arrange consultations among relevant agencies. The 15 to 21 committee members are scholars, experts, and entrepreneurs experienced in successfully reinventing private enterprises. Under this committee are three task forces, one charged with reinventing organization, one with personnel, and one with legal affairs. These task forces are staffed by personnel from the Executive Yuan's Research, Development and Evaluation Commission; Central Personnel Administration; and Council for Economic Planning and Development. Plans formulated by these task forces were sent to various government agencies for imple-

mentation after being approved by the Executive Yuan Council in June 1998.

Further Reading
(in Chinese unless otherwise noted):

Chung-hua min-kuo hsing-cheng kai-kuang 中華民國行政概況 (*Annual Review of Government Administration of the Republic of China*; in Chinese and English editions). Taipei: Research, Development and Evaluation Commission, Executive Yuan, annual.

Chung-hua min-kuo fa-lu hui-pien 中華民國法律彙編 (Compendium of Laws in the Republic of China). 10 vols. Taipei: Legislative Yuan.

Chung-hua min-kuo hsien-hsing fa-kui hui-pien 中華民國現行法規彙編 (Compendium of Current Laws and Regulations in the Republic of China). 1981– . Taipei: Compendium Compilation Steering Committee 中華民國現行法規彙編編印指導委員會印行.
This is a looseleaf edition with supplementary editions issued quarterly.

Control Yuan, Republic of China (in English). Taipei: Secretariat, Control Yuan.

1999 Directory of Taiwan, Republic of China (in English). Taipei: China News.

The Examination Yuan of the Republic of China (in English). Taipei: Examination Yuan.

Tai-pei shih yi-hui chien-chieh 臺北市議會簡介 (*A Guide to the Taipei City Council*; Chinese-English bilingual). Taipei City Council.

Chien-cha-yuan kai-kuang 監察院概況 (An Introduction to the Control Yuan). Taipei: Control Yuan.

Kao-hsiung shih hsing-cheng kai-kuang 高雄市行政概況 (An Introduction to Kaohsiung Municipal Administration). Kaohsiung: Kaohsiung Municipal Government.

Chung-hua min-kuo kao-hsuan hsing-cheng kai-kuang 中華民國考選行政概況 (An Introduction to the Examination Administration in the Republic of China). Taipei: Ministry of Examination.

Chung-hua min-kuo cheng-fu tsu-chih yu kung-tso chien-chieh 中華民國政府組織與工作簡介 (An Introduction to ROC Government Organizations and Their Tasks). Taipei: Research, Development and Evaluation Commission, Executive Yuan.

Chung-hua min-kuo szu-fa-yuan 中華民國司法院 (The Judicial Yuan of the Republic of China). Taipei: Judicial Yuan.

Legislative Yuan, Republic of China (in English). Taipei: Legislative Yuan.

Li-fa-yuan kung-pao 立法院公報 (Legislative Yuan Gazette). Taipei: Legislative Yuan, semiweekly.

Chung-hua min-kuo kuo-min ta-hui 中華民國國民大會 (*The National Assembly of the Republic of China*; Chinese-English bilingual). Taipei: Secretariat of the National Assembly.

Statistics on Chinese Examination and Personnel Administrations (Chinese-English bilingual). Taipei: Examination Yuan, annual.

Chung-hua min-kuo nien-chien 中華民國年鑑 (Yearbook of the Republic of China). Taipei: ROC Yearbook Publishers, annual.

6

Political Parties and Elections

The Central Election Commission (CEC) is responsible for conducting national elections and supervising local elections in the Republic of China. The second direct election of the President and Vice President was the most important task of the CEC in 2000.

What's New

1. Figures updated
2. More information on the 1998 "Three-in-One" elections
3. 2000 presidential election information

T he Republic of China has, in the past decade or so, moved rapidly to become a full-fledged democracy. Elections for important posts in the government have been held regularly and political parties have flourished, participating vigorously in elections. Never before have ROC citizens enjoyed such a large say in the affairs of their nation. Although some observers have pointed out problems in Taiwanese politics, no one can deny the fact that the ROC has become quite democratic in recent years.

In fact, while the United States may hold the record for frequency of elections and the number of elected offices, more posts are filled by election in Taiwan than in many other democratic countries in the world. Taiwan voters, however, differ from their American counterparts in at least one important respect—voter participation. Turnout rates in ROC elections consistently hover around 70 percent of eligible voters, lower than in some European countries, but much higher than in the United States.

Voting eligibility is defined broadly: the minimum age is 20, and there are no gender, property, or educational qualification requirements. Voter registration is automatic. The government notifies every enrolled voter of an impending election and distributes a bulletin or gazette that identifies and describes all candidates and their platforms.

Normally, voting is scheduled for Saturdays, which are usually made holidays in places where elections are held. A large group of workers, typically teachers and other dedicated locals, administer paper ballots at convenient polling stations. The workers count the votes reliably and quickly, and report the results just a few hours after the polls close. By any standard, election administration in Taiwan is efficient.

Central Election Commission

Founded in 1980, the Central Election Commission 中央選舉委員會 (CEC) under the Executive Yuan 行政院 is responsible for holding and supervising national and local elections, screening candidate qualifications, recalling elected officials, and drafting or amending laws concerning elections. The CEC is led by a chairman and consists of 11 to 19 commissioners who, after nomination by the premier and then approval by the president, serve a term of three years. To guarantee the impartiality of the CEC, the *Public Officials Election and Recall Law* 公職人員選舉罷免法 rules that commissioners from any single political party shall not constitute more than two-fifths of the whole commission.

Electoral Systems

The electoral mechanism in Taiwan varies, depending on the type of office. For such executive posts as president and vice president; special municipality mayors 直轄市市長; county magistrates 縣長 and provincial municipality mayors 省轄市市長; rural and urban township magistrates 鄉鎮長; and county municipality mayors 縣轄市市長; each voter casts only one vote in a single-member district, and the candidate who receives the most votes (not necessarily an absolute majority) is elected.

For the election of members to the National Assembly 國民大會, Legislative Yuan 立法院, special municipal councils 直轄市議會, county or city councils 縣市議會, and township councils 鄉鎮市民代表會, what has been dubbed the single non-transferable vote (SNTV) is employed. Normally, several representatives are elected from a single constituency which is demarcated essentially on the existing administrative boundaries. In a given constituency, each voter casts only one vote, and several leading candidates are elected.

Since the National Assembly election of 1991 and the Legislative Yuan election of 1992, a certain number of seats have been reserved for a national constituency and the overseas Chinese communities. These seats are allocated by proportional representation (PR). Prior to the election, each party submits two lists of candidates, one for the national constituency and the other for overseas Chinese communities. However, Taiwan voters do not vote directly for candidates on the party lists. Instead, they simply vote in their respective SNTV districts, and the votes obtained by the candidates are aggregated nationally according to party affiliation. The seats for the national constituency and overseas Chinese communities are then distributed proportionally among the parties which capture at least 5 percent of total valid votes nationwide. At present, 22 percent of the seats in the Legislative Yuan and 30 percent of those in the National Assembly are filled this way.

In general, both the SNTV and PR systems benefit the smaller parties, for as long as they win a certain number of votes, they are able to secure at least a few seats. In elections for administrative offices, however the situation is quite different. Normally, only the two largest parties emerge victorious in these single-seat contests, and smaller parties are very much at a disadvantage.

As of August 1999, a total of 88 political parties had registered with the Ministry of the Interior, but most are insignificant in electoral politics. The three significant parties are the Kuomintang (KMT) 中國國民黨, the Democratic Progressive Party (DPP) 民主進步黨, and the New Party (NP) 新黨. All three have won seats in various legislative bodies, but only the KMT and the DPP have been able to secure administrative offices. In the National Assembly election of 1996, the Green Party 綠色本土清新黨 won a seat. Not long ago, the Taiwan Independence Party (TAIP) 建國黨 was formed, which included many former DPP members and supporters who were dissatisfied with recent DPP policy changes. It also captured one seat in the Legislative Yuan election of 1998. The newly formed New Nation Association 新國家連線, Democratic Alliance 民主聯盟, and Non-Party Alliance 全國民主非政黨聯盟 won one, four, and three seats, respectively, in that election.

In the past few years, the National Assembly has amended the ROC Constitution five times, changing the electoral mechanism in Taiwan. First, the terms of office for the ROC president and for National Assemblymen were shortened from six years to four (the term for Legislative Yuan members remained three years), and proportional representation was introduced to the Legislative Yuan and National Assembly elections. Second, the offices of president and vice president are now elected directly by all citizens eligible to vote in the territory under the effective jurisdiction of the ROC, rather than indirectly by the National Assembly as in the past; furthermore, a presidential and vice presidential ticket has only to win a plurality, not a majority, to be elected. Third, the mechanism through which members of the Control Yuan 監察院 are selected was changed. Previously, Control Yuan members were elected by provincial assemblies and special municipal councils. Now, they are nominated by the president and approved by the National Assembly. This reform has transformed the Control Yuan from a parliamentary body to a semi-judicial institution. Fourth, in accordance with the constitutional amendment passed in mid-1997, the provincial government was streamlined. As a result of this decision, the provincial governor and the Taiwan Provincial Assemblymen are no longer directly elected by the general populace.

The SNTV system currently in use for the legislative elections has been criticized by many for bringing about corruption and factional politics in Taiwan. Thus, there have been talks on changing this system. Indeed, this topic was put on the agenda for recent negotiations on constitutional reform. However, no changes were made because the political parties could not agree on an alternative system. All three major parties were in favor of mixed systems, but the KMT insisted on the Japanese model, a combination of single-member districts and PR, while the DPP and the New Party favored the German model, which was essentially a variant of PR.

Political Parties

The Kuomintang

The Kuomintang 中國國民黨 is also known as the Nationalist Party. Having celebrated its one hundredth anniversary on November 24, 1994, the KMT has widespread appeal, boasting a membership of approximately 2.1 million. At the grassroots level, members are organized into cells. Moving upwards, there are district, county, and provincial congresses and committees. The highest level includes the National Congress 全國代表大會 and the Central Committee 中央委員會.

The National Congress is the highest authority of the party. Its delegates are selected to serve four-year terms. The congress amends the party charter, determines the party platform and other important policies, elects the party chairman and the Central Committee members, and approves candidates nominated by the chairman to serve as vice chairmen and members of the Central Advisory Council 中央評議委員會. When the National Congress is in recess, the supreme party organ is the Central Committee, which holds a plenary session every year.

The Central Standing Committee 中央常務委員會, which represents the Central Committee when that body is not in session, is the most influential organ in the KMT. It meets every Wednesday morning to deliberate and approve important policies for the party and the government, and to nominate people for important party and government positions, including ministers, vice ministers, and various commissioners.

The day-to-day affairs of the party are managed by the secretariat. The current secretary-general is Lin Fong-cheng 林豐正. His staff manages the various party departments and commissions. At lower levels, party organizations have their own secretariats and administrative staffs. All of these organizations, from the national to the local levels, are funded to a large extent by profits from party-owned and operated business enterprises, ranging from newspapers and TV stations to electrical appliance companies and computer firms.

The first meeting of the KMT's 14th National Congress held in August 1993 approved significant changes to the conduction of party affairs. It decided that the party chairman was to be elected by the National Congress through secret ballot. ROC President Lee Teng-hui 李登輝 won 83 percent of the votes cast and was reelected chairman of the party. In addition, four vice-chairmen were added to the Central Committee after being nominated by the chairman and approved by the National Congress. It also decided that the chairman would appoint only 10 to 15 of the 31 members of the Central Standing Committee, with the remaining members elected by the Central Committee. Finally, it decided to hold the National Congress every two years instead of four years. The second meeting of the 14th National Congress was held in August 1995 to nominate the party's presidential candidate for the election held in March 1996 (see section on Presidential Election in this chapter).

In August 1997, the 15th National Congress was convened. President Lee Teng-hui was reelected chairman of the party with 93 percent of the votes. The congress also approved four vice-chairmen, one of whom was Vice President Lien Chan 連戰, and elected 230 Central Committee members. In the first plenary session of the 15th Central Committee held immediately after the congress, 17 members were elected to the enlarged Central Standing Committee, along with 16 appointed by the chairman. In August 1998, a new Central Standing Committee was elected in the second plenary session of the 15th Central Committee.

In August 1999, the second meeting of the 15th National Congress ratified the nomination of Lien Chan and Vincent C. Siew as the KMT's presidential and vice-presidential candidates for the 2000 presidential election. At the third plenary session of the 15th Central Committee held later, the Central Standing Committee was reorganized.

Democratic Progressive Party

The Democratic Progressive Party 民主進步黨, formed on September 28, 1986, now has approximately 200,000 members. The party's organizational structure closely resembles that of the Kuomintang. The DPP's National Congress elects 31 members to the Central Executive Committee 中央執行委員會 and 11 members to the Central Review Committee 中央評議委員會. The Central Executive Committee in turn elects the 11 members of the Central Standing Committee 中央常務執行委員會. The members of these committees all serve two-year terms.

Previously, the party chairman was elected by the National Congress. At the second plenary meeting of the seventh National Congress held in September 1997, the stipulation that the chairman be directly elected by party members was formally adopted. The present chairman, Lin I-hsiung 林義雄, was elected in June 1998. He garnered 62 percent of the vote cast by party members, far ahead of his competitors. The chairman must appoint a secretary-general, one to two deputy secretaries-general, and a number of department directors. Yu Shyi-kun 游錫堃 is the current secretary-general of the DPP.

The methods used for nominating the party's candidates for public offices have been changed quite frequently. At the party's sixth National Congress, held in April and May of 1994, a two-tier primary system was initiated under which ordinary members of the DPP vote for candidates in one primary election and party cadres vote in a second primary. The results of the two would then be combined, with equal weight given to both.

At the second plenary meeting of the sixth National Congress held in March 1995, the nomination process for the presidential and gubernatorial candidates was modified to add open primaries for DPP members and nonmembers alike. It was also decided that candidate slots on the party's list of national constituency representatives for the Legislative Yuan and National Assembly would be allotted equally among three groups: scholars and experts, representatives of disadvantaged groups, and politicians.

At the seventh National Congress held in June 1996, further changes were made to the nomination of candidates for public offices. It

was decided that the primary reserved for the party leadership would be abolished. Instead, for the nomination of candidates for such offices as president, provincial governor, special municipality mayors, county magistrates, provincial municipality mayors, Legislative Yuan members, National Assemblymen, and special municipal councilmen, a two-stage process involving a closed primary for party members and an open primary for all eligible voters, with each given equal weight, would be employed.

Such a scheme was overturned at the provisional meeting of the seventh National Congress, however, held in December 1996. The second stage, an open primary for all eligible voters, was replaced by opinion polls. It was further decided at the meeting that the party chairman would be elected directly by all members of the party starting in 1998.

At the second meeting of the eighth National Congress held in May 1999, a special rule was adopted for the 2000 presidential election: A qualified candidate must be recommended by more than 40 party leaders, and if there is only one such candidate, the National Congress must be convened to ratify his or her nomination by a three-fifths majority. At the provisional meeting of the National Congress in July, the former Taipei City Mayor Chen Shui-bian was officially nominated to represent the DPP in the 2000 presidential race.

Perhaps what most distinguishes the DPP from the two other major parties is its support of Taiwan independence, or the permanent political separation of Taiwan from the Chinese mainland. Although the DPP has incorporated Taiwan independence into its official platform, the urgency accorded to its realization is a source of factional contention within the party. In more recent elections, the mainstream DPP leadership has tended to downplay the party's independence theme in an attempt to broaden voter support. This treatment of the issue, as well as the DPP's recent warming to interparty cooperation, has led to dissatisfaction among the more radical advocates of independence for Taiwan. Several of these disaffected DPP members thus left the party, and together with other independence supporters, established the Taiwan Independence Party and the New Nation Association. Whether these parties will become viable political forces in the future remains to be seen.

New Party

In August 1993, shortly before the Kuomintang's 14th National Congress, a group of KMT "Young Turks," including six Legislative Yuan members and one former lawmaker, broke away from the KMT to establish the New Party 新黨. According to their statement, the seven quit in protest against the "undemocratic practices of the KMT" as well as due to ideological differences. Such prominent personalities as the former Finance Minister Wang Chien-shien 王建煊 and former head of the Environmental Protection Administration Jaw Shau-kong 趙少康 were among the founders of the party, which adopted an anticorruption platform and championed social justice. The goal of the NP was to attract voters who were dissatisfied with the performance of the ruling KMT and opposed to the DPP's advocacy of Taiwan independence. The NP now claims a registered membership of nearly 68,500.

The New Party differs from the KMT and the DPP in organizational structure, stressing the leadership of those holding public office. At the head of the party is the National Campaign and Development Committee 全國競選暨發展委員會. The convener of the committee, a position currently filled by Lee Ching-hua 李慶華, serves as the leader of the party. In early 1998, the NP set up a separate campaign office, headed by Jaw Shau-kong, to take charge of campaign matters. Under Jaw's leadership, the NP adopted an open primary system for nominating its candidates for the year-end elections.

In August 1999, the party took almost everyone by surprise through the nomination of renowned writer Li Ao 李敖 as its presidential candidate for the 2000 presidential election.

Elections

There has been a long history of elections in the ROC. Even during the period of martial law, elections for county magistrates, municipality mayors, provincial assemblymen, county and city councilmen, etc. were held quite regularly. With the exception of 1978, when the United States announced that it would sever diplomatic ties with the ROC, supplementary elections for members of the Legislative Yuan and the National Assembly have been held regularly since 1969.

In 1986, under the leadership of President Chiang Ching-kuo 蔣經國, political reform was accelerated. After Chiang passed away, his successor, President Lee Teng-hui, continued to carry out liberalization and democratization programs. One result of these reforms was the retirement of all the senior members of the First National Assembly, Control Yuan, and Legislative Yuan, who had remained in office since the late 1940s, when they were elected both on the Chinese mainland and Taiwan as representatives of all China. Beginning with the National Assembly election of 1991 and the Legislative Yuan election of 1992, all members of the national legislative bodies have been elected by the general public in the Taiwan area on a regular basis.

The following sections will outline elections in the ROC, beginning with an account of the ROC's first-ever direct presidential election and a survey on the elections for the Third National Assembly, which were both held in March 1996; a summary of the elections for county magistrates and city mayors held in 1997; a discussion of the elections for county councilors, city councilors, and township magistrates held in early 1998; a report on the "three-in-one" elections for legislative, mayoral, and city council members held in December 1998; an explanation of the by-election for Yunlin county magistrate held in November 1999; and finally, an abstract of the 2000 presidential election.

First Direct Presidential Election

Democratic reforms in the ROC have been gathering momentum over the last decade. Ever since steps were first taken to liberalize and expand the political process, each election has carried politics on Taiwan closer to the goal of full democracy. On March 23, 1996, this evolution reached yet another milestone when voters went to the polls to cast their ballots in the ROC's first-ever direct presidential election.

As mentioned earlier in this chapter, the legal foundation which provides for the direct popular election of the president and vice president can be found in recent amendments to the ROC Constitution. These amendments also specify that the winning candidate need only a plurality rather than an outright majority. In addition to the changes to the Constitution, a number of supporting laws have been passed to ensure that presidential elections are carried out smoothly and fairly. In July 1995, the Legislative Yuan passed the *Presidential and Vice Presidential Election and Recall Law* 總統副總統選舉罷免法, which legislates that presidential and vice presidential candidates may be nominated by any political party gaining at least 5 percent of the vote in the most recent provincial-level or higher election, or by collecting the signatures of no less than 1.5 percent of eligible voters in the most recent parliamentary election. The law also requires that the Central Election Commission provide no less than 30 minutes of national television time for each candidate. Furthermore, when two or more candidates agree to participate, the committee will provide funding for nationally televised presidential debates.

As the race to become the first directly elected president unfolded, four teams of candidates emerged. The ruling KMT nominated President Lee Teng-hui, who picked Premier Lien Chan as his running mate. The DPP, after a fierce primary process, nominated a longtime political dissident and professor, Peng Ming-min 彭明敏, as its presidential candidate. Peng then chose prominent legislator Frank Hsieh as his running mate.

While the KMT and DPP candidates were both nominated, two other candidates entered the race via petition. One was Lin Yang-kang 林洋港. He and his running mate Hau Pei-tsun 郝柏村 were both former vice chairmen of the KMT, but decided to run as independents, with the endorsement of the New Party. The fourth team was Chen Li-an 陳履安 and Wang Ching-feng 王清峰. Chen was also a member of the KMT and the president of the Control Yuan, but gave up both of these positions when he announced his candidacy. He picked Wang, a female member of the Control Yuan, as his running mate.

The KMT ran a very successful campaign. Almost from the very beginning, the Lee-Lien ticket was well ahead of the other three. Lee Teng-hui, as the ROC's first native Taiwanese president, not only received the backing of traditional KMT supporters, but was also supported by some in the DPP camp. The military exercises and missile tests that the mainland staged off the coast of Taiwan prior to the election further increased support for Lee by motivating people to "rally around the flag."

On March 23, slightly over 76 percent of eligible voters turned out to cast their ballots and reelected Lee Teng-hui, giving him an impressive 54 percent of the vote. He was trailed by the DPP's Peng Ming-min, who captured 21.1 percent. Lin and Chen obtained 14.9 percent and 10 percent of the vote, respectively.

Third National Assembly

Voters at the polls on March 23, 1996, were not only deciding who would become the ROC's first directly elected president; they were also electing members to the Third National Assembly. Although this contest was largely overshadowed by the much more prominent presidential election, many parties fielded candidates, and several constituencies saw hotly contested races.

In the end, the KMT captured 49.7 percent of the vote and remained the largest party in the new Assembly. Of the 334 seats being contested, ruling party candidates won 183, or 54.8 percent. While the KMT retained its majority, the result still represented a significant decline from the 75.4 percent of the seats it had held in the previous Assembly. As for the DPP, it added considerably to the 66 Assembly seats it won in 1991. DPP candidates walked away with 29.9

The three major candidates for the 2000 presidential election actively carry out campaign activities. From top to bottom are the KMT candidate Vice President Lien Chan, independent candidate James Soong, and the DPP candidate Chen Shui-bian.
(Photo by the Central News Agency)

percent of the vote on March 23 and captured 99 seats, or 29.6 percent of the total. For the New Party, the 1996 election was its first National Assembly race. The party's candidates captured 46 seats, or 13.8 percent of the total, and 13.7 percent of the vote—a result similar to the NP's performance in the Legislative Yuan election in December 1995. Of the remaining seats, one went to a candidate backed by the newly-formed Green Party 綠色本土清新黨, while five others went to independents.

The ROC Constitution states that a constitutional amendment must be passed by at least three-fourths of the delegates present at a meeting attended by a quorum of two-thirds of the entire National Assembly. Thus, in the new National Assembly, no political party is now able to single-handedly amend the Constitution.

County Magistrates and City Mayors

The outcome of the November 29, 1997, elections for county magistrates and city mayors took many by surprise, including senior officials of both the ruling KMT and the largest opposition party, the DPP. This is due to the fact that, out of the 23 seats at stake, the KMT lost almost half of its previous 15 seats, keeping only eight of them. Meanwhile, the DPP doubled its number of seats from 6 to 12. Although the DPP won only a marginal victory over the long-standing ruling Kuomintang by 43 percent to 41 percent of the vote, the results were still quite impressive because of the fact that the DPP has only been around for 11 years, whereas the KMT commemorated its 100th anniversary in 1994. In reality, the DPP was now able to exercise administrative power over 70 percent of the country's population.

For the KMT, the exasperating outcome of this election meant more than just the shrinkage of its administrative realm. It also marked the beginning of a new era in which the central government, when trying to implement policies, was very likely to encounter mounting resistance from subordinate local governments held by the DPP. In addition, the KMT had more to worry about than just the DPP. Independent candidates also performed better in this round of local government elections, increasing their number of seats from two to three. Independents were elected to head Chiayi City, as well as Miaoli and Nantou counties. One of them was a former member of the KMT while the other was formerly from the DPP.

The two smallest of Taiwan's four major parties, the New Party and the Taiwan Independence Party, both failed to win a single seat in this round of mayoral and county magistrate elections. The New Party, plagued by internal friction and the inability to nominate anyone in many counties and cities, garnered merely 1.4 percent of the total votes, a sharp contrast to the 13 percent it won in the election for the Third Legislative Yuan in 1995.

County and City Councilors and Township Magistrates

Immediately following the election for county magistrates and city mayors, elections were held for county and provincial municipality councils, rural and urban township magistrates, and county municipality mayors. These elections were held on January 24, 1998; and altogether, there were 890 legislative seats and 319 executive offices at stake. Although the KMT lost to the DPP in the election for county magistrates and city mayors two months previous, it regained some ground in the new elections. Indeed, the results demonstrate once again how Taiwan remains, at the local level, a one-party state (see section on Cities and Townships under County Government in Chapter 5, Government).

Kuomintang candidates captured 58.9 percent of the county and city council seats, slightly down from their performance four years ago. Its candidates also won 73.3 percent of the township magistrates and county municipality mayors, an actual increase from earlier gains. In fact, these figures underestimate the KMT's strength in the elections because many independents who successfully ran were KMT members who had failed to receive their party's nomination.

The Democratic Progressive Party won 12.7 percent of council seats and 8.8 percent of magisterial positions. While these results represented an increase from the party's previous showings, the DPP had yet to win a majority of seats in a single county or city council.

The New Party won ten council seats (1.1 percent), but no magisterial positions. The Taiwan Independence Party captured only one council seat. The remaining 27.2 percent of council seats and 9 percent of magisterial and mayoral seats went to independent candidates, who outperformed DPP nominees and were the KMT's main competitors.

The 1998 "Three-in-One" Elections

On December 5, 1998, the ROC witnessed the smooth and successful completion of the "three-in-one" elections. This special name was derived from the fact that elections for legislative, mayoral, and city council members were all held simultaneously on the same day. In the Fourth Legislative Yuan election, the KMT, as expected, retained a majority of the seats, improving its performance over the same election three years earlier. It captured 46.43 percent of the vote nationwide, with 123 seats (54.67 percent) out of a total of 225 open seats; benefiting, to a large extent, from the decline of the New Party, which was embroiled in internal bickering. The NP obtained only 7.06 percent of the vote–much less than the 13 percent gained in 1995 and won 11 (4.89 percent) of the total seats. The DPP did not fare well, either. With 29.56 percent of the vote, it captured 70 seats (31.11 percent). The DPP's setback had much to do with an internal split and the formation of the TAIP and the New Nation Association. These two groups obtained one seat each.

In addition, KMT candidate Ma Ying-jeou 馬英九 managed to retake Taipei City for the ruling party by defeating incumbent DPP Mayor Chen Shui-bian 陳水扁. However, in the Kaohsiung mayoral election, DPP candidate Frank Hsieh 謝長廷 ousted the KMT incumbent, Wu Den-yih 吳敦義, by a mere 4,565 votes.

In the elections for Taipei and Kaohsiung city councils, the KMT also gained strength by winning 23 (44.23 percent) and 25 (56.82 percent) seats, respectively. The DPP obtained 19 seats (36.54 percent) in Taipei, and 9 seats (20.45 percent) in Kaohsiung. The New Party obtained 9 seats (17.31 percent) in Taipei and a single seat in Kaohsiung.

The By-Election for Yunlin County Magistrate

On November 6, 1999, independent candidate Chang Jung-wei 張榮味 won the by-election for county magistrate in Yunlin, southern Taiwan, ending the KMT's five-decade grip on power in that constituency. Chang garnered 137,106 votes, or 37.59 percent, followed by the DPP's Lin Chung-li 林中禮, who received 129,271 votes, and the KMT's Chang Cheng-hsiung 張正雄, who obtained 96,334 votes. The voter turnout rate reached 69.15 percent.

Chang took the position left by the late Yunlin county magistrate, Su Wen-hsiung 蘇文雄 (KMT), who passed away in August 1999. The by-election, originally scheduled for October 16, was postponed due to the September 21 earthquake that ravaged counties in central and southern Taiwan, including Yunlin. Receiving much attention from the media, the by-election was seen by some political analysts as a litmus test for the ROC's presidential election in March 2000.

2000 Presidential Election

Democratic Progressive Party candidate Chen Shui-bian 陳水扁 and his running mate Hsiu-lien Annette Lu 呂秀蓮 were elected president and vice president of the Republic of China on March 18, 2000, ending the Kuomintang's 50-year hold on the presidency in Taiwan. Chen and Lu received 4,977,697 votes, or 39.3 percent of the total, followed by independent candidate James Soong 宋楚瑜 and his running mate Chang Chao-hsiung 張昭雄, with 4,664,972, or 36.84 percent.

Kuomintang candidate Lien Chan 連戰 and his running mate Vincent Siew 蕭萬長 lagged behind in third place with 2,925,513 votes, or

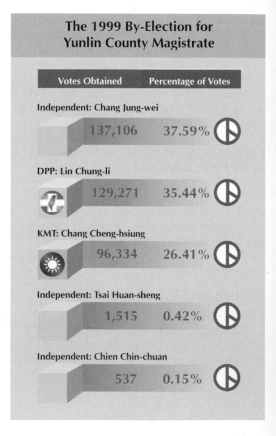

The 1999 By-Election for Yunlin County Magistrate

	Votes Obtained	Percentage of Votes
Independent: Chang Jung-wei	137,106	37.59%
DPP: Lin Chung-li	129,271	35.44%
KMT: Chang Cheng-hsiung	96,334	26.41%
Independent: Tsai Huan-sheng	1,515	0.42%
Independent: Chien Chin-chuan	537	0.15%

23.1 percent. Independents Hsu Hsin-liang 許信良 and Chu Hui-liang 朱惠良 won 79,429 votes, while New Party Li Ao 李敖 and his running mate Fung Hu-hsiang 馮滬祥 received 16,782.

The Central Election Commission noted that a total of 12,786,671 voters participated in the second direct presidential election. The voter turnout rate was 82.69 percent, approximately 6 percentage points higher than the presidential election four years ago.

Chen's victory marked a major political comeback. Elected as Taipei's first opposition mayor in 1994, he lost the Taipei mayoral race to the KMT challenger Ma Ying-jeou by 78,305 votes in 1998. Chen Shui-bian, 49, will be the youngest president of the Republic of China under the 1947 Constitution, while vice president Annette Lu will be the highest-ranking woman in the ROC's political history.

Recalls and Referendums

According to the Constitution, ROC citizens have the rights of election, recall, initiative, and referendum. In practice, however, only the right of election has been frequently exercised. Indeed, legislation to regulate the exercise of the rights of initiative and referendum have yet to be passed. Nevertheless, there have been occasional attempts to recall elected officials and representatives, and even referendums have been held in certain areas despite the lack of supporting laws. Obviously, without a detailed legal framework, the results of these referendums are advisory at best.

Two attempts at recall occurred in November 1994 and January 1995 in Taipei County and the southern district of Taipei City, respectively. In both incidents, the targets of recall were KMT members of the Legislative Yuan who were accused of reneging on campaign promises by voting in favor of the construction of a nuclear power plant. Turnout rates in both incidents were very low. In Taipei County, only 21.4 percent of eligible voters turned out to vote, and in the southern district of Taipei City, the turnout rate was 8.6 percent. As the *Public Officials Election and Recall Law* requires that a majority of eligible voters turn out to vote in order to recall elected officials or representatives, both attempts failed.

As for referendums, three recent attempts also centered around the construction of a new nuclear power plant. The first was held in May 1994 in Taipei County's Kungliao Township 台北縣貢寮鄉, the proposed site of the new plant. More than 58 percent of Kungliao's eligible voters went to the polls, and an astounding 96.1 percent expressed disapproval of the plan to construct the plant in their township. Another nuclear power plant referendum was held by the government of Taipei County in November of the same year, and while 87.1 percent of the ballots cast were against the power plant, only

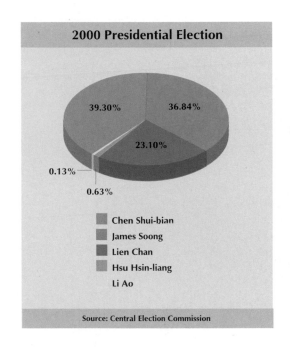

Source: Central Election Commission

18.5 percent of eligible voters participated. The most recent referendum held on the issue was undertaken by the government of Taipei City in March 1996. Fifty-eight percent of eligible voters cast their ballots, and 51.5 percent opposed the construction of the new nuclear power plant.

Another referendum was held in March 1995 by the government of Hsichih Township in Taipei County 台北縣汐止鎮 to decide on public works proposals. The turnout rate was only 17 percent, but 95 percent of the ballots cast were in favor of the local government's proposals.

In the "three-in-one" elections of 1998, three counties and cities also held referendums. These included a referendum on Taiwan independence; one on the construction of a new airport in Tainan City; the use of a parcel of public land in a ward in Neihu district of Taipei City臺北市內湖區; and again, the construction of the new Fourth Nuclear Power Plant in Taipei County. The turnout rates for these referendums ranged from 25 percent in Tainan to around 60 percent in the Neihu district.

Mainland Affairs and National Unification Policy

Heated TV debates between the DPP and New Party on cross-strait relations in August 1999 focused public attention on this critical issue.
(Photo by the Central News Agency)

Potential conflict in the Taiwan Strait still poses a serious threat to world peace and stability in the Asia-Pacific region. The Chinese civil war, beginning in 1927, brought death and destruction to untold millions of people. After the government of the Republic of China relocated to Taipei in 1949, major battles erupted during the 1950's, and lesser incidents continued to arise throughout the 1960s. Even today, when trade, business, and people-to-people contacts between the two sides of the Taiwan Strait are flourishing, the authorities on the Chinese mainland have never renounced the use of force against Taiwan.

Consequently, the historical context of seven decades of strife between the Republic of China and the Chinese communists makes the peaceful unification of China one of the world's greatest challenges. Nonetheless, guided by the principles of reason, peace, parity, and reciprocity, the government of the Republic of China has consistently and creatively sought new approaches in solving the complications and difficulties related to a divided China.

The Status of a Divided China

The Republic of China was founded in 1912, and it has since maintained sovereignty over the territories that have been administered by a succession of Chinese governments down through the ages. The international community referred to these territories as "China."

Ten years after the founding of the Republic of China, the Chinese Communist Party was established under the aegis of international communist activists. In 1949, the Chinese communists gained control of the Chinese mainland through military force, and on October 1, 1949, they proclaimed the establishment of the People's Republic of China. The ROC government was compelled to move to the island of Taiwan, and China was thus divided. Since that time, two distinct societies, with different ideologies and contrasting political, economic, and social systems, have existed simultaneously on opposite sides of the Taiwan Strait.

For many years after gaining control of the Chinese mainland, the Chinese communists sought to "liberate" Taiwan by force. Beginning in the early 1950s, they launched a series of military attacks against areas controlled by the ROC government in an effort to achieve reunification by force: the artillery bombardment of Kinmen (Quemoy) 金門 in 1958 is one of the most well-known of these incidents. Beijing changed its policy toward Taiwan, after establishing diplomatic relations with the United States in 1979, and began pursuing a course of peaceful confrontation. Although references to "liberation" in propaganda concerning Taiwan were dropped in favor of the term "peaceful reunification," Beijing has, to this day, refused to renounce the use of military force to solve the "Taiwan problem." In Taiwan, the pace of economic liberalization, social pluralization, and political democratization accelerated throughout the 1980s, and, with the lifting of martial law in July 1987, the government adopted a more open policy toward the Chinese mainland. In November 1987, the ROC government, for humanitarian considerations, began to allow people residing in the Taiwan area to visit relatives on the Chinese mainland. This decision moved cross-strait relations away from a state of complete estrangement and opened the door for private-level exchanges.

The people-to-people exchanges, the indirect trade and investment, and the cultural exchanges between the two sides of the Taiwan Strait, which blossomed in the wake of this thaw, have engendered a range of issues that necessitated a more systematic approach to bilateral contacts. The ROC government thus established a legal and organizational foundation through which the development of relations between Taiwan and the Chinese mainland could be pursued.

Unification Guidelines

The ROC government and the majority of the people of Taiwan earnestly hope for the peaceful unification of China. The termination of the Period of National Mobilization for the Suppression of the Communist Rebellion 動員戡亂時期 by President Lee Teng-hui on May 1, 1991, signifies the ROC government's determination not to use force to achieve national unification. Beijing, however, has pointedly refused to respond in kind to this friendly gesture.

To articulate its position as clearly as possible, the ROC government has devised a blueprint for this process, the *Guidelines for National Unification* 國家統一綱領, which outline the principles and positive steps that both sides can take to expedite China's unification. According to this gradual, sequential plan, China's unification is imperative not only for the sake of territorial unity, but also for the political freedom and equitable distribution of wealth for all Chinese.

The guidelines state that China's unification should be achieved in three phases: a short-term phase of exchanges and reciprocity, a mid-term phase of mutual trust and cooperation, and a long-term phase of consultations and unification. The phased approach was chosen with the full realization that the unification of China will be a long and arduous process. China's unification will not be achieved overnight, because the two sides have divergent social, political, and economic systems, not to mention vast differences in lifestyles. However, there is no fixed time frame for each stage. Progress may be slow or fast, depending on the pace with which the mainland authorities respond to the ideas outlined in the guidelines.

In the short-term phase, neither side should deny the other's existence as a political entity, and both sides should expand unofficial people-to-people contacts. In addition, the guidelines call for Beijing to renounce the use of force against Taiwan and respect Taiwan's position in the international community.

The first task in the medium-term phase is to set up channels for official communication between the two sides on the basis of parity. The goals of the second-term phase also include the establishment of direct postal, commercial, and transportation links across the Taiwan Strait, as well as exchange of visits by high-ranking officials from both sides. Only after the goals of this phase have been achieved can the process of national unification be brought into active consideration.

In the long-term phase, a bilateral consultative body should be established to jointly discuss the overall political and economic structure of a unified China, in accordance with the wishes of the people on both sides of the Taiwan Strait. A China that realizes peaceful, democratic unification, and prosperous growth will have a significant stabilizing effect on the Asia-Pacific region, in particular, and on world peace, in general.

Currently, relations between the two sides are in the short-term phase, although exchanges in many areas have already moved into the second stage.

Statute Governing Relations

The ROC is a constitutional democracy, and all major governmental policies are formulated in accordance with due process of law. The evolving policy toward the Chinese mainland and the mainland authorities is no exception. At present, the most significant piece of legislation in this regard is the *Statute Governing the Relations Between the People of the Taiwan Area and the Mainland Area* 台灣地區與大陸地區人民關係條例. The statute, which was promulgated in September 1992, covers administrative, civil, and criminal affairs and recognizes the rights of the people living under the control of the authorities in the mainland. Thus, with certain exceptions necessary to maintain the economic and social stability of Taiwan, the people living on the Chinese mainland are basically the same as those living in Taiwan, in the eyes of the law.

Organizational Structures

In addition to a clear set of principles and laws to guide the development of relations, appropriate channels of communication are also an obvious necessity. This has led to the establishment of specific institutions which are authorized to handle relations with the Chinese mainland. In 1990 and 1991, the ROC government set up a three-tier network of government and private-sector institutions. The first, the National Unification Council (NUC), was established in September 1990. Then, in January 1991, the Executive Yuan's Mainland Affairs Council (MAC) was formed. In February 1991, the MAC approved the formation of a private non-profit organization, the Straits Exchange Foundation (SEF).

National Unification Council

The National Unification Council 國家統一委員會 functions as an advisory board and provides the president with research findings and ideas. The NUC is currently headed by the president himself, with the vice president and two opposition party members as deputies. The president has also invited respected civic leaders in Taiwan to sit on the NUC. The tenure for NUC members is one year, renewable at the president's discretion. As a non-partisan board, the NUC forges a consensus among various interest groups regarding the reunification of China.

Mainland Affairs Council

The Mainland Affairs Council 行政院大陸委員會, a formal administrative agency under the supervision of the ROC premier, is responsible for the overall planning, coordination, evaluation, and partial implementation of the ROC government's policy toward the Chinese mainland. As a decision-making body, it also oversees rules and measures proposed by various ministries concerning cross-strait relations. The MAC is headed by a chairman and three vice chairmen and is organized into seven departments and three divisions. Its members include most of the ROC cabinet ministers and related commissioners or council chairmen.

Straits Exchange Foundation

The Straits Exchange Foundation 海峽交流基金會, headed by a chairman and draws its funds from both the private sector and the government, is the only private organization empowered by the government to handle relations with the mainland. Nevertheless, the SEF currently deals only with matters of a technical or business nature that might involve the government's public authority, but would be inappropriate for the ROC government to handle under its policy of no official contacts with the mainland authorities. Accordingly, the SEF is not authorized to deal with political issues. "Policy dialogue," as exemplified by talks concerning the establishment of direct postal, commercial, and transportation links, is however an area of relations that the MAC may commission the SEF to conduct on its behalf.

Cross-strait Consultations

On December 16, 1991, a little over ten months after the establishment of the SEF, the Beijing government set up its Association for Relations Across the Taiwan Straits (ARATS) 海峽兩岸關係協會, with Wang Daohan 汪道涵 as its chairman. In April 1993, SEF chairman Koo Chen-fu 辜振甫 and the ARATS chairman met in Singapore and held the first discussions between Taipei and Beijing since 1949. This first round of Koo-Wang talks resulted in several agreements dealing with document authentication, the handling of mail, and future meetings. Provisions were made for regular and non-periodic meetings between SEF and ARATS officials.

Following the meeting in Singapore, Taiwan and the Chinese mainland held seven rounds of functional talks and three rounds of secretary-general-level talks through the SEF and the ARATS. These meetings focused largely on practical issues and led to a number of agreements in areas such as the repatriation of hijackers, illegal entrants, and fishing disputes. Dates for future talks were also settled. At a preparatory meeting held in May 1995, it was decided that a second round of Koo-Wang talks would be held in Beijing on July 20, 1995. Both sides agreed that the talks would cover such issues as the implementation of accords signed during the first round of Koo-Wang talks, Taiwan investment rights

Ancient relics, dating back thousands of years, from the Shu Kingdom in Sichuan Province on the Chinese mainland were featured in the "Sanxing-dui Legend" exhibition at Taipei's National Palace Museum in 1999.
(Photo by the Central News Agency)

on the Chinese mainland, and a wide range of unofficial exchanges.

Unfortunately, the mainland authorities postponed indefinitely this second round of Koo-Wang talks in June 1995, and began test-firing missiles near the Taiwan Strait the following month. Predictably, relations between Taiwan and the Chinese mainland at the semi-official level suffered.

But the ROC's consistent stance has remained unchanged. Since then, ROC government leaders have made 114 public appeals calling on the mainland authorities to resume communications and consultations as soon as possible.

In February 1998, the Beijing authorities finally expressed their consent to resume communications and consultations in an official letter to Taipei. In the latter half of April 1998, one of the deputy secretaries-general of Taipei's Straits Exchange Foundation led a delegation to Beijing to visit their mainland counterparts from the Association for Relations Across the Taiwan Straits and resume cross-strait consultations that had been suspended for nearly three years. On the eve of US President Bill Clinton's visit to the Chinese mainland to meet with PRC President Jiang Zemin 江澤民 at the end of June, the issue

of Taiwan and mainland relations has once again emerged as the focus of world attention. The SEF and the ARATS finally agreed that SEF Chairman Koo Chen-fu would visit the Chinese mainland during October 14-19, the same year.

It was Chairman Koo Chen-fu's first visit to the mainland since the foundation's establishment in 1991. Also, the trip made Koo the highest-level negotiator from Taiwan to visit the mainland since the Chinese civil war divided the two sides 50 years ago.

Koo's 12-member delegation visited Shanghai and Beijing during the trip. In Shanghai, Koo met with his mainland counterpart, ARATS chairman Wang Daohan. During the stop in Beijing, he held discussions with mainland Chinese President Jiang Zemin, Vice Premier Qian Qichen 錢其琛, and Chen Yunlin 陳雲林, director of the Taiwan Affairs Office of the State Council.

During their meetings in Shanghai, Koo and Wang agreed on four points conducive to bringing about closer cross-strait ties. Their consensus calls for Wang to visit Taiwan at an appropriate time and for the two intermediary bodies to resume contacts and negotiations. It was also agreed that the SEF and the ARATS should help reinforce Taiwan-mainland exchanges at various

117

levels. The fourth point was that the two organizations should provide more assistance on matters concerning protection of the property and personal safety of visitors from both sides.

Despite this Koo-Wang consensus, no significant breakthroughs were achieved on the thorniest issues during the meetings on the mainland. The two sides continue to present different definitions of the "one China" principle. Also, the mainland authorities still refuse to acknowledge that the two sides of the strait are ruled separately. Moreover, Beijing has kept intact its threat of military force against Taiwan, as a possible means of unification.

Defining Cross-strait Relations

In an interview with a German radio station in July 1999, President Lee Teng-hui stated that relations between the two sides of the Taiwan Strait should be characterized as a "special state-to-state relationship."

President Lee's declaration carries a three-fold significance. First, it is pragmatic. Although the Chinese communists established the People's Republic of China in 1949, its jurisdiction has never extended over Taiwan, Penghu, Kinmen, and Matsu, the area ruled by the government of the Republic of China. It is an indisputable political and historical fact that the ROC and the PRC are separate governments ruling, respectively, the Taiwan area and the mainland area. Second, President Lee's declaration is primarily a clarification of the current state of cross-strait relations. There has been no significant change or revision in our mainland China policy. Third, it is innovative. In the Guidelines for National Unification published in 1991, the ROC declared that the two sides of the Taiwan Strait are two equal political entities. This definition was established to temporarily set aside disputes over sovereignty, and create extended opportunities for interactions between the two sides. Subsequently, the ROC adopted a series of policy adjustments, including terminating the Period of National Mobilization for Suppression of the Communist Rebellion, promoting consultations, and expanding exchanges.

The cross-strait relationship is "special" because it involves the national sentiment and cultural factors, which are present in no other relationships. Thus, an equal and normalized cross-strait relationship should be better and closer than other country-to-country relationships. President Lee's redefination of cross-strait relationship will provide an important basis for the cross-strait relations in the next century.

Some people have oversimplified President Lee's remarks as a "two states theory," which not only distorts his original meaning but also leads to misunderstandings and speculations. President Lee's remark of the "special relationship" at this juncture is primarily meant to lay a foundation of parity between the two sides across the Taiwan Strait to elevate the level of dialogue and to help build a mechanism for democracy and peace. Therefore, government leaders at various levels have reiterated that there is no change in the government policy on promoting cross-strait dialogue, implementing bilateral agreements (including those reached at the Koo-Wang talks) and pursuing the ROC's stated goal of a new China unified under democracy, freedom, and prosperity in the future.

Unofficial Exchanges

Public opinion in the ROC has always welcomed Taiwan-mainland exchanges. Polls commissioned by the MAC in August 1996 indicated that 55.2 percent of respondents felt that the pace for the relaxation of cross-strait exchanges was just right, while 21.6 percent felt it was too fast, and 14.9 percent felt it was too slow. In a similar poll in August 1997, the figures changed slightly to 51.4, 22.2, and 12.5, respectively. However, by September 1998, figures in a similar poll had substantial changes: 35.5 percent felt it was just right, while 25.9 percent felt it was too fast, and 14.6 percent felt it was too slow.

The rapid expansion of exchanges between the two sides since 1987 seems to have imparted a certain momentum to their continued development. For the entire year of 1998, exchanges in almost all areas were up over 1997 levels. Social exchanges continue to grow steadily. According

Exchanges Between Taiwan and the Chinese Mainland in 1998

Category	Quantity	Annual change
Total cross-strait trade[1]	US$23.97 billion	-9%
Mainland trade dependence on Taiwan[1]	7.40%	—
Taiwan trade dependence on the mainland[1]	11.13%	—
Taiwan investment in the mainland[2]	US$2.04 billion	-52.8%
Cross-strait remittances[3]	US$966.57 million	+28.1%
Remittances to the mainland[3]	US$758.21 million	+14.8%
Remittances to Taiwan[3]	US$208.36 million	+121%
Cross-strait postal exchanges[4]	14.68 million	-9.9%
Letters to the mainland[4]	5.75 million	-4.4%
Letters to Taiwan[4]	8.93 million	-13.2%
Cross-strait telephone exchanges[5]	369.79 million min.	—
Calls to the mainland	236.14 million min.	—
Calls to Taiwan	133.65 million min.	—
Cross-strait travel[6]	1.51 million	-20.4%
Taiwan visits to the mainland	1.43 million	-22.55%
Mainland visits to Taiwan	83,435	+23.91%

[1] MAC estimates based on ROC and Hong Kong customs data
[2] Investment Commission, Ministry of Economic Affairs, ROC 經濟部投資審議委員會
[3] Foreign Exchange Department, Central Bank of China, ROC 中央銀行外匯局
[4] Directorate General of Posts, Ministry of Transportation and Communications (MOTC), ROC 交通部郵政總局
[5] Directorate General of Telecommunications, MOTC 交通部電信總局
[6] China Travel Service 中國旅行社 in Hong Kong and the Bureau of Entry and Exit, National Police Administration, Ministry of the Interior, ROC 內政部警政署入出境管理局

to China Travel Service in Hong Kong, 1.8 million Taiwan visitors went to the mainland during the year 1997. The number during the same period in 1998 dropped 22.22 percent to 1.4 million. On the other hand, 67,731 mainlanders (not including visitors for cultural and educational exchanges) came to Taiwan in 1997 and 83,435, in 1998, registering a 23 percent growth.

The number of mainland visitors for cultural and educational exchanges grew from 7,232 in 1997 to 10,660 in 1998, registering an all time high. The most rapid growth was in the number of those who attended athletic activities, technological researches, and religious activities.

Investment and trade continued active growth. According to the statistics provided by the Ministry of Economic Affairs, Taiwan investment on the Chinese mainland in 1998 registered US$2.04 billion in direct investment that

year. And Taiwan-mainland trade amounted to US$23.97 billion in 1998.

Indirect Trade

Indirect shipments between the two sides of the Taiwan Strait find their main entrepot in Hong Kong. In 1998, Taiwan-mainland trans-shipment trade through Hong Kong dropped 12.6 percent to US$10.01 billion. In 1998, exports to the mainland through Hong Kong were stagnant at US$8.36 million. Imports from the mainland through Hong Kong dropped slightly to US$1.65 billion. The Hong Kong Customs statistics showed that Taiwan still enjoyed a US$6.71 billion trade surplus with the mainland.

Hong Kong and Macau

Chinese reunification cannot be discussed without mentioning Hong Kong and Macau, which are also integral parts of the Chinese nation. The ROC government realizes that the people of Hong Kong and Macau have carved remarkable niches for themselves in the East Asian economy and have contributed to positive change on the Chinese mainland. The ROC will therefore actively work to preserve the rights and achievements of these two areas.

History of Hong Kong

Hong Kong was separated from the rest of the Chinese nation for over 150 years. After losing the Opium War, the Ching dynasty government was compelled to sign the unequal Treaty of Nanking in 1842 and to cede Hong Kong Island to Britain. Another military defeat ended with the 1860 Convention of Beijing, under which the Ching rulers leased southern Kowloon and Stonecutters Island to the British. Finally, the New Territories and 235 outlying islands were leased to Great Britain for 99 years under the Convention for the Extension of Hong Kong, signed on June 9, 1898. (In this chapter, the term Hong Kong refers to Hong Kong Island proper, southern Kowloon, the New Territories, and the offshore islands, that is, the whole area administered by the British since 1898.)

In 1982, Britain opened negotiations with the authorities on the Chinese mainland to discuss the return of Hong Kong. On September 24, 1984, London and Beijing signed a joint declaration in which they agreed that Hong Kong was to be returned to the mainland authorities on July 1, 1997, after 150 years of British rule. Beijing made plans to establish the Hong Kong Special Administrative Region and promised to keep Hong Kong's capitalist system intact for 50 years after 1997. In April 1990, the mainland authorities drew up and promulgated the *Basic Law of the Hong Kong Special Administrative Region* 香港特別行政區基本法. In March 1996, a provisional legislature was selected to take the place of Hong Kong's popularly elected Legislative Council, and in December of the same year, Tung Chee-hwa 董建華, a shipping magnate, was appointed as Chief Executive by Beijing to run Hong Kong when it switched from British to Chinese rule in July 1997. The handover of Hong Kong is a significant event even within the lengthy course of Chinese history. The transition, along with the return of Macau in 1999, will mark the end of Europe's colonial presence in Asia, as the region strides confidently into the 21st Century.

History of Macau

Like Hong Kong, Macau has also experienced a history separate from that of the rest of China for over a century. Macau consists of a small peninsula projecting from the province of Guangdong, as well as the islands of Taipa and Coloane, with a total area of only 21 square kilometers. In physical terms, it is 1/63 the size of Hong Kong. At the end of 1998, Macau's resident population totalled 500,000, composed of 70 percent Chinese, 28 percent Portuguese, and 2 percent others. The Portuguese leased Macau from China during the 16th, 17th, and 18th centuries and used the port as an entrepot for trade with China and Japan. Under a treaty signed in 1887, the Ching rulers ceded Macau to the Portuguese. In August 1979, Portugal established diplomatic relations with the authorities on the Chinese mainland and redefined Macau as a part of China temporarily administered by Portugal. In 1987, Lisbon and Beijing issued a Joint Declaration stating that Macau would be returned to China on December 20, 1999.

With the signing of this Joint Declaration, the period of transition began. The *Basic Law of the Macau Special Administrative Region* 澳門特別行政區基本法 was approved by the National People's Assembly and promulgated by the President of the People's Republic of China on March 31, 1993. It functions as a mini-constitution, containing the fundamental statutes concerning the territory's autonomy; the exclusive powers of the Chinese central authorities; the statute and rights of the permanent residents of the Macau SAR; the political structure; and the economic, cultural, and social affairs of the region.

The second phase of the period of transition, from the beginning of 1993 to the end of 1995, was marked by the completion of various large infrastructure projects including the new Macau-

Macau's major historical tourist attraction is the facade of St. Paul's Church, all that remains of this centuries-old landmark, which was built by Jesuit missionaries during the period 1602-1629 and was destroyed by a fire in 1835.

Taipa bridge, the Outer Harbor Ferry Terminal, and the airport. The emphasis has since been placed on education, including technical training and advanced education, cultural development, and social welfare, with the intention of improving the quality of life. The founding of the University of Macau, which replaced the previous private University of East Asia, was the first step in a process which has seen the expansion of higher education. The creation of the Polytechnic, the Tourism Training Institute, and the establishment of courses run by the University of the United Nations have since followed.

Edmund Ho Hau-wah 何厚鏵 was elected by the Selection Committee and then appointed by Beijing as the Chief Executive of the Macau Special Administrative Region on May 20, 1999. The transfer of jurisdiction was smooth, and hopefully Macau will continue to enjoy the high degree of autonomy, prosperity, and stability.

Policy toward Hong Kong and Macau

The ROC maintains very close ties with both Hong Kong and Macau. In terms of the flow of people alone, Taiwan residents made 1.74 million trips to Hong Kong in 1998, while residents of Hong Kong made 194,116 trips to Taiwan. Economic ties are also strong. According to statistics published by the Ministry of Finance, the volume of trade between Taiwan and Hong Kong was US$ 26.79 billion in 1998; while Taiwan-Macau trade grew to US$360.8 million. In the same year, there were 48 Taiwan-to-Hong Kong investment cases, totaling US$68.64 million; and 67 Hong Kong-to-Taiwan investment projects, totaling US$257.62 million. In addition to Hong Kong's importance as a site for direct investment, the territory also serves as a transshipment point for cross-strait trade. Hong Kong customs officials estimated that in 1998, US$10.01 billion in Taiwan-mainland trade passed through Hong Kong. Capital goods and funds for investment on the Chinese mainland are also typically transferred through the territory.

In light of such close and comprehensive links, it should come as no surprise that policy concerning Hong Kong and Macau is a high priority of the ROC government. The ROC responded to the negotiations between Britain and the mainland authorities by forming a special Hong Kong Affairs Task Force in August 1983.

After London and Beijing signed the Joint Declaration, the Task Force was upgraded to a Coordination Panel, under the direct supervision of the vice premier of the ROC government. Following the signing of the Sino-Portuguese Joint Declaration in July 1987, the name of the Hong Kong Affairs Task Force was changed to the Hong Kong and Macau Affairs Task Force 行政院港澳小組. At the end of January 1991 when the ROC government set up the MAC, the Task Force was incorporated into the new organization as its Department of Hong Kong and Macau Affairs 港澳處 to coordinate ROC government policies toward the two areas. The ROC government has stated that it will retain its agencies in Hong Kong and Macau, and the MAC has formulated plans regarding the post-handover names, status, structures, and functions of these agencies. The number and types of services provided by these agencies have largely gone unchanged, and responsibility for Hong Kong and Macau affairs has been redistributed to reflect the change in Hong Kong's legal and political status. The MAC will take charge of the overall planning and administration of Hong Kong and Macau affairs, after responsibilities currently handled by the Ministry of Foreign Affairs are transferred.

In order to establish a legal basis for the ROC's relations with Hong Kong and Macau after Beijing assumes control, the MAC has drafted the *Statute Governing Relations with Hong Kong and Macau* 香港澳門關係條例, which was passed by the Legislative Yuan on March 18, 1997, and promulgated by the president on April 2 of the same year. The operative principle behind the statute is that, as long as the two territories retain a high degree of autonomy, the ROC government will regard them as special regions separate from the rest of the Chinese mainland. The statute addresses a number of issues, including travel, finance, trade, and trans-

portation. According to the statute, people from Taiwan entering Hong Kong and Macau will follow normal regulations and will not be subject to special restrictions, while residents of Hong Kong and Macau may enter Taiwan after receiving approval. Calling for "free transportation links in principle, and restriction or prohibition in exceptional cases," the statute aims to preserve direct transportation and trade links. As for business and finance, the statute permits direct investment in Hong Kong and Macau by individuals and corporations from the ROC, and provides for such investment to be handled according to existing foreign investment and technical cooperation measures. The statute also indicates that investment in Taiwan by individuals and corporations from Hong Kong and Macau is to be handled according to existing laws on investment and technical cooperation by overseas Chinese.

Looking to the Future

A stable and democratic China is in the interest of both the Chinese people and the world. The ROC government has repeatedly emphasized that its participation in the international community does not challenge the existing interests of the People's Republic of China. The ROC must strive for the necessary international contacts to ensure its reasonable existence and development.

As for bilateral interaction, the two sides should avoid the use of force and instead apply the principles of reason, peace, reciprocity, and mutual benefit to improve the cross-strait relationship systematically and advance toward the goal of uniting China under freedom, democracy, and equitable prosperity. Only in this way can Taipei and Beijing bring the greatest possible benefit to the people on both sides and contribute to the long-term peace and stability of the East Asian region.

8

National Defense

The ROC Air
Force provides
the nation's first
line of defense.
Top to bottom:
French Mirage
2000-5 fighter,
Taiwan Ching-kuo
Indigenous
Defense Fighter,
US E-2T AWACS,
Taiwan-built
F-5E fighter, and
US F-16 fighter.

What's New

1. *Draft of the Organic Law of the MND*
2. Shortening the length of service for conscripts
3. Developing an anti-missile system

The primary objective of the ROC's defense policy is to defend the area currently under ROC control, which includes Taiwan, Penghu, Kinmen, and Matsu. This entails establishing a fighting force of sufficient readiness to guard the nation and protect its people. The direct and most serious threat to the ROC's national security remains the unwillingness of Peking to renounce the use of military force against Taiwan. Thus, while ROC national defense strategy calls for balanced development of the three armed forces, naval and air supremacy receive first priority. In addition to current defensive preparations, a long-term policy of developing an elite fighting force and self-sufficiency in defense technology is also being strictly followed. This calls for restructuring the armed forces, streamlining command levels, renovating logistical systems, merging or reassigning military schools and upper-ranking staff units, and reducing the total number of men in uniform.

Budgetary Reduction Trend

The defense budget for the ROC military has generally been trimmed each year over the past decade, and an increasing percentage has become open to public scrutiny. The defense budget for July 1, 1999 to Dec. 31, 2000 amounted to US$12.6 billion (NT$402.9 billion), or 18 percent of the total national budget during the same period, maintaining an overall downward trend (Please note that the beginning of the fiscal year has been changed from July 1 to January 1, thus the above figures cover an 18-month period).

Doing More with Less

The thinking behind changes to the ROC's Armed Forces over the past few years reflects a shift from equally stressing offense and defense to simply assuring defense. This strategic principle, as implemented under the Ten-Year Troop Reduction Plan 十年兵力精簡方案, has led to a targeted force of less than 400,000 troops by the year 2003 and an increase in the ratio of combat troops to overall military manpower.

Facing the threat of high-tech warfare from the Chinese mainland, the ROC's Armed Forces have not only streamlined their organization and introduced cost effectiveness measures by de-centralizing organizational levels, shortening the chain of command, accelerating reaction times, and promoting increased efficiency, but they have also reformed management and the processing mechanism, thus shortening process flow times, fostering the creativity of grassroots units and individuals, and eliminating outdated approaches, in order to establish a new military organization.

The allocation of resources among the three services will give priority to air superiority and control of the seas in defensive operations, as well as to coastal defense. Accordingly, a ten-year program to develop a practicable table of organization for the three services is being implemented in three phases. This program will facilitate training and carry out peacetime missions, eliminate the overlapping of staff units in the three major services, consolidate the General Staff Headquarters of the Ministry of National Defense (MND) and the general headquarters of the three services, and transfer non-military tasks to organizations outside the MND.

Second-generation weapon systems used by the three armed services are also being actively updated. These include E-2T air defense warning systems, the Ching-kuo indigenous defense fighter 經國號戰機 (IDF) squadron, the commissioning of the Taiwan-built Cheng-kung 成功號 class missile frigates, French-built Lafayette (Kang-ting 康定號) class missile frigates, and US-rented Knox class missile frigates. Other new equipment includes F-16 and Mirage 2000-5 fighter planes, a second batch of AH-1W attack helicopters and OH-58D reconnaissance helicopters.

Command Structure

Article 36 of the *ROC Constitution* stipulates that the president of the republic "shall have supreme command of the land, sea and air forces of the whole country," and Article 3 of the *Organic Law of the Executive Yuan* 行政院組織法 states that "the Executive Yuan shall establish (among others) a Ministry of National Defense." According to the *Organization Law of the MND* 國防部組織法, the ministry shall be in charge of the defense affairs of the whole country.

Within the Ministry of National Defense is the General Staff Headquarters (GSH), under which are the various services, including the Army, Navy, Air Force, Combined Services Forces, Armed Forces Reserve Command 軍管區司令部, Coast Guard Command, and Military Police Command 憲兵司令部. The GSH is headed by a chief of the general staff who is in charge of military affairs; in the military command system, he acts as the chief of staff to the president for operational matters, while in the administrative system, he serves as chief of staff to the minister of national defense.

Ministry of National Defense

The Ministry of National Defense 國防部 is responsible for formulating military strategy, setting military personnel policies, devising draft and mobilization plans, delineating supply distribution policies, arranging the research and development of military technology, compiling the national defense budget, setting military regulations, conducting court martial proceedings, and administering military law. The ministry itself has a Minister's Office 部長辦公室; Departments of Manpower 人力司, Materials 物力司, and Law 法制司; a Bureau of the Comptroller 主計局, and the Judge Advocates Bureau 軍法局.

General Staff Headquarters, MND

The General Staff Headquarters, MND 國防部參謀本部 is in charge of the planning and supervision of joint war activities, political warfare, personnel, military intelligence, operations,

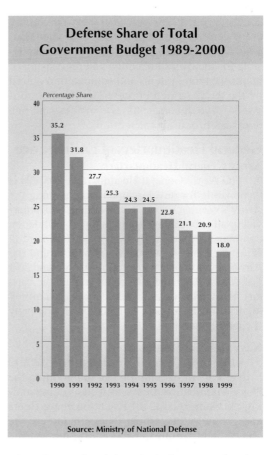

Defense Share of Total Government Budget 1989-2000

Percentage Share

Source: Ministry of National Defense

education and training, logistics, organization and equipment calibration, communications, military archives management, and medical services. It contains the Office of the Chief of the General Staff 參謀總長辦公室; the Department of Supervision and Inspection 督察部; the General Political Warfare Department 總政治作戰部; Offices of the Deputy Chiefs of the General Staff for Personnel 人事參謀次長室, Intelligence 情報參謀次長室, Operations 作戰參謀次長室, Logistics 後勤參謀次長室, and Planning 計劃參謀次長室; the Bureau of Communications and Electronics 通信電子局; the Military History and Translation Bureau 史政編譯局; the Military Medical Bureau 軍醫局; and the General Affairs Bureau 總務局.

On July 1, 1995, various military purchasing units were integrated into the Procurement Bureau, MND 國防部採購局, which became responsible for the overall planning and purchasing of major weapon systems and equipment required by the ROC Armed Forces. The Bureau consists of five departments, two offices, and one overseas procurement section.

General Headquarters of Each Service

Army General Headquarters

The Army General Headquarters 陸軍總部 is responsible for developing and maintaining the Army's combat power, commanding and supervising all subordinate troops and units. Under its command are the Army Logistics Command 後勤司令部, Army Commands 軍團司令部, and the Airborne and Special Operations Command 空降特戰司令部. Also under its command are the various Army units (in descending order) of army 軍團, division 師, brigade 旅, battalion 營, company 連, and platoon 排.

Navy General Headquarters

The Navy General Headquarters 海軍總部 is in charge of developing and maintaining the Navy's combat readiness, as well as commanding and supervising all its subordinate fleets and ground units. Under its command are the Naval Fleet Command 艦隊司令部, the Marine Corps Headquarters 陸戰隊司令部, the Navy Logistics Command 後勤司令部, Headquarters of the Naval Area Command 軍區司令部, the Area Service Office 地區勤務處, the Naval Base Command 基地指揮部, and the Bureau of Maritime Survey 海洋測量局. The subordinate Navy units are under the direct supervision of the Naval Fleet Command 艦隊司令部 and are organized into the fleet 艦隊, group 戰隊, and ship 艦 levels. The Marine Corps units, like those of the Army, extend from the Marine Corps Headquarters 陸戰隊司令部; in descending order, they consist of: division 師, regiment 團, battalion 營, company 連, and platoon 排.

Air Force General Headquarters

The Air Force General Headquarters 空軍總部 is responsible for the Air Force's combat strength and commands and supervises all subordinate troops and units. The units include the Air Force Operations Command 作戰司令部, the Air Force Logistics Command 後勤司令部, the Air Defense Artillery Command 防砲警衛司令部, and various tactical wings 聯隊. Under the wing in descending order are the group 大隊, squadron 中隊, and flight 分隊.

Combined Services Force General Headquarters

The Combined Services Force General Headquarters 聯勤總部 is in charge of ordinance, military maps, and communication equipment for the ROC Armed Forces. It also provides support and services commonly needed by all Armed Forces services, such as finance, surveying, engineering, rear echelon administration, purchase and procurement, and armament appraisal and testing.

Armed Forces Reserve Command and Coast Guard Command

Shortly after the ROC government announced the lifting of the *Emergency Decree* 戒嚴令 and the termination of the Period of National Mobilization for Suppression of the Communist Rebellion 動員戡亂時期, the Taiwan Garrison General Headquarters 警備總部 (TGGH) was deactivated, and two new commands were created to assume partial responsibility for tasks formerly performed by the TGGH: the Armed Forces Reserve Command 軍管區司令部 (AFRC), which is mainly in charge of reservist management and mobilization affairs; and the Coast Guard Command 海岸巡防司令部 (CGC) . For more details, see the sections on Manpower Structure and Military Mobilization below.

Coast Guard Command

The second new command to be formed from the TGGH, the Coast Guard Command 海岸巡防司令部 (CGC), is responsible for eight local coast guard commands and 25 coast guard battalions. These secure and protect the coastline from intrusion and smuggling by providing coastal patrol and defense through such activities as air patrols, inshore patrols, harbor inspections, and inland inspections.

The primary mission of Coast Guard forces is to safeguard coastal areas; but in peacetime, they also detect and interdict smuggling and infiltration in conjunction with other law enforcement units, such as military authorities, police units, and custom houses. In wartime, the Coast Guard forces have a ground-fighting mission.

Military Police Command

The Military Police 憲兵 guard military and certain governmental installations, enforce military law, maintain military discipline, support combat troops, and serve as supplementary police when necessary to maintain public security. The Military Police have five sub-commands and one training center. The Military Police Command 憲兵司令部 has a Department of Political Warfare 政治作戰部 and offices of Personnel 人事署, Intelligence 情報署, Police Affairs 警務署, Logistics 後勤署, Planning 計畫署, Comptroller 主計處, Judge Advocates 軍法處, and General Affairs 總務處.

Military Structure Reorganization

In August 1999, the Executive Yuan passed a revised draft of the *Organic Law of the MND*, which is intended to centralize military administration and command. The General Headquarters of the Army, Navy, Air Force and the Military Police will be directly under the command of the MND, instead of the General Staff Headquarters. Because of increasingly sensitive relations between the two sides of the Taiwan Strait, the MND will establish an assessment office to study the high-level strategic environment, analyze threats, and assess weapons research and development. The MND's organization will expand from six to ten units: the Departments of Manpower(人力司), Resources (資源司), Judge Advocate (軍法司), Strategic Planning (戰略規劃司), Reserve Affairs (後備軍務司); Office of the Minister of Defense (部長室), Alignment and Assessment (整合評估室), Military History and Translation (史政編譯室), Supervision and Inspection (督察室); and Military Law Bureau (法制局). The draft also clearly states that the General Staff Headquarters (GSH) will be a unit to assist the Minister (who should be a civilian) and will be the organization to direct the Armed Forces for joint combat. Responsibilities of the GSH include: proposing needs for military build-up for combat preparedness, suggesting distribution of military resources, supervising combat readiness and organization of troops, training troops, determining the order of battle, formulat-

In addition to defending the country, ROC soldiers also engage in natural disaster relief work. After the 921 earthquake, these soldiers entertained children in Taichung County.
(Photo by the Central News Agency)

ing and executing combat plans, and other matters concerning command of troops.

Moreover, the draft of this legislation fulfills the spirit of the constitution, in that the military should transcend personal, regional, and party ties and remain administratively neutral. The future structure of the defense system will be formed by the President, the National Security Council, and the Ministry of National Defense, in coordination to provide a national defense.

The draft of the revised *Organic Law of the MND* provides that the President may bypass the Premier to give orders directly to the Minister of the MND, who in turn can instruct the Chief of the General Staff to execute orders.

Manpower Structure

A person in the ROC military may be an officer 軍官, a noncommissioned officer (NCO) 士官, or an enlisted man 士兵. He may be serving on either a volunteer 志願役 or a conscript 義務役 basis, and may be on active duty 常備 or reserve 後備 status.

Officers

Officers in the ROC military generally come from three backgrounds. They might be graduates of military academies who become career officers 正期軍官, graduates of different specialized military schools who serve shorter terms of duty 專科軍官, or college graduates who have passed a written test to become reserve officers 預官.

Approximately 15 percent of the officers commissioned each year are graduates from different military academies; another 45 percent are graduates of specialized military schools; and the remaining 40 percent are reserve officers.

The ratio of officers to NCOs is about 1:2.4, while that to enlisted men is 1:2.6. Thus, the ratio of officers to soldiers as a whole in the ROC Armed Forces is around 1:5, which is close to the 1:6 ratio of the US Armed Forces, and almost equals that of the Japanese Self-Defense Force (1:4.98).

Noncommissioned Officers (NCO)

NCOs constitute the backbone of basic units of the Armed Forces, and are increasingly de-

pended upon to train troops and develop their combat performance. In recent years, however, most senior NCOs have retired, leaving the current proportion of career NCOs too low and the percentage of NCO reservists in service too high. Reservists are on active duty for a very limited period of time, making it difficult for them to keep up with changes in the operation and maintenance of evermore sophisticated weapons and equipment. Solutions to this problem lie in reconfiguring the NCO organizational structure and recruiting new NCOs.

Conscripts

The *Military Service Law* 兵役法 of the ROC stipulates that all males in the Republic of China shall fulfill military service. Article 3 of the law states: "Male persons shall be liable for military service on January 1 of the year immediately following the year during which they reach the age of 18, and shall no longer be drafted for service beginning on December 31 of the year during which they reach the age of 45." Citizens who have been sentenced to imprisonment for longer than seven years are prohibited from entering the military.

Under the *Military Service Law*, military conscription is administered jointly by the Ministry of National Defense and the Ministry of the Interior 內政部. The former is responsible for securing an adequate number of conscripts and training them, while the latter determines the sources of the conscripts and ensures their rights and benefits. Generally, conscripts undergo a minimum of two months of basic training before receiving their 22-month unit assignments.

Premier Vincent Siew announced in August 1999 that, beginning October 1, 2000, those who serve on a conscript basis can be discharged two months ahead of the originally scheduled date. Therefore, the total length of time for conscript military service will be one year and ten months. To fill vacancies, from September 1999 to August 2000, the Armed Forces will train 3,000 more new recruits each month. In addition, because of strong social demand, alternatives to military service will begin in July 2000.

Male senior high, vocational high, and college students whose studies would be interrupted by military conscription can defer their induction until after graduation. Students who are admitted to a university or college undergo two months of basic training in the summer before their freshman year. Upon graduation, they reenter the military to fulfill the remainder of their two-year commitment.

Young men in poor health are exempt from military conscription. Those in average health may serve in the National Guard 國民兵. Draftees from impoverished families may apply for service in this unit, giving them reserve status and allowing them to stay with their families. In addition, the only son of parents who are over seventy may also apply for National Guard service to fulfill his military obligation.

Manpower and Equipment

Ground Forces

Ground forces in the ROC, mainly those of the Army and the Military Police, number some 230,300. The Army is organized into combat, combat support, and service support troops—all under the command of the Army GHQ—and is organized into the following units:

- armies;
- Kinmen 金門, Matsu 馬祖, Penghu 澎湖, and Hualien 花蓮 Taitung 臺東 Headquarters;
- Tungyin Island Command 東指部 and Chukuang Island Command 莒指部;
- Airborne and Special Operations Command (airborne brigades and aviation groups);
- mechanized infantry divisions;
- infantry divisions;
- armored brigades;
- tank group;
- reserve divisions;
- mobile divisions; and
- air defense missile groups.

The primary weapon systems of the ROC ground forces include M48H and M60A3 tanks; M109 and M110 self-propelled artillery; M113, V-150, and CM-21 armored personnel carriers; UH-1H helicopters; Kung-feng 工蜂 6A rocket systems; TOW-type antitank guided weapons; Chaparral SP, Hawk, Tien-kung 天弓 (Sky Bow), and Tien-chien 天劍 (Sky Sword) air defense missile systems; as well as Hsiung-feng 雄蜂 I and Hsiung-feng II anti-ship missile systems.

Navy

The ROC Navy is charged with maintaining control and surveillance of the waters that surround Taiwan. The Navy also takes part in joint operations with the Army and Air Force. Including some 30,000 marines, the ROC Navy forces number around 63,000 officers and men. Navy GHQ oversees operational and land-based forces. The former consists of:

- destroyer fleets and frigate fleet;
- amphibious landing fleet and amphibious landing vessel fleet;
- submarine group;
- mine vessel fleet and minesweeper/layer fleet;
- logistical service fleet and logistical rescue group;
- Hai-chiao 海蛟 speedboat group;
- antisubmarine helicopter group;
- Hai-feng 海鋒 shore-based missile group; and
- marine divisions, landing tank regiment, and operational service regiment.

Logistical support is carried out by one fleet of auxiliary craft while another fleet of auxiliary craft is assigned to disaster relief duties. The Navy's coastal SAM batteries employ Hsiung-feng missiles which resemble US Harpoon missiles. It's Knox-class missile frigates are rented from the US navy, Lafayette (Kang-ting) frigates are imported from France, while Cheng-kung frigates are built in Taiwan.

Air Force

Taiwan's geographical location makes air defense crucial for overall defense of the nation. At present, the ROC Air Force has some 64,000 officers and men. Personnel are divided into operational and logistical support systems under the command of the Air Force GHQ.

The main operational units in the ROC Air Force include the following:

- tactical combat aircraft wings;
- transport/antisubmarine wing;
- tactical control wing;
- communication and ATC wing;
- weather forecasting wing; and
- air-defense artillery guards command, comprising commands, air defense artillery battalions, and guard battalions.

Units in the operational system are equipped with aircraft that include the locally-developed IDF, and F-16, Mirage 2000-5 fighters; F-5E fighter-interceptors; C-130H and C-119 transporters; AT-3 trainers; and S-70C helicopters.

The ROC Army will spend over US$385 million to deploy 200 fourth-generation Patriot missiles—the latest version. The only surface-to-air radar-guided antimissile system ever tested in combat, Patriot missiles were used in the 1991 Persian Gulf War to defend against Scud missile attacks. Patriot missiles are installed in missile batteries around Taiwan.

Military Mobilization

The ROC defense strategy calls for maintaining a minimum force in peacetime and mobilizing a large number of troops in the event of war. In peacetime, the primary mobilization missions are to test the preparedness of reservists for instant action.

At present, registered reservists in the ROC number about 3.8 million, or more than 18 percent of the general population. After a man is discharged from active duty, he must report to his local military reserve unit, a subunit under the Armed Forces Reserve Command. Reservists are organized into different units according to their military occupational specialty 軍職專長 (MOS). Of the total, about 800,000 to one million serve annually in the reserve, testing the muster to ensure that mobilization for war can be quickly and easily realized.

Since a prolonged mobilization recall might adversely affect both the livelihood of a reservist and the overall economic development of the country, annual reservist training is usually conducted through recalls. An MOS refresher training course is conducted, and each reservist is notified of his unit's combat mission and relative location.

The purpose of muster call is to maintain readiness by practicing immediate report on call-up, and to keep reserve data up-to-date. Ways to streamline call-up procedures and maximize public convenience are reviewed from time to time.

Military Education

Military education of officers is conducted along two developmental lines: the universal track 通才發展路線 for career soldiers and the professional track 專業發展路線 for specialized military personnel. The universal track is the general military education for career soldiers provided at the three service academies. Graduates of the three receive a bachelor's degree, which is considered the basic educational level for career soldiers. Career soldiers may then receive additional intermediate training on a short-term basis at a number of the military branch schools, such as the infantry, armor, and artillery branch schools of the Army. Candidates for full colonel (captain) or major general 少將 (rear admiral) have to receive advanced military education at the Armed Forces University 三軍大學.

The professional track is for specialized military personnel, including medical personnel, engineers, and technicians. Training for specialized military personnel is dispensed at various specialized military schools, such as Fu Hsing Kang College, the Chung-Cheng Institute of Technology, and the National Defense Medical College.

The Legislative Yuan has already passed the "Regulations for Military Education," making military education part of the national educational system. Extensive re-examinations will be given to integrate military academies, centralize educational resources, economize educational investment, and establish departments for special fields of studies to implement the concept of "training for use" and "training and use are one." Recently, the military has initiated cooperation with academic and cultural organizations to provide lifelong learning channels for military personnel, in order to elevate the quality of the Armed Forces as a whole.

Military Academies

The Chinese Military Academy 陸軍軍官學校 (CMA), founded by Dr. Sun Yat-sen in 1924 at Whampoa 黃埔, Guangdong Province, relocated to Fengshan 鳳山, Kaohsiung County, Taiwan in 1950. The large campus features modern educational facilities and equipment to cultivate future army officers and develop military science. The CMA has a tradition of stringent educational requirements, accepting and training only the most qualified candidates.

In 1954, the CMA began placing increased emphasis on education in scientific, technological, and other nonmilitary fields. Cadets are required to complete 130 university-level credits in subjects such as political science, social science, mathematics, physics, chemistry, mechanics, civil engineering, electrical engineering, information management, and foreign languages over a period of four years. Right after graduation, the young lieutenants receive further training in a branch specialty, such as infantry, armor, artillery (missiles), engineering, transportation, communications (electronics), chemistry, or the military police.

The Chinese Naval Academy 海軍軍官學校 (CNA) offers cadets courses similar to those in civilian colleges of science and engineering. During their four-year training period, these cadets take special military courses on navigation, marine engineering, and equipment maintenance. They also must serve an apprenticeship aboard a ship.

Just prior to graduation, CNA cadets sail abroad in an armada dubbed the "Fleet of Friendship" 敦睦艦隊 for two months of hands-on training. In recent years, the "Fleet of Friendship" has sailed as far as the Middle East and South Africa. During the long voyage, future naval officers are given a chance to practice their combat skills and tactics and to enrich their navigational experience.

The Chinese Air Force Academy 空軍軍官學校 (CAFA) trains pilots for jet fighters and other combat and transport aircraft. Cadets learn aeronautic navigation, combat tactics, and related skills in a program that lasts four years. They participate in supervised flight operations dur-

The armed forces' weapon systems are being constantly modernized. French-built Lafayette (Kang-ting) class missile frigates significantly increase ROC Navy combat capability.

ing their second year. At the beginning of their junior year, cadets are divided into five sections to receive specialized training in flight skills, aeronautic machinery, electronic communication, antiaircraft warfare, and air control.

Fu Hsing Kang College 政治作戰學校 (FHKC), located in the Peitou 北投 district of Taipei, was established in 1951 to train competent political warfare cadres for the Armed Forces. There are three levels of education at FHKC: basic, advanced, and graduate. The college has 11 departments and a graduate school offering both master's and doctoral degree programs.

The National Defense Medical College 國防醫學院 (NDMC) trains military medical specialists, providing a basic college education plus medical training in such fields as dentistry, pharmacology, nursing, and public health. It also has 11 graduate-level, including master's and doctoral programs. The Tri-Service General Hospital 三軍總醫院 is the main teaching hospital of the NDMC.

The Chung-Cheng Institute of Technology 中正理工學院 conducts research and development of weapon systems, maintains arms and equipment, and educates technical military officers. It has one doctoral program, six master's degree programs, and 11 undergraduate departments.

The National Defense Management College 國防管理學院 is responsible for educating the planning, decision-making, and management personnel of the Armed Forces. It has a Graduate School of Information Management 資訊管理所, a Graduate School of Law 法律研究所, and departments of accounting, statistics, business management, information management, and law.

The Chung-Cheng Armed Forces Preparatory School 中正國防幹部預備學校, founded in 1976, provides senior high school education to students who wish to continue in one of the three service academies or FHKC following graduation. It combines the ordinary education of a senior high school with basic military training and innovative teaching methods.

The ROC Armed Forces also operate a number of branch schools, such as the Infantry 陸軍步兵學校, Armor 陸軍裝甲兵學校, and Artillery 陸軍炮兵學校 branch schools of the Army, as well as specialized schools, such as the Air Technical School 空軍機械學校 and the Air Communications and Electronics School 空軍通信電子學校.

The Armed Forces University, formerly the Army Officers School, was founded in 1906, six years before the establishment of the Republic of China. It is now the highest-level institution in the ROC military education system. It is responsible for training strategic-level command and staff officers, as well as specialists in national defense administration and military intelligence. It also conducts research into the development of war strategies and political warfare. The university includes four colleges: the War College 戰爭學院, the Command and Staff Colleges for the Army 陸軍指參學院, Navy 海軍指參學院, and Air Force 空軍指參學院.

Defense R&D

Research and development of national defense technology is crucial to national modernization. While the ROC industrial sector has made considerable progress over the past decade, most of it has in fact been confined to machining components and light manufacturing. The MND has long made use of the National Defense Industrial Development Fund 國防工業發展基金 to assist public and private enterprises in cultivating qualified technical personnel, purchasing facilities, transferring advanced technology, and developing a more sophisticated production base that one day promises a fully self-reliant defense industry.

The MND has issued the *Defense Science and Technology Development Plan* 國防科技發展方案 to strengthen cooperation between the academic and industrial sectors, and has, along with several cabinet-level institutions such as the National Science Council 國家科學委員會, the Ministry of Education 教育部, and the Ministry of Economic Affairs 經濟部, set up the Executive Committee for the Development of Defense Science and Technology 國防科技發展推行委員會 (ECDDST). With its two subdivisions, the Academic Cooperation Group 學術合作小組 and the

Industrial Cooperation Group 工業合作小組, the ECDDST taps academic resources for researching defense technology and makes use of the industrial sector to develop and manufacture weaponry and armaments.

In an interview with the Financial Times (UK) in October 1999, Defense Minister Tang Fei said that even without foreign assistance, Taiwan would develop its own anti-missile system, since a strong military threat from the Chinese mainland remains. The Minister said the Chinese mainland has seven missile bases equipped with M-9 and M-11 missiles aimed at Taiwan. Under these circumstances, Taiwan has no choice but to develop its own anti-missile system.

Chungshan Institute of Science and Technology

As the leading institution for the research, development, and design of defense technology in the ROC, the Chungshan Institute of Science and Technology 中山科學研究院 (CIST) contains some 6,000 scientists and more than 8,000 technicians.

With its headquarters in Lungtan 龍潭, Taoyuan County 桃園縣, the CIST has facilities stretching over nearly 6,000 acres scattered throughout Taiwan, and is divided into four major research divisions: aeronautics, missiles and rockets, electronics, and chemistry. The CIST has six centers for systems development, systems maintenance, quality assurance, materials R&D, aeronautic development, and missile manufacturing. Each research division or research center has a director in charge of the research and development of its specialty, while planning units have project chairmen responsible for R&D program management and system integration. The CIST jointly conducts independent research and development of weapon systems with the Aero Industry Development Center 航空工業發展中心, which is now under CIST supervision; some manufacturing units of the Combined Services Force; academic institutions; and public and civilian industries.

To date, a number of weapon systems have been domestically designed, tested, and produced on a mass scale by the CIST. These include the Kung-feng 6A rocket, the Hsiung-feng I and Hsiung-feng II SAMs, artillery fire control systems, naval sonar systems, naval electronic warfare systems, and the Tzu-chiang trainer aircraft 自強訓練機. The CIST has produced or plans to produce Tien-kung I and Tien-kung II SAMs, and Tien-chien AAMs. The institute is also developing the Tien-chien II AAM system.

The ROC Navy has also been developing a second generation of missile frigates and missile patrol boats. The first domestically built missile frigate (FPG-2) was built and handed over to the ROC Navy in May 1993, with the expectation that one such frigate would be produced every 11 months from then on.

Aerospace Development

A proposal to privatize the Aero Industry Development Center was approved by the Legislature 立法院 on May 16, 1995. This conversion from military to private status, under the supervision of the Ministry of Economic Affairs, facilitated the transfer of ROC military aeronautic knowhow to the private sector while enabling the center to form joint ventures with high-tech foreign manufacturers. This, in turn, aided the acceleration of advanced aviation technology in Taiwan, accelerating the growth of the nation's aerospace industry.

9
Foreign Relations

As first proposed
by founding father
Dr. Sun Yat-sen,
the ROC continues
its policies of
sharing economic
development
experiences and
contributing to
the international
community. To
further close and
friendly ties,
President Lee met
with leaders of
Latin American
leaders at the 1999
Taipei summit.
(Courtesy of the Office
of the President)

What's New

1. Figures and information updated
2. Humanitarian aid
3. The establishment of diplomatic ties between the ROC and Macedonia

The Republic of China has been an independent and sovereign state since its founding as the first Asian republic in 1912. After the Chinese Civil War, the People's Republic of China was established on the Chinese mainland in 1949, while the Republic of China, retained its sovereign state status, and exercised full authority over the remaining territory, including Taiwan, Penghu, Kinmen, and Matsu. Both states across the strait have since then functioned separately, with neither subject to the other's rule.

The international community fully understands the fact that the ROC is an established state which rules a defined territory, has its own constitution, national flag, legal system, and armed forces. All members of the United Nations also know that the ROC conducts it own foreign relations with other countries, and that the ROC government represents the 22 million people living on Taiwan, over whom no other government in the world has any legitimate authority. Hence, the recognition of the international and legal status of the ROC within the ever-changing world order is entirely in accord with the principles, obligations, and values professed in the UN Charter.

Continued exclusion of the ROC from formal diplomacy is detrimental to world peace. Foreign relations in the post-Cold War era have been characterized by multilateralism and the development of regional organizations dedicated to promoting both economic and security issues. Exclusion of any single state in the Asia-Pacific region severely compromises the integrity and effectiveness of multilateralism. Unable in many cases to join international bodies, to participate in multilateral forums, or to join international

conventions, the ROC finds itself forced to resort to an indirect form of bilateralism. The ROC could deal much more effectively with issues ranging from international aid to the conservation of endangered species, if it were a signatory to relevant international conventions and allowed to attend the multilateral forums within the United Nations framework.

Obstruction

For many years, the PRC has sought to obstruct the ROC's relations with the world community, by asserting that China is ruled by the Marxist-Leninist Chinese Communist party in Beijing. The Chinese Communists have even attempted to denigrate the ROC government as a "renegade province." The objective is to compel the people in the Taiwan area to accept the rule of a communist dictatorship and to deny them the right to pursue their own foreign policy. Peking continuously threatens to sever or downgrade relations with any country establishing or strengthening relations with the ROC. In an attempt to exclude the ROC from international organizations, the Chinese communists have relentlessly incited discord in political, economic business, scientific, and cultural forums over issues such as the ROC's right of representation and membership nomenclature in international organizations and activities.

The ROC acknowledges the fact that Taiwan is currently separated from the Chinese mainland and that the ROC government and the Chinese communists must coexist peacefully. Worldwide diplomatic recognition of the two states on both sides of the Taiwan Strait would be a fundamental step toward true reconciliation and, eventually, peaceful unification. It would also contribute to regional peace in the Asia-Pacific region.

Multilateralism

Over the past year, the ROC's efforts to participate in international organizations have produced significant results. The ROC enjoys membership in a number of inter-governmental organizations such as the Asian Development

Bank (ADB), the International Cotton Advisory Committee (ICAC), the Asian Productivity Organization (APO), the Afro-Asian Rural Reconstruction Organization (AARRO), and the Central American Bank for Economic Integration (CABEI). The ROC also holds membership in 953 international non-governmental organizations.

The UN Issue

The Republic of China was one of the founding members of the United Nations, as delegates from the ROC signed the UN Charter in San Francisco on 26 June 1945. For over 20 years, the ROC served as a permanent member of the Security Council. From 1950 to 1971, the UN attempted to resolve the dispute over the seat for China, which had been divided into two antagonistic political entities since 1949, each with its own territory, people, and government. The passing of Resolution 2758 by the 26th session of the UN General Assembly in October 1971, which substituted the People's Republic of China for the Republic of China in the UN, did not result in the disappearance of the ROC. On the contrary, the ROC continued to be an active member of the international community and now maintains close and friendly relations with more than 150 nations. The government and people of the Republic of China are seeking to participate in the United Nations, so that they can more constructively contribute to the international community.

Since the Republic of China's departure from the United Nations in 1971, the issue of its participation in the UN has remained highly sensitive. The ROC started its UN campaign in 1993, in order to help the international community more clearly understand the implications of the ROC's exclusion from the UN.

From 1993 to 1996, the ROC's allies requested that the United Nations establish an ad hoc committee to study the issue of the right of the ROC's citizens to participate in the UN, thus allowing member states more time to discuss and exchange views on this issue and help create a friendlier atmosphere for the ROC in the UN.

ROC Membership in International Non-governmental Organizations	
Nature of Organization	*Number*
Science and Technology	90
Medicine and Hygiene	204
Agriculture, Forestry, Fisheries and Animal Husbandry	42
Religion	59
Charity and Social Welfare	44
Education	20
Journalism	3
Culture and Arts	30
Law and Police Administration	10
Labor	80
Transportation and Tourism	20
Leisure and Recreation	26
Women, Family, and Youth	8
Business, Finance, and Economics	66
Engineering	16
Industrial Technology	29
Electronics and Mechanical Science	11
Mining and Energy	12
R&D and Management	69
Wildlife Conservation and Environmental Protection	17
Sports	97
Total	953

In 1997 and 1998, the ROC continued its UN campaign and focused on drawing the attention of the UN members to the injustice imposed upon the people of the Republic of China resulting from Resolution 2758. In 1998, fifteen countries sponsored a proposal requesting that the UN General Assembly reexamine General Assembly Resolution 2758, with the view of restoring the right to participate in the activities of the UN to the people on Taiwan. The proposal was extensively debated in the General Committee and drew considerable attention from the members of the United Nations.

During the 53rd session of the UN General Assembly, twenty-five countries voiced their encouragement and support for the ROC's UN bid. They were Belize, Burkina Faso, Chad, Costa Rica, the Czech Republic, Dominica, the Dominican Republic, El Salvador, Fiji, The Gambia, Grenada, Guatemala, Haiti, Honduras, Latvia, Liberia, Malawi, Nicaragua, Paraguay, Saint Christopher and Nevis, Saint Vincent and the Grenadines, Senegal, the Solomon Islands, São Tomé and Principe, and Swaziland.

In 1997, the ROC government began to seek observer status in the World Health Organization (WHO), one of the specialized agencies of the United Nations. Since then, a proposal titled "Inviting the Republic of China (Taiwan) to Participate in the World Health Organization (WHO) as an Observer" has been put forward to each annual World Health Assembly (WHA) for consideration.

Regrettably, the proposal was not considered by the WHA. However, the ROC believes that, as a global health organization, the WHO should not exclude any state. The Republic of China is determined to continue its efforts to secure participation in the WHO.

Economic Organizations

The Republic of China is an active member of many international economic organizations. To fulfill its commitment to the world community, the ROC is expanding its role in many international economic forums. One such example is the World Trade Organization (WTO). Although the ROC was one of the founding members of the WTO's predecessor, the General Agreement on Tariffs and Trade (GATT), it lost its membership following the communist takeover of the Chinese mainland. The ROC returned to GATT as an observer in 1965, but was forced out again in 1972, shortly after the Chinese mainland replaced the ROC in the United Nations. In 1987, the ROC sought re-entry to GATT, and in 1990 filed a formal application for membership under the name of the "Separate Customs Territory of Taiwan, Penghu, Kinmen and Matsu." On September 29, 1992, GATT established a working party to examine the ROC's Foreign Trade Memorandum and to draft a protocol of accession. Meanwhile, GATT of-

---

Ministry of Foreign Affairs On-line

The ROC Ministry of Foreign Affairs 外交部 set up its own World Wide Web site in August 1996 in order to provide access to information on the organization of the MOFA; the ROC's diplomatic relations; ROC embassies, consulates, and representative offices overseas; and press releases and statements. The site is located at *http://www.mofa.gov.tw*.

---

fered the ROC observer status, which allowed the ROC to participate in related meetings before becoming a full member. On January 1, 1995, the WTO replaced GATT, and the ROC was granted observer status on January 31, 1995. On December 1, 1995, the ROC, switched its membership application from GATT to the WTO.

Conducting bilateral consultations with WTO member states has been a prerequisite for any applicant's entry to the WTO. By the end of July 1999, the Republic of China had reached bilateral agreements with all 26 WTO members who had registered to negotiate with the ROC.

The ROC has also played a significant role in various other multilateral economic activities. It is an active member of the Pacific Economic Cooperation Council (PECC) and the Pacific Basin Economic Council (PBEC). As a full member of the Asia Pacific Economic Cooperation (APEC) forum—as "Chinese Taipei"—the ROC also wholeheartedly participated in various APEC forums and conferences. Currently, the ROC holds the position of Lead Shepherd in three APEC Working Groups: Trade Promotion (WGTP), Agricultural Technical Cooperation (ATC), and Marine Resource Conservation (MRC). Also, the ROC co-chairs with New Zealand APEC's Food System Steering Group. Over the past years, the ROC has made significant contributions to and has thus won widespread recognition in APEC.

Humanitarian Aid

The Republic of China, as a responsible member of the international community, never hesitates to help others in need. For example, after

Hurricane Mitch ravaged Central America in late October 1998, the ROC donated US$52 million in cash and US$3 million worth of medical supplies, food, and clothing to Honduras, Nicaragua, El Salvador, and Guatemala.

In 1999, when Macedonia's economy suffered the influx of more than 140,000 refugees from the war in Kosovo, the ROC sent medical groups to help improve health conditions in refuge camps. Morever, in a June 7 announcement, ROC president Lee Teng-hui announced a US$300 million humanitarian aid package to help the Kosovo refugees, including emergency relief and rehabilitation assistance.

Bilateral Relations

The Republic of China has full diplomatic relations with 29 countries, in which its 29 embassies and three consulates general promote bilateral cooperation. On the basis of pragmatic diplomacy, the ROC is continuing its endeavors to establish or substantially enhance relations with countries which do not maintain full diplomatic ties with the ROC. In order to strengthen its relations with those countries, the ROC now maintains 98 representative offices. Among these offices, 62 are located in the host countries' capitals, and 13 carry the official name of the "Republic of China."

Representative offices can offer some but not all, of the services usually provided by embassies and consulates general. At present, most of the ROC representative offices in Europe and North America use either the name "Taipei Economic and Cultural Office" or "Taipei Representative Office."

Reciprocally, 47 countries that do not have diplomatic relations with the ROC have set up 53 representative offices, or visa-issuing centers in Taiwan. (For a complete list of ROC representative offices abroad and foreign offices in the ROC, see appendices IV and V.)

Asia and the Pacific

The Republic of China is an Asian nation located on the Pacific Rim. Given its geographical and cultural proximity to other Asia-Pacific countries, it is only natural that the ROC attaches great importance to expanding and upgrading ties with the nations of this region.

In the past few years, relations between the ROC and Southeast Asia countries have been

Mr. Chiang Pin-kung (third from left), the ROC's minister-without-portfolio, attending the 1999 APEC's Economic Leaders Meeting in New Zealand on behalf of President Lee Teng-hui.

greatly reinforced. Since the ROC government initiated a Southward Investment Strategy南向政策 in 1993, trade with ASEAN member states has intensified dramatically. In 1998, the value of the ROC's trade with Southeast Asia exceeded US$24.4 billion. By the end of 1998, the ROC had invested US$39 billion in Southeast Asian countries, the leading destination for outbound ROC investment.

Australia

The Republic of China's economic achievements have encouraged the Australian government and private enterprises to intensify their economic and trade relations with the ROC. Since 1992, the ROC and Australian governments have signed seven important bilateral agreements, including memoranda of understanding pertaining to scientific cooperation, the protection of intellectual property, the promotion of investment and technology transfers, the avoidance of double taxation, the prevention of income tax evasion, the temporary admission of goods, the application of competition and fair trading laws, and cooperation in aviation safety.

The two-way trade between the ROC and Australia totaled US$4.54 billion in 1998, down from US$5.92 billion in 1997. This made the ROC Australia's fifth largest market for exports and ninth largest supplier of imports. Direct air links between Taipei and Sydney were inaugurated in October 1991. Today there are five international airlines providing direct air services between Taiwan and major Australian cities. The number of ROC tourists visiting Australia reached 153,500 in 1998. The exchange of visits by high-ranking government officials continues to play a pivotal role in fostering stronger bilateral relations.

Japan

The ROC's relations with Japan have grown substantially in recent years. In September 1994, the ROC and Japan signed an aviation agreement allowing EVA Airways and Air Nippon, a subsidiary of All-Nippon Airways, to fly the Taipei-Fukuoka route, and, beginning April 1, 1998, the Taipei-Osaka route. The continual

growth in bilateral trade, investment, cultural exchanges, and tourism is also reflected in the flow of people between the two countries: some 1.5 million trips were made back and forth in 1998 alone.

Though the total amount of bilateral trade was slightly down in 1998, the Republic of China's trade deficit with Japan remains a chronic problem. In 1998, the value of two-way trade between the ROC and Japan totaled US$36.3 billion, with the ROC's trade deficit increasing to US$17.7 billion. Bilateral economic and trade talks have been held annually to try to resolve this problem. The ROC's Ministry of Economic Affairs and other governmental trade and economic units are also implementing plans to reduce the trade deficit between the ROC and Japan and promote technology transfers from Japan to help upgrade ROC industries.

Major political parties in Japan jointly established the Sino-Japanese Parliamentarian Cordial Association comprised of about 300 representatives and councillors. This association in the Diet serves as an excellent channel for friendly communication between the ROC and the Japanese government. Currently, there are 35 Sino-Japanese Councilman Cordial Associations in the Prefectural Assemblies and City Assemblies.

The ROC's four representative offices in Japan are located in the cities of Tokyo, Yokohama, Osaka, and Fukuoka. On May 20, 1992, the name of these offices operate was changed from the Association of East Asian Relations to the Taipei Economic and Cultural Representative Office. The new name refers to the ROC more specifically than the vague East Asian designation. Effcetive June 8, 1998, the Japanese government restored the 72 hours non-visa transit for ROC nationals travelling to Japan.

Malaysia

The Republic of China maintains close relations with Malaysia. In 1998, the ROC invested US$263.4 million in Malaysia, pushing the total ROC investment in that country up to US$8.598 billion and making the ROC the third largest foreign investor after the USA and Japan. The value of two-way trade reached US$5.91 billion in 1998, in spite of the regional financial crisis. In order to further enhance relations, the ROC and Malaysia hold a ministerial-level economic cooperation conference annually. In addition, there are high-level exchange visits, and the two countries have also signed many bilateral agreements for the promotions of tourism, investment, etc.

New Zealand

Direct air links between Taipei and Auckland were initiated in September 1992. In December 1992, the ROC and New Zealand held their first trade talks since severing diplomatic relations in 1972. In 1998, bilateral trade amounted to US$549 million.

Oceania

Relations between the Republic of China and the island nations of the Oceania are developing steadily. Currently, the ROC maintains diplomatic ties with four island countries in this region: Solomon Islands, Marshall Islands, Tuvalu, and Nauru. In addition, Papua New Guinea, the Fiji Islands and Vanuatu have given their full recognition to the Republic of China. The ROC has sent six agricultural and technical delegations to those countries to assist with development.

The Philippines

The systematic channels of communication and the exchange of high-level official visits underline the close ties existing between the ROC and the Philippines. Bilateral relations between the Philippines and the ROC moved a step forward at the conclusion of the Seventh Joint ROC-RP Economic Conference in August 1998, with agreement to further strengthen bilateral economic cooperation. The ROC government has been encouraging the private sector to launch more investment projects in the Philippines, especially in the Subic Bay area. Bilateral relations have also been strengthened through frequent exchanges of visits between high-ranking officials.

The value of two-way trade in 1998 reached US$3.75 billion, an increase of 4 percent over the previous year. According to ROC statistics from 1959 to 1998, ROC businesses had invested a total of US$749.92 million in the Philippines, making the ROC its fifth largest foreign investor. Moreover, 120,000 Philippine workers are currently employed in the ROC, thereby providing much-needed job opportunities for the people of the Philippines.

Singapore

Singapore is the ASEAN country which maintains the closest relationship with the ROC. Friendship between government leaders has also helped to strengthen bilateral relations between the two countries, and many agreements have been signed to promote trade, investment, shipping, technical cooperation, etc. Relations between the Republic of China and the Republic of Singapore are further strengthened through frequent interactions between high-ranking government officials. In November 1997, the two countries held their sixth annual ministerial-level economic and technical conference in Singapore and concluded bilateral negotiations for the ROC's accession to the WTO.

The 1998 Sino-Singaporean two-way trade volume stood at US$5.965 billion, making Singapore the ROC's fifth largest trading partner. By the end of 1998, the ROC had invested a total of US$1.301 billion in Singapore. Tourism also continued to boom with more than 248,000 ROC citizens visiting Singapore in 1998.

South Korea

Three ROC-ROK Fruit Trade Conferences, held from 1994 to 1996, resulted in the signing of agreements. Bilateral consultations on ROC agricultural products and accession to the WTO were concluded at the ROC-ROK Fruit Trade conference in 1995. However, due to South Korea's violation of the agreement, the ROC did not continue talks on fruit trade. Nevertheless, the ROC-ROK Automobile Trade Conference was concluded and an agreement was reached in Geneva in December 1996.

Currently, the ROK is the sixth largest trading partner of the ROC. The bilateral trade volume between the ROC and ROK reached US$7.15 billion in 1998. However, the ROC's trade deficit with the ROK reached US$4.18 billion.

Thailand

The ROC maintains close relations with Thailand. The value of two-way trade between the two nations surpassed US$3.8 billion in 1998. ROC investors pumped funds into a number of industries, including electronics, plastics, latex, textiles, and chemicals. An investment protection agreement was signed in 1996, while an aviation agreement and a double taxation agreement were inked in 1998.

By the end of 1998, the ROC had invested a total of US$9.7 billion in Thailand, making the ROC Thailand's fourth largest foreign investor. The ROC has helped to alleviate Thailand's problem of unemployment in the wake of regional financial crisis by employing more than 140,000 Thai workers .

Indonesia

The Republic of China maintains close ties with the Republic of Indonesia. In recent years, bilateral relations have been further strengthened and ROC investments have increased. The ROC and Indonesia have signed several important bilateral agreements, including memoranda of understanding pertaining to scientific, agriculture, and energy cooperation; agreements on protection and promotions of investment; and on avoidance of double taxation.

The ROC is the fifth largest investor in Indonesia, with investment volume reaching US$16.7 billion as of September 30, 1999. From January to May 1999, the bilateral trade volume of both countries was US$940 million. Frequent exchange of official visits and systematic channels of communication and consultation existing between the two countries are also important elements of the bilateral relations.

Vietnam

Relations between the Republic of China and the Socialist Republic of Vietnam grew rapidly after the ROC established a representative office in Hanoi and a branch in Ho Chi Minh City in 1992. Vietnam reciprocated in 1993 by establishing an office in Taipei. By the end of 1998, total ROC investment in Vietnam reached US$4.5 billion, making the ROC its second largest foreign investor. Bilateral trade amounted to US$1.5 billion in 1998. The two countries also signed two important agreements: (1) the investment protection agreement and (2) an agreement on the avoidance of double taxation and the prevention of evasion of taxes on income agreement, respectively in 1993 and 1998. Agreements on agricultural cooperation and labor service cooperation will be signed in the near future.

India

Relations between the ROC and India blossomed in 1995, when the two exchanged representative offices under the names of the Taipei Economic and Cultural Center in New Delhi and the India-Taipei Association in Taipei, respectively. The New Delhi office represents the ROC's first opening in South Asia.

Bilateral trade has intensified gradually in recent years. In 1998 it totaled US$987.8 million, and ROC enterprises had invested a total of US$36 million. The sixth Joint Conference of ROC-India Business Councils, co-sponsored by the Chinese National Association of Industry and the Commerce and the Federation of Indian Chambers of Commerce and Industry in May 1998 in Taipei, sought to promote bilateral trade between the two countries.

West Asia and the Middle East

Commonwealth of the Independent States (CIS) Countries

From the early 1950s to the late 1980s, contacts between the Republic of China and the Union of the Soviet Socialist Republics (USSR) were completely prohibited by the two governments. However, things changed when the drastic ideological and political transformation taking place in the Soviet Union prior to its disintegration convinced the ROC government to lift its ban on direct trade and investment in the Soviet Union in 1990. The ROC also relaxed limitations on non-governmental exchanges between the two countries.

Subsequently, a number of high-ranking ROC officials, legislators, and citizen's groups have exchanged visits with counterparts in the former USSR. In the past few years, substantive relations between the ROC and the Commonwealth of the Independent States (CIS) have greatly improved. In 1998, trade between the ROC and the CIS countries amounted to over US$1.3 billion. The Russian Federation was the ROC's major trading partner in this region. In 1998, total trade between the ROC and Russia reached US$981.6 million, followed by Ukraine, with US$250.2 million.

The ROC government is currently in the process of developing substantive relations with the CIS countries through all available channels, placing particular emphasis on Russia, Belarus, Ukraine, and Kazakhstan, and some progress has been made in this respect. In July 1996, the ROC set up the Taipei Economic and Trade Mission in Minsk. Vice President Lien Chan visited Ukraine in August 1996. Russia representative office, the Moscow-Taipei Economic and Cultural Coordination Commission, was set up in Taipei in December 1996.

Jordan

Relations between the Republic of China and the Hashemite Kingdom of Jordan leapt forward in April 1995 when President Lee Teng-hui visited the country. In February 1998, Vice President Lien Chan traveled to Jordan to receive an honorary doctorate form the University of Jordan, and to meet with Crown Prince El-Hassan bin Talal and the Prime Minister of Jordan. In recent years, the ROC's support for science and technology-based activities in Jordan, including contributions to the development of mechanical enginee's ring and the Princess Summaya University College for Technology at the Royal Scientific Society, has strengthened cooperative ties between the two countries.

King Abdullah II was crowned in February 1999 after King Hussein passed away. President Lee dispatched . Yao Eng-chi, Vice President of the Legislative Yuan, as his special envoy to Jordan to extend both his condolences and sincerest congratulations.

In 1998, bilateral trade between the ROC and Jordan reached US$74.3 million.

Saudi Arabia

Substantive relations between the Republic of China and the Kingdom of Saudi Arabia continue to develop. Four ROC technical cooperation teams are now stationed in Saudi Arabia, where they are providing long-term technical assistance. The 16th Session of the Saudi-Chinese (Taipei) Joint Committee for Technical and Economic Cooperation was held in Riyadh in October 1998, to discuss further economic, technological and investment cooperation between the two countries.

The ROC Haji Mission joined a pilgrimage to the Holy City of Mecca in March 1999. It was warmly received by Saudi government officials and Muslim leaders.

In 1998, the value of two-way trade between the ROC and Saudi Arabia reached US$1.622 billion, of which ROC imports of petroleum and related products made up US$1.204 billion.

Africa

The Republic of China maintains diplomatic relations with eight African countries: Burkina Faso, Chad, The Gambia, Liberia, Malawi, São Tomé and Principe, Senegal and Swaziland. In addition to her official embassies in those states, the ROC has also set up representative offices in Angola, Madagascar, Mauritius, Nigeria and South Africa to promote bilateral trade and economic relations.

Friendly relations with countries in Western and Southern Africa were reinforced by the visit of the ROC Vice Foreign Minister Dr. David Ta-wei Lee to Malawi and Swaziland in March 1999, and Burkina Faso and São Tomé in June 1999. Discussions on future relations and topics of mutual concern were held in a cordial, friendly, and constructive atmosphere and consensus was reached on certain issues. While extolling the substantial democratic reform and economic progress made by the ROC, leaders of these countries expressed their appreciation for the assistance and friendship of the ROC over the past years and the hope that bilateral relations will be enhanced in the near future.

Burkina Faso

The ROC and Burkina Faso restored their diplomatic relations in February 1994. The bilateral relationship has grown steadily since then, thanks to the goodwill of both governments and their strong desire to develop close cooperation.

A joint commission, consisting of officials and specialists from both sides, meets every two years for a comprehensive review of the existing bilateral cooperation programs. The latest session, held on June 23-24, 1999, was successfully concluded and agreement on full-scale cooperation initiatives encompassing political, agricultural, medical, economic, and other cooperation was reached.

H.E. Blaise Compaore was re-elected as President of Burkina Faso in Novermber 1998. To congratulate President Compaore on his success, President Lee Teng-hui designated Mr. Ding Mou-shih, Secretary General of National Security Council, as his special envoy heading a delegation to Burkina Faso to attend President Compaore's inauguration ceremony.

Liberia

In February 1997, H.E. Charles Taylor, Vice Chairman of the Liberian Council of State, paid an official visit to the ROC. In July the same year, he was elected as President of the Republic of Liberia in elections held under the observation of the United Nations and other international community representatives. At the invitation of President Lee Teng-hui, H.E. President Charles Taylor visited the ROC in the following November. In addition, Mr. Nyudueh Norkonmana, President of the National Assembly; Monie R. Captan, Minister of Foreign Affairs and Brahima Kaba, Minister of Industry and Commerce, visited the ROC in 1998 and early 1999, respectively.

The Second Session of the Joint Commission between the Republic of China and the Republic of Liberia was held in Taipei on June 15-17, 1999. A high-ranking delegation led by Minister of Foreign Affairs Monie R. Captan attended the Joint Commission. Discussions on various cooperation programs were held and agreement was reached during the three-day meeting, which turned out to be a success for both sides.

Relations between the ROC and Liberia have been growing steadily, and most of the bilateral cooperation projects are on course.

São Tomé and Principe

The Republic of China established diplomatic relations with the Democratic Republic of São Tomé and Principe in May 1997. Since then, various cooperation projects in the fields of medicine, agriculture, human resource development, and infrastructure reconstruction were initiated and successfully implemented.

Swaziland

The Republic of China and the Kingdom of Swaziland established diplomatic relations in September 1968. There have been frequent exchanges of visits by high-ranking officials of the two countries. The special relationship has been enhanced by H.M. King Mswati III paying state visits to the ROC in October 1989, May 1995, May 1996, October 1997 and again in October 1998.

The fifth Swazi-ROC Joint Ministerial Conference on Economic and Technical Cooperation was held in Taipei in March 1999. At about the same time, Dr. David Ta-wei Lee, Vice Minister of Foreign Affairs, visited the Kingdom of Swaziland where he presided over the annual African regional conference, a round-table meeting in which all ROC chiefs of missions in Africa participate. The conference was aimed at mapping out action plans for closer relations between the ROC and the African countries.

Malawi

The Republic of China has enjoyed longstanding cordial relations with Malawi. The two countries established full diplomatic relations in 1966, right after the Republic of Malawi celebrated its second anniversary of independence. President Muluzi paid state visits to the ROC in April 1995 and October 1996, to strengthen the relations between the ROC and Malawi. To further enhance bilateral agricultural relations, the two countries renewed the agreement on agricultural technical cooperation and signed a memorandum of understanding on technical and vocational training in September 1998.

With President Muluzi's success in the presidential election of June 1999, a special delegation led by Dr. Fredric F. Chien, President of the Control Yuan, was dispatched to the Republic of Malawi to attend President Muluzi's inauguration ceremony on June 21, 1999.

The Gambia

The Republic of China reestablished full diplomatic relations with the Republic of The Gambia in July 1995. In October 1995 the two countries signed a medical cooperation agreement and high-ranking officials visits have been exchangd. President Jammeh made state visits to the ROC in November 1996 and November 1998, while a delegation headed by Dr. P. K. Chiang, Chairman of Council for Economic Planning and Development, visited The Gambia in January 1999. Through the exchange of the visits, relations between the ROC and the Gambia have been strengthened.

Senegal

The Republic of China resumed diplomatic relations with the Republic of Senegal in January 1996. Since then, official visits between the two countries have increased significantly. Several agreements have been signed to reinforce bilateral relations in the fields of agricultural cooperation, economic and technical cooperation, and promotion and protection of investments. With the implementation of a series of cooperation projects, bilateral relations between the ROC and Senegal have become closer and stronger.

In January 1999, a delegation headed by Dr. P. K. Chiang, Chairman of Council for Economic Planning and Development, visited Senegal where he held the successful seminar "Sharing the Taiwan Experience ."

Chad

Full diplomatic relations between the Republic of China and the Republic of Chad were restored in August 1997. Since then, cooperation programs between the two countries have been broadened to medical, agricultural, infrastructure reconstruction, and other areas.

Assistance and Cooperation

The Republic of China has extended assistance to African countries in the fields of agri-culture, medicine, and handicrafts. As of June 1999, the ROC had dispatched eight agricultural technical missions to Malawi, Swaziland, Liberia, Burkina Faso, Chad, The Gambia, São Tomé, and Senegal; three medical missions to Chad, Burkina Faso, and São Tomé; and one handicraft mission to Swaziland.

To strengthen cooperation ties, the ROC signed agricultural technical cooperation agreements with Burkina Faso, Senegal, Liberia, São Tomé, Swaziland, Chad, and The Gambia. A joint-communiqué with Senegal was signed in January 1996, and a medical cooperation agreement with São Tomé in May 1997.

Europe

In Europe, the Republic of China maintains full diplomatic relations with the Holy See and the Republic of Macedonia. The ROC has established 26 representative offices in Europe, while 18 European countries operate representative offices in the ROC. These carry a variety of names but, in most cases, they fulfill virtually the same functions as embassies or consulates. For a long time, Europe was the ROC's third largest trading partner after the United States and Japan. In 1998, the ROC's two-way trade with Europe totaled US$40.28 billion, surpassing Japan to become the ROC's second largest trading partner.

On January 27, 1999, the governments of the Republic of China and the Republic of Macedonia announced that the two countries were establishing formal diplomatic relations, which made Macedonia the 28th country in the world and the 2nd country in Europe to have formal diplomatic ties with the ROC. The ROC hopes that this major diplomatic breakthrough may open a new window to expand its relationships in Southeastern Europe.

European Union

With the launch of the Euro on January 1, 1999 and plans for its enlargement, the EU has ushered in the boldest chapter of European integration. Hence the EU is expected to have a more significant role in the international community. The ROC and European countries already enjoy strong economic and trade relations. In view of further European integration, the ROC is attaching more importance to its relations with the EU.

The ROC's trade with the EU has grown steadily in the past four years from US$23 billion in 1995 to US$36 billion in 1998, representing approximately 89.8 percent of the ROC's total trade with Europe.

Since the first ROC-EU (then the EEC) trade consultations were initiated in 1981, a bilateral framework for promoting economic and trade relations has been established. In April 1998, the 13th ROC-EU trade consultation was held in Taipei. Through the years, the range of issues discussed in the consultations has widened from pure economic and trade issues to other areas, such as scientific cooperation, technology transfer, environmental protection, etc.

Business cooperation between private sectors has also expanded rapidly. The first ROC-EU Industrial Roundtable was convened on June 24, 1996, in Taipei. Commissioner Martin Bangemann of the European Commission and ROC Minister of Economic Affairs Wang Chih-kang 王志剛 co-hosted the meeting, in which numerous senior executives from top companies in Europe and the ROC participated. To strengthen further industrial cooperation between the ROC and the EU, Minister Wang led a delegation of some 50 industrialists and business leaders to the second ROC-EU Industrial Roundtable held in Brussels in July 1998.

In recent years, the European Parliament has shown particular interest in the ROC's international status and the well-being of its citizens. It has passed a series of resolutions to support the ROC's request for proper representation in the United Nations and other international organizations. During the missile crisis in February and March of 1996, it also passed emergency resolutions demanding that mainland China cease its military threats against the Republic of China on Taiwan.

Following the exchange of visits among parliamentarians, this friendship has led to the formation of friendly parliamentary groups on both sides, namely the ROC-EU Inter-parliamentary Amity Association and the EP-Taiwan Inter-

group. Through their efforts, exchanges of visits have been facilitated and mutual understanding has been enhanced.

West European Countries

The Holy See

The Holy See is at present one of the two European states that maintain diplomatic ties with the Republic of China. As the leader of global Roman Catholicism, the Holy See exerts much influence in promoting world peace, cooperation, and altruism. Since the Republic of China and the Holy See share the same ideals and principles, the relationship between the two has always been cordial and will continue to grow and flourish in the future.

In January 1998, Bishop Paul K.H. Shan 單國璽 of Kaohsiung was elevated to Cardinal by Pope John Paul II. In November 1998, Msgr. Thomas Yeh Sheng-nan 葉勝男 was designated as apostolic nuncio to Sri Lanka and elevated to the rank of archbishop by the Pope. These appointments were indeed timely encouragements not only to the Catholic community, but also to those in other walks of life in the Republic of China.

France

Relations between France and the ROC have been developing steadily since 1991, the year when the French Minister of Industries, M. Roger Fauroux, made an unprecedented visit to the ROC. Other French ministers and political dignitaries, including a former president and several former prime ministers, subsequently visited the ROC.

France ranks as the ROC's second largest trading partner in Europe. The two-way trade volume jumped to US$6.70 billion in 1998 from the previous year's level of US$6.12 billion. The ROC-France Economic Cooperation Conference has been held alternately in Taipei and Paris each year since 1984.

In February 1993, the French representative offices in Taipei were restructured as L'Institut Français, with more functions and staff. Direct air links between Taipei and Paris, operated by EVA

Airways, are facilitating greater interaction and closer cooperation between the two countries.

In addition to trade and industrial cooperation, France and the ROC enjoy frequent exchanges in cultural, educational, academic, technological, and agricultural fields. An exhibition of "Memories of the Empire: Fabulous Beauty of the Artwork of the National Palace Museum in Taipei," consisting of some 350 masterpieces of art, was successfully held at the Grand Palais in Paris from October 20, 1998 to January 25, 1999. It attracted some 205,000 visitors from all over Europe certainly, a grand occasion for Sino-European cultural exchange.

United Kingdom

The UK is the ROC's fourth-largest trading partner in Europe, with two-way trade at US$4.99 billion in 1998.

Direct air links between London and Taipei were inaugurated in March 1993. In October 1993, the Anglo-Taiwan Trade Committee, the representative office of the UK in the ROC, was reorganized and renamed the British Trade and Cultural Office.

The UK is currently the ROC's top destination for investment in Europe. An estimated 15,000 students from the ROC are now studying in the UK.

In the British Parliament, the British-Taiwan Parliament Group was reorganized in July 1997, following the British general election. Bilateral relations between the UK and the ROC are expected to be further enhanced through a variety of measures.

Germany

In 1998, the two-way trade between Germany and the ROC totaled US$9.23 billion. Germany has been the ROC's largest trading partner in Europe since the 1970s.

Relations in trade, culture, and investment between Germany and the ROC have been steadily strengthened following the initiation of direct air links in 1993.

In March 1992, an existing parliamentary friendship group in the Bundestag (Parliament) was formally recognized and began exchanging visits with its counterpart in the ROC. Several high-ranking officials, including a vice chancellor, ministers, and vice ministers, have visited the ROC in recent years.

The German Trade Office, the representative office of Germany in the ROC, was reorganized in May 1994, with the German Cultural Centre as its arm handling cultural and educational affairs. With the relocation of the German Parliament and Government, "Taipeh Vertretung in der BRD," the representative office of the ROC in Germany, was moved from Bonn to Berlin in the fall of 1999.

Italy

With two-way trade at US$2.83 billion, Italy ranked as the ROC's fifth-largest European trading partner in 1998. The Italian Trade Office in Taipei, set up in September 1989, was reorganized in 1994, with strengthened functions and representation, and renamed the Italian Economic and Cultural Promotion Office.

The direct air links between Rome and Taipei were established on July 17, 1995, which have been instrumental in strengthening contact and cooperation between the two countries.

The Netherlands

The Netherlands was the first European country to establish direct air links with the ROC in 1983. The Netherlands' bilateral trade with the ROC has also increased each year since then.

In 1998, two-way trade with the ROC reached US$5.96 billion. More than one hundred and forty Dutch companies are now operating in the ROC, with an accumulated investment value of US$1.2 billion, leading all other European nations.

The ROC-Netherlands Economic Cooperation Conference has been held annually since 1982, alternating between capitals. In Taipei, the Netherlands Trade and Investment Office promotes bilateral relations with the ROC.

Spain

Spain's bilateral trade with the ROC was US$1.03 billion in 1998, ranking ninth among the ROC's European trading partners. This was deemed as disproportional to the size of Spain's

147

GNP, and Spain has expressed a keen desire to seek more business opportunities in the ROC.

The Spanish Chamber of Commerce in Taipei has been authorized by the Ministry of Exterior Relations to issue visas in Taipei since July 1997. Spain is expected to strengthen its representation in the ROC to further promote bilateral relations.

Sweden

Sweden's bilateral trade with the ROC was US$1.11 billion in 1998, ranking seventh among the ROC's European trading partners and largest among the Nordic countries.

Conferences on economic cooperation (since 1986) and transportation and communications (since 1993) have been held annually, alternating between Stockholm and Taipei. Sweden was the first European country to sign an agreement on environmental protection with the ROC. In 1982, the Swedish Trade Council was set up in Taipei to promote relations between the two countries.

Switzerland

Switzerland established diplomatic relations with the PRC on January 17, 1950. Currently, the ROC's representative office in Bern, the Delegation Culturelle et Economique de Taipei, and Switzerland's Trade Office of Swiss Industries in Taipei, promote bilateral relations. In 1995, both countries signed an agreement on air traffic rights, and Swiss Air currently has two roundtrip flights between Zurich and Taipei every week.

In 1999, two-way trade reached US$1.5 billion, the ROC's imports from Switzerland were US$1.1 billion, and exports were 401.8 million. Switzerland currently has a trade surplus with the ROC of US$703.7 million.

Central, Eastern Europe and the Baltic States

Since the disintegration of the former USSR, the Central and Eastern European countries (the CEECs, including the three Baltic states) have been undergoing a period of economic, social, and political transformation. The ROC, with its economic achievements and political development, is looked to by the CEECs for investment and train-

ing in managerial skills, as well as sharing experiences in political and social reconstruction.

The ROC has representative offices in Hungary (opened in 1990), the Czech Republic (1991), Poland (1992), and Latvia (1992). The Czech Republic, Poland and Hungary have also set up representative offices in the ROC in 1993, 1995, and 1998, respectively.

In June 1998, Dr. Jason C. Hu, Minister of Foreign Affairs of the ROC, visited the Czech Republic, where he met with high-ranking government officials. Minister Hu also visited Poland and was keynote speaker at a seminar held by the Stefan Batory Foundation. The first lady of the Czech Republic, Madame Dagmar Havlova, visited the ROC in June 1998. One year later, Madame Lee Tseng Wen-fui, the first lady of the ROC, was invited to visit the Czech Republic.

In 1989, bilateral trade between the ROC and the CEECs was only US$288 million, but in 1998 the figure reached US$865.1 million. Bilateral agreements on industrial and commercial cooperation between the ROC and the Czech Republic, Hungary, and Poland have been signed in recent years, and bilateral economic cooperation conferences are held regularly.

Over the past decade, the International Economic Cooperation Development Fund (reorganized as the International Cooperation and Development Fund on July 1, 1996) has offered various programs to assist the CEECs in training technicians and specialists in various fields. In September 1991, the ROC cooperated with the European Bank for Reconstruction and Development, donating US$10 million to set up the Taipei China-European Bank Technical Cooperation Fund to assist the CEECs in developing their economies. The fund has since been replenished twice, reaching a total of US$20 million.

The National Science Council of the ROC has signed cooperation agreements with its Czech, Slovak, and Latvian counterparts for cultural and scientific exchanges. The ROC provides scholarships to CEEC students to study in the ROC. Since 1991, more than 100 CEEC recipients have benefited from such scholarships. The Czech Republic and Poland are now reciprocating with student exchange programs for ROC students.

The establishment of diplomatic relations between the ROC and the Republic of Macedonia on January 27, 1999, is one of the major breakthroughs of the ROC's pragmatic diplomacy in recent years. To the amazement of the world, Beijing then not only severed diplomatic relations with Skopje in February but also retaliated against Macedonia by vetoing deployment of the UN peacekeeping forces along Macedonia's border with the troubled province of Kosovo, thus impeding regional peacekeeping efforts. The irresponsible behavior of the People's Republic of China incurred worldwide criticism, and Beijing's self-proclaimed image as a peace promoter to the Balkans has been greatly damaged.

Soon after the announcement of the establishment of diplomatic ties between the ROC and Macedonia, exchanges of high-level officials started. Distinguished visitors from the Macedonian side include: Prof. Vasil Tupurkovski, Foreign Affairs Minister Aleksandar Dimitrov (January), the Minister of Information Rezxep Zllatku (February), and the Minister of Environment Toni Popovski (July).

The official visits of H. E. Savo Klomovski, President of the Macedonian National Assembly (March), and H.E. Lubco Georgievski, President of the Macedonian Government (June), are milestones in bilateral relations between the two countries. To reciprocate the goodwill, several important ROC delegations visited Skopje, including Dr. Jason C. Hu, Foreign Affairs Minister (March), H.E. Wang Jin-pyng, President of the Legislative Yuan, and H. E. Vincent Siew, Premier of the Republic of China. As a consequence of those official visits, a number of bilateral agreements were concluded, including:

(1) Agreement on the Exchange of News and Information Between the ROC and the ROM (August 6, 1999);

(2) Agreement on Technical Cooperation Between the Government of the ROC and the Government of the ROM (May 13);

(3) Agreement Between the Government of the ROC and the Government of the ROM on the Promotion and Reciprocal Protection of Investments (June 9);

(4) Protocol on Cooperation Between the Ministry of Foreign Affairs of the ROC and the Ministry of Foreign Affairs of the ROM (June 9);

(5) Agreement Between the Government of the ROC and the Government of the ROM for the Avoidance of Double Taxation and the Prevention of Evasion of Taxes on Income (June 9);

(6) Agreement on Economic Development Cooperation Between the Government of the ROC and the Government of the ROM (June 9).

These agreements provide a firm legal foundation for further development of bilateral ties.

Macedonia suffered greatly during the Kosovo crisis with the sudden influx of hundreds of thousands of Kosovo refugees into the country. The Republic of China was the first country to provide financial assistance to Macedonia to help with the refugee problem. The Government of the Republic of China also sent a special envoy with an extra US$5 million worth of medical supplies and other necessities to Skopje to demonstrate support. The relief mission, including a sizable medical team from the ROC, was highly praised by the Macedonian government and people, as well as by international organizations.

North America

The United States of America

The relationship between the Republic of China and the United States of America has continued to progress in a wide variety of fields. The Taiwan Relations Act of 1979, the "Six Assurances" of 1982 and the policy review of 1994 form the basis of the bilateral relations. In the policy review of 1994, the US made some adjustments in the way ROC-USA relations were conducted. Accordingly, sub-cabinet economic dialogues at the under-secretary (minister) level were held regularly, and the US government was authorized to send cabinet-level officials to visit the ROC. The US is also committed to more actively supporting the ROC membership in international organizations in which statehood is not required, and identifying ways for the ROC's voice to be heard in other international organizations.

In US-PRC summits held in October 1997 and June 1998, President Clinton and ranking US officials reiterated that US policy and commitments toward the ROC remain unchanged; that any improvement in US-PRC relations would not be made at the expense of the ROC ; and that US arms sales to the ROC would not be affected. In response, the ROC government urged the US to take more positive measures to further enhance US-ROC bilateral relations.

In spite of the changes in the US-PRC relationship, the US Congress continued to show its firm support of the ROC by holding public hearings, making floor statements, sending letters to the administration, and passing relevant resolutions. In the 106th Congress, both the Senate and the House of Representatives had adopted several resolutions favorable to the ROC.

During 1999, many US dignitaries visited the ROC. In addition to the former President Jimmy Carter and former Secretary of Defense William Perry, Director of the Office of Personnel Management Janice R. Lachance, Chairman of the Merit Systems Protection Board Ben L. Erdreich, Managing Director of the American Institute in Taiwan Richard Bush, Senator Jay Rockefeller, and Chairman of East Asian and Pacific Affairs of the Senate Committee on Foreign Relations Craig Thomas also visited Taipei.

As of the end of June 1998, 80 state legislative bodies in 44 US states and 16 American cities and counties had passed resolutions supporting the ROC's participation in the United Nations.

The ROC and the US have signed more than 100 agreements, covering education, customs duties, postal service, air transportation, and technological cooperation.

Trade between the two countries reached US$49 billion in 1998, a significant rise compared to 1978, when the US switched its diplomatic recognition from Taipei to Peking. The ROC ranked 7th largest among all US trading partners, while the US was the ROC's largest

trading partner in 1998. As of the end of 1998, there were 1,683 approved ROC investment projects with an approximate value of US$4.1 billion in the US. In terms of 1998 US agricultural exports, the ROC market ranked 5th, showing the importance of the ROC market for US goods. In 1998, the ROC market was 1.25 times that of mainland China. In each of the last five years, Taiwan imported from the US an average of 1.09 times as much as the Netherlands and 1.23 times as much as France did.

Canada

Canada is the ROC's 16th largest trading partner, while the ROC is Canada's 8th largest, with two-way trade reaching a record high of US$2.73 billion in 1998. Canada's Bombardier Aerospace was the ROC's third largest supplier of commercial aircraft, with dozens of Dash-8's operated by Great China Air. The Ministry of Economic Affairs signed a letter of intent for a strategic alliance with Bombardier in March 1998. Five Canadian banks, one trust company, and two insurance companies were operating actively in the ROC's financial market. In addition, Canada was one of the ROC's top emigration destinations. The ROC became Canada's 8th largest source of tourists (excluding the US), with 124,000 ROC citizens traveling to Canada in 1998.

As of the end of June 1999, the ROC and Canada had signed 16 Memoranda of Understanding (MOUs), including one on aviation safety cooperation.

During 1998, many Canadian dignitaries visited the ROC, including John Manley, Minister of Industry, and three parliamentary delegations.

Latin America and the Caribbean

The ROC maintains diplomatic relations with and has set up embassies in 14 Latin American and Caribbean countries, namely, Belize, Costa Rica, Dominica, the Dominican Republic, El Salvador, Grenada, Guatemala, Haiti, Honduras, Nicaragua, Panama, Paraguay, Saint Kitts and Nevis, and Saint Vincent and the Grenadines. The ROC has also set up 15 technical missions and 1 hydroelectric plant technical mission with more than 200 technicians in these countries. Except Belize, Dominica, Grenada, Saint Kitts and Nevis, Saint Vincent and the Grenadines, nine of the 15 nations have established embassies in the ROC.

In order to promote substantive relations with nations having no formal ties, the ROC has established representative offices in Argentina, Bolivia, Brazil, Chile, Colombia, Ecuador, Mexico, Peru, Uruguay, and Venezuela. Among these, six nations, including Argentina, Bolivia, Brazil, Chile, Colombia, Mexico and Peru, have set up trade and commercial offices in Taiwan.

To enhance bilateral and multilateral cooperation with the above-mentioned diplomtic allies, the ROC government in 1998 held a number of bilateral and multilateral conferences: "The Tenth Sino-Paraguayan Economic Cooperation Conference," "The Seventh Sino-Centroamerican Committee for the Ministers of Foreign Affairs Conference," "The Second Meeting of the Foreign Ministers of the Republic of China, the Commonwealth of Dominica, Grenada, Saint Kitts and Nevis, and Saint Vincent and the Grenadines." Through these conferences, the ROC government not only strengthened economic, cultural, agricultural, and technical cooperation with these diplomatic allies, but also won their unanimous support in its bid for participation in the United Nations and other international organizations.

To expand technological cooperation with Latin American and Caribbean countries, the ROC government renewed many agreements in 1998, including the agricultural technical agreements with the Republic of Guatemala and Salvador and the hydro-electric power plants agreement with the Dominican Republic. The ROC dispatched overseas volunteers missions to the Republic of Costa Rica.

In the sports field, the ROC government answered the needs of the governments of Costa Rica, Guatemala, and Paraguay by sending one table tennis coach to each country to train their national teams.

The Hang Kuang Acrobatic Team visited the Republic of Panama, El Salvador, Costa Rica, Guatemala, Nicaragua, Peru, Bolivia, Argentina, Paraguay, Brazil, and Venezuela to promote cul-

Children are the hope of the future. This primary school, built jointly by the ROC and Grenada, symbolizes the expectations of the two countries for the next generation.

tural exchanges. From February to June, the ROC government held painting exhibitions in the Republic of Haiti, Dominica, St. Kitts and Nevis, Panama, Costa Rica, Guatemala, Honduras, Nicaragua, and El Salvador. These events have greatly helped strengthen cooperation and communication between the ROC and its allies.

Leaders from the ROC and allied countries in Central and South America and the Caribbean have exchanged many high-level visits. Ranking visitors to the ROC include Salvadoran Vice President Enrigue Borgo Bustamente, Minister of Foreign Affairs Raul Ernesto Gonzalez, Haitian President Rene Preval, Grenadian Prime Minister and Minister of Foreign Affairs Keith Mitchell, and Paraguayan Minister of Foreign Affairs Dido Florentin Bogado.

Vice President Lien Chan led a delegation to the inauguration ceremony of President Miguel Angel Rodriguez of the Republic of Costa Rica in May 1998. Huang Kun-hui, Secretary General to the President, led a delegation to the inauguration ceremony of President Raul Cubas of the Republic of Paraguay. In September, Vice Minister of Foreign Affairs Francisco H.L. Ou visited Belize and attended the Opening Ceremony of the Parliament. Later, Vice President Lien Chan led a delegation in a visit to the Republic of Honduras, Guatemala, El Salvador, and Nicaragua.

Overseas Chinese

Aside from pragmatic diplomatic endeavors and attempts to participate in international organizations, the ROC government has in recent years stepped up contacts with overseas Chinese around the world and strengthened efforts to serve their interests. By tradition, any person of Chinese descent living outside the borders of the Republic of China is considered a *hua chiao* 華僑 ,or an overseas Chinese. Earlier overseas Chinese consisted mainly of emigrants who left China to make their fortunes or pursue higher studies abroad during the 19th and early 20th centuries. In the past few decades, emigrants from Taiwan have increased, initially for academic reasons and more recently for business as the ROC has

Major Destinations for ROC Emigrants					
	1994	1995	1996	1997	1998
USA	6,380	7,605	10,111	8,263	7,001
Canada	6,500	6,700	5,543	9,631	7,159
New Zealand	4,984	3,955	5,379	588	537
Australia	626	1,115	1,709	1,535	1,496
Total	18,490	19,375	22,742	20,017	16,193

Source: Ministry of the Interior

continued to experience rapid economic growth and growing prosperity. These relatively new overseas Chinese 新僑, comprising mainly of intellectuals and businessmen, face different challenges in their new environment compared with those encountered by the old overseas Chinese 舊僑.

Therefore, while equal attention will still be given to both old and new emigrants, the ROC government has adjusted its overseas Chinese policy to meet new demands arising from this demographic change in the overseas Chinese population. Previously, the emphasis was on preserving ethnic ties with the overseas Chinese by maintaining contact, providing education to new generations born overseas, offering economic assistance to overseas Chinese businessmen, and encouraging investment in the ROC. Recent trends have led to a policy shift toward planned and guided emigration by Taiwan residents, as well as the integration of the business interests of the established overseas Chinese with those of recent emigrants who are completely unfamiliar with their new adopted cultures. Meanwhile, the earlier focus on keeping overseas Chinese informed of domestic developments has been replaced by an effort to increase domestic understanding of Chinese residing overseas.

Emigration Trends and ROC Policy

There is historical evidence of Chinese people emigrating from China prior to the 14th century A.D. It was not until the early 19th century, however, that a population explosion, famines, and political instability within China swelled the ranks of people seeking greener pastures elsewhere. As more and more Chinese began arriving in places like Hanoi, Malacca, and San Francisco, communities of overseas Chinese sprang up and gradually became more prosperous than the hometowns left behind.

By the end of the 19th century, overseas Chinese communities had become havens for young Chinese intellectuals escaping persecution at the hands of the Ching dynasty. The Founding Father of the ROC, Dr. Sun Yat-sen 孫中山, who himself had been educated at a mission school on the Hawaiian island of Oahu, was able to garner financial support from influential overseas Chinese for his efforts to overthrow the Ching dynasty. From among the thousands of overseas Chinese students in Japan, Dr. Sun Yat-sen formed his Revolutionary Alliance 同盟會. This organization, which was the forerunner of today's ruling Kuomintang 中國國民黨, organized several uprisings against the Ching dynasty. Thirty-nine of the 72 valiant young men martyred in the abortive Canton uprising 廣州起義 in the spring of 1911 were overseas Chinese who had returned to China to help establish Asia's first democratic republic, the Republic of China. It was overseas Chinese such as these that earned Dr. Sun's praise as "the vanguard of the national revolution" 華僑爲革命之母. Throughout the eight-year war of resistance against Japan 抗日戰爭, the communist rebellion, and the development of the Taiwan area, overseas Chinese communities have been a source of unfailing support for the Republic of China.

According to OCAC statistics, some 8.7 million Chinese were living overseas in 1948. By 1968, the number exceeded 18 million. By 1988, it had exploded to 30 million. The latest figures indicated that over 34 million Chinese resided outside China at the end of 1998 (not including Hong Kong). About 80 percent make their homes in Asia, mainly in Indonesia, Thailand, Hong Kong, Malaysia, and Singapore. A little over half of the 15 percent of overseas Chinese who live in North or South America are concentrated in the United States. Europe is home to a little

less than 2.8 percent, while Oceania and Africa are home to about 1.7 percent and 0.4 percent, respectively. Most overseas Chinese come from Guangdong and Fujian, followed by Taiwan and Shandong. By profession, the majority are engaged in engineering or business.

Statistics show that nearly 800,000 people have emigrated from Taiwan since 1950. Prior to 1961, the ROC government prohibited emigration from Taiwan, and only students pursuing advanced studies abroad were permitted to travel overseas. Between 1962 and 1989, the emigration policy was relaxed and citizens could accept employment or emigrate to live with relatives in foreign countries. In 1989, the ban was completely lifted and ROC citizens could travel overseas without being subject to regulation. In view of this open policy and other factors such as the ROC's pragmatic diplomacy, Taiwan residents have shown a greater interest in emigrating overseas. The past five years have seen between 20,000 and 25,000 ROC citizens emigrate annually. A survey shows that 27 percent of new Taiwan emigrants to the US thought it would benefit their business interests to do so.

Among the 9,328 overseas Chinese associations which were registered with the OCAC as of December 1998, about 28 percent maintain close contact with the commission. Approximately 55 percent of the associations were formed by old immigrants, while the rest have been established by new immigrants from Taiwan. Interestingly, the number of associations formed by emigrants from Taiwan has increased rapidly over the past 20 years.

These developments have prompted the ROC government to make adjustments in the selection of the 180 delegates to the OCAC who are chosen from among overseas Chinese to serve as a bridge between the ROC government and Chinese residing abroad. Younger and more educated delegates have been chosen, and Taiwanese and women are better represented. Guidance is provided to potential emigrants to help them make plans for their settlement overseas. Overseas Chinese and emigration lawyers have been in-

Overseas Chinese Affairs Commission

In 1926, the ROC government established the Overseas Chinese Affairs Commission (OCAC) 僑務委員會 to ensure the welfare and interests of overseas Chinese, and it was placed under the Executive Yuan in 1932. The OCAC is organized into eight divisions: an overseas Chinese student center, an overseas Chinese passport and visa office, four departments, and two subsidiaries—the Overseas Chinese News Agency 華僑通訊社 and the Chung Hwa Correspondence School 中華函授學校.

The student center is known as the Office for Overseas Chinese Students Guidance 僑生輔導室 and is in charge of overseas Chinese studying in the ROC. The center also provides guidance, counseling, and post-graduation services. Areas handled by the passport and visa office, known as the Overseas Passport and Visa Service Office 華僑證照服務室, include the approval and transfer of entry and exit applications, applications to travel or settle in Taiwan, matters relating to military service, applications for re-entry visas, and the issuance of overseas Chinese ID cards and name chop certificates.

As for the OCAC's four departments, the first department is in charge of keeping track of the number of overseas Chinese, as well as providing services to overseas Chinese communities and to overseas Chinese on homecoming visits. The second department is responsible for fulfilling the formal educational, social service, and mass communication needs of overseas Chinese, as well as for promoting cultural and educational programs. Assisting overseas Chinese to invest in the ROC and providing economic and banking assistance to overseas Chinese enterprises are included in the third department's duties. The fourth department takes care of general affairs.

The Overseas Chinese News Agency provides news and media services pertaining to overseas Chinese affairs. The Chung Hwa Correspondence School provides educational services for overseas Chinese.

---

vited to OCAC-sponsored seminars dealing with emigration to a number of countries to address issues such as living environments, education, business opportunities, investment markets, and emigration laws.

Since the 1989 Tienanmen Incident erupted in Peking, the number of democracy activists, scholars and students from the Chinese mainland seeking political asylum overseas has increased dramatically. According to statistics compiled by the US Immigration and Naturalization Service, at least 80,000 people in this category were granted permanent resident status between 1995 and July 1, 1997. Other statistics show that more than 600,000 people from the Chinese mainland have emigrated to the US either legally or illegally within the last ten years, most of them from Fujian Province. The growth in the number of new emigrants from the Chinese mainland is particularly significant in North America, such emigrants now account for 70 percent of the local Chinese population. These new immigrants are very capable of adapting to the new environment and language and have thus become increasingly influential in overseas Chinese associations. Given the changing makeup of overseas Chinese associations over recent years, the OCAC is poised to extend its services to these new immigrants from the mainland.

Reception Services

Every year, large numbers of overseas Chinese from countries and areas around the globe attend the ROC's Double Tenth National Day celebration in Taiwan on October 10. In 1997, over 7,000 overseas Chinese from 50 countries came to celebrate both Double Tenth National Day and Chiang Kai-shek's birthday (October 31). To facilitate the visits of these overseas Chinese, the OCAC runs a special reception center during this period.

To encourage greater participation by overseas Chinese in these and other activities, the OCAC has been improving entry and exit services. The OCAC has reduced the amount of paperwork required for entry and exit applications and has made a special effort to provide the most friendly and efficient reception services possible. The same applies to overseas Chinese applying for overseas Chinese ID cards and name chop certificates. In 1998, the total number of entries and exits by overseas Chinese was 26,763. Issuance of overseas Chinese ID cards and name chop certificates totaled 31,870.

Cultural Solidarity

Maintaining cultural solidarity among overseas Chinese is one of the Overseas Chinese Affairs Commission's primary missions. The OCAC has 16 overseas Chinese cultural and educational centers in major US cities, Toronto, Manila, Sydney, Melbourne, Paris, and Bangkok. The Overseas Chinese Culture and Education Foundation 海華文教基金會, set up with a US$15 million fund provided by the OCAC, subsidizes outstanding overseas Chinese youths in the areas of education, arts, and culture. In 1998, arts festivals were sponsored in 27 cities and areas with large overseas Chinese populations.

The OCAC also subsidizes the establishment and management of Chinese TV and radio stations overseas. Its subsidiary, the Overseas Chinese News Agency 華僑通訊社, provides the latest information on current events in the Taiwan area to the overseas Chinese publications. The agency also puts out press releases to local news agencies to keep Taiwan residents well-informed of overseas Chinese affairs. Finally, the OCAC has set up a World Wide Web site (http://www.ocac.gov.tw) in order to provide the latest OCAC information.

Education

Traditionally, overseas Chinese education has been aimed at teaching cultural traditions—particularly Chinese customs, the Chinese family system, and Chinese literature—to new generations of foreign-born Chinese. For as long as Chinese have been emigrating and establishing themselves in new areas, they have set up schools to pass on their cultural heritage. Currently, there are about 2,916 overseas Chinese-language schools. The OCAC provides free teaching materials, subsidizes school facilities, and assists in training school teachers. In order to meet the growing need for Chinese education resulting from the increasing number of Chinese emigrants, the OCAC established an overseas Chinese volunteers' education group in September 1997 in Taiwan, which assigns domestic volunteers (mostly retired teachers) to overseas Chinese-language schools to assist in training teachers. In addition, the OCAC has commissioned domestic academic institutions to sponsor training programs for teachers of overseas Chinese-language schools. So far, 500 teachers from abroad have participated in such programs.

An alternative form of Chinese education for overseas Chinese is the Chung Hwa Correspondence School 中華函授學校, which was formally established in 1940. Mandarin lessons, vocational training, and general educational courses are provided free of charge. In 1998, more than 11,266 students from around the world registered for courses. Educational programs are broadcast via two international shortwave broadcast stations—the CBS Radio Taipei International and the Voice of Asia. The OCAC has also made available on its web page information regarding overseas Chinese-language schools, various Mandarin teaching materials and Chinese culture.

Economic Integration

For many decades, overseas Chinese have been contributing financially to the development of the ROC. As the world moves towards economic alignment, and more and more Taiwan businessmen invest overseas, the OCAC has become aware of the need to integrate the business strength of Taiwan entrepreneurs. Toward this end, the OCAC has guided the establishment of Taiwan chambers of commerce, the number of which now stands at 146 worldwide. In order to help coordinate the activities of regional Taiwan chambers of commerce, a continental council was set up in North America in 1987, and in 1994, a World Taiwanese Chambers of Commerce 世界臺灣商會聯合總會 was established. Four additional continental councils were set up between 1994 and 1995 to coordinate regional Taiwan chambers of commerce in Asia, Europe, Africa, and Central and South America. Any businessman from the Taiwan area who has invested overseas may participate in these chambers of commerce. Because most Taiwan investments are in export-oriented areas, and as the earlier emigrant Chinese are largely engaged in local trade, the integration of these two groups could foster economic strength among overseas Chinese, which in turn could help the ROC achieve further economic growth.

The scope of the Overseas Chinese Credit Guarantee Fund 華僑貸款信用保證基金 has been expanded in the last few years to enhance the economic status of overseas Chinese. Originally set up to encourage overseas Chinese investment in the Taiwan area and to offer credit guarantees to overseas Chinese businesses which lacked collateral and bank credit lines, the fund has extended its services to include Taiwan investors overseas.

The Fund now has 115 service stations in North and South America, Europe, Asia, Australia, and Africa. From its inception to the end of 1998, the fund had concluded 2,006 credit guarantee cases worth a total of US$315 million. The fund also helped overseas Chinese to obtain US$466 million from various financial institutions to develop their businesses during the same period. In 1998 alone, the number of cases handled by the fund rose 1 percent from 1997 to 327 cases.

Overseas Chinese have continued to invest in Taiwan. According to the Investment Commission under the Ministry of Economic Affairs 經濟部投資審議委員會, 81 new overseas Chinese investment projects worth a total of US$185 million were approved in 1998. These projects were concentrated primarily in Taiwan's service, financial, and insurance sectors, as well as electronics and electrical appliances, textiles, and the paper industry. Between 1952 and 1998, a total of 2,661 overseas Chinese investment projects in Taiwan, worth a total of US$3.6 billion, were approved. To encourage even greater participation from overseas Chinese investors and professionals in the ROC's Asia-Pacific Regional Operations Center 亞太營運中心 plan, the government has improved the overall investment environment in Taiwan by amending the *Regulations Governing the Investment by Returning Overseas Chinese* 華僑回國投資條例.

Political Participation

Article 10 of the *Additional Articles of the ROC Constitution* 中華民國憲法增修條文 promulgated on July 21, 1997, states that "the state shall accord to nationals of the Republic of China residing overseas protection of their rights to political participation." Article 1 and 4 of the *Additional Articles* provide respectively that 20 overseas Chinese (who must, however, retain ROC citizenship) shall be elected to the National Assembly 國民大會 and, beginning with the 1998 election of the fourth Legislature Yuan, eight of the 225 members shall be elected to the Legislature 立法院. As the result of the 1998 legislative election, eight members including four Kuomintang, three Democratic Progressive Party, one New Party were elected from among the Chinese citizens residing abroad. Overseas Chinese who hold ROC passports and who are not citizens of a foreign country have the right to take ROC civil service exams and serve in government posts. The right to vote is regulated by the ROC's *Public Officials Election and Recall Law* 公職人員選舉罷免法 and the *Nationality Law* 國籍法. A special clause was also included in the *Presidential and Vice Presidential Election and Recall Law* 總統副總統選舉罷免法 to allow overseas Chinese to return to vote in the direct popular election of the ROC president. Overseas Chinese who no longer hold an ROC passport can participate indirectly in ROC politics by becoming advisory members of the Overseas Chinese Affairs Commission.

10
The Economy

As the world's third-busiest container port, Kaohsiung Harbor handles two-thirds of Taiwan's annual import and export tonnage.

I n 1998, the Republic of China was still suffering from the effects of the Asian financial crisis, as exports declined and domestic demand weakened. To bolster domestic demand, the government launched a series of major public infrastructure projects and attempted to stimulate private investment. As a result, the ROC's economy grew 4.57 percent in 1998, while consumer prices rose by only 1.7 percent. Although the expansion was modest compared to some previous years, Taiwan still substantially outperformed most other economies of Asia.

Information and high-tech industries continued to dominate the manufacturing sector in 1998, raising their share of manufacturing to 27.7 percent from 25.3 percent of the previous year. With the further opening of the domestic telecommunications market, the transportation and communications sector expanded by 9.6 percent. These developments underlined the growing importance of high technology in Taiwan's economy.

In 1998, the ROC's gross national product (GNP) was US$268.6 billion, making it the 18th largest in the world. Per capita GNP declined to US$12,333 due to a 14 percent depreciation of the New Taiwan dollar against the U.S. dollar, but was still the 25th highest worldwide. This chapter profiles the ROC's economy in five sections: macroeconomic indicators, trade, services, industry, and energy. An introduction to the ROC's small- and medium-sized enterprises, which have made substantial contributions to the economy over the past few decades, is also included.

Macroeconomic Indicators

Gross Domestic Product

Taiwan's GDP increased by 4.57 percent in 1998, much lower than the 6.68 percent of 1997, but was still the highest in Asia. Since the mid-1980s,

owing to increasing consumer spending fueled by a considerable accumulation of personal wealth, domestic demand has been growing strongly. The service sector was particularly robust, generating more than 50 percent of Taiwan's GDP since 1988. Of a GDP worth US$267.1 billion in 1998, the industrial sector accounted for 34.06 percent, and agriculture only 2.74 percent. Continuing strong-growth, the service sector generated 63.2 percent of the GDP for the year.

Private consumption, which has been the driving force behind Taiwan's GDP growth for the past few years, registered a real growth rate of 8.6 percent. Government consumption recorded an 8.8 percent real growth in 1998, much higher than 1997's 5.8 percent. Food and beverages took up over a quarter of private consumption, while rentals, entertainment, and education also occupied important places.

Wholesale Price Index & Consumer Price Index

In 1998, the New Taiwan dollar depreciated 14 percent against the US dollar and a hike in

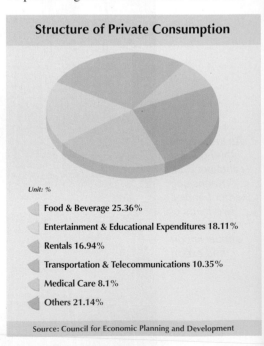

Structure of Private Consumption

Unit: %

Food & Beverage 25.36%

Entertainment & Educational Expenditures 18.11%

Rentals 16.94%

Transportation & Telecommunications 10.35%

Medical Care 8.1%

Others 21.14%

Source: Council for Economic Planning and Development

Major Economic Indicators

Item	Unit	1996	1997	1998
Economic growth rate (real GDP increase)	%	6.10	6.68	4.57
Gross national product (GNP)	US$ billion	282.9	292.6	268.6
Per capita GNP	US$	13,225.0	13,559.0	12,333.0
Changes in consumer prices (CPI)	%	3.1	0.9	1.7
Exchanges rate (end of the year)	NT$ per US$	27.491	32.638	32.216
Unemployment rate	%	2.6	2.7	2.7
Foreign exchange reserves (end of the year)	US$ billion	88.0	83.5	90.3

Source: Council for Economic Planning and Development

wholesale and commodity prices seemed likely. However, this pressure was relieved due to a drop in prices for imported agricultural and industrial raw materials and the slack demand of the domestic economy, causing the wholesale price index to grow a modest 0.6 percent. Throughout the year, the consumer price index also fluctuated moderately and inched up by 1.7 percent. Among the seven basic categories, food prices increased the most by 4.4 percent, while prices for clothing and transportation decreased.

Trade

In 1998, Taiwan's foreign trade decreased 8.9 percent to US$215.4 billion, as a result of the Asian financial crisis. Total exports for the year contracted 9.4 percent to US$110.6 billion, and the trade surplus shrank to US$5.9 billion, a decrease of 23 percent from the previous year. As a percentage of industrial exports, electronics and information-industry products have increased considerably, from 19.3 percent in 1988 to 27.7 percent in 1998. Imports declined 8.5 percent to US$104.7 billion because of sluggish domestic demand and a drop in prices for imported agricultural and industrial raw materials. Over the last few decades, exports have played a vital role in the ROC's economy.

Brisk foreign trade in the 1970s and 1980s enabled the ROC to amass huge surpluses that swelled the island's foreign exchange reserves. Annual trade surplus peaked at US$18.7 billion

in 1987. Taiwan's perennial trade surpluses soon evoked protests from major trading partners, the United States in particular, which demanded that the ROC remove trade barriers and allow more foreign products to enter the domestic market at reduced import tariffs. In 1992, Taiwan's trade surplus plunged to only US$9.5 billion, down nearly 30 percent from the preceding year. This downward trend continued through the 90s all the way until 1996, when the ROC trade surplus began to increase again. These trade surpluses have allowed Taiwan to accumulate vast sums of foreign exchange reserves, which at the end of 1998 stood at US$90.3 billion, the third highest in the world.

Exports

Exports totalling US$110.6 billion decreased 9.4 percent in 1998. The United States, Hong Kong, and Japan continued to remain the top buyers of Taiwan's exports, accounting for over 57 percent. Other major recipients of Taiwan exports include Europe and Southeast Asia.

In 1998, exports to the United States decreased slightly by 0.6 percent to US$29.38 billion. Mechanical appliances and accessories, electronics and electrical appliances, personal computers and peripherals, metal products, transportation equipment, furniture, and garments comprised the bulk of Taiwan's exports to the United States. For decades, the US market has been the most important export destination for the ROC, and this has resulted in huge trade surpluses in the ROC's favor. The

importance of the US market decreased dramatically, however, when the ROC government began to pursue liberalization and internationalization of its economy in the early 1990s. Over a decade ago, nearly 40 percent of Taiwan's total exports were destined for the United States; today, 26.6 percent of the island's exports go to the US market. Due to these changes, the ROC's trade surplus with the United States dropped from nearly US$9 billion in 1991 to less than US$5.5 billion in 1995; however, the trade surplus rose significantly to US$9.7 billion in 1998.

The ROC's exports to Hong Kong decreased 13.4 percent to US$24.84 billion in 1998, due to the slow development of exports to the Chinese mainland. In 1990, Hong Kong supplanted Japan to become the second-largest export destination for Taiwan products, and it has remained in second place ever since. There are two main reasons for Hong Kong's increased importance to Taiwan's foreign trade. The first reason is the successful implementation of the ROC government's policy to diversify its export market. The second is Taiwan's trade with mainland China, which must be carried out indirectly via a third party, usually Hong Kong. Major items exported to or via Hong Kong include electrical and electronic equipment and peripherals, machinery, accessories, raw plastic materials, and textiles.

In 1998, Hong Kong accounted for 22.5 percent of Taiwan's exports, only slightly behind the US, which took 26.6 percent. Taiwan also enjoyed a US$22.89 billion trade surplus with Hong Kong,

down 14.2 percent over the previous year. However, Hong Kong was still the region with which Taiwan enjoyed the largest trade surplus in 1998.

Exports to Japan in 1998 decreased 20.2 percent to US$9.33 billion, mainly the result of slack Japanese market demand during the year.

Europe was another target of the ROC's market diversification policy. In 1998, Taiwan's exports to Europe grew by 6.7 percent to reach US$19.64 billion. Europe was the best performing region for the ROC's export during the year. Germany, France, the United Kingdom, and the Netherlands were the four top European buyers of Taiwan products, accounting for more than 60 percent of Taiwan's exports to the continent.

To cope with the trade barriers created by the European Union's (EU) single market, a dozen of Taiwan's largest firms gained access to the EU by establishing factories or by merging with companies that already existed in the United Kingdom, the Netherlands, and Germany. Investment in Europe has mostly centered around electric appliances, electronics, and information technology products.

Southeast Asia has also emerged as a strong trade alternative, becoming the second most-favored place for Taiwan foreign investment after the Chinese mainland. Many Taiwan enterprises have established factories in this region to take advantage of abundant and cheap labor, raw materials, and significantly lower land prices. Most of the key components of the products in these countries, as well as the machinery used for

Government Oversight of the Economy

The Ministry of Economic Affairs 經濟部 oversees the nation's economic administration and development. It has the departments of Mines 礦業司, Commerce 商業司, International Cooperation 國際合作處, Industrial Technology 技術處, and an International Trade Commission 貿易調查委員會. Also under its jurisdiction are the Industrial Development Bureau 工業局, Board of Foreign Trade 國際貿易局, Intellectual Property Office 智慧財產局, Bureau of Commodity Inspection and Quarantine 商品檢驗局, Energy Committee 能源委員會, Bureau of Water Resources 水資源局, Small and Medium Enterprise Administration 中小企業處, Export Processing Zone Administration 加工出口區管理處, Central Geological Survey 中央地質調查所, Commission of National Corporations 國營事業委員會, Investment Commission 投資審議委員會, Committee for Aviation and Space Industry Development 航太工業發展推動小組，an Industrial Development and Investment Center 投資業務處 and a Professional Training Institute 專業人員研究中心.

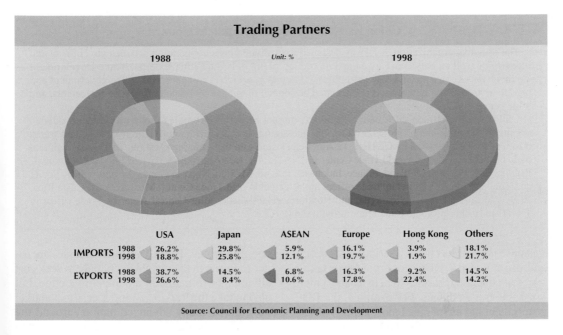

Trading Partners

Unit: %

1988   1998

		USA	Japan	ASEAN	Europe	Hong Kong	Others
IMPORTS	1988	26.2%	29.8%	5.9%	16.1%	3.9%	18.1%
	1998	18.8%	25.8%	12.1%	19.7%	1.9%	21.7%
EXPORTS	1988	38.7%	14.5%	6.8%	16.3%	9.2%	14.5%
	1998	26.6%	8.4%	10.6%	17.8%	22.4%	14.2%

Source: Council for Economic Planning and Development

production, were imported directly from Taiwan. This has contributed to the importance of Southeast Asian nations as a destination for Taiwan exports. In 1986, only 5 percent of the ROC's exports went to Southeast Asia; however, by 1998 the figure had already jumped to 10.6 percent, or US$11.67 billion.

In 1998, Taiwan ran a trade deficit of US$885 million with ASEAN, as a result of the Asian financial turmoil that broke out in mid-1997.

Imports

The ROC's economy has been able to thrive and sustain a high-level growth because of an export-oriented policy adopted by the government since the 1960s. For decades, imports—which actually constitute one-third of the island's foreign trade—have been actively discouraged by the government through the use of various barriers, such as high import tariffs and the control of foreign exchange reserves. Over the past decade, however, political democratization and economic liberalization have brought about a more prosperous Taiwan. As a result, the spending power of both the government and the private sector has

increased immensely. This is easily seen by examining the value of imports, which has quintupled during the period.

In 1998, the aggregate value of Taiwan's imports was US$104.74 billion, down 8.5 percent from the previous year. The demand for raw industrial and agricultural materials, the preponderance of Taiwan's imports, decreased as a result of slow economic growth, registering a 13.4 percent decline to US$66.83 billion. Consumer product imports also declined 12.6 percent to US$13.59 billion. However, capital good imports increased 11.9 percent to reach US$24.31 billion.

Over a quarter (US$27.02 billion) of Taiwan's 1998 imports were from Japan. Major import items included machinery, auto parts, electrical appliances, electronics, chemicals, and metal products. Many of Taiwan's industries rely heavily on the supply of key parts and the transfer of technology from Japan, especially the information and automobile industry (see sections on Information Technology Industry and Automobile Industry). Each year, much of Taiwan's trade surplus with other nations is offset by its deficit with Japan. Unabated growth of over 10 percent annually in

China External Trade Development Council

The principal organization in Taiwan designed to facilitate closer cooperation between government and industry as well as between Taiwan and its trading partners is the China External Trade Development Council (also known as CETRA) 中華民國對外貿易發展協會, which is co-sponsored by the government and private industrial and business organizations. The council maintains 38 branch offices, design centers, and trade centers in 28 countries.

CETRA gathers trade information, conducts market research, promotes made-in-Taiwan products, organizes exhibitions, promotes product and packaging designs, offers convention venues, and trains business people. Assisted by CETRA, 12 American states and the American Institute in Taiwan maintain trade offices at the Taipei World Trade Center 臺北世界貿易中心 (see Appendix V). An additional 13 nations—Bolivia, Canada, Chile, Finland, France, Indonesia, Ireland, Mexico, Nigeria, Oman, the Philippines, Spain, and Thailand—have also set up trade offices at the Taipei World Trade Center. Most recently, Costa Rica, El Salvador, Guatemala, Nicaragua, and Honduras established a joint Central America Trade office in TWTC to further promote trade relations with the ROC.

Japanese imports has led to a serious trade deficit and prompted the ROC government to take a series of concrete measures to help restore a more favorable trade balance. For example, the ROC government has encouraged more exports of Taiwan-made products to the Japanese market. In addition, endeavors have been made to attract more Japanese investment and joint-ventures to Taiwan, with output from such cooperative projects then being exported back to Japan to reduce the trade imbalance. Despite all these efforts, Taiwan's deficit with Japan again increased 2.1 percent to reach US$17.68 billion in 1998.

The second largest source of Taiwan's imports was Europe. European products comprised 19.7 percent (US$20.64 billion) of Taiwan's imports in 1998, down 4.5 percent from 1997, resulting in a trade deficit of US$994 million with the region. The United States was third, with overall imports from the country reaching US$19.68 billion, down 15.3 percent from 1997.

Economic Ties with Mainland China

The year 1997 marked the tenth anniversary of the beginning of private-sector exchanges between Taiwan and the Chinese mainland. In the past decade, economic relations between the two sides have developed from sporadic trading activities by Taiwanese small and medium-sized enterprises to large-scale investments, involving millions or even billions of US dollars by Taiwanese conglomerates. These Taiwan businesses are eager to invest in the mainland not only to seek cost advantages to maintain a competitive edge, but also to take the lead in gaining access to a market coveted by many advanced nations around the world. Despite the absence of direct transportation links, economic ties between Taiwan and the Chinese mainland have never been closer than in recent years. In 1992, investment in the mainland by Taiwanese businesses was legalized, quickly pushing the Chinese mainland to the top of the list of major recipients of Taiwan's foreign investment. Cross-strait economic ties have served as an essential link between Taipei and Peking. The two economies are so intertwined now that breaking them off would be next to impossible, as the Chinese mainland has emerged as the primary source of the ROC's trade surplus in recent years. In 1987, Taiwan had a trade surplus of just over US$1 billion with the Chinese mainland, but, by 1998, the surplus had reached US$15.7 billion.

When the ROC first lifted its ban on cross-strait exchanges by the private sector in 1987, the government expected that this would create more favorable conditions for reunification. If interaction between the people on both sides could be gradually increased, then ideological conflicts could eventually be set aside and differences in the ways of thinking and living could be ameliorated. Unfortunately, much to the disappointment of the ROC government, this was not to be the case. As the years went by, Peking authorities voraciously absorbed capital and technology from their Taiwanese compatriots, while, at the same time sparing no effort to suppress Taiwan in the international community.

In light of these strained relations between Taipei and Peking (see also Chapter 7, Mainland Affairs and National Unification Policy), as well as the danger of having Taiwan's economy too dependent on the Chinese mainland, the ROC government decided to put a brake on cross-strait economic ties. In 1996, the government presented a new policy which called for "patience over haste 戒急用忍." This policy was opposed by both business and academic circles within the ROC. In the aftermath of the Asian financial crisis, the ROC government reiterated that it will continue the policy in the future as the region's financial situation remains unstable.

According to the ROC's Mainland Affairs Council 大陸委員會, the value of two-way trade between Taiwan and the Chinese mainland amounted to US$23.95 billion in 1998. Over 82 percent of the indirect trade was exports from Taiwan, which totaled US$19.84 billion, down 11.67 percent from 1997. Major export items to the mainland included industrial machinery and equipment, electronic parts, plastics, man-made fibers and industrial textiles, etc.

Imports from the Chinese mainland soared 4.85 percent to US$4.11 billion in 1998. The bulk of the imports were agricultural and industrial raw materials.

Taiwan's worry over trade dependence on the mainland is rising. Approximately 11.13 percent of Taiwan's 1998 trade was with the mainland. Export dependency stood at 17.94 percent, and import dependency at 3.93 percent.

Inward and Outward Investment

In recent years, the ROC government has improved the investment climate by removing obstacles, implementing a "one-stop window" 單一窗口 policy, and encouraging participation by the private sector in public construction projects. Twenty-six infrastructure projects, including the high-speed rail line in Taiwan's western corridor and 8 private power plants, have been approved. These Build-Operate-Transfer (BOT) projects, with a total investment amount of US$47.9 billion, will help capitalize on private resources and accelerate national development. In 1998, private investment increased by 10.33 percent to reach US$34.2 billion.

During the same year, there were 918 approved inward foreign investments, totaling US$3.2 billion. Compared to the previous year, the total number of approved inward foreign investments increased by 235 and was 34 percent higher than 1997; but the amount of investment fell by US$970 million, representing a decrease of 22.8 percent. Most of Taiwan's inward foreign investments in 1998 came from British territories in Central America (mainly British Virgin Islands and British Cayman Islands), the United States, Japan, Hong Kong and Singapore. The total amount from these areas equaled about 71 percent of the total amount of inward foreign investment in 1998.

Approved Mainland Investments by Sector between 1991 and 1998

Unit: %

Electronics & Electrical Products 26.72%

Food & Beverage 11.27%

Metal Products 10.85%

Plastic Products 10.1%

Chemicals 8.25%

Others 32.81%

Source: Ministry of Economic Affairs

163

The top five sectors for foreign investment were electronics and electrical appliances, financial and insurance, international trade, wholesale retailing, and service, accounting for about 75 percent of the total inward foreign investment. Although the amount of investment decreased marginally from 1997, due to the impact of the Asian financial crisis, it was still the second highest in recent years. Obviously, foreigners still consider Taiwan a priority area for investment.

Overseas investments (not including those in the Chinese mainland) by Taiwanese businesses also surged by 13.9 percent to reach US$3.29 billion in 1998. In terms of the area of investment, Taiwan's outward investment focused on the British territories in Central America, the United States, Singapore, Thailand, and Vietnam.

Between 1991 and 1998, the ROC government had approved some US$13.24 billion worth of mainland investments, covering over 21,646 applications. According to statistics released by the mainland authorities, investment agreements through 1998 indicated that Taiwanese entrepreneurs assented to invest in some 41,017 projects worth a total of US$40.4 billion, thereby making Taiwan the fourth-largest mainland investor after Hong Kong, Japan, and U.S. Statistics released by the ROC Ministry of Economic Affairs showed there were 641 approved indirect investments in mainland China in 1998, totaling US$1.5 billion. Compared to 1997, the number of investments decreased by 87 or 11.9 percent, while the amount decreased by US$95 million or 5.9 percent. A large number of Taiwan manufacturers in labor-intensive industries have set up factories on the Chinese mainland to take advantage of the cheap labor and low overhead costs. Many of these manufacturers receive orders in Taiwan, produce their goods in the mainland, and ship the goods from the mainland to their overseas buyers.

As the market on the Chinese mainland becomes more open and lucrative, more of Taiwan's large enterprises, including firms in the information technology, plastics, and food and beverage industries, are beginning to undertake large-scale

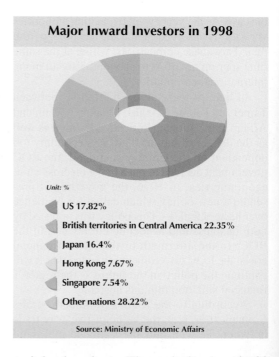

Major Inward Investors in 1998

Unit: %

- US 17.82%
- British territories in Central America 22.35%
- Japan 16.4%
- Hong Kong 7.67%
- Singapore 7.54%
- Other nations 28.22%

Source: Ministry of Economic Affairs

mainland projects. The majority (nearly 83 percent) of Taiwanese investors like to concentrate their investments on the southeastern coast of the mainland, as transportation facilities in this area are far more developed than in the interior. However, Taiwan investment is spreading beyond the eastern coast of Fujian and Guangdong provinces. Taiwan businessmen are also beginning to invest in activities other than export manufacturing, setting up mainland offices to handle real estate, insurance, banking, and tourism.

On July 15, 1997, the Ministry of Economic Affairs (MOEA) released the revised Review Guidelines for Investment and Technological Cooperation in the Mainland Area 在大陸地區從事投資或技術合作審查原則. These guidelines went into effect immediately upon release and stipulated that each individual investment case in the Chinese mainland must be reported to the relevant authorities. They further stipulated that such investments cannot exceed US$50 million without first receiving special approval from the appropriate government agencies. The MOEA also widened the scope of prohibited investments, preventing Taiwan businesses from investing in major infrastructure projects on the Chinese mainland, including such projects as railways, highways, harbors, airports, mass transit systems, incineration projects, power plants, and industrial zones. Real estate, insurance, and 17 other manufacturing products are also included in the prohibition. Despite the large number of new restrictions, tourism, leasing, and a number of entertainment businesses have been given investment authorization.

Services

In the Republic of China, the service sector is divided into seven main categories: (1) finance, insurance, and real estate; (2) commerce, which includes wholesale, retail, food and beverage, and international trade; (3) social and individual services; (4) transportation, storage, and telecommunications; (5) commercial services, including legal, accounting, civil engineering, information, advertising, designing, leasing, etc.; (6) governmental services, and (7) others. During the 1960s and 1970s, the rapid growth of industry almost caught up with Taiwan's sluggish service sector in terms of GDP percentage. Roughly two decades ago, however, Taiwan's service sector was revitalized and steadily increased the gap between the service sector and the industrial sector. In 1998, the service sector accounted for 63.2 percent of Taiwan's GDP, a percentage very similar to that of many advanced nations. The total GDP value for the service sector that year reached US$164.7 billion, up 6.09 percent over the preceding year.

Finance, insurance, and real estate continued to comprise the bulk of the service sector, accounting for just over 32 percent.

Commerce rebounded to account for 27 percent of the service sector, with wholesale, retail, and international trade all performing better than the year before. Of these, retail was the strongest sector, recording a 6.8 percent growth rate.

Asia-Pacific Regional Operations Center

Global economic activity is becoming increasingly oriented toward the Asian-Pacific region as it emerges as a counterpart to the North American and European markets. With an eye toward capitalizing on this trend, the ROC government has declared its intention to develop Taiwan into an Asia-Pacific Regional Operations Center (APROC) 亞太營運中心, promoting Taiwan as the location of choice for multinational enterprises wishing to set up headquarters from which to manage their operations in the Asia-Pacific.

Six sub-operations centers—including manufacturing, sea transportation, air transportation, financial, telecommunications, and media centers—have been envisioned within the regional operations center. While the Council for Economic Planning and Development (CEPD) [see Governmental Economic Planning inset] is responsible for the overall planning and coordination of the project, the sub-operations centers are being handled by the Ministry of Economic Affairs 經濟部, the Ministry of Transportation and Communications 交通部, the Ministry of Finance 財政部, the Central Bank of China 中央銀行, and the Government Information Office 新聞局.

The APROC plan is being implemented in three phases. In the first phase (January 1995-June 1997), laws and administrative orders were amended or enacted to support facilities. In the second phase (July 1997-December 1999), the APROC efforts will be engineered toward creating increased business opportunities in Taiwan. Administrative agencies overseeing the development of the six specific operations centers will be setting up "quantitative and non-quantitative" indices to monitor progress. The third phase starts with the beginning of the next century. At that time, Taiwan will posses one of the best established trade and financial operations centers in the Asia-Pacific region, thus, optimizing its competitiveness and consolidating its economy.

In March 1995, the Coordination and Service Office for Asia-Pacific Regional Operations Center under the CEPD 經濟建設委員會亞太營運協調服務中心 was set up to serve international companies that are interested in taking advantage of the opportunities created by this project.

Of the remaining categories, only the social and individual service sectors and the transportation, storage, and telecommunications sectors showed any major changes. The social and individual service sectors registered a moderate 7.84 percent growth, while the transportation, storage, and telecommunications sectors recorded a 9.63 percent growth.

Taiwan's thriving service sector, particularly in the financial and stock market areas, has attracted many young people eager to find careers in recent years. In 1988, the service sector surpassed the industrial sector in attracting more of the total work force. By the end of 1998, over 53 percent of the island's 9.28 million employees were working in the service sector.

Industry

Industry has long been outpaced by the service sector in terms of GDP percentage. In 1986, industry still accounted for nearly half of Taiwan's GDP. By the end of 1987, it had dropped to slightly over 40 percent of the GDP. This downward trend has continued ever since. In 1998, industry accounted for 34.06 percent of Taiwan's GDP, a further plunge over the same period of last year.

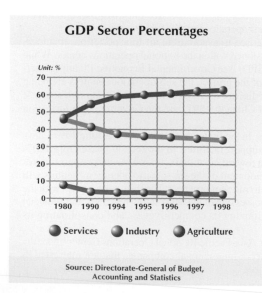

GDP Sector Percentages

Unit: %

Source: Directorate-General of Budget, Accounting and Statistics

Except for textiles, which rose 1.62 percent, production of processed foods, leather products, and wood and bamboo products, which once dominated exports, continued to decrease in 1998. These labor-intensive industries have gradually been replaced by capital- and technology-intensive industries, such as the production of chemicals, petrochemicals, information technology, electrical equipment, and electronics, all of which experienced moderate to strong growth rates in 1998 despite a general recession in the industrial sector. Electronics and information technology have evolved into the mainstay of industry, accounting for nearly 30 percent of the nation's manufacturing in terms of production values. With respect to production output, manufacturing output constituted over 78 percent of the total industrial production and engaged over 26 percent of the national work force.

In the 1960s, an abundance of well-trained local workers and inexpensive manufacturing sites were the two major factors attracting many foreign companies to set up production branches in Taiwan. By 1987, however, the stock market had become overheated due to excessive savings in the private sector and a lack of investment channels. As a result, a large portion of the population started to play the market, causing a shortage of labor (especially blue-collar workers) in nearly all industrial and business sectors. A steep hike in land prices further aggravated the overall manufacturing environment, forcing many small and medium-sized firms, as well as labor-intensive enterprises, to scale down, shut down, or move their businesses. Those firms that moved often relocated to the Chinese mainland or Southeast Asia, leading to a decline in their relevant sectors.

Fortunately, the establishment of overseas production sites by such technology- and capital-intensive industries as machinery, chemicals, precision equipment, and electronics and information technology products, has not created the aftereffect of reducing the growth of their parent companies in Taiwan. These companies have been able to avoid harmful side effects by streamlining

Taiwan is the world's third-largest manufacturer of information technology hardware, with its information and electronics industries now accounting for almost 30 percent of the island's manufacturing output.

operations and management, thereby increasing international competitiveness and making production more efficient.

Information Technology Industry

In 1998, Taiwan's hardware information technology industry (domestic and overseas combined) had a total production value of US$33.8 billion, up 11.9 percent from US$30 billion of the previous year, making it the ROC's most important foreign exchange earner. Taiwan has been the world's third-largest computer hardware supplier since 1995, trailing only the United States and Japan. Taiwan's 900 computer hardware manufacturers provide jobs for approximately 100,000 employees. In 1998, laptop computers, monitors, desktop PCs, and motherboards accounted for about 80 percent of the production value of the information technology industry. Taiwan manufacturers have a large share of the world market because of their competitive prices and high quality. According to statistics released by the Institute for Information Industry 財團法人資訊工業促進會, Taiwan has already supplanted Singapore to become Japan's second largest supplier of information products, second only to the United States.

Amid the generally lackluster performance of the domestic economy, Taiwan's hardware information technology industry still managed to register significant growth. This can be attributed to many factors, including the rapid growth of Internet use around the world, the increased popularity of multimedia computers, and the expansion of production by local PC manufacturers. Taiwan's information technology industry has grown from a minor role in the overall economy to a major contributor to the island's flourishing exports. This is partly a result of governmental inducements and partly because of the extreme flexibility of domestic small and medium-sized enterprises. This flexibility possessed by Taiwan's SMEs allows them to quickly follow and adapt to the latest market trends, and adjust their production accordingly. Nevertheless, the industry still faces problems that are common to all manufacturing sectors: labor shortages and high overhead costs.

The structure of Taiwan's information technology industry is best described as a pyramid. A handful of companies at the top of the pyramid commit themselves to product innovation through costly and time-consuming R&D (see Chapter 18, Science and Technology), while small and

SMEs

For decades, Small and Medium-sized Enterprises (SMEs) have been the backbone of the ROC's economic development. Unlike many advanced nations, where conglomerates dominate the economy, Taiwan's manufacturing and foreign trade is built up and fortified by countless SMEs.

SMEs began emerging after World War II, when Japanese conglomerates withdrew from Taiwan and the local market fell into the hands of state-run enterprises and large private companies. The island's SMEs focused on foreign markets to survive. At first, agricultural products and agricultural processed goods made up the bulk of exported items. These were eventually replaced by light industrial products, especially after the government set up several export-processing zones to spur on the economy. An export-oriented policy in the 1960s also created a favorable environment for SMEs to penetrate international markets. SME entrepreneurs are characterized by high adaptability to market trends, hard work, thrift, and a tendency to pass their businesses on to their children. According to the Ministry of Economic Affairs, over 98 percent of Taiwan's 1,024,435 registered enterprises are SMEs. These SMEs employ nearly 80 percent of the total work force and account for half of the island's aggregate export value.

The 1995 revision to the *Small and Medium-sized Enterprise Development Statute* 中小企業發展條例 defines small and medium-sized enterprises by sector, paid-in capital/annual turnover, and the number of employees. Industries, including manufacturing, construction, and mining and quarrying, that have a paid-in capital not exceeding NT$60 million (an equivalent of US$1.76 million) or hire less than 200 regular workers, are categorized as SMEs. Companies in the commercial, service, and transportation sectors with an annual turnover not exceeding NT$80 million (an equivalent of US$2.35 million) or that hire less than 50 employees are also considered SMEs. Most SMEs (60 percent) are in the commercial sector, followed by manufacturing (15 percent).

In terms of sales turnover, commercial sector accounted for over 43 percent of SME aggregate turnover, while the manufacturing took up 35 percent in 1997. The two, though distinguished by sector, are complementary in that many SMEs in the commercial sector rely on manufacturers to supply goods. At the same time, a large number of manufacturers also work closely with trading companies to export products.

For decades, Taiwan has been an Asian production outpost for many renowned multinational conglomerates, proof that Taiwan can produce high-quality goods. Today, made-in-Taiwan products, ranging from packaging to toys and from garments to personal computers, are found in shops around the world. A large number of Taiwan's SMEs still rely heavily on OEM and ODM orders, tending to avoid relatively long-term investments and investments in R&D. On average, SMEs spend no more than 3 percent of their annual operating income on R&D, mainly because these companies are reluctant to invest in arduous processes that have no guarantee of successful results. Another factor that influences SME's willingness to invest lies in their difficulty in acquiring bank loans. Although banks generally consider many SMEs financially unstable, they still provide 34 percent of the capital resources for SMEs. Roughly 82 percent of SME funding for R&D projects comes from the companies themselves, while only 11 percent comes from bank loans.

Nevertheless, SMEs constitute a large portion of Taiwan's investment overseas as the ROC has emerged to become a major investor worldwide. During the pioneering stage, most SMEs tended to invest in the Chinese mainland or in other Southeast Asian nations due to their proximity, with funds that usually did not exceed US$2 million. This has changed in the last couple of years, however, with access to the market and convenient service becoming the two primary factors concerning SMEs in their attempt to consolidate or even expand their post in the world market.

Due to the worldwide economic slump, Taiwan's SMEs have encountered many hardships in exporting goods. A shortage of laborers, increases in wages, and prohibitive prices for land acquisition have also plagued both large-scale firms and SMEs. Fluctuating exchange rates and keen competition from other nations are other major factors that have directly impacted SME operations.

In light of the continuing importance of SMEs in Taiwan's overall economy, the government has made five revisions to the *Small and Medium-sized Enterprise Guidance Regulations* 中小企業輔導準則, first stipulated in 1967. The revisions are geared to create a sounder environment for SMEs to increase productivity. Other government measures to assist SMEs include a development fund that provides assistance in case of recession and indemnification for damages caused by natural disasters as well as programs to promote automation and computerization. In addition, seminars to cultivate marketing and managerial expertise have been held, and the functions of the SME service centers located in 22 cities and counties around the island have been strengthened.

The ROC's per capita GNP reached US$13,248 by the end of 1999.

medium-sized enterprises at the base of the pyramid form the vast majority (85 percent) of the actual output. The latter comprise a weak and unstable downstream foundation. As in other manufacturing sectors, SMEs generally produce goods on an OEM (original equipment manufacturer) and ODM (original design manufacturer) basis, and therefore spend a negligible percentage of their annual turnover on R&D. This has led to the inability of these companies to make in-depth assessments regarding investment, production, and marketing of new and innovative products. Moreover, heavy reliance upon the imports of key parts and advanced technology from the United States and Japan has tied Taiwan's information technology industry to the economic strength of these countries, thereby offsetting a good portion of Taiwan's trade surplus each year.

Automobile Industry

Taiwan is currently home to 13 automobile manufacturers, the majority of which have contractual joint ventures with foreign makers, mostly from Japan. These companies both produce and import automobiles. The production value of the automotive industry reached US$9.93 billion in 1998, the equivalent to 5.08 percent of Taiwan's aggregate manufacturing production value of that year. Approximately 402,000 automobiles were produced in Taiwan in 1998.

Due to limited parking space and the operation of several mass rapid transit system lines in urban districts, total automobile demand in Taiwan dropped from 542,000 units sold in 1995 to approximately 476,000 in 1998. Sedans for private use continued to dominate the demand, accounting for nearly 80 percent. Whereas the number of domestically made sedans sold in 1998 rose 7 percent to reach 292,000 units, the number of imported units fell 7 percent from the previous year. Domestically-made vans for commercial use accounted for about 94 percent of the market. Over the last couple of years, competition between locally made and imported vehicles has

169

gradually declined and a 4:1 market share ratio has taken shape. In 1998, the domestic automobile industry, threatened by the imports from Japan and the U.S., still managed to capture around 84 percent of the market, proving that the quality of the MIT automobile has been accepted by local consumers.

In 1998, over 70 percent of the 292,000 domestically made sedans were supplied by three companies: Ford Lio Ho Motor Co., Ltd. 福特六和汽車股份有限公司(20.3 percent), Yulon Motor Co., Ltd. 裕隆汽車製造有限公司(28.6 percent), and Kuozui Motors Ltd. 國瑞汽車股份有限公司(22.4 percent). In the commercial vehicle market, China Motor Corporation 中華汽車工業股份有限公司 maintained its traditional top position, producing over 50 percent of the 115,700 commercial vehicles sold.

Although the ROC imposes a quota on autos imported directly from Japan, Japanese vehicles have, like many other commercial products, successfully penetrated the Taiwan market and built a solid customer base. In 1998, nearly a quarter of the imported vans were Japanese brands that had been made in American factories. Toyota alone took 21 percent of the Taiwan market share of imported sedans. Of the top ten best sellers in the Taiwan market, all were either products of Sino-Japanese joint ventures, or they directly carried Japanese brand names. Domestic automobile manufacturers have long worried that once Taiwan's door for imported cars is officially opened with reduced tariffs (from the current 30 percent down to 20 percent), or once Taiwan is admitted into the WTO, foreign vehicles will flood the market and threaten the survival of domestic manufacturers.

Like many other domestic industries, Taiwan's automobile industry, with decades of government protection, is short on R&D. It needs to develop its own technology in engines, computerized gearing systems, and several other components, and enhance its design capability. For example, Taiwan's reliance on foreign engines has for years hampered its plans to export vehicles. Consequently, in preparation for the impact that the ROC's admission to the WTO will have on the island's automobile industry, the Ministry of Economic Affairs has already begun to allocate budget resources to encourage R&D. Under the joint efforts of the MOEA, the Chungshan Institute of Science and Technology 中山科學研究院, and the private sector, the government will upgrade local automobile manufacturers' capabilities to produce key parts, such as engines and airbags, that would otherwise have to be imported from Japan.

Textiles

In the past five decades, Taiwan has successfully developed from an agricultural backwater to an industrialized nation. During this process, the textile industry has been one of the most important factors in Taiwan's economic growth. Comprised primarily of small, family-run businesses, the textile industry was a key element in the government's export-oriented policy. It occupied an eminent place in exports, earning large amounts of foreign exchange for the nation.

Since the second half of the 1980s, several problems, including the sharp appreciation of the NT dollar, labor shortages, increasing overhead costs, prohibitive land prices, and the environmental protection, forced textile businesses to

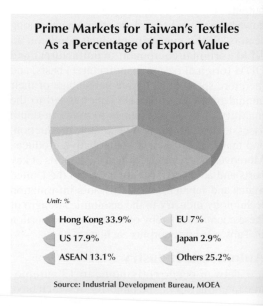

Prime Markets for Taiwan's Textiles As a Percentage of Export Value

Unit: %

Hong Kong 33.9%   EU 7%

US 17.9%   Japan 2.9%

ASEAN 13.1%   Others 25.2%

Source: Industrial Development Bureau, MOEA

relocate part or even all of their production to Southeast Asia and the Chinese mainland in order to maintain their competitiveness. Textiles have been dubbed one of Taiwan's labor-intensive "sunset industries." Those textile companies which have stayed in Taiwan have initiated reforms. Small, family-run businesses have been transformed into medium-sized or even large enterprises, with cost-effective measures and innovative management, introduced to raise quality and productivity. Since Taiwan is not blessed with cotton, wool, silk, linen and other natural raw materials, the domestic textile industry has developed man-made fabrics, which have proven to be an excellent alternative to natural products.

Today, Taiwan's man-made fibers have earned a prominent place in the textile industry throughout the world. In 1998, Taiwan produced over 3.2 million tons of man-made fiber, ranking third in the world. Polyester was 80 percent of the total output and placed Taiwan as the world's largest producer of this fiber. In that same year, Taiwan exported and imported over US$17.7 billion worth of textiles, including fiber, yarn, fabric, garments, and accessories. Hong Kong was the primary destination for Taiwan's textile exports, followed by the US and ASEAN. The industry has also been one of Taiwan's prime contributors to its favorable trade balance, accounting for nearly US$11.4 billion of the nation's surplus in 1998.

Petrochemicals

Taiwan's petrochemical industry integrates 45 upper- and middle-stream manufacturers located in Kaohsiung's special chemical zone. In 1998, the industry had a production value of US$11.3 billion (excluding textile and plastics-related industries), of which 82 percent is sold on the domestic market. However, Taiwan's petrochemical production capacity (as measured by ethylene output) could only satisfy about 53 percent of actual domestic demand in 1998; therefore, the Formosa Plastics Group (FPG) 臺灣塑膠工業股份有限公司, a renowned plastics conglomerate in Taiwan, applied for government approval to build a sixth naphtha cracking plant 第六輕油裂

解廠. The company launched the project several years ago in Yunlin County's Mailiao 麥寮. The mammoth project was built in an industrial zone that encompasses a total of 39 plants, including an oil refinery, naphtha cracking plant, cogeneration plant, coal-fired power plant, heavy machinery plant, boiler plant, wafer fabrication plant, and petrochemical-related plants. It is noteworthy that this industrial zone of 2,100 hectares of land area is reclaimed land, a great portion of which lies below sea level.

The FPG began its initial operations in the industrial zone at the end of 1998 and is expected to produce 450 thousand tons of ethylene annually. When the US$8.7 billion project is completed, it is estimated that Taiwan's ethylene self-sufficiency will jump to 79 percent.

Energy

Taiwan lacks sufficient energy resources. Its coal reserves amount to only 98 million tons, most of which are distributed throughout the northern part of the island. Oil and natural gas reserves, found mostly in the northern Taiwan counties of Hsinchu and Miaoli, and near the southern city of Kaohsiung, total 0.4 million tons and 2,400 billion cubic feet, respectively. Total hydropower reserves have been estimated at 5,047 megawatts, of which 1,973 megawatts have been developed, primarily along several major rivers. Given such limited natural resources, Taiwan must import fossil fuels to meet the bulk of its energy needs.

Supply

The total energy supply in Taiwan increased from 29 million kiloliters of oil equivalent in 1978 to 92 million kiloliters in 1998, with an average annual growth of 6 percent. Over the past two decades, local energy supplies have accounted for a progressively smaller portion of annual usage, dropping from 19 percent in 1978 to 4 percent in 1998; therefore, the imported energy share has had to rise correspondingly. Of the total energy supply, oil accounted for 51 percent and nuclear power accounted for 10 percent.

Expenditures for imported energy totaled US$6.4 billion in 1998, of which imported oil accounted for 66 percent or US$4.2 billion. Imported energy accounted for 6.1 percent of the total value of imports in 1998 and 2.4 percent of GDP, with per capita energy imports at US$293.

Consumption

Taiwan's annual energy consumption increased from 25 million kiloliters of oil equivalent in 1978 to 81 million kiloliters in 1998, an average growth rate of 6.1 percent per year. By comparison, GDP grew by an average of 7.3 percent during the same period, with an energy demand elasticity of about 0.84. Per capita energy consumption increased from 1,456 liters of oil equivalent in 1978 to 3,725 liters in 1998, an annual growth rate of 4.8 percent.

Over the past 20 years, the industrial sector has been the greatest energy consumer; however, its share of total energy consumption dropped from 65 percent in 1978 to 55 percent in 1998. Energy consumption for transportation increased from 11 percent in 1978 to 17 percent in 1998; for agriculture, it declined from 3 percent to 2 percent; for residential use, it increased from 10 percent to 12 percent; for commercial use, it increased from 2 percent to 6 percent; for other sectors, it dropped from 7 percent to 6 percent. Non-energy use was close to 2 percent in 1998.

Since the second worldwide energy crisis, coal has accounted for a growing percentage of Taiwan's overall energy consumption, rising from 10 percent in 1978 to 12 percent in 1998. By contrast, petroleum products accounted for only 39 percent of overall energy consumption in 1998, down from 49 percent in 1978.

Oil and Natural Gas

Taiwan is heavily dependent on imported oil. In 1998, approximately 62 percent of imported crude oil came from the Middle East. The other 38 percent came from Indonesia, the Congo, and Australia. Consumption of petroleum products totaled 38.8 million kiloliters of oil equivalent in 1998, of which 33 percent was for industrial use, 35 percent for transportation, 18 percent for power

---

Governmental Economic Planning

The Council for Economic Planning and Development 行政院經濟建設委員會 succeeded the former Economic Planning Council. Its functions are to coordinate the financial and economic sectors in advancing the economy and to study the world economic situation and trends in the domestic economic structure. It has eight departments: Overall Planning 綜合計劃處, Sectorial Planning 部門計劃處, Economic Research 經濟研究處, Urban and Housing Development 都市及住宅發展處, Financial Analysis 財務處, Manpower Planning 人力規劃處, Performance Evaluation 管制考核處, and General Affairs 總務處. A coordination and service office for building Taiwan into a regional operations center is also under the CEPD's jurisdiction since 1995.

---

generation, 2 percent for agriculture, 4 percent for residential use, and 8 percent for other purposes.

The state-owned Chinese Petroleum Corporation 中國石油股份有限公司 (CPC) is solely responsible for exploring, producing, importing, refining, and marketing petroleum and natural gas in Taiwan. The CPC owns two oil refineries with a total capacity of 770,000 barrels per day and recently has made considerable investment to increase the output of low-sulfur fuel oil to improve air quality.

In 1987, the government began allowing the installation of privately operated gas stations to sell gasoline and diesel oil. At the end of 1998, there were 1,720 gas stations, 1,146 (67 percent) of which were privately owned. In 1998, domestic petroleum production amounted to 38.6 million kiloliters of oil equivalent and 879 million cubic meters of gas, respectively.

To liberalize the oil market, the government authorized the establishment of petroleum refining enterprises and granted them permission to engage in petroleum production, import/export, and marketing in June 1996. The importation of fuel oil, jet fuel, and LPG was opened in January 1999, and the complete opening of petroleum products imports is expected by the end of June 2000.

To diversify the types of energy consumed, the CPC has imported 1.5 million tons of liquefied natural gas (LNG) from Indonesia every year since 1990, and, beginning in 2001, the quantity will increase to 1.84 million tons under a new contract. The CPC also started importing 0.5 million tons of LNG from Malaysia in 1995. This amount is expected to increase to 2.35 million tons at the beginning of the next century. Natural gas consumption in 1998 totaled 5,869 million cubic meters, of which 31 percent was for industrial use, 54 percent for power generation, 12 percent for residential use, and 3 percent for commercial use.

Coal

Coal production continued to decline, dropping from five million tons in 1968 down to 0.08 million tons in 1998. The local coal industry was once the prime source of energy, constituting over 60 percent of industrial energy use in the 1950s, and employing some 65,000 coal miners in over 400 mines around the island. Due to the high costs of coal production under increasingly difficult mining conditions, as well as competition from imported coal, the number of coal mines and miners in Taiwan has decreased dramatically. Today, there are 3 coal mines in Taiwan which employ approximately 300 workers. Tougher times lie ahead for the industry, as the younger generation look for white collar occupations. In addition, once the ROC is admitted into the World Trade Organization, the government must annul rules that protect local coal production. Subsequently, the remaining coal mines will most likely be forced to close within five years.

Coal supply totaled 37 million tons in 1998. Of this, 0.2 percent was domestically produced, while the remaining 99.8 percent was imported from Australia, Indonesia, South Africa, the Chinese mainland, and the United States. In 1998, some 58 percent of the total coal consumption of 21 million tons went to power generation, 5 percent to the cement industry, 15 percent to steelworks, and 22 percent to other industries and users.

Electricity

In 1998, gross power generation by the Taiwan Power Company臺灣電力公司(Taipower),

totaled 145 billion KWH, a 8.6 percent increase over 1997. Of the total, 7.3 percent was generated by hydropower, 39.8 percent by coal, 18 percent by oil, 9.6 percent by LNG, and the remaining 25.2 percent by nuclear fission. Power cogeneration by auto producers totaled 17.9 billion KWH in 1998. Electricity consumption in 1998 rose to 146.8 billion KWH, up 6.5 percent over the preceding year. At present, nearly all of the population has electricity service.

Taiwan Power Company is the agency responsible for developing, generating, supplying, and marketing electric power for almost the entire Taiwan area. By the end of 1998, the Taiwan area had 16 EHV substations (345/161 KV), with a capacity of 25,500 MVA; 88 primary substations (161/69 KV), with a capacity of 32,724 MVA; and 44 primary distribution substations (161/22-11 KV), with a capacity of 8,464 MVA. A total of 39 hydropower, 18 thermal, and three nuclear plants supply power to these stations. Taipower installed capacity totaled 26,680 megawatts, of which 16.6 percent was hydropower, 30.4 percent coal-fired, 14.7 percent gas-fired, 19.1 percent oil-fired, and 19.3 percent nuclear. By the end of 1998, the installed capacity of auto producer cogeneration was 2,865 megawatts, equivalent to 11 percent of Taipower's installed capacity.

With the continuous growth of the domestic economy, the peak load in 1998 reached 23,830 MW, up 7.2 percent over 1997. The average load was 15,904 MW, a 8.7 percent increase compared with the previous year. Facing an increasing requirement for power supplies, the government has already taken several steps to alleviate future potential shortages. In September 1994, the government promulgated the Guidelines for the Opening of the Independent Power Generation Industry 開放發電業作業要點 to encourage private sector power production. By the end of 1998, eight applications for independent power plants had been approved . Also in 1998, units five, six, seven, and eight of the Taichung Thermal Power Plant 臺中火力發電廠, unit five of the New Tienlun Hydro Power Plant 新天輪水力發電廠, and five units of combined cycle at the Hsinta Power Plant

興達發電廠 were all put into operation, generating an additional 1,900 megawatts.

In June 1999, Mailiao Power Corp., located in the Yunlin County naphtha cracker complex established by the Formosa Plastics Group, began its initial commercial operations, with a power generating capacity of 1,200 megawatts. The new independent power plant is expected to alleviate the island's power shortage during the summer time. In addition, companies operating at the Hsinchu Science-based Industrial Park (HSBIP) suffered a loss of over US$0.3 billion due to the power outage resulting from the devastating September 21 earthquake in 1999. Consequently, the government instructed the Science-based Industrial Park Administration to construct a second cogenerator in HSBIP to supply electricity to the park.

Nuclear Power

The six nuclear units in Taiwan provided 17 percent of the total installed capacity (5,144 megawatts out of 29,545 megawatts), but produced 22.4 percent of Taiwan's total electrical output in 1998. The six nuclear units are housed in three nuclear power stations, all of which are owned and operated by Taipower. With increasing demands for electricity, especially for industrial use, the government began plans to construct a fourth nuclear power plant in 1980. Support for the project has been slowly undermined, however, by the general public's environmental concerns and increasingly vehement protests against nuclear power. These protests have generated negative votes against the budget for the power plant, especially by legislators representing constituencies where the plant is slated to be built. In December 1997, the Legislative Yuan approved a proposal by opposition parties to eliminate US$2.12 million from Taipower's budget as a feedback fund for its construction of the fourth nuclear power plant, which is scheduled to be completed in 2004.

Renewable Energy Sources

Taiwan's subtropical location gives it great potential to develop solar energy resources. A number of solar, thermal, and photovoltaic testing systems are already in service in Taiwan, with the total area

---

Fourth Nuclear Power Project Chronology

1980　Taipower first broaches the plan to build a fourth nuclear power plant, scheduled to be completed by 2004. Total budget for the project is US$6.3 billion.

1983　A 480-hectare land at Yenliao 鹽寮 in Kungliao Rural Township 貢寮鄉, Taipei County, in the northern part of Taiwan is acquired for the six-unit plant.

1985　The Executive Yuan 行政院 instructs Taipower to postpone the plan and step up public relations for the project.

1987　The Legislative Yuan 立法院 freezes budget for the plan passed between 1982 and 1986.

1992　The Budget Committee 預算委員會 of the Legislature releases the budget upon the request of the Executive branch.

1995　Taipower opens bidding for the contracts. No successful result is achieved because quotations submitted by international contractors exceed the set price cap by 20 percent or more.

1996　On May 24, the Legislature votes to overturn the budget for the nuclear power plant. On the same day, General Electric Company of the United States wins the US$1.8 billion contract for the plant's two reactors. On October 18, the Legislature votes to revive the project.

1999　The Cabinet-level Atomic Energy Council issued an official license for the construction of the nuclear power plant.

---

of solar collectors reaching 800,000 square meters at the end of 1998. In addition, two 100-kilowatt wind turbines are presently in service on Chimei Island 七美嶼 in the Pescadore Islands. Technologies for biogas purification and the assembly of biogas power generators have been investigated over the last decade, and a number of pig farms already have biogas power generators in operation. In 1998, these generators produced 6 megawatts.

Energy Prices

The price structure for electrical power is configured to reflect the cost of supplying energy at different seasons (seasonal rates) and different times of the day (TOU rates). Seasonal rates and TOU rates are designed to encourage peak clipping, valley filling, and/or load shifting. Currently, the electrical service is divided into three categories: lighting, combined lighting and power, and power (metered and flat-rated). Seasonal rates are applied to all customer classes except flat-rated customers. TOU rates are mandatory for those with a contracted capacity of 100 KW and are voluntary for those with a contracted capacity below 100 KW. At present, TOU rates are applied to all customer classes except lighting customers.

Low-tension metered lighting service is applicable to residential as well as small commercial and noncommercial customers. Charges for metered lighting service are calculated solely upon the KWH consumed. Low tension combined lighting and power service is applicable to medium commercial and noncommercial customers. Low tension metered power service is applicable to small and medium-sized industrial/agricultural customers. High or extra-high tension service is applicable to customers with a contracted capacity of around 100 KW. Charges for power service and combined lighting and power service are separated into demand charge and energy charge (a two-part rate). Demand charge is billed on the contracted KW, and energy charge is calculated according to the KWH consumed.

In order to reduce the summer peak load directly, Taipower also offers a menu of interruptible rates (seven options) on a voluntary basis to customers taking high or extra-high tension service. Interruptible rates are designed to reflect capacity cost savings for customers' interruptible loads. The rates require that customers reduce their peak demand to a predetermined level in accordance with the contract in return for demand credits. The latest rate schedules for electrical service came into effect on June 1, 1995.

Domestic oil prices have been allowed to reflect the cost of imported oil as world prices fluctuate. The government also routinely considers the substitutability and heating values of petroleum products and natural gas before setting their prices. In November 1999, the Chinese Petroleum Corporation adjusted its prices for petroleum products in accordance with an oil-price formula. Oil prices were as follows: US$0.57 per liter for most tanked premium gasoline, US$0.56 for 95-octane

General Statistics on the Economy

Economic Growth Rate (%)

1999	5.74	f
1Q	4.26	r
2Q	6.54	p
3Q	5.95	f
4Q	6.16	f
2000	5.96	f

GNP (at current prices, US$ million)

1999	283,097	f
1Q	69,059	r
2Q	67,286	p
3Q	72,555	f
4Q	74,197	f
2000	306,198	f

Per Capita GNP (US$)

1999	12,874	f
1Q	3,155	r
2Q	3,068	p
3Q	3,293	f
4Q	3,358	f
2000	13,770	f

Foreign Trade (US$ million)
Exports

1999 May	10,628	r
June	9,862	p
July	9,987	p

Imports

1999 May	8,816	r
June	9,065	p
July	9,498	p

Notes:
  (f): forecast
  (r): revised
  (p): preliminary
Source: Directorate-General of Budget, Accounting and Statistics

unleaded gasoline, US$0.53 for 92-octane un-leaded gasoline, US$0.41 for premium diesel oil, and US$0.37 for kerosene.

Energy Conservation

Energy conservation is a major part of energy policy. The Measures for Energy Conservation 節約能源措施 and the Energy Management Law 能源管理法 mandate a set of incentives for energy customers to conserve energy. So far, energy productivity has risen from US$2.69 per kg of oil equivalent in 1978 to US$3.38 in 1998.

2000 Forecast

Due to the devastating earthquake in September 1999, the Directorate-General of Budget, Accounting and Statistics under the Executive Yuan 行政院主計處 expects Taiwan's overall economy to grow only 5.4 percent in 1999. According to the statistics revealed by the Council for Economic Planning and Development, the quake is expected to reduce private consumption by about US$820 million, which, in turn, will seriously affect economic growth. To revive the economy, the ROC government began to boost consumption and encouraged participation in the reconstruction projects by the private sector to help foster growth. The negative impact resulting from the quake was expected to start waning in the second quarter of the year 2000, and domestic demand reviving after the third quarter. The DGBAS also puts the economic growth forecast for 2000 at about 6 percent.

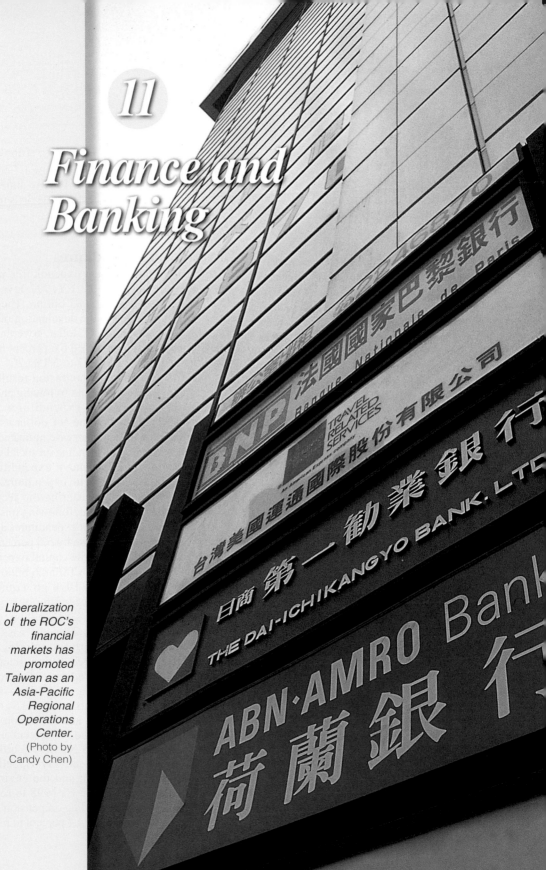

11

Finance and Banking

Liberalization of the ROC's financial markets has promoted Taiwan as an Asia-Pacific Regional Operations Center.
(Photo by Candy Chen)

The Asian financial crisis continued to trouble the Republic of China's financial markets during 1998, as an outbreak of defaults among some listed domestic firms dampened domestic economic prospects. The Taiwan Stock Exchange composite index, which rose to 9,300 points in February 1998, took a drastic plunge that pushed it below the 7,000 mark. Meanwhile, the New Taiwan dollar depreciated to an 11-year low against the US dollar, at one point reaching an exchange rate of NT$35:US$1. Imports and exports continued to decrease while overseas orders placed in terms of US dollars also declined in 1998. Beginning in the second half of 1998, several listed corporations defaulted on loans, as a result of highly leveraged stock speculation. All of these developments were strong indicators that the Asian financial crisis had taken its toll on the ROC.

The year 1998 was not without its bright side, however. The ROC government continued its plans to participate in the World Trade Organization and develop Taiwan into a major financial center for the Asia-Pacific region. Agreements were reached with the United States to accelerate the opening of domestic banking, insurance, and securities markets. On July 21, 1998, a new milestone was set in the financial market, when Taiwan International Mercantile Exchange inaugurated stock futures trading, targeted on the weighted index of the spot market. Furthermore, the long-delayed plans to privatize three government-owned commercial banks were finally completed, further liberalizing Taiwan's financial sector.

In this chapter, we use an average exchange rate of US$1:NT$28.7 for the year 1997 and US$1:NT$33.46 for 1998. As for the fiscal year 1997 (from July 1, 1996 to June 30, 1997), an average rate of US$1:NT$25.57 is used. For the fiscal year 1998 (from July 1, 1997 to June 30, 1998), an average rate of US$1:NT$31.56 is used.

Public Finance

Government Expenditures

In FY1998, government expenditures were down 6.9 percent from the FY1997 level of US$74.96 billion to US$69.82 billion. The decrease was mainly due to the devaluation of the NT dollar. In terms of the NT dollar, government expenditures actually increased 6.6 percent from NT$2.067 trillion in FY1997 to NT$2.204 trillion in FY1998. (To avoid confusion resulting from currency fluctuations, the following analysis regarding government expenditures and revenues will be based on the NT dollar as the unit of calculation unless otherwise indicated.)

With the exception of spending on social welfare, the increase in government expenditures occurred across-the-board, with expenditures for economic development registering the second highest growth at 13.2 percent, following miscellaneous expenditures. Current expenditures at all levels of government also rose by 5.6 percent to reach NT$1.545 trillion, while capital expenditures climbed 9.2 percent to NT$658.6 billion.

A breakdown of the FY1998 government expenditures showed that spending on social welfare fell 4.1 percent to NT$282.8 billion compared to the previous year. This decrease reflected a change in policy priorities during the financial crisis. Funding for education, science, and culture—which accounted for 18.7 percent of total government spending in FY1998—rose 9.5 percent from FY1997 to reach NT$411.5 billion. Spending on general administration and national defense also increased 5.1 percent and 7 percent in FY1998 to reach NT$257.3 billion and NT$312.3 billion, respectively. Spending on community development and the environment climbed 9.1 percent in FY1998 to reach NT$74.9 billion; while spending on pension and survivors' benefits increased 4.4 percent to reach

NT$187.7 billion. Finally, the figure for debt obligations was up 8 percent from FY1997 to NT$328.0 billion.

Government Revenues

With increases in revenues from surpluses of public enterprises, profits of public properties, and taxes levied, the total revenue for all levels of government jumped 12.1 percent in FY1998 to reach NT$2.325 trillion. However, revenues from bonds, loans, and monopolies were down. This reflected that governments, as a whole, were somewhat limited in issuing new bonds, given its current debt status.

Revenues from taxes, which accounted for 57.6 percent of government revenues, increased 10.4 percent in FY1998 to reach NT$1.34 trillion. Surpluses from public enterprises and public utilities showed a large increase of 90.5 percent from the previous year to hit NT$361.6 billion, while profits of public properties also rose 114.4 percent to NT$42 billion. Revenues from fees, fines and indemnities, donations and contributions, proceeds from sales of properties, and recalled capital all increased to a lesser extent in FY1998. However, revenues from monopolies declined 1.3 percent from FY1997 to reach NT$57.4 billion. Proceeds from issues of public debts and receipts from loans for economic construction also fell 56 percent and 11.9 percent, reaching NT$59.9 billion and NT$176.3 billion, respectively.

Debt Obligations

In contrast to the deficit that occurred in FY1997, all levels of government actually managed to maintain a surplus of NT$121.7 billion in FY1998—a result of the government's determination to cut the fiscal deficit and the delay of infrastructure projects.

Money & Banking

Money Supply

In the first half of 1998, the economy was feeling the impact of the Asian financial crisis as exports started to fall. However, active trading in the Taiwan Stock Exchange saw the

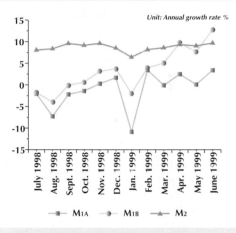

Money Supply

Unit: Annual growth rate %

Source: Central Bank of China

growth rate of the widely defined money supply aggregate M₂ fall from 9.37 percent in January to 8.13 percent in March, and then rebound to 8.45 percent in May.

Beginning in the second quarter, however, the economy declined further and caused the demand for capital to decline. Trading in stock markets also decreased. In addition, the NT dollar began to depreciate against the US dollar. To mitigate the speed of depreciation, the Central Bank of China 中央銀行 (CBC) sold US dollars to defend the NT dollar. As a result, the growth rate of the M₂ dropped to 7.76 percent in June, the lowest monthly growth figure of the year.

This decline was amplified by an outflow of capital. The financial account in the Balance of Payments recorded a net outflow of US$1.3 billion in the second quarter and a further net outflow of US$3.7 billion in the third quarter.

The annual growth rate of the M₂ probably would have continued to fall had the CBC not intervened. On August 2, the CBC lowered the required reserve ratio for banks, thus injecting NT$46.7 billion into the economy. On September 28, the CBC again lowered the required reserve ratio to release another NT$36.1 billion. The CBC also cut the rediscount rate from 5.25

percent to 5.125 percent and the prime rate for secured loans from 5.625 percent to 5.5 percent.

These relaxed monetary measures produced the desired effect and boosted the growth rate of the M_2 to 9.82 percent in October and attained an overall average growth rate of 8.76 percent for 1998. This average was slightly higher than the 8.26 percent of 1997 and was well within the target zone of 6 to 12 percent set up by the CBC for the annual growth rate of the M_2. In 1999, the supply of the M_2 returned to a steady rate of growth, rising from 7.37 percent in January to 9.32 percent in May.

The growth rate of the narrowly defined money supply aggregate M_{1b}, on the other hand, continued to fall throughout most of 1998— mainly because of the boom-and-bust performance of the stock market, which caused individuals to switch from demand deposits to time deposits. The M_{1b} declined from a peak of 11.52 percent in January to 2.64 percent in August, and then rose again to 2.87 percent in December. The average growth rate of the M_{1b} was 2.58 percent in 1998, well below the 13.82 percent reached in 1997.

Despite lagging trends in 1998, a rejuvenated stock market helped the M_{1b} growth rate to increase sharply in 1999 from 0.33 percent in January to 9.23 percent in May. The 9.23 percent growth rate was above the median of the target zone, and

the CBC therefore adjusted its monetary policy stance from expansionary to neutral.

Financial Institutions

By the end of December 1998, the number of financial institutions in Taiwan, including monetary institutions and the Postal Savings System, had decreased by eight from the previous year to reach a total of 499. The reduction of institutions included one new local branch of a foreign bank and three new domestic banks formed either from the combining of credit cooperatives or from the merging of credit cooperatives with existing banks. In addition, the long-delayed plans to privatize three large commercial banks owned by the Taiwan Provincial Government were finally completed in the first half of 1998.

The first half of 1998 witnessed a continuing slowdown in Taiwan's economy. The annual growth rate of loans granted by major financial institutions remained on the decline, dropping from 13.32 percent at the beginning of 1998 to 5.34 percent by the end of 1998. It finally reached 2.9 percent in January 1999—a record low since October 1996—before slowly climbing back up to 5.22 percent in May 1999. On the other hand, the growth rate for portfolio investments increased from 13.13 percent in January 1998 to an annual high of 42.11 percent in September 1998. This was a result of efforts by the Ministry of Finance 財政部 (MOF) to encourage banks to buy stocks in order to

Financial Institutions							
Domestic Banks		Medium Business Banks		Taiwan Branches of Foreign Banks		Credit Cooperatives	
Head Office	Branches	Head Office	Branches	Head Office	Branches	Head Office	Branches
1991	17	756	8	290	36	47	74	425
1994	34	1,174	8	403	37	57	74	530
1998	42	2,052	6	352	46	72	54	446

Note: For foreign banks, the number of head offices indicates the number of multinational banks that have branch offices in Taiwan.
Source: Central Bank of China

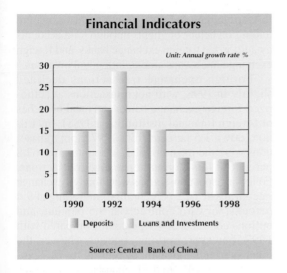

Financial Indicators

Unit: Annual growth rate %

Deposits   Loans and Investments

Source: Central Bank of China

prevent the weighted index from further sliding. After the stock market recovered in March 1999, the monthly growth rate hit 15.85 percent in May 1999.

The non-performing loan ratio for domestic financial institutions rose from 4.16 percent in March 1998 to 5.1 percent in March 1999. This reflected the continued sluggishness of Taiwan's economy and the poor performance of the real estate market. In May 1999, the CBC announced six measures to reduce the non-performing loan ratio for domestic financial institutions; and as stock markets started to recover in the second quarter of 1999, the non-performing loan ratio for domestic financial institutions decreased.

Money Markets

The money market became an important source of short-term capital for companies. Both transactions in the interbank call-loan market and in short-term bills expanded rapidly. During 1998, transactions worth a total of NT$14.598 trillion were completed in the interbank call-loan market, up 31.8 percent from 1997. Short-term bills valued at NT$13.691 trillion were issued in 1998, representing a 20.6 percent increase over 1997, and the outstanding balance on short-term bills was up 16.8 percent to NT$2.386 trillion. Transactions in short-term bills were 37 percent higher than in 1997, reaching NT$85.071 trillion

in 1998. Commercial paper accounted for the majority of those transactions, taking a lion's share of 92.2 percent.

In the first half of 1998, active trading on the Taiwan Stock Exchange and the CBC's moderate stabilization operations kept interest rates stable. This trend continued in the second half of the year, when Taiwan's economy appeared to deteriorate and the CBC moderately relaxed its monetary policy. With the CBC's double reduction of the required reserve ratio and the steady growth of money supply, short-term interest rates declined substantially. The annual average interest rate for the overnight call-loan market was 6.56 percent, down from 6.85 percent in 1997. The weighted average of 31 to 90-day Commercial Paper (CP) rates in the secondary market also declined from 6.83 percent in 1997 to 6.81 percent in 1998.

Bond Markets

As a result of decreases in the government deficit and a slowdown of infrastructure projects, the primary bond market saw a sharp decline with the issuance of a mere NT$146 billion worth of bonds (excluding treasury bills) in 1998, down from the NT$174 billion issued in 1997. As a result, the outstanding balance for bonds issued by all levels of government was only NT$1.044 trillion, a slight increase of 0.88 percent from the previous year. On the other hand, corporate bonds issued by private enterprises rose 93.9 percent from 1997 to US$6.45 billion in 1998, due to heavy trading on the Taiwan stock market, the outbreak of the Asian financial crisis, and a drop in short-term interest rates. In December 1998, the outstanding balance for corporate bonds was US$14.11 billion, an increase of 62.1 percent over 1997.

Transactions in the secondary bond market recorded an all-time high in 1998, with US$1.642 trillion worth of securities changing hands to attain a 36.1 percent increase over 1997. The main factors contributing to this development included the sluggish economy, the weak performance of the stock markets, the loose monetary policies implemented by the CBC to keep interest rates low, and an increase in repurchase (repo) and short-term bond transactions. Repo transactions, up 26.6 percent from 1997, made up the largest portion of these factors, accounting for US$1.430 trillion.

Interest Rates

The money supply in the first half of 1998 was relatively loose and remained so throughout the second half of the year, primarily because of the weakened economy and the depreciation of the NT dollar against the US dollar. In order to stabilize the foreign exchange market and avoid further slides in the stock market, the CBC lowered the rediscount rate three times from 5.25 percent to 4.75 percent. In addition, the prime lending rate for major commercial banks was lowered from 7.955 percent in the first half of the year to 7.704 percent in December 1998.

Foreign Exchange Market

The New Taiwan dollar remained stable in the first half of 1998, suffered a moderate devaluation against the US dollar in the middle of the year, and gradually appreciated in the latter half. The average exchange rates were NT$33.04:US$1 and NT$33.63:US$1 in the first two quarters of 1998, dropping to NT$34.54: US$1 in the third quarter. This devaluation was mainly due to a sharp depreciation in the Japanese yen and the CBC's decision to float the NT dollar. On June 10, 1998, the foreign exchange rate fell below the NT$35:US$1 mark to reach an 11-year low. It finally bottomed out following strong defensive actions by the CBC and the stabilization of the Japanese yen. In the fourth quarter, the average exchange rate of the NT dollar rose to NT$32.61:US$1. The annual average exchange rate for the year was NT$33.44: US$1, a depreciation of 16.68 percent compared to 1997.

In order to prevent speculation in the foreign exchange market and alleviate devaluation pressure on the NT dollar, three measures were implemented by the CBC toward the end of May 1998. These measures included bans on nondelivery forward trading (NDF) by domestic firms, margin trading on behalf of clients through joint accounts by authorized foreign exchange banks, and foreign exchange rate swaps among individual investors.

Foreign exchange transactions declined slightly in 1998, with net transactions at authorized foreign exchange banks and local branches of foreign financial institutions at US$1.169 trillion, down 1.5 percent from 1997. Spot transactions were the most popular, accounting for 63.8 percent of total foreign exchange transactions. Following spot transactions were foreign exchange rate swaps at 14.2 percent, margin trading at 9.4 percent, forward contracts at 8.5 percent, and options contracts at 4.1 percent. Compared with 1997, however, options contracts showed the most substantial growth, increasing by 78.7 percent. This was due to the high volatility of the NT dollar against the US dollar caused by the Asian financial crisis and the tumult on Wall Street following the Long-Term Capital Management Company (LTCM) crisis.

Stock Market

The Taiwan Stock Exchange (TSE) started on a brisk note in 1998 before gradually slowing down for the rest of the year. Recovering Asian economies and the subsequent appreciation of their currencies, a booming US stock market, and the high dividend policies announced by Taiwan's listed electronics companies all pushed the TSE composite index from 8,085 points on January 22 to 9,277 points on March 2. The index reached a high of 9,300 in April, but then gradually dropped to below 7,000 in mid-June. This boom-and-bust performance was attributable to many factors: the weaker profits of hi-tech US stocks, disappointing movements in the prices of Taiwan's listed stocks after dividend payments were made to shareholders, a higher number of purchases on margin, continued financial instability in East Asia, growing pressure for further devaluation of the NT dollar, and a deterioration in the external trade sector in the first quarter of 1998. With the exception of a short-term boost in July due to the opening of the Taiwan Stock Index futures market and the record-breaking Dow Jones Industrial

Average, the TSE composite index continued to gradually fall for the rest of the year, eventually hitting 6,418 points at the end of 1998.

To stabilize the stock market and restore investors' confidence, the MOF announced five measures on November 13: establishing an ad hoc fund to stabilize the market; encouraging financial institutions to buy stocks when necessary; temporarily halting the trading of stocks owned by troubled firms; investigating rumors unfavorable to the market; and punishing those who engaged in illegal activities that placed firms in financial disorder.

The TSE composite index continued its downward trend in 1999, hitting a low of 5,400 points in February. However, it has since rebounded quite strongly due to the recovery of the global economy, Taiwan's strong export performance, and the continuous inflow of foreign capital. By June, the TSE had increased 60 percent from its low point in February to reach 8,600 points.

The total trading value of the market was US$885.2 billion in 1998, a decrease of 20.5 percent from 1997. Even though the number of listed companies increased from 404 in 1997 to 437 in 1998, the total market value reached only US$250.4 billion, down 13.6 percent from 1997.

Financial Restructuring

The ROC economy grew at a phenomenal pace throughout the 1970s and 1980s. The rapid accumulation of assets which accompanied this growth led to a tremendous increase in financial activity and brought about profound structural changes in the local financial market. Increasing labor costs and the appreciation of the NT dollar in the 1980s sped up the globalization of Taiwanese capital by encouraging investment and other financial involvements in overseas financial markets. This trend, in turn, exerted competitive pressure on the domestic financial system and forced the ROC to liberalize itself more to attract foreign investors and financial institutions to Taiwan.

The ROC's financial system has been undergoing restructuring since 1987. Among the many changes which have been made is the relaxation

In February 2000, the Taiwan Stock Exchange composite index rose above 10,000 points, the level it reached ten years ago.

of restrictions on cross-border capital flows. Interest rates have also been gradually liberalized, beginning with discount rates on CDs and bank debentures in 1980 and expanding to include deposit interest rates. In 1989, the revised *Banking Law* 銀行法 was passed, lifting all restrictions on interest rates and bringing an end to Taiwan's long history of interest rate controls. In addition, the island has developed its short-term money market and long-term capital market to help meet the requirements of supply and demand, thereby allowing market mechanisms to play a more active role in the financial system.

When the ROC set up its money market in 1975, it was limited to interbank call loans and other short-term monetary instruments. Since then, it has evolved into the second largest money market in Asia with an annual turnover exceeding US$1.6 trillion. The size of the bond market also expanded drastically after 1989 due to the heavy issuance of government bonds for economic development. As for the stock market, the revised *Securities Transaction Law* 證券交易法 of 1989 allowed new entries into the brokerage business and loosened restrictions on inward remittances of foreign capital for portfolio investments, thereby making Taiwan's financial markets much more competitive internationally.

Taiwan has strengthened financial re-regulation and supervision in response to changes in the financial environment. The rapid expansion of financial markets; the deregulation of financial activities, financial innovations, and new entries in the financial sector; and the possible disorder associated with financial realignment have all made re-regulation necessary. In line with the Bank of International Settlements, the ROC has set its capital adequacy ratio at 8 percent of risk assets. The government also established the Central Deposit Insurance Corporation 中央存款保險公司 in 1987 to provide a better safety net for depository institutions. The *Banking Law* of 1989, while allowing new entrants into the banking industry, also tightened regulations dealing with problem banks. Regulating some areas while deregulating others has been the most important task of financial restructuring in Taiwan.

After a number of runs on local credit cooperatives in the past few years, the CBC and the MOF decided to form a temporary joint committee to monitor all banking institutions. The MOF also made a proposal to revise the *Statute of Deposit Insurance* 存款保險法, requiring all financial institutions to participate in a system of compulsory deposit insurance.

To promote an active market of corporate bonds and to introduce more positive competition among banking institutions, the first credit rating company began its operation in May 1997. With the passage of the *Statute of Futures Trading* 期貨交易法, the local futures exchange was opened in October 1997 and the Taiwan International Mercantile Exchange (TAIMEX) was inaugurated in July 1998. As further trading on indexes of electronic and financial stocks are scheduled to open in the near future, firms and individuals will be able to hedge their risks against the volatility of commodity prices, exchange rates, interest rates, and stock prices. Several new financial instruments, including warrant contracts on approved stocks, exchange rate options, and foreign exchange futures, were also listed on the Taiwan Stock Exchange or allowed to be traded over-the-counter in 1997.

In 1998, a few domestic firms inappropriately engaged in the excessive use of high leveraged funds for speculation. This led to financial disruptions and caused the entire economy to suffer a severe setback. To prevent similar events from happening again, the government has proposed a unified supervisory agency to reinforce financial regulation. Also, consideration is being given to limit the chairman of the board of directors in financial institutions to only those individuals with financial specialty backgrounds, so as to preclude the chairman from taking personal advantage of funds. To improve the quality of bank assets and to allow an accelerated write-off of nonperforming loans, the Ministry of Finance reduced the business tax rate on financial institutions, including securities firms and insurance companies, from 5 percent to 2 percent. Other important measures passed include revising the regulations on stock holding by subsidiaries and the encouragement of mergers and acquisitions among financial institutions. In the future, Taiwan will continue its liberalization process and employ the newest technology, such as e-commerce, in the financial system, allowing it to adapt more quickly to the challenging and rapidly changing world of finance.

12
Agriculture

After the autumn harvest, rice fields in Taiwan are often planted with rape to replenish the soil. With two crop seasons, rice remains the island's most valuable crop.

Brilliant green rice paddies set against a misty backdrop of bamboo and bananas, cicadas droning loudly under the heat of the noontime sun—these are the images of old Taiwan, where once over 90 percent of the island's residents lived in farming villages growing rice, sugar cane, tea, jute, and other crops. This picture has rapidly faded in the wake of industrialization, however, and today Taiwan's farmers make up only 8.9 percent of the workforce and produce less than 3 percent of the island's GDP. Farmers in Taiwan are now confronting falling incomes, rising costs, and increased foreign competition, and they are becoming fewer and older as younger generations abandon farming for city life. As Taiwan gears up for entry into the World Trade Organization (WTO), the predicament of farmers is likely to worsen before getting better.

If the sector is to avoid becoming an anachronism on the margins of Taiwan's modern economy, it must completely reinvent itself. The Century-spanning Agricultural Development Plan 跨世紀農業建設方案 implemented in July 1997 is designed to serve this purpose for the next four years. In accordance with this plan, the annual growth rate of the GDP for the agricultural industry will be maintained at 0.5 percent; efficient farming operations will be carried out to increase total agricultural production from US$14.95 billion in 1995 to US$18.36 billion in 2001; and the annual income of each farming household will be raised from US$22,655 in 1995 to US$32,727 in 2001. The plan also calls for agricultural agencies to address environmental problems arising from agricultural development. An estimated US$12.7 billion will be needed to carry out this plan through the year 2000.

Farmers

In 1998, there were nearly 859,000 hectares of farmland worked by more than 782,000 farming households, meaning that each household on average tilled a plot of land only 1.1 hectares (2.7 acres) in size. For the past decade, Taiwan farmers have derived over 60 percent of their annual income from non-farming activities. The rise of part-time farming households, which have accounted for over 80 percent of all farming households since 1980, concerns economic planners, who argue that only full-time farmers are likely to divert the capital and training investment needed to develop large and profitable businesses.

Efficient farming is also being hindered by the rapidly aging agrarian workforce. The number of farmers over the age of 65 has increased annually, and in 1998 they accounted for around 10 percent of the total farming population. Many youths are choosing to leave family farms for the better wages found in cities. Farming incomes have grown, but they have not kept pace with the gains made in other sectors.

To plug the youth drain, the Council of Agriculture 農業委員會 (COA) has taken a number of measures to persuade graduates of agricultural institutes and young members of farming families to stay on the farm. Local agricultural authorities encourage potential young farmers to improve farm management and raise farm income after determining that they are capable of farming on their own. Rural development projects are also being developed to make rural life more compatible with the lifestyles and needs of today's youth.

Invariably though, the only long-term solution is to gradually downsize the farming workforce as older farmers retire and raise the efficiency of those that remain. To help farmers displaced by this trend, the COA and the Council of Labor Affairs 行政院勞工委員會 have been conducting training programs and job counseling over the past several years in accordance with the *Agricultural Development Act* 農業發展條例. Recognizing the difficulty of training farmers who are advanced in age and the need to provide alternative forms of assistance to this group, the government promulgated on May 31, 1995, a temporary statute to grant elderly farmers a monthly stipend of US$87. Eligible farmers include those who:

- have reached the age of 65;
- have been covered by the farmers' health insurance program for more than six months;
- are not receiving any old-age pensions from social insurance (such as labor insurance), living allowances, or other types of government;
- are solely employed in the agricultural sector;
- have lands and houses (private farmlands and farmhouses excluded) whose value does not exceed US$185,185; and
- have an individual income that does not exceed the annual basic wage.

In an effort to enhance the welfare of farmers even further, the Legislative Yuan passed several revisions to the temporary statute in October 1998. Items 3, 4, 5, and 6 above were removed, and the act was expanded to include fishermen. These changes made an additional 150,000 people in the farming and fishing industries eligible to receive the stipend. As of June 1998, nearly US$563 million had been granted to nearly 436,000 farmers, and applications for the stipend were still being accepted and reviewed.

Land

In mountainous Taiwan, farming is largely restricted to the island's arable western slope lands and alluvial plains. Farming plots tend to be small: 75 percent of all farming households have less than one hectare of cultivable land. The small average size of farming plots has created a huge obstacle to Taiwan's agricultural modernization, since advanced methods of farm mechanization and management depend on scale to be cost-efficient. As a result, advances in farming efficiency have not kept pace with other sectors, and in many cases, the land has ceased to be profitable for farming. Roughly 10 percent of Taiwan's total farmland is left fallow because it is no longer profitable to farm it.

To address this situation, the government has been working in cooperation with farmers' organizations and other agencies to convert unprofitable farmland to other uses, consolidate plots into larger areas of land that are easier to farm, and gradually reduce excess farmland. On July 11, 1996, the Executive Yuan passed amendments to the *Agricultural Development Act*, lifting restrictions on the transfer, inheritance, and division of farmland.

Farmland Rezoning

On August 4, 1995, the Executive Yuan passed the Farmland Release Program 農地釋出方案 to ease restrictions on farmland rezoning. Some 160,000 hectares of farmland have been targeted for release, including 78,000 hectares of coastal subsidence area, 50,000 hectares of polluted area, and 27,000 hectares of low productive farmland. Fish farms in subsidence areas are given priority for release with the goal of reducing the present 50,000 hectares by 40 percent over the next ten years.

The minimum area for plots released for the construction of laborer housing is five hectares; for industrial and commercial use, at least five hectares; and for residential use, at least ten hectares. To ensure safe and efficient land use, all development on rezoned farmland must follow the government's environmental and development policies.

To prevent windfall profits, those who transfer farmland to industrial or commercial use are required to pay a usage fee of up to 12 percent of the

current assessed price of the transferred land. Half of this money is donated to government agricultural agencies while the other half is given to local governments. At the same time, 30 percent of the land must be donated to the government for "green belts or infrastructural projects." To encourage businesses to move to eastern Taiwan and to accelerate offshore island development, farmland released in Ilan 宜蘭, Hualien 花蓮, Taitung 臺東, the Penghu Islands 澎湖群島, Kinmen 金門, and Matsu 馬祖 is exempt from usage fees. As of December 1998, some 14,392 hectares had been released under the Farmland Release Program, and an additional 4,316 hectares were in the process of being released.

Farmland Consolidation

The farmland consolidation program 農地重劃 is designed to combine odd-shaped plots of scattered farmland into one large "pie," which can then be cut into slices that are easier to farm. The reshaped plots of land are then redistributed, giving each farmer a plot of land about the same size as the one he formerly owned but much better proportioned. Under the program, some 380,000 hectares of farmland were consolidated between 1958 and 1998, and an additional 1,454

> ### Farming Households
>
> A farming household is a family of which at least one member grows agricultural products or raises domesticated animals, honey bees, or silk worms. Such a family must meet at least one of the following five criteria. It must:
> - manage at least 0.05 hectares of cultivated land, which need not be owned by the family, but may be rented, borrowed, or share-cropped;
> - raise at least one large animal, such as a dairy cow, a head of beef cattle, or a deer;
> - raise at least three medium-sized animals, such as pigs or goats;
> - raise at least 100 poultry, such as chickens, ducks, geese, pigeons, or quail; or
> - sell or consume agricultural products worth more than US$740 annually.

> ### Farmland
>
> According to Article 3, Item 10 of the *Agricultural Development Act,* farmland includes any property necessary to the farming, forestry, animal husbandry, or aquaculture industries—such as farm houses, animal stalls or coops, storage facilities, drying areas, collection areas, farm roads, irrigation ditches, and catchment areas. It also includes land used for warehouses, refrigeration facilities, equipment centers, silkworm houses, and collection centers that have been provided by farmers' associations or agricultural cooperatives and stations.

hectares are slated for consolidation in 1999. Farm roads and irrigation ditches that serve these areas are also being improved, rebuilt, and repaired. This program is helping to overcome a few of the shortcomings of small-scale farming by reducing production and marketing costs and increasing operational efficiency.

Farmland Utilization Project

The COA, in cooperation with the now defunct Taiwan Provincial Department of Agriculture and Forestry, enacted a long-term General Farmland Utilization Project 農地利用綜合規劃 in 1992. This project guides county and city governments and grassroots organizations in setting up collective agricultural production districts to meet the needs of farmers based on environmental, economic, and technical requirements. In fiscal 1999, the COA spent US$3.2 million on the project in districts encompassing over 60,000 hectares of farmland.

Water

Farming is dependent on large quantities of clean water, and although Taiwan seems to be fairly rainy with an annual average precipitation of 2,515 millimeters, its water resources are unevenly distributed. Regional and seasonal water shortages necessitate careful planning and conservation of all water resources. The Water Resources Bureau 水資源局 (WRB) under the Ministry of

Economic Affairs estimated Taiwan's water usage in 1998 to be 18.03 billion cubic meters (bcm); and of that amount, agriculture accounted for the lion's share, consuming 13.51 bcm or 74.9 percent of the total. In comparison, the residential and industrial sectors consumed 16.16 percent and 8.95 percent, respectively, of the total water used in 1998.

Crops

Both the types and quantities of crops produced in Taiwan are changing rapidly. The ROC's pending acceptance into the WTO has given farmers impetus to diversify away from traditional crops—which cannot be farmed competitively in an unprotected market—and into horticulture, agritourism, exotic fruits and vegetables, chemical-free organic produce, new cultivars, and other high-value products. These moves have also been made in response to the people's changing dietary habits, with people on Taiwan beginning to eat more wheat-based foods and dairy products and consuming less rice. The island's rising standard of living has also boosted demand for luxury products, such as exotic flowers and processed foods.

Rice ranked as Taiwan's most valuable crop in 1998, followed by betel nuts, corn, sugar cane, mangoes, watermelon, tea, pineapples, pears, and grapes. In terms of harvested area, rice again ranked first, followed by corn, betel nuts, sugar cane, peanuts, bamboo shoots, tea, mangoes, watermelon, and sorghum.

Rice

According to the COA, there were 358,000 hectares of ricefields in Taiwan in 1998. Some 1.49 million tons of brown rice were produced during the island's two crop seasons, which exceeded the island's annual demand. This surplus was largely attributed to changes in people's dietary habits, which caused per capita rice consumption to plunge by more than 50 percent between 1974 and 1997, dropping from 134 kilograms to 58 kilograms. As Taiwan opens its doors to rice imports in preparation for entering the WTO, foreign competition will further exacerbate the problem of oversupply and intensify the downward pressure on rice prices.

To help Taiwan rice growers adapt to these trends, the government is working to bring rice supply in line with falling demand through the Rice Production and Ricefield Diversion Program 稻米生產及稻田轉作計畫 and the initiation of several programs for rice purchasing. In May 1997, a *Grain Control Law* 糧食管理法 was put into effect to further stabilize the price, upgrade the quality, and regulate the supply and demand of rice.

Ricefield Diversion Program

In July 1984, the ROC government implemented the Rice Production and Ricefield Diversion Program to reduce rice production in Taiwan. This program encouraged farmers, through subsidies and incentives, to leave rice paddies fallow, rotate crops, or fully convert their land to other, more profitable uses. The program was concluded at the end of June 1997 and replaced with the Program for Rezoning Paddy Fields and Dry Farmland 水旱田利用調整計畫 a month later to further balance the supply and demand of rice. By 1998, these two programs combined had diverted nearly 142,000 hectares of paddies, of which about 84,000 hectares were laid fallow and the remainder was planted with other crops; reduced the total area of rice cultivation from 429,000 hectares in 1991 to about 358,000 hectares in 1998; and dropped rice yields by 156,000 metric tons to 1.49 million metric tons.

Rice Purchasing Program

Since April 1974, the government has been buying rice from farmers by means of the Food Stabilization Fund 糧食平準基金. Altogether, the government has purchased 15.1 million metric tons of rice for US$7.9 billion between 1974 and 1998, increasing growers' income by US$1.3 billion. In 1998 alone, some 398,000 metric tons of rice were purchased in this manner for US$252 million, directly increasing growers' total income by nearly US$33 million. Since the government buys this rice and then sells it at a loss, by fiscal 1998 the Food Stabilization Fund had accumulated a deficit of US$3.1 billion.

Rice Quality Improvement

The High-quality Rice Production and Marketing Program 良質米產銷計畫 was enacted in fiscal 1986 and included in the Six-Year National Development Plan 國建六年計畫 of fiscal 1992. In fiscal 1999, 29 farmers' associations participated in this program to improve rice quality, and 73 grain traders contracted with farmers to produce high-quality rice.

Vegetables

In 1998, some 178,000 hectares of land were devoted to vegetable cultivation, down from a high of 240,000 hectares in 1986, but still considerably higher than the 1945 figure of 35,000 hectares. The main vegetable producing areas were concentrated in Yunlin, Changhua, Chiayi, and Tainan counties. The leading vegetables grown in 1998 with respect to planted area were bamboo shoots, watermelon, leafy vegetables, vegetable soybeans, cabbage, cantaloupe, garlic, scallions, celery cabbage, Chinese cabbage, and radishes. Due to international trade liberalization, most vegetables produced in Taiwan are now for domestic consumption.

Vegetable production in 1998 was 2,872,571 metric tons. Through technological improvements such as new cultivars, growth regulators, and mechanization, crop yields per hectare of land jumped from 8,600 kilograms in 1945 to 16,384 kilograms in 1998. Taiwan's biggest vegetable crops in 1998 by value were watermelon, bamboo shoots, garlic, cantaloupe, cabbage, scallions, radishes, edible mushrooms, leafy vegetables, and radishes. Currently, more than 100 kinds of vegetables are produced in Taiwan. In northern Taiwan, radishes, Chinese cabbage, leaf-mustard, and garlic thrive in the cooler climate. In southern Taiwan, tomatoes, cauliflower, bamboo shoots, and beans are cultivated. Ginger is grown in central Taiwan.

Fruits

Around 30 types of fruit are cultivated in Taiwan. Deciduous varieties like apples, pears, and peaches thrive at high elevations, while citrus fruits, bananas, pineapples, lychees, longans,

mangoes, papayas, persimmons, loquats, and guavas dot the lower plains and undulating slope lands. The main crops are citrus fruits, mangoes, lychees, bananas, pineapples, wax apples, and Asian pears. In 1998, almost 2.6 million metric tons of fruit were grown in Taiwan on a total planted area of nearly 170,000 hectares. Processed products enjoy stable domestic and international markets: for instance, canned pineapples and lychees are exported, while a wide selection of fruit juices are offered to satisfy local tastes.

Local fruit growers have suffered tremendously from imported foreign produce, which has

Modern technologies have greatly improved the quality and quantity of vegetable production in Taiwan. At present, more than 100 kinds of vegetables are produced in Taiwan.

Asian Vegetable Research and Development Center

The Asian Vegetable Research and Development Center 亞洲蔬菜研究發展中心 (AVRDC) was established in Tainan County's Shanhua Township 臺南縣善化鎮 in October 1973. The goal of this international nonprofit organization was to help farmers in the tropics increase crop yields by developing better, stronger vegetables that were more resistant to insects and diseases, as well as more tolerant of heat and flooding. Occupying a 98-hectare research farm, the center carries out its mission through three different programs: crop improvement, production systems, and international cooperation. These research and development programs are led by internationally recruited professionals from 13 different countries, and employee over 250 mid-level researchers and administrative staff.

The center's gene bank, with over 45,500 accessions, is one of the world's largest for tropical germplasm and focuses on such globally and regionally important vegetables as tomatoes, peppers, eggplant, onions, garlic, shallots, soybeans, mung beans, and cabbage. Researchers collect seeds, grow new varieties, document their results, and share their findings with other researchers and organizations worldwide. As of the end of 1998, the center had officially released a total of 239 new breeding lines in 90 countries and sent out some 422,000 seed samples to cooperators in 193 countries and territories.

The AVRDC assists Taiwan farmers by training them in insect and disease management; teaching them intercropping; showing them how to use agricultural inputs more effectively; and developing technologies that allow them to overcome seasonal stresses in vegetable production. Among the improved techniques developed by the center are raised beds to enhance drainage and improve soil aeration during the monsoon season; straw mulching to suppress weeds and retain soil moisture; and fertilization and composting to improve the fertility of tropical soils.

The center can look back on a number of triumphs. One of the biggest achievements involved tomatoes. Over the last decade, researchers have increased the summer tomato yield for Taiwan farms from 5 metric tons per hectare to 40. The center has produced 95 high-yielding, heat-tolerant, disease-resistant, high-quality tomato varieties for release in 34 countries. Nearly 25 percent of Taiwan's vegetable soybean fields are planted with strains (Kaohsiung Nos. 1, 2, and 3) developed at the center, and much of the island's Chinese cabbage production can also be credited to the AVRDC.

---

flooded the domestic market in response to the reduction—and in some cases elimination—of tariffs on imported fruit. To face this growing competition, Taiwan fruit growers have applied advanced horticultural technology to modernize their operations. Through the effective control of diseases, adjustments to fruit maturation periods, the cultivation of improved fruit strains, and the implementation of multiple annual harvests, the fruit sector has witnessed both profitability and growth. Orchards are also diversifying into the lucrative agritourism business (see section on Agritourism below).

Sugar Cane

Taiwan's sugar industry has lost some of its former vitality due to a stagnation in global sugar prices and the importation of sugar into the domestic market. Both of these signs spell "transition" for the state-run Taiwan Sugar Corporation 臺灣糖業公司 (TSC), which has expanded its product line and diversified into biotechnology, land development, and overseas investments in order to remain competitive.

Taiwan used to be one of the world's leading sugar exporters. In the 1950s and 1960s, the island boasted some 100,000 hectares of sugar cane fields and produced over one million metric tons of sugar annually. By 1998, however, farm labor shortages and a steady decline in world prices had reduced Taiwan's sugar cane fields down to 48,000 hectares, half of which were owned by the TSC. These decreases in domestic sugar production led to a subsequent increase in sugar imports, and Taiwan now imports almost 190,000 metric tons of sugar annually.

In an effort to bring down sugar prices even further, the Executive Yuan passed the Sugar

Taiwan Area Tea Industry
(unit: metric tons)

Year	Local Production	Imports	Exports
1990	22,299	2,604	6,194
1991	21,380	6,045	5,696
1992	20,164	6,752	5,577
1993	20,515	10,237	5,606
1994	24,485	10,685	4,948
1995	20,892	8,354	4,150
1996	19,955	7,365	3,475
1997	23,505	7,692	2,918
1998	22,641	9,034	3,188

Source: Council of Agriculture

Industry Management Policy and Sugar Price Adjustment Program 糖業經營策略與糖價調整方案 in June 1996 to progressively reduce domestic production and increase imports.

Tea

Tea, a product symbolic of China, was once one of the mainstays of Taiwan's early economy. At one time, Taiwan was exporting some 80 percent of its tea production. In 1973, tea exports topped 21,000 metric tons. This situation has reversed since then, however, and the island has been a serious tea importer since 1991. More than 9,000 metric tons of tea were imported in 1998. The transformation of Taiwan from seller to buyer has been driven by local demand.

According to the Council of Agriculture, ever since the government opened Taiwan's market to Southeast Asian tea in 1990, annual tea imports have nearly tripled in weight. In 1998, tea imports increased to 9,034 metric tons while local production dropped to 22,641 metric tons (see chart). Taiwan has transferred tea processing techniques to Vietnam, Indonesia, and Thailand in order to take advantage of these nations' lower labor costs, and the tea produced in these countries is usually exported back to the Taiwan market.

Flowers

With a wide variety of fresh, beautiful flowers to choose from, it is no wonder that Taiwan's floriculture industry has been flourishing in recent years. Between 1986 and 1998, output value ballooned from about US$74 million to US$340 million; export value skyrocketed from US$3.7 million to US$41.5 million; and as sales soared, the farmland used for raising flowers expanded from 3,500 hectares to 10,000 hectares. Major markets for export include Japan, Hong Kong, and the US. On most flower farms, half of the planting area is usually devoted to producing cut flowers while the other half is used for nursury production. Annual production for cut flowers stands at 1.4 billion stems, and for potted plants, 25 million.

Recreational Agriculture

Agritourism

From 1982 to 1999, some 2,005 hectares of land yielding 16 crops were officially converted into tourist farms 觀光農園 where visitors could pick their own fruits and vegetables. In 1990, the government began to encourage traditional farm owners to transform their farms into recreational farms 休閒農場. Recreational farms were similar to tourist farms, but also offered visitors picnicking, bird watching, and other low-impact activities aside from the opportunity to harvest their own agricultural products. In the early 1990s, however, it became clear that the agritourism industry was developing to an extent and in a direction that violated a few environmental protection laws and land utilization regulations.

In an effort to bring tourist and recreational farms under the rule of law, the COA drew up a revised set of *Recreational Agriculture Guidance Measures* 休閒農業輔導辦法 in April 1999 for review by the Executive Yuan. The purpose of these rules and measures was to protect the environment; utilize land in a wise and appropriate fashion; and promote agricultural, educational, and recreational activities to increase the income of farmers and strengthen farm communities.

Fishing Industry

Over the past half-century, the island's fishing industry has developed from small-scale coastal fishing to deep-sea commercial fishing.

In 1945, only a hundred or so trawlers were tied up at Taiwan's piers to unload an annual catch of about 40,000 metric tons. By 1998, the island's fishing fleet totaled 27,163 ships (of which 25,156 were powered craft) and brought home an annual haul of some 1,090,000 metric tons.

In 1998, Taiwan produced US$2.9 billion worth of fish. Of this, 62 percent came from deep-sea fishing, 20 percent from aquaculture, 15 percent from offshore fishing, and 3 percent from coastal fishing. More than 33 percent of Taiwan's total production was exported, with the biggest export items being skipjack and eel.

The expanding role of deep-sea fishing in Taiwan's fishing industry was largely a product of declining fish stocks close to home caused by overfishing and pollution from industrial and household waste. In 1990, the government began to work on restoring its declining fish stocks. By 1998, a total of US$40 million had been allocated to set up 26 fishery conservation zones, 75 artificial reefs, and 70 reef protection zones along the coasts of Taiwan proper and the Penghu Islands 澎湖群島. Sea bream, abalone, and kuruma shrimp were then released into these areas to restore depleted fish stocks.

The COA is also working to reduce the size of Taiwan's fishing fleet through a boat buy-back program. Approximately 2,327 old boats have been bought back since the program's initiation, and displaced fishermen have been retrained to work in other occupations. Furthermore, the ROC government has played an active role in international fishery management organizations and worked to promote international fishery cooperation. As of 1998, the ROC had signed official or private fishery agreements with 27 countries.

Aquaculture

The role of aquaculture in Taiwan's overall fishing industry has been growing steadily over the years. Its annual production of 280,000 tons accounts for more than one-fifth of Taiwan's total seafood production. Taiwan's geography and climate are ideal for aquaculture, offering fish farmers tropical, temperate, and frigid conditions to raise a wide variety of fish. Even the North American rainbow trout can be cultivated in some of Taiwan's mountains.

Taiwan's most important farmed fish is eel. Annual production of eel has fluctuated around 17,000 metric tons and is worth more than

More than 60 percent of Taiwan's catch is from deep-sea fishing, which plays an increasingly important role in the fishing industry.

193

US$180 million. Taiwan also to be a large producer of grass shrimp, with a peak output of 80,000 metric tons in 1987. Unfortunately, diseases have drastically reduced the grass shrimp population, and in 1998 the aquacultural industry only produced some 4,850 metric tons.

Aquacultural development has not come without environmental cost. Freshwater aquaculture operations draw off huge amounts of groundwater, sometimes causing land to shift or cave in (for details, see the section on Land Subsidence in Chapter 13, Environmental Protection). To tackle this problem, the Ministry of Economic Affairs and the COA have jointly promoted recycling systems that use fresh water more efficiently. Furthermore, they have encouraged aquaculturists to switch to marine ranching.

Livestock Industry

Starting from backyard farms in poor villages in the 1950s, the livestock industry in Taiwan has grown into a multi-billion dollar business and become a mainstay of the agricultural sector. In 1998, livestock production was valued at more than US$3.6 billion, accounting for 41.56 percent of Taiwan's total agricultural production value. Hog production still ranks first in the livestock industry with respect to value, followed by broiler, chicken eggs, and milk.

In an effort to readjust the structuring of both hog farming and the broiler industry, the Executive Yuan approved a program mapped out by the COA to abandon the livestock business. So far, some 6,751 hog farmers and 974 broiler farmers have applied to join this program.

With the assistance of several animal protection groups, the Animal Protection Law was promulgated in October 1998. In addition, the Animal Husbandry Law 畜牧法 went into effect in June 1998 to better balance animal production and consumption, thereby ensuring a steadier income for farmers.

Agricultural Prospects

Perhaps the single biggest challenge confronting Taiwan farmers today is the increased competition they will face after the ROC is admitted into the World Trade Organization (WTO). To meet WTO requirements, the ROC government has been systematically reducing the trade barriers on its traditionally well-protected agricultural goods market. The current average tariff on Taiwan's agricultural imports is 20 percent; after gaining admittance to the WTO, the ROC will reduce this average to 14.1 percent by the first year and 12 percent by the sixth year. After accession, all area restrictions will be completely eliminated, tariffs will be cut substantially, and products currently subject to import control will be subject to tariff-based conversion measures instead.

Currently, 90 percent of the agricultural products consumed in Taiwan are open to imports. According to the COA, Taiwan's US$4.6 billion trade deficit in agricultural products for 1998 was a direct result of tariff reductions and the Asian financial crisis. That year, agricultural exports declined 21 percent to US$3.2 billion and imports decreased 22 percent to US$7.8 billion. To meet the challenge of liberalization, the government has taken legal steps to soften the impact of imports on local farmers, with the COA promulgating the *Agricultural Producer Import Damage Compensation Guidelines* 農產品受進口損害救助基金管理運用辦法 on January 31, 1996.

13
Environmental Protection

Educational initiatives have increased public awareness of such environmental issues as air, noise, and water pollution; waste disposal; nature reserves; and wildlife preservation, which are now priority policy issues for the central and local governments.

Following four decades of rapid industrial development, growing public and governmental awareness of the severe extent and ultimate cost of pollution is propelling the environmental protection movement in the Taiwan area today. A number of factors have conspired to shift the focus of policymaking: First, the predominant concern in the 1960s and 1970s of stimulating economic growth has given way over the last decade or so to a more balanced consideration of the needs for additional growth versus the short- and long-term environmental costs. Second, as Taiwan today approaches developed-nation status, its people are starting to demand a quality of life commensurate with their level of economic achievement. Finally, the acceleration toward democracy over the past few years in the Republic of China has heightening public awareness of the people's environmental responsibilities and prerogatives.

The fight to clean up and preserve Taiwan's environment has brought about some improvements in recent years; however, to raise the issue to the next level, the ROC government has put new urgency into a major initiative for 1998. The demands on Taiwan's environment stem from a dense population of more than 21.8 million people on 36,000 square kilometers of land, as well as from the impact of rushing to become an industrialized nation over the last couple of decades. Effective environmental protection measures have taken on added significance in recent years because Taiwan--now a major world trader--is facing greater pressure from the international community to protect the environment and step up its wildlife conservation efforts.

In all respects, the key to continued improvement is strict enforcement of already existing laws, coupled with a sustained campaign to inculcate a positive environmental protection and wildlife conservation ethic among the public. This chapter recounts the vicissitudes of environmental protection and wildlife conservation in Taiwan and describes the mandates, as well as legal and financial resources, at the disposal of the various government agencies that work to preserve the environment, conserve Taiwan's natural resources, and protect the island's wildlife.

Air Quality

Air pollution is one of the most serious problems in Taiwan, chiefly because of the heavy traffic and high concentration of industrial plants on the island. The Environmental Protection Administration 環境保護署 (EPA [see inset below]) reported in 1999 that there were 4.22 registered factories and 445 motor vehicles for every square kilometer in the Taiwan area. Overall, there were some 16 million vehicles (5.47 million cars and 10.57 million motorcycles) registered in the Taiwan area, nearly three for every four people. According to the EPA, vehicular exhaust comprises more than 95 percent of the air pollution in Taipei, Taiwan's largest city.

According to EPA measurements of air quality in 1998, ozone and suspended particles were

Environmental Protection Administration

The only government agency at the national level that is devoted solely to protecting the environment is the Environmental Protection Administration (EPA) under the Executive Yuan 行政院環境保護署. The EPA sets standards by which to measure the pollution of Taiwan's environment and drafts laws to elicit environmentally friendly behavior. The EPA had a budget of US$540 million in fiscal 1999. As of 1998, the EPA was employing 582 full-time employees, 262 environmental investigators charged with collecting evidence in pollution cases, and 85 lab technicians responsible for analyzing test samples of pollutants brought back to the EPA's National Institute of Environmental Analysis 環境檢驗所.

the primary air pollutants in the Taiwan area, accounting for 54 percent and 46 percent, respectively. The percentage of days in 1996 where the Pollution Standards Index (PSI) was greater than 100 for the Kaohsiung and Pingtung areas was 18%. Thus, in August 1997, the EPA established an office in the area and began the Air Pollution Improvement Project. The purpose of this office was to conduct total quality control and assist local government's environmental protection bureaus to eliminate pollution from stationary, mobile, and fugitive sources. By the end of 1999, the percentage of days in these areas with PSI values greater than 100 had been lowered to 12.8%.

To more effectively monitor air pollution, the EPA set up the Taiwan Area Air Quality Monitoring Network 臺灣地區空氣品質監測網, which began formal operations in September 1993. By 1998, the network comprised 72 automatic air quality monitoring stations, 2 monitoring vans, 1 air quality assurance laboratory, and 5 remote work stations. In January 1996, the EPA divided Taiwan into eight air quality prediction areas and began issuing next-day air quality forecasts islandwide.

On July 1, 1995, the EPA began collecting a broad surcharge on fuel in the form of an air pollution control (APC) fee. Under this scheme, a per-liter fee of US$0.006 was imposed on both high-grade diesel fuel and leaded gasoline. APC fees were also levied on exhausted NO_x 氮氧化物 (US$0.094-0.375 per kg) and exhausted SO_x 硫氧化物 (US$0.016-0.313 per kg) in air pollution control zones. In fiscal year 1999, the APC fee system generated almost US$124 million.

The funds collected from APC fees are earmarked for carrying out air pollution control programs, such as implementing air quality improvement plans at the local level, establishing environmental conservancy parks, subsidizing the purchase of electric motorcycles, and converting automobile engines to allow them to run on liquefied petroleum gas (LPG). The first LPG station for such converted automobiles was opened in Taipei City on March 15, 1996, and today there are four LPG stations in Taiwan.

Noise Pollution

Article 8 of the *Enforcement Rules of the Noise Control Act* 噪音管制法施行細則 requires all counties and cities in the Taiwan area to establish noise monitoring sites. In view of the serious noise pollution caused by numerous vehicles in urban areas, the EPA drew up plans in fiscal 1996 for a comprehensive, islandwide environmental and traffic noise monitoring network to complement the existing noise monitoring sites. This plan originally called for 28 noise monitoring stations—at least one station for every county—to be set up in Taiwan to collect vital data on the environmental and noise pollution caused by traffic. After the completion of these stations, Taipei City added two more stations, bringing the total number of noise monitoring stations to 30.

Although the use of firecrackers is quite extensive in Taiwan, it is prohibited between 11 p.m. and 5 a.m. under the *Noise Control Act* 噪音管制法. On January 1, 1996, the Civil Aeronautics Administration under the Ministry of Transportation and Communications began collecting an Airport Noise Control Fee 機場噪音防制降落費 from 11 airports throughout the ROC in accordance with the *Civil Aeronautic Act* 民用航空法. Revenues from this fee are not only used for noise control, but also to improve the environmental quality of schools, hospitals, and communities in areas affected by aviation noise.

Water Resources

Most of Taiwan's rivers and coastal waters have been seriously polluted for some time now. Urban communities are major culprits, primarily because of the island's failure to develop sewage systems. Most industrial, agricultural, and residential wastewater drains directly into rivers, seriously polluting the water downstream. According to the EPA, most advanced nations have completed 95 percent of their sewage systems, while Taiwan has built only 6.25 percent—far behind most East Asian countries, and even some African countries. Even in Taipei

Government Entities with Missions in Environmental Protection or Resource Conservation

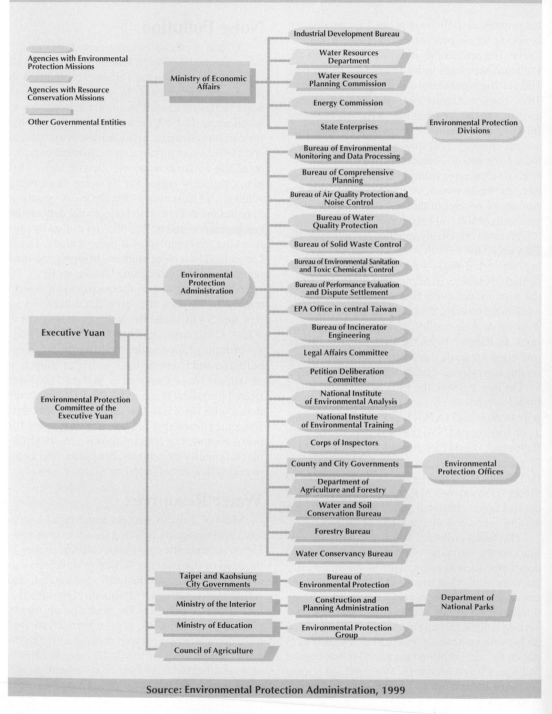

City, where the ROC government began building a sewage system in 1972, only 665,000 households (43.96 percent) had been connected by June 1999. The cities of Taiwan thus urgently need to build adequate sewage systems in order to stem water pollution.

There are 21 primary, 29 secondary, and 79 ordinary rivers in the Taiwan area. As of 1999, there were 282 river and stream water quality sampling stations and 103 ocean water quality sampling stations in Taiwan Province. Thirty-six river water quality sampling stations have been set up in Taipei's Tamsui River 淡水河 basin alone. Environmental protection agencies have regularly monitored the water quality of primary and secondary rivers, measuring levels of dissolved oxygen, biochemical oxygen demand, suspended solids, ammonia nitrogen, and some other parameters. According to the EPA, 35.7 percent of primary and secondary rivers are polluted to various degrees, and the Peikang River 北港溪 tops the list of the 50 rivers that are most heavily polluted. Industrial wastewater and waste are the main pollutants.

To more effectively control water pollution, the EPA in May 1991 promulgated amendments to the *Water Pollution Control Act* 水污染防治法 that stipulate daily fines of between US$2,000 and US$20,000 for polluting water. July 1994 saw the enactment of two major water pollution laws: the *Oceanic Effluent Standards* 海洋放流水標準 and the *Supervisory Guidelines for Industrial Wastewater Pollution Control Measures and Urban Effluent Discharge* 事業水污染防治措施及排放廢(污)水管理辦法. Furthermore, the EPA renewed the Integrated Environmental Protection Project for River Basins 流域整體性環保計畫 for fiscal years 1996 through 2001 and allocated nearly US$5.5 million to dredge ten primary rivers in fiscal 1998. The Taiwan Provincial Government's Department of Environmental Protection 臺灣省政府環境保護處 drew up a pollution treatment program for river basins in July 1995 and budgeted US$1.44 billion to manage pollution control in the Kaoping River 高屏溪 and the Tungkang River 東港溪. Thirty river-quality monitoring stations have already been set up on these two rivers to take monthly measurements.

Legislative Developments

The Environmental Protection Administration (EPA) under the Executive Yuan has taken the system of laws and regulations regarding environmental protection and separated them into five different categories: basic laws, administrative organizations, prevention, control, and relief. With the exception of the *Basic Environmental Protection Law*, whose draft is still being reviewed by the Legislative Yuan, the remaining four categories have more or less completed the principal structuring of their laws and regulations. Drafts are currently being formulated for the *Soil Pollution Control Act*, the *Ocean Pollution Control Act*, and the *Recycling and Reuse of Resources Act*. At the same time, revisions are being made to the *Solid Waste Disposal Act*, the *Noise Control Act*, and several other related environmental protection laws that require modification due to changes in the official function and organization of the Taiwan Provincial Government. A total of 136 pieces of legislation were completed between June 1996 and June 1999, including 12 laws and amendments and 124 regulations and administrative orders. The twelve environmental protection laws and amendments passed thus far consist of: (1) the *Environmental Impact Evaluation Law*, (2) the *Air Pollution Control Act*, (3) the *Noise Control Act*, (4) the *Waste Pollution Control Act*, (5) the *Amendment to the Solid Waste Disposal Act*, (6) the *Amendment to the Toxic Chemical Control Act*, (7) the *Amendment to the Drinking Water Management Act*, (8) the *Environmental Agents Control Act*, (9) the *Amendment to the Public Nuisance Dispute Settlement Law*, (10) *Amendment to the Regulations Governing the Structure of the EPA under the Executive Yuan*, (11) the *Regulations Governing the EPA's Institute for Training Environmental Protection Personnel under the Executive Yuan*, and (12) the *Regulations Governing the EPA's National Institute of Environmental Analysis under the Executive Yuan*.

Condition of Taiwan's Primary and Secondary Rivers

	Primary		Secondary	
	km	%	km	%
Unpolluted	1,279.2	61.6	608.7	72
Lightly Polluted	202.4	9.7	70.1	8.3
Moderately Polluted	342.7	16.4	99.6	11.8
Heavily Polluted	264	12.3	67.3	7.9
Total	2,088.3	100.0	845.7	100.0

Source: Environmental Protection Administration, 1998

There are 40 reservoirs in the Taiwan area, and the water quality at 20 primary reservoirs is regularly monitored. In 1998, 14 of the 20 primary reservoirs were heavily polluted and eutrophic. The following three reservoirs remained heavily polluted for two consecutive years: Akungtien Reservoir 阿公店水庫, Fengshan Reservoir 鳳山水庫, and Cheng Ching Lake Reservoir 澄清湖水庫. The Sun Moon Lake Reservoir 日月潭水庫 and the Feitsui Reservoir 翡翠水庫 had the best water quality.

The development of industrial zones, golf courses, and real estate presents yet another challenge. Mountain deforestation has severely damaged watersheds. Soil in upstream areas is washed away, turning into silt and filling the reservoirs downstream, thereby reducing both the quantity and quality of water available for use. There seems to be no easy remedy for such upstream pollution beyond spending more money on downstream water cleanup or finding new water sources.

With this in mind, the Ministry of Economic Affairs 經濟部 (MOEA) plans to add 9 new reservoirs to the island's current 40. However, environmentalists worry about environmental degradation resulting from reservoir construction, and reservoir proposals almost always provoke public protest. To win over the public, the MOEA in April 1996 drafted the *Water Resource Development and Conservation Incentive Regulations* 水資源開發保育回饋條例, which establish an incentive fund for residents near new reservoirs. Furthermore, the MOEA and Taiwan Provincial Government's Department of Water Conservancy 臺灣省水利處 will jointly implement a five-year, US$1.55 billion integrated reservoir conservation program to clean up 38 reservoirs in the Taiwan area between 1997 and 2001. The EPA has also provided funds for local governments to carry out reservoir pollution control programs.

Land Subsidence

Lured by profits, many farmers in the coastal areas of Yunlin 雲林, Changhua 彰化, Pingtung 屏東, Chiayi 嘉義, and Ilan 宜蘭 have expanded into aquaculture. Aquaculturalists have dug 170,000 illegal wells and pumped out excessive amounts of precious groundwater because it is cheap and stable in temperature. In addition to being used in aquaculture, groundwater is also pumped for industrial, residential, and standard agricultural uses. Recent data shows that while 5.94 billion cubic meters of groundwater is being pumped annually, only four billion cubic meters is being replaced. This deficit has caused land in many areas to subside, especially along Taiwan's southwestern coast and on the Ilan Plain 宜蘭平原. Overall, almost 865 square kilometers of Taiwan's plains, or a full 8 percent, tend to subside. The most serious subsidence has occurred around Chiatung 佳冬 in Pingtung County, where sites have sunk by as much as 3.06 meters.

Environmental Nuisance Complaints

In 1998, environmental protection agencies in the Taiwan area registered 85,768 complaints about environmental nuisances, most of which concerned waste disposal. The public has not only become increasingly intolerant of companies that do not offer environmentally-friendly products or services, but has also become more willing to do something about pollution control now that the government has set up channels for handling complaints and resolving disputes.

The *Public Nuisance Dispute Settlement Law* 公害糾紛處理法 was promulgated in February 1992 and amended in June 1998; its enforcement rules were announced in February 1993. This legislation provides a legal basis for the Public Nuisance Arbitration Panel 公害糾紛裁決委員會 under the EPA and all of the subordinate public nuisance mediation committees 公害糾紛調處委員會 in every city, county, and provincial government in the Taiwan area. These committees are open to public participation and are usually made up of academic and environmental specialists to insure objectivity. Decisions reached by the mediation committees and/or the EPA's arbitration panel are reviewed by the courts, and thus carry the weight of legal judgments.

Yearly Tabulation of Selected Environmental Nuisance Complaint Categories

	Waste Disposal	Noise	Air Pollution	Noxious Odors	Total* Complaints
1991	31,322	15,726	12,966	3,814	67,438
1992	29,805	20,328	16,916	5,603	77,547
1993	32,319	19,165	18,676	8,186	84,273
1994	34,855	20,265	12,957	10,049	86,517
1995	52,462	21,149	12,277	11,950	117,788
1996	51,557	19,432	10,962	12,655	114,431
1997	43,015	20,546	12,454	13,072	95,711
1998	31,702	19,343	14,575	14,309	85,768

*Includes categories not listed
Source: Environmental Protection Administration

The average rate of subsidence in the coastal areas is between 5 and 15 centimeters per year.

In November 1995, the Executive Yuan 行政院 passed a land subsidence control program drawn up jointly by its Council of Agriculture 行政院農業委員會 and the MOEA. This program calls for US$56 million to be spent from July 1995 to June 2000 to control land subsidence in seven counties and cities. Efforts in Yunlin, Chiayi, and Pingtung will be given the priority in the first two years.

Solid Waste Disposal

There has been a great increase in solid waste generation as a result of rapid industrial and economic developments in the Taiwan area. According to the EPA, the amount of household garbage produced in Taiwan has nearly doubled in just over a decade, from 0.67 kilograms per person per day in 1985 to 1.16 kilograms in 1998. A daily average of 24,740 metric tons, or 9.03 million metric tons annually, of household garbage was collected in 1998. Overall, 20,645 metric tons of garbage are properly treated in landfills or by incineration every day; the rest is disposed of in landfills that do not meet EPA standards. In addition, the industries produce on average 18 million metric tons of waste each year, of which only 52 percent is properly treated.

Another problem is that many landfills are either full or nearing their capacity; however, constructing replacements is difficult since available land resources are extremely scarce in Taiwan. In

1998, 66 of the island's 316 garbage treatment sites had reached full capacity, leaving more than half of Taiwan's rural and urban townships with no place to dispose of their garbage. The third stage of the Taiwan Area Solid Waste Disposal Project 臺灣地區垃圾處理第三期計畫, initiated in July 1997, calls for the construction of 8 regional landfills, 135 local sites, and 19 large-scale incinerators. At the close of the second stage of this project at the end of 1996, 9 regional landfills, 161 local sites, and 2 large-scale incinerators had already been completed.

Recycling

A study performed by the EPA shows that about 40% of Taiwan's garbage is recyclable, including paper, glass, plastics, and metals. Recycling of these materials can not only lessen environmental burdens, lower the costs of waste disposal, and reduce dependence on resources, it can also create job opportunities and increase our GDP. Thus, the ROC has spent a great deal of effort on formulating regulations and programs for waste reduction and resource recycling in recent years. After Article 10.1 of the *Waste Disposal Act* was amended on March 28, 1997, a new system for recycling resources was put into force. Through the market mechanism, the manufacturing and recycling systems are now integrated to the effect that communities, local garbage collection teams, scrap dealers, and the recycling fund all work together to carry out recycling activities.

The Four-in-One Resource Recycling Program 資源回收四合一計畫, which has been promoted since January 1997, combines the efforts of the industry, auditing groups, scrap dealers, the government, and the public. In accordance with stipulations made by the Review Committee of Recycling Fee Rates, all responsible parties must pay fees to a recycling fund. Independent auditing groups selected by the EPA examine the recycling rate and determine its value by taking into account materials, volume, weight, recycling value, and the recycling rate in the previous year. Based on the stipulated fee rate and their revenue, the responsible parties pay fees to a designated bank to form a recycling

fund, which is managed by eight councils responsible for different aspects of the recycling program: waste containers, waste vehicles, waste tiers, waste lubricant oil, waste lead acid batteries, waste agricultural pesticide containers, waste electronic appliances, and waste computers. Established by the EPA, the councils consist of members selected from relevant government agencies, academia, and non-governmental organizations, who are then appointed by the EPA's administrator. Still, many legislators and several non-governmental organizations have suggested that the management and use of the recycling fund be made more transparent and supervised by the Legislative Yuan; accordingly, the EPA integrated the eight councils managing the recycling fund. In FY1999, the EPA divided the collected recycling fund into two parts: a trust fund and a non-commercial fund.

Hazardous Waste Disposal

In 1997, nearly 147,000 metric tons of hazardous industrial waste were produced by factories, farms, ranches, power plants, waterworks, and medical facilities in the Taiwan area. As early as 1989, the EPA had already recognized the need to dispose of hazardous waste properly and proposed the establishment of a waste disposal center inside Kaohsiung's Tafa Industrial Zone 大發工業區. In September 1994, the Ministry of Economic Affairs decided to invest US$74 million to establish the center. An environmental impact assessment was carried out and the project received EPA approval, but public protests have thus far prevented timely implementation of the plan.

1998 Recycling Amount (Ton)	
General Packaging	128,007.60
Lubricant Oil	7,751.00
Agricultural Pesticide Packaging	628.63
Lead Acid Batteries	26,163.74
Tiers	55,512.35
Waste Motorcycles	10,768.56
Waste Cars	41,624.80

Source: Environmental Protection Administration

After being melted down in a furnace, recycled aluminum cans are turned into ingots of usable raw material.

Nearly 20,000 chemical substances are used regularly in the Taiwan area, of which 6,000 are highly toxic. Pursuant to the *Toxic Chemicals Control Act* 毒化物管理法, the EPA released a list of 114 toxic chemicals for which the production, import, export, sale, or use must first be approved. Under another EPA program aimed at gathering information on pollution sources, all enterprises that use toxic substances or discharge waste gas, wastewater, or industrial waste are required to file plans covering the proper disposal of all toxins. Companies are then assigned deadlines for setting up disposal systems. A company that has filed a report and received a deadline is off the hook until the deadline passes. A company that does not file a plan and is found to be polluting the environment is subject to the heaviest fine under the law, which ranges from US$11,111 to US$37,037. Under the *Solid Waste Disposal Act* 廢棄物清理法, manufacturers must assume responsibility for managing waste, and violators face fines of between US$2,222 and US$5,556. Those who dump hazardous waste resulting in the loss of life may be sentenced to life imprisonment. Fortunately, the ROC government has not needed to carry out such a drastic punishment.

Wildlife Conservation

Over the past decade, the ROC government and private environmental groups in Taiwan have been acting to stop international traffic in outlawed wildlife products. Beginning with the promulgation of the *Wildlife Conservation Law* 野生動物保育法 in 1989 and continuing through 1995 with the formation of an interministerial task force for the investigation and supervision of wildlife conservation to crack down on the smuggling of wildlife products, Taiwan has repeatedly demonstrated its commitment to domestic conservation and support for global wildlife protection efforts. However, some well-intentioned environmental groups feel that Taiwan's conservation efforts have come "too little, too late."

Criticism of Taiwan's conservation record came to a head on March 25, 1994, when the Convention on International Trade in Endangered Species (CITES) concluded at its standing committee meeting in Geneva that Taiwan's proposed actions "toward meeting minimum requirements have not yet been [carried out]." Following the decision by CITES, the United States invoked the Pelly Amendment to impose trade sanctions on Taiwan in April 1994, and

Whale Conservation

In line with the world trend toward protecting whales, the Ministry of Economic Affairs licensed whaling and prohibited uncontrolled hunting in 1981. Whalers who returned their licenses to the government not only receive assistance with establishing alternative businesses, but their decommissioned whaling ships would also be bought and disassembled for them by the Council of Agriculture. Pursuant to the *Wildlife Conservation Law*, the COA classified 23 species of whales as endangered. From 1990 through 1995, this list grew to include all species of whales. During the same period, the government investigated several cases involving violations of conservation laws, and about 40 people were charged with whaling and selling whale meat in connection with these cases. In 1996 and 1997, the COA launched several national whale conservation campaigns, distributing posters and pamphlets to relevant agencies; which, in turn, distributed them to the public. Currently, no whaling activities are conducted in Taiwan.

went on to announce a ban on imports of wildlife and wildlife products from Taiwan, effective August 19, 1994. To avert international trade sanctions, the ROC legislature pushed through amendments to the *Wildlife Conservation Law* and toughened penalties against violators. The government also made an even greater and more visible effort to abide by international agreements to halt the trafficking of endangered species and illegal wildlife products.

Taiwan has enacted legislation which, as closely as possible, complies with CITES requirements. Close contact is maintained with officials at CITES, the Worldwide Fund for Nature, the Trade Records Analysis of Flora and Fauna in Commerce, the World Conservation Union, and numerous other international conservation groups. As a result, Taiwan has won recognition for its efforts and progress in policing illicit trade in wildlife and wildlife products over the past three years. On June 30, 1995, the United

States lifted its trade sanctions on Taiwan. A little over a year later, on September 11, 1996, Taiwan's achievements were further confirmed when the US announced that Taiwan was being removed entirely from the Pelly Amendment's "watch list." The United States cited the ROC government's comprehensive efforts and cooperation with international endeavors as being behind the decision.

Legal Framework

Trafficking in certain wildlife products in Taiwan is proscribed by the *Cultural Heritage Preservation Law* 文化資產保存法, enacted in 1981, and the *Wildlife Conservation Law*. The former mandates the creation of a system of nature reserves and designates 11 species of rare and valuable plants and 23 species of rare and valuable animals for protection; the latter classifies over 1,045 species of rare flora and fauna into three levels of protection. Species listed either as "endangered" 瀕臨絕種 (meaning that their population size is at or below a critical level) or as "rare and valuable" 珍貴稀有 (referring to endemic species or those with a very low population) may not be disturbed, abused, hunted, captured, traded, exchanged, owned, killed, or processed. Species considered to "require conservation measures" 應予保育 may be utilized once the population has reached a sustainable level as determined by the Council of Agriculture (see inset, next page).

1998 Wildlife Conservation Law Enforcement

Cases brought to trial	149
Persons involved	173
Persons sentenced	152
one to two years	12
six months to one year	86
two to six months	50
detention	4
Persons found not guilty	21

Source: Ministry of Justice

The original *Wildlife Conservation Law* had a number of shortcomings. It lacked provisions for effective punishment of holders of unregistered rhino horns or tiger bones, mandated no punishments for people who falsely claim that their products contain materials derived from endangered species, and was lax on wildlife smuggling. A newly revised *Wildlife Conservation Law* went into effect on October 29, 1994. The revised law is among the most severe in Asia: The trade or display for commercial purposes of protected, endangered, or rare and valuable wildlife products, as well as the unauthorized import or export of live protected wildlife or products made from protected wildlife, is punishable by a prison term of between six months and five years and/or a fine of between US$9,000 and US$45,000. Habitual offenders face prison terms of between one and seven years and/or fines of between US$15,000 and US$75,000. A person who falsely labels merchandise as containing protected wildlife or protected wildlife products shall be subject to a fine of between US$4,500 and US$22,500.

Further progress was achieved with the promulgation of the *Wildlife Conservation Law Implementation Regulations* 野生動物保育法施行細則 on April 29, 1995. The regulations stipulate that the Wildlife Conservation Advisory Committee 野生動物保育諮詢委員會 shall review the classification of endangered species at least once a year.

Enforcement of Wildlife Conservation Laws

The ROC government has redoubled its efforts to investigate and punish violators of the *Wildlife Conservation Law* and other conservation-related legislation. A six-member Wildlife Protection Unit 野生動物保護小組 (WPU), set up on November 26, 1993, is in charge of investigations. The WPU is assisted by more than 350 police officers who have completed special training in wildlife conservation. Since it was established, the unit has conducted extensive undercover operations and overseen investigations into more than 10,640 traditional Chinese pharmacies.

The Taiwan Provincial Government has continued to coordinate the implementation of the *Wildlife Conservation Law* at the local government level by maintaining frequent contact and organizing training workshops and conservation-related activities. All local governments have established joint enforcement task forces, which coordinate affairs among different agencies at the county level and hold review meetings to improve enforcement efforts.

In 1998, local governments investigated at least 2,035 wildlife-related cases and found 274 violations of the *Wildlife Conservation Law*. Customs officials uncovered 51 cases of wildlife product smuggling. At the same time, local police investigated 128 violations of the *Wildlife Conservation Law*, all of which were referred to the prosecutor's office for prosecution. During the same period, the WPU investigated 48 wildlife-related cases itself and the eight district offices of the Taiwan Forestry Bureau under the Taiwan Provincial Government made 209

Council of Agriculture

As opposed to the EPA, which is in charge of environmental protection, the Executive Yuan's Council of Agriculture 行政院農業委員會 (COA) is the highest government agency responsible for enforcing Taiwan's conservation laws. The COA devises the nation's conservation policies and oversees its implementation. The COA spent approximately US$8.8 million of its budget on wildlife conservation in fiscal year 1999, and has allocated US$12.8 million for fiscal 2000. A Wildlife Conservation Investigation and Supervisory Force 野生動物保育查緝督導小組 was set up in September 1993 to coordinate conservation activities at various national and local government agencies, boost conservation awareness, train conservation personnel, and strengthen crackdowns on illicit traffic in wildlife products. The task force, which is composed of vice ministerial officials from selected government ministries and convened by the chairman of the COA, meets regularly to coordinate government work plans for strengthening wildlife conservation.

investigations and seized 2,079 illegal hunting, trapping, and fishing gears.

The coastguard, local police officers, customs agents, and state investigators are all working together to enforce the *Wildlife Conservation Law* and to confiscate smuggled wildlife and wildlife products at airports, seaports, along the coast, and in open waters. For example, on April 1, 1998, the Ministry of Justice's Investigation Bureau (MJIB) and the Keelung Customs Bureau jointly seized 190 ivory tusks and ivory ornaments at a cargo ground in the northeastern port city of Keelung. The ivory originated from Nigeria and was hidden inside a shipping container for timber. On April 9, 1998, the MJIB seized eight ivory tusks and ivory products in Chiayi County. In another case, on September 28, 1998, the Coast Guard of the Ministry of National Defense 國防部 (MND) uncovered an animal smuggling case involving 17 ostriches, 580 chipmunks, 80 squirrels and 160 lizards at Hsinchu Harbor.

Wildlife Products in Traditional Chinese Medicine

Although tigers became extinct in Taiwan long ago and rhinos have never inhabited the island at all, both tiger parts and rhino horn have been used for thousands of years by Chinese pharmacists as ingredients in traditional remedies. Tiger and rhino products were seen as prestige items because of their scarcity, and therefore demand for them in Taiwan was very high. After the importation of tiger parts and rhino horn was outlawed in August 1985, a black market for these goods and in counterfeit copies began to flourish. Some traditional Chinese pharmacies in Taiwan were still selling such products in the early 1990s. As a result, international environmental groups became alarmed and began a public relations campaign against Taiwan. Some environmentalists called for a boycott of products produced in Taiwan until the authorities passed tougher legislation and began devoting more manpower to enforcement.

In response, the ROC government revised the *Wildlife Conservation Law*, beefed up enforcement, and established a registration system for rhino horn. By December 1994, a total of 458 kilograms of rhino horn had been accounted for and marked with tamper-proof identification labels. Photographs and other measurements were also taken, and all registration information was entered into a computer database to facilitate future reviews. This system has significantly strengthened the position of conservation officials. In March 1994, 6.5 percent of the traditional Chinese pharmacies investigated were found to have violated conservation laws; by August and September of that same year, this figure had dropped to nil.

In addition to the establishment of a computer database to better manage registered rhino horns and tiger parts, the local governments also conducted regular and random checks for such products. In 1998, they conducted 274 rechecks of registered rhino horns and tiger parts. Together with the Department of Health under the Taiwan Provincial Government, the local governments also inspected 4,474 traditional Chinese medicine stores and found no selling of rhino horns or tiger parts.

Despite recognizing the ROC government's overall effort to crack down on the illegal importation of endangered wildlife products, some US wildlife conservation institutions have continued to list Taiwan among the world's major consumers of bear parts. However, all bear species, including American black bears, are now listed as protected species under the *Wildlife Conservation Law*. In 1998, custom officials uncovered five bear gall bladders and a total of 22.5 kg of suspected bear gall bladders in powder form. In an effort to boost public awareness of bear conservation, the Department of Health (DOH), the COA, and the Government Information Office have turned to employing various advertising means such as phone cards, post cards, magazines and newspapers, product packages, TV screens at the CKS International Airport, and rest stations along the freeway.

Habitat Conservation

One of the best ways to protect wild animals is to preserve their natural habitat. Unfortunately, this is not easily done in Taiwan, since it contains roughly 590 people per square kilometer and nearly as many motor vehicles as people, making it one of the most crowded places in the world. While the ROC government has been able to put a cap on serious pollution problems, the fact remains that much of Taiwan's unique habitat has suffered from human encroachment.

Taiwan's location between three major climatic zones and its diverse topography have, however, endowed the area with a wide range of flora and fauna. Some 70 species of mammals, around 450 species of birds (40 percent of which reside on Taiwan year-round), 90 species of reptiles, 30 species of amphibians, nearly 170 species of freshwater fish, and 17,600 named species of insects (including 400 butterfly species) are known to exist in the Taiwan area. Regarding flora, there are 610 species of ferns, 28 species of gymnosperms, and 3,400 species of angiosperms.

The different land formations, climates, and forest types, not to mention the impact of large-scale human development, have combined to create ecological havens within the physical entity that is Taiwan. To protect these ecological havens, the ROC government has set aside 12.6 percent of Taiwan's total land area as part of a multitiered conservation system that includes six national parks 國家公園, 18 nature reserves 自然保留區, 23 forest reserves 國有林自然保護區, and 11 wildlife refuges 野生動物保護區.

Three laws specifically authorize the designation and protection of natural areas and wildlife refuges: the *Cultural Heritage Preservation Law*, which authorizes the creation of nature reserves and identifies endangered species of flora and fauna; the *Wildlife Conservation Law*, which establishes wildlife refuges; and the *National Park Law* 國家公園法, which allows for the designation of national parks. The central government agencies that supervise Taiwan's refuges are the Ministry of Interior's Department of National Parks 內政部國家公園組 and the Council of Agriculture. Answerable to the COA are the Taiwan Forestry Bureau 農委會林務局 under the Taiwan Provincial Government; the Taiwan Forestry Research Institute 農委會林業試驗所 under the Council of Agriculture; the Bureaus of Reconstruction 建設局 under the Taipei and Kaohsiung city governments; and the agriculture bureaus 農業局 of all city and county governments in the Taiwan area.

National Parks

The Republic of China has created a comprehensive national park system that balances conservation, recreation, and research. This has taken only ten years to implement, compared to over a hundred years for many other countries. Since the process was not begun until the island's population density was already quite high, park officials have faced a constant tug of war over land rights. Ownership of park land has been contested by businesses that previously occupied it, aborigines who claim it as ancestral land, investors who would like to develop hotels and other tourist facilities there, and even a veterans' agency that runs a farm in the middle of one of the parks.

The quick and continuous development of land did not give Taiwan the luxury of building its park system gradually. Instead, it has done the best it could, pushing through an ambitious park program that has placed 8.5 percent of its land area under protection (see map, Protected Areas). Additional land acquisitions together with the 52 existing protected nature and wildlife areas will eventually push the proportion of protected territory to over 12 percent of Taiwan's total area.

Taiwan's national park system was inaugurated in 1984 with the establishment of Kenting National Park 墾丁國家公園 at the southern tip of the island. In 1985 and 1986, Taiwan moved swiftly to set up Yushan National Park 玉山國家公園, Yangmingshan National Park 陽明山國家公園, and Taroko National Park 太魯閣國家公園 in central, northern, and eastern Taiwan, respectively. In 1992, Shei-Pa National Park 雪霸國家公園 was established in north-central Taiwan, and in October 1995, a sixth national park—Kinmen National Park 金門國家公園, occupying 25.5 percent of the Quemoy islands—was opened to the public.

National Park Facilities

Each national park has a national park headquarters, which is supervised by the Department of National Parks. In fiscal 1999, the combined budget for all the national park headquarters and the Department of National Parks exceeded US$104 million. Each national park has at least one visitor center and one nature display center. Most of the parks also have trailhead nature centers. Guided tours may be arranged by contacting the park headquarters in advance.

Taiwan's national parks received 11.5 million visitors in 1998. To minimize the impact of large crowds, the parks are divided into management zones. These zones identify the best use for each area within a park, classifying them as general protection areas, recreational areas, scenic areas, ecological protection areas, or cultural and historical sites.

Nature Reserves and Wildlife Refuges

The Council of Agriculture administers land protected under two designations: nature reserves and wildlife refuges. The COA has overseen the establishment of 18 nature reserves in Taiwan. These reserves range from a five-hectare plot to protect volcanic land forms in Kaohsiung to the 47,000 hectare forest reserve surrounding Mount Tawu 大武山. Altogether more than 63,200 hectares of land have been designated as nature reserves. Eleven of the nature reserves are directly managed by the Taiwan Forestry Bureau under the Council of Agriculture. The other nature reserves are managed by such agencies as the Taipei City Government's Bureau of Reconstruction 臺

北市建設局, the Penghu County Government 澎湖縣政府, and the Taiwan Forestry Research Institute. Each of these managing bodies is responsible to the COA, which ensures that the reserves are run in full accordance with the law.

In addition to nature reserves, 11 wildlife refuges encompassing over 11,700 hectares of land have been established in the Taiwan area. The first to be established was the Cat Islets Seabird Refuge 貓嶼海鳥保護區. Located in the southwest corner of the Pescadores 澎湖群島, the refuge encompasses both the Greater and Lesser Cat Islets. The islets serve as a rookery and breeding ground for thousands of terns, and over 16 families and 26 kinds of sea birds—most of them migratory—have been sighted here. Designated as a seabird refuge in May 1991, the Cat Islets refuge is a little over 36 hectares in area.

Next to be established was the Nantzuhsien River Wildlife Refuge 楠梓仙溪野生動物保護區 in Kaohsiung County's Sanmin Township 高雄縣三民鄉. This refuge is home to 10 species of freshwater fish and 80 species of birds, including the plumbeous water redstart, the little forktail, the gray-throated minivet, and the Formosan whistling thrush. The Nantzuhsien refuge covers 274 hectares and was set up in May 1993.

The Wuwei Harbor Waterbird Refuge 無尾港水鳥保護區 is located near Suao 蘇澳 in Taiwan's northeastern county of Ilan. Surrounded by diverse coastal forests, the 102 hectare site was designated as a bird refuge in September 1993 to protect its wetlands and bird habitats. Lakes, marshes, and streams within the site create an ideal environment for wildfowl such as the migratory ducks and geese that stop in Taiwan during the winter. According to one survey, close to 140 kinds of birds frequent the Wuwei Creek site. Every winter, from November to February, some 3,000 ducks and geese from 12 different species rest here.

The Taipei City Waterbird Refuge 臺北市野雁保護區 is home to 79 species of waterfowl and 41 species of plants. This 203 hectare wildlife refuge, set up in November 1993, serves as a natural classroom for Taipei citizens during the bird-watching season. Another urban area refuge is the Ssutsao Wildlife Refuge 四草野生動物保護區 in Tainan City. An important wetland site in southern Taiwan, this refuge is the permanent home to some 40 species of wild birds, and an additional 21 endangered and rare species of birds have been sighted here. Designated as a wildlife refuge in November 1994, the 515 hectare site also contains three kinds of rare mangroves.

Kenting Uplifted Coral Reef Nature Reserve is one of the 18 nature reserves established in Taiwan.

Nature Reserves

Taiwan Pleione Nature Reserve
臺灣一葉蘭自然保留區

Chatienshan Nature Reserve 插天山自然保留區

Chuyunshan Nature Reserve 出雲山自然保留區

Hapen Nature Reserve 哈盆自然保留區

Kenting Uplifted Coral Reef Nature Reserve
墾丁高位珊瑚礁自然保留區

Kuantu Nature Reserve 關渡自然保留區

Miaoli Sanyi Huoyenshan Nature Reserve
苗栗三義火炎山自然保留區

Nanao Broadleaved Forest Nature Reserve
南澳闊葉樹林自然保留區

Penghu Columnar Basalt Nature Reserve
澎湖玄武岩自然保留區

Pinglin Taiwan Keteleeria Nature Reserve
坪林臺灣油杉自然保留區

Taitung Hungyeh Village Taitung Cycas
Nature Reserve 臺東紅葉村臺東蘇鐵自然保留區

Tamsui River Mangrove Nature Reserve
淡水河紅樹林自然保留區

Tawu Taiwan Amentotaxus Nature Reserve
大武事業區臺灣穗花杉自然保留區

Tawushan Nature Reserve 大武山自然保留區

Watzuwei Nature Reserve 挖子尾自然保留區

Wushanting Mud Volcano Nature Reserve
烏山頂泥火山自然保留區

Wushihpi Coastal Nature Reserve
烏石鼻海岸自然保留區

Yuanyang Lake Nature Reserve
鴛鴦湖自然保留區

In addition to the Cat Islets refuge, Penghu County also contains the Wangan Island Green Turtle Refuge 望安島綠蠵龜產卵棲地保護區. Since the number of green turtles in the Taiwan area has fallen due to environmental degradation and poaching, the 23 hectare refuge was set aside in January 1995 to serve as a breeding ground and refuge for nesting green turtles. Wangan Island is one of the few green turtle habitats still largely untouched by human intrusion.

The Tatu River Mouth Wildlife Refuge 大肚溪口野生動物保護區, which straddles the border between Taichung County 臺中縣 and Changhua County 彰化縣, is a diverse collection of coastal waters, rivers, sandbanks, tidal flats, farmland, and fish farms. The wide plains and abundance of nourishing organisms brought in by the tides attract an enormous number of migratory birds, and 24 protected species have been sighted here. Established in February 1995, the 2,670 hectare refuge serves as an outdoor classroom for the residents of central Taiwan.

The Mienhua Islet and Huaping Islet Wildlife Refuge 棉花嶼花瓶嶼野生動物保護區 is located in the waters north of Keelung City 基隆市. Home to rare bird species and characterized by fascinating geology, the two uninhabited islets were classified as major wildlife habitats in June 1995 and then upgraded to wildlife refuges in March 1996.

Established in September 1996, the Lanyang River Mouth Waterbird Refuge 蘭陽溪口水鳥保護區 is located on the Lanyang Plain at the confluence of the Lanyang, Ilan, and Tungshan Rivers in Ilan County. The 206 hectare site is characterized by a wide range of topographical features, including coastal waters, rivers, sand bars, and fertile land. This wetland area attracts a great number of migratory birds every year because of its abundant food sources, and with some 231 bird species already sighted here, it is one of the best refuges for bird watching.

In October 1997, the Taichung County government announced the establishment of the Formosan Landlocked Salmon Refuge 櫻花鉤吻鮭野生動物保護區. A member of the glacial relic species, the Formosan landlocked salmon inhabits cold, high mountain streams as a result of the alternating effect of the geological changes that occurred during the Ice Age. Exhaustive fishing, water pollution, and other human factors over the years have done great damage to the salmon's natural habitat, causing the distribution and population to shrink dramatically. At present, the salmon is only found in the Chichiawan Stream 七家灣溪 at the Wuling 武陵 section of the upper reaches of the Tachia River

大甲溪 and in certain sections of the river on Mount Snow. In 1989, the COA declared the Formosan landlocked salmon an endangered species in accordance with the *Wildlife Conservation Law*.

Forest Reserves and the Taiwan Forestry Bureau

According to the most recent survey, about 72 percent of the 1.57 million hectares of national forestland in Taiwan is natural forest. The Taiwan Forestry Bureau (TFB) has classified the forests under its jurisdiction into 459 compartments based upon forest distribution, traffic conditions, and the degree to which the forests have been damaged in the past. Two to three rangers patrol each zone to prevent people from illegally felling trees, dumping refuse, or otherwise damaging the forests. These rangers also work to prevent and fight forest fires.

Forest reserves are national forest lands recognized as possessing unique natural characteristics. While these reserves are subject to the multiple-use policies of the TFB, managers of these areas are expected to emphasize preservation over development. In the past, several forest reserves have been promoted to nature reserve status, and this practice is expected to continue.

The basic law regulating the preservation of forests in Taiwan is the *Forest Law* 森林法. In accordance with this law, the TFB began a forest conservation program in 1965. This program includes surveying and studying rare plants and animals, as well as drafting plans for long-term studies, experimentation, and educational tourism within protected nature areas. TFB workers are continuing to survey the forests of Taiwan to identify different kinds of representative ecosystems

---

Forest Reserves

Alishan Coniferous and Broadleaved Forest Reserve 阿里山針闊葉樹林自然保護區

Chachayalaishan Taiwan Amentotaxus Reserve 茶茶牙賴山臺灣穗花杉自然保護區

Chiahsien Ssute Fossil Reserve 甲仙四德化石保護區

Chiaohsi Taiwan Keteleeria Reserve 礁溪臺灣油杉自然保護區

Chinshuiying Broadleaved Forest Reserve 浸水營闊葉樹林自然保護區

Erhshui Formosan Rock Monkey Reserve 二水臺灣獼猴自然保護區

Sheishankenghsi Forest Reserve 雪山坑溪自然保護區

Juiyenhsi Forest Reserve 瑞岩溪自然保護區

Kuanshan Taiwan Wingnut Reserve 關山臺灣胡桃自然保護區

Kuanshan Formosan Date Palm Reserve 關山臺灣海棗自然保護區

Kuanwu Taiwan Sassafras Reserve 觀霧臺灣擦樹自然保護區

Kuanyin Coastal Reserve 觀音海岸自然保護區

Liukuei Shihpalohanshan Landscape Reserve 六龜十八羅漢山自然保護區

Lulinshan Coniferous and Broadleaved Forest Reserve 鹿林山針闊葉樹林自然保護區

Peitawushan Coniferous and Broadleaved Forest Reserve 北大武山針闊葉樹林自然保護區

Sheipa Forest Reserve 雪霸自然保護區

Shuangkuei Lake Forest Reserve 雙鬼湖自然保護區

Taitung Coastal Mountain Range Broadleaved Forest Reserve 臺東海岸山脈闊葉樹林自然保護區

Taitung Coastal Mountain Range Taitung Cycas Reserve 海岸山脈臺東蘇鐵自然保護區

Taitung Formosan Rock Monkey Reserve 臺東臺灣獼猴自然保護區

Takuanshan Forest Reserve 達觀山自然保護區

Tawu Taiwan Keteleeria Reserve 大武臺灣油杉自然保護區

Yuli Wildlife Reserve 玉里野生動物自然保護區

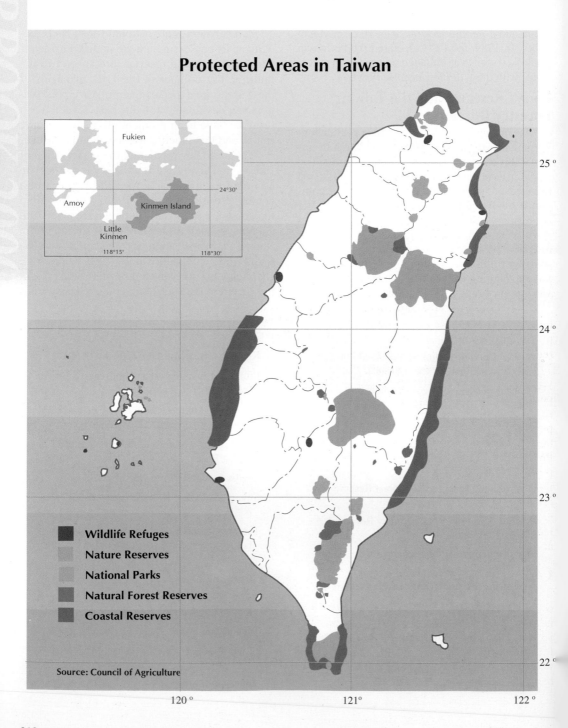

Protected Areas in Taiwan

Fukien

Amoy

Kinmen Island

Little
Kinmen

118°15'   118°30'   24°30'

25°

24°

23°

22°

Wildlife Refuges
Nature Reserves
National Parks
Natural Forest Reserves
Coastal Reserves

Source: Council of Agriculture

120°   121°   122°

and rare flora and fauna. In addition to entering all data into a computer network and setting up management survey stations for researching and protecting wild plants and animals, the TFB also posts educational information along the perimeters of forest reserves.

Until 1989, the TFB was financed through logging operations; however, forest management programs are no longer tied to timber harvest receipts. With a staff of more than 4,000, the TFB spent nearly US$88 million in fiscal 1998, yet the administration's income during that same period was just under US$4.5 million. Eighty-seven percent of this difference in funding was provided for by the central government, while the remaining 13 percent came from the Taiwan Provincial Government. The TFB also operates a network of hostels in forest areas that are more than a day's journey from any city, increasing the accessibility of such isolated regions. Such hostels are open to the public for a fee that depends on the quality of services available and the length of stay.

Cultivating a Conservation Ethic

Many government agencies and private conservation groups are working to carry out a massive educational campaign aimed at cultivating a conservation ethic in Taiwan. At the forefront of conservation education is the COA, which sponsors research projects, hosts international symposia, and subsidizes publicity campaigns. The COA also commissions other government agencies to provide conservation-related publications. Meanwhile, the Ministry of Education 教育部 (MOE) has training teachers to teach courses on wildlife conservation and introduced wildlife conservation into the public school curriculum. In 1998, 16 new textbooks introducing conservation concepts were written for students of all ages.

Targeting the general public, the Government Information Office under the Executive Yuan 行政院新聞局 has made wildlife conservation a major part of its informational campaigns. In July 1995, the GIO went on the Internet (*http://www.gio.gov.tw*) with a new database—available in both Chinese and English—of facts and figures about Taiwan, including the island's efforts in the area of wildlife conservation.

In 1998, more than 1,180 conservation-related activities were held in Taiwan. These activities included "Adopt a River," cleaning Taiwan's beaches, a national forestation campaign, a program for the protection of bears, a program for the conservation of fireflies, lake restoration projects, and so on. That same year, the GIO arranged eight nature-related films to be frequently aired on all four network TV stations. The Department of Health also arranged two conservation films to be aired on cable TV stations. In 1998, the COA sponsored a number of booklets with topics on wildlife regulations, enforcement, resources, and other areas. Government agencies also sponsored a number of books with topics on wildlife inventory, wildlife identification, and habitat protection. These are a few of the ROC government's many efforts to cultivate a conservation consciousness amongst the people.

International Cooperation

The ROC has an established record of cooperation with international conservation organizations. In 1998, the COA donated US$454,000 to support international conservation activities and projects, such as the IUCNSSC Cat Specialist

Group's project titled "Current Distribution of Tiger Populations in East and Southeast Asia"; the Biodiversity Research and Application Association's project titled "Rehabilitation and Reintroduction of Cape Pangolins Confiscated from Traders in Namibia"; and the two projects from the Friends of Animals titled "Plan for Assistance to Park Rehabilitation and Anti-Poaching Patrols-Niokolo Koba National Park, Senegal" and "Plan for the Translocation of Scimitar-Horned Oryx from Israel to Senegal for Purposes of Conservation Breeding Reintroduction of the Species to Nature." The ROC government's donations toward international wildlife conservation efforts have continued into 1999.

Stray Dog Control

The Animal Protection Law 動物保護法, which was drafted by the COA with the assistance of both the Animal Protection Association of the ROC and the ROC Life Conservation Association 關懷生命協會, was passed by the Legislative Yuan in October 1998. This bill not only ensures that all animals are given complete legal protection, it also devotes a specific section to the management of pets, providing the government with a major weapon in its arsenal for dealing with irresponsible pet owners. The regulations stipulated by the Animal Protection Law include:

• Certain pets must be registered and given IDs by supervising agencies. Registration includes a complete record of the animal's birth, acquisition, transference, loss, and death. In addition, a program for sterilization and microchip implantation will be implemented for more effective management of such pets—which, according to the Council of Agriculture, will focus on pet dogs and cats in its first stage.

• All animal keepers—including private pet owners, kennel owners, veterinarians, pet stores, pounds, shelters, and the like—must supply the animals in their care with sufficient quantities of food and water. Safe, sanitary, and adequate living space with proper ventilation, lighting, and temperature must also be given. Animal keepers may not abuse, harass, torture, harm, or maltreat their animals.

• Animal keepers must provide proper medical care to their animals in the event of injury or illness. Any treatment or operation performed must be carried out by a qualified, licensed veterinarian.

• Pet owners who no longer want their pets are required to send them to a licensed shelter; they cannot simply abandon them.

• Whenever animals are being transported, proper attention must be given to their food, water, excretion, environment, and safety. They should also be kept free from shock, pain, and harm during their journey.

• The euthanasia of animals must be carried out in a humane fashion by a veterinarian or under a veterinarian's supervision. Care should be taken to ensure minimal pain for the animal.

Years ago, a lack of proper training and experience on the part of some kennel keepers employed by local governments led to a few cases of inhumane treatment towards the animals in their care. These incidents triggered well-intentioned criticism of the ROC government from Taiwan's animal-loving friends in the international community. The ROC government responded immediately, heeding the good advice contained in the investigative reports released by the ROC Life Conservation Association and the World Society for the Protection of Animals (WSPA) stationed in the UK. Since then, the ROC government has taken effective measures to improve step by step the stray dog management of local governments. For example, from fiscal years 1995 to 1997, the ROC government allocated nearly one million US dollars to conduct a humane dog-catching project; and in fiscal year 1998, a similar amount was appropriated to improve the treatment of stray dogs nationwide.

At present, local governments are in charge of handling the stray dog problem. These governments work under the direct supervision of the central government's COA and EPA in accordance with the *Rules for the Management of*

Domestic Dogs and the *Regulations for Destroying Abandoned Dogs*. The central government assists them by providing money, training, and equipment, such as by setting up incinerators for cremation. In addition, as the newly passed *Animal Protection Law* stipulates, an animal protection committee will be established under a central supervising organization in order to draw up animal protection policies and examine the enforcement of relevant regulations, especially those concerning the management of stray dogs.

In order to reduce the number of dogs in Taiwan, veterinary research units offer discounts on performing sterilization operations. These discounts are made possible through local government subsidies and help to provide pet owners with an incentive to have their dogs sterilized. Furthermore, in an effort to more effectively identify dogs with their respective owners, the COA has entrusted research units to develop the technique of implanting radio-frequency microchips into dogs. This new technique is currently being put on demonstration and promoted; and with the passing of the *Animal Protection Law*,

the rights and safeguards regarding the well-being of animals in Taiwan have been strengthened even further.

Pet Registration

To resolve the problem of stray or lost dogs, the COA publicly proclaimed the "Pet Licensing Program," which took effect September 1, 1999. Under this regulation, all pet owners must apply for a pet license from a pet registration station in their residential area. The COA developed this pet licensing program in cooperation with the Institute for Information Industry, which developed the microchips to be implanted in dogs. Once the pet registration has been completed and the microchips implanted, the data will be processed to a central system. On the report of a missing pet, the data will then be automatically transferred to the "Lost Pet Recovery Service." According to Article 13 of the *Animal Protection Law*, a pet owner who does not register their pet within a specific period of time will be fined. If the owner refuses to register, he will be fined each time he is reported to the authorities.

Many famous film stars and singers participated in the Companion Animal Chip Implantation Activity held in Taipei to promote public awareness of this new requirement.
(Photo by the Central News Agency)

China Airlines
Heralding a New World of Service

Wherever business or leisure leads you, China Airlines is ready to take you on your way.

In the air. On the ground.

In Asia. Across the globe.

We're creating a fresh, new name for service as one of the world's most reliable airlines.

Elegance, comfort and convenience.

- Famed hospitality aloft with all the amenities.
- Fully reclining seats in first class; 50-inch span in business cla
- Spacious 747-400s and 737-800s mean more room to unwin

Flying towards a bright future.

- One of the world's youngest fleets with more than 80 aircraft the year 2003.
- Expert cargo service to five continents. Official shipper of the ROC's China One Satellite.
- The region's largest maintenance facility - the Three-Bay Hangar Complex in Taoyuan - certified for ISO-9002 inspections as well as those of nine leading regulatory agencies.

It's a whole new world. *For you...*

CHINA AIRLINES

CHINA AIRLINES CARGO

Like an endless summer, EVA Air, the wings of Taiwan

Bask in EVA Air's service, as inviting as it is relaxing

After only eight years, EVA Air has gained a reputation for remarkable comfort and friendly service. In the process, it has also earned numerous international honors and awards. This is no surprise to the savvy and selective frequent flyers who enjoy EVA Air's superior amenities, flight after flight. These travelers appreciate EVA Air's attention to the finer details, from a comforting pillow adjustment to an irresistible game no child can resist. And, more and more travelers are discovering EVA Air every day.

Isn't it about time you experienced EVA Air's service for yourself. From its home in Taiwan, EVA Air takes tropical warmth and tradition to new heights.

EVA AIR — THE WINGS OF TAIWAN

THE WINGS OF TAIWAN

EVERGREEN GROUP

EVA Air has ISO 9002 Certification.

For reservations please call : Taipei(02)2501-1999   Taichung(04)329-95(
Kaohsiung(07)536-9301   or contact your local travel age
FAX Back No.(02)2501-8999/2501-8599 (For Taiwan area only)   http://www.evaair.com.

Unhindered Worldwide Service

With "Punctual, Speedy, Reliable and Economical" transportation,
Yangming helps you grasp every business opportunity.

 **YANG MING LINE**
陽明海運股份有限公司

271 Ming De 1st Road, Chidu, Keelung, Taiwan 206, R.O.C.
TEL: 02-24559988 Telex:31572 YANGMIN FAX: 02-24559958
Internet Web Site: http://www.yml.com.tw.
E-mail address: cs@lmail.yml.com.tw

14
Transportation

The 117-km
Second Northern
Freeway
connects to the
Sun Yat-sen
Freeway in two
locations at
Hsichih and
Hsinchu.
(Photo by Berlin Chi)

A well-developed transportation network is essential to the Republic of China's export-oriented economy. Transportation has therefore always been an important priority in national development programs, from the Ten Major Construction Projects 十大建設 of the 1970s through the Six-Year National Development Plan 國家建設六年計畫 of the 1990s. With the official approval of the Asia-Pacific Regional Operations Center plan 亞太營運中心計畫 on January 5, 1995, the expansion and improvement of the island's transportation infrastructure has become even more critical. The plan, which targets the six major sectors of manufacturing, air transportation, sea transportation, finance, telecommunications, and media, will to transform Taiwan into a center of business and investment in the Asia-Pacific region. Considerable resources are thus being devoted to achieving the plan's sea and air goals to ensure that businesses in Taiwan enjoy the advantages of an extensive and efficient transportation network. This chapter reviews the organization of the ROC's railways, harbors and shipping, civil aviation, freeways and highways, and urban transportation systems, as well as recent developments that are shaping the new face of transportation industry in the country.

Railways

Taiwan's modern railway system provides frequent and convenient passenger service between all major cities on the island. By December 1998, Taiwan's railway network totaled 2,363 kilometers, an equivalent of 1.11 km per 10,000 people, or 66 meters per sq. km of land. These 2,363 km of rail transported 17.1 million tons of freight in 1998, for a total of 1.6 billion ton-km, 0.8 percent more than in 1998. The number of passengers carried increased 4 percent to a total

of 172 million. Railways in Taiwan are operated by the Taiwan Railway Administration 臺灣鐵路管理局 (TRA), the Taiwan Sugar Corporation 臺灣糖業公司, and the Taiwan Forestry Bureau 農委會林務局. The TRA provides passenger and freight services to the general public, while the Taiwan Sugar Corporation and the Taiwan Forestry Bureau haul their own products and offer limited passenger service, respectively.

Several types of passenger train services are available: the fastest express class is the Tzu-chiang express 自強號, which only stops at the major stations; the next fastest express class, with more frequent stops at lesser, but still large stations, is the Chu-kuang express 莒光號. The third class of trains, the Fu-hsing express 復興號, includes ordinary trains that only exclude the smallest stops, and electric commuter trains 通勤電車 which stop at every station on a designated commuter route. Finally, local trains—both with air conditioning 平快車 and without 普通車 —serve mostly long routes, stopping at every station and generally yielding to higher-priority Tzu-chiang, Chu-kuang, and Fu-hsing trains.

The TRA has upgraded equipment and facilities. In October 1995, the administration purchased 810 cars (344 electric commuter cars, 400 push-pull electric cars, 66 diesel rail cars) and began putting them in operation in December 1995. The TRA also completed a computerized ticketing system and implemented an automated phone ticketing system linking 42 stations. This new phone system has greatly reduced the hours-long lines common in the past, especially during long weekends and holidays. To allow for the operation of new trains, platforms at all stations have been raised to 86 centimeters, and all but the smallest stations have been paved with special guiding tiles for the sight-impaired.

While recent modernization projects have definitely resulted in a higher levels of service, several areas still need improvement. Routing and switching are done manually along most of the rail network, and even at major stations, delays in arrivals or departures are often only disclosed at the last minute. The TRA is attempting to

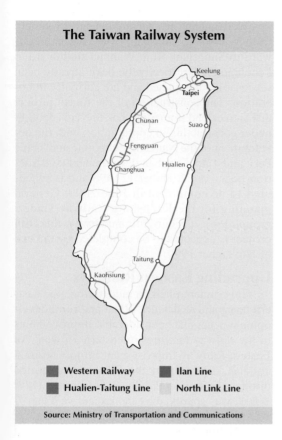

The Taiwan Railway System

Keelung

Taipei

Chunan

Suao

Fengyuan

Changhua

Hualien

Taitung

Kaohsiung

■ Western Railway   ■ Ilan Line

■ Hualien-Taitung Line   ■ North Link Line

Source: Ministry of Transportation and Communications

expedite commuter ticket purchases by install-ing additional ticket dispensing machines at ma-jor stations. However, passengers are still confronted by a confusing number of buttons to push (none of which are marked in English) before a ticket is issued. With the installation of such machines, the requirement that a ticket be bought before boarding is increasingly being enforced, despite often slow-moving lines at at-tended ticket booths and automated machines.

Nonetheless, station personnel are generally making an effort to serve passengers with more positive and courteous attitudes. Non-Chinese speakers will find most personnel on the train and at information and ticket booths very will-ing to help them with scheduling questions and ticketing problems.

Round-island travel in just one day has been possible since December 1992, when the TRA completed the South Link Railway 南迴線 and finished increasing the track gauge between Hualien and Taitung. Travel between Taipei near the northern tip of the island and Kaohsiung in the south takes just four-and-a-half hours by ex-press train and six hours by regular train, with 75 round-trip services each day. At the end of 1998, a one-way ticket from Taipei to Kaohsiung by express train cost a little less than US$25. Infor-mation on current fares can be obtained by call-ing the Taipei Railway Information Desk 臺灣鐵路局台北站服務臺 (02 2371-3558, 02-2381-5226) or the Kaohsiung Railway Information Desk 臺灣鐵路局高雄站服務臺 (07-221-2376, 080-711-333).

High-speed Railway

The ROC government has already begun the development of a high-speed railway (HSR) in Taiwan. The Bureau of Taiwan High Speed Rail 高速鐵路工程局 (BOTHSR) under the Min-istry of Transportation and Communications 交通部 (MOTC) is responsible for the implemen-tation of this project.

The planned HSR route, 340 km in length, will pass through the western corridor of the island. Ten stations will be located in Taipei, Taoyuan 桃園, Hsinchu 新竹, Miaoli 苗栗 Taichung 臺中, Changhua 彰化, Yunlin 雲林, Chiayi 嘉義, Tainan 臺南, and Kaohsiung 高雄. The overall construc-tion cost of the HSR project is estimated to be US$13.05 billion, with initial operation in 2005. The travel time from north to south will be cut from four and one-half hours by existing train or highway vehicles to 90 minutes by HSR.

In May 1995, the Legislature approved the HSR project to be implemented through the Build-Operate-Transfer (BOT) model. The HSR will thus be the first major infrastructure project in Taiwan to be undertaken by the pri-vate sector. The invitation to tender BOT bids for the HSR was officially announced on Octo-ber 29, 1996. Two private entities–China De-velopment Corporation and Taiwan High Speed Rail Consortium–submitted their proposals. The

BOTHSR held frequent discussions and negotiations with these two qualified applicants starting in March 1997 to draft the contract terms.
In September 1997, BOTHSR selected the Taiwan High Speed Rail Consortium (THSRC) for
the project, and, in July 1998, contracts were
simultaneously signed between the two for the
construction, operation, and station development of the HSR.

The overall venture will create as many as
486,000 jobs on the island, spread out over a
five-year construction period. Currently, around
99 percent of the 900 hectares of land set aside
for the construction project have been leveled.
In addition to funds for the HSR itself, the MOTC
also plans to allocate US$1 billion for the con-
struction of roads connecting the train stations to
neighboring commercial areas to assist in the
development of the regions along the railway.

Moving Underground in Taipei & Kaohsiung

In order to eliminate crossings in the Taipei
metropolitan area, downtown traffic bottlenecks,
decrease noise pollution, and promote a cleaner,
healthier environment, the Taipei Railway Underground Project was initiated in conjunction
with the Taipei Mass Rapid Transit System
and the High Speed Rail projects. The first, second, and third (north side tunnel) portions, which

involved building an underground railway system
from Wanhua to Huashan, from Huashan eastward to Sungshan, from Wanhua southward to
Panchiao area, respectively, have already been
successfully completed and are currently in operation. The construction of the fourth project
that is to extend from Sungshan to Nankang 南港,
under constructing in coordination with the development of the Nankang Economic and Trade
Park and Taipei's urban development construction began on Novmber 1, 1998 and is scheduled to be completed in June 2009. General
planning for the Kaohsiung Railway Underground Project is currently underway, this fifth
project is expected to be completed by the end
of November 1999.

Upgrading Eastern Railways

Government plans to industrialize the eastern coast and to balance urban and rural development necessitate considerable improvements
in the railway facilities in eastern Taiwan. An
Eastern Railway Improvement Project 東部鐵路
改善計畫, drawn up by the TRA and submitted
through the Taiwan Provincial Government 臺灣
省政府, was approved by the Executive Yuan 行
政院 in January 1991 and became part of the Six-
Year National Development Plan. The project
focuses on modernizing the 337 km of railway
comprising the Ilan line, the North Link line,

Transportation Administration

Transportation facilities are administered by several government agencies, including the national Ministry
of Transportation and Communications (MOTC) and various municipal-level agencies. Each agency has
different responsibilities depending on the type of transportation.

The MOTC has eight offices, departments, and divisions, three of which are devoted to various modes of
transportation: Railways and Highways 路政司, Posts and Telecommunications 郵電司, and Navigation and
Aviation 航政司. Numerous other MOTC committees are responsible for making and administering
transportation and communications policies. The Taiwan Provincial Government is especially active in the
highway and railway portion of land transportation. Local municipal units are primarily responsible for
developing adequate municipal transportation facilities but have significant power over provincial and
national transportation facilities located within their city limits.

Private sector participation can be found in many areas of transportation, but it is especially prominent in
the airline, airport, and shipping sectors at this stage of development. Private sector influence is certain to
expand, as the government moves toward greater privatization and encourages increased private investment.

Kaohsiung Harbor, the largest harbor in Taiwan, has a water area of around 12.4 sq. km, and can accommodate 151 ships at a time, greatly benefiting industry and transportation.

and the Hualien-Taitung line. Construction started in July 1991 and is scheduled to be completed in June 2003 at a total cost of US$1.51 billion. Improvements will include electrification, double tracks, heavy rails, a centralized traffic control system, new locomotives, repair facilities, and the relocation of the Hualien depot.

Harbors and Shipping

Maritime transportation is vital to Taiwan's trade-oriented economy. Statistics at the end of 1998 show that the ROC's 120 shipping lines have a fleet of 255 vessels (over 100 gross tons), totaling 8.72 million dead weight tons and 5.51 million gross tons. The ROC's fleet of container ships was listed at the top of world. The largest operator in Taiwan is Evergreen Marine Corporation 長榮海運公司, which is the second largest container operator in the world. Yangming Marine Transport Corporation 陽明海運公司, another giant shipping line, now ranks as the sixteenth largest container carrier in the world.

Taiwan has six international harbors—Keelung, Suao, Taichung, Hualien, Anping, and Kaohsiung. The total cargo handled by those ports amounted to 161.9 million metric tons in 1998.

Kaohsiung Harbor

Kaohsiung Harbor 高雄港 handled nearly 6.27 million TEUs (Twenty-foot Equivalent Units; cargo measured in terms of standardized 20-foot containers) in 1998, making it the third largest harbor in the world (after Hong Kong and Singapore) in terms of the volume of container cargo processed. Kaohsiung Harbor has 115 operating piers totaling 25,800 meters in length. With a water area of about 12.4 sq. km, the port can accommodate 151 ships at a time. The harbor has five container terminals, 23 container wharves, 57 gantry cranes, and 224 hectares of container yard. The harbor handled 98.2 million tons of cargo in 1998.

The government has built an 80,000-ton grain silo at Kaohsiung Harbor. A ten-year development project is underway to construct Container Terminal Number 5 第五貨櫃中心, including eight container wharves, in the Tajen Commercial Harbor Area 大仁商港區 of Kaohsiung Harbor. This project is scheduled to be completed by the end of 1999, at an estimated cost of nearly US$420 million.

Anping Harbor

Anping Harbor 安平港 is located on the western coast of southern Taiwan. The sixth and latest addition to Taiwan's group of international harbors, Anping has a channel depth of 7.5 meters and is capable of supporting ships under 6,000 dead weight tons. There are currently only three wharves in operation—a 320-meter wharf that goes to a depth of 3.5 meters, a 530-meter wharf that goes to a depth of 7.5 meters, and a 320-meter wharf that goes to a depth of 9 meters. However, expansion of the harbor as part of a periodical plan to develop the Taiwan area and spur on Tainan's industrial and economic growth is currently underway. Anping's main purpose will be to serve the Asia Pacific region, including northeast and southeast Asia, the Chinese mainland, Hong Kong, and various smaller coastal islands. It will also serve to boost tourism in the area by providing support for both sightseeing and pleasure boating.

Keelung Harbor

Located near the northern tip of Taiwan, Keelung Harbor 基隆港 has 57 berths and 3 mooring buoys capable of handling vessels in the 50,000-ton range (within the limits of a 13.5 meter draft). In addition, its three container terminals with 14 berths totaling 3,235.4 meters in length and its 25 container gantry cranes are capable of concurrently accommodating 14 container ships in the 30,000-ton range. Including the open yard, total storage capacity for the harbor his about 484,511 tons. This includes 184,378 square meters of marshaling yards (84,046 square meter for rent) capable of storing 276,569 tons and a 50,500-ton capacity grain silo equipped with three pneumatic vacuums.

Total imports and exports handled by Keelung Harbor exceeded 76 million tons in 1998. In order to meet the requirements of globe shipping and strengthen the competitiveness of Keelung Harbor, a dredging project for the basin and channel is now being implemented, to enable Keelung Harbor to accommodate 60,000 DWT conventional cargo ships and post-panamax type container ships. In addition, conversion of some conventional cargo berths into container piers is also in the works. The Keelung Harbor Bureau opened cargo handling in the port area to private stevedoring companies on January 1, 1999, to promote operational efficiency and service quality.

Taichung Harbor

Taichung Harbor 臺中港 is a man-made port covering a total area of about 5,000 hectares. Located on the west coast in central Taiwan, the harbor was projected to cope with the fast growing needs of the national economic development. It not only helps to relieve some of the shipping traffic from the heavily used Keelung and Kaohsiung ports, but aids in balancing the population and economic development of Taiwan itself.

Taichung Harbor's main channel and harbor basin both reach a depth of 14 meters below sea level during low tide. At present, there are 39 deep-water wharves in the port. With the most automated and efficient equipment, Taichung Harbor handled over 70 million tons of cargos in 1998, including 880,000 TEUs handled by the 8 container piers.

Taichung's operational concept is "strengthening port business by cooperation and coordination, offering best services by active engagement and involvement." Based on past experiences, a significant growth rate each year can still be anticipated in the future.

Hualien Harbor

Located on Taiwan's east coast, Hualien Harbor 花蓮港 is a relatively small port with 25 deep-water berths totaling 4,742 meters in length. With the completion of the fourth extension in 1991, Hualien Harbor is capable of simultaneously berthing one 100,000-ton class vessel in a special terminal for unloading coal, six 60,000-ton ships, two 30,000-ton ships, fourteen 5,000- to 15,000-ton ships, and two ships under 5,000 tons. It also has 504 meters of shallow-water wharves that are capable of accommodating fishing boats and other small vessels. In 1998, the harbor handled 12.2 million tons of cargo.

Suao Harbor

Suao Harbor 蘇澳港 is situated on the northeast coast of Taiwan, serving as Keelung Harbor's

Airlines Providing Scheduled International Services to/from Taiwan

Air Orient
Air Canada
Canadian Air
Air Macau
Air Micronesia
Air New Zealand
Air Nippon
Ansett Australia
British Asia Airlines
Canadian Airlines International
Cargolux Airlines International*
Cathay Pacific Airways
China Airlines
Continental Micronesia
Hong Kong Dragon Airlines
EVA Airways
Evergreen International Airlines*
Far Eastern Air Transport Corp.*
Federal Express Airways*
Japan Asia Airways

KLM Royal Dutch Airlines
Malaysian Airlines
Mandarin Airlines
Martinair Holland*
Northwest Airlines
Pacific Airlines
Pacific East Asia Cargo Airlines *
Philippine Airlines
Qantas Ltd.
Polar Air Cargo*
Royal Brunei Airways
Saudi Arabia Airlines*
Singapore Airlines
Swiss Air Asia
Thai Airways International
Transasia Airways
UNI Airways*
United Airlines
United Parcel Service*
Viet Air
*non-passenger services

auxiliary port. The total water area of the harbor is about 2.9 sq. km. Currently, the harbor has 13 operating berths, with an annual capacity of 10 million tons. In 1998, imports and exports passing through Suao Harbor totaled over 6.3 million tons.

Taipei Harbor

Taipei Harbor 臺北港 serving as Keelung Harbor's auxiliary port, is located at the south bank of Tamsui river, nearby Hsun Tang village, Pali township, Taipei County. Two berths, with a total length of 340m and 9m in depth, and a 70-hectare stacking yard have been completed in the first phase of construction. The construction of an outer breakwater of 3,810 m commenced in July 1997 and is scheduled to be finished by December 2001. In order to provide complete berthing facilities to serve international vessels and relieve the heavy cargo traffic burden of Keelung Harbor, the second phase of construction has been started since 1997, with its three phases of constructions to be completed by 2011. In accordance with the policy of privatization

and enhancement of the port's competitiveness, there is a plan for leasing out port facilities and business might possibly be opened to public and private investment.

Civil Aviation

As of 1998, a total of 48 airlines were providing flight services to destinations in the ROC. Among these, 34 foreign carriers and six ROC-based airlines (EVA Airways, Mandarin Airlines, China Airlines, Transasia Airways, UNI Airways and Far Eastern Air Transport Corp.) operate scheduled international air services to and from Taiwan.

ROC Domestic Airlines

China Airlines 中華航空公司
Far Eastern Air Transport 遠東航空公司
Mandarin Airlines 華信航空公司
Transasia Airways 復興航空公司
U-Land Airlines 瑞聯航空公司
UNI Airways Corporation 立榮航空公司
Daily Air Corporation 德安航空公司
Asia Pacific Airlines 亞太航空公司

U-Land Airlines—also ROC-based carriers—offers international charter services. There are eight companies (including two helicopter operators) with domestic passenger flights in the ROC.

There are currently two international airports in the Taiwan area: Chiang Kai-shek International Airport 中正國際機場 at Taoyuan in northern Taiwan, and Kaohsiung International Airport 高雄國際機場 in the south. In addition, there are several domestic airports: Taipei, Hualien, Taitung, Hsinchu, Taichung, Tainan, Chiayi, Pingtung 屏東, Makung 馬公, Chimei 七美, Orchid Island 蘭嶼, Green Island 綠島, Wangan 望安, Kinmen 金門, and Matsu (Peikan 北竿). It is estimated that over the next five years domestic air traffic will grow by over 10 percent annually; therefore, work is currently under way to expand capacity. Airport facilities have been expanded at Tainan, Hualien, Chiayi, Makung, Kinmen and Orchid Island. New navigational aids have been installed at CKS, Kaohsiung, Taipei, Chiayi, and Pingtung airports. Also projects have been made for construction of a new airport at Matsu (Nankan) and Hengchun, as well as a new terminal at Hsinchu.

Due to economic recession around the world, the number of inbound and outbound international passengers decreased 8.69 percent to 49 million less than the 1997 figure of 54 million. The amount of air freight handled also slightly decreased from around 1.31 million tons in 1997 to 1.3 million tons in 1998. In addition to passengers and cargo, the number of flights decreased from 714,403 in 1997 to 638,344 in 1998.

However, in order to meet the prospective demands by 2010, a US$700 million expansion project at the Chiang Kai-shek International Airport began in 1989. The project includes the construction of a second passenger terminal, aircraft bays, airport connection roads, car parks, and a people mover system. It is scheduled for completion by 2000. The planned facilities are designed to allow the airport to handle an additional 14 million passengers annually.

In addition to work at the CKS airport, a US$300 million expansion project was under construction for years at the Kaohsiung International Airport. After a new international passenger terminal building was opened on January 11, 1997, further expansions of airport facilities are continuing. The project is designed to increase capacity at the airport by 6.4 million international passengers per year.

ROC authorities have been working diligently to obtain additional air traffic rights for ROC carriers that operate international air services. In 1998 and the first half of 1999, the ROC revised or renewed agreements with Canada, Thailand, Australia, Cambodia, Russia, etc. As a result, EVA Airways started services to Vancouver in June 1999. China Airlines commenced scheduled all-cargo flights between Taipei and Sydney in July 1999. The ROC also plans to sign aviation accords with Brazil, India, Turkey, Spain, and other countries with market potential.

Highways and Freeways

Highway traffic, both in terms of passengers and cargo, was down in 1998. Traveling on Taiwan's 19,684 km of highways were a total of 1.16 billion passengers, or roughly 34 million less than in 1996. Passenger-kilometers fell 4.6 percent to 9.06 billion, and the 307 million tons of freight carried on highways in 1997 represented a one percent decrease from the previous year. Although these figures may give the impression of

Taiwan Highway Classifications

Highways in Taiwan are classified according to the level of government having jurisdiction over them. Thus, highways are either national 國道, provincial 省道, county 縣道, township 鄉道, city 市道, or special highways 專用公路. There are six different kinds of highways: the freeway 高速公路, the round-the-island highway 環島公路, the cross-island highway 橫貫公路, the longitudinal highway 縱貫公路, the coastal highway 濱海公路, and the connecting highway 聯絡公路. The Taiwan Highway Bureau 臺灣省交通處公路局 is responsible for the construction and maintenance of Taiwan's highway system.

Taiwan Highway Network

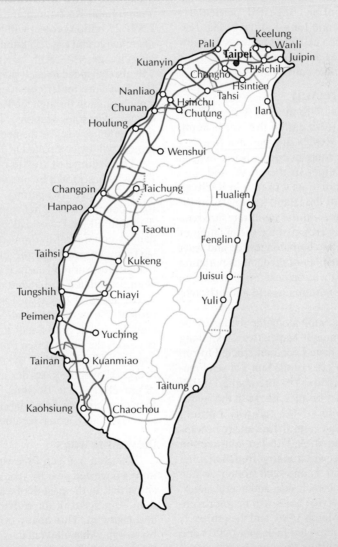

Keelung
Wanli
Pali
Juipin
Taipei
Kuanyin
Hsichih
Changho
Hsintien
Nanliao
Tahsi
Chunan
Hsinchu
Houlung
Chutung
Ilan
Wenshui
Changpin
Taichung
Hualien
Hanpao
Tsaotun
Fenglin
Taihsi
Kukeng
Juisui
Tungshih
Chiayi
Yuli
Peimen
Yuching
Tainan
Kuanmiao
Taitung
Kaohsiung
Chaochou

	East-West Highways			Western Coastal Expressway
	Sun Yat-sen Freeway (the North-South Freeway)			Taipei-Ilan Freeway
	Second Freeway			Planned Routes

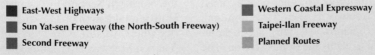

Source: Ministry of Transportation and Communications

an improving traffic situation, the opposite is generally true. With more than 13.12 million vehicles and 21.7 million people in Taiwan, major highways are often congested, particularly during weekends and long holidays. The sections below describe existing highways and new and future projects aimed at making highway travel faster and more convenient.

Sun Yat-sen Freeway

Inaugurated in 1978, the Sun Yat-sen Freeway 中山高速公路 (also called the North-South Freeway) was the ROC's first national freeway. The 373-km long route connects Kaohsiung in the south with Taipei in the north, and then continues northward to its terminus in Keelung. The freeway is still the island's primary north-south thoroughfare, and the rapid rate at which the traffic load has grown since the opening of the freeway has led to both congestion and wear and tear. Thus, a number of recent transportation projects and plans focus on ensuring that the Sun Yat-sen Freeway remains a safe and efficient traffic corridor.

To relieve congestion along the section of the freeway running through Taipei, two 21-km long elevated viaducts have been constructed to run parallel along both sides of the Sun Yat-sen Freeway from the Hsichih 汐止 interchange in the north to the Wuku 五股 interchange in the south.

Several sections of the freeway running through northern and central Taiwan are becoming heavily congested. A 27.6-km long section of the four-lane freeway running from Yangmei 楊梅 to Hsinchu 新竹 is one such stretch. A lane will thus be added to each side, and interchanges, toll stations, and service areas will be improved. Bidding began in March 1996, and the project is scheduled to be completed in January 2003 at a cost of US$162 million. Another heavily used section of the freeway is the 112 kilometers from Hsinchu to Yuanlin 員林. One lane is therefore being added to each side of this section. The US$790 million project, which began in November 1994, is scheduled to be completed in December 2001.

Since the Sun Yat-sen Freeway is also becoming saturated in southern Taiwan, preliminary plans were drawn up to widen the section between Yuanlin and Kaohsiung at the end of 1997. The US$1.27 billion project will begin at the Yuanlin interchange and run 158 kilometers to the Wuchia interchange 五甲交流道 in Kaohsiung. One lane will also be added to each side of the freeway, and two lanes are under consideration for a 4.3-km stretch running through the Kaohsiung metropolitan area. For some sections, bidding and construction started as early as the beginning of 1997. The project will be completed in 2007.

The volume of traffic on the Sun Yat-sen Freeway has grown by an average of 11 percent annually since its opening. This heavy traffic load, coupled with a hot tropical climate, abundant rainfall, and overloaded trucks and trailers, causes considerable damage to the freeway's surface. To maintain the quality of the road, many five-year road surface repair projects have been formulated and undertaken since 1982.

In addition to expansion and maintenance projects, some major repair work has also been completed. The Sino-Saudi Arabian Bridge 中沙大橋 carries the Sun Yat-sen Freeway across central Taiwan's Choshui River 濁水溪. The river bed has deepened over the years due to excessive removal of gravel as well as flooding following typhoons. Pier protection and the stabilization of the river bed have thus become paramount concerns.

New Freeways

The Sun Yat-sen Freeway became increasingly congested year by year in 1980's. Statistics show that in the past the freeway handled more than 70 percent of the traffic between Keelung and Hsinchu. This heavy traffic load has since been somewhat alleviated by the construction of the Northern Second Freeway 北部第二高速公路. With a total length of 117 km including connecting roads, this new freeway connects the Sun Yat-sen Freeway at Hsichih, extends southward, and rejoins the Sun Yat-sen Freeway at Hsinchu.

In August 1993, the southern 65 km between Chungho 中和 and Hsinchu were opened to traffic, and the opening of the northernmost section running between Hsichih and Mucha 木柵 followed in March 1996. The final middle section, which links Mucha to Chungho, was completed in August 1997. The total cost of the Northern Second Freeway was about US$52 billion.

To facilitate traffic flow in central and southern Taiwan, the construction of the central and southern sections of the Second Freeway 中南部第二高速公路, with a total length of 388 km including connecting roads, has commenced. These two sections are expected to be finished in the year 2002. When completed, the second freeway will run southward from Taipei to Pingtung. Being the second main artery in the country, the Second Freeway will certainly be a relief to the heavily congested Sun Yat-sen Freeway.

Construction of the Taipei-Ilan Freeway 北宜高速公路, 31 km of length commenced in July 1991. Beginning at Nankang 南港 with a tunnel to the picturesque Ilan, the freeway is scheduled for completion by mid-2003, making the current three-hour drive from Taipei to Ilan only 40 minutes long. In addition, a new east-west expressway in Taipei City is slated for completion in 1999.

The government has begun the construction of 12 East-West Expressways 東西向快速公路. Once completed, the 12 E-W Expressways will connect the Western Coastal Expressway 西部濱海快速公路 with local transportation systems. Two of the 12 east-west lines, the northernmost and southernmost, will not link directly with the Western Coastal Expressway, but will instead hook into the larger highway network and provide

---

Taipei Taxi Cabs

At the end of 1998, there were over 38,544 registered taxi cabs cruising the streets of Taipei City. Of these, 20,472 were operated by a total of 1,434 taxi companies. Another 8,827 were individually owned and operated taxis, 5,549 radio-dispatch taxis, and 5,421 cabs associated with, but not operated by, taxi companies.

The last fare increase approved by the Taipei City Government in July 1998 added a NT$5 (US$0.15) surcharge to the old base fare of NT$65, making the effective base fare NT$70, or about US$2. Since this increase did not involve a recalibration of taxi meters (i.e., the other factors affecting the fare were not changed), the fare taxi passengers should pay at the end of a ride is always NT$20 higher than the total indicated on the meter.

Many major hotels now record the number of the taxicab on a card for their guests. This ensures that should there be any problem with the trip, the passenger has meaningful information to report to the passenger hotline listed below.

Effective Taipei Taxi Fares (with surcharge figured in the base rate) as of August 15, 1999

	Daytime (6 A.M.–11 P.M.)	Nighttime (11 P.M.–6 A.M.)
Base fare	NT$70 (1,650 meters)	NT$70 (1,375 meters)
Distance Increment	NT$5 (350 m)	NT$5 (290 m)
Time Increment	NT$5 every 3 min. under 5 km/hr.	NT$5 every 2.5 min. under 5 km/hr.

Regular additions to total fare:
    NT$10 for a dispatched cab
    NT$10 for each luggage placed in the taxi trunk.
The nighttime fare is charged all day during the Chinese New Year's holiday.

Complaints about Taxi Service

Passenger Hotline—Taipei City Police Headquarters 臺北市警察局 2394-9007
Bureau of Transportation, Taipei City Government 臺北市交通局 2725-6888
Office of Motor Vehicle Inspection, Taipei City Government 臺北市監理處 2767-8217

Islandwide Parking Problem

The number of motorcycles and cars has continued to soar in recent years as strong overall economic growth and rising personal incomes have made the purchase of motor vehicles commonplace. By 1997, there were 14.27 million motor vehicles in the Taiwan area, a little less than 4.2 million of which were passenger cars. By way of comparison, there were only 8.7 million vehicles and 1.04 million passenger cars ten years ago. With such skyrocketing growth, parking is already a problem, and it will become increasingly serious in the near future. Accordingly, the MOTC has recommended in its revision of the *Highway Law* 公路法 (which has been submitted to the Legislature 立法院 for approval) that every car buyer should be required to have a personal parking space. Even so, alleviating the serious shortage of parking spaces in the ROC will take time.

The five-year (1995-1999) Public Parking Lot Construction Plan 政府興建公共停車場五年投資計畫 calls for building 360 new parking lots. The total cost of the project is estimated at roughly US$2.44 billion.

---

express east-west routes in their respective localities. The 12 links, from north to south, are Wanli 萬里 to Juipin 瑞濱, Pali 八里 to Hsintien 新店, Kuanyin 觀音 to Tahsi 大溪, Nanliao 南寮 to Chutung 竹東, Houlung 後龍 to Wenshui 汶水, Changpin 彰濱 to Taichung, Hanpao 漢寶 to Tsaotun 草屯, Taihsi 臺西 to Kukeng 古坑, Chiayi to Tungshih 東石, Peimen 北門 to Yuching 玉井, Tainan to Kuanmiao 關廟, and Kaohsiung to Chaochou 潮州. The 12 E-W Expresssways will ease traffic congestion, promote the development of specific regions and improve access to certain areas.

Freeway Traffic Control

During holidays, the volume of traffic is generally 30 to 50 percent above usual traffic loads. Accordingly, the Taiwan Area National Freeway Bureau (TANFB) under the Ministry of Transportation and Communications 交通部臺灣區國道高速公路局 has adopted a ramp metering control system 匝道儀控管制系統 to maintain an acceptable flow of traffic. This system was introduced on four national holidays in 1993, and, since it proved fairly effective, the TANFB gradually extended the system to include long holidays, weekends, and normal weekdays. The TANFB has implemented a fully automated ramp metering control system over the entire Sun Yat-sen National Freeway, at a cost of US$14.1 million.

To increase the effectiveness of the ramp metering control system and smooth the flow of traffic on the freeway during long holidays, High

Occupancy Vehicle Control 高乘載車輛專用通行時段管制 has been in force since the 1995 Chinese New Year holiday. The system involves allocating different time slots during which vehicles of various carrying capacities are allowed onto freeways. High Occupancy Vehicles (HOV), such as buses and cars carrying at least four people, are given priority. As a result, congestion on the freeways during holidays has been reduced.

Tolls

There are ten toll stations along the Sun Yat-sen Freeway and two on the Northern Second Freeway. Standard tolls are NT$40 (US$1.18) for cars, NT$50 (US$1.47) for buses and small trucks, and NT$65 (US$1.91) for trailer trucks.

To help vehicles pass through quickly, there are "No Change" toll lanes at every toll station. Drivers are also encouraged to use coupons, which can be conveniently purchased at post offices, gas and toll stations, rest areas, the Land Bank of Taiwan 臺灣土地銀行, and the Medium Business Bank of Taiwan 臺灣中小企業銀行.

Traffic Control

Traffic control is the joint responsibility of the Traffic Division of the National Police Administration 內政部警政署交通組, the Highway Police Bureau 公路警察局, the Taiwan Provincial Highway Police Corps 公路警察大隊, and all local police departments. The Airborne Squadron 空中警察隊 assists when necessary.

Urban Traffic

Traffic in Taiwan's major cities is very congested. Urban planners in all of Taiwan's metropolitan areas must cope with a similar set of challenges: a soaring number of new motorcycles and cars, a limited number of streets, and the complexities of acquiring very scarce space for improvements. Fortunately, countermeasures such as the mass rapid transit systems and swift and convenient bus services are finally on the way.

Taipei's Traffic Challenge

Compared to other major cities in Taiwan, Taipei City undoubtedly has the busiest traffic. Growing numbers of private cars and construction projects are placing an increasingly intolerable burden on Taipei's already-saturated roads and streets. According to the volume data in 1998, there are 681,386 automobiles and 904,232 motorcycles operating on Taipei's limited land space. An average of 11,832 additional automobiles and motorcycles take to Taipei's streets each month.

To encourage the use of the public bus system, the Taipei City Government set aside certain lanes of eight streets for exclusive use by buses, on Sungchiang Road 松江路, Hsinsheng South Road 新生南路, Hsinyi Road 信義路, Jenai Road 仁愛路, Nanching East Road 南京東路, Minchuan East and West Road 民權東西路, Tunhua South and North Road 敦化南北路, and Chungshan South and North Road 中山南北路. There are a total of 47.6 kilometers of such bus lanes. Although they are generally reserved for urban buses, the government has agreed to allow commuter buses owned by schools, companies, and other organizations with a seating capacity of at least 20 persons to use them. By the end of 1997, 263 commuter buses were using the bus-only lanes, and the number of bus passengers had increased by 4.9 percent annually. Research shows a positive influence of the bus-only lanes system.

Research has shown these lanes as improving local traffic flow. Based on a 1996 survey, the average travel speed of cars during rush hour was 15 percent higher than two years ago. Furthermore, after their implementation, the average travel speed of buses during rush hour increased 35 percent.

Preparations for the Taipei Rapid Transit Systems 臺北大眾捷運系統 (TRTS) began back in early 1986, when the Executive Yuan 行政院 completed preliminary plans for the network and approved their implementation. The initial network, spanning a

The newly-opened Taipei Mass Rapid Transit System has eased traffic congestion, shortened commuting time, and improved the city's quality of life.

Taipei Rapid Transit Systems

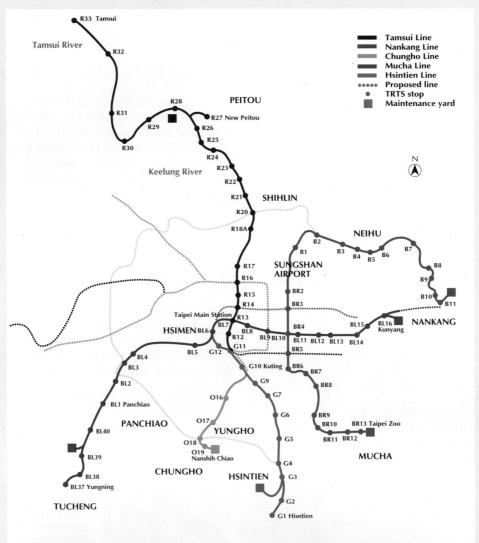

Legend:
- Tamsui Line
- Nankang Line
- Chungho Line
- Mucha Line
- Hsintien Line
- Proposed line
- TRTS stop
- Maintenance yard

Red Line (Tamsui Line)
R12 NTU Hospital
R13 Taipei Main Station
R14 Chungshan
R15 Shuanglien
R16 Minchuan W. Rd.
R17 Yuanshan
R18A Chientan
R20 Shihlin
R21 Chihshan
R22 Mingte
R23 Shihpai
R24 Chili An
R25 Chiyen
R26 Peitou
R27 Hsin Peitou
R28 Fuhsing Kang
R29 Chungyi
R30 Kuandu
R31 Chuwei
R32 Hung Shulin
R33 Tamsui

Blue Line (Nankang Line)
BL37 Yungning
BL38 Tucheng
BL39 Haishan
BL40 Nantzu
BL1 Panchiao
BL2 Hansheng Rd.
BL3 Hsinpu
BL4 Chiangtzu Tsui
BL5 Lungshan Temple
BL6 Hsimen
BL7 Taipei Main Station
BL8 Shantao Temple
BL9 Chunghsiao Hsinsheng
BL10 Chunghsiao Fuhsing
BL11 Chunghsiao Tunhua
BL12 Sun Yat-sen Memorial Hall
BL13 Taipei City Hall
BL14 Yungchun
BL15 Houshan Pi
BL16 Kunyang
BL17 Nankang

Orange Line (Chungho Line)
O16 Tinghsi
O17 Yung-an Market
O18 Ching-an
O19 Nanshih Chiao

Brown Line (Mucha Line)
BR2 Chungshan Middle School
BR3 Nanking E. Rd.
BR4 Chunghsiao Fuhsing
BR5 Ta-an
BR6 Technology Building
BR7 Liuchang Li
BR8 Linkuang
BR9 Hsinhai
BR10 Wanfang Hospital
BR11 Wanfang Community
BR12 Mucha
BR13 Taipei Zoo

Green Line (Hsintien Line)
G1 Hisntien
G2 Hsintien City Hall
G3 Chichang
G4 Ta Pinglin
G5 Chingmei
G6 Wanlung
G7 Kungkuan
G9 Taipower Building
G10 Kuting
G11 CKS Memorial Hall
G12 Hsiao Nanmen

*The section of Brown Line from station B1 to station B11 has yet to receive final approval.
Source: Department of Rapid Transit Systems, Taipei City Government.

Taipei Rapid Transit Systems Initial Network (2005 Completion except Neihu Line)

Tamsui Line 淡水線
Runs at grade, elevated, and underground tracks from Tamsui to Taipei Main Station, passing Peitou 北投, Shihlin 士林 and Yuanshan 圓山—22.8 km, 20 stations, Mass Rapid Transit (MRT)

Hsintien Line 新店線
From Taipei Main Station runs underground along Roosevelt Road 羅斯福路 and Peihsin Road 北新路 to Hsintien—10.3 km, 11 stations and a stabling yard MRT

Mucha Line 木柵線
Runs on elevated tracks from the Taipei Zoo 臺北市立動物園 in Mucha to the intersection of Hoping East Road 和平東路 and Fuhsing South Road 復興南路, and then along Fuhsing South and North Road to Minchuan East Road 民權東路—10.9 km, 12 stations, Medium Capacity Transit (MCT)

Nankang Line 南港線
Runs underground along Chunghsiao (E. and W.) Road 忠孝東西路 from Nankang Railway Station 南港車站 to Chunghua Road 中華路, and then on to Hsimen Station 西門站—10.3 km, 12 stations, MRT

Panchiao Line & Tucheng Line 板橋線及土城線
Runs underground from the terminus of the Nankang Line at Hsimen Station to Hoping W. Road, then crosses under the Hsintien River 新店溪 to Panchiao and runs along Nanya S. Road, Chungyang Road to Tucheng 土城—12.6 km, 9 stations and a maintenance depot, MRT

Chungho Line 中和線
Runs underground from Chungho and Yungho 永和 and then crosses under the Hsintien River to join the Hsintien Line at Kuting Station 古亭站—5.4 km, 4 stations, MRT

Neihu Line 內湖線
DORTS is currently analyzing socioeconomic and construction factors on route selection. The appropriate system technology is also being evaluated at the present time.

Maintenance Link 維護軌
Runs underground from Hsimen to the Chiang Kai-shek Memorial Hall 中正紀念堂 and provides a route for Nankang and Panchiao line cars to reach the Peitou depot—1.6 km, 1 station, MRT

Long-term Network Hsinchuang Line 新莊線
DORTS has set the year 2021 as the target year for the completion of a long-term network that will expand the initial TRTS network to include the Hsinyi Line 信義線, Sungshan Line 松山線, Hsinchuang Line 新莊線, Luchou Extension Line 蘆洲支線, a medium-capacity orbital line, an eastward extension from the Nankang Line, and an extension to Tamhai New Town 淡海新市鎮 around Tamsui.

total length of 86.8 km, is scheduled to be completed by the year 2005 at a cost of US$18 billion. French contractor MATRA started work on the first TRTS line—the Mucha Line—in July 1988. The Mucha Line began revenue service on March 28, 1996. The first section of the Tamsui Line opened on March 28, 1997, and the entire line opened on December 25, 1997. The Chungho Line and the northern section of the Hsintien Line began service in December 1998. The entire Hsintien Line, the western section of the Nankang Line, and the northern section of the Panchiao Line opened at the end of 1999.

These mass transit systems were initially designed to alleviate urban traffic in downtown Taipei and to encourage people to move from the metropolitan area to the outlying areas. Not unexpectedly, property values along the five routes have increased dramatically. Housing prices have more than tripled in the suburban areas of Mucha, Peitou, and Nankang since 1987, when the Taipei City Government formally established the Department of Rapid Transit Systems 臺北市政府捷運工程局 (DORTS). DORTS is responsible for the construction project, while operation is the responsibility of the Taipei Rapid Transit Corporation (TRTC) 臺北捷運公司.

The TRTS lines all share the common feature of being able to transport large numbers of passengers. With the exception of the Mucha Line, which runs four-car trains, all other lines handle six-car trains, with a maximum capacity of 2,200 passengers per train. Hourly capacity will thus vary between 20,000 and 60,000 people in one direction. In the case of Mucha Line, the computerized run trains currently have a capacity of 10,000 to 25,000 passengers per hour in one direction, because its headway ranges from two to ten minutes. Train speeds range from 25 to 80 kilometers per hour, and the distance between stations varies from between 800 and 1,000 meters downtown to between 1,000 and 2,000 meters in the suburbs.

Rapid Transit in Other Cities

Following Taipei's lead, many other cities in Taiwan, including Kaohsiung, Taichung, Tainan, and Taoyuan, initiated plans for their own metropolitan rail transit systems. A feasibility study for a rapid transit system in Hsinchu has also been undertaken. However, the only project to have made it past the planning stage so far is Kaohsiung's.

Kaohsiung is Taiwan's largest harbor and second-largest city. Rapid industrial development and population growth have accentuated the need for efficient metropolitan transportation. The Kaohsiung City Government 高雄市政府 has accordingly mapped out the Kaohsiung Metropolitan Area Mass Rapid Transit System Development Plan (First Term) 高雄都會區大眾捷運系統第一期發展計畫, which was approved by the Executive Yuan in January 1994. The Kaohsiung MRT system is being designed to integrate high-speed and regular railway and city bus systems, thus providing a comprehensive mass transportation network. Already finalized plans call for the construction of a Red Line and an Orange Line—with 37 stations and a total length of 42.7 km—at an estimated cost of US$6 billion. Two additional lines and extensions to the Red and Orange lines are currently in the planning stage. Although bidding for the construction of the Orange Line was originally scheduled for 1996, the funding for the system was not passed by the Kaohsiung City Council 高雄市議會 until December 1997. Following the Executive Yuan's B.O.T. (Build-Operate-Transfer) policy and instruction, the Kaohsiung MRT (KMRT) project will use B.O.T. approach. The construction of KMRT project is expected to begin in October 2000, with partial operation is in December 2004, operation of the northern section of the Red Line in December 2005, and the full operation of the Red Line and Orange Line in December 2006.

15
Public Health

For decades, religious organizations have provided important health care services in the Taiwan area. Hualien's Mennonite Christian Hospital 基督教門諾會醫院 in Eastern Taiwan was initially established in 1948 as a mobile medical service station, and now is a fully-equipped hospital with a capacity of more than 500 beds.

What's New

1. Figures updated
2. Reorganization of the public health administration
3. New categorization of communicable diseases
4. Drug injury relief

S hifting demographic patterns and changes in modern lifestyles have affected health care in Taiwan. The graying of the population has highlighted pension issues and long-term care for the elderly, and the recent influx of large numbers of foreign laborers has exacerbated the problem of providing health care for foreign workers. Serious pollution and smoking problems have triggered a high rate of lung cancer, especially in the urban areas of Taipei, Kaohsiung, Keelung 基隆, and Tainan. Industrial development and growth in urban traffic have resulted in an alarming rate of occupational and traffic accidents. Of the 10,973 fatal accidents recorded in 1998, 6,203 cases (or 58.83 percent) were transportation-related fatalities, constituting the leading cause of death for people under the age of 44 in this category. More than 95 percent of fatalities (5,903 persons) were due to motorbike-related traffic accidents. A major youth health concern that has arisen is the unprecedented number of students using amphetamines. Health authorities are also concerned about the sanitation standards of Taiwan's many unregulated eateries, roadside stalls, lunch box caterers, and galleries of food vendors.

Overall, the control of infectious diseases in the ROC has greatly improved. Forty years ago, acute infectious diseases were the number one killer in the Taiwan area; today they are no longer among the top ten causes of death in Taiwan. Bubonic plague, smallpox, and cholera were all eradicated long ago; and not a single case of rabies has been discovered since 1959. In 1965, the World Health Organization of the United Nations (WHO) declared malaria nonexistent in

Plans and Programs

The public health policies in the Taiwan area were mainly formulated by the Department of Health 衛生署 (DOH). In fiscal 1998, three primary plans and nine secondary programs were drawn up under the directions of the Executive Yuan and the Department of Health in order to improve the health conditions of the people and the efficiency of the public health care system. The plans and programs, respectively, to be implemented according to schedule are as follows: the *Reinforcement Plan for the Control of TB* 加強結核病防治方案, the *Plan for the Second Stage of New Family Planning* in the Taiwan Area 台灣地區新家庭計畫第二期計畫, and the *Third Term Promotion Plan for the Follow-up of the National Health Information Network* 全國醫療資訊網後續推廣計畫第三期計畫; the *Third Term Program for the National Health Network* 醫療網第三期計畫, the *Second Term Program for the Eradication of Poliomyelitis, Congenital Rubella, Measles and Neonatal Tetanus* 根除三麻一風第二期計畫, the *Fourth Term Program for Reinforcing the Control of Hepatitis* 加強肝炎防治第四期計畫, the *Second Term Program for the Control of AIDS* 後天免疫缺乏症候群防治計畫第二期計畫, the *Second Term Intermediate Stage Program for the Control of Dengue Fever* 登革熱防治第二期中程計畫, the *Five-Year Program for the Control of Leprosy* 癩病防治五年計畫, the *Program for the Prevention and Control of Tobacco Hazards in the Taiwan Area* 台灣地區菸害防制計畫, the *Program for the Control of Cancer in Women* 婦女癌症防治計畫, and the *Occupational Diseases Control Program* 職業病防治計畫.

Taiwan. Other infectious diseases such as diphtheria, pertussis, neonatal tetanus, poliomyelitis, Japanese encephalitis, and tuberculosis are now under strict control. Major immunization drives in 1995 focused on eradicating poliomyelitis, measles, congenital rubella, and neonatal tetanus. Since 1998, a pioneering plan has been initiated to protect senior citizens 65 years or older against flu with free vaccinations.

The increase in economic prosperity of the Taiwan area has brought greater access to health

Medical Infrastructure

Manpower

At the end of 1998, there were more than 144,070 medical personnel in the Taiwan area. On average, there was one doctor of Western medicine for every 811 persons, one doctor of Chinese medicine for every 6,509 persons, and one dentist for every 2,766 persons. There are currently 11 medical schools, 11 paramedical junior colleges, and 13 paramedical vocational schools in the ROC. In 1997, these institutions trained 950 physicians, 290 dentists, 963 medical technicians, 1,139 pharmacists, and 14,025 nurses and midwives. Physicians may apply for a medical specialist license after being certified in such specialties as family medicine, internal medicine, pediatrics, obstetrics and gynecology, orthopedics, neurology, neurosurgery, urology, ENT, ophthalmology, dermatology, psychiatry, rehabilitation medicine, anesthesiology, radiology, pathology, and nuclear medicine. A specialist license is valid for only five to six years, after which physicians must undergo a short period of retraining, to ensure that physicians have been keeping up with the new advances in technology and are familiar with new systems and equipment. After completion, physicians may extend their licenses for another term. This system was first set up in 1988, and by the end of 1998, 26,511 specialists had been certified.

Manpower imbalances pose major problems for the ROC's medical care system. A shortage of qualified nurses is especially serious, given the growing medical needs of an aging population. To improve the quality of medication and

Medical Personnel in the Taiwan Area 1998	
Type	Number in Service
Physicians	27,168
Doctors of Chinese Medicine	3,461
Dentists	7,900
Dental Assistants	93
Pharmacists	14,807
Pharmacist Assistants	7,954
Medical Technologists 醫檢師	5,282
Medical Technicians 醫檢生	301
Registered Professional Nurses	40,062
Registered Nurses	31,153
Midwives	704
Medical Radiography Technologists (Technicians) 醫用放射線技術師(士)	2,485
Physical Therapist & Assistants	1,720
Dieticians	575
Occupational Therapists & Assistants	405
Total	144,070

Source: Department of Health

care resources and enabled the government to launch the National Health Insurance 全民健康保險 (NHI) program, which officially began on March 1, 1995. By December 1998, more than 96 percent of the Taiwan population or 20.76 million persons were insured under the new program.

The health situation in Taiwan has already made impressive gains over the past 40 years. For example, average life expectancy from 1951 to 1997 has jumped from 53.38 years to 71.93 years for males, and from 56.33 years to 77.81 years for females. The crude death rate dropped from 18.15 per 1,000 persons in 1947 to 5.64 per 1,000 persons in 1998, and the infant mortality rate also dropped from 44.71 per 1,000 live births in 1952 to a low of 4.80 per 1,000 in 1993. However, in 1996 infant mortality increased to 6.66 mainly due to the implementation of a new, more efficient nationwide registration system for reporting newborns. In 1998, the rate dropped again to 6.57.

Teaching Hospitals in Taiwan

Of the 556 hospitals with three-year accreditation in Taiwan, 125 are teaching hospitals 教學醫院. Teaching hospitals are classified into five categories: medical centers 醫學中心, regional hospitals 區域醫院, district hospitals 地區醫院, specialty teaching hospitals 特殊功能醫院, and psychiatric teaching hospitals 精神專科教學醫院.

lower the doctor-patient ratio to 1:575, the DOH has proposed to increase medical student enrollments by 100. The number of medical technicians capable of operating more sophisticated, advanced medical equipment has also been decreasing.The number of technicians and technologists in radiology and medicine, as well as dentists, have already exceeded the number of physicians. In 1997, the number of pharmaceutical graduates increased to more than twice that of the previous year. The government's plan to prohibit sales of prescription medicine by physicians may lead to greater demand for pharmacists.

Rural and remote areas are still terribly short of qualified medical personnel. The government, therefore, offers incentives, such as increased pay and commuting subsidies to medical personnel serving in these areas. Beginning in 1999, medical school graduates who have studied on government scholarships are assigned to remote areas or special medical branches for one year. According to the *Measures for the Improvement of Medicare in the Mountain and Remote Areas and Outlying Islands,* St. Paul's Hospital in Taoyuan, and 12 other hospitals have provided medical services to 13 areas considered inaccessible. Transportation subsidies are provided for patients who require transfer to cities.

The Taiwan Provincial Government is now pushing its third ten-year program (1991-2000) to train doctors and supporting staff for work in rural hospitals and clinics.

Foreign nationals with licenses recognized by the ROC government may apply to take a written exam in Chinese which, if passed, will allow them to obtain a license to practice medicine in Taiwan.

Medical Facilities

A wide network of hospitals and clinics serves the people in the Taiwan area. At the end of 1997, the combined total of public hospitals, private hospitals, and clinics in the ROC numbered more than 17,731. These facilities provided 124,564 short-term and long-term care beds, averaging nearly 56.8 beds per 10,000 people.

Public medical care institutions consist of 97 hospitals and 497 clinics, including provincial, municipal, county and city hospitals, medical school hospitals, veterans hospitals and clinics, clinics affiliated with government institutions, and civil departments of military hospitals. Private medical care institutions consist of 622 hospitals and 11,235 clinics, including proprietary hospitals, hospitals affiliated with private medical schools, corporate hospitals and clinics, and private clinics. Medical institutions in the Taiwan area provide a total of more than 1,242,900 beds, about 65 percent of which are provided by private medical institutions.

Accreditation and Licensing

A hospital accreditation system has been in operation since 1978 to assure quality hospital in-patient care and rank the service and quality of Taiwan area hospitals. Currently, hospitals are evaluated on the basis of the quality of personnel, facilities, hospital management, and community services, as well as the quality of medical care in various departments, such as internal medicine and surgery, radiological diagnosis and therapy, laboratory testing, nursing care, pharmaceutical service, ward management, infection control in hospitals, emergency care, and psychiatric care. The accreditation is valid for three years, after which a hospital must apply for reassessment. By June 1999, a total of 556 hospitals in the Taiwan area had received three-year accreditations.

Clinics are not subject to accreditation procedures, but instead must apply to the local health station for an operating license. The requirements for obtaining such a license are set by each individual health station, which ensure that the clinics are maintaining high standards at all levels, ranging from the quality of the facilities to the credentials of the medical staff. Once clinics obtain their operating licenses, they are subject to periodic inspections by local health station personnel. Such routine checks help to maintain the high standards and must be passed in order for the clinics to renew their licenses.

Information Exchange

In 1991, the Department of Health commissioned the Institute for Information Industry 資訊工業策進會 to set up a computerized information exchange system in Hsinchu 新竹 between local medical institutions and hospitals. This Public Health Information Exchange was originally a three-year (1991-93) experimental project to improve medical services in Hsinchu; however, owing to its success, the local project was extended in 1993 to cover the entire Taiwan area. By August 1995, regional centers had been established in Hsinchu, Taipei, Kaohsiung, and Taichung.

The Public Health Information Exchange incorporates three subsystems: the Health Administration Information System (HAIS), the Administration System of General Affairs (ASGA), and the National Health Information Network (NHIN). The HAIS covers the exchange of medical affairs, pharmaceutical affairs, food sanitation, communicable disease control, and health promotion, and the ASGA is primarily concerned with speeding up the administrative efficiency of public health. The NHIN provides the latest general profiles of national medical resources, shows the current certification for all medical personnel and management, displays information exchanges between medical institutions and medical administration units, and provides consulting services for the general public (relevant medical legislation and bulletin boards). This network was fully operational by the end of 1997, allowing all health stations to exchange information concerning medical records, insurance histories, medical personnel resumes, etc.

Public Health Administration

Before July 1, 1999, public health administration in the ROC was organized at four levels: national, provincial/special municipality, county and city, as well as township. At the national level, the Department of Health under the Executive Yuan is the highest authority, and determines national health policies, formulates programs, and both supervises and coordinates health services at all levels. Beginning July 1, 1999, in coordination with the reengineering of the government organization and the streamlining of the Taiwan Provincial Government, the DOH established the Central Taiwan Office to replace the former provincial department of health. At the same time, the DOH made some adjustments in the organization of the central public health system. Five bureaus oversee medical affairs 醫政處, pharmaceutical affairs 藥政處, food sanitation 食品衛生處, health promotion 保健處, and health planning 企劃處. In addition to seven newly established departments, the DOH has 48 subordinate agencies. The new departments are: the Center for Disease Control 疾病管制局, the National Bureau of Controlled Drugs 管制藥品管理局, the Institute of Family Planning 家庭計劃研究所, the Maternal & Children's Health Institute 婦幼衛生研究所, and the National Institute of Public Health 公共衛生研究所. Other subordinate agencies are: the National Laboratories of Food & Drugs 藥物食品檢驗局, the National Health Insurance Supervisory Committee 全民健康保險監理委員會, the National Health Insurance Disputes Review Committee 全民健康保險爭議審議委員會, the Committee for the Negotiation of Medical Fees 全民健康保險醫療協定委員會, the Committee on Chinese Medicine & Pharmacy 中醫藥委員會, the Bureau of National Health Insurance 中央健康保險局, 27 hospitals (including branch hospitals), five sanatoria, and four chronic disease prevention units. The three DOH-affiliated organizations include the National Health Research Institute 國家衛生研究院, the Taiwan Joint Commission on Hospital Accreditation 醫院評鑑暨醫療品質策進會, and the Center for Drug Evaluation 醫藥品查驗中心.

At the special municipality government level are the Taipei City Department of Health 臺北市政府衛生局 and the Kaohsiung City Health Department 高雄市政府衛生局, along with their subordinate district health stations in each district within Taipei and Kaohsiung cities. These agencies are responsible for implementing health and medical care programs in their respective administrative areas.

At the county and city level, health bureaus are the responsible health units, and health stations are located in each urban or rural township. In mountain areas and outlying islands health rooms 衛生室 or small-scale health posts 衛生站 have been set up to provide primary health services, to improve health conditions, and raise the quality of medical care services at the grassroots level.

With implementation of the National Health Insurance plan in 1995, the development of a more comprehensive, overall medical information network that would link NHI units with community dispensaries became one of the top priorities of the DOH.

Medical Care Network

Rapid industrialization and urbanization, as well as the aging of the population in recent years, have highlighted the need for better health care and medical services, which have long been unevenly distributed. To balance medical resources, the DOH in July 1985 launched a 15-year project designated the Establishment of Medical Care Network 醫療保健計畫—籌建醫療網計畫 in the Taiwan area. This three-phase project divides the Taiwan area into 17 medical care regions, each of which serves as the basic unit for developing medical manpower, facilities, and an emergency care network. These 17 medical regions are further subdivided into 63 subregions, based on population, geographic conditions, and transportation facilities. Each subregion is equipped with regional or district hospitals, as well as primary medical care units (i.e., private practitioners, group practice centers, and health stations). By December 1995, 174 group practice centers had already been established under the first phase of the 15-year project.

The second phase of the Establishment of Medical Care Network project also seeks to distribute medical resources more evenly by restricting the establishment or expansion of hospitals in regions with plentiful medical resources and setting up a Medical Care Development Fund to encourage the private sector to establish health care institutions in regions lacking sufficient medical facilities. The Medical Care Development Fund subsidized a total of 201 hospitals and 105 clinics between fiscal 1992 and 1999, making the 37 regions previously lacking medical facilities now sufficient.

The first phase of the Establishment of Medical Care Network was completed in 1990, and the second phase was completed in December 1996. The third phase, which started in January 1997, targets primary medical care in the mountain areas and offshore islands by expanding the emergency medical care network and developing health services for the chronically and mentally ill. In 1998, the Medical Care Network has put more emphasis on catering to the needs of an aging society, emergency care, mental health care, long-term medical care service, improvement of medical personnel, and quality of medical care.

Health Stations

Residents in mountain areas and offshore islands rely heavily on the medical services provided by local health stations 衛生所, which, along with health rooms 衛生室, provide general outpatient treatment and emergency medical care. Educational programs provided by the health stations include courses on maternal and child health, family planning, and the prevention and control of geriatric, acute, and chronic diseases. Surveys show that 70 to 90 percent of the visits to community health stations are for infant and child immunizations. In 1945, there were only 15 health stations in the entire Taiwan area; however, by the end of 1998, there were 369 health stations and 507 health rooms throughout the Taiwan area, with 12 district health stations in Taipei City and 11 in Kaohsiung City; four health stations in Kinmen County, and four in Lienchiang County.

Health stations form the basis of primary health care in the Taiwan area. As of December 1995, these health centers were staffed with nearly 4,900 medical personnel, including physicians, dentists, pharmacists, nurses, and laboratory technicians. On the average, each health station has one to two doctors, with 37 percent having a pharmacist, and 15 percent, a dentist. Even health stations and health rooms in remote areas feature basic medical equipment. By December 1995, 249 of the health stations in Taiwan were equipped with X-ray machines, 128 had dental X-ray machines, and almost all of the group practice centers were equipped with automatic biochemical analyzers.

A health station with supporting hi-tech equipment to strengthen emergency care services has been set up in each township in the mountain areas, outlying islands, and other areas with relatively limited medical resources. This includes 39 health stations established in 30 aboriginal townships scattered throughout 12 counties in Taiwan proper, the Pescadores, Liuchiu (in Pingtung County), and Green Island (off the coast of Taitung). Furthermore, approximately 200 health rooms have also been set up to serve residents in inaccessible areas. Since 1979, the government has been sending mobile medical teams to remote villages on a regular basis. In the Pescadores, where there is no health station, a telecommunications medical care program was initiated in 1988 to provide emergency medical care for the island's residents. Later, 145 other points of service in various mountainous areas and other offshore islands also joined this telecommunications medical care network.

To provide prompt and accurate information for the health stations around the island, a health station information system was inaugurated in 1983. By the end of 1998, a total of 357 health stations had implemented this computerized system.

Health Insurance

Prior to March 1995, only 59 percent of Taiwan's population had health insurance, all under 13 public health insurance plans. In view of the rapidly growing medical care costs and the increasing number of the elderly, the ROC government launched the National Health Insurance program on March 1, 1995, to provide universal medical care. This system incorporates the medical insurance coverage provided by the original 13 public health insurance plans and further extended coverage to the 7.99 million citizens who were formerly uninsured, mainly the elderly, children, students, housewives and the disabled. At the end of 1998, there were 20,757,185 people covered by the NHI program; 264,868 persons more than the previous

---

Public Health Policy Report

A new version of the ROC's *White Paper on Health Care—Health Care Development Beyond 2000* 衛生白皮書—跨世紀衛生建設 was published in August 1997. As part of the ten-year national development plan projected by the Council of Economic Planning and Development, this 350-page document (consisting of six sections and 33 chapters) spells out the government's health care policies for the rest of the decade.

Due to rapid social changes and problems that emerged after the implementation of the National Health Insurance program, targets to be attained during the period include:
* Seeking stable development of the National Health Insurance program (to keep medical growth in NHI expenses under 10 percent, to provide a more effective NHI program for insurants, and to give more protection to disadvantaged groups);
* Reinforcing health promotion programs (genetic health; oral health; visual health; geriatric health; improvement of physical strength; control plans on cancer, smoking and betel nut chewing; and preventive measures on accidents);
* Fortifying the medical care system (computerization);
* Strengthening preventive measures against communicable diseases;
* Promoting the quality and safety of foods and medicines;
* Installing medical facilities for the purpose of long-term care of patients with chronic diseases;
* Developing medicare technologies; and
* Enhancing international cooperation (ROC's bid for WHO participation).

---

year and representing 96 percent of the total population. The average age was 32.65.

The implementation of NHI has benefited everyone, especially the 362,168 people suffering from serious or terminal illnesses who, in the past, had to shoulder the bulk of the expenses for medical care themselves or burden their family with high medical costs. The NHI has also cushioned the high hospitalization expenses incurred from premature babies, thereby alleviating the huge financial stress normally placed on their families.

Under the *National Health Insurance Act* 全民健康保險法, participation in the NHI program is mandatory for all ROC citizens who have resided in Taiwan for more than four months, with the exception of servicemen and prison inmates, who receive free medical care from the government. Foreign nationals employed in Taiwan who possess valid Alien Resident Certificates 外僑居留證 are also eligible to participate, along with their family members.

As NHI is compulsory and an important part of social security, the Bureau of National Health Insurance 中央健康保險局 cross-checks the lists of uninsured persons with the government agencies overseeing household registration, internal revenue, and labor insurance to assist in locating and enrolling them in the NHI program.

By the end of 1998, 16,122 of the medical institutions in the Taiwan area had joined the NHI program, including 645 western medicine hospitals and 8,483 clinics, 73 Chinese medicine hospitals and 1,878 clinics, and 5,043 dentists. In addition, some 3,364 community pharmacies, 236 medical labs, 191 home health care institutions, 24 midwife clinics, and 23 community rehabilitation centers for psychiatric patients are all providing services to participants in the NHI program.

Under the schedule for premiums and rates that was approved in July 1994, employees pay 30 percent of the premium, employers 60 percent, and the government 10 percent. Thus, a typical worker, earning just over US$943 a month, with a spouse and two children, will pay about US$42 a month. The law specifies a first-year premium rate of 4.25 percent of the monthly wage, which can be raised to no more than 6 percent thereafter.

The *National Health Insurance Act* requires an evaluation of the health insurance program within two years of its implementation, especially regarding the source of its finance. At the end of 1998, the NHI program experienced a budget deficit of US$47 million. In order to reduce costs, a co-payment system based on pharmaceutical costs and frequent users was introduced on August 1, 1999. Some prospective payment schemes have been tried out on a small scale. A universal payment method has been implemented for dental service on a pilot basis since 1997. Up to 50 inpatient service items are now reimbursed on case payments. A capitation system has been initiated in remote areas and outlying islands and is applicable to certain diseases.

The *National Health Insurance Act* was revised (effective July 1999) to increase the number of dependents per household who are not required to pay the premium from three to five. For example, a household with more than three dependents does not need to pay the premium for the fourth and fifth dependents. The lowering of the premium-free threshold and the strengthening of medicare for low-income groups and residents in remote areas has benefited more than two million people. In addition, medical subsidies are provided to aborigines below the age of 20 and above 55.

Integration with Existing Programs

Before the National Health Insurance program was implemented, there were 13 public health insurance plans that served as the primary sources of medical insurance. The majority of these plans were categorized under three main systems: labor insurance, government employees' insurance, and farmers' insurance. Although the medical coverage portions of these programs have been subsumed by the National Health Insurance program, the original programs still continue to provide benefits for various categories of extraordinary financial hardships.

The Labor Insurance program 勞工保險, for example, still provides benefits for workers, such as industrial workers, journalists, employees in nonprofit organizations, government employees and teachers not eligible for civil servant or teachers insurance, fishermen, and persons receiving vocational training in institutes registered with the government.

Labor insurance covers payments under two criteria: ordinary payments and compensation

National Health Insurance Premium Shares

	Insured Status Category*	Insurant	Rate Shared % Employer	Government
I	Civil servants Government employees	40	60	0
	Private school employees	40	30	30
	Wage & salary workers of public & private firms with specific employers	30	60	10
	Employers, self-employed, licensed professional practitioners & technicians	100	0	0
II	Members of occupational associations Sailors recruited overseas	60	0	40
III	Farmers, fishermen, & members of irrigation associations	30	0	70
IV	Dependents of servicemen	40	0	60
V	Low-income households	0	0	100
VI	Veterans Dependents of the deceased veterans Others	0 30 60	0 0 0	100 70 40

*Unless stated explicitly otherwise, all of the above categories include dependents.
Source: Bureau of National Health Insurance, DOH

for occupational and industrial damage. Ordinary payments include cash benefits for maternity, subsidies for those who have no income during hospitalization, compensation for the disabled, lump-sum payments for old age, and funeral grants for survivors. Since January 1999, an unemployment subsidy has been provided for those who are involuntarily unemployed. Compensation for occupational injuries include medication and payments to workers during their hospitalization and compensation for workers killed or disabled on the job. After March 1995, the NHI program covered almost all health care services under one program. Labor insurance became supplementary in sharing part of the patients'

out-of-pocket payments for hospital care. Supplemental health maintenance and treatment services are provided as a preventive measure on an annual basis for 23 health conditions to detect occupational diseases and injuries. The ordinary premium rate for labor insurance is 6.5 percent of the participant's wages, and 0.08 to 3 percent for occupational injury. By May 1999, there were 7,586,830 persons enrolled in labor insurance through 386,345 insuring units.

The benefit packages in each of the nine Government Employees' Insurance (GEI) programs vary in content, but generally include cash benefits for disability, old age, and death, as well as funeral allowances for dependents. Each program covers a

different range of people. For example, the *Government Employees' Insurance Law* 公務人員保險法 covers all civil servants currently employed by the government, the *Retired Government Employees' Insurance Law* 退休人員保險法 covers civil servants who have already retired (as well as their dependents), and the *Insurance Code for Private School Teachers and Administrative Staff* 私立學校教職員保險條例 covers private school teachers and administrative staff. By October 1999, a total of 624,831 people were covered under one GEI program or another. All GEI programs are under the purview of the Examination Yuan's Ministry of Civil Service 考試院銓敘部 and are insured by the Central Trust of China 中央信託局, a government-owned financial enterprise.

As of March 1998, the Comprehensive Farmers' Health Insurance program 農民健康保險 covered 1.81 million farmers. This insurance program is administered at the national level by the Ministry of the Interior 內政部, and at the local level by the respective provincial, county, and city governments. All farmers over 15 years of age, who engage in agricultural work for more than 90 days a year and who are members of a farmers' association, are eligible for coverage under the Comprehensive Farmers' Health Insurance program. The coverage includes compensation in the event of illness and injury, and cash benefits for disability, maternity, and funeral expenses. In August 1999, there were 1,804,648 farmers enrolled in the Comprehensive Farmers' Health Insurance program.

Other plans include insurance for professional groups, which are eligible for group life insurance sponsored by the Central Trust of China. Each professional group forms an insurance unit that pays two-thirds of the premium, while those insured pay the remainder. Military personnel also have their own insurance plan, with officers paying special low premiums and all enlisted men receiving free coverage. Comprehensive accident insurance for students 學生團體保險 is also provided by the government, covering 4,113,443 students as of June 1999. The insurer, Taiwan Life Insurance Co., Ltd. 台灣人壽保險股份

有限公司, is supervised by the Taiwan Provincial Government and either the Taipei or Kaohsiung City Government, depending on the acquirement of the bid for students' insurance. The government partially subsidizes the program, and students pay a token premium every semester. The government also subsidizes the full cost of premiums for aboriginal and offshore island students. Other government-sponsored insurance programs include the Ocean Fishermen Group Accident Insurance 海上作業漁民團體保險 and the Miners Group Accident Insurance 煤礦礦工團體平安保險, which had 100,000 and 167 enrollees in 1998, respectively.

Health Promotion Programs

Maternal and Child Health Care

Ever since the first health care programs for mothers and children were begun in 1952, infant deaths caused by birth trauma and infection have been decreasing. The infant mortality rate was 6.57 per 1,000 live births in 1998. Unfortunately, the relative number of accidental injuries, premature births, and birth defects have increased since 1952. As estimated, about 8 to 10 percent of the 300,000 live births were premature, therefore, it is important that comprehensive health services cover all stages of development, from conception through childhood.

The current NHI program provides prenatal and postnatal care for early detection and treatment of pregnancy-related diseases, ensures safe deliveries, and maintains the health of both infants and mothers. Ten free prenatal checkups and a "handbook for pregnant women" are provided to record the health conditions of expecting mothers. Breast-feeding is also encouraged. As a result, the health of mothers and children in the Taiwan area has greatly improved. In 1965, the number of women who died from childbirth was 75 per 100,000. This figure had dropped to 9.41 by 1986, and to 8.84 by 1998.

The infant mortality rate has also fallen. In 1965, it was 24 per 1,000; by 1994, the rate had decreased to 5.07 per 1,000. The figure rose to

6.57 per 1,000 in 1998, but the increases was mainly the result of an underestimation of infant and neonatal mortality rates due to the registration system in use prior to 1994. This discrepancy has now been corrected through the implementation of a more efficient and accurate birth registration system.

Over 99.95 percent of all deliveries were assisted by qualified personnel in 1997, a marked improvement in health service over past years, but a surprising 34.51 percent of all deliveries were done by Caesarean section (C-section), with only 20 percent of these operations performed out of medical necessity. The reason for the increase in the number of C-sections is strongly believed to be twofold. Although women who died of obstetric causes were at a low 8.84 per 100,000 live births, women regularly asked for this procedure to secure the health of their babies. Furthermore, the expenses for this method of delivery are fully covered by the NHI program. On the other hand, it is believed that hospitals were promoting C-sections out of a desire to increase their surgical fee income.

A strong preventive health care program has been implemented in Taiwan with health stations around the island offering free vaccinations to infants and children for hepatitis B, poliomyelitis, measles, mumps, rubella, Japanese encephalitis, tuberculosis, diphtheria, pertussis, and tetanus. Comprehensive health programs and preventive health care services include six health examinations and a handbook of health for all infants and children up to three years of age. These examinations are conducted at clinics and hospitals islandwide. In October 1998, the Taipei City Government began to subsidize Taipei's children under six for medical care not provided under the NHI program. Growth and development norms, as well as recommended daily dietary allowances, have also been charted; thus, health care information in kindergartens and nurseries is now available for preschool children to detect growth anormalities at an early age.

Comprehensive measures have been taken to educate preschool teachers, parents, and expectant mothers on the importance and techniques of oral hygiene. Educational activities on injury prevention of accidents and injuries are conducted every year on Children's Day (April 4).

To secure national health quality and to address health problems at an early age, the Ministry of Education 教育部 and the DOH have decided that a complete health record for all elementary school students will be completed biannually, starting from the 1998 school year. The examination will include a record of the students' height and weight, eyesight, auditive power and ENT conditions, oral hygiene, spine and chest, skin, cardiac and pulmonary system, and abdomen, as well as a check for eye diseases, parasites, diabetes, and other health problems. Parents and local health units will each receive a copy of the student's health records for follow-up inquiries and future reference.

Genetic Health Program

Congenital defects were the second most common cause of neonatal and infant deaths in 1997, accounting for nearly 29.79 percent of all neonatal and infant mortalities. Although the infant mortality rate has declined as a result of improved health services, the percentage of babies born with congenital abnormalities has not fallen, with percentage of newborns with congenital defects at 1.15 percent in 1998. According to experts, it was estimated that 3 to 4 percent of all newborns were categorized as severely deformed, adding more than 10,000 infants to the group annually.

The government has long been aware of this problem, and in 1980 initiated the Congenital Malformation Registration and Follow-up Project 先天性缺陷兒登記追縱計畫 to study the prevalence, causes, and care of birth defects. There are 256 medical institutions participating in the project to report cases of congenital abnormalities. Genetic health counseling centers have been set up at the National Taiwan University Hospital, Tzu Chi Buddhist General Hospital (Hualien), the Taipei Veterans General Hospital, and the Kaohsiung Medical College Hospital. There are currently 22 certified cytogenetics laboratories operating

in Taiwan, and, in 1998, approximately 99 percent of all newborns were screened for congenital metabolic disorders.

The *Genetic Health Law* 優生保健法 provides a legal basis for health services, such as premarital health examinations, prenatal diagnosis, neonatal screening for congenital metabolic disorders, and genetic counseling. In 1998, there were more than 750 institutions providing one or more of these services and about 98 percent of the newborns were screened. The promotion of genetic health programs by the Medical Genetic Advisory Committee is also provided for under the *Genetic Health Law*.

In 1998, some 21,109 pregnant women received cytogenetic examinations. Among them, 12,104 were over 34 years old, accounting for 55.73 percent of expectant mothers in the age group of 35 years old and over. Some 2.8 percent of the fetuses were found to have chromosome disorders through amniocentesis. To detect thalassemia major and other complications during pregnancy, screenings for thalassemia have been provided for pregnant women since July 1993. In 1998, 872 couples were found MCV abnormal, and among them, 389 couples were carriers of the same genes. Of the fetuses examined, 103 were found of thalassemia major, approximately 60 percent of the 169 thalassemia major new borns in a year. In 1998, 17,564 potential mothers received rubella vaccinations as a measure to prevent birth defects.

Family Planning

The use of contraceptives by married women between 22 and 39 years of age in the Taiwan area has increased from 24 percent in 1965 to 74.86 percent in 1998. Statistics also show that women are having fewer and fewer children. For example, a survey of women between the ages of 40 and 49 revealed that the average number of children per woman declined from 6.1 in 1975 to 2.79 in 1998. The percentage of women in this same age group having four or more children has declined from 18.8 percent in 1975 to 3.7 percent in 1997, and the number of women having only one or two children has increased from 61.8 percent to 80.5 percent during that same time period.

The proportion of women who married between the ages of 20 and 34 years has declined from 67.3 percent in 1960 to 54 percent in 1997. The average age at first marriage during this time period increased from 22.7 to 28.4 years for women, and from 27.1 to 31.51 years for men. All of these factors have significantly lowered the birth rate in the Taiwan area. In 1998, the birth rate and death rate were 12.43 and 5.64 per 1,000 persons, respectively, with the natural population growth rate at 6.79 per 1,000 persons.

The aging of the population, the declining marriage rate among women between the ages of 20 and 34, and the falling birth rate have all raised concerns about a situation where the "dependent people are in the majority and the productive (young) people are in the minority" 食之者眾，生之者寡. Therefore, starting in 1990, the government adjusted its family planning policy to provide reproductive health services and education to married couples, potential mothers, and special groups (such as the disabled, infertile couples, youths, and residents in outlying areas).

Advanced developments in medical science and technology have enabled infertile couples to have their own babies through artificial means. The medical practices concerning artificial fertilization and implantation have to be regulated very carefully in order to safeguard individual rights, as well as to ensure the quality and correct application of artificial reproductive technologies. Relevant legislation promulgated thus far includes the *Ethical Guidelines for Practicing Artificial Reproductive Technologies* 人工生殖技術倫理指導綱領, *Regulations Governing Artificial Reproductive Technologies* 人工協助生殖術管理辦法, *Accreditation Standards for Institutions Providing Artificial Reproductive Technological Services* 施行人工協助生殖技術機構評估要點, and *Operational Explications to Data Concerning the Donation of Eggs and Sperm* 捐贈精卵資料作業說明. To date, 60 medical institutions have been accredited, enabling them to provide such services.

Teenage Pregnancy

The fertility rate among adolescents between the ages of 15 and 19 in the Taiwan area at 15 per 1,000 was higher than in some other Asian countries in 1997. The fertility rate for married teenagers in this age group was even higher than that of the United States: 746 per 1,000 in 1997. Unexpected pregnancies and pregnant brides could help to explain this high fertility rate. More than 14,000 children are born annually to teenage mothers in the Taiwan area. According to a study conducted by the Taiwan Provincial Government titled "Teenage Sexuality, Pregnancy and Abortion in Taiwan." A study comparing the results of a 1984 survey with the results of a survey conducted in 1994 showed a 264 percent increase in premarital sexual activities among teenagers. In 1994, approximately 10 percent of teenage girls in Taiwan had sexual experience. Two-thirds of those who had engaged in sex for the first time did not use any form of contraception, and 11 percent became pregnant. Eight percent of the pregnant girls chose to have an abortion, and the vast majority of the rest became teenage mothers. As social values and behavior change, the problem of unwed teenage mothers may worsen.

The DOH has responded to this phenomenon by offering sex education and counseling services in schools, factories, and communities. In addition, civic organizations like the ROC Public Health Association 中華民國公共衛生學會, the School Health Association 中華民國學校衛生學會, the Mercy Memorial Foundation 財團法人杏陵醫學基金會, the Youth Guidance Foundation 中國青少年輔導基金會, Teacher Chang 張老師 and the Maternal and Child Health Association 中華民國婦幼衛生協會 have all cooperated with the DOH to develop educational materials, train professional counselors, and provide consultation services for teenagers. The Mercy Memorial Foundation and the Family Life and Sex Education Center 家庭生活與性教育中心 have gone one step further, by providing sex education training to school administrators and teachers. In 1998, some 20 youth health promotion clinics 青少年保健門診 were established in both city medical centers and in teaching hospitals to provide counseling services and sex education for young people.

Adult and Geriatric Health

The aging population has increased the need for adult and geriatric health care. In 1997, persons aged 65 and over constituted 8.16 percent of the population (1.78 million people), an increase of 1.71 percent over the previous year. Although not a significantly large increase, when combined with the fact that the population aged 15 and below dropped by 11.6 percent over the past decade, then it can be seen why geriatric health care will become relatively more important in the future. It is estimated that by the year 2000, people aged 65 and over will account for 8.4 percent of the total population, qualifying the Taiwan area to be termed an "aged society," in United Nations parlance.

As the ratio of elderly people in society increases, chronic cardiovascular diseases have replaced infectious diseases as the major causes of death among adults. In 1998, for instance, cerebrovascular diseases, heart diseases, diabetes mellitus, and hypertensive diseases were the second, third, fifth, and ninth leading causes of death, respectively, representing 27.5 percent of all deaths that year.

Currently, all persons over 65 are entitled to free blood pressure and blood sugar tests at local health stations, and family health records are kept at all health stations for efficient follow-up. Cases of cardiac disease, diabetes, and hypertension are generally referred to adult or chronic disease clinics in public hospitals for treatment. After being discharged from public hospitals, patients are usually referred to local health stations for follow-up care. The primary health centers also provide home nursing services to persons aged 65 and above.

Local governments have appropriated special funds to subsidize medical expenditures for the aged. Guidelines on the control and treatment of hypertension, diabetes, and hyperlipidemia have been established to provide standard treatment

procedures for these medical groups in the Taiwan area. Likewise, a series of educational materials on the control of chronic diseases have also been circulated among clinics. Finally, 49 education units for diabetes have been established in medical centers islandwide to provide comprehensive care for diabetic patients.

Long-term Care

Elderly people who are discharged from hospitals but still require some medical attention, or those who are chronically ill, usually require home health care. This service is provided by 148 hospital-based and 18 freestanding home care institutions in the Taiwan area. For less than US$56 per visit, elderly people can receive the medical care they need on a regular basis, usually twice per month. At the end of August 1999, the DOH also commissioned 220 medical institutions to provide out-of-hospital services as well as 20 day care centers. Supportive services are provided to families with members who are chronically ill. In addition, the Sun Yat-sen Cancer Center provides home care specifically for cancer patients. (Information on other welfare services for the elderly can be found in Chapter 19, Social Welfare.)

Health Control Programs

Myopia Control

For more than ten years, Taiwan has had the world's highest incidence of myopia. A DOH survey conducted between mid-1995 and early 1996 revealed that while only 12.1 percent of first graders in elementary schools suffered from nearsightedness, the figure jumped to 55.4 percent for sixth graders, and 85 percent for twelfth graders. Vision screenings are now conducted in schools a month after school starts. By 1998, some 258 ophthalmologists were providing special outpatient services for students experiencing vision problems. The DOH has implemented a vision protection and screening program that includes preschool children and special occupational groups. Since 1995, visual screening has been conducted in every city and county, allowing the early detection of strabismus and amblyopia for preschool children from five to six years old.

Since 1986, visual health centers have been set up in major hospitals around the island, including the National Taiwan University Hospital, the Taipei and Taichung Veterans General Hospital, the Kaohsiung Medical College Hospital, and the Hualien Tzu Chi Buddhist General Hospital.

Cancer Control

Cancer has been the leading cause of death in the Taiwan area since 1982. In 1998, over 29,000 people died of cancer, accounting for 24 percent of all deaths. In Taiwan the five most common forms of cancer for men are liver, lung, colorectal, stomach, and oral cancer, while women are mainly afflicted with cervical, breast, colorectal, lung, and liver cancer. The DOH has initiated cancer control programs targeting the prevention and control of the more common cancers, including cervical, liver, colorectal, oral cancer, and breast cancer. Major medical research organizations, such as National Taiwan University's College of Public Health, are conducting studies on the effectiveness of different screening intervals of some common cancers.

The high incidence of oral and cervical cancer has been a serious problem for Taiwan residents. In 1998, 9.57 out of every 100,000 women had cervical cancer, resulting in 1,017 deaths that year. If detected and treated at an early stage, however, cervical cancer can be cured in 95 percent of the cases. Since July 1, 1995, National Health Insurance has covered cervical smear tests for women aged 30 and over, and in 1997 testing was conducted on 16 percent of women in this age group. In 1998, oral cancer caused 1,167 deaths.

In 1998, breast cancer killed 995 people. Breast cancer programs focus on preventive measures, with the current emphasis on increasing the current rate of women who conduct self-examinations. Each year since 1993, approximately 250,000 women have learned how to conduct self-examinations.

The DOH offers free screenings for family members of liver cancer patients to detect live

Ten Leading Causes of Death by Illness in the Taiwan Area, 1998

Cause of Death	% of All Deaths	Mortality per 100,000
All Causes	100.00	558.47
Malignancies	23.99	134.00
Cerebrovascular Diseases	10.42	58.18
Heart Diseases	9.04	50.51
Accidents & Adverse Effects	9.00	50.25
Diabetes Mellitus	6.18	34.49
Chronic Liver Diseases & Cirrhosis	4.05	22.62
Pneumonia	3.65	20.37
Nephrites, Nephrotic Syndrome & Nephrosis	2.82	15.73
Hypertensive Diseases	1.86	10.41
Suicide	1.79	9.97
Subtotal	72.80	406.54
Other Causes	27.20	151.93

Source: Department of Health

cancer in its early stages. If family members are diagnosed as having chronic hepatitis and cirrhosis of the liver, or if they are found to be carrying either the hepatitis B or hepatitis C antibodies, free rescreening is available once every six to 12 months. In 1997, 4,374 family members of liver cancer patients received screenings at the nine medical centers in Taiwan that offer such screenings. The government also offers free colon cancer screening for people in high risk groups. This program covered screenings for approximately 1,170 patients in fiscal 1996. To lower the death rate and strengthen early detection of cervical, breast, and oral cancer, the DOH formulated a community cancer-screening spot check plan. The goal of the plan is to provide free cervical smear tests to 3.45 million women over 30 years old, conduct examinations of up to one million women over 35 years old, and check 500,000 habitual betel nut chewers for oral submucosal fibrosis.

Occupational Disease Prevention

In Taiwan, the most common diseases or disorders attributable to work environment include blood poisoning by heavy metals, gas narcosis, black lung disease, skin disorders, trauma, and dysbarism. Between 1995 to 1998, of the 8,283 cases of occupational diseases that were reported, 8,2761 of them were confirmed. According to the Council of Labor Affairs, between 1989 to 1998, labor insurance payments were made to 974 victims, including 595 victims of pneumoconiosis, 43 for hearing loss, and 765 for herniation of intervertebral disk.

There are six occupational health centers in the following institutions: the National Taiwan University's College of Public Health 國立台灣大學公共衛生學院, National Defense Medical College Hospital 國防醫學院附設醫院, Taipei Veterans General Hospital, China Medical College Hospital, National Cheng Kung University's College of Medicine 國立成功大學附設醫院, and Kaohsiung Medical College Hospital. The occupational health centers provide diagnoses, treatments, follow-up assessments, and referrals. In addition, they offer consultation services at no charge to public and private enterprises. Another 36 medical institutions are able to provide special outpatient services for occupational diseases. In 1998, some 446 medical institutions were qualified to detect black lung disease and to conduct ordinary

"Save your life in six minutes," a program to promote cervical smear tests, is part of the DOH's community cancer screening sites plan for early detection of cervical, breast, and oral cancer.

and special health examinations for workers. The DOH also holds seminars on occupational diseases to improve the quality of medical services by increasing the knowledge of medical personnel.

Anti-Smoking Campaign

The smoking rate in Taiwan is alarmingly high. Approximately one out of five persons, some four million people, in Taiwan smoke, including about 27 percent of the population over 18 years of age in1998. Categorized by gender, about 48 percent of male adults and 5 percent of female smoke tobacco products regularly, while only 3.3 percent of women smoke. Studies show that in 1994, among those more than 20 years old, 10,268 deaths were related to smoking. A recent survey of public health conducted by National Taiwan University (NTU) revealed that an average of over 10,000 Taiwan residents die each year from smoking related causes, including more than 4,490 who die of lung cancer. By sex, 12 percent of male deaths and 8 percent of female deaths in Taiwan are related to smoking. Economic loss due to sickness caused by tobacco products was estimated to exceed US$1.84 billion in 1994.

According to the NTU survey, 43.7 percent of the smokers consume between half a pack and one pack each day, 37.4 percent smoke less than half a pack, and 15.3 percent smoke more than one pack. Since the government lifted the ban on the importation of foreign cigarettes to Taiwan in 1987, the number of smokers has increased by 4.6 percent and has broadened to include a larger portion of the teenage and female populations. A 1994 survey estimated that more than 16 percent of junior high school students and 10 percent of senior high school students smoke.

With so many smokers in Taiwan, it should come as no surprise that more than 96 percent of the nonsmoking female and child populations, including almost 75 percent of pregnant women were frequently exposed to secondhand smoke. According to a survey conducted by Academia Sinica 中央研究院, 22 percent of nonsmoking female lung cancer victims are frequently exposed to secondhand smoke.

In July 1990, the DOH launched an antismoking campaign. Under the project, free distribution of cigarettes to military personnel was terminated in July 1991, and more warnings against the health hazards of smoking have been printed on cigarette packs. Antismoking literature and films have also been distributed nationwide. The project has yielded some progress. By June 1995, all Taiwan-based airlines had prohibited smoking on both domestic and international flights.

Despite these government measures, concern over the hazards of smoking continued to increase in 1994. The Taiwan Tobacco and Wine Monopoly Bureau's 臺灣省菸酒公賣局 loss of its 40-year monopoly over alcohol and tobacco sales in June 1995 (to speed up Taiwan's entry into the World Trade Organization) has raised fears that the influx of foreign cigarettes will exacerbate an already grave health problem. Health authorities, therefore, submitted to the legislature a draft of the tough *Tobacco Hazards Prevention Act* 菸害防制法, which would outlaw the sale of cigarettes to minors (those under the age of 18), ban advertising and promotion by cigarette companies, and require the labeling of nicotine and tar contents on cigarette products. This draft was passed by the Legislature on March 19, 1997, and the new law came into effect on September 19.

This law restricts smoking in public places, including any kind of school, medical facility, or library. In addition, smoking is also forbidden in financial institutions, art galleries, public transportation vehicles, and places where highly flammable materials and products are manufactured, stored, or sold. Well-ventilated smoking areas must be designated in places, such as restaurants, department stores, government offices, and etc.

Punishments for violators of this law vary according to the type of violation and the perpetrator of the crime. For instance, underage smokers could simply be made to attend smoking cessation courses. On the other hand, tobacco companies and/or newspapers, magazines, could be fined as much as US$10,000 for placing or carrying ads of tobacco products.

Antismoking and consumer-interest groups like the John Tung Foundation 董氏基金會 have taken a more active role in increasing public awareness about the hazards of smoking. For example, the John Tung Foundation initiated a "Dear Legislator" campaign to ask lawmakers to support the revised version of the *Tobacco Hazards Prevention Act*. The Department of Health awarded the Foundation a large grant for its antismoking campaign, which centers on a cartoon character named Hsu Tse-lin 徐則林 (a pun on Lin Tse-hsu 林則徐, the famous Ching dynasty official who fought the import of opium into China some 150 years ago). The cartoon character is drawn as a "hip" guy sporting a ponytail reminiscent of the long braids Chinese men wore during the Ching dynasty. He can be spotted carrying an antismoking sign in made-for-TV videos, and on stickers, pamphlets, and placards in public places around Taiwan. The John Tung Foundation also tailored a new slogan to coincide with the implementation of the *Prevention Act*: "Take this opportunity to quit smoking, as the *Tobacco Hazards Prevention Act* is in force!" The lengthy revision process of the *Act* took five years. Since smokers are reluctant to break this law for fear of being fined between US$36 and US$109, harm from secondhand smoke has been reduced.

The *Prevention Act* also stipulates that four years after its implementation, the nicotine and tar content of a single cigarette cannot exceed 1.5 mg and 15 mg, respectively. In 1999, more than 83 percent of the cigarettes produced in Taiwan meet one or both of these standards. Ten years after the implementation of the *Prevention Act*, the content will be further reduced to 1.2 mg and 12 mg, respectively.

The Betel Nut Problem

The seed of the betel palm has long been used by Chinese doctors to treat parasitic infections and other intestinal disorders. Only when taken in excess does this pulpy nut have negative side effects; however, the betel nut widely chewed in Taiwan as a stimulant often contains unhealthy additives.

Experts estimate that 88 percent of oral cancer patients and 96 percent of mucous membrane fibrosis patients in the Taiwan area habitually chew betel nut. Statistically, the likelihood of contracting oral cancer is 28 times higher for betel nut chewers than for those who do not, and the risk is 89 times higher for people who both chew betel nuts and smoke. Furthermore, those who chew, smoke, and drink heavily are 123 times more likely to contract nasopharyngeal

cancer than those who do not indulge in any of these habits. Oral cancer deaths in the ROC have increased from 1.25 per 100,000 people per year in 1976 to 2.25 in 1991, and 5.34 in 1998. In 1997, there were an estimated three million betel nut chewers in the Taiwan area, spending up to US$3.45 billion on betel nuts annually.

Especially worrisome to health officials is the increasing popularity of betel nuts and the changing demographics of the betel nut chewing population. In the past, most betel nut chewers were adult laborers concentrated in eastern and southern Taiwan. Today, young and educated urbanites and suburbanites are taking up the habit in unprecedented numbers. To cater to the demand of the chewers, betel nut farming has grown, becoming the fourth largest crop in Taiwan. In response to this shift, the government is now targeting anti-betel nut campaigns at the younger generation. The hazards of betel nut chewing are being publicized in the form of TV ads, video programs, and leaflets distributed amongst high school and college students. Also, a substitute called "healthy betel nut" 健康檳榔, which does not contain the toxic components in the pulpy nut and its additives, has been developed to compete with the more harmful one.

Prevention of Accidents and Adverse Effects

In 1998, deaths from accidents and adverse effects, including suicide, averaged 60.22 per 100,000 people. They accounted for 11 percent of the 13,150 deaths reported in that year, making it the fourth largest cause of death in the Taiwan area. Nearly half (47.17 percent or 6,203 deaths) of the people died in transportation-related accidents, with 3,908 of the victims between 20 and 64 years of age. According to a survey covering the period 1988 to 1996, about 60 percent of skull injuries occurred in traffic accidents, with 72 percent of them being motorbike riders and 30 percent around the age of 20. Over the past years, more than US$28 million has been spent on medical care for those who

were left with brain damage from traffic accidents. Since a large number of accidents involving motorbikes resulted in death or permanent injury, the Ministry of Transportation and Communications 交通部 made wearing a helmet compulsory for all motorcyclists starting June 1, 1997.

To prevent the financial burden that often accompanies traffic accidents, third-person automobile insurance to cover those injured or killed in car accidents has become mandatory in 1998. This has also been strongly advocated for years by victims, their families, and consumer-interest groups. In 1999, such insurance has become mandatory for motorbikes as well.

Suicide constituted the tenth leading cause of death in the ROC. Just over 2,170 people took their own lives in 1997. According to DOH statistics, 164 youths between the ages of 15 and 25 took their own lives in 1998, making suicide the third major cause of death for this age group. The mortality rate for this age group was 4.23 per 100,000 persons. The mental health of the young and elderly is, in fact, a problem of society, and both age groups must be treated as equally important.

Communicable Diseases

An islandwide surveillance system involving a network of some 700 physicians has been set up to report diseases. All the physicians involved are connected to the network and provide weekly updates by phone. The latest information and medical updates are then made available to other physicians in the monthly *Epidemiology Bulletin* 疫情報導, which is circulated to medical centers islandwide. Currently, ten disease surveillance centers and quarantine stations under the National Quarantine Service have been set up in the central, southern, and eastern parts of the Taiwan area to administer the control and prevention of communicable diseases. An enterovirus infections outbreak in 1998 accounted for the deaths of 78 persons. The infections caused a panic among parents since 78 of the victim were below 15 years old.

The *Law of the Communicable Disease Control* 傳染病防治條例 is a new piece of legislation governing the control of epidemics. In the past, communicable diseases which required being reported were divided into specified and unspecified communicable diseases. Under the new law, any cases of the 38 infectious diseases listed must be reported, patients treated, and epidemic areas disinfected. Infectious diseases are now divided into four categories and are closely watched. The first category includes: cholera, plague, yellow fever, rabies, and ebola marburg. The second category includes: a) typhus fever, diphtheria, meningoccal meningitis, typhoid, paratyphoid, and anthrax; b) poliomymelitis, dysentery bacillary, amoebic dysentery, and open tuberculosis. The third category includes: a) dengue fever, malaria, measles, acute hepatitis A, enterohemorrhagic E. Coli, and enteroviral carditis (or meningitis); b) tuberculosis (except open tuberulosis), Japanese encephalitis, leprosy, rubella, congenital rubella syndrome, pertussis, scarlet fever, tetanus, tsutsugamushi disease, acute hepatitis (except hepatitis A), mumps, smallpox, legionellosis, haemophilus influenza B, syphilis, gonorrhea, and influenza. The fourth category includes other infectious diseases not listed or newly discovered.

This new categorization has been more inclusive of those infectious diseases more susceptible to Taiwan residents such as influenza and enterovirus, and also some diseases in the future, such as anthrax and legionellosis. Generally speaking, most of these diseases have been either eradicated or brought under control in the Taiwan area. However, in 1998 a total of 21 cases of amoebic dysentery, 424 cases of bacterial dysentery, 79 cases of typhoid and paratyphoid, 12 cases of meningococcal meningitis, 232 cases of scarlet fever and one case of cholera were reported.

More than 15,000 cases of TB and 64 cases of rubella were reported in 1998. That same year, more than 2,400 cases of syphilis, 547 cases of acute hepatitis, and 334 cases of dengue fever were confirmed by the DOH. In addition, the DOH requires that any disease, parasitic infection, or unusual symptom related to pets be reported, especially in cases that both the owner and pet become ill.

Local health authorities routinely carry out vaccination programs for polio, measles, mumps, rubella, diphtheria-pertussis-tetanus (DPT), tuberculosis, Japanese encephalitis, and hepatitis B. The coverage rates for these vaccinations, with the exception of measles, have reached approximately 90 percent. In 1992, the DOH initiated the first stage (1992-1996) plan for the eradication of polio, neonatal tetanus (NNT), measles, and congenital rubella syndrome (CRS), with excellent results. No cases of polio, CRS, and NNT were reported in 1998, but there were sporadic occurrences of rubella (64 cases) and measles (49 cases) that year. There was a decrease in the occurrence of acute flaccid paralysis cases from 153 (1997) to 127 (1998). In order to eliminate polio by the year 2000 in accordance with World Health Organization policy, the DOH decided to continue with the second stage (1996-2001) of the plan with the intent of attaining vaccination coverage of 95 percent, strengthening the disease reporting network, and computerizing vaccination records to minimize the likelihood that diptheria-pertussis-tetanus (DPT) and oral polio vaccination series would be discontinued. Other health measures include education on disease and sanitation and vector control.

Enterovirus

In 1998, the outbreak of enterovirus infections killed 78 persons and put the whole preventive medicine system on alert. After the first case was detected in February, 4053 cases of enterovirus infections had been discovered by December 1998. Seventy-one of the 78 persons died of the disease were children under five. Those between one to three years old numbered over half of the total deaths. Most victims lost their lives within five days after being infected. The disease reached its height during the period of May and June, decreasing slightly during the summer vacation, but climbing again in southern Taiwan after the

holiday. Under closed supervision of the government and cooperation of parents, the disease was brought under control.

Poliomyelitis

Free vaccinations against communicable diseases are available for infants and preschool children. In May 1994, the DOH launched the largest immunization drive ever: an islandwide campaign to administer Sabin oral polio vaccine to the estimated 1.8 million children under six years of age in Taiwan. All such children were required to be inoculated, and the polio immunization coverage rate reached 102.5 percent in 1995. No case of polio has been discovered since 1992.

AIDS

The *Acquired Immune Deficiency Syndrome (AIDS) Control Act* 後天免疫缺乏症候群防治條例 was promulgated in December 1990 to provide free screening and treatment for patients, and to deal with cases of those who are HIV-infected and yet knowingly transmit the disease to unsuspecting others. As of June 1999, over 20 million blood tests had been conducted to screen for the human immune deficiency virus (HIV) antibody. From 1984 to September 1999, a total of 2,504 people had been detected as HIV positive; among these, 2,254 (or 90 percent) were ROC nationals. In 1997 and 1998, the number of HIV positive victims has increased at an average of more than one case discovered per day. More than 84 percent were thought to have been infected through sexual contact with an HIV-infected, and 55 married people were infected by their spouses. Among infected ROC nationals, 82.8 percent of the HIV-infections were in the 20 to 49 age group, 19.7 percent of victims were unemployed, and 32 percent were businessmen and workers. Around 42 percent of HIV-positive cases in Taiwan were male heterosexuals, with 27.6 percent male homosexuals, and 16.7 percent bisexuals.

According to the DOH, the typical male HIV carrier in Taiwan is single, employed, around 34 years old, and has frequented prostitutes. Female HIV carriers are typically married and around 35 years old. Many are housewives who have been infected by their husbands. By September 1999, HIV-infected males outnumbered females 11.5 to 1. Among the 173 females infected with HIV, 37 were foreign brides. Alien workers are also considered high-risk group. To date, 85 legal alien workers and 12 foreign language instructors have tested HIV positive and were subsequently deported.

Despite its efficiency, the screening procedure has encountered setbacks. For fear of being discriminated against by hospital employees or having a positive HIV record in their hospital records, many people who suspected that they were HIV positive refused to be tested in a hospital. Instead they turned to donating blood as a free and confidential method of testing, as health authorities would notify them if their blood test indicated the presence of the virus. As a result, the DOH called for legislation that would impose strict penalties on people who donate their blood for this purpose, because the DOH feared that infected blood may be donated when the virus is still undetectable. Since then, relevant legislation has been passed, and the results of blood tests from donated blood are no longer released to the donor.

People who suspect that they might be infected are now encouraged to go to public health centers across the island or to the 25 hospitals authorized by the DOH to conduct free HIV tests. The DOH authorized hospitals detected almost 64.5 percent of HIV positive cases and around 20 percent were detected at health stations or hospitals at the provincial level. HIV screening is actually required for servicemen (military service is compulsory for almost all ROC men), inmates, and alien workers.

The DOH also publishes pamphlets, booklets, and manuals on AIDS, which are distributed to medical personnel and the general public in selected areas. The government also produces TV programs and films to educate the public. To raise the survival rate of the patients, free antiretroviral therapy is provided by the DOH for all HIV-infected nationals.

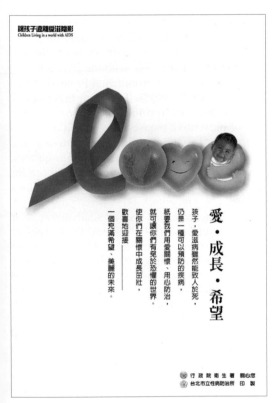

孩子，愛滋病雖然能致人於死，仍是一種可以預防的疾病，祇要我們用愛關懷、用心防治，就可讓你們有免於恐懼的世界。使你們在關懷中成長茁壯，歡喜地迎接一個充滿希望、美麗的未來。

愛・成長・希望

行政院衛生署 關心您
台北市立性病防治所 印製

The number of HIV-positive victims has increased at an average of more than one new case discovered per day. Male HIV-carriers have usually contracted the illness from prostitutes.
(Courtesy of the Taipei Municipal VD Control Institute)

Hepatitis

Around 90 percent of the people over 40 years of age in the Taiwan area are infected with the hepatitis B virus, and between 15 to 20 percent of the total population are estimated to be hepatitis B carriers. Therefore, liver cancer, which has been linked to hepatitis, has for years been the number one killer in the ROC. An islandwide program to control the spread of hepatitis B that was initiated in 1984 and was completing its third and final phase in 1997. This immunization program covers all newborns, preschool children, elementary school children, young adults, medical personnel, and family members of carriers. Around 1,800 hospitals and clinics in 1999 administered 35,661 doses of hepatitis B vaccines (three shots being required for each vaccination) to preschool and elementary school children. During that same period, some 344,645 underwent an antenatal test for hepatitis B. Nearly 15,600 doses of hepatitis B immunoglobulin were provided to newborns of carriers, and 1,232,838 doses of hepatitis B vaccine (HBV) were used to immunize the newborns of non-carriers. For the rest of the population, vaccinations are available at a reasonable cost and are also offered at health stations and clinics islandwide.

The Republic of China is the first country in the world to implement the hepatitis B immunization program, which after 12 years has been a complete success. One study shows that hepatitis B carriers under six years of age were at an all-time low of 1.7 percent. Reduced incidents of liver cancer in children between six to 14 years old has been another benefit of the immunization program. The rate of liver cancer in the six to 14 age group was 0.7 in 100,000 persons from 1981 to 1986, and the rate dropped to 0.36 between 1990 and 1994. Children between six to nine years old, who have been vaccinated, have the lowest rate of liver cancer at 0.13 per 100,000 children. Before the implementation of the hepatitis B immunization program, the rate of liver cancer in the same age group was 0.52 per 100,000 children.

Hepatitis C, or post-transfusion hepatitis, is transmitted by body fluids, especially blood or blood products 80 percent of the time. It can also be transmitted as a result of sharing needles in tattooing or intravenous drug use. The hepatitis C anti-HCV prevalence rate in the Taiwan area was between 1 and 2 percent. The DOH requires that blood used for transfusions be tested for hepatitis C antibodies to prevent the transmission of the disease.

Poor sanitary conditions usually account for the transmission of hepatitis A. The infection rate

in urban areas is low (less than 5 percent for preschool children), but the rate is 76 and 95 percent for elementary and junior high students, respectively, in mountain areas because of poor living conditions and hygiene habits. Two immunization programs were instituted in mountain areas in 1995 and 1996, bringing the infection of hepatitis A under control. In 1995, 851 cases of hepatitis A were reported, dropping to 167 in 1998.

Tuberculosis

Tuberculosis was one of the leading causes of death in the 1950s. In 1947, the TB death rate was 294.44 per 100,000 people. Accordingly, a TB survey has been taken once every five years since 1957. That year, the prevalence rates of pulmonary tuberculosis and bacteriologically infectious tuberculosis were 5.15 and 1.02 percent, respectively, making TB the third leading cause of death by illness in Taiwan. By 1982, these rates had dropped to 0.88 and 0.15 percent, respectively. However, by the 1987 survey, the rate for pulmonary TB had increased to 1.29 percent, while bacteriologically infectious TB continued to fall to 0.11 percent. Although the TB death rate was only 6.93 per 100,000 in 1998, with 1,513 reported deaths and 14,0866 patients, it was still high compared with that of advanced nations.

A five-year project running from 1994 to 1998 aims to enhance TB control by refurbishing treatment facilities, controlling chronically active cases, and implementing a surveillance system for TB risk groups, especially in the aboriginal communities, where TB was the eighth leading cause of death in 1998. Beginning in April 1995, the DOH implemented the Mountain Area TB Inpatient Subsidy Plan 山地鄉結核病人住院治療補助計畫 and the Chronic TB Patient Accommodation Plan 慢性開放性結核病人收容管理計畫, with 28 hospitals participating. Since 1996, a surveillance system to control TB, based on the data provided by the NHI medication record, has been in operation to locate those cases not reported. Since April 1995, 674 persons applied for TB medication, and 138 patients of chronic open TB received inpatient services.

Dengue Fever

A center for the control of dengue fever, which is caused by a mosquito-borne virus, was set up in December 1988 with the joint effort of the DOH and the Environmental Protection Administration 環境保護署. The joint taskforce is responsible for the formulation and implementation of preventive measures, a surveillance system, vector surveying, insecticide spraying, and eliminating the breeding grounds of mosquitoes. The taskforce provides medication to those infected and supervises disease control measures of local governments.

In 1998, there was a small scale outbreak of dengue fever in southern Taiwan. There were 80 confirmed cases (64 domestic, 16 imported) reported from Kaohsiung City, 30 confirmed cases (24 domestic, six imported) in Kaohsiung County, and 138 cases (135 domestic, three imported) in Tainan City. Compared with the 1,938 cases in 1988, the disease has been brought under control. The results of a monthly density index of vector mosquitoes and larvae must be recorded and reported to the relevant units for evaluation. Frequent examination of the vector index and intensive environmental sanitation education after typhoons and floods are the most important work of the taskforce.

Quarantine

Quarantine procedures help to prevent the entry and spread of communicable diseases from abroad. Travelers, aircraft crew members, airport workers, and imported produce are targeted for scrutiny at ports of entry. International health regulations stipulate that all interference with modern transportation be minimized during the screening procedures, and the DOH makes every effort to comply while rendering efficient service.

The DOH consolidated the nation's seven quarantine stations and two substations into the National Quarantine Service in 1989. The service includes quarantine, port sanitation management, and disease surveillance divisions.

Since April 1995, travelers entering Taiwan from highly infected areas in Southeast Asia have been required to submit a Health Declaration Form to monitor infectious diseases. Travelers showing symptoms of the diseases are contacted by public health workers to identify cases for prompt treatment and to prevent further transmission. In 1998, some 2,972 suspected cases had been checked and 21 confirmed. All of the confirmed cases were diarrheal infections, such as shigellosis, salmonellosis, and vibrio parahaemolyticus.

Field Epidemiology

The DOH administers a two-year field epidemiology instruction program at the Center of Disease Control, in collaboration with the US Center for Disease Control and Emory University. Physicians, dentists, and researchers in related fields are chosen annually for on-site training in epidemiological investigations and long-term study projects. Since its inception, the program has trained 36 physicians, 25 dentists, and 70 public health specialists. Forty-nine of them now serve in public institutions, and 81 long-term projects have already been completed.

Food & Restaurant Regulation

Since Chinese people love to eat out, to make sure this enjoyable pastime is also a safe one, the Department of Health monitors sanitary standards in the ubiquitous eating places around the island. On a day-to-day basis, local health authorities conduct routine spot checks of food establishments on the island using 13 basic diagnostic devices to test food. Educational materials are also distributed. More than 179,400 spot checks were conducted in 1998, with 16,821 of food establishments failing to meet sanitary requirements. Those that fail are given a grace period to improve sanitary conditions. Of those that failed in 1998, over 99 percent passed the second time around. Those 1,035 failed a second time were fined, with 95 establishments having their licenses suspended. All establishments that pass are issued a plaque to display on the restaurant wall, and the restaurant names are published to help consumers locate safe eating places.

The DOH, in collaboration with the Council of Labor Affairs, is also promoting a licensing system for food technicians. In 1994, the DOH released a new set of requirements for chefs at six types of restaurants to be licensed within the next five years to ensure better hygiene. The plan will affect about 80 percent of the chefs at hotel restaurants, school cafeterias, banquet halls, catering services, airline caterers, and public cafeterias in the Taiwan area. Currently, there are more than 78,570 licensed chefs in Taiwan.

Widespread sanitary practices have reduced the number of cases of food poisoning and hepatitis A. Disposable tableware is now available in many restaurants. Consumers can also purchase inspected processed food products labeled as meeting the Chinese Agricultural Standard 中國農業標準 (CAS) or general food products with the seal Food Good Manufacturing Practices 優良食品製造標準 (FGMP). By June 1999, 345 factories producing 3,570 food products had been authorized as Good Manufacturing Practices 優良製造標準 (GMP) factories, and 36 factories were

Number of Chinese Medicine Hospitals and Clinics, December 1998			
	Hospitals	*Clinics*	*Total*
Taiwan Area	72	2,258	2,330
Taiwan Province	57	1,826	1,883
Taipei City	6	272	278
Kaohsiung City	9	160	169
Source: Department of Health			

producing 392 frozen food products bearing the CAS seal. Similarly, 2,074 meat products and 49 food processing plants qualified for the CAS label. Around 5,600 licenses were issued for imported food additives and over 1,650 licenses for domestically produced additives. Starting from July 1999, all processed food products are required to list nutrition facts.

The expanding food processing industry and international trade have complicated food safety, so current laws and regulations need to be strengthened to cope with the new situation. The DOH Bureau of Food Sanitation oversees the amendment of laws and related regulations and is also responsible for the review and approval of special dietary foods, the registration and premarket approval of food additives, and domestically produced low-acid canned foods. By coordinating with the Council of Agriculture (COA) and the Ministry of Economic Affairs (MOEA) which oversee the importation of agricultural products, the DOH could respond quickly when crises arose. In June 1999, Belgium produce such as eggs, dairy products and meat products which had been suspected of being polluted were prohibited from entering Taiwan's market before investigation and evaluation had been made. Inspection, sampling, testing, supervision of foods, and food sanitation are handled by local health authorities.

Pharmaceutical Regulation

All medicines and medical devices, both imported and locally produced, must be registered and licensed by the DOH before they are marketed in the Taiwan area. Local health authorities conduct regular and unscheduled inspections, sampling medicines and cosmetics that are manufactured, imported, or sold in their areas. Manufacturers and purveyors of medicines and cosmetics that fail to pass inspections are punished according to the *Pharmaceutical Affairs Law* 藥事法 and the *Cosmetics Sanitary Control Law* 化妝品衛生管理條例.

By 1999, the DOH and the Ministry of Economic Affairs 經濟部 had jointly issued the GMP

seal to 236 certified pharmaceutical factories. An ongoing GMP monitoring program helps to maintain the integrity of the ROC pharmaceutical industry, as well as the quality of drug products in the market. All GMP drug manufacturers are inspected at least once every two years. Factories which do not meet GMP standards are fined between US$910 and US$4,545. Those which fail to make improvements may also be shut down by health authorities, and their applications for registration and market permits suspended during the probation period.

The DOH also monitors the safety of new medicinal products. During the monitoring period, manufacturers should submit records of safety monitoring in designated teaching hospitals for their newly licensed drugs and immediately report any side effects observed. Test results of domestic clinical trials are also required. In July 1998, the Center for Drug Evaluation 財團法人醫藥查驗中心 was established to conduct research and develop standards on the safety, effectiveness, and labeling of all drug products and review and evaluate new drug and new medical device premarket approval applications. As of December 1997, 263 new chemical substances and 480 new pharmaceutical formulas were being monitored. On April 12, 1996, in preparation for entry into the World Trade Organization (WTO), the DOH promulgated ten basic standards for the registration and examination of imported medicines.

The DOH is currently conducting a truth-in-advertising campaign. Provincial and municipal health authorities strictly review applications for advertisements. According to the newly amended *Pharmaceutical Affairs Law*, media that run advertisements exaggerating the efficacy of medical products are subject to heavy fines.

The ROC's pharmaceutical market registers sales of US$1.47 billion per year. Hospitals accounted for the largest share at 66.7 percent (US$0.98 billion) of the market, while dispensaries and clinics held 21.6 percent (US$317 million) and 11.7 percent (US$172 million) of the market, respectively. After the separation of medical and pharmaceutical professions, however, more patients have actually preferred to see pharmacists for their medical needs. Thus, in recent years dispensaries and pharmacies have been growing and taking an ever increasing share of this market. It has been estimated that this sector will almost double in size to reach a value of US$588 million. At present, National Taiwan University Hospital alone dispenses 4.45 percent of the medicine consumed nationwide, but hospitals, dispensaries, and clinics must adjust to the practice of patients opting to see pharmacists rather than doctors.

The separation of the medical and pharmaceutical professions is one of the most important tasks in restructuring health services in Taiwan. Effective March 1, 1997, Taipei and Kaohsiung Cities were designated areas to first implement this separation. Gradually, the plan will encompass the entire Taiwan area. Effective July 6, 1998, the separation policy also covers the cities of Keelung, Hsinchu, Taichung, Chiayi, and Tainan; and the counties of Taipei, Ilan, Taoyuan, Hsinchu, Miaoli, Taichung, Changhua, Nantou, Yunlin, Chiayi, Tainan, Kaohsiung, and Pingtung. By June 1999, about 3,400 community pharmacies which adhere to "Good Dispensing Practice" were under contract with the DOH as part of the health care delivery system. The DOH is also helping to upgrade the quality of pharmaceutical personnel through on-the-job training and by helping to set up computerized patient profiles.

Drug Injury Relief

The *Key Points for Drug Injury Relief* 藥害救濟要點 effective January 12, 1999, have been formulated to safeguard the interests of patients and pharmaceutical manufacturers. A drug injury review committee composed of experts has been set up under the Department of Health to examine and investigate all drug injury cases petitioned.

According to the *Key Points for Drug Injury Relief*, drug injury relief is based on no-fault liability insurance and covers drug injuries ranging from medical expenses for cases of reversible injury to compensation for fatal drug injuries.

As stated, a maximum of US$62,500 in compensation can be given for a fatal case.

In addition, a relief fund has been established among pharmaceutical companies, with operational fees subsidized by the government. Some 131 pharmaceutical companies have joined and contributed to the fund. In most cases, around one-thousandth of the value of the company's annual domestic pharmaceutical sales is contributed. Thus far, the drug injury relief fund has raised US$560,000.

A special logo provided to participating pharmaceutical manufacturers or sellers informs consumers that they are covered by the relief fund in the case of accidental drug injuries. To substantiate the implementation of the *Key Points for Drug Injury Relief*, the ROC government has encouraged medical institutions, hospitals, and pharmacies to purchase products from participating manufacturers and sellers.

Substance Abuse

Until last decade, Taiwan's drug problem was considered minor in comparison with its neighboring areas, such as Japan and Hong Kong, but that began to change in the early 1990s, as evidenced by the increasing number of drug-related criminal arrests. Previously, such arrests accounted for 5 percent or less of the total number of arrests made per year; however, this rate increased to 13 percent in 1991, climbed to 19 percent in 1992, and jumped to nearly 32 percent in 1993. By December 1994, drug offenders had replaced burglars as the largest group in Taiwan prisons, accounting for 63 percent of Taiwan's inmate population. The situation turned around in 1995, where there was a 7 percent decrease in drug-related criminal arrests, dropping another 4.6 percent in 1998.

It appears that, substance and drug abuse in Taiwan is headed toward harder drugs. In the 1970s, sporadic cases of glue sniffing were reported, and, in the 1980s, incidences of sedative abuse were occasionally uncovered. By the early 1990s, the drug of choice was amphetamines, with recent increases in addition to heroin. Although there were fewer than 21,000 addicts in

the Taiwan area in 1998, it is estimated that more than 200,000 people (or nearly 1 percent of the total population) are currently abusing at least one substance, primarily methamphetamine or heroin. In contrast to the 2,886 kilograms of amphetamines (including raw materials and semi-products) seized in 1998, only 150 kilograms of other illegal drugs were confiscated, down 23 percent from the previous year. Thus, amphetamines have moved to the forefront of current drug abuse concerns in Taiwan. In addition, the incidence of the abuse of new substitutes, such as FM2 (a sedative) and MDMA (a type of methamphetamine), has been discovered in the past year.

Currently, there are four drug detoxification centers and 145 hospitals to treat drug addicts in the Taiwan area. Convicted drug abusers are sent for treatment before serving their sentences. There are also four special jails for inmates sentenced for drug-related offenses. Following the US DAWN model, a network for the survey of the prevalence of drug abuse and case reporting for the Taiwan area has been set up. However, these detoxification, rehabilitation, and medical care facilities are insufficient for the estimated 200,000 drug addicts in Taiwan and need to be expanded.

Traditional Chinese Medicine

Chinese medicine is just as valued today by Chinese people as it has been for thousands of years and is enjoying new-found respect from modern western medical researchers. In Taiwan, the main research body specializing in traditional Chinese medicine is the Committee on Chinese Medicine and Pharmacy (CCMP), whose members are selected from the ranks of the nation's most distinguished practitioners of Chinese medicine. As of December 1998, there were 8,438 licensed doctors of Chinese medicine in the Taiwan area, although only 3,461 of them were actually practicing. There were 3,330 Chinese medicine hospitals and clinics, as well as 9,510 licensed dealers and 257 manufacturers of herbal medicines.

In Taiwan today, treatment through Chinese medicinal practices, including acupuncture, moxibustion 艾灸 (burning of a medicinal plant close to acupuncture points 穴脈 to restore the body's "energy flow" 行氣 throughout what Chinese medicine refers to as the 12 meridians 經絡), and herbal remedies, is readily available. Treatment through Chinese medicine is also covered by the National Health Insurance program.

Around one hundred prescriptions of Chinese medicine have been tested for their efficacy and standardized.

Training in Chinese Medicine

Doctors of Chinese medicine can receive training at China Medical College Hospital 中國醫藥學院附設醫院, which offers a seven-year Chinese medicine program and a five-year post-baccalaureate Chinese medicine program to train modern Chinese medicine doctors. Since 1998, the Chang Gung University 長庚大學 has offered a seven-year program of Chinese medicine. Candidates can then take the national examination offered by the Examination Yuan to qualify as Chinese medicine doctors. Candidates who have passed the written examination are qualified Chinese medicine practicioners. Non-Chinese Chinese medicine candidates have to pass another special examination and must receive eight months of training in basic medical sciences, followed by ten months of clinical practice before they can be certified as doctors of Chinese medicine.

The Taipei Municipal Chinese Medical Hospital 臺北市立中醫醫院 and the Kaohsiung Municipal Chinese Medicine Hospital 高雄市立中醫醫院 were established to promote the department of Chinese medicine, and teaching hospitals are encouraged to set up affiliated departments of Chinese medicine. The advantages of western and Chinese medicine are thus able to work side-by-side to improve the health of people in the ROC. The 26 teaching hospitals with departments of Chinese medicine include the Chang Gung Memorial Hospital (Linkou) 長庚醫院林口分院, China Medical College Hospital 中國醫藥學院附設醫院, and Tzu Chi Buddhist General Hospital (Hualien) 慈濟綜合醫院, as well as the six regional hospitals supervised by the DOH (Taipei Hospital 行政院衛生所台北醫院, Keelung Hospital 行政院衛生所基隆醫院, Chiayi Hospital 行政院衛生所嘉義醫院, Hsinying Hospital 行政院衛生所新營醫院, Hualien Hospital 行政院衛生所花蓮醫院, Penghu Hospital 行政院衛生所澎湖醫院). In addition are the following: Taipei Municipal Hoping Hospital 臺北市立和平醫院, Taipei Municipal Chunghsiao Hospital 臺北市立忠孝醫院, Taipei Municipal Chungshing Hospital 臺北市立中興醫院, Taipei Municipal Jen-ai Hospital 臺北市立仁愛醫院, Taipei Municipal Yangming Hospital 臺北市立陽明醫院, Taipei Municipal Wanfang Hospital 臺北市立萬芳醫院, Tainan City Hospital 臺南市立醫院, Hsiu Chuan Memorial Hospital 秀傳紀念醫院 (Changhua), Cardinal Tien Center 耕莘醫院, Mennonite Christian Hospital 門諾會醫院 (Hualien), St. Mary's Hospital 羅東聖母醫院 (Lotung), and Min-Shen General Hospital 敏盛綜合醫院 (Taoyuan).

Chinese medicine is eliminating the stigma of being unscientific by combining age-old practices with modern technology. At the Foundation for East-West Medicine 國際醫學科學研究基金會 in Taipei, doctors are using an electro-dermal screening device (ESD) to pinpoint the source of an illness. The ESD measures what traditional Chinese medicine refers to as the "energy flow" in a patient's body by probing the acupuncture points. Acupuncture is applied in the dentistry department, for example, to locate problems by tracking the places of energy stasis in the mouth. Once the problem area is detected, dental instruments are used to pinpoint and treat the problem.

The ROC is the vanguard in research on Chinese medicines, acupuncture, and other Chinese medical practices. Many research projects have been conducted to evaluate the effects of Chinese medicine and acupuncture on various types of illnesses and diseases. The China Medical College 私立中國醫藥學院, for instance, has undertaken studies on the effects of Chinese medicine and acupuncture on hepatitis, sciatica, and other chronic diseases. Similar research studies have been done on the effects of Chinese medicine on nephrosis. Chinese herbal remedies have also been developed for diseases like systemic lupus erythematosus, intestinal ulcers, and bronchial asthma.

Since 1996, the CCMP underwrote 284 research projects on Chinese medicine. Twenty-three research projects have examined the tranquilizing effects of acupuncture, 30 on clinical studies of Chinese medicinal practice, 28 research projects developing supportive devices for diagnosis, 125 studies on the pharmacological efficacy of Chinese medicine, 58 projects on the standards and quality control of Chinese drug products, 14 on the resources of herbal medicine, two on substitutes for endangered fauna in Chinese medicine, and four on the evaluation of manpower in the field. Such efforts are helping to incorporate Chinese medicinal knowledge and techniques into the mainstream of modern medicine. Other projects include the publishing of research which uses modern scientific technologies to interpret important but abstruse classics on Chinese medicine. These are compiled in the *Chinese Medicinal Yearbook* 中醫藥年報 published by the DOH. Information concerning Chinese medicine can be obtained on-line at *http://www.ccmp.gov.tw* or by sending electronic mail to *ykou@ccmp.gov.tw*.

The Department of Health and the China Medical College study the distribution and cultivation of medicinal plants in the Taiwan area. With the assistance of the agriculture and forestry agencies, some rare medicinal plants of high economic value have been cultivated on a trial basis. If the results of these trials are satisfactory, the plants will be farmed on a large scale to safeguard the supply of raw materials. In the meantime, Kaohsiung Medical College and the China Medical College have been requested to evaluate and assess the efficacy of the available Taiwan-grown herbs to establish a data base on raw materials for Chinese medicine. Since a program to standardize some 337 Chinese medicine prescriptions was started in July 1990, about one hundred prescriptions have been standardized for use. The program also authorizes factories to produce Chinese medicine. In addition, the China Medical College is hosting a project to promote the cross-strait exchange of Chinese medicine doctors and pharmacists.

16
Mass Media

Satellite television programming has increased the number of Taiwan's cable TV selections to more than 90 channels.

Virtually all media markets in the Republic of China have changed dramatically in recent years, partly in response to technological advances, but perhaps more in concert with the lightning pace of democratization. New cable service authorizations and broadcast frequency allocations have greatly increased the diversity of radio and television stations available to domestic audiences. Taiwan enjoys a flourishing multimedia and information industry. The domestic publishing industry is also thriving in this favorable media environment which has become even more liberalized since the repeal of the 69-year-old *Publication Law* 出版法 in January 1999. With increasing joint use of resources and global competition, more and more media operators are engaging in multimedia as well as international cooperation. This chapter discusses the most significant changes in the ROC media industry in recent years, including the proliferation of print media, the growth of cable TV, the release of new broadcast allocations, and efforts by the government and private sector to strengthen the industry.

Print Media

News Agencies

Taiwan's news agencies are mostly concentrated in Taipei and are generally small in scale. Most of them focus on economic and financial news and developments in the stock market. They serve the print and electronic media, government agencies, financial organizations, the industrial and commercial sectors, and local schools.

The oldest and largest news agency is the Central News Agency 中央通訊社 (CNA), which was established in Canton in 1924. It was relocated to Taiwan in 1949 and reorganized as a body incorporate in January 1996. Fully computerized in 1990 (the first media organization in the ROC to do so), CNA operates on a 24-hour basis and maintains 35 overseas offices, which file stories on Chinese and Asian affairs, political events, and economic news from major areas around the world in both Chinese and English.

The Central News Agency provides complete services in three areas of news coverage—domestic, overseas Chinese and international. CNA provides a daily average of 230,000 words in general news to all newspapers, radio and TV stations on Taiwan, while its economics and financial wire transmits another 300,000 words daily to business-oriented clients. In its service to over 100 Chinese-language newspapers worldwide, CNA provides daily information on current Chinese-related affairs and feature stories, informing more than 22 million overseas Chinese of the events of the past 24 hours in the ROC, the Chinese mainland and other areas around the globe. CNA also offers general English-language news to foreign media and Spanish-language news to Latin American countries.

Among other CNA operations are a business news service offering up-to-the-minute global business and financial information as well as a computerized newspaper-clipping data service for clients at home and abroad. CNA also conducts opinion polls on important issues. Since 1997, its Internet website has become one of the most popular Internet portals, attracting millions of visitors from home and abroad seeking information about Taiwan.

Like CNA, the Overseas Chinese News Agency 華僑通訊社 provides information on overseas Chinese affairs to the domestic and international media. The agency is an affiliate of the Overseas Chinese Affairs Commission 僑務委員會. The Military News Agency 軍事新聞通訊社 (MNA), which was founded under the Ministry of National Defense 國防部 in 1946, is the only domestic news agency that specializes in military news. Besides news releases, MNA also provides video programs for television.

Another popular news source is the China Economic News Service 中國經濟通訊社 (CENS) founded in 1974 by the *United Daily News* 聯合報. With a 140-member staff, CENS provides domestic and foreign economic news in English on international financial updates and information on Taiwan's export industries. It also has two websites, one focusing on the latest developments in Taiwan's export sector, and the other providing daily coverage of Taiwan's economic, financial, and trade news.

Newspapers

In the 1950s, Taiwan's newspaper industry faced the formidable situation of operating in an agrarian society with low purchasing power. By the 1960s, however, Taiwan's successful transition to an industrialized society led to increased newspaper circulation and a doubling of the number of pages (although only eight pages). Competition began to intensify, not just within the newspaper industry itself, but also with the television media which had just taken off in Taiwan. By the mid-1980s, newspaper size had expanded to 12 pages, although perhaps still not providing enough information to meet the needs of the public.

When restrictions were eased on newspaper licensing and publishing in January 1988, the papers continued to expand to 32 and even 40 pages per issue. News coverage became more professional and in-depth and specialized reporting become an established trend. Recent economic slowdowns and the rapid proliferation of the Internet, however, have stunted the growth of the newspaper industry. The resultant competition, further intensified by new rivals and rising price wars, has led many newspapers to add new sections or shuffle existing sections. A few newspapers have even shut down, slashed salaries, or offered early retirement packages to reduce overhead costs. On the optimistic side, more and more newspapers have gone online, allowing readers to access news reports via the Internet.

What follows is a look at several Taipei-based, Chinese-language newspapers which together show the diversity of the ROC newspaper industry.

Representative Publications

The Chinese-language newspaper market is dominated by two general-interest dailies, the *China Times* 中國時報 and the *United Daily News* 聯合報. The longstanding competition between the two is no longer limited to the print edition; it has recently expanded into their electronic on-line versions as well.

The *China Times* is part of a chain of publications, including the *China Times Weekly* 時報週刊, the *China Times Express* 中時晚報, the *Commercial Times* 工商時報, and the Taiwan edition of the French magazine *Marie Claire* 美麗佳人. Its affiliated publishing companies include the China Times Publication Company 時報文化出版公司, the Infotimes Company 時報資訊公司, and the Shih Kuang Company 時廣企業有限公司. In September 1995, the enterprise went digital with the China Times website 中國時報系全球資訊網, providing daily electronic newspapers through the Internet to Chinese-language readers worldwide.

The *United Daily News* is the flagship publication of another major family of publications, including the Taiwan-based *Economic Daily News* 經濟日報, *Min Sheng Daily* 民生報, *United Evening News* 聯合晚報, *Unitas* 聯合文學 literary monthly, and *Historical Monthly* 歷史月刊, in addition to the *World Journal* 美洲世界日報 in New York, the *Europe Journal* 歐洲日報 in Paris, and the *Universal Daily News* 世界日報 in Bangkok. Its affiliated companies include the China Economic News Service, the Linking Publishing Company Ltd. 聯經出版事業公司, United Informatics Inc. 聯經資訊公司, and the World Television Corporation in New York.

The *Liberty Times* 自由時報 is currently the third largest national newspaper in the ROC. In addition to publishing a US edition through its Los Angeles branch, it also publishes an English daily in Taiwan called the *Taipei Times*, which hit the domestic market with its first issue in

June 1999. The *Central Daily News* 中央日報, the official news organ of the Kuomintang 中國國民黨, is known for its comprehensive coverage of ROC politics. In contrast to the *Central Daily News*, the *Independence Evening Post* 自立晚報 assumes a liberal approach in its news coverage.

While Taipei's major papers provide extensive coverage of national issues and approach the news more objectively, local dailies based in Kaohsiung perhaps reflect a stronger sense of the local identity of the people in southern Taiwan. Aggressive and provocative, the Kaohsiung press places a heavy emphasis on political news as well as the culture, literature, and history of the southern region. Leading Kaohsiung papers, the *Commons Daily* 民眾日報, the *Taiwan Times* 臺灣時報, and the *Taiwan Shin Wen Daily News* 臺灣新聞報, are peppered with expressions unique to the Taiwanese dialect.

In addition to these more traditional, general-interest newspapers, recent entrants into the market have taken a more specialized approach, targeting younger age groups with colorful and more daring layouts styled after the *USA Today*. The *Great News* 大成報 publishes two special morning editions every day: one on entertainment and lifestyle, and the other on sports and recreation. *Power News* 勁報, on the other hand, is a late afternoon newspaper that gives equal importance to words and graphics; its content and layout are designed mainly to attract consumers living or working in metropolitan areas.

The *Mandarin Daily News* 國語日報 and the *Children's Daily News* 兒童日報 are two children's papers published regularly. They carry news features and fictional stories written for elementary school students. Their texts feature Mandarin phonetic symbols as pronunciation glosses for each Chinese character.

In 1999, competition intensified in Taiwan's English-language newspaper market, previously dominated by the *China Post* and the *China News*, which changed its name to *Taiwan News*. These two dailies were joined in mid-June by the *Taipei Times*, a new affiliate of the *Liberty Times*. These English dailies are not only popular

learning tools for students studying the English language, their increased economic and financial news coverage has allowed them to meet the growing needs of an expanding foreign business community in Taiwan.

The Government Information Office publishes the *Taipei Journal* (*TJ*) in English once a week, and French and Spanish journals every ten days. The *TJ* can also be accessed via the Internet and the Oklahoma-based DataTimes International Online Network.

Magazines

By 1998, Taiwan's magazine industry had settled down somewhat from the heated competition triggered by the emergence of several new periodicals in the preceding years. Newly established trends showed a shift from general-interest magazines to specialized periodicals catering to learning interests and consumer concerns, such as *Ez Talk* 美語會話誌, which targets those eager to improve their spoken English, and *Smart* 理財生活, which offers advice on personal financial management. The interest in leisure that came with Taiwan's new alternating two-day weekends initially spurred the growth of magazines covering food and recreation, and this interest has since expanded to the realms of culture and the art. Among the newest magazines on music and arts are *Play* 流行月刊, a music publication that debuted in April 1998, and *Art China* 新朝藝術, which came out in October 1998.

The ROC magazine industry, like the other print media, has been gradually losing its readership to the TV industry, and has responded by entering into joint ventures with well-known international magazines, publishing Chinese editions of *Esquire, Living, Marie Claire, Net* and the likes. Many magazines have also established Internet websites to provide readers with a selection of articles from each issue.

General-interest Journals

General-interest journals in Taiwan mainly cover current events, social morals, and political issues. The *Reader's Digest* 讀者文摘 is widely read by all ages throughout Taiwan. The content of the Taiwan edition includes translations from the original English edition, supplemented by original Chinese-language essays of particular interest to Taiwan readers. The *Global Views Monthly* 遠見雜誌 is another established general-interest magazine. Covering political, economic, social, and other domestic issues, this magazine helps to keep its readers well-informed of current developments in Taiwan.

Among the most popular political magazines is *The Journalist* 新新聞週刊, a weekly magazine established in 1987. Over the past decade, it has with its hard-hitting writing style, sculpted an image for itself as a sharp critic of ROC political matters. Another widely read magazine reflecting a strong local identity is the *New Taiwan Weekly* 新台灣新聞周刊, which focuses mainly on political issues and other domestic developments.

Special-interest Magazines

Recent surveys have shown that the most widely read magazines in Taiwan are about finance, computers, health, cars, women's lifestyle, and parenting. Over the past few decades, Taiwan's business-oriented society has shown a strong demand for financial magazines. These now form the largest class of magazines, standing at about one-fifth of the total published in Taiwan.

Among the most popular financial magazines is the *CommonWealth* 天下雜誌, established in 1981 and highly respected for its attractive design, excellent business image, and concern for the well-being of society. Its coverage of macroeconomic trends and modern management concepts carries much prestige in the commercial sector. It has also reached out overseas, particularly in Southeast Asia, and is now accessible to Internet users throughout the world. *Wealth* 財訊, although the size of a thick paperback, is considered a "must read" by many stock investors, entrepreneurs, and politicians in Taiwan because of its insightful articles. Other popular magazines focusing on personal finance include *Money* 錢雜誌 and *Smart* 理財生活, which were founded in 1986 and 1998, respectively.

Growing prosperity in Taiwan has taken care of the people's basic needs, leading to a widespread interest in fitness and health. In response, publications have begun to cater to these new-found interests. *Evergreen* 常春, a monthly magazine

---

National Press Council

The National Press Council of the ROC 中華民國新聞評議委員會 (NPC), founded in 1974, currently consists of eight news groups, the News Editors Association 中華民國新聞編輯人協會, the News Agency Association 中華民國新聞通訊事業協會, the National Association of Broadcasters, ROC 中華民國廣播電視事業協會, the ROC Television Association 中華民國電視學會, Taiwan Province Press Association 臺灣省報紙事業協會, Taipei Press Guild 臺北市報業公會, Kaohsiung City Press Association 高雄市報紙事業協會, and Taipei Journalists Association 臺北市新聞記者公會, to safeguard press freedom, promote press discipline, and raise the standards of media ethics. The NPC review board comprises veteran journalists, scholars of journalism, legal experts, and prominent civic figures. The panel regularly assesses the quality of media production in the Taiwan area in accordance with the Code of Ethics for Chinese Journalists 中國新聞記者信條, the Code of Ethics for the ROC Press 中華民國報業道德規範, the Code of Ethics for ROC Radio Broadcasting 中華民國無線電廣播道德規範, and the Code of Ethics for ROC Television 中華民國電視道德規範. The NPC reviews complaints raised by the public or other concerned parties and announces its conclusions after exhaustive investigations and hearings.

The NPC publishes a monthly magazine and numerous books exploring news issues. The council cooperates with the electronic and print media to promote the exchange of public views, and produces a ten-minute news evaluation program, *News Bridge* 新聞橋, which is broadcast on Taiwan's over-the-air television stations every Sunday evening. In 1990 the council began presenting the ROC Outstanding Journalists Award 中華民國傑出新聞人員研究獎. Each recipient obtains a research scholarship equivalent to as much as US$18,500 to study abroad for a period of three to six months. The council also offers programs for advanced studies at home.

Foreign Media Represented in the ROC

As of October 1999, a hundred correspondents and photographers representing 62 foreign mass media organizations were stationed in the Republic of China. The accredited foreign correspondents were from the following enterprises:

News Agencies

- Agence France-Presse (France)
- AFX-Asia Financial News (Hong Kong)
- Associated Press (United States)
- Associated Press Television (United States)
- Black Star Photo Agency (United States)
- Bloomberg Financial News (United States)
- Bridge News (United States)
- Dow Jones Newswires (United States)
- EFE News Agency (Spain)
- German Foreign Trade News (Germany)
- Jiji Press (Japan)
- Kyodo News (Japan)
- Pan-Asia Newspaper Alliance (Japan)
- Reuters (United Kingdom)
- Reuters Television (United Kingdom)
- United Press International (United States)

Newspapers and Magazines

- *Air Finance Journal* (United Kingdom)
- *Asahi Shimbun* (Japan)
- *Asian Business* (Hong Kong)
- *Asian Sources Electronic* (Hong Kong)
- *The Asian Wall Street Journal* (Hong Kong)
- *Asiaweek* (Hong Kong)
- *The Australian* (Australia)
- *Bike Europe* (the Netherlands)
- *Business Traveler* (Hong Kong)
- *Business Week* (United States)
- *Cheng Ming Monthly* (Hong Kong)
- *The Chunichi Shimbun* (Japan)
- *The Economist* (United Kingdom)
- *Electronic Business Asia* (Hong Kong)
- *Emphasis Inflight* (Malaysia)

- *Far Eastern Economic Review* (Hong Kong)
- *Financial Times* (United Kingdom)
- *Journal Chines Americana* (Brazil)
- *Lianhe Zaobao* (Singapore)
- *Lonely Planet* (Australia)
- *Mainichi Shimbun* (Japan)
- *Ming Pao Daily News* (Hong Kong)
- *Moku* (Japan)
- *Nanyang Siang Pau* (Malaysia)
- *New Times* (Russia)
- *Nihon Keizai Shimbun* (Japan)
- *Oriental Press* (Hong Kong)
- *Ossietzky* (Germany)
- *Sankei Shimbun* (Japan)
- *Sin Chew Jit Poh* (Malaysia)
- *Sing Tao News* (Hong Kong)
- *Straits Times* (Singapore)
- *The Sun* (Hong Kong)
- *Time* (United States)
- *Tokyo News Service* (Japan)
- *The Trend* (Hong Kong)
- *Yazhou Zhoukan* (Hong Kong)
- *Yomiuri Shimbun* (Japan)

Radio and Television

- CNBC Asia (Singapore)
- Hong Kong Commercial Broadcasting (Hong Kong)
- NHK (Japan)
- North America Television (United States)
- Phoenix Satellite Television (Hong Kong)
- Radio France Internationale (France)
- Radio Free Asia (United States)
- Voice of America (United States)

---

published by a commercial television station, offers the average reader extensive knowledge about common diseases and health conditions, as well as how to keep fit through exercise and a proper diet. Another magazine, *Common Health* 康健雜誌, which published its first issue in September 1998, covers in everyday language a wide range of health and psychological issues,

especially those related to working men and women. In contrast to these two magazines, the established periodical *Health World* 健康世界 offers in-depth coverage of diseases and detailed articles discussing medical and health issues.

In recent years, as major cosmetics companies from abroad have penetrated the Taiwan market, international women's magazines have also launched Chinese editions on the island. *Harper's Bazaar* 哈潑時尚, *Cosmopolitan* 柯夢波丹, *Elle* 她, and *Vogue* 時尚雜誌 are among them. Despite the influx of foreign competition, locally owned women's journals, such as *Beauty* 美人誌, remain the leaders in domestic market sales.

Among other popular women's magazines is *Lady Ann* 安少女, which provides the latest on movie stars, fashion, romance, fortune-telling, and the daily routines of young people. *Mademoiselle* 女性雜誌 attracts readers with articles on fashion, famous personalities, cultural activities, travel, and food.

With the flourishing of the ROC computer industry and the arrival of the Internet in Taiwan, computer science magazines have become very popular among local readers. For instance, launched in February 1996, *PC Home* 電腦家庭 has witnessed a meteoric rise to prominence. *The Third Wave* 第三波 is published by Taiwan computer giant, the Acer Group 宏碁關係企業集團 and targets people who are new to computers. *PC Magazine* 微電腦傳真 provides information on industrial computerization and also reviews new products and emerging technologies. *Amazing Computer Entertainment* 電腦玩家, a Chinese-language publication licensed by the US *PC Gamer* magazine, introduces and analyzes new computer games and software. A free CD-ROM is included inside each issue.

Convenience stores and corner newsstands in Taiwan carry periodicals on baseball, golf, cars, stereo equipment, religion, pets, gourmet cooking, the film industry, broadcasting, travel, leisure, and much more.

English-language periodicals and magazines which juxtapose Chinese and English texts are an entertaining way for Taiwan readers to learn a foreign language. Currently, about ten such periodicals are published in Taiwan. Among them, *Studio Classroom* 空中英語教室, one of the most popular, is also available on CD-ROM, and half of its readers are college students.

Other English or bilingual magazines in Taiwan include the *Taipei Review* (formerly the *Free China Review*, and available in English, French,

The varied interests of Taiwan's readers are reflected in the diverse and growing magazine industry.

German, Russian, and Spanish editions), *Sinorama* 光華 (available with English, Spanish, or Japanese texts juxtaposed with Chinese), *Taiwan International Trade*, and *This Month in Taiwan*.

Books

The year 1998 was significant for the ROC's book publishing industry as it marked the end of the 69-year-old *Publication Law* 出版法. It also marked the government's shift from a regulatory and supervisory role to one of guidance and encouragement. In response to this historic change, recent political and economic developments, and new consumer fads, ROC publishers released more than 30,000 new titles that year. The expansion of the book market has paralleled the rising affluence and purchasing power of the Taiwan public. Also, the government's campaign to promote a more culture-conscious and literary society in Taiwan has added fuel to the growth of the publishing industry.

Book publishers in Taiwan can be classified into three groups: governmental, semigovernmental, and private. The Taiwan Book Store 臺灣書店 is a government agency under the Taiwan Provincial Department of Education 臺灣省教育廳 responsible for editing and publishing elementary and high school textbooks. Semigovernmental units include the Cheng Chung Book Co. Ltd. 正中書局, which is run by the Kuomintang, and the Youth Cultural Enterprise 幼獅文化事業 of the China Youth Corps 中國青年反共救國團. As for private publishers, about 80 percent of them are located in northern Taiwan. Most are small or medium-sized businesses with 10 to 50 employees; only a few have more than 100 full-time workers. Many newspapers and magazines have special columns introducing and critiquing new books. Informa-

tion on Taiwan's book market is available from the National Central Library's International Standard Book Number Center 國家圖書館國際標準書號中心 and ISBN newsletter.

The demand for a tremendous number of textbooks over the past 50 years has nurtured the development of the printing and publishing industries in Taiwan. Cheng Chung has long been a leader in this market, and about ten private publishers have also played important roles. Since 1996, the government's market liberalization policy has enabled private publishers to grab a bigger share of the textbook market. Several large-scale companies that publish reference books operate their own printing and binding factories as a means of reducing production costs and raising competitiveness.

With Taiwan focusing on globalization and appropriating vast sums of money for research purposes, the market for imported Western books is poised for solid growth. Many foreign publishers are actively promoting their books in Taiwan. Among them, Simon & Schuster, Oxford, Longman, Thomson, and McGraw-Hill have set up Taiwan branches and sent representatives to manage their sales on the island.

Books on finance, trade, business management, and computers continue to be at the top of the production schedules of local publishing houses. But easier access to overseas destinations has given rise to more books on foreign countries, unfamiliar cultures, and self-help travel tips. In addition, publishers have responded to the growing public concern for better health and spiritual growth amid Taiwan's ever-more-hectic lifestyles and increasing materialism. Also in recent years, the production of electronic books and CD-ROM products has expanded rapidly, further diversifying Taiwan's publishing sector.

One of the major goals of the ROC publishing industry is to integrate the Chinese-language publications printed in Taiwan, Hong Kong, and mainland China. However, there are numerous barriers to overcome, not the least of which is the rising cost of production, contributor, translation, and royalty expenses and fees for works from abroad.

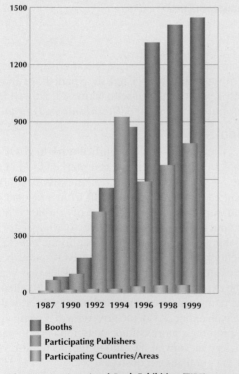

Taipei International Book Exhibition

1987 1990 1992 1994 1996 1998 1999

■ Booths
■ Participating Publishers
■ Participating Countries/Areas

The Taipei International Book Exhibition (TIBE) was a biennial event first held in December 1987. In 1998, it became an annual event. As Asia's largest book exhibition, TIBE serves as a channel for the exchange of market information and the development of business relationships.

Source: Taipei International Book Exhibition Organizing Committee

Bookstores and Bestsellers

When Kingstone Book Store 金石堂書店 enterprise launched its chain of stores in 1983, it marked the first remarkable change in Taiwan's retail book market. Since then, Q Book Center Corporation 永漢國際書局, New-Schoolmate Book Co. Ltd. 新學友書局, and Caves Books Ltd. 敦煌書局 have followed suit and opened fleets of spacious, bright, and comfortable chainstores to attract customers. The Eslite corporation 誠品書局 arrived on the scene in 1989, representing another innovation in the marketing of books in Taiwan. Presenting a highly professional image, Eslite extended its cultural function beyond the selling of books to include the holding of art exhibitions, lectures, and musical performances in its stores.

The large-scale chains have changed the purchasing habits of Taiwan consumers and have become a major retail force. In 1984, Kingstone again broke new ground by compiling for customers a regular list of its 100 bestselling books, and other retailers soon followed. Most bookstores in Taiwan today promote self-compiled "top 100" lists. Taiwan's convenience stores also display bestsellers on their racks. The promotion of bestsellers has helped make books fast-moving commodities in Taiwan.

The publishing industry set another new milestone in 1994 with the opening of Taiwan's first women's bookstore, Fembooks 女書店, in downtown Taipei. Its shelves are filled with a variety of books for women, about women, and by women. Meanwhile, the introduction of e-commerce into Taiwan in recent years has led to the establishment of online bookstores and the emergence of a new generation of writers creating works specifically for the Internet. It will probably be sometime, however, before these online services successfully draw consumers away from traditional bookstores.

Children's Books

Over the past ten years, the market for children's books in Taiwan has witnessed substantial growth. In 1988 and 1989, the lifting of restrictions on publications stimulated the exchange of children's literature between Taiwan and the Chinese mainland. Taiwan publishers began purchasing reprint authorization from mainland publishers in addition to cooperating with mainland authors and translators. Around that time, about 20 children's periodicals put out their first issues in Taiwan. Also, popular comic strips started appearing in book form, covering subjects ranging from science and history to biographies and languages. In 1990, local writers became interested in writing books for children. Within a short time, children's books created in Taiwan were winning recognition on the world stage in Bologna, Italy, and Catalonia, Spain.

Since 1993, the quality of Taiwan's *hui-pen* 繪本, or illustrated books, has improved rapidly. Several of these publications have won international prizes, while others have even sold copyrights to publishers in other countries. In view of such favorable acclaim, Taiwan publishers are actively encouraging local writers to create new novels or retell historical stories for children. Even so, at present more than 70 percent of the children's books on the Taiwan market are foreign publications. Taiwan and mainland China publications share the rest of the market. Many private organizations and government agencies, including the Government Information Office, Ministry of Education, and Taiwan Provincial Government have established funds and awards to encourage more local writers and publishers to create children's literature.

Broadcasting

The addition of cable and satellite broadcasting in Taiwan during the past two decades has brought significant changes to the broadcasting industry. In mid-1999, Taiwan had 3.61 radio receivers and 1.37 television sets per household. Terrestrial telecasting reached 99.47 percent of all households and cable penetration was as high as 80 percent.

In 1993, the ROC government implemented the *Cable Television Law* 有線電視法 to govern the cable systems that had proliferated around

Taiwan. In February 1999, a revised version of the law, renamed the *Cable Radio and Television Law* 有線廣播電視法, was promulgated, liberalizing foreign investment in cable operations, prohibiting monopolistic developments, and supporting the interests of cable subscribers.

The *Satellite Broadcasting Law* 衛星廣播電視法 was also recently promulgated to provide the legal basis for satellite broadcasting signals received via cable or satellite dishes. In addition to ensuring the appropriate content of satellite programming, the law also liberalizes direct satellite broadcasting, eliminating the reliance on cable systems.

Radio

Prior to 1993, there were only 33 radio broadcasting companies in the Taiwan area. By October 1999, the number had increased to 118 while another 27 were under construction. In another liberalizing move, the ROC government released in mid-1999 a batch of 72 frequencies, including 42 for regional stations and 30 for community stations. Of these 72 frequencies, seven were allocated to the National Education Radio 國立教育廣播電台, four were designated for aboriginal programming, and five were earmarked for Hakka programming. Aside from the seven frequencies given to the National Education Radio, the remaining 65 radio frequencies attracted approximately 500 applications from the private sector. The winning applicants are expected to be announced in mid-2000.

Programming

The broadcast industry in Taiwan has come a long way since the 1950s, when dramatic, cultural, educational and children's programs on the radio were the mainstays of household entertainment. The advent of TV broadcasting in Taiwan in the 1960s brought revolutionary change to local entertainment habits; however, another major change occurred in the 1980s—radio stations adopted policies to specialize in order to secure target audiences. Currently, many radio stations focus almost exclusively on such specialty

areas as current news, light music, traffic updates, stock market reports, or agricultural news. Throughout the 1990s, news stations have diversified their programming to include regular features and studio and telephone interviews. Also, newspapers, with their vast resources, have started working in cooperation with radio stations to bring the latest news into local homes as quickly as possible.

The ROC's increasing social diversity and growing public assertiveness have led to a proliferation of radio call-in programs. Listeners are eager to express their views on the air about national developments and to put questions to government officials who visit the studios to answer inquiries about government policy. Call-in programs cover a wide range of topics, everything from health care to traffic laws. Radio broadcasting in Taiwan includes regular domestic programming by medium-wave AM and VHF FM stations, medium- and shortwave broadcasts to the Chinese mainland, and specialized programming via shortwave transmissions to other countries. Programs in various Chinese dialects and English are also available.

Station Facilities and Services

The Broadcasting Corporation of China 中國廣播公司 (BCC), the pioneer of the ROC's broadcasting industry, was founded in Nanking in 1928 as the Central Broadcasting Station 中央廣播臺 and reorganized under its present name in 1947. Two years later, it established a foothold in international radio with its broadcast of the Voice of Free China 自由中國之聲 over short-wave channels. The BCC set up the ROC's first FM station in 1968 and was also the first to broadcast in stereo over AM channels in 1987.

The BCC operates a flagship station in Taipei, nine regional stations, and two professional stations which specialize in agricultural programs and traffic reports. The BCC has six national and five regional simulcast programming streams. These networks offer popular music, national news, industrial and commercial services, educational and religious programs, stock market reports, and programs in the Southern Fukienese 閩南語 dialect. Its news and popular music broadcasts are also available via streaming audio on its website.

In January 1998, the Central Broadcasting System 中央廣播電臺 (CBS) was reorganized as the ROC's national radio station under the *Central Broadcasting System Establishment Statute* 中央廣播電臺設置條例 by merging the CBS, formerly under the Ministry of National Defense, and the BBC's international department. The CBS operates a variety network and a news network in Mandarin Chinese; a dialect network that is broadcast in seven dialects, including Southern Fukienese, Cantonese, Hakka, Mongolian, and Tibetan; the Radio Taipei International 台北國際之聲, which is broadcast in 11 foreign languages; and the Voice of Asia 亞洲之聲, which is broadcast in English, Mandarin, Thai, and Indonesian. The CBS broadcasts news of developments in the ROC's governmental policies, business activities, tourism, and education to the mainland and the global community.

The Cheng Sheng Broadcasting Corporation Ltd. 正聲廣播公司 (CSBC) operates one FM and eight AM stations islandwide. The stations gear their programming to the needs of Taiwan's agricultural, fishing, and labor communities. Programs are broadcast in the Southern Fukienese and Hakka dialects as well as in Mandarin. In October 1994, CSBC launched a new service called the Information Broadcasting Company 生活資訊調頻臺. Since October 1995, the company has been using an Integrated Services Digital Network (ISDN) to broadcast its "Super Sound" music program and simulcasts with KAZM AM 1300, a Chinese-language radio station in Los Angeles. The ISDN is also used to facilitate audience call-ins on the CSBC's news program aired in cooperation with the *China Times*.

The Public Radio System 警察廣播電臺 (PRS) specializes in traffic reports and social services. Besides its headquarters station in Taipei, the PRS has seven regional stations across the island. Its traffic-news networks are located in the cities of Taipei, Taichung, Kaohsiung, and

---

Major Awards for the Media

- Golden Bell Awards 金鐘獎: Founded in 1965 to honor excellence in over-the-air broadcasting, and presented annually, alternating each year between the radio and television industries.
- Golden Horse Awards 金馬獎: Presented annually since 1962 to advance the art of motion pictures and recognize outstanding achievements in Chinese-language film production.
- Golden Melody Awards 金曲獎: Presented annually since 1990 to recognize outstanding performances in and contributions to pop, classical, and folk music.
- Golden Tripod Awards 金鼎獎: Founded in 1976 and presented annually since 1981 to individuals and publishers for outstanding achievements in four major categories—newspapers, magazines, books, and audio recordings.
- Golden Visual Awards 金視獎: Held annually since 1997 to recognize and encourage outstanding work in local cable television programming.
- Little Sun Awards 小太陽獎: Presented annually since 1996 to recognize writers' and publishers' efforts to produce books for outside reading for elementary and junior high school students.

Hualien. The PRS also operates an Evergreen Network 長青網 to provide middle-aged and elderly citizens with cultural programs and information on medicine, health, and retirement. Through a computerized network, PRS stations receive and distribute round-the-clock reports on road conditions and traffic snarls in local areas and on the freeways. The traffic updates are interspersed with music and special features.

International Community Radio Taipei (ICRT), owned and operated by the Taipei International Community Cultural Foundation, is Taiwan's only predominantly English-language radio station. Its FM and AM channels broadcast separate programming, including popular Western music, talk shows, and community service segments. ICRT is also available via streaming audio on its Internet website.

Television

The past decade has witnessed unprecedented challenges for Taiwan's television industry with the establishment of a public television system, the legalization of private cable operations, increased popularity of satellite broadcasting, the promotion of digital television, and the employment of new information technology by the broadcasting industry. In November 1998, it sponsored its first National Conference on Radio and Television Affairs 全國廣播電視會議 to prepare for the coming of digital TV and satellite technology and to discuss the management problems that might arise from it. The conference drew government attention to the fact that new legislation was necessary to deal with future broadcasting techniques and market changes, as well as increase the global competitiveness of the domestic broadcasting industry.

Commercial Television

A landmark development in the history of Taiwan's television industry was the inauguration of a fourth over-the-air television station in June 1997. Kaohsiung-based Formosa Television 民間全民電視臺 (FTV) joined the three existing companies, Taiwan Television Enterprise 臺灣電視公司 (TTV) established in 1962, China Television Company 中國電視公司 (CTV) in 1969, and Chinese Television System 中華電視臺 (CTS) in 1971. FTV is affiliated with the opposition Democratic Progressive Party and telecasts on VHF low-band.

Taiwan's over-the-air TV stations are being severely threatened as more and more viewers are tuning in to cable TV. They are feeling intense pressure to preserve their market share by improving programming and technical facilities. Regulated cable television operation arrived relatively late on Taiwan. When the *Cable Television Law* was passed in August 1993, illegal cable systems were already serving viewers throughout Taiwan, some improving reception of over-the-air television broadcasts in hilly areas and some offering a wide selection of satellite and videotape programming. These cable systems have since then registered with the GIO and will remain in temporary service until authorized cable systems under the *Cable Television Law*—which was revised and renamed the *Cable Radio and Television Law* in 1998—begin to provide programming in the service areas concerned. As of October 1999, a hundred of these cable systems were still in operation, while another 32 cable systems had already received authorization under the *Cable Radio and Television Law* and had begun offering services.

Taiwan's cable systems usually offer subscribers a fixed package of over 70 channels at a fixed monthly rate. These channels include news and information, Chinese and foreign movies, cartoons, religious programs, sports, music, and

---

Digital Television

In November 1992, the ROC government adopted a plan to develop the high-definition television industry. In the following year, a special task force was set up to coordinate related matters. However, market factors both in Taiwan and around the world indicated that the first step toward developing high-definition television would be to promote digital TV.

The digitalization project was thus included under the National Information Infrastructure 國家資訊通信基本建設 (NII). Incentive measures and channel allocation plans were drawn up and a timetable was worked out for the digitalization of over-the-air television beginning in 1999. Digital TV broadcasting is expected to become nationwide in the year 2001 and the frequencies for conventional analog TV broadcasting will be returned to the government for reallocation in 2006.

Meanwhile, related laws have to be revised to keep pace with these developments in the television industry. Once this ambitious project is implemented, viewers around Taiwan will receive sharper pictures, CD-quality sound, and movie-quality signals.

a variety of other entertainment programming, as well as talk shows and home-shopping services. In October 1999, a total of 62 companies were offering 109 satellite channels in Taiwan, including a number of foreign channels like NHK from Japan; Home Box Office (HBO), Disney, and Discovery from the United States; as well as groups of specialized, satellite-based channels operated by local media conglomerates, such as Eastern Multimedia Group 東森媒體事業群, Sanlih Entertainment Television 三立電視台, and Videoland 緯來電視台. The major news and information channels include TVBS-N 無線衛星電視新聞台, FTV news, the Chinese Television Network 傳訊電視中天頻道(CTN), Eastern Television 東森新聞台, the Cable News Network (CNN), the Discovery Channel, and National Geographic. The more popular foreign movie channels are HBO, AXN, Sun Movie, and Cinemax, all of which feature Chinese subtitles. For sports fans, live telecasts of Taiwan's professional baseball and basketball leagues along with a wide selection of other sports programming are available on several channels. Other popular channels include TVBS 無線衛星電視台; the Disney channel, which is popular with children; MTV, which features rock music videos; and Star Plus, which airs both cartoons and TV serials. The programming distributed by satellite TV services through cable TV operators continues to eat away at the viewership and advertising profits of the over-the-air TV stations in Taiwan.

Public Television

After 18 years of delay, the Public Television Service 公共電視臺 (PTS) finally began broadcasting on July 1, 1998. The creation of public-interest television was first proposed in 1980, and four years later the Government Information Office established a task force to produce public-interest programs to be aired on a rotation basis on the three commercial stations—TTV, CTV and CTS. In 1990, a 22-member committee was set up to draft a *Public Television Law* 公共電視法 as a framework for establishing

Every week, the Public Television Service airs a special program, "Face to Face with the Tribes," covering indigenous cultures and issues.
(Courtesy of the Public Television Service)

the hardware requirements, programming policies and financial resources of the PTS. The bill was submitted to the Legislative Yuan 立法院 for review in 1992 and, after five years of debate, was passed in May 1997.

The PTS offers educational programs, documentaries, dramas, cultural programs, news shows for indigenous peoples and a range of investigative reports. It serves the interests of minority groups as well as the greater public, and is commercial-free, as required by the *Public Television*

Asia-Pacific Media Center

In 1995, the ROC government launched a massive project to transform Taiwan into an Asia-Pacific media center. The aim of the project is to develop a regional media industry incorporating satellite and cable television, raise the proportion of made-in-Taiwan Chinese-language programming on cable television, and encourage the construction of at least two high-technology media parks on the island.

The Government Information Office began laying plans in January 1995 to establish a framework for a complete and comprehensive media system covering the electronic and print media. The first stage of the plan stressed the development of the motion picture and television industries. The second stage, which began in 1998, underlines the establishment of a complete environment for the production of Chinese-language media, including print media.

The government has taken a series of measures to improve the environment for media industry development: The legal system related to the media industry is being strengthened, import tariffs are being reduced on professional motion picture and television equipment, tax incentives and preferential measures are being formulated, assistance is being provided for the cultivation and training of professional talent, and media industry exchanges are being promoted with the Chinese mainland.

Efforts are also under way to promote the planning and construction of several high-tech media parks. These parks, which are to be commerce-oriented and financed by the private sector, will serve as specialized areas for the production of motion pictures, television programs, and TV commercials. The first of these parks, the ERA High-tech Media Park 年代高科技媒體園區 in Chiayi, is scheduled to begin operations in 2006.

Law. As with other public television stations worldwide, the PTS does not focus on market share but instead strives for excellence in programming and aims to increase the public's cultural awareness. The PTS is subsidized by the government in its first year of operation. The subsidy will be gradually reduced in subsequent years.

Motion Pictures

Taiwan's film industry has shown serious signs of decline since the mid-1990s, in part due to the aggressive marketing of Hollywood filmmakers and in part because of the ROC's continued relaxation of restrictions on film imports. Although liberalization has had a negative effect on domestic film production, it has also spurred the growth of cinema multiplexes in metropolitan areas. The excellent consumer services offered by multiplexes, such as their wide selection of available films in small screening halls, have forced many community theaters to merge into large complexes or improve their facilities in order to remain competitive.

In 1998, the domestic film industry produced a total of 21 feature films and one animated film.

Most were low-budget action films that were not even screened in cinemas, but were instead released directly to video or through cable television outlets. As in the past several years, the Domestic Film Guidance Fund 國片輔導金 continued to play an important role providing investment funding for high-quality domestic films. Budgeting for this fund has increased eight-fold since 1990, reaching US$3.75 million in 1998. The fund has supported a total of 88 films, many of which have represented the ROC and won major awards in international film festivals.

In 1998, Taiwan films participated in 52 international film festivals, actively competing in 19 of them. Among the seven films honored with awards was *The Hole* 洞, which won the International Critics Prize at the Cannes International Film Festival in 1998. This movie also won several honors, including the award for best film, best director, and best actress in the 1999 Singapore International Film Festival. Another Taiwan film that captured the international spotlight was *Light and Darkness* 黑暗之光, which won four awards—the Tokyo Grand Prix, the Tokyo Gold Prize, the Governor of Tokyo Award, and the Asian Film Award—at the Tokyo International Film Festival in November 1999. In order to promote domestic films in the global market, the Government Information Office has worked with foreign film organizations to sponsor Taiwan Film Festivals overseas. These cultural activities have been held in many countries, including Canada, Japan, South Africa, Hungary, Senegal, Burkina Faso, France, and Denmark.

Domestically, the GIO works together with the local film industry to plan exclusive screenings of domestic productions. Every year, it holds the Golden Horse Awards 金馬獎, which recognizes outstanding Chinese-language films in a number of categories, including features, shorts, documentaries, and animation. The Taipei Golden Horse International Film Festival 臺北金馬國際影展 is held around the same time and features a non-competitive showcase of a wide range of foreign films, with roughly 100 foreign entries participating in the 1998 festival.

Film Imports

In October 1994, restrictions on the import of mainland Chinese movies and videotapes were lifted to allow the release of feature films and ten categories of videotaped programs in Taiwan. These ten categories include: science and technology, business management, nature and animals, geography and scenic locations, culture

and the arts, sports, language instruction, and medicine and health, variety programs, and dramatic films. The GIO promulgated guidelines on the import quota, categories, and viewing hours allotted to Chinese mainland movies and videotapes in the Taiwan market. The annual import of mainland Chinese films is limited to ten different titles with 36 copies of each. In May 1999, the number of copies of each foreign film permitted into Taiwan was increased from 50 to 58; and as of September 1999, such films could only be screened simultaneously by 18 theaters in Taipei and Kaohsiung, and ten theaters in the counties and other cities, with a maximum of three screens per theater showing a particular film.

Telecommunications

Telecommunication Sector Reconfigured

Taiwan's telecommunication sector underwent structural change in 1996 in line with the trend of technological development and policies of economic liberalization and internationalization. On July 1, 1996, the Directorate-General of Telecommunications 電信總局 (DGT), which is supervised by the Ministry of Transportation and Communications, stopped serving the dual capacity of regulator and operator. Under the

	Telephone Subscribers		Mobile Phone Subscribers		Radio Pager Subscribers		Pay Stations	
	Number	*Per 100 population*	*Number*	*Per 100 population*	*Number*	*Per 100 population*	*Number*	*Per 100 population*
1988	5,332,285	26.72	--	--	200,237	1.00	99,992	0.50
1990	6,300,755	30.88	83,482	0.41	792,419	3.88	106,979	0.52
1992	7,418,277	35.66	384,779	1.85	1,169,460	5.62	112,206	0.54
1994	8,503,201	40.15	584,326	2.76	1,729,030	8.16	121,538	0.57
1996	10,010,614	46.52	970,473	4.51	2,300,766	10.69	126,118	0.59
1998	11,500,361	52.45	2,179,741	9.94	2,259,901	10.31	135,183	0.62

Telecommunications Statistics

Source: Ministry of Transportation and Communications

revised *Telecommunications Act* 電信法 promulgated on February 5, 1996, the DGT is now an independent regulator responsible for devising national telecommunications policies, regulating the telecommunications market, and allocating radio broadcast frequencies.

Telecommunications services are now provided by the Chunghwa Telecom Co. Ltd. 中華電信股份有限公司 (CHT). This fully state-run enterprise has seven branch offices that are responsible for local, long-distance, international, mobile, radio paging, and data and communications satellite services.

The first step to telecommunications deregulation goes as far back as June 1989 when value-added network (VAN) services were partly liberalized. In the years that followed, several other services have also been liberalized. By mid-1999, there were seven mobile telephone, six radio paging, six mobile data, nine trunked radio, five CT-2, and four satellite program relay service providers serving Taiwan consumers. Other services to be opened to the private sector include the satellite communications business, fixed networks, digital television, live satellite broadcasting, and digital audio broadcasting.

Telecommunications Services

Over the past five decades, the DGT has undertaken a number of telecommunications development projects to meet Taiwan's steadily growing information needs. Important international ventures include the financing and emplacement of undersea fiber-optic cables to develop a national information infrastructure. The world's longest undersea cable network, and the sixth such global venture that the ROC has participated in, is scheduled to begin operation at the end of 1999. It will upgrade Taiwan's international telephone services, video transmissions, teleconferencing, and other digital functions. Another undersea cable system boasting the world's largest transmission capacity and linking the ROC directly with the US is also expected to be operational by the end of 1999. These projects will consolidate Taiwan's role as an Asia-Pacific telecommunications center.

Telecommunications liberalization has spurred the growth of the mobile phone industry, with rapid expansion in subscribers and increased services. The photo above shows large crowds at a mobile phone exhibition in Taipei.

Important ventures have also been implemented locally, such as the modernization of Taiwan's local communication networks by implementing digitized telephone switches. DGT is developing an Integrated Services Digital Network (ISDN) to significantly enhance the quality and diversity of services. Taiwan's ISDN commercial service made its local debut on May 16, 1995, providing end-to-end voice and non-voice transmissions.

Mobile telephone services in Taiwan have been growing at a tremendous pace since their inauguration in July 1989. Chunghwa Telecom has been joined by six strong competitors, which have added a wide variety of functions and services to increase their market share in Taiwan. Because the analog Advanced Mobile Phone System was almost fully loaded, the DGT started a new Global System for Mobile Communication (GSM) cellular telephone service in July 1995 to accommodate the pressing demand. The DGT has also set up international GSM roaming services with a number of countries around the world.

The first phase of the project to develop the Intelligent Network 智慧型網路 was completed on April 27, 1996, to promptly offer advanced free phone, mass calling, and credit telephone services. The DGT's Telecommunications Laboratories 電信研究所 have developed ATM VPX prototypes and will further develop an ATM/BEX-VCX. These products form the backbone of the broadband service trial network. The services to be provided include: point-to-point videoconferencing, LAN interconnection, video on demand, multimedia database retrieval, and E-mail.

To meet growing demands for a stronger national information infrastructure in the ROC, an Asynchronous Transfer Mode virtual path switch multiplexer and local area network has been established. The National Information Infrastructure was launched on July 14, 1995, at the Hsinchu Science-based Industrial Park 新竹科學工業園區 in northern Taiwan. The initial services of the NII include a multimedia database, cable TV services, electronic data interchange, automated customs clearance, distance learning, and distance medical treatment. The NII also renders technical assistance to domestic research organizations and the private sector for the development of a broadband network, video on demand, multimedia applications, network security, and field trials.

By mid-1999, Taiwan's active Internet users exceeded four million, representing an increase of one million from December 1998. Statistics from July 1999 show that the ROC, with 413 million users, ranked eighth in the world in terms of the number of Internet users; ninth, at 18.8 percent, in terms of Internet penetration; and seventh in the world (third with regard to the Asia-Pacific region, just after Japan and Australia) in terms of Internet hosts, which totaled nearly 677,000, up 30 percent from January 1999 (see also section on National Information Infrastructure in Chapter 18, Science and Technology).

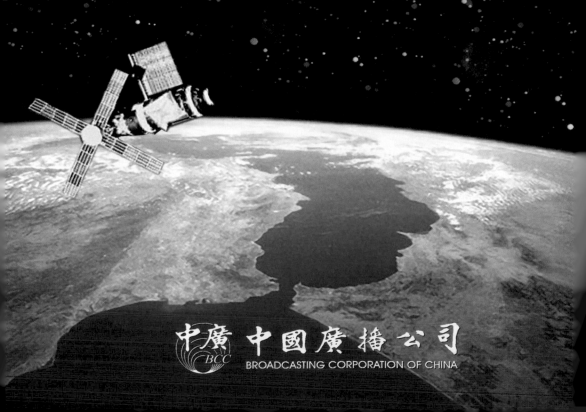

CBS Invites You to Enjoy Our Programs

in the New Millennium

Reaching every corner of the world,

the national radio station of the ROC introduces Taiwan's arts,

news and culture through medium and

short wave broadcasts

We welcome your support of the world's window on Taiwan.

▼

55, PEI—AN ROAD ,TAIPEI 104, TAIWAN ,R.O.C   TEL: 886-2-25918161   FAX∕886-2-25850741   http∕www.cbs.org.tw. E-mail∕rtim@cbs.org.tw

ISDN

整體服務數位網路
INTEGRATED SERVICES DIGITAL NETWORK

按影指定 NO PROBLEM

輕鬆搞定 NO PROBLEM

中華電

穿上 CEFIRO，成就事業版圖。

California
4ELF515
SESQUICENTENNIAL · 150 YEARS

NISSAN
new CEFIRO

100～150 萬尊貴房車第一品牌

17 Education

After nine years of compulsory education, most junior high school graduates choose to continue their studies in either the vocational track (senior vocational schools) or the academic track (senior high schools). Senior high graduates now have several options to enter college.

(Courtesy of the Department of Information, Taipei City Government)

What's New
1. Figures updated
2. Changes in the administrative framework
3. More about the National Central Library

Education is strongly emphasized in the Republic of China, as it has been through out Chinese history. As such, the ROC Constitution allocates a lion's share of national expenditures for educational purposes (Article 164). In the last decade or so, the ROC's educational development was focused on higher education. Around 22.54 percent of the education budget was allocated for 915,921 students in the higher education system, whereas 38.29 percent was spent amongst the 2,919,990 elementary and junior high students in the compulsory education system in school year 1998. This uneven distribution caused the government to shift its focus and place greater emphasis on a quality compulsory education, resulting in several major changes to the ROC Constitution. On July 18, 1997, the second session of the Third National Assembly passed a provision to Paragraph 8, Article 10, of the *Additional Articles of the Constitution of the Republic of China* (for a complete version of the ROC Constitution, see Appendix II). Promulgated three days later on July 21, the provision states: "Priority shall be given to funding for education, science, and culture, and in particular funding for compulsory education, the restrictions in Article 164 of the Constitution notwithstanding."

Therefore, although this provision gives compulsory education higher priority with respect to funding within the education budget, it also removes the minimum expenditure requirements for different levels of the government stipulated in Article 164 of the ROC Constitution. Thus, after the implementation of the *Additional Articles*, the government will have more freedom in allocating budget resources for different government functions. For fiscal 1999, government spending for education, science, and culture exceeded US$17.33 billion, or about 6.51 percent of the GNP or 15.57 percent of government expenditures and roughly US$619 per citizen. (The drop in educational expenses was due to an appreciation of the US dollar during the period, rather than a cut in the actual budget. The figures stated here are based on the exchange rate of one US dollar to 32 New Taiwan dollars.)

Nine years of education has been compulsory since 1968, and there is a wide range of other educational options for citizens of all ages. In the 1999 school year from August 1, 1998, to July 31, 1998 (hereafter, SY1998), more than 97.8 percent of all elementary school-age children (age six to 11) were in school. The total enrollment rate of the population aged between six and 21 was 80.04 percent, and more than one-fifth of the total population was attending an educational institution of some type. In 1998, there were 7,731 registered schools, with an average of 36.41 students per class and a student-teacher ratio of 20.30. Statistics indicate that 237.85 persons per thousand studied in some type of educational institutions. The national illiteracy rate has further fallen to 5.34 percent.

Even though a larger proportion of the population now receives higher education, the education system in general has been criticized for its inflexibility and for failing to address the needs of Taiwan's rapidly changing society. As a result, educational reform has become a major issue, and in the last few years, measures have been adopted to tackle problems in different aspects of the educational system. Measures have focused on the establishment of a more comprehensive compulsory education, universal preschool education, improvement of higher education, pluralistic and refined vocational education, a system of life-long education and information education, more thorough promotion channels for continued study, a new supportive students counseling system, and a program for fostering pedagogic talents and on-the-job training. Furthermore, family education, aboriginal education, special education, and

Educational Tracks in the ROC

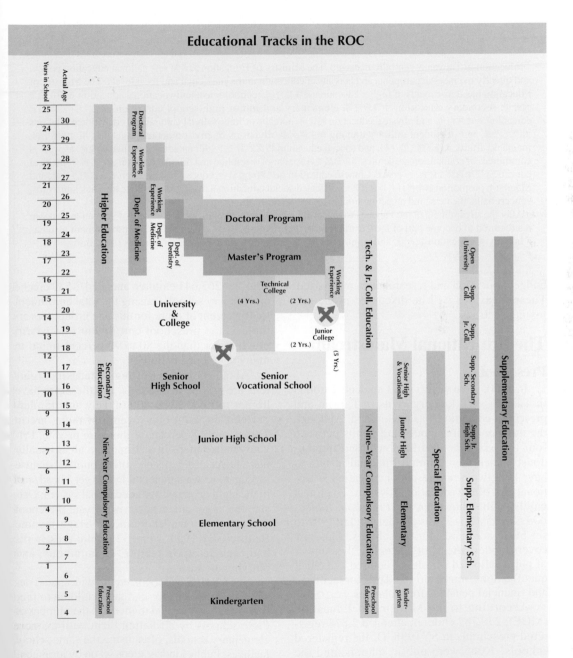

Source: Ministry of Education

Administrative Framework

Education in Taiwan is centrally managed. The Ministry of Education 教育部 sets national education policy, and directly oversees departments and bureaus of education at the municipal and local levels. The Ministry of Education has departments of higher education 高等教育司, technological and vocational education 技術及職業教育司, secondary education 中等教育司, elementary and junior high school education 國民教育司, social education 社會教育司, and physical education 體育司; bureaus of international cultural and educational relations 國際文教處, and of student military training 學生軍訓處; divisions of environmental protection 環境保護小組, mainland affairs 大陸事務工作小組, and special education 特殊教育工作小組; an advisory office 顧問室; as well as committees or councils on academics 學術審議委員會, school discipline and moral education 訓育委員會, medical education 醫學教育委員會, overseas Chinese education 僑民教育委員會, educational research 教育研究委員會, and Mandarin promotion 國語推行委員會. Other affiliated social educational institutions include libraries, museums, concert halls, theaters, and an acting troupe.

After the streamlining of the Taiwan Provincial Government, the provincial Department of Education has been restructured to become part of the Central Regional Office 中部辦公室. Each municipal government also has a bureau of education 教育局, and county or city governments have education bureaus or sections.

budget allocation and research are emphasized. These measures will be discussed in the following sections.

The Educational Mainstream

Preschool

In 1950, there were 17,111 students enrolled in Taiwan's 28 kindergartens in Taiwan and preschool education was uncommon. Although the number of preschools and pupils between four and six years old has increased tremendously since then, limited financial resources have kept two-year preschool education an optional part of the educational system. To protect pupils' rights, however, the *Preschool Education Law* 幼稚教育法 was promulgated in 1981 to set basic standards for preschools. This law covers kindergartens' organization, the number of pupils allowed per class, required personnel qualifications, minimum standards for facilities, and financial penalties for violations.

According to the Ministry of Education (MOE), 238,787 children attended 2,874 registered preschools in SY1998. Of the registered schools, 1,065 were public schools, and the remaining 1,809 were private. Registered kindergartens accommodated 24.56 percent of the three- to five-year-olds eligible for schooling.

Another 263,641 children attended 2,539 crèche and nursery schools, raising the total enrollment to 40 percent or more for this age group. Nevertheless, the preschool enrollment rate is still much lower than the 80 to 90 percent found in many developed nations.

About 63 percent of registered kindergartens are private institutions, and therefore have higher tuition. Some 409 of Taiwan's kindergartens, or about one-seventh of them, are in Taipei, and 68 percent of them are private. Private kindergartens in metropolitan areas usually have fewer problems recruiting pupils, because most parents want their children to get a head start in the highly competitive educational system. Outside the larger cities, however, private preschool fees are often a burden for most average-income families. By 1999, some 37 public preschools had been set up in remote, mountainous, and outlying areas.

The MOE has recognized the widespread desire among parents to send their children to preschool, and it has tried to increase the number of these schools by affiliating them with existing elementary schools, often using the same school facilities. Public kindergartens set up by local governments are also encouraged. The central government hopes that preschool enrollment will reach 80 percent of the age group as soon as possible.

As noted in *A Report on ROC Education* 中華民國教育報告書 published in 1995 by the MOE, about 20 percent of private kindergartens in operation are not registered, and therefore unregulated. Although they help to overcome the shortfall in needed schools, many have poor teaching quality and learning conditions that can jeopardize the rights and safety of their pupils. To redress the situation, the MOE helps private, unregistered kindergartens to restructure in accordance with the law.

In 1983, the MOE first formulated the *Measures for Encouraging Private Preschool Development* 私立幼稚園獎勵辦法 to stimulate positive growth of well-established preschools. This adjusted the preschool system in several ways, such as restricting the number of pupils per class and providing more on-the-job training programs for teachers. This has greatly improved the pupil-to-teacher ratio (13.95 pupils to one teacher in SY1997). The MOE lowered the number of students again to 25.26 per class in 1998.

In 1995, the MOE promulgated the *Establishment Standard for Universities and Colleges Offering Teacher Education* 大學校院教育學程師資及設立標準, which created a regular channel for training teachers in the preschool system. Twelve on-the-job training courses were conducted at normal colleges for more than 1,200 teachers.

In 1999, a mid-range plan for the development and improvement of preschool education was formulated to strengthen related legislation, administration, teaching quality, evaluation and the supervisory system. The MOE is constantly reviewing preschool curricula to ensure that these schools fulfill the purposes stipulated in the *Preschool Education Law*. Preschool education helps to foster good habits, promote basic physical and mental development, and enrich children's living experiences.

Fundamental Education

The *Constitution of the Republic of China* entitles all children to at least six years of basic education. Building upon this constitutional right, the *National Education Law* 國民教育法,

Public schools seek to provide a well-rounded and high-quality education to students. These students at Taipei's Min-tsu Elementary School are attending an outdoor art class.

promulgated in 1979, stipulates that all school-age children (between six and 15) must attend six years of public elementary school and three years of junior high school. Exceptions to this rule are children with special educational needs, students who spend time in the supplementary education track, and a small number of students in experimental schools (all discussed elsewhere in this chapter).

In 1982, when the *Statute of Compulsory School Attendance* 強迫入學條例 was revised, the law expressly stated that parents or guardians of children between six and 15 are obliged to send them to school or be subjected to fines and other penalties. To enforce this statute, the Compulsory Attendance Committee 強迫入學委員會 was set up at different levels of local governments.

In SY1998, the net enrollment rate of students eligible for universal education was 99.94 percent. Almost all (99.69 percent) children eligible to begin the first year of elementary school enrolled that year as required by the ROC government, leaving only 972 children unenrolled. Also that year, 99.60 percent of the elementary school graduates went on to junior high, and 93.94 percent of the junior high school graduates continued their studies.

During the same school year, Taiwan had 1.91 million students attending 2,557 regular elementary schools, more than 1.01 million students enrolled in 715 regular junior high schools, and small numbers attending experimental elementary and junior high schools. Although the compulsory education system is the training ground for all children, a larger percentage of students are now continuing their education. In 1950, about 94 percent of all students were in either elementary or junior high schools (i.e., only 3.7 percent were in high school programs or above); in 1998, only 55.98 percent were.

After taking exams that are open to all students, 93.94 percent of those who completed their compulsory education in SY1998 pursued their studies further. Even though the remaining 6.06 percent of them (less than 23,000 students) are expected to enter the unskilled labor market or work at marginal jobs, the MOE has designed a program to help these former students acquire more skills (see section on Junior High School).

Elementary Education

Elementary schooling is the first formal education children receive, and the paramount aim is literacy. In 1952, about 42 percent of the Taiwan population could not read and write, elementary school graduates accounted for 77.5 percent of the total number of graduates. In the 15 years that followed, the population's general educational level improved as more and more children went on to secondary education. By 1998, the illiteracy rate had dropped to 5.34 percent, and it is still falling.

The implementation of universal elementary education has been a success. In 1967, about 97.52 percent of the students aged six to 12 were enrolled in school. By SY1998, the enrollment rate was 99.94 percent, with an average of less than 32 students per class.

In 1968, when the government introduced nine-year compulsory education, elementary school graduates accounted for 57.35 percent of Taiwan's total graduates. By SY1998, they accounted for 25.65 percent of the total, a strong indication that the general level of education has been raised. In 1998, the government spent about US$2,117 on each elementary school student, roughly 4.1 times as much as was spent a decade ago. Of the 1,910,681 students in 2,557 elementary schools in SY1998, about 99.18 percent of those that graduated continued on to junior high. Despite the high promotion rate, that still leaves approximately 1,250 children (with 310,968 graduates) who dropped out of the educational system at an early age.

1998-99 Mainstream Fundamental and Secondary Educational Resources

	Preschool	Elementary School	Junior High	Senior High	Senior Vocational
Schools	2,874	2,557	715	242	201
Students	238,787	1,910,681	1,009,309	311,838	493,033
Faculties	9,455	59,869	27,007	7,105	10,854

Source: *Education Statistics of the ROC 1999*, Ministry of Education.

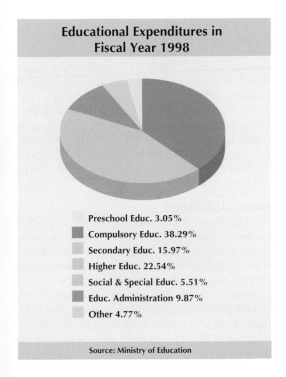

Educational Expenditures in Fiscal Year 1998

Preschool Educ. 3.05%

Compulsory Educ. 38.29%

Secondary Educ. 15.97%

Higher Educ. 22.54%

Social & Special Educ. 5.51%

Educ. Administration 9.87%

Other 4.77%

Source: Ministry of Education

Junior High School

In the ROC educational system, the three-year junior high school program is similar to grades seven through nine in the United States. Before 1968, junior high school education was optional. Students at this level accounted for less than 15 percent of the total graduates in 1950, and less than one-quarter in 1968.

Junior high school, often referred to as "intermediate education" in Taiwan, is divided into academic and vocational tracks. The future of each child is profoundly affected by the decisions made by educational authorities during these intermediate years. After completing three years of junior high school courses, graduates of both tracks must pass open examinations in their respective tracks in order to enter senior high school or senior vocational school, both of which are also three-year programs. It is no longer difficult for students to transfer from one track to the other. Junior graduates of both tracks can choose to transfer to senior high school, senior vocational school, and five-year college by application, recommendation and selection, or through examination.

According to the *National Education Law*, any ROC citizen between 12 and 15 years of age is eligible for public junior high school education, but also have the option of attending private schools. In SY1998, there were 1,009,309 students attending 715 junior high schools, with most classes containing 38.68 students. With regard to private schools, only 92,141 students were registered in the nine private schools around the island.

In SY1998, about 93.94 percent of all junior high graduates continued their studies in either senior high or vocational schools. A total of 223,244 people sat for the joint public senior high-school entrance examinations 公立高中聯招, and roughly 35 percent were accepted.

The junior high vocational program was abolished in 1970 after the implementation of nine-year compulsory education two years earlier. Some of the vocational courses were merged into the junior high curriculum, in line with Article 7 of the *National Education Law*. This law states that junior high school curricula must meet both academic and vocational needs, and stipulates that technical courses should be included in junior high schools. Although specialized preparation for college or career usually begins at this level, specific vocational training is not particularly emphasized.

In 1992, the MOE implemented a program called the Prolonged National Education Based Upon Vocational Education 延長以職業教育為主的國民教育. In 1993, the program became an extension of the nine-year compulsory education system. Technical training courses begin in the third year for junior high students who do not wish to study further in a general education curriculum. Upon graduation, they may also enroll in vocational schools that provide a minimum of one more year of vocational training. In 1995, this program was transformed into the Practical Technical Program 實用技能班. Some 46,266 junior high graduates attended the program in SY1998.

In an attempt to reduce the pressures caused by keen competition in senior high school entrance examinations, the MOE is planning to introduce the *Implementation Policies for Pedagogic Innovations at the Elementary and Secondary Levels* 加強輔導中小學正常教學實施要點. These policies will set up alternatives to the entrance exams by establishing experimental bilateral (combined vocational and academic) high schools 綜合高中 and comprehensive junior-senior high schools 完全中學, as well as a program entitled the *Voluntary Promotion Scheme for Junior High School Graduates Entering Senior High Schools* 國民中學畢業生自願就學輔導方案. These alternatives will give students a more diversified educational system with different channels for completing their junior high and senior high education.

Secondary Education

The secondary school in the ROC is a comprehensive institution that provides students with various types of educational programs for their intellectual development and career interests. The system of schooling after the nine-year compulsory curriculum is a multilateral system in which students are assigned to different types of schools based on a range of factors. The majority of students in the mainstream educational system will enter one of three types of institutions after junior high school. Programs vary in length, although those geared for college entrance are usually the longest and most difficult, terminating with rigorous examinations in the student's late teens.

In SY1998, there were 364,455 junior high graduates: 29.69 percent (108,214 students) entered senior high schools, 41.93 percent (152,824 students) went to three-year senior vocational schools, and 7.07 percent (28,051 students) studied at supplementary senior vocational schools, 9.45 percent (34,438 students) went directly to five-year junior colleges 五專, which also cover a student's high school years, and 18,839 (5.17 percent) went on to attend the Practical Technical Program. Only about 6 percent of the students who completed their nine years of compulsory education did not continue their schooling. Senior high schools focus primarily on training students to pass the Joint University Entrance Examinations 大學聯考 (JUEE) after 12th grade, which is a requirement for all students wanting to enter college. Entrance into all of these institutions, except for the Practical Technical Program and a few other experimental cases, is by competitive examination. The MOE is planning on making the Practical Technical Program a compulsory tenth year of education for those who do not continue their studies.

Senior High School

The three-year senior high school program prepares students aged 15 to 18 for learning special fields of knowledge, as well as for college study. In 1950, there were 62 senior high schools serving 18,866 students islandwide. Beginning in the 1970s, senior high schools entered a period of phenomenal growth. By 1972, there were 203 senior high schools with an enrollment of 197,151 students, more than ten times the number of students in 1950.

From 1971 to 1982, the number of students admitted to senior high schools was gradually reduced, while the number of students entering senior vocational schools increased. This was done in order to meet the growing demand for skilled workers needed to sustain the rapid economic development of the time. Later, when demands for high-quality professional laborers increased, educational policies were reversed, cutting down on the supply of senior vocational school students and increasing the number of students admitted into senior high schools.

By SY1998, senior high school students totaled 311,838, and the ratio of senior high school students to those in senior vocational schools was 38.7:61.3. Under the current education system, senior high graduates have two main options: either pursue study at a university or college, or attend a two-year junior college after one year of work experience, provided that they have passed the relevant entrance examinations. About 67 percent of senior high school graduates chose to pursue higher education in 1998.

The population of college students has increased dramatically in recent years as the number of universities rose to 39 as of 1998. College life is no longer the exclusive domain of the younger generation.

In line with the policy of providing all students the opportunity for secondary education, the ROC has made an effort to democratize the educational system. This would allow all levels of training to be integrated while maintaining ~~ugh~~ variety to meet the many different needs ~~of~~ students. The *Voluntary Promotion Scheme for Junior High School Graduates Entering Senior High Schools* calls for a unitary system in which experimental classes or schools would provide students with the option of attending a comprehensive junior-senior high school. Basically, this would allow students to progress uninterruptedly from the first year of junior high school through senior high school without having to take the competitive entrance examinations.

Senior Vocational School

The purpose of vocational schools is to equip youths between the ages of 15 and 22 with vocational knowledge and skills. In 1950, there were 77 vocational schools, comprising one senior vocational school, 44 junior vocational schools, and 32 junior-senior vocational schools enrolling a total of 335,524 students. The number of junior vocational schools and students dropped in the subsequent years, and by 1968, all junior vocational schools had stopped enrolling new classes. With the abolishment of the junior high vocational program in 1970, the only vocational schools now are senior vocational schools.

In SY1998, a total of 493,055 students attended 201 senior vocational schools and 90 senior high schools with vocational classes. Specialized high schools include those particularly designed for the study of art, music, business, agriculture, specific trades, and industrial occupations, as well as paraprofessional occupations such as nursing and midwifery. About 42 percent of the students majored in engineering, 38.84 percent in commerce, 3.68 percent in agriculture, and 15.65 percent in maritime and marine products, medical care, home economics, and the arts.

A senior vocational school graduate may choose to either take a job or continue with their studies, assuming they pass the relevant entrance examinations. Continued studies include attending a four-year institute of technology, a university, an independent college, or a two-year junior college. In 1998, about 24.74 percent of senior vocational school graduates entered an institution of advanced education or a noncollegiate postsecondary school.

Current wisdom suggests that the ideal proportion of senior high school students to senior

vocational school students is 38.7:61.3, and that admissions and facilities should be adjusted accordingly. Some vocational classes are already being affiliated with senior high schools, and there has been considerable expansion in the vocational courses offered in all secondary schools.

Bilateral High School

Since 1996, several experimental bilateral high schools have combined vocational and academic programs under the same roof. This development has enabled students to select from a much wider range of courses before distinguishing an aptitude for either the academic or vocational tracks. Subjects to be covered in bilateral high schools as part of the general education for junior high students include: a first and second language, mathematics, social and natural sciences, the arts, domestic science, physical education, extracurricular activities, and vocational education. Various technical courses are provided for students taking skilled trades and semiprofessional careers. Plans have been made to further include junior college and college courses at this stage while a minimum of 160 credits are required for students upon graduation. Nevertheless, all students of such experimental bilateral schools must still fulfill the same general requirements for graduation as in other high schools.

There are several prospective options for students with this background: they may either enter the labor market immediately after graduation, or take the joint entrance exams for college, four-year institutes of technology, two-year junior colleges, or enter the above institutions through recommendatory selection and recommendatory examination. As of SY1998, there were 34,851 students enrolled in the 62 experimental bilateral high schools nationwide.

Higher Education

Higher education, also called post-secondary education or tertiary education, includes a variety of programs beyond secondary schools. In the ROC, such education is offered at junior

Higher Education Institutional Growth 1988/1998		
	1988	*1998*
Schools	109	137
Students	496,530	915,921
Faculties	23,809	40,149

Source: Ministry of Education

colleges, colleges, universities, and graduate programs. College and university enrollment in SY1998 was 40.66 per 1,000 of the total population, ranking the ROC comparatively high in the world.

Junior colleges focus primarily on applied sciences, providing well-trained technicians for the labor market. Other than the five-year junior colleges, which usually enroll students straight out of junior high schools, there are also two-year junior colleges, technical and other colleges, and universities for senior high graduates. All colleges and universities must be entered by passing the JUEE, although exams will vary depending on the particular program. For example, engineering programs are entered through a nationwide joint examination, whereas business programs are entered via a regional joint examination.

In theory, students can test into any of these institutions from either senior high or senior vocational schools. Moreover, students who complete any junior college program may retake the JUEE to enter college or university as freshmen. If the college or university offers it, they may also transfer in by taking tests held by the individual departments, entering as sophomores or juniors. Private medical colleges enroll transfer students through a joint entrance examination.

Finally, ROC universities and colleges offer a wide variety of master's and doctoral programs which are also entered through competitive examination. Students may also go directly from university or college into these programs.

In 1950, seven institutions offered higher education programs serving 6,665 students. One university had three graduate-level departments. Since then, the government has established additional colleges and universities, and has also allowed the private sector to set up such institutions. By 1974, 13 public and 19 private higher education institutions had been opened. The number of higher education institutions in SY1998 had reached 137, including 39 universities, 45 independent colleges, and 53 junior colleges. Approximately 915,921 undergraduates were enrolled in these institutions, and 841 graduate programs for 53,870 graduate students attached to them.

Junior College

Fifty-three of Taiwan's 57 junior colleges are private. They are categorized according to their specialization, with the main ones being industry and business, paraprofessional, commerce, industrial and business management, maritime affairs, pharmacy, medical care, foreign languages, and food catering. By SY1998, 8.67 percent of students at different levels of the educational system were in junior colleges, a dramatic contrast with 0.12 percent in 1950.

Five-year Junior College

A junior college under this category admits junior high school graduates for five years of specialized or paraprofessional training, except for those majoring in pharmacy, veterinary medicine, marine engineering, or navigation, who are required to take an additional year of training. There are 47 junior colleges providing five-year courses. In SY1998, 197,855 students were enrolled in 3,986 classes, with 33,902 students graduating in SY1997. Less tha~ ~nt percent of the total number of students stud~ in public institutions.

Three-year Junior College

Three-year junior colleges have shrunk in number and importance and stopped enrolling freshmen in SY1996. Most three-year junior colleges

are being upgraded to become independent colleges. In SY1998, only a few students were still in this category. After their graduation, there will be no three-year junior colleges in operation.

Two-year Junior College

This category admits senior vocational school graduates majoring in different subjects, such as business administration, engineering, math, computer science, medical care, agriculture, forestry, fishery, and home economics. Students with work

Taiwan Area Libraries

National Library	1
Public Libraries	435
College Libraries	158
Senior High & Vocational School Libraries	440
Junior High School Libraries	719
Elementary School Libraries	2,540
Professional Libraries	537
Total	4,830

Note: Branches libraries are not included.
Source: *Libraries Survey in the Taiwan and Fukien Areas*, National Central Library.

National Central Library, Taiwan Branch

By the end of 1998, there were 4,830 libraries and information centers in the Taiwan area. The National Central Library (NCL) under the Ministry of Education handles the collection, storage, and review of ROC books and literature, as well as general research and guidance for all Taiwan's libraries. By 1998, the NCL had a collection of 1,618,058 books (including books in Chinese and other languages, old rare books, and non-book documents), 30 LD databases, four on-line databases, about 2,000 electronic magazines, 24,304 periodicals, and 418 newspapers. The NCL has large collections of rare books, Chinese calligraphic writings, governmental publications, and microfilms.

In 1981, the NCL established a Center for Chinese Studies 漢學研究中心, collecting global information on Chinese cultural studies. In 1988, the NCL implemented a library information network program and established a national catalog center. Since 1991, its network has connected the libraries of Taiwan's colleges and universities. In August 1993, the NCL began to issue its Chinese catalogue and Chinese-language periodicals. At present, the development of the National Bibliographic Information Network (NBINet) has reached its second phase since its establishment in December1994, sharing and cooperating with 32 libraries in compiling a 1.03 million-item catalog. Due to increasingly frequent cross-strait exchanges, the NCL has set up a Mainland China Information Center.

On January 9, 1996, the Legislature amended *the Organic Law of the National Central Library* 國家圖書館組織條例 and changed the Chinese name of the NCL to *Kuo-chia t'u-shu-kuan* 國家圖書館, the English name has not changed. Since July 1989, the NCL has provided a free-of-charge ISBN system to publishers. As of June 1999, 4,629 publishers were using the system. To promote the internationalization of the ROC publishing industry, the NCL assists ROC publishers in participating in major international book fairs.

---

experience can also seek admission. The civil engineering program requires an additional year of training. In SY1998, there were 254,427 students studying in 4,836 classes. A total of 79,956 students graduated from two-year junior colleges in 1997.

University, Graduate School, and Other Options

Most college and university programs last four years, with the exception of teachers and civil engineering (which require five years) and undergraduate law and medical programs (which last from five to seven years). In 1998, 368,940 students were registered in 39 universities, 20 of which were national universities. Meanwhile, another 45 independent colleges served the needs of 94,635 students.

Generally, institutes of technology recruit students through examinations, with two-year institutes of technology admitting junior college graduates and four-year institutes of technology admitting senior vocational school graduates.

A five-year post-bachelor's degree program of Chinese medicine recruits college graduates

who have a minimum of four credits in each of the subjects of biology, organic chemistry, physics, and mathematics. Graduate programs usually admit students only after they have passed relevant examinations. Junior college graduates with relevant work experience are also allowed to take part in graduate school entrance exams.

Master's degree programs last one to four years. Doctorate programs admit master's degree holders or college graduates majoring in medicine. Such programs require at least two to seven years to finish. In 1998, there were 53,870 students studying in 841 graduate schools, with 10,845 studying for doctorates. In SY1997, 1,282 doctorates, 14,146 master's degrees, and 85,802 bachelor's degrees were awarded.

Alternatives to Mainstream Education

Special Education

This category includes programs and facilities for gifted children, as well as those with special needs due to handicaps or learning disabilities. Special schools in the latter category focus on blind, deaf, physically handicapped, and mentally retarded students. For the most part, these schools are run by the government and parallel the mainstream educational system, extending from preschool through senior vocational school. In SY1998, there were 5,588 students in 20 such schools. In addition, 2,345 mainstream schools offered 4,196 classes for another 81,632 special students (disabled or gifted).

In SY1998, three schools for the blind had an enrollment of 468 students, four schools for the deaf enrolled a total of 1,111 students, nine schools for mentally retarded pupils had 3,417 students, and one school for the physically handicapped had 395 students, and three special schools for 197 students with learning problems.

Additionally, based on the *Resourceful Education Program* 資源教育方案 has helped establish 679 resource rooms 資源班 providing facilities for 24,914 students of special needs at the elementary and high school levels. At the undergraduate level, 1,153 students benefited from the supportive system provided in junior colleges, colleges, and universities.

In SY1998, a total of 136 schools offered classes for "gifted" students 資賦優異生 and another 344 schools provided classes for "talented" students 才藝優異生. Most gifted and talented children are still educated in regular schools, but have special provisions to meet their needs. Gifted students are classified as those who have superior abilities in either mathematics or the sciences, whereas talented students are those who excel in such areas as music, fine arts, dance, or sports.

Since the formulation of the *Special Education Law* 特殊教育法 in 1984, handicapped children or those with other health problems have been allowed to receive their education at home. In SY1998, home study services were provided to 384 special students, 180 of which were in Taipei City.

Social Education

The Ministry of Education supports a number of social education programs in line with the *Social Education Law* 社會教育法. These programs include support for supplementary education, adult education, and other services such as museums, libraries, exhibition centers, social education centers, and cultural centers. With respect to training, social education programs include courses in Mandarin Chinese (for native speakers of regional dialects) and family education.

Supplementary Education

Supplementary schools may be private or public. Most students receive certificates upon graduation, and some may receive diplomas equivalent in level to those in the mainstream system by passing examinations. The top schools in the supplementary system are open universities. National Open University 國立空中大學 has been in operation since 1987 while the new Open University of Kaohsiung 高雄市立空中大學 in south Taiwan started to enroll undergraduates in 1997.

Supplementary education can be divided into three types: compulsory, advanced, and short-term. Supplementary schools are attached to regular schools at their corresponding levels in the mainstream either as correspondence or night schools. Weekend classes are also offered. The supplementary system does not include courses with university equivalence.

Supplementary compulsory education, also known as continuing education, is a formal educational activity for adults, and includes elementary through junior high school level courses. Supplementary advanced education, or extension education, enrolls students at three different levels: senior high school and senior vocational school, junior college, and college. After completing the prescribed courses of study and passing the qualification exams, graduates earn mainstream-equivalent diplomas. Finally, those enrolled in short-term supplementary education are in either general or technical educational courses.

This gardening class at one of the many new community area colleges, is part of the government's commitment to continuous adult education.

In SY1998, 330,544 students attended 936 supplementary schools: approximately 46,700 were in 716 elementary and junior high schools; 5,306 senior high and 138,713 (the majority) senior vocational students enrolled in 229 schools, 45,589 were enrolled in 36 junior colleges, 837 students studied in two supplementary colleges, and 44,622 were with the two open universities. There are three kinds of undergraduates in open universities; regular students, students of electives, and independent students. Regular students to be admitted must be aged 20 or over and have required senior high or equivalent qualification. Students of electives are admitted through application and must be at least 18 years of age. In SY1998, there were 44,622 regular students, 1,154 of whom were graduates. Short-term supplementary education restricted the term to 18 months and only provide technical courses and art and science courses.

In addition, 48,872 students participated in the Practical Technical Program which aimed at providing practical skills and craftsmanship for those who do not wish to continue academic studies.

Short-term Supplementary Classes

Large numbers of private cram schools 補習班 exist to prepare students for the senior high school and university entrance examinations. Other cram schools specialize in such subjects as foreign languages, children's classes, preparation for the civil service exams, and preparation for TOEFL and other exams required for study abroad. As of 1998, there were 5,536 such schools registered with the government (a much larger number operate without licenses). About 17 percent were in Taipei City, 14 percent in Kaohsiung City, and 10.31 percent in Taipei County. The metropolitan areas have the largest market for short-term supplementary education.

Approximately 1,891,100 students studied in cram schools in SY1998. It is also a large number of students attended review classes at such schools in order to gain academic assistance in general subjects, with the aim of passing entrance examinations. Cram schools fulfill a definite need in Taiwan's educational system, and as such, the government is exercising closer supervision of their safety and educational standards.

International Exchanges

Cultural Exchanges

The Ministry of Education also sponsors activities which help to enhance international cultural and educational exchanges. In 1998, the MOE offered grants to domestic participants in 74 international academic meetings overseas. A thousand outstanding foreign professionals were invited to share their expertise with scholars and students in Taiwan. Sponsored by the MOE, cultural exchanges were promoted through the sending of good will missions overseas. In the last few years, famous performance groups such as the Cloud Gate Dance Troupe have been invited to perform in the United States and Europe.

Scholastic Exchanges

Cultural exchange agreements have also been signed with friendly nations to strengthen scholastic exchanges. Scholarships have been offered as well as donations of books and other publications. In SY1998, 5,109 foreign students coming from 87 countries studied in the ROC. About 69 percent of these students from Asia, and approximately 92 percent of them majored in the humanities.

Before 1989, government permission was required for all students studying abroad. According to official records, the number of ROC students studying abroad increased annually between 1973 and 1989. In 1988, 6,382 of the 7,122 ROC students going abroad went to the United States. According to US statistics, around 31,000 Taiwan students are studying in the US.

Other Educational Options

Adult education classes are offered in such areas as writing skills, practical mathematics, and civics. Technical classes in basic job skills are also available at training centers. In addition, the National Open University offers classes through radio and correspondence that can lead to a bachelor's degree. The Open University of Kaohsiung is the second such university with such courses and is the first to be located in southern Taiwan. These open university programs are available to all senior high school graduates or equivalently qualified secondary education students. The Educational Broadcasting Station 教育廣播電台, Chinese Television System 中華電視股份有限公司, and school-on-the-air 空中教學 also offer educational classes.

ROC Educational Reform

Mixed Success

The ROC educational system is, by many standards, a mixed success. On the one hand, literacy is high and educational opportunities are varied and widely accessible. A full one-fifth of the total population is enrolled in some form of educational institution or program, and students generally emerge from the mainstream system skilled, well-informed, and self-disciplined.

On the other hand, however, calls for sweeping reform of the educational system are quite common. In particular, the Joint University Entrance Examinations often come under frequent criticism. At present, the MOE is investigating ways to reduce the pressure of such examinations, as well as give more room to colleges and universities to govern themselves and set their own curricula.

Institutional reform has been under study for some time now. In July 1994, the Seventh National Education Conference 第七屆全國教育會議 pointed out the need for pluralized cultural development and improved education. Among the highlighted issues are the distribution of educational resources, revising the structure and flexibility of the curriculum, improving teacher quality, enhancing lifelong education, beefing up physical education courses, and promoting cross-strait academic exchanges.

Educational reform received a boost with the formation of the Commission on Educational Reform 教育改革審議委員會(CER) in late 1994, headed by Nobel laureate Lee Yuan-tseh 李遠哲. The commission was responsible for diagnosing the problems of the present education system and suggested possible reforms. The commission's report was made public at the end of 1996 and included several reforms, such as the implementation of pluralistic channels to provide students with other means to advance to higher levels of education without having to rely solely on examinations. In the past, all junior high graduates were required to pass joint examinations in order to enter senior high schools; however, starting in SY1998, Taipei City has become one of the first designated cities to implement educational reforms allowing junior high school students to advance to senior high school without passing an entrance exam (through a comprehensive junior-senior high school program). The report also discussed the establishment of a comprehensive six-year high school secondary education. The key concept underlying these reform efforts is flexibility, as the existing system is considered to be too rigid. Other areas examined include the optimal allocation of educational resources, adult education (including retraining), revised teacher training with innovative teaching techniques, and curriculum changes.

Inordinate Emphasis on Examinations

There is growing dissatisfaction with the emphasis on examinations, especially the university entrance exam system. Currently, students are offered uniform national examinations depending upon the type of institution they hope to enter and the field (social science, medicine, and etc.) they wish to study.

A major criticism is that this highly competitive system places tremendous stress on young people. A typical college-bound 17-year-old will devote at least a year or two of his or her life to test preparation, often attending both regular senior high school and cram schools at the same time. Many students who fail to gain admission to the school or their chosen field will usually choose to spend another full year preparing in cram schools in order to retake the exam.

Another main criticism is that the exams emphasize rote memorization of texts. Critics of the system, as well as many students, feel that exam-takers are forced to memorize vast amounts of disconnected trivia which are regurgitated during the exams and then forgotten. The emphasis on preparation for examinations based on rote memorization is, in fact, a problem that permeates the entire school system. Reformers say that students are denied the opportunity to develop their imagination and capacity for independent thinking, arguing that these skills, rather than the self-discipline for memorization and the deference to authority taught by the existing system, are more suited to contemporary needs.

Shortage of Resources and Opportunities

Many of the problems of the school system center around the inadequacy of resources, especially complaints about high student-to-teacher ratios and high student-to-classroom ratios. These ratios partially reflect the instruction quality and the resources and facilities students can utilize. Although the student-to-classroom ratios remain rather high (25.26 for preschool, 31.91 for elementary, 37.37 for junior high, 43.89 for senior high, and 45.43 for senior vocational schools), improvement in the student-to-teacher ratios have been made. By SY1998, the preschool student-to-teacher ratio was 13.42, 20.11 for elementary, 16.80 for junior high, and 20.04 for senior high.

The state of intense competition for entry into high schools and universities is fundamentally the result of a demand for far more places than currently exist in these institutions. In recent years the government has allowed many colleges to expand and upgrade to university status in an effort to alleviate these demands. Moreover, plans are currently being discussed to restructure the ratio of students in senior high schools as compared to those in senior vocational schools. Currently, the ratio is roughly 38.7:61.3; reformers wish to adjust it to 50:50. (For related data, see the sections on Fundamental Education and Junior Colleges.)

Reform Measures

New Paths for Advancement

A few experimental programs to provide alternative routes to higher education are now being tested. The experimental comprehensive junior-senior high schools and bilateral high schools are in many ways considered breakthroughs in secondary education and are expected to begin operation in SY1999. There are now a number of other experimental programs for senior high school entrance: by being assigned in accordance with the *Voluntary Promotion Scheme* or by promotion within the same schools. Special education students may be recommended in accordance with the *Special Recommendation Measures of Advancement Governing the Age and Years of Study for Special Students* 特殊教育學生入學年齡修業年限及保送甄試升學辦法.

Senior high schools or high schools in the designated experimental districts are free to join in the experimental programs, and positions are being made available to junior high school graduates. In some experimental programs, advancement to successive levels is determined by each student's in-school performances (cumulative grades at the rate of 20 percent for first-year grades and 40 percent for each of the next two years), achievement test scores, or assessment of early promotion test scores. Other experimental methods combine grades with examinations. Most of the experimental high schools are required to either set up a senior high school admission board or be placed under the auspices of a district board.

For higher education, 71,890 students passed the JUEE in 1998, with 6,949 senior high school graduates entering college through recommendation and selection. High school graduates recommended and selected are required to pass the general *Scholastic Attainment Test of College-Bound Seniors* 學科能力測驗 and the *College Testing of Proficiency for Selected Subjects of College-Bound Students* 指定項目甄試. In 1998, about 330 seniors were admitted to college via special recommendation which benefit special and disadvantaged students. And 585 applicants were admitted by 20 colleges in the same school year.

Curriculum Revisions

New teaching methods and textbooks are also being introduced. In 1992, the MOE introduced an experimental interactive teaching method for mathematics designed by a group of math teachers and other educators interested in reform. These methods were somewhat successful and are still being implemented today. Social science and history textbooks are being greatly rewritten, and ever since SY1996, the MOE has given elementary school administrators a free hand to select their own textbooks. Aside from the standardized version of elementary textbooks edited and published by the government, privately published texts, which are approved by the competent authorities, are now in use as well.

One important change is that there is now less emphasis on general Chinese history, with more attention being devoted to Taiwan's culture and history as well as world topics. Discussions are continuing about phasing out those parts of the JUEE system which deal exclusively with the Three Principles of the People and the thoughts of Dr. Sun Yat-sen. While Dr. Sun remains a revered historical figure, it is thought that the time has come for schools to broaden discussion of political ideology.

Greater Number of Choices

Students are beginning to have more opportunities to choose electives, rather than be rigidly limited to a single curriculum. Perhaps the clearest example of this increased flexibility, is the MOE's announcement that it is selecting schools for an experimental program in which students would not have to define their major fields of study during their first year or two in college. Such a program would allow students to avoid being stuck with a major they had chosen while still a high school senior. This reform should also make schools more responsive to market demands for various fields, and thus better able to meet the needs of society.

The MOE is also continuing its policy, begun in 1993, of gradually reducing class sizes for all junior high and elementary schools. For junior high schools, a target of 35 pupils or fewer is being set, while for elementary schools a class size limit of 35 or fewer is being sought. All measures are of course subject to the availability of financial resources, teachers, and the land for school construction. At the elementary school level, the high priority goal to reduce the class size of first graders has been reached. By the SY1998, the class size of over 95 percent of all first grades had been reduced to 35 students or less.

Non-governmental reform efforts are also underway. Two well-known experimental elementary schools, the Forest School 森林小學 and the Caterpillar School 毛毛蟲學苑, have both been established with small class sizes, low student-teacher ratios, and a curriculum that stresses creativity, personal growth and dignity, independent thinking, and harmony with nature. Civic reform groups are also currently lobbying the government to make it easier to establish such private educational institutions below the university level.

A Mixed Reform Outlook

The demand for increased educational resources will inevitably compete with other demands on the state budget, such as increased social welfare and environmental protection. Infrastructural changes in the budgetary allocation for educational purposes are foreseeable with the adoption of the new *Additional Articles of the Constitution of the Republic of China* in 1997. Indeed, after 1997, even national universities will have to raise part of their own funding so that more resources can be allocated to fundamental (compulsory) education. In 1999, there were 24 universities joining in fund-raising. A beginning target of 20 percent self-raised funding has been encouraged. In the beginning stages this will be accompanied by a 2 percent decrease in government budget annually. Any funding that exceeds that rate will not lead to further cuts in government budgetary support up to 25 percent. That is, 75 percent of the budget will still be provided by the government as a stable source of financial support.

While alternative schools may come close to providing ideal, flexible, humanistic, and pluralistic education, they are also very expensive. Moreover, despite the flaws of the monolithic exam system with its demands for rote memorization, its universality and uniformity does create a level playing field for all higher education aspirants. In an attempt to find a balance, the narrow gate of JUEE was opened wider in SY1999 to allow more people into higher education. In that year about 59.83 percent of the people who took the JUEE passed. These figures, combined with increases in the number of universities, colleges, and junior colleges to a total of 137, has allowed the once highly competitive JUEE to fulfill the needs of more and more people. It is clear that reform is the wave of the future, and more and more changes in the educational system will surely follow.

18
Science and Technology

Taiwan ranks
number one in
the world in
nine categories
of information
technology
products,
including com-
puter moth-
erboards, mice,
image scanners,
keyboards, power
supplies, moni-
tors, network
cards, modems,
and graphic cards.

News of that handy device, the wheelbarrow, took almost 1,000 years to reach Europe from China. Similarly, fourteen centuries elapsed before something as simple as a screw was brought to China from the West. The tremendous lag in the diffusion of fundamental technology slowed the economic and intellectual growth of both East and West. Such a sluggish pace of technology transfer would be unpardonable in the late 20th century when the ability to design, develop, and produce state-of-the-art technology is a crucial component of economic progress and national strength.

The Republic of China is certainly aware of the need to stay abreast of scientific development. The ROC government has allocated an ever increasing portion of its budget and manpower to the research and development of new technologies. Indeed, the government's education, national defense, and economic policies all focus, to some extent, on the development of scientific expertise. The absolute and relative amounts of funding for R&D in both the public and the private sectors have grown rapidly over the last decade. In 1997, national R&D expenditures totaled 1.91 percent of the GNP. The figure is expected to reach 2.5 percent by the year 2000.

This commitment is born out of pragmatism. Land and natural resources, two essential factors of production, are limited in the Taiwan area. A third factor of production, labor, is becoming increasingly expensive. Where does Taiwan turn for comparative advantage? Brain power.

More people in Taiwan than ever before are graduating with bachelor of science degrees, master of science degrees, or Ph.D.s in hard sciences. More ROC scientists are traveling abroad and more non-Chinese scientists are visiting Taiwan. There are more R&D institutes, more experiments, and more scientific publications in Taiwan than ever before.

Direct scientific research in Taiwan is motivated first by profit—Taiwan's freewheeling market economy provides plenty of incentives for R&D in profitable technology; and second, by the National Science Council, the highest ROC government office charged with coordinating national science and technology policy, which closely coordinates all R&D activities, and funds public-sector scientific and technological research projects through grants and subsidies (see inset, next page).

One major stride taken toward building Taiwan into a high-tech island is the Science and Technology White Paper 科技白皮書, issued by the government for the first time in June 1997. R&D work will be intensified so as to advance the goal of building Taiwan into an Asia-Pacific regional research stronghold by the year 2000. To lay a legal foundation for facilitating science-technology development, the *Basic Law of Science and Technology* 科技基本法, was promulgated on January 20, 1999.

Public Sector Research
NSC-supported

The National Science Council's fiscal 2000 (July 1, 1999, through Dec. 31, 2000) budget registered US$816.8 million. The lion's share of the budget is to be spent on basic and vanguard research projects launched in cooperation with academic institutions, and facility construction and equipment procurement for selected advanced technologies. To support academic research, a total of US$220.54 million worth of grants have been appropriated to projects ranging from natural sciences to humanities and social sciences. In 1998, an amount of US$185 million was given to support 10,550 research projects . At the National Science Council and its subsidiary research centers, some US$408.1 million has been allocated for the following expenses: US$12.84 million for administration,

NSC Research Appropriations

	Support
Natural Sciences & Mathematics	24%
Engineering & Applied Sciences	33%
Life Sciences	24%
Humanities & Social Sciences	13%
Science Education	6%

Source: National Science Council

US$95.4 million for aerospace technology R&D, US$36.71 million for synchronous radiation technology R&D, US$11.27 million for the management of the Science and Technology Information Center 科學技術資料中心, US$5.23 million for experimental animal research, US$11.21 million for the development of precision instruments, and US$18.19 million for the Center for High-performance Computing 高速電腦中心. Furthermore, the NSC has appropriated US$20.37 million for the management of the Hsinchu Science-based Industrial Park 新竹科學工業園區. Remaining funds were deposited in a preparatory fund.

MOEA-supported

While a large portion of the NSC's annual budget goes to financing academic research, the Ministry of Economic Affairs 經濟部 is committed to industry-oriented scientific advancement in order to maintain continuous growth of manufacturing, expedite the transformation of traditional industries and promote technology-intensive industries. In 1998, the MOEA allocated some US$436 million to public and private nonprofit research institutes for applied industrial research as part of its broad-ranging Sci-tech R&D Project 科技研究發展專案計畫. The funds were distributed among the Industrial Technology Research Institute 工業技術研究院 (see ITRI section), with special emphasis on electronic and information technology research, the Chungshan Institute of Science and Technology 中山科學研究院 (CIST, see also Chapter 8, National Defense), and the Institute for Information Industry 資訊工業策進會 (see inset, next page). The MOEA expects that the CIST will take an increasingly larger share of its annual expenditure for sci-tech projects because plans are underway to integrate defense technology into economic development and to open up CIST R&D and production facilities to the private sector. The MOEA also set up an Industrial Technology Information Services Office 產業技術資訊服務推廣計畫專案辦公室 in 1990 to provide a wide range of information covering products, technology, and companies in industries such as aerospace, electronics, mechanics, automation, food, metal, biochemistry, industrial materials, optoelectronics, chemistry, industrial safety, semiconductors, consumer electronics, information technology, shipbuilding, communications, measurement instrumentation, and textiles. Users may access the database at *http://140.96.1.11*.

National Science Council

The National Science Council 國家科學委員會 (NSC) is the highest government organ responsible for promoting and planning overall scientific and technological development in the ROC; setting national science policies; recruiting experts in scientific fields; providing stipends and incentives for researchers; coordinating the scientific and technological research and development projects of other government ministries; reviewing the annual science and technology reports of these ministries; and developing science-based industrial parks.

The National Science Council consists of the heads of government offices that have science or technology projects, the ministers without portfolio 政務委員 in charge of reviewing scientific or technological development, the president of Academia Sinica 中央研究院, the secretary-general of the Executive Yuan 行政院, and noted scientists.

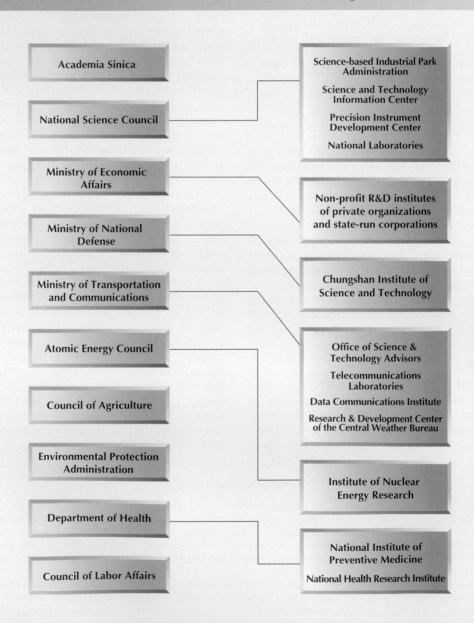

Scientific Research Institutions and Agencies

Academia Sinica

National Science Council

Ministry of Economic Affairs

Ministry of National Defense

Ministry of Transportation and Communications

Atomic Energy Council

Council of Agriculture

Environmental Protection Administration

Department of Health

Council of Labor Affairs

Science-based Industrial Park Administration

Science and Technology Information Center

Precision Instrument Development Center

National Laboratories

Non-profit R&D institutes of private organizations and state-run corporations

Chungshan Institute of Science and Technology

Office of Science & Technology Advisors

Telecommunications Laboratories

Data Communications Institute

Research & Development Center of the Central Weather Bureau

Institute of Nuclear Energy Research

National Institute of Preventive Medicine

National Health Research Institute

Source: Directorate-General of Budget, Accounting and Statistics

Close Public/Private-sector R&D Cooperation

ROC economic policy in recent years has increasingly stressed a cooperative and complementary relationship between government and the private sector in developing Taiwan's economic future. In the area of technology, this generally involves specific, goal-oriented, and time-limited government subsidies. In some cases, the concerted commitment of government-founded research facilities and organizations, to develop further technologies considered key to national development and increased global competitiveness. For the most part, the goal of such government-subsidized research is to develop competitive technology in sufficient time for transfer to the private sector so that Taiwan-based companies can produce increasingly competitive high-tech products and services while private industry works to ultimately shoulder more of the R&D burden itself.

Close cooperation between local industry and government-funded agencies produced particularly promising results in the field of electronics. MOEA appropriations for the Electronics Research and Service Organization (ERSO) under the ITRI amounted to more than US$49.7 million for fiscal 1999. The main projects undertaken by ERSO include the Five-year Deep Sub-micron Technology Development Program 深次微米製造技術發展五年計畫, the Four-year Flat Panel Display Technology Development Program 平面顯示器技術發展四年計畫, and the Four-year Microelectronics System Key Technology Development Program 微電子系統關鍵技術發展四年計畫, and the Four-year RFIC Technology Development Program(射頻積體電路技術發展四年計劃). These four programs consumed nearly 56 percent of the total budget of ERSO, reflecting the high priority placed on continued development in these fields of high-tech industrial growth in the ROC.

The ERSO has enjoyed notable success in its Sub-micron Process Technology Development Project (from the fiscal years 1990-95), which attracted over US$15 billion in investment in 8 inch wafer fabrication as well as memory production capabilities in the local semiconductor indus-

Institute for Information Industry

Founded in 1979 under the Ministry of Economic Affairs, the Institute for Information Industry (III) serves to develop and promote the information industry as part of the overall process of spurring economic development in the ROC. With 1,212 employees (over 55 percent of whom have a master's degree or higher degree in a pertinent field), the III coordinates the efforts of government agencies, the private sector, and academic institutions to build a sound base for the development of Taiwan's information industry. The significance of the III can be seen by the US$110 million in revenue it had generated by mid-1999. The III also provides a variety of training courses for school teachers, computer professionals, and employees of private companies to increase their overall knowledge of information technologies and facilitate computerization in both the public and private sectors. In the past 20 years, over 220,000 people have benefited from the III's training programs.

try. Following this success, the ERSO started the Deep Sub-micron Process Technology Development Project in July 1996, which focuses on the development of the 0.18 µm process and copper/low-K multi-level interconnect technologies. In 1999, excellent results were achieved in the following areas of research: dual damascene etch technology, post-etch cleaning technology for the Cu process, low K polymer etch technology, the DUV photolithography process, low K dielectric process technology, CMP process technology, multilayered Cu interconnect process integration, and low K dielectric process integration.

In the area of flat panel display technology, the ERSO has made the development of Thin Film Transistor Liquid Crystal Display (TFT LCD) a top priority. The ERSO has over the past successfully developed a 3" to 6" color panel for both direct view and projection applications and 10.4" full color, wide-view angle and reflective type TFT LCD modules and systems. A major achievement in 1998 was the development of a

Government Agency Budgets for R&D (in US$ millions)

Government Agency	FY 00	FY 99
Academia Sinica	195	114
Ministry of Economic Affairs	913	561
Ministry of Transportation and Communications	20	13
National Science Council	817	473
Atomic Energy Council	33	17
Council of Agriculture	91	54
Ministry of Education	48	29
Department of Health	72	42
Environmental Protection Administration	2.5	2
Ministry of the Interior	8.0	5
Council of Labor Affairs	6.7	4
Public Construction Commission	1.4	0.3
Research, Development, and Evaluation Commission	--	4.5
Total R&D Budget	2,207	1,319

12.4" Engineering Workstation (EWS), full color TFT LCD module and system. In 1999, this program made many technological breakthroughs; for instance, its large area, low temperature Poly-Si TFT (thin film transistor) devices have a leakage current that is one-tenth that of other world competitors. In addition, micro-slant reflector LCD technology has achieved 32% reflectivity and a 30:1 contrast ratio; MVA and IPS wide view angle LCD technology has reached 75% light efficiency and a viewing angle greater than 70 degrees; and 12.4" SXGA low temperature Poly-Si TFT LCD modules have been successfully designed and created. Plans for future development include: research into an active matrix organic EL display device, wide view angle technology and reflective process, high aperture ratio, high resolution technologies, and thick film field emission display (FED), Crystallized-Silicon light valve LCD technology, and plastic LCD technology.

Research topics in the microelectronics system key technology project include communication and electronic components, image sensors, digital signal processing, and power integrated circuits. Four projects were successfully developed

in 1999: the 3.3V 12bits 2.5MHz ADC (Analog Digital Converter) IC, the 0.35 μm CMOS 128x1024 Active Pixel Sensor (APS), the Voltage Mode PWM Controller IC, and the 3.3V 900MHz CMOS RF IC chipset. Research on the last project, the RF IC chipset, was actually started in July 1998 and was vital to the wireless and mobile communications industry. Its development included a low noise amplifier, mixer, power amplifier, and FSK demodulator. Also achieved in 1999 was the high-frequency (above 25GHz), double poly-bipolar technology IC process.

The above examples represent just a tiny fraction of the entire ERSO research effort in 1996 and 1997. This, in turn, was merely one part of the larger MOEA-sponsored Sci-tech Research Project involving a complex consortium of public and private research institutions conducting research in a number of other areas of key technological development. To further clarify the rich mosaic of technological development research efforts in which various government agencies interact with the public and private research sector in the ROC, several prominent examples of Taiwan's public-sector research institutions and facilities are introduced below.

Public Sector Research Facilities

Science-based Industrial Parks

The first of what is envisioned to be a series of high-technology industrial parks, the Hsinchu Science-based Industrial Park, has been in operation since 1980. Located near National Chiao Tung University 國立交通大學, National Tsing Hua University 國立清華大學, and the Industrial Technology Research Institute, the park is designed as a comprehensive research environment. It contains educational, sports, entertainment, residential, and shopping facilities designed to appeal to engineers of Chinese origin with overseas educational and working experience—especially that gained in the United States. Financial incentives are offered to induce companies to set up operations in the park.

Administered by a division of the National Science Council, the Science-based Industrial Park Administration 科學工業園區管理局, the park has put Taiwan on the world map of such high-tech industries as IC manufacturing and key information industry components. Over the past decade, the park has witnessed remarkable growth in both the number of companies set up in the park and the combined sales these firms have achieved. In 1998, aggregate sales of the 272 firms in the park topped US$13.7 billion, a 2 percent decrease over the preceding year. The 112 IC manufacturers in the park concentrate on producing DRAM and SRAM chips, as well as the development of Application Specific Electronic Module (ASEM) and Multichip Module (MCM) foundry services. IC manufacturing at the park gets a boost from a full range of support industries that handle materials, design, testing, and packaging. Today, these with a turnover of US$6.9 billion companies produce 7.7 percent of the world's IC production value, making Taiwan the fourth largest supplier worldwide after the United States, Japan, and South Korea. The importance of computers and computer peripherals to Taiwan's foreign trade has naturally risen over the past decade, and currently Taiwan ranks number one for global market share in six categories of information technology products,

including notebook PC, mouse, scanner, monitor, card, and modem. For more information on the economic aspects of the ROC's information industry, please see Chapter 10, The Economy.

For the third phase of expansion at the Hsinchu Science-based Industrial Park, basic infrastructure on a 190-hectare site has been completed. Despite the ongoing success of the park, growth at the facility has run up against the realities of land acquisition in Taiwan today. Thus, the Executive Yuan has approved plans to develop a science-based industrial park in adjacent Miaoli County as the fourth phase of the Hsinchu Science-based Industrial Park. The Miaoli facility will primarily be geared toward serving biotechnology.

To ensure that high-tech manufacturers have room to grow, the National Science Council has designated a site in southern Taiwan for a second science-based industrial park. The Tainan Science-based Industrial Park 臺南科學工業園區 will be located on a 638-hectare site between

---

Public Research Enterprises

One of the largest government-run enterprises is the Chinese Petroleum Corporation 中國石油股份有限公司, which has set up a Refining and Manufacturing Research Center 煉製研究中心 and an Exploration Development Research Institute 探採研究中心. The China Petrochemical Development Corporation 中國石油化學工業開發股份有限公司 conducts applied research as does the China Steel Corporation 中國鋼鐵公司. The Taiwan Power Company 臺灣電力公司, usually known as Taipower, has one research institute, the Power Research Institute 電力綜合研究所. The Taiwan Sugar Corporation has two such organizations, the Taiwan Sugar Research Institute and the Animal Industry Research Institute 畜產研究所. The Taiwan Fertilizer Company 臺灣肥料公司, the Taiwan Salt Works 臺灣製鹽總廠, the Taiwan Machinery Manufacturing Corporation 臺灣機械公司, the China Shipbuilding Corporation 中國造船股份有限公司 and Aerospace Industrial Development Corporation 漢翔航空工業股份有限公司 all run research laboratories.

Hsinshih rural township新市鄉 and Shanhua urban township善化鎮 in Tainan County. The choice of locality is meant to capitalize on the agricultural resources of Taiwan's south, and the technological support of institutions nearby, such as the Asian Vegetable Research and Development Center 亞洲 蔬菜研究發展中心 and the Taiwan Sugar Research Institute 臺灣糖業研究所.

The preparatory office of the Tainan Science-based Industrial Park was officially set up on July 8, 1997, and the office has begun operations since June 1998. The park represents part of the government's plan to build Taiwan into a "science and technology island." Presently, plans call for the park to initially focus on serving companies from six major industries: semiconductors, computers and peripherals, telecommunication, optoelectronics, precision machinery, and biotechnology. Efforts are being made to avoid the crowding experienced at the first park by selecting a much larger initial area, and to develop the surrounding neighborhood to accommodate the 70,000 personnel who are projected to eventually work in the new park. As of June 1999, 32 firms of these industries had already received approvals to move into the park, and the MOEA estimates that factories at the park will produce an annual total of US$32.72 billion in goods by the year 2010. The park is also expected to draw substantial investment from the service sector.

Industrial Technology Research Institute

The Industrial Technology Research Institute (ITRI), the largest of Taiwan's non-profit research institutes, has its headquarters in Hsinchu near the Science-based Industrial Park and branch offices throughout Taiwan. ITRI has about 6,073 employees, 76 percent of whom are engineers or scientists.

Founded in 1973 by the Ministry of Economic Affairs, ITRI serves primarily to develop industrial technologies and transfer them to domestic private enterprises to sharpen the competitive edge of Taiwan industry in the international market. ITRI's research projects cover a broad spectrum of industries from traditional to

emerging, and from labor-intensive to high-tech. One example is the integrated circuit industry. During the mid-1970s, ITRI began to provide Taiwan's IC manufacturers with the technology transfers necessary to acquire seven micron CMOS technology. Today, Taiwan is a major producer of eight-inch DRAM chip wafers, producing over US$2.21 billion worth of DRAM/SRAM chips in 1998. Taiwan's declining textile industry is another beneficiary of ITRI's R&D commitment. With ITRI's micro-fiber technology, local textile manufacturing has been able to improve polymerization and high-speed spinning processes to raise productivity.

ITRI's 1999 budget stood at US$487 million, with 50 percent of funding coming from government-sponsored projects and the other 50 percent from the industrial sector for contract research, joint development, and technical services. ITRI has thus achieved its aim of reaching a one-to-one ratio of funding from government projects to revenue from contracts and services. In fiscal 1999, ITRI transferred new technology to 538 scientific and technical companies in Taiwan, hosted over 1,104 conferences and exhibits, and published 645 reference papers and 659

Organizations under the ITRI Umbrella

Underneath ITRI are the Union Chemical Laboratories (UCL)化學工業研究所, the Mechanical Industrial Research Laboratories (MIRL)機械工業研究所, the Electronics Research and Service Organization (ERSO) 電子工業研究所, the Computer and Communications Research Laboratories (CCL) 電腦與通訊工業研究所, the Energy and Resources Laboratory (ERL) 能源與資源研究所, the Materials Research Laboratories (MRL) 工業材料研究所, the Optoelectronics and System Laboratories (OES) 光電工業研究所, the Center for Measurement Standards (CMS) 量測技術發展中心, the Center for Industrial Safety and Health Technology (CISH) 工業安全衛生技術發展中心, the Center for Aviation and Space Technology (CAST) 航空與太空工業技術發展中心, and the Biomedical Engineering Center (BMEC) 生醫工程中心.

Taiwan's vibrant market economy provides plenty of incentives for R&D in new technology.

conference papers. Most indicative of its success was the number of patents it was awarded in fiscal 1999—a total of 537, of which 307 were foreign patents. In the same year, the institute provided technical services to around 27,800 science-oriented and technical companies in Taiwan.

Patents

More than 54,000 applications for patents were received by the MOEA's National Bureau of Standards 經濟部中央標準局 (NBS) in 1998. Of these, ROC citizens filed nearly 63 percent, while foreign nationals submitted the remainder. The NBS approved nearly 25,100 applications in 1998, down 4,305 applications or 15 percent from the previous year. Approximately 66 percent of these were awarded to ROC citizens.

The NBS distinguishes between patents for new inventions, for new designs, and for new utility models. Foreign nationals have consistently filed several times as many successful patent applications for new inventions as ROC citizens have. In 1998, 8,478 patent applications for new inventions were approved, among which ROC citizens were awarded 1,598, or 19 percent.

According to the US organization Intellectual Property Owners (IPO), the U S government issued 3,850 new patents to ROC manufacturers in 1998, making the ROC the fifth largest patent holder in the US. The number of patents awarded to a country by the US has long served as an indicator of that country's level of scientific and technological advancement and global competitiveness. The IPO figures show that the ROC's progress in science and technology has boosted the competitive edge of local manufactures.

On January 26, 1999, the National Bureau of Standards was reorganized and renamed the Intellectual Property Office (IPO, 經濟部智慧財產局). The new responsibilities of the IPO include the governing of patents, trademarks, IC layouts, and copyrights; partaking in anti-counterfeiting activities; and managing other affairs related to Intellectual Property Rights (IPR).

Research Work Force

At publication time, the latest available ROC research work force figures were from 1997. That year, over 129,165 people in Taiwan were working on R&D related projects. More than 76,588 were researchers, i.e., persons with a

B.S., M.S., Ph.D., or associate degree and more than three years of research experience outside the classroom, engaged in R&D activities.

The number of researchers decreased by 2 percent from 1996. The corporate sector employed over 43,291 in 1997. Colleges and universities employed nearly 15,904, an increase of 4 percent from 1996. Research institutes employed 17,393 in 1997, or 10 percent more than the year before.

ROC researchers in 1997 were assisted by more than 34,021 technicians, i.e., people who perform technical tasks under the supervision of scientists and engineers, and are typically high school, vocational school, or junior college graduates with less than three years of working experience. Both researchers and technicians rely heavily on supporting personnel (administrators, accountants, secretaries, and maintenance workers), nearly 18,556 of whom were employed at scientific or technical institutes in 1997.

National Information Infrastructure

An ad hoc inter-ministerial steering committee meets monthly to monitor the development of the ROC's national information infrastructure. Minister without Portfolio 政務委員 Dr. Yang Shih-chien 楊世緘 is chairman. There are six subcommittees: resources planning (run by the Council for Economic Planning and Development 行政院經濟建設委員會), network construction (Ministry of Transportation and Communications 交通部), applied technology and promotion (Ministry of Economic Affairs), manpower development and basic applications (Ministry of Education 教育部), international cooperation (MOEA) and general administration (Science and Technology Advisory Group [see inset on p.321 next column]). A consultative committee with 30 members from leading private companies has also been formed to facilitate such development. Under the NII scheme, the government hopes to build ROC into an Asia-Pacific telecommunications center and establish the island as a global Chinese Internet center. Plans call for such concrete goals such as increasing the number of active Internet users in the ROC to three million within three years and providing one multimedia computer for every 20 students by the year 2000.

The information industry today is the ROC's largest industry as well as its most prolific foreign exchange earner. New information industry products are to be developed, utilized, and promoted by private businesses. The government's role is primarily to encourage investment and innovation through suitable tax and legislative measures. Tariff rates on data leased-lines will be lowered to encourage private investment. The project plans to give advance notice of major-item equipment procurement in large-scale computer and communication development projects to allow the private sector sufficient time to prepare bids.

Results to Date

The first concrete result from the project has been the Experimental Hsinchu Broadband Network Region 新竹寬頻試驗網路, which began operation on July 14, 1995. A similar network began operation in Taipei during September 1995. This project has required the cooperation of a number of government agencies. The Chunghwa Telecom

Co., Ltd. 中華電信公司 (a company divided from the Directorate General of Telecommunications 交通部電信總局 since July 1996) is laying a nationwide fiber-optic cable network. The equivalent of more than US$5.4 billion will be invested by Chunghwa Telecom in the project. In June 1999, 99.2 percent of Taiwan's trunk circuits were converted to optical fiber, together with a full 100 percent of international submarine cable. Meanwhile, Chunghwa Telecom has completed 28.7 percent of opticalization for subscriber loops and is scheduled to reach 100 percent in 2011. The plan also calls for integrating existing narrow-band networks, including an AT&T No. 5 ESS, an Alcatel System 1240, a Taicom-T (Siemens EWSD) digital switching system, and Taiwan's recently established ISDN (see Chapter 16, Mass Media).

One application of the network to date is a remote tele-medicine pilot system to transmit medical history images and data, as well as remote medical instructions. Developed jointly by National Taiwan University Medical College 國立臺灣大學醫學院, National Cheng Kung University Medical College 國立成功大學醫學院, Veterans General Hospital 臺北榮民總醫院 (Taipei), and Taichung Veterans General Hospital 臺中榮民總醫院, the system may ultimately be extended to provide medical consultation to the more remote parts of the Taiwan area.

Another example of applying the network to everyday life is e-mail service between the public and government inaugurated in July 1995. Government agencies at every level have set up Internet homepages, allowing Taiwan's growing number of Internet users easy access to information on government services and providing a convenient channel for feedback and communication through e-mail. As of July 1999, there were over 4.13 million active Internet users in the Taiwan area. Although over 100 independent Internet service providers now operate in Taiwan, Internet access on the island continues to be dominated by three large providers, namely HiNet (run by Chunghwa Telecom), SEEDNet (run by the Institute for Information Industry), and TANet (run by the

Science and Technology Advisory Group of the Executive Yuan

(行政院科技顧問組)

To actively promote the development of science and technology, the Executive Yuan promulgated the "Science and Technology Development Program" in 1979 as a guide for ministerial efforts. A board of advisors consisting of internationally renowned leaders from various scientific and technological fields was invited to the Office of the Premier to give the premier advice. In December of that same year, a mission-oriented organization called the "Science and Technology Advisory Group" was established to ensure the effective operation of the board. The convener of is a minister without portfolio selected by appointment. There are currently 10 to 15 advisors in the group, with one serving as the chief advisor. An executive secretary, a deputy executive secretary, and several researchers from the various science and technology fields implement all decisions. The group's primary responsibilities include assessing national projects and programs involving science and technology and then giving recommendations on national policy regarding their further research and development. Regular group board meetings are held to carry out these tasks, as well as to coordinate inter-ministerial policies.

Ministry of Education). Both HiNet and SEEDNet are commercial operations, while TANet provides access to academic and government users. HiNet leads the market with over 740,000 subscribers. SEEDNet is also a popular choice, with over 40 thousand hits per day on its homepage.

The project most recently initiated as part of the NII's efforts to build the ROC's information superhighway is a trial program for the integration of cable television and telecommunications networks. The program, which was inaugurated on July 16, 1997, will employ cable modems, fiber optics and the latest telecommunications technology to test the feasibility of advanced multipurpose broadband networks. Plans call for initial small-scale trials in two districts of Taipei City.

The Food Industry Research and Development Institute in the northern Taiwan city of Hsinchu is one of many active private research institutes in Taiwan.

Other Developments

Biotechnology

As part of the government's plan to build Taiwan into the Asia-Pacific manufacturing center, biotechnology and pharmaceuticals are being promoted as key industries. To encourage related research, the government plans to provide more subsidies for development of biotech in Taiwan. Government R&D expenditures in the field of biotechnology in fiscal 1999 totaled US$97.4 million, but this figure is expected to rise to at least US$110 million over the next decade. Responsibility for basic research (including genetic engineering, gene therapy, transgenic animals and plants, enzyme engineering, protein engineering, and pharmaceutical development) lies with the National Science Council. The MOEA's Industrial Development Bureau 工業局 (IDB) is also involved in biotech R&D. In 1998FY, IDB projects included the development of paclitaxel (an anticancer agent), hypolipemics, and biopolymers (including gene chips).

Aeronautics and Space Technology

One of the primary objectives of the government's efforts to develop space technology is to upgrade Taiwan's overall competitiveness, as the versatile nature of space technology itself will inevitably pave the way for further developments in other fields, including experimental research, communications, conservation, transportation, and agriculture. It was under such considerations that the National Space Program Office (NSPO) was born in October 1991. The NSPO is responsible for carrying out the ROC's 15-year space technology development program with a budget of US$615.63 million. In its initial stage, the NSPO is concentrating on a satellite project known as ROCSAT which consists of three different satellite ventures. The first venture involved the ROC's first satellite, the ROCSAT-1, which was successfully launched on January 27, 1999, from Cape Canaveral, Florida. ROCSAT-1 was an experimental, low-earth orbit science satellite that contained three instruments onboard: the Ionospheric Plasma Electrodynamics Instrument (IPEI), the Ocean Color Imager (OCI), and the Ka-band Experimental Communications Payload (ECP). Daily operations of ROCSAT-1 are being managed by the NSPO operations team, which controls the satellite from its NSPO Mission Operations Center located in Hsinchu, Taiwan.

ROCSAT-2 is a smaller satellite designed for remote sensing and contains an electron-optical imager and a Sprite imager to complete its tasks. The electron-optical imager can simultaneously capture four panchromatic, multi-spectrum images and then transmit this data to government agencies, private sector companies, and research organizations. The applications of such remote sensing include governing the use of land, agriculture, natural disaster assessment, environmental monitoring, scientific research, and educational activities. In addition to its remote sensing mission, ROCSAT-2 also has the scientific mission of investigating various lighting phenomena in the upper atmosphere. The launch date for the ROCSAT-2 is currently scheduled for the end of 2002. The ROCSAT-3 Program is a collaboration project between the University Corporation of Atmospheric Research (UCAR) in the United States and the NSPO. The goal of ROCSAT-3 is to develop a constellation of eight low-earth orbiting satellites for operational weather prediction, space weather monitoring, and climate research. Each of the eight satellites will carry a GPS/MET instrument to measure atmospheric refractivity through the use of a GPS emitted signal passing through the earth's atmosphere. The global data collected from this constellation of satellites will then be inputted into a sophisticated model and used for worldwide weather forecasting. The expected launch date for ROCSAT-3 is the middle of 2003.

With a joint effort, Taipower and the people of Republic of China are continuing to develop our land into a place of vigor, brightness, and prosperity.

TAIWAN POWER COMPANY
REPUBLIC OF CHINA
242 Roosevelt Rd., Sec. 3, Taipei, Taiwan
TEL:886-2-23651234 / FAX: 886-2-23651509
http://www.taipower.com.tw

" Winbond –

The Name to Trust. "

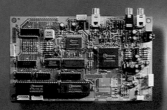

INTERNATIONAL TRADE SHOWS
TAIPEI 2000

TAIPEI FURNITURE   March 8-12
Taipei Int'l Furniture Show

TAITRONICS SPRING   March 22-26
Taipei Int'l Electronics Spring Show

TAIPEI CYCLE   April 7-10
Taipei Int'l Cycle Show

TaiSPO   April 15-18
Taipei Int'l Sporting Goods Show

Giftionery Taipei   April 21-25
Taipei Int'l Gift & Stationery Spring Show

TAIPEI AUTOMAT   May 9-13
Taipei International Automation &
Precision Machinery Show

AMPA   May 17-20
Taipei Int'l Auto/Motorcycle Parts &
Accessories Show

COMPUTEX TAIPEI   June 5-9
Taipei Int'l Computer Show

FOOD TAIPEI   June 15-18
Taipei Int'l Food Show

FOODTECH TAIPEI   June 22-26
Taipei Int'l Food Machinery Show

Taipei Telecom   Aug. 31-Sept. 3
Incorporating **Networking**
Taipei Int'l Telecommunications Show

SEMICON Taiwan   Sept. 13-15

**TAITRONICS –
Components & Equipment**   October 9-13
Taipei Int'l Electronics Show

**TAITRONICS –
Finished Products**   October 17-21
Taipei Int'l Electronics Show

Giftionery Taipei   October 25-28
Taipei Int'l Gift & Stationery Autumn Show

**Taipei Health
Promotion Show**   Nov. 2-5

MEDIPHAR TAIPEI   Nov. 9-12
Taipei Int'l Medical Equipment &
Pharmaceuticals Show

• **Subject to change without notice.**

TWT

Organizer:
China External Trade
Development Council (CETRA)
http://www.cetra.org.tw

Sponsor:
Taipei World
Trade Center

Venue:
Taipei World Trade
Center Exhibition Hall   5 Hsinyi Rd., Sec. 5, Taipei, Taiwan 110, R.O.C.
Tel: 886-2-2725-1111   Fax: 886-2-2725-1314

http://TaipeiTradeShows.cetra.org.t

Bright Future for Taipei Transit

The Taipei Rapid Transit Systems (TRTS) network seeks to meet the transportation needs of Taipei residents, strengthen links between downtown Taipei and satellite towns, and promote the overall development of the Taipei metropolitan area.

Eight major corridors of the initial network will eventually span a total of 86.8 kilometers in Taipei city and county, with 57.1 kilometers already in active service.

A long-term plan for a more extensive network is also underway, with a completion target of 2021.

Efficient, fast, and comfortable transportation. Building a bright future for Taipei.

DEPARTMENT OF RAPID TRANSIT SYSTEMS, TCG

7 Lane 48, Sec. 2, Chung Shan N. Rd., Taipei, Taiwan, R.O.C.
Tel: 886-2-25215550   Fax: 886-2-25115335

19
Social Welfare

Children up to four years of age are eligible for six free health examinations in addition to standard medical services provided by the National Health Insurance program.

The vast majority of ROC citizens in the Taiwan area now enjoy a greater quality of life than ever before, such as equal access to education, jobs, housing, medical care, travel, and political participation. These are the result of profound social and political changes accompanying the astounding economic success of recent years that has capped Taiwan's transformation over the past four decades from a traditional agricultural economy into a modern industrial entity. However, this restructuring of society has also given rise to new social ills, which have made life more hazardous in many ways, especially for disadvantaged groups. This chapter highlights services provided by the government and private sector in Taiwan to children, juveniles, women, the elderly, people with mental and/or physical handicaps, and the poor.

Changing Welfare Sources

Extended families were once the fundamental source of welfare services in Chinese society. Traditionally, all members of a farming family lived together in one household, caring for each other's needs. Three generations cohabiting was common, and five generations living together was seen as ideal. Each family member had certain responsibilities according to his or her age and gender. Young men worked in the fields, and women cooked, managed the home, and took care of the family. Grandparents provided wisdom, guidance, and childcare, and children did light chores. When all members fulfilled their duties, everyone's needs were met, and the family was said to be in harmony.

The traditional conception of family-based support has been challenged by the emergence

of a modern, post-agricultural economy in Taiwan. By 1998, only 8.9 percent of the working population was employed in agriculture. Many young people have left the farming households in which they grew up and established nuclear families in urban areas (50 percent of the population lives in either Taipei, Taichung, Tainan, or Kaohsiung). It is now common for both parents to work full-time outside the home. Children are often cared for by the school system, and grandparents are only visited during major holidays.

The metamorphosis of extended farming families into nuclear urban families has resulted in growing numbers of children, juveniles, women, handicapped people, and senior citizens who require assistance from non-family sources. Coinciding with this increased need for outside assistance are two new phenomena: heightened demand for government services and the proliferation of private organizations that provide welfare services.

In fiscal 1999, the ROC central government spent US$5.08 billion, or 12.4 percent of its total expenditures, on what it broadly defines as "social welfare," a budget heading that includes social insurance expenses (6.2 percent), social relief expenses (0.8 percent), welfare services (4.9 percent), national employment expenses (0.1 percent), and medical care expenses (0.4 percent). The ROC government is not attempting to be the sole source of welfare services in Taiwan despite its large allocated budget. Instead, the government sees its role as a facilitator and coordinator of welfare activities in local communities.

As can be imagined, communication between various government agencies, academic institutions, private charities, and care recipients is of crucial importance. In a typical scenario, the Ministry of the Interior's Department of Social Affairs 內政部社會司 (DSA) formulates welfare policies and drafts related legislation. The DSA then briefs local welfare offices on the latest policies. These offices commission universities or individual scholars to survey the actual demand for specific services in the local community. Once community demand has been assessed, local welfare officials invite representatives from each of the private charities active in the area to attend seminars in which the new government guidelines are explained, community needs discussed, and responsibilities and priorities set. For their part, special interest groups, charities, the media, and the more than 700 professional social workers in Taiwan provide constant feedback to policymakers at the highest levels of government.

Over the last decade, a vast array of public and private agencies has arisen to assist disadvantaged people in Taiwan. While all of these Samaritan groups face shortages of manpower and funding, the number of people, the amount of media attention, and the total value of services devoted to helping people in need are continuing to rise rapidly. In addition, charitable organizations are now learning to form coalitions in which each member group provides a specific service. These coalitions of care are increasingly organized, focused, and effective.

Children's Welfare

Nearly 17.5 percent of the people in Taiwan are children (under 12 years of age, as defined in the *Children's Welfare Law* 兒童福利法). Experts agree that the pressures faced by most children in Taiwan, while not extreme, nevertheless demand immediate attention. For example, children today have fewer siblings and less outdoor space to play in, but face increased pressure from academic competition at an early age. More often than ever, they are raised by a single parent who must spend most of his or her time working outside the home.

The *Children's Welfare Law* was first promulgated in 1973, and revised in 1993 in light of the 1989 UN Convention on the Rights of the Child. Under the law, a pregnant woman may not smoke, drink, take drugs, chew betel nuts (see section on betel nuts, Chapter 15, Public Health), or engage in any other activity that might endanger her fetus. The law also mandates subsidies for the medical care of premature babies and seriously ill children. Health care professionals, daycare workers, teachers,

and the police are required to report cases of child abuse. The revised *Children's Welfare Law* also prohibits parents from leaving children who are under the age of six or who require special attention unattended. Parents violating this regulation must attend a minimum of four hours of a parental responsibility course. Fines of US$44 to US$222 are charged for each refusal to attend the classes. Under the revision, courts are able to assign a child to another guardian if both parents are deemed incompetent. As an added measure, the revised *Children's Welfare Law* empowers authorities to make public the name of anyone who violates provisions of the law and to fine them up to US$11,111.

Child Protection

According to the Department of Social Affairs, reported cases of child abuse have increased steadily from 1,235 in 1993 to over 3,165 in 1998. Article 18 of the *Children's Welfare Law* mandates that child abuse cases must be reported within 24 hours of discovery. At the end of 1995, a toll-free round-the-clock telephone hotline was set up in Taiwan Province in order to promptly uncover cases of child abuse. In 1998, among the 4,112 children up to the age of 18 protected by the Child and Youth Protection Center, physical abuse was the most common complaint (38.1 percent), followed by neglect (24.7 percent), and substandard parenting (18.9 percent).

According to the law, all reports of child abuse must be investigated. A social worker is dispatched to the site, sometimes accompanied by police. When a serious case of child abuse is confirmed, and if the parents are unable to guarantee the safety of the child, the child is then removed and placed in a safe environment. According to the *Children's Welfare Law,* the protective custody may not exceed 72 hours in duration without a direct court order. Almost 57 percent of the said 4,112 persons monitored by social workers received family counseling, of whom 26.92 percent were placed with relatives, temporary foster homes, or children's homes, and 11.84 percent in permanent foster care.

In order to clarify what constitute child abuse, the government has established a referential index, classifying child abuse into four categories, namely, physical, mental, sexual, and negligence. This detailed index specifying the severity of a child's physical injuries and behavioral abnormality provides guidelines in identifying child abuse cases.

Medical Care

All children are covered under the National Health Insurance 全民健康保險 (NHI) program, which came into effect on March 1, 1995. In addition to standard medical services, this comprehensive health program provides six free health examinations for children up to four years of age.

On December 25, 1995, children under three who are registered in Taipei City began to enjoy subsidies from the city government for medical care not covered under the NHI program. In October 1998, this subsidy program of the Taipei City Government was further extend to include children under the age of six. In addition to nine free health checkups, eligible children can apply for subsidies for early diagnosis and treatment of certain illnesses and vaccination for chicken pox. However, the granting of this subsidy is subject to budgetary limitations.

Childcare

The demand for childcare has risen rapidly in the ROC with the increase in the number of single parent families and nuclear families in which both parents work outside the home. The *Children's Welfare Law* and its enforcement rules, the *Nursery Establishment Measures* 托兒所設置辦法 and the *Foster Care Measures* 兒童寄養辦法 mandate the establishment of child welfare centers in all cities and counties in Taiwan. As of December 1998, there were a total of 288 public nurseries, approximately 1,993 private nurseries, and nearly 168 community nurseries in the Taiwan area. The number of children accommodated by these institutions rose slightly from the previous year to 248,517. A growing number of private corporations and government organizations now provide nurseries for staff children.

A program initiated on July 5, 1995, called for strengthening the professional training of kindergarten teachers. As of December 1998, some ten child welfare centers were serving the Taiwan area, while 42 homes for foundlings and orphans were caring for about 2,455 children.

To match the schedules of working mothers, elementary schools hold after-school classes for children up to eight years of age. Full-day childcare centers must meet legally mandated standards for basic facilities, personnel qualifications, space allotted, and staff size. To accommodate children from low-income families, all daycare centers must admit at least 10 percent of their students free of charge. Under the *Social Service Promotion Incentive Guidelines* 加強推展社會福利獎助作業要點, local social welfare bureaus offer grants and awards to outstanding daycare centers.

Juvenile Services

As of December 1998, the segment of Taiwan's population aged 12 to 17 amounted to 2.18 million youths. Most ROC citizens graduate from the nation's nine-year compulsory education system by age 15. These young people face abrupt and difficult choices, such as whether they will take the competitive examinations to enter a senior high school or senior vocational school, enroll in a cram school to prepare for the exams (see Chapter 17, Education), or look for employment. Young people who are unable to pass the competitive examinations or who purposely forsake educational opportunities realize that life without a high school diploma will be difficult. Not surprisingly, rates of petty crime, drug dependence, and suicide are rising among this group.

Juvenile delinquency is still a major problem. The MOI's National Police Administration 內政部警政署 (NPA) statistics indicate that 14.54 percent of all crime suspects in 1998 were juveniles between the age of 12 and 18, down from 17.8 percent in 1992. Accordingly, the juvenile crime rate has also been reduced from 1,311 per 100,000 juveniles in 1992 to 1,037 per 100,000 in 1998 thanks to the government's consistent effort to maintain law and order. Burglary, violent crimes, and drug violations dominated juvenile delinquencies in 1998. In percentage, the arrest were 61.1, 11.53 and 12.1, respectively.

Another disturbing trend is the drop in the mean age of delinquents. In the past, most juvenile delinquents in Taiwan were either 17 or 18 years of age, but since 1986 the number of 14- and 15-year-old delinquents has been rising quickly.

The NPA reports that in 1998, police charged 41,945 people with drug violations (including amphetamine-related charges). Of those charged, 31 percent were young people between the ages of 12 and 23.

The rate of amphetamine and other drug abuse has reached major proportions over the past several years. The abuse of amphetamines (usually in the form of crystal methamphetamine) by youngsters in Taiwan appears to be even more common than in Japan, Korea, Singapore, or Hong Kong.

Campaign Against Drug Abuse

To combat the increase in drug usage and drug-related crimes, then Premier Lien Chan 連戰 formally declared a war on drugs on May 12, 1993. As almost all drugs used on the island come from overseas, the government has mobilized every available force, including the military, to protect the island from the influx of illegal drugs. In addition to law enforcement agencies, customs authorities, and the judiciary, agencies working in such diverse areas as health, education, finance, and agriculture also contribute to the common effort to attack this scourge on all fronts. The government is running advertisements to convince youngsters to stay away from drugs. Drug violations have seen a gradual decrease since the launch of the campaign. However, an increasing rate of drug recidivism is now a main target of the NPA that aims to further strengthen a tracking scheme monitoring former drug users.

With a view to curbing drug-related crimes that tend to grow increasingly organized and high-tech, *Money Laundering Control Law* 洗錢防制法 was promulgated on October 23, 1996. *Narcotics Elimination Act* 肅清煙毒條例 was also revised and renamed *Narcotics Endangerment Prevention Act* 毒品危害防制條例 in May 1998 to work more effectively against narcotics.

Youth Counseling and Guidance

Young people in need do have a place to turn for help. Counseling and psychiatric services for youths are readily available at community health centers and psychiatric health clinics at major hospitals. The government subsidizes 33 youth welfare centers in the Taiwan area which provide youths with counseling, psychiatric advice, emergency aid, school and employment assistance, and recreational opportunities.

Hotlines in north, central, and south Taiwan also serve people in need. One such hotline is named "Teacher Chang" 張老師. Set up by the China Youth Corps (see inset) in 1969, the Teacher Chang hotline is a free counseling service that recruits volunteers from all walks of life to provide professional phone counseling to youths.

Rewriting the Law

The *Law Governing the Disposition of Juvenile Cases* 少年事件處理法, first promulgated in 1962 and amended in 1980, was further amended in October 1997. The newly revised law strengthens the protective and counseling functions of the judicial system for juveniles and provides for the establishment of juvenile courts at various locations around the island. The law now empowers judges to sentence parents or legal guardians of convicted juvenile offenders to between eight and 50 hours of parental counseling and instruction. The judges are also allowed to order juveniles to work or to remand them to the appropriate reformatory or welfare institutions after they are released from detention or parole. Juveniles who commit misdemeanors will have the offenses struck from their records two years after their sentences are served, after the completion of three years of probation, or when no trial is deemed necessary.

Teenage Prostitution

According to the *Penal Code* 刑法, any person who has sexual intercourse with an individual aged 14 or under is guilty of statutory rape and is subject to a mandatory sentence of at least five years' imprisonment. A person who has sex with an adolescent aged 15 or 16 is also guilty of rape and must be sentenced to one to seven years in jail. But these provisions are based on the condition that a complaint must be filed either by the victim or the victim's guardian, not just by the public prosecutor. Most parents of young victims are reluctant to seek redress in a public court of law, usually preferring out-of-court settlements.

In July 1995, the Legislative Yuan passed the *Child and Youth Sexual Transaction Prevention Act* 兒童及少年性交易防制條例. This law targets teenage prostitution, supplementing the *Penal Code* and compensating for its inadequacy with respect to sexual exploitation of adolescents. Pursuant to the new law, public prosecutors can now independently press charges against pimps or patrons. The act stipulates that a sexual patron of a prostitute aged under 16 can be sentenced to a maximum of three years' imprisonment and a maximum fine of US$2,857. Patrons of prostitutes aged 16 or 17 are subjected to the same fine but no imprisonment. Pimps can be sentenced to life imprisonment and fined US$571,429.

Halfway houses provide rescued adolescent prostitutes with shelter, food, clothing, medical care, and counseling. These young women are encouraged to go back to school or helped to seek a socially acceptable job. In Taipei City, teenage prostitutes are sent to the Occupation Training Center for Women at the Taipei Municipal Kuangtzu Po Ai Institution 臺北市立廣慈博愛院. Its counterpart in Kaohsiung City and County is the 802 Military General Hospital 國軍802總醫院. In Taiwan Province, teenage prostitutes are cared for by the Taiwan Provincial Yunlin Institute 臺灣省立雲林教養院 and the Taiwan Provincial Jen Ai Vocational Training Center 臺灣省立仁愛習藝中心. In all, these public facilities can accommodate about 230 people. Their stay in these institutions ranges from 72 hours to one year, depending on the court decision.

Several halfway houses are operated by private foundations such as the Good Shepherd Sisters 善牧基金會, a Catholic foundation, and the Garden of Hope Foundation 勵馨基金會. Their full capacity totals 75 people. In addition to this, they also accept teenage girls who are victims of incest and sexual abuse.

Women

Over the last decade, new definitions of women's roles have been formed as more Chinese women have received higher education, joined the work force, begun to compete with men, and become financially independent. Chinese women are resisting the traditional view that women are inferior to men and that, in male-female relationships, a woman should be submissive. Many women in Taiwan complain that they are unfairly burdened with both traditional and modern roles. It is, many women say, difficult to be simultaneously wage earners, good mothers, dutiful daughters-in-law, and dutiful wives.

In 1998, there were 10.69 million women in the Taiwan area, compared to a male population of 11.24 million. On average, first-time brides were 28.1 years old that year, up from 25.8 in 1990. Almost half of Taiwan's women are regular wage earners and help support their families financially.

For thousands of years, all Chinese women were expected to marry, and all married women in China had to give birth to and take care of several children in addition to caring for their parents-in-law. At one time, most welfare agencies at the local level of government in Taiwan believed that women's welfare meant helping women meet these traditional obligations. According to this relatively conservative outlook, subsidies for the daycare, medical expenses, and education of children and elderly people supposedly reduced the burden on women. To the extent that women are still required to fulfill traditional roles, these welfare services do indeed

Drug Seizure and Persons Arrested for Drug Abuse

Item	1989	1990	1991	1992	1993	1994	1995	1996	1997	1998
Narcotics (kg)*	4.66	36.68	154.52	90.82	814.18	526.99	105.58	47.69	110.08	618.8
Number of Cases	945	1,072	3,072	4,701	14,269	11,608	5,896	6,065	7,474	31,033
Number of People Charged	1,196	1,446	4,436	6,378	19,997	16,145	8,394	8,458	10,045	41,945
Age 12-17	27	44	156	214	614	523	258	243	218	2,807
Age 18-23	107	184	896	1,200	3,603	2,791	1,350	1,282	1,510	10,401

Note:*Includes opium, poppy and seed, marijuana, morphine, cocaine, heroin, codeine, other derivatives and synthetic drugs.
Source: National Police Administration, Ministry of the Interior

benefit women. Nonetheless, the activism of feminist groups and recent media reports of domestic violence and rising divorce rates have challenged local authorities to change their parochial attitudes towards women.

Women's Educational Attainment

In ancient China, naivety was considered a feminine virtue, and consequently, few women were taught to read and write. Today, however, more and more women receive higher education. According to the Ministry of Education, at the end of 1998, some 56 percent of junior college graduates, 51 percent of university and college graduates, and 26 percent of graduate school graduates were women. For the first time, the number of female graduates from junior college, university, and college surpassed the number of male graduates. Two decades earlier, the corresponding figures were 32, 24, and 15 percent, respectively. Clearly, women are enjoying better education opportunities, with female graduates from university, college and graduate school having increased by 50 percent in 20 years.

Women's Service Networks

In the last 15 years, numerous women's organizations have arisen to help women cope with these problems, and to clarify liberalized roles for both men and women. The government has adopted measures to protect women's welfare by setting up a women's protection hotline, Women's Rights Promotion Committee under the Executive Yuan 行政院, and Sexual Violation Prevention Committee under the Ministry of the Interior. *Domestic Violence Prevention Act* 家庭暴力防治法 is currently being drafted by the Ministry of the Interior. City governments also set out to allocate specific budget for providing women services. In Taipei for example, an annual budget of US$3.5 million has been earmarked for women's welfare. Many local governments, under the supervision of the Ministry of the Interior, have organized regional coalitions of groups aiming to help women. These coalitions have generated public awareness about gender issues and provided medical, legal, psychological, educational, and vocational assistance to an ever growing number of women. Furthermore, they empower women by providing them with avenues for action and a collective voice. The most mature and successful women's welfare coalition is the Taipei Women's Service Network (see inset, next page).

In 1998, the Taiwan area boasted 83 comprehensive welfare centers offering counseling, vocational training, seminars, and other services to disadvantaged women. Halfway houses and shelters for women in need numbered 30 that year, up 13 from 1994. With a maximum capacity of 339 persons, they accommodated 579 in 1998.

Taipei Women's Services Network

Legal Consultation
The Taipei Citizen's Service Center 臺北市政府聯合服務中心 2725-6168

Domestic Violence
Domestic Violence Prevention Hotline 080-024995, 080-000600

Emergency Hotline
Suicide Prevention Center 生命線 2505-9595

Rape
Hotline 080-024995, 080-000600

Halfway Houses
The Garden of Hope Foundation 勵馨基金會 2550-9595
Good Shepherd Sisters Social Welfare Services 善牧基金會 2381-5402

Family Problems
Taipei Family Education Service Center 臺北市社會教育館家庭教育服務中心 2578-1885
Mackay Counseling Center 馬偕協談中心 2571-8427

Psychological Problems
Huaming Counseling Center 華明心理輔導中心 2382-1885
Peace Line of the Mackay Counseling Center 馬偕協談中心平安線 2531-8595, 2531-0505
Christian Cosmic Light Holistic Care Organization 財團法人基督教宇宙光全人關懷機構 2362-7278,
2363-2107

Unwed Mothers
Cathwel Service 財團法人天主教未婚媽媽之家 2311-0223
Christian Salvation Service 財團法人台北市基督徒救世會社會福利事業基金會 2729-0265

Child Abuse
Child Protection Hot Line, Taipei City Government
臺北市政府兒童保護專線 080-024995

Forced Labor
Taipei Women's Rescue Foundation 婦女救援基金會 2700-9595

Job Counseling
Public Employment Service Center, Bureau of Labor Affairs, Taipei City Government
臺北市政府勞工局國民就業輔導中心 2591-4654

Vocational Training
Taipei Women's Development Center of the Presbyterian Church 臺灣基督長老教會
臺北婦女展業中心 2369-8959
Vocational Training Center, Bureau of Labor Affairs, Taipei City Government 臺北市政府勞工局
職業訓練中心 2872-1940

Medical Issues
Medical Information & Service Association, ROC 中華民國醫療諮詢服務協會 2314-1515

Divorcées and Widows
The Warm Life Association for Women 晚晴婦女協會 2708-0126
Single Parent Service Center 單親家庭服務中心 2558-0170

Note: These telephone numbers are staffed by personnel who do not necessarily speak English.

Female Employment Assistance

The *Employment Promotion Measures* 促進就業措施 initiated in 1985 by the Employment and Vocational Training Administration of the Council of Labor Affairs 行政院勞工委員會職業訓練局 (EVTA) target women, people 45 years old and above, the disabled, aborigines, low-income households, and dislocated workers. These measures involve promoting job equality between the sexes, providing women with vocational training, surveying the demand for part-time and freelance work to enlarge the employment market for women, and even offering daycare center for preschool children, after-school classes for elementary students, and daycare for the elderly to alleviate the burden on women.

From July 1998 to June 1999, some 2,380 women have completed training courses from Taiwan's 13 vocational training centers as full-time students, and 4,750 as evening-class students. The government paid all school-related expenses for the full-time students and subsidized half the expenses for the evening-class students. During the same period, another 7,337 completed vocational programs organized by local county or city governments.

Rising Sun Project

Since July 1, 1991, a comprehensive youth guidance program—the Rising Sun Project 旭日方案—has been underway. Through this program, special task forces to help youth aged from 12 to 18 have been established in police departments around the island.

Activities within this program include informal visits to police departments, lectures and panel discussions on legal affairs and youth issues, hiking, camping, and mountain climbing. All teenagers, regardless of whether or not they have criminal records, are encouraged to attend. In this way, those who do have criminal records are able to interact with their more fortunate peers and receive correctional education in a healthy environment. Additionally, task force members visit delinquents in their homes, offering assistance to the teenagers as well as their guardians.

From July 1998 to June 1999, the EVTA provided job-hunting assistance to 30,777 women, 3,354 people over 45, 6,093 handicapped, 2,275 aborigines and 199 people from low-income households.

Today's women enjoy better educational opportunities and are taking more important positions in business.

China Youth Corps

The China Youth Corps 中國青年反共救國團 (CYC) is a non-government organization aimed at guiding youth in their growth and development through various activities. Established in 1952, in addition to the counseling hotline, the CYC holds lectures and seminars to educate youth. Its most popular activities are the outdoor recreational programs during summer and winter vacations, designed for teenagers and young adults.

The organization also sponsors youth good will missions around the world, seeking to broaden young people's horizons. Since July 1992, the CYC has organized youth cultural and education exchanges with the Chinese mainland. From January 1998 to August 1999, a total of 615 ROC youths had traveled to the mainland in 20 CYC groups, and 507 young mainlanders had come to visit the ROC.

Young Chinese who were born overseas and foreign youth are not excluded from CYC programs. During summer vacations, youth of Chinese descent can come to Taiwan to learn Chinese language, culture, and customs. In addition, each year groups of young foreigners are invited to Taiwan for cultural and academic exchanges with their Chinese counterparts.

These cross-strait and intercultural exchanges are either partially or completely funded by government agencies, including the Ministry of Education 教育部, Overseas Chinese Affairs Commission 僑務委員會, Mainland Affairs Council 行政院大陸委員會, and Ministry of Foreign Affairs 外交部, among others.

Divorce

Nothing illustrates the ongoing reevaluation of women's roles in Taiwan better than the issue of divorce. A few decades ago, divorce was a relatively rare occurrence. During the 1980s, an increasing number of women in Taiwan began to earn their own paychecks. The experiences of women working outside the home have allowed them greater access to information and ideas about alternative lifestyles. Hence, their growing independence gives them more freedom to reject dysfunctional marriages. Data released by the Department of Population 戶政司 under the Ministry of the Interior 內政部 indicate that the divorce rate in the Taiwan area has more than quadrupled in the last 25 years while the marriage rate has only undergone a barely discernible increase. The divorce rate stood at two couples per 1,000 people in 1998, compared to 0.37 in 1970, and 0.77 in 1980. However, the marriage rate only showed a slight overall increase, having risen from 7.50 per 1,000 people in 1970 to 9.68 in 1980, and then fallen back to 6.69 by 1998. Thus, in 1998, divorced people accounted for 3.71 percent of the 15-and-over population, compared to 0.89 percent in 1970 and 1.07 percent in 1980.

In general, Taiwan society still demonstrates little sympathy for divorced women. The founder of the Warm Life Association for Women 晚晴婦女協會, an organization that helps divorced and widowed women and seeks to eliminate discrimination against divorcées while fighting for their equality in the eyes of the law, says that divorced women in Taiwan face more emotional problems than divorced men. Founded in Taipei in 1988, Warm Life now has branches in Taichung and Kaohsiung as well. The organization provides professional legal advice and psychological counseling, and operates telephone hotlines in Taipei, Taichung, and Kaohsiung that provide emergency counseling for women coping with dysfunctional marriages or divorce.

Women's attitudes with regard to marriage are changing much more quickly than may be apparent from currently available statistics. More and more women are resisting parental pressure to marry and have children early, seeing marriage and married life as risky, unnecessary, or simply not worth the trouble.

Rewriting the Law

Many women's groups have been lobbying lawmakers to change Book IV of the *Civil Code* 民法, which concerns family matters. This section of the *Civil Code* went into effect in May 1931 and was only partially revised once in 1985. It covers divorce-related issues such as child custody, child support and alimony, and the division of property. The language of this section clearly favors men.

On September 6, 1996, several landmark revisions were made to Book IV by the Ministry of Justice 法務部. Article 1051, which automatically gave the father custody in the case of divorce by mutual consent, was struck from the books. Article 1055 was amended to stipulate that, when a court is ruling on a divorce, it must do so in the interest of any children involved, weigh all circumstances, and take into consideration all interview reports from social workers. Article 1089 was amended to give both parents equal priority with regard to parental rights and obligations to minor children, and to give the court—rather than the father—final say in resolving disputes. This revision was crucial to filling in the legal void left after the Council of Grand Justices 大法官會議 ruled on September 23, 1994, that the original wording of Article 1089 giving fathers priority in the enforcement of parental rights violated the ROC Constitution.

Changes were also made with regard to property rights. Prior to the 1985 revision of the *Civil Code,* any property registered under a married woman's name belonged to her husband. The 1985 revision gave the wife full rights over property registered under her name, but these rights were extended only to women who married after the revision came into effect. The September 6, 1996, amendments extended this right retroactively to all married women, regardless of their date of marriage.

On June 24, 1998, a *Domestic Violence Prevention Law* 家庭暴力防治法 went into effect. This law stipulates that the Ministry of the Interior and all levels of local government must organize domestic violence prevention committees. Resources such as judicial, police, medical, educational, and volunteer service organizations shall be integrated into a complete prevention system. The new law also provides for timely and thorough protection to victims of domestic violence.

The Elderly

People who attain the grand age of 65 in Taiwan are apt to fully discover the advantages of filial piety, or reverence for one's parents, which has been the highest virtue in Chinese ethical relations since well before the time of Confucius. Chinese people today still feel a strong moral obligation to care for the elderly. The law in Taiwan reflects this moral compunction by mandating a broad range of services for anyone over the age of 65, from subsidized transportation and entertainment to free medical care and housing. Nevertheless, the government is not the primary source of support for most senior citizens: More than 64 percent of the 1.81 million people in Taiwan who are over the age of 65 are still personally cared for by their children in their own homes.

Welfare for the elderly is defined by the Ministry of the Interior as providing basic subsistence aid and health care to poor and helpless senior citizens. The government advocates that elderly people live with or near their children. In-home care is provided for senior citizens who live by themselves and have difficulties in performing everyday activities.

As the average life expectancy rises in Taiwan—to 77.81 and 71.93 years in 1998 for women and men, respectively—elderly people are making up a growing proportion of the population. In December 1998, some 8 percent of the population was over 65. By the year 2000, a full 8.5 percent of the total population is expected to be over 65. As the population grays, there will be proportionally fewer wage earners to provide for the aged (see Chapter 2, People, and Chapter 15, Public Health).

Elderly Pensions

Elderly residents of Taipei City and County, Ilan County, Hsinchu County, Tainan County, Chiayi City, Kaohsiung County, and Penghu County benefit from organized pension systems. Residents of these areas who are 65 years of age or older and do not receive other forms of pension or subsidy from the government are entitled

to a pension ranging from US$88 to US$176 per month, depending on the county or city of residence. This welfare policy is budgeted separately by each county or city government, and is not universal throughout the Taiwan area.

Medical Services

Since March 1, 1995, senior citizens with low incomes have received free inpatient and outpatient medical assistance through the National Health Insurance program. The government also provides free in-home medical care for the indigent elderly. Low-income elderly residents who are hospitalized because of severe illnesses are entitled to US$23 to US$47 of medical subsidy per day. In addition, 50 nursing homes, 33 medical institution-affiliated homes for the elderly, and 14 homes for retired servicemen have brought serenity and security to many seniors who do not have any family in Taiwan. In 1998, social workers and volunteers paid a total of 224,222 visits to the elderly around the island.

Elderly Daycare

Daycare for the elderly has become more important as younger family members go out for work. In May 1988, the Taipei City Government 臺北市政府 inaugurated the Taiwan area's first daycare center for people over 65, the Neihu District Elderly Service Center 內湖老人服務中心. Now, this center and the Taipei Municipal Kuangtzu Po Ai Institution 臺北市立廣慈博愛院 together can accommodate about 70 people per day. These centers conduct regular physical checkups and provide breakfast, lunch, and entertainment during working hours on weekdays and Saturdays. Five additional daycare centers are currently being planned in Taipei. Ideally, these will be located in every district, so that users will not need to travel far from home, and for the convenience of family members. Similar institutions are now operating throughout the Taiwan area. Altogether, elderly people paid nearly 314,358 visits to daycare centers in 1998.

Over 4,000 senior-citizen recreation centers and organizations such as the Evergreen Academy 長青學苑, Community Longevity 社區長壽俱樂部,

and Pine Clubs 老人文康中心 serve senior citizens and provide activities such as folk dancing, Chinese "shadowboxing" 太極拳, folk music, opera, chess, and handicrafts. In 1998, nearly 74,976 people enrolled in classes provided by the 202 Evergreen Academies. Lung-shan Elderly Service Center 龍山老人服務中心, inaugurated in Taipei in June 1996, is the first service center for the elderly operated by the private sector using government facilities. It is expected that future centers will follow this model.

Independent Housing

Although Taiwan's 108 retirement homes and nurseries accommodated over 10,785 elderly people in 1998, there is a desperate shortage of housing for elderly people who find it necessary to live independently of their family or who have no family. The private Kaohsiung County Senior Citizens' Apartments 崧鶴樓, which began operating in July 1995, has set a fine example for residential complexes catering exclusively to senior citizens. This Kaohsiung County facility has a 350-person capacity. Similar institutions which together will accommodate about 500 people are under construction in Tainan City and Taipei County.

In Taipei City, the Yangming apartment building for the elderly 陽明老人公寓 began operation in November 1998. The building provides living quarters for about 200 people, and include small single- and double-occupancy residential units, indoor recreational facilities, and plenty of outdoor space. Only people who are over 65, healthy, and able to handle daily chores qualify for residency. The planning of another similar building, Chulun 朱崙, is underway.

In addition, the self-paid nursing home in Taipei's Wenshan District 文山區 serves 380 old people who are able to take care of themselves. Two other such facilities, one in Mucha 木柵 and one in Yangmingshan 陽明山, will join the Wenshan facility to serve an additional 1,168 elderly people.

The Taipei Municipal Kuangtzu Po Ai Institution provides comprehensive care for needy old people, women, and children. Benefits include free room and board, and even pocket money.

Disabled People

As of 1998, about 571,125 people held Handicapped Certificates 身心障礙手冊 in the Taiwan area, up 2.6 percent since the end of 1997. Long-term observers of the social welfare movement in Taiwan note that advocates for the rights of disabled people are perhaps the best organized and most effective of all the special-interest groups competing for recognition and services. The ROC government spent about US$127 million on subsidies for disabled people in 1998, including more than US$95 million in living-expense subsidies.

The *Protection Law for the Handicapped and Disabled* 身心障礙保護法 stipulates that welfare services must be provided for the autistic and for people with serious facial injuries or major organ malfunction. The law also states that all private enterprises with more than 100 employees must hire at least one disabled worker. In other words, any medium or large private enterprise must reserve one percent of its job positions for the disabled. Government offices, public schools, and public enterprises with 50 or more employees are held to a doubly stringent standard. Two percent of their employees must be disabled people. Thus, a police station with a staff of 150 ought to have at least three disabled employees.

In June 1999, the Department of Social Affairs under the Ministry of the Interior indicated that 7,848 private or government employers in Taiwan are large enough to be subject to the provisions of the law and thus must hire a set number of disabled personnel. If each employer could meet the quota exactly, a total of 28,561 disabled people would be employed. About 33,510 disabled people had been hired as of June 1999, with all employers having met or exceeded the minimum requirements.

This high cooperation may be partly attributed to the successful enforcement of the *Protection Law for the Handicapped and Disabled* which provides a clear set of punishments and inducements to encourage employer cooperation, and to fund services for the disabled. Employers who do not meet the quota must pay US$319 every month for each handicapped person they have not yet hired. The money obtained is paid into a Special Account for Handicapped Welfare 身心障礙者就業金專戶 set up and monitored by the Social Services Department 社會局 of the county or city where the employer is located. In June 1999 the Taipei City Special Account had a net balance of US$ 144 million. Employers who fail to pay the fine are prosecuted.

The money in this special account is used to make work places more accessible to disabled people, to pay the full salaries of disabled employees during their first three months of probationary employment, and to underwrite half the salary of each disabled employee who is hired after an employer has already met his quota.

Vocational Training

Seven consultation service centers around Taiwan handle telephone consultations, correspondence management, one-on-one sessions, and interviews for disabled people who wish to take classes, receive special medical care, or seek employment. The centers also host seminars, recreational activities, and social gatherings. Thirty-eight public and private vocational training institutions for the disabled provide classes in practical skills to help disabled people lead independent lives.

The first-ever civil service examination for disabled people took place in July 1996. The exam was open exclusively to disabled people aged between 18 and 55 with educational backgrounds from junior high school to graduate school. A total of 779 passed the exam and were admitted into the civil service.

Medical Care and Subsidies

Under the National Health Insurance program, people with severe disabilities pay no premium and receive free treatment for serious injuries. People whose disabilities are not so severe pay a discounted premium and a flat rate of US$2 for basic outpatient services. Prior to

the implementation of the NHI program on March 1, 1995, subsidies for medical treatment and rehabilitation expenses were granted to disabled people on the basis of financial need. Disabled people received medical subsidies totaling US$16.6 million during 1998. Severely disabled people are also eligible to receive long-term care at the 128 welfare institutions for the handicapped located across the island.

Education of the Disabled

Disabled people are integrated into regular educational institutions as much as possible. Many regular schools, from the elementary to the senior high and senior vocational level, offer special classes for the disabled. In addition, as of the 1997-98 school year, the Taiwan area boasted 17 government-established special education schools exclusively for handicapped students (see Chapter 17, Education).

Indigenous Peoples

The welfare of the various indigenous peoples in the Taiwan area, who numbered nearly 390,244 at the end of 1998, is among the top priorities of the ROC social welfare system. Several new government organizations whose mission is to

serve the aborigine population were created in recent years. On March 16, 1996, the Taipei City Government established its Commission for Native Taiwanese Affairs 原住民事務委員會. On December 10 of the same year, a cabinet-level Council of Aboriginal Affairs under the Executive Yuan 行政院原住民委員會 was established. On July 1, 1997, the Kaohsiung City Government also set up the Commission for Native Taiwanese Affairs. As mandated by the *Additional Articles of the ROC Constitution*, the government actively seeks to protect the aborigines' rights, and to assist and encourage them in many areas (see Chapter 2, People).

The government provides low-interest housing loans to aborigines. Under this program, aborigines can borrow up to US$55,556 at an annual interest of 4.5 percent, repayable over a 20-year period. Aborigines are accorded special status when taking entrance exams for the high-school level and above. An extra 35 percent is added to the exam score of aborigines participating in the senior high school and senior vocational high school entrance examinations. Any aborigine who passes these tests and enters school is also entitled to receive the same government

The ROC government has established 17 special education schools for the handicapped, from preschool through senior vocational school. Here, students of the Cheng-kung Developmental Disabilities School present "The Dream of the Crystal Ball Princess." (Courtesy of Kaohsiung Municipal Cheng-kung Developmental Disabilities School)

subsidies as students in the ROC's normal universities. Aboriginal students who participate in the college and university entrance examinations receive an additional 25 percent on their final test scores. There are also scholarships for aborigines from low-income families, and tuition is waived for aborigines who take part in government-sponsored vocational training programs. They also receive a monthly US$73 food stipend and a US$222 living-expense stipend from the Council of Aboriginal Affairs. The Council also provides an additional US$148 monthly stipend to those who receive training for three months or more. A special civil-service examination for aborigines is administered biennially. By the end of 1999, the exam had been held a total of 19 times, with 1,740 aborigines passing.

Volunteer Services

The warm participation of the private sector plays an important role in the ROC social welfare scheme. In July 1995, the Ministry of the Interior initiated the Hsiang Ho Program 祥和計畫 to consolidate and strengthen volunteer work. In addition to recruiting volunteers through media campaigns, this program strives to balance the distribution of volunteer services so that those in need can receive proper care regardless of geographic location. Another purpose is to consolidate volunteer resources and provide volunteers with high-quality training and education. Volunteer workers who complete the programs with excellent records and work as volunteers for more than one year with a total of 200 hours of service may apply for a Volunteer Service Certificate from the Ministry of the Interior.

Beginning July 1997, the National Youth Commission (NYC) under the Executive Yuan launched a program to recruit people from 15 to 45 years of age to join the volunteer services. As of the end of 1998, more than 40,000 young people have joined the program and received training. On average, these volunteers render more than 120,000 trips of service every year to those in need.

Soon after the devastating earthquake that struck Taiwan on September 21, 1999, the NYC set up a volunteer coordination center to coordinate all volunteer services carried out as part of the relief work. Every day, 3,538 volunteers offered direct and efficient services in the stricken areas, and 1,442 volunteers helped transporting relief goods and taking calls at the rescue and relief centers.

Low-income Households

The ROC government provides several types of special subsidies and assistance to individuals and families having low incomes, including assistance in finding jobs, educational aid for children, stipends during traditional festivals, and child and maternal nutritional programs, as well as other cash and noncash benefits. Most of the programs base eligibility on individual, household, or family income, and a few offer help on the basis of presumed need. To determine eligibility, each fiscal year a figure for "monthly minimum expenses" based on the consumer price index and variations in regional income distribution is assigned by the government. This figure differs from area to area: for example, for fiscal year 2000, in Taipei City the monthly minimum expenses is set at US$337, in Kaohsiung City it stands at US$265, in Taiwan Province it is US$220 and in Kinmen County, US$171. Families whose average monthly income does not reach this amount are classified as low-income families. In 1999, only 129,968 people (56,720 households), or 0.5 percent of the population of Taiwan, were considered members of low-income families.

Starting in July 1993, the ROC government began providing a monthly subsidy to low-income elderly throughout the Taiwan area. The amount of this subsidy does not vary from locality to locality. All ROC citizens over the age of 65 whose average family income is less than or equal to 1.5 times the minimum monthly expenses are qualified to receive a monthly subsidy of US$174. Elderly people whose average family income is between 1.5 and 2.5 times the minimum expense are eligible for a monthly relief subsidy of US$87. Through May 1999, some 198,000 elderly people had benefited from this policy. In addition, the government pays the full premium for low-income households to enter NHI program. Emergency aid is also available to those in need.

Some low-income families with children qualify for an additional monthly subsidy. Again, the standards vary depending on the locality. Children of families whose average monthly income does not exceed the minimum are entitled to a monthly subsidy. In Taiwan Province, the subsidy is US$52 per child, with each household being limited to a maximum of two children to be eligible. In Kaohsiung City, each child qualifies for a monthly sum of US$52. Taipei City, with deeper pockets, is somewhat more generous: households with children below the age of two, and between the ages of 12 and 17, are eligible to collect US$150 per child. Children between the ages of two and 11 qualify a household for US$90 per month. In Taiwan Province, two-thirds of the cost of the subsidy program is borne by the central government, with the rest falling on the shoulders of the local government. A local government is allowed to pay more, but not less, than its allotted share.

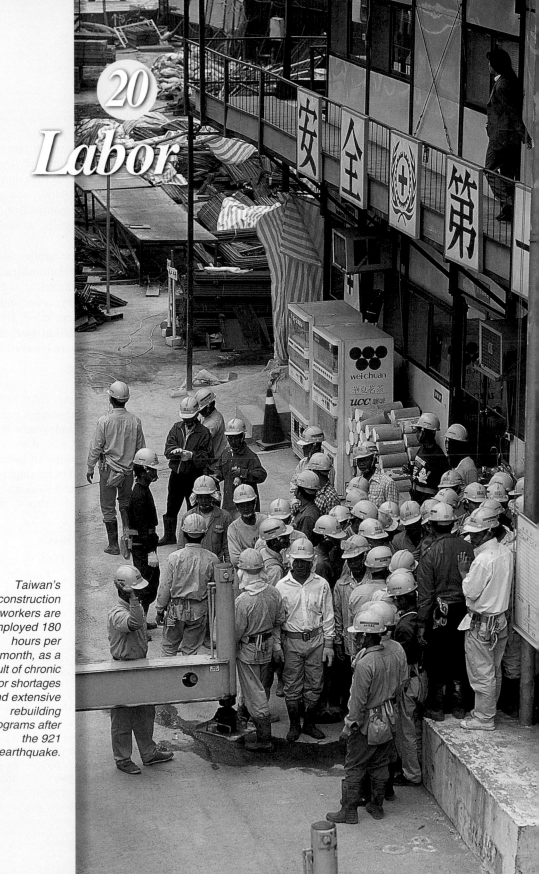

20
Labor

Taiwan's construction workers are employed 180 hours per month, as a result of chronic labor shortages and extensive rebuilding programs after the 921 earthquake.

安全 ✚ 第

What's New

1. Figures updated
2. Gender equality law under legislative review

The ROC's economic growth over the past 50 years has been powered by a well-educated and highly motivated work force, which has given it a lead in science and technology and a competitive edge in high value-added manufacturing. The ROC has a diversified and skilled work force of roughly 9.7 million people, with a comparatively low unemployment rate of less than 3 percent; approximately 6.6 million are paid workers, as opposed to those who are self-employed or have some other working status.

During 1998, as in previous years, the government has sought to maintain a productive and qualified work force. Legislative priorities have focused on the rights of workers, including workers' welfare, gender equality, labor-management relations, safety and health, and appropriate quotas for foreign workers.

Labor Rights

Legal Framework

Legislative provisions for workers' welfare are prescribed in the ROC Constitution as a fundamental part of national policy. According to Article 153 of the Constitution, "the State, in order to improve the livelihood of laborers and farmers and to improve their productive skill, shall enact laws and carry out policies for their protection." Under this constitutional provision, the legal framework accords all workers equal opportunity to work as well as guarantees their rights.

Labor Standards Law

The key labor law in the ROC, the 1984 *Labor Standards Law* 勞動基準法, defines such terms as worker, employer, wages, and contract. It delineates the rights and obligations of workers and employers, prescribes the minimum requirements for labor contracts, and has provisions on wages, work hours, leave, and the employment of women and children. The law protects against unreasonable work hours and forced labor, and grants workers the right to receive compensation for occupational injuries and layoffs, as well as a pension upon retirement.

The *Labor Standards Law* applies to virtually all employer-employee relationships; however, some sectors, such as theatrical and other arts, the entertainment industry, community services, and civil service are excluded. By mid-1999, approximately 5.5 million workers (84 percent of the work force) were covered by the *Labor Standards Law*.

Employment Services Act

The *Employment Services Act* 就業服務法, promulgated on May 8, 1992, guarantees equal job opportunities and access to employment services for all. It also calls for a balance of manpower supply and demand, efficient use of human resources, and the establishment of an employment information network. To protect workers' rights during times of economic slowdown, the act

ROC Labor Force

Unit: thousand

Year	Male	Female
1991	5,355	3,214
1993	5,497	3,377
1995	5,659	3,551
1997	5,731	3,701
1999	5,812	3,856

Labor Force Participation Rate

Unit: %

Year	Overall	Male	Female
1991	59.11	73.80	44.39
1993	58.82	72.67	44.89
1995	58.71	72.03	45.34
1997	58.33	71.09	45.64
1999	57.93	69.93	46.03

Source: Council of Labor Affairs

stipulates that the central government should encourage management, labor unions, and workers to negotiate on the possibility of work hour reductions, wage adjustments, and in-service training to avoid layoffs.

The *Employment Services Act* also regulates public and private employment service agencies. The act calls for the offering of employment guidance to the handicapped, indigenous peoples, low-income families, female heads of households, those who are more advanced in years, and the unemployed. Public agencies compile and analyze labor market information such as wage fluctuations and manpower supply and demand, offer advice on the setting up of professional training programs, and recommend jobs or training for the unemployed.

As of mid-1998, employment discrimination evaluation committees 就業歧視評議委員會 have been established under the *Employment Services Act* in the cities of Taipei, Kaohsiung, Hsinchu, Taichung, Chiayi, and Tainan, and the counties of Taipei, Taoyuan, Miaoli, Taichung, Changhua, Yunlin, Nantou, Chiayi, Kaohsiung, Ilan, Tainan, Hualien, and Pingtung. These committees, formed by government, labor, and management representatives, as well as scholars and experts, ensure equal employment opportunities and determine if any discriminatory actions have been taken by an employer against an employee.

The employment of foreign workers is also regulated under the *Employment Services Act*. Foreign workers may be employed on the condition that they do not limit job opportunities for ROC citizens or adversely affect labor conditions, national economic development, or social stability. Nine categories of workers are permitted to work in Taiwan, including workers with specialized or technical expertise, foreign language teachers, sports trainers, coaches, domestic helpers, caretakers, crews on fishing boats, and workers in construction and manufacturing industries. The act lays down rules on working permits, extension of working permits, maximum duration of permits, and supervision of foreign workers.

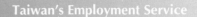

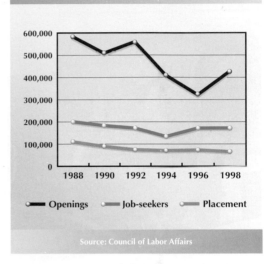

Taiwan's Employment Service

Openings   Job-seekers   Placement

Source: Council of Labor Affairs

Recent Legal Developments

The labor welfare system has been modified by the revision of several labor-related laws. A notable development has been the drafting of the *Gender Equality Labor Law* 兩性工作平等法, currently under legislative review, to encourage more women to join the work force and to ensure a healthy work environment for both men and women.

Protecting Labor Rights

Labor Insurance

The *Labor Insurance Act* 勞工保險條例 was promulgated in 1958 to provide insurance coverage to workers in the private sector, including industrial workers, journalists, employees of non-profit organizations, fishermen, persons receiving vocational training in institutes registered with the government, and members of unions. Teachers and employees working in government agencies who are not eligible for teachers' or civil servants' insurance are also covered under this law. When the labor insurance program was first launched in 1950 under provincial regulations, there were 554 insured units and a total of

Fishermen are covered by a group accident insurance program as well as by the Labor Insurance Act.

128,625 insured laborers in Taiwan. By March 1999, there were 385,169 insured units, and the number of workers covered by the program had grown to approximately 7.6 million.

Labor insurance coverage consists of two types: ordinary labor insurance with seven kinds of benefits—maternity, injury, sickness, disability, old-age, death, and unemployment; and occupational injury insurance with four kinds of benefits—injury and sickness, medical care, disability, and death. The *Labor Insurance Act* was partially revised in February 1995, with the transferring of the medical care aspect of ordinary labor insurance to the National Health Insurance 全民健康保險 program in March of that same year

(see section on Health Insurance in Chapter 15, Public Health). Regulations for unemployment benefits, now available to selected categories of insured ROC workers, were implemented on January 1, 1999.

Premium rates for ordinary labor insurance are 6.5 to 11 percent of the beneficiary's reported monthly salary, with the maximum monthly salary limited to US$1,292 for the purpose of premium calculations. The responsibility of paying for the premium is generally shared by employees, employers, and the government in the proportion 2:7:1. For occupational injury insurance, premiums are paid by employers. The rates differ among the 52 categories of businesses covered, ranging from 0.08 percent to 3 percent of reported wages and averaging 0.34 percent.

Occupational Safety and Health

The *Labor Safety and Health Law* 勞工安全衛生法 was revised and promulgated in 1991 to cover workers in mining and quarrying; manufacturing; construction; electricity, gas, and water; transportation; and other industries designated by the central authorities, including agriculture, forestry, fisheries, and animal husbandry; restaurants and hotels; machinery and equipment rental and leasing; mass media services; and repair services. The amendments included many new requirements on the installation of safety and health equipment in work places such as dockyards and fireworks factories. It also prohibited women and employees under the age of 16 from working in dangerous or harmful environments. As of December 1998, the *Labor Safety and Health Law* covered over 224,000 businesses and some 3.91 million laborers in the Taiwan area. The Council of Labor Affairs is currently drafting a law to enhance preventive measures against occupational accidents and related diseases.

In 1998, the occupational accident rate in the ROC stood at 3.86 per 1,000 workers, with a mortality rate of 0.094 percent, up 13.19 points from 1997. About 46 percent of all fatal occupational injuries were the result of motor vehicle accidents, and approximately 69 percent of serious disabilities were the result of human error.

To prevent occupational diseases, some 500 hospitals islandwide are authorized by the government to offer annual medical checkups for workers. In 1998, about 87 percent of the 39,738 workers engaged in especially hazardous work received medical examinations.

The Council of Labor Affairs established the Institute of Occupational Safety and Health 勞工安全衛生研究所 in 1992, as part of an effort to ensure workers' safety and health. The institute comprises five divisions: Occupational Safety, Occupational Hygiene, Method Development and Analysis, Occupational Medicine, and Occupational Safety and Health Exhibitions. The institute surveys the work environment and conditions, evaluates and prevents occupational injuries and diseases, and conducts technological research on occupational safety and health management and personal protective equipment.

Labor Inspections

The *Labor Inspection Law* 勞動檢查法 was promulgated on February 3, 1993, to replace the *Factory Law* 工廠法. It empowers the Council of Labor Affairs and local governments to inspect labor conditions in the workplace and thereby safeguard the health and safety of workers. The scope of inspections carried out under the law covers labor health and safety, labor insurance, employee welfare funds, and the hiring of foreign workers. The approval of labor inspectors is required before workers are allowed to work at potentially dangerous sites. These include petroleum cracking plants; agrochemical, firework and gunpowder manufacturers; locations with containers holding gases under high pressure; construction sites; and sites where dangerous or harmful materials are manufactured or handled. In the event of a major occupational accident or disaster, the site is immediately inspected to determine the cause. Work at such sites may be completely or partially suspended should conditions be deemed too hazardous to workers.

A team of 217 inspectors oversees labor conditions at the 224,014 enterprises on the CLA's inspection list. Enterprises where hazardous working conditions are prevalent are a primary focus of inspections. Averaging three visits a day for each inspector, the team covered 7.4 percent of all enterprises in 1998. Over 24,000 visits were made in 1998 to workshops with high

accident rates, such as firework factories, construction sites, and worksites with high levels of noise and air pollution or where toxic or explosive substances were handled. The CLA is assisted by 22 authorized private and public inspection agencies, which have 800 qualified personnel trained to conduct thorough health and safety inspections. Violators of safety codes are fined between US$923 and US$4,615.

Labor Unions and Industrial Relations

Within the ROC's legal framework, three labor laws—the *Labor Union Law*, the *Collective Agreement Law*, and the *Settlement of Labor Disputes Law*—protect the rights of workers to

Labor Inspections

Source: Council of Labor Affairs

Vocational Training and Occupational Skill Testing

Between 1981 and 1998, a total of 13 public vocational training institutes offered entry-level and advanced courses to more than 360,000 trainees.

Many local businesses now offer on-the-job training courses. In 1998, approximately 197,000 workers receive on-the-job training conducted either by businesses or training institutes operating under government contracts. In 1998, the CLA assisted private enterprises in setting up a total of 46 vocational training centers. In addition, the CLA held courses to train supervisors and technical personnel for public and private institutions, and completed training for 17,852 workers in 1998. The CLA also offered vocational training to 160 foreign workers employed by investors based overseas.

Occupational skill testing in the ROC serves as a guideline for determining the qualifications of workers. Examinees who pass are issued certificates designating the level of expertise attained. According to the *Vocational Training Act* 職業訓練法, laborers' skills are classified as A, B, or C level. Exams are offered by the Employment and Vocational Training Administration in 162 occupational categories. To date, a total of 1,434,984 examinees have passed these exams. In 1998, a total of 638 workers from 39 different occupations participated in the 29th National Vocational Training Competition 全國技能競賽.

The expansion of Taiwan's high-tech industrial sector has increased job opportunities at all levels.
(Photo by the Central News Agency)

organize labor unions, reach consensus on labor issues, protect their collective interests, and voice their grievances and opinions. As of 1998, a total of 1,176 industrial unions and 2,464 craft guilds had been formed, representing more than half of the six million paid employees in Taiwan. Under the CLA's efforts to strengthen labor-management relations, 13,847 enterprises had established work rules as of 1998, a 20 percent increase from 1997. Of these, 1,119 had implemented stock option plans for their employees, a 4.9 percent increase from 1997.

To better define labor relations, a revision of the *Collective Agreement Law* now awaiting legislative approval will designate labor unions as the sole labor representative in the signing of collective agreements. Such agreements will promote labor-management cooperation and cover labor conditions such as wages, work hours, layoffs, pensions, compensation for occupational injuries, and the handling of labor complaints and disputes. In 1998, a total of 296 government and private businesses had entered into collective agreements with employees.

There were 1,254 labor disputes in the first quarter of 1999, a 48 percent increase compared to the same period of 1998. In terms of the 5,277 workers involved, however, the figure was up 67 percent from the same period in 1998.

Elderly Workers and Pensions

According to the *Labor Standards Law* and the *Rules for the Allocation and Management of Workers' Retirement Fund* 勞工退休準備金提撥及管理辦法, a retiree is entitled to a maximum pension equal to 45 times his average wage in the

Average Monthly Income per Industry in 1998	
	US$
Mining and Quarrying	1,301
Manufacturing	1,115
Electricity, Gas, and Water	2,640
Construction	1,166
Commerce	1,124
Transportation, Storage, and Communications	1,541
Finance, Insurance, and Real Estate	1,804
Business Services	1,494
Social and Personal Services	1,175

Source: Directorate General of Budget, Accounting and Statistics

Information and Service Centers

An islandwide network of 62 employee service centers offers career counseling, information on labor-management disputes, labor welfare, career planning, insurance, pensions, and labor education services to workers in the Taiwan area. Some 79,000 employees were served in 1997.

Every city and county government in Taiwan has established a regional Labor Education Promotion Team 勞工教育輔導小組 to offer career training courses. In 1997, these teams offered a total of 43,716 training programs to 1,720,000 laborers.

A labor issues hotline for the Taiwan area [(02)87701860-1 or, toll free, (080) 211-459] averages between 700 and 800 calls per month. In addition, the *Labor Education Handbook* 勞工教育手冊 contains information on most of the ROC labor laws and the occupational rights of ROC workers, and is available free of charge to all workers in the ROC.

are required to pay 0.025 percent of the insurance wages for each employee. As of April 1999, about 95 percent of the 249,263 eligible firms in the Taiwan area were contributing to the fund and had set aside a total of US$134.4 million by April 1999.

Foreign Workers

Since 1990 when the ROC liberalized its foreign labor policy to remedy a labor shortage, 270,620 foreign workers have been recruited to work in domestic industries. Approximately 62 percent of these workers are employed in the manufacturing industry, and 18 percent are working in construction. The majority come from Thailand—about 133,400 in 1998. As of March 1999, some 11,000 foreign maids, mostly from the Philippines, were employed as domestic helpers in families with dependents under six or over 75 years of age. Another 45,000 foreign workers were legally employed in the nursing and caretaking sectors.

The employment of these foreign workers in nine occupational categories is provided for by the *Employment Services Act*. Foreign workers can stay in Taiwan for a maximum period of two years. Employers may apply for a one-year extension of work visas only once. An additional six

six months prior to retirement. Each month, employers must pay between 2 to 15 percent of their employees' total monthly wage aggregate into the wage retirement fund. This fund is monitored by a supervisory committee made up of labor and management representatives.

The retirement fund allocation requirement was included in the 1984 *Labor Standards Law* to improve workers' welfare. As of April 1999, about 35,000 businesses—of which over 70 percent are from the manufacturing industry—had established retirement funds for their employees. Beginning in July 1993, the CLA has been offering subsidies to businesses that hire elderly workers (those over 60 years of age). By mid-1997, subsidies have also been offered to businesses that employ workers between 45 and 65 years of age. Currently, the CLA provides a subsidy of US$154 per elderly worker per month.

To ensure that workers receive due wages should their employers file for liquidation, the government has set up a Wage Arrears Repayment Fund 積欠工資墊償基金, to which employers

Duration of Paid Leave

Unit: working days, unless otherwise noted
Annual
  7 (1-3 years)
  10 (3-5 years)
  14 (5-10 years)
  14 plus 1 additional day for every additional
  year over 10 years to a maximum of 30 days
Maternity (weeks)
  8 (childbirth)
  4 (miscarriage)
Funeral
  3-8 (length of leave depends on worker's
  relationship to the deceased)
Wedding
  8

months' extension is available under special circumstances for foreign workers engaged in major construction projects.

However, foreign workers have in some cases been viewed as a threat to local workers. Recent disputes over the substitution of local workers by foreign laborers have focused attention on claims that foreign workers are no longer playing the supplementary role which had originally been envisioned for them. Meanwhile, employers argue that domestic workers have shown little interest in the kind of work in which foreign laborers are engaged. Thus, local businesses now offer foreign workers greater incentives, and as a result, their average monthly salary is fast approaching that of their local counterparts. Statistics show that after less than two years on the job, foreign workers already earn wages as high as 96 percent of the local standard.

To protect the rights of legal foreign workers and help them adjust to life in Taiwan, 13 foreign worker counseling and service centers have been established islandwide. These centers offer foreign workers information on pertinent laws and regulations, provide psychological counseling, and mediate disputes. Hotlines have also been set up to offer guidance and other services.

Almost all enterprises provide programs and services for foreign employees, such as insurance coverage under the government's labor insurance program and through private group insurance. Other programs and forms of assistance include recreational activities on weekends, cultural and recreation centers, counseling sessions, weekend religious activities, and Chinese language training.

Due to the slight slowdown in economic growth in recent years, the Council of Labor Affairs now allows foreign workers to apply for a change of employer in the event that a company shuts down, suspends production, lays off employees, or automates production to save on labor costs. Foreign employees may also be transferred to other businesses or factories owned by the same employer, or may work for the new owners of a business in the event of a takeover.

Foreign workers in Taiwan also have the right to strike. To exercise this right, they must be working in either agriculture, forestry, fisheries, and animal husbandry; mining and quarrying; manufacturing; construction; water, electricity and gas; transportation, warehousing, and telecommunications; or mass communications. They must also belong to a local labor union. Domestic maids and teachers of foreign languages do not fall under these categories, but are instead protected by employment contracts drawn up in accordance with the ROC *Civil Code* 民法. Foreign maids may strike if they have joined a domestic services union; however, foreign teachers have no such union to join, and thus may not strike.

DON'T COUNTERFEIT;
PROTECT INVENTIONS

拒絕仿冒
保護創作

**Protecting Intellectual Property Rights
is Promoting National Economic Strength.**

中 華 民 國 全 國 工 業 總 會
保 護 智 慧 財 產 權 委 員 會

INTELLECTUAL PROPERTY PROTECTION COMMITTEE, R.O.C.

台北市復興南路一段390號12樓   TEL:886-2-2706-0223 FAX:886-2-2704-2477
12TH FL., 390 FU HSING S. RD., SEC. 1, TAIPEI, TAIWAN, R.O.C.
http://www.industry.net.tw   E-mail:intell@mail.cnfi.org.tw

98 無鉛汽油勁驥上路

發揮愛車強勁馬力

高科技產品，跨世紀頂級汽油

汽車是現代生活中最便捷的交通工具，重視外型美觀、平穩舒適、勁靂有力，隨著引擎科技進步，汽車對於高辛烷值汽油的需求日益殷切，針對此一趨勢，中油公司陸續推出高科技跨世紀頂級汽油-98無鉛汽油。

發揮強勁馬力，使愛車比汗血馬更有力

98無鉛汽油是高壓縮比高性能汽車引擎使用的頂級汽油，可充份發揮原引擎設計之高馬力與高扭力，讓愛車比漢代的戰馬—大宛汗血馬更強勁有力。

保護愛車，珍惜環境

使用98無鉛汽油可減少爆震發生機率，提高駕駛舒適性，可展現愛車最佳性能，是保護愛車，珍惜環境的最好選擇。

汗血馬小檔案

汗血馬是漢朝為加強戰力，從西域大宛國引進的戰馬，是西域天馬的一種，強壯有力，驃悍無比，馳騁時，汗如血色自兩頰揮灑而下，故名汗血馬。

 中國石油股份有限公司
CHINESE PETROLEUM CORP

PROTECTING THE EARTH IS
EVERYONE'S RESPONSIBILITY

Conservation is a global effort, and the Republic of China on Taiwan is doing its part to conserve nature's bounty. The government agency in charge of the nation's wildlife conservation program is the Council of Agriculture. We at the Council of Agriculture look forward to working with you to protect our planet.

**COUNCIL OF
AGRICULTURE
EXECUTIVE YUAN**

37 NANHAI RD.
TAIPEI,TIAWAN 100
REPUBLIC OF CHINA
TEL: 886-2-2312-4065
FAX: 886-2-2312-0337
E-mail: rc0000@mail.coa.go

Taipei Review

21
The Arts

"The Twelve Women," by the Taipei Folk Dance Troupe, incorporates elements from classical and modern dance into a lively and colorful performance.

Traditional and contemporary, Eastern and Western, local and international—Taiwan's artists in both visual and performing arts are exploring styles across the spectrum, combining elements from different periods and traditions. In fact, one characteristic that marks the art of Taiwan today is an increasingly sophisticated and successful blending of such seemingly opposite sensibilities.

Aboriginal Arts

While the culture of Han Chinese is dominant on Taiwan, the island is also enriched by the cultures of nine aboriginal peoples—the Atayal 泰雅族, Saisiyat 賽夏族, Ami 阿美族, Bunun 布農族, Tsou 鄒族, Rukai 魯凱族, Puyuma 卑南族, Paiwan 排灣族, and Yami 雅美族—whose ancestors arrived here perhaps 15,000 years ago. Arts such as woodcarving, weaving, and basketry, as well as ceremonial dances and songs have long played a central role in aboriginal life, with each people developing its distinct artistic style.

Recent years have seen a growing interest in preserving and developing the aboriginal arts. Tribal members themselves have been involved in a number of projects, such as recording their songs and dances, as have researchers and individuals in the Han Chinese community. The government is also making efforts to promote tribal culture. In the last few years, the Council for Cultural Affairs' annual National Festival of Culture and Arts 中華民國全國文藝季 has included performances, exhibitions and seminars on aboriginal arts. A major contribution was made by businessman Safe C.F. Lin 林清富, who in 1994 established the Shung Ye Museum of Formosan Aborigines 順益臺灣原住民博物館 across the street from the National Palace Museum. Housing a private collection, the four-floor museum is the first to be dedicated solely to Taiwan's tribal cultures. In addition to its displays of artifacts, costumes, musical instruments, household utensils, and weapons, the museum also provides extensive information on aboriginal history, lifestyles, social relationships, and religious beliefs and customs.

The museum has also helped to promote research of Taiwan's indigenous peoples, including grants to the Academia Sinica and to writers and filmmakers involved in recording aboriginal culture. It has also funded research projects at the University of California, Berkeley, and the University of Tokyo. In addition, the museum has provided money for university scholarships for aboriginal students.

The collections at the Shung Ye Museum, the Taiwan Museum 國立臺灣博物館, the museum of Academia Sinica's Institute of Ethnology 中央研究院民族學研究所博物館, and the National Museum of Natural Science 國立自然科學博物館 in Taichung provide good introductions into the artistic traditions of the various peoples.

Woodcarving

The Paiwan and Rukai, which may have once been a single people, are known especially for their woodcarvings. The homes of important members of the people, for example, are embellished with relief carvings of simplified human figures, zigzag or triangular patterns, and the all-important hundred-pace snake with its menacing diamond-shaped head. The snake is particularly prominent in Paiwan and Rukai art, being revered as the incarnation of the tribal ancestors.

Woodcarving skills are also highly developed among the Yami, who live primarily on Orchid Island, off the southern coast of Taiwan. The Yami are best known for their sturdy hand-built canoes, which can carry ten or more people and are made without nails or glue. They are decorated in delicately carved relief designs that feature a concentric sun-like motif and stylized human figures accented with spiral formations. The canoes are then painted white, red, and black, before undergoing an elaborate launching ceremony.

Weaving

Another art form central to aboriginal culture is weaving, which is especially well-developed among the Atayal. Using simple back-strap looms, Atayal women create rectilinear patterns of squares, diamonds, and triangles, using mostly red, blue, black, and white. Some designs also incorporate strings of thin shell beads or rows of small bronze bells.

Architecture

The aboriginal peoples also have unique architectural traditions. Some of the best places to view these traditions are at the Formosan Aboriginal Cultural Village 九族文化村, a privately run facility close to Sun Moon Lake 日月潭 in central Taiwan, and the Taiwan Aboriginal Culture Park 臺灣山地文化園區, set up by the provincial government in the south-island county of Pingtung. Although commercialized and intended for tourists, both have sections that have carefully reproduced traditional homes of the different aboriginal peoples. Among the most interesting are Rukai houses, traditionally made of stacked slate, and Yami houses, which are situated partly underground as protection against typhoons.

Music and Dance

No discussion of aboriginal culture would be complete without including dance and music—perhaps the richest legacy of Taiwan's tribal peoples.

Communal dances, performed at regular ceremonies and rituals, consist mostly of simple but harmonious walking and foot-stomping movements, often performed in unison and accompanied by melodic choruses. The sound of small bells or other metal ornaments attached to the dancers' colorful costumes or to ankle bracelets add to the celebratory atmosphere.

Aboriginal dance rituals usually go on for several days and are performed in connection with specific customs or legends. The *Ilisin* spring festival of the Ami, for example, involves the annual rite of passage of the members of various age groups. The three-day *Pastáai* ceremony of the Saisiyat (the Ceremony of the Dwarfs 矮人祭), held every other year in the tenth lunar month, is performed to appease a legendary race of dwarfs who are believed to have taught the Saisiyat people how to farm. The Yami perform rituals every year to mark the launching of new boats and to celebrate the season of the flying fish, one of their staple foods. The latter ritual includes an impressive "hair dance," in which women swing their long hair back and forth through the air.

Even more than dance, aboriginal music is intimately connected to nearly every aspect of tribal life, from daily chores to religious rites, and has been studied by ethnomusicologists and other scholars from around the world. The songs have been divided into four groups, according to theme: harvests, daily work, love, and tribal legends.

There are four types of aborigine musical instruments: drums, simple stringed instruments, woodwind instruments (such as flutes), and other percussion instruments (rattles, wooden mortars and pestles). One interesting example is a kind of Jew's harp used by the Atayal, which consists of a piece of bamboo with one or more small metal strips that are played by moving a thread back and forth with the mouth. The Paiwan have a unique double-piped flute that is played with the nose.

A number of efforts have been made in recent years to preserve and pass on tribal dance and music, and also to introduce it to general audiences. Many of the peoples have been involved in re-enacting their dance and song rituals on stage. The National Institute of the Arts 國立藝術學院, working in conjunction with the Institute of Ethnology at Academia Sinica, has also recorded dances of several tribes in Labanotation (an internationally recognized way of depicting dance movements on paper) and has reconstructed these for staged performances. Some private groups, including the Cloud Gate Dance Theater Foundation 財團法人雲門舞集文教基金會, have also produced high-quality cassettes and CD recordings of authentic aboriginal singing.

One of the most important developments has been the creation of the Formosa Aboriginal Dance Troupe 原舞者 in April 1991. The troupe is made up of young people from several different tribes who work directly with elder tribe members to learn the dances and songs of a particular ritual, often doing their fieldwork in conjunction with qualified ethnologists. The troupe has also undertaken several overseas tours, including performances in New York, France, Spain and Hungary.

Folk Arts

Preserving Folk Arts

While handicrafts such as paper cutting, knotting, and dough sculpture continue to be fairly common in Taiwan, other apprentice-oriented folk arts are struggling to survive. In addition to the challenge of competing with inexpensive machine-made goods, folk crafts also find it difficult to attract young people to the professions of woodcarving, lantern making, and other crafts. Few are willing to endure the lengthy period of training which results in only modest financial rewards. Traditional performing arts such as puppetry, dragon and lion dances, folk dance, folk opera, and traditional acrobatics have had an even tougher time competing with TV, movies, and karaoke (see sections on Puppetry, Dance, and Opera).

Still, many folk arts have benefited from a revival of interest in the past five to ten years, with government, scholars, artists, and private individuals joining in preservation and promotion efforts. One of the first steps in government support came in 1980, when the Ministry of Education sponsored a survey of the island's folk arts. The survey discovered 70 types of crafts and 56 types of traditional performing arts still being practiced, by some 4,000 artists. In 1981, the Council for Cultural Affairs 行政院文化建設委員會 (CCA) was set up with the responsibility of giving equal attention to fine arts and folk arts. It has sponsored a number of folk arts festivals, publications, and other projects.

Ripped-paper art by Hsieh Shu-hui, which depicts a string of firecrackers and the festival of the Chinese New Year.
(Courtesy of Hsieh Shu-hui)

The *Cultural Heritage Preservation Law*, passed in 1982, gave even more substance to the government's commitment to preserve and promote folk arts. It paved the way for such programs as the Folk Art Heritage Award 民族藝術薪傳獎, set up in 1985 to honor outstanding folk art masters, and the prestigious title of Folk Arts Master 重要民族藝術藝師, established in 1989. The latter has provided leading woodcarvers, puppeteers, traditional musicians, and other craftspeople and performers with a monthly stipend and helps recruit and subsidize apprentices and training programs for these masters to pass on their skills. Other government efforts have included recording performances on videotape and transcribing dialogues of traditional puppet plays.

One of the most extensive efforts to preserve, promote and reintroduce folk arts back into the community has been the CCA's National Festival of Culture and Arts. In recent years, the annual festival has focused primarily on traditional arts, working in conjunction with private organizations and county cultural centers to organize folk art exhibitions and performances around the island. Festival events have showcased everything from paper umbrellas and lanterns, to Hakka yodeling songs, drum dances and carnival skits. Such activities as temple preservation seminars, tea-picking festivals, and folk operas have also been on the festival agenda.

Private organizations such as the Chinese Folk Art Foundation 中華民俗藝術基金會 have also been instrumental in promoting traditional crafts and performing arts. Besides its many local activities, the foundation promotes Taiwan folk arts overseas. In 1999, for example, it sponsored the International Yunlin Puppet Theatre Festival, and several international seminars.

Other private efforts include the Taiwan Folk Art Museum 臺灣民俗北投文物館 at Peitou 北投, near Taipei, which houses an extensive collection of folk arts as well as Chinese clothing and embroidery. The Tso Yang Workshop 左羊工作坊 in Lukang 鹿港 is another group that focuses on trying to increase public appreciation of the island's traditional art forms.

Temple Arts

Not only have temples been a traditional venue for many folk art displays and performances, particularly lantern-making competitions, puppet shows, and folk operas, but some of the buildings themselves are a virtual repository of some of the most important of the island's folk crafts. Examples of traditional stone-carving, colorful ceramic figurines (known as *chien-nien* 剪黏), and embroidered banners of legendary scenes are just some of the many arts that can be viewed at a well-preserved temple.

The most predominant form of temple craftsmanship, however, is woodcarving. From the entranceway to the back altar, nearly every beam, lintel, and other wooden support structure is covered with elaborate carvings of legendary figures and stories from history, literature, and folklore. Also common are symbolic animals, including birds, dragons and other mythical creatures. The subject matter chosen is often not directly related to the religious function of the temple, but tends to promote traditional ethical values such as loyalty, chastity, filial piety, and patriotism.

Like most traditional crafts, exquisite handcarvings are in danger of being replaced by simpler, machine-tooled decorations. Woodcarving, as well as other temple crafts, have gotten a boost, however, through several temple reconstruction projects. One of the most significant has been the 200-year-old Tsushih Temple 祖師廟 in Sanhsia 三峽, which has been undergoing extensive renovation for 50 years and has employed some of the island's top craftspeople.

Among those who have worked on the Tsushih Temple was Huang Kwei-li 黃龜理, who died in 1996 at the age of 94. In 75 years as a woodcarver and a national Folk Art Master, he created thousands of carvings for more than 80 temples around the island, with many of his works depicting complex battle scenes from history or literature. Like most temple woodcarvers, Huang was heavily influenced by the Taiwanese opera performances that were traditionally performed at temples as part of religious festivities. This shows in the scenes depicted as well as the dramatic poses of the figures.

Another well-known woodcarver is Lee Sung-lin 李松林, also in his nineties and known for his temple figurines. His works can be seen at the Tsushih Temple and the Tienhou Temple 天后宮 in Lukang. Among the younger generation of carvers is 47-year-old Chen Cheng-hsiung 陳正雄, who has worked on the Tsushih reconstruction for more than a decade.

Woodblock Printing

An additional folk art that has benefited from renewed interest is woodblock printing 版畫, used to make colorful Chinese New Year hangings. Traditional woodcut prints in Taiwan are of a simple, rural style brought over by early immigrants from Fujian Province in mainland China.

Common images are the God of Wealth 財神, the Kitchen God 灶神, and Door Gods 門神—who often appear in the form of elaborately dressed and fierce-looking generals. These images are usually printed on red or orange paper in prominent black outlines filled in with several colors.

Among the handful of woodcut artists left is Pan Yuan-shih 潘元石, who has been a key figure in passing on the art to children as well as university students and teachers. Exhibitions and annual competitions sponsored by the Council for Cultural Affairs are also helping to keep the art of New Year printmaking alive. These events promote both traditional and modern methods—including lithography, silkscreening, and etching—as well as a wider variety of subject matter.

Puppetry

Up until the 1960s—before television had arrived in Taiwan—puppet shows were one of the primary forms of entertainment. Nearly any festive occasion, whether a wedding, holiday, or temple festival, called for a puppet performance. Numerous troupes were active throughout the island, and in the early days they often traveled from village to village by foot, carrying their stage, musical instruments, and trunks full of puppets on poles over their shoulders.

The styles of puppetry common in Taiwan—glove puppets 布袋戲, shadow puppets 皮影戲, and marionettes 傀儡戲—were brought here by immigrants from southeastern China in the early 19th century. Although the forms have evolved into distinct local styles and have also adopted modern innovations, they still retain many of the original characteristics, especially in their similarities to Chinese opera. As in opera, a puppet's costume and facial "makeup" indicate the type of character portrayed. Specific roles such as the young scholar, the refined woman, or the fierce general are also drawn from opera.

In glove puppetry, the stage is covered with intricate carvings that are painted gold, resembling the entrance to a traditional Chinese temple. The elaborate setting is ideal for presenting the finely embroidered costumes, exquisite headdresses, and delicately carved faces of the puppets, which stand nearly a foot high. Shadow puppets, which stand one to two feet in height, are expertly cut out of leather, then engraved, dyed, and painted in bright colors. With joints to allow movement, the puppet characters are pressed against a white screen lit from behind, thus creating a colorful and lively performance for audiences. Marionette puppets, about two feet high and manipulated by 11 to 14 strings, are usually presented in front of a simple backdrop. As in Chinese opera, many of the stories used in puppet shows are adapted from classical literature or ancient legends. Some popular examples are *The Tale of the White Serpent* 白蛇傳 and the *Journey to the West* 西遊記. As in opera, traditional puppet performances are always accompanied by live music.

Master Puppeteers

In the hands of several masters, puppetry in Taiwan developed along its own lines into a regional style distinct from puppetry in mainland China. This is especially true of glove puppetry. However, among the 200-some puppet troupes still active around the island, only a handful continue to work primarily in the traditional regional style. One of the most popular was the late Lee Tien-lu 李天祿, whose life was immortalized in Hou Hsiao-hsien's 侯孝賢 award-winning film *The Puppetmaster* 戲夢人生 (1993, see section on Film). Lee, a national Folk Arts Master, first became famous in the 1950s and '60s for his serial dramas based on kungfu novels. Lee was especially popular for his innovative martial arts sequences, acrobatic stunts, and use of modern slang mixed with classical Chinese. Along with his two sons, Lee has also helped to set up two children's puppet troupes, the Wei Wan Jan 微宛然 and the Cheau Wan Jan 巧宛然, both of which have been highly praised. In addition, Lee's own troupe, I Wan Jan 亦宛然, has performed throughout Asia and in the United States and Europe, winning awards at puppetry festivals in New York and France. The beloved puppet master passed away on August 13, 1998, at the age of 90.

Another key figure in glove puppetry is Hsu Wang 許王, whose Hsiao Hsi Yuan 小西園 has also toured extensively abroad, including trips to mainland China, Japan, Canada, and the United States. Hsu also keeps up a busy local schedule, often performing about twice a month. The Chinese Folk Art Foundation also frequently invites Hsu to perform at temples and other venues around the island.

One more acknowledged master is Huang Hai-tai 黃海岱, whose melodramatic tales of ancient swordsmen full of action-filled battle scenes were highlighted by elegant and highly literary dialogue. Huang's son, Huang Chun-hsiung 黃俊雄, was at the forefront of a trend that started in the 1960s to modernize puppet theater and adapt it for television. Using his father's chivalry repertoire, he added popular music and fantastic lighting and other visual effects to create *chin-kuang* 金光 or gold light puppetry. The Huang family now runs its own cable TV channel, devoted exclusively to puppet shows.

The less common forms of shadow and marionette puppetry have had a much harder time surviving than glove puppetry. Among the more prominent representative of shadow puppetry that still perform are the family of Chang Te-cheng 張德成. Chang, who died in 1996, was named a national Folk Art Master. Chang's son, Chang Fu-gwo 張榑國, represents the sixth generation to carry on the family puppet troupe. Also of note is shadow puppeteer Hsu Fu-neng 許福能, whose group Fo Hsing Ko 復興閣皮影劇團 has earned two Folk Art Heritage Awards. The troupe has also toured abroad, to Asia, Europe and North America. Hsu has been highly active in efforts to pass on his art, regularly giving lessons and demonstrations to students across the island.

Painting

There was only a limited amount of traditional Chinese painting practiced in 18th and 19th century Taiwan. Works produced at the time were mostly amateur paintings of landscapes and flowers by scholars or government officials sent from the mainland. This art would have little influence on later artistic developments.

Western-style Oil Painting and Impressionism of the Japanese Era

The first artists of any note came out of the Japanese era (1895-1945), during a time when there were few if any cultural influences from mainland China affecting Taiwan. Painters such as Chen Cheng-po 陳澄波, Li Shih-chiao 李石樵, Li Mei-shu 李梅樹, and Yang San-lang 楊三郎 studied Western-style oil painting in Japan, mainly at the Tokyo Fine Arts Institute, where they absorbed artistic techniques such as fixed perspective and a naturalistic rendering of light and shade. Strongly influenced by French Impressionism (as it had filtered through Japan), these artists were eager to capture and depict the flavor and hues of the Taiwan landscape. Their subject matter often centered on common, daily scenes of the island's villages, farms, and rural areas. The oil painters would have an important influence on future artistic developments, as many of them became influential teachers and leading figures in artistic circles. They also dominated the two most important annual exhibitions of the time, the Taiwan Fine Arts Exhibition 臺灣美術展覽會, first held in 1927, and the Taiyang Arts Show 臺陽美展, which began in 1934. Through their influence at these exhibitions, the Taiwan impressionists ensured that Western-style painting would hold an important place in the future development of Taiwan art.

The works of this group represented what came to be known as nativist art 鄉土藝術, which also had a parallel development in literature. Characterized by a conscious desire to depict images that evoked Taiwan's unique identity, the nativist sensibility also proved to have a long-lasting influence. It would surface again in the 1970s, in both art and literature, and subsequently in music and film.

1950s: Traditional Chinese Painting

While many of the nativist impressionists were reaching their prime, an influx of traditional Chinese ink painters arrived with the ROC government in its move from the mainland. With the government eager to reintroduce Chinese culture to Taiwan, landscape artists such as Huang Chun-pi 黃君璧 and Fu Chuan-fu 傅狷夫 enjoyed official backing, and by the early 1950s their genre of painting had replaced Western styles at official art exhibitions, competitions and in school curriculums.

The most important figure to emerge from the mainland emigre artists was Chang Dai-chien 張大千, who went far beyond the conventional precepts of Chinese painting. Before arriving in Taiwan, he had already made a significant contribution to the Chinese art world with his more than 200 detailed copies of the ancient Buddhist murals in China's Dunhuang Caves 敦煌石窟, which he painted in the early 1940s. Chang's mature paintings, which earned international recognition, were marked by his unique splash-ink technique. Using broad strokes and deliberate blotches of color—often deep greens and blues—he created powerful landscapes that were often monumental in size.

1960: Abstract Art

By the late 1950s and early 1960s, many younger artists were beginning to feel disillusioned with traditional Chinese painting and also unable to identify with the Japanese-trained impressionists. Social changes of the post-war era were begging for a new vehicle of expression. These younger artists, most of them also of mainland origin, were drawn to contemporary Western trends, especially abstract art.

The rising young modernists were very outspoken in their criticism of the older traditionalists. They banded together in private art groups, the most prominent of which were the Eastern Art Group 東方畫會 and the Fifth Moon Group 五月畫會, both formed in the mid-1950s. The most influential among the pioneers of Taiwan abstract art was Li Chung-sheng 李仲生. Once established, some of the more prominent artists of this generation sought to find a synthesis between modern abstraction and traditional painting. Liu Kuo-sung 劉國松 and Chuang Che 莊喆, for example, sought to create a new, modern form of Chinese landscape art.

By the late 1960s, artists were working in a much greater variety of modernist styles as more Western movements filtered into Taiwan. American trends such as pop art, minimalism, and optical art all had their local followers. European trends such as surrealism and especially dada art also found avid supporters. Many modernist painters of the 1960s emigrated to the United States and Europe in order to fully develop their Western-oriented art skills.

1970: New Nativist Art

Artists in the late 1960s and 1970s began rejecting the idolization of Western-style art in search of something that was more in touch with their own environment and their own culture. What emerged was a new nativist movement in Taiwan's arts.

The new movement found its expression most among those who had been trained in Western-style oil painting as well as those with backgrounds in Chinese ink painting. A number of artists who had left Taiwan to find inspiration in America or Europe returned at this time. Among this group was Hsi Te-chin 席德進, who gave up his earlier devotion to abstraction and in 1966 began sketching and painting local scenery and architecture and exploring the island's folk art traditions. His change in direction had significant influence on younger artists of the time.

Another influential artist of this time was Wu Hao 吳昊, whose folk-like woodblock prints were often colorful and nostalgic renditions of the Taiwan countryside. At much the same time, Cheng Shan-hsi 鄭善禧 provided a new direction to traditional ink painting. He focused on local landscape scenes rather than idealized memories of mainland scenery, and also left behind the refined brushstrokes of old in exchange for a more colorful and down-to-earth vitality. In the calligraphic inscriptions on his works, he replaced classical poetic lines with vernacular descriptions.

An important inspiration was also found in the work of "native" artists such as Ju Ming 朱銘 (see section on Sculpture) and Hung Tung 洪通. The latter had no training as a painter but possessed a rich imagination nurtured on Taiwanese

folk traditions. His intriguing, childlike paintings, full of colorful patterns and simplistic figures and animals, became the talk of the art world, especially after the influential *Hsiung Shih Art Monthly* 雄獅美術 published a Hung Tung special issue in 1973.

Contemporary Trends

Artists of the 1980s and '90s encompass a much greater variety of styles and subject matter than in the past.

Taiwan consciousness was an important starting point for the influential 101 Art Group 一○一 現代藝術群, founded in 1982. These artists often expressed their sense of local identity with symbolic or metaphorical images. Wu Tien-chang 吳天章 and Yang Mao-lin 楊茂林, for example, fill their canvases with primitive-looking images that often suggest social events. Working often in monumental scale and with a harsh black and white palette, Wu has also produced works commemorating the February 28 Incident 二二八事件 or commenting on other events and figures from Taiwan's past. By comparison, Yang's *Made in Taiwan* 臺灣製造 series often presents a quieter juxtaposition of subjects native to the island, such as sweet potatoes, sea shells, images of Taiwan's aboriginal peoples, or references to the 17th century Dutch occupation of Taiwan. His approach presents a more subtle vision of Taiwan history and society.

Chinese ink painting has also continued to have a solid standing in Taiwan. Many artists, such as Chiang Chao-shen 江兆申, the late deputy director of the National Palace Museum 國立故宮博物院, remain fairly well-grounded in the traditional style, although many incorporate subtle innovations. Yu Cheng-yao 余承堯, who only began painting after he retired from a long military career, ignores the traditional brushstroke lexicon and instead works over his mountains and trees with closely knit, interwoven strokes that create a richly textured surface.

Other painters have departed from tradition not only in their brushstrokes, but in their subject matter. Lo Ching 羅青, for example, in his *Palm Tree Boulevard* 棕櫚大道 , replaces the standard pine or willow with palm trees and mountains, or waterfalls with an asphalt road. In his inscriptions, he replaces traditional metaphors with modern-day references. Lo and other ink painters have also embraced the exploration of a Taiwan consciousness, drawing much of their inspiration from a local reality rather than from distant memories of mainland China.

Plastic Art

Sculpture

There was no strong formal tradition of sculpture brought from mainland China as in painting. Before the 1920s, temple and folk sculpture were the only sculptural forms thriving in Taiwan, and it was not until the 1970s that sculpture was widely accepted as a fine-art genre.

Taiwan's first fine-art sculptor was Huang Tu-shui 黃土水, born in 1906. Like many painters of his generation, he studied Western-style techniques at the Tokyo Fine Arts Institute. His most celebrated works are of water buffaloes, an animal that symbolizes the heart of the Taiwan countryside. Marked by realism and rational composition, these works are gracefully rendered in low relief, using media ranging from plaster to bronze. After Huang, there were still very few professional sculptors in Taiwan, the most renowned being Chen Hsia-yu 陳夏雨. Chen was also trained in Japan and returned to Taiwan after World War II to create realistic portraits and figures, often of women in pensive poses.

The tide of Western-oriented abstraction that swept the local art world in the 1960s produced the first Taiwan sculptor to gain world attention. Yuyu Yang,who died in 1997, (also known as Yang Ying-feng 楊英風) was most famous for his stainless steel sculptures, which often convert traditional Chinese symbols like the phoenix and dragon into fluid abstract forms. His works are sometimes monumental in size and have been erected in cities around the world. His *East West Gate* 東西門 (1973) stands on Wall Street in Manhattan, and the 23-foot *Advent of the Phoenix* 鳳凰來儀 (1970) can be found in Osaka. In 1996, Yang held a major retrospective of his work in England, at the invitation of the Royal Society of British Sculptors.

The back-to-roots movement of the 1970s (see section on Painting) gave rise to Ju Ming, who was initially trained as a folk sculptor, then went on to study with Yuyu Yang. Ju was initially admired for his rustic, simple figures carved from wood, including the monumental *Tai Chi Series* 太極系列. In recent years, he has explored a variety of materials, including painted bronze and rolled stainless steel sheets, creating abstract figures of athletes, ballerinas, and people in everyday poses. Like Yuyu Yang, Ju has also exhibited worldwide, in Hong Kong, England, New York, and elsewhere.

Although there are not nearly as many sculptors as painters in Taiwan, several, however, are internationally recognized in their field.

Ceramics

Taiwan is also known for its high-quality reproduction ceramics, an industry that got its start in the late 1940s. Several talented figures, such as Lin Te-wen 林德文 and Tsai Hsiao-fang 蔡曉芳, became known for their skill at imitating ancient porcelain. Today, there are a number of kilns in the north-central city of Miaoli 苗栗 and in Yingke 鶯歌鎮, a small town southwest of Taipei, that are known worldwide for their reproductions of Ming and Qing dynasty ceramics.

In the early 1950s, several ceramists—primarily Lin Pao-chia 林葆家, Wu Jang-nung 吳讓農, and Wang Hsiu-kung 王修功—made the first efforts to develop Taiwan's ceramics into a contemporary art form. These men began their careers by working in ceramics factories, helping to revive the industry after its decline during the Japanese occupation. Eventually they broke away to pursue their own creative ideas and to establish teaching studios. Although they remained within the traditional framework of functional ceramics—making vases, bowls, and pots—their works represented a creative venture into unusual shapes and experimental glaze effects.

It was not until the late 1960s, however, that creative ceramists began to gain widespread recognition, thanks in large part to exhibitions at the National Museum of History, which continues to play a central role in promoting the art form. In 1968, the museum held the island's first major solo ceramics show, featuring Wu Jang-nung. In the following decade, ceramic exhibitions at private galleries also gradually became more common. A key figure during this era was Chiu Huan-tang 邱煥堂, who studied ceramics in Hawaii and returned to introduce to Taiwan contemporary ideas from abroad. Ceramist Sun Chao 孫超 also started to gain renown during this time for his crystalline glazes 結晶釉. After a career in the National Palace Museum, Sun began applying his experiments into ancient glazing techniques to his own work. In recent years, he has moved from making decorative crystal patterns on vases and bowls to large, flat glaze "paintings" that combine the sensibility of Chinese ink landscapes with abstract expressionism.

After 1981, ceramic art quickly came into its own, boosted by the 1983 opening of the Taipei Fine Arts Museum, which included ceramics in its opening show. In 1986, the National Museum of History held its first biennial ceramic show, which continues to play a key role in promoting ceramic art. The Chinese Ceramics Association was formed in 1992, and the following year held the first ceramist festival, which featured indoor and outdoor exhibitions, demonstrations, and lectures by prominent ceramic artists.

Seal Carving

Carving name chops, or Chinese seals, with names or other calligraphic inscriptions was once a necessary skill to master for any well-rounded literati artist. It followed right along with painting and calligraphy. Although machine-carved name chops are commonly used for many business transactions, only a handful of artists specialize in hand-engraving name chops. Among them are Wang Pei-yueh 王北岳, who teaches seal carving at the art department of National Taiwan Normal University. Among the younger generation of chopmakers is Huang Ming-hsiu 黄明修, who was recognized in the 1994 Provincial

Art Contest for his work. Name chops are made of wood, jade, or soft precious stones such as *tien huang* 田黃. The body of the chop may be a plain rectangle or it may be sculpted into a lion, dragon, or other symbolic image. Besides their use in business transactions, name chops are also stamped on traditional paintings and calligraphy, both to identify the artist and to add an aesthetic touch.

Museums and the Art Market

Art Museums

Taiwan's best-known museum is, of course, the National Palace Museum in Taipei, a repository for traditional art from mainland China. In 1933, the numerous treasures in the museum's collection started traveling from Peking to Taiwan in a harrowing 12,000-kilometer journey around China over the course of 16 years, evading both the Japanese army and the Chinese communists. The Taipei museum itself finally opened in 1965, and is recognized for having one of the world's best collections of Chinese art, from ancient bronze castings, calligraphy and scroll paintings to porcelains, jade, and rare books. The museum's current collection numbers some 640,000 items, a collection so large that only about 1 percent can be accommodated for display at any one time while the rest is kept in storage.

In 1996, the Palace Museum greatly enhanced its international image with a spectacular US tour of 452 of its finest works of art. The exhibition, "Splendors of Imperial China," ran from March 1996 through April 1997, with stops at the Metropolitan Museum of Art in New York city, the Art Institute of Chicago, the Asian Art Museum of San Francisco, and the National Gallery of Art in Washington, D.C. Curators and scholars in the United States hailed the exhibition, which attracted 900,000 viewers, as a once-in-a-lifetime experience that could very well give new impetus to the study of Chinese art, just as a smaller-scale 1961 exhibition inspired many of today's Chinese art scholars. In 1999, the Palace Museum held a special joint exhibition with the

Szechwan Kuanghan San-hsing-tui Museum on the Chinese mainland, providing a better understanding of the life style of the prehistoric Chinese kingdom of Shu.

The National Museum of History 國立歷史博物館, also located in Taipei, is known for its impressive collection of ancient bronzes, pottery, and ceramic burial figurines. The museum regularly exhibits the works of major Chinese artists of the 20th century. In 1999, the National Museum of History held five exhibitions in Estonia, US, and Latvia, introducing Taiwanese artists.

The Taipei Fine Arts Museum, since its opening in 1983, has been a major catalyst for the development of modern art. It has showcased many local artists and hosted important foreign exhibitions, including the 1999 Outdoor Sculpture of the 20th century, supported by Paris Musees, in the newly opened Taipei Art Park nearby. It also hosts annual and biennial competitions, as well as invitational exhibitions. Modern art museums have also been established in Taichung, and most recently in Kaohsiung. The Kaohsiung Museum of Art, which opened in 1993, is billed as the largest fine arts museum in Asia.

The Chang Foundation Museum 鴻禧美術館, which opened in 1991, is the island's first private museum showing Chinese art. Although relatively small, with about 16,000 square feet of exhibition space, it has an impressive collection that features traditional painting, exquisite porcelain, and other ceramics. In 1999, it showed its private collection of historical Chinese tea utensils in Paris, in cooperation with the Centre Culturel et d'Information de Taipei à Paris, successfully bringing masterpieces of Chinese crafts to the capital of France.

Galleries

The gallery scene in Taiwan has grown tremendously in the past 15 to 20 years from a single enterprise, the Lungmen Gallery 龍門畫廊 in 1975, to about 150 galleries today. The Lungmen has retained its prominence among the galleries and show works by artists from Taiwan as well as overseas. The Hanart Gallery

漢雅軒, which has a home gallery in Hong Kong, has also played an important role in promoting Taiwan's younger generation of artists.

Among the scores of other galleries, some that stand out include the Galerie Elegance 愛力根畫廊, the Eslite Gallery 誠品畫廊, the Taiwan Gallery 臺灣畫廊 and Home Gallery 家畫廊 which focus on contemporary art, and the Caves Art Center 敦煌藝術中心 and the Pristine Harmony Art Center 清韻藝術中心 which focus on Chinese ink paintings by both traditional and not-so-traditional artists. IT Park 伊通公園, on the other hand, is an alternative gallery for artists looking for a non-commercial environment. It has provided a much-needed venue for installation and performance artists.

Several galleries in central and southern Taiwan are also beginning to establish themselves in the art market. Some of the best known include Gallery Pierre 臻品藝術中心, East Gallery 東之畫廊, and Modern Art Gallery 現代藝術空間 in Taichung; New Phase Art Space 新生態藝術環境 in Tainan; the Up Gallery 阿普畫廊 and Duchamp Gallery 杜象藝術中心 in Kaohsiung; and Venus Gallery 維納斯藝廊 in Hualien 花蓮.

The boom in art galleries around the island has been partly due to the great increase in art collecting in the 1980s, which in turn has been driven by a boom in the stock and real estate markets. Taiwan collectors have also become involved in the art markets in Hong Kong and New York, prompting such high-profile auction houses as Sotheby's and Christie's to provide previews of their Hong Kong and New York auctions in Taiwan to attract buyers. This eventually led both houses to hold auctions in Taiwan beginning in the early 1990s, with varying success. They have focused primarily on traditional Chinese painting and works by Taiwan's Japanese-trained impressionists such as Chen Cheng-po, whose 1931 painting *Sunset at Tamsui* 黃昏淡水 (see section on Painting) sold for US$380,000 in 1993, a record-breaking price for a Chinese painting sold by Sotheby's.

Another major development has been the annual Taipei Art Fair International 臺北國際藝術

博覽會, begun in 1992, which serves to promote the local art market both regionally and internationally. Organized by the ROC Art Galleries Association 中華民國畫廊協會, the 1997 fair included 45 galleries, not only from the ROC, but also from the US, Australia, Singapore, Hong Kong, and Finland.

Music

The great variety and rich tradition of music in Taiwan has been highlighted by such events as "100 Years of Taiwanese Music" 臺灣音樂一百年, a major festival and conference held in 1995. Performances included Taiwanese folk songs, Fujian and Hakka music, as well as contemporary compositions by some of Taiwan's leading composers (see section below on Composers). Other big music events, such as the 1996 Taipei International Music Festival 臺北國際樂展, and the 1998 Asian Composers' League Conference and Festival 亞洲作曲家聯盟大會暨音樂節, held in Taipei, have also encompassed a wide range of music, traditional and contemporary, Chinese and Western.

Traditional Chinese Music

The four main professional groups performing primarily Chinese music are the Taipei Municipal Chinese Classical Orchestra (TMCCO) 臺北市立國樂團, the National Experimental Chinese Orchestra 國立臺灣藝術學院實驗國樂團, the Kaohsiung Experimental Chinese Orchestra 高雄市實驗國樂團, and the Chinese Orchestra of the Broadcasting Corporation of China 中國廣播公司國樂團. In addition, about ten smaller ensembles perform regularly around the island. One of the more prominent is the Ensemble Orientalia of Taipei 臺北民族樂團, which has performed in the United States and Australia. The ensemble is also involved in fieldwork, including researching and transcribing traditional music from throughout Taiwan.

While the musicians in these groups play mostly traditional Chinese instruments, they sometimes perform Western compositions or Chinese works that incorporate Western-style rhythms or harmonies. The TMCCO, for example, has performed such well-known classical works as Ludwig van Beethoven's Symphony No. 5 in C Minor and Franz Schubert's Symphony No.8 in B Minor ("Unfinished") on Chinese instruments. And the National Experimental Chinese Orchestra has presented works by Aaron Copeland and Randall Thompson in conjunction with a Western-style chorus.

Increased cultural contacts with mainland China have brought new ideas to Chinese music in Taiwan. Since the late 1980s, a number of groups from the mainland (representing by Western-style and traditional music) have performed here, including major orchestras such as the Shanghai National Music Orchestra and the China Central Ensemble of National Music, as well as smaller ensembles such as the Shanghai Quartet and the Shanghai Chinese Traditional Folk Music Ensemble.

Cross-strait exchange has also included performers from Taiwan visiting the mainland, although these are mainly Western-style musicians.

Pei-Kuan and Nan-Kuan

While many traditional Chinese musicians are drawing on Western influences, others have shown a renewed interest in preserving the traditional quality of several types of ancient music—including pei-kuan 北管, a fast-tempo music that was once commonly played as an accompaniment at operas and traditional puppet shows, and nan-kuan 南管, which has a more delicate and soothing sound. The interest in nan-kuan music has been especially prominent. This musical form is thought to have flourished in southern China during the Tang dynasty and first appeared in Taiwan during the 16th century. A major performer of nan-kuan music today is the Han Tang Classical Musical Institute 漢唐樂府, founded in 1983 by Chen Mei-o 陳美娥, which has performed in the United States, Europe and Asia, and has released a number of CDs. The group later established the Liyuan Dance Studio 梨園舞坊, which draws its inspiration from "The Musical Theater of the Pear Orchard" 梨園戲, a form that also flourished during the 8th century and was brought to Taiwan in the 18th century. The two often perform together at Han Tang's own theater in Taipei, which offers a small, traditional teahouse-like setting.

Other main figures in passing on the tradition of nan-kuan music have been singer Wu Su-ching 吳素慶 and musician Lee Hsiang-shih 李祥石, who has been honored with the Folk Arts Master Award (see section on Folk Arts). Wu and Lee were both invited to teach in a special Nan-kuan Performance Program set up in 1988 at the National Institute of the Arts. The Changhua County Cultural Center 彰化縣立文化中心 has also maintained a Nan-kuan and Pei-kuan Center 南北管音樂劇曲館 since 1990.

Western Classical Music

While traditional Chinese music—whether it adopts foreign influences or maintains its original flavor—has an important position in Taiwan, Western classical music still predominates. In fact, many more musicians are trained in Western music than in Chinese music. Young classical musicians from Taiwan, along with their counterparts elsewhere in Asia, have been making a strong mark in international music circles in recent years. Violinists Lin Chao-liang 林昭亮, Hu Nai-yuan 胡乃元, and Edith Chen 陳毓襄 are just three of the many Taiwan-born musicians who have attended elite music schools abroad, winning prestigious competitions, and become prominent on the international concert circuit. Another prominent figure is conductor Lu Shao-chia 呂紹嘉, a graduate of the Vienna Conservatory and now the opera conductor for the Komische Oper Berlin. While these young talents often go on to successful careers abroad, many more are now returning to Taiwan, both as visiting musicians and as regular members of orchestras and chamber groups.

Taiwan's main Western-style orchestras are the National Symphony Orchestra 國家音樂廳交響樂團, now under the artistic direction of Jahja Wang-chieh Lin 林望傑, and the Taipei City Symphony Orchestra 臺北市立交響樂團, conducted by Chen Chiu-sheng 陳秋盛. Outside of Taipei are the Taiwan Symphony Orchestra 臺灣省立交響樂

團, based in Taichung, and the semi-professional Kaohsiung City Symphony Orchestra 高雄市實驗交響樂團.

The largest privately run orchestra is the Taipei Sinfonietta and Philharmonic Orchestra 臺北愛樂室內及管弦樂團, founded in 1985 by conductor Henry Mazer. With some of the island's most talented musicians among its members, the group has toured the United States, Canada, and Europe.

Perhaps the busiest ensemble on the island is the Ju Percussion Group, directed by Ju Tsung-ching 朱宗慶. The group performs more than 100 times every year, at performance halls as well as at schools and outdoor venues, and holds many educational demonstrations for teachers and the general public. The group's music is often a hybrid of Western and Chinese, and its instruments are both traditional and experimental, ranging from drums, gongs, and xylophones to empty beer bottles, sawed-off steel pipes, and even bursting balloons. The affiliated Ju Percussion Foundation 財團法人打擊樂文教基金會 oversees a research center for traditional Chinese percussion music and runs educational centers for children around the island. In 1996, the foundation organized the second International Percussion Convention. In 1997, the group performed in Washington, D.C., New York, Los Angles, Seoul and Beijing.

Western Opera

Thanks to such groups as the Taipei Opera Theater 臺北歌劇劇場, under Tseng Tao-hsiung 曾道雄, and the Taiwan Metropolitan Opera 首都歌劇團, directed by internationally known tenor William Wu 吳文修, Western opera has also established a foothold in Taiwan. The Taipei Opera Theater has performed such works as Gounod's *Faust*, Mozart's *Magic Flute*, and Verdi's *Rigoletto*. The Taiwan Metropolitan Opera has presented Puccini's *Madame Butterfly*, Leoncavallo's *Cavalleria Rusticana*, and *Pagliacci*, as well as *The Great Wall* 萬里長城 a Western-style opera sung in Chinese and narrating a Chinese story. Another active opera promoter has been the Taipei City Symphony Orchestra, which in 1995 presented Verdi's *Aida* and in January 1997 Wagner's *The Flying Dutchman*, both featuring international casts.

Composers

Taiwan has played host to the annual conference and festival of the highly regarded Asian Composers' League (ACL), most recently in 1998. Hsu Chang-hui 許常惠, considered by many to be the pioneer for local composers, was one of the founders of the ACL in 1973. Hsu, who studied in France, founded the Music Creative Group 製樂小集, which in the 1960s played an important role in promoting the development of local music composition. He also introduced to local music circles new, experimental developments from the West, such as Arnold Schoenberg's serialism. In addition, Hsu has also been involved for many years in extensive research of Taiwan folk music.

Other composers with strong reputations, locally as well as regionally and internationally, include Ma Shui-long 馬水龍, whose works have been performed in Europe, the United States, South Africa, and Southeast Asia, and Pan Huang-lung 潘皇龍, who has introduced some avant-garde ideas for composition to local audiences.

Many local organizations and performing groups have made extensive efforts to promote Taiwan composers. In 1996, for example, the Council for Cultural Affairs and the Chiang Kai-shek National Concert Hall 國家音樂廳 sponsored the Taipei Composition Competition 臺北作曲比賽, which featured an international jury and offered exposure to some of Taiwan's younger composers.

Drama

Chinese Opera

Chinese opera is one of Taiwan's premier art forms. Although performances are not as frequent as they once were, they can still be seen on a weekly basis at opera schools, community theaters and temples, and on television, as well as in major seasonal productions at the National Theater 國家戲劇院. While the form includes many regional styles, the most common in Taiwan are Peking opera, which first reached maturity in the Ching dynasty, and Taiwanese opera (see section on Taiwanese Opera below), which was influenced by operatic forms of southern China. Most regional forms of Chinese opera are sung in the dialect of their region of origin, hence Taiwanese opera is performed by speaking and singing in Southern Fukienese. Beijing opera is an exception, however. Dialogue is in the Beijing dialect, but the arias are recited or sung in an artificial stage dialect that combines phonetic features of various parts of the Chinese mainland from which it was synthesized in the 18th century.

Beijing Opera

Although traditionally performed on an empty or nearly empty stage, Beijing opera is a colorful and often lively form of drama. Plots are adapted from enduring tales in Chinese history and classical literature where the theatricality of a particular point in the narrative can be successfully exploited on stage. The demands of this theatrical spectacle ensure the inclusion of at least one exciting battle scene or acrobatic display per performance. Plot development reflects traditional Chinese Confucian moral values, such as loyalty, filial piety, and patriotism, although human foibles are also well represented. All characters in a given play are developed within the confines of traditional character roles, with each actor specializing in a specific type of character, such as the *hsiao-sheng* 小生, a handsome and scholarly young man, the *wu-tan* 武旦, a beautiful female warrior, or the *chou* 丑, a clown-like figure who brings comic relief. Each role is marked by a specific range of gestures and a codified style of makeup. Singing is highly stylized, with some characters requiring a high-pitched falsetto (since traditionally, only men appeared on stage, even in female roles). Live musical accompaniment is closely integrated with the action, with the conductor regulating the pace of performance and cueing actors through his control of the basic percussive beat. Traditional string and wind instruments accompany the singing, while percussion comments on virtually all stage movements, marks stage entrances and exits, and serves to bring additional excitement to fighting and acrobatic scenes.

Taiwan's major Beijing opera troupes are the National Kuo Kuang Chinese Opera Company 國光劇團 and the National Fu-Hsing Chinese Opera Theater 復興劇團. The former, which is funded by the Ministry of Education, was established in 1995 following the shutdown of three major military-sponsored opera troupes; performers from those groups merged into the new one. Kuo Kuang maintains a highly traditional repertoire. Although most of the company's productions are long-established opera scripts, its most recent, in October 1996, featured a new script, which was based on a scenario originally written by opera great Mei Lan-fang 梅蘭芳.

The Fu-Hsing company is affiliated with the National Fu-Hsing Dramatic Arts Academy 國立復興劇藝實驗學校, the island's main training school for Chinese opera. The company is known for being more adventuresome in its productions, which tend to be new scripts that often combine traditional and modern ideas. Its 1996 fall production, *When Chang O Meets Armstrong* 當嫦娥碰上阿姆斯壯, was billed as a Beijing opera for children. Another 1996 production, *The Story of Ah-Q* 阿Q正傳, was based on an early 20th century short story by mainland writer Lu Hsun 魯迅.

One of the first to begin experimenting, although on a more modest scale of modernization, was Kuo Hsiao-chuang 郭小莊, who founded the Ya-yin Ensemble 雅音小集 in 1979. Kuo attracted many younger audience members by bringing a stronger visual dimension to her productions, adding more props, dramatic lighting effects, and revolving platforms to the nearly bare, evenly lit stage of traditional opera. The troupe has not been active in the last several years, although Kuo does continue to perform on occasion in mainland China.

Another important innovator has been the Contemporary Legend Theater 當代傳奇劇場, founded by opera actor Wu Hsing-kuo 吳興國 in 1984. The internationally acclaimed group is best known for its Beijing opera adaptations of Western classics such as Shakespeare's *Macbeth*

and Euripides' *Medea*. These adaptations incorporate elements of Western drama, including dramatic stage and costume designs, and greater psychological character development than is generally found in traditional Chinese opera. Using tragic stories that raise moral questions rather than provide conventional answers, is also a distinct departure from tradition. Due to financial difficulties, the group stopped performing in late 1998.

Taiwanese Opera

Taiwanese opera 歌仔戲, the theatrical art form believed to have originated in Taiwan, was once performed on nearly any auspicious occasion, including weddings, birthdays, and temple festivals. By tradition, the form is said to have its roots in short songs originating in Ilan County 宜蘭縣 which purportedly was influenced by the narrative music of Taiwan's aboriginal peoples, evolved into a powerful musical form. These "Ilan folk songs" are distinguished by an orchestra consisting of the *san-hsien* 三絃, a three-stringed Chinese banjo; the *pipa* 琵琶, a four-stringed vertical lute; the *tung-hsiao* 洞簫, a vertical flute; the *sona* 哨吶, a trumpet-belled, double-reeded horn; and, various percussion instruments, including gongs and drums. However, various regional Chinese music theater forms clearly had an influence on Taiwanese opera, particularly the pei-kuan and nan-kuan music theater brought to Taiwan by early immigrants from southern China. This is evident in its colorful makeup and costumes, stage props, and stylized gestures. Taiwanese opera was a full-fledged musical genre by the 1930s.

The role of Ilan in the development of Taiwanese opera continues to be important today. Several major troupes are based there, including one sponsored by the Ilan County Cultural Center, which also houses a Taiwanese opera museum. Today, there are nearly 200 troupes performing around the island, but only a handful of professional calibre. The best-known is the highly popular Ming Hwa Yuan Theater Troupe 明華園歌劇團, established in 1929. Like other Taiwanese opera troupes, Ming Hwa Yuan started out playing only on outdoor stages, often set up in front of temples, but today it also performs at prestigious venues such as the National Theater. The troupe has also toured overseas, performing in Paris as well as mainland China.

Other important companies include the Ho Lo Taiwanese Opera Troupe 河洛歌仔戲團, the Han Yang Troupe 漢陽歌劇團, and the Lan Yang Troupe 蘭陽戲劇團.

Another important name in Taiwanese opera is Yang Li-hua 楊麗花, the genre's most celebrated actress. With a career spanning some 30 years, she continues to periodically present her own productions. Like many Taiwanese opera actresses, Yang is known for playing only male roles.

Television performances of Taiwanese opera have also played an important role in the form's development since the 1960s. Although many TV troupes have resorted to a soap opera mentality, complete with electronic music and pop songs, the Yeh Ching Taiwanese Opera Troupe 葉青歌仔戲團 is one that has worked to keep the basic traditional form intact. Actress Yeh Ching has developed an islandwide following through her TV performances and has won numerous prizes.

Other Regional Opera Forms

The Kuo Kuang company 國光劇團豫劇隊, has a section for Henan opera 河南梆子, which is sung in a natural voice rather than the falsetto common to Peking opera. Taiwan audiences have also been introduced to Hakka opera, which incorporates traditional tea-farming folk songs, through the Rom-shing Hakka Teapicker Opera Troupe 榮興客家採茶劇團. In keeping with tradition, the majority of its productions are presented outdoors, although it also performs at major venues such as the National Theater.

Another winner of the Heritage Award is the Hsin Mei Yuan Troupe 新美園劇團, the only professional pei-kuan opera group on the island.

An opera form that has been regaining attention is kun opera 崑曲, which preserves late Ching dynasty musical scores and singing techniques from the longest extant tradition of Chinese music theater, possibly dating back to the late 12th or early 13th century. Compared to Beijing opera, Kun opera features more delicate and complex music and singing, and employs more poetic language. Although there are currently only two amateur groups performing kun opera in Taiwan, a major project is under way to establish a professional troupe. Under the sponsorship of the Kuo Kuang opera school and the private Chinese Folk Arts Foundation 中華民俗藝術基金會, 20 students have been chosen for a three-year training program; the group will train under a series of kun masters from the Chinese mainland.

Spoken Drama

Non-musical Theater

The first Western-style spoken drama in Taiwan was based on the realistic styles of 19th and early 20th century playwrights such as Ibsen, Chekhov, and Eugene O'Neill. The only plays produced, however, were dull and didactic performances by government-sponsored troupes that attracted little attention.

The beginnings of the dynamic theater scene of today began in the 1960s, with what is known as the Little Theater Movement 小劇場運動. Thanks to the enthusiasm and talent of several new dramatists, including Li Man-kuei 李曼瑰 and Yao Yi-wei 姚一葦, the repertoire of locally written plays expanded and took a more creative direction. Li alone wrote more than 50 plays, including full-length dramas, one-act works, and children's performances. These have been compiled in a volume entitled *Collection of Chinese Plays* 中華戲劇集.

The first professional stage play produced by an independent (rather than government-sponsored) troupe was Yao Yi-wei's *Red Nose* 紅鼻子, which became a classic among local plays, and was later staged in Peking and Japan as well. The 1970 debut of *Red Nose* helped to usher in the prolific era of the 1970s, when private minitheaters proliferated and directors began experimenting more freely with staging techniques and imaginative interpretations of both local and Western plays.

Early Innovators

Among other things, the Lan-ling Drama Workshop 蘭陵劇坊, founded in 1977 by Wu Ching-chi 吳靜吉, was the first theater group to recast a Chinese opera in modern colloquial language. This involved a very experimental approach that emphasized strong physical movement and the importance of body language. Lan-ling's groundbreaking 1977 production *Ho-chu's New Match* 荷珠新配, adapted from a well-known Peking opera story, was a contemporary social satire on the new bourgeoisie. This play paved the way for a new theatrical genre in Taiwan, with future theater groups staging contemporary adaptations of other Beijing operas. Other Lan-ling productions were even more avant-garde, such as its 1986 adaptation of the ancient Chinese poetry anthology, *Nine Songs* 九歌, which dispensed with both plot and dialogue, in favor of improvisation, rhythmic movements, chanting, and other elements of ritualism. Although Lan-ling is no longer active, it continues to have an influence on theater in Taiwan.

Another pioneer in the theater world was the New Aspect Art Center 新象藝術中心, established in 1978. Although New Aspect never maintained an actual theater group (it has since developed into an arts agency, bringing a wide variety of performing arts to Taiwan from abroad), it has produced a number of major plays and presented some new dramatic forms to the local theater world. In 1982, it introduced a new multimedia approach associated with epic theater in the landmark production of *Wandering in the Garden and Waking from a Dream* 遊園驚夢. Taiwan's first homegrown musical, *The Chess King* 棋王, was also a New Aspect production.

The Performance Workshop

The early efforts of Lan-ling and New Aspect helped set the stage for the mid-1980s, which saw the establishment of several leading theater companies that are still active today. Most prominent is the Performance Workshop 表演工作坊, set up in 1984 by Stan Lai 賴聲川, who introduced collective improvisational theater to

Taiwan. Lai's ideas about collective theatre have been heavily influenced by Shireen Strooker's Amsterdam Werkteater.

The group's first production to attract more than just a student audience was *The Night We Became Hsiang-sheng Comedians* 那一夜我們說相聲. The play marked the first time that the highly stylized *hsiang-sheng* 相聲, a traditional form of fast-paced comic dialogue (cross-talk), was expanded into a full-length play.

Performance Workshop's other productions have also offered reflections on modern Taiwan society. For example, *The Island and the Other Shore* 回頭是彼岸 (1989) and *Look Who's Cross-talking Tonight* 這一夜誰來說相聲 both grapple with the island's complex and controversial relationship with mainland China. In the 1994 play *Red Sky* 紅色的天空, the troupe revealed the experiences of Taiwan's elderly population. The two week performance of *The Complete History of Chinese Thought-Cross Talk Version* in 1997 at the National Theater again ran to capacity audiences. Performance Workshop director Stan Lai has ventured into filmmaking, with one of his movies based on his play *The Peach Blossom Land* 暗戀桃花源 (see section on Film, The Second New Wave).

Like the Performance Workshop, the Pin-Fong Acting Troupe 屏風表演班, set up in 1986, has become widely popular among local audiences. Directed by Li Kuo-hsiu 李國修, who formerly worked with the Lan-ling as well as the Performance Workshop, the troupe presents mainly comedies, often of a slapstick nature. But underneath the pranks and wisecracks are satirical comments on Taiwan society.

The Godot Theater Company 果陀劇場, set up in 1988, often combines theater, music and dance. The company has staged Taiwan-oriented adaptations of such works as *Our Town* and Shakespeare's *The Taming of the Shrew*. The Godot's 1996 production was a martial arts drama called *Chiao Feng, the End of Destiny* 天龍八部之喬峰, adapted from a Chinese swashbuckler novel written by Chin Yung 金庸 about a beggar king.

Another unusual group is the U Theater 優劇場, founded by Liu Ching-min 劉靜敏 and dedicated to creating a form of contemporary theater that expresses a unique Taiwanese identity. To absorb the traditions of the culture, the actors and actresses take part in a strict physical training program that includes martial arts and have also worked with a variety of folk artists, such as Taiwanese opera performers and traditional drummers.

Recent years has also seen a rise in theater companies based in central and southern Taiwan. These include the Hwa Teng Troupe 華燈劇團 in Tainan, the Taitung Theater Troupe 臺東劇團, and the Nan Feng Theater Troupe 南風劇團 of Kaohsiung.

Dance

The dance world in Taiwan today is surprisingly diverse, considering it really got its start only in the late 1960s. However, there are some early pioneers that should be mentioned, especially in modern dance. Tsai Jui-yueh 蔡瑞月 and Lee Tsai-o 李彩娥, having studied European-influenced modern dance in Japan, began giving performances in the 1940s. But soon after, when the Nationalists moved to Taiwan in 1949, modern dance began to take a back seat in favor of Chinese folk dance, which the government encouraged as a means for promoting traditional Chinese culture on the island.

In the 1960s, local dancers and audiences began to get a taste of new styles, thanks to tours by American companies such as Alvin Ailey and Paul Taylor. Modern dance again began to come to the forefront.

Mother of Modern Dance

One of the first to introduce modern dance to Taiwan was Liu Feng-hsueh 劉鳳學, whom many today consider the matriarch of the dance world. Using dancers from her own studio, established in 1967, and from her students in the physical education department at National Taiwan Normal University, Liu began presenting showings of modern choreography. In 1976, she formed the Neo-Classic Dance Company 新古典舞團, which continues to perform today. Her choreographic style is heavily influenced by Rudolf Laban, whose famous system of dance notation she studied in Germany in the 1970s. As a result, many of her works, such as *Carmina Burana* (1993), appear very mathematical, with an emphasis on structural concepts of space and group formation.

The Cloud Gate Dance Theater

At the same time that Liu was beginning to make her mark in the early 1970s, Lin Hwai-min 林懷民 was forming the Cloud Gate Dance Theater 雲門舞集, which would go on to become Taiwan's premier dance company, gaining a devoted local audience as well as an international reputation in numerous overseas tours. After studying under Martha Graham, Lin returned to Taiwan in 1973 and began using modern techniques along with Chinese opera movement. His early works had strong Chinese themes, as in *The Tale of the White Serpent*, an updated version of a classic story.

Similar to the nativist artists and writers (see section on Painting, and Chapter 24, Literature) of the 1970s, Lin was eager to express a local identity. Cloud Gate's signature work, *Legacy* 薪傳 (1978), told the dramatic story of the first Chinese pioneers to arrive in Taiwan. *Crossing the Black Water* 渡海, one segment of *Legacy* that has been performed on its own numerous times, is a spellbinding portrayal of the pioneers crossing the Taiwan Strait, with a huge billowing white sheet acting as the treacherous water. Later works dealt with more contemporary concerns. *The Rite of Spring* 春之祭 (1983), for example, took a harrowing look at the plight of urban existence. The 1984 *Dreamscape* 夢土, and its 1995 reproduction, explored the Chinese conflict between modern life and traditional culture.

In recent years, Lin has begun to combine more universal inspirations into his choreography. The 90-minute *Nine Songs* 九歌 (1993), which was re-staged at New York's Kennedy Center in 1995, draws on the work of ancient Chinese poet Chu Yuan 屈原 and contains many references to gods and goddesses, as well as traits found in Indian and Javanese dance and Chinese opera movement. References can also be found to historical tragedies, such as executions by the Japanese and Chinese governments in Taiwan, and the massacre at Tienanmen Square. In 1997, the troupe performed *Songs of the Wanderers* in Paris, Copenhagen, and Hamburg.

Lin Hwai-min's new work *A Moon in the Water* 水月 (1998) premiered in November 1998 along with the highly acclaimed *Songs of the Wanderers* as part of the *Spiritual, Quiet Journey* 靈，靜之旅 series. This work assimilates gestures of taichi and meditative philosophy into dances that dwell on the theme of "nothingness."

Diverse Dance Styles

Since the 1980s, a number of smaller dance companies have started up, many of them founded by former Cloud Gate members. Among the most prominent is Lin Hsiu-wei's 林秀偉 Taigu Tales Dance Theater 太古踏舞團, known for its meditative dances based on Asian philosophical thought. With an emphasis on poetic expression and soul-searching, her works are stirring and cathartic, often with a primitive quality akin to the modern Japanese dance form Butoh. Another former Cloud Gate dancer is Liu Shao-lu 劉紹爐, who also studied with Liu Feng-hsueh early in his career and started his own group, the Taipei Dance Circle 光環舞集, seven years ago. Liu's best known work, *Olympics* 奧林匹克, is based on an innovative technique in which dancers with oiled bodies spin and slide on an oiled floor to create a surprisingly poetic display of motion. In 1998, he was granted the second National Award of Culture and Arts for dance.

Working in a very different style is the Dance Forum Taipei 舞蹈空間, founded in 1989 by Ping Heng 平珩. Under artistic director Sunny Pang 彭錦耀, originally from Hong Kong, the group presents a wide mixture of styles, but is best known for works that combine a postmodern sensibility with a Chinese or Asian frame of reference.

Although ballet has held a less prominent position in Taiwan's dance world, there are several schools and small companies that perform it.

One of the better known is the Taipei Chamber Ballet 臺北室內芭蕾舞團, which presents annual summer concerts choreographed by Yu Nengsheng 余能盛, also a dancer with the Osnabruck Ballet in Germany.

Folk Dance

Dances drawing inspiration from Taiwan's folk tradition have seen a major flowering in Legend Lin Dance Theater's 無垢舞蹈劇場 *Mirrors of Life* 醮, by Lin Li-chen 林麗珍, which was invited to France's Avignon Art Festival in July and August 1998. This work, with its strong local flavor, features the vivacity of Taiwan's folk culture and brilliantly demonstrates Taiwan's originality in choreography. Inspired by Taiwan's folk rituals, especially the great sacrificial feasts of the Ghost Festival set out in temples to appease wandering ghosts, the highly stylistic *Mirrors of Life* transcends the limits of culture and convention and attains universality through its enticing quietude, harmony, mystery, and wildness. This work explores the relation between (wo)man and (wo)man, between (wo)man and environment, as well as between (wo)man and unnamable, intangible forces.

Several children's folk dance troupes have also disseminated Chinese culture abroad. The best-known internationally is the Lan Yang Dancers 天主教蘭陽舞蹈團. Established in 1966 by Catholic missionary Gian Carlo Michelini, the troupe has been received by Vatican popes on six occasions and has performed in more than 20 countries, including a performance in Brazil in October 1997. (See also, the Formosa Aboriginal Dance Troupe in the section on Aboriginal Arts.)

Cinema

One of the most talked-about developments in the international film world in recent years has been the surge in award-winning works by Asian directors and producers—and much of the conversation has centered around Taiwan.

Since the late 1980s, Taiwan films have secured a regular place in film festivals and award ceremonies around the world. The honors have included the prestigious Golden Lion for best film awarded by the Venice International Film Festival to *City of Sadness* 悲情城市 (1989) by Hou Hsiao-hsien, and *Vive l'Amour* 愛情萬歲 (1994) by Tsai Ming-liang 蔡明亮; the Golden Bear awarded by the Berlin International Film Festival to *The Wedding Banquet* 喜宴 (1993) by Ang Lee 李安; the Jury Prize awarded by the Cannes Festival to Hou Hsiao-hsien's *The Puppetmaster* (1993); and a nomination of *The Wedding Banquet* for best foreign film at the 1994 Academy Awards.

Taiwan cinema continued to make a mark in 1996, with a particularly impressive showing at the Asia-Pacific Film Festival: a best director's award to Hou Hsiao-hsien for *Good Men, Good Women* 好男好女, best screenplay to Lee Khan 李崗 and Sylvia Chang 張艾嘉 for *Tonight, Nobody Goes Home* 今天不回家, and a special juror's award for *Ah Chung* 忠仔, directed by Chang Tso-chi 張作驥. In 1997, *The River* 河流, directed by Tsai Ming-liang, won a special jury prize of the Golden Berlin Bear. In 1998, Hou Hsiao-hsien's *Flowers of Shanghai* 海上花 and Tsai Ming-liang's *The Hole* 洞 were among the Features in Competition at the Cannes Festival.

It is only in the last dozen years, however, that Taiwan cinema has come into its own. Although during the late 1960s and early 1970s the island's film industry was one of the strongest in Asia, the scene was dominated by syrupy romances, grade-B kungfu movies, and moralistic or propaganda-oriented dramas. In time, the public and the media began to grow weary of the limited variety of domestically produced films. People were also being exposed to high-quality foreign movies through film festivals held by the National Film Archives 電影資料館 (originally the Motion Picture Library 電影圖書館), set up in 1977, and through the increasing availability of movies on videotape. Opportunities for scholarships and awards for young filmmakers and scriptwriters through the Motion Picture Development Fund 中華民國電影事業發展基金, established in 1975, also helped create a better environment for quality cinema. Another plus was the Golden Horse Awards 金馬獎, Taiwan's version of the Oscars. Although established in 1962, the awards first started to attract attention in 1980, and since then have become a prestigious affair in the Taiwan film world.

New Wave Cinema

The real breakthrough for Taiwan cinema came in 1982 with *In Our Time* 光陰的故事, a four-part film produced by the Central Motion Picture Corporation 中央電影公司 that featured four talented young directors (Edward Yang 楊德昌, Tao Te-chen 陶德辰, Ko I-cheng 柯一正, and Chang Yi 張毅). The film won over audiences by replacing melodrama and escapism with a realistic look at life in Taiwan.

This new approach paved the way for what came to be known as the New Cinema, or New Wave Cinema, which has been compared stylistically to the Italian neo-realism. Initially inspired by Taiwan's nativist literature of the 1960s and 1970s (see also Chapter 24, Literature), New Wave directors such as Hou Hsiao-hsien, Edward Yang, and Wang Tung 王童 created a cinema with a unique Taiwanese flavor by focusing on realistic and sympathetic portrayals of both rural and urban life.

Many New Cinema films were actually based on famous nativist novels. This was in fact the continuation of an established tradition of adapting literary works to the screen. From 1965 to 1983, for example, a total of 50 films were adapted from the romance novels of Chiung Yao 瓊瑤. But the New Wave directors were interested not only in stories of these novels, but also in their realistic, down-to-earth style and spirit. They wanted to give a genuine local flavor to their films. Like the nativist writers, they also took a critical look at some of the central issues facing Taiwan society—the struggle against poverty, the conflicts with political authority, the growing pains of urbanization and industrialization.

One of the first films in this mode was *The Sandwich Man* 兒子的大玩偶 (1983), a three-part movie by directors Hou Hsiao-hsien, Tseng Chuang-hsiang 曾壯祥, and Wan Jen 萬仁. It was adapted from short stories by the famous writer Huang Chun-ming 黃春明 that deal with the struggles of working class people in 1960s Taiwan.

As evident in *The Sandwich Man*, the New Cinema directors took a highly introspective approach in examining the effects of the tremendous political, social, and economic changes that Taiwan had experienced in the past 50 or more years. Their works thus offer a fascinating chronicle of the island's social transformation in modern times. For example, Wang Tung's *The Strawman* 稻草人 (1987) and *Hill of No Return* 無言的山丘 (1992) portray the tragic, work-burdened lives of rural Taiwanese during the Japanese occupation. Wang's latest work is *The Red Persimmon* 紅柿子 (1996), the story of a mainland family that escaped to Taiwan in 1949. Hou Hsiao-hsien's *The City of Sadness* takes place in the same era, focusing on the conflicts between the local Taiwanese and the newly arrived Nationalist government that came to a climax in the February 28 Incident of 1945 (for historical details, see section concerning the ROC on Taiwan in Chapter 4, History). Another of Hou's film's *A Time to Live and a Time to Die* 童年往事 (1985) examines life in rural Taiwan in the 1950s and 1960s, and his more recent *Good Men, Good Women* covers political developments from the end of World War II to the present day. In contrast, the works of Edward Yang, such as *Taipei Story* 青梅竹馬 (1985), *The Terrorizers* 恐怖份子 (1986) and *Confucian Confusion* 獨立時代 (1994), reflect the clash of traditional values and modern materialism among young urbanites of the 1980s and '90s.

Second New Wave

While New Wave films have continued to win critical acclaim, the initial enthusiasm of local audiences began to wear off in the late 1980s. The genre soon gave rise to many low-quality imitations, and viewers, growing tired of New Wave seriousness, became drawn to the escapist, entertainment-oriented films of Hong Kong, which soon began to dominate the market.

Local directors found it increasingly difficult to secure financing for auteur films that were not big box-office draws.

Nevertheless, during the lean years of the late '80s and early '90s, a number of talented new filmmakers started to create a "Second New Wave" for Taiwan cinema, one which is still going strong today. Compared with the older generation, these new directors are offering up a much greater variety, in both content and style, although they still appear strongly committed to portraying a uniquely Taiwan perspective. They also tend to reject the nostalgic, historical approach of older filmmakers, being drawn instead toward exploring the pain and absurdities of contemporary life.

One of the major figures of the Second New Wave is Tsai Ming-liang, whose films *Rebels of the Neon God* 青少年哪吒 (1992) and the 1994 Venice winner *Vive l'Amour* take an existentialist approach to the plight of urban teenagers and young adults who are on the margins of today's affluent society. The latter also won praise for its unique style of filmmaking; it includes no music or soundtrack, only the background noises of the city, and a minimum of dialogue, relying instead on the power of simple but ambiguous images.

Second New Wave director Stan Lai (also a key figure in Taiwan's stage theater; see section on The Performance Workshop) has also brought an experimental as well as light-hearted touch to his films. *The Peach Blossom Land* (1992), which won prizes at the Tokyo and Berlin film festivals, is an adaptation of one of Lai's stage productions; the tragicomic story revolves around two groups of actors who take turns rehearsing two very different plays on the same stage. His 1994 film *The Red Lotus Society* 飛俠阿達 juxtaposes a fantastic story—about a young man who is determined to fly like the martial arts masters of ancient China—against the realistic setting of modern-day Taipei.

The films of Ang Lee, another Second New Wave director, take a more realistic approach, yet still deal with current-day concerns. For example,

Pushing Hands 推手 (1991), *The Wedding Banquet* and *Eat Drink Man Woman* 飲食男女 (1994) look at the generational and cultural conflicts confronting modern Chinese families.

Other new names have also begun to make an impression on Taiwan's film world in the last few years. Among them are Wu Nien-chen 吳念真, who already had a solid reputation as one of the island's top screenwriters before making his debut as a director. His 1994 *A Borrowed Life* 多桑 was awarded best film at the Turin International Film Festival, and *Buddha Bless America* 太平天國 (1996) was shown at the Venice Festival. Another new director, Chen Yu hsun 陳玉勳, was awarded the Blue Leopard Prize at Switzerland's Locarno Film Festival for *Tropical Fish* 熱帶魚 (1995). Hsu Hsiao-ming 徐小明, Steve Wang 王獻箎 and Lin Cheng-sheng 林正盛 are also among the latest generation of Taiwan directors whose works have been shown at prestigious film festivals around the world.

Cross-Strait Collaboration

As with many areas, the film world has been affected by the ROC government's relaxation on contacts with mainland China in recent years. Some of the first contacts were at international film festivals in the mid-1980s. In 1991, the ROC allowed actors from Taiwan to attend the Golden Rooster awards in Peking, and mainland directors Chen Kaige 陳凱歌 and Peng Xiaolian 彭小蓮 to attend the Golden Horse awards in Taipei. Soon after, actors and directors from both sides were regularly exchanging visits, and Taiwan directors were beginning to shoot footage, or even entire films, in the mainland—something that was once forbidden. The most recent examples are Wang Shau-di's 王小棣 *Accidental Legend* 飛天 (1996), shot in China, and Hou Hsiao-hsien's *Good Men, Good Women*, which includes several mainland scenes.

Perhaps the most significant cross-strait development in the cinema has been the surge in Taiwan financing of mainland films. Mainland director Chen Kaige's *Farewell to My Concubine* 霸王別姬, which won the Golden Palm at Cannes in 1994 and was nominated (along with *The Wedding Banquet*) for an Academy Award, was financed by Taiwan actress-turned-producer Hsu Feng 徐楓. Hsu also backed Chen's 1996 production, *Temperance Moon* 風月.

ERA International 年代影視 is another Taiwan company that has supported mainland directors. ERA collaborations include two highly successful films by Zhang Yimou 張藝謀: *Raise the Red Lantern* 大紅燈籠高高掛, which won the 1992 Silver Lion Award in Venice and an Academy Award nomination, and *To Live* 活著, winner of the Jury Grand Prize at Cannes in 1994. More recent Taiwan-backed mainland films include Huang Jianxin's 黃建新 *Wooden Man's Bride* 驗身 (1995) and Wu Ziniu's 吳子牛 *Don't Cry Nanking* 南京一九三七 (1995), both produced by Taiwan's Long Shong International 龍祥影視.

Public Art

"Public art" is a rather new concept in Taiwan. In 1992, the *Statute on Encouraging and Rewarding Cultural and Art Enterprises* 文化藝術獎助條例 marked a new era for the development of public art in Taiwan. Article 9 of the statute stipulates that "the owner of public buildings should set up artworks with the expenditure of no less than one percent of that for such buildings in order to beautify the buildings and environment," and that "large-scale government projects of public construction should include the installment of artworks for more beautiful environment." In accordance with this regulation, *Public Art Establishment Measures* 公共藝術設置辦法, drafted by the Council for Cultural Affairs, were promulgated and implemented in January, 1998.

In 1994, the Council for Cultural Affairs began to work on the Public Art Demonstrative (Experimental) Establishment Project 公共藝術示範（實驗）計劃, wherein nine sites were chosen for the demonstration of public art. These demonstration sites include the cultural centers in Hsinchu City, Hsinchu County, Chiayi City, Kaohsiung County, and Hualien County, the Center of Arts and Culture of Puli Township 埔里鎮藝文中心 in Nantou County, the Public No.11

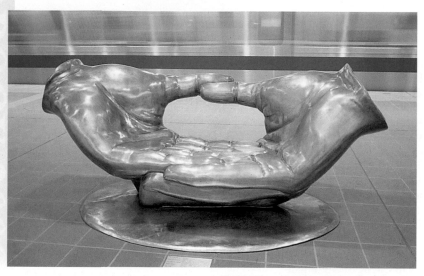

"Small Park" (250x110x100cm): The theme Suite of Hands *was chosen for display at the NTU Hospital MRT Station. Increasingly common in Taiwan's cities, public art raises aesthetic and social consciousness, while improving the visual environment.*

Parking Lot 公十一停車場 in Tainan City, the Athletic Park 運動公園 in Pingtung County, the Aboriginal House 原住民會館 in Taitung County. This project has been completed except for some modifications to be made in a few cases.

In recent years, public art has been promoted by both central and local governments, as well as by private organizations. In May 1997, an international contest of public artworks hosted for the first time by private enterprise, was held with the purpose of promoting urban renovation, reshaping the cityscape, consolidating the union between public art and buildings, encouraging and nurturing talented artists, and gratefully making contributions to society.

The year 1997 was designated by the Taipei city government as the Year of Public Art. Public buildings which occupy more than 1,500 square meters or have construction expenditures of over US$14.7 million must allocate one percent of their budget to the establishment of pulic artworks. Rewards will be offered to encourage private enterprises that are willing to follow this regulation. Public buildings or construction projects which are required to set up public artworks but fail to do so will be unable to receive a construction license from the Taipei city government.

Further Reading

(in Chinese unless otherwise noted):

The Art of Classical Chinese Flower Arrangement (in English). The Women's Garden and Art Club of the Republic of China, ed. Taipei: Council for Cultural Affairs, Executive Yuan, 1986.

Chang Shao-tsai 張少載. *Chinese Architecture* (Chung-kuo te chien-chu yi-shu 中國的建築藝術). Taipei: Grand East Enterprise, 1979.

Chen Chi-lu 陳奇祿. *Woodcarving of the Paiwan Tribe of Taiwan* (Pai-wan-tsu mu-tiao wen-wu-chan 排灣族木雕文物展). Taipei: Council of Chinese Culture Renaissance, 1992.

Lydia Chen 陳夏生. *Chinese Knotting* (in English). Taipei: Echo Publishing Co., Ltd., 1982.

Chiu Kun-liang 邱坤良. *Music in Traditional Chinese Opera* (Chung-kuo te chuan-tung hsi-chu yin-yueh 中國的傳統戲曲音樂). Taipei: Yuan Liu Publishing Co., 1981.

Contemporary Ceramics from the Republic of China (Chung-hua min-kuo tang-tai tao-tzu-chan 中華民國當代陶瓷展; Chinese-English bilingual). Taipei: Council for Cultural Affairs, Executive Yuan, 1988.

Contemporary Sculpture Exhibition: ROC, 1991 (Yi-chiu-chiu-yi chung-hua min-kuo tang-tai tiao-su-chan 一九九一中華民國當代雕塑展; Chinese-English bilingual). Taipei: Taipei Fine Arts Museum, 1991.

Chuang Po-ho 莊伯和. *Chinese Sculpture* (Chung-kuo te tiao-ke yi-shu 中國的雕刻藝術). Taipei: Council for Cultural Affairs, Executive Yuan, 1988.

Current Concerns: Humanistic Focus in Modern Taiwan Clay (Tang-hsia-kuan-chu: Tai-wan-tao te jen-wen hsin-ching

當下關注：臺灣陶昀人文新境; Chinese-English bilingual). Taipei: Taipei Fine Arts Museum, 1995.

The Development of Modern Art in Taiwan (Tai-wan ti-chu hsien-tai mei-shu te fa-chan 臺灣地區現代美術的發展). Taipei: Taipei Fine Arts Museum, 1990.

A Guide to the Taiwan Folk Arts Museum (Tai-wan min-chien yi-shu hsin-shang 臺灣民間藝術欣賞; Chinese-English bilingual). Taipei: Taiwan Folk Arts Museum, 1989.

International Conference, China: Modernity and Art (Chung-kuo hsien-tai mei-shu kuo-chi hsüeh-shu yen-tao-hui lun-wen-chi 中國現代美術國際學術研討會論文集; Chinese-English bilingual). Taipei: Taipei Fine Arts Museum, 1991.

International Print Exhibition: 1983 ROC (Chung-hua min-kuo kuo-chi pan-hua-chan 中華民國國際版畫展). Taipei: Council for Cultural Affairs, Executive Yuan, 1983.

Ju Ming Sculptures (Chu-ming tiao-ke 朱銘雕刻; Chinese-English bilingual). Singapore: Ministry of Community Development, 1986.

Juan Chang-jui 阮昌銳. *The Sculptural Art of Taiwan's Aborigines* (Tai-wan shan-pao tiao-ke yi-shu 臺灣山胞雕刻藝術). Nantou: Department of Education, Taiwan Provincial Government, 1991.

T.C. Lai, *Chinese Seals* (in English). Seattle: University of Washington Press, 1976.

Lin Hsing-yüeh 林惺嶽. *The Vicissitudes of Taiwanese Art Over 40 Years* (Tai-wan mei-shu feng-yun ssu-shih nien 臺灣美術風雲四十年). Taipei: The Independence Evening Post, 1991.

Liu Liang-yu 劉良佑. *Chinese Handicrafts* (Chung-kuo chi-wu yi-shu 中國器物藝術). Taipei: Hsiung Shih Art Books Company, 1972.

Local Folk Arts (Hsiang-tu te min-tsu yi-shu 鄉土的民族藝術).

Taipei: Council for Cultural Affairs, Executive Yuan, 1988.

The Origins and Development of Chinese Calligraphy (Chung-hua shu-fa yuan-liu 中華書法源流). Yunlin: Association for the Promotion of the Welfare of the Hearing and Speaking Impaired in Taiwan Province, 1972.

An Overview of the Chinese Film Industry (in English). Taipei: Kwang Hwa Publishing Company, 1991.

So Yu-ming 索予明. *The Best of Classical Chinese Handicrafts* (Ku-tien kung-yi ching-hua 古典工藝精華). Taipei: Council for Cultural Affairs, Executive Yuan, 1984.

Sung Lung-fei 宋龍飛. *The Exquisite Art of Chinese Porcelain* (Ching-ya chüeh-lun chung-kuo tzu-chi 精雅絕倫中國瓷器). Taipei: Council for Cultural Affairs, Executive Yuan, 1988.

Taipei Biennial: The Quest for Identity (Yi-chiu-chiu-liu shuang-nien-chan: tai-wan yi-shu chu-ti-hsing 一九九六雙年展：臺灣藝術主體性; Chinese-English bilingual). Taipei: Taipei Fine Arts Museum, 1996.

Talks on Dance and the Cloud Gate Dance Company (Yun-men wu-hua 雲門舞話). Taipei: Yuan Liu Publishing Co., 1976.

Teng Sui-ning 鄧綏寧. *Chinese Drama* (Chung-kuo te hsi-chu 中國的戲劇). Nantou: Department of Information, Taiwan Provincial Government, 1969.

Tu Yun-chih 杜雲之. *Chinese Cinema* (Chung-kuo te tien-ying 中國的電影). Taipei: Crown Publishing Co., 1978.

"Yu Peng and the Postwar Generation of Chinese Painters in Taiwan," *Yu Peng a Contemporary Chinese Painter* (in English). Towson, Maryland: Asian Arts Center, Towson State University, 1991.

Yuyu Yang in Stainless Steel (Yang Ying-feng pu-hsiu-kang tiao-su 楊英風不鏽鋼雕塑; Chinese-English bilingual). Singapore: The Ministry of Information and the Arts, 1991.

100 Years of Taiwanese Music: 1895–1995 (Tai-wan yin-yueh yi-pai-nien 臺灣音樂一百年). Taipei: The Egret Cultural and Educational Foundation, 1995.

The Beauty of Taiwan Crafts

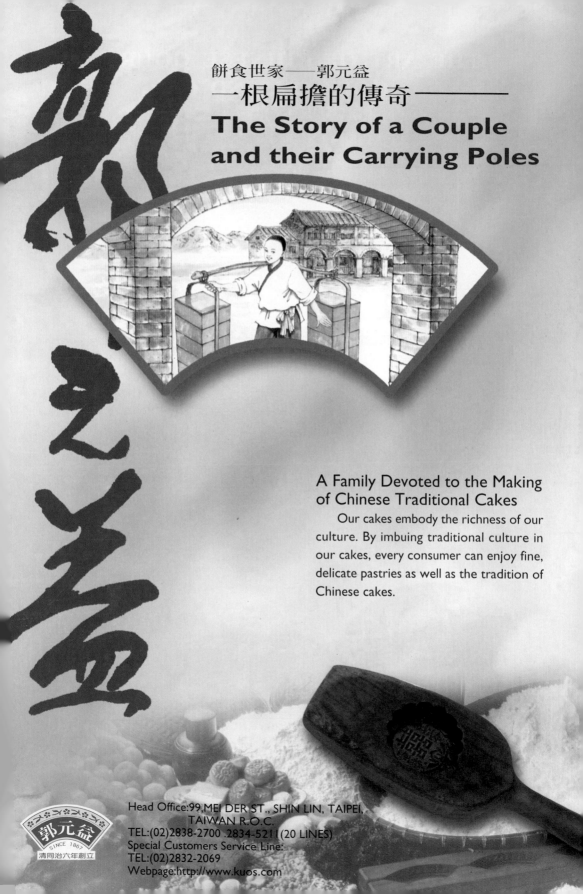

餅食世家──郭元益

一根扁擔的傳奇─────

The Story of a Couple and their Carrying Poles

A Family Devoted to the Making of Chinese Traditional Cakes

Our cakes embody the richness of our culture. By imbuing traditional culture in our cakes, every consumer can enjoy fine, delicate pastries as well as the tradition of Chinese cakes.

Head Office:99,MEI DER ST., SHIN LIN, TAIPEI, TAIWAN R.O.C.
TEL:(02)2838-2700 .2834-5211 (20 LINES)
Special Customers Service Line:
TEL:(02)2832-2069
Webpage:http://www.kuos.com

郭元益
SINCE 1867
清同治六年創立

THE ART OF CHINESE GOURMET GOES ON AND ON.

SHISEIDO

HAIR ENERGIZING COMPLEX

SHISEIDO
hair energizing complex
complexe énergisant
pour les cheveux

『髮力』維持頭髮自然規律
讓頭髮健康亮麗的祕密

生堂髮力」富含多種精華成份，經常使用讓髮絲健康亮麗。歷經多年研發而成的 TETRACOSAMINE精華，能深入滋潤頭髮。而自天然胡蔾萃取的
提煉物，能使頭髮充滿活力。每一滴「資生堂髮力」都精純無比，能溫柔呵護你的頭髮；持續使用，讓頭皮和髮絲保持良好狀態。每天以 「資生
力」輕輕充分的按摩頭皮，你將會有意想不到的驚喜。

區>太平洋SOGO、中興、遠東寶慶、大葉高島屋、德安、新光三越/站前/信義/南西、豐群來來、永和太平洋 基隆地區>裝苑 桃竹苗地區>新光三越、豐群來來、桃闐遠東、中
、太平洋SOGO、新竹中興 台中地區>中友廣三SOGO、豐群來來、豐原太平洋 嘉義地區>遠東、衣蝶 台南地區>新光三越、遠東/公園/成功、東帝士 高雄地區>漢神、太平
O、大立伊勢丹、新光三越、大統和平店 屏東地區>太平洋、領南

SHISEIDO 國際櫃　　消費者諮詢專線：080-001-080　魅麗之網WWW.shiseido.com.tw 衛署中部妝廣字第8811046號

22
Tourism

Dazzling
lanterns and
floats attracted
huge crowds
to the annual
Taipei Lantern
Festival, which
opened on
March 1, 2000,
at the Chiang
Kai-shek
Memorial.

VEARBOOK 2000

What's New

1. Visitors arrivals in 1998, and the first half of 1999
2. ROC's outbound travellers
3. Two major tourism events in 1998
4. The East Rift Valley 花東縱谷

Exotic culture, breathtaking scenery, priceless art, the entire range of Chinese cuisine, and hospitable people make the Republic of China an excellent destination for tourists. Travelers to the ROC can enjoy themselves in comfort with fast and convenient transportation, excellent hotels, and clean restaurants. Unfortunately, many visitors to Taiwan never go far beyond Taipei the capital, and thus deprive themselves of some rich cultural experiences and the enjoyment of the island's scenic wonders.

Northern Taiwan: Where Ancient and Modern Coexist

The ROC's "economic miracle" has put a modern face on Taipei, but the city is still Chinese at heart. Its underlying current of traditional lifestyles and vibrant contemporary culture makes it fascinating for visitors.

Taipei's National Palace Museum 國立故宮博物院 houses the world's largest collection of Chinese art treasures, spanning over five millennia of Chinese history. Much of the immense collection of jade, porcelain, paintings, and bronzes is regularly rotated, making each visit unique. The museum has regular guided tours in several foreign languages, including English and French. English-language tours are given daily at 10:00 A.M. and 3:00 P.M., and self-guided tape tours in English and Japanese are also available.

The Chiang Kai-shek Memorial Hall 中正紀念堂 in Taipei is the island's most impressive monument to the late president. The memorial hall's massive marble edifice dominates beautiful gardens, graceful pavilions, and placid ponds.

A Ming-style arch at the main entrance is flanked by two buildings: the National Theater 國家劇院 and the National Concert Hall 國家音樂廳.

To appreciate the vitality of Chinese temples, the Lungshan Temple 龍山寺, one of the city's oldest and most famous, with striking ornamentation is highly recommended. Stone columns, alive with figures dancing on the backs of intricately carved dragons, support a heavily-ornamented roof.

The World of Yesterday 昨日世界 offers visitors displays of mythology, ancient toys and games, and handicrafts. Chinese opera and demonstrations of crafts and folk arts are presented on Sundays and holidays. The World of Yesterday is located across from the Taipei Fine Arts Museum 臺北市立美術館, host to exhibitions by international and domestic artists, on Chung Shan North Road.

The Lin Family Garden 林本源園邸 is Taiwan's best example of Pre-Republican Chinese architecture and gardens. Originally a Fujian merchant's house, the garden is landscaped with exquisite pavilions, towers, cottages, bridges, artificial mountains, and placid pools, and offers views of distant mountains.

Directly north of Taipei is Yangmingshan National Park 陽明山國家公園, where visitors can find waterfalls, volcanic craters, lakes, steaming hot springs, and, in the springtime, cherry and azalea blossoms. Well-maintained walkways and trails lead to the park's main scenic spots, which offer picnic and recreation areas.

Other areas of northern Taiwan beyond the borders of Taipei City are rich in country beauty. The natural rock formations at Yehliu 野柳, or "wild willows," on the northern coast west of Keelung 基隆, are a striking example. Weather, erosion, and other natural forces have carved the rocks into a variety of shapes.

The coastline east of Keelung, set aside as the Northeast Coast National Scenic Area 東北角海岸風景特定區, is one of the loveliest regions on the island. A notable feature of this area is the magnificent sandstone promontory that rises from the sea at Lungtung 龍洞. Farther down the coast, pure white sand and azure waters make the Fulung Seaside Park 福隆海濱公園 one of Taiwan's best beaches. Wooden pavilions and walkways lend an intensely Chinese character to the Yenliao Seaside Park 鹽寮海濱公園. The scenic area also boasts a Ching dynasty footpath. Sailing, surfing, camping, and fishing equipment can be rented in places.

Taiwan's largest camping area was opened in 1991 in the most beautiful part of the Northeast Coast National Scenic Area. Lungmen Riverside Camping Resort 龍門露營渡假基地, a short distance from Yenliao and Fulung, provides sightseeing, water sports, camping, and bicycling.

A historic fort, fresh seafood, and beautiful sunsets make the quaint seaside town of Tamsui 淡水 a popular day trip from Taipei. Old-fashioned shops along the main road give visitors a feel for the town's history. Oxford College and the Mackay Hospital, which were built in the late 1800s by Western missionaries, remain to this day. Fort San Domingo, which came to be known as the "Red-haired Barbarian Fort" 紅毛城 once it came into Dutch possession, was built by the Spanish in 1629, occupied by the Dutch in 1642, leased to the British in 1867, and bombarded by the French in 1884.

Tamsui has many fine seafood restaurants with large selections of fresh delicacies on display. Some of the restaurants are built along the Tamsui River to provide diners with a riverside view of Tamsui's sunset.

Wulai 烏來, just south of Taipei, is an aboriginal enclave where visitors can witness the traditional dances and ceremonies of Taiwan's Atayal tribe and view a powerful waterfall cascading through lush vegetation.

Just an hour south of Taipei, you can take a one-stop tour of China's Great Wall, Peking's Forbidden City, and the Temple of Heaven. The place is Window on China 小人國, which captures 130 of the best-known structures in both Taiwan and the Chinese mainland in miniature. A recently added section features famous buildings from all over the world. With careful attention to detail, thousands of living trees and shrubs are shaped and grown to sizes proportional to the various buildings. Window on China also has a classical Chinese garden, restaurants, snack bars, a tea house, amusement park, and souvenir shops.

Buddhist temples, shrines, and monasteries, evoking the flavor of ancient China, are perched on the cool, verdant hills of Lion's Head Mountain 獅頭山, about halfway between Taipei and Taichung.

A short trip through the lush countryside southwest of Taipei brings you to a small town that produces hand-painted replicas of elegant Ming (1368-1644) and Ching (1644-1911) vases. Yingke 鶯歌 is Taiwan's pottery center, and the narrow streets are lined with shops selling an endless variety of ceramics, from simple earthenware tea sets to delicate statues. Some of the factories provide tours, allowing visitors to watch potters working the clay and artists painting vases. The information desk at the Yingke Town Hall can help arrange tours of factories.

For tourists who enjoy shopping and munching on savory Taiwanese snacks, night markets are a good choice. Markets, offering fun, and a lot of local color, generally sell a variety of products, casual clothes, fruit, snacks, and novelty items.

Night markets with the best bargains in food, fashions, and curios in the Taipei area include the Shihlin 士林 night market, north of the Grand Hotel; the Kungkuan 公館 night market, near National Taiwan University; the Shihta 師大 night market, on Shih Ta Road off Hoping East Road; the Hua Hsi Street 華西街 night market, also known as Snake Alley; the Tung Hua Street 通化街 night market, near the World Trade Center; the Jao Ho Street 饒河街 night market, in the Sungshan district; and the Chingkuang 晴光 market, off Chung Shan North Road.

Central Taiwan: Enchanting Cascades and Snowy Peaks

The central region of Taiwan displays the full range of the island's beauty: mountain lakes and shining seas, roaring rivers and steaming hot

General Information for Visitors to the Taiwan Area

Climate
Taiwan's climate is subtropical, with an average annual temperature of 21.7°C (71.2°F) in the north and 24.1°C (75.7°F) in the south. Summers, which last from May through September, are usually hot and humid with daytime temperatures from 27°C to 35°C (in the 80s and 90s Fahrenheit). Winters, from December through February, are short and mild. Snow falls only on the island's higher mountains.

Currency
The Republic of China's unit of currency is the New Taiwan Dollar (NT$). The exchange rate, around NT$33 to US$1 in mid-1999, has fluctuated greatly in recent years. Foreign currencies can be exchanged at government-designated banks, hotels, and shops. Receipts are given when currency is exchanged, and travelers wishing to exchange unused NT dollars before departure must present these receipts. Traveler's checks can be cashed at hotels or at the local branches of the issuing banks.

Time Differential
All territories under ROC government control, including Taiwan, the Pescadores, Quemoy, Matsu, Orchid Island, and Green Island, are in one time zone, which is UTC +8 hours. The ROC observes the same time standard all year, i.e., there is no daylight savings time during the summer months. Thus, Taiwan's relative time differential, with a given part of the world, usually increases by an hour in the spring and correspondingly decreases by an hour in the fall.

Language
The national language of the ROC is Mandarin Chinese. Many people can speak some English and Japanese (the most widely studied foreign languages), but most taxi drivers do not.

Credit Cards & Traveler's Checks
Major credit cards (including American Express, Carte Blanche, MasterCard, Diners Club, and Visa) are accepted, and traveler's checks may be cashed at international hotels, tourist-oriented restaurants, souvenir shops, and most department stores.

Tipping
The standard tip is NT$50 per piece of luggage at airports. A 10 percent service charge is automatically added to room rates and meals at hotels and most restaurants. All other tipping is optional.

Business Hours
Most of the island's people work a half-day on the first and third Saturday of each month. Banks are open from 9 A.M. to 3:30 P.M. Monday~Friday and from 9 A.M. to noon on these Saturdays. Most commercial firms are open from 9 A.M. to 5:30 P.M. Monday~Friday and from 9 to noon these Saturdays. Department stores are open daily from either 10:30 or 11 A.M. to 9:30 P.M., and most other stores are open daily from 9 or 10 A.M. to 9 or 10 P.M. Government offices are open from 8:30 A.M. to 12:30 P.M. and 1:30 to 5:30 P.M. Monday~Friday, and from 8:30 A.M. to 12:30 P.M. on working Saturdays.

Electricity & Water
Electrical power used throughout Taiwan is 110-volt, 60-cycle AC. Drinking water served at hotels and restaurants is distilled or boiled.

Vaccinations
Vaccinations are not normally required for entry into Taiwan.

Visa Information

Tourist visas for the Republic of China can be obtained from the ROC Ministry of Foreign Affairs and ROC embassies, consulates, and designated representative offices in foreign countries (see Appendix IV, Directory of ROC Representatives Abroad).

Foreign nationals may obtain a visitor visa, if they hold a foreign passport or travel document valid for more than six months and wish to stay less than six months in the Republic of China for the purpose of business, sightseeing, family visits, study or training, visits by invitation (with letter of invitation), transit, technical assistance, medical treatment, and other legitimate activities.

Visa requirements include one completed application form, incoming and outgoing travel tickets (or a letter of confirmation from a travel agency), three photos, documents verifying the purpose of the visit (except for transit or sightseeing), and, in some cases, a letter of guarantee.

Those holding a visitor visa for tourism purposes may stay in the ROC for two weeks to 60 days and, unless restricted to two weeks, may apply for a maximum of two extensions of 60 days each, for a total of six months. The visa may be single- or multiple-entry and valid for up to one year (or up to five years for citizens of those countries that have signed reciprocal agreements with the ROC) for stays of up to six months. Holders of a visitor visa for tourism are not permitted to assume employment in the ROC.

Participants in major international meetings, and VIP visitors invited by the ROC government, may be issued visas upon arrival if their names are on an approved list.

Citizens of 18 countries, including the United States, Japan, Sweden, Spain, Portugal, Austria, France, Germany, the United Kingdom, the Netherlands, Belgium, Luxembourg, Canada, Australia, New Zealand, Costa Rica, Italy, and Greece may enter the ROC visa-free for stays of up to 14 days, so long as their passports are valid for at least six months from the date of entry and they possess onward or return tickets with confirmed seats.

Complete information on ROC visas can be obtained from:

Bureau of Consular Affairs
Ministry of Foreign Affairs
3F, 2-2 Chinan Rd., Sec. 1
Taipei, Taiwan, ROC
Phone: 886-2-2343-2888

---

springs, lofty snow-capped peaks and lush tropical valleys, emerald forests and craggy ravines.

Taichung is the major city in this region and is one of Taiwan's main business centers. Taichung's location, quality hotels, museums, cafes, and convenient transportation make it a good starting point for trips to many of the island's tourist sites.

Encore Garden 亞哥花園, a masterpiece of landscape gardening, is located just ten kilometers northeast of Taichung. In addition to a tremendous variety of flowering plants, the garden also has snack bars, a children's playground, hiking trails, camping, and barbecue sites. In the evenings, a fountain lit by multicolored lights pulses to the rhythm of music.

A giant statue of a Buddha sits on Pakua Hill 八卦山 overlooking the small city of Changhua 彰化, southwest of Taichung. Inside the hollow statue, dioramas illustrate Buddhist teachings, and visitors can view the surrounding area through the statue's eyes. The Taiwan Folk Village 臺灣民俗村 near Changhua features old buildings from all over Taiwan, which have been reconstructed after removal from their original sites. Here, the visitor can watch traditional weddings and puppet shows as well as other performances. Just past Changhua is the quaint old town of Lukang 鹿港 or "deer harbor," one of Taiwan's most important historical and cultural towns, noted for its impressive Matsu and Lungshan temples, as well as for the annual four-day Lukang Folk Arts Festival, which begins three days before the Dragon Boat Festival.

The Central Cross-island Highway 中橫公路, Asia's most beautiful mountain road, winds its way from just outside of Taichung over the Central Mountain Range and through Taroko National Park 太魯閣國家公園 to the island's east coast. This route offers broad vistas across cloud-filled valleys, mist-shrouded peaks, starry skies, beautiful sunrises, delightful forest walks, rushing mountain streams, and hot springs.

Southeast of Taichung lie some of the region's most popular scenic spots. Emerald waters and jade mountains, temples, hiking, boating, and a picturesque pagoda are all in the vicinity of Sun Moon Lake 日月潭. At the nearby Formosan Aboriginal Culture Village 九族文化村, groups from Taiwan's nine indigenous tribes perform traditional songs and dances with ancient musical instruments and use traditional tools to make handicrafts. Beauty and serenity make the Hsitou Forest Recreation Area 臺大溪頭實驗林場, south of Sun Moon Lake, a favorite getaway.

Nearby Mount Ali (Alishan) 阿里山 is well known for its view of the sunrise over a sea of clouds.

Blue peaks rise from a fleecy gray ocean, which is gradually painted in vivid colors by the sunrise as the clouds dissipate. Visitors can reach Mount Ali from the city of Chiayi by rail or bus, but the scenery along the 72-kilometer railway from Chiayi is worth the three-hour trip.

Some 15 kilometers away from Mount Ali is Mount Jade (Yushan) 玉山, which at 3,952 meters is Northeast Asia's highest peak. Yushan National Park 玉山國家公園, which is dominated by Mount Jade's massive slopes, is Taiwan's largest national park. Mount Jade's towering main peak can be reached from Mount Ali or via an ancient trail known as the Patung Pass Road 八通關古道.

The 9-21 earthquake, which caused extensive damage in the central part of Taiwan, devastated the well-known scenic resort of Sun Moon Lake. Lalu Island in the center of Sun Moon Lake was split in half toppling structures on the island. All 18 of the major hotels around Sun Moon Lake were damaged, and four completely collapsed. The site is now closed for reconstruction.

During his visit to the disaster area, President Lee announced a plan to rebuild the Sun Moon Lake area as a national park.

The Chingching Farm, located high in the hills of central Taiwan, has become a scenic tourist area.

Pertinent Customs Regulations for Inbound Passengers

Each person may bring into the ROC one liter of alcoholic beverages, 25 cigars, 200 cigarettes, or one pound of other tobacco products duty-free.

A written declaration is required when bringing dutiable articles into the ROC. Duty is charged on gold in excess of 62.5 grams in weight. No more than NT$40,000 in cash may be brought into the country by each passenger. Undeclared New Taiwan currency in excess of this amount will be confiscated. Incoming passengers who want to bring in more than NT$40,000 in cash should apply for a permit from the Ministry of Finance prior to entry. Any amount of foreign currency may be brought in, but amounts in excess of US$5,000 must be declared.

There are severe penalties for the importation, use, possession, or sale of the following prohibited articles:
- Counterfeit currency or forging equipment;
- Gambling apparatus or foreign lottery tickets;
- Obscene or indecent materials;
- Firearms or weapons of any kind (including air guns) and ammunition;
- Controlled substances (drugs or narcotics) of a non-prescription and non-medical nature (including marijuana);
- Toy guns;
- Articles infringing on the patents, designs, trademarks, or copyrights of another person;
- Contraband articles, as specified by other laws, e.g., fruit, animals, and pets.
  Pursuant to the provisions of Paragraph 2 of Article 87 of the *Copyright Law* 著作權法:
- Importation of any audio-visual work for archival purposes by an organization operated for scholarly, educational, or religious purposes and not for private gain shall be limited to one copy.
- Importation of any work other than an audio-visual work for library lending or archival purposes by an organization operated for scholarly, educational, or religious purposes and not for private gain shall be limited to no more than five copies.
- Importation of any work for the importer's private use and not for distribution shall be limited to one copy of a work at any one time.
- Importation of any work forming part of the personal baggage of any person arriving from outside the territory shall be limited to one copy of a work at any one time.

Source: Ministry of the Interior

Visitors are advised to contact the ROC's Tourism Bureau or check the Internet before traveling to central Taiwan's scenic spots (see box, page 386).

Southern Taiwan: Bucolic Scenes from the Past

Southern Taiwan is a study in contrasts. Bustling modern cities with all the latest amenities are surrounded by the pastoral panorama of old Taiwan.

Tainan, the island's oldest and fourth largest city, has the unhurried atmosphere of a small country town. Famous today for its unusual snacks, it is also filled with reminders of the city's past: gates, memorial arches, remnants of forts, and temples that date back three centuries or more.

More than 200 temples provide some of the best remaining examples of southern Chinese architecture in Taiwan. They range from the serene Confucius Temple 孔廟, built in 1666, to the elaborate new Temple of the Goddess of the Sea 聖母廟 at Luerhmen 鹿耳門, a complex built by some of Taiwan's finest artisans.

Tainan's other major historical sites include Fort Zeelandia 安平古堡 and Fort Provintia 赤崁樓, both originally built during the Dutch occupation in the 1600s, and the "new" Eternal Fortress 億載金城, built by the Chinese in 1876.

Due south of Tainan is the vibrant city of Kaohsiung, Taiwan's second largest city, foremost industrial center, and largest international port. Offering excellent shopping, dining, and night life, Kaohsiung is close to many notable tourist attractions. The hillside temples, pavilions, shaded terraces, and city view make Mount Longevity 壽山 worth a stop. Cheng Ching Lake 澄清湖, just north of Kaohsiung, features a pagoda, islands, pavilions, tree-lined pathways, and a variety of recreational facilities. Both the graceful Spring and Autumn Pavilions 春秋閣 and the nearby Dragon and Tiger Pagodas 龍虎塔 stand in the placid waters of Lotus Lake 蓮池潭. Beside the lake are temples dedicated to Confucius and the God of War.

About an hour's drive northeast of Kaohsiung, the island's tallest image of a Buddha gazes over the surrounding rice paddies in the countryside. The huge 120-meter gilded statue is surrounded by 480 life-size gold-colored Buddha images near the entrance to the Light of Buddha Mountain (Mt. Fokuang) 佛光山, home to one of Taiwan's largest temple complexes and the island's center of Buddhist scholarship. The complex was recently closed to visitors for an indefinite period.

The southernmost point of Taiwan, about two hours from Kaohsiung, forms a crescent known as the Hengchun or "eternal spring" Peninsula 恆春半島. Kenting National Park 墾丁國家公園, the ROC's first national park, encompasses much of the peninsula and offers spectacular shorelines with coral and rock formations. Kenting also has some of Taiwan's best beaches, with clean white sand and water sports. Pleasant wooded paths wind through a large botanical garden, which contains a variety of exotic plant life. Visitors can wander through unusual dryland coral formations or rest at pavilions and enjoy the view by the sea. Facilities include an international-class resort hotel, as well as economical lodgings.

Moon World 月世界, an area of banana and jujube orchards, bamboo groves, and fish ponds, is named for its lunar landscape of sharp-peaked clay hills with steep, deeply eroded slopes and sawtooth ridges. One of the most interesting sites here is the unpredictable "mud volcano," a small crater filled with thin, cold mud through which gas bubbles occasionally rise to the surface. A deep rumble gives a warning just before the gas bursts through and whips the mud into a bubbling gray mass that spills out of the crater.

The Penghu Archipelago 澎湖群島, also known as the Pescadores, consists of 64 separate islands, situated in the Taiwan Strait, roughly midway between Taiwan and the Chinese mainland. Fishing is the major source of income, and a meal of fresh seafood is a must for visitors. The islands offer fascinating sightseeing opportunities, with ancient temples, picturesque farms, windswept fishing villages, friendly people, fine beaches, and rugged coastlines. Fishing, swimming, snorkeling, scuba diving, wind surfing, and boating are the major recreational activities in the archipelago. The government established the Penghu National Scenic Area 澎湖風景特定區 here in July 1995.

Eastern Taiwan: Unspoiled Natural Beauty

Eastern Taiwan has some of the island's most beautiful and accessible attractions, notably Taroko Gorge, the East Coast National Scenic Area 東部海岸風景特定區, and the East Rift Valley National Scenic Area 花東縱谷風景特定區 .

Taroko Gorge, a spectacular marble-walled cleft that runs for 19 kilometers through the mountains near the east coast, is the focus of Taroko National Park. At the head of the gorge is the village of Tienhsiang 天祥, known for its suspension bridge, pagoda, and new five-star hotel.

Located at the eastern end of the Central Cross-island Highway, the city of Hualien 花蓮 is renown for producing the best marble products on the island. The vast marble deposits in the area are sculpted into an amazing range of products such as animal figures, chess sets, wine and coffee sets, bookends, ash trays, kitchen utensils, and furniture.

Hualien is also popular for performances of song and dance by the island's indigenous people.

Nearly 80,000 reside in the area, most from the Ami tribe 阿美族. The annual Ami harvest festivals, held at more than 20 villages in Hualien and Taitung counties on various days in July and August, are elaborate spectacles of color, costume, music, and dance. Tribal dances are performed regularly at the Ami Culture Village 阿美文化村, about a 15-minute drive from Hualien.

Along most of its length, the coastal road from Hualien to Taitung in the south runs through the East Coast National Scenic Area, an isolated, unspoiled region where development is strictly controlled to preserve the area's natural beauty. The coastal highway's attractions include picturesque temples inside mountain caves, venerable banyan trees, coral reefs, fantastic rock formations, and deserted beaches that stretch for miles.

The East Rift Valley National Scenic Area covers the inter-mountain valley in Hualien and Taitung counties, but does not include nine urban planning areas within the valley of the National Dong Hwa University 國立東華大學 special district. The total area is 138,368 hectares. The East Rift Valley National Scenic Area Administration 花東縱谷管理處 was established on April 15, 1997, to take responsibility of the area's development work, and a total of NT$100 million had been invested through fiscal year 1998.

Just south of Taitung is the Chihpen Hot Springs 知本溫泉 resort, which offers several interesting sites for tourists. First is the Chihpen Hot Spring itself, which is open to the public. Nearby hotels provide more private bathing. A short distance from the hotels, a path leads to the beautiful White Jade Waterfall 白玉瀑布. On a

Customs Regulations for Outbound Passengers

Except in the following cases, completion of the Outbound Passenger's Declaration Form is optional. Outbound passengers must declare to Customs in writing when:
- Carrying foreign currencies, New Taiwan Dollar notes, or gold or silver ornaments in excess of the designated amounts (see below);
- Carrying gold and/or silver ornaments and, when leaving the country within six months of arrival, the unused portion of foreign currencies in excess of the designated amounts (see below) which were declared to Customs on entry;
- Carrying commercial samples and/or dutiable items (cameras, tape recorders, calculators, etc.) which will be brought back duty-free in the future;
- Carrying computer information storage media, including magnetic tapes, magnetic disks, diskettes, punched cards, and punched tapes.

Passengers who do not make a declaration to Customs and are found, on their departure from the ROC, to be carrying gold, silver, New Taiwan Dollar notes, and/or foreign currencies in excess of the designated limits, shall have the excess amount confiscated. They may also be subject to punishment under the law.

The designated limits on gold and/or silver ornaments and currency which a passenger is allowed to carry on departure from the ROC are as follows: Up to 62.5 grams (or two market taels) of gold ornaments or coins; up to 625 grams (or 20 market taels) of silver ornaments or coins; up to US$5,000 in notes or the equivalent in foreign currencies; and up to NT$40,000 in notes and 20 coins (of the types in circulation) of New Taiwan Dollar specie.

Articles that may not be taken out of the country include unauthorized reprints or copies of books, records, and videotapes; genuine Chinese antiques, ancient coins, and paintings; and items prohibited from entry, such as firearms, drugs, counterfeit currency, and contraband.

For further Customs information, contact:

Directorate General of Customs
13 Tacheng St., Taipei, Taiwan, ROC
Phone: 886-2-2550-5500

Visitor Information Sources

• *The Tourism Bureau, Ministry of Transportation and Communications (MOTC)*
  9th Fl., 280 Chung Hsiao E. Rd., Sec. 4, Taipei
  Phone: 886-2-2349-1635
  Internet Address: http://www. tbroc. gov. tw
• *Taiwan Visitors Association*
  5th Fl., 9 Min Chuan E. Rd., Sec. 2, Taipei
  Phone: 886-2-2594-3261
• *The Tourist Information Hot Line*
  Phone: 886-2-2717-3737

  The Tourism Bureau's Tourist Information Hot Line provides a wide range of assistance and information in Chinese and English (and other languages as needed) to callers from anywhere in the ROC or the world. The hot line operates every day of the year from 8 A.M. to 7 P.M., local time (UTC +8 hours).

• *Travel Information Service Centers*

  The Tourism Bureau's Travel Information Service Center provides information to inbound and outbound tourists. There are service centers at Chiang Kai-shek International Airport in Taoyuan, Sungshan Domestic Airport in Taipei, and these other locations:

Taipei:
345 Chung Hsiao E. Rd., Sec. 4
Phone: 886-2-2717-3737

Taichung:
4th Fl., 216 Min Chuan Rd.
Phone: 886-4-227-0421

Tainan:
10th Fl., 243 Min Chuan Rd., Sec.1
Phone: 886-6-226-5681

Kaohsiung:
5th Fl.-1, 235 Chung Cheng 4th Rd.
Phone: 886-7-281-1513

---

lane off the main road from Chihpen to Inner Hot Spring 內溫泉 is Chingchueh Temple 清覺寺, which boasts two large Buddha images: one of bronze from Thailand and the other of jade from Burma. Inner Hot Spring, two kilometers down the main road from Chihpen Hot Spring, boasts newer hotels and a mineral water swimming pool. A suspension bridge leads to the Chihpen Forest Recreation Area 知本森林遊樂區, perched on a mountainside covered with bamboo groves and dense forests. The recreation area offers a riverside picnic spot, campground, bonfire area, flower garden, and footpath to a waterfall. Near the top is a huge banyan tree with long, gnarled roots that half surround a restful pavilion.

Green Island 綠島, off the Pacific coast of Taiwan, is now part of the East Coast National Scenic Area. The island is known for its saltwater hot spring (said to be one of only three in the world), coral, and spectacular coastal scenery. The reefs, waters, and beaches around the island are great for fishing, swimming, and scuba diving.

Just south of Green Island lies Orchid Island 蘭嶼, which takes its name from the wild orchids that grow in the hills. It is inhabited by the Yami, Taiwan's smallest indigenous tribe. They do some farming but live mainly by fishing. The tribe's intricately painted wooden boats are built entirely by hand and joined together by wooden pegs (for more about the Yami, see Chapter 2, People).

Chinese Festivals

The Chinese lunar calendar is crowded with traditional festivals, which are celebrated with verve and color throughout Taiwan. (see Appendix VII, National and Popular Holidays).

The first major festival of the year is Chinese New Year, often called Lunar New Year 春節, the most important of annual festivals, followed by the Lantern Festival 元宵節 on the first full moon of the lunar calendar (usually during the month of February on the solar calendar). Next on the calendar is the birthday of Matsu, Goddess of the Sea, celebrated with elaborate rites at Matsu temples throughout Taiwan. Tourists should visit Peikang 北港 or "north harbor" to see the annual pilgrimage and elaborate celebrations. Boat races and the eating of *tsongtse* during the Dragon Boat Festival 端午節 commemorate a drowned poet-statesman. The Ghost Festival 中元節, when the gates of Hell open and spirits visit the land of the living, is marked by temple ceremonies, feasts for wandering ghosts, and other activities. The Mid-Autumn or Moon Festival 中秋節 celebrates the full harvest moon with family reunions, barbecues, gazing at the moon, and eating rich pastries known as "moon cakes" 月餅. Confucius' Birthday, also celebrated as Teachers' Day 教師節, features an ancient dawn ceremony of dance, costume, music, and rites.

The last major festival of the year is Double Ten National Day 雙十節, which commemorates the anniversary of the October 10, 1911, revolution which led to the overthrow of the Ching dynasty and the founding of the Republic of China. Huge parades in front of Taipei's Presidential Office Building, displays of martial arts, folk dances, and other cultural activities attract enormous crowds of well-wishers.

Cuisine

Because of China's widely diverse geography, each region has developed its own distinctive cuisine. Those diverse cuisines found their way to the island, during the major waves of immigration from the mainland to Taiwan in the last century, and especially following World War II.

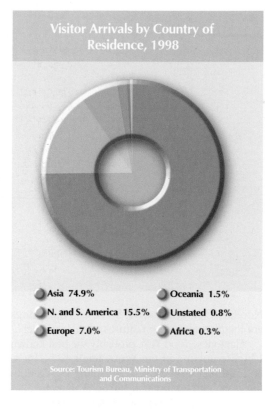

Visitor Arrivals by Country of Residence, 1998

Asia 74.9%
N. and S. America 15.5%
Europe 7.0%
Oceania 1.5%
Unstated 0.8%
Africa 0.3%

Source: Tourism Bureau, Ministry of Transportation and Communications

At Taipei's top restaurants, visitors can savor the true taste of Chinese cuisine.

Sichuan cuisine 川菜, which along with its cousin, Hunan cuisine 湘菜, favors liberal use of garlic, scallions, and chilies. Sichuan food is distinguished by its hot peppery taste, while Hunan food is richer, either spicy and hot or sweet and sour. Chicken, pork, river fish, and shellfish are all common ingredients.

Jiangsu-Zhejiang cuisine 江浙菜 is the best known branch of the eastern Chinese style. Because of the area's proximity to the ocean, major lakes, and rivers, this culinary style is renowned for superb seafood. For the most part, these dishes are lightly spiced and fairly oily, with rich and slightly sweet sauces.

Basically mild Peking cuisine 北平菜 was developed in the area of the imperial palace and uses wheat rather than rice as a basic staple.

People on Taiwan enjoy cuisine from all over China.

Noodles, steamed breads, buns, and dumplings are the distinguishing features of this cuisine.

Cantonese food 粵菜, probably the best known Chinese cuisine in the West, tends to be more colorful and less spicy. It is usually stir-fried to preserve both texture and flavor. A noon meal of dim sum 點心, featuring snack-sized servings, is a great way to pick and choose a large variety of items, yet not feel overly full.

Taiwanese cooking 臺菜 is a branch of the eastern Chinese style: light, simple, easy to prepare, and often liberally spiced with ginger. Like its Shanghai cousin, Taiwanese cuisine features seafood.

ROC Tourism in 1998-1999

Following a 14.97 percent growth in 1994, a 9.62 percent increase in 1995 and a mere 1.13 percent increase in 1996, Taiwan's visitor arrivals fell further to 0.59 percent in 1997 to reach 2,372,232. Tourism officials expect growth to continue at a slow rate for the next few years, with the numbers rising at rates of no more than 5 percent annually.

Tourism industry sources say that the high rates of growth in 1994 and 1995 were the result of a natural increase following the institution of a visa-free entry program at the beginning of 1994. This program initially covered citizens of 12 countries for stays of up to five days. In 1995, three more countries were added, and the length of stay was boosted to 14 days. Another factor in the rapid growth was an additional US$2 million, which the government allocated to the Tourism Bureau for international promotion in fiscal 1996 (July 1995-June 1996). The international promotion budgets for fiscal 1997 and 1998 were cut, however, and further reductions are expected.

The Tourism Bureau is making the most of its limited promotion budget by going to the Internet with a homepage and by demanding more effective efforts from its overseas branches. The Seoul branch, which had been closed following the rupture of diplomatic ties with South Korea, was reopened in 1995, and a Hong Kong branch was inaugurated in June 1996. This brought the total number of its overseas offices to nine.

In 1998, Japan still contributed the largest number of visitors to the ROC with 826,632, a 8.71 percent drop from 1997. The United States remained Taiwan's second-largest source of visitors totaling 308,407, an increase of 1.57 percent

Hong Kong continues to be Taiwan's third largest source of visitors, as arrivals increased a 7.80 percent in 1997.

Visitors from Singapore increased by 6.34 percent to 87,022. Arrivals from Indonesia totaled 47,967, and from the Philippines, 126,282. However, a large portion of that number was made up of contract workers. Visitors from Thailand, another major source of contract workers, totaled 128,541, a slight growth of 5.26 percent; while arrivals from Malaysia dropped 9.39 percent to 49,291.

Visitors from Europe saw an overall increase of 0.76 percent in 1998, with Belgium providing the largest growth increase of 5.37 percent; however, arrivals from Belgium account for only 4,117, far less than other European countries.

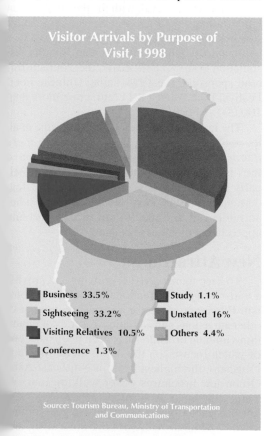

Visitor Arrivals by Purpose of Visit, 1998

Business 33.5%
Sightseeing 33.2%
Visiting Relatives 10.5%
Conference 1.3%
Study 1.1%
Unstated 16%
Others 4.4%

Source: Tourism Bureau, Ministry of Transportation and Communications

Germany constituted the largest source of European visitors to the ROC, with 35,343, a 3.65 percent growth, followed by the United Kingdom at 33,628, an increase of 2.24 percent. France ranked third with 23,595, followed by Italy (11,743) and the Netherlands (11,222).

Visitors from Australia and New Zealand decreased more than 4 percent in 1998, with arrivals from Australia totaling 29,028 and New Zealand totaling 5,190. The number of visitors from Canada also increased 4.2 percent to 34,201, while visitors from South Africa declined 11.8 percent to 4,024. Korean visitors also declined by 36.42 percent to 63,099 and visitors from India increased by 1.82 percent to 11,717.

In the first half of 1999, a total of 1,281,911 visitors arrived in the ROC, an overall increase of 158,030 or 14.06 percent from the 1,123,881 of the same period last year. Overseas Chinese visitors accounted for 160,766 or 12.54 percent, with overseas Chinese visitors from Hong Kong accounting for 87.20 percent of the total overseas Chinese visitors.

Japan was still the largest source of visitors to the ROC in the first half of 1999, with 454,163 or 35.43 percent of the total. Visitors from the United States, still the second largest number, accounted for 174,624 or 13.62 percent, followed by Thailand and Philippines with 72,512 and 69,669, respectively.

Compared to the same period last year, the largest increase, however, was from Indonesia and Korea, with a 69.27 percent and 34.15 percent respectively. A total of 36,403 Indonesians and 40,080 Koreans came to Taiwan in the first half of 1999.

Visitors from Canada increased by 10.04 percent to 25,454, while 18,694 Australians and 3,642 New Zealanders visited the ROC, marking an increase of 11.25 percent and 10.26 percent, respectively.

Visitors from Europe totaled 109,617, with an overall increase of 5.25 percent. Visitors from the Netherlands increased by 14.86 percent, 6.61 percent from France, 5.42 percent from the United Kingdom, but there was a decline of 3.40

percent from Germany. In the first half of 1999, a total of 31,118 Britons, 20,117 Germans, 15,494 French and 8,216 Dutch visited the ROC. Visitors from South Africa registered a growth of 1.01 percent to reach 2,097.

After growing at double-digit rates for years, the increase in outbound travel dropped to 7.85 percent in 1997 and further to 4.05 percent in 1998, bringing the total outbound travelers to 5,912,383. The number of overseas trips taken by Taiwan residents thus equals more than one-fourth of the entire population.

The destinations of outbound travelers is not completely clear, since ROC citizens going abroad are no longer required to fill out departure cards stating their destination. In compiling destination figures, therefore, officials must rely on the first landing point of the flights on which travelers leave Taiwan, leaving much latitude for inaccuracy. It is clear, however, that most passengers travel to destinations in Asia, especially Hong Kong (where most transit to their final destinations in mainland China) and Japan. Taiwan residents traveling to Hong Kong numbered 1,746,524 in 1998, down 10.36 percent, while visits to Japan rose by 3.45 percent, to 674,089. Travel within Asia as a whole totaled 4,467,828, down 3.47 percent, but still accounting for the vast majority of all outbound travelers.

The United States attracts the third largest group of outbound travelers with visits by Taiwan residents totaling 577,178 in 1998, up 1.99 percent. Travel to Canada rose by 9.21 percent, to 127,393. Trips to Europe, as a whole, increased by 4.45 percent for the year to 195,871, with the greatest number traveling to the Netherlands (66,909), followed by Germany (36,924), and United Kingdom (35,457). Travel to New Zealand was down 1.5 percent in 1999, and the year 1998 saw a drop of 22.28 percent. Trips to Australia decreased over 42 percent in 1997, and dropped a further 1.23 percent in 1998.

In the first half of 1999, outbound travel increased by 10.26 percent, bringing the total number of overseas trips for the period to 3,203,259. Except for trips to Africa, which totaled zero, all outbound travel by ROC citizens registered a positive growth: 8.90 percent for Asia, 4.43 percent for the Americas, 7.96 percent for Europe, and 18.35 percent for Oceania.

To attract more foreign tourists, while providing local residents with a greater diversity of cultural and recreational activities, the Tourism Bureau sponsored two major annual events in 1998: the Taipei Lantern Festival 臺北燈會 and the Taipei Chinese Food Festival 臺北美食節.

The Taipei Lantern Festival is held two weeks after the Chinese New Year, when the moon is full for the first time of the lunar year, usually in February. This cultural extravaganza takes place at the Chiang Kai-shek Memorial and features displays of traditional and modern decorative lanterns, folk arts performances, handicraft demonstrations, and religious processions. The 1998 Taipei Lantern Festival, with the theme of "Great Undertakings with a Great Spirit," 浩氣展宏圖 was held on February 11-15.

In association with the Taiwan Visitors Association 財團法人台灣觀光協會, the Tourism Bureau sponsored the 1998 Taipei Chinese Food Festival from August 8-11, attracting more than 100,000 visitors.

The festival focuses on Chinese cuisine in all its regional variations, but is becoming more international in scope every year. In addition to the display and sale of a vast number of artistically presented dishes, the festival also offers demonstrations, contests, workshops, and other activities, all designed to advance the art and appreciation of Chinese cuisine.

New Attractions

To keep tourist arrivals growing and provide a wider range of recreational choices, the Tourism Bureau promotes an increasing number of other attractions and activities. A series of mountain-climbing brochures has been published, one of which focuses on the 3,952-meter Mt. Jade (Yushan), the highest peak in Northeast Asia. Other new brochures cover walking tours of Taipei, the quaintly scenic Chichi 集集 railway line in Nantou County 南投縣, the old gold-mining town of Chiufen 九份, not far from Taipei, an the southern port city of Kaohsiung. These brochures are aimed not only at general tourists but also business travelers, who have extra time on their hands during their stay in Taiwan. A CD-ROM entitled "An Interactive Guide to Taiwan" has also been published.

Among the bureau's other responsibilities are the development and management of national scenic areas, and construction of infrastructural facilities, such as parking lots, pavilions, beach amenities, hiking trails, toilets, marinas, food and beverage outlets, visitor centers, and display halls. The private sector is then encouraged to invest in hotels, restaurants, and recreational facilities in the national scenic areas.

There are currently five national scenic areas: the Northeast Coast, the East Coast, Penghu (Pescadore) Islands, the Dapeng Bay 大鵬灣 in southwestern Taiwan, and the East Rift Valley 花東縱谷 that runs between Hualien and Taitung in eastern Taiwan.

The fortress island of Quemoy (Kinmen), situated less than two kilometers (at low tide) off the coast of Chinese mainland, was opened to tourism in 1992. Quemoy was the focus of fierce attacks by Chinese communist forces in 1949 and of artillery battles in the late 1950s, the failure of which discouraged the communists from attempting to invade Taiwan proper, in addition to its historical significance, Quemoy is also a fascinating repository of traditional Chinese architecture and culture. Fascinating granite "wind lion" 風獅爺 statues and remarkably preserved houses, built in the old Fukienese style, attract many visitors, while the island's renowned pottery and *kao-liang* 高粱, a fiery sorghum liquor, make popular souvenirs. The ROC's newest national park, which serves both as a war memorial and nature reserve, was established on Quemoy in 1995.

In addition to tourism, growing numbers of foreign visitors come to Taiwan for international meetings and conventions. The Taipei International Convention Center 臺北國際會議中心, opened in 1991 and is praised as one of the best such facilities in the world. The TICC is managed by the China External Trade Development Council, which is also in charge of the adjoining Taipei World Trade Center Exhibition Hall.

Construction of Taiwan's largest and much-delayed theme park, Yamay, is expected to begin soon. The first stage of the 198-hectare park, to be located in the central part of the island, was scheduled to open in mid-1999. Completion of the third and final stage of the Disneyland-type park, with an Oriental flavor, is set for 2006.

Travel Services

Services for Inbound Tourists

The CKS International Airport Tourist Service Center maintains three travel service counters, one each in the greeter's lobby and the north and south inbound concourses. Service personnel offer services in a variety of languages. Travel information is provided around the clock on seven display racks at the three service counters, transit lounge, and inbound arrivals area. There is also an interactive multimedia travel information inquiry system for travelers' use in the greeter's lobby. The Kaohsiung International Airport Tourist Service Center was established on January 15, 1997, with the opening of the new terminal at the airport, and provides travel information and related inquiry services to international travelers arriving in southern Taiwan.

Accommodations

Hotels in Taiwan were once rated by a plum blossom system analogous to the star system used internationally. The Tourism Bureau has long planned to revise this system to provide a clearer ranking of the island's hotels. However, many hoteliers resisted the change, fearing downgrading, and the plum-blossom system was therefore abandoned. Tourist hotels in Taiwan today are officially classified in just two categories, each of which encompasses a vast range of properties: tourist class and international tourist class. In addition to the officially rated hotels recognized by the Tourism Bureau, there are also large numbers of unrated ones, some of which are quite luxurious and expensive. Others are inexpensive hostels and youth activity centers, which vary widely in facilities, service, and price.

In addition to the usual guest rooms, shopping arcades, swimming and exercise facilities, entertainment systems, and business centers, Taiwan's hotels also offer fine dining. While most of the best Chinese restaurants on the island are independent establishments, some are also found in international tourist-class hotels. Top hotels frequently offer the best quality Western cuisine.

Transportation

Surface travel in the ROC is both convenient and reasonably priced. Express buses link all cities, towns, and scenic spots, and the railway line reaches all the way around the island. Rental cars are widely available, although the major international car rental agencies have not yet succeeded in setting up their own fleet operations in the local market. Renting a car in Taiwan requires an international or ROC driver's license plus a major credit card or, frequently, a sizable deposit. Visitors who are reluctant to drive themselves can hire drivers along with their cars.

Major urban areas have comprehensive and convenient public bus services. Taxis are extremely plentiful, but few drivers speak any non-Chinese language. The second line of the island's mass rapid transit system began operation on March 28, 1997, offering service from Taipei to the town of Tamsui. Another line, the 5.4 km-long Chungho Line has begun operation since December 1998. Additional lines are under construction in Taipei, and more MRT systems are being planned for other large cities. Convenient local and international air services are provided by more than 50 domestic and international airlines (for additional information see Chapter 14, Transportation).

23

Sprots and Recreation

As a result of the ROC's growing economic prosperity, Taiwan's people now have more time for healthy leisure activities, such as outdoor sports and camping.

What's New

1. Figures and information updated
2. Three plans for indigenous people
3. Cross-strait sports exchanges

The six-day work week and predilection of ROC citizens to put in long work hours may be the hallmark of the Taiwan "economic miracle"; however, as the standard of living on Taiwan continues to rise, citizens are increasingly seeking a more balanced lifestyle of sports and recreational activities to provide a suitable physical and spiritual counterpoise to the frenetic pace of national development. Therefore, the government has implemented a plan that gives its employees every other Saturday off. This has provided everyone with more quality time to spend with their family or to pursue hobbies and recreational activities.

Healthy habits of proper exercise acquired early in life by students, and plentiful, well-appointed recreational facilities readily accessible to old and young alike, have become more and more prominent goals in educational reform proposals and government plans. The growing value placed on exercise and leisure is also apparent at the individual consumer level. According to the Directorate-General of Budget, Accounting and Statistics 行政院主計處 (DGBAS), spending on sports and recreation by ROC citizens has increased by an average of 10 percent each year over the last decade. This chapter seeks to provide a reasonably balanced overview of the ROC's sports and recreation programs by giving a brief introduction of all of the options available to the public. First, though, it describes the sports and recreation infrastructure in the Taiwan area and details major government programs to bring sports to all the people.

Sports Facilities

In densely populated Taiwan, it takes time, money, and determination to participate in a sport. Just finding a place to play tennis or go

Number of Sports Facilities in Taiwan

Type of Sports	Number of Facilities	
	Number	%
Total	55,603	100.0
Track & Field	3,524	6.3
Swimming	1,841	3.3
Judo	175	0.3
Taekwondo	385	0.7
Cycling	87	0.1
Croquet	250	0.4
Basketball (standard)	3,181	5.7
Basketball (simple)	4,055	7.3
Volleyball	1,404	2.5
Soccer	498	0.9
Baseball or softball (standard)	124	0.2
Baseball or softball (simple)	586	1.1
Table tennis	3,966	7.1
Handball	324	0.6
Tchoukball	114	0.2
Tennis	1,400	2.5
Gymnastics	747	1.3
Kendo	64	0.1
Dance (including yoga, folk dance)	2,487	4.5
Weightlifting	169	0.3
Boxing	29	0.0
Shooting	24	0.0
Crossbow	36	0.1
Horsemanship	25	0.0
Bowling	657	1.2
Billiard rooms	3,131	5.6
Golf	83	0.2
Golf (driving range)	209	0.3
Beach	26	0.0
Sports park	15,239	27.4
Ice skating	704	1.3
Roller skating	14	0.0
Beach	26	0.0
Badminton	1,864	3.4
Football	29	0.0
Karate	141	0.2
Outdoor multi-purpose sports grounds	4,303	7.7
Indoor multi-purpose sports grounds	2,208	4.0
Rock-climbing	28	0.0
Dodge ball	18	0.0
Fitness	259	0.5
Physical strength and game playing	963	1.7
Field events	59	0.1
Ball game practice	62	0.1
Tai chi chuan	85	0.2

ROC Government Units in Charge of Sports

Over the past few decades, sports have been subsumed under the government-run educational system. Accordingly, the government budget for sports has also been inextricably linked with the budget for education, and government educational units at each level of government are responsible for overseeing sports and sports-related activities in their jurisdictions. However, in order to cope with increasing international sporting events and the need for training world-class athletes, the National Council on Physical Fitness and Sports 體育委員會 under the Executive Yuan was set up and started operations in July 1997.

The Ministry of Education 教育部 (MOE) has a Department of Physical Education 體育司, which is responsible for testing, implementing, and offering guidance on physical education-related policies in schools. It also has a Committee for Physical Education that is responsible for policymaking.

The special municipalities of Taipei and Kaohsiung have Departments of Education 教育局. Bureaus of education under county and city governments have physical education and health care sections. Rural townships, townships, cities, and districts all have officials in charge of local sports activities.

In addition to government units, the Republic of China also has private physical education organizations which accept governmental guidance and promote various kinds of sporting events; physical education funds set up by sports enthusiasts to promote physical education; large enterprises which sponsor company teams for competition; and service groups such as the China Youth Corps, Lions Clubs, Rotary Clubs, and the Kiwanis, which commonly hold sports-related events.

jogging is often a major undertaking. The government, therefore, places a high priority on providing sports facilities. The Taiwan area has 46 major public stadiums with artificial tracks at various locations. Each county and major city in Taiwan has school playgrounds and a network of baseball parks.

Under the "sports for all people" 全民運動 campaign begun in 1979, a total of 72 public sports centers have been built around the island, each with a track, swimming pool, gymnasium, and tennis courts. An additional 4,000 elementary schools, 2,000 junior high schools, 400 senior high schools, and 130 colleges open their facilities to the public for at least a few hours each day. Twenty-five seminars were held during the "sports for all people" campaign, with a total of 4,700 physical education workers at the basic level participating. "Regular and weekend-holiday community recreation and sports activities" were held in 16 counties and cities. In 1999, 555 recreation and sports activities were held for public employees in 25 counties and cities in the Taiwan area, attracting some 300,000 participants.

Other facilities available to serious athletes in Taiwan include first-class living and training facilities at the Tsoying National Sports Training Center 左營運動訓練中心 and the Northern National Sports Training Center 北部運動訓練中心. In 1998, the two training centers put 4,000 athletes through a rigorous one- to two-month training program to prepare for international competitions overseas. Taiwan has one stadium for soccer in Taipei, Chungshan Soccer Stadium 中山足球場, and two major competition arenas for track and field, Taipei Municipal Stadium 臺北市立體育館 and Kaohsiung Municipal Stadium 高雄市立體育館. The island's largest competition-level indoor facility for basketball burned down in 1988, but was replaced by a much improved facility constructed at the National College of Physical Education and Sports 國立體育學院 in Linkou, a suburb of Taipei. In 1999, the central government provided US$20.27 million in assistance to local governments for building 482 sports grounds, including 11 county and city sports grounds, 4 town sports grounds, 7 town swimming pools, 6 sports parks, 244 community sports grounds, lighting facilities for 97 sports grounds, and other projects. A survey conducted between 1998 and 1999 found that Taiwan had a total of 55,603 sports grounds, with 11,334 in Taipei alone. The majority of these facilities are sports parks (See charts).

Baseball fans are eagerly awaiting the construction of a domed stadium in Taipei. It is to be built on the site of the current Taipei City Baseball Stadium 臺北市立棒球場 and finished by the year 2001. A smaller indoor stadium is also being built in Tienmu 天母 on the outskirts of Taipei. This 16-hectare sports stadium, which will include a baseball stadium, track and field, swimming pools, and tennis courts, had its opening ceremony in February 2000 and will be open to the public in June. During winter vacation, around 7,300 recreational sports activities were held on weekends and holidays for teenagers and youth, as well as 120 winter sports and recreation camp activities, 14 activities that included foreign visits for recreation and sports, and 11 activities that provided various recreational and sports services.

Sports in the Schools

Physical education is a required subject in every elementary school, secondary school, college, and university. However, in reality, physical education instruction programs in schools have traditionally been kept to a minimum in order to allow students more time to prepare for the all-important high school and college entrance exams. In practice, junior and senior high school students are only required to take two hours of P.E. class per week. Although they can also choose athletics for their two hours of weekly electives, most students use this time to study. In order to alter this situation, it has been suggested that physical fitness be included in the entrance evaluations to senior highs and colleges.

Regular P.E. courses cover physical hygiene and sports physiology. The courses are also designed to cultivate skills in a wide variety of sports, including tennis, track and field, baseball and the martial arts. In practice, although the limited time available does not allow many students to become proficient at any particular sport, they do, however, get a good introduction to a variety of sports skills and games.

Currently less than 20 percent of Taiwan's population regularly engages in sports or exercise. This is low when compared to the US and European rate of 40 to 50 percent. To improve this situation, the ROC government enacted a Five Year Medium-term Plan for Physical Education (1998-2002) to cultivate the concept of lifelong sports and exercise into Taiwan students. It is expected that the percentage of students taking regular exercise will increase from the current 25 percent to 35 percent in the year 2002. The total budget for this plan is US$180 million.

New Steps for Developing Athletic Talent

To discover and start training potentially outstanding athletes at an early age, the government has set up athletic aptitude classes in elementary and high schools throughout Taiwan. National sports foundations are responsible for selecting and training young people with superior athletic talent for participation in large-scale international competitions such as the Olympics and the Asian games. The ROC government rewards successful athletes with the Chungcheng Physical Education Award 中正體育獎章 or the Kuokuang Physical Education Award 國光體育獎章, and provides these athletes with educational or vocational guidance. In fiscal 1998-1999, some US$16.7 million was awarded to local athletes through these prestigious awards.

Increased funding from the Ministry of Education for school athletic teams made it possible to maintain 570 primary school baseball teams in 1996. The ministry's plan also includes selecting various primary and junior high schools to specialize in a specific sport. For example, the Keelung Girls' High School 基隆女中 is building its taekwondo team while Taipei's Yucheng Elementary School 玉成國小 is expanding its swimming program. Starting in 1998, Taitung's Hsinsheng Junior High School 臺東縣新生國中 began developing a baseball program. The ministry hopes to foster cooperation between these selected schools and the various national sports associations. In 1991, the MOE and the ROC Amateur Archery Association 中華民國射箭協會 began developing an archery program at Minglien Elementary School 明廉國小 in Hualien 花蓮.

The government has had more success with programs that focus on physical health. It is currently reviewing the physical education curriculum and revising physical education textbooks. As part of its push to promote student health, the government implemented the Five-year Plan to Develop and Improve School Lunches 發展與改進學校午餐五年計畫 and established a student health checkup system. Currently, about 68 percent of the elementary schools around the island supply pupils with lunch.

Baseball is the most popular extracurricular activity. Little League baseball is now offered to both boys and girls in about 47 percent of elementary and junior high schools, 16 percent of high schools, and a small fraction of colleges. Basketball is also popular. In 1997, nearly 60 percent of junior high schools and 42 percent of high schools participated in basketball league matches. Other extracurricular sports range from softball, volleyball, table tennis, and badminton to judo, taekwondo, and kendo. Most schools also have their own dance clubs, marching bands, drill teams, and ping-pong clubs.

Sports After Graduation

After graduating from high school, athletes have relatively little chance to continue their sporting careers. Most dedicated athletes have to choose between taking exams or training. Since 1992, the best players have been able to attend one of nine colleges specializing in sports. Other universities and colleges can also recruit outstanding athletes as needed. In practice, this option has remained limited since athletes are only admitted if they happen to meet the needs of the school's sports teams. Most athletes end up majoring in physical education at one of the sports colleges.

Many in Taiwan believe that creating more options for athletes would make individual competitors happier and would also speed the development of Taiwan's college sports by spreading the best athletes throughout the school system. The result would be a more equal development of sports and a more competitive field for athletes.

Chinese Taipei Olympic Committee

Officially recognized by the International Olympic Committee, the Chinese Taipei Olympic Committee 中華奧林匹克委員會(CTOC) is the sole sports organization with exclusive powers to organize and field representative delegations from the ROC at the Olympic Games, the Asian Games, and other international sports competitions recognized by the International Olympic Committee.

The mission of the Chinese Taipei Olympic Committee is to promote the Olympic Movement in the Republic of China in accordance with the Olympic Charter. CTOC members are approved by the CTOC Executive Board upon recommendation from the CTOC president. Currently, there are 58 members, the majority of whom are presidents of national sports associations.

The CTOC works hand-in-hand with the International Olympic Committee, the Olympic Council of Asia, the Association of National Olympic Committees, the General Association of International Sports Federations, and the Asian, Pacific and Oceania Sports Assembly. It also maintains close relations with other national Olympic committees worldwide.

In June 1998, a total of 267 students graduated from the National College of Physical Education and Sports 國立體育學院. For the majority of them, however, the end of school meant the end of their athletic careers.

Amateur Sports in the ROC

The ROC Sports Federation

The Republic of China Sports Federation 中華民國體育運動總會 is the primary body in charge of amateur sports in the ROC. The federation is under the jurisdiction of and receives funding from the National Council on Physical Fitness and Sports.

The primary functions of the Sports Federation are to provide its member sports associations with technical and administrative assistance, to raise their sports standards and administrative efficiency, to increase participation in international competitions, and to train good athletes.

The following 53 sports are represented by national sports associations that belong to the federation: aikido, airsports, alpine sports, archery, badminton, baseball, basketball, billiards, bodybuilding, bowling, boxing, canoeing and kayaking, crossbow, cycling, dancing sports, equestrian, fencing, folk sports, football (soccer), gateball, golf, gymnastics, handball, hockey, judo, karate, kendo, korfball, kuoshu, luge and bobsledding, pentathlon and biathlon, powerlifting, roller skating, rowing, rugby, shooting, skating, skiing, softball, soft tennis, swimming, table tennis, taekwondo, tai chi chuan 太極拳, tchoukball, tennis, tug-of-war, volleyball, water skiing, track and field, weightlifting, wrestling, and yachting. Sports associations serving the armed forces, district sporting associations (Taiwan Province, Taipei, Kaohsiung, and Quemoy 金門), and associations of athletic trainers and the disabled are also members of the federation.

The Sports Federation operates the Tsoying National Sports Training Center and the Northern National Sports Training Center to train national team members preparing for international competition. These centers provide accommodations, coaching, training facilities, and

Promotion of Sports in the Schools

Since the late 1980s, the Ministry of Education has taken several significant steps toward promoting sports in the schools. The ministry launched a US$740 million *National Physical Education Development Medium-Range Plan* 國家體育建設中程計畫 from 1989 to 1993 that calls for the construction of 100 athletic facilities at schools islandwide and 36 basic recreation centers and parks in various counties and cities. To date, 100 stadiums have been constructed at elementary and secondary schools.

In an effort to establish an integrated system for the training of athletes, the government set up the National Taitung Experimental Senior High School of Physical Education 國立臺東體育實驗高級中學 in 1995. To better guide and reward highly-gifted athletes, government education units revised the *Regulations for the Counseling and Academic Advancement of Athletically Gifted Students at the Secondary School Level* 中等學校運動成績優良學生升學輔導辦法.

pocket money for athletes, as well as academic tutoring when necessary.

The Sports Federation has also been engaged in sports science research aimed at furthering athletic performance and prevention and care of

Kuoshu, or "Chinese martial arts," is a generic name for more than 20 different styles of martial arts, including the better-known tai chi chuan.

injuries. The federation also participates in international sports exchanges and has signed official sports exchange agreements with Hungary, Korea, Germany, Peru, Guatemala, Paraguay, Argentina, Italy, Costa Rica, Nicaragua, Uruguay, and Vietnam.

International Competition

Since the 1984 Olympics, the Republic of China has competed in international competitions under the banner of "Chinese Taipei." Today, ROC athletes compete all over the world.

From July 1998 to June 1999, 3,586 ROC athletes participated in international tournaments and competitions. Among them, 1,768 athletes attended 136 international championships in 76 sports and 1,818 team members competed in 196 invitational tournaments in 112 events. In total, ROC athletes took home 269 gold, 264 silver, and 225 bronze medals from these events. In addition, the ROC sponsored ten international sports conferences and exchanges. A total of 272 ROC delegation members have participated in 142 international and Asian general annual conferences and other important conferences.

Training Facilities

The facilities at the three sports colleges and at university sports departments vary widely. At the National Taiwan College of Physical Education 國立臺灣體育學院 and the Taipei Physical Education College 臺北市立體育學院, much of the equipment is older. In contrast, the nine-year-old National College of Physical Education and Sports is equipped with international-class training facilities. Located on a 66-hectare site near the northern town of Linkou, this school is considered Taiwan's best sports institution. Students can earn undergraduate degrees in health, physical education, or sports technique, and graduate degrees in physical education or sports science. Entrance into the undergraduate health program is by written examination, but applicants must also be top athletes for admission to the physical education and sports science programs.

1998 World Youth Games

The Chinese Taipei team that participated in the 1998 World Youth Games held in Moscow from July 11-19, 1998, consisted of 106 athletes. The delegation won one gold, five silver, and six bronze medals. Of the 125 participating countries, the ROC team ranked 15th.

1998 Asian Games

In December 1998, around 580 athletes from the Chinese Taipei team participated in the Asian Games held in Bangkok, Thailand. Taking sixth place overall, the ROC team returned with 19 gold medals, 17 silver medals, and 41 bronze medals. Both the variety and number of medals won exceeded those obtained four years ago during the Asian Games held in Japan. Considered the greatest success achieved by ROC teams thus far, this accomplishment enabled outstanding athletes and their trainers to earn prizes totaling US$13 million.

Other International Championships

In November 1999, Chinese Taipei's women's football team defeated Japan and won second place in the Asian Cup held in the Philippines.

In July 1999, at the 8th World Police Administration and Fire Fighting Games held in Sweden, the 39-member ROC team won 18 gold, 10 silver, and 9 bronze medals in 10 fields of competition, such as bowling, golf, tennis, and track and field.

During the 2nd Olympic Hope Summer Games held in Sofia, Bulgaria, in April 1999, 30 ROC athletes competed in track and field, swimming, boxing, archery, and wrestling. The delegation won second place among 7 participating countries and bagged 28 gold, 18 silver, and 7 bronze medals.

An 11-member Chinese Taipei team also attended the 4th Winter Asian Games in South Korea. In July 1999, another Chinese Taipei team competed in Spain at the 20th World College Games, winning two gold and two silver medals.

Dragon Boat Racing

Dragon boat racing originally started out as a festival to commemorate the death of the patriotic poet Chu Yuan 屈原, who committed suicide on the fifth day of the fifth lunar month in 277 B.C. (see Chinese Festivals in Tourism). Today, however, dragon boat racing has emerged as one of the most popular sports worldwide. In many countries, competitions are no longer held only during the lunar festival in the summer, but rather are held almost year round.

In 1999, 12 counties and cities held dragon boat races and related activities, with more than 1.5 million spectators and participants. In addition, the international dragon boat races held in Taipei attracted teams from Indonesia, the United States, Japan, the Philippines, Thailand, Hong Kong, Macau, and the Chinese mainland, with 50,000 spectators.

World Sports Events in the ROC

The ROC hosts a growing number of international competitions in Taiwan, furthering international exchange and providing top-notch competition for Taiwan sports fans. First held in Taiwan in 1977, the annual R. William Jones Cup International Basketball Tournament features national teams from all over the world. In 1998, teams from the ROC, Japan, Korea, Senegal, Thailand, United States, Costa Rica, Jordan, Malaysia, the Philippines, Saudi Arabia, and the UAE competed for the title in this tournament, which has become one of the ROC's most popular sporting events. Both the men's and women's teams of the ROC won second place in this tournament.

In June 1999, the Chinese Taipei Olympic Committee (CTOC) held a ten-mile marathon in Taipei. A total of 3,400 runners participated, including competitors from Macedonia, North Korea, and Thailand.

Sixty gymnasts from eleven countries, including Russian star Yelena Dolgopolova, attended the "1999 China Motor International Gymnastic Cup" held in Kaohsiung, southern Taiwan.

National Games

In 1998 it was decided that beginning in 1999, the Taiwan Area Games 臺灣區運動會, with a history of 25 years, would be replaced by the National Games and held every two years. Competition categories would be limited to those at the Asian and Olympic Games. The purpose of this change was to internationalize, professionalize, and standardize the National Games. The last Taiwan Area Games were held in Tainan County in southern Taiwan in 1998; the first National Games were held in December 1999 in Taoyuan County in northern Taiwan.

Beginning in 2000, the National College Games will be renamed the ROC National College Games and held each year between March and May, lasting four to six days. Competitions will include track and field, swimming, and six to ten other selected categories.

Kuoshu

The development of traditional Chinese sports is vital to the preservation of Chinese culture. Kuoshu 國術, or "Chinese martial arts," is a collective name for more than 20 different styles of martial arts, including the better known tai chi chuan. Kuoshu is a recognized sport in the Asian Games. Reflective of Taiwan's commitment to kuoshu, the Chinese Taipei Kuoshu Federation 中華國術總會 receives funding directly from the National Council on Physical Fitness and Sports, and the ROC is the headquarters of the International Chinese Kuoshu Federation 中華民國國術國際聯盟總會. In November 1997, the Chinese Taipei Kuoshu Federation participated in the 1997 World Chinese Kuoshu Invitational Tournament held in Rome, Italy. The team won four medals: one gold, two silver, and one bronze. Also in 1997, the ROC Tai Chi Association participated in the 13th San Francisco Bay Area Chinese Sports Meet where five of the team members won first place, two won second place, and two took third place positions.

Training Amateur Athletes

Compared with some neighboring countries, the ROC has not achieved a high level of excellence in international sport competition. For example, the ROC has never won an Olympic gold

ROC Track and Field National Records

Men's Events

Sports	Record	Units	Athlete	Date
100M	10.37	sec	Cheng Hsin-fu 鄭新福	6/28/86
200M	20.93	sec	Tao Wu-hsun 陶武訓	10/16/94
400M	46.72	sec	Chang Po-chih 張博智	10/26/98
800M	1:47.24	min/sec	Wang Jung-hua 王榮華	5/3/80
1,500M	3:46.4	min/sec	Huang Wen-cheng 黃文成	6/11/83
5,000M	14:04.0	min/sec	Chang Chin-chuan 張金全	6/13/75
10,000M	29:12.10	min/sec	Hsu Chi-sheng 許績勝	11/28/93
110M hurdle	13.90	sec	Wu Ching-chin 吳清錦	11/5/83
400M hurdle	50.15	scc	Chen Tien-wen 陳天文	12/15/98
3,000M steeplechase	8:43.61	min/sec	Huang Wen-cheng 黃文成	9/18/82
400M relay	39.27	sec	Lai Cheng-chuan 賴正全 Cheng Hsin-fu 鄭新福 Lin Chin-hsiung 林金雄 Hsieh Tsung-tse 謝宗澤	10/3/90
1,600M relay	3:07.61	min/sec	Chen Tien-wen 陳天文 Chang Po-chih 張博智 Lin Chin-fu 林進福 Lee Ching-yen 李清言	12/19/98
high jump	2.22	meters	Liu Chin-chiang 劉金鎗	10/29/82
long jump	8.34	meters	Nai Hui-fang 乃慧芳	5/14/93
pole vault	5.30	meters	Lee Fu-en 李福恩	10/29/90
triple jump	16.65	meters	Nai Hui-fang 乃慧芳	11/17/89
shot put	18.02	meters	Lu Ching-i 呂景義	4/29/94
discus	53.68	meters	Lin Tsung-cheng 林宗正	8/10/85
hammer	65.62	meters	Hou Chin-hsien 侯金賢	4/30/97
javelin	72.92	meters	Lin I-shun 林義順	3/17/90
decathlon	8,009	pts	Yang Chuan-kwang 楊傳廣	4/27-4/28/63

medal. A key reason, as in many countries, is a lack of funding. While the National Council on Physical Fitness and Sports gives large cash rewards to some champions (e.g., each member of the silver medal-winning 1992 Olympic baseball team earned US$190,000), government funding for most national sports associations only covers costs and training for selected international competitions. Meager funding is allocated to train athletes; thus, they cannot reach international competitive levels or have a realistic chance of winning medals. As a result, there is little money available for the coaching, facilities, and support necessary for developing and training elite athletes.

A lack of facilities in Taiwan that meet international standards is another problem. The two facilities operated by the Sports Federation are only available for short-term use, forcing many athletes to share crowded, ill-equipped facilities with the general public. To help overcome this problem, the Sports Federation began a program to train 470 athletes between the ages of 10 and 20 who had been recommended by national sports associations. Under the program, athletes are trained at short-term camps during winter and summer vacation in order to identify naturally talented or highly skilled athletes.

ROC Track and Field National Records (continued)

Women's Events

Sports	Record	Units	Athlete	Date
100M	11.22	sec	Chi Cheng 紀政	7/18/70
200M	22.56	sec	Wang Huei-chen 王惠珍	10/30/92
400M	52.74	sec	Chi Cheng 紀政	7/29/70
800M	2:04.74	min/sec	Lee Ya-huei 李雅惠	7/21/98
1,500M	4:22.80	min/sec	Lee Chiu-hsia 李秋霞	5/17/75
3,000M	9:37.68	min/sec	Lee Su-mei 李素梅	6/24/79
5,000M	17:28.64	min/sec	Chiang Chiu-ting 江秋婷	11/22/96
10,000M	36:29.75	min/sec	Su Tzu-ning 蘇子寧	10/22/93
100M hurdle	12.93	sec	Chi Cheng 紀政	7/12/70
400M hurdle	55.71	sec	Hsu Pei-ching 徐佩菁	10/14/98
400M relay	44.58	sec	Gao Yu-juan 高玉娟	10/16/94
			Hsu Pei-ching 徐佩菁	
			Chen Shu-chen 陳淑珍	
			Wang Huei-chen 王惠珍	
1,600M relay	3:39.88	min/sec	Hsu Ai-ling 徐愛齡	9/29/85
			Shen Shu-feng 沈淑鳳	
			Cheng Fei-ju 鄭妃汝	
			Lai Li-chiao 賴利嬌	
high jump	1.86	meters	Su Chiung-yueh 蘇瓊月	4/23/89
triple jump	13.51	meters	Wang Kuo-hui 王國慧	4/29/98
long jump	6.56	meters	Wang Kuo-hui 王國慧	11/5/97
pole vault	3.71	meters	Chang Ko-hsin 張可欣	3/29/99
shot put	14.89	meters	Tsai Mei-ling 蔡美玲	5/12/98
discus	48.48	meters	Fang En-hua 方恩華	10/3/93
javelin	55.02	meters	Fang En-hua 方恩華	4/25/95
hammer	54.76	meters	Huang Chih-feng 黃芝鳳	3/30/99
heptathlon	5,786	pts	Ma Chun-ping 馬君萍	10/11/94

Aboriginal Athletes

Without doubt the most famous athlete in ROC history is Yang Chuan-kwang 楊傳廣. Yang, of the Ami indigenous tribe, won the silver medal in the decathlon at the 1960 Rome Olympics. Recognizing his achievement and that of the Ami team from Taitung County 臺東縣, which won the ROC's first World Little League Baseball championship, the ROC Sports Federation organizes special programs to help cultivate the talents of aboriginal athletes. One of these programs, supported by the Chinese Taipei Amateur Baseball Association 中華民國棒球協會, is the Pacific League 太平洋聯盟, which started in 1993. With the participation of aboriginal professional baseball players, the Pacific League organizes baseball games and clinics for children in Ilan, Hualien 花蓮, and Taitung counties.

Three plans were formulated in 1999 to assist and guide sports for indigenous peoples and contribute to raising the quality of life. These plans were aimed at promoting sports activities for aborigines, discover and train aboriginal sports talents, and improve the sports environment of aboriginal schools and communities.

Sports activities held in 1999 for indigenous peoples included volleyball championships for Paiwan tribal youth in Pingtung, sports games for aboriginal senior citizens, the Sixth Aboriginal Games, and the 1999 Aboriginal Sports Meet. Altogether, about 50,000 aboriginal peoples participated in these events. In addition, seminars on promoting sports for indigenous peoples were held throughout the island.

Coaching

One of the biggest obstacles facing local athletes is the lack of a comprehensive professional coaching system. Coaching school athletes has only recently become a full-time job and permanent career. In 1989, the MOE established a full-time school-coach training system wherein recruits receive three months of training before being assigned full-time coaching positions at a school, sports association, or the Tsoying National Sports Training Center. Since coaches still receive lower salaries and have less job security than teachers, most prefer teaching positions instead. Consequently, most school teams are coached on a volunteer basis by teachers who enjoy sports. Many national associations choose to hire coaches on a part-time or contractual basis. These coaches hold short-term contracts and go back to their positions as P.E. teachers or coaches of professional teams after a particular event is over.

Most national associations and their athletes, however, cannot afford coaching. Therefore, athletes must rely on coaches willing to volunteer their time. In order to help alleviate the shortage of coaches, the ROC Sports Federation has invited distinguished coaches and athletic trainers to Taiwan from Australia, the Chinese mainland, Germany, Hungary, Japan, Russia, South Korea, the Philippines, and the United States to provide instruction in swimming, weightlifting, archery, shooting, diving, judo, taekwondo, track and field, equestrian, golf, table tennis, gymnastics, softball, boxing, baseball, badminton, kuoshu, fencing, basketball, and soccer.

Sports for Disabled People

The Chinese Taipei Sports Association for the Disabled 中華民國殘障體育運動協會 assists with athletic training and sponsors many competitions for disabled athletes. The association is a member of the International Paralympic Committee and other international sports federations for the disabled.

At the 1999 multi-games competitions for the mentally and physically disabled in the Far East and the South Pacific area, the ROC delegation won 16 gold, 17 silver, 20 bronze medals. In addition, the Chinese Taipei team came home with 20 gold, 19 silver, and 21 bronze medals from the 1999 Summer Special Olympics.

The ROC government has spent US$312,500 to assist and subsidize 21 schools to promote special athletic games for the disabled and help discover and cultivate new talents for international competitions. In addition, in 1999, the Chinese Taipei Sports Association for the Disabled, the Chinese Taipei Special Olympics, and the Chinese Taipei Sports Association for the Hearing Impaired held more than 200 sports activities for disabled people, with attendance in excess of 200,000.

Special Olympics

The ROC is a member country of the Special Olympics International. The Chinese Taipei Special Olympics 中華民國智障者體育運動協會 publishes newsletters, sponsors coaching workshops, and initiates local, area, and national games for people with mental handicaps. At the 1993 Fifth Winter Special Olympics in Salzburg, Austria, the Chinese Taipei team collected seven gold, three silver, and six bronze medals. In July 1995, the Chinese Taipei team sent 24 athletes to the Ninth Summer International Special Olympics at Yale University in Connecticut, USA. The team came home with 16 gold, 10 silver, and 15 bronze medals. This number was a large increase over the ten medals won two years earlier.

Professional Sports

Professional Golf

Three simultaneous taps on dragon drums by President Lee Teng-hui and professional golfer Ernie Els opened the 1999 Jonnie Walker Classic at the Ta Shee Country Club in Taoyuan County on Nov. 9, 1999. Foreign golf players included Tiger Woods, Ernie Els, Nick Faldo, Frank Nobilo, Mark McNulty, Vijay Singh, Jim Fuyrk, and Sandy Lyle. For the professional-celebrity tournament, other participants included names of celebrities from both Hong Kong and Taiwan.

Professional Baseball

If the ROC could be said to have a national sport, it would certainly have to be baseball. Taiwan fans pack local stadiums each season to watch the six teams in the Chinese Professional Baseball League 中華職棒聯盟: the Brother Elephants 兄弟象, Weichuan Dragons 味全龍, President Lions 統一獅, Mercury Tigers 三商虎, Sinon Bulls 興農牛, and China Trust Whales 和信鯨. Each team plays more than 300 regular season games between March (February in 1998) and October. Fans islandwide can see the action, with games in Taipei, Hsinchu 新竹, Taichung, Tainan, Kaohsiung, and Pingtung. In the 1999 season, the Weichuan Dragons again outperformed the other five teams; however, at the end of the season, both the Mercury Tigers and the Weichuan Dragons announced the dismissal of their respective teams.

Taiwan Major League Professional Baseball 臺灣大聯盟 made its debut in the 1997 pro-baseball season. The league has four teams: Gida 太陽隊, Agan 金剛隊, Luka 勇士隊, and Fala 雷公隊, all with team names taken from aboriginal languages. Their debuts in the 1997 pro-baseball season with 96 regular games promised fierce competition and widespread popularity, as reflected in the record US$57.7 million bid to broadcast their games for the 1997-99 seasons. By 1999, the number of regular season games had increased to 168. Agan outplayed the other three teams that year to win the championship.

Professional Basketball

Professional basketball made its debut on November 12, 1994, with the inception of the Chinese Basketball Alliance 中華職業籃球股份有限公司. The 1997-1998 season saw six teams battle for the title: the Mars 戰神, Hungkuo Elephants 宏國象, Yulon Dinosaur 裕隆龍, Luckipar 幸福豹,

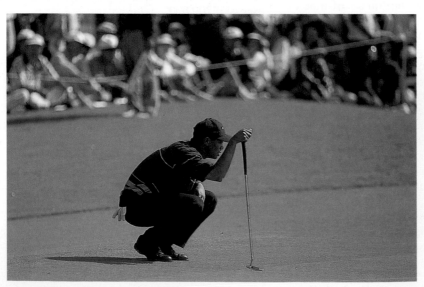

Tiger Woods and other champion golfers competed in the 1999 Johnnie Walker Classic at the Ta Shee Country Club in northern Taiwan.

Hungfu Rams 宏福公羊, and Dacin Tigers 達欣虎. In a repeat of the 1996-1997 season, the Hungkuo Elephants and the Mars again swept the first and second place titles, respectively. The past five years of professional basketball have been a success in Taiwan, and audiences predominately teenagers captivated by the outstanding talent of the league's many players. In the 1998-1999 season, around 250,000 attended 150 basketball games. However, at the close of the season in March 1999, the league was reorganized in preparation for the beginning of six-year seasonal matches.

Cross-Strait Sports Exchanges

The government has assisted and guided local associations and organizations to proceed with sports exchanges with the Chinese mainland. In addition, a team was organized and flew to Shenyang 瀋陽 to attend the 1st Asian Sports Festival from August 29 to September 9, where the ROC team won 11 gold, 4 silver, and 5 bronze medals.

Recreation

Taipei appears exciting enough to a first-time visitor, but it is not exactly leisure-friendly. Major thoroughfares are jammed with traffic, and the sidewalks are crammed with people and parked motorcycles. There are few places to go to ride a bike, jog, or even just take a stroll without having to weave through a maze of clutter. Taipei, like the island's other urban centers, has a distinctive recreational style that has developed in response to rapid urbanization. The biggest single shift is that recreation has become increasingly constrained by diminishing physical space and limited free time. Except for a handful of private companies, all businesses require employees to work at least a half-day on every other Saturday. This leaves little spare time for leisure activities.

Another factor that reduces leisure time in urban centers is traffic. In metropolitan Taipei, rush-hour traffic frequently triples normal commuting time. It can be even worse on holidays and long weekends; during Chinese New Year, for example, a one-hour drive to a neighboring town can easily extend to three or four hours. Although

Taiwan boasts six national parks, accounting for 8.5 percent of the island's land mass, many people seldom visit them for fear of traffic problems. Consequently, many people stick close to home.

A growing class of people who have money to spend but demand convenient places to spend it, has fueled a boom in indoor, easy-to-reach, urban activities. Thus, no matter where a person lives or works, there are nearby restaurants, discos, KTVs (see next page), and clothing boutiques down the street, next door, or even downstairs. To attract patrons who work long hours, most leisure spots are open late into the night. Bookstores and clothing boutiques are commonly crowded with browsers until 10 P.M. on week nights, and night markets (streets where outdoor vendors set up shop in the evenings) are packed with people of all ages until long after midnight.

Recently, Taiwan has seen an increased participation in cultural activities. In 1998, a total of 18,658 cultural activities, ranging from art exhibitions, music, dance, and theater performances, to folk arts, were held in the Taiwan area. Among those, 76 percent were sponsored by the government. The total attendance of these activities registered at 74.3 million.

Whether eating out alone or treating friends and family, getting a bite to eat is probably the most popular entertainment islandwide. Consequently, most neighborhoods have a wide range of restaurants. The Taipei City Department of Public Health 臺北市政府衛生局 estimates that Taipei alone has between 5,000 and 6,000 restaurants.

More easily accessible entertainment options seem to be on the way, including exercise. In order to make better use of the government's alternating five-day work week plan, which began in 1998, the National Physical Education Council launched an "everyone works out" 陽光健身方案 campaign on October 1, 1997. This campaign is a coordinated effort by the Ministry of Education, city and county governments, and schools at every level. By creating more sports facilities and making both the already existing and new ones available to the public, the council hopes to encourage Taiwan's population into exercising more often to become stronger and healthier.

KTV

KTV, or Karaoke television, is the ideal indoor entertainment of choice for thousands of people in Taiwan. It may be the fantasy element, the chance to be with friends, or the fact that there simply are not many other leisure activities available—no one can say quite why, but KTV has become an islandwide craze.

Karaoke, a term coined by the Japanese, is a combination of *kara*, which means "none" in Japanese; and a modification of *orche*, the initial letters of the word "orchestra," which the Japanese pronounce as "okay." Literally, the term means "an orchestra without instruments." In fact, it is a microphone hooked up to a tape or videocassette player. As a singer sings into the mike, the sound is mixed with the taped music. No matter how hoarse or off-key one's voice might be, it will emerge from the speaker sounding professional.

Karaoke (minus the video) first showed up in local coffee shops and restaurants in 1976 as an import from Japan. Soon it swept the island, becoming immensely popular in both urban and rural areas. A second boom started in 1988, when the government cracked down on pirated videotapes. Many of the island's numerous MTV parlors, which rent videos for customers to watch in private rooms, were forced to stop showing pirated movies. To stay in business, many MTVs added karaoke equipment and switched a letter on their signboard to become KTVs. Thus, a new trend was born. A high percentage of families in Taiwan have their own karaoke sound equipment to entertain family and guests.

KTV patrons include people of all ages and occupations, from teenagers to retirees, housewives to business people. Even high-ranking government officials have been known to pick up a microphone and perform on occasion.

Outdoor Recreation

"Adventure sports" such as surfing, scuba diving, and sailboarding, although still on a small scale in Taiwan, are gaining popularity around the island as a result of interest generated by classes, rental shops, and clubs. Even gutsier activities such as paragliding and bungee jumping are attracting brave souls not scared off by the danger or expense. Since the island's first bungee jumping group set up operations in November 1991, thousands of people have paid a US$80 fee for the thrill of hurling themselves off a bridge while hooked to an elastic cord. A less thrilling but equally trendy sport that has become a lure to children and adults alike is roller blading. People, particularly children, wearing roller blades and skating to their heart's content is now a common scene in parks and playgrounds. A variety of fishing activities have also gained in popularity since the *Recreational Fishing Regulatory Measures* 休閒漁業管理辦法 took effect in 1993. Sea parks and aquariums have also been set up around the island.

In 1993, the National Taiwan College of Physical Education 國立臺灣體育學院 located in Taichung established the first and only Department of Recreational Sports in Taiwan. The Department's goal is to train specialists in recreational sports coaching, planning, management, and promotion. Students choose from a variety of courses, including diving, bowling, skiing, surfing, and yachting. They also work in local recreational businesses. Private associations have also been formed to conduct research on leisure-related topics and to promote outdoor recreation through seminars, lectures, and group activities. In 1988, the Outdoor Recreation Association of the ROC 中華民國戶外遊憩學會 was founded. This association has sponsored hiking lectures by botanists, geologists, and other nature specialists, allowing participants to learn as they picnic or hike.

Organized recreational activities are offered all year round by groups like the China Youth Corps 中國青年反共救國團. On weekends and holidays and during summer and winter vacations, the corps offers young people diverse outdoor activities like parachuting, rafting, skiing, and mountaineering. Each year it also organizes mock military exercises, back country hiking and camping, talent camps, and safari-style adventures for teenagers and young adults alike. For those who prefer indoor activities, the corps arranges arts and craft courses, such as guitar workshops, knitting courses, and painting classes. There are also self-improvement programs, including management courses, vocational workshops, and psychological counseling.

The China Youth Corps holds activities throughout the Taiwan area—in major cities, the countryside, and even on the offshore island of Penghu 澎湖. Altogether, the corps has 23 youth activity centers and hostels, complete with recreational, educational, and camping facilities. The Taipei International Youth Activity Center 臺北國際青年活動中心 previously provided services and programs especially for young foreigners traveling or studying in the Taipei area. Starting in 1995, though, this function was taken over by the Chientan Overseas Youth Activity Center 劍潭海外青年活動中心.

For those who are able to get away from the city for a whole afternoon, golf is yet another tremendously popular form of recreation in Taiwan, and many international-standard courses dot the island. There are currently 25 registered golf courses in the Taiwan area. While the price of membership in one of the more prestigious golf clubs on Taiwan can be very high, people still flock to the greens on the weekends. The basic cost for playing 18 holes, not including rentals, caddie fees, and gratuities, ranges from US$50 to US$100.

Ultimately, however, the Chinese city park provides the best idea of how Chinese people seek exercise and relaxation. If one strolls through any park in Taipei early in the morning, one will witness people dancing folk dances, practicing kung fu, playing Chinese chess, doing aerobics, jogging, stretching, singing, and even taking their birds "for a walk." After spending fifteen minutes in this peaceful microcosm, one gains a better understanding of the traditional Chinese concept of health through harmony.

For a change of atmosphere, many people retire to one of the numerous traditional teahouses or "tea art" shops all over Taiwan. Chinese teahouses are an unusual blend of contemplative serenity and buzzing activities. A casual afternoon at a teahouse will bring one to the heart of the social, artistic, intellectual, and political activities brewing in Taiwan. A number of such teahouses have been local trend setters for arts and culture, hosting art exhibitions, ceramic displays, antique shows, and teapot collections.

Many of these teahouses, set in elegant cultured gardens, are ideal hideaways where tea drinkers can sample a wide selection of first-class teas. Tea drinking in Taiwan is akin to the high art of wine tasting in the west, and tea drinkers gladly pay between US$40 and US$80 for a half kilogram of good tea. On weekends, mountainside tea-art shops and restaurants offering open-air tea drinking, dining, and scenic views have become favorite destinations for Taipei residents. Perhaps the most notable of these are the teahouses in the Mucha 木柵 district of Taipei.

⊘ GIANT.
BICYCLES

IT GIVES BICYCLING A WHOLE NEW TWIST!

Introducing Lafree. The electric bicycle with a twist!
Lafree is the first bicycle to incorporate Giant's
patented Variable Power Control (VPC) feature,
giving the rider freedom to apply power to the pedals when
and where desired. With a simple twist of the wrist
to Lafree's handlebar throttle,
the bicycle instantly delivers increased force to the pedals,
easily conquering steep hills and strong head-winds.

Lafree's modular design has been custom-crafted specifically
with the demands of the electric bicycle in mind.
A "total design" approach resulting in an electric bicycle
that is as easy to maintain as it is to ride.
For more information on Lafree email:
lafree@giant-europe.com

Lafree.
ELECTRIK

A Proven Track Record

Now 16 years since the Howard Plaza Hotel Taipei's 1984
opening and still leading the field.
Taiwan's first five star hotel chain,
the group has expanded to business
hotels in Taipei, Taichung and Kaohsiung,
and luxury resorts in Pacific Green Bay,
Shihmen Dam and Kenting.
 Well established island-wide
our state of the art services
mean we've got all the
angles covered.
At work or at play,
wherever you are,
giving you the choice.

Howard
HOTELS & RESORTS
INTERNATIONAL
福華大飯店

Howard Plaza Hotel Taipei
886-2-27002323
Howard Prince Hotel Taichung
886-4-4632323
Howard Plaza Hotel Kaohsiung
886-7-2362323
Howard Beach Resort Pacific Green Bay
886-2-24926565
Howard Lake Resort Shihmen Dam
886-3-4111234
Howard Beach Resort Kenting
886-8-8862323

Corporate Sales Office Tel : 886-2-23267527   Fax : 886-2-27082376
Automated Voice Service : 886-2-27019288   160, Jen Ai Road, Sec. 3, Taipei Taiwan 106, R.O.C.
E-mail : howard@ howard-hotels.com   URL: http ://www.howard-hotels.com

24
Literature

Traditional Chinese architecture incorporated decorative poetry in building design for both aesthetic and literary purposes.

What's New

According to the 1998 Annual of Literature in Taiwan 一九九八年臺灣文學年鑑 published by the Council for Cultural Affairs, the ten foremost literary events in Taiwan for 1998 were:

1. On March 31, the Chiu Ko Publishing Company 九歌出版社 celebrated its 20th anniversary. One of the most important publishers of literary works in Taiwan, the Chiu Ko Publishing Company announced at its celebration festivities the publishing of the *Chiu Ko Anthology of Taiwanese Literature* 臺灣文學廿年集 1978-1998 and the reprinting of the works of four senior writers, including Liang Shih-chiu 梁實秋.

2. On May 3, the May Fourth Literature and Art Gathering 五四文藝雅集 was held at the Howard Plaza Hotel. Organized by *Wen Hsun Magazine* 文訊雜誌 and sponsored by the Kuomintang Central Committee Cultural Department, this gathering featured the first May Fourth Awards, which were given to six veterans in the fields of literary editing, literary education, literary criticism, literary activity, literary exchange, and youth literature.

3. On May 9, the first National College Student Literary Awards 全國大專學生文學獎 were held at the NTU student activity center. Planned by the Council for Cultural Affairs and cosponsored by National Taiwan University (NTU) and the *United Daily News*, this ceremony rewarded the writing of 31 students in various categories, such as new poetry, prose, novels, playwriting, and literary criticism. In the future, local colleges and universities will take turns sponsoring this award.

4. In August, *The Complete Works of Tzeng Ching-wen's Short Novels* 鄭清文短篇小說全集 was published by the Rye Field Publishing Company 麥田出版社. This collection of 7 volumes contains 68 short novels, including the first novel he ever published, *The Lonely Heart* 寂寞的心. Tzeng Ching-wen's works have frequently appeared in Taiwan's prominent annual literary selections. Having spent 40 years focusing his writing on the land and people of Taiwan, Tzeng Ching-wen has been coined "the purest native writer" by the former editor-in-chief of the *Chinese Pen,* NTU English professor Chih Pang-yuan 齊邦媛.

5. In January, *The Complete Works of Chang Shen-chieh* 張深切全集 was published by Cosmax Publishing Company 文經社. Chang Shen-chieh was instrumental in pioneering the new Taiwan literature movement during the period of Japanese occupation and founded the Taiwan Literary League 臺灣文藝聯盟. The editing and publishing of his works is regarded as a milestone in the history of Taiwanese literature, especially regarding studies on the period of Japanese occupation.

6. Japanese literature fever in Taiwan witnessed a rebirth, starting with the enthusiastic response given to the Chinese edition

of *Lost Paradise* 失樂園, a Japanese novel which was subsequently turned into both a movie and a TV serial drama. The publishing of works and novels by new-generation Japanese women writers, as well as pop novels for conversion into dramas for television, quickly became a fad for Taiwan publishers, giving them a new line of products to market. Reading Japanese literature on the Internet also became quite vogue; for instance, the China Times Publishing Company set up a website devoted to the works of Japanese writer Murakami Haruki.

7. On October 29, the Conference of Cross-Strait Writers Prospecting 21st Century Literature 兩岸作家展望廿一世紀文學研討會 was held in the international conference room of the National Central Library. Jointly sponsored by the Nan Hua University 南華大學, the literary supplement of the *United Daily News*, the National Central Library, and *Wen Hsun Magazine*, this landmark event included attendance by a nine-member "dream team" of Chinese mainland literary figures from the past 20 years.

8. The fame of Chinese chivalry novelist Chin Yung 金庸 rose to new heights in 1998. Chosen as Man of the Year in Publishing by Kingstone Bookstores 金石堂書店 (one of the leading bookstore chains in Taiwan), Chin Yung continued to write outstanding novels which often remained on the "long-term best sellers" list for extended periods of time. Two international conferences—one in Taipei and the other in the United States—were held on the Chin Yung phenomena, whose works appeared in almost every type of media conceivable: books, movies, television, video games, cartoons, and even the Internet.

9. In January 1999, the nearly 70-year-old Publication Law 出版法 was abolished. The main functions of this law were issuing registration certificates, penalizing pornographic publications, and subsidizing worthy publications. A gradual loosening in the qualifications required for publishers made the issuing of registration certificates obsolete, and other laws and regulations replaced the need to penalize and subsidize publications. Thus, the regulatory agency for this law, the Government Information Office, recommended its abolishment, feeling that the domestic publishing industry would thrive in a more liberalized media environment.

10. On November 11, 1998, the bill to establish the National Taiwan Literature Institute 國立臺灣文學館 was passed by the Executive Yuan. This institute will consist of four sections: a research section for studying, research, and translation; an archival section for collecting materials, preservation, and reproduction; an exhibition section for programming exhibitions; and a promotional section for inter-institutional cooperation, cultivation of literary talent, and publishing. The institute will be located in Tainan City and is scheduled to open by 2001.

To recognize the rich legacy of Chinese Literature and its significant impact on Taiwan's literary consciousness, a description of Chinese Literature before 1949 will follow that of Taiwanese literature per se.

Early Taiwanese Literature

Aboriginal Traditions

The aboriginal peoples settled on the island of Taiwan thousands of years ago, and have since developed their distinctive oral narratives, languages, customs, and cultures. For centuries, aborigines on Taiwan have been marginalized in the expression of Taiwanese culture. As each tribe has its own language and customs, intertribal communication or coordination is weak. Only until recently was some progress made for such intertribal purposes, and the major event that drew different tribes together was the 1985 Wu Feng Incident 吳鳳事件, in which the statue of Wu Feng, a fictional deity invented by the Han-Chinese to domesticate the "barbaric" aborigines, was crushed. Quite a few aboriginal intellectuals joined their people in the demonstration, urging the government to drop the ethnocentric Wu Feng mythology in the primary school textbooks and to pay more attention to the crisis the aboriginal population was facing.

Since 1980, aboriginal intellectuals have tried to recreate their own past by re-expressing the oral traditions. A large body of oral narratives about creation myths and tribal heroes have been transcribed and circulated in the form of parallel texts in which the original aboriginal languages are spelled out in romanization, accompanied by Chinese translation. The texts are not only intended for Chinese-speaking audiences, but are also primarily used as textbooks for the younger generations in the aboriginal population. For many aboriginal intellectuals, such texts literally constitute the last utopian hope for their traditions to be transmitted in the struggle for cultural survival, fully aware of the brutal fact that even their children are resisting the use of the native tongue. As a result, indigenous languages and literatures are on the verge of disappearance.

Chinese Immigrant Literature

Between 1612 and 1844, quite a few Chinese intellectuals visited or stayed in Taiwan, most notably the Ming poet Shen Kuang-wen 沈光文, who was forced to land on the island by a typhoon in 1662 and afterwards played an important role in forming a Taiwanese Poets Society under the name of *Tung-yin* 東吟. Like Koxinga 鄭成功, who came with his soldiers and conquered the island in 1661, Shen was a royal subject to the Ming emperors, even though China had by then been taken over by the Ching rulers. His poetry was mostly composed in regulated verse, expressing his patriotic feelings and nostalgia for the empire lost. Shen was thus instrumental in planting the seeds of classical Chinese literature on the island. Students were trained to familiarize themselves with the grand Chinese literary tradition. The lyric subjects were often on exotic landscapes or the poet's own inscapes of consciousness that had little to do with the social reality of Taiwan. As a consequence, in more than two hundred years, there were only a few memorable pieces composed in prose narrative by high officials who happened to be in Taiwan for a brief period. Examples are *Chu-lo-hsien chih* 諸羅縣志 by Chen Meng-lin 陳夢林 (who arrived in Taiwan in 1716) and *Hsiao-liu-chiu man-chih* 小琉球漫誌 by Chu Shih-chieh 朱士玠 (who stayed from June 1763 until August 1764).

Several local Taiwanese poets began to make their names known during the mid-19th century, among them Tsai Ting-lan 蔡廷蘭 (1811-1870), Chen Chao 陳肇, Huang Ching 黃敬, Cheng Yung-hsi 鄭用錫 (1787-1858), and Lin Chan-mei 林占梅 (1816-1865). They were literati and cultural elites writing in the mode of classical Chinese lyrics, and as intellectuals who played important roles in Taiwan's history, their influence on local culture remains strong. In response to the colonial world of the late Ching period and in reaction to their precursors, Taiwanese poets of the next two decades became more devoted to everyday subjects and were often committed to expressing nationalist sentiment. Tang Ching-sung 唐景崧 and Chiu Feng-chia 丘逢甲 were two prominent officials and poets who got deeply involved in establishing the Democratic Taiwan Nation 臺灣民主國 on May 25, 1895, upon hearing the news that the Ching court had ceded Taiwan to Japan. Other major poets of this generation, such as Chen Wei-ying 陳維英 and Wang Kai-tai 王凱泰, were equally interested in describing ordinary people and popular culture. In many ways, they opened paths toward a more dynamic and democratic era of literary production, the period of Taiwanese literature under Japanese rule (1895-1945).

Early Colonial Literature

On April 7, 1895, in the Treaty of Shimonoseki which put an end to the first Sino-Japanese War, the Ching empire ceded Taiwan and the nearby Pescadores to Japan. Subsequently, the Japanese army landed on Taiwan on May 29, 1895, but met fierce resistance from the Taiwanese, who had proclaimed independence. The Taiwan Republic established by a group of cultural elites and local people lasted only ten days; however, the Taiwanese fought the Japanese troops for four months before surrendering Tainan City in October 1895. Sporadic guerrilla resistance to the colonizer continued for some 20 years. The casualties on both sides were quite heavy; more than 10,000 Taiwanese died. As a result, the Japanese gradually modified their policies to seek the acquiescence of the Taiwanese elites and began to introduce modern technology and social reforms, instead of resorting to military or political force.

Between 1895 and 1913, a minor group of national elites, mostly poets writing in the classical Chinese tradition, returned to China, thinking that they could not survive colonialism. The remaining local elites tried, on the other hand, to preserve their cultural heritage, retain ties with other provinces, and develop their distinctive arts of improvisation in the midst of colonial banality and brutality. Hung Chi-sheng 洪棄生 was probably the most famous writer of the period. He refused to cut off his queue, withdrew from public life, and wrote in classical Chinese, to make the point that he was identifying himself with the Ching. In his poetical and prose works, Hung constantly referred to the society and culture of Taiwan of the time to reveal his patriotism and nationalism. However, the most important literary event in the first 20 years under Japanese occupation was the establishment of a Li Poetry Society 櫟社, of which the key members included Lien Ya-tang 連雅堂, Lin Chih-hsien 林痴仙, Lin Hsien-tang 林獻堂, and many others. The society was responsible for publishing an influential journal on poetry and poetics, *Taiwan Wen-i Chiu-chih* 臺灣文藝舊誌; it was also instrumental in supporting nationalist movements. Lien's monumental work on Taiwan's history, *A Comprehensive History of Taiwan* 臺灣通史, remains a classic in the field.

In 1911, Liang Chi-chao 梁啓超 visited Taiwan and brought with him ideas of Western enlightenment and new experimental literature. Even though Taiwanese writers of the time were versed in the classical Chinese tradition, they were forced to confront the colonial reality and to work in more realistic modes of literary expression. This made a shift toward modern literature inevitable.

Taiwanese New Literature

The Colonial Context

Whereas most literature in Taiwan prior to 1920 was written in the style of the classical Chinese tradition, a new strand of modern Taiwanese literature emerged in the early 1920s in a process commonly referred to as the Taiwanese New Literature movement 臺灣新文學運動. Compared with its mainland counterpart, Taiwanese New Literature displayed two distinctive features that seem to universally characterize colonial cultural products, its multi-linguisticity and its overriding political import. In addition to Chinese-language works, many of the literary products of this movement—especially in the later stage—were written in Japanese. There was also a viable Taiwanese Language movement 臺灣話運動 in the early 1930s, advocating the use of a new written language based on spoken Taiwanese, which is a version of the southern

Fukienese dialect used by the majority of population in Taiwan. From the beginning, Taiwanese New Literature was an integral part of a new phase of sociopolitical resistance by the Taiwanese people against Japanese colonial rule. In the 1920s, the Taiwanese intelligentsia, revolving around the Taiwanese Cultural Association 臺灣文化協會 (1921-1931), launched a large-scale cultural reform program with various sorts of political agendas, in lieu of the futile and often brutally suppressed armed revolts in the first two decades of the Japanese period. Key figures of the early stage of the movement, such as Lai He 賴和 (1894-1943), frequently regarded as the "Father of Taiwanese New Literature," Chen Hsu-ku 陳虛谷 (1896-1965), and Tsai Chiu-tung 蔡秋桐 (b. 1900), were also active members of the Cultural Association, participating in its well-known islandwide mass education lecture tours. Not surprisingly, nationalistic sentiments were expressed through their literary works. Even after 1931, when a harsh crackdown by the colonial government put an end to the lively resistance activities of the previous decade, the New Literature movement, nourished by the sociopolitical movements of the twenties, continued to grow among the increasingly bilingual intellectual class of Taiwan. The legacy of resistance to colonialism, too, persisted, in either overt or covert forms, until the very end of the Japanese period.

However, the broadly defined political nature of Taiwanese New Literature refers not only to explicit criticism of the colonizers, in works by such undaunted anti-imperialist fighters as Lai Ho and Yang Kui 楊逵 (1906-1985), but also to the cultural hybridity in later works of the Taiwanese New Literature movement written in the colonizer's language, which was by definition a political product and carries with it imprints of an unjust power relationship. Whereas the first generation of Taiwanese New Literature writers, most of whom were born after the Japanese takeover, still exhibited a characteristically Chinese cultural and artistic outlook, there was a notable shift in the second generation of

Taiwanese New Literature writers. The overall increase in the degree of hybridity in Taiwanese culture in the second half of the Japanese period may be explained by changes in the colonizer's governing policies.

Beginning in 1918-1919, the Japanese adopted an effective assimilation policy 內地延長主義, (which would translate as "the principle of treating Taiwan as an extension of Japan proper"), which shifted from high-handed police control and differential treatment of the Taiwanese to more enlightened civil governing, emphasis on education, and cultivation of a more congenial relationship between Japanese and Taiwanese. As the new colonial situation steadily took shape and Japanese language education became more effectively implemented, a greater number of students in the colony went to study in Japan. Those among them who enrolled in college literary departments and had contact with famous Japanese writers later played influential roles in the literary scene of Taiwan. An even more drastic change was that, during the last phase of the Japanese period (1937-1945), as Japan declared war with China, the colonial government mobilized huge amounts of social resources to enforce an intensified Japanization program 皇民化運動, (literally, "the movement of converting Taiwanese into loyal subjects of the Japanese Emperor"), which included a ban on Chinese-language publications.

The hybrid nature of this colonial literature reflects Taiwan's colonial past and its relatively unusual experience as a Japanese colony. A territory of Han 漢 settlers since the 17th century and a province of the Manchurian-governed China since 1885, Taiwan was incorporated by Japan into a different geopolitical and economic system in the early part of the 20th century, and as a result went through the initial stages of modernization via its East Asian colonizer, which had itself recently modernized after the Western model. The kind of society produced in Taiwan by this process was inevitably of a hybrid nature, with modern and traditional institutions of different ethnic origins coexisting side by side.

Taiwan occupied a strategic position in Japan's imperialist project, serving as a base for Japan's further advancement into South China and Southeast Asia. For this reason, it is said to have received relatively benign treatment from the Japanese (as compared to Japan's other colonies, such as Korea), considerably mitigating the hostility between colonizer and colonized. The colonial condition in Taiwan is thus a product of the extremely intricate political and cultural negotiations between the colonial government and the local elite, articulated by progressive intellectuals who often served as spokesmen for the elite. Fine Taiwanese writers of the later period, such as Chang Wen-huan 張文環 (1909-1978), Lu Ho-jo 呂赫若 (1914-1950), Yang Kui, and Lung Ying-tsung 龍瑛宗 (b. 1911), achieved their distinctive art under the influence of Western artistic trends through Japanese literary institutions.

Taiwanese New Literature Movement

As stated earlier, the Taiwanese New Literature movement began as part of a larger cultural reform movement during the 1920s. A brief introduction of this cultural movement, sometimes called the Taiwanese New Culture movement 臺灣新文化運動, may be in order. The first events of this movement took place in 1920, when some Taiwanese expatriates in Tokyo organized the New People Association 新民會, followed by a student-based Taiwanese Youth Association 臺灣青年會. The two organizations published a journal called *Taiwanese Youth* 臺灣青年 to propagate progressive ideas and voice opinions about the current state of affairs in Taiwan. The zeal for cultural reform soon spread to the island itself and was carried on by the Taiwanese Cultural Association. There are significant parallels between the Taiwanese New Culture movement and the Chinese mainland's May Fourth movement 五四運動. First of all, intellectuals in both societies, faced with the imperative to modernize, identified the cultural sediments of Neo-Confucian moralism and the feudalist social order as reactionary forces obstructing progress. Inspired by democratic ideals of modern Western society,

both groups had come to associate the "old" with the conservative mentality of the gentry class, and the "new" with ways of the "modern citizen"— and sought to transform the masses through popular education and cultural enlightenment 文化啓蒙. The popular idea of social Darwinism, which equated rejuvenation of national culture with survival of the people, added to the urgency of the task of cultural reform as a means of national self-preservation. Secondly, the new intellectuals of both societies were influenced by the dynamics of progressive discourse on national emancipation and socialist revolution in the years following the First World War. Such currents of thought created an imaginary alliance among the "weak and oppressed" nations of the world and provided a powerful rationale for nationalistic resistance by victims of imperialist aggression, as obviously the Chinese mainland and Taiwan both were. Thus, a patriotic discourse combining the two components of sociocultural modernization (cultural enlightenment) and anti-imperialism (national salvation and anti-colonialism) was developed in the 1920s and shared by the new intellectuals on both the Chinese mainland and Taiwan.

Although in the first two issues of *Taiwanese Youth* there were already articles on language reform and the need for rejuvenating contemporary Taiwanese literature, it was not until the heated New Versus Old Literary Debate 新舊文學論戰, which began with Chang Wo-chun's 張我軍 attack on traditional poets in 1924 and lasted till 1926, that the Taiwanese New Literature movement was formally launched. In this debate, new literary concepts—mainly those centering around the advantage of adopting the vernacular as a new literary medium and the social functions of literature in a modern age—were introduced, criticized, and defended. Traditional poets were castigated for using literature to incur social gains and political favor, their literary style criticized as hackneyed and insincere. Advocates of new literature, on the other hand, were branded as shallow and ignorant charlatans, their literary views ungrounded in solid learning. As in the case of many literary debates in modern times, the heated antagonism between opposite camps prevented a meaningful exchange of ideas. Rather, the debate performed an important ritualistic function: after the debate, traditional literary activities were increasingly confined to poetry clubs that continued to thrive but with limited social reach, while New Literature was legitimized as a powerful social institution. Through this institution, the new intellectuals denounced their Chinese cultural heritage—partly by taking traditional men of letters and their world views as scapegoats—and endorsed a vision of "modern civilization." These denouncements and this new vision constituted the major content of Taiwanese New Literature for at least a decade.

If the two New Culture movements on the Chinese mainland and Taiwan were analogous but separate, the relationship between the Chinese and Taiwanese New Literature movements was actually much closer. In the early stages, literary reform in the Taiwanese New Literature movement virtually mirrored its slightly earlier Chinese counterpart (1917-1925). When Chang Wo-chun wrote the polemical essays that triggered the Old Versus New Literary Debate, he was a student of Peking Normal University. During the debate, the major tenets for the May Fourth literary revolution, such as Hu Shih's "Principle of Eight Don'ts" 八不主義 from his "Preliminary Suggestions for Literary Reform" were introduced with slight modifications. Even the harsh style of the way Chang Wo-chun castigated the traditional poets was immediately reminiscent of the radical Chinese reformist Chen Tu-hsiu. Furthermore, throughout the decade of the 1920s, creative works by Chinese New Literature writers, such as Lu Hsun, Hu Shih, Kuo Mo-jo 郭沫若, Ping Hsin 冰心, Wang Lu-yen 王魯彥, and Ling Shu-hua 凌淑華, were reprinted in Taiwanese journals and undoubtedly served as models for literary practice.

However, within a decade, this dependent relationship began to change. Apparently, during this time the deepening of Japanese colonization had begun to structurally transform Taiwan society and steer it further away from the cultural orbit of the Chinese mainland. Consciousness of this new reality among the Taiwanese intellectuals manifested itself in two consecutive literary debates in 1931-32, the Nativist Literature Debate 鄉土文學論戰 and the Taiwanese Language Debate 臺灣語文論戰, which represented a turning point in the Taiwanese New Literature movement.

The Nativist Literature Debate testified to the prominent leftist presence in Taiwan's literary circles. The literary program proposed by its chief advocate Huang Shih-hui 黃石輝—suggesting that writers target their creative works at the working-class mass—was clearly modeled upon the leftist concept of proletarian literature. And the split of the Taiwanese Cultural Association in 1927 was primarily a result of disagreement in resistance strategies between the nationalist right wing and the socialist left wing. After the split, the association was controlled by left-wing members, led by Lien Wen-ching 連溫卿 and Wang Min-chuan 王敏川. The more moderate members formed the Taiwanese People's Party 臺灣民眾黨 and continued to fight for greater constitutional rights for the Taiwanese people. Yet, the political climate in the colony was so disillusioning that even the Taiwanese People's Party later displayed a leftward leaning tendency and was forced to dissolve by the colonial government in 1931.

Initially, the Taiwanese New Culture movement focused on cultural enlightenment to address the society's internal needs to modernize, and the main targets of its attack were old Chinese customs and lingering social ills of feudalism. As Taiwan proceeded along the course of modernization, however, the worldwide economic depression of the late 1920s exacerbated social problems, such as unemployment and class exploitation, thus leading to a rise in support for socialist ideology and Taiwan nativism.

Primarily concerned with internal social problems and conflicts between classes, leftist intellectuals called for a Taiwan-centered view in literary creation. Aside from a class-oriented literary view, Huang Shih-hui also was known for forcefully arguing that Taiwanese writers should write in their own language and about things on their own homeland. Termed by historians as following the direction of "self-improvement based on one province (Taiwan)" 一島改良主義, advocates of the Nativist Literature clearly envisioned a "Taiwanese consciousness" as something to be distinguished from the more inclusive "Chinese consciousness," or the ethnic consciousness of the Han race 漢民族意識.

This Taiwanese consciousness was the core spirit of Kuo Chiu-sheng's 郭秋生 campaign for Taiwanese language in the following year. The Taiwanese Language Debate, with the literary journal Nan-yin 南音 as its major forum, revealed the anxieties and ambivalent feelings of a colonized people in their attempts to develop a national language. In an effort to assert Taiwanese subjectivity, the movement had effectively served the Taiwanese intellectuals' emotional ties with China. First and foremost, the movement called attention to the fact that early advocates of the Taiwanese New Literature movement had followed the Chinese model of the May Fourth movement too closely. They had thus unwittingly mistaken the latter's problematics and strategies for their own, without giving proper attention to the objective circumstances of Taiwan.

To facilitate popular education in a country with an extremely high illiteracy rate, advocates of the May Fourth movement proposed to replace the difficult, obsolete classical Chinese language with modern Chinese vernacular as the official written language. The basic theoretical assumption was that since there would be a close correspondence between the spoken and written versions of modern Chinese, as reflected in the famous slogan "我手寫我心" (My hand writes what my heart feels), the efforts required to become literate in Chinese would be greatly lessened. In reality, however, a standard Chinese vernacular was yet to be popularized within the country; people from different regions still predominantly used dialects for daily communication, and some Chinese dialects are even mutually unintelligible (see section Dialects, Chapter 3, Language). There was, to be sure, a considerable disparity between the standard Chinese vernacular and the southern Fukienese dialect used by the majority of Taiwanese. Moreover, as Taiwan had already been politically separated from China for over two decades, its people had far fewer channels for learning the standard Chinese vernacular through public institutions such as an education system, publications, or a state bureaucracy.

Nevertheless, early advocates of the Taiwanese New Literature movement still favored the adoption of Chinese vernacular as the medium for Taiwanese New Literature. The fact that this position was uncontested at the time shows that by then the ethnic-cultural identity of Taiwanese intellectuals was still predominantly Chinese. One popular argument they espoused was that since most of the Taiwanese gentry class members were still tutored in the written language of classical Chinese in their childhood, minimal additional efforts would be needed to enable them to use the Chinese vernacular as a literary medium. The advantage of this was that it would facilitate the circulation of Taiwanese literary works in the larger Chinese community, since obviously Chinese recognition was still highly regarded by Taiwanese intellectuals. In practice, however, despite the goodwill on the part of most Taiwanese New Literature writers, the disadvantages are by no means negligible. It is said that Lai He had to write his works in classical Chinese first, then translate it into the Chinese vernacular, and finally revise it with more life-like Taiwanese colloquialisms. Yang Shou-yu 楊守愚 (1905-1959), a writer well-versed in the Chinese vernacular because of special personal background, had to regularly rewrite works submitted for publication when he served as the editor for the literary section of the Taiwanese People's Newspaper 臺灣民報. Such a cumbersome and laborious process works against the fundamental principle of realistic literary writing, which explains why the kind of reevaluation offered by the Taiwanese Language Movement was well-received even by Lai He, a writer with ostensible Chinese consciousness.

Without political enforcement, however, the goals of the Taiwanese Language Movement were very difficult to materialize. The fact that many words in the Taiwanese spoken language are not believed to have corresponding Chinese characters made the development of a new writing system an enormous project beyond the reach of private groups. It is said that Lai He, after extensively using the Taiwanese language in writing his short story "A Letter of Criticism from a Comrade" 一個同志的批評信 (1935), was so frustrated with the experiment that he completely stopped writing fiction in the New Literature style. The colonial government, not surprisingly, only tried to hinder such a nationalistically motivated project as an obstacle to the implementation of Japanese as the official language in Taiwan. The Taiwanese Language Debate thus reveals a typical dilemma facing colonized people: as the effort to develop a new national language based on the native tongue was seen by the Japanese colonial rulers as mainly a linguistic strategy of resistance and a means to assert one's own subjectivity, it was not likely to gain the political support required for its success. Despite failure, however, the Taiwanese Language Movement must be regarded as a significant turning point in the Taiwanese New Literature movement. There was a marked decline in the number of works by Chinese New Literature writers reprinted in Taiwanese journals after 1931. From this point on, the development of Taiwanese New Literature began to consciously depart from the Chinese model, embarking on a path of its own.

Maturation and Growth

The crackdown of leftist organizations and the general suppression of sociopolitical movements in 1931 ironically heralded a period of maturation and growth for Taiwanese New Literature, which lasted for over a decade. Various literary organizations were formed and new literary journals mushroomed. Having passed its initial, experimental stage, the evolution of the new literary form, particularly in the technical

respect, made impressive progress during this period. Whereas the first generation of Taiwanese New Literature writers continued to be productive, a group of young talents also joined the ranks. There was, however, a notable gap between the two generations of Taiwanese New Literature writers in such respects as cultural outlook, aesthetic preference, and vocational orientation. This apparent disjuncture in the relatively brief history of Taiwanese New Literature is particularly noteworthy, as it points to a rapidly changing cultural landscape in the second half of Taiwan's Japanese colonial period.

It has been argued that, by the time when the New Literature movement began, despite the fact that Taiwan had already been colonized by the Japanese for more than two decades, the cultural identity of Taiwanese intellectuals was still predominantly Chinese. Members of an ordinary Taiwanese gentry family were still sufficiently exposed to the Chinese cultural tradition, as children were still sent to private tutorial classes, or *shu-fang* 書房, to study classical Chinese. Most of the first generation of Taiwanese New Literature writers, being members of the traditional gentry class, were well-versed in classical Chinese and competent in traditional Chinese poetry writing, a practice to which some of them returned after Chinese publications were banned in 1937. The fact that there were no substantial changes in the ethnic content of cultural production and reproduction in the society is attributable to the special kind of colonial policies that were applied to Taiwan during the first two decades of the Japanese colonial period. Acknowledging that the colony had a separate history of its own, the Japanese were primarily concerned with maintaining social stability, rather than culturally assimilating the Taiwanese people. The cultural upbringing and community imagination of Taiwanese writers whose formative years fell into the first half of the colonial period were therefore not fundamentally transformed by colonial rule, even though most of them also received formal education in Japanese and were equipped with modern knowledge. Lai He, for example, went to a modern-style medical school and knew the Japanese language well, but he never used it in his creative writing. More importantly, as evidenced both by his writing and the role he played in the literary community, he was in many ways an exemplary traditional Chinese intellectual.

Significantly influenced by the Chinese May Fourth movement and its reformist ideology, the historical role played by this generation of Taiwanese writers was primarily that of new intellectuals in a pre-modern society struggling to break away from the past and to usher in progressive social visions. The past, however, was still very much with them. It can be easily demonstrated that, compared to their younger followers, this generation of Taiwanese writers carried over a considerable cultural legacy from the Chinese tradition in their New Literature-style works. Many of their works criticized a "spiritual disease" of Taiwanese society directly reflecting the Neo-Confucian moralist world view. The formal dimension of literary works by writers of this generation also displays a characteristically transitional character. The omniscient narrative point of view and episodic plot structure were obvious traits inherited from Chinese vernacular fiction. Since the modern short story, the novel, and free verse were essentially forms imported from the West, this generation of Taiwanese writers' assimilation of Western literary techniques and artistic conceptions was largely superficial.

The situation, however, was very different with writers born at later dates (Yang Kui was born in 1906; Weng Nao 翁鬧, 1908; Chang Wen-huan, 1909; Lung Ying-tsung, 1911; and Lu Ho-jo, 1914). In their formative years, the colonial cultural institutions were increasingly consolidated, and there was consequently a marked decrease in the value of Chinese learning as cultural capital. Generally speaking, unlike their immediate predecessors, the generation of Taiwanese writers active in the 1930s and 1940s lacked a solid background in traditional Chinese learning and demonstrated a more characteristically hybrid cultural identity. (As Hsu Chun-ya

許俊雅 has pointed out, the use of Japanese in literary creation gradually increased since 1933, and, by the time around 1936 and 1937, there were actually very few works written in Chinese.) At the same time, rapid social change, already a norm in 20th-century non-Western countries, was greatly accelerated by Taiwan's colonial authorities. The gap between the social visions of the two generations of writers was even more remarkable, as the younger writers were raised in a society at a considerably more advanced stage of modernization than their predecessors. Several critics have pointed out that Lai He seemed to be obsessed with the abusive power of laws and regulations enforced by the colonial government and its agents. These critics often justified Lai He's criticism with the fact that police control was notoriously harsh in Taiwan during the Japanese colonial period. Nevertheless, judging from many passages in Lai He's fiction in which he meditated on the demarcation line between justice and law from various philosophical points of view, one gets the impression that his ideals and framework of reference were still derived from a pre-modern, Confucianist world view. The fact that younger writers tended to present both the evil and the benign sides of the law indicates that these writers held a more realistic view of the modern judicial system, despite discriminatory practices in the colonial context. Thus, in many ways these two generations of Taiwanese writers perceived the relationship between the individual and society quite differently.

Another significant factor is that the younger generation of writers were oriented to the literary profession in an entirely different manner from their predecessors. The 1930s saw the emergence of a new cohort of writers who had studied in Japan, a group that constituted the majority of second-generation Taiwanese New Literature writers. While in Japan, these aspiring young Taiwanese writers found themselves on the periphery of an entirely different system of cultural production, and many of them began to earnestly seek membership in Japanese literary institutions. They enrolled in university literary classes, attended salons revolving around famous writers, and, above all, joined literary contests, which seemed to be an effective way of earning recognition from mainstream Japanese literary circles (often referred to as *Chung-yang wen-tan* 中央文壇). Yang Kui, Lu Ho-jo, and Lung Ying-tsung were winners of literary prizes in the mid-1930s. As Japanese assimilation of the West surpassed that of the Chinese in the same period, the Taiwanese writers' knowledge of Japanese seemed to have enabled them to have a firmer grasp of Western artistic concepts, and, more important, of the kind of vocational vision that artists in a modern society often take for granted. As they came to perceive themselves as professional artists, with technical expertise and individualistic aesthetic visions, it is less conceivable that they would ever become such spiritual leaders as Lu Hsun or Lai He, whose status as major writers was derived from personal charisma and outstanding moral character as well as literary talent.

Apparently, the younger writers enjoyed access to a wide range of literary models, mainly from the West, as evidenced by the remarkable diversity their works have shown in both artistic mode and ideological outlook. To give a few better known examples: Yang Kui adhered to a more orthodox leftism and dedicated his literary works to humanitarian criticisms of class exploitation, imperialism, and general evils in a capitalist society. Chang Wen-huan's approach was more humanistic in a liberal vein. His interest in the mystic power of the individual's inner self, projected onto Nature, resulted in some beautifully written lyrical pieces. Lu Ho-jo successfully emulated naturalism, offering realistic portraits of Taiwan's degenerated gentry class through "typical characters." Lung Ying-tsung's works showed influences of Symbolism, delicately aesthetic, with visible touches of decadence.

It is perhaps ironic that, whereas early advocates of the Taiwanese New Literature movement insisted on using the Chinese vernacular to ensure a place in the Chinese literary world, two out of three Taiwanese stories first collected in anthologies published in China—"The Newspaper Man" 送報夫 by Yang Kui, and "The Ox Cart" 牛車 by Lu Ho-jo (the other story selected was the Chinese language "The Ill-fated" 薄命, by Yang Hua 楊華, 1900-1936)—were translated from Japanese. And significantly, too, the high reputation these two stories enjoyed was clearly derived from the fact that they had won prizes in literary contests sponsored by important Japanese magazines. Furthermore, Hu Feng 胡風, the editor of the Chinese collections in which these stories were found, *Mountain Spirit: Short Stories from Korea and Taiwan* 山靈：朝鮮臺灣短篇小說集 and *Anthology of Stories from Weak and Small Nations in the World* 世界弱小民族小說選, was a renowned leftist literary theorist. The fact that Hu selected Yang and Lu's stories in recognition of their anti-imperialist spirit points to an extremely complex relationship between the Taiwanese authors and their Japanese colonizers, who were simultaneously oppressors and bestowers of cultural prestige. Such facts eloquently speak to the profoundly ambivalent cultural positions in which the second-generation Taiwanese New Literature writers found themselves in the 1930s.

End of an Era

After the Sino-Japanese War broke out in 1937, the colonial government in Taiwan started an intensive Japanization program, and banned the Chinese-language sections in newspapers and magazines. The impact of the harsh reality of war was not, however, fully felt until 1941, when Japan launched the Pacific War. The year 1937, for example, still saw the publication of a literary magazine *Wind and Moon* 風月報 (the only Chinese-language magazine of this period), which featured popular types of literati writings, such as pulp romance, familiar essays, and occasional pieces of traditional scholarship, and enjoyed wide circulation. A literary organization consisting mainly of Japanese writers published in 1940 an aesthetically-oriented journal *Literary Taiwan* 文藝臺灣. With the onslaught of the Pacific War, however, the Japanese stepped up their war campaign efforts and began to actively mobilize people in the colony to make a contribution to the "Warfare of the Great East Asia" 大東亞戰爭. Between 1941 and 1942, *Literary Taiwan* chimed in with the colonial government's call for arms and published such stories as Chou Chin-po's 周金波 (b. 1920) "Volunteer Conscript" 志願兵 and other unabashedly propagandist poems and plays. Several well-known second-generation writers of Taiwanese New Literature, disapproving of both the political stance and artistic orientation of *Literary Taiwan*, formed their own literary organization and began to publish *Taiwanese Literature* 臺灣文學 in 1941. Before the two journals were forced to merge by the government under the new name *Taiwanese Literature and Art* 臺灣文藝 in 1944, *Taiwanese Literature* published perhaps the most important works of second-generation Taiwanese New Literature writers: such as "Capon" 閹雞 and "Night Monkeys" 夜猿 by Chang Wen-huan; "Wealth, Offspring, and Longevity" 財子壽, "Peace for the Entire Family" 閣家平安, and "Guava" 石榴 by Lu Ho-jo; "A Village Without Doctors" 無醫村 by Yang Kui; and "Rapid Torrents" 奔流 by Wang Chang-hsiung 王昶雄 (b. 1916).

The contention between *Literary Taiwan* and *Taiwanese Literature* between 1941 and 1944 represented a significant turn of events, as second-generation Taiwanese New Literature writers began to directly confront oppressive relationships within the colonial structure. For these writers, who had been partially nourished by Japanese culture in their formative years and to which they held various degrees of allegiance, this experience must have been simultaneously disillusioning and educating. Above all, it became clear to them that artistic approaches were not ideologically innocent. One thing that the Taiwanese writers objected to was the Japan-centered, typically colonist point of view of *Literary Taiwan* which treated Taiwan as an exotic "foreign" place to be romanticized for the connoisseurship of readers in Japan. To the Taiwanese writers, such a literary approach was obviously complicitous in the colonial government's effort to involve culture in the process of political domination by way of diverting people from sociopolitical concerns to purely aesthetic ones. Such realizations are undoubtedly behind the tactics used by writers of *Taiwanese Literature* in their endeavors to champion realism as opposed to the exquisite aestheticism and romanticism of *Literary Taiwan*. Aside from works directly informed by leftist ideology, such as those by Yang Kui, it is said that some writers of the *Taiwanese Literature* group consciously shifted to more detailed depictions of local customs, rural life, and folk traditions of Chinese/Taiwanese origin in order to register their resentment of the Japanization program.

The nationalistic orientation of *Taiwanese Literature*, however, failed to attract some of the ardent writers of an even younger generation, such as Yeh Shih-tao 葉石濤 (b. 1925) and Chou Chin-po, who published in *Literary Taiwan* and expressed either aestheticism or political loyalty to the colonizer. Yeh even wrote the controversial essay "Shit Realism" 糞寫實主義, which provoked a heated response from colleagues of *Taiwanese Literature*. However, it was not until the next period that some of this younger generation of writers began to deeply reflect upon the complicated issues surrounding colonial subjectivity.

The unusually convoluted trajectory traveled by Taiwanese New Literature writers may also be illuminated by a brief examination of their intriguingly different attitudes toward the issue of modernity. The wholehearted embrace by many first-generation writers of modernity as an advanced stage of civilization was expressed in vacant terms, for essentially they never had any real experience of a truly modernized society. Most of the second generation, pressured by wartime literary policies, engaged in indirect resistance by means of asserting nativism, to the effect of notably decreasing their criticism of traditional, feudalist traits of the Taiwanese society. However, if some of them consciously denigrated modern urban civilization, symbolically represented by the

Japanese metropolis, still others held exactly the opposite stance. In works of Chen Huo-chuan 陳火泉 (b.1915) and the younger writer Chou Chin-po, who opted to side with progress, a prominent theme was the urgency to modernize in view of the obvious benefits that modernity could have brought to the Taiwanese people. As Japan was equated with civilization, they ardently supported Japanization, albeit not without doubts from time to time.

In artistic terms, the modern literary form of the Taiwanese New Literature movement significantly departed from the classical Chinese tradition, but its evolution was brought to an abrupt cessation at the end of the Second World War when Taiwan was returned to China. Several years later, the Nationalists, having lost the Chinese mainland to the communists in the civil war, relocated to Taiwan and started an entirely new era. The drastic changes such historical events brought to Taiwanese society caused most of the Taiwanese New Literature writers to halt their creative activities. Many artistic potentials were therefore never allowed to develop to their fullest extent, and the movement ended before any genuinely masterful works of art could ever appear.

The legacy of the Taiwanese New Literature movement was suppressed in the postwar years, as the dominant culture was now constituted by the mainland Chinese tradition. But there were still some significant works written and published, and the exploration of colonial subjectivity continued to be the dominant concern of works written by writers directly nourished by the Taiwanese New Literature of the Japanese colonial period, such as *The Orphan of Asia* 亞細亞孤兒 by Wu Cho-liu 吳濁流 (1900-1976), "The Oleander Flowers" 夾竹桃 by Chung Li-ho, *The Man Who Rolls On the Ground* 滾地郎 by Chang Wen-huan, and later works by Yeh Shih-tao. Despite their largely marginal position, these writers would play a crucial role in Taiwan's postwar literary history by offering alternative visions to the dominant culture, and their impact was increasingly felt in the Nativist 本土化 movement of the last two decades.

Post-1949 Literature in Taiwan

Shifting Literary Trends

Taiwan's post-1949 era began when China's Nationalist government, led by Chiang Kai-shek, settled on the offshore island-province of Taiwan after the mainland fell to the Chinese communists. The 40-year period under the rule of two presidents from the Chiang family was characterized by remarkable social, political, and cultural continuity and homogeneity. Drastic structural changes have been occurring at all levels of the society since the mid-1980s, as direct consequences of the lifting of martial law, the recognition of opposition parties, the removal of the ban on establishing newspapers, and the resumption of communication with mainland China at the nonofficial level. New intellectual and artistic currents have emerged, many with the explicit or implicit motive of reexamining existing orders. Nonetheless, it is undeniable that literary accomplishments of writers from the earlier post-1949 decades laid solid groundwork for Taiwan's vital and pluralistic cultural development in the 1990s.

As China split into two political entities with different sociopolitical systems after 1949, the tradition of Chinese New Literature 新文學 traveled along divergent paths in these two Chinese societies. Writers in post-1949 Taiwan have been selective in developing their literary heritage: whereas revolutionary literature and "critical realism" were suppressed, the more inoffensive lyrical-sentimental strand enjoyed great popularity. From the anticommunist propaganda of the cold war decade of the 1950s, through the Modernist and the Nativist literary movements of the 1960s and 1970s, to the expression of today's pluralism and the burgeoning of market-oriented mass culture, literary currents in post-1949 Taiwan have closely mirrored the country's larger sociopolitical transitions.

The Western-influenced Modernist literary movement of the sixties and the populist, Nativist literary movement of the 1970s may appropriately be regarded as "alternative" and "oppositional" cultural formations in Taiwan during this period. As the Modernists adopted literary concepts developed in Western capitalist society, they simultaneously longed for an ideological transformation, taking such bourgeois social values as individualism, liberalism, and rationalism as correctives for the oppressive social relations derived from a traditional system of values. The Nativist literary movement, by contrast, with its use of literature as a pretext to challenge the dominant sociopolitical order, may be properly considered as counterhegemonic. The movement was triggered by the nation's diplomatic setbacks in the international arena during the 1970s, and provided a forum for native Taiwanese intellectuals to vent their discontent with the socioeconomic problems that have accompanied the country's accelerated process of industrialization since the 1960s.

For different reasons, both movements dominated Taiwan's literary scene only for a relatively brief period of time. By the late 1970s and early 1980s, the influence of both the Modernists and the Nativists had sharply declined, and some of their inherent shortcomings had become obvious with the passage of time. As most of the Modernist writers advocated artistic autonomy and were politically disengaged, the subversive elements of their works were easily co-opted by more powerful cultural forces and their critical impact was consequently diluted. The more radical adherence to aestheticism by certain writers, moreover, was deeply at odds with the predominantly lyrical sensibility of ordinary Chinese readers. Even though the essential dynamics of the Modernist movement were not entirely exhausted by the loss of popular favor, both critics and general readers received the movement's most mature output in the 1980s with nonchalance. In the meantime, the militant political agenda of the Nativists both threatened and bored middle-class readers. The resistant activities of the more radical Nativists, moreover, were increasingly channeled into direct political involvement. The subsiding of these contending literary voices thus paved the way for the rise of a "serious" literature more popular in nature and a resurgence of the lyrical and sentimental strain of the 1980s. The younger generation of writers of this decade assimilated the technical sophistication of the Modernists and displayed a social awareness as a result of the Nativist influence. Their vocational visions, however, significantly departed from those of their mentors and were much more deeply conditioned by the market logic of Taiwan's increasingly commercialized cultural setting.

Fifties Mainland Emigre Literature

After Taiwan was returned to rule by a Chinese government in 1945, Mandarin Chinese replaced the Taiwanese dialect and Japanese as the official spoken language of the province. Creative activities of middle-aged native Taiwanese writers were greatly hampered by this language barrier. Political fear is another factor that silenced native Taiwanese writers, as many Taiwanese intellectuals were persecuted during and after the February 28 Incident in 1947 (see pertinent section of Chapter 4, History). The literary scene in Taiwan during the 1950s was therefore virtually dominated by mainland writers who followed the Nationalists to Taiwan around 1949. These emigre writers were frequently mobilized in the state-sponsored cultural programs and produced a literature that has often been characterized as anticommunist.

In addition to political propaganda, writers of the 1950s have been frequently faulted for their amateurism, which is partly the product of a special institution in Taiwan, the *fu-kan* 副刊, or literary supplement to newspapers. The *fu-kan* undeniably has been the most significant sponsor of literary activities in contemporary Taiwan; nevertheless, with its large demand for works of immediate popular appeal, it at the same time fostered casual, lightweight writing and pandered to middlebrow literary tastes. As literary writing became less professional, the distinction between artistic and journalistic genres was often blurred.

Although the general climate of the 1950s was not conducive to the production of serious art, works of considerable artistic merit by a number of writers deserve greater critical attention than is usually given to them. Two broad categories of writings by these writers, traditionalist prose and realistic fiction, may be discussed as representative of literature in this decade.

Traditionalist prose

Contrary to the situation in the People's Republic of China, where gentry literature of China's feudal past was sometimes renounced for ideological reasons and where numerous political idioms designed to mobilize the masses were added to the vocabulary, the prose style in post-1949 Taiwan tended to be more literary, retaining a great many more archaic expressions and allusions to classical literature. The proliferation of traditionalist prose 散文 in Taiwan during the 1950s, in the forms of familiar essay and the hybrid genre of essay-fiction, was apparently a continuation of an earlier trend on the mainland during and after the Sino-Japanese war. The decade's best-known essayists—Chang Hsiu-ya 張秀亞, Chung Mei-yin 鍾梅音, Hsu Chung-pei 徐鍾珮, Liang Hsuan 亮軒, and Chi-chun 琦君—were therefore all mainland writers.

Realistic fiction

Having in their formative years been exposed to the works of Lu Hsun, Mao Tun 茅盾, Pa Chin 巴金 , and Lao She 老舍, mainland emigre writers active in the 1950s and 1960s by and large carried on the Chinese "realist" tradition— a somewhat atrophied version of 19th-century European realism—established during the May Fourth era and the thirties. For political reasons, however, they consciously or unconsciously modified those realistic conventions that might have been offensive to the dominant culture of post-1949 Taiwan: revolutionary and proletarian themes were taboo, and references to class consciousness were avoided. Nevertheless, the nature of literary conventions is such that their suppression can never be as complete as it appears on the surface.

The 1960s saw the publication of several well-written, "anticommunist" realistic novels, such as *Rice-sprout Song* 秧歌, *The Whirlwind* 旋風, and *The Ti Village* 荻村傳. Although important in their own right, these stories were set exclusively in pre-Revolution China, and their authors either never resided in Taiwan (e.g., Eileen Chang 張愛玲 , 1921-95), or were marginal to Taiwan's literary scene (e.g., Chiang Kui 姜貴 and Chen Chi-ying 陳紀瀅), thus diminishing their significance in Taiwan's post-1949 literary history. Far more relevant are such writers as Wang Lan 王藍, Meng Yao 孟瑤, Pan Jen-mu 潘人木, Lin Hai-yin 林海音, Nieh Hua-ling 聶華苓, Peng Ko 彭歌, Chu Hsi-ning 朱西寧, Tuan Tsai-hua 段彩華, Ssu-ma Chung-yuan 司馬中原, and Chung Chao-cheng 鍾肇政, writers who established their literary reputations around the mid-1950s and who have continued to play prominent roles in Taiwan's literary scene.

Although the fiction of these writers is also filled with nostalgic recollections of the mainland past, their works are nevertheless unique products of the contemporary cultural and political environment. Unmistakably, the emancipation ethos, a legacy of pre-1949 realist literature, has informed a number of their writings set in the past on subjects such as the oppression of women, the repressive nature of the traditional Chinese family system, and the condition of working-class people and domestic servants. In addition, the realistic codes were rewritten and the critical messages mitigated or displaced rightist political convictions and active support of the present government frequently caused these writers to domesticate the revolutionary spirit with counterdevices and to shift the thematic focus from the sociohistorical to private domains. The rise of the young Modernists, with their liberalism and new aesthetic conceptions, challenged not only these older writers' artistic visions, but also the dominant culture's ideological control over creative writers. The change brought forth by the Modernists in the artistic realm formed the basis for more radical cultural critiques found in later decades.

Modernist Literary Movement

The dominant culture in post-1949 Taiwan carries on many traditions established in China during the Republican era (1911-1949). The Modernist literary movement is an expression of the predilection by Chinese intellectuals of the time to emulate Western high culture. Ever since the end of the 19th century, shocked by the devastating effect of China's encounters with Western culture, modern Chinese intellectuals have attempted various kinds of cultural rejuvenation, the most potent formula of which has been the assimilation of Western cultural products. Taiwan's Modernist literary movement, as one of the latest in a series of such efforts, inevitably displays some of its essential characteristics. Second, an important link can be perceived between this movement and the liberal strand of thought in China's pre-Revolution era, especially that of the Anglo-American wing of intellectuals. It is readily observable that ideas of important literary figures of post-1949 Taiwan, such as Liang Shih-chiu 梁實秋, former member of the Crescent Moon Society 新月社, Hsia Chi-an 夏濟安, mentor of a core group of Modernists, and Yen Yuan-shu 顏元叔, leading critic of the '60s who introduced New Criticism to Taiwan, are all fundamentally rooted in the Western liberal-humanist tradition. Yen Yuan-shu's proposition that "literature has the dual function of being the dramatization and criticism of life," in particular, closely echoes both Matthew Arnold and the Literary Studies Association's 文學研究社 famous tenet, "art for life's sake." Taiwan's Modernists particularly stressed the principle of artistic autonomy, among other liberal conceptions of literature, and, by and large, have more thoroughly adhered to this principle than their pre-1949 liberal predecessors.

From the point of view of literary history, however, the epoch-making significance of Taiwan's Modernist literary movement rests primarily in terms of its generation of new dynamics among contemporary writers and its redirecting of their artistic mode of expression.

New Thematic Conventions

In terms of theme and subject matter, writers of Taiwan's Modernist fiction endeavored to explore new spheres of human experience beyond the confines of traditional literature. In doing so, they continued the efforts of their early-20th century May Fourth Movement predecessors and even surpassed them in depth. To comprehend and analyze the complexity of human experience in the modern world, they generally favored rationalism, scientism, and serious, if at times immature, philosophical contemplation. We have thus witnessed the establishment of a set of thematic conventions that supposedly incorporate advanced knowledge of human behavior made available by the modern sciences. For example, apparently influenced by popular versions of Freudian psychoanalysis, young writers at the early stage of the Modernist literary movement were particularly fascinated with non-traditional or even abnormal interpersonal relationships. These writers have included Wang Wen-hsing 王文興, Pai Hsien-yung 白先勇, Ou-yang Tzu 歐陽子, Chen Jo-hsi 陳若曦, Shui Ching 水晶, Chen Ying-chen 陳映眞, to name just a few. Their sincerity and bold, honest self-analysis broke new ground in Taiwan's cultural context, and have redefined the boundaries of normality in human behavior, thus presenting challenges to the conservative middle-class mentality that has been the backbone of the dominant culture in post-1949 Taiwan.

Some truly radical cultural examinations are found in the movement's later more mature stages. For example, with a common theme of father-son conflict, two of Taiwan's most significant modernist novels, Pai Hsien-yung's *Crystal Boys* 孽子 (1983) and Wang Wen-hsing's *Family Catastrophe* 家變 (1973), offered bitter protests against the traditional ethical norms that are crystallized in the Confucianist notions of loyalty 忠 and filial piety 孝, and thus called into question fundamental underpinnings of the superstructure of contemporary Taiwan society. Notably, in both works, the battle against the social retention of traditional values is waged with the aid of Western conceptual frames. *Family Catastrophe* features as its central theme the conflict of bourgeois individualism with the concept of filial piety in a financially strapped modern Chinese family. That the hero is portrayed as a fanatic rationalist shows the degree to which the author is skeptical of the real efficacy of such an ideological transfer. *Crystal Boys* projects a more idealistic vision influenced by the countercultural movement of the 1960s in the United States, with its anarchic assertion of the emancipatory power of the Dionysian impulse, its celebration of youth and beauty in their ephemeral physical forms, and its romantic affirmation of the redeeming virtue of love. The author has further enriched the symbolic level of this book by infusing this vision with mythical themes from the Chinese classic *Dream of the Red Chamber* 紅樓夢. The underground homosexual community of New Park 新公園 in *Crystal Boys,* like residents of the Garden of the Grand Vision 大觀園 in the famous traditional novel, is ruled by the supreme order of sentimentality 情 and the heart 心, which can be both salvational and damning. This microcosm, however, is extremely vulnerable, as it is forever overshadowed by the law of the father—the dominant order of the patriarchal, Confucianist society outside the garden. The prominence of the father-quest motif in both *Family Catastrophe* and *Crystal Boys*—heroes in both novels are constantly searching for paternal surrogates—betrays their authors' anxiety over the general corruption of the terms governing human relationships in contemporary Taiwan society, terms that in history were solidly built on the patriarchal order.

Formal Innovations

Particularly eye-catching in the initial stages of the Modernist literary movement was the temporary surge of an avant-garde trend. One prominent feature of the self-styled avant-garde writers of the 1960s was their infatuation with the intellectual current of existentialism. As Franz Kafka was introduced early in the movement, the use of obscure plots and bizarre language quickly became a fad, and the basic tenor of works by many young writers—Chi-teng Sheng 七等生, Tsung Su 叢甦, and Shih Shu-ching

施叔青 among them—seemed to be dominated by nihilism, agonism, and an anxiety over the absurdity of existence.

The upsurge of aesthetic iconoclasm in the 1960s represented a significant moment in post-war Taiwan's literary history. The vigorous dynamics of newly introduced artistic conceptions associated with modernism called into question conventional forms and criteria of literary excellence. The more enduring efforts generated by this initial enthusiasm eventually ushered in a new era of modern Chinese literary history.

Most other Modernist fiction writers in Taiwan stayed within the general confines of realism, but they were no less experimental. Their conscious explorations of language and voice brought forth fundamental changes in rhetorical conventions of modern Chinese narrative. Since, as some scholars have observed, the attempts of earlier modern Chinese writers to offer realistic portraits of life were frequently hampered by the dominance of the subjective voice in the work's rhetorical structure, the Modernists tried to redress this deficiency by introducing a new "objective form." They strove to present an "impartial" picture of reality so that readers may be given the privilege of forming their own opinions and moral judgments. To be sure, these ideas are more reminiscent of the realists' concept of literary representation than the modernist view of literature as self-referential discursive practice. Throughout the 1960s, in fact, the majority of critical writings introducing Western literary concepts focused on basic technical rules and critical criteria that have long been naturalized and taken for granted in the West. Authoritative US-trained scholars and critics such as Yen Yuan-shu, Chu Li-min 朱立民, and Wai-lim Yip 葉維廉 systematically expounded the fundamentals of a whole set of Western literary codes, and their influence on creative writing and practical criticism in Taiwan was immeasurable. Such a phenomenon is actually not very difficult to understand, given that literary genres of the short story and the novel (in the strict sense) have been imported from the West only in this century.

It is also true, however, that the appropriation of foreign literary codes necessarily involves larger, more complicated networks of artistic and ideological systems. Given that the most noteworthy formal feature popularized by the Modernists is widened distance between author and text, their efforts may be seen as having continued the general trend in modern Chinese literary history away from the traditional expressive view toward the mimetic view of literature. With their denunciation of sentimentalism and express interest in the hidden complexities of the human psyche, personal emotions are no longer treated as the source or origin of literature, but rather as objects for detached observation.

It is arguable that, despite the fact that Taiwan's Modernist literary movement has taken place in a "postmodern" period from the standpoint of the West—in the 1960s and 1970s—and despite the fact that many newer artistic trends and techniques have been incorporated by the Modernist writers into their work, the dominant tendency of this movement nevertheless is closest to the early phase of Western modernism in the late 19th century and early 20th century. In other words, in the extremely compressed timetable of Taiwan's Modernist literary movement, one nevertheless discerns features such as the reversal of the conventional content-form hierarchy and the radical rejection of traditional writing techniques that can only be the result of a burgeoning skepticism about language and meaning. Most of the Modernists' explorations of language unmistakably reflect Western influences. However, more original experiments have also been made, which result from a new awareness of the unstable relationship between language and its referents, as well as of a reawakened sensitivity toward the ideographic nature of the Chinese language. These experiments, especially those found in Wang Wen-hsing's two novels *Family Catastrophe* and *Backed Against the Sea* 背海的人 (1981), and Li Yung-ping's latest story series *Chronicle of Chi-ling* 吉陵春秋 (1986), mark the apex of the development of modernist aestheticism in contemporary Chinese literature.

Nativist Literary Debate

In the late 1960s and early 1970s, as the Modernist fiction writers began to mature artistically, the resistance to modernism's dominance of Taiwan's literary scene also began. The precursor to a large-scale denunciation of the Modernist literary movement was the 1972 Modern Poetry debate 現代詩論戰, which involved a number of academic critics and Modernist poets who discussed specific Western-influenced features in contemporary Taiwan poetry. The consensus reached in this debate seemed to be that, despite its other merits, the currently practiced Modern Poetry suffered from such unhealthy qualities as semantic obscurity, excessive use of foreign imagery and Europeanized syntax, and evasion of contemporary social reality. These features, furthermore, were considered symptomatic of the faulty style generally promoted in Taiwan's Modernist literary movement.

While it may not be unusual in literary history for critics and writers to periodically reexamine and revolt against the current dominant style, the Modern Poetry debate bore a special social implication in that it was closely tied to the Taiwan intellectuals' growing consciousness of their endangered Chinese cultural identity. In what was later known as the "return to native roots" 回歸鄉土 trend around the turn of the 1970s, progressive intellectuals criticized the blind admiration and slavish imitation of Western cultural models, and exhorted their compatriots to show more respect for their indigenous cultural heritage, as well as greater concern for domestic social issues. Many liberal scholars, especially returnees from the United States, played important roles in igniting this new current, which at first revolved around several universities and intellectual magazines.

Shortly after the Modern Poetry debate, a group of critics began to renounce publicly the foreign-influenced Modernist work and to advocate a nativist, socially responsible literature. This trend reached its apex with the outbreak of a virulent Nativist Literature Debate in 1977 and 1978 and suddenly declined when, in 1979, several key figures of the Nativist camp exited from the literary scene and became directly involved in political protests. The tradition of Nativist literature as a creative genre—the main features of which are use of the Taiwanese dialect, depiction of the plight of country folk or small-town dwellers caught up in economic difficulty, and resistance of the imperialist presence in Taiwan—can be traced back to the Nativist literary trend during the Japanese colonial period. While inheriting the dominant nationalist spirit from this earlier trend, the Nativist literature champions of the 1970s had their own political agenda as well.

Viewed retrospectively, the Nativist camp was the first oppositional formation at a critical juncture in Taiwan's post-1949 history. After two decades of political stability and steady economic growth, the country suffered a series of diplomatic setbacks at the turn of the decade—beginning with its expulsion from the United Nations in 1971, followed by Richard Nixon's visit to the Chinese mainland and the termination of the ROC's diplomatic relations with Japan in 1972—which caused not only international isolation, but also a confidence crisis among Taiwan intellectuals.

Unlike the majority of the country's liberal intellectuals who demanded democratization while supporting capitalist-style economic modernization, the Nativists believed that the socioeconomic system of Taiwan must be changed. They fiercely attacked the ROC government's economic dependence on Western countries (especially the United States), deplored the infiltration of "decadent" capitalist culture into the ordinary lives of Taiwan's people, expressed indignance on behalf of Taiwan's farmers and workers who paid a high economic price for the nation's urban expansion, and attempted to draw public attention to the adverse effects of the country's overall economic development.

The regionalist sentiment implied in the Nativist project immediately touched on an extremely sensitive issue, the "provincial heritage problem" 省籍問題. Tensions between native Taiwanese and mainlanders always existed, especially given the perceptions of an unbalanced distribution of political power at the time. As a consequence, even though some of the leading Nativist critics were socialists or nationalists rather than separatists promoting Taiwan independence (Chen Ying-chen, for example, has always been a staunch advocate of the future unification of China), the Nativist critical discourse as a whole could not but be part of the ongoing political strife.

It is therefore undeniable that literary nativism was used by a special group of people at a particular historical moment to challenge the existing sociopolitical order. However, it appears that ideological debates in modern Chinese society inevitably generate widespread polemics around literature, as evidenced by numerous such disputes in the May Fourth period, in the thirties, and during the entire communist reign on the mainland. The traditional Chinese pragmatic view of literature and the legacy of a gentry ideology, which assigns to intellectuals, especially writers, lofty social missions, have combined to make literary discourse a genuine political space. As a result, the attacks launched by the Nativists on the Modernist writers, whose literary ideology is a conspicuously apolitical one, have largely centered on the latter's default of their social responsibilities as members of the intelligentsia.

The home base for the anti-Modernist critics was the journal *Literary Quarterly* 文季, founded in 1966. With Yu Tien-tsung 尉天聰 as the central mover, the journal's founding members included several writers already known for their Modernist works, such as Chen Ying-chen, Liu Ta-jen 劉大任, Shih Shu-ching, and Chi-teng Sheng. The journal had, furthermore, discovered two important writers, Huang Chun-ming 黃春明 and Wang Chen-ho 王禎和, whose fiction significantly departed from the current Modernist fads and depicted rural life with unaffected realism. Although both writers refused to label their works as "Nativist," the literary reformers on the journal's editorial board were ready to use them as weapons in their fight against the Modernist hegemony.

In 1973, Tang Wen-piao 唐文標, a visiting math professor closely associated with the *Literary Quarterly*, criticized the Modernists' elitist tendency and neglect of the masses. The straightforward accusations so startled the liberal critics that Yen Yuan-shu referred to this critical attack as the "Tang Wen-piao Incident." However, even more vehement militancy was to be seen when the Nativist critics chose individual writers as targets. Almost simultaneously with the Tang Wen-piao Incident, the *Literary Quarterly* organized a series of seminars to examine the thematic implications of Ou-yang Tzu's fiction, and branded it "corrupt and immoral." By the mid-1970s, Taiwan's literary writers were already deeply split into opposing camps.

The literary climate in this decade became truly unpleasant with the increasing politicization of critical discourse. With the founding of a radical magazine *Summer Tide* 夏潮 in 1976 and its provocative use of such taboo terms as "proletarian literature" (literally, literature of workers, peasants, and soldiers) and "class consciousness," the deep-seated anticommunist sentiments of the liberals were incited. In the summer of 1977, the country's leading Modernist poet Yu Kuang-chung 余光中 wrote a short essay entitled "The Wolf Is Here" 狼來了 openly accusing the Nativists of being leftists. This fatal charge ignited highly emotional responses and retaliations from all sides, and polemical writings about literature and politics began to flood the country's newspapers and literary magazines. This so-called Nativist literary debate came to an end only in the middle of 1978 as a result of threatened government intervention.

Placed within a larger historical context, the Modernist-Nativist split is part of the continual struggle in modern Chinese history between liberal and radical intellectuals with different reform programs and different views of literature's social function. The new paradigm of ideological writing as established in the mid-1970s moved in a direction diametrically opposed to that of the introspective, humanist, and universalist approach of the Modernists and deliberately focused on the historical specificity of contemporary Taiwan society. In addition to later works by Huang Chun-ming on imperialism, such writers as Yang Ching-chu 楊青矗 and Wang To 王拓 explored capitalist exploitation as it affected urban factory workers and fishermen. These literary efforts were also backed by some serious theoretical thinking, although most of the Nativist literary debate itself was virtually divorced from contemporary literary practice.

Wang To's 1977 essay, "It should be 'literature of the here and now,' not 'nativist literature'" 是現實主義文學，不是鄉土文學 stood out among numerous polemical writings precisely because of its accurate representation of the reality of recent literary practice. The main argument Wang proposes in this essay is that, instead of writing about rural regions and country people, Nativist literature is concerned with the "here and now" of Taiwan society, which embraces a wide range of social environments and people. Nativist literature thus should be defined as a literature rooted in the land of Taiwan, one that reflects the social reality and the material and psychological aspirations of its people. By using the term *hsien shih* 現實 (contemporary reality, the "here and now") rather than *hsieh shih* 寫實 (realism), and by enlarging the scope of Nativist literature to include all levels of social reality in Taiwan, Wang stressed high-priority Nativist issues. The essay, therefore, represented an important step in the Nativists' process of self-definition.

The critical evaluation of Nativist works produced in the 1970s, however, is in general not very positive. Although the change in thematic conventions since the seventies met the approval of most critics, excessive ideological concern is considered to have detracted from their literary achievement. Even though Huang Chun-ming is often regarded as such an exception, many have felt that his art, too, deteriorates in direct proportion to the increase in social commentary in his later works. However, just as Modernist literature continued to evolve after the rise of Nativist literature, the practice of Nativist literature did not come to an end even though the Nativist literary debate folded toward the end of the 1970s. In the continuing efforts made by such Nativist ideological writers as Chen Ying-chen, Sung Tse-lai 宋澤萊, Li Chiao 李喬, and Wu Chin-fa 吳 錦發 in the 1980s, one can discern a sharp increase in formal consciousness as well as attempts to experiment with innovative techniques.

Eighties Pluralism

In a sense, the articulation of dissident views during the Nativist literary debate paved the way for more intense struggles toward democratization, which rapidly gained momentum in the early 1980s. Eventually, with the formation in 1987 of an opposition party, the Democratic Progressive Party, literature was largely relieved of its function as a pretext for political contestation. It became, however, even more inextricably involved in the country's booming mass media. Most notably, the two competing media giants, the *United Daily News* 聯合報 and *China Times* 中國時報 each claiming the loyalty of a group of writers, invested heavily in their literary pages for marketing purposes. The annual fiction contests they sponsored between the mid-1970s and mid-1980s gave creative writing a solid boost— an overwhelming majority of the writers of the baby-boom generation rose to literary prominence by winning one of these contests.

The Nativist theorists may have felt both frustrated and vindicated in the 1980s, as the "spiritual corruption" of capitalist society, which they had predicted, appeared along with the ascendancy of materialism and a sharp rise in the crime rate. The overall cultural environment also became heavily consumer-oriented. Not without a touch of irony, even the Nativist literature itself was largely co-opted by the cultural establishment, especially between the late 1970s and early 1980s. Newspaper supplements and literary magazines were inundated by pseudo-Nativist works, which displayed Taiwanese local color but contained little ideological content.

As public fervor for both the Modernist and the Nativist causes subsided, the literary scene of the 1980s was largely dominated by the baby-boom generation, whose vocational visions were drastically different from those of their predecessors. Rather than treating creative writing as an intellectual project or a political quest, they were more concerned with popularity and with various problems affecting Taiwan's middle-class urbanites, especially the new social affluence and the relaxation of moral standards. Some writers, such as Huang Fan 黃凡 and Li Ang, with a cynical intellectual pose, offered critiques of materialism and the cultural impoverishment it caused; while others, such as Hsiao Sa 蕭颯 and Liao Hui-ying 廖輝英, with down-to-earth pragmatism, examined the new social factors that had changed ordinary people's way of life, showing particular interest in liberated sexual views and the problem of extramarital relationships; and still others, such as Yuan Chiung-chiung 袁瓊瓊, Chu Tien-wen 朱 天文, and Su Wei-chen 蘇偉貞, falling back on the sentimental-lyrical tradition, focused their attention on subjective, private sentiment with a posture of complacency in regard to sociopolitical issues. Whether progressively or conservatively inclined, the new generation of writers seemed to share a common response to the emergence of new political situations. As knowledge about the Chinese on the other side of the Taiwan Strait suddenly became available, and with the public debate over the nature and pace of unification with the Chinese mainland intensifying on a daily basis, many of the writers of the baby-boom generation tended to deliberately stress their unique cultural identity, rooted in the specific sociohistorical realities of Taiwan's post-1949 era.

Writers' approaches to literature in this decade were certainly pluralist. While writers of the Modernist generation published their more mature works during this decade, literary products of the younger generation were marked by a rich diversity— *chuan tsun* 眷村 (residential military community) literature, works about life in business corporations, political fiction (with a special sub-genre on the February 28 Incident), neo-Nativist literature, resistance literature, feminist works, and science fiction—a phenomenon that may be aptly characterized as the orchestration of a multitude of discordant "voices."

The broadly defined "return to native roots" trend carried over into the early 1980s beyond the Modernist-Nativist contention. After the Nativist literary debate, new interest in an indigenous literary heritage fostered a trend of cultural nostalgia. Several former Modernist writers made notable contributions to this trend. Shih Shu-ching and Li Ang, for example, consciously turned to folk traditions and native subject matter in their writing. Lin Huai-min 林懷民, a former Modernist writer who had studied under Martha Graham while in the US, founded the first Chinese modern dance troupe, produced the well-received "Cloud Gate Dance Ensemble" 雲門舞集 and incorporated both classical Chinese and folk Taiwanese elements in his choreography (see section, Dance, in Chapter 21, The Arts). Their accomplishments set the tone for creative endeavors of the new decade, even while encouraging commercial exploitation of traditional and native cultural signs.

As the indigenous came to replace the foreign as the primary source of exotic imagination, and "Chinese/Taiwan cultural identity" came to occupy a prominent place in the public consciousness, "postmodernism" came into vogue after the mid-1980s and again raised issues about Western influences on contemporary Chinese literature. In a pattern closely resembling that by which such earlier Western literary trends as Romanticism, Realism, and Modernism were appropriated by Chinese writers, the postmodern mode of writing has become a new fad and its surface markers, such as double endings, juxtaposition of the factual and the fictional, and the technique of pastiche, among others, have appeared profusely in works by both greater and lesser writers. Such imitative literary products cannot but recall works written during the earliest phase of the Modernist literary movement and not surprisingly are considered to be of dubious value by some veteran Modernists.

Although the younger writers of the 1990s consciously subscribed to the more cynical, "postmodern" ideology—as evidenced by their emphasis on difference, tolerance of pluralistic coexistence of the incommensurable, and, above all, their appetite for the indeterminacy that is uncongenial to the Modernist temperament, there were also similarities between the two generations of writers: their intellectual disposition, their globalism, and the way they looked to the West—or Western-influenced literary traditions such as those of East Europe and Latin America—for literary models. As prescribed by "post-modern" ideology, however, the younger writers were more keenly aware of the self/other dichotomy and thus did not endorse universalism as the Modernists did.

Nineties Multiculturalism and Postidentity Politics

Taiwan has undergone an interpretive turn in terms of national identity and critical multiculturalism in the 1990s. Taiwanese literature of the '90s tends to use mixed genres and multilingual devices, drawing on a wide range of global/local cultural codes, idioms, and traditions, to express the fluid, albeit disoriented, structure of feelings.

Into the '90s, Chu Tien-wen and Chang Ta-chun 張大春 are still prominent figures in the field of political fiction or nostalgic narrative on the dissolution of a certain culture within government housing compounds. Chang is reputed for his technique of intermixing various genres—history, dream text, diary, with news report, for example—and voices. Chu's Notebooks from the Wasteland 荒人手記 won the 1994 China Times best fiction award. Although the second-generation mainlanders as subjects of the novel reappear as if in a repetition compulsion, Chu's sensitivity to the ethnic tensions, rupture of tradition, and societal psychopathologies is nicely matched by her literary style and narrative coherence. As a writer appropriating all news and media events, Chang has gradually moved from writing cynical diaries and "factual fiction" based on the tragic death of a navy officer to producing public TV programs and increasingly becoming a media person. In between Chu and Chang stands a young talent Yang Chao 楊照, who has successfully blended romance with saga, collapsing the distinction between public and private, the personal and the social. Yang is currently a Harvard Ph.D. candidate, cultural critic, political activist, and novelist. His multiple roles in contemporary Taiwanese public culture as well as his impressive talent in fusing personal and interpersonal histories are self-evident in one of his trilogies, *A Dark Alley on a Confusing Night* 暗巷迷夜.

In contrast to Li Ang, who has severely criticized the patriarchal system of domination, younger women writers emerging in the '90s, such as Lo Yi-chun 駱以軍 or Cheng Ying-shu 成英姝, are more playful in their treatment of sexual liaisons in bars (often gay or lesbian), of the object-choice "medial woman," of fantasies and frustrations of the so-called "New Human Species" 新新人類 in relation to the new unsettling social milieu that has yet failed to take shape. Writers like Cheng are on the way to expressing postidentity politics, celebrating postmodern flexibility and unpredictability in the global cyberspace of easy accessibility. Their counterpart in the field of poetry is late Lin Yao-te 林燿德,who employs the language of the fax machine and computer terminal to describe the fluid human relations in a transnational capitalist society. Lin was very active in the '80s in promoting postmodern poetry about urban culture and cityscapes, following poets like Lo Men 羅門, Lo Ching 羅青, and others. These poets are far from the humanist tradition set up by Lo Fu 洛夫, Wai-lim Yip, Ya Hsien 亞弦, and later on revised by Chien Cheng-chen 簡政珍, Hsu hui-chih 許悔之, and Chiao Tung 焦侗, with a phenomenological, psychoanalytical, or even poststructuralist twist.

To question Chinese nationalism, quite a few writers try to highlight several issues associated with the Taiwan independence movement, minority discourse, political feminism, and environmental protection. Reportage, science fiction, and biography are the most popular modes of literary expression or ethnographic exploration of everyday political subjects among these writers. Ku Ling 苦苓 is a most celebrated political satirist who never fails to make fun of statesmen, as Yu Fu 魚夫 does in his political cartoons. A prolific poet writing on related subjects is Li Min-yung 李敏勇. However, it is in the mini theater 小劇場 that serious political satires intermingle with comic relief. The stages for mini plays can take many forms; they can be in the theater, on the street, in city hall, or even in front of the Legislature. Some differing and milder versions of post-avant-garde theater, on the other hand, are offered by playwrights like Stan Lai 賴聲川, Li Kuo-hsiu 李國修, and Chung Ming-te 鍾明德, who draw inspiration from a range of Chinese-Western drama—both ancient and modern (see Spoken Drama and Traditional Music Theater sections, Chapter 21, The Arts).

An important trend in the '90s has been to revive the local vernacular tradition. As localization processes take root, Taiwanese (southern Fukienese) or Hakka is often looked upon as a preferred linguistic medium for literary expression. In this regard, Chang Chun-huang 張春凰 has been hailed, since the publication of her pioneering prose work *Paths to Youth* 青春之路途 in 1995, as the first prose writer in Taiwanese. From the perspective of a mother, the narrator attempts to introduce her son to the beauties of pronouncing everyday objects in Taiwanese. The work represents a crucial step toward rearticulating one's literary tradition and toward a more promising future in which linguistic nuances and cultural differences may be appreciated and cherished. After all, it is the diversity of languages and customs on the island that has enriched the literary expressions of the people of Taiwan.

Online Literature 網路文學

The proliferation and dissemination of information technology in Taiwan has led to the emergence of new literary vehicles unique to the computer era. The electronic bulletin boards (BBS), the World Wide Web (WWW) on the

Internet, and electronic mail (e-mail) have not only diversified the means of circulation of literary works but also created a new aesthetic dimension for literature arising from the manipulation of online techniques such as animation, multimedia, hyperlink, and interactive writing. Works probing into the virtual reality of cyberspace, categorized as hypertext literature, are distinguished by their creative form from those appearing in the traditional print-based media (and from those works going online without hypertextual elements). They illustrate an "organized stream of consciousness," as one of the supportive statements for hypertext literature goes. The Garden of Forking Paths 歧路花園 (benz.nchu.edu.tw/~garden/garden.htm) is one of the sites devoted to the creation and promotion of hypertext literature.

The recent developments of online literature in Taiwan include the establishment of online bookstores, professional literary sites and intermedia sites (e.g. the literary supplements of the newspapers such as the *China Times* and the *Central Daily News* are online). Another phenomenon is the appearance of literary sites, organizational and personal, on the WWW, changing the scene of online literature formerly dominated by the BBS.

One of the most significant characteristics of online literature is its immediacy, as well as its expansion across social, racial, sexual and any other hierarchical boundaries. For one thing, the writer can bypass publishers or editors to reach readers directly through the ideally indiscriminate world of cyberspace without joining in the marketing system of popular culture. According to some literary theorists, the free flow and easy access of online literary resources will vigorously challenge the "cultural hegemony" of traditional media.

While there are still considerable controversies and even anxieties over the would-be paradise of cyber literature (the overflow of online works, the infringement of copyright, and the intervention of commercialism have posed problems or complication), the function of digital

The "Way of Poetry" homepage, sponsored by the Council of Cultural Affairs, contains the works, translations, and multimedia materials of Taiwan's most important modern poets.

archives on the internet makes an indisputable contribution, as the availability of literary materials will surely aid in literary research and appreciation. One such effort is the Contemporary Authors Full-Text & Image System 當代文學史料影像全文系統 established by the National Central Library, which collects personal information, brief biographies, manuscripts, photos, chronicles of works, critical sources, translation sources, famous words, and records of literary awards of around 1,000 modern writers in Taiwan. Another example is the "Way of Poetry" 詩路 project by the Council for Cultural Affairs and the Online Alliance of Taiwan's Modern Poetry 臺灣現代詩網路聯盟 which works to gather the works, translations, and multimedia materials of Taiwan's important modern poets.

Earliest Chinese Literary Traditions

The beginnings of Chinese literature go back thousands of years. The earliest pieces in the Book of Songs 詩經 date to the 12th century B.C.. A number of scholars believe that writings in the *Book of History* 書經 (or 尚書) tradition should be classified as history rather than literature.

Furthermore, private accounts, as opposed to government archives, have since the time of Confucius been classified as expositions of thought. Official archives were relegated to the realm of history, and private writings to that of philosophy, leaving only works belonging to the *Book of Songs* 詩經 tradition to literature. Because the *Book of Songs* is an anthology of poetry, Chinese literature came to be regarded as a basically lyrical tradition.

The prevalence of this way of thinking has led some scholars to insist that China has no epic tradition, no fiction until the seventh century A.D., and no drama until the 13th century. This ignores the fact that public and private writings "recording words and events" have been produced in China without interruption since the *Book of History*, and that they have always enjoyed the status of fine literature. They often disregard the narrative tradition comprised by the numerous fables that appeared in histories after the *Book of History* and in philosophical works such as the *Chuang Tzu* 莊子, the *Mencius* 孟子, the *Han Fei Tzu* 韓非子, the *Spring and Autumn Annals of Mr. Lu* 呂氏春秋, and the *Lieh Tzu* 列子, all written after the fourth century B.C., along with the myths from earlier ages that were preserved in these and similar works.

The earliest fiction in China—be it in the form of a continuation of mythical narrative or an imitation of official history called *yeh-shih* 野史 ("unofficial history")—was created in the spirit of the fable. The narrative tradition—comprising history, myth, fable, and fiction—balanced and supplemented the lyrical tradition of poetry produced subsequent to the *Book of Songs*.

"Recording words," the other expressed feature of the *Book of History*, in turn influenced philosophical works and essay-type prose 散文. Philosophical works produced since the sixth century B.C., like the *Analects* of Confucius 論語, are basically collections of quotations or records of a master's sayings, inseparable in content and style from the personalities, speech habits, and biographical experiences of the masters themselves. This style of writing, which fuses reason and emotion, served as a model for the essay in later ages. The essay thus became the most important genre in Chinese literature, and *san-wen* (prose) even became a synonym for literature itself, while poetry was considered a specialized branch of literature.

In contrast to the personalism of the essay, Chinese poetry gradually departed from the spoken language and came to stress formalistic rules. Poetry thus became relatively objective and impersonal and, while still lyrical in nature, it was often more symbolic and constructive than prose.

The Literary-Vernacular Split

Related to the division of Chinese literature into the traditions of the *Book of Songs* and the *Book of History* is the fact that the spoken and written Chinese language are actually two independent representational systems. Chinese writing, having evolved from pictographs, is an ideographic script that expresses meaning directly through the forms of the characters themselves. The Chinese system stands in contrast to the phonetic alphabets and syllabaries of Japan, Korea, and the West, which express meaning through phonetic representation. As a result, Chinese writing constitutes a notational system that is partially independent of the phonemic nature of the Chinese spoken language; and the relative independence of this notational system has had a major effect on Chinese literature.

One example of this effect can be seen in the *Book of Songs* tradition, which during the several centuries of its evolution gradually broke away from music in pursuit of its own metrical form. The combination of an independent writing system with the Chinese spoken language—which in early times was mainly monosyllabic—produced neat lines of four, five, or seven characters, and sometimes three or six. Tonal theory evolved in the fifth and sixth centuries, based on a new apprehension that Middle Chinese syllables had tonal or pitch distinctions that affected meaning. Thus, "even" 平 and "deflected" 仄 tones were matched and contrasted, and words of parallel or antithetical meaning were aligned. Literary forms almost completely divorced from the spoken language developed, such as parallel prose 駢文 and regulated verse 律詩. This formalistic beauty, which derived from a neat matching of written characters, became an important aesthetic characteristic of traditional Chinese poetry.

Poetry often broke away from the speaking subject, and became a structural object in itself, objectivizing and collectivizing the lyrical self. This paved the way for the subsequent fusion of emotion 情 and scene 景 that resulted in a progression from an aesthetic "expression of self" 言志 to a "spiritual resonance" 神韻 over the first to eighth centuries.

Following territorial expansion and the establishment of a unified empire encompassing a large number of local dialects, the maintenance of the *Book of History* tradition depended increasingly on scholars and officials learning a form of written communication called *ku-wen* 古文 (classical prose). In early antiquity, the classical prose style may have reflected the contemporary spoken language, but it eventually evolved into a purely literary style that allowed the literary language to experience no major syntactic changes for 2,000 years.

Around the fifth century A.D., the spoken language began to gradually evolve from being mainly monosyllabic in nature toward bisyllabicity or polysyllabicity, as the Old Chinese consonant clusters were gradually lost and originally distinct vowels merged. The unchanging stability of the literary language, *or wen-yen* 文言, thus led to a gradual split with the vernacular language, or *pai-hua* 白話.

The simultaneous development toward balance and parallelism in belletristic writing further widened the gulf between the written language of the literati and the oral literature of the common people. Oral literature is by its very nature not easily preserved. But the tradition in China of writing down ballads and salon ditties to popular tunes of the time, combined with the growth of cities after the tenth century and a flourishing entertainment industry, led to the spread—through writing and printing—of the *tzu* 詞 (lyric),

music drama, and fiction. These were all popular oral literary genres that originated with storytellers and performing artists.

The vernacular literature of the common people, consisting for the most part of fiction and drama, developed parallel to the literature of the scholars, which was composed mainly of poetry and essays written in classical Chinese. Literature written in the classical language received official sanction by becoming the testing material for the examination system, while vernacular literature owed its increasing popularity mainly to growth in the popular entertainment industry.

An Outline of Traditional Chinese Literature

Traditional Chinese literature can be divided into four periods: early antiquity, from the 12th century B.C. to 206 B.C.; middle antiquity, from 206 B.C. to 618 A.D.; late antiquity, from 618 to 1279; and the pre-modern era, from 1279 to 1911.

Early Antiquity

The literature of early antiquity includes the classics preserved from the Chou 周 dynasty and organized by Confucian scholars; the works of philosophers from the Spring and Autumn 春秋 period and the Warring States 戰國 period; the *Songs of the South* 楚辭; and the early myths, which were compiled from various sources. Together these works laid the spiritual foundation of Chinese literature and culture. The *Book of Songs* from northern China and the *Songs of the South* represent the fundamental dichotomy of Chinese poetry: realism and lyricism versus romanticism and imagination.

The early myths are scattered among a number of works, chiefly the *Chuang Tzu*, the *Mountain and Sea Classic* 山海經 and the poem "Heavenly Questions" 天問 in the *Songs of the South*. The concept behind creation myths such as those of Pan Ku 盤古 and the goddess Nu Wa 女媧 that "the myriad things arise from the same source" had a profound influence on the intimate identification of the Chinese people with nature and on their pursuit of harmony, both of mankind and the universe as a whole. More importantly, this concept established in Chinese poetry the method of indirect metaphor 起興 and the fusion of emotion and scene.

The myths of Kun 鯀 and Yu 禹 controlling floodwaters and Hou I 后羿 shooting the nine suns illustrate the awakening of human consciousness and mankind's awareness of the need to control nature for his own purposes. Invention myths, such as Fu Hsi 伏羲 drawing the eight trigrams, reflect an awareness of the origins of civilization. Although the narratives are incomplete, the early myths had a fundamental influence on the way the Chinese people view the universe, mankind, nature, and civilization.

A total of 305 poems are preserved in the Book of Songs. They describe all aspects of social life, and include hymns from ancestral temples, sagas of nation-building, political satires and encomia, and simple love songs. The book is divided into three groups of sung 頌 (hymns), two of ya 雅 (odes), and 15 of kuo-feng 國風 (songs). The hymns were apparently composed to accompany ceremonial dances at ancestral temples in praise of Heaven and the virtuous achievements of former rulers, and in hope of continued blessings. The ta-ya 大雅 (greater odes) are generally classified as odes of the royal court, many of which laud the founding of the Chou dynasty. The hsiao-ya 小雅 (lesser odes) are thought to have been performed at feasts and banquets, and many contain political messages criticizing society and the life of the nobility. The songs are folk songs from various nation-states around the empire, expressing love between man and woman and the life experiences of the common people. The Book of Songs can thus be viewed as a composite portrait of the life of the people.

The richly imaginative Songs of the South contains poems from the southern kingdom of Chu 楚. The anthology includes religious pieces which reflect a worship of nature far different from the worship of ancestors and the theoretical God posited in the Book of Songs. Poems in the Songs of the South were written by Chu Yuan 屈原 and other writers influenced by him.

Chu Yuan was China's first major poet. He secularized the originally religious songs of Chu, producing a complete vision of human life that encompasses myth, history, nature, society, and politics. In his masterpieces, "Encountering Sorrow" 離騷 and "Nine Chapters" 九章, he repeatedly examines the ideals of human existence and the crises and degeneration to which they are subject.

From the Book of History tradition of recording the words of the early kings developed both the narratives of the historians and the speculative works of the philosophers. The most important works of history are the Spring and Autumn Annals of Mr. Lu, the Tso Commentary 左傳, and the Conversations from the States 國語. Corresponding to the recording of words in the Book of History is the recording of deeds in the Spring and Autumn Annals. This work records in concise language—often only a single sentence—major historical events in chronological order. It uses the method of "according praise or censure in a single word" to make penetrating ethical judgments about the events it relates. The Kung-yang Commentary 公羊傳, the Ku-liang Commentary 穀梁傳, and the Tso Commentary explicate the ethical appraisals of the Spring and Autumn Annals with commentary. The first two stress moral and ethical judgments, while the Tso Commentary supplements the Spring and Autumn Annals with detailed narratives. It is with the Tso Commentary and the Conversations from the States that narrative literature in China became fully mature, fusing the twin traditions of recording words and recording deeds. These works used the techniques of recording deeds and rendering ethical appraisals from the Spring and Autumn Annals as models for their treatment of narrative and subject matter. They also applied the technique of recording words from the Book of History in creating dialogs that illumined the psychology and motivations of characters to thereby depict and morally judge historical events.

Thinkers of the ancient era prior to the third century B.C. not only made major contributions to the development of Chinese thought, but also had a lasting effect on Chinese aesthetics and literature. The effect of the Confucian thinkers is reflected in an emphasis on ethical, social, and political concerns. Taoist influence can be seen in a striving for transcendental, universal meaning, and in an awareness of an eternal, metaphysical significance of life beyond history and society, achieved through an appreciation and description of one's natural surroundings.

The works of these ancient philosophers, through their method of illustrating morals through fables, established narrative models for characterization and plot development, which was a break with the recording of words and deeds of outstanding historical figures in historical narrative. The various styles that evolved along these lines subsequently influenced the development of Chinese prose. The *Analects* of Confucius and the *Classic of The Way and Its Power* 道德經 of Lao Tzu made terseness and profundity the foremost criteria of prose style. The *Mo Tzu* 墨子 advanced the methods of logical exposition, while the *Chuang Tzu* established the model of an exuberantly imaginative composite form that defied classification. The *Mencius* made full use of the expressive powers of the spoken language in forging an eloquent verbal style. Hsun Tzu 荀子, in addition to being the first writer of Chinese *fu* 賦 (prose-poems), made full use of the isolating character of the Chinese writing system to develop a regulated aesthetic of parallelism and antithesis. All these works became sources and models for later literature, both spoken and written.

Middle Antiquity

The major political development of middle antiquity was the conclusion of the feudal system of the Chou dynasty and the establishment of a stable, unified empire under the Han. In the area of philosophical thought, the effect of this development was the triumph of Confucianism; in literature, it was the independence of literature from philosophy, and a striving for formal aesthetics and emotional experience. Its first literary product was the prose-poem, and the *Songs of the South.*

The prose-poem is a literary form that is recited rather than sung. Tied less to musical form than poetry, the prose-poem combined visual and aural elements in its attention to formal rules and euphony. Because it developed in response to the preferences and patronage of the emperor, its earliest subjects were invariably praise and glorification of the splendor of the imperial palace, the capital, parks, and hunting grounds. Out of this arose a tradition of exhaustive description, often accompanied by the coining of new Chinese characters, which catered specifically to the ruler's consciousness of possessing the empire, the world, the universe, and everything in it. Works of this type which were presented to the emperor are called *ta-fu* 大賦 (greater prose-poems).

As writers came to realize that a consciousness of totality must be connected with a sense of individuality to have value and meaning, they began to experience anxiety over individual existence. Thus, "the scholar born out of his time" became a basic theme of the *hsiao-fu* 小賦 (lesser prose-poem). Chia I 賈誼 and Szu-ma Hsiang-ju 司馬相如 in the second century B.C., and Chang Heng 張衡 and Wang Tsan 王粲 in the second century A.D., were the most important writers of prose-poems, a genre which would continue to develop right up until the end of the 19th century.

Shih 詩, or poetry of lines of equal length, was still identified with song when the *Yueh-fu* 樂府 (Music Bureau) was established during the reign of Emperor Wu Ti 武帝 (140-86 B.C.) in the Han 漢 dynasty. The amalgams of song and poetry produced then were generally referred to as *Yueh-fu shih* (Music Bureau ballads). Often originating among the common people, these pieces were rich in narrative content and filled with laments over social issues, especially the gap between rich and poor, the posting of soldiers to distant regions, the plight of widows and orphans, and the vicissitudes of life and time. Poems that reflected social realities and contained a sharp consciousness of moral crisis continued to be created under the name of *yueh-fu* in later times. Although they were no longer set to music, they preserved the external form of early *yueh-fu*, with its lines of unequal length.

Another literary development during the nearly 400 years of the Han dynasty era was the appearance of poems written in neat five- or seven-character lines that were unbound to music. The inspiration for replacing the harmonic effects of music with a strictly regulated form may have come from the prose-poem. Poetry consisting of lines of five or seven characters later became the universally acknowledged fundamental poetic form. The rules for matching and balancing characters in parallel constructions became increasingly refined, and ultimately resulted in the regulated verse of the seventh century onward. Middle antiquity can be considered the period of formalization of Chinese literary aesthetics. From the third century onward, the method of writing prose-poems was extended to the writing of essays, culminating in the blossoming of parallel prose in the sixth century.

The five-character line 五言詩 form of poetry emerged after the period of the lesser prose-poem. Anxiety over life and death became a basic theme for this new poetic form as well. Representative examples are found in the *Nineteen Ancient Poems* 古詩十九首 collection of the first century, the most important work in this genre of the time. Finding consolation in Taoist thinking to dispel the cares of existence, poets gradually turned to the subject of fields, gardens, hills, and streams, discovering and reveling in the natural beauty of landscapes. The most important poets of this period were Tsao Chih 曹植, Juan Chi 阮籍, Tao Chien 陶潛, and Hsieh Ling-yun 謝靈運.

Middle antiquity was also a fruitful period for the narrative tradition. First and foremost of works in this genre was Szu-ma Chien's 司馬遷 *Records of the Grand Historian* 史記. The *Records*, written during the first century B.C., was the first comprehensive work to recount China's ancient and recent history. It also established a model for historical writing centered around biography. Szu-ma Chien shifted the focus from unity of plot evident in the *Tso Commentary*

and the *Conversations from the States* to a unity of character. Official Chinese historians after him all adopted the biography as the chief form of their works. Subjects chosen for his biographies included not only great figures of history but also individuals he considered noteworthy because of their special talents or personalities, such as jesters and assassins. His writing helped pave the way for the *chuan-chi* 傳奇 (classical tales) of the eighth and ninth centuries.

Pan Ku's 班固 *History of the Former Han Dynasty* 漢書 was the first history devoted to a single dynasty. Pan Ku's work, together with Fan Yeh's 范曄 *History of the Later Han Dynasty* 後漢書, Chen Shou's 陳壽 *Records of the Three Kingdoms* 三國志, and the *Records of the Grand Historian*, are traditionally considered the pillars of Chinese historical writing.

Although its narrative roots can be traced back to the *Chuang Tzu*, *Hsun Tzu*, and *Tso Commentary*, Chinese fiction is often said to have begun its development under the influence of the romantic and supernatural adventures related in the biographies of diviners and imperial concubines in the *Records of the Grand Historian*. This genre consisting of depictions of courtly affairs and supernatural occurrences was referred to as *chih-kuai* 志怪 ("recording the strange") fiction. Among the earlier examples of this sort of fiction were the *Private Life of Lady Swallow* 飛燕外傳 and the *Intimate Biography of Han Emperor Wu* 漢武內傳 of the fourth century.

Late Antiquity

A milestone in the development of Chinese society was the establishment of the bureaucratic examination system in the seventh century. This system produced a new class of officials who played a leading role in society both politically and culturally. The literature of late antiquity was the activity and expression of this new class. Unlike the old aristocracy, the members of the new class owed their entrance to officialdom to success in the examinations. They had to form factions to avoid isolation, and when policies changed or power alliances shifted, they had to worry about demotion or exile. The effect of this situation was twofold. On the one hand, the new officials felt a strong sense of self-awareness as individuals, and did not identify solely with the family; on the other, they traveled widely throughout the country, whether in exile or in official service. As a result, the literature of late antiquity is characterized by a high degree of mobility, autobiography, and sense of regionalism.

During the seventh through ninth centuries, examination candidates were tested in poetry, which led to the widespread development of that genre, whereas during the tenth through 12th centuries, they were tested in essays on public policy, which led to a flourishing of the literary language. The seventh century saw the refinement of regulated verse, in response to the needs of the examination system. Its most popular themes were closely tied to the efforts of the new class to advance as officials, and its basic spirit was emotional experience 感遇. The course of an official career might include a posting to the frontier headquarters of a commander, or temporary retirement to the countryside to cultivate one's reputation in hopes of being recruited for a higher office, or a trip to the capital to court powerful patrons and establish one's name as a scholar. Such experiences were brought out in particular in poems with border, forest, and banquet themes. Seventh through ninth century poetry generally strived for a consciousness of human existence through descriptions of natural beauty:

Stars loom over the broad plain's sweep;
The moon swells in the Great River's flow.
Fame—how will my writings ever win me that?
Career—old age and sickness prompt me to retire.

> 星垂平野闊
> 月湧大江流
> 名豈文章著
> 官應老病休

(from "Lu-yeh shu-huai" 旅夜書懷 ["Traveling at Night, Writing My Feelings"] by Tu Fu 杜甫)

Wang Wei 王維, Li Pai 李白, Tu Fu, Pai Chu-i 白居易, Han Yu 韓愈, and Li Shang-yin 李商隱 are the most important poets of the Tang 唐 dynasty (which spanned the seventh through ninth centuries) and are major figures in the history of Chinese poetry.

The Sung 宋 dynasty poets of the 11th and 12th centuries introduced philosophy into poetry, and discourse and reasoning became important characteristics of their works. To the technique of conveying emotion through scenic description, they added the poetic metaphor:

Human life, everywhere,
what is it like?
It might be compared to a flying goose
stepping in the snow;
It leaves behind a random patch
of claw prints in the slush;
And after it's flown away, who can tell
whether east or west?

> 人生到處知何似
> 應似飛鴻踏雪泥
> 泥上偶然留指爪
> 鴻飛那復計東西

(from "Ho Tzu-yu Min-chih Huai-chiu" 和子由澠池懷舊 ["Matching Tzu-yu's Poem Recalling the Past at Minchih"] by Su Shih 蘇軾)

They also added comic touches:

> *The road was long, we were beaten,*
> *and the lame mule wheezed.*

> 路長人困蹇驢嘶

(from the same Su Shih poem)

Tang and Sung poetry became the twin paradigms of Chinese poetry in later ages. Ou-yang Hsiu 歐陽修, Wang An-shih 王安石, Su Shih (Su Tung-po 蘇東坡), Huang Ting-chien 黃庭堅, and Lu Yu 陸游 are the major representatives of Sung poetry.

The medieval era of the seventh through ninth centuries was a time of cultural fusion. Not only was there a melding of the contrasting cultures of earlier dynasties from the fourth through sixth centuries when China was politically divided, but the administration of the western regions and reopening of the Silk Road led to the absorption and popularity of music and dance from Central Asia.

447

The lyric 詞, a poem originally set to music and with lines of unequal length, became the dominant poetic genre. Poems (i.e. *shih*) of the literati had by this time moved toward strict regulation (both in formal "neatness" and in tonal contraposition) due to the examination system, and had become increasingly alienated from the spoken language. The art of the lyric, on the other hand, was cultivated at banquets and entertainment activities among merchants and the common people.

The lyric genre began to attract the attention of the literati during the ninth and tenth centuries, and by the 11th century, had become the second most important poetic genre among literati. Due to the differing lengths of its lines and its origins among the common people, it preserved to a considerable degree characteristics of the spoken language. Because it was popular at performances and banquets attended by both men and women, its basic themes were love and feminine emotions. And even though poets later turned to this genre to express their thoughts about life, human experience, the nation, and history, it never fully broke away from its mild and gracious original character, and its minute observations of women's quarters, courtyards, and seasonal changes. The following example is typical of this style:

Free and easy flying blossoms
light as a dream;
Limitless the threadlike rain,
slender as sorrow.
The jeweled curtain loosely hangs
from tiny silver hooks.

自在飛花輕似夢
無邊絲雨細如愁
寶簾閒掛小銀鉤

("Huan-hsi sha" 浣溪沙 [To the tune of "Sand of the Washing Stream"] by Chin Kuan 秦觀)

For poets of the Sung dynasty, the poem came to express the rational and public aspect of the writer's spirit, and the lyric, his emotional and private side. The most important lyricists were Wen Ting-yun 溫庭筠, Wei Chuang 韋莊, Feng Yen-szu 馮延巳, Li Yu 李煜, Liu Yung 柳永, Su Shih, Chou Pang-yen 周邦彥, Hsin Chi-chi 辛棄疾 and Chiang Kuei 姜夔.

Another major literary development of late antiquity was the revival of the classical literary language, or *ku-wen*. *Pien-wen* 駢文, or parallel prose, had been criticized as being beautiful in form but shallow in substance ever since the late sixth century. The reform of prose writing, however, had to await the mid-eighth century, when Han Yu and Liu Tsung-yuan 柳宗元 began to promote the classical literary language. Their models were the *Mencius* and the *Records of the Grand Historian*. They ultimately succeeded in developing a new, more comprehensive style of writing that reflected the life of people outside the class of officials and returned to the tenets of Confucian thought as a main theme.

This type of writing emphasized narration and argument, which became autobiographical and lyrical vehicles of expression by lending prominence to the writer as a subjective entity. The classical literary language achieved unprecedented success during the 11th century and became the main form of prose writing in China thereafter. Major writers in this genre during the Sung dynasty were Ou-yang Hsiu, Wang An-shih, Su Hsun 蘇洵, Su Shih, Su Che 蘇轍, and Tseng Kung 曾鞏.

The career ups and downs experienced by the new class of officials inspired a narrative form that conveyed change. The form gradually encompassed social realities and human life, but was at the same time influenced by the *chih-kuai* (reportage) genre of fiction of the fourth century onward, and the *Records of the Grand Historian* tradition that emphasized outstanding individuals. By the eighth century, this type of fiction was called the *chuan-chi* (classical tale). These stories often added elements of the mysterious and fantastic to everyday occurrences.

Such tales might feature an overnight lodging turning into a dragon's palace; a fiancee revealing herself to be a fox spirit, an ant princess, or a dragon king's daughter; or some other extraordinary individual who changes the fate of the protagonist. The classical tale was typically based in reality but interwoven with fantasy and descriptions of a mysterious, imaginary world. Representative classical tales include the *Chen-chung Chi* 枕中記 by Shen Chi-chi 沈既濟, the *Nan-ko Tai-shou Chuan* 南柯太守傳 by Li Kung-tso 李公佐, and *Ying-ying Chuan* 鶯鶯傳 by Yuan Chen 元稹, and *Chang-hen-ko Chuan* 長恨歌傳 by Chen Hung 陳鴻.

The Pre-Modern Era

The Mongolian invasion represented the end not only of the Sung dynasty, but also of the cultural patterns of late antiquity, which centered on a class of officials selected through the examination system. The imperial examinations were halted for some 80 years during the Great Mongol Empire, known in China as the Yuan 元 dynasty, and the social status of the Confucianists plummeted. Commerce and world-class cities, on the other hand, thrived in this age. This led to the growth of the entertainment industry and an unprecedented flourishing of vernacular literature aimed at the petty bourgeoisie. A vernacular narrative genre called *pien-wen* 變文 ("changed writing"), which was partly recited and partly sung, arose from the reciting of Buddhist sermons in temples from the seventh century onward. At the start of the 12th century, a form of *chantefable* involving a medley of tunes called the *chu-kung-tiao* 諸宮調 ("all keys and modes") was created. It was designed to be sung and narrated, and so was structurally organized around suites of poetic songs sung to popular tunes of the age. A work of oral storytelling, it was part of a professional storytelling tradition that seems to have developed by the ninth century, and was already highly popular in Pienliang and other cities during the 11th and 12th centuries. The most complete surviving example of this genre is available in English translation under the title *Master Tung's Romance of the Western Chamber* 西廂記諸宮調.

The musical influence on plot structure inherited from the *chantefable*, combined with the verbal repartee of the *yuan-pen* 院本 genre of dramatic skits of the 11th century, formed the basis for the earliest known form of completely developed music drama in China, the *Yuan tsa-chu* 元雜劇, or Yuan Music Drama of the 13th century. Less than 170 complete examples of this genre have survived, with plots ranging from melodrama and crime to comedy and spiritual redemption. Among these theatrical works are intensely melodramatic works, such as Kuan Han-ching's 關漢卿 *Injustice to Tou O* 竇娥冤, Pai Pu's 白樸 *Rain on the Wu Tung Tree* 梧桐雨, Ma Chih-yuan's 馬志遠 *Autumn in the Han Palace* 漢宮秋, and Chi Chun-hsiang's 紀君祥 *Orphan of Chao* 趙氏孤兒. Most of the musical comedies were social satires, such as fantasies about scholars climbing the bureaucratic ladder, often through love and at the expense of merchants. One of the most influential romantic music comedies from the 14th centuries was the *Romance of the Western Chamber* 西廂記, traditionally attributed to Wang Shih-fu 王實甫, which had an enormous impact on the plot structure of later music drama and fiction with its popularization of the *chia-jen tsai-tzu* 佳人才子 ("Beauty-Scholar") motif.

The literary heart and soul of all three of these theatrical forms, the *chantefable*, *yuan-pen*, and Yuan Music Drama, was a new kind of poetry called the *chu* (ditty) based on a new song form that appeared in the north of China during the 12th and 13th centuries. The lyrics of the ditty also became an independent poetic form in their own right, originally sung to the tune of the ditty in a manner like the *lieder* settings of 18th and 19th century German poetry by Franz Schubert and other contemporary Viennese composers. The major difference was that these composers created music to match an already existing poetic text, while the 12th and 13th century Chinese ditty poets created text to match an already existing ditty melody. By the 14th century, the original northern ditty melodies were gradually lost, yet ditty lyrics were still successfully set to what succeeding generations preserved as their original tune matrix, and new music from southern China was ultimately created to again allow musical performance.

A special characteristic of the ditty was that filler words could be freely added outside the fixed metrical pattern for euphonic effect. The metrical pattern itself was flexible within certain musically proscribed limits. This freedom gave the ditty a strikingly colloquial nature. Furthermore, several or even a score of ditties in the same mode could be combined into a ditty sequence 套數. This enabled it to be freely extended to a length that surpassed the scope of ordinary poetry, and endowed it with a special vividness:

I'm a ring-a-dang-ding brass pea
that won't steam tender
won't cook soft
won't pound flat
and won't fry pop!

You brothers in vice,
who told you to go poking him
can't-be-hacked-through
can't-be-chopped-down
can't-be-worried-loose
can't-be-thrown-off
oh-so-slow thousand-loop brocade slipknot?

我是個蒸不爛煮不熟

搥不扁炒不爆

響璫璫一粒銅豌豆

恁（您）子弟每（們）

誰教你鑽入他

鋤不斷砍不下

解不開頓不脫

慢騰騰千層錦套頭

("Pu-fu-lao" 不伏老 ["Not Bowing to Old Age"] by Kuan Han-ching)

Verbal effects like these were possible only in ditties. As the above two verses show, ditty writers in either music dramas or independent verses often flirted with the comic and risqué, although nostalgic and angry ditties were also written. In addition to the Yuan playwrights who frequently wrote ditties outside the context of music dramas, major ditty poets included Chang Yang-hao 張養浩 and Chiao Chi 喬吉.

Earlier kinds of poetry, the *shih* and lyric, were part of the fabric of vernacular fiction in its earliest manifestation, prompt books 底本 or *hua-pen* 話本.

These seem to have arisen, either directly or indirectly, through imitation from the oral storytelling tradition whose roots extended back to the 11th or 12th centuries during the Sung dynasty. All three kinds of poetry played an integral role in short, medium, and full-length vernacular fiction until the 19th century. The vernacular fiction genre flourished in the 14th through 16th centuries of the Ming 明 dynasty, thanks to the expansion of commercial printing.

The most outstanding extant examples of short story collections from this period are Feng Meng-lung's 馮夢龍 *Three Collections of Words [to Awaken the World]* 三言 and Ling Meng-chu's 凌濛初 *Two Collections of Striking the Table [in Amazement]* 二拍. There are four great works of extended fiction, major editions of which date from the 15th and 16th centuries of the Ming: *The Romance of the Three Kingdoms* 三國演義; *Water Margin*, also translated as *All Men are Brothers* 水滸傳; *Journey to the West* 西遊記, also translated as *Monkey*; and *Golden Lotus* 金瓶梅.

Unlike earlier ninth through 12th century classical literary tales written in the literary language about scholars, courtesans, semi-mythical characters, fox-spirits, and ghosts, the vernacular short story generally featured characters in an urban, middle-class setting. Money, marriage, social and business ethics, and the vagaries of fortune often constituted the principal plot concern. Of the four great works of extended fiction, *The Romance of the Three Kingdoms, Water Margin,* and *Journey to the West* were all products of a long and gradual process of revision and embellishment by storytellers and editors over the centuries leading up to the Ming dynasty, so they can be considered collective national creations, even if their later Ming versions primarily reflect a single literary mind. This process of collective revision could even be said of *Golden Lotus*, which circulated in manuscript form among various Ming literati prior to appearing in several different editions. In their Ming manifestations, all four great works of extended fiction reflect a growing sense of literary irony in their retelling of the traditional story plot. This may be an expression of growing literati

dissatisfaction with the moral and political climate of the Ming court and society.

The Ming also witnessed the flourishing of a new kind of literati music drama called *chuan-chi* 傳奇 (Grand Music Drama), the same Chinese name as the literary tales of the eighth century onward, but otherwise a completely separate literary genre. Unlike Yuan Music Drama, which continued to be written during the Ming, albeit in increasingly modified form, Grand Music Drama evolved from an early popular form of music drama in southern China known as *nan-hsi* 南戲 (Southern Music Drama) into a highly sophisticated theatrical genre that came to rival the prevailing Yuan Music Drama in literary quality. Grand Music Drama plots were more complex and expansive than the neat, highly structured Yuan Music Drama which organized acts around suites of ditties in the same key or mode. Instead of being dominated by musical considerations, the structure of Grand Music Drama plots often became bipolar, with two major strands of plot development interwoven through the length of the play. The dominant plot strand was almost always a variation on the "Beauty-Scholar" theme so prevalent in both drama and fiction throughout

the Ming. Various actors on the stage could sing roles at the same time, unlike the northern Yuan Music Drama which restricted the singing role to a single star throughout the drama.

The most influential early example of Grand Music Drama was *The Lute* 琵琶記 by Kao Ming 高明, which has even appeared in a highly modified version on the Broadway stage as *The Lute Song*. By its more extensive use of imagery and poetic diction than ever before, the 14th century Ming original set a new standard for the Southern Music Drama tradition, lifting it beyond the ken of casual theatergoers. As a result, Grand Music Drama after *The Lute* gradually evolved into a new, highly complex musical tradition which took its name and some of its characteristics from the music of Kun-shan 崑山. *Kun-chu* 崑曲 (Kun Music Drama), as Grand Music Drama had then come to be called, reached its peak of popularity during the 16th century when Tang Hsien-tsu 湯顯祖 wrote his cycle of four dream plays, including *The Peony Pavilion* 牡丹亭. Although a famous scene from *The Peony Pavilion* is often performed today as one of the few remaining examples of Kun Music Drama, Tang Hsien-tzu was in fact less concerned for musical effect than for achieving highly theatrical effects through the lyrical intensity and figural density in his poetic imagery.

The fall of the Ming dynasty and the ultimate consolidation of political power under the Manchus in the 17th century are reflected in the plot of the most famous 17th century Kun Music Drama, *Peach Blossom Fan* 桃花扇 by Kung Shang-jen 孔尚任. The *Peach Blossom Fan* also bears witness to the increasing distance between the musical and literary dimensions of Kun Music Drama which culminated in the virtual demise of the form by the 18th century. But a century earlier, the genre reached the climax of its literary development in Hung Sheng's 洪昇 *Palace of Eternal Sorrow* 長生殿. Appropriately, it took as its plot kernel a well-known narrative poem by the ninth century poet Pai Chu-i titled "Song of Eternal Sorrow," 長恨歌 depicting the story of the eighth century Emperor Hsuan-tsung 唐玄宗 and the loss of his favorite imperial consort, Yang Kuei-fei 楊貴妃. While echoing the era of medieval Chinese poetry when vernacular fiction and drama may have first taken form, the *Palace of Eternal Sorrow* also invoked the "Beauty-Scholar" theme, which usually resulted in the union of male and female principal leads by the final scene, in a more poignant, ironic way. Thus, 17th and 18th century Kun Music Drama achieved a literary richness beyond that of its predecessors, but in its greatest works, also conveyed a sense of despair and irrevocable loss indicative of the age.

This same mixture of literary qualities can be found in increasing intensity among the majority of 17th through 19th century works of extended fiction, such as Wu Ching-tzu's 吳敬梓 *The Scholars* 儒林外史, Li Ju-chen's 李汝珍 *Flowers in the Mirror* 鏡花緣, and Tsao Hsueh-chin's 曹雪芹 *Dream of the Red Chamber* 紅樓夢 or as it is alternatively known, *The Story of the Stone* 石頭記. The extended fiction of the 19th and early 20th centuries generally displayed a growing sense of despair at the moral lethargy of contemporary society. Among them were Wu Yen-jen's 吳趼人 *Strange Events Witnessed in the Past Twenty Years* 二十年目睹之怪現狀, Li Po-yuan's

李伯元 *Bureaucracy Exposed* 官場現形記, and Liu O's 劉鶚 *The Travels of Lao Tsan* 老殘遊記.

Although fiction became increasingly popular from the 13th century onward, this was mainly as leisure reading among the literati and merchant class. After the Mongols were driven out in the 14th century and Han Chinese rule reestablished, efforts were made to return to the views and values of two earlier great periods of Han Chinese rule, the Han and Tang dynasties. The formalistic eight-legged essay 八股文 (so named because it was divided into eight parts) also got its start at this time. The eight-legged essay was the form adopted for the explication of the Confucian classics, which formed the basis for a reinstatement of the examination system. Thus, the eight-legged essay and imitations of the classical literary language of the earlier eras of Chinese cultural greatness became the major written genres of the time. There were no further breakthroughs in literary writing, except for a style of artistically heightened descriptions of everyday life experiences, called *hsiao-pin* 小品 ("little sketches"), which emerged in the 15th and 16th centuries.

Fiction in the form of jottings 筆記, written in the literary language, also regained popularity at this time. The most important fiction collections in this genre were Pu Sung-ling's 蒲松齡 *Strange Stories from a Chinese Studio* 聊齋誌異 and Chi Hsiao-lan's 紀曉嵐 *Jottings from the Thatched Hall of Close Observations* 閱微草堂筆記. Although vernacular literature developed greatly during the 14th through 19th centuries, literature written in the classical literary language by scholars still constituted the cultural mainstream, given that literacy was still primarily their specialized province. This situation remained essentially unchanged up until the emergence of the New Literature Movement.

Modern Chinese Literature

The New Literature Movement

After attempts by the Western powers, Japan, and Russia to carve up or annex China in the late

19th and early 20th century, several professors at National Peking University initiated the New Culture Movement with the founding of the monthly magazine *Hsin Ching-nien* 新青年 *(La Jeunesse; New Youth)*. *New Youth* criticized traditional culture and welcomed the arrival of "Mr. Democracy" and "Mr. Science" from the West.

The new literature was to herald social reform. Hu Shih 胡適 raised the curtain for the literary revolution with his 1917 essay, "A Modest Proposal for the Reform of Literature." In another essay, "On a Constructive Literary Revolution," Chen Tu-hsiu 陳獨秀, Chien Hsuan-tung 錢玄同, and Hu Shih advocated "...a literature in the national language, and a national language of literary quality." They hoped that a nation with more than 2,000 different dialects could adopt a unified "national language" 國語, and that the written literary language of the scholarly class be discarded in favor of this national language, the ordinary speech of everyday, as the basis for writing (see Chapter 3, Language). In his *History of Vernacular Literature*, Hu Shih reevaluated the Chinese literary tradition, and attempted to raise the vernacular literature of the people from its previous position as a subbranch of literature to the mainstream. His goal was for vernacular literature to replace the classical literature of the scholars, which he pronounced "dead writing."

The early period of new literature was fraught with contradiction: individual freedom was encouraged so as to oppose traditional society, but was at the same time to be abandoned in the name of social justice, social concern, and the building of modern organizations. Rejecting the traditional culture and literature of the scholars, the reformers insisted that vernacular literature was the only living literature. Yet because vernacular literature grew out of the professional storytelling tradition, they also viewed it as backward and primitive. And, except for a few great works rich in cultural criticism, they adopted a largely negative attitude towards the vernacular tradition because it had originated as popular entertainment.

Chou Tso-jen 周作人 and others faced the dilemma of advocating a vernacular literature while being unable to identify with either the form or content of traditional Chinese vernacular literature. To solve this dilemma, Hu Shih, Chen Tu-hsiu, and others proposed using the genres, forms, and spiritual consciousness of Western literature as models for imitation. Translation became a required intermediary in the creation of the new literature. The first translators had no scruples about remolding the Chinese language along European lines, and the foreign flavor of their writing became one of its major characteristics. Thus, a deliberate "horizontal transfer" of literature was advocated as part of the movement to modernize China. Actual literary works of the time, however, were not simply imitations of foreign models. Lu Hsun's 魯迅 story, *Diary of a Madman* 狂人日記, for example, was obviously influenced by Gogol, but the thrust of its contents—its denunciation of the overly severe and demanding ethics of traditional culture—was an expression of a uniquely Chinese situation. Its style approached that of the fables of Chuang Tzu, Lieh Tzu, Han Yu, and Liu Tsung-yuan.

The New Literature: Early Period

The new literature experimented with different genres and drew on varied sources, and as a result was eclectic and multifaceted in nature. Works such as Lu Hsun's novella *The True Story of Ah Q* 阿Q正傳 and Lao She's 老舍 novel *Rickshaw Boy* 駱駝祥子 are told in a satirical tone filled with sorrow and pity. They seem to recall stories of the early vernacular short story tradition that describe the fickle fate of the lower classes, in contrast to the entertainment-oriented themes of the "Beauty-Scholar," itinerant swordsman, or detective-officials fictional works popular in the 17th and 18th centuries. These early works of modern fiction were also influenced to a certain degree by left-wing Western thinking and by the tradition of the Confucian scholars of pleading to the emperor on behalf of the people.

The neat five-and seven-syllable lines of traditional poetry were replaced in this period by the cadences of spoken Chinese, modeled after the line patterns of Western poems. Even more notable was the discord that resulted from the introduction of intellectual argumentation and search for meaning and freedom into the traditional themes of love and natural scenery. Whether through ardent passion or cold critique, these poems signaled an end to gentleness and ingenuousness, to the fusion of emotion and scenery, and to the original harmony of man and nature. They announced the beginning of an aesthetics of bitterness and anguish.

Prose writers such as Lin Yu-tang 林語堂 and Liang Shih-chiu 梁實秋, who were intimately acquainted with the Western tradition, wrote informal essays in the style of Montaigne and Lamb. Excepting for their use of the colloquial language, they generally followed the classical prose style of the ninth through 12th centuries, mixing reason with emotion, and musing on minor events of daily life. Chu Tzu-ching 朱自清, Hsia Mien-tsun 夏丏尊, Feng Tzu-kai 豐子愷, and Hsu Chih-mo 徐志摩 were all masters of this genre of writing.

The impassioned critiques of Liang Chi-chao 梁啓超, the cogent lucidity of Hu Shih, and the caustic wit of Lu Hsun were often expressed in "wars of the pen." Standing in contrast to this high level of social involvement were writers such as Chou Tso-jen and Lin Yu-tang, who rediscovered the informal essays of the 16th and 17th centuries. They advocated an easygoing humor and the *savoir-vivre* of sipping tea and copying old books; but were at the same time conversant with Freud and D.H. Lawrence. Although both types of essays were written in the colloquial language, their spirit was still rooted in the old culture of the scholar. The writers themselves, however, were not government officials but college professors, publishing house editors, journalists, and high school teachers.

Leftism in the New Literature

Owing to continued internal turbulence and constant power struggles among the warlords, a number of writers (mainly members of the Creation Society 創造社 literary group) followed up the literary revolution with a call for a "revolutionary literature," advocating that literature should serve the revolution. The Chinese Communist Party (CCP) set up the League of Leftist Writers 左聯. By the eve of the War of Resistance against Japan, the CCP had, through the power of organized party struggle, effectively stifled creativity and freedom of expression in many writers. Following the Japanese invasion, literature became totally subservient to the war effort, and the vigor and diversity of the early period of modern literature drew to a halt.

In the process of fanning the flames of patriotism and nationalistic fervor during the War of Resistance, a higher reassessment was made of traditional Chinese culture and literature. Many writers began adopting methods from folk drama and storytelling in their propaganda campaigns, presaging the literature of workers, peasants, and soldiers later espoused by the Chinese communists. Immediately following the Japanese surrender, China was plunged into all-out civil war. After the Chinese mainland fell into Chinese communist hands, socialist realism and Mao Zedong's talks on art and literature at Yen'an set the narrow confines within which writers on the mainland could operate. At the same time, the withdrawal of the ROC government to Taiwan began a new chapter in modern Chinese literature.

The New Literature:

The Later Period

To accurately catalogue the enormous array of literary works written every year since 1949 throughout the entire Chinese nation would be a herculean task. The difficulty presented by the sheer magnitude of such works is compounded by the fact that at present the Chinese mainland is not under the administrative control of the ROC government, and the power of literature to expose and criticize social and political ills is still greatly dreaded by Chinese communist authorities, resulting in the suppression of a large number of literary works over the years. Hence data regarding these works and their writers is either incomplete or unreliable.

Further Reading

(in English unless otherwise indicated):

Birch, Cyril, ed. *Anthology of Chinese Literature*. New York: Grove Press, 1965.

——, tr. *Stories From a Ming Collection*. New York: Grove Press, 1958.

Brewitt-Taylor, C.H., tr. *Romance of the Three Kingdoms*. 2 vols. Rutland, Vt.: Charles E. Tuttle, 1959.

Chang Chien 張健, ed. *Chung-kuo wen-hsueh pi-ping lun-chi* 中國文學批評論集 (A Collection of Chinese Literary Criticism; in Chinese). Taipei: Heavenly Lotus Publishing Company, 1979.

Chen, Li-li, tr. *Master Dung's Western Romance, A Chantefable*. Cambridge: Cambridge University Press, 1976.

Chen Jo-hsi 陳若曦. *Spirit Calling: Tales about Taiwan*. Taipei: Heritage Press, 1962.

——*The Execution of Mayor Yin* 尹縣長 *and Other Stories from the Great Cultural Revolution*. Bloomington: Indiana University Press, 1978.

——[Chen Ruoxi]. *The Old Man* 老人 *and Other Stories*. Renditions paperback. Hong Kong: Chinese University of Hong Kong, Research Centre for Translation, 1986.

Chen Ying-chen 陳映眞. *Exiles at Home: Stories by Chen Ying-chen* 陳映眞. Trans. Lucien Miller. Ann Arbor: University of Michigan, Center for Chinese Studies, 1986.

Chi Pang-yuan, ed. *An Anthology of Contemporary Chinese Literature*. Seattle: University of Washington Press, 1989.

Crump, J.I. *Chinese Theater in the Days of Kublai Khan*. Tucson: The University of Arizona Press, 1980.

Egerton, Clement, tr. *The Golden Lotus*. 4 vols. London: Routledge & Kegan Paul, 1972.

Chung-kuo ku-tien wen-hsueh lun-tsung: tse-erh, wen-hseh pi-ping yu hsi-chu chih pu 中國古典文學論叢：冊二，文學批評與戲劇之部 (Essays on Chinese Literature: Vol. 2, Literary Criticism and Drama; in Chinese). Taipei: Chung Wai Literary Monthly, 1976.

Chung-kuo ku-tien wen-hsueh yen-chiu tsung-kan: san-wen yu lun-ping chih pu 中國古典文學研究叢刊：散文與論評之部 (Essays on Classical Chinese Literature: Prose and Criticism; in Chinese). Taipei: Chu Liu Book Company, 1979.

Chung-kuo wen-hsueh chiang-hua 中國文學講話 (On Chinese Literature; in Chinese). Taipei: Chu Liu Book Company, 1982. 6 vols.

Lo Lien-tien 羅聯添, ed. *Chung-kuo wen-hsueh shih lun-wen hsuan-chi* 中國文學史論文選集 (Essays on the History of Chinese Literature; in Chinese). Taipei: Student Book Company, 1985. 5 vols.

Hawkes, David, and John Minford, trs. *The Story of the Stone*. Middlesex, Penguin, 1973-1982.

Hsieh Wu-liang 謝無量. *Chung-kuo fu-nu wen-hsueh shih* 中國婦女文學史 (History of Chinese Women's Literature; in Chinese). Taipei: Chung Hwa Book Company, 1973.

Hu Shih 胡適. *Pai-hua wen-hsueh shih* 白話文學史 (A History of Chinese Vernacular Literature; in Chinese). Tainan: Tunghai Publishing Company, 1981.

Hu Yu-huan 胡毓寰. *Chung-kuo wen-hsueh yuan-liu* 中國文學源流 (The Origins of Chinese Literature; in Chinese). Taipei: Commercial Press, 1967.

Hwa Yen 華嚴. *Lamp of Wisdom* 智慧的燈. Taipei: *Woman Magazine*, 1974.

Huang Chun-ming 黃春明. *The Drowning of an Old Cat* 溺死一隻老貓 *and Other Stories*. Trans. Howard Goldblatt. Bloomington: Indiana University Press, 1980.

Ke Ching-ming 柯慶明, Lin Ming-te 林明德, ed. *Chung-kuo ku-tien wen-hsueh yen-chiu tsung-kan: hsiao-shuo chih-pu* 中國古典文學研究叢刊：小說之部 (Essays on Classical Chinese Literature: Novels; in Chinese). Taipei: Chu Liu Book Company, 1979.

Kung Shang-jen. *The Peach Blossom Fan*. Trans. Chen Shih-hsiang and Harold Acton. Berkeley: University of California Press, 1976.

Kuo, Gloria Liang-hui 郭良蕙. *Taipei Women*. Hong Kong: New Enterprise Company, 1983.

Lau, Joseph S.M., ed. *Chinese Stories from Taiwan, 1960-1970*. New York: Columbia University Press, 1976.

Li Ang 李昂. *The Butcher's Wife* 殺夫: *A Novel by Li Ang*. Trans. Howard Goldblatt and Ellen Yeung. San Francisco: North Point Press, 1986.

Lin Hai-yin 林海音. *Green Seaweed and Salted Eggs* 綠藻與鹹蛋. Taipei: Heritage Press, 1963.

Lin Wen-keng 林文庚. *Chung-kuo wen-hsueh fa-chan Shih* 中國文學發展史 (The Development of Chinese Literature; in Chinese). Taipei: Ching Liu Publishing Company, 1976.

Liu Chen-lu 劉振魯, ed. *Tang-chien Tai-wan so-chien ke-sheng hsi-chu hsuan-chi* 當前臺灣所見各省戲曲選集 (Selected Local Drama from Various Provinces Still Performed in Taiwan Today; in Chinese). Taichung: Taiwan Provincial Historical Commission, 1982. 2 vols.

Liu O 劉鶚. *The Travels of Lao Tsan*. Trans. Harold Shadick. Ithaca: Cornell University Press, 1966.

Liu Wu-chi, ed. *An Introduction to Chinese Literature*. Bloomington: Indiana University Press, 1966.

——, ed. *Sunflower Splendor: Three Thousand Years of Chinese Poetry*. Bloomington: Indiana University Press, 1975.

Ma, Y.W. and Joseph S.M. Lau, eds. *Traditional Chinese Stories, Themes and Variations*. New York: Columbia University Press, 1978.

McNaughton, William, ed. *Chinese Literature: An Anthology from the Earliest Times to the Present*. Rutland: Charles E. Tuttle Company, 1974.

Mulligan, Jean, tr. *The Lute, Kao Ming's Pi-pa chi*. New York: Columbia University Press, 1980.

Nieh, Hua-ling 聶華苓, ed. *Eight Stories by Chinese Women*. Taipei: Heritage Press, 1962.

——. *Mulberry and Peach* 桑青與桃紅: *Two Women of China*. London: Women's Press, 1986, c1981.

Nienhauser, William H., ed. *The Indiana Companion to Traditional Chinese Literature*. Bloomington: Indiana University Press, 1986.

Pai Hsien-yung 白先勇. *Wandering in the Garden, Waking from a Dream* 遊園驚夢: *Tales of Taipei Characters*. Trans. Pai Hsien-yung and Patia Yasin. Ed. George Kao. Bloomington: Indiana University Press, 1982.

——. *Crystal Boys* 孽子: *A Novel by Pai Hsien-yung* 白先勇 Trans. Howard Goldblatt. San Francisco: Gay Sunshine Press, 1990.

Peng Ko 彭歌. *Black Tears* 黑色的淚, *Stories of War-Torn China*. Trans. Nancy Ing. Taipei: Chinese Materials Center Publications, 1986.

Shih Nai-an 施耐庵. *Outlaws of the Marsh*. Trans. Sidney Shapiro. Bloomington: Indiana University Press, 1981

Shih, Shu-ching 施叔青. *The Barren Years* 那些不毛的日子 *and Other Short Stories and Plays*. Trans. John M. Mclellan. San Francisco: Chinese Materials Center, 1975.

Tang Xianzu, *The Peony Pavilion (Mudan Ting)*. Trans. Cyril Birch. Bloomington: Indiana University Press, 1980.

Tseng Yung-i 曾永義. *Shuo hsi-chu* 說戲曲 (On Drama; in Chinese). Taipei: Linking Publishing Company, 1976.

Yeh Ching-ping 葉慶炳. *Chung-kuo wen-hsueh shih* 中國文學史 (The History of Chinese Literature; in Chinese). Taipei: Student Book Company, 1987. 2 vols.

Yip Wai-lim 葉維廉, ed. *Chung-kuo hsien-tai wen-hsueh pi-ping hsuan-chi* 中國現代文學批評選集 (An Anthology of Contemporary Chinese Literary Criticism; in Chinese). Taipei: Linking Publishing Company, 1976.

Wang Chiu-kuei 王秋桂, ed. *Chung-kuo wen-hsueh lun-chu yi-tsung* 中國文學論著譯叢 (Essays on Chinese Literature; in Chinese). Taipei: Student Book Company, 1985.

Wang Shih-fu 王實甫. *The Romance of the Western Chamber*. Trans. S. I. Hsiung. New York: Columbia University Press, 1968.

Wang, Wen-hsing 王文興. *Family Catastrophe* 家變. Trans. Susan Dolling. Honolulu: University of Hawaii Press, 1995.

——. *Backed Against the Sea* 背海的人 Trans. Edward Gunn. Ithaca: Cornell East Asia Program, 1993.

Wen Hsun Magazine 文訊雜誌社, ed. *1997 wen-hsueh nien-chien* 一九九七臺灣文學年鑑 (1997 Annual of Literature in Taiwan; in Chinese). Taipei: Council of Cultural Affairs, 1997.

Wu Cheng-en 吳承恩. *The Journey to the West* (Translated into English by Anthony C. Yu). 4 vols. Chicago: The University of Chicago Press, 1980.

25
Religion

Taiwan's widely
practiced folk
religion has
been strongly
influenced by
Buddhism and
Taoism.

What's New

1. Figures updated
2. Religious community's contributions to the 9-21 Earthquake relief
3. Alternative military service
4. Establishment of the first Taiwan Association for Religious Studies (TARS)
5. The birthday of Buddha declared a national holiday
6. The Taipei Grand Mosque is designated as Taipei City's first religious heritage site
7. A non-religion-affiliated university to establish a graduate school in religious studies

Age-old religious customs, icons, and beliefs permeate all levels of Taiwan's Chinese culture. Almost all adults in Taiwan, even those not formally subscribing to a religious belief or worshiping regularly at a particular temple, engage in religious practices stemming from one or a combination of traditional Chinese folk religions. It is very common in Taiwan to see homes and shops include a lighted shrine with incense burning to honor a deity, hero, or ancestor. Most families perform the filial duties of ancestral worship; and on important occasions, as when a son or daughter takes the university entrance examination, a visit to the temples is made to present petitions and solicit divine assistance. Many taxi drivers in Taiwan decorate their cars with charms, amulets, statuettes, and religious slogans for protection against accidents and harm. Yet strictly speaking, these people are not necessarily Buddhist, Taoist, officially affiliated with any certain temple, or registered with a religious organization.

The latest figures released by the Ministry of the Interior in December 1998 indicate that about 11.8 million people in Taiwan—more than half of the population—are religious believers (see chart, next page). Altogether, some 47,400 temples and churches dot the island serving the spiritual needs of the people on Taiwan.

Polytheistic and syncretic, Chinese society is dominated by ancestor worship, Taoism, and Buddhism, but has never excluded the addition and development of other indigenous and foreign religions. Although each religion may appear to postulate an independent doctrine, some cannot be strictly differentiated. For example, the Taiwan folk deity Matsu 媽祖, Goddess of the Sea, and Kuanyin 觀音, the Buddhist Goddess of Mercy, are often worshiped together in the same temple. This reveals the special character of the Chinese religious outlook, which can accommodate seemingly contradictory beliefs simultaneously.

Freedom of religion is a fundamental right of every citizen in the ROC: "The people shall have freedom of religious belief," states Article 13 of the ROC Constitution. People of all recognized religions can publicly proselytize, evangelize, and congregate as long as they do not violate ROC laws and regulations, public morals, and social systems. To be recognized, however, these groups must apply and register with the Department of Civil Affairs of the Ministry of the Interior 內政部民政司 after meeting stipulated requirements, including a minimum number of local believers, organizations, and churches. Currently, there are 13 religions recognized by the government: Buddhism, Taoism, Catholicism, Protestantism, Hsuan-yuan Chiao 軒轅教, Islam, Li-ism 理教, Tenrikyo 天理教, Baha'i faith 巴哈伊教, Tien Dih Chiao 天帝教, Tien Te Chiao 天德教, I-kuan Tao 一貫道, and Mahikarikyo 眞光教.

Religious groups have traditionally been the backbone of community services in Taiwan. As of December 1998, religious groups were operating 52 hospitals, 69 clinics, 27 retirement homes, 24 centers for the mentally retarded, 8 handicapped welfare institutions, 5 rehabilitation centers, 10 orphanages, and 34 nurseries in Taiwan. These groups have established 386 kindergartens, 22 primary schools, 48 high schools, 13 colleges, 19 universities, and 86 monasteries and seminaries. They have also set up 163 libraries, 156 publishing houses, and 272 publications.

Aside from sharing a common concern for the poor and disaster victims, religious organizations have also diversified into medical services, free health checkups, community projects, and visitations to homes and hospitals. Churches in Taiwan have also taken the lead in organizing cultural and recreational activities. Whereas the Protestant church has focused on promoting youth activities, Taoist organizations have channeled much of their efforts into preserving and staging traditional Chinese dramas while Buddhist groups have offered a wide range of self-improvement seminars.

Another important factor influencing religion in Taiwan is the extremely eclectic nature of the Chinese. The religions currently practiced in Taiwan are for the most part combinations of elements from several religions. Even Taoism, which is rooted in traditional Chinese philosophy, has absorbed many aspects of non-Chinese dogmas. Unlike the Jewish and Christian religions of the West, which require that believers adhere only to their particular doctrines, the Chinese have seldom felt it necessary to exclude aspects of other faiths from their personal or collective religious beliefs.

The 921 Earthquake Relief Measures

Immediately following the 921 Earthquake on September 21, 1999, the religious community contributed immensely to relief efforts with great compassion and efficiency. They were among the first to reach out to victims in the disaster areas, bringing hope, comfort, food, materials, and monetary assistance. Particularly noteworthy were the Buddhist Compassion Tzu Chi Relief Foundation 佛教慈濟慈善事業基金會; Fo Guang Shan 佛光山 (FGS) and its affiliate, the Buddha's

Light International Association 國際佛光會 (BLIA), which formed a 921 Earthquake United Relief Fund/Center 佛光山國際佛光會聯合救災基金 / 中心; and the Association of Dharma Drum Mountain Cultural and Educational Organizations 法鼓 山文教基金會.

The Tzu Chi Foundation's earthquake relief efforts were conducted in three stages: The first stage was devoted to immediate emergency relief, providing sleeping bags, tents, daily necessities, and cooked meals to the victims. The Foundation also provided psychological counseling and spiritual consolation. Total expenditures exceeded US$6.3 million.

In the second stage, the Tzu Chi Foundation built 2,000 prefabricated houses, complete with basic home conveniences, and provided basic living allowances of US$94 each to 3,000 homes. They also conducted 14 large-scale religious memorial services to comfort victims in the disaster areas. Total expenditures exceeded US$37.5 million.

During the third stage, the Tzu Chi Foundation began reconstruction of 25 schools at an estimated cost of about US$128.1 million. Total earthquake relief projects by the Tzu Chi Foundation are estimated to be nearly US$187.5 million.

Fo Guang Shan and its affiliate, the Buddha's Light International Association, formed the United Relief Center to aid earthquake victims. More than 50,000 Fo Guang Shan venerables and Buddha's Light International Association members have participated in earthquake relief activities, offering medical aid, prayer and consolation, temporary shelters, food, and daily necessities.

In the preliminary stages, the FGS opened more than 80 of its branch temples to provide accomodations and meals to those who had lost their homes in the quake; its Ta Tzu Children's Home 大慈育幼院 accomodated homeless children; and resting places were provided for ashes of the deceased at six of its mausoleums.

In addition, the FGS adopted three shelters: the Tungshih Forestry Department 東勢林務處, the Tunghsing Junior High School 東興國中, and the Tungshih Military Hospital 東勢分院(軍醫院); while the BLIA sponsored three elementary

Religious Populations 1998		
	Believers (thousands)	Percentage of Total Population
Buddhist	4,864	22.11
Taoist	4,505	20.48
I-Kuan Tao	983	4.47
Protestant & Catholic	727	3.30
Other	809	3.68
Total	11,888	54.04

schools: the Tungshih Chung Ko Elementary School 東勢中科國小, Chungliao Shuang Wen Elementary School 中寮爽文國小, and the Tsaotun Ping Lin Elementary School 草屯平林國小. The total cost for rebuilding these schools is estimated to exceed US$31.3 million.

In cooperation with the Ministry of Education, both of these Buddhist groups provided 1,800 students in disaster areas with free lunches for three months and donated 30,000 copies of *I Will Be Up Again* 我會再站起來 to help students cope with the disaster in a positive fashion.

The FGS has also offered 1,200 units of temporary housing for victims of the earthquake, which will be distributed to the cities of Nantou 南投, Tsaotun 草屯, Chungliao 中寮, Chichi 集集, and Chushan 竹山.

By October 11, 1999, donations collected by the BLIA had reached US$2.1 million, and relief goods distributed by the group included: 80 truckloads of miscellaneous foods, 10 truckloads of bottled drinking water, 20 truckloads of rice, 10 truckloads of instant noodles, 10 truckloads of miscellaneous supplies, 1 truckload of medical supplies (including US$8,532 worth of medicines), 10 truckloads of clothing, 12,000 blankets and bedding, 2,000 Dharani Sutra Quilts,

12,000 sleeping bags, 8,500 tents, 2 million batteries, 3,000 bottles of saline solution, 1,000 cremation urns, 700 coffins, and 1,000 body bags.

The United Relief Center provided families with US$313 to US$1,563 for every relative lost in the quake; US$94 to US$156 to people with injuries; and US$156 to US$3,125 to families whose houses had been damaged or destroyed.

The Association of Dharma Drum Mountain Cultural and Educational Organizations mobilized 15,000 people to help in disaster areas, pray for the deceased, and care for the sick and injured in hospitals. The organizations also donated US$9.4 million worth of food and materials, provided coffins for the deceased, and gave 150 tents and 5,000 raincoats to protect homeless victims from winter winds and rain. A million copies of the booklet *Settled Heart* 安心手冊 by Master Sheng-yen were also donated to victims in the disaster areas.

Catholic churches in Taiwan set up a 921 Earthquake Relief Center 臺灣天主教九二一賑災救助中心 headed by Cardinal Paul Shan 單國璽樞機主教 of Taiwan. Churches and church institutions were opened for temporary housing of refugees and as centers to provide emergency relief and medical services, among other measures.

Volunteer workers of the Buddhist Compassion Tzu Chi Relief Foundation build temporary housing for victims of the 921 Earthquake.

Catholic hospitals and clinics provided emergency medical aid, especially to remote areas, and Catholic institutions offered to provide adoption services to 300 homeless elderly and orphans.

Bank accounts were set up for donations from various sectors, receiving more than US$50,000 for earthquake relief.

The Chinese Christian Relief Association of Taiwan 中華基督教救助協會 (CCRA) set up a Taiwan Christian United Rescue Action for the 921 Earthquake 九二一地震救助行動, and as of October 31, 1999, had collected US$40.6 million from both domestic and foreign donors. Except for US$1.88 million specifically allocated to the Ling Lueng Church 靈糧堂 for use in the construction of prefabricated houses, the funds were to be used by the CCRA for disaster relief. Of this amount, the CCRA subsidized US$78,000 for churches damaged in the disaster areas and churches that had adopted disaster area reconstruction projects; US$423,000 for hardware development of churches in the disaster areas; US$406,000 for the counseling, guidance, and assistance of elementary and junior-high school children and teenagers; and US$313,000 for poor earthquake victims. The CCRA also helped in resettling orphans, widows, and families broken apart by the quake; training churches to organize relief groups and resources; and producing audio-visual spiritual guidance tapes, videotapes, and booklets for distribution in the disaster areas and for broadcasting.

Taoism

Taoism developed from the philosophy of Lao Tzu 老子, who lived in the sixth century B.C. He and his disciples emphasized individual freedom, laissez-faire government, human spontaneity, and mystical experience. Taoist philosophy takes *The Way and Its Power* 道德經 as its central text.

The themes of Taoism as a religion coalesced in the third century B.C., but Taoism itself did not become an organized religious movement until the second century A.D. The fundamental aim of Taoism as a religion (not as a philosophy) was the attainment of immortality. Accordingly, people who lived in harmony with nature were said to become "immortals" 仙. Lao Tzu, founder of the philosophy of Taoism, eventually was deified as a Taoist god at the head of a huge pantheon of "immortal" folk heroes. Famous generals and sages made up the rest of the pantheon once they had ascended to immortal status. The Taoist pursuit of everlasting life ultimately led to a search for immortality pills or potions. Medieval Taoist rituals to some extent mirrored alchemical research in Europe during the same period.

Taoism was adopted as the religion of the imperial court during the seventh through the ninth centuries, and Taoist mystical elements were codified. In the ensuing centuries, the Taoist religious community was increasingly fractionalized. Taoism became interlaced with elements of Confucianism, Buddhism, and folk religion. The particular forms of Taoist religion brought to Taiwan some 300 years ago (then regarded as an outlying frontier area) are considered typical of the fragmented Taoist traditions. The most distinctive feature of the present practice is the worship of one's forebears alongside Taoist deities.

During the period of Japanese occupation (1895-1945), the Japanese colonial government implemented a policy of suppressing Taoism in Taiwan, because it was associated with Chinese patriotism. Many religious images in Taoist temples were burned, and various repressive measures were directed against Taoist followers.

After Taiwan's retrocession to China in 1945, Taoist temples that had been registered as Buddhist under pressure from the Japanese colonial government returned to the Taoist fold. Taoist priests from the Chinese mainland, including Chang En-pu 張恩溥, a 63rd generation Taoist priest of the Cheng I 正一 sect of Lung Hu Mountain 龍虎山, began moving to Taiwan in increasing numbers. In 1950, Chang En-pu established a Taoist fellowship in Taiwan, assuming the position of director. This was the beginning of organized Taoism in Taiwan.

In the past, much emphasis was put on constructing luxurious temples and holding frequent, lavish festivals. Today, adherents and priests pay more attention to preaching through mass media. Some Taoist leaders have turned to the strategy of using temple associations to unite the various "generic" temples under the umbrella of a common main deity, while at the same time trying to win over temple diviners from small local or home temples 神壇 and offering them guidance.

As of 1998, approximately 8,557 Taoist temples and 33,200 Taoist clergy were meeting the spiritual needs of some 4.65 million Taoist faithful living in Taiwan. Two Taoist seminaries, one each in Taipei and Kaohsiung, provided instruction in Taoist doctrine and rites. There were also 1 college, 59 kindergartens, 3 retirement homes, 1 hospital, 19 clinics, 16 libraries, 9 publication houses, and 160 publications.

Buddhism

Buddhism is a pan-Asian religion which originated in India and was brought to China sometime before the sixth century. Buddha was an Indian prince named Siddhartha Gautama who renounced his royal family and luxurious lifestyle to search for religious understanding and release from the human condition. It is said that he achieved enlightenment through self-denial and meditation, and thereafter instructed his followers on the nature of dharma, the true way. Buddha preached a doctrine envisioned in the "Four Noble Truths": life is fundamentally difficult and disappointing; suffering is the result of one's desires; to stop disappointment one must control one's desires; and the way to stop desire is through right views, intention, speech, conduct, livelihood, effort, mindfulness, and concentration.

Buddhism spread south to Ceylon, Cambodia, and Laos to become Theravada or Hinayana (Little Vehicle 小乘) and north to China, Korea, and Japan, where it developed into Mahayana (Great Vehicle 大乘). Hinayana is concerned more with individual salvation through contemplation and self-purification, while Mahayana teaches compassion and universal salvation.

Mahayana adherents believe in powerful godlike bodhisattvas, enlightened individuals who are capable of saving all sentient beings and transporting them to a state of release (nirvana) from the human condition. Bodhisattvas possess the natural disposition to attain enlightenment and become Buddhas, a potential which is inherent in all men. Mahayana adherents also believe in a cycle of lives which continues until one attains nirvana and becomes a Buddha.

Several Mahayana concepts, such as a life of suffering, many powerful godlike figures, and possible transcendence to a higher state of being, meshed well with similar ideas in Taoism and folk religion already widely accepted in China. As a result, Mahayana Buddhism became the most popular form of Buddhism in China, and indeed, in all of Northeast Asia.

Although Buddhism originated in India, since its introduction to China almost two millennia ago it has undergone thorough Sinification. In terms of thought system, canons, and ceremonies, the Buddhism practiced in China today is distinctly Chinese, and few Chinese people consider it a foreign religion.

Buddhism was introduced into Taiwan in the late 16th century. By the time Ming loyalist Koxinga 國姓爺 escaped to Taiwan and drove out the Dutch, Buddhist monks were already coming to Taiwan with official sanction. Buddhist temples were built with the support of Koxinga and his followers. By the 17th century, several Buddhist temples had been erected by officials, the gentry, and local people; however, Buddhist missionary work at the time seems to have been limited in scope. Some Buddhist temples were used as temples of folk religion by the people, and thus received popular support.

Japanese Buddhism was introduced into Taiwan during the period of Japanese occupation at the turn of the 20th century. Eight Buddhist sects, namely, the Tendai 天臺, the Shingon 眞元, the Pure Land 淨土, the Soto 曹洞宗, the Rinzai 臨濟宗, the Shin 眞, the Nichiren 日蓮, the Hokke 法華, and the Agon 阿含, came to Taiwan to proselytize. Buddhist sects already established in Taiwan responded to the incursion by accommodating the newcomers. By 1925, a large number of Japanese monks were in leading positions in

Taiwan's established Buddhist temples. Buddhism in Taiwan gradually took on a Japanese cast, particularly in the areas of moral and disciplinary codes and education.

During the Japanese occupation, Buddhist groups in Taiwan separated into the northern, central, and southern schools. The monk Shan-hui 善慧 founded the Yueh-mei Mountain 月眉山 school of Keelung 基隆 (the northern school), and the monk Chueh-li 覺力 established the Fa-yun Szu 法雲寺 school of Miaoli 苗栗 (the central school) and the Kai-yuan Szu 開元寺 school of Tainan (the southern school). Most Buddhist temples of this era belonged to one of these three schools. Towards the end of the Japanese occupation, many monks actively engaged in proselytizing activities and established Buddhist organizations. In 1947, Master Chang-chia 章嘉 established the Buddhist Association of the ROC 中國佛教會 in Nanking. Large numbers of Chinese monks followed the Chinese Nationalist government to Taiwan and established the Taiwan provincial chapter of the Buddhist Association of the ROC. Monks from the Chinese mainland headed the association at first, and temples throughout the island became association members.

Postwar Buddhism in Taiwan has witnessed the reestablishment of the Chinese Mahayana tradition, renewed stress on moral and disciplinary codes and the ceremony of ordination 傳戒大典, emphasis on Buddhist education and the establishment of Buddhist institutes, and active proselytizing. As of 1998, Buddhists in the ROC had registered 3,961 temples, 32 seminaries, 5 universities, 3 colleges, 4 high schools, 44 kindergartens, 29 nurseries, 6 orphanages, 5 retirement homes, 1 center for the mentally retarded, 60 institutions for proselytizing, 3 hospitals, 3 clinics, 115 libraries, and 32 publishing houses with 24 publications. There were also around 9,200 Buddhist clergy serving the 4.86 million Buddhists of Taiwan.

Since the 1950s, the Buddhist Association of the ROC has held ordination ceremonies for Buddhist monks, nuns, and lay people. Temples recognized by the association hold an annual third-level ordination ceremony 三壇大戒, with monks and nuns receiving one month of stringent training before ordination. A total of about 10,000 monks and nuns have been ordained in this ceremony at various temples and monasteries over the past four decades.

Since 1980, Tantric Buddhism, an esoteric sect that developed between the second and fourth centuries A.D. in India, has become increasingly popular in Taiwan. In recent years, exiled Tibetan monks of the Tantric sect have come to Taiwan, rapidly attracting a large following and thereby exercising a significant effect on Taiwan's religious culture.

On March 22, 1997, the Nobel Prize winning religious and political leader of Tibet, the Dalai Lama, set foot again on Chinese soil for the first time in 38 years, ever since his exile in 1959. Invited by Master Ching Hsin 淨心長老 of the Buddhist Association of the ROC, the 14th Dalai Lama held two public talks and a Buddhist consecration ceremony, met with religious leaders, and ended his five-day visit to Taiwan on March 27 by meeting with President Lee Teng-hui.

On April 16, 1998, the Tibet Religious Foundation of His Holiness the Dalai Lama 財團法人達賴喇嘛西藏宗教基金會 was formally established. Although religious in name, the Foundation serves as a de facto Tibetan representative office in Taiwan.

On May 3, 1998, the Dalai Lama conducted a dialogue session in New York with the highly-respected Master Sheng Yen 聖嚴 of the Association of the Dharma Drum Mountain Cultural and Educational Organizations 法鼓山文教基金會 of Taiwan. The two discussed Chinese and Tantric Buddhism.

On April 8, 1998, a 200-member delegation led by Master Hsing Yun 星雲 and Presidential Advisor Wu Poh-hsiung escorted to Taipei on a chartered China Airlines flight a sacred tooth of the Buddha, said to be one of the three teeth salvaged from the Buddha's ashes after his cremation 2,000 years ago.

The sacred tooth had been kept in India for 30 years by a Tibetan monk in exile, who decided last February to donate the relic to the Venerable

Master Hsing Yun, whose Buddha's Light International Association 國際佛光會 is the world's largest Buddhist organization.

On April 11, the Buddha's tooth was given a grand reception in the square of the Chiang Kai-shek Memorial Hall. More than 30,000 Buddhists from Taiwan and overseas attended the event. The mass reception was presided over by Premier Vincent Siew with other high-ranking ROC officials in attendance. Among them were Vice President Lien Chan and Presidential Advisor Koo Chen-fu.

Invited by the Nanhua Management College of Fokuang University 佛光大學南華管理學院 and the Straits Exchange Foundation 海基會, five officials from mainland China's Bureau of Religious Affairs 國家宗教局 arrived in Taiwan on July 28, 1998, for a twelve-day visit. The group toured various religious centers, temples and churches of the Buddhist, I-kuan Tao, Catholic and Protestant religions. The purpose of the visit was to promote exchanges and research on Taiwan's religious development.

Education

The road traveled by Buddhist education has not been a smooth one. Its beginning in post-retrocession Taiwan dates from the invitation by the Buddhist Master Miao-kuo 妙果 of the Yuan-kuang Temple 圓光寺 in Chungli 中壢 to the Buddhist Master Tzu-hang 慈航 from the Chinese mainland to establish a Buddhist institute in Taiwan. Master Tzu-hang later founded a Maitreya monastery in Hsichih 汐止, Taipei County. Next, Master Yin-shun 印順 assumed the directorship of a Buddhist institute in Hsinchu 新竹. Subsequently, over 50 Buddhist institutes were founded islandwide. Many of these institutes functioned intermittently; only a portion of them were able to maintain unbroken operations. One explanation for this is that Buddhist and other religious institutes were not officially recognized by the Ministry of Education. Another is that many Buddhist figures founded independent educational institutes instead of uniting to establish one large institute. The Buddhist-sponsored Tzu Chi Junior College of Nursing 慈濟護理專科學校 opened in

1989, the Huafan College of Humanities and Technology 華梵人文科技學院 opened the following year, the Tzu Chi Medical College 慈濟醫學院 began enrolling students in 1994, and the College of Humanities and Sociology of Fokuang University 佛光大學人文社會學院 is presently under construction in Ilan 宜蘭. The Nanhua Management College of Fokuang University 佛光大學南華管理學院 located in Chiayi 嘉義, which began enrolling students in October 1996, was renamed in 1999 as Nanhua University 南華大學. Dharma Drum College 法鼓人文社會學院 and the Shuan Tsang College of Humanities and Social Sciences 玄奘大學人文社會學院 are both currently under construction.

In February 1999, National Changhua University of Education 國立彰化師範大學 became Taiwan's first non-religious university to offer courses in religion.

Pending the passing of a final review, National Chengchi University 國立政治大學 will also be establishing a graduate school in religious studies in 2000, becoming the only university unaffiliated with any religious groups to set up a graduate program in religion.

Trends

Buddhists are becoming more missionary in outlook. Over the past few years, television proselytizing has gained popularity, and lectures on Buddhism have begun to draw large crowds. Some of the leading figures in Buddhism have even expanded their missions to North America. The famous Master Hsing Yun directed the construction of the Hsi-lai Temple 西來寺, completed in 1988, in Los Angeles. He also directed the construction of Nan-tien Temple 南天寺 (registered under the International Buddhist Association of Australia, Inc.) in Sydney, Australia, completed in 1995 and reputed to be the largest Buddhist temple in the southern hemisphere.

Responding to the Buddhists' drive to designate Buddha's birthday a national holiday, President Lee declared the birthday of the Buddha a national holiday, which is April 8th on the Lunar calendar. Both the Buddha's birthday and Mother's Day share the same day, which falls on Sunday.

In addition to the chanting of mantras and sutras—the more traditional form of worshiping—meditation is gaining a foothold among believers. Buddhists have established centers to offer courses on meditation to the public. The practice is also becoming popular among politicians and businessmen as a means of relieving tension.

Intellectuals have been drawn to Buddhism from the beginning, for both academic and religious reasons. Some have become renowned monks and nuns. By stressing "Buddhism for this world," Buddhist leaders have also managed to attract people outside of academia who have contributed significant amounts of financial and spiritual support to Buddhist organizations.

Taiwan's first religious association, the Taiwan Association for Religious Studies (TARS), was established on April 18, 1999, by a group of scholars and academics. The association researches mainstream and folk religions in Taiwan, and publishes a monthly newsletter.

Alternative Military Service

In coordination with the implementation of alternative military service beginning in July 2000, the Ministry of the Interior has agreed that conscripts inducted into the military in 1999 may apply for a one year postponement due to religious reasons, but must produce a certificate of proof from a legitimate religious group. According to Conscription Department (MOI) 內政部役政司 records, 23 conscripts have been sentenced by the military court for refusal to serve in the military or to carry weapons of war. The largest number of these conscripts are Jehovah's Witnesses. All these disputes, however, should be resolved by the year 2000 with the implementation of alternative military service.

Confucianism

Confucianism is a philosophy with a religious function. It is named after Confucius, whose discourses on ethical behavior have been passed down from generation to generation to become the definitive marker of things Chinese. It embraces some elements of traditional Chinese religion, such as a reverence toward heaven and the worship of ancestors. Moreover, it concerns the cultivation of an ethical life in order to establish harmonious relationships with other individuals and with society. It does not assert the existence of a deity. Most Chinese do not identify Confucianism as a religion; rather they view it as a philosophy. They regard Confucian temples more as halls to honor Confucius rather than places of worship. Visitors may witness an elaborate ceremony to honor Confucius at Taipei's Confucian Temple 孔廟 every year on his birthday, September 28, which is also designated as Teachers' Day 教師節 in the ROC.

Folk Religion

The majority of Taiwan's people believe in Chinese folk religion, a faith whose theology, rituals, and officiants are widely diffused into other secular and social institutions. Taiwan's difficult pioneer environment of the past two centuries created a strong need for religion, and folk religion was the choice of virtually all Chinese immigrants to the island. They brought from the mainland images of gods and traditional religious beliefs. While transplanting their religion, they adapted it functionally to their new society, sometimes even creating new gods and rituals to meet their needs for security and survival. The resulting mixture of beliefs is called folk religion for the sake of convenience.

Like Taoism, folk religion has a broad pantheon of gods and goddesses. Relations between gods and people, and between gods and gods, are of paramount importance. Like Buddhism, folk religion offers salvation, or at least temporary aid, for true believers. Although folk religion has been significantly influenced by Buddhism and Taoism, it is neither Buddhist nor Taoist. People associated with Taoism often place folk religion in the same category as Taoism; however, they concede that folk religion includes a number of gods that Taoism does not recognize.

In folk religion, the supreme deity is the God of Heaven 天公, who is recognized as a personification of justice. Below this supreme deity are hundreds of lesser gods. Almost every neighborhood in Taiwan has a temple for the Earth God 土地公, and many families make offerings to the House God 地基主 when they move into a house.

One of the most popular deities is Matsu 媽祖, the patron goddess of the sea and fishermen. Meizhou, a Fujian Province 福建省 islet, is where worship for the Meizhou Matsu originated. In 1987, worshipers celebrated the 1,000th anniversary of Matsu's ascent to heaven with a round-the-island parade of her image. Her birthday is regularly celebrated with great pomp as worshipers carry her image in a procession through cities around Taiwan. On January 24, 1997, amid the sounds of gongs, drums, and traditional Chinese music, the Meizhou Matsu 湄洲媽祖, an 800-year-old wooden statue, arrived from the Chinese mainland and visited major temples islandwide over the following 100 days. These religious exchanges are narrowing the distance between people of the two sides of the Taiwan Strait..

Some deities in Taiwan folk religion were originally normal people who, through their actions or accomplishments in life, later became gods. The brave warrior Kuan Yu 關羽 from the Period of the Three Kingdoms 三國時代; General Koxinga, who drove the Dutch colonists off Taiwan in the 17th century; and the renowned healer Hua Tuo 華陀, who lived sometime between the first and third century A.D., all have faithful followings in Taiwan.

Taiwan's Wang Yeh 王爺 are believed to be celestial emissaries sent by the heavens to ensure the safety of mankind by driving away evil spirits and eradicating epidemics. There are said to be 360 Wang Yeh in Taiwan, but the religious practices surrounding each of these celestial lords is different, depending on the locality and the time of year. Wang Yeh are often worshiped together in groups of three or five.

While the Wang Yeh are worshiped mainly by those originally from Fujian Province, the San Shan Kuo-wang 三山國王, literally, the Three Kings of the Mountains, are revered by Chinese of Hakka descent (an ethnic and linguistic subset of Han Chinese culture). Legendary stories surrounding

the two groups of deities are similar, the only difference being that the San Shan Kuo-wang originated from the worship of mountains. With the outward spread of Hakka Chinese from the Hsinchu and Miaoli areas throughout Taiwan, the three gods have been separated and are often worshiped individually instead of as a group.

Meanwhile, traditional magical calculations, such as geomancy 風水 and physiognomy 看相, are not only still in fashion, they are also changing with the times. Forecasts based on magical calculations are made to strike it rich in the stock market.

I-kuan Tao

The Chinese words I-kuan Tao 一貫道 can be roughly translated as the Religion of One Unity. The name belies I-kuan Tao's nature as a religious doctrine that draws upon both traditional Chinese teachings and each of the world's major religions. I-kuan Tao is a modern, syncretic faith, and the third most popular religion in Taiwan.

According to I-kuan Tao adherents, this religion attempts to identify common principles underlying Taoism, Buddhism, Christianity, Islam, Judaism, and Hinduism. I-kuan Tao faithful believe that by uncovering a single set of universal truths, the "increasing chaos" of modern times can be defeated and the world can live peacefully in harmony. They believe in a God beyond all other gods, called Ming-ming Shang-ti 明明上帝 (the God of Clarity).

I-kuan Tao evolved from Hsien-tien Tao 先天道, which was founded by Huang Te-hui 黃德輝 of the Ching dynasty (during the Shun-chih period, which lasted from 1644 to 1661). Huang Te-hui combined the three main belief systems of China with the belief in the *Wu-Sheng Lao-Mu* 無生老母 ("Lifeless Old Mother") deity to form the Hsien-tien Tao.

As a religion, I-kuan Tao was highly accessible to Chinese. One reason for its rapid spread throughout China over the years was that, although I-kuan Tao claimed to be a universal religion, its basic writings, forms of religious observance, and moral precepts were all couched in traditional Chinese terms. By drawing heavily on Confucian, Buddhist, Taoist, and folk religious terminology, I-kuan Tao was readily understandable in traditional Chinese religious terms. Consequently, however, it was less appealing to non-Chinese.

To some extent, this still holds true today. While I-kuan Tao boasts large numbers of faithful in Australia, Canada, the United States, South Africa, France, Italy, and elsewhere, it is widely embraced only by the overseas Chinese communities in these countries, and only limited fragments of I-kuan Tao scripture have been translated into non-Chinese languages.

I-kuan Tao adherents more or less follow the rituals of Confucianism and engage in ancestor worship. Services are usually held at family shrines and are aimed at both cultivating personal character and regulating family relations—two key concepts in Chinese culture. By 1998, there were 31,108 large or medium-sized I-kuan Tao temples in Taiwan with some 2,257 temple priests serving approximately 983,000 believers. By increasing the number of I-kuan Tao temples, the faithful believe they are bringing the Buddhist "Western Paradise" to earth and creating a world of brotherhood and universal love as envisioned by Confucian teachings.

The goodness of personal sublimation and the grace of a life of service are key tenets in the I-kuan Tao moral scheme, and adherents devote a great deal of resources to social work. In Taiwan, there are 4 I-kuan Tao seminaries, 34 kindergartens, 4 retirement homes, 21 hospitals, 8 clinics, 30 publishing houses, and 32 publications. This service ethic is closely related to the order's tradition that each believer should "give his heart to the universe and contribute his life to humanity."

In the 40-some years since it was brought to Taiwan, I-kuan Tao has established many cultural and educational units. These units train an average of 10,000 I-kuan Tao devotees each year. Over half of the vegetarian restaurants around the island are run by I-kuan Tao adherents, who are required to follow a strict vegetarian diet.

Proselytism of I-kuan Tao has not always been such an open matter. Indeed, I-kuan Tao teachings incorporate a tradition of secrecy inherited from the various clandestine religious sects that have thrived during periods of chaos in Chinese history.

In their day-to-day lives, I-kuan Tao followers strive to uphold the precepts of not killing, stealing, committing adultery, lying, or drinking alcohol, while putting into practice the I-kuan Tao ideals of benevolence, righteousness, courtesy, wisdom, and faith.

Other Independent Religions

There are several other independent religions in Taiwan that generally fall into one of the following four categories: religions brought to Taiwan from the Chinese mainland; religions brought in from foreign countries; new religions developed from existing ones; and new religions created in Taiwan.

Included in the first category are Chai Chiao 齋教, Hsia Chiao 夏教 (Chai Chiao and Hsia Chiao are not recognized by the ROC government as religions), Li-ism, and Tien Te Chiao 天德教. Chai Chiao entered Taiwan during the 17th century, and is divided into three major schools: Lung Hua 龍華, Chin Chuang 金幢, and Hsien Tien 先天 (a forerunner to I-kuan Tao). It is a modified form of Buddhism combined with elements of Confucianism, Taoism, and folk beliefs. Chai Chiao adherents worship Buddha and the goddess Kuanyin. As vegetarians who neither shave their heads nor don the monk's robes, they worship in the home, thus giving Chai Chiao the common title "Lay Buddhism." During the Japanese occupation of Taiwan, the group joined the Soto sect of Buddhism to escape Japanese suppression, and the religion greatly declined as a result.

Hsia Chiao was founded by Lin Chao-en 林兆恩 in the 16th century, and was brought to Taiwan during the Japanese occupation. When praying, adherents burn four incense sticks—instead of the usual folk practice of burning three—to venerate Confucius, Lao Tzu, the Buddha, and the founder of the religion. Hsia Chiao has three temples and several hundred followers.

Li-ism (doctrine of order) was founded by Yang Lai-ju 楊來如 in the 17th century. Its creed stresses traditional Chinese morals and ethics, such as the loyalty and filial piety of Confucianism, the world salvation and forgiveness of Buddhism, and the natural way and inaction of Taoism. It is, in fact, the synthesis of Confucianism, Buddhism, and Taoism given a new dimension by the worship of Kuanyin. Though Li-ists worship Kuanyin, they do not reject deities of other religions. They believe the providence may be revealed in the form of other deities and prophets. Li-ists abide by the great law of Li-ism called *Fa Pao Tieh Wen* 法寶牒文 (precious and official decrees), written by Yang.

Some Li-ist clergy came to Taiwan from the Chinese mainland in 1949. The Association of Li-ism 中華理教總會 was officially reestablished in Taiwan in 1950, with headquarters in Taipei. Today, Li-ism has spread to Korea, the United States, Hong Kong, Japan, and the Philippines. In 1952, Sheng-li College 聖理書院 was established for Li-ists to study the classics. Today, there are nearly 631 Li-ist clergy in 129 temples islandwide serving about 168,000 adherents. There are also 4 Li-ist seminaries, 3 kindergartens, 14 institutes for Li-ist proselytizing, 6 clinics and 1 publishing house. Adherents enthusiastically provide the needy with relief in winter, free medication, and scholarships.

Tien Te Chiao was founded in 1923 in China by a young shaman, Hsiao Chang-ming 蕭昌明, now known to his followers as the "celestial worthy." Tien Te Chiao is a synthesis of the two major religio-philosophical traditions of China—Confucianism and Taoism—and three world religions—Buddhism, Christianity, and Islam. Adherents are required to strictly follow 20 principles: loyalty, forbearance, honesty, openness, virtue, uprightness, righteousness, faith, endurance, fairness, universal love, filial piety, benevolence, kindness, consciousness, moral integrity, frugality, truth, courtesy, and harmony. Tien Te Chiao adherents also practice various methods of self-cultivation, health preservation, and psychic healing. They are trained to tap acupuncture points to cure ailments. Believers learn to meditate under the guidance of their masters in order to search for their original being, which is free and untainted from worldly ties and yearnings.

Since Tien Te Chiao was introduced into Taiwan in 1953, worship and medical service centers have been set up throughout Taiwan. Tien Te Chiao was officially recognized by the government in 1989. By 1998, there were 5 Tien Te Chiao temples and 31 masters for its more than 200,000 believers in Taiwan. Members must be at least 20 years of age. There are also 22 institutes for Tien Te Chiao proselytizing, 2 Tien Te Chiao libraries, 1 publishing house and 3 publications.

Religions from Abroad

Foreign religious groups in Taiwan include Baha'i, Judaism, and Tenrikyo (Islam and the various sects of Christianity are discussed separately later in this chapter).

The first Taiwan convert to the Baha'i faith was an overseas student in the United States in 1949. An Iranian husband-wife team came from mainland China in 1954 to do pioneer work and established Taiwan's first Baha'i center in Tainan. There are currently about 16,000 Baha'i followers, 2 Baha'i places of worship, 60 foreign missionaries, and 1 publishing house to help serve the faithful in Taiwan. The local Baha'i headquarters, the National Spiritual Assembly of the Baha'is of Taiwan 財團法人巴哈伊教臺灣總靈體會, is located in Taipei.

Baha'i communities all over the world target urgent social issues in each region. In Taiwan, the local Baha'i assemblies have singled out environmental protection as their main area of social concern. Since 1990, the Baha'i community has launched joint projects with government organizations to promote environmental education amongst kindergarten and elementary school teachers around the country. Baha'i teams visit schools all over Taiwan, organizing simulation games designed to teach basic environmental principles. The Baha'i community has produced 30-odd radio programs and a videotape on environmental issues, as well as published a book on environmental education in collaboration with the Homemakers' Union and Foundation 主婦聯盟環保基金會.

Jews from Persia and other areas began to settle in China about 1,000 years ago during the Tang dynasty. Thriving communities developed in many large cities, but particularly in Kaifeng 開封, which became the center of Chinese Jewish life. Due to gradual assimilation, however, these communities had virtually disappeared by the middle of the 19th century. During the 20th century, China again received an influx of Jews, this time refugees from persecution in Europe— first from Russia, and later from eastern European countries taken over by the Nazis. The largest groups of Jews settled in Harbin in Manchuria and in Shanghai; however, after World War II, most of this population moved to the West due to the communist threat in China.

Today, the small Taiwan Jewish community of about 40 families consists of expatriates (mainly Americans, but also Israelis and Europeans) who are either long-term Taipei residents or assigned here on tours of duty by multinational corporations, academic institutions, or international organizations. The community is affiliated with the Asia-Pacific Jewish Association based in Australia. Activities include religious observances, religious instruction for children, holiday celebrations, and cultural events. Most activities are held in a community center maintained in the Tienmu 天母 district of Taipei.

Tenrikyo 天理教 was founded in Japan in 1838 by a farm woman, Miki Nakayama. The religion was first introduced into Taiwan during the period of Japanese occupation. The doctrine of Tenrikyo stresses respect for ancestors, filial piety, self-cultivation, and service to mankind, and thus resembles traditional Chinese ethics and the concept of universal brotherhood. The religion was therefore readily accepted in Taiwan, continued to develop, and was formally recognized by the Ministry of the Interior in 1973. As of 1998, there were 150 Tenrikyo temples and 32 foreign clergymen serving 23,000 believers in Taiwan, with 3 publications.

Mahikarikyo 眞光教 was founded in 1959 by Yosikazu Okata, a former Japanese army officer. It was registered with the Ministry of the Interior on April 8, 1996, under the title of Foundation Corporation Taiwan General Meeting of Funds for Mahikari Organization 財團法人眞光教團臺灣總會基金會. Supervised by the above organization, as of 1998 Mahikarikyo had 10 clergymen and 7 foreign clergymen, 9 institutes for proselytizing, and 1,000 believers in Taiwan. Mahikarikyo advocates respect for nature, love among human beings, and spiritual purification through religious teachings.

New Extensions

A large number of new religions in Taiwan were developed on the basis of previously existing ones. The main representatives of this group are Confucian Spirit Religion 儒宗神教 and Tienti Chiao 天帝教. Both religions practice spiritual and psychic healing.

Instead of temples or churches, the Confucian Spirit Religion has "phoenix halls" 鳳廳 in which "phoenix writing" is created by means of "spirit writing." The central deity in these phoenix halls is the Jade Emperor 玉皇大帝. Other deities vary from hall to hall, and include such figures as the warrior Kuan Yu 關羽 and Prime Minister Kung Ming 孔明 from the Period of the Three Kingdoms. Although not all phoenix halls belong to the same organization, they remain in frequent contact with one another and occasionally work together.

Tienti Chiao was founded by Li Yu-chieh 李玉階 in the mid-1980s after he split with Tien Te Chiao. The doctrines of Tienti Chiao emphasize the cultivation of one's moral self, and it has "20 True Words" 二十字眞言 that serve as "required daily homework" for its followers. Believers in Tienti Chiao are especially concerned about nuclear war. Since its founding, Tienti Chiao has established 54 temples with 133 clergymen. These temples are concentrated mainly in Taipei, Taichung, Tainan, Pingtung and Hualien. It currently claims a following of 212,000 believers in Taiwan. The religious group has five foreign clergymen, two seminaries, one university, one kindergarten, two institutes for proselytizing, one library, and two publishing houses. Temples have also been opened overseas in Los Angeles and San Francisco, USA.

Religions Founded in Taiwan

Few religions fall into the fourth category of new religions founded in Taiwan. A typical example is Hsuan-yuan Chiao 軒轅教, which was formally founded in Taiwan in 1957 by 82-year-old legislator Wang Han-sheng 王寒生. Hsuan-yuan Chiao attempts to raise people's sense of nationalism and to organize and unite the religious thoughts of China over the ages, including Confucianism, Taoism, and Mohism. Its main creed is respect for heaven and ancestors. Hsuan-yuan Chiao is named after the ancient legendary founder of the Chinese nation, whose name was Hsuan-yuan.

The religion was inspired by Wang's grief over the loss of the Chinese mainland to the Chinese communists. Wang attributed the loss primarily to the absence of national spirit, which could only be restored by a renewal of Chinese culture. Hsuan-yuan Chiao is an attempt to revive national spirit through an unnamed religion that dates from Hsuan-yuan to the Western Han dynasty. The religion inherits orthodox Chinese traditions from Hsuan-yuan to Dr. Sun Yat-sen. Adherents abide by the principles set forth in the Hsuan-yuan Chiao scriptures, the *Huang Ti Ching* 黃帝經.

Hsuan-yuan Chiao affirms the existence of a creator who can be identified as the "Tao" or Way. Hsuan-yuan Chiao holds that man can become divine through self-cultivation and enlightenment in the Tao. The highest state attainable in the new religion is "the union of heaven and man" where "the self is denied and yet is omnipresent." This progress can only be accomplished through self-purification, cultivation of illustrious virtues, and helping others to achieve salvation.

As of 1998, Hsuan-yuan Chiao had 18 temples and 109 clergy serving 136,000 believers, 1 seminary, 1 retirement home, 8 institutes for proselytizing, 3 clinics and 1 publishing house.

Christianity

Christianity came to Taiwan with the Dutch in 1624. The first missionary in Taiwan was Georgius Candidius of the Reformed Church of Holland. Six Ping-pu 平埔 aborigine communities near modern day Tainan were the center of his mission activities. (The Ping-pu tribe was later assimilated by Han settlers.) Robert Bunius continued Candidius' mission work in southern Taiwan, where he lived for 14 years. By 1643, over 6,000 aborigines had been converted to Christianity. Mass conversions were typical of his evangelistic style.

In 1626, a Spaniard, Father Martinez, in the company of Spanish troops, brought with him four Dominican missionaries from the Philippines to the Keelung 基隆 and Tamsui 淡水 areas to do mission work. The Spanish army occupied a portion of northern Taiwan, and ruled there for 16 years. Missionaries actively spread Roman Catholicism at this time, during which they won approximately 4,000 aborigines over to their faith.

In 1642, the Dutch forces occupying southern Taiwan pushed northward to rout the Spaniards, arresting them and driving them out of Taiwan. It is not known what became of the Roman Catholic converts, since no trace of them was to be found. All that remains from this period of Roman Catholic missionary activity are a few historical records. By the time the Chinese general Koxinga 國姓爺 drove the Dutch off the island, this scantily documented page in the history of Christianity in Taiwan had more or less come to an end. By the year 1714, when the Roman Catholic Jesuits came to Taiwan for map-making, they found a few descendants of these early Christians who had still preserved some remnants of their forebears' beliefs. In 1859, the Spanish Dominican Father Fernando Sainz and Father Angel Bofurull arrived in Kaohsiung from the Philippines via Amoy, and founded the first Roman Catholic church in Kaohsiung, the Holy Rosary Church 玫瑰聖母堂. Father Sainz later conducted mission work in the Kaohsiung, Tainan, and Pingtung areas. In 1861, he founded the Immaculate Conception Church in what today is Wanchin Village 萬金村 in Wanluan 萬巒. This is the oldest extant Roman Catholic church in Taiwan.

Catholic missions operate many elderly care centers around the island.

In 1860, British missionaries Reverend Carstairs Douglas and Reverend H.L. Mackenzie came to Tamsui and Mengchia 艋舺, now called Wanhua 萬華, in Taipei to preach the gospel. In 1864, Dr. James L. Maxwell was officially sent to Taiwan by the English Presbyterian Mission to preach Christianity. With Tainan as his base, he concentrated his efforts in southern Taiwan. In 1872, the Canadian Presbyterian Church dispatched George L. Mackay to northern Taiwan to do mission work, choosing Tamsui as his center.

Prior to the Japanese occupation of Taiwan in 1895, there were 97 Protestant churches, 4,854 believers, about 90 mission workers, and 13 foreign missionaries in Taiwan. During the period of Japanese occupation, the colonial government exercised control over churches and had them absorb Japanese Christian groups. The Japanese also strictly forbade Christian mission work among the aborigines. When the Japanese left in 1945, Taiwan had about 238 Protestant churches and 60,000 believers.

Roman Catholicism also experienced a relatively slow development during the Japanese occupation. Some theorize that this was due to suppression by the Japanese colonial government; however, there is no concrete evidence to support this. By 1945, there were only about 10,000 Roman Catholics (some records report 8,000), 52 churches or missions, and 20 missionaries in Taiwan.

Christianity in Taiwan developed in a new direction after the mainland fell to communism and the central government relocated to Taiwan in 1949. Churches of numerous denominations flocked to Taiwan, and the number of Christian denominations active in Taiwan went from just three in 1945 to approximately 40 in 1955.

Taiwan's Protestant churches experienced rapid growth between 1950 and 1964, but after the mid-1960s, they entered a phase of sluggish and even negative growth. By 1998, the congregation had expanded to approximately 423,000 with nearly 2,683 churches, 2,554 ministers and 1,109 foreign ministers.

Roman Catholicism made a remarkable comeback in Taiwan after retrocession. In 1948, the number of believers stood at 13,000. When the central government moved to Taiwan in 1949, multitudes of Roman Catholic clergy and believers followed, infusing Roman Catholicism in Taiwan with new strength and vigor. The number of converts grew rapidly in the 1953-1963 period, going from 27,000 to 300,000. The number of practicing Roman Catholics peaked in 1969, when the total reached nearly 306,000, and seven dioceses were formed: the Taipei archdiocese, and the Hsinchu, Taichung, Chiayi, Tainan, Kaohsiung, and Hualien dioceses. Since then, the Roman Catholic church of Taiwan has faced a period of stagnancy.

On January 18, 1998, Bishop Paul Shan 單國璽 of the Catholic diocese in Kaohsiung was appointed to the status of cardinal by Pope John Paul II. Shan officially assumed this position on February 21, when the College of Cardinals congregated at the Vatican. Shan is the only Taiwanese to be conferred the title of cardinal in the past 20 years and is the fifth Chinese cardinal in the history of the Roman Catholic Church. The last cardinal from Taiwan was Cardinal Yu Pin, who was elevated to cardinal status in Nanjing before he relocated to Taiwan in 1950.

Among the leading schools founded by the Catholic church in Taiwan are Fu Jen University 輔仁大學, the Cardinal Tien School of Nursing & Midwifery 耕莘高級護理助產職業學校, the Blessed Imelda's School 靜修女子高級中學, the Kuangjen middle and primary schools, the Providence University 靜宜大學, the Taichung Viator High School 臺中市私立衛道高級中學, and the Wentsao Ursuline Junior College of Modern Languages 文藻外國語文專科學校. As of 1998, there were some 793 Catholic churches, 1,834 clergymen, and 652 foreign missionaries in Taiwan serving about 304,000 believers.

While mainstream Protestant churches and the Roman Catholic Church have enjoyed a head start in their evangelical work, independent churches are also growing consistently by emphasizing fundamentalist theology, flexible administration, and self-supporting financial power. Popular independent churches include the True Jesus Church, the Mandarin Church 國語禮拜堂, and the Ling Leung Church 靈糧堂.

The first missionaries from the Church of Jesus Christ of Latter Day Saints, also known as the Mormon Church, arrived in Taiwan in 1956. By 1963, the book of the Mormon Church had been translated from English into Chinese by Hu Wei-I

胡唯一, and a branch of the Mormon Church had been established locally. Since then, the Mormon gospel has been spread to even the most remote reaches of Taiwan. Today the Mormon Church has a local membership of more than 26,000 members.

Some 390 full-time Mormon missionaries, including 44 locals, are proselytizing and performing community services in Taiwan. In Taipei alone, there are 147 full-time missionaries, and 145 in Taichung and 139 in Kaohsiung. In most areas, foreign missionaries also offer free English conversation classes to the public, and a handful of full-time church workers provide assistance to those in need. Although assisted by a steady rotation of foreign missionaries, all Mormon churches in Taiwan are headed by local Chinese leaders.

The Jehovah's Witnesses came to Taiwan in 1950 and registered with the Ministry of the Interior in 1964. As of December 1998, they had 53 congregations around the island, with 60 foreign missionaries and more than 3,500 faithful.

The Unification Church, registered as the Holy Spirit Association for the Unification of World Christianity 財團法人世界基督教統一神靈協會, came to Taiwan in 1971. At present, there are 31 congregations with more than 50,000 believers in the Taiwan area. In November 1997, 336 couples from Taiwan participated in a mass wedding of 3.6 million couples conducted by the Rev. Sun Myung Moon. The main ceremony was held in Washington, D.C. and conducted via satellite. Blessing '98, in which 120 million married couples reaffirmed their marriage vows, was held on June 13, 1998, at Madison Square Garden in New York City with the Rev. Sun Myung Moon and several world religious leaders presiding. Six hundred and twenty-three unwed youths from Taiwan participated in this event.

Christian missions, along with their evangelical intent, have contributed to Taiwan's education and social work as well. The Roman Catholic Church has been very successful in Taiwan. As of 1998, it operated 3 universities, 1 seminary, 36 high schools, 10 elementary schools, 199 kindergartens, 10 retirement homes, 3 rehabilitation centers, 21 centers for the mentally retarded, 4 handicapped welfare institutions, 1 institute for spreading church teachings, 12 hospitals, and 15 clinics.

The Protestants are involved with 40 seminaries, 10 universities, 9 colleges, 8 high schools, 11 elementary schools, 46 kindergartens, 4 nurseries, 3 orphanages, 4 retirement homes, 2 rehabilitation centers, 2 centers for the mentally retarded, 4 handicapped welfare institutes, 15 hospitals, 15 clinics, 4 libraries, and 78 publishing houses producing 52 publications.

Various international Christian organizations have established branches in Taiwan. Working with local groups that have sprung up, these organizations provide a network of welfare and social services to various target groups in society. World Vision of Taiwan 臺灣世界展望會 has been instrumental in providing aboriginal and child welfare; Campus Crusade and Navigators are active on college campuses; the Garden of Hope Foundation 勵馨基金會 runs halfway houses for teenage prostitutes; Mackay Counseling Center 馬偕協談中心 offers family and psychological counseling services; and Cathwel Service 財團法人天主教未婚媽媽之家 and Christian Salvation Service provide assistance for unwed mothers.

Islam

The troops that Koxinga led to Taiwan in the mid-17th century included a number of Muslims. Some of them made Taiwan their permanent home, leaving historical traces which are still visible in Lukang 鹿港 and Tamsui, among other places. By the time of Taiwan's retrocession to China, however, most of the descendants of these early Mohammedan soldiers no longer embraced Islam; at best, only a few Islamic burial traditions were still observed.

Approximately 20,000 Muslims accompanied the central government to Taiwan in 1949; most were soldiers, civil servants, or food service workers. Two Muslim organizations reestablished themselves in Taiwan to preach Islamic doctrines and build mosques: the Chinese Muslim Association 中國回教協會 and the Chinese Muslim Youth League 中國回教青年會.

Differences in everyday habits and customs—such as food and drink or religious ceremonies and activities—led to diminished contact between Muslims and Han Chinese in Taiwan during the 1950s. Believers in Islam depended to a large extent on a liaison network that regularly met in a house on Lishui Street 麗水街 in Taipei. By the 1960s, realizing that return to the mainland would not be likely in the immediate future, Muslims in Taiwan began to engage in permanent occupations. Although there was still a considerable degree of interdependence in the Islamic community, Muslims began, primarily out of professional need, to have increasingly frequent contact with Han Chinese.

Limited by a non-Muslim environment, Muslims in Taiwan today struggle to observe orthodox Islamic practices. Only a few Muslim women have adopted the traditional veil; and a handful of halal butchers and restaurants prepare meat according to the strict Islamic food observances. The busy urban lifestyle in the cities poses many constraints. For example, it is virtually impossible to keep the Islamic Sabbath, which falls on Fridays, or to faithfully perform the salat, a set of prayers repeated five times a day. In addition, all prayers are conducted in Arabic, which means that every adherent must master the language despite cultural and linguistic constraints.

Three new Arabian-style mosques, constructed in Kaohsiung, Taichung, and Lungkang 龍崗, have recently joined Taipei's two mosques in meeting the needs of Muslim faithful. These new facilities cost a total of US$2.7 million, half of which was funded by overseas donations, predominantly from the Middle East.

The Taipei Grand Mosque, on the verge of being demolished several times because of disputes over land deeds, is now recognized as Taipei City's first religious heritage site after being surveyed by academics and scholars. The mosque will be preserved where it stands.

As of 1998, Taiwan was home to a Muslim population of approximately 53,000, including 33 Mullahs, 6 mosques, 5 libraries, 1 foreign Mullah, and 1 publishing house with 4 publications.

Further Reading

(in Chinese unless otherwise noted):

Cheng, Chih-ming 鄭志明. *Tai-wan te tsung-chiao yu mi-mi chiao-pai* 臺灣的宗教與秘密教派 (Religions and Clandestine Religious Sects of Taiwan). Taipei: Tai-uain Publishing Co., 1991.

Chiang, I-cheng 姜義鎮, comp. *Tai-wan te min-chien hsin-yang* 臺灣的民間信仰 (Folk Beliefs of Taiwan), 3rd ed. Taipei: Woolin Publishing Co., Ltd., 1990.

Chien-lung Chu-shih 潛龍居士. *Chung-kuo min-chien chu-shen chuan* 中國民間諸神傳 (Stories of the Folk Gods of China). Taipei: Chuan Yuan Publishing Co., 1992.

Chu, Hai-yuan 瞿海源. *Tai-wan ti-chu Min-chung te tsung-chiao hsin-yang yu tsung-chiao tai-tu* 臺灣地區民眾的宗教信仰與宗教態度 (Religious Beliefs and Religious Attitudes of People in the Taiwan Area). *Pien-chien-chung te tai-wan she-hui* 變遷中的臺灣社會 (Taiwan Society in Transition) ed. by Yang, Kuo-shu 楊國樞 and Chu, Hai-yuan. Taipei: Institute of Ethnology, Academia Sinica, 1987.

Fang, Li-tien 方立天. *Chung-kuo fo-chiao yu chuan-tung wen-hua* 中國佛教與傳統文化 (Traditional Culture and Chinese Buddhism). Taipei: Laureate Book Co., Ltd., 1990.

I-kuan Tao chien-chieh 一貫道簡介 (Introduction to I-kuan Tao). Tainan: Tien Jiuh Book Store, 1988.

Nan, Huai-chin 南懷瑾. *Tao-chiao mi-tsung yu tung-fang shen-mi-hsueh* 道教密宗與東方神祕學 (Tantric Religions of Taoism and Oriental Mystic Study). Vols. I & II, 7th ed. Taipei: Lao Ku Cultural Foundation Inc., 1990.

Ping, Chuan-chang 平川彰 (Hsu, Ming-yin 許明銀, tr). *Fo-chiao yen-chiu ju-men* 佛教研究入門 (An Introduction to the Study of Buddhism). Taipei: Dharma-tatha, 1990.

Religions in the Republic of China (in English). 4th ed. Taipei: Kwang Hwa Publishing Co., 1991.

Tsung-chiao chien-chieh 宗教簡介 (Introduction to Religion). Taipei: Ministry of the Interior, 1991.

Yao, Li-hsiang 姚麗香. *Tai-wan te tzu-szu yu tsung-chiao* 臺灣的祠祀與宗教 (Worship and Religion in Taiwan). 2nd ed. Taipei: Taiwan Publishing Co., 1990.

Yang, Sen-fu 楊森富. *Chung-kuo chi-tu-chiao shih* 中國基督教史 (The History of Christianity in China). Taipei: The Commercial Press Ltd., 1991.

中國輸出入銀行
The Export-Import Bank
of the Republic of China

A SPECIALIZED BANK
THAT OFFERS

Medium-And Long-Term Loan
For Purchase of
Machinery, Equipment And
Turnkey Plants From The ROC

Our low-interest loans with repayment periods of up to seven years make it easy for overseas buyers to procure machinery, equipment and turnkey plants from the ROC.

Head Office	8th Fl., 3 Nan Hai Road. Taipei, Taiwan, R.O.C. Tel: (02)2321-0511 Fax: (02)2394-0630 Tlx: (02)26044
Kaohsiung Branch	8th Fl., 74, Chung Cheng 2nd Road, Kaohsiung, R.O.C. Tel: (07) 224-1921 Fax: (07)224-1928
Taichung Branch	5th Fl., 1-18, Sec. 2, Tai Chung Kan Road, Taichung, R.O.C. Tel: (04) 322-5756 Fax: (04)322-5755
Taipei Branch	2F-2A15, 5 Hsinyi Rd., Sec. 5, Taipei, R.O.C. Tel: (02) 8780-0181 Fax: (02)2723-5131
Representative Office in Jakarta	Wisma Dharmala Sakti 11th Fl., Ji Jendral Sudirman No. 32 Jarkarta Indonesia Tel: 6621-5704320, 6621-5701136 Fax: 6621-5704321
Representative Office in Budapest	7th Fl., Karoly Korut 11, 1075 Budapest, Hungary Tel:361-2697893, 361-2697894 Fax: 361-2697895

Who's Who
in the ROC

Who's Who in the ROC
Abbreviations Used

AARRO	Afro-Asian Rural Reconstruction Organization
Acad.	Academy; Academic; Academia
Acct.	Accountant; Accounting
Add.	Address
Adm.	Admiral
Admin.	Administration; Administrative; Administrator
Adv.	Advisor; Advisory
AEAR	See TECROJ
AEC	Atomic Energy Council, Executive Yuan
Aff.	Affairs
Affi.	Affiliation
Agr.	Agriculture; Agricultural
Alt.	Alternate
Am.	America(n)
Amb.	Ambassador
APACL	See APLFD
APLFD	Asian Pacific League for Freedom and Democracy (Known as Asian Pacific Anti-Communist League, APACL, before Apr. 1, 1991)
APPU	Asian-Pacific Parliamentarians' Union
Apt.	Apartment
Ass.	Assembly
Assc.	Associate(d)
Assn.	Association(s)
Asst.	Assistant(s)
b.	born
B.	Bachelor
BA	Bachelor of Arts
BBA	Bachelor of Business Administration
BCC	Broadcasting Corporation of China
BCE	Bachelor of Civil Engineering
BCiS	Bachelor of Civil Science
BCoS	Bachelor of Commercial Science
Bd.	Board
BD	Bachelor of Divinity
BEE	Bachelor of Electrical Engineering
BFA	Bachelor of Fine Arts
BJ	Bachelor of Journalism
Bk.	Bank(s); Book(s)
Bldg.	Building
B.Lit.	Bachelor of Literature; Bachelor of Letters
Bn.	Battalion
BPS(BPs)	Bachelor of Political Science (or Politics)
Br.	Branch
Brig.	Brigade; Brigadier

BS	Bachelor of Science
BSA	Bachelor of Science in Agronomy
BSE	Bachelor of Science in Education
BSEE	Bachelor of Science in Electrical Engineering
B.Th.	Bachelor of Theology
Bu.	Bureau
c.	child; children
CAC	Central Advisory Committee
Calif.	California
Can.	Canada; Canadian
CAPD	See COA
Capt.	Captain
CBC	Central Bank of China
CC	Central Committee
CCA	Council for Cultural Affairs, Executive Yuan (Known as Council for Cultural Planning and Development, Executive Yuan, CCPD, before July 16, 1995)
CCoun.	City Council
CCNAA	Coordination Council of North American Affairs (Known as TECO/TECRO after Oct. 10, 1994)
CCPD	Council for Cultural Planning and Development, Executive Yuan (See CCA)
CDN	Central Daily News
CEC	Central Executive Committee
CElC	Central Election Commission, Executive Yuan
Cent.	Center; Central
CEO	Chief Executive Officer
CEPD	Council for Economic Planning and Development, Executive Yuan
Cert.	Certificate(s)
CETRA	China External Trade Development Council
CFD	Central Finance Department
CG	Commanding General
CGSC	Command and General Staff College
Ch.	Chinese; China
Chem.	Chemistry; Chemical
Chmn.	Chairman
CIECD	Council for International Economic Cooperation and Development
C-in-C	Commander-in-Chief
CITC	Committee of International Technical Cooperation, Executive Yuan
CLA	Council of Labor Affairs, Executive Yuan

Cmd.	Command		DE	Doctor of Engineering
Cmdg.	Commanding		DGBAS	Directorate General of Budget, Accounting & Statistics, Executive Yuan
Cmdr.	Commander			
Cmdt.	Commandant		Def.	Defense
Cml.	Commercial		Del.	Delegate; Delegation
CNA	Central News Agency		Dem.	Democrat(ic); Democracy
CNRRA	Chinese National Relief and Rehabilitation Administration		Dep.	Deputy
			Dept.	Department; Departmental
Co.	Company		Dev.	Development(al); Developing
COA	Council of Agriculture, Executive Yuan (Known as Council for Agricultural Planning and Development, Executive Yuan, CAPD, before Sept. 20, 1984; Also known as Joint Commission on Rural Reconstruction, JCRR, before Mar. 16, 1979)		Dip.	Diplomat(ic); Diplomacy
			Dir.	Director(s)
			Dist.	District
			Disting.	Distinguished
			Div.	Division
			D.Lit.	Doctor of Literature; Doctor of Letters
CoCoun.	County Council		DMS	Doctor of Medical Science
Col.	Colonel		DOH	Department of Health, Executive Yuan
Coll.	College		DPP	Democratic Progressive Party
Com.	Commerce; Commission		DPS(DPs)	Doctor of Political Science (or Politics)
Comm(s).	Communication(s)		Dr.	Doctor(al); Doctorate
Comr.	Commissioner		Dr.PH	Doctor of Public Health or Public Hygiene
concur.	concurrently		D.Sc.	Doctor of Science
Conf.	Conference(s)		DSEE	Doctor of Science in Electrical Engineering
Cong.	Congress		E.	East
Consl.	Consulate; Consular		Ea.	Eastern
Const.	Constitution(al); Constituency		ECAFE	Economic Commission for Asia and the Far East
Corp.	Corporation(s); Corporate			
Corr.	Correspondent; Corresponding		Econ.	Economic(al); Economy; Economics
Coun.	Council; Councilor		Ed.	Editor; Editorial
Counsl.	Counselor		Ed.B.	Bachelor of Education
CPA	Central Personnel Administration, Executive Yuan		Ed.D.	Doctor of Education
			Ed.M.	Master of Education
CPC	Central Planning Committee		educ.	education(al)
CRC	Central Reform Committee		EE	Electrical Engineer (Engineering)
CRRA	Chinese Refugees Relief Association (Known as Free China Relief Association, FCRA, before Aug. 16, 1991)		Elec.	Electric; Electrical
			Elect.	Electronic(al); Electronics
			Emb.	Embassy
C/S	Chief-of-Staff		Eng.	England; English
CSC	Central Standing Committee		Engr.	Engineer; Engineering
CSF	Combined Service Forces		Ent.	Enterprise(s)
CTC	Central Trust of China		EPA	Environmental Protection Administration, Executive Yuan
CTS	Chinese Television System			
Cttee.	Committee		EPC	Economic Planning Council
CTV	China Television Company		Exam.	Examination
Cul.	Culture; Cultural		Exec.	Executive
CUSA	Council for United States Aid		FAO	United Nations Food and Agriculture Organization
CWAAL	Chinese Women's Anti-Aggression League			
d.	daughter(s)		FCRA	See CRRA
DCS	Doctor of Commercial Science		Fed.	Federation
DD	Doctor of Divinity		Fel.	Fellow; Fellowship(s)

FETC	Foreign Exchange and Trade Commission	MAC	Mainland Affairs Council, Executive Yuan
FETCC	Foreign Exchange and Trade Control Commission	Mach.	Machine(ry)
		Mag.	Magazine
Fl.	Floor	Magis.	Magistrate
For.	Foreign	Maj.	Major
Found.	Foundation	M.Arch.	Master in Architecture
GA	General Assembly	Math.	Mathematics; Mathematical
Gen.	General	MB	Bachelor of Medicine
Geog.	Geographic; Geography	MBA	Master of Business Administration
Geol.	Geology; Geological	MCE	Master of Civil Engineering
GHQ	General Headquarters	MCL	Master of Comparative Law
GIO	Government Information Office, Executive Yuan	MD	Doctor of Medicine
		Mech.	Mechanical; Mechanics; Mechanism
Gov.	Governor	Med.	Medical; Medicine
Govt.	Government	MEE	Master of Electrical Engineering
Grad.	Graduate; Graduated	Mem.	Member
Hist.	History; Historical	Metro.	Metropolitan
Hon.	Honor(able); Honorary	Mfg.	Manufacturing
Hosp.	Hospital	Mfr.	Manufacture; Manufacturer(s)
Hqs.	Headquarters	Mgr.	Manager
ICOM	International Council of Museums	Mil.	Military
Ind.	Industrial; Industry	Min.	Minister; Ministry
Info.	Information	MIT	Massachusetts Institute of Technology, USA
Ins.	Insurance	ML	Master of Laws
Insp.	Inspector	M.Lit.	Master of Literature; Master of Letters
Inst.	Institute; Institution(al)	MND	Ministry of National Defense, Executive Yuan
Instr.	Instructor	Mng.	Managing; Management
Int.	Interior	MOC	See MOTC
Intl.	International	MOE	Ministry of Education, Executive Yuan
JCRR	See COA	MOEA	Ministry of Economic Affairs, Executive Yuan
J.D.	Doctor of Jurisprudence	MOF	Ministry of Finance, Executive Yuan
Jour.	Journalism; Journalist; Journal(s)	MOFA	Ministry of Foreign Affairs, Executive Yuan
Jr.	Junior	MOI	Ministry of the Interior, Executive Yuan
Jud.	Judicial; Judiciary	MOJ	Ministry of Justice, Executive Yuan
KMT	Kuomintang	MOTC	Ministry of Transportation and Communications, Executive Yuan (Known as Ministry of Communications, Executive Yuan, MOC, before July 31, 1991)
Lab.	Laboratory		
Lang.	Language(s)		
Lectr.	Lecturer		
Legis.	Legislative; Legislator	MPA	Master of Public Administration
Lib.	Library; Librarian; Liberal	MPH	Master of Public Health
Lit.	Literature; Literary	MPS(MPs)	Master of Political Science (or Politics)
LHD	Doctor of Humanities	MS	Master of Science
LL.B.	Bachelor of Laws	MSEE	Master of Science in Electrical Engineering
LL.D.	Doctor of Laws	MTAC	Mongolian and Tibetan Affairs Commission, Executive Yuan
LL.M.	Master of Laws		
Lt.	Lieutenant	M.Th.	Master of Theology
Ltd.	Limited	Mun.	Municipal; Municipality
m.	married	N.	North
M.	Master	NA	National Assembly
MA	Master of Arts	Nat.	National(s)

NCCU	National Chengchi University	Regt.	Regiment
NCHU	National Chung Hsing University	Rel.	Relation(s)
NCKU	National Cheng Kung University	Rep.	Representative
NCTU	National Chiao Tung University	Repub.	Republic(an)
NCU	National Central University	Res.	Research; Researched
NMC	National Military Council	Resr.	Reseacher
No.	Number	Rev.	Revolution; Revolutionary
NP	New Party	Rm.	Room
Nr.	Northern	ROC	Republic of China
NSC	National Security Council	ROCAF	ROC Air Force
NScC	National Science Council, Executive Yuan	ROCN	ROC Navy
NTHU	National Tsing Hua University	Rwy.	Railway
NTNU	National Taiwan Normal University	S.	South
NTU	National Taiwan University	s.	son(s)
NUC	National Unification Council, Office of the President	Sc.	Science(s); Scientific
		Sch.	School
NYC	National Youth Commission, Executive Yuan	Sec.	Secretary; Security; Securities
OCAC	Overseas Chinese Affairs Commission, Executive Yuan	Sect.	Section
		SEF	Straits Exchange Foundation
Off.	Office; Officer(s)	Sess.	Session(s)
Op.	Operation(s)	S.J.D.	Doctor of Juridical Science
Org.	Organization	So.	Southern
Outsdg.	Outstanding	Soc.	Society; Social
Ovs.	Overseas	Sp.	Special; Specialist
PA	Public Administration	Spkr.	Speaker
PCRM	Planning Commission for the Recovery of Mainland China (was withdrawn in 1991)	Sr.	Senior
		St.	Saint; Street
PDAF	Provincial Department of Agriculture and Forestry	STAG	Science & Technology Advisory Group, Executive Yuan
Penn.	Pennsylvania	Sup.	Supervisor(y); Supervision
Pers.	Personnel	Supt.	Superintendent
Ph.D.	Doctor of Philosophy	TCG	Taipei City Government
Phys.	Physical; Physician; Physics	Tchr(s).	Teacher(s)
Pol.	Political; Politics	Tech.	Technical; Technician; Technology
PPRC	Political Party Review Commmittee, Ministry of the Interior (PPRC was under the auspices of the Executive Yuan before Sept. 1, 1992)	TECO	Taipei Economic & Cultural Office
		TECRO	Taipei Economic & Cultural Representative Office (Known as Coordination Council of North American Affairs, CCNAA, before Oct. 10, 1994)
Pres.	President		
Prin.	Principal		
Prod.	Product; Production	TECROJ	Taipei Economic and Culture Representative Office in Japan (Known as Tokyo Office, Association of East Asian Relation, AEAR, before May 30, 1992)
Prof.	Professor; Profession(al)		
Prog.	Program		
Prov.	Province; Provincial		
Pub.	Publisher; Publishing	Telecom.	Telecommunications
Publ.	Publication(s)	Tng.	Training
Recon.	Reconstruction; Reconnaissance	TPA	Taiwan Provincial Assembly
Rd.	Road	TPG	Taiwan Provincial Government
RDEC	Research, Development and Evaluation Commission, Executive Yuan	Trans.	Transportation; Transport
		Transl.	Translated; Translation
Regln.	Regulation(s)	TTV	Taiwan Television Enterprise Ltd.

TV	Television	V.	Vice
Twn.	Taiwanese; Taiwan, Republic of China	VAC	Veterans Affairs Commission, Executive Yuan (Known as Vocational Assistance Commission for Retired Servicemen, Executive Yuan, VACRS, before Jan. 1, 1997)
U.	University(-ies)		
UC-Berkly.	University of California-Berkeley, USA		
UCLA	University of California at Los Angeles, USA		
USAEC	United States Atomic Energy Commission	VACRS	See VAC
UN	United Nations	Voc.	Vocational
UNESCO	United Nations Educational, Scientific and Cultural Organization	Vol.	Volume(s)
		W.	West
UNGA	United Nations General Assembly	WACL	See WLFD
UNICEF	United Nations International Children's Emergency Fund	We.	Western
		WHA	World Health Assembly
UNIRO	United Nations International Refugee Organization	WHO	World Health Organization
		WLFD	World League for Freedom and Democracy (Known as World Anti-Communist League, WACL, before Apr. 1, 1991)
UNRRA	United Nations Relief and Rehabilitation Administration		
USA	United States of America	YMCA	Young Men's Christian Association
USSR	Union of the Soviet Socialist Republics	YWCA	Young Women's Christian Association

Who's Who in the ROC I

(The list and general profiles of the heads of Cabinet-level agencies in this section are based on information released before May 1, 2000. The latest information about Cabinet members can be obtained on-line at *http://www.gio.gov.tw*).

Sample I

[1] LEE, YUAN-TSEH 李遠哲
[2] Pres., Acad. Sinica 94-, Mem. 80-; **[3]** *b.* Twn. Nov. 29, '36; **[4]** *m.* Wu, Bernice; **[5]** 2 *s.*, 1 *d.;* **[6]** *educ.* BS, NTU 59; MS, NTHU 61; Ph.D., UC-Berkly. 65, Postdr. Fel. 65-67; **[7]** Res. Fel., Harvard U. 67-78; Asst. Prof., U. of Chicago 68-71, Assc. Prof. 71-72, Prof. 73-74; Fel., Am. Phys. Soc.; Mem., Nat. Acad. of Sc., USA, Am. Acad. Arts & Sc., & Am. Chem. Soc.; Prof. of Chem., UC-Berkly. 74-94; Nobel Prize in Chem. 86; Nat. Medal of Sc., White House, USA 86; Peter Debye Award for Phys. Chem., ACS 86; Faraday Medal 92; Nat. Policy Adv. to the Pres. 91-95. **[8]** *Publ.:* Numerous articles on chem. phys. to prof. jour.; **[9]** *Add.* Acad. Sinica, Nankang, Taipei.

Item

[1] Name
[2] Occupation
[3] Vital statistics
[4] Marriage
[5] Number of children
   or sons and daughters

[6] Education
[7] Experience
[8] Publication
[9] Address

AU, HO-NIEN 歐豪年
Artist; Prof., Ch. Cul. U. 70-, Chmn., Dept. of Fine Arts 83-; *b.* Kwangtung Aug. 6, '35; *m.* Chu, Moo-lan; *educ.* Ph.D., Ch. Acad.; Art exhibitions held at Nat. Museum of Hist. 68, 74, 78, 81, & 84; US Cul. Cent., Hong Kong 68; Nara Museum, Japan 76; San Jose Museum of Art, USA 76; Tokyo Cent. Museum of Art, Japan 77, 78, & 82; San Diego Museum of Art, USA 79; Spink Gallery, UK 84; Art Gallery of Greater Victoria, Can. 85; Fung Ping Shan Museum, U. of Hong Kong 87; Museum Cernuschi, Paris 90; Rijksmuseum Voor Volkenkunde, Leiden, Netherlands 90; Museum für Volkerkunde, Wien 90; Taipei City Arts Museum 90; Bersee-Museum, Bremen 91; Bomand Museum, Lelle, Germany 91. *Works:* 10 selections of works of art published by Nat. Museum of Hist. 78; Ni Cen Sha Co., Japan 82; Mitsukoshi Gallery, Japan 83; Art Bk. Co., ROC 84; Art Gallery of Greater Victoria 85; Fung Ping Shan Museum 87; GIO 89; Museum Cernuschi 90; Rijksmuseum Voor Volkenkunde 90; Pacific Cul. Found., ROC 91; *Add.* 9th Fl., 133 Sung Ping Rd., Taipei 110.

BAI, HSIU-HSIUNG 白秀雄
Dep. Mayor, Taipei City 94-; *b.* Twn. Sept. 27, '41; *m.* Han, Chu-teh; 1 *s.*, 2 *d.; educ.* LL.B. & LL.M., NCCU; Assc.

Prof., Dept. of Sociology, NCCU & Prof., Dept. of Soc. Work, Tunghai U. 71-81; Adv., Kaohsiung City Govt. 79-81, Dir., Bu. of Soc. Aff. 81-86; Dir., Bu. of Soc. Aff., TCG 86-93, & Dept. of Soc. Aff., MOI 93-94. *Publ.: Soc. Welfare in ROC* 80; *Soc. Work* 92; *Soc. Welfare Admin.* 93; *Welfare for the Aged* 96; *Social Admin.* 99; *Add.* 1 Shih Fu Rd., Taipei 110.

CHAI, CHOK-YUNG 蔡作雍
Mem. & Sr. Investigator, Inst. of Biomed. Sc., Acad. Sinica 82-; *b.* Canton Feb. 17, '28; *m.* Shih, J.Y.; 2 *s.,* 1 *d.; educ.* MD, Nat. Def. Med. Cent. (NDMC) 53; Ph.D., Columbia U. 66; Assc. Prof., NDMC 62-67; Visiting Assc. Prof., Columbia U. 68; Prof. & Chmn., Biophys. Dept., NDMC 68-75, Dean of Faculty 72-75, Dir. 75-82. *Publ.:* Over 160 papers on physiology & pharmacology in nat. & intl. sc. jour.; *Add.* 16 Alley 5, Lane 24, Ting Chou Rd., Sect. 3, Taipei 100.

CHAI, TRONG R. 蔡同榮
Mem., Legis. Yuan 93-; Chmn., Formosa TV 96-, & Found. for Plebiscite in Twn. 97-; *b.* Twn. June 13, '35; *m.* Chai, Lylian; 2 *d.; educ.* BS, NTU 58; MS, U. of Tennesee 62; DPS, U. of So. Calif. 69; Founding Pres., World United Formosans for Independence 70-71; Full Prof., City U. of New York 78-93; Chmn., Formosan Assn. for Public Aff. 82-83, & Assn. for Plebiscite in Twn. 92; *Publ.: Parliamentary Biweekly* 93-96; *Add.* 7 Fl.-7, 7 Tsingtao E. Rd., Taipei 100.

CHEN, CHAO-WEI
(See CHEN, REGIS C.W. 陳朝威)

CHAN, CHI-HSIEN
(See CHAN, CHI-SHEAN 詹啓賢)

CHAN, CHI-SHEAN 詹啓賢
Dir.-Gen., DOH 97-2000; Bd. Mem., Hosp. Assn. of the ROC 91-; *b.* Twn. July 9, '48; *m.* Lee, Lee-hung; 1 *s.,* 1 *d.; educ.* MD, Chungshan Med. & Dental Coll. 72; Chief Resident Surgeon, St. Raphael Hosp. (Yale U.) 75-77, & Mercy Catholic Med. Cent. (Jefferson Med. Coll.) 77-80; Attending Surgeon, Pomona Med. Cent. Hosp., USA 80-89, Chief, Dept. of Surgery 86-89; Bd. Mem., Pomona Health Found., USA 86-89; Supt., Chi-Mei Found. Hosp. 90-97; Pres., Non-govt. Hosp. & Clinics Assn., ROC 93-96; Mem., Nat. Health Insurance Adv. Bd., Exec. Yuan 96-97, & Evaluation Cttee., Dept. of Health, TPG 97; *Add.* 14th Fl., 100 Ai Kuo E. Rd., Taipei 100.

CHAN, HOU-SHENG 詹火生
Chmn., CLA 98-2000; Prof., NTU 88-; *b.* Feb. 10, '49; *m.* Ying, Chan; *educ.* BA, NTU 71; Sp. Diploma, Oxford U.

76; MS, Econ., Wales U. 77, Ph.D. 84; Visiting Assc. Prof., NTU 84-86, Assc. Prof. 86-88, Prof. 88-; Dir. & Prof., Grad. Inst. of Soc. Welfare, NCCU 89-90; Prof. & Chmn., Dept. & Grad. Inst. of Sociology, NTU 90-93; V. Chmn., CLA 95-97; Min. without Portfolio 97-98. *Publ.:* "Soc. Welfare in Twn." in *Soc. Welfare in Asia* 84; *Theories on Soc. Welfare* 88; *Soc. Change & Soc. Welfare* 92; "Aging in Twn." in *Aging in E. & S.E. Asia* 92; *Add.* CLA, 15th Fl., 132 Ming Sheng E. Rd., Sect. 3, Taipei 105.

CHAN, HSIEN-CHING 詹憲卿
Rep., TECO, Philippines 95-; *b.* Twn. Oct. 17, '39; *m.* Chan, Jenny; 1 *s.; educ.* LL.B., NCCU 62; Staff, MOFA 64-67; 3rd & 2nd Sec., Emb. in Brazil 67-74; Sect. Chief, Protocol Dept., MOFA 74-77; 1st Sec., Emb. in S. Korea 77-81; Dep. Dir., Dept. of Cent. & S. Am. Aff., MOFA 81-83; Consul-Gen. in Cape Town 83-89; Dir., Dept. of Pers., MOFA 89-91; Dir., Dept. of Consl. Aff. 91-92; Dir.-Gen., CCNAA, San Francisco 92-94; Rep., TECO, Brazil 94-95; *Add.* P.O. Box 1097, Makati Cent. Post Off., 1250 Makati, Metro Manila, Philippines.

CHAN, HUNG-CHIH
(See JAN, HUNG-TZE 詹宏志)

CHAN, HUO-SHENG
(See CHAN, HOU-SHENG 詹火生)

CHAN, I-CHANG
(See CHAN, YIH-CHANG 詹益彰)

CHAN, SHAO-HUA
(See CHAN, SHAO-HWA 詹紹華)

CHAN, SHAO-HWA 詹紹華
Nat. Policy Adv. to the Pres. 96-; Pres., Hsinchu Bank Intl. Business Group 97-; *b.* Twn. Sept. 20, '12; *m.* Chan Hu, Yen-wan; 2 *s.,* 4 *d.; educ.* Grad., Taipei Second Tchrs. Coll. 32; Tchr., Hsinchu First Public Sch. 38-39; Mem., Hsinchu County Coun. 53-55; Pres., Hsinchu Bank 59-90, Chmn. of Bd. 90-96; Chmn., ROC Small- & Medium Business Bank Assn. 92-97; *Add.* 93 Hsin Hsueh St., Hsinchu 300.

CHAN, SUNNEY I. 陳長謙
Mem., Acad. Sinica 88-, V. Pres. 99-; Hoag Prof., Biophys. Chem., Calif. Inst. of Tech. 92-; *b.* USA Oct. 5, '36; *m.* Tam, Irene Yuk-hing; 1 *s.; educ.* BS, UC-Berkly. 57, Ph.D. 60; Grad. Teaching Asst., UC-Berkly. 57-58; Nat. Sc. Found. Postdr. Fel., Harvard U. 60-61; Asst. Prof., U. of Calif., Riverside 61-63; Asst. Prof., Calif. Inst. of Tech. 63-

64, Assc. Prof. 64-68, Prof., Chem., Phys., & Biophys. Chem. 68-92; John Simon Guggenheim Fel., Oxford U. 68-69; Visiting Scholar, UC-Berkly. 76; Acting Exec. Off., Chem. 77-78; Exec. Off., Chem. 78-80; Visiting Prof., Stanford U. 81; Chmn. of the Faculty, Calif. Inst. of Tech. 87-89; Exec. Off., Chem. 89-94; Wilson T.S. Wang Int. Disting. Prof., Ch. U. of Hong Kong 93; Dir., Inst. of Chem., Acad. Sinica 97-99. *Publ.:* 200 sc. papers on chem., phys., & biochem.; *Add.* 128 Yen Chiu Yuan Rd., Sect. 2, Taipei 115.

CHAN, TIEN-HSING
(See CHAN, TIEN-SHING 詹天性)

CHAN, TIEN-SHING 詹天性
Chmn., *CDN* 99- & *Ch. Daily News* 94-; *b.* Twn. July 1, 42; *m.* Chen, Shan-lie; 1 *s.; educ.* BS, NCHU; LL.M., NCCU; Mem. & Dir., Ch. Youth Corps 67-79; Sp. & Dir., Dept. of Cul. Aff., KMT 80-81, Chmn., Pingtung County Charter 81-82, Sec. & Sp., Dept. of Cul. Aff. 82-86; Pres., *Ch. Daily News* 86-94. *Publ.: Modernization & Mass Media; Newspaper Op. & News Gathering; Words of Ch. Entrepreneurs; Traffic Lights; Add.* 260 Pa Te Rd., Sect. 2, Taipei 105.

CHAN, YIH-CHANG 詹益彰
Mem., Control Yuan 99-; *b.* Twn. Jan. 1, '39; *m.* Chien, Kuei-chia; 1 *s.,* 1 *d.; educ.* LL.B., NTU 62; Grad. Studies, Meiji U. 71; Dep. Dir., Dept. of Labor Aff., MOI 81-85, Dir., Dept. of Population Admin. 85-88, Gen. Sec. 88-91; Dep. Sec.-Gen., CEIC 91-92; Gen. Sec., MOI 92-93; Counsl., Control Yuan 93-96; Dir., 1st Bu., Off. of the Pres. 96-99; *Add.* 122 Chungking S. Rd., Sect. 1, Taipei 100.

CHANG, AN-PING
(See CHANG, NELSON AN-PING 張安平)

CHANG, C.P. 張昌邦
Chmn., Business Mng. Cttee., KMT 2000-; Attorney-at-Law; Adjunct Prof., Fu Jen Catholic U. 71-; *b.* Twn. Nov. 13, '46; *m.* Huang, Chuan-chuan; 1 *s.,* 1 *d.; educ.* LL.B., Fu Jen Catholic U. 68; LL.M., NCCU 71; Visiting Scholar, Harvard Law Sch. 86; Sect. Chief, Laws & Reglns. Cttee., Exec. Yuan 73-76; Sr. Sp., Secretariat, MOF 77, Exec. Sec., Laws & Reglns. Cttee. 77-82, V. Chmn., Sec. & Exchange Com. (SEC) 82-88, & Chmn., SEC 88-93; Admin. V. Min. of Finance 93-95; Dep. Sec.-Gen., Exec. Yuan 95-96; Pol. V. Min. of Econ. Aff. 96-2000. *Publ.: Thesis on Tax Collection & Assessment Law; A Res. on Burden of Proof in Criminal Procedure; Add.* 11 Chung Shan S. Rd., Taipei 104.

CHANG, C.Y. 張慶衍
Amb. to the Honduras 96-; *b.* Chekiang Feb. 28, '34; *m.* King, Theresa; 1 *d.; educ.* LL.B., Soochow U.; Grad. Sch., Law Cent., Georgetown U.; V. Consul, Honolulu 65-68; Sect. Chief, MOFA 69-71; Counsl., Emb. in USA 71-78; Div. Dir., CCNAA, Washington, D.C. 79-83; Sec.-Gen., CCNAA 84-88; Dir.-Gen., CCNAA, Chicago 88-89, & CCNAA, Los Angeles 89-94; Amb. to the Bahamas 94-96; *Add.* Apartado Postal 3433, Tegucigalpa, M.D.C., Honduras.

CHANG, CHANG-CHI
(See CHANG, CHUN-CHIG 張昌吉)

CHANG, CHANG-PANG
(See CHANG, C.P. 張昌邦)

CHANG, CHAO-HSIUNG
(See CHANG, CHAU-HSIUNG 張昭雄)

CHANG, CHAU-HSIUNG 張昭雄
Independent Candidate, 2000 Election for ROC V. Pres. (10th term); V. Chmn., People First Party 2000-; *b.* Kaohsiung Feb. 3, '42; *m.* Lee, Fang-hui; 2 *s.; educ.* MD, NTU 67; Part-time Attending Physician, NTU Hosp. 76-77; Chief, Dept. of Surgery, Chang Gung Memorial Hosp. 76-79, Chief, Sect. of Cardiovascular & Thoracic Surgery 79-91, Supt. 79-97; Pres., Chang Gung U. 97-99. *Publ.:* Author of 16 & co-author of 167 sc. citation index papers; *Add.* 5 Fu Hsing St., Kueishan Hsiang, Taoyuan County 333.

CHANG, CHE-CHEN
(See CHANG, CHE-SHEN 張哲琛)

CHANG, CHE-SHEN 張哲琛
Dir.-Gen., Finance Aff. Cttee., KMT 2000-; *b.* Shanghai May 14, '45; *m.* Wong, Deh-hwa; 2 *s.,* 1 *d.; educ.* B., NTU 70; M., Cent. Michigan U. 75; Sp., MOF 76-77; Asst. Dir., DGBAS 77-79, Sect. Chief 79-85, Dep. Dir., 1st Bu. 87-90, Dir., 1st Bu. 90-92; Dep. Dir.-Gen., DGBAS 92-96; Dep. Sec.-Gen., Exec. Yuan 96-99; Dir.-Gen., CPA 99-2000. *Publ.: Improvement of the Compilation of the ROC Govt. Budget; An Assessment of the ROC Govt. Budget Structure & Decision-making; Add.* 11 Chung Shan S. Rd., Taipei 104.

CHANG, CHEN-CHENG
(See CHANG, CHIN-CHEN 張眞誠)

CHANG, CHI-CHUNG 張啓仲
Nat. Policy Adv. to the Pres.; Pres., ROC Cooperative Union, ROC Credit Cooperative Union, & Taichung Bus

Co.; Chmn., Twn. Regional Dev. Inst., & 7th Credit Cooperative, Taichung; *b.* Twn. May 10, '16; *m.* Lee, Chiu-rong; 2 *s.,* 4 *d.; educ.* Grad., Japan Med. U. 42; Pres., Chi Jen Hosp. 48-64; Spkr., Taichung CCoun. 55-58; Mayor, Taichung City 64-67; Mem., Legis. Yuan 73-81; Chmn., Prov. Bus Fed. Twn. 78-84; Gov., Dist. 300, Lions Club Intl. 79-80; Adv., Exec. Yuan 81-90; *Add.* Rm. 710, 150 Chi Lin Rd., Taipei 104.

CHANG, CHIA-CHU
(See CHANG, CHIA-JUCH 張家祝)

CHANG, CHIA-JUCH 張家祝
Admin. V. Min. of Trans. & Comms. 95-; *b.* Twn. June 25, '50; *m.* Chen, Eugenia; 1 *s.,* 1 *d.; educ.* BS, Civil Engr., NCKU 73; MS, Civil Engr., Calif. State U., San Jose 76; Ph.D., Purdue U. 79; Asst. Prof., Dept. of Civil Engr., Marquette U., USA 79-81; Assc. Prof., Inst. of Traffic & Trans., NCTU 81-82, Prof. & Dir. 82-87; Dir.-Gen., Inst. of Trans., MOTC 87-95. *Publ.:* Over 90 papers on trans. in prof. jour.; *Add.* 2 Changsha St., Sect. 1, Taipei 100.

CHANG, CHIEH-CHIEN 張捷遷
Mem., Acad. Sinica 64-, & New York Acad. of Sc.; Prof. Emeritus, Catholic U. of Am.; *b.* Peking July 21, '13; *m.* Chang, Than-chie; 3 *c.; educ.* BS, N.E. U. 32; MS, Calif. Tech. 41, Ph.D. 50; Guggenheim Fel. 52-53; Instr., NTHU 34-40; Assc. Prof., Johns Hopkins U. 47-52; Res. Prof., U. of Maryland 52-54; Prof., U. of Minnesota 54-62; Chmn. & Prof., Catholic U. of Am. 62-77. *Publ: Real Fluid Mech.; Ed. Process of Plasma Space Sc. System;* & over 100 sc. papers; *Add.* 2122 Galewood Place, Silver Spring, MD 20903, USA.

CHANG, CHIEN-PANG
(See CHANG, CLEMENT C.P. 張建邦)

CHANG, CHIN-CHENG 張眞誠
Dir., Sc. & Tech. Adv. Off., MOE 98-; Prof., Nat. Chung Cheng U. 95-; *b.* Twn. Nov. 12, '54; *m.* Huang, Ling-hui; 1 *s.,* 2 *d.; educ.* BS, Applied Math., NTHU 77, MS, Computer & Decision Sc. 79; Ph.D., Computer Engr., NCTU 82; Assc. Prof., Dept. of Computer Engr., NCTU 82-83; Assc. Prof., Inst. of Applied Math., NCHU 83-85, Prof. 85-89; Prof. & Dir., Inst. of Computer Sc. & Info. Engr., Nat. Chung Cheng U. 89-92, Dean, Coll. of Engr. 92-95; Acting Pres., Nat. Chung Cheng U. 96-97. *Publ.:* 12 acad. bks. & over 400 published acad. papers; *Add.* 160 Sanhsing Village, Minhsiung, Chiayi County 621.

CHANG, CHIN-KOU
(See CHANG, JIN-GOU 張金鈎)

CHANG, CHING-YEN
(See CHANG, C.Y. 張慶衍)

CHANG, CHING-YU
(See CHANG, KING-YUH 張京育)

CHANG, CHUAN-CHIUNG 張傳炯
Mem., Acad. Sinica 76-; Prof., Pharmacology, NTU 65-; *b.* Twn. Oct. 23, '28; *m.* Chen, Wang-shyu; 1 *s.,* 2 *d.; educ.* BS, NTU 50; Ph.D., U. of Tokyo 65; Assc. Prof., NTU 60-65; Fel., NIH Res. 62-64. *Publ.:* Over 100 original articles on the discovery of ß-Bungarotoxin & synaptic transmission of the nervous system; *Add.* 3rd Fl., 3 Lane 60, Chou Shan Rd., Taipei 106.

CHANG, CHUN-CHIG 張昌吉
V. Chmn., CLA 97-; *b.* Twn. Sept. 7, 57; *educ.* LL.B., NCCU 80, MS, Grad. Sch. of Pol. Sc. 85; MS in Policy Sc. (major in Econ.), U. of Maryland, USA 88, Ph.D. 91; Asst. Res. Fel., Inst. for Econ., Acad. Sinica 91-92; Assc. Prof. & concur. Dir., Inst. for Labor Res., NCCU 92-96, Prof. 96-97, *Add.* 15th Fl., 132 Min Sheng E. Rd., Sect. 3, Taipei 105.

CHANG, CHUN-HSIUNG 張俊雄
Sec.-Gen., Off. of the Pres. 2000-; *b.* Mar. 23, '38; *educ.* LL.B., NTU 60; Lawyer; Mem., CC, DPP, Exec. Mem., CSC 87-89; Convener & Exec. Dir., DPP Caucus, Legis. Yuan; Convener, Jud. Cttee., Legis. Yuan 91, Home & Border Aff. Cttee. 92, & Trans. & Comms. Cttee. 95 & Mem. 97; Mem., Legis. Yuan 83-2000; *Add.* c/o Off. of the Pres., Taipei 100.

CHANG, CHUN-YEN 張俊彥
Pres., NCTU 98-, Chair Prof. 69-; Nat. Chair Prof., MOE 97-; Mem., Acad. Sinica 96-; *b.* Twn. Oct. 12, '37; *m.* Lee, Shun-mei; 3 *s.; educ.* BS, NCKU 60; MS, NCTU 62, Ph.D. 70; Visiting Prof., U. of Florida 87 & Stuttgart U. 89; Dean of Res. 90-93; Dean, Coll. of Engr., NCTU 90-94 & Coll. of EE & Computer Sc. 94-95; Pres., Nat. Nano Device Labs., NScC 90-97; Dir., Microelec. & Info. Systems Res. Cent., NCTU 96-98 & Res. Cent. 96-98; *Add.* 1001-1 Ta Hsueh Rd., Hsinchu 300.

CHANG, CHUN-YEN 張俊彥
Sec.-Gen., Kaohsiung City Govt. 99-; *b.* Twn. Feb. 7, '41; 2 *s.,* 1 *d; educ.* B., Dept. of Intl. Trade, Feng Chia U. 75; M., Grad. Inst. of Public Admin., NCCU 77; Dir., Dept. of

Finance, Tainan City Govt. 81-85; Adv., Kaohsiung City Govt. 85-88, Dir., Dept. of Personnel 88-94 & Dept. of Civil Aff. 94-96, Sec.-Gen. 96-98; Chmn., Kaohsiung City Bk. 98-99. *Publ.: Res. of Budget System; The Theory of Admin. Mng.; Add.* 2 Ssu Wei 3rd Rd., Lingya, Kaohsiung 802.

CHANG, CLEMENT C.P. 張建邦

Sr. Adv. to the Pres. 97-; Mem. & Chmn., Presidium, CAC, KMT 97-, Comr., Evaluation & Discipline Com. 94-; Prof., Grad. Inst. of Am. Studies, Tamkang U. 91-; Pres., WLFD 99-; *b.* Twn. Mar. 15, '29; *m.* Chiang, Carrie W.T.; 2 *d.; educ.* BA, Econ., St. John's U., Shanghai 49; MS, Agr. Econ., U. of Illinois 52, Ed.D., Educ. Admin. 81; Prof., Agr. Econ., NTU 55-65 & Econ., Tamkang Coll. 58-65; Pres., Tamkang Coll. of Arts & Sc. 64-80; Dep. Spkr., Taipei CCoun. 69-81, Spkr. 81-89; Chmn., YMCA in the ROC 72-90; Founder, Tamkang U. 80, Pres. 80-86; Prof., Educ., NCCU 82-86; Mem., CSC, KMT 84-93; Chmn., Bd. of Trustees, Tamkang U. 86-89, Dir. 91-95; Pres., WACL, ROC Chapter, & APACL 88 89; Min. of Trans. & Comms. 89-91; Mem., CC, KMT 93-97; Sr. Adv., NSC 95-97. *Publ.: Educ. in a Changing Soc.* (4 Vol.); *What I Have Seen in the USA under Eisenhower Fellowships* 74; *The Characteristics & Models of Governance of Coll. & U.* 80; *A Study of Bureaucratic Collegial & Pol. Models of Governance in Six U. in Twn.* 81; *Introduction to Futures Studies* (co-author) 96; *Add.* 5 Lane 199, Chin Hua St., Taipei 100.

CHANG, DAVID H.C. 張希哲

Nat. Policy Adv. to the Pres.; Prof., NCCU; Hon. Chmn., Sino-Indonesia Assn., Sino-Ryukyuan Cul. & Econ. Assn., Amateur Roller Skating Assn.; Chmn., Ovs. Ch. Assn., & Friends of Hong Kong & Macau Assn.; *b.* Kwangtung Oct. 14, '18; *m.* Liu, Hui-shao; 2 *s.,* 5 *d.; educ.* LL.B., NCCU; Nat. War Coll.; Postgrad. Studies, U. of Washington; Hon. DPS, Konkuk U. 81; Mng. Ed., *Chungshan Daily News* 41-44; Pub., *Canton Daily News* 46-49; Mem., Canton Mun. Coun. 45-48; Adv., Kwangtung Prov. Govt. 48-49; Dir., 1st Dept., Min. of Info., KMT 49-50, & Dept. of Gen. Aff., MOE 50-51; Mem., Legis. Yuan 50-91; Prof., NCCU 58-62; Mem., CPC, KMT 62-72; Pres., Fengchia Coll. of Engr. & Business 63-73; Mem., CC, KMT. *Publ.: Planned Govt. & Planned Econ.; Election System in US; Cong. & Pol. Parties in Various Countries; Const. Tendency of Post-War Countries; Ovs. Ch. Policy & Work of the Ch. Communists; The Ideal & Practice of Higher Educ.; The KMT Party of Ch. & Party Pol.; Add.* 10 Lane 70, Min Tsu St., Peitou, Taipei 112.

CHANG, DING-CHONG 張鼎鍾

Mem. (ministerial rank), Exam. Yuan 90-; Ed., *Jour. of Lib. & Info. Sc.* 74-; *b.* Nanking Feb. 4, '34; *m.* Fung, John; 1 *s.,* 2 *d.; educ.* BA, NTU 55; M., Lib. Sc., Marywood Coll. 59; Ph.D., Indiana U. 83; Dep. Dir., Lib., Ch. U. of Hong Kong 66-67; Assc. Prof., NTU 69-74; Assc. Prof., NTNU 74-80, Dir., Lib. 77-80, Prof. 80-84; Visiting Prof., U. of Illinois 84-87; Exec. Dir., Wang Inst. of Grad. Studies, USA 85-87; Res. Assc., Fairbank Cent., Harvard U. 85-95; Adv., Boston U. 87-90; Ed., *Digest for Ch. Studies* 87-89; Visiting Prof., NTU 88-90; Prof., Nat. Chung Cheng U. 90-97 & NCCU 90-98. *Publ.: Lib. & Info.* 79; *On Lib. & Info. Sc.* 82; *Guide to Info. Sc.* 84; *The Evolving Soc. Mission of the Nat. Cent. Lib. in Ch. 1928-1966* 84; *A Primer of Lib. Automation* 87; *Reflections on Civil Service & Lib./Info. Sc.* 96; & many articles on educ., lib. & into. sc.; *Add.* P.O. Box 2-53, Mucha, Taipei 116.

CHANG, FREDERIC P.N. 張平男

Dep. Dir.-Gen., GIO 97-; *b.* Twn. Jan. 10, '42; *m.* Huang, Chi-chung; 2 *s.,* 1 *d.; educ.* BA, For. Lang. & Lits., NTU 64, Grad. Studies, Inst. of For. Lang. & Lits. 66-70; Admin. Asst., JCRR 73-79; Asst., CAPD 79-81, Sp. Asst. 81-84, Sec. 84; Sect. Chief, COA 84-87, Sr. Sp. Asst. 87-92, Counsl. 92-93; Dep. Dir.-Gen., 1st Bu., Off. of the Pres. 93-96, Dir.-Gen., Dept. of Sp. Aff. 96-97. *Publ.: Solzhenitsyn: A Documentary Record* (transl.) 74; *Practical Eng.* (ed.) 75; *A Passage to India* (transl.) 75; *The Open and Closed Minds* (transl.) 78; *Mimesis: The Representation of Reality in We. Lit.* (transl.) 80; *Add.* 2 Tientsin St., Taipei 100.

CHANG, FU-MEI
(See CHEN CHANG, FU-MEI 張富美)

CHANG, FU-MEI
(See CHANG, FWU-MEI 張芙美)

CHANG, FWU-MEI 張芙美

Pres., Tzu Chi Coll. & Tech. 99-; *b.* Twn. July 20, '39; *m.* Chen, Shang-chi; 2 *s.; educ.* BS, Nat. Def. Med. Cent. 63; MBA, Oklahoma City U. 86; Ed.D., Drake U. 93; Nurse, Army 805 Gen. Hosp. 63-64 & Army 803 Gen. Hosp. 64-67; Instr., Chung Shan Med. & Dental Coll. 67-68; Instr. & Assc. Prof., Hungkuang Coll. of Tech. 68-90; Pres., Tzu Chi Coll. of Nursing 90-99. *Publ.: Res. on the Dev. of Mil. Tng. Edu. in the ROC on Twn.* 99; *Res. on the Will-ingness of Aboriginal Jr. High Students in Hualien County to Continue Study* 97; *Attitude of the Freshmen Toward the Handicapped* 94; *Add.* 880 Chien Kuo Rd., Sect. 2, Hualien 970.

CHANG, HONG-CHIA 張宏嘉
Chmn., Holmsgreen Holdings Co Ltd. 97-, F.C. Lai Lai Dept. Store Co. Ltd. 97-, Circle K Convenience Store (Twn.) Ltd. 97-, Makro Twn. Ltd. 97-, & Serena Confectionary Co. Ltd. 97-; *b.* Taipei Dec. 20, '51; *educ.* BS, Nat. Taipei Inst. of Tech. 72; MBA, U. of So. Calif. 81; Mech. Engr., San Yang Ind. Co. Ltd. 74-78, Dir., Audit Dept. & Head, Computer Dept. 81-85, Marketing Dir. 85-86; Pres., F.C. Lai Lai Dept. Store Co. Ltd. 86-97; V. Chmn., Holmsgreen Holdings Co. Ltd. 86-97; *Add.* 2nd Fl., 260 Tun Hua N. Rd., Taipei 105.

CHANG, HONG-JEN 張鴻仁
V. Min., DOH 99-, Dir.-Gen., Cent. for Disease Control 99-; *b.* Twn. Apr. 10, '56; *m.* Liao, Li-ying; 1 *d.; educ.* MD, Nat. Yangming Med. Sch. 82; MPH, NTU 84; MS, Sch. of Public Health, Harvard U. 87; Dep. Dir., Bu. of Health Promotion & Protection, DOH 89, & Bu. of Pharmaceutical Aff. 89-94, Sp. Gen. 94-95, Dir. Gen., Bu. of Communicable Disease Control 95-98; V. Pres., Bu. of Nat. Health Ins. 98-99; *Add.* 14th Fl., 100 Ai Kuo E. Rd., Taipei 100.

CHANG, HORNG-JINH 張紘炬
Pres., Tamkang U. 98-; *b.* Twn. Mar. 15, '49; *m.* Lin Chuan-ling; 2 *d.; educ.* BS, Dept. of Math., Tamkang U 71, MS, Grad. Inst. of Math. 73, Ph.D., Grad. Inst. of Mng. Sc. 80; Chmn., Dept. of Statistics, Tamkang U. 81-84, Dean, Evening Sch. 84-89, Dir., Grad. Inst. of Mng. Sc. 84-89, Dean, Coll. of Grad. Studies 86-89, V. Pres., Financial Aff. 89-96, V. Pres., Acad. Aff. 96-98. *Publ.: Statistics;* 58 periodical articles, nine symposium papers, & 165 res. papers on public approval ratings; *Add.* 151 Ying Chuan Rd., Tamsui, Taipei County 251.

CHANG, HSI-CHE
(See CHANG, DAVID H.C. 張希哲)

CHANG, HSIAO-YUEH
(See CHANG, KATHARINE S.Y. 張小月)

CHANG, HSIN-HSIUNG 張信雄
Pres., So. Twn. U. of Tech. 89-; *b.* Twn. Mar. 3, '40; *m.* Wu, Ching-mei; 3 *s.; educ.* BA, Intl. Trade, NCCU 63, MBA 66; Ph.D., Grad. Sch. of Agr. Econ., Tokyo Agr. U. 92; Sr. Asst., Ch. Productivity & Trade Cent. 66-68; Sr. Asst. to the Pres., Formosa Plastics Corp. 68-72; Part-time Assc. Prof., NCKU 72-77, Part-time Prof. 78-88; V. Pres., Nan-Tai Inst. of Tech. 86-89. *Publ.: Intl. Marketing; The Theory & Practice of Sales Mng.; Add.* 1 Nan Tai St., Shangting Li, Yungkang, Tainan County 710.

CHANG, HSU-CHENG
(See CHANG, PARRIS HSU-CHENG 張旭成)

CHANG, HUNG-CHIA
(See CHANG, HONG-CHIA 張宏嘉)

CHANG, HUNG-CHU
(See CHANG, HORNG-JINH 張紘炬)

CHANG, HUNG-JEN
(See CHANG, HONG-JEN 張鴻仁)

CHANG, I-FAN 張一蕃
Pres., Fooyin Inst. of Tech. 95-; *b.* Shanghai Feb. 27, '46; 2 *s.; educ.* Ph.D., Applied Phys., Cornell U. 72; Assc. Prof. & Prof., NCTU 72-78; Prof., Nat. Twn. Inst. of Tech. 78-84; Dir., Voc. & Tech. Educ., MOE 80-84; Dean, Coll. of Sc. & Dean of Acad. Aff., NCU 84-89; V. Pres., Yuan Ze Inst. of Tech. 89-95; *Add.* 151 Chin Hsueh Rd., Yungfang Village, Taliao Hsiang, Kaohsiung County 831.

CHANG, JAMES WEN-CHUNG 張文中
Rep., Rep. Off. in Moscow for the Taipei-Moscow Econ. & Cul. Coordination Com. 97-; *b.* Szechwan Dec. 24, '35; *m.* Chang, Chin-ning; 2 *d.; educ.* LL.B., NTU 58; 3rd Sec., Emb. in Senegal 64-65; 3rd & 2nd Sec., Emb. in the Togolese Repub. 65-68; Sect. Chief & Dep. Dir., Dept. of African Aff., MOFA 68-73; Consul, Consl. Gen. in New York City 73-76; 1st Sec., Emb. in USA 76-78; Dir., Service Div., CCNAA, Washington, D.C. 79-83; Counsl., Emb. in S. Africa 83-84; Dir., Dept. of Consl. Aff., MOFA 84-88; Dir.-Gen., CCNAA, Seattle 88-90, & Boston 90-93; Dep. Rep., CCNAA 93-94; Dep. Rep., TECRO 94-96; Dep. Sec.-Gen., NSC 96-97; *Add.* 4th Fl., Gate 4, Korpus 1, 24/2 Tverskaya St., Moscow 103050, Russian Fed.

CHANG, JEFFREY P. 張伯毅
Mem., Acad. Sinica 74-; Hon. Prof., Peking Union Med. Coll.; Prof. Emeritus, U. of Texas Med. Br., Galveston 87-; *b.* Hunan Oct. 10, '17; *m.* Tang, Sulaine; 3 *s.,* 2 *d.; educ.* BS, NCU; MS & Ph.D., U. of Illinois; Res. Assc., U. of Kansas Med. Sch. 52-55; Asst. Prof., Assc. Prof., & Prof., U. of Texas, Houston 55-72; Prof., U. of Texas Med. Br., Galveston 72-87; Invented fresh frozen sectioning technique for pathologic diagnosis; Dev. open-top cryostat; Invented sect. freeze substitution, monolayer flat embedding, mitochondia staining technics; Established Chang hepatoma cell lines; Proposed tublin-cilia formation hypothesis. *Publ.* Over 150 sc. papers; *Add.* 6th Fl.-1, 236 Chung Hsiao E Rd., Sect. 3, Taipei 106.

CHANG, JIN-GOU 張金鉤

Amb. to the Kingdom of Swaziland 99-; *b.* Twn. Mar. 8, '41; *m.* Chang Li, Sue-jue; 2 *s.,* 1 *d.; educ.* BA, NTNU 66; Res. at Victoria U. of Wellington, New Zealand 71; Sec., E. Asia Trade Cent., Auckland, New Zealand 75-80; Sect. Chief, W. Asian Aff. Dept., MOFA 80-84; 1st Sec. & Counsl., ROC Emb. in Korea 84-90; Asst. Dir.-Gen. & Dep. Dir.-Gen., Dept. of E. Asian & Pacific Aff., MOFA 90-91; Dep. Rep., Taipei Rep. Off. in Singapore 91-93; Dir.-Gen., TECO in Sydney 93-97 & Dept. of E. Asian & Pacific Aff., MOFA 97-99; *Add.* P.O. Box 56, Mbabane, Kingdom of Swaziland.

CHANG, JUNG-KUNG 張榮恭

Dir.-Gen., Dept. of Mainland Aff., CC, KMT 98-; *b.* Taipei Jan. 1, '50, m. Lee, Chi-min; 2 *s.; educ.* LL.B., Fu Jen Catholic U. 72; LL.M., NCCU 75; Ed., CNA 77-86; Dep. Ed.-in-Chief, *Cent. Monthly* 83-85; Dir., Mainland News Dept., CNA 86-98; Lectr., Fu Jen Catholic U. 87-91; Dep. Ed.-in-Chief, CNA 93-98; *Add.* 8th Fl., 11 Chung Shan S. Rd., Taipei 100.

CHANG, JUNG-WEI 張榮味

Spkr., Yunlin CoCoun. 99-; Prov. Rep., Construction Assn. 88-; Chmn., Chianglungchung Construction Co. 87-; *b.* Twn. July 10, '46; *m.* Wang, Yueh-hsia; 1 *s.,* 2 *d.; educ.* Studied at Nat. Chia-Yi Inst. of Agr. Sch.; Apprentice, Sanyuan Lumber Yard 62-64; Homei Store 64-76; Spkr., Yunlin CoCoun. 90-97; *Add.* 2 Ho Ping St., Tuku, Yunlin County 633.

CHANG, KAI-YOEN 張凱元

Pres., Hsuan Chuang Coll. of Humanities & Soc. Sc. 97-; *b.* Kwangtung July 22, '40; *m.* Che, Christine C.Y.; 1 *d.; educ.* Diploma, World Coll. of Jour. 64; BA, Fu Jen Catholic U. 72; MA, Tennessee Tech. U. 75; Ed.D., U. of Tennessee 79; Tchr., Prov. Pingtung Ind. Sch. 65-68; Teaching Asst. & Sec., World Coll. of Jour. 68-69, Dean of Studies 80-81, Pres. 81-90; Prof., Ming Chuan U. 90-97. *Publ.: A Comparison of the Personal Dev. of Am. & Ch. Coll. Students within an Eriksonian Framework; A Study of the Personality Dev. of Ch. Students from 1979 to 1991; The Effects of Two-Step Flow of Comm. on Ch. Tourist Behavior;* etc.; *Add.* 48 Hsuan Chuang Rd., Hsinchu 300.

CHANG, KAI-YUAN

(See CHANG, KAI-YOEN 張凱元)

CHANG, KATHARINE S.Y. 張小月

Amb. to St. Christopher & Nevis, & Commonwealth of Dominica 97-; *b.* Twn. Feb. 12, '53; *m.* Ho, Jei-fu; *educ.* B., NCCU 75; M., Long Island U. 85; Desk Off., Dept. of Intl.

Org., MOFA 76-80; Sec., CCNAA, New York 80-89; Sect. Chief, Dept. of N. Am. Aff., MOFA 89-91, 2nd Dep. Dir. 92-93, Dep. Dir. 93-94; Dir.-Gen., TECO, Seattle 95-97; *Add.* P.O. Box 119, Basseterre, St. Kitts, West Indies.

CHANG, KING-YUH 張京育

Nat. Policy. Adv. to the Pres. 99-; Prof., NCCU 75-; *b.* Hunan Apr. 27, '37; *m.* Yu, Grace Yu-dih; 2 *s.; educ.* LL.B., NTU 58; LL.M., NCCU 61; MCL, Columbia U. 64, Ph.D. 71; Hon. LL.D., Sung Kyun Kwan U., S. Korea 90; Lectr., Hofstra U. 68-69; Asst. Prof., We. Illinois U. 72; Assc. Prof., NCCU 72-75, Dir., Dept. of Dip. 74-77, Dean, Grad. Sch. of Intl. Law & Dip. 75-77; Visiting Fel., Johns Hopkins U. 76-77; Dep. Dir., Inst. of Intl. Rel., NCCU 77-81, Dir. 81-84; Disting. Visiting Scholar, Inst. of E. Asian Studies, UC-Berkly. 83; Dir.-Gen., GIO 84-87; Dir., Inst. of Intl. Rel., NCCU 87-90, Pres., 89-94; Min. without Portfolio 94-96; Chmn., MAC 96-99. *Publ.: Intl. Rel. & Intl. Pol.; Looking at the World from Taipei; A Framework for Ch.'s Unification; Add.* c/o Off. of the Pres., 122 Chungking S. Rd., Sect. 1, Taipei 100.

CHANG, KUANG-CHENG

(See CHANG, SAMUEL K.C. 張光正)

CHANG, KUANG-CHIH

(See CHANG, KWANG-CHIH 張光直)

CHANG, KUN 張琨

Mem., Acad. Sinica 72-; Prof., Oriental Lang., U. of Calif.; *b.* Honan Nov. 17, '17; *m.* Shefts, Betty; *educ.* BA, NTHU 38; Ph.D., Linguistics, Yale U. 55; Asst. Prof., Assc. Prof., & Prof., U. of Washington, Seattle 51-63. *Publ.: A Comparative Study of the Kathinavastu; A Manual of Spoken Tibetan; The Proto. Ch. Final System & the Chieh-yun; Spoken Tibetan Texts; Add.* Dept. of E. Asian Lang., UC-Berkly., CA 94720, USA.

CHANG, KUO-CHAO

(See CHANG, LOUIS K. 張國照)

CHANG, KWANG-CHIH 張光直

Mem., Acad. Sinica 74-, Adjunct Res. Fel., Inst. of Hist. & Philology; John E. Hudson Prof., Archaeology, Harvard U. 84-; *b.* Peiping Apr. 15, '31; *m.* Li, Hwei; 1 *s.,* a *d.; educ.* BA, NTU 54; Ph.D., Harvard U. 60; Lectr., Harvard U. 60-61; Instr., Yale U. 61-63, Asst. Prof. 63-66, Assc. Prof. 66-69, Prof. 69-77, Chmn., Dept. of Anthropology 70-73; Chmn., Coun. on E. Asian Studies 75-77 & 86-89; Prof., Anthropology, Harvard U. 77-84, Chmn., Dept. of Anthropology 81-84. *Publ.: The Archaeology of Ancient*

Ch.; Art, Myth & Ritual; & about 150 articles & 40 bk. reviews; *Add.* Peabody Museum, Harvard U., Cambridge, MA 02138, USA.

CHANG, LEROY L. 張立綱
Mem., Acad. Sinica 94-; V. Pres. & Prof., Hong Kong U. of Sc. & Tech. 98-; *b.* Kirin Jan. 20, '36; *m.* Chang, Helen H.; 1 *s.,* 1 *d.; educ.* BS, NTU 57; MS, U. of S. Carolina 61; Ph.D., Stanford U. 63; Staff Mem., IBM Watson Res. Cent. 63-68; Assc. Prof., MIT 68-69; Res. Mgr., IBM Watson Res. Cent. 69-92; Dean of Sc., Hong Kong U. of Sc. & Tech. 93-98. *Publ.: Molecular Beam Epitaxy & Heterostructures* 85; *Synthetic Modulated Structures* 85; *Resonant Tunneling in Semiconductors: Phys. & Application* 91; *Add.* Hong Kong U. of Sc. & Tech., Clear Water Bay, Kowloon, Hong Kong.

CHANG, LI-KANG
(See CHANG, LEROY L. 張立綱)

CHANG, LIANG-JEN 張良任
Dep. Sec.-Gen., SEF 96-2000; *b.* Anhwei Aug. 21, '46; *m.* Chen, Alice; 1 *s.,* 1 *d.; educ.* BA, Dip., NCCU 68; MA, Grad. Sch. of E. Asian Studies, NCCU 71; MA, Harvard U. 84; Ed., TTV 73-75; Dir., Div. of Info. & Protocol, GIO 86-88, & Dept. of Compilation & Transl. 88-91; Dir., Dept. of Info. & Liaison, MAC 91-93, Dept. of Cul. & Educ. Aff. 93-96, & Dept. of Hong Kong & Macau Aff. 96; *Add.* 17th Fl., 156 Min Sheng E. Rd., Sect. 3, Taipei 104.

CHANG, LIN-SHENG 張臨生
Dep. Dir., Nat. Palace Museum 91-2000; Res. Fel., Nat. Unification Assn. 95-; V. Pres., Ch. Assn. of Museums 96-; *b.* Shantung July 3, '46; *m.* Mei, Kuang; 1 *s.; educ.* BA, NTU 68; MA, Ch. Cul. U. 72; Grad. Studies, Harvard U. 72-74; Asst. Curator, Nat. Palace Museum 74-76, Assc. Curator 76-79, Sr. Res. Fel. 79-82, Curator, Dept. of Antiquities 83-91. *Publ.:* "Yun Shou-p'ing, a Great Ch'ing Dynasty Artist," *Nat. Palace Museum Quarterly (NPMQ)* 75; "The Dating of the We. Chou Bronze '90 Meng Kuei' & a Transl. of Its Inscription," NPMQ 77; "Chien Ware: A Suggestion for a Revised Dating in the Light of Our Knowledge of the Tea Drinking Contests of the Nr. Sung Period," *NPMQ* 78; "On the Function of Ho and Yi Bronze Vessel-types as Ceremonial Water Vessels," *NPMQ* 82; & numerous other articles; *Add.* Nat. Palace Museum, Waishuanghsi, Shihlin, Taipei 111.

CHANG, LOUIS K. 張國照
Pres., Dahan Inst. of Tech. 99-, & Dahan Jr. Coll. of Eng. & Business 94-; Standing Bd. Dir., ADI Corp. 91-; *b.* Twn. July 8, '40; *m.* Chang, Diana K.; 1 *s.* 1 *d.; educ.* Ed.B.,

NTNU 63; Ed.M., Pennsylvania State U. 79, Ed.D. 83; Tchr., Twn. Prov. Taichung Ind. Sch. 63-74; Instr., Twn. Prov. Tchr. Coll. 74-77; Instr., Dept. of Ind. Educ., Pennsylvania State U. 79-82, Assc. Res., HPCL 83-89; Visiting Assc. Prof., NTNU 89-91. *Publ.: Varification a Curriculum Model for V-I Educ. in Twn.; Curriculum Dev. for V-I Edu.; A Study on Behavior Objectives for Drawing; Add.* 1 Shu Jen St., Tahan Village, Hsin Cheng, Hualien County 971.

CHANG, NELSON AN-PING 張安平
Pres., Chia Hsin Cement Corp.; V. Chmn., Ch. Mng. Systems Corp.; Exec. Dir., Ch. Nat. Assn. of Ind. & Com. 90-; *b.* Twn. June 8, '52; *m.* Koo, Huai-ju; 2 *d.; educ.* BA, Princeton U.; MBA, New York U.; V. Pres., Chia Hsin Cement Corp. 78-88; Sup., Ch. Trust Co. 85-89; Pres., Ch. Mng. Systems Corp. 81-89; Pres. & CEO, Ch. Sec. Co. 88-89; Bd. Chmn., Channel Intl. Corp. 89-90; *Add.* 96 Chung Shan N. Rd., Sect. 2, Taipei 104.

CHANG, PARRIS HSU-CHENG 張旭成
Prof. Emeritus, Pol. Sc., Penn. State U.; Mem., Legis. Yuan 93-; Pres., Twn. Inst. for Pol. Econ. & Strategic Studies 94-; Dir., Twn. DPP Mission in the USA 95-; Columnist, *Newsweek* (Intl.); *b.* Twn. Dec. 30, '36; *m.* Lin, Shirley Hsiu-chu; 3 *c.; educ.* BA, NTU 59; MA, U. of Washington 63; Ph.D., Columbia U. 69; Asst. Prof., Penn. State U. 70-72, Assc. Prof. 72-76, Prof. 77-97; Visiting Fel., Australian Nat. U. 77-78; Visiting Prof., Inst. for Sino-Soviet Studies, George Washington U. 79, Columbia U. 85, & Tokyo U. of For. Studies 86-87. *Publ.: Power & Policy in Ch.; Elite-Conflict in Post-Mao Ch.; Radical & Radical Ideology in Ch. Cul. Rev.; If Ch. Crosses the Twn. Strait: The Intl. Response* (co-author) 93; & over 100 articles in *Asian Aff., Asian Survey, Ch. Quarterly, Current Hist., Far Ea. Econ. Review, Mil. Review, Newsweek, Orbis, Problems of Communism;* etc.; *Add.* 3-2 Tsingtao E. Rd., Taipei 100.

CHANG, PATRICK PEI-CHI 張北齊
Amb. Extraordinary & Plenipotentiary of the ROC to the Repub. of Liberia 98-; *b.* Twn. Oct. 3, '39; *m.* Chang, Peggy; 1 *s.,* 1 *d.; educ.* LL.B., Intl. Law & Dip., NCCU 64; Studied, Grad. Sch. of the Intl. Law & Dip., NCCU 69; Studied, Grad. Sch. of Public Policy, U. of Washington, Seattle 77; 3rd Sec., Emb. of the ROC in Liberia 69-72; Dir., For. Aff. Dept., TPG 73-76; Consul, Consl.-Gen. of the ROC, Seattle 76-77; Consul, Consl. of the ROC, Portland 77-79; Sec., CCNAA Off., Washington, D.C. 80; Dep. Dir., Info. Off., CCNAA, New York 80-83; Dir., Info. Off., Toronto 83-86; Sr. Sp., N. Am. Aff. Dept., MOFA 86-88; Dir., Hong Kong & Macau Aff. Task Force, Exec. Yuan

88-90; Dir.-Gen., Taipei Off. in Berlin 90-98; *Add.* Emb. of the ROC, Tubman Boulevard, Congo Town, P.O. Box 5970, Monrovia, Liberia.

CHANG, PEI-CHI
(See CHANG, PATRICK PEI-CHI 張北齊)

CHANG, PETER 昌彼得
Dep. Dir., Nat. Palace Museum 84-2000; *b.* Hupei Jan. 24, '21; *m.* Fan, Ching-ju; 1 *c.; educ.* BA, NCU; Ed. & Head, Sp. Collections Dept., Nat. Cent. Lib. 45-70; Curator, Dept. of Bk. & Documents, Nat. Palace Museum 68-83. *Publ.: Comments on Bk. by Chin-an; A Study of Shuo Fu; Descriptive Bibliography to Woodblock Editions* (2 Vol.); *Add.* 7th Fl., 5-3 Alley 12, Lane 190, Chung Shan N. Rd., Sect. 7, Taipei 112.

CHANG, PI-TE
(See CHANG, PETER 昌彼得)

CHANG, PING-NAN
(See CHANG, FREDERIC P.N. 張平男)

CHANG, PO-I
(See CHANG, JEFFREY P. 張伯毅)

CHANG, PO-LONG 章博隆
Nat. Policy Adv. to the Pres. 96-; *b.* Twn. Nov. 10, '25; *m.* Chen, Chin-lien; 3 *d.; educ.* Prov. Taitung Agr. Sch.; LL.B., Kinki U; Mem., Taitung CoCoun. 50-60, & TPA 60-77; Comr., Twn. Prov. Coun. 78-81; *Add.* 171 Chuan Kuan Rd., Taitung 950.

CHANG, PO-LUNG
(See CHANG, PO-LONG 章博隆)

CHANG, PO-YA 張博雅
Min. of the Int. & concur. Gov. of the TPG 2000-; *b.* Twn. Oct. 5, '42; *m.* Chi, Tsan-nan; 1 *s.,* 1 *d.; educ.* MD, Kaohsiung Med. Coll. 68; MPH, Inst. of Public Health, NTU 70; MPH, Johns Hopkins U. 74; Ph.D., Kyorin U. 94; Prof. & Dir., Dept. of Public Health, Kaohsiung Med. Coll. 80-83; Mayor, Chiayi City 83-89; Mem., Legis. Yuan 90; Dir.-Gen., DOH 90-97; Mayor, Chiayi City 97-2000. *Publ.: Study of Occupational Lead Poisoning in S. Twn., ROC* 87; *Add.* 5 Hsuchow Rd., Taipei 100.

CHANG, SAMUEL K.C. 張光正
Pres., Chung Yuan Christian U. 91-; *b.* Chungking Feb. 8, '46; *m.* Kuo, Datong; 2 *d.; educ.* BS, Meteorology, NTU 68; MS, State U. of New York, Albany 72, Ph.D., Atmospheric Sc. 77, MBA 79; System Analyst, New York State Ass. Off. of Mng. & Budget 79-80; Chmn. & concur. Dir., Dept. of Business Admin., Chung Yuan Christian U. 81-84; Visiting Scholar, Sch. of Business, UC-Berkly. 84-85; Dean, Coll. of Business, Chung Yuan Christian U. 85-91. *Publ.:* "Am. & Ch. Mgr. in US Co. in Twn.: A Comparison," *Calif. Mng. Review* 85; "Managerial Attitude & Leadership Power in US Co. in Twn., ROC," *Intl. Jour. of Comparative Sociology* 87; "Paradigm Shift of Mng. Educ.-Holistic Educ. Perspective," *Mng. Review* 96; *Observations of Gen. Educ. in Am. U.: A Report* 97; "Gen. Educ. & the Realization of Hoistic Educ.—The Experience of Chung Yuan Christian U.," *The Educ. Philosophy of U. & Prof. Ethics* 99; *Add.* Chung Yuan Christian U., Chungli, Taoyuan County 320.

CHANG, TAO-MIN
(See CHANG, TAO-MING 張導民)

CHANG, TAO-MING 張導民
Nat. Policy Adv. to the Pres. 88-; *b.* Hupei Jan. 1, '08; *m.* Tsai, Shiao-i; 4 *s.,* 4 *d.; educ.* Grad., Chung Hua U., Wuchang; London U.; Dir., Kwangtung Tax Bu., MOF 39-41; Comr. of Finance, Kwangtung Prov. Govt. 41-45; Chief, Land Tax Dept., Min. of Food 46-49; Adv., CBC 50-57; Dep. Dir.-Gen., DGBAS 57-63, Dir.-Gen. 63-68; Auditor-Gen., Nat. Audit Off., Control Yuan 69-87; Standing Mem., Const. Res. Coun., NA; *Add.* 24 Lane 62, Hsin Sheng N. Rd., Sect. 3, Taipei 104.

CHANG, TE-MING
(See CHANG, TEH-MING 張德銘)

CHANG, TE-TZU 張德慈
Mem., Acad. Sinica 96-; For. Assc., Nat. Acad. of Sc. (USA); Fel., Nat. Acad. of Agr. Sc. (India), Third World Acad. of Sc., & Pontifical Acad. of Sc.; *b.* Shanghai Apr. 3, '27; *m.* Hwa, Szu-mei; 2 *s.; educ.* BSA, U. of Nanking 49; MS, Cornell U. 54; Ph.D., U. of Minnesota 59; Jr. Sp., JCRR 49-52, Sr. Sp. 59-61; Geneticist/Prin. Scientist, Intl. Rice Res. Inst., Philippines 61-91; Sp. Consultant, CITC 94-97; Expert, APEC-ATC 96. *Publ.: Plant Genetic Resources—Key to Future Plant Prod.* 97; & over 250 tech. papers on plant genetics, conservation of plant germ, plasm, evolution & improvement of rice, appearing in jour., bk., proceedings, encyclopedia pub. in the US, UK, Netherlands & other sources; *Add.* 2nd Fl., 2 Alley 13, Lane 131, Sha Lun Rd., Tamsui, Taipei County 251.

CHANG, TEH-MING 張德銘
Mem., Control Yuan 93-; Tchr. 90-; *b.* Twn. Nov. 1, '38; *m.* Yeh, Li-tzu; 2 *s.,* 1 *d.; educ.* LL.B., NTU; Attorney-at-Law; Mem., Legis. Yuan 75-77, & Taipei CCoun. 85-89; *Add.* Control Yuan, 2 Chung Hsiao E. Rd., Sect. 1, Taipei 100.

CHANG, TIEN-CHIN
(See CHANG, TIEN-JIN 張天津)

CHANG, TIEN-JIN 張天津
Pres., Nat. Taipei U. of Tech. 94-; Chmn., Soc. of Mfg. Engr., Taipei Chapter 94-, & Ch. Taipei U. Sports Fed. Table Tennis Cttee. 94-; ATEA Bd. of Trustees representing the Asia Region; Mem., Acad. Cttee., Intl. Voc. Educ. & Tng. Assn. (IVETA) 90-; *b.* Twn. Apr. 13, '40; *m.* Tu, Kuei-hui; 5 *d.; educ.* BS, Ind. Educ., NTNU 65; Ph.D., Ind. Educ., Penn. State U. 74; Pres., Tower Inst. of Tech. 74-78; Assc. Prof., NTNU 78-80, NTU & NTHU 77-80; Pres., Twn. Prov. Hai-san Sr. Ind. Voc. Sch. 79-80; Pres., Nat. Yunlin Inst. of Tech. 80-89; Chmn., IVETA 89-90; Pres., Nat. Taipei Inst. of Tech. 89-94. *Publ.: Admin. & Sup. in Voc. Tech. Educ.; Tool Design; Mech. Drawing; Mach. Mfg.; Heat Treatment; Jigs & Fixtures; Metal Working; Add.* 1 Chung Hsiao E. Rd., Sect. 3, Taipei 106.

CHANG, TING-CHUNG
(See CHANG, DING-CHONG 張鼎鍾)

CHANG, WAN-LI 張萬利
Pres., ROC Sports Fed. 97-, Nat. Educ. Assn. of the ROC 96-, Jin Wen Inst. of Tech. 90-, & Jin Wen Ent. 80-; *b.* Twn. Oct. 4, '33; *m.* Tsai, Yuen-kuei; 2 *s.,* 3 *d.; educ.* Taipei Mun. Tchrs. Coll. 52; NTNU 61; Dr. with Hon. in Educ., Columbia Coll. 88; Pres., Taipei Mun. Athletic Assn. 93-98; V. Pres., ROC Sports Fed. 93-97; Pres., Ch. Taipei Gymnastics Assn. 94-98; *Add.* Rm. 209, 20 Chu Lun St., Taipei 104.

CHANG, WEN-CHUNG
(See CHANG, JAMES WEN-CHUNG 張文中)

CHANG, WEN-HSIEN
(See CHANG, WEN-SHIANN 張文獻)

CHANG, WEN-HSIUNG
(See CHANG, WEN-SHION 張文雄)

CHANG, WEN-SHIANN 張文獻
Nat. Policy Adv. to the Pres. 95-; *b.* Twn. Jan. 28, '34; *m.* Hu, Ching-yueh; 1 *s.,* 3 *d.; educ.* LL.B., NTU 56; Mem.,

TPA 63-68, Legis. Yuan 73-81, & Control Yuan 81-93; *Add.* 10th Fl., 237 Fu Hsing S. Rd., Sect. 1, Taipei 105.

CHANG, WEN-SHION 張文雄
Pres., Nat. Yunlin U. of Sc. Tech. 97-; *b.* Taipei June 10, '38; *m.* Liu, Michelle M.H.; 3 *d.; educ.* BS, Chung Yuan Christian U. 61; MS, Waseda U. 65, DE 69; Acting Chmn., Union Ind. Res. Inst., MOEA 69-72; Dean of Acad. Aff., Nat. Kaohsiung Normal U. 72-78; Pres., Nat. Kaohsiung Inst. of Tech. 78-84, & Nat. Taipei Inst. of Tech. 84-89; Dir., Preparatory Off., Nat. Yunlin Inst. of Tech. 89-91, Pres. 91-97. *Publ.: A Study of the Org. & Function of Tech. Sch.* 96; *A Study of the Curricula in Tech. Coll.* 99; & over 88 publ. on bio-tech. & engr. educ.; *Add.* 123 U. Rd., Sect. 3, Touliu, Yunlin County 640.

CHANG, WEN-YING 張溫鷹
Mayor, Taichung City 97-; *b.* Twn. July 26, '50; *m.* Chen, Wen-hsien; 1 *s.,* 1 *d.; educ.* BA, Kaohsiung Med. Sch.; MD, Chung Shan Med. & Dental Coll.; Mem., CEC, DPP, Exec. Cttee., Twn. Assn. of Human Rights, & TPA 89-97; *Add.* 5th Fl., 17 Lane 217, Min Chuan Rd., Taichung 400.

CHANG, YU-FA 張玉法
Mem., Acad. Sinica & concur. Res. Fel., Inst. of Modern Hist. 75-; Prof., Inst. of Hist., NTNU 75-95, & NCCU 78-95; *b.* Shantung Dec. 28, '36; *m.* Li, Chung-wen; 1 *s.,* 1 *d.; educ.* BA, Dept. of Hist. & Geog., NTNU 59; MA, Jour., NCCU 64; MA, Hist., Columbia U. 70; Assc. Res. Fel., Inst. of Modern Hist., Acad. Sinica 71-75, Assc. Dir. 82-85, Dir. 85-91. *Publ.: Const. Parties in Late Ch'ing Ch.* 71; *Rev. Parties in Late Ch'ing Ch.* 75; *The Modernization of Ch.: The Case of Shantung Prov. (1860-1916)* 82; *Pol. Parties in the Early ROC* 85; *Ind. Hist. of Modern Ch. (1860-1916)* 92; *Collected Papers on the 1911 Rev. of Ch.* 93; *Draft Hist. of the ROC* 98; *Dem. Hist. of Modern Ch.* 99; *Add.* Inst. of Modern Hist., Acad. Sinica, 128 Yen Chiu Yuan Rd., Sect. 2, Taipei 115.

CHANG, YU-HENG
(See CHANG, YU-HERN 張有恆)

CHANG, YU-HERN 張有恆
Dir.-Gen., Civil Aeronautics Admin., MOTC 98-; Prof., NCKU 88-; *b.* Twn. Jan. 25, '54; *m.* Lin, Yee-shin; 2 *s.,* *educ.* BS, Dept. of Mech. Engr., NCKU 76; MS, Inst. of Traffic & Trans., NCTU 78; Ph.D. in Trans. Mng., Dept. of Civil Engr., U. of Pennsylvania 84; Chmn., Inst. of Trans. & Comm. Mng. Sc., NCKU 91-95; Dir. Gen., Inst. of Trans. & Comms., MOTC 95-97. *Publ: Logistics Mng.; Urban*

Transit Systems & Tech.; Design & Mng. of Transit Systems; Econ. of Trans.; Trans.; Urban Public Trans.; Op. & Mng. of Mass Transit Systems; Op. & Mng. of Trans. Ind.; Evaluation & Decision Making of Trans. Projects; Business Logistics; Trans. Policy Analysis; Air Trans. Mng.; Add. 340 Tun Hua N. Rd., Taipei 105.

CHANG, YU-HUEI 張有惠
Min. without Portfolio 2000-; Mem., CC, KMT 97-; *b.* Jan. 13, '41; *m.* Huang, Hsiang-ju; 2 *s.,* 1 *d.; educ.* Diploma, Nat. Tainan Tchrs. Coll. 59; BA, Childhood Educ., NTNU 64; B., PA, Tamkang U. 70; Doctoral Prog., Coll. of Pol. & Soc. Scs., Universidad Complutense de Madrid, Spain; Tchr. & Dean of Student Aff., elementary & jr. high schs. 59-69; Sp. Asst., Cent. Pers. Admin., Exec. Yuan 69-75; Planning Off., Com. of Nat. Corp., MOEA 69-75, Sect. Chief, 75-77, Dir., Pers. Off., Com. of Nat. Corp. 77-79; Dept. Dep. Dir. & Adv., Twn. Sugar Corp. 79-88; Counsl. & Adv., MOEA 88-90; Pres. & Chmn., Twn. Aluminum Corp. 90-92; Pres., Twn. Sugar Corp. 92-95, Chmn. 95-97; Sec.-Gen., Exec. Yuan 97-99; Bd. Chmn., CTC 99-2000; *Add.* Exec. Yuan, 1 Chung Hsiao E. Rd., Sect 1, Taipei 100.

CHANG, YU-HUI
(See CHANG, YU-HUEI 張有惠)

CHANG, YU-SHENG 張豫生
Pres., Pacific Cul. Found. 87-; Mem., CC, KMT 93-; *b.* Fukien Feb. 4, '29; *m.* Yang, Shi-jy; 2 *s.,* 1 *d.; educ.* LL.B., NTU 53; MA, Dip. & Intl. Law, NCCU 59; MA, St. John's U., USA 66; CEO, Fed. of Free Ch. Youth for Anti-communism 51-52; Assc. Prof., Tamkang U. 67-74; Sec. & Dep. Chief, CC, KMT 68-78, Dir.-Gen., Dept. of Youth Aff., CC 78-84; Dep. Dir.-Gen., Ch. Youth Corps 84-87; Assc. Prof., NTU 78-92; *Add.* 38 Chungking S. Rd., Sect. 3, Taipei 100.

CHAO, BEI-TSE 趙佩之
Mem., Acad. Sinica, & US Nat. Acad. of Engr.; Fel., Am. Soc. of Mech. Engrs., Am. Assn. for the Advancement of Sc., & Am. Soc. for Engr. Educ.; Consultant to Ind. & Govt. Agencies 50-; *b.* Kiangsu Dec. 18, '18; *m.* Kiang, May; 2 *c.; educ.* BEE, NCTU 39; Ph.D. (Boxer Indemnity Scholar), Victoria U., UK 47; Asst. Engr., Tool & Gauge Div., Cent. Mach. Works, Kunming 39-41, Assc. Engr. 41-43, Mgr. 43-45; Res. Asst., U. of Illinois, Urbana 48-50, Asst. Prof., Dept. of Mech. Engr. 51-53, Assc. Prof. 53-55, Prof. 55-87, Head, Thermal Sc. Div. 71-75, & Dept. of Mech. & Ind. Engr. 75-87; Assc. Mem., U. of Illinois (Cent.

for Advanced Study) 63-64; Russell S. Springer Prof., UC-Berkly. 73; Mem., Reviewing Staff Zentralblatt für Mathematik, Berlin 70-82; Mem., US Engr. Educ. Del. to Mainland Ch. 78; Mem., Adv. Screening Cttee. in Engr., Fulbright-Hays Awards Prog. 79-81, Chmn. 80 & 81; Mem., Cttee. for US Army Basic Sc. Res., NRC 80-83; Prince Disting. Lectr., Arizona State U. 84; Bd. Mem., Aircraft Gear Corp., Rockford, Illinois 89-94. *Publ.: Advanced Heat Transfer;* & numerous articles on mech. engr. in prof. jour.; *Add.* 101 W. Windsor Rd., Apt. 6103, Urbana, IL 61801-6697, USA.

CHAO, CHANG-PING 趙昌平
Mem., Control Yuan 93-; *b.* Twn. Feb. 1, '40; *m.* Chien, Yu-yun; 2 *s.,* 1 *d.; educ.* Grad., Taipei Mun. Tchrs. Coll. 59; Passed Sp. Exam. for Jud. Pers.; Grad., Judges & Prosecutors Tng. Cent. 73; Sup., Prosecutors' Off., Taipei Dist. Court 83-84; Prosecutor, Twn. High Court 84-86; Chief Prosecutor, Kinmen Dist. Court 86-89, Taitung Dist. Court 89-91, & Ilan Dist. Court 91-93; Chmn., Presidium, NA 86-92; Mem., APPU 84; Convener, 1st Cttee., Const. Res. Cttee. 81-89; *Add.* Control Yuan, 2 Chung Hsiao E. Rd., Sect. 1, Taipei 100.

CHAO, CHING-CHUAN
(See CHAO, HELEN C.J. 趙鏡涓)

CHAO, HELEN C.J. 趙鏡涓
Dir.-Gen., Public Radio System 91-; *b.* Hunan May 28, '41; *m.* Tang, Pan-pan; 1 *s.,* 1 *d.; educ.* BJ, Fu Hsing Kang Coll. 64; Public Aff. Reporter, Public Radio System 66-76, News Dir. 76-84, Prog. Dir. 84-87, Dep. Dir.-Gen. 87-91; *Add.* 17 Kuang Chou St., Taipei 100.

CHAO, LI-YUN
(See CHAO, NANCY LI-YUN 趙麗雲)

CHAO, LOUIS R. 趙榮耀
Mem., Control Yuan 93-; *b.* Twn. Aug. 17, '43; *m.* Hu, Sally; 1 *s.,* 1 *d.; educ.* BEE, NTU 65; Ph.D., Duke U. 71; Dir., Computer Sc. Dept., Tamkang U. 71-73, Dean, Engr. Coll. 73-78, Dean of Acad. Aff. 78-84, V. Pres. 84-89, Pres. 89-93. *Publ.: Introduction to Computers; Numerical Analysis; Advanced Numerical Analysis; Add.* 2 Chung Hsiao E. Rd., Sect. 1, Taipei 100.

CHAO, NANCY LI-YUN 趙麗雲
Chairperson, Nat. Coun. on Phys. Fitness & Sports, & concur. Adv., Exec. Yuan 97-2000; Mem., CC, KMT 93-, & Bd. of Gov., Intl. Coun. for Health, Phys. Educ., Recreation, Sport & Dance (ICHPERSD) 82-; Prof., Ch. Cul. U.

99-; *b.* Twn. Aug. 8, '52; *m.* Chien, Feng-wen; 1 *d.; educ.* Ed.B., NTNU 75, Ed.M. 77; Ed.D., Columbia U. 87; Lectr., Fu Jen Catholic U. 77-84; Staff, Sp., & Sect. Chief, Dept. of Phys. Educ. & Sports, MOE 78-85, Sr. Sp., Dep. Dir., & Dir. 85-89; Assc. Prof., Nat. Coll. of Phys. Educ. & Sports 87-89, & NTNU 88-91; Dir., Nat. Inst. for Compilation & Transl. 92-97. *Publ.: A Descriptive Study of Teaching: Pupil Motor Engagement Time in Phys. Educ. Classes in Taipei City* 87; *Sports for All Movement in the ROC* 91; *Sports Promotion & Strategy for 21st Century* 98; *Add.* 11th Fl., 20 Chu Lun St., Taipei 104.

CHAO, PEI-CHIH
(See CHAO, BEI-TSE 趙佩之)

CHAO, SHOU-PO 趙守博
Dir.-Gen., Dept. of Org. Aff., KMT 2000-; Mem., CSC, KMT 96-, & CC 80-; Chmn., Bd. of Dir., Memorial Found. of the 228 Incident 97-; *b.* Twn. Mar. 1, '41; *m.* Lu, Miaoshen; 2 *s.,* 1 *d.; educ.* LL.B., Cent. Police Coll.; MCL & S.J.D., U. of Illinois; Prof., Law, Cent. Police Coll. 72-76; Dir., Dept. of Sch. Youth Service, Ch. Youth Corps 75-76; Comr., Dept. of Info., TPG 76-79, Comr. 79-81; Mem., Bd. of Intl. Assn. for Community Dev. 81; Dep. Dir.-Gen., Dept. of Cul. Aff., CC, KMT 79-83; Comr., Dept. of Soc. Aff., TPG 81-87; Dir.-Gen., Dept. of Soc. Aff., CC, KMT 87-89; Chmn., CLA 89-94, Pres., Nat. Water Life Saving Assn., ROC 95-; Pres., Coun. of Soc. Welfare, ROC 95; Sec.-Gen., Exec. Yuan 94-97; Min. without Portfolio 97-98; Gov., TPG 98-2000. *Publ.: Getting Involved; A Comparative Study of the Choice of Law in Domestic Rel.; Law & Innovation; Soc. Policy, Family Welfare & Community Dev.; Soc. Problems & Soc. Welfare; Labor Policy & Labor Problems; Add.* 11 Chung Shan S. Rd., Taipei 104.

CHAO, SHU-TE
(See CHAO, SHWU-DER 趙淑德)

CHAO, SHWU-DER 趙淑德
Mem. (ministerial rank), Exam. Yuan 96-; *b.* Beijing Aug. 22, '41; *m.* Chang, Ming-wen; 2 *s.,* 1 *d.; educ.* BA, NCHU; Prof., NCHU 83-, Head, Dept. of Land Econ. & Admin. 87-92; Dir., Cent. for Land Econ. & Admin. Res. 92-96; Pres., Ch. Inst. of Land Appraisal 91-93, Real Estate Res. & Dev. Assn. of Ch. 94-96, & Jour. of Modern Land Admin. Assc. 87-96. *Publ.: Hist. of Ch. Land System; Study of Twn. Urban Readjustment; From Rural Land Usage to See Twn. Population Problem; The Practices of Housing Purchase; How to Ensure Mortgage Debt; Land Law; Add.* 1 Shih Yuan Rd., Wenshan, Taipei 116.

CHAO, TZE-CHI 趙自齊
Sr. Adv. to the Pres. 92-; Hon. Pres., WLFD 99-; *b.* Jehol Jan. 1, '15; *m.* Cheng, Li-zrin; 3 *s.,* 2 *d.; educ.* Nat. Nankai U.; Mil. Acad.; Sun Yat-sen Inst. on Policy Res. & Dev.; Nat. War Coll.; Hon. Ph.D., Kyung Hee U., S. Korea 79; Mem., Legis. Yuan 48-91; Mem., Jehol Prov. Cttee., KMT 55-56; Chmn., San-Min Chu-I Youth Corps in Jehol Prov. 56-59; Comr., Jehol Prov. Govt. 58-60; Chmn., Taichung City Cttee., KMT 55-64; Mem., KMT Caucus, Legis. Yuan 68-70, CAC, KMT 74-80, CC 74-94, & CAC 94; Dep. Sec.-Gen., Policy Coordination Cttee., CC, KMT 70, Sec.-Gen., CC 70-88, Dir.-Gen., Dept. of Org. Aff., CC 78; Prof., Ch. Cul. U. 76-77; Lectr., Nat. War Coll. 82-84; Chmn., Lung Kong World Fed. 88-92; Mem., CSC, KMT 84 & 88-94; Comr., NUC 90-91; Pres., WLFD/APLFD, ROC Chapter 89-97. *Publ.: The Refugees' Mng. of Recovery of the Mainland; US, Don't Wander Again; Six Hours in E. Berlin; Add.* 6 Lane 176, Ssu Wei Rd., Taipei 106.

CHAO, TZU-CHI
(See CHAO, TZE-CHI 趙自齊)

CHAO, YANG-CHING 趙揚清
Chmn., Fair Trade Com., Exec. Yuan 96-; *b.* Kiangsu Dec. 14, '49; *educ.* BC, Tamkang Coll. 72; LL.M., NCCU 75; Sect. Chief, Taxation & Tariff Com., MOF 82-85, Sr. Sp. & Dir., Dept. of Nat. Treasury 85-90, Coun. 90-91; Dep. Exec. Sec., Dev. Fund, Exec. Yuan 90-91; Dep. Dir.-Gen., Dept. of Nat. Treasury, MOF 91-95, Dir.-Gen. 95-96; *Add.* 14th Fl., 2-2 Chi Nan Rd., Sect. 1, Taipei 100.

CHAO, YI 趙怡
Dir.-Gen., GIO & Govt. Spokesman 99-2000; *b.* Twn. Apr. 12, '50; *m.* Lin, Li-chuan; 1 *d.; educ.* BBA, NCCU 72; MA in Jour. & Mass Comm., U. of Minnesota 77; Ph.D. in Comm. Arts & Sc., U. of So. Calif. 87; Reporter, CTV 77; Dir., Ch. Cul. Service Cent., Off. in Los Angeles, Dept. of Ovs. Aff., CC, KMT 77-81; V. Pres. & Gen. Mgr., Ch. Times Inc. (N. Am.) 81-84; Asst. Prof., Comm. Dept., Pasadena City Coll., USA 87; Assc. Prof., NCCU 87-99; Dep. Mgr., Mgr., & Dir., CTS 89-95; Gen. Mgr., AIM Media (Taipei) Co., Ltd. 95-96 & Global Broadcasting Co., Ltd. 96-98; Comr., RDEC 96-99; V. Pres., Hsuan Chuang U. 98-99; Chief Adv. & V. Chmn. of the Bd., Ea. Multimedia Co., Ltd. 98-99; *Add.* 2 Tientsin St., Taipei 100.

CHEN, BOR-SEN 陳博現
Prof., EE, NTHU 87-; *b.* Twn. Apr. 7, '47; *m.* Tsay, Shiow-fan; 1 *s.,* 1 *d.; educ.* BS, Tatung Inst. of Tech. 70; MS, NCU 73; Ph.D., EE, U. of So. Calif. 82; Lectr., Tatung Inst. of

Tech. 73-76, Assc. Prof. 76-83, Prof. 83-87. *Publ.:* Over 100 articles on control & signal processing published in intl. jour.; *Add.* Dept. of EE, NTHU, Hsinchu 300.

CHEN, CHANG-CHIEN
(See CHAN, SUNNEY I. 陳長謙)

CHEN, CHANG-WEN
(See CHEN, CHARNG-VEN 陳長文)

CHEN, CHAO-KUANG 陳朝光
Prof., NCKU 76-; Nat. Chair Prof., MOE 98-; *b.* Fukien Oct. 17, '34; *m.* Chang, Liang; 1 *s.*, 1 *d.; educ.* BS, NCKU 58, MS 64; MS, Georgia Inst. of Tech. 70; Ph.D., U. of Liverpool 87; Mech. Engr., CPC 60-66; Instr., NCKU 66-71, Assc. Prof. 71-76, Head, Inst. of Mech. Engr. 90-93. *Publ.:* Over 300 mech. engr. papers; *Add.* Dept. of Mech. Engr., NCKU, Tainan 700.

CHEN, CHAO-MIN 陳肇敏
Gen. C-in-C, ROCAF 98-; *b.* Twn. July 10, '40; *m.* Tien, Jung-chi; 1 *s.*, 1 *d.; educ.* Ch. Air Force Acad. 61; Regular Class, Air Force Cmd. & Staff Coll. 76; War Coll., Armed Forces U. 85; Maj./Gen., DCS/Op., GHQ, ROCAF 91-92; Lt./Gen., Cmdr., E. Area Cmd., ROCAF 92-93; Lt./Gen., Supt., Ch. Air Force Acad. 94-95; Lt./Gen., Cmdr., Air Combat Cmd. 95-96; Lt./Gen., V. C-in-C, ROCAF 97-98; *Add.* P.O. Box 90251-1, Taipei.

CHEN, CHAO-WEI
(See CHEN, REGIS C.W. 陳朝威)

CHEN, CHAO-YANG
(See CHEN, CHAU-YANG 陳朝洋)

CHEN, CHARNG-VEN 陳長文
V. Pres., Red Cross Soc. of the ROC 88-; Sr. Partner, Lee & Li, Attorneys-at-Law 72-; Mem., Taipei, Hsinchu & Kaohsiung Bar Assn.; Adv., Exec. Yuan 88-; Legal Consultant, CBC 88-, & MOFA; Gen. Counsl., MND; Mem., Cttee. on Review & Drafting of Socioecon. Laws, CEPD; Gov., Cml. Arbitration Assn. of the ROC; Adv., Ch. Aviation Dev. Found.; Hon. Pres., Harvard Club of the ROC 87-; Adjunct Prof., Law, NCCU, & Soochow U. 72-; *b.* Ch. Oct. 25, '44; *m.* Chen, Suzy K.W.; 1 *s.*, 1 *d.; educ.* LL.B., NTU; LL.M., U. of British Columbia, Can.; S.J.D., Harvard Law Sch.; Mem., Am. Bar Assn.; Coun. Mem., Asian Patent Attorneys Assn. *Publ.: Public Intl. Law; World Unfair Competition Law;* & numerous textbk. & articles; *Add.* 7th Fl., 201 Tun Hua N. Rd., Taipei 105.

CHEN, CHAU-YANG 陳朝洋
Pres., Tajen Inst. of Tech. 99-; *b.* Tokyo Dec. 24, '34; *m.* Chen Lin, Lan; 1 *s.*, 3 *d.; educ.* BS, Chung Yuan Coll. 59; BS in Pharmacy, Taipei Med. Coll. 64, MS in Pharmaceutic Sc. 67, Dr. of Pharmaceutical Sc. 70; Teaching Asst., Chung Yuan Coll. 59-61; Prof., Chung-san Med. Coll. 70-71, & Ch. Med. Coll. 71-74; Dean of Acad. Aff., Chia-nan Jr. Coll. 74-78; Prof., Twn. Coll. of Educ. 78-83; Chmn., Dept. of Pharmacy, Taipei Med. Coll. 83-89 & Grad. Inst. of Pharmaceutical Sc. 89-96, Dean of Acad. Aff. 96-97. *Publ.:* More than 50 res. papers; *Add.* 20 Wei Hsin Rd., Hsin Erh Village, Yenpu, Pingtung 907.

CHEN, CHECHIA 陳啓家
Pub., *Great Entertainment Daily & Great Sports Daily* 97-; *b.* Shanghai Jan. 6, '35; *m.* Chen, Pi-chih; 1 *s.*, 2 *d.; educ.* LL.B., NCCU 59; Reporter, *Twn. Shin Sheng Daily News* 60-71, City Ed. 71-78; Dep. Ed.-in-Chief, *Min Sheng Pao* 78-84, Ed.-in-Chief 84-90, Dep. Dir. 90; Pub., *Great News Daily* 90-97; *Add.* 216 Cheng Te Rd., Sect. 3, Taipei 104.

CHEN, CHEN-HSIANG 陳鎮湘
C-in-C, ROC Army 99-; *b.* Anhui Oct. 10, '42; *m.* Huang, Chi-mei; 2 *d.; educ.* Ch. Mil. Acad. 65; Army CGSC, Armed Forces U. 74; Mil. Res. Inst. of War, CGSC 83; Co., Bn., Brig., Div., Corps Cmdr.; Cmdr., Airborne & Sp. Warfare Cmd.; C/S, ROC Garrison Cmd. Hqs.; Cmdr., Field Army 94-96; Cmdr., Kinmen Def. Cmd. 96-98; C-in-C, Armed Forces Reserve Cmdr. & Coast Guard Cmd. 98-99; *Add.* P.O. Box 90601 Lungtan, Taoyuan 325.

CHEN, CHEN-KUEI
(See CHEN, MICHAEL J.K. 陳振貴)

CHEN, CHENG-HSIUNG
(See CHEN, DAVID T.H. 陳澄雄)

CHEN, CHENG-KUEI
(See CHEN, MICHAEL J.K. 陳振貴)

CHEN, CHI-CHIA
(See CHEN, CHECHIA 陳啓家)

CHEN, CHI-HSIUNG 陳吉雄
Dep. Sec.-Gen., Control Yuan, 98-; *b.* Twn. Aug. 3, '44; *m.* Chen, Shu-man; 2 *s.*, 1 *d., educ.* BA, NCHU 68; Admin. Asst., Bu. of Pers. 69-73; Sec. & Dir., Pres. Off., Control Yuan 73-91, Sec. Dir. 91-98, Acting Sec.-Gen. 95-96; *Add.* 2 Chung Hsiao E. Rd., Sect. 1, Taipei 100.

CHEN, CHI-LU 陳奇祿
Nat. Policy Adv. to the Pres. 88-; Mem. & Coun., Acad. Sinica; V. Chmn., Coun. of Ch. Cul. Renaissance; Mem., Preparatory Cttee., Ch. Public TV; Pres., Ch. Folklore Soc., & Ch. Cul. Property Preservation Soc.; *b.* Twn. Apr. 27, '23; *m.* Chang, Jo; 4 *s.; educ.* St. John's U., Shanghai; Grad. Sch., U. of New Mexico; Visiting Scholar, London U.; Ph.D., Sociology, U. of Tokyo; Res. Asst., Assc. Prof., Prof. & Chmn., Dept. of Archaeology & Anthropology, NTU 49-69; Curator, Dept. of Anthropology, Twn. Prov. Museum 58-63; Visiting Prof., Michigan State U. 69-70; Dir., Inst. of Am. Cul., Acad. Sinica 74-77; Dean, Coll. of Lib. Arts, NTU 75-77; Dep. Sec.-Gen., CC, KMT 75-77; Min. without Portfilio 77-82; Chmn., CCPD 81-88, Preparatory Cttee., Ch. Public TV 88-96, & Nat. Cul. & Arts Found. 96-97. *Publ.: Woodcarving of the Paiwan Tribe of Twn.; Soc. Org. of the Thao of Sun Moon Lake, Formosa; Material Cul. of the Formosan Aborigines; Studies of the Cul. of Twn. Aborigines; Add.* 6th Fl., 88 Min Chuan E. Rd., Sect. 6, Taipei 114.

CHEN, CHI-NAN 陳計男
Grand Justice, Jud. Yuan 94-; Adjunct Prof., Soochow U. 87-, & NCCU 88-; *b.* Twn. Aug. 28, '37; *m.* Ko, Ching-chih; 2 *s.,* 1 *d.; educ.* LL.B., NTU 60; Justice, Supreme Court 79-86; Div. Chief Justice, Admin. Court 86-94. *Publ.: Law of Bankruptcy; Law of Civil Procedure I & II; A Study of the Law of Procedure I & II; Add.* 4th Fl.-2, 2 Lane 163, Yen Ping S. Rd., Taipei 100.

CHEN, CHIEN-CHUNG 陳建中
Sr. Adv. to the Pres.; Mem., CAC, KMT; Bd. Chmn., ROC-Japanese Rel. Res. & Dev. Found.; V. Chmn., Assn. for the Promotion of Nat. Unification & Reconst. of the ROC; Standing Bd. Mem., CRRA; Bd. Chmn., Tahua Jr. Coll. of Tech. & Com.; *b.* Shensi Oct. 12, '13; *m.* Fan, Ching-jun; 2 *s.,* 4 *d; educ.* BA, Shanghai U.; Ph.D., Tankuk U., S. Korea; Mem., CC, KMT, Exec. Yuan Planning Com., & 1st NA; Sec.-Gen., NA; V. Chmn., Const. Reform Res. Cttee.; *Add.* 9th Fl., 237-1 Fu Hsing S. Rd., Sect. 1, Taipei 106.

CHEN, CHIEN-JEN 陳建仁
Mem., Acad. Sinica 98-; Prof., Grad. Inst. of Epidemiology, NTU 94-, Dean, Coll. of Public Health 99-; *b.* Twn. June 6, '51; *m.* Lo, Fong-ping; 2 *d.; educ.* BS, NTU 73, MPH 77; D.Sc., John Hopkins U. 82; Prof., Grad. Inst. of Public Health, NTU 86-94; Res. Fel., Inst. of Biomed. Sc., Acad. Sinica 88-96; Visiting Res. Fel., Columbia U 89-90; Adjunct Prof., Tulane U. 94-99; Prof. & Dir., Grad. Inst. of Epidemiology, NTU 94-97; Dir.-Gen., Div. of Life Sc.,

NScC 97-99. *Publ.:* coauthor, *Malignant Neoplasms Among Residents of a Blackfoot Disease-endemic Area in Taiwan: High-arsenic Artesan Well Water & Cancers* 85, *Arsenic & Cancers* 88, *Universal Hepatitis B Vaccination in Twn. & the Incidence of Hepatocellular Carcinoma* 97; etc.; *Add.* Grad. Inst. of Epidemiology, 1 Jen Ai Rd., Sect. 1, Taipei 100.

CHEN, CHIEN-JEN 程建人
Rep., TECRO, USA 2000-; *b.* Kiangsu Aug. 11, '39; *m.* Ho, Yolanda; 1 *s.,* 1 *d.; educ.* LL.B., NCCU 60, Grad. Sch. of Intl. Rel. 62; LL.B., U. of Cambridge 65; Res. Fel., U. of Madrid 66; Sp., Info. Dept., MOFA 67-69, Sect. Chief 69-71; Adjunct Lectr., Intl. Law, NCCU 68-71; 3rd Sec., Emb. in USA 71-74, 2nd Sec. 74-76, & 1st Sec. 76-79; Dir., Public Aff., CCNAA, Washington, D.C. 79-80, & Dept. of N. Am. Aff., MOFA 80-82; Adjunct Lectr., Intl. Rel., NCCU 80-82; Adv., CCNAA, Washington, D.C. 82, Dep. Rep. 82-89; Admin. V. Min. of For. Aff. 89-93; Alt. Mem., CC, KMT 88-93; Convener, For. Aff. Cttee., 1st, 2nd & 4th Sess., Legis. Yuan 93-96; Dir.-Gen., Dept. of Ovs. Aff., CC, KMT 93-96; Pol. V. Min. of For. Aff. 96-98; Dir.-Gen., GIO & Govt. Spokesman 98-99; Min. of For. Aff. 99-2000; *Add.* 4201 Wisconsin Avenue, NW, Washington, DC 20016-2137, USA.

CHEN, CHIEN-MIN 陳健民
Min. without Portfolio 97-2000; *b.* Chekiang Oct. 5, '42; *educ.* LL.B., NTU 64; Judge, Taipei Dist. Court 69-79, Chief Judge 79-80; Judge, Twn. High Court 80-84; Pres., Kinmen Dist. Court 84-86, Hualien Dist. Court 86-90, Chiayi Dist. Court 90-91, & Tainan Dist. Court 91-92; Sec.-Gen., MOJ 92-93; Mem., Legis. Yuan 93-97; *Add.* 1 Chung Hsiao E. Rd., Sect. 1, Taipei 100.

CHEN, CHIEN-NIEN 陳建年
Magis., Taitung County 93-; *b.* Twn. Oct. 10, '47; *m.* Huang, Yu-hsia; 1 *s.,* 2 *d.; educ.* BS in Pharmacology, Kaohsiung Med. Coll. 72; Mem., Taitung CoCoun. 82-86; Charter Mem., Naruwan Jaycees 83-84; Mem., TPA 86-93, & Twn. Prov. Cttee., KMT 87-93; Dir., Taitung Off., VAC 93-99; Dep. Dir., Taitung Cttee., Ch. Youth Corps 94-98; *Add.* 36 Alley 360, Chuan Kuang Rd., Taitung 950.

CHEN, CHIN-HUANG 陳錦煌
Min. without Portfolio 2000-; *b.* Twn. May 19, '52; *m.* Chen, Ching-chou; 2 *s.,* 1 *d.; educ.* B., Sch. of Med., NTU 77; Passed the Sr. Exam. for Med. Pers. 77; Pediatric Residency, NTU Hosp. 79-81; Practice at Dr. Chen's Clinic Hsinkang Rural Township, Chiayi County 81-2000; Pres for 5 sess., Hsin Kang Found. of Cul. & Educ., Chiay

County 87-2000; Public opinion leader; Mgr. of cul. regeneration campaigns in Hsinkang area; Outsdg. Alumni of Chiayi High Sch. (1st sess.) 94; Mem., 1st Bd. of Dir., Nat. Endowment for Cul. & Arts 96-98; Sup., Community Bldg. & Mng. Soc. of the ROC 97, Standing Sup. 99; "One of the 200 Most Influential Figures in Twn.," *Commonwealth Mag.* 98; Mem., Review Cttee. of Life-long Learning Project, MOE 98; Consultative Mem. of Public Health Dev. in Community, DOH 99; The Found. d'Entreprise Montblanc de la Cul. Award 2000; *Add.* Exec. Yuan, 1 Chung Hsiao E. Rd., Taipei 100.

CHEN, CHIN-HSIUNG 陳金雄

Pres., Nat. U. Preparatory Sch. for Ovs. Ch. Students 98-; *b.* Twn. June 28, '39; *m.* Huang, Yu-mei; 1 *s.*, 1 *d.*; *educ.* Twn. Prov. Tainan Tchrs. Coll. 59; BA, NTNU 66; Elementary Sch. Tchr. 59-62; Jr. High Sch. Tchr. 66-71; Lectr., Nat. Kaohsiung Inst. of Tech., Assc. Prof., Prof., Dir., Off. of Gen. Aff., Dir., Night Sch. 71-80; Sec., Sc. & Tech. Counsl. Off., MOE 80-81; Prof., NCKU, Dean, Off. of Gen. Aff., Sec.-Gen., Dir., Night Sch. 81-98; Sec.-Gen., Nat. Space Prog. Off., NScC 91-93; Res., NScC, STAG 91-93; Sec.-Gen., MOE 96-98. *Publ.: Supplementary Proofs to Wang Yi's Annotation of the Connectives in the Odes of Chiu Yuan & Song Yuh* 85; *The Study of Yen Jy-tuei* 88; *The Analytical Study of the Expletives in Hsun Tzu* 91; *Comments on Song Yuh & His Works* 96; *Add.* 46 Hsin Liau Rd., Linkou, Taipei County 244.

CHEN, CHIN-JANG

(See CHEN, CHING-JANG 陳金讓)

CHEN, CHIN-LI

(See CHERN, JINN-LIH 陳進利)

CHEN, CHING-HSIU 陳清秀

Spkr., Yunlin CoCoun. 98-; *b.* Twn. Apr. 5, '45; 1 *s.*, 1 *d.*; *educ.* Tounan High School; Borough Chief, Hsitun Bourough, Huwei, Yunlin County 73-82; Dep. Spkr., Yunlin CoCoun. 82-90, Mem. 90-98; *Add.* 73 Fu Chien St., Touliu, Yunlin County 640.

CHEN, CHING-JANG 陳金讓

Acting Spkr., NA 99-, Mem. 96-; Mem., CSC, KMT 99-; *b.* Twn. Feb. 1, '35; *m.* Pai, May-yun; 1 *s.*, 4 *d.*; *educ.* LL.B., Soochow U. 58; Spkr., Yungho Rep. Conf. 64-72; Mem., NA 73-87; Dep. Dir.-Gen., Dept. of Org. Aff., CC, KMT 79-84, Chmn., Taipei Mun. Cttee. 84-88, V. Chmn., Policy Coordination Cttee., CC 88-90, Dir., Secretariat 90, Dir.-Gen., Dept. of Org. Aff. 90-92; Sec.-Gen. & Mem., NA 92-96, Dep.

Spkr. 99; Mem., CSC, KMT 93-97; Min. of Exam., Exam. Yuan 96-99; *Add.* 53 Chung Hua Rd., Sect. 1, Taipei 100.

CHEN, CHING-TAN 陳鏡潭

Comr., TPG 94-; *b.* Twn. Jan. 4, '29; *m.* Chen Kau, Shu-jung; 1 *s.*, 2 *d.*; *educ.* BS, NTNU; MS, Tohoku U., Japan; Ph.D., Tokyo U., Japan; Assc. Prof., NTHU 70-75; Prof. & Chmn., Dept. of Chem., NTNU 75-80, Prof. & Dean, Coll. of Sc. 80-86; Pres., Nat. Taipei Tchrs. Coll. 86-94. *Publ.:* "Biosynthesis of Elsinochrome" in *Chem. Pharm. Bull.* 66; "Analysis of 5-chloro-7-iodo-8-quinolinol Conjugates by High Performance Liquid Chromatography" in *Chem. Pharm. Bull.* 75; "Serum Levels of 5-chloro-7-iodo-8-quinolinol and Its Toxicity in Various Animals" in *Chem. Pharm, Bull.* 76; "The Educ. Interchange in Chem. between Japan & the ROC—Overview & Prospects" in *Chem. & Educ.* 90; "Chem. Educ. in Twn." in *Chem. & Chem. Ind.* 93; *Add.* 8-2 Alley 2, Lane 217, Chung Hsiao E. Rd., Sect. 3, Taipei 106.

CHEN, CHIU-SEN 陳秋盛

Music Dir., Taipei City Symphony Orchestra; *b.* Twn. July 9, '42; 2 *d.*; *educ.* Grad., Tamkang U.; Staat Hochschule für Musik und Darstellung, München; Prof., Nat. Twn. Acad. of Arts 72-77; Conductor, Twn. Symphony Orchestra 77-79; *Add.* 7th Fl., 25 Pa Te Rd., Sect. 3, Taipei 105.

CHEN, CHIU-SHENG

(See CHEN, CHIU-SEN 陳秋盛)

CHEN, CHIUNG-LING 陳瓊玲

Dir.-Gen., Directorate Gen. of Posts, MOTC 96-; *b.* Twn. Dec. 1, '34; 3 *s.*, 2 *d.*; *educ.* BA, NTNU; Chief, Acct. Div., Taipei Post Off. 70-77; Chief, Acct. Div., Twn. Post Admin. 77-79; Dep. Dir., Acct. Dept., Directorate Gen. of Posts 79-85; Dir., Data Processing Cent., Directorate Gen. of Postal Remittances & Savings Bk. 85-88, Secretariat of Planning & Evaluation Cttee., Directorate Gen. of Posts 88-89, & Acct. Dept. 89-90; Regional Postmaster Gen., Twn. Cent. Region Head Off. 90-92; Dep. Dir., Directorate Gen. of Postal Remittances & Savings Bk. 92-96; Dep. Dir., Directorate Gen. of Posts 96-96; *Add.* 55 Chin Shan S. Rd., Sect. 2, Taipei 106.

CHEN, CHU 陳菊

Chairperson, CLA 2000-; *b.* Twn. June 10, '50; *educ.* Grad., Dept. of Lib. & Info. Studies, Shin Hsin U. 64-68, Grad. Sch. of Soc. Transformation Studies 97-98; Studying, Inst. of Public Aff. Mng., Nat. Sun Yat-sen U. 98-; Mem., Bd. of Trustees, Ea. Asian Assn. for Human Rights 79; Off. Dir.,

Sec.-Gen. & Pres., Twn. Assn. for Human Rights 86-92; Mem., NA 91-93; Dir., Bu. of Soc. Aff., TCG & Kaohsiung City Govt. 95-98 & 98-2000. *Publ.: Imprisonment as One's Dowry—Love & Fight of a Twn. Woman* 93; *A Beautiful Dream About Olive—Twn. Chrysanthemum & Twn. Passion;* 95; *Add.* 15th Fl., 132 Ming Sheng E. Rd., Sect. 3, Taipei 105.

CHEN, CHUAN 陳川
Sec.-Gen., NA 96-, Dep. Sec.-Gen., KMT Caucus 85-, Mem. 81-; Mem., CC, KMT 93-; *b.* Twn. June 29, '34; *m.* Tsai, Ray-in; *2 s., 2 d.; educ.* LL.B., Land Admin. Dept., NCHU 59; Staff, Land Admin. Bu. 57-61; Dir., Wufeng Dist. Land Admin. Off. 61-70; Sect. Chief, Taoyuan Land Admin. Dept. 70-82; Dep. Dir., Secretariat, NA 82-85; Dep. Sec.-Gen., NA 90-96; *Add.* 9th Fl.-9, 107 Chung Hua Rd., Taoyuan 330.

CHEN, CHUN-HSIUNG 陳俊雄
Prof., Dept. of EE, NTU 72-; *b.* Twn. Mar. 7, '37; *m.* Chen Ho, Tzu-yen; *4 c.; educ.* Ph.D., Grad. Inst. of EE, NTU; Instr., NTU 63-68, Assc. Prof. 68-72, Chmn., Dept. of EE 82-85; Visiting Prof., U. of Houston, USA 86-87. *Publ.:* 120 papers on EE; *Add.* 1 Roosevelt Rd., Sect. 4, Taipei 106.

CHEN, CHUNG-HUA 陳重華
Comr., Chiang Kai-shek Memorial Hall 95-; *b.* Fukien May 15, '35; *m.* Chen, Guey-shiang; *1 s., 1 d.; educ.* BSE, NTNU 59; Dep. Dir., Employment & Voc. Tng. Admin., MOI 87-94; Coun., CLA 95. *Publ.: Heaven, Earth, Human Beings* 82; *Add.* 21 Chung Shan S. Rd., Taipei 100.

CHEN, CHUNG-SHENG 陳聰勝
V. Chmn., NYC 94-; *b.* Twn. Jan. 21, '44; *m.* Wu, Yin-hwa; *2 s.; educ.* BPS, NTU 66; MPS, NCCU 70, Ph.D. 78; Sect. Chief, Exec. Yuan 78, Counsl. 78-81; Counsl., MOI 82-83, Dir., Dept. of Soc. Aff. 84, Dep. Dir.-Gen., Employment & Voc. Tng. Admin. 84-87; Dir.-Gen., Employment & Voc. Tng. Admin., CLA 87-94. *Publ.: A Study of the Org. of Twn.'s Farm Assc.* 79; *Voc. Tng., License System, & Employment Services of Service Ind. in Germany, Switzerland & Austria* 85; *Reform & Dev. of Voc. Tng. in Korea & Japan* 87; *Voc. Tng. & Employment Assistance in the ROC; A New Milestone in Dev. Voc. Tng. to Meet the Changing Times* 93; *Voc. Tng. System in the Main Country* 97; *Add.* 14th Fl., 5 Hsuchow Rd., Taipei 100.

CHEN, DAVID T.H. 陳澄雄
Exec. Dir., Twn. Musical Cul. Educ. Found. 92-; Music Dir., Nat. Symphony Orchestra 91-; *b.* Twn. Aug. 26, '41;

m. Wu, Margaret Kuei-mei; *2 s.; educ.* Grad., Nat. Twn. Acad. of Arts; Music Dept., Nat. Akademie Mozarteum, Salzburg; 1st Flutist, Nat. Symphony Orchestra 63-65; Assc. Prof., Nat. Twn. Acad. of Arts 68-77; Music Dir., Taipei Mun. Tchrs. Coll. 79-83, & Taipei Mun. Ch. Orchestra 83-91; Pres., ROC Band Assn. 88-92. *Publ.:* Theses & articles on music; *Add.* 3rd Fl., 7-5 Lane 22, Hsin Sheng S. Rd., Sect. 3, Taipei 106.

CHEN, DING-NAN 陳定南
Min. of Justice 2000-; *b.* Sept. 29, '43; *m.* Chang, Chao-yi; *2 s.; educ.* LL.B., NTU; Ilan County; Magis., Ilan County 81-89; Mem., Budget Cttee., Legis. Yuan 94, Home & Border Aff. Cttee., & Organic Laws Cttee. 97; Mem., Legis. Yuan 93-2000; *Add.* 130 Chungking S. Rd., Sect. 1, Taipei 100.

CHEN, DING-SHINN 陳定信
Mem., Acad. Sinica 92-; Prof., Coll. of Med., NTU 83-; Dir., Hepatitis Res. Cent., NTU Hosp. 88-; *b.* Taipei July 6, '43; *m.* Hsu, Hsu-mei; *1 s., 1 d.; educ.* MD, Coll. of Med., NTU 68; Lectr., Dept. of Internal Med., Coll. of Med., NTU 75-78, Assc. Prof. 78-83, Dir., Grad. Inst. of Clinical Med. 85-91. *Publ.:* Over 400 sc. papers published in intl. jour. & ed. of 2 bk.; *Add.* Hepatitis Res. Cent., NTU, 7 Chung Shan S. Rd., Taipei 100.

CHEN, DU-CHENG 陳篤正
Dir., Nat. Twn. Arts Educ. Inst. 96-; *b.* Twn. Nov. 27, '40; *m.* Wu Yue-fen; *1 s., 1 d.; educ.* Twn. Prov. Tchr. Coll. 65; BS, Tamkang U. 73; Res. at NCCU 86; Dir., Pers. Off., NTHU 78-79; Sp., MOE 88-92; Dep. Dir., Nat. Dr. Sun Yat-sen Memorial Hall 92-94, & MOE 94-96. *Publ.: Admin. Reform Begins from Improving the Bidding System; Add.* 47 Nan Hai Rd., Taipei 100.

CHEN, FEI-KUN 陳慧坤
Oil painter 77-; *b.* Twn. June 25, '07; *m.* Chen Chuang, She-chi; *1 s., 2 d.; educ.* Taichung First High Sch. 22; Tokyo Arts Coll., Japan 28; Tchr., Taichung Com. Sch. 34-45, Taichung Second Girls' High Sch. 41-45, Shih Chien Coll. 58-72, Nat. Twn. Art Coll. 65-76, & NTNU 47-77. *Publ.: A Trip of Art to the Europe; Van Gogh; Add.* 3rd Fl., 43 Lane 101, Roosevelt Rd., Sect. 2, Taipei 106.

CHEN, GEORGE S.Y. 陳世圯
Pol. V. Min. of Trans. & Comms. 97-2000; *b.* Kiangsi May 13, '38; *m.* Chiu, Shiow-mei; *2 s.; educ.* BE, Civil Engr., Chung Yuan Christian U. 70; ME, Trans. & Traffic Engr., Asian Inst. of Tech. 72; MBA, Sch. of System Mng., U. of So. Calif. 77; Highway Engr., Twn. Highway Bu., TPG 56-

70; Engr. & Dir., Nat. Freeway Bu., MOTC 70-87; Dep. Dir., Dept. of Rapid Transit Systems, TCG 87-90; Dir., Twn. Highway Bu., TPG 90-96, Comr., Dept. of Trans. 96-97. *Publ.: A Study of the Dangerous Sects. of the Nat. Freeways; Add.* 2 Changsha St., Sect. 1, Taipei 100.

CHEN, GORDON S. 陳樹

Chmn., Sec. & Exchange Com., MOF 95-; Dir., 4th Div., EY, & Secretariat; *b.* Twn. Mar. 10, '54; *m.* Fang, Shu-chin; 1 *s.,* 2 *d.; educ.* MA, Inst. of Public Finance, NCU 79; Ph.D. in Mng., NTU; Assc. Prof., NCCU & Ch. Cul. U. 86-94; Dir. & V. Chmn., Sec. & Exchange Com., MOF 95. *Publ.: The Theory & Practice of Convertible Bonds; Add.* 1 Chung Hsiao E. Rd., Sect. 1, Taipei 100.

CHEN, HAN 陳涵

Nat. Policy Adv. to the Pres. 98-; Adv., MOJ 97-; Prof. of Law, NCCU & Cent. Police U. 97-; State Public Prosecu-tor-Gen. emeritus, Public Prosecutor Off., Supreme Court 92-; *b.* Kwangtung May 6, '27; *m.* Wu, Tsai-hsiu; 3 *s.,* 1 *d.; educ.* LL.B., NCU 52; Chief Judge, Kinmen Dist. Court 72-74; Presiding Judge, Tainan Br., Twn. High Court 75-76; Chief Public Prosecutor, Public Prosecutor's Off., Chiayi Dist. Court 78-79; Dir., Dept. of Prosecution Aff., MOJ 79-82; Chief Public Prosecutor, Public Prosecutor's Off., Taipei Dist. Court 82-85; Admin. V. Min. of Justice 85-86; Public Prosecutor-Gen., Public Prosecutors' Off., Twn. High Court 86-92. *Publ.: Oughtopia; Add.* 122 Chungking S. Rd., Sect. 1, Taipei 100.

CHEN, HSI-FAN
(See CHEN, STEPHEN S.F. 陳錫蕃)

CHEN, HSI-HUANG 陳希煌

Chmn., COA 2000-; *b.* Taipei Dec. 18, '35; *m.* Liu, Hsin-yu; 1 *s.,* 3 *d.; educ.* BS, Agr. Econ., NTU 59; MS, Agr. Econ., U. of Georgia 71, Ph.D. 74; Teaching Asst., NTU 61-62; Res. Asst., Rural Econ. Div., JCRR, Taipei 62-64, Jr. Sp. 65-69, Sp. 74-75, Sr. Sp. 75-79, Chief 79-82; Prof., Dept. of Agr. Econ., NTU 82-2000, Head 87-93; Mem., Ed. Adv. Bd. of Agr. Econ., *Jour. of Intl. Assn. of Agr. Economists* 92-97. *Publ.:* "Issues & Strategies of Raising Agr. Competitiveness in Twn.," COA res. report 98; *A Dynamic Multi-targets Policy-making Model for Agr.—A Study for Strengthening Credit System of Farmers' Finan-cial Inst.* (a NScC report) 97; *A Vista of Agr. Reform on the Ch. Mainland & the Implementation of Agr. Exchange Cross-Strait* (a NScC report) 96; *An Econ. Analysis of Econ. & Trade Polices Cross-strait* (A COA report) 94; *Problems of ROC-Germany Produce Trade & Agr. Policy of the ROC—A Comparative Study* (A COA report) 93; "Tech. Strategy of Twn. Agr. Dev." presented in the Seminar on the Dev. of Modern Agr. Tech. held by the Ch. Rural Plan-ning Soc. 95; & over 37 res. & conf. papers about agr. dev. in Twn., Ch. mainland, & Asia; *Add.* 37 Nan Hai Rd., Taipei 100.

CHEN, HSI-TSAN 陳錫燦

Amb., Emb. of the ROC in Malawi 99-; *b.* Anhwei Oct. 24, '35; *m.* Yun Mei-ling; 1 *s.,* 1 *d.; educ.* B. of PA, NCU 65; Desk Off., MOFA 67-70; 3rd Sec., Emb. in Swaziland 71-74, 2nd Sec. 75; Sect. Chief, Protocol Dept., MOFA 76-79, Sec., Secretariat 80-81, Sr. Sec. 82-86; Dep. Dir-Gen., CCNAA, Off. in Los Angeles 87-90, & Off. in Seattle 90-96, Sec.-Gen., CCNAA 97-99; *Add.* Area 40, Plot No. 9, Capital City, Lilongwe, Malawi.

CHEN, HSING-LING 陳桑齡

Strategy Adv. to the Pres. 91-; *b.* Peiping Aug. 9, '24; *m.* Tang, Chiao-chung; 2 *s.,* 4 *d.; educ.* Ch. Air Force Acad.; Pilot Tng. Sch., Luke Field, USA; War Coll., Armed Forces U.; Group Cmdr., 3rd Tactical Fighter Group, ROCAF 64-66, Wing Cmdr. 72-74; Asst. to DCGS/Planning, MND 77; Dep. C/S for Op., Hqs., ROCAF 77-79; CG, Combat Air Cmd., ROCAF 79-80; Dir., Pol. Warfare Dept., Hqs., ROCAF 80-82; Dep. C-in-C, ROCAF 82-83; V. Chief of the Gen. Staff, MND 83-86; C-in-C, ROCAF 86-89; Chief of the Gen. Staff, MND 89-91; *Add.* 5 Lane 118, Jen Ai Rd., Sect. 3, Taipei 106.

CHEN, HSING-SHEN
(See CHERN, SHIING-SHEN 陳省身)

CHEN, HSIUNG-FEI
(See TCHEN, HIONG-FEI 陳雄飛)

CHEN, HUI-FA
(See CHEN, WAI-FAH 陳惠發)

CHEN, HUI-KUN
(See CHEN, FEI-KUN 陳慧坤)

CHEN, JUI-LUNG
(See CHEN, STEVE RUEY-LONG 陳瑞隆)

CHEN, KAI-MO 陳楷模

Supt., Cathay Gen. Hosp. 96-; Prof. Emeritus, NTU 96-; Adjunct Prof., NTU Hosp. 96-; Pres., T.Y. Lin's HCC Res. Found. 92-; *b.* Twn. Aug. 29, 29; *m.* Hsu, Tsuei-lien; 2 *s.,* 3 *d.; educ.* MB, NTU 56; Prof., Coll. of Med., NTU 75-96;

Dir., Emergency Service, NTU Hosp. 75-82, Chmn., Dept. of Anesthesiology 82-84, & Dept. of Surgery 84-90; Pres., Surgical Society of Gastroenterology, ROC 88-90, Surgical Assn., ROC 90-92, & E. CICD 92-96. *Publ.:* More than 170 med. papers; *Add.* 280 Jen Ai Rd., Sect. 4, Taipei 106.

CHEN, KANG-CHIN 陳庚金
Chmn., Twn. Prov. Cttee., KMT 98-; Mem., CC, KMT 93-; *b.* Twn. Feb. 2, '39; *m.* Liu, Jin-feng; 1 *s.,* 2 *d.; educ.* BPS, NCCU 65, MPA 69; Sect. Chief, RDEC 69-76; Dir., Dept. of Soc. Aff., CC, KMT 77-80; Magis., Taichung County 81-89; Admin. V. Min. of Exam., Exam. Yuan 90, Pol. V. Min. of Exam. 90-93; Dir.-Gen., CPA 93-97; Nat. Policy Adv. to the Pres. 97-98. *Publ.: Current System for the Appointment of Govt. Employees; Mng. in Theory & Practice; Applied Behavioral Sc. on Mng.; Human Rel. & Mng.; Add.* 109 Huai Ning St., Taipei 100.

CHEN, KENG-CHIN
(See CHEN, KANG-CHIN 陳庚金)

CHEN, KUEI-HUA 陳桂華
Nat. Policy Adv. to the Pres. 95-; *b.* Kwangtung July 19, '18; *m.* Yi, Kuei-chen; 1 *s.,* 1 *d.; educ.* 11th Class, Mil. Acad.; 18th Class, Army Coll.; 1st Sp. Class, CGSC, USA; 1st Class, Pragmatism Inst.; Div. Cmdr., 8th Reserved Div. & 32nd Div., ROC Army; C/S, 2nd ROC Army Corps; Dean, Pragmatism Inst.; V. C/S, GHQ, ROC Army; Dir.-Gen., Pers. Admin., MND 66-68, Dept. Chief, Gen. Staff for Pers. 68-72; Dir.-Gen., CPA 72-84; Min. of Pers., Exam. Yuan 84-94. *Publ.: A Study of Hitler's Unsuccessful Aggression on Russia; Add.* 1 Shih Yuan Rd., Taipei 116.

CHEN, LARRY L.G. 陳龍吉
Sec.-Gen., TPG 99-; Chmn., Twn. Environmental Sanitation Assn. 97-; Comr., Ch. Inst. of Engr. 98-; Assc. Prof., NTU 84-; *b.* Twn. Jan. 2, '45; *m.* Lo, Amy S.C.; 1 *s.,* 1 *d.; educ.* BS, NTU; MS & DE, Asian Inst. of Tech.; Sect. Chief, Dept. of Environmental Protection, TCG 76-84, Sec.-Gen. 85-86, Dep. Dir.-Gen. 86-87; Comr., Ch. Inst. of Engr. 92-96; Chmn., Ch. Inst. of Environmental Engr. 92-94, Acoustic Assn. of the ROC 92-96, & Fund of Resources Recovery 93-95; Dep. Admin., EPA 87-96; Comr., Dept. of Environmental Protection 96-99; Comr., TPG 98-99. *Publ.: Water Quality Modeling of the Hsintien River in Twn.; Study of Refuse Storage & Collection Systems; Futekeng Sanitary Landfill Projects; The Status of Hazardous Waste Mng. in Twn.; Water Pollution Control in Twn.; Add.* 1 Sheng Fu Rd., Chunghsing New Village, Nantou 540.

CHEN, LI-CHUN
(See CHEN, LIH J. 陳力俊)

CHEN, LIH J. 陳力俊
Dean, Coll. of Engr., NTHU. 99-, Prof., Dept. of Material Sc. & Engr. 79-; Pres., Ch. Soc. for Materials Sc. 95-; Ed., *Materials Chem. & Phys.* 92-; MOE Chair Prof.; *b.* Chekiang Aug. 13, '46; *m.* Wu, Hsiang; 2 *s.; educ.* Ph.D., Phys., UC-Berkly. 74; BS, Phys., NTU 68; Chmn. & Dir., Dept. of Materials Sc. Cent. 84-85. *Publ.:* 251 referred papers in intl. jour.; 303 papers in conf. proceedings; 74 bk., monographs & others; *Add.* Dept. of Materials Sc., NTHU, Hsinchu 300.

CHEN, LUNG-CHI
(See CHEN, LARRY L.G. 陳龍吉)

CHEN, MICHAEL J.K. 陳振貴
Pres., Providence U. 99-, & Catholic Nat. Coun. of the Lay Apostolate, ROC 99-; Adv. Bd. Mem., NYC 97-; *b.* Twn. Dec. 6, '47; *m.* Huang, Feng-chu; 1 *s.; educ.* BA, Foreign Lang. & Lit. NCKU 71; MA, Am. Studies, Tamkang Coll. of Arts & Sc. 74; MA, Smith Coll., USA 77, Ed.D., Nova U. 91; Exchange Prof., Pasadena City Coll., USA 81-82; Assc. Prof., Shih Chien Coll. 78-81, Prof. & Dean of Academic Aff. 85-87; Adjunct Prof., MBA prog., Northrop U., USA 88-90; Prin. & Bd. Mem., Catholic Ming Yuan Inst., Calif. 87-93; Prof., V. Pres. & Dean of Acad. Aff., Shih Chien U. 93-99. *Publ.: The Influence of Henry A. Kissinger on the Decision-making of US Foreign Policy* 85; "The Am. Community Coll.," *Shih Chien Youth* 85; *Practical Business* (co-author) 87; *A Little White Paper on Catholic Envangelization in Twn.* 99; *Add.* 200 Chung Chi Rd., Shalu, Taichung County 433.

CHEN, MENG-LING 陳孟鈴
V. Pres., Control Yuan 99-; Mem., Control Yuan 93-; *b.* Twn. May 1, '34; *m.* Liou, Sin-chuan; 1 *s.,* 1 *d.; educ.* BA, Eng. Lit., Tamkang U. 58; Tchr., Dean, & Prin. 58-73; Magis., Taichung County 73-81; Comr., TPG 81-84, Comr., Dept. of Civil Aff. 84-87; V. Chmn., Twn. Prov. Cttee., KMT 87-90; Admin. V. Min. of the Int. 90; Pol. V. Min. of the Int. 90-93. *Publ.: Standard Eng. Grammar* (4 Vol.); *Res. of Soc. Worker System of Twn. Prov.; Add.* 2 Chung Hsiao E. Rd., Sect. 1, Taipei 100.

CHEN, MING-BANG 陳明邦
Dir.-Gen., Intellectual Property Off., MOEA 97-; *b.* Twn. Oct. 20, '41; *m.* Liu, Ching-hsien; 1 *s.,* 1 *d.; educ.* B., Intl. Trade, NCCU 65; MBA, Okolahoma City U. 88; Sect.

Chief, Dept. of Customs Admin., MOF 77-81, Sr. Sp. 82-87; Dep. Dir.-Gen., Dept. of Com., MOEA 87-91, Exec. Sec., Investment Com. 91-94, Dir.-Gen., Dept. of Com. 94-97; *Publ.:* Various publ. on IPR protection in Twn.; *Add.* 3rd Fl., 185 Hsin Hai Rd., Sect. 2, Taipei 106.

CHEN, MING-PANG
(See CHEN, MING-BANG 陳明邦)

CHEN, MING-TE
(See CHEN, ROBERTO MING-TEH 陳明德)

CHEN, MING-YI
(See CHEN, MING-YIE 陳明義)

CHEN, MING-YIE 陳明義
Attorney; Standing Mem., Bd. of Trustees, ROC Bar Assn. 96-; Pres., Tainan Labor Mng. Found. 92-; Pres., Tainan Assn. of Conscription 81-; *b.* Twn. Mar. 22, '36; *m.* Chen Chiang, A-mci; 1 *s.*, 2 *d.*; *educ.* LL.B., NTU 59; Supporting Consultant, immediate action service center, Tainan City Govt. 79-99; Dir., Civilian Law Service Cent., Tainan Bar Assn. 88-91; Standing Mem. & Sup., Tainan Bar Assn. 91-99; Chmn., Judicial Reform Cttee., Tainan Bar Assn. 96-99; Mem., Discipline Cttee., Twn. Bar Assn. 98-99; *Add.* 8 Kai Shan Rd., Tainan 700.

CHEN, MU-TSAI 陳木在
Chmn., Farmers Bk. of Ch. 98-; *b.* Twn. Dec. 18, '45; *m.* Wang Yu-mei; *educ.* BA, Tunghai U. 68; MA, NTU 72; Sect. Chief, Dept. of Monetary Aff., MOF 76-78, Asst. Dir. 78-80; Dir. & Sr. V. Pres., Taipei Bk. 80-84; Dep. Dir.-Gen., Dept. of Monetary Aff., MOF 84-89, Dir.-Gen. 89-91, Dir.-Gen., Bu. of Monetary Aff. 91-95; Admin. V. Min. of Finance 95-98; Eisenhower Exchange Fel. 97. *Publ.: US Tax System Reform—Also of ROC's Tax System* 73; *Essays on Twn. Finance & Price Level* 73; *Money & Finance During Econ. Fluctuation* 77; *Twn.'s Financial Dev. & Strategies After the Retrocession* 78; *Issue of High Denominated Paper Money & Improving Combination of NT Dollar Denomination* 83; *Gen. Overview of ROC's Econ. Dev. Strategies* (2 Vol.) 87; *Add.* 85 Nanking E. Rd., Sect. 2, Taipei 104.

CHEN, PAO-CHUAN 陳寶川
Nat. Policy Adv. to the Pres. 90-; Adv., CBC 87-; Standing Sup., Const. Soc., ROC; Standing Sup., Constitutionality Soc., ROC; Chmn., Unity & Self-Reliance Assn., ROC; *b.* Twn. Mar. 22, '17; 2 *s.*, 2 *d.*; *educ.* Grad., Nat. Taipei Inst. of Tech. 37; Grad., Dept. of Law, N.E. U. 41; 2-year Res.,

Kyoto Imperial U.; Assc. Prof., Twn. Prov. Coll. of Laws & Com. 45-47; Assc. Prof., NTU 46-50; Mgr. & Sect. Chief, Planning & Inspecting Sect., Chang Hwa Cml. Bk. 50-53; Gen. Mgr. & Dir., Medium Business Bk. of Taipei 53-64; Chmn., Kuohua Life Ins. Co. 64-71; Mem., NA 69-91; Chmn., Medium Business Bk. of Twn. 71-77, Chang Hwa Cml. Bk. 77-83, & First Cml. Bk. 83-87. *Publ.: Res. of Entrepreneurialization of Govt. Bk.; Implementation of the Const. & Twn. Econ.; A Study of the Promotion of Twn. as the Trade & Monetary Cent. in the Far E.; Add.* 34 Lane 279, Fu Hsing S. Rd., Sect. 1, Taipei 104.

CHEN, PENG-JEN 陳鵬仁
Dir., Hist. Com., CC, KMT 96-; Part-time Prof., Pol. Sc., Ch. Cul. U. 89-; *b.* Twn. Dec. 2, '30; *m.* Yen, Lily; 5 *d.*; *educ.* B., Econ., Meiji U. 61, M., Pol. Sc. 65; MA, Seton Hall U., USA 71; Ph.D., Intl. Rel., U. of Tokyo 97; Off., ROC Army 54-55; Ed.-in-Chief, *Ea. Digest* 60-61; Pres., *Modern Rev.* 63-66, *Ch. Youth Quarterly* 70-73; Columnist, *Ch. Daily News* 68-70; Pres., Twn. Welfare Assn. 69-73; Sec. Gen., KMT Off., Japan 73-74; Chief, Ovs. Ch. Aff. Sect., Tokyo Off., AEAR 74; Columnist, *Youth Warrior Daily* 77-78. *Publ.: Dr. Sun Yat-sen & the Japanese Friends* 73; *Japanese Thought and Pol. After World War II* 76; *Kung Chi Tao Tien on Sun Yat-sen & Huang Hsing* 77; *Pres. Elections & Pol. in Am.* 77; *An Analysis of Ovs. Ch. Problems in Japan* 79; *What Are the Three Principles of the People?* 80; *Tanaka's For. Policy Toward Ch.* 81; *The Japanese Soldiers on the Ch. Mainland During World War II* 83; *An Inside Story of Japan's Invasion of Ch.* 84; etc.; *Add.* 7th Fl., 11 Chung Shan S. Rd., Taipei 100.

CHEN, PIN-CHUAN
(See CHEN, ROBERT PIN-CHUAN 陳品全)

CHEN, PO-CHANG 陳伯璋
Pres., Nat. Hualien Tchrs.' Coll. 93-; *b.* Twn. Dec. 20, '48; *m.* Lu, Meei-quay; 1 *s.*; *educ.* Ed.B., NTNU 72, ED.M. 77, Ph.D. 84; Asst. Resr., NTNU 75-77, Instr. 77-85, Assc. Prof. 85-91; Postdr., London U. 85-86; Prof. & Dir. of Extension, NTNU 91-93. *Publ.: Secondary Educ.* 82; *Hidden Curriculum Res.* 85; *Curriculum Res. & Educ. Innovation* 87; *Ideology & Educ.* 88; *Neil & Summerhill Sch.* 89; *Open Educ.* 91; *Res. on Educ. Issues* 87; *New Trend of Educ. Res.-Quantitative Method* 89; *Add.* 123 Hua Hsi, Hualien 970.

CHEN, PO-CHIH 陳博志
Chmn., CEPD 2000-; Prof., Econ., NTU; *b.* Twn. Feb. 1, '49; *m.* Chiu, Hsiu-chin; 1 *s.*, 1 *d.*; *educ.* Ph.D., Econ., NTU 79; Dir. & Chmn., Econ. Dept., NTU 88-90; Sec.-Gen., Ch.

Econ. Assn. 90-93; Res. Cttee. Mem., NUC; Bd. Dir., CBC; Adv., MOEA & Twn. Inst. of Econ. Aff.; Mem., Consulting Cttee. on Ind. Dev., MOEA & concur. Convener, Com. of Ind. Policy; Mem., Review Cttee. of Nat. Income, DGBAS; Bd. Dir., Twn. Inst. of Econ. Res. *Publ:* "Changing Patterns of Trade in Goods & Services: The Case of Twn.," *Changing Pattern of Trade in Goods & Services in the Pacific Region*, (Osaka) Japan Cttee. for Pacific Econ. Outlook 94; "For. Investment in the So. Ch. Growth Triangle," *Growth Triangles in Asia* (M. Thant & I.I. Kakazu eds.; Oxford U. Press) 94; *The Impacts of the Devaluation of S.E. Asian Currencies on the Industries of Twn.,* Proceedings for the Conf. on S.E. Asian Currency Crisis at Taipei held by the Banking Inst. of the ROC 97; "The Substitution Among the Exports of E. Asian Countries," *The Retrospects & Prospect of E. Asian Econ. Dev.* (Chang Ching-si ed.; NTU) 99; *Add.* 7th Fl., 2-2 Chi Nan Rd., Sect. 1, Taipei 100.

CHEN, PO-HSIEN
(See CHEN, BOR-SEN 陳博現)

CHEN, REGIS C.W. 陳朝威
Bd. Chmn., Ch. Petroleum Corp. 97-; *b.* Fukien Feb. 9, '47; *m.* Chen, Lori M.; 1 *s.,* 1 *d.; educ.* M., Econ., Ch. Cul. U. 72; Mem., Commodity Price Sup. Bd., MOEA 74-88, Twn. Salt Works 88-89, Com. of Nat. Corp. 89-91; Bd. Chmn., BES Engr. Corp. 91-95 & Taipei Rapid Transit Corp. 95-97; *Add.* 83 Chung Hua Rd., Sect. 1, Taipei 100.

CHEN, ROBERT PIN-CHUAN 陳品全
Pres., Shu-Te Inst. of Tech. 97-; Prof., Dept. of Eng., 97-; *b.* Kiangsu Aug. 14, '35; *m.* Chen, Carrie Chia-li; 1 *s.,* 1 *d.; educ.* LL.B. (Dip.), NCCU 59, LL.M. 64; M. of Lib. Sc., U. of Pittsburgh 67; Ph.D., Lib. & Info. Sc., Indiana U., Bloomington 76; Assc. Prof., Ea. Illinois U. 76-82; Visiting Assc. Prof., NTU 77-78; Prof., Ea. Illinois U. 82-97; Exchange Prof., Nat. Kaohsiung Normal U. 91-93, 94-96. *Publ.: The Acquisition, Org., & Utilization of Ch. Govt. Publ. in Lib. in Twn.* 87; *Lib. Resources for Am. Studies in Twn.: A Reassessment* 94 & 95; *Add.* 59 Hun Shan Rd., Yenchau, Kaohsiung County 824.

CHEN, ROBERTO MING-TEH 陳明德
Dir.-Gen., TECO, Miami 96-; *b.* Taipei Nov. 1, '51; *m.* Ramos, Manuela; 2 *s.; educ.* BA, NCCU 73; MA 77, Ph.D. 80, U. Complutense de Madrid ; 3rd, 2nd, 1st Sec., Emb. in Uruguay 82-86; Sect. Chief, 2nd Dep. Dir.-Gen., Dep. Dir.-Gen., Cent. & S. Am. Aff., MOFA 86-92; Rep. to Uruguay 92-94; Dep. Dir.-Gen., Cent. & S. Am. Aff., MOFA 94-96. *Publ.: Econ. Aspects of British For. Policy Toward the*

Spanish Civil War; Add. 2333 Ponce de Leon Boulevard, Suite 610, Coral Gables, FL 33134, USA.

CHEN, SHEN-LING
(See CHEN, HSING-LING 陳燊齡)

CHEN, SHIH-I
(See CHEN, GEORGE S.Y. 陳世圮)

CHEN, SHOU-AN
(See CHEN, SHOW-AN 陳壽安)

CHEN, SHOU-SHAN 陳守山
Nat. Policy Adv. to the Pres. 91-; *b.* Twn. Feb. 20, '21; *m.* Huang, Shu-nu; 1 *s.,* 5 *d.; educ.* 16th Class, Mil. Acad. 40; 6th Class, Army CGSC 55; 13th Regular Class, Armed Forces Joint Staff Coll. 65; 11th Class, Nat. War Coll. of Res. 70; Gen. Off. Course, War Coll., Armed Forces U. 72; Cmdt., Fu Hsing Kang Coll. 73-75; Exec. Off., Pol. Warfare Dept., MND 75-76; CG, Army Tng. & Combat Dev. Com. 78-79; CG, 8th Field Army 79-81; Dep. C-in-C, ROC Army 81; C-in-C, Twn. Garrison GHQ, & concur. CG, Twn. Corps Area Cmd. 81-89; V. Min. of Nat. Def. 89-91. *Publ.: Prospects & Retrospect of the Build-up of the ROC Armed Forces in the Past 60 Years; A Study of the Dev. of E. Twn.; Add.* P.O. Box 90001, Taipei.

CHEN, SHOW-AN 陳壽安
Prof., Dept. of Chem. Engr., NTHU 74-; Ed., *Jour. of Polymer Res.* 94-; Nat. Chair Prof. 99-2001; *b.* Fukien Apr. 8, '40; *m.* Pi, Chuan-chih; 2 *d.; educ.* BS, NCKU 62; D.Sc., Washington U. 69; Sr. Chemist, UniRoyal Inc. 69-70; Res. Scientist, W.R. Grace & Co. 70-73; Assc. Prof., Dept. of Chem. Engr., NTHU 73-74; Dir., Dept. of Chem. Engr., NTHU 79-82. *Publ.:* 165 articles & 9 patents on the structure/properties of polymers, conjugated conductive polymers, polymerization kinetics & engr., thermodynamics of solutions; *Add.* 101 Kuanf Fu Rd., Sect. 2, Hsinchu 300.

CHEN, SHU
(See CHEN, GORDON S. 陳樹)

CHEN, SHUI-BIAN 陳水扁
Pres., ROC 2000-; Mem., CSC, DPP; *b.* Twn. Feb. 18, '51; *m.* Wu, Shu-chen; 1 *s.,* 1 *d.; educ.* LL.B., NTU 74; Hon. Dr. Degree of Laws, Kyungnam U., Korea 95; Hon. Dr. Degree in Econ., Plekhanov Russian Acad. of Econ., Russia 95; Chief Attorney-at-Law, Formosa Intl. Marine & Cml. Law Off. 76-89; Mem., Taipei CCoun. 81-85; Mem., CSC, DPP 87-89, Mem., CEC 87-89 & 91-96; Mem., Legis.

Yuan 89-94, Exec. Dir., DPP Caucus 90-93, Convener, Nat. Def. Cttee. 92-94, Convener, Rules Cttee. 93, Mem., Jud. Cttee. 94; Chmn., Formosa Found. 90-94; V. Pres., Taipei N. Gate Rotary Club 93; Mayor, Taipei City 94-98. *Publ.: Series on Justice* (4 Vol.); *Conflict, Compromise & Progress; Nat. Def. Black Box & White Paper; Through the Line Between Life & Death; Add.* c/o Off. of the Pres., Taipei 100.

CHEN, SHUI-MU 陳水木
Spkr., Kinmen County Coun. 98-; Pres., Hsiu-zhong Co. 95-; Pres., Harvard Lang. Inst. 96-; *b.* Fukien Apr. 22, '48; *m.* Chuang, Neng-hsiu; 1 *s.,* 2 *d.; educ.* Chmn., Parents' Assn., Kinmen County's Chung Cheng Elementary Sch. 84-86; *Add.* Kinmen County Coun., 17 Chin Shan Rd., Chincheng, Kinmen County 893.

CHEN, SHUI-PIEN
(See CHEN, SHUI-BIAN 陳水扁)

CHEN, SHUI-TSAI 陳水在
Magis., Kinmen County 93-; *b.* Fukien Oct. 8, '48; *m.* Chai, Mei-yu; 2 *s.,* 1 *d.; educ.* LL.B., Pol. Staff Coll. 66, Studied, Advanced Course 73, & Pol. Warfare Res. 79; Pol. Staff Off., Gen. Pol. Warfare Dept., Twn. Garrison Cmd. 84-85, Chief, Counter Intelligence Unit (Col.) 85-86, Dep. Dir., 4th Sect. 86-87; Dir., Pol. Warfare Dept., Taipei Garrison Div. 87-90; Dep. Dir., Sect. 4, Gen. Pol. Warfare Dept., MND 90-91; *Add.* 60 Min Sheng Rd., Chincheng, Kinmen County 893.

CHEN, STEPHEN S.F. 陳錫蕃
Rep., TECRO, USA 97-2000; *b.* Nanking Feb. 11, '34; *m.* Chen, Rosa Te; 2 *s.,* 1 *d.; educ.* BA & MA, U. of Santo Tomas, Manila; Passed the For. Service Exam. 60; Served in Emb. in the Philippines 53-60; Sp. Asst., MOFA 60-63; 2nd & 1st Sec., Emb. in Brazil 63-69; Chief, 2nd Sect., Dept. of Latin Am. Aff., MOFA 69-71; Counsl., Emb. in Argentina 71-72; Chargé d'affaires, Emb. in Bolivia 72-73; Consul-Gen., Atlanta 73-79; Dir., CCNAA, Atlanta 79-80; Dir., CCNAA, Chicago 80-82; Consul-Gen. attached to the Secretariat, MOFA 82-84, Dir., Dept. of Treaty & Legal Aff. 84-86, Dir., Dept. of Intl. Org. 86-88.; Dir.-Gen., CCNAA, Los Angeles 88-89, Dep. Rep., CCNAA, Washington, D.C. 89-93; Admin. V. Min. of For. Aff. 93-96; Dep. Sec.-Gen. to the Pres. 96-97. *Publ.: A Critical Study of Sino-Filipino Rel.; Random Notes on Transl.; Add.* 4201 Wisconsin Avenue, N.W., Washington, D.C. 20016, USA.

CHEN, STEVE RUEY-LONG 陳瑞隆
Dir.-Gen., Bd. of For. Trade, MOEA 97-; *b.* Twn. June 15, '48; *m.* Chiang, Margaret Mei; 1 *s.; educ.* BA, Econ., NCHU

70; Dir., Taipei Trade Off. in Zurich 87-96; Rep., Representation of the Separate Customs Territory of Twn. Penghu, Kinmen & Matsu to WTO (Geneva) 93-96; Dep. Dir.-Gen., Bd. of For. Trade, MOEA 96-97; *Add.* 1 Hu Kou St., Taipei 100.

CHEN, STEVEN Y. 陳堯
Bd. Chmn., Chunghwa Telecom. Co. Ltd. 96-; Mem., CC, KMT 93-; *b.* Twn. Mar. 7, '34; *m.* Chou, Tsai-hsing; 3 *s.; educ.* B., NCKU 59; M., NCCU 66; Studied, Am. U. 72; Dir., Pers. Dept., Directorate Gen. of Telecom. 68-74, Dep. Insp.-Gen. 74-75, Exec. Sec., Res. & Planning Cttee. 75-81, Dir., Traffic Dept. 81-82, Insp.-Gen. 82-85, V. Chmn., Res. & Planning Cttee. 85-87; Mng. Dir., Cent. Twn. Telecom. Admin. 87-89; Dep. Dir.-Gen., Directorate Gen. of Telecom. MOTC 89-93, Dir.-Gen., 93-96; Pres., Ch. Inst. of Elec. Engr. 95-96. *Publ.: The Application of Behavior Sc. on Business Mng.; Add.* 31 Ai Kuo E. Rd., Taipei 106.

CHEN, TAN-SUN 陳唐山
Chmn., NScC 2000-; Adv., Cent. for Twn. Intl. Rel. 88-; *b.* Twn. Sept. 16, '36; *m.* Lin, June; 3 *s.; educ.* BS, NTU 59; Ph.D., Purdue U. 72; Pres., Twn. Assn. of Am. 78-79, Fed. of Twn. Assn. 79-83, Formosan Assn. for Public Aff. 84-86, & Twn. Found. 87-91; Mem., Legis. Yuan 93; Magis., Tainan County 93-2000. *Publ.: Returning to the Motherland—Twn.; Add.* 17th-22nd Fl., 106 Ho Ping E. Rd., Sect. 2, Taipei 106.

CHEN, TANG-SHAN
(See CHEN, TAN-SUN 陳唐山)

CHEN, TIEN-MAO 陳田錨
Sr. Adv. to the Pres. 99-; Mem., CC & CSC, KMT 93-; Pres., Our Cml. Bk. 92-; V. Pres., Twn. Cement Corp. 94-; Pres., Shin-Kao Gas Co. Ltd. 83-; *b.* Twn. Apr. 16, '28; *m.* Huang, Shu-hui; 2 *s.,* 1 *d.; educ.* Grad., Kinki U., Japan; Mem., Kaohsiung CCoun. 58-73, Dep. Spkr. 64-68, Spkr. 68-73; Bd. Mem., Twn. Cement Corp. 82-85 & 89-91, Standing Mem. of the Bd. 91-94; Spkr., Kaohsiung CCoun. 81-99; *Add.* 12th Fl., 58 Chung Cheng 2nd Rd., Kaohsiung 802.

CHEN, TING-AN 陳聽安
Mem. (ministerial rank), Exam. Yuan 96-; Prof., NCCU 72-; Consultant, CEPD 78; *b.* Kiangsu Oct. 8, '33; *m.* Sy, Chung-ao; 2 *s.; educ.* BA, NCHU 61; Res., Freburg U., Germany; Dr. in Econ., Münster U. 69; Dir., Grad. Sch. of Public Finance, NCCU 73-81, Dean, Sch. of Law & Com. 81-84, Dir., Grad. Sch. of Econ. 85-87; Chmn., Tax Reform Com. 87-89; Visiting Prof., Cambridge U. & Harvard

U. 89-90 & 90-91. *Publ.: The Relationship Between Population & Tax Policies* 76; *Fiscal Reform & Econ. Dev.* 81; *A Study of the European Single Market* 91; *New Trend of Econ. Regln. Toward the 21st Century* 95; *Add.* Exam. Yuan, 1 Shih Yuan Rd., Wenshan, Taipei 116.

CHEN, TING-HSIN
(See CHEN, DING-SHINN 陳定信)

CHEN, TING-NAN
(See CHEN, DING-NAN 陳定南)

CHEN, TSO-CHEN 陳佐鎮
Dir.-Gen., Bu. of Commodity Inspection & Quarantine, MOEA 97-; *b.* Twn. Aug. 1, '42; *m.* Chang, Kuo-ying; 2 *s.; educ.* LL.B., NCHU 75; Chief, Trademarks Div., Nat. Bu. of Standards (NBS), MOEA 78-80, Dep. Dir. 82-84, Dir. 84-88, Dir., Patents Dept. 88; Dep. Dir.-Gen., NBS, MOEA 88-94, Dir.-Gen. 94-97. *Publ.:* Various publ. concerning IPR protection in Twn.; *Add.* 4 Chi Nan Rd., Sect. 1, Taipei 100.

CHEN, TU-CHENG
(See CHEN, DU-CHENG 陳篤正)

CHEN, WAI-FAH 陳惠發
Mem., Acad. Sinica 98-; Dean, Coll. of Engr., U. of Hawaii 99-; *b.* Nanking Dec. 23, '36; *m.* Hsuan, Lily; 3 *s.; educ.* BSCE, NCKU 59; MSCE, Lehigh U. 63; Ph.D., Brown U. 66; Prof., Lehigh U. 66-76; Prof., Purdue U. 76-98. *Publ.:* Limit Analysis & Soil Plasticity 75; Theory of Beam-Columns 76-77; Plasticity in Reinforced Concrete 82; Constitutive Equations for Engr. Materials 85, 96; Stability Design of Steel Frames 91; George E. Goodwin Disting. Prof. of Civil Engr. 92-99; Stability Design of Semi-rigid Frames 96; *Add.* U. of Hawaii, Coll. of Engr., 2540 Dole St., Honolulu, HI 96822, USA.

CHEN, WEI-CHAO
(See CHEN, WEI-JAO 陳維昭)

CHEN, WEI-JAO 陳維昭
Pres., NTU 93-; Prof., Surgery & Public Health, NTU 83-; *b.* Twn. Nov. 15, '39; *m.* Tang, Shiang-yang; 1 *s.*, 1 *d.; educ.* MD, NTU 65; DMS, Tohoku U., Japan 73; MPH, Johns Hopkins U. 89; Resident, NTU Hosp. 66-69, Chief Resident 69-70, Visiting Staff 70-72; Lectr., Coll. of Med., NTU 75-79, Assc. Prof. 79-83; Visiting Res. Assc. Prof., U. of Cincinnati 81-82; Dep. Dir., NTU Hosp. 87-91; Dean, Coll. of Med., NTU 91-93. *Publ.: Ah-jen, Ah-i & I—A Story About the Separation of Siamese Twins;* & over 150 sc. publ.; *Add.* 5th Fl., 15 Hsin Yi Rd., Sect. 2, Taipei 100.

CHEN, WEN-HUA
(See CHEN, WEN-HWA 陳文華)

CHEN, WEN-HWA 陳文華
Prof., Dept. of Power Mech. Engr., NTHU 81-; *b.* Twn. Aug. 15, '48; *m.* Chang, Hsiao-chen; 2 *s.; educ.* BS, Engr., NCKU 71; Ph.D., Georgia Inst. of Tech. 77; Head, Dept. of Power Mech. Engr., NTHU 81-88, Chmn., Cttee. of Res. & Dev. 88-92; Dean, Coll. of Engr., NTHU 92-98; Ed.-in-Chief, *Ch. Jour. of Mech.* 86-94, & *Proceedings of NScC*, Series B, ROC 94-96. *Publ.:* Over 100 res. papers in mech.-related areas; *Add.* Coll. of Engr., NTHU 300.

CHEN, WU-HSIUNG 陳武雄
V. Chmn., COA 99-; *b.* Twn. Mar. 11, '44; *m.* Lee, Maw-jing; 1 *s.*, 1 d; *educ.* B., NCHU 66, M. 70; Ph.D., U. of Illinois 80; Dir., 1st Div., Bu. of Agr., MOEA 80-84; Chief, Planning & Programming Div. COA 84-90; Dep. Dir., Farmers' Services Dept., COA 90; Dir., Econ. & Planning Dept. COA 90-96; Dep. Comr. & Acting Comr., Dept. of Agr. & Forestry, TPG 96, Comr. 96-98; Sec.-Gen. & Spokesman, TPG 98-99. *Publ.: A Study of the Feasibility of Orderly Production & Marketing for Red Bean Ind. in Twn.* 77; *SDRs: Current Situation & Further Expansion* 77; *Promotion of Agr. Trade Between ROC & USA* 78; *Simulation Experiment of Rice Price Policy in Twn.* 82; *A Stochastic Control Approach to Buffer Stoch Mng. in Twn.* 82; *Comparison of Public Expenditures on Agr. in Asia* 87; *Contributions of Agr. to Food Sec.* 90; *Add.* 37 Nan Hai Rd., Taipei 100.

CHEN, YAO
(See CHEN, STEVEN Y. 陳堯)

CHEN, YI-YANG
(See CHEN, YIH-YOUNG 陳義揚)

CHEN, YIH-YOUNG 陳義揚
Pres., Nat. Open U. 91-; *b.* Chekiang Sept. 15, '43; *m.* Cheng, Jui-shan; 3 *s.; educ.* BEE, NCKU 65; MEE, NCTU 68, & Washington U. 70; Ph.D., EE, Tulane U. 74; Assc. Prof., Coll. of Engr., NCTU 74-77, Prof. 77-83; Dept. Dir. NYC 78-82; Dir., Bu. of Intl. Cul. & Educ. Rel. 82-83; V. Pres., St. John's U. 83-84; Dean of Student Aff., NCTU 85-87, Dean of Acad. Aff. 87-91. *Publ.: Automation of Pathology Labs.* 74; *Add.* 172 Chung Cheng Rd., Luchou, Taipei County 247.

CHEN, YING-HAO
(See CHEN, YING-HAU 陳英豪)

CHEN, YING-HAU 陳英豪

Mem. (Ministerial Level), Exam. Yuan 99-; *b.* Twn. June 17, '37; *m.* Huang, Mei-huei; 3 *c.; educ.* Grad., Twn. Prov. Pingtung Tchr. Coll. 56; BA, NTNU 63; MA, U. of N. Colorado, USA 73, Ed.D. 75; Postdr., U. of Minnesota 84; Assc. Prof. & Chmn., Dept. of Educ., Nat. Kaohsiung Tchr. Coll. 75-78, Prof. & Chmn., Dept. of Educ. & Grad. Inst. of Educ. 78-82, Prof. & Dean of Students Aff. 82-84; Pres., Twn. Prov. Tainan Jr. Tchr. Coll. 84-87; Pres., Nat. Tainan Tchr. Coll. 84-92; Comr., TPG 92-99. *Publ.: Teaching of Moral Educ.; Theory & Practice of Testing; Teaching on Creative Thinking; Add.* Exam. Yuan, 1 Shih Yuan Rd., Wenshan, Taipei 116.

CHEN, YING-LIN
(See CHEN, ENG-RIN 陳瑩霖)

CHEN, YU-CHANG
(See CHEN, YUH-CHANG 陳裕璋)

CHEN, YU-CHU 陳毓駒

Rep., Taipei Rep. Off. in Denmark 94-; *b.* Hupei Aug. 17, '32; *m.* Yang, Chiu-ping; 3 *s.,* 1 *d.; educ.* BPS, NTU; 3rd Sec., Emb. in S. Korea 61-62; 2nd Sec. & Consul, Emb. in the Philippines 65-67; Consul, Consl. Gen. in Los Angeles 67-74; Sect. Chief, Dept. of N. Am. Aff., MOFA 74-77, Dep. Dir. 77-80; Dep. Dir.-Gen., CCNAA, Los Angeles 80-82; Dir.-Gen., CCNAA, Seattle 82-85, CCNAA, Houston 85-87; Dir., Dept. of Info. & Cul. Aff., & Spokesman, MOFA 87-90; Rep., Taipei Rep. Off. in Singapore 90-94; *Add.* Amaliegade 3, 2, 1256 Copenhagen K, Denmark.

CHEN, YU-HSIU
(See TCHEN, YU-CHIOU 陳郁秀)

CHEN, YU-WU 陳友武

Pres., Chung Shan Inst. of Sc. & Tech. 98-; *b.* Chekiang Jan. 7, '45; *m.* Wang, Lucy; 1 *s.; educ.* B. Ch. Army Acad. 67; MBA, Chadwick U., Birmingham, Alabama 92; Dep. Chief of Staff, TAC Wing, ROCAF 85-87, Dep. Cmdg. Off. 87-90, Cmdg. Off. 92-93; Dir., Bu. of Comms. & Elect., MND 93-98; *Add.* P.O. Box 90008, Lungtan, Taoyuan 325.

CHEN, YUH-CHANG 陳裕璋

Sec.-Gen., TCG 98-; *b.* Twn. Sept. 18, '55; *m.* Chen, Chia-hsin; 1 *s.,* 1 *d.; educ.* BCoS, NTU 77, M. 82; Resr., Exec. Yuan Dev. Fund 82-83; Insp., Dept. of Nat. Treasury, MOF 83-84; Sect. Chief, Dep. Div. Dir., Div. Dir., Mem., Sec. & Exchange Com., MOF 84-92; Dir., Fair Trade Com., Exec.

Yuan 92-96; Dir., 4th Dept., Exec. Yuan 96-98. *Publ: A Study of the Computerization of Sec. & Stock Market; A study of the Clearance Systems of Sec. & Stock Market; &* etc; *Add.* 11th Fl., 1 Shih Fu Rd., Taipei 110.

CHEN CHANG, FU-MEI 張富美

Min., OCAC 2000-; *b.* Oct. 10, '38; *educ.* LL.M., Northwe. U. 61; Ph.D., Harvard U. 70; Bd. Mem., Formosan Assn. for Public Aff., USA 87-91; Founding Pres., N. Am. Twn. Women's Assn. 88-89; Res. Fel., Hoover Inst., Stanford U. 78-94; Mem., NA 92-99, Convener, DPP Caucus, 94-95; Exec. Dir., Com. for Examining Petitions & Appeals, TCG 94-98; Mem., Control Yuan 99-2000; *Add.* 15th-17th Fl., 5 Hsuchow Rd., Taipei 100.

CHENG, AN-KUO 鄭安國

V. Chmn., MAC 99-2000; Mem., CC, KMT 99-; *b.* Kwangtung Oct. 16, '46; *m.* Cheng Wu, Sheue-sheue; 2 *s.; educ.* LL.B. & MA, NCCU 68 & 73; Corr., *Ch. Daily News* 71-75; Adjunct Lectr., NCTU 73-74; Div., Ovs. students service cent., New York 75-81; Dir., Los Angeles Ch. Cul. Service Cent. 81-84; Div. Dir., Dept. of Ovs. Aff., CC, KMT 84-86, Sup.-Gen., USA Aff. 86-92; Dir., Dept. of Res. & Planning & Dept. of Hong Kong & Macau Aff., MAC 92-93 & 93-95; Pres., Chunghwa Travel Service (Rep. Off. in Hong Kong), Hong Kong 95-99; Dir.-Gen., Bu. of Hong Kong Aff., MAC 97-99. *Publ.: A Study on the Process of Personnel Admin. Reform in the ROC; Add.* 16th Fl., 2-2 Chi Nan Rd., Sect. 1, Taipei 100.

CHENG, CHEN-KUANG 鄭成光

Spkr., Hsinchu City Coun. 98-; *b.* Twn. April 5, '49; 5 *s.,* 1 *d.; educ.* Chien Hua Jr. High Sch.; Village Rep., 9th term, Hsinchu County 78-82; Coun., 1st., 2nd 3rd terms, Hsinchu CCoun. 82-94, Dep. Spkr., 4th term; *Add.* 122 Chungcheng Rd., Hsinchu City 300.

CHENG, CHIA-LIN 成嘉玲

Pres., Shih Hsin U. 97-; *b.* Tientsin Sept. 17, '37; *m.* Chow, Liang-yen; 1 *s.,* 1 *d.; educ.* B., Econ., NTU 61; Ph.D., Agr. Econ., U. of Hawaii 68; Asst. Prof., NCHU 68-69; Head, Dept. of Econ., Soochow U. 77, Dir. 78-79, Dean, Sch. of Business 83-90; Pres., World Coll. of Jour. & Comm. 91-97. *Publ.: A Comparative Study of Employment & Income of Public & Private U. Grad.—An Analysis of the Utility of Govt. Investment in Public & Private U.; Add.* 1 Lane 17, Mu Cha Rd., Taipei 116.

CHENG, CHIA-LING
(See CHENG, CHIA-LIN 成嘉玲)

CHENG, CHIEN-JEN
(See CHEN, CHIEN-JEN 程建人)

CHENG, CHUNG-MO 城仲模
V. Pres., Jud. Yuan 99-; *b.* Twn. Oct. 30, '38; *m.* Pan, Grace S.H.; *2 s.; educ.* LL.B., Soochow U. 62; LL.M., Waseda U. 66; Res., U. of Tokyo 67; LL.D., U. of Vienna 70; Res., Law Sch., U. of Wisconsin 71; Lectr., Mil. Law Sch. 62-63; Sect. Chief, Sr. Sp., & Adv., Exec. Yuan 71-73; Prof. & Chmn., Law Dept., Fu Hsing Kang Coll. 73-77; Prof. & Chmn., Law Dept., NCHU 77-79; Prof. & Dean, Grad. Sch. of Law, NCHU 79-82; Guest Prof., U. of Vienna 80-81; Comr., TPG 82-90, & Exam. Yuan 90-94; Grand Justice, Jud. Yuan 94-98; Min., MOJ 98-99. *Publ.: Basic Theory of Admin. Law; Essay of Compensational Law System; Collection of Admin. Laws I; Admin. Law in the Past 40 Years; The Gen. Legal Principles of the Admin. Law* (ed.) (2 Vol.) 94 & 97; *Selected Hundred Sentences of the Admin. Law* (ed.) 96; *On Constitutionalism & Rule of Law* 98; *Add.* 14 Lane 89, Shih Tung Rd., Shihlin, Taipei 111.

CHENG, DAVIS YEN-WEI 鄭炎爲
Chmn. & CEO, Hitron Tech. Inc. 94; *b.* Twn. Dec. 10, '53; *m.* Chang, Pi-chi; *2 d.; educ.* Grad., Elect. Engr., Nat. Taipei Inst. of Tech. 76; Sales Mgr. & Dir., Heighten Corp. 70-75; Pres., Hitron Tech. Inc. 75-83; Project leader, Twn. Telecom. Ind. Co. 78-80; *Add.* Wuku Ind. Dist., 40 Wu Kung 5th Rd., Wuku, Taipei County 248.

CHENG, FENG-SHIH 鄭逢時
Dir.-Gen., Dept. of Party Rel., CC, KMT 93-; Mem., Legis. Yuan 93-; *b.* Twn. Dec. 27, '41; *m.* Wang, Lin-hui; *1 s.; educ.* Grad., Supplementary Open Jr. Coll. for PA, NCCU; MPA, Tunghai U.; Mem., Taipei CoCoun. 68-73, NA 73-79, & TPA 81-93; Dep. Dir., Twn. Prov. Cttee., KMT 89-93; *Add.* 158 Chung Shan Rd., Sect. 1, Panchiao, Taipei County 220.

CHENG, KUO-SHUN
(See CHENG, KUO-SHUNG 鄭國順)

CHENG, KUO-SHUNG 鄭國順
Pres., Nat. Chung Cheng U. 97-; *b.* Twn. Jan. 2, '46; *m.* Cheng Yeh, Jin-fung; *1 s., 1 d.; educ.* BS, Physics, NTU 68; Ph.D. in Physics, State U. of New York—Stony Brook 74; Head, Dept. of Applied Math., NCTU 77-80, Dir. 80-85, Dean, Coll. of Sc. 84-85, Prof. 86-89; Dir., Grad. Inst. of Applied Math., Nat. Chung Cheng U. 89-90, Dean, Acad. Aff. 89-95; Dir., Adv. Off., MOE 96-97. *Publ.:* "Classical Lagrangian Theory with Radiative Reaction: Extension of Rohrilich 2-field Formalism to include Monopolies," *Phys.*

Review 78; "Constraints of the Lorentz-Dirac Equation," *Jour. of Math. Phys.* 78; co-author: "Necessary & Sufficient Conditions for the Existence of Metric in 2-Dimensional Affine Manifold," *Ch. Jour.of Physics* 78; "Analysis of Gen. Cml. Fishing Model," *Jour. of Environmental Econ. & Mng.* 78; *Add.* Nat. Chung Cheng U., 160 San Hsin Village, Minhsiung, Chiayi County 621.

CHENG, PETER 鄭博久
Consl., Emb. of the ROC in Macedonia 99-; *b.* Twn. Dec. 5, '41; *m.* Cheng, Helen P.; *1 s., 1 d.; educ.* B., Dip., NCCU 65, MA 68; Desk Off., Asian Aff., MOFA 68-71; 3rd Sec., Emb. in Belgium 71-72; 2nd Sec., Emb. in Spain 72-74; 1st Sec., Emb. in Vatican, Holy See 74-80; Sect. Chief, Dept. of European Aff., MOFA 80-83; Chargé d'Affaires, Emb. in St. Vincent & the Grenadines 83-89; Rep., Cml. Rep. Off. of the ROC in Jordan 89-94; Dir.-Gen., Dept. of W. Asian Aff., MOFA 94-95, Dir.-Gen., Dept. of Asia-Pacific Aff. 95-96, Dir.-Gen., Dept. of Info. & Cul. Aff. & MOFA Spokesman 96-97; Dep. Rep., TECRO, USA 97-99; *Add.* Skopje, Rep. of Macedonia, Salvador Aljende 73.

CHENG, PO-CHIU
(See CHENG, PETER 鄭博久)

CHENG, SHU-MIN
(See CHENG, SU-MING 鄭淑敏)

CHENG, SU-MING 鄭淑敏
Chmn. & CEO, CTV 96-; Acting Dir., Twn. Nat. Cttee. for the Intl. Press Inst., ROC 97-; Dir., Intl. Coun. for the Nat. Acad. of TV Arts & Sc. 98-; *b.* Taipei Apr. 7, '46; *m.* Wei, Duan; *educ.* BA, NCKU 68; MA, Mass Comms., Université Catholique de Louvain, Belgium 72; Studied, Yale U. 77; Ed. & Screener, CTS 72-75, Producer, CTS 75-79; Pub. & Ed.-in-Chief, *Ch. Times Mag.* 79-83; Dep. Dir., Dept. of Compilation & Transl., GIO 83-84; Dep. Mgr., CTS 84-88; Exec. V. Pres., CTS Cul. Ent. 88-91; Mgr., CTS 91-94; Chmn., CCA 94-96, Nat. Endowment for Cul. & Arts 94-96. *Publ.:* Numerous articles & bk.; *Add.* CTV, 120 Chung Yang Rd., Nankang, Taipei 115.

CHENG, TIEN-SHOU 鄭天授
Dir.-Gen., TECO, Boston 96-; *b.* Fukien July 11, '46; *m.* Tung, Wen-wen; *2 s.; educ.* BA, NCCU 68; MA, NTU 73; MS, Georgetown U. 83; Counsl., Chargé d'Affaires, Emb. in the Commonwealth of Dominica 84-88; Dir., FETO, Bangkok 88-89; Dep. Dir., Pers. Off., MOFA 89-90; Dir., CCNAA, Washington, D.C. 90-93; Dir.-Gen., TECO Toronto 93-96; *Add.* 99 Summer St., Suite 801, Boston MA 02110, USA.

CHENG, TIEN-TSO
(See TSONG, TIEN T. 鄭天佐)

CHENG, TING-WANG
(See CHENG, TING-WONG 鄭丁旺)

CHENG, TING-WONG 鄭丁旺
Pres., NCCU 94-; *b.* Twn. Feb. 15, '42; *m.* Chen, Yueh-hua; 3 *d.; educ.* BA, NCCU 64, MA 68; MA, U. of Mis-souri-Columbia 70, Ph.D. 74; Asst. Prof., Indiana U. 74-75; Assc. Prof., Prof., Dept. Chair, & Grad. Prog. Chair, NCCU 75-84, Prof. & Dean, Coll. of Com. 85-91, Prof. & Provost 92-94. *Publ.: Current Value Acct.* 79; *Advanced Acct.* 94; *Intermediate Acct.* 97; *Introductory Acct.* 97; *Add.* 64 Chih Nan Rd., Sect. 2, Wenshan, Taipei 116.

CHENG, WEN-HUA
(See TZEN, WEN-HUA 鄭文華)

CHENG, WEN-TUNG 鄭文銅
Spkr., Nantou CoCoun. 94-; Bd. Chmn., Puli Farmers' Assn. 93-; *b.* Twn. June 19, '48; *m.* Wang, Meng-hua; 2 *s.; educ.* Ling Tung Coll.; *Add.* 663 Chung Hsing Rd., Nantou 540.

CHENG, YEN-WEI
(See CHENG, DAVIS YEN-WEI 鄭炎爲)

CHENG YEN 證嚴
Dharma M.; Pres., Buddhist Compassion Relief Tzu Chi Assn.; Chmn., Tzu Chi Found., Tzu Chi Gen. Hosp., Tzu Chi Jr. Coll. of Nursing, & Tzu Chi Coll. of Med.; *b.* Twn. May 14, '37; *educ.* Tien Long Buddhist Acad.; Hon. Dr., Sociology, Ch. U. of Hong Kong 93. *Publ.: Still Thoughts* (2 Vol.); *3 Essentials for Buddhahood; Treasure Hunt; Lectures on 37 Principles of Enlightenment; Still Thoughts, Wisdom, & Love; On the Sutra of 8 Great Ways of En-lightenment; A Mind of Equanimity; 20 Difficulties for Attain-ing Buddhahood; Morning Talks; Tzu Chi Lamp of Heart; Kindness & Compassion; Sympathetic Joy & Total Dedica-tion; Pure & Clean Wisdom; Dharma M. Cheng Yen's Lotus of the Heart; Morning Sermons; Return to the Spiritual Home; Joyful & Even-Minded; Tzu Chi Lotus of the Heart; Wisdom of Life; Words for the Tzu Chi World; Spring of Wisdom; Bodhisattvas in This World; Joyful & at Ease; The Master Tells Stories; Sutra of Profound Gratitude to Parents; Add.* 21 Kanglo Village, Hsincheng, Hualien County 971.

CHENG, YUNG-CHI 鄭永齊
Mem., Acad. Sinica 94-; Prog. Dir., Dev. Therapeutical Chemotherapy, Yale Comprehensive Cancer Cent. 90-, Prof. of Pharmacology & Internal Med. 89-; Henry Bronson Prof. of Pharmacology, Sch. of Med., Yale U. 89-; *b.* En-gland Dec. 29, '44; *m.* Cheng, Elaine H.C.; 2 *s.; educ.* BS, Tunghai U. 66; Ph.D., Brown U.; Postdoctoral Res. Staff in Pharmacology with Dr. W.H. Prusoff, Yale U. 72-73; Res. Assc., Dept. of Pharmacology, Sch. of Med., Yale U. 73-74; Asst. Prof., Dept. of Pharmacology, State U. of New York 74-77, Assc. Prof. 77-79, Sr. Cancer Res. Scientist, Roswell Park Memorial Inst. 74-76; Am. Leukemia Soc. Scholar 76-81; Cancer Res. Scientist, Dept. of Experimen-tal Therapeutics, Roswell Park Memorial Inst. 77-79; Head, Drug Dev. Prog., Linberg Cancer Res. Cent., USA 79-89; Prof., Dept. of Pharmacology & Med., U. of N. Carolina 79-89; Sp. Chair, Inst. of Biomedical Sc., Acad. Sinica 87. *Publ.:* Over 200 articles on related fields; *Add.* 961 Baldwin Rd., Woodbridge, CT 06520, USA.

CHERN, JINN-LIH 陳進利
Mem., Control Yuan 93-; *b.* Twn. Sept. 7, '42; *m.* Wang, Jung; 1 *s.,* 2 *d.; educ.* B., Agr., NCHU 66; M., Agr., Kyushu U., Japan 73, Ph.D. 78; Assc. Prof., Dept. of Biology, Nat. Chang Hua U. of Educ. 78-81, Dir. 80-86, Prof. 82-93; Visiting Prof., U. of Wisconsin 86-87; Bd. Chmn., Assn. for the Promotion of Ab-origines' Welfare 88-93; Adv., CC, KMT 89-93; Visiting Prof., Grad. Sch. of Agr., Kyushu U. 90-91. *Publ.: Phylo-genetic Studies on Sect. Sativa by Use of Electrophoretic Patterns; Electrophoretic Estimation of Progenitor of the C Genome Species Constituting Tetraploid-Punctata (BBCC); RFLP Analysis of Introgressed Segment in a Near Isogenic Line of Rice for the Bacterial Blight Resistance Gene Xa-10; Add.* 2 Chung Hsiao E. Rd., Sect. 1, Taipei 100.

CHERN, SHIING-SHEN 陳省身
Mem., Acad. Sinica 48-; Emeritus Math. Educator; Prof. Emeritus, U. of Calif. 79-; Dir. Emeritus, Math. Sc. Res. Inst. 84-; Fel., Third World Acad. of Sc.; Mem., NAS, Am. Math. Soc., Am. Acad. of Arts & Sc., New York Acad. of Sc., Am. Philosophical Soc., Indian Math. Soc., Brazilian Acad. of Sc., Royal Soc. of London, Acad. Peloritana, Lon-don Math. Soc., Acad. des Sc. of Paris, Acad. der Lincei of Rome; *b.* Chekiang Oct. 26, '11; *m.* Chern, Shih-ning; 1 *s.,* 1 *d.; educ.* BS, Nankai U. 30; MS, NTHU, Peiping 34; D.Sc., U. of Hamburg 36, Hon. D.Sc. 72; Hon. D.Sc., U. of Chicago 69, & State U. of New York-Stony Brook 85; LL.D. Honoris Causa, Ch. U. of Hong Kong 69; Hon. Dr. Math., Eidgenossische Technische Hochschule, Switzer-land 82; Hon. D.Sc., U. of Notre Dame, USA 94; Prof., Math., NTHU, Peiping 37-43; Mem., Inst. for Advanced Study, Princeton 43-45; Acting Dir., Inst. of Math., Acad. Sinica 46-48; Prof., Math., U. of Chicago 49-60, & UC-Berkly. 60-79;

Dir., Math. Sc. Res. Inst. 81-84; Dir., Inst. of Math., Tientsin; *Add.* 8336 Kent Ct., El Cerrito, CA 94530, USA.

CHI, CHENG 紀政
Bd. Chmn., Hope Cul. & Educ. Found. 93-; *b.* Twn. Mar. 15, '44; *m.* Chang, Bor-fu; 2 *d.; educ.* BS, Calif. State Polytech. U.; Bronze Medal Winner in the 80M low hurdles, Mexico Olympics 68; Dir., Women's Athletics, U. of Redland 74-76; Sec.-Gen., ROC Track & Field Assn. 77-89, Chmn., 89-93, Bd. Dir. 98-99; Mem., Legis. Yuan 80-89; *Add.* 3rd Fl., 188 Ta Tung Rd., Sect. 3, Hsichih, Taipei County 221.

CHIA, FU-MING 賈馥茗
Nat. Policy Adv. to the Pres. 98-; *b.* Hopei May 5, '26; *educ.* BA, Twn. Tchrs. Coll.; Ed.M., NTNU; MS, U. of Oregon, USA; Ed.D., UCLA; Tchr., Taipei Normal Girls' Sch. 50-55, Instr. 57-58, Assc. Prof. 64-67; Prof. & Dir., Grad. Inst. of Educ., NTNU 67-72; Mem., Exam. Yuan 72-90. *Publ.: Psychological & Creative Dev.; Introduction to Educ.; Gifted Educ.; Philosophy of Educ.; Add.* 14th Fl., 1 Lane 8, Ta Kuan Rd., Hsintien, Taipei County 231.

CHIANG, ANTONIO 江春南
Pub. & Ed.-in-Chief, *Taipei Times* 99; Pub., *Twn. Daily* 96-; *b.* Twn. Apr. 24, '44; *m.* Chou, Tong-shing; 1 *s.,* 1 *d.; educ.*MA, Pol., Tunghai U., 68; MA, Pol., NCCU 72; Studied in Media Inst. of Berlin & Hawaii E.W. Cent. 89; Corr., *Ch. Times* 72-79; Ed. Writer, *Independence Evening Post* 76-83; Ed.-in-Chief, *The Eighties'* Mag. 79-87; Pub., *The Jour. Weekly* 91-92; Dir. & Ed.-in-Chief, *Capital Morning News* 91-92; *Add.* 5th Fl., 137 Nanking E. Rd., Taipei 104.

CHIANG, CHIA-HSING 蔣家興
V. Chmn., RDEC 94-2000; *b.* Twn. July 15, '39; *m.* Lee, Chiou-yueh; 1 *s.; educ.* Nat. Taipei Inst. of Tech. 60; MS, Materials Engr., N. Carolina State U. 73, Ph.D. 77; Assc. Prof. & Head, Mech. Engr. Dept., Tamkang U. 78-81; Sr. Staff Engr., CEPD 81-84; Dir., Ovs. Ch. Scholars & Students Service Cent., NYC 84-87, Acting Chmn. 87-94. *Publ.: Compressive Behavior of Angle-wound Fiber Composites; Influence of Graphite on Young's Modulus of Cast Iron;* etc.; *Add.* 7th Fl., 2-2 Chi Nan Rd., Sect. 1, Taipei 100.

CHIANG, CHING-CHIEN 江清棣
Lieutenant Gov., TPG 98-; *b.* Twn. Dec. 17, '42; *m.* Shih, Ming-ying; 1 *s.,* 2 *d.; educ.* B., PA, NCHU 65; MPA, NCCU 69; Exec. Sec., Res., Dev. & Evaluation Cttee., TPG 82-85, Dep. Dir., Dept. of Comm. 85-90; Pres., Twn. Prov. Bus Trans. Co. 90-93; Dep. Sec.-Gen., TPG 93-96; Dir., Bu. of Housing & Urban Dev. 96-97; Admin. V. Min.

of the Int. 97-98; *Add.* 1 Sheng Fu Rd., Chunghsing New Village, Nantou 540.

CHIANG, CHUN-NAN
(See CHIANG, ANTONIO 江春南)

CHIANG, CHUNG-LING 蔣仲苓
Sr. Adv. to the Pres. 99-; Mem., CSC, KMT 99-, Mem., CC 93-; *b.* Chekiang Sept. 21, '22; *m.* Wu, Su; 4 *s.,* 1 *d.; educ.* 16th Class, Mil. Acad. 40; 6th Class, Army CGSC 55; Gen. Off. Course, War Coll., Armed Forces U. 76; 26th Infantry Div. Cmdr. 68-72; 9th Corps Cmdr. 73-75; 6th Field Army Cmdr. 77-79; CG, Kinmen Def. Cmd. 79-81; C-in-C, ROC Army 81-88; Exec. V. Chief of the Gen. Staff, MND 88-89; Personal C/S to the Pres. 89-92; Nat. Policy Adv. to the Pres. 92-94; Min. of Nat. Def. & concur. Min. of State 94-99; *Add.* 6 Lane 112, Hsing Yi Rd., Peitou, Taipei 112.

CHIANG, HUNG-I 蔣洪彝
Bd. Chmn., Ch. Airlines 94-; *b.* Kiangsu Oct. 12, '26; *m.* Hsu, Kuei-chen; 1 *s.,* 2 *d.; educ.* Studied, Air Tech. Sch., ROCAF 48, Air Force Inst. of Tech., USA 64, Armed Forces Warfare Coll. 72, CGSC 81; Group Cmdr., 5th Maintenance & Supply Group, ROCAF 75-77, Sect. Chief, Maintenance Sect. of DCS/LOG, Ch. Airlines Hqs. 77-78; Div. Chief, 4th Div., Off. of the Dep. Chief of the Gen. Staff for Logistics, MND 78-80; Asst., DCS/LOG, ROCAF Hqs. 80; Cmdr., 1st Air Logistics Area Cmd., ROCAF 81-83; Dep. Cmdr., Logistics Cmd. 83-84, Cmdr. 85-87; V. Pres., Ch. Airlines 88-90; Gen. Mgr., Far E. Air Trans. Corp. 89-94; *Add.* 131 Nanking E. Rd., Sect. 3, Taipei 104.

CHIANG, KAI-SHEK, MADAME
(See SOONG, MAYLING 宋美齡)

CHIANG, NANCY ZI 蔣徐乃錦
Former Sup., Nat. YWCA of the ROC 97-; Hon. Chmn. Chronide Sec. Investment Trust Co. Ltd. 95-; Pres., Ch.-German Cul. & Econ. Assn. 95-, Ch.-German Cul. & Educ Found. 95-, & Ch. Women's Assn. 96-; 1st V. Pres., FAWA 96-; Bd. Mem., Kingvic Investment Co. Ltd. 88-, & Chinesisch-Deutscher Kultur- und Wirtschaftsverband 88-; Bd Mem., Taipei Intl. Community Cul. Found., & Chmn., Prog Cttee. 84-; Exec. Dir., Raw Materials Ltd. 78-; *b.* Shang hai Mar. 29, '38; *m.* Chiang, Alan Hsiao-wen (deceased) 1 *d.; educ.* BA, NTU; MS, U. of So. Calif.; Lectr., Ch Cul. U. 52-53; 1st V. Pres., Intl. Women's Club 64-65 & 66-67, & Taipei YWCA 69-70 & 73-75; Exec. Sec., Intl Aff. Off., CTC, & Producer 73-80; Chief Ed., *Bi-monthl' Update* 74-76; Chmn., L'Escargot Co. Ltd. 77-82, &

Europa Haus Co. Ltd. 78-87; 1st V. Pres., Nat. YWCA of the ROC 78-87; Adv., Admin., & Planning Coun., Nat. Theater & Nat. Concert Hall 83-86; Pres., Taipei YWCA 83-89; Mem., Exec. Cttee., World YWCA 87-95; V. Chmn., Kingvic Intl. Dev. & Investment Co. Ltd. 88-92; Bd. Mem., World Vision of Twn. 89-96; Pres., Nat. YWCA of the ROC 91-97; *Add.* 6th Fl., 7 Tsingtao W. Rd., Taipei 100.

CHIANG, PENG-CHIEN 江鵬堅

Mem., Control Yuan 96-; *b.* Taipei Apr. 25, '40; *m.* Peng, Fong-mei; 1 *s.,* 2 *d.; educ.* LL.B., NTU 62, Studied, Grad. Sch. of Law 63-64; Attorney-at-Law 65; Sec.-Gen., Ch. Comparative Law Soc. 76-77; Mem., Legis. Yuan 84-87 & 95-96; Founding Pres., Twn. Assn. of Human Rights 84-86, & DPP 86-87; Sr. Fel., Cent. of Dev. Policy, Washington, D.C. 88; Sec.-Gen., DPP 92-93. *Publ.: Recall Soc. Justice 82; Pamphlet on Human Rights 82; Viva Human Rights 83; Vote Vs. Bullets 87; Add.* 2 Chung Hsiao E. Rd., Sect. 1, Taipei 100.

CHIANG, PIN-KUNG 江丙坤

Chmn., CEPD 96-2000; Min. without Portfolio 98-; Dir.-Gen., So. Twn. Joint Services Cent., Exec. Yuan 98-; Mem., CC, KMT 93-, CSC 99-; *b.* Twn. Dec. 16, '32; *m.* Chen, Mei-huey; 3 *c.; educ.* Ph.D., Agr. Econ., U. of Tokyo 62-71; Asst. Cml. Attaché, Emb. in Japan 67-74; Cml. Attaché, Consl. Gen. in Johnnesburg 74-79; Econ. Counsl., Emb. in S. Africa 79-81; Dep. Dir.-Gen., Bd. of For. Trade (BOFT), MOEA 82-83; Sec.-Gen., CETRA 83-88; Dir.-Gen., BOFT, MOEA 88-89; Admin. V. Min. of Econ. Aff. 89-90; Pol. V. Min. of Econ. Aff. 90-93; Min. of Econ. Aff. 93-96. *Publ.: Study of Twn. Land-tax Reform; Add.* 3 Pao Ching St., Taipei 100.

CHIANG, PING-KUN
(See CHIANG, PIN-KUNG 江丙坤)

CHIANG, WEI-PING
(See KIANG, WEBSTER WEI-PING 江偉平)

CHIANG HSU, NAI-CHIN
(See CHIANG, NANCY ZI 蔣徐乃錦)

CHIAO, HSIUNG-PING
(See CHIAO, HSIUNG-PING PEGGY 焦雄屏)

CHIAO, HSIUNG-PING PEGGY 焦雄屏
Prod. & Dir., Twn. Film Cent. 95-; Assc. Prof., Nat. Inst. of the Arts 87-; Adjunct Assc. Prof., NCU 88; *b.* Twn. Aug. 8,

'53; *educ.* BA, NCU 75; MA, Radio-TV Film, U. of Texas, Austin 81; Film Dept., UCLA 85-86; Screenplay, Actress 92; Adjunct Prof., Ch. Cul. U. 81-86, Fu Jen Catholic U. 85-86, Nat. Twn. Acad. of the Arts 82-83; Coordinator, *Ch. Times* Film Award 88-95; Mng. Dir., Nat. Film Year 93-94. *Publ.: Twn. New Cinema 88; Hong Kong Cinema 75-87; Reading Mainstream Cinema 90; Anthropology of Film Writings 91; Authors & Genre: A Study of Twn. & Hong Kong Cinema 91; Hou Hsiao-hsien 93; Musicals 93; The Five Years That Changed Twn. Film History: A Study of Kuo Lien Studio 93; HHH: Await of Hou Hsiao-hien 97; Hong Kong Memoir: Still Love You After All These 98; Hong Kong Memoir: As Times Goes By 98; The River 98; Add.* 4th Fl., Lane 2, 19 Wan Li St., Wenshan, Taipei 116.

CHIAO, JEN-HO 焦仁和

Min., OCAC 98-2000; Mem., CC, KMT 93-; Prof., Law, Ch. Cul. U. 74-; *b.* Chekiang Nov. 11, '48; *m.* Tan, Hai-chu; 1 *s.,* 2 *d.; educ.* LL.B., Ch. Cul. U. 70; MCL, So. Methodist U. 72; J.D., Ohio Nr. U. 74; Res., London Sch. of Econ. & Pol. Sc. 79; Dean of Student Aff., Ch. Cul. U. 75-78, Dean of Studies 79-80; Dir., Secretariat, Yang Ming Inst. 80-82, Dir., Guidance Sect. 82-83; Counsl., Off. of the Pres. 84-85, Dep. Dir., 1st Bu. 85-88, Dir., Confidential Aff. & concur. Press Sec. 88-93; V. Chmn., MAC 93; V. Chmn. & concur. Sec.-Gen., SEF 93-98. *Publ.: A Comparative Study on Products Liability; A New Approach on the Study of Private Intl. Law; Add.* 16th Fl., 5 Hsuchow Rd., Taipei 100.

CHIAO, TING-PIAO 焦廷標

Hon. Chmn., Walsin Lihwa Corp. 86-; *b.* Peking Mar. 3, '14; *m.* Hung, Pai-yun; 4 *s.,* 1 *d.; educ.* Grad., High Sch.; Tech., Kuang Hua Rubber Factory 43-48, & Yung Kuang Elec. Cable 48-50; Plant Mgr., First Pacific Elec. Cable 50-63; Chmn., Walsin Lihwa Corp. 78-86, Dep. Chmn. & Pres. 68-86; *Add.* 12th Fl., 117 Min Sheng E. Rd., Sect. 3, Taipei 104.

CHIEN, CHIH-HSIN 簡志信

Chmn., *Ch. Times Weekly; b.* Hupei Oct. 3, '35; *m.* Huang, Yueh-kuei; 1 *s.,* 1 *d.; educ.* Studied, Nat. Twn. Coll. of Arts; BA, Tamkang U.; Prog. Host, Air Force Broadcasting System; Reporter, Ed. & Dep. Ed.-in-Chief, *Ch. Times;* Ed.-in-Chief & Pub., *Ch. Times Weekly; Add.* 5th Fl., 25 Min Chuan E. Rd., Sect. 6, Taipei 114.

CHIEN, CHUN-AN 簡春安

Pres., Chang Jung Christian U. 97-; Chmn., Bd. of Trustees, Chung Tai Christian Seminary 94-; Pub., *Ch. Christian*

Monthly 93-; *b.* Twn. July 28, '48; *m.* Huang, Hsiu-pao; 1 *s.,* 1 *d.; educ.* BA, Tunghai U. 71; MA, Soc. Work, U. of Hawaii 76; Ph.D., Case We. Reserve U. 83; Dir., Taichung Lifeline Assn. 84-86, & Family Wellness Cent. 87-91; Chmn., Dept. of Soc. Work, Tunghai U. 88-93, Dean of Labor Educ. 93, Gen. Sec. 94. *Publ.: Eden of Happiness; Marriage 100; Analysis & Handling of Extramarital Aff.; Marriage & Family; Add.* 396 Chang Jung Rd., Sect. 1, Kueijen, Tainan County 711.

CHIEN, EDWARD H.T. 簡弘道
Chmn., Hua Nan Cml. Bk., 98-; *b.* Twn. Oct. 28, '33; *m.* Lin Sue-tzu; 2 *s.,* 1 *d.; educ.* LL.B. in Econ., NTU 56; M., in Econ., U. of Nebraska, 61; Dep. Gen. Mgr., Loan Dept., Bk. of Am. (Taipei Br.) 66-75; Dep. Gen. Mgr., Intl. Banking Dept., Hua Nan Bk. 75-77, Gen. Mgr. 77-82; Dep. Dir., Dept. of Monetary Aff., MOF 82-87; Exec. V. Pres., Hua Nan Bk. 87-94, Pres., 94-98; *Add.* 38 Chungking S. Rd., Sect. 1, Taipei 100.

CHIEN, EUGENE Y.H. 簡又新
Dep. Sec.-Gen., Off. of the Pres. 2000-; Mem., CC, KMT 88-; *b.* Twn. Feb. 4, '46; *m.* Wang, Kuei-jung; 2 *s.,* 1 *d.; educ.* BS, Mech. Engr., NTU 68; MS, Aeronautics & Astronautics, New York U. 71, Ph.D. 73; Prof. & Chmn., Dept. of Aeronautical Engr., Tamkang U. 76-78, Prof. & Dean, Coll. of Engr. 78-84; Mem., Legis. Yuan 84-87; Admin., EPA 87-91; Min. of Trans. & Comms. 91-93; Rep., Taipei Rep. Off. in the UK 93-98; Mem., Consultative Cttee., NSC, Off. of the Pres. 98-2000; *Add.* c/o Off. of the Pres., Taipei 100.

CHIEN, FREDRICK FU 錢復
Pres., Control Yuan 99-; Mem., CSC, KMT 88-, CC 76-; *b.* Peiping Feb. 17, '35; *m.* Tien, Julie; 1 *s.,* 1 *d.; educ.* BA, NTU 56; MA, Yale U. 59, Ph.D. 62; Hon. LL.D., Sung Kyun Kwan U., S. Korea; Hon. D.Lit., Wilson Coll., USA; Hon. LL.D., Boston U., Idaho State U., & Caribbean Am. U.; Hon. D. of Public Service, Florida Intl. U.; 10th Class, Nat. War Coll.; Sec. to the Premier, Exec. Yuan 62-63; Visiting Assc. Prof., NCCU 62-64; Sp. & Sect. Chief, Dept. of N. Am. Aff., MOFA 64-67, Dep. Dir. 67-69, Dir. 69-72; Visiting Prof., NTU 70-72; Dir.-Gen., GIO 72-75; Admin. V. Min. of For. Aff. 75-79; Pol. V. Min. of For. Aff. 79-82; Rep., CCNAA, Washington, D.C. 83-88; Chmn., CEPD & concur. Min. without Portfolio 88-90; Min. of For. Aff. 90-96; Spkr., NA 96-98. *Publ.: The Opening of Korea: A Study of Ch. Dip. 1876-1885; Speaking as a Friend; More Views of a Friend; Faith & Resilience: The ROC Forges Ahead; Opportunity & Challenge; Add.* 53 Chung Hua Rd., Sect. 1, Taipei 100.

CHIEN, FU
(See CHIEN, FREDRICK FU 錢復)

CHIEN, GEORGE L.T. 錢龍韜
Bd. Chmn., Hu Chiang High Sch. 93-; Exec. Dir., Ch. Latin-Am. Cul. & Econ. Assn.; Coun., KMT 93-; *b.* Chekiang Sept. 9, '22; 3 *s.,* 1 *d.; educ.* BA, U. of Shanghai; Rep. & Comr., Shansi Prov. Govt. 45-47; Econ. Sp., MND 47-48; Dep. Mgr., Kaohsiung Br., Bk. of Twn. 49-50, Dep. Mgr., Treasury Dept. 50-57, & Mgr. 58-61; Dir., Twn. Navigation Co. 58-61; Gen. Mgr., Treasury Dept., CBC 61-82; Adv., Bk. of Twn. 62-63; Bd. Mem., City Bk. of Taipei 70-83; Chmn., Chung Kuo Ins. 82-89, & Ch. Bills Finance Corp. 89-93; Chmn. of the Bd., Bills Finance Assn. of Taipei 92-93; Exec. Dir., Taipei Bills Finance Assn. 93-96; Adv., Ovs. Ch. Bk. 93-96; *Add.* 9th Fl.-3, 43 Hsin Yi Rd., Sect. 3, Taipei 106.

CHIEN, HSU
(See CHIEN, SHU 錢煦)

CHIEN, HUNG-TAO
(See CHIEN, EDWARD H.T. 簡弘道)

CHIEN, JEN-TEH
(See CHIEN, JEN-TER 簡仁德)

CHIEN, JEN-TER 簡仁德
Dir.-Gen., Directorate Gen. of Telecomms., MOTC 97-; *b.* Twn. Oct. 17, '44; *m.* Chen, Su-ching; 1 *s.,* 2 *d.; educ.* B., Dept. of Ind. Engr., Nat. Chung Cheng U. 68; M. of Op. Res., Naval Postgrad. Sch., USA 74; Dr. of Mng. Sc., Tamkang U. 81; Prof., Dir. & Dean, Nat. Def. Mng. Coll. 81-87; Dir., Comprehensive Planning Bu., EPA 87-89, Environmental Monitoring & Data Processing Bu. 89-90; Dir., Gen. Aff. MOTC 91-93, Counsl. 93-96, Dir., Posts & Telecomms. 96-97; *Add.* 16 Chi Nan Rd., Sect. 2, Taipei 100.

CHIEN, LUNG-TAO
(See CHIEN, GEORGE L.T. 錢龍韜)

CHIEN, MAO-FA
(See CHIEN, MAW-FA 簡茂發)

CHIEN, MAW-FA 簡茂發
Pres., NTNU 99-; *b.* Twn. Feb. 25, '41; *m.* Chien Ou Tsing-yi; 1 *s.,* 2 *d.; educ.* Ed.B., NTNU 64, Ed.M. 68, Ed.D., U. of Northern Colorado, USA 73; Asst., Dept. of Educ., NTNU 65-69, Instr., Dept. of Educ. Psychology 69-70, Assc. Prof., Grad. Inst. of Educ. 73-78, Prof. 78-81, Dir

81-87; Pres., Nat. Taichung Tchrs. Coll. 87-93; Dean of Studies, NTNU 93-97, V. Pres. 97-99. *Publ.: Res. Methods in Educ.; Educ. Psychology; Psychological Testing & Statistical Methods; Add.* 162 Ho Ping E. Rd., Sect. 1, Taipei 106.

CHIEN, MAO-NAN
(See CHIEN, MO-NA 簡茂男)

CHIEN, MO-NA 簡茂男
Chmn., Chailease Finance Co., Ltd. 98-; V. Chmn., Factors Chain Intl., Amsterdam 97-; V. Chmn., Ch.-Philippine Business Coun. 97-; *b.* Twn. Feb. 20, '44; *m.* Chien Lu, Hsueh-yun; 3 *d.; educ* BS, Agr. Econ., NTU 67; Grad., MIT Alfred P. Sloan Sch. of Mng. (Prog. for Sr. Exec.) 93; Chmn., Taipei Leasing Assn. 95-98, Chailease Resources Trading Co. 98, Grand Pacific Co. 98, Otto-Chailease Mailorder Co. 98-99; *Add.* 4th Fl., 56 Tun Hua N. Rd., Taipei 105.

CHIEN, SHU 錢煦
Mem., Acad. Sinica 76-, Chmn., Adv. Cttee., Inst. of Biomed. Sc. 93-; Mem., Nat. Acad. of Engr., USA 97-; Chmn., Adv. Cttee., Nat. Health Res. Inst. 93-; Founding Fel., Am. Inst. of Med. & Biological Engr. 92-; Mem., Inst. of Med., USA 94-; Prof., Bioengr. & Med., & Dir., Inst. for Biomed. Engr., U. of Calif., San Diego 88-; Chair, Dept. of Bioengr. 94-; *b.* Peiping June 23, '31; *m.* Hu, Kuang-chung; 2 *d.; educ.* MB, NTU 53; Ph.D., Columbia U. 57; Instr., Physiology, Columbia U. 56-58, Asst. Prof. 58-64, Assc. Prof. 64-69, Prof. 69-88, Dir., Div. of Circulatory Physiology 74-88; Dir., Inst. of Biomed. Sc., Acad. Sinica 87-88; Pres., Am. Physiological Soc. 90-91; Pres., Fed. of Am. Soc. for Experimental Biology 92-93. *Publ.:* 8 bks. & over 300 original sc. papers; *Add.* 9445 La Jolla Farms Rd., La Jolla, CA 92037-1128, USA.

CHIEN, TAI-LANG 簡太郎
Admin. V. Min. of the Int. 99-; Mem., NA 96-; *b.* Twn. Feb. 15, '47; *m.* Yang, Ling-chin, 2 *s.; educ.* BA, Sociology, NCHU 70; Studied, U. of Calif. —Long Beach 84; Chief Sec., Kaohsiung City Govt. 82-86; Dep. Dir., Dept. of Pop. Admin., MOI 86-88, Dir. 88-96; Sec.-Gen., CEIC 96-99; *Add.* 5 Hsuchow Rd., Taipei 100.

CHIEN, YU-HSIN
(See CHIEN, EUGENE Y.H. 簡又新)

CHIEN, YUEH-WEI
(See KAN, YUET-WAI 簡悅威)

CHIN, CHUNG-HSUN
(See CHIN, TSUNG-SHUNE 金重勳)

CHIN, HSIAO-YI 秦孝儀
Dir., Nat. Palace Museum 83-; Chmn., Nat. Cul. & Arts Found. 97-; *b.* Hunan Feb. 11, '21; *m.* Hsu, Hai-ping; 3 *s.,* 1 *d.; educ.* Grad., Law Dept., Shanghai Law Coll.; Hon. Dr., Humane Letters, Oklahoma City U.; Exec. Sec. to Pres. Chiang Kai-shek 50-75; Dep. Sec.-Gen., CC, KMT 61-75, Mem. 63-93; Prof., Grad. Inst. of San-Min-Chu-I, NTU 74-88; Chmn., Party Hist. Com., CC, KMT 76-91; Pres., Ch. Hist. Assn. 84-91, & Ch. Assn. of Museums 90-95. *Publ.: Basic Courses in Dr. Sun Yat-sen's Thought; The Spring of Advancing Virtue; Pres. Chiang Kai-shek's Thorough Understanding & Forthright Application of Dr. Sun Yat-sen's Thought; Add.* 7 Lane 138, Chih Shan Rd., Sect. 1, Waishuanghsi, Shihlin, Taipei 111.

CHIN, SHU-CHI
(See KING, CHARLES SHU-CHI 金樹基)

CHIN, TSUNG-SHUNE 金重勳
Prof., Dept. of Materials Sc. & Engr., NTHU 88-; Exec. Dir., Tze-chiang Found. of Sc. & Tech. 91-; *b.* Twn. Oct. 18, '48; *m.* Chun, Alice; 2 *s.; educ.* BS, NCKU 71, MS 73, D.Sc. 82; Assc. Res. Scientist, Metal Res. Lab., Ind. Tech. Res. Inst. 75-79, Res. Scientist 79-81; Lectr., Dept. of Metallurgy & Materials Engr., NCKU 81-82, Assc. Prof. 82-86, Prof. 86-88; Visiting Scientist, Dept. of Materials Sc. & Engr., MIT 84-85. *Publ.: Materials Engr.;* 78 referred papers on magnetic materials, ceramics, & metals; 84 conf. papers; 3 bk. (transl.); *Add.* 4th Fl., 65 W. Yuan, NTHU, Kuang Fu Rd., Sect. 2, Hsinchu 300.

CHIN, WEI-CHUN
(See JIN, WEI-TSUN 金惟純)

CHIN, YAO-CHI
(See KING, AMBROSE Y.C. 金耀基)

CHING HSIN 淨心
Chmn., Ch. Buddhist Assn. 94-, World Ch. Buddhist Sangha Cong. 92-; V. Pres., World Buddhist Sangha Coun. 81-; Bd. Dir., Lin Chi Chan Temple 89-, & Shih Pu Temple 89-; *b.* Twn. July 22, '29; *educ.* BA, Bukkyo U., Japan 77; Abbot, Kuang Te Temple 63, Buddhist Lotus Assn. in Kaohsiung 66, Lin Chi Chan Temple 67, Buddhist Lotus Assn. in Taipei 71, Hsuan Chuang Temple 91; *Add.* Kuang Teh Temple, 76 Kan Hou Valley, Alien Hsiang, Kaohsiung County 822.

CHIOU, I-JEN 邱義仁
Dep. Sec.-Gen., NSC, Off. of the Pres. 2000-; *b.* Twn. May 9, '50; *m.* Chiang, Mei-ling; 1 *s.; educ.* MPS, U. of Chicago;

Dep. Sec.-Gen., CC, DDP, Sec.-Gen.; *Add.* c/o Off. of the Pres., Taipei 100.

CHIOU, JONG-NAN 邱榮男
Amb. to Haiti 97-; *b.* Twn. Oct. 6, '39; *m.* Chen, Jacqueline; 1 *s.,* 1 *d.; educ.* LL.B., NTU 62; Dep. Dir., Dept. of European Aff., MOFA 77-79; Rep. to Switzerland 79-85; Dir., Dept. of European Aff., MOFA 85-90; Rep., Taipei Rep. Off. in France 90-96; *Add.* P.O. Box 655 Port-au-Prince, Haiti.

CHIOU, LIAN-GONG 邱聯恭
Nat. Policy Adv. to the Pres. 96-; Prof. of Law, NTU 83-; Mem., Cttee. for Proposed Amendments to the Code of Civil Procedure at the Judicature 83-; Nat. Policy Adv. to the Pres. 96-; Nat. Chair 98-; *b.* Twn. Apr. 10, '38; *m.* Lin, Ya-ying; 1 *s.,* 1 *d.; educ.* LL.B., NTU 61; ML, U. of Tokyo 73, Ph.D. 81; Judge, Tainan Dist. Court 65-66, & Taipei Dist. Court 66-70; Mem., Cttee. for Proposed Amendments to the Code of Notary Public Law 89-95. *Publ.: The Role of Lawyer in Modern Soc.; Der Zweck des Zivilprozesses; Über die Prozesshindernde Einrede des Schiedsvertrages; Über Funktionen der Verfahrensgarantie im Zivilprozess; Add.* 3rd Fl., 10 Lane 92, Shih Ta Rd., Taan, Taipei 106.

CHIU, CHENG-HSIUNG
(See CHIU, PAUL CHENG-HSIUNG 邱正雄)

CHIU, CHENG-TUNG
(See YAU, SHING-TUNG 丘成桐)

CHIU, CHEYNE J.Y. 邱進益
Min. of Civil Service, Exam. Yuan 96-2000; Mem., CC, KMT 93-; *b.* Kiangsu Nov. 19, '36; *m.* Cheng, Jean; 2 *s.; educ.* LL.B., NCCU 60; Grad. Studies, NCCU 61-64, Vienna U. 65-66, & Bonn U. 74-76; Staff Mem., MOFA 62-65, Sect. Chief, Dept. of European Aff. 72-74, Dep. Dir. 79-81; Chargé d'Affaires, Emb. in Malta 70-72; Rep. to Sweden 81-83; Dir., Protocol Dept., MOFA 83-85, Spokesman, MOFA 85-87; Amb. to Swaziland 87-88; Dep. Sec.-Gen. to the Pres. 88-93; Spokesman, Off. of the Pres. 90-93; Convener, Res. Cttee., & Exec. Sec., Secretariat, NUC 90-93; V. Chmn. & concur. Sec.-Gen., SEF 93; Nat. Policy Adv. to the Pres. 93-96; Rep., Taipei Rep. Off. in Singapore 94-96; *Add.* 1 Shih Yuan Rd., Wenshan, Taipei 116.

CHIU, CHIN-I
(See CHIU, CHEYNE J.Y. 邱進益)

CHIU, CHIN-SUNG
(See CHIOU, JIN-SONG 邱金松)

CHIU, CHUANG-HUAN 邱創煥
Mem., CC, KMT 76-, CSC 79-; Sr. Adv. to the Pres. 96-; V. Chmn., KMT 97-; *b.* Twn. July 25, '25; *m.* Pai, Ling-yu; 2 *s.,* 2 *d.; educ.* MPS, NCCU; Dir., 3rd Dept., Min. of Pers., Exam. Yuan 65-67; Dep. Dir., 5th Sect., CC, KMT 67-69; Comr., Dept. of Soc. Aff., TPG 69-72; Dir.-Gen., Dept. of Soc. Aff., CC, KMT 72-78; Min. without Portfolio 76-78; Dep. Sec.-Gen., CC, KMT 78; Min. of the Int. 78-81; Chmn., CEIC 78-81; V. Premier 81-84; Gov., TPG 84-90; Sr. Adv. to the Pres. 90-93; Pres., Exam. Yuan 93-96; Acting V. Chmn., KMT 96-97. *Publ.: Thoughts Regarding Soc. Welfare in the Three Principles of the People; A Summary of Ch. Soc. Welfare System; Soc. Welfare & People's Livelihood; A Treatise of Civil Service System; Add.* 122 Chungking S. Rd., Sect. 1, Taipei 100.

CHIU, CHUNG-JEN
(See CHIU, JONG-JEN 邱仲仁)

CHIU, HUNGDAH 丘宏達
ROC Amb.-at-Large 98-; Prof., Sch. of Law, U. of Maryland; Ed.-in-Chief, *Ch. Yearbk. of Intl. Law & Aff.* 81-; Mem., NUC; Pres., Ch. Soc. of Intl. Law 93-; Pres., Intl. Law Assn. 98-00; *b.* Shanghai Mar. 23, '36; *m.* Hsieh, Yuan-yuan; 1 *s.; educ.* LL.B., NTU; MA, Long Island U. 62; LL.M., Harvard U. 62, S.J.D. 65; Assc. Prof., NTU 65-66; Res. Assc., Law Sch., Harvard U. 66-70 & 72-74; Prof., NCCU & NTU 70-72; Assc. Prof., U. of Maryland 74-77; Observer, Intl. Law Assn. to the 3rd UN Conf. on the Law of the Sea 76-82; Pres., Assn. of Ch. Soc. Scientists in N. Am. 84-86; Pres., Am. Assn. for Ch. Studies 85-87; Min. without Portfolio 93-94; Bd. Dir., SEF 93-95; Sp. envoy to the 20th anniversary of the independence of Grenada 94. *Publ.: The Capacity of Intl. Org. to Conclude Treaties; Ch. & the Question of Twn.; Documents & Analysis; Ch. & the Twn. Issue; Ch.: 70 Years After the 1911 Hsinhai Rev.; Criminal Justice in Post-Mao Ch.; The Future of Hong Kong, Toward 1997 & Beyond; Survey of Recent Dev. in Ch. (Mainland & Twn.) 85-86; The US Const. & Constitutionism in Ch.; The Draft Basic Law of Hong Kong: Analysis & Documents; Intl. Law of the Sea: Cases, Documents & Readings; Modern Intl. Law* (Ch.); *Reference documents on modern Intl. Law* (Ch.); etc.; *Add.* 500 W. Baltimore St., Baltimore, Maryland 21201, USA.

CHIU, HUA-YEN
(See CHIU, HWA-YEN 邱華演)

CHIU, HUNG-TA
(See CHIU, HUNGDAH 丘宏達)

CHIU, HWA-YEN 邱華演

Pres., Forward Enterprise Co. Ltd. 74-; Leading Mng. Dir., Bd. of Trustees, Twn. Printing Ind. Assn. 92-; Mng. Dir. of the Bd., Printing Tech. Res. Inst. 93-; *b.* Twn. Mar. 19, '39; *m.* Chen, Shiou-chen; 1 *s.,* 2 *d.; educ.* BA, Econ., Soochow U.; Asst. Mgr., Chung Hua Wire & Cable Co.; Mgr., Ting Hou Enterprise; Mgr., Ch. Rebar Co.; *Add.* 65 Chung Shan Rd., Tucheng, Taipei County 236.

CHIU, I-JEN
(See CHIOU, I-JEN 邱義仁)

CHIU, JONG-JEN 邱仲仁

Amb. to the Repub. of Chad 97-; *b.* Twn. Oct. 20, '48; *m.* Teng Mci-hua; 1 *s.,* 1 *d., educ* B., Dept. of Dip., NCCU 70; DPS, Université de Paris 78; Sp., Dept. of European Aff., MOFA 79-81, Sect. Chief, Dept. of Protocol 81-84; Counsl., Del. to the Luxemborg 84-90; Dep. Dir.-Gen., Dept. of Treaty, MOFA 90-94; Sp. Del., Délégation Spéciale de la Republique de Chine an Madagascar 94-97. *Publ.: La Politique étrangärie de la Ch. Communiste pendant la Révolution culturelle, Paris* 78; *Impact of Mainland Ch. on the ROC-We. Europe Rel. in the 90s* 93; *Add.* Ambassade de la République de Ch., B.P. 1150 N'DJAMENA TCHAD.

CHIU, JUNG-NAN
(See CHIOU, JONG-NAN 邱榮男)

CHIU, KUN-LANG
(See CHIU, KUN-LIANG 邱坤良)

CHIU, KUN-LIANG 邱坤良

Pres., Nat. Inst. of the Arts 97-; *b.* Twn. Feb. 13, '49; *m.* Chang, I-lin; 1*d.; educ.* MA, Ch. Cul. U. 73; Ph.D., U. of Paris VII 86; Assc. Prof., Dept. of Theater, Ch. Cul. U. 82-83; Fulbright Scholar to Columbia U. 83; Dir., Traditional Arts Res. Cent., Nat. Inst. of the Arts 86-90, Head, Dept. of Theater 93-97; Postdr. Res., UCLA 90-91. *Publ.: Open Stage—Participation in Twn. Opera* 80; *Folk Opera in Modern Soc.* 83; *The Ceremonial Perspective of Ch. Operas* (French) 91; *Twn. Operas During Japanese Occupation* 93; *Twn. Opera Live—Antagonism & Identification* 97; *Twn. Theater & Cul. Change* 97; *Add.* 1 Hsueh Yuan Rd., Peitou, Taipei 112.

CHIU, LIEN-KUNG
(See CHIOU, LIAN-GONG 邱聯恭)

CHIU, MAO-YING
(See TJIU, MAU-YING 邱茂英)

CHIU, PAUL CHENG-HSIUNG 邱正雄

Min. of Finance 96-2000; Mem., CSC, KMT 99-; *b.* Twn. Feb. 19, '42; *m.* Chang, Mei-pao; 2 *s.; educ.* BA, NTU 64; MA & Ph.D., Econ., Ohio State U. 71-78; Eisenhower Fel. 88; Assc. Prof., NTU 73-75; Dep. Gen. Mgr., Banking Dept., CBC 75-76, & For. Exchange Dept. 76-81, Gen. Mgr., Banking Dept. 81-88; Pres., Hua Nan Cml. Bk. 88.; Dep. Gov., CBC 88-96. *Publ.: Optimal Open Market Strategy: A Generalized Kareken-Muench-Wallance Model in Econ. Essays* 73; *Optimal Monetary Policy Indicator—An Application of Kalman Filter to the St. Louis Equation & the Minnie Equation of the US Econ. in Econ. Essays* 78; *The 2-Stage Decision Rule for the Conduct of Monetary Policy* 78; *Performance of Financial Inst. in Twn. in Conf. on Experiences & Lessons of Econ. Dev. in Twn.* 81; *"Money & Financial Markets: The Domestic Perspective,"* in *Twn.: From Dev. to Mature Econ.* 92; "Prices, Money & Monetary Policy Implementation under Financial Liberalization: the Case of Twn." in *Financial Opening: Policy Issues & Experiences in Dev. Countries* 93; *Add.* 2 Ai Kuo W. Rd., Taipei 100.

CHIU, YING-NAN 丘應楠

Mem., Acad. Sinica 86-; Prof., Catholic U. of Am. 70-; Fel., Am. Phys. Soc. 86-; *b.* Canton Nov. 25, '33; *m.* Chow, Lue-yung; 2 *c.; educ.* NTU 50-52; BS, Berea Coll. 55; MS, Yale U. 56, Ph.D. 60; Res. Fel., Columbia U. 60-62; Res. Assc., U. of Chicago 62-64; Asst. Prof., Catholic U. of Am. 64-66, Assc. Prof. 66-70, Prof. & Chmn., Dept. of Chem. 70-80; Alfred P. Sloan Fel. 69-71; Hillebrand Prize, Chem. Soc. of Washington 84. *Publ.:* 123 res. articles in referred jour.; *Add.* Dept. of Chem., Catholic U. of Am., Washington, D.C. 20064, USA.

CHIU, YING-TIAO
(See CHIU, YING-TIAU 邱英桃)

CHIU, YING-TIAU 邱英桃

Pres., Yu-Da Inst. of Business Tech. 99-; *b.* Twn. Oct. 13, '39; *m.* Chiu Ke, Jing-yi; 1 *s.,* 2 *d.; educ.* BA, Intl. Trade, Ch. Cul. U.; MA, Com., Takushoku U., Japan, Studied, Business Sch., Japan-Asia U.; Ph.D. Candidate, Account Dept., Financial Coll. of Tianjin, Ch.; Instr., Takming Jr. Coll. of Com. 73-76; Assc. Prof., Tamsui Oxford U. Coll. 76-78; Assc. Prof. & class dir., Hsing Wu Jr. Coll of Com. 78-79; Prof. & class dir., Chih Lee Coll. of Business 79-93; Prof. & Dept. Head, Chang Jung Christian U. 93-97, Dept. Head 98-99; Prof., Chao Yang U. of Tech. 97-98. *Publ.: Deferred Assets; Market Mng.; Study of Abacus; Auditing; Add.* 600 Wu Jih Chieh Lake, Tanwen Village, Chaochiao, Miaoli County 361.

515

CHO, ALFRED Y. 卓以和

Mem., Acad. Sinica 90-; Dir., Semiconductor Res., Bell Labs., Lucent Tech., USA; Bd. Mem., Instruments SA Inc., USA 84-; Adjunct Prof., Dept. of EE, U. of Illinois 87-; *b.* Peking July 10, '37; *m.* Willoughby, Mona Lee; 1 *s.,* 3 *d.; educ.* BSEE 60; MSEE 61; Ph.D., U. of Illinois 68; Mem., Tech. Staff, Materials Sc. Res. Dept., AT&T Bell Labs. 68-84, Head, Elect. & Photonic Res. Dept. 84-87, Dir., Materials Processing Res. 87-90. *Publ.:* Over 400 publ. & 49 patents; *Add.* Bell Labs., Lucent Technologies, 600 Mountain Avenue, Murray Hill, NJ 07974, USA.

CHO, I-HE

(See CHO, ALFRED Y. 卓以和)

CHOU, CHANG-HUNG 周昌弘

Mem., Acad. Sinica 94-; Fel., Third World Acad. of Sc. 93-; Chmn., Nat. Cttee., Intl. Union of Biological Sc., SCOPE 88-, V. Pres. 97-; Prof., NTU 76-; Adjunct Prof., NTNU 76-; Fel. Prof., Acad. Sinica 76-; V. Pres., Nat. Sun Yat-sen U. 99-; Mem., Exec. Bd., PSA 99-; *b.* Twn. Sept. 5, '42; *m.* Yang, Liang-hui; 1 *s.,* 1 *d.; educ.* BS, Botany, NTU 65, MS, Botany 68; Ph.D., Plant Ecology, U. of Calif., Santa Barbara 71; Res. Asst., U. of Calif., Santa Barbara 68-71; Postdr. Fel., U. of Toronto 71-72; Prof., Res. Fel., & Dir., Inst. of Botany 89-96; Dir., Life Sc. Res. Promotion Cent., NScC 89-96. *Publ.: Plant Ecology;* over 220 allelopathic res. papers, 12 monographs, & over 12 review articles; *Add.* Inst. of Botany, Acad. Sinica, Taipei 115.

CHOU, LIEN-HUA

(See CHOW, LIEN-HWA 周聯華)

CHOU, SHENG-YUAN 周盛淵

Pub., *Cml. Times* 98-; *b.* Hupei Sept. 20, '46; *m.* Su, Pei-ling; 1 *s.; educ.* BA, Soochow U. 69; V. Pres., *Ch. Times* 89-98, & Ch. Times Group 82-98; V. Gen. Mgr., *Ch. Times* 77-79; Gen. Mgr., *Cml. Times* 79-85, & *Ch. Times* 85-86; *Add.* 132 Ta Li St., Taipei 108.

CHOU, SHIH-PIN 周世斌

Bd. Chmn., CTS 95-; *b.* Szechwan Sept. 6, '30; *m.* Hwang, Sheue-er; 1 *s.,* 1 *d.; educ.* Ch. Army Acad. 53; CGSC, Führungsakademie, Bundeswehr, W. Germany 67; War Coll., Armed Forces U. 79; Div. Cmdr. 75-77; Cmdt., Chung-cheng Armed Forces Preparatory Sch. 77-81; Corps Cmdr. 81-83; Cmdt., Cent. Police Coll. 83-87; Dep. C-in-C, Twn. Garrison GHQ 87-90; Sec.-Gen., VAC 90-91, V. Chmn. 91-93, Chmn. 93-94; Mem., CC & CSC, KMT 93-97; *Add.* 100 Kuang Fu S. Rd., Taipei 106.

CHOU, TSE-CHUAN 周澤川

Prof., NCKU 80-; Bd. Mem., Ch. Inst. of Chem. Engr. 95-; Ed. 95-; Bd. Mem., Kaohsiung Div., Ch. Chem. Associety 95-; *b.* Twn. Aug. 21, '41; *m.* Tsai, Hsiu-lien; 2 *s.; educ.* BS & MS, Chem. Engr., NCKU; Ph.D., Chem. Engr., Purdue U.; Instr., NCKU 69-75, Assc. Prof. 75-80; Visiting Prof., Rensselaer Polytechnic Inst. 81-82; Visiting Resr., Tokyo Inst. of Tech. 84; Visiting Prof. & Dean of Student Aff., Yuan Tze Inst. of Tech. 89-90; Prof. & Chmn., Dept. of Chem. Engr., NCKU 90-93; Coordinator, Intl. Symposium on Organic Reaction 91-93; Cttee.-in-Assc. Chief, Kaohsiung Div., Ch. Chem. Associety 92-95; Assc. Dean, Engr. Coll., NCKU 97-99. *Publ.:* 143 refer jour. papers, 11 review papers, 131 conf. presentation papers, 76 res. reports, 9 patents & 11 bk.; *Add.* 1 Ta Hsueh Rd., Tainan 701.

CHOU, WEN-HSIEN

(See CHOU, WEN-SHEN 周文賢)

CHOU, WEN-SHEN 周文賢

Pres., Kung Shan Inst. of Tech. 97-; *b.* Twn. Sept. 6, '33; *m.* Lin, Yu-tzu; 2 *d.; educ.* BS, NTNU 67; MA, Statistics, Brigham Young U., USA 75; Ph.D., Statistics, Oklahoma State U. 82; Prof. & Dean of Student Aff., Mingchi Inst. of Tech. 78-80, Prof. of Ind. Mng. & Pres. 82-94; Prof. & Dir., Dept. of Tech. Cooperation, Nat. Yunlin Inst. of Tech. 94-97. *Publ.:* 24 papers for acad. jour., conf. presentation, etc.; *Add.* 949 Ta Wan Rd., Yungkang, Tainan County 710.

CHOU, YEN-HSIN

(See CHOW, YIEN-SHING 周延鑫)

CHOU, YUAN-SHEN

(See CHOW, YUAN-SHIH 周元桑)

CHOW, GREGORY CHI-CHONG 鄒至莊

Mem., Acad. Sinica 70-; Fel., Econometric Soc., Am. Statistical Assn.; Prof. of Econ. & Class of 1913 Prof. of Pol. Econ., Princeton U. 70-, Dir., Econometric Res. Prog.; *b.* Kwangtung Dec. 25, '29; *m.* Chen, Paula K.; 2 *s.,* 1 *d.; educ.* BA, Cornell U.; MA & Ph.D., U. of Chicago; Hon. Dr., Zhongshan U.; LL.D., Lingan Coll.; Asst. Prof., MIT 55-59; Assc. Prof., Cornell U. 59-62; Res. Staff, IBM Res. Cent. 62-70; Visiting Prof., Cornell U. 64-65, Harvard U. 67, & Rutgers U. 69; Adjunct Prof., Columbia U. 65-70. *Publ.: Demand for Automobiles in the US; Analysis & Control of Dynamic Econ. Systems; Econ. Analysis by Control Methods; Econometrics; The Ch. Econ.; Understanding Ch.'s Econ.; Dynamic Econ.; Sower of Modern Econ. in Ch.:*

Interview of Gregory Chow (Ch.) *Add.* Dept. of Econ., Princeton U., Princeton, NJ 08544, USA.

CHOW, LIEN-HWA 周聯華
Pastor, Kai-ko Chapel 54-; *b.* Chekiang Mar. 7, '20; *m.* Yuan, Marie; 3 *s.*, educ. BBA, U. of Shanghai 47; BD, So. Baptist Theological Seminary, USA 51, Ph.D. 54; Prof., Twn. Baptist Theological Seminary 54-75; Pastor, Grace Baptist Church 54-75; Bible Translator; Bd. Chmn., Tunghai U. 92-99. *Publ.: Systematic Theology* (2 Vol.); *The New Homiletics; Ch. Bible Commentary* (ed.); *Add.* 12 Lane 58, Hsin Sheng S. Rd., Sect. 1, Taipei 100.

CHOW, YIEN-SHING 周延鑫
Dir., Nat. Museum of Nat. Sc. 97-; Res. Fel., Inst. of Zoology, Acad. Sinica 73-; *b.* Shangtung Jan. 1, '37; *m.* Lin, Sheng-hua; 1 *s.*, 1 *d.*, educ.; BS, Dept. of Entomology & Phytopathology, NTU 56-60, MS 60-63; Ph.D., Dept. of Zoology, Auburn U., USA 66-70; Postdr. Fel., Dept. of Chem., Insect Attractants & Basic Biology Lab., USDA, Florida; Res. Asst., Inst. of Zoology, Acad. Sinica 64-66, Assc. Res. Fel., 70-73, Res. Fel. 73, Res. Fel. & Dep. Dir., 78-84, Res. Fel. & Dir., 84-90. *Publ.: Insect Biochem. & Molecular Biology; Proceedings of Acarology;* Co-author, *The Role of Calcium in the Stimulation of Ecdysteroidogenesis in Silkworm, Biology & Life Stages of Charletonia Taiwanensis; Add.* 1 Kuan Chien Rd., Taichung 404.

CHOW, YUAN-SHIH 周元燊
Mem., Acad. Sinica 74-; Prof., Statistics, Columbia U. 68-; *b.* Hupei Sept. 1, '24; *m.* Chang, Yi; 5 *c.; educ.* BS, Nat. Chekiang U. 49; MA, U. of Illinois 55, Ph.D. 58; Asst., NTU 49-54; Res. Assc., U. of Illinois 58-59; IBM Res. Mathematician 59-62; Dir., Inst. of Math., Acad. Sinica 70-77; Assc. Prof. & Prof., Purdue U. 62-68; Fel., Inst. of Math. Statistics; Mem., Intl. Statistical Inst. *Publ.: Optimal Stopping; Probability Theory; Add.* 144 Washington Avenue, Dobbs Ferry, NY 10522, USA.

CHU, C.Y. 朱建一
V. Min., OCAC 99-; *b.* Fukien Sept. 14, '38; *m.* Chen, Ping-hsiang; 1 *s.*, 1 *d.; educ.* LL.B., NCCU 61, Grad. Sch. of For. Aff. 63; V. Consul, Consl. in Houston 65-68, Consul 69-74; Sect. Chief, Dept. of N. Am. Aff., MOFA 74-76; Consul, Consl. in New York 76-79; Sr. Sec., CCNAA, New York 79-84; Sr. Adv., CCNAA, Washington, D.C. 84-86; Dep. Dir., Dept. of N. Am. Aff., MOFA 86-88; Sec.-Gen., CCNAA, Hqs. in Taipei 88-89; Dir.-Gen., CCNAA, Atlanta 89-93; Sec.-Gen., CCNAA Hqs. for TECRO 94-

96; Dir.-Gen., Bu. of Consular Aff., MOFA 96-99; *Add.* 16th Fl., 5 Hsuchow Rd., Taipei 100.

CHU, CHI-YING
(See CHU, JAMES C.Y. 祝基瀅)

CHU, CHIEN-HUNG 褚劍鴻
Nat. Policy Adv. to the Pres. 93-; Prof., Fu Jen Catholic U. 70-; Hon. Pres., Ch. Soc. of Law 93-; *b.* Kiangsu May 10, '19; *educ.* LL.B., Nat. Futan U.; Chief Prosecutor, Hualien Dist. Court 55-59, Keelung Dist. Court 59-63, & Chiayi Dist. Court 63-64; Pres., Yunlin Dist. Court 64-68, & Changhua Dist. Court 68-70; Chief Prosecutor, Taipei Dist. Court 70-72, Pres. 72-78; Chief Prosecutor, Twn. High Court 78-79, Pres. 79-87; Prof., Ch. Cul. U. 71-85; Chief Justice, Supreme Court 87-93; Pres., Ch. Soc. of Law 89-93; Convener, Cttee. for Jud. Officials' Tng. 90-93. *Publ.: Gen. Part of Criminal Code; Sp. Part of Criminal Code; Code of Criminal Procedures; Criminal Procedure Practices & Sp. Topics; Essays on Criminal Law; Add.* 4th Fl., 72 Chin Hua St., Taipei 106.

CHU, CHIEN-I
(See CHU, C.Y. 朱建一)

CHU, CHING-WU
(See CHU, PAUL CHING-WU 朱經武)

CHU, ELIZABETH Y.F. 朱玉鳳
Dir.-Gen., TECO, Kansas City 98-; *b.* Twn. July 30, '55 m. Yu Chao-wen; 1 *s.*, 1 *d.; educ.* B.Lit., Tunghai U. 77; M. of Soc. Sc., San Francisco State U. 91, M. of Econ. 92; Desk Off., Dept. of Protocol, MOFA 78-86; Asst., TECO, San Francisco 86-92; Sect. Chief, Dept. of Econ. & Trade Aff. 92-95, Asst. Counsl. & Section Chief, 95-96, Dep. Dir.-Gen. 96-97. *Publ.: Exploring the ROC's For. Aid Prog. on Tech. Asst; ASEAN Countries Econ. Dev. & the ROC's Southward Policy; Add.* TECO in Kansas, Suite 800, 3100 Broadway, Kansas City.

CHU, FU-SUNG 朱撫松
Nat. Policy Adv. to the Pres. 79-; *b.* Hupei Jan. 5, '15; *m.* Hsu, Chung-pei; *educ.* BA, Shanghai U.; Acting Dir., UK Off., Min. of Info., KMT 46-47; Dir., Dept. of Intl. Info. Service, GIO 48-49; Counsl., TPG 49-50; Sr. Sec. & Counsl., Exec. Yuan 50-54; Adv., Off. of Govt. Spokesman 50-54; Dir., Info. Dept., MOFA 52-56; Counsl. & Min., Emb. in USA 56-60; Min., Emb. in Can. 60-62; V. Min. of For. Aff. 62-65; Amb. to Spain 65-71; Amb. to Brazil 71-74; Amb. to Korea 75-79; Min. of For. Aff. 79-87; *Add.* 262 Kuang Fu S. Rd., Taipei 106.

CHU, GLORIA WAN-CHING 朱婉清

Adv., Exec. Yuan 97-2000; Chmn., Bd. of Trustees, Cent. Broadcasting System of the ROC 97-; Lectr., Tamkang U. 86-; Pres., Ch. Women Writers' Assn. 95-; V. Pres., World Assn. of Women Jour. & Writers 97-; *b.* Taipei Feb. 9, '50; *m.* Ho, Marvin Ching-hsien; 1 *s.*, 1 *d.; educ.* BA, Ch. Lit., NCHU 73; MA, St. John's U., New York 81; Studied, City U. of New York 81; Ed., *New York World Daily News* 79-81; Sp. Corr. in New York, *Shin Sheng Daily News* 79-81; Ed., *CDN* 81; Sup., CCPD 81-87; Lectr., Pol. Warfare Coll. 81-88; Chief Ed., *TV Scan Monthly,* CTV 81-92; Insp., OCAC 87-88; Sr. Sp., Dept. of Info. & Cul. Aff., MOFA 88-90; Coun., Adv., & Dir., Taipei Off., TPG 90-93; Counsl. & Dir., 6th Dept., Exec. Yuan 93-97. *Publ.: The Age of TV Simulcasting; The Theory & Application of an Aural-Oral Approach to Mandarin Ch.; Cross-sect. of So. USA—A Potpourri; The Lowest of the Low* (transl.); *Selection of Gloria Chu's Lit. Works; Selection of Contemporary Ch. Authoresses* (ed.); *Lien Chan, V. Pres. & Premier of the ROC* (ed.); *Add.* 55 Pei An Rd., Taipei 104.

CHU, JAMES C.Y. 祝基瀅

Rep., Taipei Mission in Sweden 98-; Mem., CC 93-; *b.* Fukien Apr. 3, '35; *m.* Lin, Ruth; 2 *d.; educ.* LL.B., NTU 57; MA, Jour., NCCU 60; MA & Ph.D., Jour., So. Illinois U. 70; Sect. Chief, GIO; Reporter, *Daily Repub.,* Illinois 67-68; Asst. Prof., Assc. Prof., Prof., Chmn., Comm. & Info. Res. Dept., & Dir. of Res. Cent., Calif. State U., Chico 70-88; Visiting Res. Prof., NCCU 84-86; Dep. Dir.-Gen., Dept. of Cul. Aff., CC, KMT 89, Dir.-Gen. 89-94; Dep. Sec.-Gen., CC, KMT 94-96; Min., OCAC 96-98; Nat. Policy Adv. to the Pres. 98; Mem., CSC, KMT 97-98. *Publ.: Mass Comm.* 73; *Pol. Comm.* 83; *Comm. Dev. & Modern Soc.* 85; *Comm., Soc. & Tech.* 86; *Meditation of Modern Men* 86; *2-Way Traffic* 89; *Add.* Wenner-Gren Centre, 18tr Sveavagen 166, S-113 46 Stockholm, Sweden.

CHU, JU-CHIN 朱汝瑾

Mem., Acad. Sinica 64-; Bd. Chmn. & Pres., Tech. Res. Inc., Irvine, CA 72-; *b.* Kiangsu Dec. 14, '19; *m.* Lee, Ching-chen; 3 *s.; educ.* BS, NTHU 40; D.Sc., MIT 45; Sr. Chem. Engr., Shell Chem. Corp. 46; Asst. Prof., Chem. Engr., U. of Washington 46-49; Assc. Prof., Polytechnic Inst. of Brooklyn 49-54, Prof. 54-66; Tech. Dir., Chem. Construction Corp. 56-57; Consultant, US Govt. & over 60 major chem., petroleum, propulsion, & nuclear firms in US, Britain, W. Germany, Italy, Netherlands, & Japan 48-66; Tech. Adv., Strategic Missiles Div., N. Am. Rockwell Corp., Orange, Calif. 69-70; Prof., Virginia Polytechnic Inst. & State U. 67-72. *Publ.: Distillation; Fluidixation; Weapon Systems; Envi-ronmental Pollution Control; Propulsion; Nuclear Tech.; Mass Transfer; Drying; Extraction; Engr. Thermodynamic & Kinetics; Reactor Design; Radiation Effect; Space Vehicle System & Subsystem Optimization; Cyogenics & Ind. Newly Processed Products Utilization of Agr. Products;* etc.; *Add.* 21 Yorktown, Irvine, CA 92720, USA.

CHU, MING

(See JU, MING 朱銘)

CHU, PAUL CHING-WU 朱經武

Mem., Acad. Sinica 88-, Nat. Acad. of Sc. 89-, Am. Acad. of Arts & Sc. 89-, & Third World Acad. of Sc. 90-; Dir., Texas Cent. for Superconductivity, U. of Houston 87-; T.L.L. Temple Chair of Sc., Dept. of Sc. 87-, Prof. of Phys. 79-; Mem., Intl. Adv. Cttee., Hong Kong Baptist U. 95-; Mem., Sc. Adv. Bd., Cent. for Nanoscale Sc. & Tech. (Rice U.) 95-; Mem., Adv. Bd., Intl. Inst. for Condensed Matter Phys., U. of Brasilia 93-; Mem., Bd. of Dir., Coun. on Superconductivity for Am. Competitiveness 89-; *b.* Hunan Dec. 2, '41; *m.* Chern, May P.; 2 *c.; educ.* BS, NCKU 58-62; MS, Fordham U. 63-65; Ph.D., U. of Calif., San Diego 65-68; Mem., Tech. Staff, Bell Labs., USA 68-70; Assc. Prof., Phys., Cleveland State U. 70-73, Prof. 75-79; Solid State Prog. Dir., Nat. Sc. Found. 86-87; Dir., Space Vacuum Epitaxy Cent., NASA/U. of Houston 86-88; Nat. Medal of Sc.; Comstock Award; Intl. Prize for New Mats., Medal of Sc. Merit, Phys. & Math. Sc. Award; NASA Achievement Award; Texas Instruments Founders' Prize; Leroy Randle Grumman Medal; Sigma Xi Res. Excellence Award. *Publ.:* 420 sc. papers; *Add.* Texas Cent. for Superconductivity, U. of Houston, Houston Sc. Center, Houston, TX 77204-5932, USA.

CHU, SHIH-LIEH 朱士烈

Nat. Policy Adv. to the Pres. 92-; *b.* Liaoning July 23, '15; *m.* Wu, Yu-lien; 2 *s.*, 2 *d.; educ.* LL.B., Nat. Wuhan U.; Justice, Revision Trial, Hupei & Szechwan Prov. 41-49; Justice & Admin. Chief Off., dist. courts in Twn. 49-70; Chief, Prison Dept., Min. of Legal Aff. 70-74; Public Prosecutor, Supreme Court 74-77; Lawyer 77-80 & 87-89; Chief Sec., KMT Caucas, NA 79-84 & 89-90; Dep. Sec.-Gen., Policy Coordination Cttee., CC, KMT 84-87; Sec.-Gen., NA 90-92; *Add.* 3rd Fl., 1 Lane 75, Yung Kang St., Taipei 106.

CHU, STEVEN 朱棣文

Mem., Acad. Sinica 94-; Prof., Phys. & Applied Phys., Stanford U. 87-; Mem., Nat. Acad. of Sc.; Fel., Am. Acad. of Arts & Sc.; *b.* USA Feb. 28, '48; 2 *s.; educ.* BS, Math., U. of Rochester 70, BS, Phys. 70; Ph.D., Phys., UC-Berkly. 76, Postdr. Res. Fel. 76-78; Mem., Tech. Staff, Bell Labs.,

Murray Hill 78-83; Head, Quantum Elect. Res. Dept., AT&T Bell Labs., Holmel 83-87; Morris Loeb Lectr., Harvard U. 88; Sp. Visitor to JILA 89; Visiting Prof., Coll. de France 90; Theodore & Frances Geballe Prof. of Phys. & Applied Phys., Stanford U. 90, Chair, Phys. Dept. 90-93; Nobel Prize for Phys. 97; *Add.* Dept. of Phys., Stanford U., Stanford, CA 94305-4060, USA.

CHU, TI-WEN
(See CHU, STEVEN 朱棣文)

CHU, WAN-CHING
(See CHU, GLORIA WAN-CHING 朱婉清)

CHU, WU-HSIAN 朱武獻
Dir.-Gen., CPA 2000-; Adjunct Prof., Grad. Inst. of the Three Principles of the People, NTU 92-, & Dept. & Grad. Inst. of Law, Fu Jen Catholic U. 88-; Lectr., Judges & Prosecutors Tng. Inst., & TCG's Civil Servants Tng. Cent.; *b.* Twn. June 10, '50; *m.* Tu, Man-ting; 2 *c.; educ.* LL.B., NTU 74, LL.M., NTU 79; LL.D., Universität des Saarlandes, Germany 83; Passed the Deutscher Akademicher Austauschdienst (DAAD) 79; Passed the Civil Service Sp. Exam. A for Ordinary Admin. Staff (Legal Sect.) with excellence 86; qualified lawyer 87; Counsl., Exam. Yuan & concur. Mem., Disputes Review Cttee. 86-90; Dir., Dept. of Legal Aff., MAC 90-93; Counsl. & concur. Sec.-in-Chief., Exam. Yuan 93-94, Dep. Sec.-Gen. 94-96; Visiting Prof., Universität des Saarlandes, Germany 88; Assc. & Adjunct Prof., Law Sch. & Grad. Inst., Fu Jen Catholic U.; Exec. Mem., Legal System Sect., Planning Taskforce of Const. Reform.; Lectr., Sun Yat-sen Inst. of Policy Res. & Dev. of KMT, Tng. Inst. for Pers. of Finance & Tax Admin. of MOF, Kaohsiung City Govt.'s Civil Servants Tng. Cent., & the Medium Business Bk. of Twn.; V. Chmn., Civil Service Protection & Tng. Com. 96-2000. *Publ.: Distinctions Between Admin. Orders & Admin. Rules; Grand Justices' Interpretations of the Const. & Unified Interpretations of Laws & Orders: Const. Rulings in the ROC* (in German); "Selected Res. on the Public Law I & II," *Fu Jen Catholic U. Law Series; Add.* 9th-11th Fl., 2-2 Chi Nan Rd., Sect. 2, Taipei 100.

CHU, WU-HSIEN
(See CHU, WU-HSIAN 朱武獻)

CHU, YEN 朱炎
Writer; Prof., For. Lang., NTU 71-; Res. Fel., Inst. of European & Am. Studies, Acad. Sinica; Pres., Ki Ko Cul. & Educ. Found.; *b.* Shantung June 6, '36; *m.* Hsu, Li-ching; 1

s., 1 *d.; educ.* BA, For. Lang., NTU 60; Ph.D., La Universidad de Madrid 65; Assc. Prof., For. Lang., NTU 65-71; Dir., Inst. of Am. Studies, Acad. Sinica 77-83; Dean, Coll. of Arts, NTU 84-90; V. Chmn., NScC 92-93; Pres., British & Am. Lit. Assn., ROC 92-93. *Publ.: La Dramatica Shakespeariana en Ch.; Love in the Morning; Collection of Criticisms of Am. Lit.; Bitter Growth; Sour Plum;* 10 essays on lit. & soc.; etc.; *Add.* 21 Alley 5, Lane 30, Chou Shan Rd., Taipei 106.

CHU, YU-FENG
(See CHU, ELIZABETH Y.F. 朱玉鳳)

CHUA, NAM-HAI 蔡南海
Mem., Acad. Sinica 88-; Andrew W. Mellon Prof. 88-; Prof. & Head, Lab. of Plant Molecular Biology, Rockefeller U. 81-; Fel., Royal Soc. 88-; Assc. Fel., Third World Acad. of Sc. 88-; *b.* Ch. Apr. 8, '44; *m.* Suat-Choo (Pearl); 2 *d.; educ.* BS, U. of Singapore 65; MS, Harvard U. 67, Ph.D. 69; Lectr., Biochem. Dept., U. of Singapore Med. Sch. 69-71; Res. Assc., Cell Biology Dept., Rockefeller U. 71-73; Asst. Prof. 73-77, Assc. Prof. 77-81; Hon. Mem., Japan Biochem. Soc. 92. *Publ.:* 220 sc. papers; *Add.* Lab. of Plant Molecular Biology, Rockefeller U., 1230 York Avenue, New York, NY 10021-6399, USA.

CHUAN, HAN-SHENG 全漢昇
Mem. & Res. Fel., Acad. Sinica 84-; Dir., New Asia Inst. of Advanced Ch. Studies 83-; *b.* Kwangtung Nov. 19, '13; *m.* Hwang, Hui-fang; 2 *s.; educ.* BA, Nat. Peking U. 35; Res. Fel., Harvard U. 44-45 & 62-63; Visiting Scholar, Columbia U. 45-47; Visiting Scholar, U. of Chicago 61-62; Prof., Econ. Dept., NTU 49-65, Dir. 52-57; Dir.-Gen., Acad. Sinica 58-61; Sr. Lectr. & Reader, New Asia Coll., Ch. U. of Hong Kong 65-77, Pres. 75-77. *Publ.: Collected Essays on Ch. Econ. Hist.; Studies on the Econ. Hist. of Ch.; Add.* 7th Fl.-1, 39 Chien Chung 1st Rd., Hsinchu 300.

CHUANG, CHIN 莊晉
Pres., Van Nung Inst. of Tech. 83-; Cttee. Mem., Found. of the Staff's Retirement & Pension of Private Sch. in the ROC; V. Chmn., Cttee. of Corps Aff. Conducting of youth Corps, Taoyuan, Twn.; *b.* Kiangsu Aug. 23, '40; *m.* Yao, Kai-luan; 1 *s.; educ.* B., Math., 64; MBA, New Coll. of Calif. 80, Ed.D. 85; Tchr., Sungshan Jr. High Sch. 62-67; V. Pres., Chiaohsin Textile Co. 68-76; Lectr., Van Nung Inst. of Tech. 72-77, Assc. Prof. 77-83; *Add.* 1 Wan Neng Rd., Chungli, Taoyuan County 320.

CHUANG, FANG-JUNG
(See JUANG, FANG-RUNG 莊芳榮)

CHUANG, HENG-TAI 莊亨岱
Nat. Policy Adv. to the Pres. 93-; Mem, CAC, KMT 97-; *b.* Fukien Oct. 7, '26; *m.* Chou, Ming-lih; 3 *s.,* 3 *d.; educ.* 17th Class, Cent. Police Coll., & 1st Class, Advanced Course I for Sr. Police Off.; Comr., Ilan Police Bu. 75-78; Comr., Taoyuan Police Bu. 78-82; Comr., Rwy. Police Bu. 82-85, 1st Peace Preservation Corps 85-87, & Bu. of Criminal Investigation 87-90; Dir.-Gen., Nat. Police Admin., MOI 90-93; Consultant, Exec. Yuan 93-97; Mem., CC, KMT 93-97; Chmn., Po Hsin Multimedia Inc. 94-96; *Add.* 78 Ta Hu Shan Chuang St., Neihu, Taipei 114.

CHUANG, I-CHOU
(See CHUANG, YI-CHOU 莊逸洲)

CHUANG, K. CASEY 莊國欽
Chmn., Logitech Inc. & Precsion Machinery R&D Cent.; *b.* Twn. Oct. 13, '35; *m.* Cho, S.H.; 2 *s.,* 1 *d.; educ.* BS, NCKU; Ph.D., MIT 65; Consultant Engr., IBM, USA 65-68; Plan Engr., Bendix Co., USA 68-72; Gen. Mgr., Far E. Mach. Co. Ltd. 72-87; Exec. Dir., Ch. Nat. Fed. of Ind.; Chmn., Twn. Assn. of Mach. Ind.; Mem., Legis. Yuan 90-92; Chmn., Far E. Mach. Co. Ltd. & Cimtek Inc. 87-99; *Add.* 8th Fl., 56 Nanking E. Rd., Sect. 4, Taipei 105.

CHUANG, KUO-CHIN
(See CHUANG, K. CASEY 莊國欽)

CHUANG, LUNG-CHANG
(See CHUANG, JUNG-CHANG 莊隆昌)

CHUANG, MING-CHE
(See TSUANG, MING T. 莊明哲)

CHUANG, MING-YAO 莊銘耀
Sec.-Gen., NSC, Off. of the Pres. 2000-; *b.* Twn. Nov. 16, '29; *m.* Hsu, Hsiu-ying; 2 *s.,* 2 *d.; educ.* Ch. Naval Acad., Class 1952; Naval Staff Coll., Class 1968; War Coll., Class 1973; Capt., Landing Ship Tank, Destroyer Escort, & Destroyer 63-75; Cmdr., Recruit Tng. Cent., ROCN 75-76; Dir., Service Bu., ROCN 76-79; Cmdr., 142 Fleet Squadron 79-80; Asst. Dep. Chief of the Gen. Staff for Intelligence, MND 80-83; Dir., Pers. Dept., ROCN 83-84; Cmdr., Fleet Tng. Cmd. 84-86; C/S, GHQ, ROCN 86-89, Dep. C-in-C 89-91; V. Min. of Def. 91-92; C-in-C, ROCN 92-94; Strategy Adv. to the Pres. 94-95; Nat. Policy Adv. to the Pres. 95-99; Rep., TECRO, Japan 96-2000; *Add.* c/o Off. of the Pres., Taipei 100.

CHUANG, PO-HO 莊伯和
Dir., Twn. Prov. Cul. Found. 97-; Dir., Public TV Service Found. 98-; *b.* Twn. May 19, '47; *m.* Chang, Chiung-huei; *educ.* BA, NTNU 69; MA, Ch. Cul. U. 74; Res., Grad. Sch. of Humanities & Sc. 76-77; Tchr., Kaohsiung Sanmin Jr. High Sch. 69-71; Clerk, Chang Hwa Bk. 71. *Publ.: Twn.'s Forms of Folk Art; Reports on Folk Art; Ch. Forms; Permanent c.'s Face; Interest in Appreciating Beauty; Display & Beautification of Celebration Ceremony; Traditional Handicrafter of Twn.; Add.* 3rd Fl., 11 Lane 50, Chung Cheng Rd., Sect. 2, Shihlin, Taipei 111.

CHUANG, SHUO-HAN
(See CHUANG, SUO-HANG 莊碩漢)

CHUANG, SUO-HANG 莊碩漢
Pol. V. Min. of Civil Service, Exam. Yuan 96-; *b.* Twn. Oct. 24, '55; *m.* Chu, Chin-yan; 1 *d.; educ.* BA, Pol. Sc., NTU 77; MA, Pol. Sc., Nr. Illinois U. 81; Ph.D., Pol. Sc., U. of So. Calif. 89; Res. Fel., Inst. for Nat. Policy Res. 89-90; Assc. Prof., PA, Tamkang U. 90-91; Assc. Prof. & Dean of Student Aff., World Coll. of Jour. & Comm. 91-93; Dep. Sec.-Gen., Nat. Cul. Assn. 93-96; Dep. Dir., Dept. of Youth Aff., CC, KMT 95-96; *Add.* 1 Shih Yuan Rd., Wenshan, Taipei 116.

CHUANG, YI-CHOU 莊逸洲
Nat. Policy Adv. to the Pres. 96-; Dir., Admin. Cent., Chang Gung Memorial Hosp. 88-; Assc. Prof., Chang Gung U. 94-, Dean, Sch. of Mng. 96-; *b.* Kaohsiung Oct. 20, '49; *m.* Chang, Chiao-mei; 1 *s.,* 4 *d.; educ.* MHA, Hosp. Adm., Ch. Med. Coll. 94; Asst. Mgr., Formosa Chem. & Fibre Corp.; Mgr., Chang-Gung Hosp.; Sp. Asst., Chang-Gung Hosp. *Publ.:* Many articles published in *Ch. Jour. of Public Health; Add.* 199 Tun Hua N. Rd., Taipei 105.

CHUNG, CHAO-CHENG
(See CHUNG, CHAU-CHENG 鍾肇政)

CHUNG, CHAU-CHENG 鍾肇政
Novelist; *b.* Twn. Jan. 20, '25; *m.* Chang, Chiu-mei; 2 *s.,* 3 *d.; educ.* Attended Dept. of Ch. Lit., NTU; Instr., Dept. of Japanese, Soochow U. 74-77; Chief, *Twn. Lit. Mag.* 76-82; Ed.-in-Chief, *Commons Daily* 78-80. *Publ.: Troubled River: A Triology; Twn. Hist.: A Triology; Expecting the Spring Wind;* etc.; *Add.* 53 Lung Hua Rd., Lungtan, Taoyuan County 325.

CHUNG, CHIN 鍾琴
Dir.-Gen., GIO & Govt. Spokesperson 2000-; *b.* Chekiang Nov. 8, '53; *m.* Tai, Hua; 1 *s.; educ.* BS, Econ., NTU 72-76; Res., E.-W. Cent., U. of Hawaii 80-81; MS, Econ., Cornell U. 81-85, Ph.D. candidate in Econ. 85; Ed., Buffalo Bk. Co., Ltd. 76-77, & Chung-Hua Cent. for Lang. & Audio-

visual Educ. 77-80; Asst. Res. Fel., Mainland Ch. Div., Chung-Hua Inst. for Econ. Res. 87-92, Assc. Res. Fel. 92-97, Exec. Sec., Cent. for Small & Medium-sized Ent. 97-98, Res. Fel., Mainland Ch. Div. 97-2000, Convener, Group on Intl. Econ. & Finance 99-2000. *Publ.:* More than 50 articles & res. papers on mainland econ. aff., cross-strait interactions, intl. trade, local ind. policies, & etc.; *Add.* 2 Tientsin St., Taipei 100.

CHUNG, FU-SHAN 鍾福山

V. Chmn., Coun. of Aboriginal Aff., Exec. Yuan 97-; *b.* Twn. Nov. 12, '37; *m.* Shih, Ai-hsiang; 2 *d.; educ.* Nat. Hsinchu Tchrs. Coll. 56; LL.B., NTU 65; Tchr., elementary & jr. high sch. 56-61; Sp. Asst., CPA 66-69; Sect. Chief, Secretariat, Taipei Water Dept. 70-82, Sec.-Gen., Engr. Corps 83-86; Sec.-Gen., Bu. of Taipei Feitsui Reservoir Admin. 86-87; Sr. Sp., Dept. of So. Aff., MOI 87-88, Dep. Dir., Dept. of Pers. 89-90, Dept. of Civil Aff. 90-91, Dir. 91-96; *Add.* 17th Fl., 4 Chung Hsiao W. Rd., Sect. 1, Taipei 100.

CHUNG, YAO-TANG

(See JONG, YAW-TARNG 鍾曜唐)

DING, MOU-SHIH 丁懋時

Sec.-Gen., Off. of the Pres. 99-2000; Mem., CSC, KMT 99-, Mem., CC 93-; *b.* Yunnan Oct. 10, '25; *m.* Shih, Mei-chang; 1 *s.,* 1 *d.; educ.* Paris U.; Reporter, CNA 56-58; Consultant, MOFA 58-60, Sect. Chief, Dept. of W. Asian Aff. 60-62; 1st Sec., Ch. Mission to the European Off. of the UN 62; Chargé d'Affaires, Emb. in Rwanda 62-64; Amb. to Rwanda 64-67; Amb. to Zaire 67-71; Alt. Rep., ROC Del. to the 24th & 25th Sess. of UNGA 69-70; Dir., Dept. of African Aff., MOFA 72-74; Govt. Spokesman & Dir.-Gen., GIO 75-79; Dir., Dept. of Cul. Aff., CC, KMT 77-79; Admin. V. Min. of For. Aff. 79; Amb. to S. Korea 79-82; Pol. V. Min. of For. Aff. 82-87; MOFA 87-88; Rep., TECRO, Washington, D.C. 88-94; Sec.-Gen., NSC 94-99; Sr. Adv. to the Pres. 99; *Add.* 122 Chungking S. Rd., Sect. 1, Taipei 100.

DING, MOW-SUNG 丁懋松

Consultant on British & US laws, Ding & Ding Law Off.; *b.* Yunnan Feb. 25, '38; 1 *s.,* 1 *d.; educ.* LL.B., Tokyo U. 59; LL.M., Yale Law Sch. 65; Barrister-at-Law, Inner Temple, UK 67; Attorney-at-Law, New York State 73, & Calif. State 74; Asst. Prof., Nanyang U., Singapore 69-71; Attorney-at-Law, Winthrop, Stimson, Putnam & Roberts, New York 68-69 & 71-74, & Graham & James, San Francisco 75; Partner, Kirkwood, Kaplan, Russin & Vecchi,

Washington 76-78; *Add.* Ding & Ding Law Off., 10th Fl., 563 Chung Hsiao E. Rd., Sect. 4, Taipei 110.

DUO, JEONG-FEONG 杜炯烽

Pres., Nat. Pingtung Inst. of Com. 91-; *b.* Twn. Oct. 21, '48; *m.* Duo Lee, Tsiu-chieng; 1 *s.,* 2 *d.; educ.* MS, Ind. Tech., U. of Wisconsin, Platteville 76-77; Ph.D., Voc. Educ., Penn. State U. 78-82; Head, Dept. of Ind. Engr., Nat. Taipei Inst. of Tech. 82-85; Visiting Scholar, Dept. of Ind. & Op. Engr., U. of Michigan 85-86; Dir., Computer Cent. of Coll. of Law & Com., NCHU 89-90; Preparatory Off. Dir., Nat. Pingtung Inst. of Com. 91; *Add.* 51 Min Sheng E. Rd., Pingtung 900.

FAN, CHI

(See FAN, KY 樊畿)

FAN, KY 樊畿

Mem., Acad. Sinica 64-; Prof. Emeritus, U. of Calif., Santa Barbara 85-; Hon. Prof., Peking U. & Peking Normal U. 89-; Mem., Ed. Bd., *Linear Algebra & Its Application* 68-, *Topological Methods in Nonlinear Analysis* 93-; *Set-valued Analysis* 93-; *b.* Chekiang Sept. 19, '14; *m.* Yen, Yu-fen; *educ.* BS, Peking U. 36; Docteur ès Sc. Math., U. of Paris 41; Docteur Honoris Causa, U. Paris IX Dauphine 90; Chargé de Recherches, Cent. Nat. de la Recherche Scientifique, France 42-45; Mem., Inst. for Advanced Study, Princeton U. 45-47; Asst. Prof., U. of Notre Dame 47-49, Assc. Prof. 49-52, Prof. 52-60; Prof., Wayne State U. 60-61, & N.we. U. 61-65; Prof., Dept. of Math., U. of Calif., Santa Barbara 65-85, Chmn. 68-69; Dir., Inst. of Math., Acad. Sinica 78-84; Visiting Prof., U. of Texas, Austin 65, U. Hamburg 72, U. Paris IX Dauphine 81, U. Perugia, Italy 85 & 87; Mem., Ed. Bd., *Jour. of Math. Analysis & Applications* 60-92, & *Linear & Multilinear Algebra* 73-92. *Publ.:* Over 120 res. papers in various intl. math. jour.; *Add.* 1402 Santa Teresita Drive, Santa Barbara, CA 93105-1948, USA.

FANG, CHIN-YEN 房金炎

Rep., TECO, Can. 96-; *b.* Twn. Nov. 11, '31; *m.* Hsu, Hui-ying; 2 *d.; educ.* BA, NTU 54; MA, Am. U. 67, Ph.D. 77; Staff Asst., Info. Dept., MOFA 56-58; Attaché & 3rd Sec., Emb. in USA 58-65; 2nd Sec., Emb. in the Philippines 66; Sect. Chief & Dep. Dir., Dept. of Intl. Org., MOFA 66-71; Adv., Del. to 24th UNGA 69; Alt. Rep., Del. to UNIDO Sp. Conf. 71; Amb. to Nicaragua 72-76; Sr. Sec., MOFA 77, Counsl. 78-81; Assc. Prof., Soochow U. & NCCU 79-81; V. Chmn., Res. & Pol. Planning Bd., MOFA 80-81; Rep. in UK 82-90; Admin. V. Min., MOFA 90-93, & Pol. V. Min.

93-96; *Add.* Suite 1960, World Exchange Plaza, 45 O'Connor St., Ottawa, Ontario K1P 1A4 Can.

FANG, HUAI-SHIH
(See FANG, HWAI-SZE 方懷時)

FANG, HWAI-SZE 方懷時
Mem., Acad. Sinica 78-; Prof. Emeritus of Physiology, Coll. of Med., NTU 86-; *b.* Chekiang Nov. 7, '14; *m.* Loh, Kun-cheng; 1 *s.,* 1 *d.; educ.* Chekiang Prov. Med. Coll. 37; MD, Nagoya U. 52; Res. Fel., W. Virginia U. & Ohio State U. 52-53, Columbia U. 60-61; Asst. & Instr., Nat. Kweiyang Med. Coll. 38-41; Assc. Prof., Nat. Kiangsu Med. Coll. 43-47; Assc. Prof., NTU 47-50, Prof. 50-85, Dean of Student Aff., Coll. of Med. 72-78; Nat. Res. Chair, Nat. Coun. on Sc. Dev. 66-68; Visiting Prof., Columbia U. 68-70; Sr. Lectr., Tng. Unit of Aviation Safety & Mng., Coll. of Engr., NTU 73-86, Cml. Pilot Tng. Unit, & Tjing Ling Ind. Res. Inst. 96-99. *Publ.: Aviation Physiology; Altitude Convulsion; Explosive Decompression; Hypoxia & Gastrointestinal Motility;* etc.; *Add.* Inst. of Physiology, Coll. of Med., NTU, 1 Jen Ai Rd., Sect. 1, Taipei 10018.

FANG, JUNG-CHUEH
(See FANG, RONG-JYUE 方榮爵)

FANG, RONG-JYUE 方榮爵
Pres., Nat. Taitung Tchrs.' Coll. 94-; *b.* Twn. Aug. 26, '51; *m.* Hwang, Hsu-wuen; 1 *s.,* 1 *d.; educ.* B.Ed., Nat. Kaohsiung Tchrs.' Coll. 74; Ed.M., NTNU 79; MS, Ea. Illinois State U. 80; Ph.D., Penn. State U. 84; Teaching Asst., Nat. Kaohsiung Tchrs.' Coll. 74-75; Tchr., Elect., Hsilo Voc. High Sch. 77-78; Teaching Asst., Ea. Illinois U. 79-80; Res. Asst., Penn. State U. 80-84; Assc. Prof., Nat. Kaohsiung Tchrs.' Coll. 84-89, Dir., Computation Cent. 85-87; Prof., Nat. Kaohsiung Normal U. 89, Chmn., Dept. of Tech. Educ. 92-94. *Publ.:* 42 papers published in prof. jour.; 26 theses presented in acad. seminars; *Add.* 684 Chung Hua Rd., Sect. 1, Taitung 950.

FEI, PHILIP TSUNG-CHENG 費宗澄
Partner, Fei & Cheng Asscs. 74-; *b.* Kiangsu Sept. 26, '41; *m.* Fei Chao, Stella Shan; 2 *s.; educ.* BS, Civil Engr., NCKU 62, N. Carolina State U. 65; MS, Urban Planning, Pratt Inst. 73; Designer, Anne Arundle County Assc. Architects, US 64, Project Architect, Philip Johnson & Richard Foster 65-69, Sr. Assc. Pokorny & Pertz 69-73, Assc. Mgr., Parsons, Brinckerhoff Quade & Douglas Inc./Pokorny & Pertz 74; Assc. Prof., Tamkang U. 75-86; Exec. Dir., Taipei Architects Assn. 76-79; Dir., Ch. Inst. of Architect 79-81; *Add.* 9th Fl., 310 Chung Hsiao E. Rd., Sect. 4, Taipei 106.

FEI, TSUNG-CHENG
(See FEI, PHILIP TSUNG-CHENG 費宗澄)

FENG, CHING-FU 酆景福
Nat. Policy Adv. to the Pres. 93-; V. Chmn., Promotion Com. for ROC Nat. Unification & Dev.; Mem., CAC, KMT; *b.* Kiangsi Nov. 14, 1900; *m.* Fang, Fu-lin; 3 *s.; educ.* Grad., So. U., Shanghai; Sp., MOI 45-47; Mem., Control Yuan 48-93; *Add.* 2nd Fl., 6 Lane 36, Ho Ping E. Rd., Sect. 2, Taipei 100.

FENG, YUAN-CHEN
(See FUNG, YUAN-CHENG 馮元楨)

FU, HSUEH-PENG 傅學鵬
Magis., Miaoli County 97-; *b.* Twn. Apr. 4, '51; *m.* Lin, Hsiu-ying; 1 *s.,* 2 *d.; educ.* Prov. Sr. High Sch. of Miaoli; Mem., Miaoli CoCoun. 82-90; V. Spkr., Miaoli CoCoun. 90-94; Mem., TPA 94-97; *Add.* 100 Hsien Fu Rd., Miaoli 360.

FU, SHEN-LI 傅勝利
Pres., I-Shou U. 90-; *b.* Shantung Aug. 1, '45; *m.* Chang, Show-chung; 1 *s.,* 1 *d.; educ.* BS, NCKU 69, MS 72, Ph.D. 77; Assc. Prof., NCKU 77-82, Prof. 82-90, Dean of Student Aff. 87-89; Visiting Scholar, UCLA 80-81; Dir., Engr. & Tech. Promotion Cent., NScC 89-90. *Publ.:* Author & co-author of over 100 acad. papers about elect. material sc. & microelect.; *Add.* 1 Hsueh Cheng Rd., Sect. 1, Tashu, Kaohsiung County 84008.

FU, SHENG-LI
(See FU, SHEN-LI 傅勝利)

FUNG, YUAN-CHENG 馮元楨
Mem., Acad. Sinica 66-; Prof. Emeritus 90-; Hon. Chmn., World Coun. for Biomech. 90-; Mem., US Nat. Acad. of Engr. 79-, & Inst. of Med. 90-, & US Nat. Acad. of Sc. 92-; Mem., Acad. Sinica 68-; For. Mem., Ch. Acad. of Sc. 94-; Fel., Am. Inst. of Med. & Biological Engr. 92-; *b.* Kiangsu Sept. 15, '19; *educ.* BS, NCU 41, MS 43; Ph.D., Calif. Inst. of Tech. 48; Asst. Prof., Calif. Inst. of Tech. 51-55, Assc. Prof. 55-59, Prof. 59-66; Consultant, Boeing Aircraft Co. 58-62, Douglas Aircraft 60, Aerospace Corp. 62, N. Am. Aviation 63; Prof., U. of Calif., San Diego 66; Mem., Am. Heart Assn. 67; V. Pres., Intl. Soc. of Biorheology 74-83 Chmn., US Nat. Cttee. for Biomech. 80; Pres., Soc. of Biomed. Engr. 82-83; Pres., Am. Acad. of Mech. 83. *Publ.: Theory of Aeroelasticity; Found. of Solid Mech.; 1st Course in Continuum Mech.; Biomech.—Mech. Properties of Living Tissues; Biodynamics-Circulation; Biomech.: Motion*

Flow, Stress & Growth; & numerous tech. papers in prof. jour.; *Add.* 2660 Greentree Lane, La Jolla, CA 92037, USA.

HAN, KUANG-WEI 韓光渭
Mem., Acad. Sinica 90-; Chair Prof., Yuan-Ze U. 95-; *b.* Shantung Jan. 29, '30; *m.* Han, Mei-lei; 3 *d.; educ.* BS, Ch. Naval Coll. of Tech. 55; Ph.D., US Naval Postgrad. Sch. 61; Hon. Ph.D., NCTU 95; Hon. Prof. NCTU 97; Rear Adm.; Assc. Prof., Ch. Naval Coll. of Tech. & NCTU 62-64; Visiting Res. Assc., UC-Berkly. 64-65; Scientist, Chung Shan Inst. of Sc. & Tech. 55-94, Dep. Dir., System Dev. Cent. 82-95; Adjunct Prof., NCTU 62-92, & NTU 92-98; *Add.* 135 Far E. Rd., Neili, Chungli, Taoyuan County 320.

HAN, PAO-TE
(See HAN, PAO-TEH 漢寶德)

HAN, PAO-TEH 漢寶德
Pres., Tainan Nat. Coll. of the Arts 96-; Adjunct Prof., Grad. Inst. of Bldg. & Planning, NTU 81-; Weekly Columnist, *United Daily News* 74, & *Ch. Daily News* 76-; *b.* Shantung Aug. 19, '34; *m.* Han Hsiao, Sharon; 1 *s.,* 1 *d.; educ.* BS, NCKU 58; M.Arch., Harvard U. 65; M., Fine Arts, Princeton U. 67; Lectr., Tunghai U. 61-64; Prof. & Chmn., Dept. of Architecture, Tunghai U. 66-67; Visiting Prof., Calif. State Polytechnic U. 74-75; Dean, Coll. of Sc. & Engr., NCHU 77-82; Dir., Dev. Off., Nat. Museum of Natural Sc. 82-87; Dir., Nat. Museum of Natural Sc. 87-95; Design Works: Youth Hostels; Inst. of Ethnology, Acad. Sinica; S. Garden; Major Restoration Works: Changhua Confucius Temple; Lukang Lungshan Temple, Panchiao Lin Family Garden. *Publ.: Spiritual Dimension of Architecture; Architecture, Soc., & Cul.; Essays on Ancient Ch. Garden; Add.* 11th Fl., 214 Tun Hua N. Rd., Taipei 105.

HAO, YEN-PING 郝延平
Mem., Acad. Sinica 96-; Prof., U. of Tennessee 72-; Lindsay Young Prof., Hist., U. of Tennessee 84-; *b.* Nanking Dec. 22, '34; *m.* Hao T., Pin-han; 2 *s.; educ.* BA, NTU 58; Ph.D., Harvard U. 66; Asst. Prof., U. of Tennessee 65-68; Assc. Prof. 68-72. *Publ.: The Comprador in 19th-Century Ch.* 70; *The Cml. Rev. in 19th-Century Ch.* 86; *Add.* 1101 McClung Tower, Knoxville, TN 37996-0411, USA.

HAO, PO-TSUN
(See HAU, PEI-TSUN 郝柏村)

HAU, PEI-TSUN 郝柏村
Independent Candidate, 1996 Election for ROC V. Pres.; Pres., Wang Yang-ming Cul. & Educ. Found.; *b.* Kiangsu July 13, '19; *m.* Kuo, Wan-hua; 2 *s.,* 3 *d.; educ.* Ch. Mil. Acad.; Ch. Army U.; US Army CGSC; War Coll., Armed Forces U.; Hon. Dr. of Humanities, Columbia Coll. 93; Chief Instr., Artillery Sch. 53-54; Corps Artillery Cmdr. 55-57; 9th Infantry Div. Cmdr. 58-61; 3rd Corps Cmdr. 63-65; Chief Aide to Pres. Chiang Kai-shek 65-70; 1st Field Army Cmdr. 70-73; Dep. C-in-C, ROC Army 75-77; Exec. V. Chief of the Gen. Staff, MND 77-78; C-in-C, ROC Army 78-81; Chief of the Gen. Staff, MND 81-89; Mem., CSC, KMT 84-93; Min. of Nat. Def. 89-90; Premier, ROC 90-93; V. Chmn., KMT 93-95; Sr. Adv. to the Pres. 93-96. *Publ.: Ch. Communist Artillery Bombardment Against Kinmen on Aug. 23, 1958; Add.* 315 Fu Lin Rd., Shihlin, Taipei 111.

HO, CHIEN 何潛
Mem., Acad. Sinica 80-; Prof., Dept. of Biological Sc. & Dir., Pittsburgh NMR Cent. for Biomed. Res., Carnegie Mellon U. 86-, Alumni Prof. of Biological Sc. 85-; *b.* Shanghai Oct. 23, '34; *m.* Tseng, Nancy; 2 *d.; educ.* BS, Williams Coll., USA 57; Ph.D., Yale U. 61; Res. Chemist, Linde Co., Union Carbide Tonowanda 60-61; Res. Assc., MIT 61-64; Asst. Prof., U. of Pittsburgh 64-67, Assc. Prof. 67 70, Prof. 70-79; Prof. & Head, Dept. of Biological Sc., Carnegie Mellon U. 79-86. *Publ.:* Over 190 articles in sc. jour.; *Add.* 2034 Garrick Drive, Pittsburgh, PA 15235, USA.

HO, I-WU
(See HO, IRWINE W. 何宜武)

HO, ING-KANG 何英剛
Mem., Acad. Sinica 96-; Interim Assc. V. Chancellor for Res. & Grad. Studies 97-; Chmn. & Prof., Dept. of Pharmacology & Toxicology, U. of Mississippi Med. Cent. 82-; Dir., Grad. Prog., U. of Mississippi Med. Cent. 82-; *b.* Twn. May 7, '39; *m.* Ho, Patricia; 1 *s.,* 2 *d.; educ.* BS, NTU 62; Ph.D., U. of Calif., San Francisco 68; Instr., Baylor Coll. of Med. 68-70; Asst. Res. Pharmacologist, U. of Calif., San Francisco 70-73, Asst. Prof. 73-75; Assc. Prof., U. of Mississippi Med. Cent. 75-78, Prof. 78-82. *Publ.:* 295 res. papers; *Add.* 2500 N. State St., Jackson, MS 39216-4505, USA.

HO, IRWINE W. 何宜武
Sr. Adv. to the Pres.; Mem., CSC, KMT; Chmn., United World Ch. Cml. Bk., & Cul. & Charity Found.; Prof., Ch. Cul. U.; Chmn., Feng Chia U. *b.* Fukien Dec. 10, '13; *m.* Wang, Hsiu-chiao; 2 *s.,* 1 *d.; educ.* BA, Chaoyang U.; Resr., U. of Washington; Chief Sec., Dept. of Finance, TPG 45-46; Comr. & Mem., OCAC 49-61, V. Chmn. 62-72; Comr., Fukien Prov. Govt. 49-86; Sec.-Gen., NA 80-90.

Publ.: Res. on Econ. of Ovs. Ch.; Add. 65 Kuan Chien Rd., Taipei 100.

HO, MAN-TE
(See HO, MONTO 何曼德)

HO, MEI-YUEH 何美玥
Dir., 5th Div., Exec. Yuan 97-; *b.* Twn. Jan. 9, '51; *m.* Yang, Shih-hwi; 2 *s.; educ.* B., NTU 73; Tech., Ind. Dev. Bu., MOEA 75-80, Sr. Tech. 80-85, Sect. Chief 85-86, Dep. Dir. 86-90, Dir. 90-94, Dep. Dir.-Gen. 94-97; *Add.* 1 Chung Hsiao E. Rd., Sect. 1, Taipei 100.

HO, MONTO 何曼德
Mem., Acad. Sinica 78-; Dir., Div. of Clinical Res., Nat. Health Res. Inst. 97-; Prof. & Chmn. Emeritus, Dept. of Infectious Diseases & Microbiology, Grad. Sch. of Public Health, U. of Pittsburgh; Mem., Assn. of Am. Phys., & Am. Soc. of Clinical Investigation; *b.* Hunan Mar. 28, '27; *m.* Tsu, Carol; 2 *c.; educ.* A.B., Harvard Coll., USA 49; MD, Harvard Med. Sch. 54; Fulbright Sr. Scholar 67-68; Max-Planck Inst. for Virology 67-68; Josiah Macy Sr. Scholar 78-79; John Curtin Sch. of Med. Res., Canberra; Fel., Am. Assn. for the Advancement of Sc. (AAAS). *Publ.: Ho, M. Cytomegalovirus: Biology & Infection; Add.* Nat. Health Res. Inst., 128 Yen Chiu Yuan Rd., Sect. 2, Taipei 115.

HO, PENG-YOKE 何丙郁
Mem., Acad. Sinica 88-; Emeritus Prof., Griffith U., Australia; Dir., Needham Res. Inst., Cambridge, UK; Prof. & Res. Assc., U. of London; *b.* Ch. Apr. 4, '26; *m.* Ho Fung, Mei-yiu; 1 *s.,* 4 *d.; educ.* BS, U. of Malaya 50, MS 51, Ph.D. 59; Prof., Ch. Studies, U. of Malaya 64-73; Visiting Prof., Yale U. 65; D.Sc., U. of Singapore 69; Fel., Inst. of Phys., London 71; Asian Fel., Australian Nat. U. 72; Fel., Leverhulme; Visiting Prof., Keio U. 75; Fel., Australian Acad. of Humanities 76; Prof., U. of Hong Kong 81-87; Visiting Prof., NTHU 91; Hon. D.Lit., Edinburgh, UK 95; Fel. Int. Eurasian Acad. of Sc. 97. *Publ.: The Astronomical Chapters of the Chin Shu; Li, Qi & Shu: An Introduction to Ch. Sc.; Add.* Needham Res. Inst., 8 Sylvester Rd., Cambridge, CB3 9AF, UK.

HO, PING-TI 何炳棣
Mem., Acad. Sinica 55-; Fel., Am. Acad. of Arts & Sc. 79-; *b.* Tientsin Sept. 1, '17; *m.* Shao, Ching-lo; 2 *s.; educ.* BA, NTHU 38; Ph.D., Columbia U. 52; Hon. LL.D., Ch. U. of Hong Kong 75; Hon. LHD, Lawrence U., USA 78; Hon. LHD, Dennison U., USA 88; Instr., NTHU 39-45; Asst. Prof. & Prof., U. of British Columbia 48-63; Hon. Sr. Res. Fel., Ch. Acad. of Soc. Sc. 67; Pres., Assn. for Asian Stud-

ies 75-76; James Westhall Thompson Prof. of Hist., U. of Chicago 63-87; Visiting Disting. Prof., U. of Calif., Irvine 87-90. *Publ.: Studies on the Population of Ch., 1368-1953* 59; *The Ladder of Success in Imperial Ch., 1368-1911* 62; *The Cradle of the E. 5000-1000 B.C.* 75; etc.; *Add.* 5471 Sierra Verde Rd., Irvine, CA 92612-3842, USA.

HO, PING-YU
(See HO, PENG-YOKE 何丙郁)

HO, YING-KANG
(See HO, ING-KANG 何英剛)

HON, MIN-HSIUNG 洪敏雄
Prof., NCKU 82-, Dean, Res. & Dev.; *b.* Twn. Sept. 22, '43; *m.* Hon, Mann C.; 3 *d.; educ.* BS, NCKU 67; MS, N. Carolina State U. 76, Ph.D., 78; Resr., ITRI 68-78; *Add.* 1 Ta Hsueh Rd., Tainan 701.

HONG, YUH-CHIN 洪玉欽
Exec. Dir., Policy Coordination Cttee., KMT 99-; Mem., Legis. Yuan (for 7 consecutive terms) 96-; *b.* Twn. July 11, '43; *m.* Hong Shen, Mei-chu; *educ.* LL.B., Soochow U. 67; LL.M., Ch. Cul. U., LL.D. 79; Dep. Sec.-Gen., Cent. Policy Cttee., KMT 88-89; Dir.-Gen., Dept. of Intra- & Inter-Party Rel., CC, KMT & concur. Dept. of Party-Govt. Coordination of the Legis. Yuan 92-93, Mem., Cent. Policy Cttee. 93-94; Chmn., Econ. Sub-cttee. & For. Aff. Sub-cttee., Cent. Policy Cttee., KMT; Mem., Econ. Cttee., Legis. Yuan 94, For. & Ovs. Ch. Aff. Cttee. 95, & Organic Laws Cttee.; Dep. Sec.-Gen., CC, KMT 94-98, Supt., Cent. Policy Cttee., KMT 93-99; Prof., & Dept. Head, Ch. Cul. U.; V. Chmn., Soc. of ROC-US Parliamentarians, Legis. Yuan; Chief Del., visiting US Cong., Legis. Yuan 88; Guest to the Nat. Cong. of the US's Republican Party 88 & 96; Visiting US's State Dept. 89; Head, Observation Team of the US Congressional Elections 90; Leading Rep. of the ROC, APPU 92; *Add.* 11 Chung Shan S. Rd., Taipei 100.

HOU, CHIA-CHU 侯家駒
Prof., Intl. Econ., Soochow U. 74-; *b.* Anhwei Aug. 6, '28; *m.* Shen, Tsui-ying; 3 *s.; educ.* MS, NCHU; MA, Agr Econ., U. of New Eng.; Assc. Prof., Coll. of Ch. Cul. 66-67 & Soochow U. 67-72; Visiting Fel., Yale U. 73. *Publ. Introduction to Factor Prices; Marginal Analysis & Average Analysis; Hist. of Ch. Econ. Thought; Add.* 5th Fl., 101-1 Hsin Tien Rd., Hsintien, Taipei County 231.

HOU, HO-HSIUNG
(See HOU, HO-SHONG 侯和雄)

HOU, HO-SHONG 侯和雄
Exec. Dep. Mayor, Kaohsiung City 99-; *b.* Twn. Apr. 3, '44; *m.* Chen, Pai-ho; 2 *s.*, 2 *d.; educ.* BSHE, NCKU 67, MSCE 69; Ph.D., Civil & Coastal Engr., U. of Florida 76; Chief, Hydraulic Lab., Taichung Harbor Construction Bu. 70-73; Assc. Resr., Coastal & Hydraulic Lab., U. of Florida 73-76; Adjunct Prof., Inst. of Naval Architecture, NTU 76-87; Dir. & Prof., Nat. Twn. Ocean U. 78-81; Dep. Dir., Inst. of Harbor & Marine Tech. 81-85; Dep. Dir.-Gen., Inst. of Trans., MOTC 85-97, Dept. of Railways & Highways 97-98. *Publ.:* Over 300 publ. in the fields of coastal & harbor engr. planning & design, model simulation, ocean engr., high speed rail, pavement, & highway; *Add.* 2 Ssu Wei 3rd Rd., Kaohsiung 802.

HOU, HSIAO-HSIEN 侯孝賢
Film Dir.; Dir., 3H Prod. Ltd.; *b.* Kwangtung '47; *m.* Tsao, Pao-feng; 1 *s.*, 1 *d.; educ.* Grad., Film Dept., Nat. Twn. Acad. of Arts 72; Script Sup.; Screenplay Writer; Winner, Sp. Jury Award, Asia-Pacific Film Festival & Award for Best Film, Rotterdam Film Festival for *The Time to Live & the Time to Die* 85; Award for Best Dir., Award for Best Photography & Award for Best Music, Nantes Festival for *Dust in the Wind* 86; Sp. Jury Award, Durin Intl. Festival for *D. of the Nile* 87; Golden Lion of Venice Award, Venice Intl. Film Festival for *City of Sadness* 90; Jury Prize, Cannes Intl. Film Festival for *The Puppetmaster* 93; officially selected for Cannes Intl. Film Festival for *Good Men, Good Women* 95; *Goodbye S., Goodbye* 96. *Films: Cute Girl* 80; *Green, Green Grass of Home* 82; *The Sandwich Man* 83; *The Boys from Feng-kuei* 83; *A Summer at Grandpa's* 84; *Flowers of Shanghai* 98; Exec. Producer for films *Raised the Red Lanterns* & *Dust of Angel; Add.* 2nd Fl., 5 Lane 23 Wan Ning St., Wenshan, Taipei 116.

HSI, SHIH-CHI 席時濟
Chmn., Twn. Power Co. 97-; *b.* Shanghai Aug. 17, '36; *m.* Chiou, Chin-ling; 2 *s.*, 1 *d.; educ.* BEE, NCKU 57; V. Chmn., Twn. Power Co. 85-94, Pres. 94-97; *Add.* 242 Roosevelt Rd., Sect. 3, Taipei 100.

HSIA, DER-YU 夏德鈺
Chmn., AEC 2000-; *b.* Hupei Aug. 10, '49; *m.* Chen, Chia-yu; 1 *s.*, 1 *d.; educ.* BS, Nuclear Engr., NTHU 70; On-the-job tng., Health Phys. Div., Oak Ridge Nat. Lab., USA 73-74; MS, Phys., U. of Tennessee 74; Ph.D., Nuclear Engr., MIT 80; Res. Asst., Health Phys. Div., Inst. of Nuclear Energy Res. (INER), Chung-Shan Inst. of Sc. & Tech., MND 71-73, Asst. Scientist, Reactor Engr. Div., INER 74-77, Assc. Scientist (Dir., Kuosheng PRA Project; Auditor,

Maanshan FSAR Review) 80-85; Dir., Dept. of Nuclear Regln. AEC 85-92, INER 92-2000. *Publ.: Probabilistic Risk Assessment on Kuosheng Nuclear Power Station* (with the Kuosheng PRA Project Team; 4 Vol.) 85; *Add.* 67 Lane 144, Keelung Rd., Sect. 4, Taipei 106.

HSIA, HAN-MIN 夏漢民
Nat. Policy Adv. to the Pres. 96-; *b.* Fukien May 3, '32; *m.* Wang, Show-mee; 2 *s.*, 1 *d.; educ.* BS, Marine Engr., Ch. Naval Acad. 54; MS, Mech. Engr., NCKU 62; Ph.D., Mech. Engr., U. of Oklahoma 65; Prof. & Chmn., Dept. of Engr. Sc., NCKU 67-71; Pres., Prov. Kaohsiung Inst. of Tech. 72-77; Dir., Dept. of Voc. & Tech. Educ., MOE 77-79; Admin. V. Min. of Educ. 79-80; Pres., NCKU 80-88, & Ch. Inst. of Engr. 88-89; Chmn., NScC 88-93; Min. without Portfolio 93-96. *Publ.:* Over 40 publ. in the fields of heat transfer, voc. & tech. educ.; *Add.* 3rd Fl., 13-2 Lane 97, Hsin Sheng S. Rd., Sect. 1, Taipei 106.

HSIA, TE-YU
(See HSIA, DER-YU 夏德鈺)

HSIA, TIEN 夏甸
Rep., TECO, Austria 96-; *b.* Hopei Feb. 8, '29; *m.* Hsia Wang, Hsi-ming; 2 *s.*, 1 *d.; educ.* Grad., Ch. Naval Acad. 50, Class A, Fire Control, USNTC 57, Cmd. Coll., US Naval War Coll. 72, & War Coll., Armed Forces U. 73; Cmdg. Off., RCS Yung-tai (PCE 41) 63, RCS Tai-ho (DE 23) 68, & RCS Nan-yang (DD17) 70; Chief, Bu. Planning, GHQ, ROCN 75, Cmdr., Destroyer Squadron 77; Cmdt., Naval Cmd. & Staff Coll., Armed Forces U. 79; Dep. Chief of the Gen. Staff, Planning (J-5), MND 82, V. Chief of the Gen. Staff 87; Rep., Taipei Rep. Off. in the Netherlands 92-96; *Add.* Praterstrasse 31/15 OG, A-1020, Vienna, Austria.

HSIANG, WU-CHUNG 項武忠
Mem., Acad. Sinica 80-; Prof. of Math., Princeton U.; *b.* Chekiang June 12, '35; *m.* Hsiang, Pei-ying; 2 *s.; educ.* BS, NTU 57; Ph.D., Princeton U.; *Add.* Dept. of Math., Princeton U., Washington Rd., Princeton, NJ 68544, USA.

HSIANG, YEN-CHU 向延竚
Amb. to the Dem. Repub. of São Tomé e Príncipe 98-; *b.* Hunan July 29, '43; *m.* Hsiang Chi, Chung-jen; 2 *d.; educ.* BA, NCCU 66, MA 70; Sect. Chief, MOFA 80-85, Counsl., Emb. in Uraguay 86-88, Emb. in Costa Rica 88-92; Rep. in Portugal 92-96; Dep. Dir.-Gen. MOFA 96-98; *Add.* P.O. Box 839, São Tomé, República Democrática de São Tomé e Príncipe (via Portugal).

HSIANG YANG 向陽
(See LIN, CHI-YANG 林淇瀁)

HSIAO, CHENG 蕭政
Mem., Acad. Sinica 96-; Prof. of Econ., Dept. of Econ., U. of So. Calif.; Bd. Mem., Ch. Res. Inst. for Land Econ. 80-; Prof. of Econ., U. of So. Calif. 85-; Fel. & Ed., *Jour. of Econometrics* 91-; Fel., Econometric Soc. 96-; Pres., Ch. Econ. Assn. in N. Am. 98-; *b.* Chungking June 27, '43; *m.* Hsiao, Amy; 2 *s.,* 2 *d.; educ.* BA, NTU 65; B. Phil., Oxford U. 68; MS, Stanford U. 70, Ph.D. 72; Asst. Prof. of Econ., UC-Berkly. 72-77; Faculty Res. Fel., Nat. Bu. of Econ. Res., Inc. 76-77; Prof. of Econ., U. of Toronto 80-85; Visiting Prof., Princeton U. 80-81; Consultant, Bell Labs. 81-82; Disting. Visitor, Suntory-Toyota Intl. Cent. for Econ. & Related Discipline, London Sch. of Econ. 95; Visiting Scholar, Inst. for Monetary & Econ. Studies, Back of Japan 96-97; Kuo-Shu Liang Prof. of Econ., NTU 97-98. *Publ.: Analysis of Panel Data* 86; *Econometric Models, Techniques & Applications* 96; *Add.* Dept. of Econ., U. of So. Calif., Los Angeles, CA 90089-0253, USA.

HSIAO, HSIN-HUANG
(See HSIAO, HSIN-HUANG MICHAEL 蕭新煌)

HSIAO, HSIN-HUANG MICHAEL 蕭新煌
Nat. Policy Adv. to the Pres. 96-; Mem., NUC 97-; Res. Fel., Inst. of Sociology, Acad. Sinica, Dir., Prog. for S.E. Asian Area Studies 95-; Prof., Dept. of Sociology, NTU 84-; Exec. Dir., Found. for the Advancement of Outsdg. Scholarship; Bd. Mem. of Public TV Found. 98-; Nat. Cul. & Arts Found. 98-; Asia-Pacific Public Aff. Forum 97-; *b.* Taipei Dec. 26, '48; *m.* Hsiao Lee, Yu-hyang; 2 *s.; educ.* BA, NTU 71; MA, State U. of New York, Buffalo 76, Ph.D. 79; Assc. Res. Fel. & Res. Fel., Inst. of Ethnology, Acad. Sinica 79-83 & 83-95; Assc. Prof., NTU 80-84; Visiting Prof., Boston U. 83-84, Duke U. 88, & Leiden U. 94. *Publ.: In Search of an E. Asian Dev. Model; Twn.—A Newly Industrialized State; Twn. 2000; Discovery of the Middle Classes in E. Asia; Dev. & Underdev.; Middle Classes in Changing Twn. Soc.; Dev. & Exchange of Sociology in Twn., Hong Kong & Ch.; E. Asian Middle Classes in Comparative Perspective; Add.* 3rd Fl., 55 Lane 70, Yen Chiou Yuan Rd., Sect. 2, Taipei 115.

HSIAO, TENG-WANG 蕭登旺
Spkr., Chiayi CCoun. 90-; Bd. Chmn., Gen. Prov. Hsiao's Filiation Group, Chiayi Hsiao's Filiation Group; Pres., Chiayi Tienhou Temple; Hon. Chmn., Retired Servicemen Assn., Chiayi; *b.* Twn. Dec. 1, '47; *m.* Lin, Jui-man; 2 *s.,* 1 *d.; educ.* Grad., Sr. High Sch.; Hon. Chmn. of the Bd., Chiayi Chamber of Com.; *Add.* 278 Pei Kang Rd., Chiayi 600.

HSIAO, WAN-CHANG
(See SIEW, VINCENT C. 蕭萬長)

HSIEH, FRANK CHANG-TING 謝長廷
Mayor, Kaohsiung City 98-; Mem., CSC, DPP 86-; *b.* Taipei May 18, '46; *m.* Hsieh Yu, Fang-chih ; 1 *s.,* 1 *d.; educ.* LL.B., NTU 67; LL.M., Kyoto U. 72; Attorney 69-81; Mem., Taipei CCoun. 81-88; Legis. 89-95; DPP Candidate, 1996 Election for ROC V. Pres.; *Add.* 2 Ssu Wei 3rd Rd., Kaohsiung 802.

HSIEH, H. STEVE 薛香川
V. Chmn., NScC 96-2000; *b.* Twn. Dec. 12, '44; *m.* Hsieh, Mary W.; 1 *s.,* 2 *d.; educ.* BS, Agr. Chem., NTU 67; MS & Ph.D. in Nutritional Biochem., U. of Wisconsin, Madison 74; Postdr. Fel., Biochem. Dept., Florida State U. 74-77; Resr., Inst. of Dental Res., U. of Alabama in Birmingham 77-82; Sp., NScC 82-84, Dir., Div. of Planning & Evaluation 84-86, & Div. of Life Sc. 86, Dep. Dir.-Gen., Hsinchu Sc.-based Ind. Park Admin. 86-89, Dir.-Gen. 89-96; *Add.* 19th Fl., 106 Ho Ping E. Rd., Sect. 2, Taipei 106.

HSIEH, HSIN-LIANG
(See SHIEH, SHINN-LIANG 謝信良)

HSIEH, LUNG-SHENG
(See SHIEH, LUNG-SHENG 謝隆盛)

HSIEH, MENG-HSIUNG
(See SHIEH, MUNG-SHIUNG 謝孟雄)

HSIEH, MING-TSUN
(See HSIEH, MING-TSUEN 謝明村)

HSIEH, MING-TSUEN 謝明村
Pres., Ch. Med. Coll. 99-, Prof., Inst. of Ch. Pharmaceutical Sc. 85-; Dir., Lifu Med. Res. Found. 89-; Controller, Ch Pharmacy Soc. 93-; Chmn., Ch. Traditional Med. Res. & Dev. Fund 98-; Mem., Consultant, Nat. Inst. of Ch. Med 99-; *b.* Twn. Dec. 28, '39; *m.* Ko, Ai-chin; 2 *s.,* 1 *d.; educ* BS, Pharmacy, Ch. Med. Coll. 63, MD, Inst. of Ch. Pharmaceutical Sc. 76; Ph.D., Pharmacology, U. of Tokyo 82 Teaching Asst., Sch. of Pharmacy, Ch. Med. Coll. 64-68 Lectr. 68-72, Assc. Prof. 72-85, Dir., Inst. of Ch. Pharmaceutical Sc. 81-97; Mem., Cttee. on Ch. Med. & Pharmacy DOH 82-95. *Publ.: An Introduction of Ch. Med.; Ch*

Herbs Album (Vol. 12); *Prescription of Ch. Med.; Ch. Med. Formula;* & 115 papers; *Add.* 91 Hsueh Shih Rd., Taichung 404.

HSIEH, SEN-CHUNG
(See SHIEH, SAMUEL C. 謝森中)

HSIEH, SHEN-SAN 謝深山
Sec.-Gen., Exec. Yuan 99-2000; *b.* Twn. Feb. 3, '39; *m.* Chien, Shu-neu; 2 *s.,* 1 *d.; educ.* Hualien Ind. Voc. Sr. High Sch.; Mem., Standing Cttee., Twn. Railway Workers' Union 71-85; Legis. 73-94; Mem., Standing Cttee., Ch. Fed. of Railway Workers' Union 82-85; V. Pres., Ch. Taipei Baseball Assn. 84-92; Ch. Fed. of Labor 88-94; Mem., CSC 88-94; Dep. Sec.-Gen., CC, KMT 91-94; Chmn., CLA 94-98; *Add.* 1 Chung Hsiao E. Rd., Taipai 100.

HSIEH, SHUI-NAN 謝水南
Pres., Open U. of Kaohsiung 97-; *b.* Twn. Aug. 31, '46; *m.* Woo, Li-yeh; 2 *s.; educ.* Ed.B., NTNU 69, Ed.M. 75, Ed.D. 84; Prin., Twn. Prov. Taichung Sch. for the Deaf 81-87; Dean of Acad. Aff., Nat. Taichung Tchrs.' Coll. 88-90; Dir., Inst. for Elementary & Secondary Sch. Tchrs.' in Twn. 90-97. *Publ.: A Study on the Dev. of Soc. Cognitive Ability of C. in Elementary Sch.* 74; *A Study on the Effect of Different Grouping in Small-group Counseling* 90; *Add.* 436 Ta Yeh N. Rd., Hsiaokang, Kaohsiung 812.

HSIEH, TSAI-CHUAN
(See HSIEH, TSAY-CHUAN 謝在全)

HSIEH, TSAY-CHUAN 謝在全
Grand Justice, Jud. Yuan 99-; Adjunct Assc. Prof., Soochow U. 95-; Lectr., Judges & Prosecutors Tng. Inst.; *b.* Twn. Jan. 20, '44; *m.* Lin, Mei-chu; 1 *s.,* 2 *d.; educ.* LL.B., NTU 66; LL.M., So. Methodist U. 78; Judge, Twn. Taipei Dist. Court 69-79, Twn. Chiayi Dist. Court 79-80, Twn. Taichung Br. Court, Twn. High Court 80; Prosecutor, Twn. Tainan Br. Court, Twn. High Court 80-83; Judge, Supreme Court 85-89; Sr. Judge & concur. Pres., Twn. Yunlin Dist. Court 89-91, Twn. Changhua Dist. Court 91-93, Twn. Taichung Dist. Court 95-97; Dir., Civil Dept., Jud. Yuan 95-97; Dir., Judges & Prosecutors Tng. Inst. 97-99. *Publ.: Law of Property* (2 Vol.); *Theory & Practice of Internal Legal Relationship of Co-ownership of Property; Add.* 4th Fl., 124 Chungking S. Rd., Sect. 1, Taipei 100.

HSIEH, TUNG-MIN
(See SHIEH, TUNG-MIN 謝東閔)

HSIEH, YI-YUNG
(See HSIEH, YIH-YUNG 謝義勇)

HSIEH, YIH-YUNG 謝義勇
Pres., Nat. Sc. & Tech. Museum 99-; *b.* Twn. Nov. 14, '51; *m.* Kao, Yu-feng; 1 *s.,* 2 *d.; educ.*Grad., Prov. Taichung Normal Coll. 72; B. & M., Dept. of Soc. Educ., NTNU 80 & 89; Studying, Ph.D. Prog., Adult Educ. Inst., Nat. Kaohsiung Normal U. 99; Tchr., Chunkeng Elementary Sch., Nantou County 72-76; Staff, Educ. Bu., Kaohsiung City Govt. 80-80, Div. Chief 83-86; Div. Chief, Kaohsiung City Lib. 82, Preparatory Off. of the Kaohsiung Cul. Cent. 82-83; Dir., Kaohsiung City's Soc. Educ. Hall 86-89; Dir., Preparatory Off. of the Kaohsiung Museum of Fine Arts 89-90; Sec., Nat. Museum of Marine Biology (Aquarium) 92; Sr. Sp., CCA 92-93; Sec., Preparatory Off. of the Nat. Tainan Coll. of Arts 93-96; Chief Sec., Nat. Tainan Coll. of Arts 96-97; V. Pres., Nat. Sc. & Tech. Museum 97-99; *Add.* 720 Chiu Ju 1st Rd., Kaohsiung 807.

HSING, WAN-CHIAO
(See HSING, WOAN-CHIAU 辛晚教)

HSING, WOAN-CHIAU 辛晚教
Prof. Grad. Inst. of Urban (& Regional) Planning, NCHU 75-; Mem., CEPD's & CCA's consulting cttees. 96-; *b.* Twn. Nov. 25, '38; *m.* Cheng, Mei-li; 2 *s.,* 1 *d.; educ.* BA & MA, NCHU 62 & 66; M.S.C., London U. of Econ. 73; Dep. Dir.-Gen., Construction & Planning Admin., MOI 81; Bd. Chmn., Urban Planning Soc. 92-94; Dir., Grad. Inst. of Urban Planning, NCHU 75-81 & 94-97. *Publ.: City & Planning* (Ch.); *Add.* 69 Chien Kuo N. Rd., Sect. 2, Taipei 104.

HSING YUN 星雲
Buddhist M.; 48th Patriarch, Linchi Ch'an Sch.; Pres., Buddha's Light Intl. Assn.; Hon. Pres., World Fel. of Buddhists; Chmn., Sino-Tibet Assn.; Hon. Pres., World Fel. of Buddhists; Chmn., Sino-Tibet Assn.; *b.* Kiangsu July 22, '22; *educ.* Chihsia Vinaya Coll.; Chiaoshan Buddhist Coll.; Hon. Ph.D., Orient U., Calif.; M., Cttee. of Religious Aff. 53; Abbot, Shoushan Temple, Kaohsiung 53-77, & Lei-Yin Temple, Ilan; Dir., India Study, Ch. Cul. U. 67; Founder, Foguangshan, Hsi Lai Temple, Foguangshan Tsunglin Monastic U., E. Buddhist Coll., Hsi Lai U., Ch. Buddhism Res. Inst., Pumen Middle Sch., Chihkuang Middle Sch., Foguangshan Compassion Found., Foguang Clinic, Winter Relief Campaign, Cloud & Water Mobile Clinic, Emergency Aid Prog., Friendship & Care Brig., Kuanyin Life Conservation Group, Tatzu C.'s Home,

Lanyang Sr. Citizens' Home, & Foguangshan Retirement Home; TV Production: Sweet Dew; Gate of Faith; M. Hsing Yun's Seminar on Buddhist Studies; Hsing Yun's Dharma Talk; Radio Prog. Production: Voice of Buddhism; Wonders of Ch'an; Carefree Life. *Publ.: The Life of the Buddha; 10 Major Disciples of Buddha; Song of Silence; Forum of Awakening the World; Collection of Lectures* (4 Vol.); *Ch'an Talk* (4 Vol.); *Dharma Talk* (4 Vol.); *Everyday's Verse* (4 Vol.); *The Lion's Roar;* etc.; *Add.* 13th Fl., 327 Sung Lung Rd., Taipei 110.

HSIUE, GING-HO 薛敬和
Prof., Dept. of Chem. Engr., NTHU 73-; Chmn. & Prof., Dept. of Chem. Engr., NCHU; Adjunct Prof., Inst. of Med. Engr., Nat. Yang Ming Med. Coll.; *b.* Twn. Feb. 4, '39; *m.* Hsiue Lee, Su-jong; 1 *s.,* 1 *d.; educ.* BS, Ind. Chem., Nippon U., Japan 65; MS, Synthetic Chem., Tokyo U. 67; Ph.D., Polymer Chem., Tohoku U. 72; Visiting Prof. of Macromolecular Sc., Case W. Reserve U. 83-84; Visiting Scientist of the ROC NScC; Pres. of Biomaterials & Controlled Release Soc. of Twn. *Publ.: The Synthesis, Morphology & Properties of Triblock Copolymers; Experiments in Polymer Chem.; Enzyme Immobilized Polymeric Membrane for Biosensors; Studies on Polymeric Material with Microphase Separation Structure; Surface Modification of Silicon Rubber Membranes as an Artifical Cornea in Vitro and in Vivo Studies; Dev. of Ferroelectric Liquid Crystalline Polymers for Electro-optical Application;* & 190 sc. papers; *Add.* 5th Fl., 66 W. Court, NTHU, Hsinchu 300.

HSU, CHANG-HUI
(See HSU, TSANG-HOUEI 許常惠)

HSU, CHENG-KUANG 徐正光
Chmn., MTAC 2000-; Pres., Taipei Hakka's Cul. Found.; *b.* Twn. Feb. 16, '43; *m.* Chang, Hsiu-jung; 2 *s.; educ.* BA, Sociology, NTU 65; MA, Sociology, U. of Illinois 71; Ph. D., Sociology, Brown U. 84; Asst. Res. Fel., Acad. Sinica 73-78, Assc. Res. Fel. 79-84, Res. Fel. 84-2000, Head, Behaviorial Anthropology Sect. 86-87; Prof., Dept. of Sociology NTU 86-87; Prof. & Dir., Inst. of Sociology & Anthropology NTHU 86-90; Pres., Ch. Sociological Assn. 88-90; Visiting Scholar, St. Antony's Coll., U. of Oxford, UK 91-92; Dir., Inst. of Ethnology, Acad. Sinica 94-2000; Dir., *Hakka's Mag. Publ.:* "White-collar Proletarianization? The Case of Twn.," *Res. in Soc. Stratification & Mobility* & "Modernization & Changes in Extended Kinship in Taipei, Twn. 1963-1991," *Marriage & the Family in Ch. Soc.* (with Robert Marsh) 94; "Introduction: Understanding Soc. & the State of Twn.," *State & Soc. in Twn.* (with Michael

H.H. Hsiao eds.) 94; "'Lang. Problems' of the Hakka People in Twn.: A Sociological Analysis," Field Materials, *Inst. of Ethnology, Acad. Sinica, Occasional Series, No.10* 95; "Changes in Norms & Behavior: Concerning Extended Kin in Taipei, Twn. 1963-1991," *Jour. of Comparative Family Studies* 26(3) 95; "Facing New Challenges: Diversification Strategies of S.E. Asian Agr.," *Newsletter of the Program for S.E. Asian Area Studies* (forthcoming) 96; *Soc. Dev. & Soc. Movement* (forthcoming) 96; & 45 acad. papers; *Add.* 4th Fl., 5 Hsuchow Rd., Taipei 100.

HSU, CHIA-TUNG
(See SHEA, JIA-DONG 許嘉棟)

HSU, CHIEH-SU 徐皆蘇
Mem., Acad. Sinica 90-, & Nat. Acad. of Engr., USA 88-; Prof., Dept. of Mech. Engr., UC-Berkly. 64-; *b.* Kiangsu May 27, '22; *m.* Tse, Helen Yung-feng; 1 *s.,* 1 *d.; educ.* Grad., Nat. Inst. of Tech. 45; MS, Mech. Engr., Stanford U. 48, Ph.D. 50; Engr., Shanghai Naval Dockyard & Engr. Works 46-47; Res. Asst., Stanford U. 48-51; Tech. & Project Engr., IBM Corp. 51-55; Assc. Prof., U. of Toledo 55-58; Assc. Prof., UC-Berkly. 58-64, Prof. 64-91, Dir., 69-70; John Simon Guggenheim Fel. 64-65; Miller Res. Prof., UC-Berkly. 73-74; Ed., *Jour. of Applied Mech.* 76-82. *Publ.: Cell-to-Cell Mapping—A Method of Global Analysis for Nonlinear Systems* 87; 106 sc. & tech. res. papers; *Add.* 208 Yale Avenue, Berkeley, CA 94708, USA.

HSU, CHING-HUA
(See HSU, KENNETH J. 許靖華)

HSU, CHO-YUN 許倬雲
Mem., Acad. Sinica 80-; Prof. of Hist. & Sociology 70-82, U. of Pittsburgh, U. Prof. 83-98, U. Prof. Emeritus 99-; Weilun Prof. of Hist., Honor Prof. 98-, Ch. U. of Hong Kong 93-97; John Burns Prof. of Hist., U. of Hawaii 95-; Semons Disting. Prof., Duke U. 99-; *b.* Amoy (native of Kiangsu) July 10, '30; *m.* Sun, Man-li; 1 *s.; educ.* BA & MA, NTU; Ph.D., U. of Chicago; Assc. Prof. & Prof., NTU 62-70; Asst. Fel., Assc. Fel., & Fel. 60-71; Sp. Chair, Acad. Sinica 80 & 99; Mem., Phi Beta Kappa, & Bd. of Dir. Chiang Ching-kuo Found. *Publ.: Ancient Ch. in Transition; Han Agr. & Hist. of W. Chou Civilization;* etc.; *Add.* 5742 5th Avenue, Unit 103, Pittsburgh, PA 15232, USA.

HSU, DOUGLAS TONG 徐旭東
Chmn., Twn. Textile Fed. 95-, Far Ea. Textile Ltd. 91-, Asia Cement Corp. 93-, Far Ea. Dept. Store Ltd. 88-, Oriental Union Chem. Corp. 94-, & U-Ming Marine Trans. Corp.

95-; V. Chmn., Far Ea. Intl. Bk. 92-, & Intl. Business Cttee., the Metropolitan Museum of Art in New York; Hon. Pres., Intl. Textile Mfr.'s Fed. 94-; Trustee, U. of Notre Dame; Mem. of IBM Greater Ch. Adv. Bd.; Dir., Prudential/Asia Pacific Fund; Intl. Dir., The Asia Soc.; Consul-Gen., Consl. of the Rep. of Malawi & Ivory Coast in Taipei; *b.* Shanghai Aug. 24, '42; *m.* Morris, Mary Dustin; 1 *s.,* 2 *d.; educ.* BA & MA, U. of Notre Dame; Postgrad., Columbia U.; *Add.* 38th Fl., 207 Tun Hua S. Rd., Sect. 2, Taipei 105.

HSU, FRANCIS L.K. 許烺光
Mem., Acad. Sinica 78-; Author; Lectr., Consultant & Prof. Emeritus of Anthropology, N.we. U.; *b.* Liaoning Oct. 28, '09; *m.* Tung, Vera Y.N.; 2 *d.; educ.* BA, Shanghai U. 33; Ph.D., U. of London 40; Lectr., Columbia U. 44-45; Asst. Prof., Corncll U. 45-47; Prof., Anthropology, N.we. U. 47-78, Chmn., Dept. of Anthropology 57-75; Prof. & Dir., Cent. for Cul. Studies in Educ., U. of San Francisco 78-82; Pres., Am. Anthropological Assn. 78-79. *Publ.:* 16 bk. & over 110 articles; *Add.* 61 Milland Drive, Mill Valley, CA 94941, USA.

HSU, FU-SEM 許福森
Spkr., Kaohsiung CCoun. 98-; *b.* Twn. Oct. 20, '50; *m.* Hsu Shyu, mei-ing; 1 *s.; educ.* Studying, Ind. Mng. Dept., I-Shou U. 99; Chmn., Kangshan Urban Township Rep. Coun., Kaohsiung County 90-94; Mem., Kaohsiung CoCoun. 94-98; *Add.* 156 Kuo Tai Rd., Sect. 2, Fengshan, Kaohsiung County 830.

HSU, FU-SEN
(See HSU, FU-SEM 許福森)

HSU, HENG
(See HSU, HENRY HENG 徐亨)

HSU, HENRY HENG 徐亨
Nat. Policy Adv. to the Pres. 87-; Mem., CAC, KMT 88-; Pres., Red Cross Soc. of the ROC 88-; Hon. Mem., Intl. Olympic Cttee. 88-; Pub., *Twn. Daily News* 94-96, Chmn. 78-96; Chmn. & CEO, Taipei Fortuna Hotel 82-, & Universal Fortuna Investment Inc.; Corp. Gen. Partner, Fortuna Ent. L.P.; Owner, Los Angeles Airport Hilton & Towers 92-; *b.* Kwangtung Dec. 6, '12; *m.* Yue, Amy So-hing; 1 *s.,* 2 *d.; educ.* Whampoa Naval Coll. 32; LL.B., Nat. Ch. U., Shanghai 35; US Naval Tng. Cent., Cmdg. Off. Class, Miami 44; Hon. LL.D., Kyung Hee U., S. Korea 75; Hon. Dr. of Humanics, Springfield Coll., Massachusetts 95; Cmdg. Off., "Yung Ning," ROCN 45-46, Capt. 47; Rear Adm. (Retired), ROCN 78; Chmn., Fortuna Athletic Assn., Hong

Kong 53; Governing Dir., Intl. Finance Corp. Ltd., Hong Kong 54; Pres., Amateur Swimming Assn., ROC 54-65; Mng. Dir., Burlington Investment Co., Ltd., Hong Kong 60; Hon. Pres., Volleyball Assn., Hong Kong 60-69; Pres., Ch. Swimming Assn., Hong Kong 60, Hon. Pres. 61-69; Mng. Dir., Walton Investment Co., Ltd., Hong Kong 62; Pres., Sea Dragon Skin Diving Club, Hong Kong 63, Hon. Pres. 64; Hon. Pres., Hong Kong Amateur Basketball Assn. 65-69; V. Pres., Amateur Swimming Fed. of Asia 66-72; Mem., Intl. Olympic Cttee. 70-87; Mem., Legis. Yuan 72-86; Mem., CC, KMT 83-88; *Add.* Taipei Fortuna Hotel, 122 Chung Shan N. Rd., Sect. 2, Taipei 104.

HSU, HUNG
(See HSU, HONG 徐泓)

HSU, HONG 徐泓
Acting Pres., Nat. Chi Nan U. 99-, Dean of Acad. Aff. 98-; Prof., Dept. of Hist., NTU 80-; *b.* Fukien Dec., 25, '43; *m.* Hsu Wang, Genevieve; 1 *s.,* 1 *d.; educ.* BA, MA & D.Litt in Hist., NTU 65, 69 & 73; Head, Dept. of Hist., NTU 85-91, Dir., Grad. Inst. of Hist. 89-91; Prof. of Hist. & concur. Head, Div. of Humanities, Hong Kong U. of Sc. & Tech. 91-93, Acting Dean, Sch. of Humanities & Soc. Sc. 92-93; Prof. & Dir., Grad. Inst. of Hist., Nat. Chi Nan U. 96-99; *Add.* Temporary Off. of the Nat. Chi Nan U., 1 Roosevelt Rd., Taipei 106.

HSU, HSIEN-HSIU
(See SHU, HSIEN-SIU 徐賢修)

HSU, HSIN-LIANG 許信良
Independent Candidate, 2000 Election for ROC Pres.; Former Chmn., DPP 96-98; Chmn., Cul. & Educ. Found. of the Rising People; *b.* Twn. May 27, '41; *m.* Chung, Pi-hsia; 2 *s.,* 2 *d.; educ.* BPS, Pol., NCCU 63, Studied, Inst. of Pol. 67; Studied, Grad. Inst. of Philosophy, U. of Edinburgh, UK 69; Hon. Ph.D., U. of Kyongnam, S. Korea 93, & U. of Far Ea. State 97; Mem., TPA 73-77; Magis., Taoyuan County 77-79; Dir., *Formosa Mag. of Twn. Dem. Movement* 79; Dir., *Formosa Weekly of Twn. Dem. Movement* 80; Chmn., DPP 91-93. *Publ.: The Sound of Wind & Rain* 77; *The Rising People* 95; *Challenge Lee Teng-hui* 96; *Add.* 12th Fl., 22 Chung Cheng Rd., Sect. 2, Peitou, Taipei 112.

HSU, HSU-TUNG
(See HSU, DOUGLAS TONG 徐旭東)

HSU, HUI-YU
(See SHI, HWEI-YOW 許惠祐)

529

HSU, I-HSIUNG 許義雄

Chmn., Nat. Coun. on Phys. Fitness & Sports, Exec. Yuan 2000-; *b.* Twn. Nov. 11, '38; *m.* Huang, Ying-ching; 1 *s.,* 1 *d.; educ.* Grad., Prov. Tainan Tchrs.' Sch.; B., Phys. Educ. (PE) Dept., NTNU; M., PE, Tokyo Educ. U.; Dr., PE, Tsukuba U., Japan; Elementary & high sch. tchr.; Teaching asst., lectr., assc. prof., & prof. in Coll.; Sec.-Gen., V. Chmn., & Chmn., Ch. Sports Soc., ROC; Sec.-Gen., Coll. Sports Fed., ROC; Mem., Panels of Civil Service Exam (Ordinary & Advanced Level) & JUEE; Mem., Prov. Sports Cttee. for Nats.; Convener, PE Textbk. Review Panel, Nat. Inst. for Compilation & Transl.; Convener, PE Lesson, Curriculum Revision Cttee., MOE; Comr., Nat. Coun. of Phys. Fitness & Sports, Exec. Yuan; Dir., Inst. of PE & Dev. Cent., NTNU; Mem., Sportsmen election and tng. panel, Ch. Taipei Sports Fed., ROC Sports Fed.; Dir., Inst. of PE, NTNU; Ed.-in-Chief., *Sch. Sports Mag., MOE & Nat. Sports Joun. for Coll.;* Convener-in-Chief, Formulation of the *White Paper for Sports, ROC. Publ.: A Handbk. for Elementary & High Sch. Tchrs.* 95; *Child Dev. & PE* 97; *Contemporary Ch. Sports Educ.—Aims & Dev.,* (with Hsu Yuan-min) 99; "A New Mission for Coll. PE" & "The Background of Contemporary Ch. Thinking About PE," *NTNU PE Studies* 85 & 86; "New Tasks of Sports Educ. in U. from the Viewpoint of Sports Educ. in Twn. U.," presented in the FISU/CESU Conf. Proceeding, the 18th Universidale 1995 Fukuoka 95; *Add.* 10th Fl., 80 Chien Kuo N. Rd., Sect. 1, Taipei 104.

HSU, I-HSIUNG
(See HSU, YI-HSUNG 許義雄)

HSU, KE-SHENG
(See SHEU, KE-SHENG 許柯生)

HSU, KENNETH J. 許靖華
Mem., Acad. Sinica 90-; Pres., Tarim Asscs. AG. Zurich, Switzerland; For. Assc., US Acad. of Sc. 86, & Third World Acad. of Sc.; *b.* Nanking June 28, '29; *m.* Eugster, Christine; 3 *s.,* 1 *d.; educ.* BS, Nanking U. 48; MA, Ohio State U. 50; Ph.D., UCLA 54; Project Leader & Div. Chief, Shell Dev. Co. Geologist, Texas 54-63; Assc. Prof., State U. of New York 63-64, U. of Calif. 64-67; Assc. Prof., ETH ZÅrich 67-74, Prof. 74-94; Hon. Fel., Geological Soc. of Am. 79; Hon. Mem., Soc. of Econ. Paleontologists & Mineralogists 82; Orton Award, Ohio State U. 84; Hon. Prof., Ch. Acad. of Sc., Beijing 85, N.we. U. of Ch., Xian 85, Tongji U., Shanghai 85. *Publ.: Ein Schiff Revolutionist die Wissenschaft; Mediterranean was a Desert; The Great Dying; Geol. of Switzerland;* Author or ed. of over 10 bk. & 300

sc. articles; *Add.* Tarim Asscs. for Sc. Mineral & Oil Exploration AG, Frohburgstrasse 96, 8006 Zurich, Switzerland.

HSU, KUEI-LIN 許桂霖
Mem. (ministerial rank), Exam. Yuan 96-; *b.* Twn. May 4, '34; *m.* Ho, Ing-jau; 2 *s.,* 1 *d.; educ.* B., PA, NCHU 55; Chief Sec., Kaohsiung City Govt. 78-79, Dir., Dept. of Civil Aff. 79-87; Dir., Dept. of Civil Aff., MOI 87-89; Sec.-Gen., CEIC 89-96; *Add.* 1 Shih Yuan Rd., Wenshan, Taipei 116.

HSU, LANG-KUANG
(See HSU, FRANCIS L.K. 許烺光)

HSU, LI-CHIH
(See TSUI, LAP-CHEE 徐立之)

HSU, LI-KONG 徐立功
Pres., Zoom Hunt Intl. Prod. Co. Ltd. 97-; *b.* Fukien Dec. 27, '43; *m.* Yang, Wen-yun; 1 *s.,* 1 *d.; educ.* MS, Philosophy, Fu-Jen Catholic U.; Sect. Chief., Radio & TV Aff. Dept., GIO 74-80; Dir., Nat. Film Archive of ROC 80-89; Exec. Off. of Cul. Aff. Dept., KMT 89-90; V. Pres., Cent. Motion Picture Corp. 90-95, Pres. 95-96, V. Chmn. 96-97; *Add.* 10th Fl., 37 Kuang Fu N. Rd., Taipei 105.

HSU, LI-KUNG
(See HSU, LI-KONG 徐立功)

HSU, LI-NUNG 許歷農
V. Chmn., NUC 97-; *b.* Anhwei Mar. 4, '21; *m.* Chen, Ching-hwa; 1 *d.; educ.* Grad., Ch. Mil. Acad.; Army CGSC; Armed Forces Staff Coll.; Sp. Class, War Coll., Armed Forces U.; Cmdt., Fu Hsing Kang Coll. 75-77; Cmdt., Ch. Mil. Acad. 77-79; CG, Field Army 79-81, & Kinmen Def. Cmd. 81-83; Dir., Gen. Pol. Warfare Dept., MND 83-87; Chmn., VAC 87-93; Nat. Policy Adv. to the Pres. 93-97; *Add.* 122 Chungking S. Rd., Sect. 1, Taipei 100.

HSU, LI-TE
(See HSU, LI-TEH 徐立德)

HSU, LI-TEH 徐立德
Sr. Adv. to the Pres. 97-; Mem., CSC, KMT 93-; Chmn., Ch. Aviation Dev. Found. 97-; *b.* Honan Aug. 6, '31; *m.* Liu, Ching-sheng; 2 *s.; educ.* LL.M., NCCU; M., PA, Harvard U. 86; Admin. V. Min. of Finance 76-78; Comr., Dept. of Finance, TPG 78-81; Min. of Finance 81-84; Min. of Econ. Aff. 84-85; Chmn., Lien Ho Jr. Coll. of Tech. 86-88, & CFC, KMT 88-93, Dep. Sec.-Gen. 90-93; V. Premier, ROC 93-97; Chmn., CEPD 94-96. *Publ.: Theory of Modern Financial*

Policy; Theory of Modern Econ. Policy; Equity & Efficiency; Add. 122 Chungking S. Rd., Sect. 1, Taipei 100.

HSU, SHENG-FA
(See HSUI, SHENG-FA 許勝發)

HSU, SHUI-TE
(See HSU, SHUI-TEH 許水德)

HSU, SHUI-TEH 許水德
Pres., Exam. Yuan 96-; Mem., CSC, KMT 88-; b. Twn. Aug. 1, '31; m. Yang, Shu-hua; 2 s.; educ. Ed.B., NTNU; Ed.M., NCCU; Grad. Sch., U. of Tsukuba; Assc. Prof.; Adjunct Prof.; Dir., Bu. of Educ., Kaohsiung City Govt. 70-73, Chief Sec. 73-75; Comr., Dept. of Soc. Aff., TPG 75-79; Dir.-Gen., Dept. of Soc. Aff., CC, KMT 79; Sec.-Gen., Kaohsiung City Govt. 79-82; Mayor, Kaohsiung City 82-85, Taipei City 85-88; Min. of the Int. 88-91; Rep., TECROJ 91-93; Sec.-Gen., CC, KMT 93-96. Publ.: Blessing of Prudence & Tranquillity in a Misty Age—A Collection of Interviews During His Tenure of Sec.-Gen. of KMT (93-96); Breaking Through & Marching Forward—A Collection of Essays & Speeches During His Tenure of Sec.-Gen. of KMT (93-96); The Childhood Educ. of Emile; Psychology; Introduction to Psychology; Essay on Modern Educ.; A Study of High Sch. Curriculum in Japan; My Compliments—Recollections of Those Days Serving as Kaohsiung Mayor; A Thousand Sunrises & Midnights; My Scoopwheel Philosophy; A Study of Welfare Admin. for the Aged; Add. 1 Shih Yuan Rd., Wenshan, Taipei 116.

HSU, TSAI-EN 許再恩
Spkr., Taipei CoCoun. 90-; Chmn., Yungfeng Sec. Co. 90-; Adv., Ocean World; b. Taipei June 3, '42; m. Chang, Mei-ching; 1 s., 2 d.; educ. Grad., Nat. Taipei Coll. of Business; Chmn., Fu-hua Co. Ltd. & Fu-teh Co. Ltd.; Head & Corr., Hsintien Bu., Twn. Daily News; Dir. & Mgr., Changfeng Construction Co. Ltd.; Dir., Hsintien Lions Club Intl.; Dep. Dir., Soc. of Contemporary Forum; Add. 116 Wen Hua Rd., Sect. 2, Panchiao, Taipei County 220.

HSU, TSAI-LI 許財利
Spkr., Keelung CCoun. 90-, Mem. 82-; Leader, Keelung Voluntary Fire Service 90-; b. Twn. Nov. 5, '47; m. Chien, Hsiu-chin; 2 s., 1 d.; educ. Sun Yat-sen Inst. on Policy Res. & Dev. 92; Studied, Nat. Open U.; Mem., Urban Planning Cttee., Keelung 90-94; Chmn., Keelung CCoun. Mem. Assn. 91-94; Add. 5 Shou Shan Rd., Keelung 201.

HSU, TSANG-HOUEI 許常惠
Nat. Policy Adv. to the Pres. 96-; Dir., Grad. Inst. of Music, NTNU 91-, Prof. 80-; Pres., Ch. Folk Arts Found.; Chmn.,

Asian Composers League; Chmn., Asia Pacific Soc. for Ethnomusicology 90-; b. Twn. Sept. 6, '29; m. Lee, Chu-huei; 3 s.; educ. BA, Music, NTNU 53; MA, Institut de Musicologue, U. of Paris 54-59; Chmn., the Soc. for Ethnomusicology in Twn. 91-97; Chmn., Soc. of Music Education in Twn. 93-95; Dir., Grad. Inst. of Music, NTNU 91-94. Publ.: A Study of Debussy; Essays on Folk Music (3 Vol.); Colorful Music of Twn.; An Introduction to Ch. Ethnomusicology; Hist. of Music in Twn.; Compositions: Legend of the White Snake; C. of Lion Mountain; Spring for All; Ch. Festival Overture; etc.; Add. 5th Fl., 25 Lane 30, Hsin Sheng S. Rd., Sect. 2, Taipei 106.

HSU, WEN-CHENG 許文政
Nat. Policy Adv. to the Pres. 99-; Pres., Lo-Hsu Found. 69-; V. Chmn., NTU Gen. Alumni Assn. 97-; b. Twn. Feb. 5, '24; m. Hsu, Chiu-wei L.; 5 s., 1 d.; educ. MB, NTU 49; MD, Nat. Nagasaki U. 70; Chmn., Ilan Physicians' Assn. 64-70; Spkr., Ilan CoCoun. 73-81; Mem., Control Yuan 81-87; Adv., Exec. Yuan 89-98; Add. 83 Nan Chang St., Lotung, Ilan County 265.

HSU, WEN-CHIH
(See HSU, WEN-TSU 許文志)

HSU, WEN-LUNG
(See SHI, W.L. 許文龍)

HSU, WEN-PIN
(See HSU, WUN-PIN 許文彬)

HSU, WEN-TSU 許文志
Nat. Policy Adv. to the Pres. 98-; b. Twn. Sept. 30, '36; m. Lin, Su-chen; 2 s., 2 d.; educ. LL.B., Ch. Cul. U. 68; LL.B., Meiji U. 71; Magis., Yunlin County 81-89; Comr., Dept. of Recon., TPG 90-94; Sec.-Gen., TPG 94-96; Dir., Dept. of Org., CC, KMT 96-97; Add. 1st Fl., 2 Alley 1, Lane 307, Kang Ning St., Hsichih, Taipei County 221.

HSU, WUN-PIN 許文彬
Nat. Policy Adv. to the Pres. 96-; Mem., Cttee. for Nat. Health Ins. Dispute Review, DOH 95-; Sup., Nat. Lawyers Assn. of the ROC 93-; Mem., Twn. Lawyers Disciplinary Cttee. 96-; b. Twn. Nov. 3, '48; m. Liu, Yuen-ying; 1 s., 3 d.; educ. LL.B., NTU 70; Prosecutor, Twn. Kaohsiung Dist. Court 72-76; Add. 3rd Fl., 25 Jen Ai Rd., Sect. 2, Taipei 100.

HSU, YI-HSIUNG 徐義雄
Dep. Gov., CBC 98-; b. Twn. Sept. 29, '40; m. Hsu Liu, Fu-rong; 1 s., 2 d.; educ. MA, Econ., NTU 70, BBA, 63; Off., Sect. Chief, Dep. Div. Chief, Div. Chief, Asst. Dir.-Gen.,

CBC 63-86; Dep. Dir.-Gen., Econ. Res. Dept. 86-90; Dep. Dir.-Gen., Banking Exam. Dept. 90-93; Dep. Dir.-Gen., Bk. Dept. 93-96; Dir.-Gen., Bk. Exam. Dept. 96-98; *Add.* 2, Roosevelt Rd., Sect. 1, Taipei 100.

HSU, YI-HSUNG 許義雄
Pres., Sunrace Roots Enterprise Co. Ltd. 72-; *b.* Twn. Aug. 18, '41; *m.* Lin, Patty; 1 *s.,* 1 *d.; educ.* B., NCHU 67; Sales Mgr., Ta Ming Ind. 65-72; *Add.* 9 Lane 130, Kuang Fu Rd., Sect. 1, Sanchung, Taipei County 241.

HSU, YU-PU 許毓圃
Dep. Dir.-Gen., CPA 90-2000; *b.* Kwangtung Dec. 27, '34; 2 *s.,* 1 *d.; educ.* Grad., Supplementary Open Jr. Coll. for PA, NCCU 80, Grad. Prog., PA of Civil Servants 89; Staff, Dept. of Pers., Taichung City Govt. 60-64; Staff, Dept. of Finance, TPG 64-67; Sp. & Sect. Chief, CPA 67-72; Dir., Pers. Off., DOH 72-77; Sr. Sp. & Dep. Dir., CPA 77-81; Dep. Dir., Dept. of Pers., TCG 81-83; Counsl., Dir., & Chief Sec., CPA 83-90; *Add.* 10th Fl., 2-2 Chi Nan Rd., Sect. 1, Taipei 100.

HSU, YUAN-YIH 許源浴
Prof., Dept. of EE, NTU 87-; *b.* Twn. June 19, '55; *m.* Yang, Mu-jang; 1 *s.; educ.* BS, NTU 77, MS 80, Ph.D. 83; Instr., NTU 80-84, Assc. Prof. 84-87, V. Chair, Dept. of EE 92-94. *Publ.:* Over 97 intl. jour. papers & 50 reports & papers; *Add.* Dept. of EE, NTU, 1 Roosevelt, Sect. 4, Taipei 106.

HSU, YUAN-YU
(See HSU, YUAN-YIH 許源浴)

HSUEH, CHI
(See SCHIVE, CHI 薛琦)

HSUEH, CHING-HO
(See HSIUE, GING-HO 薛敬和)

HSUEH, HSIANG-CHUAN
(See HSIEH, H. STEVE 薛香川)

HSUI, SHENG-FA 許勝發
Nat. Policy Adv. to the Pres. 99-; V. Chmn., SEF 93-; Mem., NA 92-; Chmn., Prince Motors Group Corp., Cosmos Bk. 91-, & Ch. Chamber of Com. & Ind. 93-; Hon. Chmn., Ch. Fed. of Ind. 94-; *b.* Taipei Jan. 24, '25; *m.* Cheng, Wen-wen; 1 *s.,* 2 *d.; educ.* LL.B., NTU; Hon. Dr. of Business Admin., Santa Tomas U., Philippines 92; Chmn., Taipei County Ind. Assn. 75-81; Mem., Legis. Yuan 81-91, Dep. Sec.-Gen., KMT Caucus 84-86; Chmn.,

Twn. Prov. Ind. Assn. 81-87; Dep. Sec.-Gen., Policy Coordination Cttee., CC, KMT 86-88, Mem., CSC 88-93; Nat. Policy Adv. to the Pres. 95-97; *Add.* 50 Sungkiang Rd., Taipei 104.

HU, CHI-JU
(See HWU, REUBEN JIH-RU 胡紀如)

HU, CHIH-CHIANG
(See HU, JASON C. 胡志強)

HU, CHIN-PIAO
(See HU, CHING-PIAO 胡錦標)

HU, CHING-PIAO 胡錦標
Min. without Portfolio 2000-; *b.* Taipei July 1, '43; *m.* Huang, Su-yuan; 2 *s.,* 2 *d.; educ.* Ph.D., U. of Illinois 74; Assc. Prof., Civil Engr. Dept., NTU 74-76; Res. Visiting Prof., Cornell U. 77-78; Dep. Dir. & Dir., Tjingling Ind. Res. Inst. 80-89; Dir., Engr. & Applied Sc. Div., NScC 89-90.; V. Chmn., NScC 90-96; Prof., Dept. of Mech. Engr., NTU 79-99; Chmn., AEC 96-2000. *Publ.:* 4 bk. & over 70 acad. papers; *Add.* Exec. Yuan, 1 Chung Hsiao E. Rd., Sect. 1, Taipei 100.

HU, CHUN-HUNG
(See HU, CHUNG-HONG 胡俊弘)

HU, CHUNG-HONG 胡俊弘
Pres., Taipei Med. Coll. 90-; Clinical Prof., Stanford U. 91-; *b.* Taipei Jan. 1, '42; *m.* Hu, Mimi; 2 *s.; educ.* MD, Taipei Med. Coll. 66; Instr., Mayo Med. Sch. 74-75; Asst. Prof., Case We. Reserve U., USA 75-79; Dir., Dermato-pathology, U. Hosp. of Cleveland 77-79; Asst. Prof. & Assc. Prof., Stanford U. 79-90; Chief, Dermatology, Palo Alto Veterans Admin. Med. Cent. 79-85; Dir., Dermatology Clinic, Stanford U. Med. Cent. 85-90; Visiting Prof., U. of Geneva 90. *Publ.:* 45 papers, 16 abstracts, & 9 chapters; *Add.* 250 Wu Hsing St., Taipei 110.

HU, FU 胡佛
Prof., Dept. of Pol. Sc., NTU; U. Chair, NTU 98-99; Mem., Acad. Sinica 98-; *b.* Kiangsu May 14, '32; *m.* Hu Han, Hsia-ying; 4 *c.; educ.* LL.B., NTU 55; MPS, Emory U. 60; Visiting Scholar, Yale U. 69-70; Res. Fel., NScC 73-74; Visiting Scholar, U. of Chicago & Columbia U. 87-88. *Publ.: The Structure of Pol. Cul.; Issue Orientations of the Voter; Behavior of Pol. Participation of the People on Twn.; The Structural Variation & Recon. of Our Const. System; Add.* 16 Lane 61, Ta Hu Villa St., Neihu, Taipei 114.

HU, JASON C. 胡志強

Dir.-Gen., Dept. of Cul. Aff., KMT 2000-; Mem., CC, KMT 93-, Mem., CAC 98-; *b*. Kirin May 15, '48; *m*. Shaw, Shirley; 1 *s*., 1 *d*.; *educ*. LL.B., Dept. of Dip., NCCU 70; M. of Soc. Sc., Dept. of Pol., U. of Southampton 78; D.Phil., Oxford U. 84; Res. Fel., St. Anthony's Coll., Oxford U. 85; Assc. Prof., Sun Yat-sen Inst. for Interdisciplinary Studies, Nat. Sun Yat-Sen U. 86-90; Dep. Dir., 1st Bu., Off. of the Pres. 91; Chief, Conf. Dept., NUC 90-91; Dir.-Gen., GIO & Govt. Spokesman 91-96; Rep., TECRO, Washington, D.C. 96-97; Min. of For. Aff. 97-99. *Publ.: "On the Role of PLA in Post-Mao Ch. Pol.," Ch. Pol. After Mao* 77; *Add*. 11 Chung Shan S. Rd., Taipei 104.

HU, LIU-YUAN
(See WOO, SAVIO LAU-YUEN 胡溜源)

HU, MAO-LIN 胡戀麟
Pres., Nat. Chiayi Inst. of Tech. 97-; Pres., Ch. Soc. of Agronomy ; *b*. Twn. Jan. 6, '46; *m*. Chang, Li-yun; 1 *s*., 1 *d*.; *educ*. BS, NTU 68; Ph.D., Washington State U. 74; Res. Assc., Washington State U. 74; Assc. Prof., Prov. Chiayi Inst. of Agr. 75-79, Prof. & concur. Dean of Studies 80-85; Dean of Student Aff., Nat. Chiayi Inst. of Agri. 86-89, Pres. 90-97. *Publ.: Genetic Study on Semidwarfism of Wheat; Add*. 300 U. Rd., Chiayi 600.

HU, SHIH-CHEN
(See HU, SZE-TSEN 胡世楨)

HU, SZE-TSEN 胡世楨
Mem., Acad. Sinica 66-; Prof. of Math., UCLA 60-; *b*. Chekiang Oct. 9, '14; *m*. Wang, Shia-zong; 1 *s*., 1 *d*.; *educ*. BS, NCU 38; Ph.D. & D.Sc., U. of Manchester; Assc. Res. Fel., Acad. Sinica 47-48; Mem., Inst. for Advanced Study, Princeton U. 50-52; Assc. Prof., Tulane U. 52-55; Prof., U. of Georgia 55-56, & Wayne State U. 56-60. *Publ.: Homotopy Theory; Introduction to Contemporary Math.; Elements of Gen. Topology; Elements of Modern Algebra; Threshold Logic; Homology Theory; Math. Theory of Switching Circuit & Automata; Differentiable Manifolds; Calculus; Linear Algebra with Differential Equation;* etc.; *Add*. 1076 Tellem Drive, Pacific Palisades, CA 90272-2242, USA.

HU, WEI-JEN 胡爲眞
Dep. Sec.-Gen., NSC 99-2000; Adjunct Assc. Prof., NCCU 93-; *b*. Nanking Aug. 4, '47; *m*. Lin, Hui-ying; 2 *s*., 2 *d*.; *educ*. LL.B., NCU 69; MS in Foreign Studies, Georgetown U. 72; Ph.D., U. of Pretoria, S. Africa 88; Intern Prog., UN 71; Jr. & Sr. Off., MOFA 72-79; Counsl., Dir., Consul Gen.

& Dir.-Gen., MOFA off. stationed ovs. 79-91; Dir.-Gen. of MOFA dept. 91-93; 2nd Dep. Dir.-Gen., Nat. Sec. Bu. 93-97, 1st Dep. Dir.-Gen. 97-99. *Publ.: The Strategic Significance of the ROC on Twn.* 88; *Soviet Policy Toward the ROC Reflected in Its Ch. Lang. Broadcast Prog.* 78; etc.; *Add*. 122 Chungking S. Rd., Sect. 1, Taipei 100.

HUA, CHIA-CHIH 華加志
Chmn., Coun. of Aboriginal Aff., Exec. Yuan 96-2000; *b*. Twn. Apr. 2, '36; *m*. Lee, Yan-mey; 1 *s*., 2 *d*.; *educ*. Ed.B., NTNU; High sch. tchr.; Mem., TPA; Comr., TPG; Chmn., Cul. Assn. of Twn. Indigenous Peoples; Pub., *Sanhai Cul. Mag.; Add*. 17th Fl., 4 Chung Hsiao W. Rd., Sect. 1, Taipei 100.

HUANG, ALICE S. 黃詩厚
Mem., Acad. Sinica 90-, Sr. Coun. External Rel. Fac. Assc. Biology, Calif. Inst. Tech. 97-; Dean for Sc. & Prof. of Biology, New York U. 91-97; Sc. Adv., Inst. of Molecular & Cell Biology, Nat. U. of Singapore 84-; Trustee, Found. for Microbiology, New York 86-, Chair 93-; Trustee, Johns Hopkins U. 92-; *b*. Kiangsi Mar. 22, '39; *m*. Baltimore, David; 1 *c*.; *educ*. BA, Johns Hopkins U. 61, MA, Microbiology 63, Ph.D. 66; Hon. MA, Harvard U. 80; Hon. D.Sc., Wheaton Coll., USA 82, Mt. Holyoke Coll., USA 87, & Med. Coll. of Penn. 91; Postdr. Fel., Salk Inst. for Biological Studies, San Diego 67 & Postdr. Fel., Dept. of Biology, MIT 68-69, Res. Assc. 69-70; Lectr., Acad. Sinica 70; Asst. Prof., Microbiology & Molecular Genetics, Harvard Med. Sch. 71-73, Assc. Prof. 73-78, Prof. 79-91; Prof., Microbiology in Health Sc. & Tech., Harvard-MIT Prog. 79-91; Dir., Lab. of Infectious Diseases, C.'s Hosp., Boston 79-89; Trustee, U. of Massachusetts 88-92. *Publ.:* Over 100 papers on vesicular stomatitis virus; *Add*. Mail Code 1-9, Calif. Inst. of Tech., Pasadena, CA 91106, USA.

HUANG, CHEN-TAI
(See HWANG, JENN-TAI 黃鎮台)

HUANG, CHEN-YEH 黃鎮岳
Nat. Policy Adv. to the Pres. 99-; *b*. Twn. Jan. 26, '35; *m*. Hung, Mai-yeh; 2 *s*., 2 *d*.; *educ*. LL.B., Soochow U. 58; high sch. tchr. 61-63; Mem., Yunlin CoCoun. 64-73; Mem., TPA 73-93, Dep. Spkr. 81-93; Mem., Control Yuan 93-99; *Add*. 122 Chungking S. Rd., Sect. 1, Taipei 100.

HUANG, CHEN-YUEH
(See HUANG, CHEN-YEH 黃鎮岳)

HUANG, CHENG-HSIUNG
(See HWANG, JENG-SHYONG 黃正雄)

HUANG, CHENG-KU
(See HWANG, CHEN-KU 黃正鵠)

HUANG, CHENG-WANG 黃政旺
Chmn., Yakult Co. Ltd. 98-, Tailung Corp. 91-, Tai Ling Motor Co. Ltd. 74-, Bridgestone Twn. Co. Ltd. 84-, Hotung Investment Holdings Ltd. 97; V. Chmn., Fortune Motors Co. Ltd. 93-; Standing Mem., Bd. of Dir., Cathay United Bk. 97-; Standing Mem., Bd. of Sup., Importers & Exporters Assn. of Taipei 97-; *b.* Taipei Aug. 1, '30; *m.* Huang, Wu-zen; 2 *s.,* 1 *d.; educ.* MA, Econ., U. of Washington, Seattle 57; *Add.* 12th Fl., 261 Sungkiang Rd., Taipei 104.

HUANG, CHENG-WEN 黃正文
Pres., Chung-Tai Inst. of Health Sc. & Tech. 98-; V. Pres., NTU Alumni Assn. 98-; *b.* Twn. Jan. 6, '42; *m.* Lo, Su-huei; 1 *d.; educ.* B., Med. Tech. Dept., NTU 66; M., Mng. Sc., Baker U., USA 93; Med. Technologist, Naval Am. Med. Res. Unit II 68-71; V. Pres. & concur. Dir., Med. Tech. Dept., Hsun-Tien Hosp. 71-81; Chief Sec., Chung-tai Med. Tech. Coll. 71-84, Pres. 84-98; Pres., Twn. Med. Technologists Assn. 85-91; Pres., S.W. Rotary Club 85-91. *Publ.: A Survey on Med. Tech. Educ. in 5-Year Jr. Coll.* 93; *An Evaluation of Serum Carcinoembryonic Antigenetic Test—A Methodology & Clinical Approach* 83; *An Evaluation of Noraml Blood Viscosity* 85; *A Survey on Underground Drinking Water at the Foothill of Mt. Tatu, Nantun Dist., Taichung* 88; *Add.* 11 Pu Tzu Lane, Peitun, Taichung 406.

HUANG, CHI
(See HWANG, CHYI 黃奇)

HUANG, CHI-CHUAN 黃啓川
Spkr., Kaohsiung CCoun. 98-, Coun. 77-; Pres., Ta-jung Sec. Corp., Ltd. 97-; *b.* Kaohsiung June 29, '50; *m.* Huang Ho, Tsai-feng; 2 *s.,* 1 *d.; educ.* BCE, Tsenghsiu Engr. Coll. 71; Founder & Pres., Alumni Assn., Tsenghsiu Engr. Coll. 78-82; Pres., Intl. Lions Assn. Dist. 300 E 83-84; Pres., Parent Assn., Tsenghsing Elementary Sch. 88-91; *Add.* 192 Chung Cheng 4th Rd., Kaohsiung 801.

HUANG, CHIA-MING 黃嘉明
Chmn., Twn. Prov. Certified Public Accts. (CPA) Assn. 92-; Comr., Com. for the Discipline of CPA 93-; Dir., Acct. Res. & Dev. Found. 93-; CPA, Chia-ming CPA 73-; *b.* Kaohsiung May 26, '40; *m.* Chiang, Chin-feng; 1 *s.,* 2 *d.; educ.* B., Com., NCHU 69; Pers. Mng., Twn. Power Corp. 61-65; Accts. Mng., MOEA 65-73; Sup., Taipei City CPA Assn. 80-83; Dir. & Mng. Dir., Twn. Prov. CPA Assn. 83-92; Dir., Nat. Fed. of CPA Assns. (NFCPA) of ROC 89-92; NFCPA-Rep., Twn. Prov. & Taipei City CPA Assn. 86-92; Chief Comr., Com. for the Discipline of Twn. Prov. CPA Assn. 89-92; *Add.* 9th Fl.-1, 1 Nan Hai Rd., Taipei 100.

HUANG, CHIH-HSIANG
(See HUANG, JACK C. 黃致祥)

HUANG, CHING-FENG
(See HWANG, CHING-FONG 黃鏡峰)

HUANG, CHU-WEN 黃主文
Min. of the Int. 98-2000; Mem., CSC, KMT 99-; *b.* Twn. Aug. 20, '41; *m.* Huang, Shu-ling; 1 *s.,* 1 *d.; educ.* LL.B., NTU; Tng. Cent. for Jud. Off.; Public Prosecutor 68-78; Attorney-at-Law 78-81; Mem., Legis. Yuan 83-98; Dep. Exec. Dir., Policy Coordination Cttee., CC, KMT 93-98. *Publ:* 14 bks.; *Add.* 5 Hsuchow Rd., Taipei 100.

HUANG, FU-SHUN 黃富順
Pres., Nat. Chiayi Tchrs.' Coll. 96-; Sec.-Gen., Ch. Adult Educ. Assn. (Taipei) 90-; *b.* Twn. June 25,'44; *m.* Liau, Iue-li; 2 *d.; educ.* Ph.D., NTNU; Assc. Prof., Dept. of Soc. Educ., NTNU 85-88, Prof., 89-95; Dir., Adult & Continuing Educ., Nat. Chung Cheng U. 93-96. *Publ.: Motivation of Adult Learning; Comparative Adult Educ.; Adult Dev. & Learning; Adult Dev.; Aging & Health; Ch. Adult Educ. Dictionary; Add.* 85 Wenlung Village, Minhsiung, Chiayi County 621.

HUANG, HAI-TAI 黃海岱
Leading Dir., Wu-Chou Garden Glove Puppet Troupe 31-; *b.* Twn. Jan. 2, '01; *m.* Hung, Chin-kuei; 8 *s.,* 4 *d.; educ.* Studied Ch. Classics in trad. Ch. private sch.; Learnt Chuanchou's Nan-chuan puppeteering from Huang Ma 19; Apprenticed to Wang Mun-yuan (M. of Pei-chuan music) at Chin-Chun Chai 25; Specialized in performing lawsuit stories, swordman stories, & Chin-kuang stories; Performed in the US & France 93 & 95; Awarded Nat. Folk Artist 98. *Publ.:* Numerous playscripts (15 were perserved by the govt.); *Add.* 64 Cheng Kung Rd., Tungming Village, Lunpei, Yunlin County 637.

HUANG, HSIEN-JUNG
(See HUANG, HSIEN-YUNG 黃顯榮)

HUANG, HSIEN-YUNG 黃顯榮
Rep., TECO in Thailand 98-; *b.* Twn. Aug. 9, '35; *m.* Tzeng, Fang-ching; 2 *s.,* 1 *d.; educ.* Grad., Ch. Air Force Acad. 58; Squadron Off. Course 59, Regular Course 76,

Air Cmd. & Staff Coll.; War Coll., Armed Forces U. 85; Fighter Pilot, Element Leader, & Squadron Cmdr. 58-74; Dir., Pol. Warfare Dept., 828th Wing ROCAF 82-84, 455th Wing Cmdr. 86-88, Dep. Chief of Staff for Op. 88-90, V. CG, Combat Air Cmd. 90-91, Insp.-Gen. 92, CG 92-94, Dep. C-in-C 94-95; C-in-C, ROCAF 95-98; *Add.* 10th Fl., Kian Gwan Bldg. (1), 140 Witthayu Rd., Bangkok, Thailand.

HUANG, HSIN-PI 黃新璧
Rep., TECO, Poland 97-; *b.* Twn. Mar. 26, '33; *m.* Chang, Ming-tze; *educ.* LL.B., NTU 56; Grad. Sch., NCCU 58-61; Sec., Emb. in Japan 61-66; Sec. to Min., MOFA 66-69, Dep. Dir.-Gen., Off. of Records & Compilation 69-71; Consul-Gen., Fukuoka, Japan 71-72; Chief, Osaka Off., AEAR 73-75; Dep. Dir., Dept. of E. Asian & Pacific Aff., MOFA 75-78; Counsl., Emb. in Korea 78-85, Min. 85-88; Chief Sec., MOFA 89-90, Dir.-Gen., Dept. of Info. & Cul. Aff. & concur. Spokesman 90-91; Rep., TECO, Malaysia 91-97; Rep., TECO, Poland 97; *Add.* 4th Fl., Koszykowa St. 54, 00-675 Warsaw, Poland.

HUANG, HUAN-CHI 黃煥吉
Spkr., Hsinchu CoCoun. 94-; *b.* Twn. Mar. 19, '40; *m.* Wen, Yueh-mei; 3 *s.,* 1 *d.; educ.* Grad., Chutung Jr. High Sch.; Mem., Dep. Chmn., & Chmn., Chutung Rep. Conf.; *Add.* 48 Lane 664, Chang Chun Rd., Chutung, Hsinchu County 310.

HUANG, HUANG-HSIUNG 黃煌雄
Mem., Control Yuan 99-; Chmn., Twn. Res. Found. 88-; *b.* Twn. Sep. 15, '44; *m.* Wu, Yueh-er; 3 *d.; educ.* B., Pol., NTU 67; M., Pol., NTU 71; Visiting Scholar, Fairbank Cent. for E. Asian Res., Harvard U. 96-98; Mem., Legis. Yuan 81-84, 87-90, & 93-96; Rep., NA 92-93. *Publ.: On the Her-tsung & Lien-heng Strategies During the Warring States Period* 75; *Chiang Wei-shui: the Formosan Prophetic Mentor* 76; *The Hist. of Formosan Resistance Against Japanese Rule* 77; *Strategies—Twn. Marching Forward;* etc.; *Add.* 2 Chung Hsiao E. Rd., Sect. 1, Taipei 100.

HUANG, HUI-CHEN
(See HUANG, HWEI-CHEN 黃輝珍)

HUANG, HWEI-CHEN 黃輝珍
Dir.-Gen., Dept. of Cul. Aff., CC, KMT 99-2000; *b.* Twn. Dec. 1, '54; *m.* Yang, Christina; *educ.* LL.B., NCCU; Dep. Chief Ed. Writer & concur. Chief. Ed., *Ch. Times;* Exec. Dir., Inst. for Nat. Policy Res., Chang Yung-fa Found.; Publ., *CDN* 96-99; *Add.* 7th Fl., 11 Chung Shan S. Rd., Taipei 104.

HUANG, JACK C. 黃致祥
Pub. & concur. Dir., *Ch. Post* 93-; Exec. Dir., Nancy Yu Huang Found. 92-; Mem., PHILAMBDA, Intl. Advertising Assn. 94-; *b.* Taipei Mar. 7, '49; *m.* Chao, Yu; 1 *s.; educ.* BA, Ch. Lit., Soochow U. 71; MS, Jour., So. Illinois U. 76; MS, Telecomms. Mng., Golden Gate U., USA 86; Reporter & Ovs. Corr., *Ch. Post* 69-73, Dep. Dir. 76-83, Dir. 90-93; Lectr., Dept. of Mass Comm., Ch. Cul. U. 73-74 & 94-96; Business Broker, Vendorhurst 86-87; Bd. Chmn., Taipei Newspapers Assn. 97-99. *Publ.: A Study of a Day's Newspaper* 71; *Add.* 8 Fu Shun St., Taipei 104.

HUANG, JONG-TSUN 黃榮村
Min. without Portfolio 2000-; *b.* Twn. Mar. 30, '47; *m.* Hsu, Mei-kuei; 1 *s.; educ.* B., Psychology, NTU 69, M. 72, Ph.D. 76; Prof. & Dir., Dept. & Inst. of Psychology, NTU; Dir., NTU's Educ. Schedule Cent.; Convener, NTU Apr. 6th Incident Taskforce; Res. Fel., Acad. Sinica; Visiting Scholar, Harvard U., Carnegie-Mellon U. & UCLA; Chmn., Bd. of Trustees, Ch. Psychology Soc.; Standing Bd. Mem., Assn. of Promoting Coll. Educ. Reform; Mem., Educ. Reform Coun., Exec. Yuan & Implementation Cttee. of Educ. Reform; Mem., Jud. Reform Com.; Standing Dir., Civic Assn. of Jud. Reform; Dir., Humanities & Soc. Sc. Dept., NScC; Pres., Yuan-tseh Sc. Educ. Found.; CEO, Recon. Adv. Group (for rebuilding the nation after the Sept.21st, 1999 Earthquake). *Publ.:* (between 98-2000) *Visual Perception in Ch. People; Conjunction Searching as a Paradigm to Study the Interaction of the Functional Multichannel of Human Visual System* (with J.C. Yuan); *Disparity Interpolation in the Blind Spot* (with D. Tang); *Educ. Reform—Implications for Competitiveness, Equity & Democratization* (forthcoming); *The Effect of Object Type & Contour Complexity on Object Recognition* (with Wang Man-ying, forthcoming); & etc.; *Add.* Exec. Yuan, 1 Chung Hsiao E. Rd., Taipei 100.

HUANG, JUNG-TSUN
(See HUANG, JONG-TSUN 黃榮村)

HUANG, KUANG-CHIH 黃廣志
Pres., Nat. Kaohsiung Inst. of Tech. 97-; *b.* Twn. Apr. 26, '39; *m.* Liu, Pi-hsia; 1 *s.,* 1 *d.; educ.* BSEE, NCKU 62; MS, NCTU 67; Ph.D., Polytechnic Inst. of Brooklyn 70; Chmn. & Prof., Dept. of Electrophys., NCTU 73-78, Dean of Acad. Aff. 78-81; Dean, Coll. of Engr., Nat. Sun Yat-Sen U. 86-92; Pres., Nat. Kaohsiung Inst. of Tech. 92-98. *Publ.:* Over 200 papers on sc. & tech.; numerous commentaries on humanities; *Add.* 415 Chien Kung Rd., Kaohsiung 807.

HUANG, KUANG-NAN 黃光男
Dir., Nat. Museum of Hist. 95-; Prof., Grad. Sch. of Fine Arts, Nat. Inst. of the Arts, NTNU 95-; *b.* Kaohsiung Feb. 15, '44; *m.* Kuo, Chiu-yen; 2 *s.; educ.* BA, Ch., Nat. Kaohsiung Normal Coll. 81; MA, Fine Arts, NTNU 84; Ph.D., Ch. Lang. & Lit., Nat. Kaohsiung Normal U. 93; Lectr., Nat. Pingtung Tchrs.' Coll. 77-86; Assc. Prof., Fine Arts Dept., Nat. Twn. Acad. of Arts 87-93, & Grad. Sch. of Fine Arts, NTNU 88-93; Dir., Taipei Fine Arts Museum 86-95. *Publ.: Museum Marketing Strategies; Analyses of Five Twn. Painters; Painting Album of Kuang-Nan Huang* (4 Vol.); *Appreciation & Instruction of the Ch. Painting; A Study on the Style of the Flower & Bird Painting of Sung Dynasty; Aesthetics & Recognition; Museum Admin.; Temperature of Aesthetics; The Aesthetic Dynamism in Ch. Art & Lit.; Add.* 49 Nan Hai Rd., Taipei 100.

HUANG, KUN-HUEI 黃昆輝
Sec.-Gen., CC, KMT 99-2000; Mem., CSC, KMT 93-; *b.* Twn. Nov. 8, '36; *m.* Lin, Mann; 1 *s.,* 3 *d.; educ.* Ed.B., Twn. Prov. Normal U. 64, Ed.M. 67; Ed.D., U. of Nr. Colorado 71; Elementary & jr. high sch. tchr. 55-65; Teaching Asst., Dept. of Educ., Twn. Prov. Normal U. 65-67; Instr., Dept. of Educ., NTNU 67-71, Assc. Prof., Prof., & Dir., Grad. Inst. of Educ. 71-78, Dir., Dept. of Educ. 76-78; Comr., TPG 78-79; Dir., Bu. of Educ., TCG 79-81; Comr., Dept. of Educ., TPG 81-83; Dep. Dir.-Gen., Dept. of Cul. Aff., CC, KMT 83-84; V. Chmn., NYC 84-87; Dir.-Gen., Dept. of Youth Aff., CC, KMT 87-88; Min. without Portfolio 88-91; Chmn., MAC 91-94; Min. of the Int. 94-96; Sec.-Gen., Off. of the Pres. 96-99. *Publ.: Analysis of Investment in Educ.; Educ. Admin. & Educ. Issues; Theory & Practice of Educ. Admin.: Theory & Res.; Add.* 11 Chung Shan S. Rd., Taipei 104.

HUANG, KUN-HUI
(See HUANG, KUN-HUEI 黃昆輝)

HUANG, LI-CHING 黃麗卿
Dir.-Gen., Dept. of Women's Aff., CC, KMT 99-; *b.* Twn. Sept. 6, '55; *m.* Lin, Wen-hsiang; 1 *s.,* 1 *d.; educ.* LL.B., Cent. Police Coll. 78; LL.M., Munich U. 92; Dir., Dept. of Women's Aff., Taoyuan County Cttee., KMT 81-89, Chmn., Dept. of Women's Aff., CC 89-94, Dir.-Gen., Hsinchu City Cttee. 94-96, Dep. Dir.-Gen., Dept. of Women's Aff., CC, & concur. Dir.-Gen., Taoyuan County Cttee. 96-97; Dir.-Gen., Dept. of Cul. Aff., CC, KMT 97-99; *Add.* 4th Fl., 11 Chung Shan S. Rd., Taipei 104.

HUANG, LUNG-YUAN
(See HWANG, FRANCISCO L.Y. 黃瀧元)

HUANG, MAO-HSIUNG
(See HUANG, THEODORE M.H. 黃茂雄)

HUANG, NAN-TU 黃南圖
Chmn., Concord System Mng. Corp., Twn. 95-, Concord System Corp., Twn. 95-; *b.* Taipei Oct. 16, '46; *m.* Lin, Lee-Hwa; 1 *s.,* 1 *d.; educ.* MBA, U. of S. Calif.; Exec. V. Pres., Wei Chuan Foods Corp., USA 72-80; Pres., Concord Trust Corp., USA 77-80; Chmn., Wei Chuan Foods Corp., Twn. 95-98; *Add.* 16th Fl., 176 Keelung Rd., Sect. 1, Taipei 110.

HUANG, PIEN-CHIEN 黃秉乾
Mem., Inst. of Molecular Biology, Acad. Sinica 86-; Prof., Biomed., NTHU 93-, Dean, Coll. of Life Sc. 93-; Prof., Johns Hopkins U. 65-; *b.* Shanghai July 13, '31; *m.* Chow, Ru-chih; 1 *s.,* 1 *d.; educ.* BS, NTU 52; MS, Virginia Polytechnic Inst. 56; Ph.D., Ohio State U.; Fel., Calif. Inst. of Tech. 60-65; Asst. Prof. & Assc. Prof., Johns Hopkins U.; Visiting Prof., Cambridge U. 72. *Publ.:* Over 100 res. articles; *Add.* NTHU, Hsinchu 300.

HUANG, PING-CHIEN
(See HUANG, PIEN-CHIEN 黃秉乾)

HUANG, SHI H. 黃世惠
Chmn., Chinfon Group; *b.* Taipei May 7, '26; *m.* Huang, Janet; 1 *s.,* 2 *d.; educ.* MD, NTU, & Washington U.; Resident & Fel. in Neurosurgery, Washington U., Barnes Hosp. 53-59; V. Supt., Yodogawa Christian Hosp., Japan 59-74; Prof. of Neurosurgery, Washington U. 75-80; *Add.* 14th Fl., 180 Chung Hsiao E. Rd., Sect. 4, Taipei 106.

HUANG, SHIH-CHENG 黃石城
Acting Chmn., CEIC 2000-; Nat. Policy Adv. to the Pres. 96-; Pres., Ch. Taipei Football Assn. 98-; Sec.-Gen., Nat. Cul. Assn. 91-; Chmn., CEIC 94-; Pres., World Ch. Writer's Assn. 93-; *b.* Twn. Aug. 27, '35; *m.* Chen, Chau-o; 2 *s.,* 1 *d.; educ.* LL.B., Soochow U.; Hon. Ph.D., U. of Bridgeport, USA; Lawyer 66-81; Magis., Changhua County 81-89; Del., Nat. Aff. Conf. 90; Min. without Portfolio 90-96; *Add.* 5 Hsuchow Rd., Taipei 100.

HUANG, SHIH-HOU
(See HUANG, ALICE S. 黃詩厚)

HUANG, SHIH-HUI
(See HUANG, SHI H. 黃世惠)

HUANG, SHOU-KAO
(See HUANG, SHOU-KAU 黃守高)

HUANG, SHOU-KAU 黃守高
Mem., Control Yuan 99-; *b.* Taipei July 10, '38; *m.* Lin, Chiung-chen; 2 *s.,* 1 *d.; educ.* LL.B., NTU 60, LL.M. 64; Chief Sec., Min. of Pers. 75-77; Counsl., Jud. Yuan 77-78; Chief Sec., MOTC 78-82; Chief Sec., MOJ 82-85, Dept. Dir. 85-87; Chmn., Cttee. of Legal Aff. & Appeals, Exec. Yuan 87-95; Admin. V. Min. of the Int. 95-99. *Publ.: The Comparative Res. of Modern Admin. Penalty; The Soc. Mission of Modern Admin. Law; Add.* 2 Chung Hsiao E. Rd., Sect. 1, Taipei 100.

HUANG, TA-CHOU 黃大洲
Min. without Portfolio 97-2000; Pres., Ch. Taipei Olympic Cttee. 98-; *b.* Twn. Feb. 7, '36; *m.* Lin, Wen-ying; 2 *d.; educ.* BS, Agr. Econ., NTU 60, MS, 62; MS, Rural Sociology, Cornell U. 66, Ph.D., Rural Dev. 71; Instr., NTU 66-68, Assc. Prof. 71-76; Sr. Res. Fel., E.-W. Cent., Hawaii 76 & 77; Prof., NTU 76; Counsl., CEPD 77; Adv., TCG 79-81; Exec. Sec., RDEC 79-81; Dep. Sec.-Gen., TPG 81-84; Dean of Business Aff., NTU 84-87; Sec.-Gen., TCG 87-90; Fel., Eisenhower Exchange Fel. 89; Acting Mayor, Taipei City 90, Mayor 90-94; Coun. Mem., CEPD 94-96; Chmn., RDEC 96-97; Mem., CSC, KMT 93-97. *Publ.:* 38 articles & bk.; *Add.* 1 Chung Hsiao E. Rd., Sect. 1, Taipei 100.

HUANG, THEODORE M.H. 黃茂雄
Chmn., ROC & Australia Business Coun., TECO Elec. & Mach. Co. Ltd., Taian Elec. Co. Ltd.; V. Chmn., Coordinate Coun. on Sino-Japanese Business Aff.; *b.* Twn. June 19, '39; *m.* Lynn, H.H.; 2 *s.,* 1 *d.; educ.* BA, Econ., Keio U., Japan 62; MBA, Wharton Sch., U. of Penn. 64; Chmn., Twn. Chapter of Young Pres. Org., Elec. & Elect. Products Dev. Assn.; Pres., Taian Elec. Co. Ltd.; *Add.* 156-2 Sungkiang Rd., Taipei 104.

HUANG, TING-CHIA 黃定加
Nat. Chair. Prof. 97-; Prof. Emeritus, Dept. of Chem. Engr., NCKU 98-; *b.* Twn. June 1, '32; *m.* Huang Wan, Juei-chin; 2 *s.,* 2 *d.; educ.* BS, NCKU 55; Dr. of Engr., U. of Tokyo 79; IAEA Res. Fel., Japan Atomic Energy Res. Inst., Tokaimura, Ibaraki-ken 62; Res. Assc., Dept. of Chem. Engr., U. of Houston 69-70; Prof., Dept. of Chem. Engr., NCKU 68-98; Chmn. & Dir., Dept. of Chem. Engr., NCKU 81-87; Consultant, MOE 88-94; V. Pres., NCKU 95-97, Acting Pres. 96-97. *Publ.: Experimental Phys. Chem.* 63; *Chem. Engr. Thermodynamics* 71; *Phys. Chem.* 78; *Experiments in Phys. Chem.* 83; over 170 articles to prof. jour., proceedings & symposiums; *Add.* Dept. of Chem. Engr., NCKU, 1 U. Rd., Tainan 70101.

HUANG, TSUN-CHIU
(See HWANG, TZUEN-CHIOU 黃尊秋)

HUANG, WEN-HSIUNG 黃文雄
Dir.-Gen., Park Admin., Hsinchu Sc.-based Ind. Park (SIP) 99-; Prof., NTNU 92-, Dept. of Air-Conditioning & Refrigeration, Nat. U. of Tech. 98; *b.* Twn. Oct. 21, '41; *m.* Huang, Li-hwa; 1 *s.,* 2 *d.; educ.* M., Philippines' Asia Mng. Coll. 72; MS, Mech. Engr., Stanford U. 71; Dr., Engr., Tokyo U. 77; Prof. & Dir., Grad. Sch. of Mech. Engr., Tatung U. 77-88; Dep. Exec. Sec., Energy Com., MOEA 88-92; Dir.-Gen., Precision Instrument Dev. Cent. 92-99, Preparatory Off. of the Tainan SIP 98-99. *Publ.: Solar Energy; Heat Transfer;* & 80 acad. papers; *Add.* 2 Hsin An Rd., Hsinchu Sc.-based Ind. Park, Hsinchu 300.

HUANG, WEN-CHUNG
(See HUANG, WEN-JUNG 黃文忠)

HUANG, WEN-JUNG 黃文忠
V. Chmn., Nat. Coun. on Phys. Fitness & Sports, Exec. Yuan 98-2000; *b.* Twn. Dec. 10, '46; *m.* Liang, Shyh-chyn; 1 *d.; educ.* B, Ch. Cul. U.; Assc. Prof., NCU 82-89; Gen. Sec., Ch. Taipei U. Sports Fed. 93-97; *Add.* 11th Fl., 80 Chien Kuo N. Rd., Sect. 1, Taipei 104.

HUANG, YEN-CHAO 黃演鈔
Rep., Taipei Rep. Off. in Belgium 95-; *b.* Twn. Oct. 31, '34; *m.* Lin, Mei-hui; 3 *c.; educ.* LL.B., NTU; Staff, MOFA 61-64; 3rd Sec., Emb. in Italy 64-66; 2nd & 1st Sec., Ch. Mission to the European Off. of the UN 66-72; Dir., Off. in Switzerland, MOEA 75-83, Dir., Investment & Trade Service Off. in USA 83-86, Dir.-Gen., Bu. of Standard & Quality Assurance 86-93; Dir.-Gen., Bd. of For. Trade, MOEA 93-94. *Publ.: Res. on the European Common Market; Questions on the Euro Dollar; Econ. Growth & Soc. Justice; Add.* Av. des Arts, 41, B, 1040 Brussels, Belgium.

HUANG, YU-WEN 黃郁文
Spkr., Tainan CCoun. 98-; *b.* Twn. July 23, '57; 1 *s.,* 1 *d.; educ.* High Sch. Grad.; Undergrad.; Mem., Tainan CCoun. 94-98; Chmn., Baseball Assn. of Tainan City 95-99; *Add.* 2 Yung Hua Rd., Sect. 2, Tainan 708.

HUANG, YUN-CHEH 黃允哲
Rep., Taipei Cul. & Econ. Del. in Switzerland 98-; *b.* Twn. June 4, '42; *m.* Shaw, Ming-lien; 1 *d.; educ.* LL.B., For. Aff. Dept., NCU 63; 2nd Sec., Emb. in Zaire 68-72, & Emb. in Niger 72-73; Sect. Chief, Dept. of African Aff.,

MOFA 72-76, Dep. Dir. 76; 1st Sec., Emb. in Ivory Coast 76-79; Dep. Dir., Dept. of Intl. Aff. 79-82; Dir., Service Div., CCNAA, Off. in USA 82-90; Dir., 2nd Dept., Exec. Yuan 90-91; Amb. to Cent. African Repub. 91-94; Dir.-Gen., Dept. of Pers., MOFA 94-98; *Add.* Monbijoustrasse 30, 3011 Bern, Suisse, Switzerland.

HUANG CHOU, JU-CHI
(See HUANG CHOW, RU-CHIH 黃周汝吉)

HUANG CHOW, RU-CHIH 黃周汝吉
Mem., Acad. Sinica 82-; Prof., Johns Hopkins U. 75-; *b.* Nanking Apr. 2, '32; *m.* Huang, Pien-chien; 1 *s.*, 1 *d.; educ.* BS, NTU; Ph.D., Ohio State U.; Fel., Calif. Inst. of Tech. 50-55; Resr., Calif. Inst. of Tech. 60-65; Asst. Prof., Johns Hopkins U. 65-67, Assc. Prof. 71-75; *Add.* 4604 Kerneway, Baltimore, MD 21212, USA.

HUNG, CHAO-NAN 洪昭男
Dir., Policy Res. Cttee., KMT 98-; Mem. & Convener, Legis. Yuan 80-; *b.* Twn. Aug. 24, '43; *m.* Chang, Yen-ju; 2 *s.; educ.* BA, Soochow U. 65; MA, U. of Arkansas, USA 75; Sr. Official, Inspectorate Gen. of Customs, MOF 67-69; Sect. Chief, MOFA 69-79; Sec., CCNAA, Off. in San Francisco 79-81. *Publ.: Dev. & Progress of the ROC; Add.* 9th Fl., 11 Chung Shan S. Rd., Taipei 100.

HUNG, CHI-CHUN 洪吉春
Nat. Policy Adv. to the Pres.; Adv., TPG; Mem., CAC, KMT; V. Pres., ROC Sports Fed. 94-; Chmn., Twn. Prov. Sports Fed. 93-, & Taipei County Cul. Fed. 90-; *b.* Twn. Dec. 5, '31; *m.* Wang, Sheh; 3 *s.*, 2 *d.; educ.* Nat. Taipei U. of Tech.; Mem., Taipei CoCoun. 68-82, Dep. Spkr. 82-86, Spkr. 87-90; *Add.* 28th Fl., 37 San Min Rd., Sect. 2, Panchiao, Taipei County 220.

HUNG, CHI-JEN
(See HUNG, CHI-REN 洪啓仁)

HUNG, CHI-REN 洪啓仁
Dir., Shin Kong Wu Hong-su Memorial Hosp., Chief, Cardiovascular Surgery 92-; Prof. Emertius, NTU 92-; *b.* Twn. Aug. 30, '30; *m.* Hung Chan, Tsai-fan; 5 *d.; educ.* MD, NTU 56; Fel. in Cardiac Surgery, New York Columbia-Presbyterian Med. Cent. 63-65; Prof., Med. Sch., NTU; Chmn., Dept. of Surgery, NTU Hosp.; Pres., Surgical Assn., ROC, Ch. Chapter, Int. Coll. of Surgeons, & Assn. of Thoracic & Cardiovascular Surgery, ROC. *Publ.:* med. lit.; *Add.* 95 Wen Chang Rd., Shihlin, Taipei 111.

HUNG, CHIEN-CHAO 洪健昭
Rep., Ufficio di Rappresentanza di Taipei in Italia 93-; *b.* Twn. Feb. 15, '32; *m.* Lu, Li-ying; 1 *d.; educ.* BA, NTU 54; MA, So. Illinois U. 65; Ph.D., Georgetown U. 81; M. Checker, Army GHQ 58-60; Chief Press Ed., USIS, Taipei 60-64; Assc. Prof., NCCU 66-73; Mng. Dir., *Ch. Post* 65-70; Chief, Eng. Dept., CNA 71-74, Bu. Chief, Middle E. 74-77, Chief Corr., Washington, D.C. 77-80, Bu. Chief, Houston 80-83, Tokyo 83-87, & W. Europe 87-89; Pres., CNA 90-93. *Publ.: Twn. Today; Formosa Under the Cheng; Add.* Via Panama 22 PI, Int. 3, 00198 Rome, Italy.

HUNG, MIN-HSIUNG
(See HON, MIN-HSIUNG 洪敏雄)

HUNG, TUNG-KUEI 洪多桂
V. Min., OCAC 97-2000; Assc. Prof., NTNU; *b.* Twn. Dec. 6, '47; *m.* Su, Ming-teh; 1 *s.*, 2 *d.; educ.* Ed.B., NTNU 70, Ed.M. 73, Ed.D. 86; Postgrad. studies, UC-Berkly.; Lectr., Assc. Prof., Shih Chien Coll. 73-89; Assc. Prof., Ch. Cul. U. 87-89; Chief, Dept. of Alumni Assn., Sun Yat-Sen Inst. on Policy Res., & Dev. 89-91; Mem., NA 87-90; Convener, Educ. Cttee., 1st Sess., Legis. Yuan 93, Mem. 90-97. *Publ.: A Study on the Mental Health of Students at the Med. Coll.* 82; *A Study of Ch. Coll. Students' Adjustment Problems, Coping Behaviors, Preference of Help-seeking, & Related Factors* 86; *Add.* 16th Fl., 5 Hsuchow Rd., Taipei 100.

HUNG, WEN-HSIANG 洪文湘
Mem. (ministerial rank), Exam. Yuan 90-; Prof., Dept. of Acct., NTU 78-; *b.* Anhwei Nov. 12, '40; *m.* Cheng, Hsueh-ying; *educ.* BBA, NTU 63; MBA, U. of Houston 67; Instr., NTU 70-73, Assc. Prof. 73-78, Chmn., Dept. of Business Admin. 75-79, Chmn., Grad. Sch. of Business Admin. 75-79. *Publ.: Goodwill; Issue of Price Level; CPA Exam. of ROC; Add.* 1 Shih Yuan Rd., Wenshan, Taipei 116.

HUNG, YU-CHIN
(See HONG, YUH-CHIN 洪玉欽)

HWANG, CHANG-CHIEN 黃彰健
Mem., Acad. Sinica 82-, Corr. Res. Fel., Inst. of Hist. & Philology 89-; *b.* Hunan Feb. 2, '19; *m.* Peng, Wei-tzu; 3 *d.; educ.* BA, NCU; Asst., Inst. of Hist. & Philology, Acad. Sinica 44-48, Asst. Res. Fel. 48-55, Assc. Res. Fel. 55-61, Res. Fel. 61-89; Nat. Res. Chair Prof., NScC 65-69. *Publ.: Studies on the Hist. of the 1898 Reform; On the Hist. of the Ming & Ch'ing Dynasties; The Authentic Memorials by K'ang Yu-wei in 1898; New Light on the Controversie.*

Between the New-text Sch. & the Old-text Sch.; Studies on Duke Chou & Confucius; Studies on Ch. Hist. in Antiquity; Add. 1st Fl., 51 Lane 70, Yen Chiu Yuan Rd., Sect. 2, Taipei 115.

HWANG, CHEN-KU 黃正鵠
Pres., Nat. Kaohsiung Normal U. 92-; b. Chekiang Dec. 20, '37; m. Hu, Chyi-fang; 1 s., 1 d.; educ. Ed.B., NTNU; Ed.M., NCCU; Ed.D., U. of Nr. Colorado 82; Dir., Lib., Nat. Kaohsiung Tchrs.' Coll. 69-75, Dir., Counseling Cent. 77-78, Dir. of Student Aff. 78-81, Head, Secretariat 83-84, Dean of Student Aff. 84-87; Dir., Grad. Inst. of Educ., Nat. Kaohsiung Normal U. 87-88, Dean of Studies 88-92. *Publ.: Basic Theory on Mental Analysis* 67; *Infant-Parent Relationship* 73; *A Survey of Disabled Students in Twn. (ROC) to Assess the Need of Rehabilitation Services* 81; *Res. on Prof. Tng. & Occupational Guidance for the Mentally Retarded in Kaohsiung City* 90; & numerous articles in prof. jour.; Add. 116 Ho Ping 1st Rd., Kaohsiung 802.

HWANG, CHING-FONG 黃鏡峰
Nat. Policy Adv. to the Pres. 98-; Bd. Chmn., Hsin Hsin Cement Ent. Corp. 98; b. Twn. Sept. 5, '30; m. Hsu, Chiung-ying; 2 s., 3 d.; educ. Prov. Taitung Sr. High Sch.; Passed Sr. Civil Service Exam.; Passed Sp. Civil Service Exam. A; Completed 1st-term Courses on Nat. Dev., Sun Yat-Sen Inst. on Policy Res. & Dev.; Sec., Taitung County Govt. 64; Mgr., Credit Corp., Taitung County 64-68; Magis., Taitung County (2 terms); Chmn., Ch. Youth Corps Cttee., Taitung County 68-76; Dir., Twn. Prov. Food Bu., TPG 84, Comr., Dept. of Recon. 84-87, Comr. 87-89; Acting Mayor, Taichung City 89; Chmn., Kaoshiung Mun. Cttee., KMT 89-93; Dir.-Gen., Secretariat, CC, KMT 93-95; V. Chmn., VAC 95-98; Mem., NA 92-96; Add. 6th Fl., 121 Sungkiang Rd., Taipei 104.

HWANG, CHYI 黃奇
Dir., Cent. for Environmental Protection & Ind. Safety & Hygiene, Chem. Dept., Nat. Chung Cheng U. 99-; b. Fukien May 18, '52; m. Lin, Ya-jung; 2 s.; educ. BS, NCKU 76, MS 78; Ph.D. 81; Instr., NCKU 78-81, Assc. Prof. 81-87, Prof. 87-93; Prof. & Chmn., Dept. of Chem. Engr., Nat. Chung Cheng U. 93-99. *Publ.:* More than 160 acad. jour. papers; Add. 160 Sanhsing Village, Minhsiung, Chiayi County 621.

HWANG, FRANCISCO L.Y. 黃瀧元
Dir.-Gen., 3rd Bu., Off. of the Pres. 98-; b. Twn. Jan. 25, '41; m. Chen, Fu-mei; 1 s., 1 d.; educ. BA, Spanish, Tamkang U. 66; Staff Mem., MOFA 68-71; 3rd, 2nd, & 1st Sec., Emb. in Costa Rica 71-83; Sr. Sp., Chief Protocol

Sect., MOFA 84-85, Dep. Dir., Dept. of Cent. & S. Am. Aff. 85-86, Dep. Dir., Dept. of Protocol 86; Cul. Counsl., Emb. in Costa Rica 86-92; Rep., Oficina Comercial Y Cul. de Taipei en la Repubica Argentina 92-96; Dir.-Gen., Dept. of Protocol, MOFA 96-97, Dept. of Cent. & S. Am. Aff. 97-98; Add. 122 Chungking S. Rd., Sect. 1, Taipei 100.

HWANG, JENG-SHYONG 黃正雄
Dep. Sec.-Gen., CC, KMT 99-2000; b. Twn. Nov. 14, '39; m. Hsieh, Kuei-mei; 2 s., 3 d.; educ. LL.B., NCHU; Mem. & Ed., Legal Com., Exec. Yuan 66-70; Sect. Chief, Min. of Jud. Admin. 70-76; Coun., Exec. Yuan 76-78; Chmn., Changhua County Cttee., KMT 78-82; Chmn., Com. for Examing Petitions & Appeals, Kaohsiung City Govt. 82-84, Dir.-Gen., Bu. of Reconstruction 84-86, Dep. Sec.-Gen. 86-87; Mem., Legis. Yuan 87-90; Comr., TPG 90-94; Gen. Mgr., Tang Eng Iron Works Co., Ltd. 95-96; Dep. Sec.-Gen., Off. of the Pres. 96-99; Dir-Gen., Dept. of Org. Aff., KMT 99-2000; Add. 53 Jen Ai Rd., Sect. 3, Taipei 106.

HWANG, JENN-TAI 黃鎮台
Chmn., NScC 98-2000; Adjunct Prof., Chem. Dept., NTHU 91-; Bd. Mem., Ch. Chem. Soc. 91-; b. Twn. Oct. 17, '48; m. Sun, Lucy; 1 s., 1 d.; educ. BS, NTU 70; Ph.D., Columbia U. 77; Postdr. Res., Princeton U. & U. of Chicago 78-79; Assc. Prof. & Prof., NTHU 79-89; Dir. of Admin. & Planning, Tzu-chiang Res. Inst. 85-86; Dir., Div. of Natural Scs., NScC 86-89; Dir., Dept. of Higher Educ., MOE 89-90; Dir., Soc. of Explosives & Propellants, ROC 86-90; Chmn., Ch. Chem. Soc. 89-91; V. Chmn., RDEC 91-94; V. Min. of Educ. 94-95; Pres., Feng Chia U. 95-98. *Publ.:* Over 20 phys. & chem. res. papers published in local & intl. jour.; Add. 106 Ho Ping E. Rd., Sect. 2, Taipei 106.

HWANG, TZUEN-CHIOU 黃尊秋
Sr. Adv. to the Pres. 93-; b. Twn. Dec. 5, '23; m. Yuan, Tsui-lan; 3 s., 2 d.; educ. Cent. Police Coll.; Judge & Chief, Hsinchu, Kaohsiung, & Taipei Dist. Courts 56-65; Judge, Tainan High Court 65-67; Chief Prosecutor, Penghu & Taitung Dist. Courts 67-71; Chief Judge, Tainan High Court 71-73; Mem., Control Yuan 73-81, V. Pres. 81-87, Pres. 87-93; Add. 122 Chungking S. Rd., Sect. 1, Taipei 100.

HWANG, YUEH-CHIN 黃越欽
Grand Justice, Jud. Yuan 99-; b. Twn. May 30, '41; m. Wang, Shu-wan; 2 s., 1 d.; educ. LL.B., NCCU 65; LL.D., U. of Vienna 70; Assc. Prof., NCCU 70-79, Prof. 79-93; Visiting Prof., Grad. Sch. of Law, U. of Zurich 86-87; Mem., Control Yuan 93-99. *Publ.: Theses on Private Laws; Labor Laws;* Add. 124 Chungking S. Rd., Sect. 1, Taipei 100.

HWU, REUBEN JIH-RU 胡紀如
Prof. of Chem., NTHU 90-; Res. Fel., Acad. Sinica 90-; Assc. Mem., IUPAC Com. on Nomenclature of Organic Chem. 89-; Res. Consultant, State U. of New York 87-; *b.* Taipei Apr. 17, '54; *m.* Leu, Alice Show-mei; 2 *d.; educ.* BS, NTU 76; Ph.D., Stanford U. 82; Asst. Prof. of Chem., Johns Hopkins U. 82-88, Assc. Prof. 88-91; Alfred P. Sloan Fel., USA 86-90; Pres., Ch. Am. Chem. Soc. 91-93; Ed., Chem. Comms., Royal Chem. Soc., 94-97. *Publ.:* 110 sc. papers published in intl. jour.; *Add.* Dept. of Chem., NTHU, Hsinchu 300.

I, CHING-CHIU
(See YEE, CHIN-CHIU 易勁秋)

ISQAQAVUT, YOHANI 尤哈尼‧伊斯卡卡夫特
Chmn., Coun. of Aboriginal Aff., Exec. Yuan 2000-; Bd. Dir., Found. of the Gen. Ass. of the Presbyterial Church, Twn. (GAPC); Mem., Cttee. of Secular Task, GAPC; Mem., Bd. of Trustees, Assn. for the Termination of C. Prostitutes; Mem., Workshop of Awakening Consciousness of Twn. Indigenous Peoples; Sec., Alumni Assn. of the Yu-shan Theological Coll. & Seminary; Mem., Bd. of Trustees, Tribal Aff. Assn.; Sup., Ecological Environmentalists Assn.; *b.* Twn. (Bunun Tribe) July 28, '53; *m.* Lu, Shu-mei; 1 *s.; educ.* Grad., Theology, Yu-shan Theological Coll. & Seminary, GAPC; BA, Dept. of Religion & Soc. Work, Tainan Theological Coll. & Seminary, M.Divinity; Studied, Nungkalingya Coll., Australia & Cent. for Min., the Uniting Church in Australia; Exec. Mem., of GAPC 89-98; Exec. Mem., Service Cent. for Indigenous Peoples in Taichung 78-82; Dir., the Taichung's Indigenous Collegian Cent. 85-87; Bd. Mem., Yu-shan Theological Coll. & Seminary, Chmn., Alumni Assn.; Mem., Preparatory Off. of the TCG's Aboriginal Aff. Com.; Ed., *New Messenger Mag.* & *The Voice of Twn. Indigenous Peoples;* Dean of Gen. Aff., Yu-shan Theological Coll. & Seminary, GAPC 98-2000; *Add.* 16th-17th Fl., 4 Chung Hsiao W. Rd., Sect. 1, Taipei 100.

JAN, HUNG-TZE 詹宏志
Pub. & CEO, PC Home Publ. Group 95-; Chmn., Cité Publ. Group, 96-; *b.* Twn. Mar. 12, '56; *m.* Wang, Chiuan-I; 1 *s.; educ.* B., Econ., NTU 78; Ed., *United Daily* 78-79; Chief Ed., *Cml. Times* 79-80; Ed.-in-Chief, *Ch. Times Weekly* 80-81; Chief, Lit. Dept., *Ch. Times* (NY) 81-82; Mng. Dir., Yuan-Liou Pub. Co. 82-94. *Publ.: Trends Deciphered* 85; *Trends Reports* 87; *City Watch* 89; *Rebelling Against Reading* 90; *A City Lang.* 96; *Add.* 3th Fl., 64-1 Tun Hua N. Rd., Taipei 105.

JAO, CHI-MING
(See RAU, CHYI-MING 饒奇明)

JAO, YIN-CHI
(See YAO, ENG-CHI 饒穎奇)

JIN, WEI-TSUN 金惟純
Pub., *Business Weekly;* Chmn., Shang Chou Co., Ltd 87-; V. Chmn., The Business Dev. Found. of Ch. Straits 93-; *b.* Twn. Jan. 16, '52; *m.* Kao, Hsiao-chin; 1 *d.; educ.* BA, NCCU 74; Grad. Sch., NCCU 80, & New York U. 86; Columnist, *Ch. Times* 79; Writer, *Ch. Times* (US edition) 84; Ed., *Commonwealth* 86; *Add.* 21st Fl., Bldg. B, 333 Tun Hua S. Rd., Sect. 2, Taipei 105.

JOEI, BERNARD T.K. 芮正皋
Sr. Adv., MOFA 86-, Mem., Res. & Planning Bd. 94-; Sr. Adv. for UN Aff., TECO, New York 93-; Prof., Intl. Law, Ch. Cul. U. 93-; Chmn., Sino-Vietnam Ind. & Comm. Assn. 87-; Gen. Counsl., Chen & Lin Attorneys-at-Law 94-; Mem., Nat. Coluncil Assn. 93-; Ed. Writer & Columnist, *Ch. Post, CDN,* & *Independent Evening Post;* Bd. Mem., Taipei European Sch. Found. 94-; *b.* Chekiang Aug. 14, '19; *m.* Liu, Yumei; 3 *s.; educ.* LL.B., Aurora U., Shanghai; Grad., Inst. of Pol. Sc., Paris 51; Dr. of Intl. Law, U. of Paris 50; Proficiency of Eng. Cert., Cambridge U. 71; Prof. & Dir., Grad. Inst. of European Studies, Tamkang U. 84-92, Dir., Cent. for Regional Studies 84-90; Amb. to Mali 60; Amb. to Upper Volta 61-68; Amb. to Gambia 65-68; Amb. to Côte d'Ivore 68-83; Alt. Rep. to regular sess. of UNGA 65-71. *Publ.:* "Pragmatic Dip. in the ROC—Hist. & Prospects," *Quiet Revolutions on Twn., ROC; In Search of Justice—The Twn. Story;* 150 articles on intl. pol., UN Aff. Twn.'s pragmatic dip., & domestic pol. published in jour & newspapers; *Add.* 7th Fl., 176 Sung Te Rd., Taipei 110.

JONG, YAW-TARNG 鍾曜唐
Chief Justice, Admin. Court 97-; *b.* Twn. Aug. 3, '32; *m.* Ou, Rong-leou; 1 *s.,* 2 *d.; educ.* LL.B., NTU 55; Judge Tainan Dist. Court 58-61, Taipei Dist. Court 61-66; Presiding Judge, Kaohsiung Dist. Court 66-67; Judge, Twn. High Court 67-74, Presiding Judge 75-81; Chief Judge, Panchiao Dist. Court 81-87; Chief Public Prosecutor, Public Prosecutors' Off., Kaohsiung Dist. Court 87-90; Dep. Sec.-Gen. Jud. Yuan 90-92; Chief Judge, Tainan Br., Twn. High Court 92-93, & Kaohsiung Br., 93-95, Chief Judge, Twn. High Court 95-97; *Add.* 1 Lane 126, Chungking S. Rd., Sect. 1 Taipei 100.

JU, MING 朱銘
Sculptor; Prof.; *b.* Twn. Jan. 20, '38; *m.* Chen, Fu-may; 2 *s* 2 *d.; educ.* Studied traditional woodcarving with Lee Chin chuan 53; Studied with sculptor Yu-yu Yang; Exhibitions

Nat. Hist. Museum 76; Tokyo Cent. Gallery 78; Hong Kong Arts Cent. 80; Max Hutchinson Gallery, New York 81; Nat. Museum, Singapore 86; Hong Kong 87; S. Bk. Cent., London 91; Dunkerque Contemporary Art Museum, Paris 91; Yorkshire Sculpture Park, U.K. 91; Intl. Contemporary Art Fair, Yokohama 92; Glory Sculpture Park, Twn. 94; Hakone Open-Air Museum, Japan 95; ART-ASIA—Intl. Art Expositions, Hong Kong 95; Place of Vandome, Paris 97; Luxembourg City, Luxembourg 99; Vedovi Gallery, Brussels 99; *Add.* 28 Lane 460, Chih Shan Rd., Sect. 2, Taipei 111.

JUAN, KANG-MENG 阮剛猛

Magis., Changhua County 93-; *b.* Twn. Jan. 5, '51; *m.* Huang, Li-hua; 1 *s.,* 2 *d.; educ.* Grad., Prov. Taichung Tchrs. Coll.; Tchr., Changhua County Tachia Elementary Sch. 72-80; Reserve Judge, Tainan Dist. Court 80-81; Reserve Judge, Taichung Dist. Court 81-82, Judge 82-87, Judge & concur. Presiding Judge 89, Justice & concur. Presiding Judge 89-92, Presiding Judge 92-93; Judge, Shihlin Br., Taipei Dist. Court 87-89; *Add.* 416 Chung Shan Rd., Sect. 2, Changhua 500.

JUAN, TA-NIEN
(See YUAN, DANIEL TA-NIEN 阮大年)

JUANG, FANG-RUNG 莊芳榮
Dir., Nat. Cent. Lib. 98-; Asst. Prof., NTU 84-; *b.* Twn. July 16, '47; *m.* Juang Lin, Tzai-lien; 1 *s.,* 2 *d.; educ.* B., NTU 69; M., Ch. Cul. U. 74, Ph.D. 87; Sect. Chief, RDEC 75-79; Counsl., CCA 87-90; Dir., Bu. of Civil Aff. of the TCG 91-94; Counsl., CCA 94-96; Head, Preparatory Off. of Nat. Cent. for Traditional Cul. 96-98. *Publ.: A Cumulative Series Bibliography, Part II* 74; *Antiquities Mng. & Preservation* 83; *Draft of Bibliography for Ch. Encyclopedias* 83; *Federal Cul. Admin. in the US* 90; *Add.* 20 Chung Shan S. Rd., Taipei 100.

JUI, CHENG-KAO
(See JOEI, BERNARD T.K. 芮正皋)

KAKU GENJI 郭源治
Pitcher, Ch. Trust Whale Baseball Team 98-; *b.* Twn. Oct. 5, '56; *m.* Takai, Mieko; 2 *s.,* 2 *d.; educ.* B., Fu Jen Catholic U., 79; Pitcher, Pres. Lion Baseball Team 97-98; Pitcher, Sino-Japanese Dragon Baseball Team, Japan 80-96; Fu Jen Catholic U. sch. baseball team & Lu Kuang Baseball Team 78-80; Hua Hsing High Sch. "AA" & "AAA" baseball team 72-77; Golden Dragon "A" Baseball Team 69; *Add.* 6th Fl., 3 Sung Shou Rd., Taipei 110.

KAN, YUET-WAI 簡悅威
Mem., Acad. Sinica 88-; Prof., Dept. of Med. & Lab. Med., U. of Calif., San Francisco 77-, Louis K. Diamond Prof. 83-; Investigator, Howard Hughes Med. Inst. 76-; Foreign Mem., Ch. Acad. of Sc. 96-; *b.* Ch. June 11, '36; *m.* Kan, Alvera; 2 *d.; educ.* MD, U. of Hong Kong 58, D.Sc. 81; Asst. Prof., Pediatrics, Harvard Med. Sch. 70-72; Prof., Dept. of Med. & Lab. Med., U. of Calif., San Francisco 72; Investigator, Howard Hughes Med. Inst. 76-; Chmn., Croucher Found., Hong Kong; Mem., exec. cttee. & sc. adv. bd., Qiu Shi Found., Hong Kong, 92. *Publ.:* Over 230 papers in sc. jour.; *Add.* U. 426, U. of Calif., San Francisco, CA 94143-0724, USA.

KANG, NING-HSIANG 康寧祥
Chmn., Nat. Def. Cttee., Control Yuan 97-, & Mem. 93-; Mem., NA 91-, & NUC 90-; V. Pres., Inst. of Intl. Aff. 91-; *b.* Taipei Nov. 16, '38; *m.* Chen, Li-jung; 1 *s.,* 1 *d.; educ.* BPA, NCHU; Visiting Scholar, E. Asian Inst., Columbia U. 85; Mem., Taipei CCoun. 69-72; Founder, *Twn. Pol. Review* 75, *The Eighties, The Asians, & The Current* 79-86; Mem., CSC, DPP 86-88, & Legis. Yuan 72-90; Pub., *Capital Morning Post* 89-90; Chmn., Presidium & Mcm., Preparatory Cttee., Nat. Aff. Conf. 90; Chmn., For. Aff. Cttee., Control Yuan 95-97, Convener, Nat. Def. Cttee. 93-97. *Publ.: 3 Years in Parliament; 6 Years in Parliament; Problems of Const. Dem.; Crisis & Hope; Gas Station Serviceman, Ch. Petroleum Corp.; Add.* 2 Chung Hsiao E. Rd., Sect. 1, Taipei 100.

KANG, TZU-LI
(See KANG, TZE-LI 康自立)

KANG, TZE-LI 康自立
Pres., Nat. Changhua U. of Educ. 99-; *b.* Fukien Jan. 18, '40; 1 *s.,* 1 *d.; educ.* Ed.D., NTNU; MS, U. of Wisconsin; Ph.D., Iowa State U.; Prof. & Chair, Dept. of Ind. Educ., Nat. Twn. Coll. of Educ. 87-89; Dir., Cent. Voc. Educ., & Prof., Dept. of Ind. Educ. 89-93, Prof. & Chair, Grad. Sch. of Ind. Educ. U. 89-92, Prof. & Dean, Coll. of Voc. Educ. 89-95. *Publ.: Tech. Textbk. for Jr. High Sch.* (Vol. 5); 26 bk. & 121 articles on educ.; *Add.* Paisa Village, Changhua 500.

KAO, CHARLES H.C. 高希均
Founder & Pres., *Commonwealth Mag., Global Views Monthly,* & Commonwealth Pub. Co.; Prof., Dept. of Econ., U. of Wisconsin, River Falls; Dir., Cent. for Pacific Rim Studies; *b.* Nanking Apr. 16, '36; *m.* Kao, Anne; 2 *c.; educ.* BS, NCHU; Ph.D., Michigan State U. 64; Adv., CIECD 69-70; Chmn., Dept. of Econ., U. of Wisconsin, River Falls 71-80; Yuan-Tung Prof., Grad. Sch. of Business Admin.,

NTU 77-79; Visiting Prof., NTNU 82; Dir., Cent. for Quality of Life Studies, Ming-Teh Found. 80-85; Econ. Adv., Exec. Yuan. *Publ.: The Brain Drain; A Case Study of Ch.; The Role of the Agr. Sector in Twn.'s Econ. Dev.; The World of Econ.; Add.* 2nd Fl., 1 Lane 93, Sungkiang Rd., Taipei 104.

KAO, CHARLES K. 高錕
Mem., Acad. Sinica 92-; Chmn., Transtech Services Ltd. 96-; *b.* Shanghai Nov. 4, '33; *m.* Wong, May-wan; 1 *s.*, 1 *d.; educ.* BS, U. of London 57, Ph.D. 65; Engr., Standard Telephones & Cables Ltd., UK 57-60; Res. Scientist/Res. Engr., Standards Telecomms. Lab. Ltd., UK 60-70; Prof. & Chmn., Elect. Dept., Ch. U. of Hong Kong 70-74; Chief Scientist, Electro-optical Products Div., ITT, USA 74-81, V. Pres. & Dir. of Engr. 81-83; Exec. Scientists & Dir., Res., ITT Advanced Tech. Cent., USA 83-87; Adjunct Prof. & Fel., Trumbull Coll., Yale U. 86; V. Chancellor (Pres.), Ch. U. of Hong Kong 87-96. *Publ.:* 5 bk. on fiber optics & high tech.; over 100 papers on fiber optics; *Add.* Transtech Services Ltd., 17th Fl., Telecom House, 3 Gloucester Rd., Wanchai, Hong Kong.

KAO, CHIN-YEN 高清愿
V. Chmn., Pres. Ents. Corp. 89-; Mem., CSC, KMT 99-; Chief Exec. Off., Pres. Group 89-; Chmn., Pres. Chain Store Corp. 86-, Ton Yi Ind. Corp. 79-, & Ztong Yee Ind. Co., Ltd. 77-; *b.* Twn. May 24, '29; *m.* Kao, Lai-kwan; 1 *d.; educ.* Grad., Tainan County Tienchou Elementary Sch. 37; Hon. Ph.D., Lincoln U. 83; Sales Mgr., Tainan Fabric Corp. 57-67; Pres., Pres. Ents. Corp. 67-89; *Add.* 301 Chung Cheng Rd., Yungkang, Tainan County 710.

KAO, CHING-YUN
(See LIAU, MARIETTA 高青雲)

KAO, CHING-YUAN
(See KAO, CHIN-YEN 高清愿)

KAO, HSI-CHUN
(See KAO, CHARLES H.C. 高希均)

KAO, KOONG-LIAN 高孔廉
Chmn., MTAC 97-2000; Prof., Grad. Sch. of Business Admin., NCCU; *b.* Fukien Nov. 9, '44; *m.* Kao L., Halina H.C.; 2 *s.; educ.* MBA, NCCU 69; Ph.D., Louisiana State U. 75; Prof. & Chmn., Dept. of Business Admin., Soochow U. 76-81; Dept. Dir., RDEC 81-83, V. Chmn. 83-91; V. Chmn., MAC 91-97. *Publ.: Theories & Applications of Finite Markov Chains; Op. Res.: A Quantitative Approach*

to Decision-making; Planning & Control Systems; Add. 4th Fl., 5 Hsuchow Rd., Taipei 100.

KAO, KUEI-YUAN 高魁元
Strategy Adv. to the Pres.; *b.* Shantung Mar. 26, '07; *m.* Teng, Yu-chin; *educ.* Mil. Acad.; Armed Forces Staff Coll.; CGSC, US; CG, 295th Brig. 38-39; CG, 99th, 118th & 88th Divs., ROC Army 40-48; CG, 18th, 96th, & 45th Corps 49-53; Dir., Pol. Warfare Dept., Army GHQ 55-57; Dep. C-in-C, ROC Army 57-58; CG, Reserve & Replacement Tng. Cmd. 58; CG, 2nd Field Army 59-60; Dir., Gen. Pol. Warfare Dept., MND 61-65; C-in-C, ROC Army 65-67; Chief of the Gen. Staff, MND 67-70; Personal C/S to the Pres. 70-73; Min. of Nat. Def. 73-81. *Publ.: Mil. Theories & Mags.; Add.* 10 Lane 124, Pei Yi Rd., Sect. 1, Hsintien, Taipei County 231.

KAO, KUN
(See KAO, CHARLES K. 高錕)

KAO, KUNG-LIEN
(See KAO, KOONG-LIAN 高孔廉)

KAO, YING-MAO
(See KAU, YING-MAO 高英茂)

KAU, YING-MAO 高英茂
Prof. of Pol. Sc. & Dir., E. Asian Sec. Project, Brown U. 68-; Ed., *Ch. Law & Govt. Quarterly* 73-; Pres., Assn. of Ch. Soc. Sc. in N. Am. 86-, & 21st Century Found. 88-; *b.* Twn. Aug. 31, '34; *m.* Huang, Anna; 2 *s.*, 1 *d.; educ.* BA, NTU 56; MA, Cornell U. 60, Ph.D. 68. *Publ.: Critical Issues Facing Twn.'s Current Reform; The Writings of Mao Zedong; Ch.'s Unification & Communist-Nationalist Negotiation; The Twn. Experience; Mao Zedong Text; The Future of Twn.;* & 4 bk.; *Add.* 9th Fl., 380 Keelung Rd., Sect. 1, Taipei 100.

KIANG, WEBSTER WEI-PING 江偉平
V. Chmn., RDEC 96-; *b.* Kiangsu July 10, '46; *m.* Kiang, Caroline; 1 *s.*, 2 *d.; educ.* BS, NTU 68; MBA, N.we. U. 79; MS, Engr., Washington U. 72, D.Sc. 74; Staff Res. Engr., Amoco Chem. Corp. 78-81; Res. Assc., Quantum USI Div. 81-93; Mem., Ovs. Ch. Aff. Com. 85-93; Mem., Legis. Yuan 93-96; *Add.* 7th Fl., 2-2 Chi Nan Rd., Sect. 1, Taipei 100.

KING, AMBROSE Y.C. 金耀基
Mem., Acad. Sinica 94-; Pro-V. Chancellor, Ch. U. of Hong Kong 89-, Prof., Sociology 83-; *b.* Ch. Feb. 14, '35; *m.* Tao, Yuan-jan; 4 *s.; educ.* BA, NTU 57; MPS, NCCU 59; Ph.D., U. of Pittsburgh 70; Instr., NCCU 65-67; Assc. Ed., *Twn.*

Cml. Press 65-70; Ed.-in-Chief, *Ea. Miscellany* 67-70; Lectr., Sociology, New Asia Coll., Ch. U. of Hong Kong 70-74, Head, Dept. of Sociology 72-75, Chmn. & Dir. of Studies in Sociology 76-89, Head, New Asia Coll. 77-85. *Publ.: Hist. Dev. of Ch. Dem. Thought; From Tradition to Modernity: An Analysis of Ch. Soc. & Its Change; Ecology of PA; Modernization of Ch. & Intellectuals; Idea of the U.; Predicament & Dev. of Dem. in Ch.; Pol. of the 3 Ch. Soc.; Salient Issues of Ch. Soc. & Cul.; Salient Issues of Ch. Pol. & Cul.; Add.* Dept. of Sociology, Ch. U. of Hong Kong, Shatin, N.T., Hong Kong.

KING, CHARLES SHU-CHI 金樹基
Rep., Taipeh Vertretung in der Bundesrepublik Deutschland; *b.* Chekiang Nov. 11, '36; *m.* Yang, Wan-yu; 1 *s.,* 2 *d.; educ.* BS, Econ., NTU; 2nd Sec., Emb. in Thailand 68-69; 1st Sec., Emb. in Japan 69-72; Sect. Chief, Dept. of N. Am. Aff., MOFA 73-74, Dep. Dir. 74-77, Acting Dir., Dept. of Info. 77-78, Dir. 78-80; Dir.-Gen., TECO, Los Angeles 80-83; Amb. to Costa Rica 83-85; Admin. V. Min. of For. Aff. 85-89; Pol. V. Min. of For. Aff. 89-90; Extraordinary & Plenipotentiary Amb. to S. Korea 90-92; *Add.* Markgrafenstr 35, 10117 Berlin, Germany.

KO, MIN-MOU 柯明謀
Mem., Control Yuan 87-; *b.* Twn. Sept. 23, '38; *m.* Hung, Yueh-mei; 1 *s.,* 3 *d.; educ.* BCE, NCKU 62; Mem., TPA 73-85; Adv., TPG 86-87; *Add.* 2 Chung Hsiao E. Rd., Sect. 1, Taipei 100.

KO, MING-MOU
(See KO, MIN-MOU 柯明謀)

KO, SHOU-JEN
(See KUH, ERNEST SHIU-JEN 葛守仁)

KO, TSE-TUNG 柯澤東
Mem. (ministerial rank), Exam. Yuan 96-; Exec. Dir., ROC Dist., Kiwanis Intl. 92-; Prof. of Law, NTU 81-, Chmn., Dept. of Law 93-, Dean, Sch. of Law 94-; Arbitrator, Cml. Arbitration Assn. of the ROC 93-, Mem. 89-; Mem., Gen. Chamber of Com. of the ROC 90-; Bd. Mem., Twn. Fire & Marine Ins. Co., Ltd. 80-93; Chair, Judges & Prosecutors Tng. Inst. 88-90; *b.* Twn. Aug. 23, '37; *m.* Ko, Grace M.H.; *s.; educ.* LL.B., NTU 61; MPS, U. of Minnesota 66; LL.D., U. of Paris 75; Charter Pres., Kiwanis Club of Keelung 78-79; Mem., CCPD 90-91; Gov., ROC Dist., Kiwanis Intl. 91-92. *Publ.: Intl. Trade Law; Maritime Law; Environmental Law* (2 Vol.); *Add.* 1-8th Fl., 90 Fu Hsing S. Rd., Sect. 1, Taipei 106.

KO, WEI-SHIN 葛維新
V. Min., OCAC 96-; *b.* Anhwei Sept. 9, '40; *m.* Wu. Jin-shiang; 1 *s.,* 2 *d.; educ.* LL.B., NCCU 64; BBA, We. Illinois U. 72, MA 74; Sp., Nat. Youth Com. 75-78; Supt. Twn. Prov. Cttee., KMT 78-79; Sr. Sp., Dep. Dir. & Dir., Ch. Youth Corps 79-90; Dep. Dir.-Gen., Dept. of Ovs. Aff., KMT 90-96. *Publ.: Org. Change of the Ch. Communist Party During Cul. Rev.; Add.* 16th Fl., 5 Hsuchow Rd., Taipei 100.

KOH, WEI-HSIN
(See KO, WEI-SHIN 葛維新)

KOO, ANTHONY YING-CHANG 顧應昌
Mem., Acad. Sinica 68-; Prof. of Econ., Michigan State U.; *b.* Shanghai Nov. 22, '18; *m.* Wei, Delia Zung-fung; 3 *d.; educ.* BA, St. John's U. 40; MS, U. of Illinois 41; MA & Ph.D., Harvard U. 46; Asst. Prof., Assc. Prof. & Prof., Michigan State U.; Prof., U. of Michigan; Prof. Emeritus, Michigan State U.; Adjunct Prof., Florida State U. 90. *Publ.: Environmental Repercussions on Trade & Investment; Land Market Distortions & Tenure Reform; Lib. Econ. Order* (2 Vol.) 93; *Add.* 4554 Sequoia Trail, Okemos, MI 48864, USA; (winter) 1008 Mimosa Drive, Tallahassee, FL 32312, USA.

KOO, CHEN-FU 辜振甫
Sr. Adv. to the Pres. 91-; Chmn., SEF 91-; Mem., CSC, KMT; Chmn., Twn. Cement Corp., & Twn. Polypropylene Co.; Hon. Chmn., Ch. Nat. Assn. of Ind. & Com., Chinatrust Cml. Bk., & Ch. Nat. Fed. of Ind.; Hon. Pres., Confed. of Asian Chambers of Com. & Ind.; *b.* Twn. Jan. 6, '17; *m.* Yen, Cho-yun; 2 *s.,* 3 *d.; educ.* LL.B., Taihoku (Taipei) Imperial U.; Hon. Ph.D., U. of Penn., Korea U., & U. of Victoria, Can.; Chmn., Twn. Stock Exchange 62-64; Founder, Twn. Econ. Res. Inst.; Convener, Econ. Reform Cttee., Exec. Yuan 85; Nat. Policy Adv. to the Pres. 88-91; Intl. Pres., Pacific Basin Econ. Coun. 90-92; Rep. of Pres. Lee Teng-hui to APEC Leaders Econ. Meeting, Osaka 95, Subic Bay 96 & Vancouver 97. *Publ.: Collected Essays & Speeches of Koo Chen-fu; Add.* 14th Fl., 113 Chung Shan N. Rd., Sect. 2, Taipei 104.

KOO, CHENG-CHEU 顧正秋
Adv., Nat. Fu-hsing Dramatic Arts Acad.; Mem., Prog. Cttee., Nat. Theater & Concert Hall; *b.* Shanghai Sept. 3, '30; *m.* Jen, Hsien-chun (deceased); 1 *s.,* 1 *d.; educ.* Grad., Shanghai Opera Acad. 46; Performed with Tan Fu-ying in Shanghai Queen's Theater 46; Performed with Lee Tsungi in Shanghai Golden Theater 46; Founder & Dir., Koo Troupe 47-53; *Performances: The 4th M. Visits His Mother*

91, & *The Unicorn Bag* 93; *Works: Treasurable Art Pieces in Video: The Treasure Bag; The Story of Wang Chiang; The Romance of Susan; The Legend of the White Snake; Wong Bao-chuen; The Green Sparkling Sword; The Red Mark on the Palm; The Lantern of the Precious Lotus; The Meander of River Fin; The Phoenix Back to the Nest; The 4th M. Visits His Mother; The Unicorn Bag; Add.* 21th Fl., 169 Jen Ai Rd., Sect. 4, Taipei 106.

KOO, JEFFREY L.S. 辜濂松
Amb.-at-Large, ROC 98-; Nat. Policy Adv. to the Pres.; Chmn. & Chief Exec. Off., Chinatrust Cml. Bk. 92-; Chinatrust Bk., Chinatrust (Philippines) Cml. Bk., Chmn., Ch. Nat. Assn. of Ind. & Com., ROC-USA Econ. Coun., Ch. Taipei Pacific Econ. Cooperation Cttee., Twn. Inst. of Econ. Res., & Taipei Intl. Community Cul. Found. Chinatrust Cul. Found., Ovs. Investment & Dev. Corp., Euro-Asia Trade Org.; Adv., ROC Del. of Asia Pacific Eco. Coun.; Adv., ROC Del. of Asian Dev. Bk.; Hon. Pres., Confed. of Asia-Pacific Chambers of Com. & Ind.; Mem., Bd. of Trustees, Eisenhower Exchange Fel.; *b.* Twn. Sept. 8, '33; *m.* Koo, Mitzi; 3 *s.,* 1 *d.; educ.* BA, Soochow U.; MBA, New York U.; Hon. Ph.D., Business Mng., De La Salle U., Philippines; Chmn., Chinatrust Co. 88-92; *Add.* 3 Sung Shou Rd., Taipei 110.

KU, CHEN-FU
(See KOO, CHEN-FU 辜振甫)

KU, CHENG-CHIU
(See KOO, CHENG-CHEU 顧正秋)

KU, CHUNG-LIEN NELSON 顧崇廉
Rep., Taipei Rep. Off. in the Netherlands 97-; *b.* Shanghai June 6, '31; *m.* Kao, Shiun-yung; 1 *s.,* 1 *d.; educ.* Ch. Naval Acad. 54; Naval Cmd. & Staff Coll., Armed Forces U. 66; US Naval War Coll. 77; Cmdg. Off., Guided Missile Destroyer 75; Mil. Sr. Aide to the State Pres. 78-84; Cmdr., 1st Destroyer Squadron 84; Chief, Bu. of Planning, GHQ, ROCN 85; Supt., Naval Acad. 86; Cmdr., Fleet Cmd. 88; Dep. C-in-C, ROCN 90; Dep. Chief of the Gen. Staff, MND 92; V. Min. of Nat. Def. 93; C-in-C, ROCN 94-97; *Add.* Javastraat 46-48, 2585 AR, the Hague, the Netherlands.

KU, FU-CHANG 顧富章
Dir.-Gen., Bu. of Consl. Aff., MOFA 99-; *b.* Kiangsu Jul. 29, '35; *m.* Heh, Esther Ming-lin; 1 *d.; educ.* LL.B., Fu Hsing Kang Coll.; Studied at Grad. Sch. of Pol. Sc. & Admin., Lovanium U.; Asst., Fu Hsing Kang Coll. 57-59; Asst. Resr., Inst. of Intl. Rel., NCU 61-64; Staff, MOFA 64-67;

3rd, 2nd, & 1st Sec., Emb. in Abidjan, Kinshasa, & Ouagadougou 67-72; Sect. Chief, MOFA 72-75; Counsl., Emb. to the Holy See 75-81; Rep. to Switzerland 85-91; Amb. to Guinea-Bissau 91-95; Rep. to Brazil 95-98; Chmn., Res. & Planning Bd. 98-99. *Publ.: The Analysis of the Org. of the Communist Party of the Soviet Union; The Const. of the Repub. of Zaire; Add.* 5th Fl., 2-2 Chi Nan Rd., Sect. 1, Taipei 100.

KU, LIEN-SUNG
(See KOO, JEFFREY L.S. 辜濂松)

KU, YING-CHANG
(See KOO, ANTHONY YING-CHANG 顧應昌)

KU, YU-HSIU 顧毓琇
Mem., Acad. Sinica 59-; Prof. Emeritus, EE & System Engr., U. of Penn. 72-; Consultant, Gen. Elec. Co., Univac, & RCA; Personal Mem., GA, Intl. Union of Theoretical & Applied Mech. 46-; *b.* Kiangsu Dec. 24, '02; *educ.* BS, MS, & Sc.D., MIT 25-28; MA, Hon. LL.D., U. of Penn. 72; Prof. & Dir., EE Dept., Nat. Chekiang U. 29-30; Dean, Coll. of Engr., NCU 31-32; Prof. & Dir., EE Dept., NTHU, Dean, Coll. of Engr. 32-37; V. Min. of Educ. 38-44; Pres., NCU 44-45; Educ. Comr., Shanghai 45-47; Pres., NCCU 47-49; Visiting Prof., MIT 50-52; Prof., U. of Penn. 52-71; Fel., AIEE 45, IRE 61, Inst. of Elec. & EE, IEE; Mem., US Nat. Cttee. on Theoretical & Applied Mech. *Publ.: Analysis & Control of Nonlinear Systems* 58; *Elec. Energy Conversion* 59; *Transient Circuit Analysis* 61; *Analysis & Control of Linear Systems* 62; *Collected Sc. Papers* 72; *Woodcutter's Song* 63; *Pine Wind* 64; *Ch. Collected Works* (12 Vol.) 61; *Lotus Song* 66; *Lofty Mountains* 68; *The Liang River* 70; *The Hui Spring* 71; *The Si Mountain* 72; *The Great Lake* 73; *300 Recent Poems* 76; *Hist. of Chan (Zen) M.* 76; *Hist. of Japanese Zen Ms.* 77; *Hist. of Zen* 79; *The Long Life* 81; *One Family—Two Worlds* 82; *Poems After Chin Kuan* 83; *Poems After Tao Chien* 84; *303 Poems After Tang Poets* 86; *Flying Clouds & Flowing Water* 87; *Poems After Wu Wen-ying* 89; *Selected Plays* 90; *Eyebrows* 92; *Sc. Paper* 92; *Old Age* 93; *Clear Water & Beautiful Flowers* 94; *Banana Hut Poems* 95; *Add.* 1420 Locust St. (22G), Philadelphia, PA 19102, USA.

KUAN, CHUNG
(See KUAN, JOHN C. 關中)

KUAN, JOHN C. 關中
V. Pres., Exam. Yuan 96-; Assc. Prof., NCCU; *b.* Tientsin June 9, '40; *m.* Kuan, Grace C.; 1 *s.,* 1 *d.; educ.* BA, NCCU; Ph.D., Fletcher Sch. of Law & Dip., Tufts U.; Hon. LL.D

Indianapolis U. 91; Dep. Dir.-Gen., Dept. of Youth Aff., CC, KMT 77-79, Dep. Sec.-Gen., CPC 79-81, Chmn., Taipei Mun. Cttee. 81-84, & Twn. Prov. Cttee. 84-87; Chmn., NYC 87; Dir.-Gen., Dept. of Org. Aff., CC, KMT 87-89, Dep. Sec.-Gen. 89-90; Chmn., Dem. Found. 90-97; Chmn., Asia & World Inst. 90-97; Chmn., BCC 90-93; Mem., Legis. Yuan 93-94, & CSC, KMT 93-94; Visiting Prof., Stanford U., U. of Virginia, & Ohio State U.; Min. of Civil Service 94-96. *Publ.: A Review of US-ROC Rel. '49-'78; Notes on Communist Ch.'s For. Policy; The KMT-CCP Wartime Negotiation '37-'45; The Modernization of the KMT: Observations & Expectation; Democratization of Twn. & the Future of Ch. Unification; On Parliamentary Reform; Essays on Issues of Public Policy; Add.* 1 Shih Yuan Rd., Wenshan, Taipei 116.

KUAN, YUNG-SHIH 關永實
Bd. Chmn., Ch. Petrochem. Dev. Corp., Kaohsiung Monomer Co., Ltd., & Twn. Chlorine Ind. Ltd. 92-; *b.* Hopei Feb. 25, '33; *m.* Shih, Lien-chun; 1 *s.,* 2 *d.; educ.* BS, Econ., NTU 55; Staff, Kaohsiung Refinery Plant, Ch. Petroleum Corp. 56-70; Chmn., Twn. Petroleum Workers' Union 70-72; Dep. Sect. Chief, Acct. Sect., Kaohsiung Refinery Plant, Ch. Petroleum Corp. 72-75; Acct. Chief, Ch. Petrochem. Dev. Corp. 75-76, V. Pres. 76-85, Pres. 85-87; Pres., Ch. Petroleum Corp. 87-92; Mem., NA 92-96; *Add.* 8th-11th Fl., 12 Tung Hsing St., Taipei 115.

KUH, ERNEST SHIU-JEN 葛守仁
Mem., Acad. Sinica 74-; Prof., EE, UC-Berkly.; *b.* Peiping Oct. 2, '28; *m.* Chow, Bettine; 2 *s.; educ.* NCTU, Shanghai 45-47; BS, U. of Michigan 49; MS, MIT 50; Ph.D., Stanford U. 52; Tech. Staff, Bell Labs. 52-56; Chmn., Dept. of EECS, UC-Berkly. 68-72, Dean, Coll. of Engr. 73-80; Mem., Nat. Acad. of Engr., USA. *Publ.:* 4 bk.; *Add.* Dept. of EECS, UC-Berkly., CA 94720, USA.

KUNG, CHENG-TING
(See KUNG, SAINTING 龔政定)

KUNG, SAINTING 龔政定
Amb. to Burkina Faso 94-; *b.* Prague Aug. 5, '34; *m.* Lee, Theresa; 2 *s.; educ.* BA, NTU 58; LL.M., NCCU 63; 3rd Sec., Emb. in Upper Volta 63-65; 3rd & 2nd Sec., Emb. in Rwanda 66-68; Sect. Chief, Dept. of African Aff., MOFA 68-72; 1st Sec., Emb. in Togo 72; 1st Sec., Emb. in Zaire 72-73; 1st Sec., Emb. in Côte d'Ivoire 73-76; Dir., Service d'Info., Assn. pour la Promotion des Echanges Com. et Touristiques, France 76-80, Rep. 80-90; Dir., Dept. of European Aff., MOFA 90-94; Amb. concur. to Liberia 97; &

to São Tomé Príncipe 97-99; *Add.* 01 B.P. 5563, Ouagadougou 01, Burkina Faso.

KUNG, TE-CHENG
(See KUNG, TEH-CHENG 孔德成)

KUNG, TEH-CHENG 孔德成
Sr. Adv. to the Pres.; 77th lineal descendant of Confucius; Sacrificial Official to Confucius; Prof., NTU, Fu Jen Catholic U., & Soochow U.; *b.* Shantung Feb. 23, '20; *m.* Sun, Chi-fang; 4 *c.; educ.* Hon. Res. Fel., Grad. Sch., Yale U.; Hon. Ph.D., Sung Kyun Kwan U., S. Korea; The Holy Duke 20-35; Mem., Const. NA 46-48, Nat. Law-making Cttee. 47-48, & NA 48-91; Pres., Exam. Yuan 84-93. *Publ.: A Correlative Interpretation of the Various Texts of & Notes on the Ritual; An Interpretation of the Bk. of Rites; On the Rites & Customs in the Annals of Spring & Autumn Interpreted by Tso Chiu-ming; A Supplement to the List of the Characters on Bronze Bells & Tripods in Pre-Han & Han Dynasties (2205 B.C.- A.D.220); Notes on the Hieroglyphic Inscriptions on Bronze Bells & Tripods; Confucius, His Life, Thought, & Influence: A Collection of Speeches During a European Tour* 84; *Add.* 4th Fl., 129 Chung Yang Rd., Hsintien, Taipei County 231.

KUO, CHE 郭哲
Nat. Policy Adv. to the Pres. 90-; Mem., NA 92-; Ch. Pres., Refugees Relief Assn.; *b.* Shensi Dec. 15, '19; *m.* Whai, Litan; 1 *s.,* 1 *d.; educ.* Grad., Dept. of Ind. Mng., Soochow U.; Sun Yat-sen Inst. on Policy Res. & Dev.; Nat. Def. Res. Cent.; Mem., Design & Evaluation Cttee., CSC, KMT 68-69, Dep. Dir., 1st Sect., CC 69-72, V. Chmn., Twn. Prov. Cttee. 72-78, Dep. Dir.-Gen., Dept. of Org. Aff., CC 78-79, Chmn., Kaohsiung Mun. Cttee. 79-81, Dep. Sec.-Gen., CPC 81-84, Dir.-Gen., Dept. of Soc. Aff., CC 84-85, Dep. Sec.-Gen., CC 85-87; Chmn., BCC 87-90. *Publ.: Res. on Party Aff.; Soc. Construction & Soc. Problems; Tchrs.' Soc. Responsibility; Nat. Prospects & Goals; Add.* 11 Alley 17, Lane 96, Ho Ping E. Rd., Sect. 3, Taipei 106.

KUO, HSIAO-LAN 郭曉嵐
Mem., Acad. Sinica 88-; Prof. Emeritus, Meteorology, U. of Chicago 85-; *b.* Hopei Jan. 7, '15; *m.* Yen, Hsia-mei; 2 *s.,* 1 *d.; educ.* BS, NTHU 37; MA, Nat. Chekiang U. 42; Ph.D., U. of Chicago 48; Res. Assc., Acad. Sinica 37-45; Res. Assc., Sr. Sp., & Dir. of Hurricane Project, MIT 49-54 & 55-61; Prof., U. of Chicago 62-85. *Publ.: Dynamics of the Atmosphere;* over 120 papers on atmospheric dynamics & theorems of weather & climate; *Add.* 5501 S. Kimbark Avenue, Chicago, IL 60637, USA.

KUO, JU-LIN 郭汝霖

Nat. Policy Adv. to the Pres.; *b.* Anhwei Dec. 10, '20; *m.* Kuo Chen, Ming-shien; 1 *s.; educ.* Ch. Mil. Acad. 40; Ch. Air Force Acad. 43; Regular & Res. Course, Air CGSC; Gen. Grade Off. Course, War Coll., Armed Forces U. 79; Tactical Fighter Cmdr. & Wing Cmdr. 61-64 & 69-71; Supt., Air Force Acad. 75-77; C-in-C, ROCAF 81-86; V. Chief of the Gen. Staff (Exec.), MND 86-88; Personal C/S to the Pres.; Pol. Adv. to the Pres.; *Add.* 122 Chungking S. Rd., Sect. 1, Taipei 100.

KUO, KANG 國剛

Extraordinary & Plenipotentiary Amb. to the Dominican Repub. 90-; *b.* Shantung May 9, '27; *m.* Tsao, Ai-yen; 1 *s.,* 1 *d.; educ.* BA, Sociology, NCHU 60; 3rd & 2nd Sec., Emb. in Argentina 60-66; Sect. Chief & Dep. Dir., Dept. of Treaty & Legal Aff., MOFA 66-71; Counsl., Del. in UN 71-72; Counsl., Emb. in Colombia 72-75; Chargé d'Affaires, Emb. in Bolivia 75-76; Dir., 2nd Dept., Exec. Yuan 76-77; Rep., ROC's Cml. Off. in Ecuador 77-87; Dir., Treaty Dept., MOFA 87-88, Dir., Dept. of Cent. & S. Am. Aff. 88-90; *Add.* Edificio Palic-Primer 1 Piso, Avenue Abraham Lincoln, Esq. José, Amado Soler, Santo Domingo, Republica Dominicana.

KUO, SHIRLEY W.Y. 郭婉容

Min. without Portfolio 93-2000; Mem., CSC, KMT; *b.* Twn. Jan. 25, '30; *m.* Nieh, Wen-ya; 3 *d.; educ.* BA, NTU; MS, MIT; Dr. in Econ., Kobe U.; Lectr., Assc. Prof., & Prof., NTU 66-89; Fulbright-Hays Exchange Prof., MIT 71-72; V. Chmn., EPC, Exec. Yuan 73-77, & CEPD 77-79; Dep. Gov., CBC 79-88; Min. of Finance 88-90; Chmn., CEPD 90-93. *Publ.: The Twn. Econ. in Transition;* Co-author: *Growth with Equity—The Twn. Case; The Twn. Success Story—Rapid Growth with Improved Distribution in the ROC '52-'79; Macroecon.; Microecon.; Econ. Policies—The Twn. Experience, 1945-1995; Add.* 11th Fl.-1, 289 Tun Hua S. Rd., Sect. 1, Taipei 106.

KUO, TENG-CHI 郭藤吉

Pres., Tainan Women's Coll. of Arts & Tech., 97-; *b.* Twn. Jan. 18 '38; *m.* Lin, Ying-chiao; 1 *s.,* 3 *d.; educ.* Head, Dept. of Acct. & Statistics, Tainan Jr. Coll. of Home Econ. 75, Dean of Gen. Aff. 77-83, Dean of Students Aff. 83-88, Dean of Acad. Aff. 88-82. *Publ.: The Res. of Fixed Asset; The Policy & Trend of Family Financial Mng.; The Function & Problem of Student Practice Bk.; The Study of Stock Market in Twn.; Add.* 529 Chung Cheng Rd., Yungkang, Tainan County 710.

KUO, TSONG-TEH 郭宗德

Mem., Acad. Sinica 74-, Sp. Chair 97-, Res. Fel., Inst. of Botany 68-; Prof., Dept. of Botany, NTU 77-; *b.* Twn. Feb. 27, '33; *m.* Chuang, Tzu-hua; 1 *s.;* 1 *d.; educ.* BS, Twn. Prov. Taichung Coll. of Agr. 57; MS, NTU 60; Ph.D., U. of Calif., Davis 65; Res. Fel., Biology Div., Calif. Inst. of Tech. 70-71; Dir., Inst. of Botany, Acad. Sinica 71-77; Visiting Prof., Dept. of Biochem. & Biophys. Sc., Sch. of Hygiene & Public Health, Johns Hopkins U. 77; Dir., Biology Res. Cent., NScC 71-84; Acting Dir., Inst. of Molecular Biology, Acad. Sinica 94-95. *Publ.: Recent Dev. of Genetic Engr. Techniques; Loss of Sigma Factor of RNA Polymerase of Xanthomonas campestris pv. oryzae During Phage XP 10 Infection* 86; *Add.* 128 Yen Chiu Yuan Rd., Sect. 2, Nankang, Taipei 115.

KUO, TZUNG-TE
(See KUO, TSONG-TEH 郭宗德)

KUO, WAN-JUNG
(See KUO, SHIRLEY W.Y. 郭婉容)

KUO, WEI-FAN 郭為藩

Rep., Taipei Rep. Off. in France 97-; *b.* Twn. Sept. 3, '37; *m.* Lin, Mei-ho; 1 *s.,* 1 *d.; educ.* BA & Ed.M., NTNU; Ph.D., U. of Paris; Assc. Prof., NTNU 67-70, Prof. 70-72 & 77-78; Admin. V. Min. of Educ. 72-77; Pres., Ch. Sp. Educ. Assn. 73-75 & 79-81; Dir., NTNU 78, Pres. 78-84; Pres., Ch. Educ. Soc. 84-86; Min. without Portfolio 84-88; Chmn., CCPD 88-93; Min. of Educ. 93-96; Rep., Taipei Rep. Off. in the Netherlands 96-97. *Publ.: Educ. of Exceptional C. & Youth—Psychology of Self-Concept; Concepts of Educ.; Humanistic Educator in Tech. Age; Reflections on Educ. Reform; Add.* 78, rue de l'Universite, 75007 Paris, France.

KUO, YI-YU 郭一羽

Pres. & Prof., Chung Hua U.; *b.* Taipei Mar. 6, '48; *m.* Hsu Shau-lang; 2 *s.; educ.* MS & Ph.D., Kyushu U., Japan; Assc. Prof., NCTU 80-83, Prof. 83-98; Head., Dept. of Civil Engr. NCTU 84-87; *Add.* 11 Alley 9, Lane 779, Chung Hua Rd., Sect. 6, Hsinchu 300.

KUO, YUAN-CHIH
(See KAKU GENJI 郭源治)

KUO, YUN 果芸

V. Chmn. & Pres., Inst. for Info. Ind. 91-; *b.* Hopei Oct. 10 '25; *m.* Hu, Shirley; 1 *s.,* 2 *d.; educ.* Grad., Air Force Inst. for Tech. & Def. Ind. Coll., USA; Dir., Air Force Logisti Control Cent. 70-76, & Def. Mng. Cent. 76-81; Dep. Cmdr Army Logistic 81-83; Pres., Def. Mng. Coll. 83-84, & Inst for Info. Ind. 82-84; Chief of Mil. Mission in USA 84-91

Strategy Adv. to the Pres. 91-93; Adv. to the Premier 91-93; *Add.* 11th Fl., 106 Ho Ping E. Rd., Sect. 2, Taipei 106.

KUO, YUNG-CHAO
(See KUO, YUNG-CHAU 國永超)

KUO, YUNG-CHAU 國永超
Dep. Auditor-Gen., Nat. Audit Off., Control Yuan 91-; *b.* Shantung Mar. 19, '31; *m.* Yee, Yi-huey; 1 *d.; educ.* BBA, Feng Chia U. 73; Asst. Auditor, Nat. Audit Off., Control Yuan 63-73, Auditor & concur. Acting Sect. Chief 73-81, Auditor & concur. Br. Chief 81-86, Sr. Auditor 86-87, Sr. Auditor & concur. Dir., 5th Bu. 87-91; *Add.* 1 Hangchow N. Rd., Taipei 100.

LAI, FENG-WEI 賴峰偉
Magis., Penghu County 97-; *b.* Twn. Sept. 20, '53; *m.* Kuo, Mary-Jane; 2 *s.; educ.* BA, Tunghai U. 77; MA, U. of Missouri 88, Ph.D. 95; Sect. Chief, AEC 80-95; Chmn., Penghu County Cttee., KMT 95-97; *Add.* 32 Chih Ping Rd., Makung, Penghu County 880.

LAI, IN-JAW 賴英照
Grand Justice, Jud. Yuan 99-; *b.* Twn. Aug. 24, '46; *educ.* S.J.D., Harvard U. 81; Chmn., Grad. Sch. of Laws, NCHU 82-84; Dir.-Gen., Customs Dept., MOF 84-89; Admin. V. Min. of Finance 89; Pol. V. Min. of Finance 89-93; Lt. Gov. 96-98, & concur. Comr., Dept. of Finance, TPG 93-98. *Publ.: Annotations of the ROC Sec. Exchange Law* (4 Vol.); *Essays on the Corp. Law; Twn.'s Financial Map: Prospect & Retrospect; Add.* 124 Chungking S. Rd., Sect. 1, Taipei 100.

LAI, KUO-CHOU 賴國洲
Dir.-Gen., Dept. of Youth Aff., CC, KMT 98-; Producer & Host, "Authors, Readers & Bks.: A Dialogue" (TTV Prog.) 95-; Pub., *Youth Community Newspaper* 96-; Mem. & concur. Exec. Sec., TV-Cul. Res. Cttee. 92-; *b.* Twn. Nov. 3, '52; *m.* Lee, Annie; 1 *s.; educ.* BA, Pol. Sc., NCCU 75, MA, Jour. 80, Ph.D. 88; Reporter & Asst. Mgr., Reader Services Dept., *Twn. Hsin Sheng Daily* 80-81; Assc. Prof., Dept. of Soc. Sc., Soochow U. 83-98, & Dept. of Jour., NCCU 87-98; Sec.-Gen., Nat. Press Coun. of the ROC 89-97; *Add.* 8th Fl., 78 Chang An E. Rd., Sect. 2, Taipei 104.

LAI, MEI-SHU 賴美淑
CEO & Pres., Bu. of Nat. Health Ins., DOH 98-; Adjunct Assc. Prof., Coll. of Med., NTU 95-; *b.* Twn. Sept. 2, '49; *m.* Ou, Sheng-yun; 1 *s.,* 1 *d.; educ.* MD, NTU 75, Ph.D., Coll. of Public Health 94; Residency, NTU Hosp. 75-79; Res. Assc., U. of Pittsburgh 79-80, Epidemiology Phys. 81-

82; Lectr., NTU 82-90; Dep. Dir., Bu. of Health Promotion, DOH 90-95, Dir. 95-96; Dep. Dir.-Gen., DOH 96-98; *Add.* 140 Hsin Yi Rd., Sect. 3, Taipei 106.

LAI, MICHAEL M.C. 賴明詔
Mem., Acad. Sinica 92-; Prof. of Microbiology, U. of So. Calif. 83-; Investigator, Howard Hughes Med. Inst. 90-; *b.* Twn. Sept. 8, '42; *m.* Wung, Cathy Hwei-ying; 2 *d.; educ.* MD, NTU 68; Ph.D., UC-Berkly. 73; Asst. Prof., U. of So. Calif. 73-78, Assc. Prof. 78-83; Visiting Prof., Inst. of Molecular Biology, Acad. Sinica 88; Pres., Soc. of Ch. Bioscientists in Am. 91-92; Chmn., RNA Virus Div., Am. Soc. for Microbiology 92-93. *Publ.:* 230 articles published in *Sc., Nature, Proceedings of Nat. Acad. of Sc., EMBO Jour., Jour. of Virology, Virology*; etc.; *Add.* 1215 Wabash St., Pasadena, CA 91103, USA.

LAI, MING-CHAO
(See LAI, MICHAEL M.C. 賴明詔)

LAI, SHENG-CHUAN
(See LAI, STAN 賴聲川)

LAI, STAN 賴聲川
Playwright, Dir. & Filmmaker 84-; Artistic Dir., Performance Workshop Theater 84-; Prof., Grad. Sch. of Theater, Nat. Inst. of the Arts 92-; *b.* Washington, D.C. Oct. 25, '54; *m.* Ding, Nai-chu; 2 *d.; educ.* BA, Fu Jen Catholic U. 76; Ph.D., Dramatic Art, UC-Berkly. 83; Assc. Prof., Theater Dept., Nat. Inst. of the Arts 83-92, Chmn. 87-92, Dir., Grad. Sch. of Theater 90-92; Silver Award, Young Cinema Competition, Tokyo Intl. Film Festival 92; Golden Horse Award 92; Caligari Award, Berlin Intl. Film Festival 93; Best Dir., Best Film, FIPRESCI Award, Singapore Intl. Film Festival 93; *Plays (written & directed): We All Grew Up This Way* 84; *Plucking Stars* 84; *The Passer-by* 84; *The Other Evening, We Performed Xiangsheng* 85; *Bach Variations* 85; *Secret Love for the Peach Blossom Spring* 86; *Pastorale* 86; *Circle Story* 87; *The Island & the Other Shore* 89; *Look Who's Cross-talking Tonight* 89; *Strange Tales from Twn.* 91; *Red Sky* 94; *Complete Hist. of Ch. Thought (Crosstalk Version)* 97; *Open the Door, Sir!* 98; *I Me He Him* 98; *Menage Ö 13* 99; *Plays (directed): Beckett in the Classical Ch. Garden* 88; *The Seagull* 90; *Servant of Two Ms.* 95; *Angels in Am.* 96; *Spirits Play* 98; *Opera: Journey to the W.* 87; *Films: The Peach Blossom Land* 92; *The Red Lotus Soc.* 94; *TV Prog.: We Are Family* (252 episodes) 95-97. *Publ.: Stan Lai: Theatre* (16 plays in 4 Vol.) 99; *Add.* 3rd Fl., 153 Kang Ning St., Hsichih, Taipei County 221.

LAI, TZE-LEUNG 黎子良
Mem., Acad. Sinica 94-, Adv. Cttee., Inst. of Statistical Sc. 90-; Prof. of Statistics, Stanford U. 87-, External Assessor, Dept. of Statistics, Ch. U. of Hong Kong 91-; *b.* Hong Kong June 28, '45; *m.* Chow, Letitia; 2 *s.; educ.* BA, U. of Hong Kong 67; MA, Columbia U. 70, Ph.D. 71; Asst. Prof., Dept. of Math. Statistics, Columbia U. 71-74, Assc. Prof. 74-77, Prof. 77-87; External Examiner, Dept. of Math., Nat. U. of Singapore 89-93. *Publ.:* Over 170 articles & papers; *Statistics: Inference & Decisions; Add.* Dept. of Statistics, Stanford U., Stanford, CA 94305-4065, USA.

LAI, TZU-LIANG
(See LAI, TZE-LEUNG 黎子良)

LAI, YING-CHAO
(See LAI, IN-JAW 賴英照)

LAI, YUAN-HO 賴源河
Mem. (ministerial rank), Exam. Yuan 96-; Adjunct Prof., Laws Dept., NCCU 95-; *b.* Twn. Dec. 20, '38; *m.* Kang, Su-i; 3 *d.; educ.* LL.B., NTU 62; LL.M., Penn. State U.; LL.M. & LL.D., Kobe U., Japan 72 & 76; Prof. of Laws, NCCU 82-95, Dean, Sch. of Laws, & concur. Dir. & Head, Laws Dept. 93-94; V. Chmn., Fair Trade Com., Exec. Yuan 95-96. *Publ.: Concise Practical Cml. Laws; On Fair Trade Laws; Intelligence Properties under Trade Protection; Sec. Mng. Regln.; Study on Co. Laws; Add.* 1 Shih Yuan Rd., Wenshan, Taipei 116.

LAN, CHIH-MIN 藍智民
Amb. to the Repub. of Panama 98-; *b.* Fukien Aug. 27, '39; *m.* Hung, Chiu-fang; 1 *s.*, 1 *d.; educ.* BA, Tunghai U. 61, & U. of Chile 66; Sp., Sect. Chief & Dep. Dir.-Gen., Dept. of Cent. & S. Am. Aff., MOFA 67-70, 77-80 & 80-82; 3rd & 2nd Sec., Emb. in Uruguay 70-77; Dep. Dir.-Gen., TECO in Spain 82-83; Counsl., Emb. in Paraguay 83-84; Rep., TECO in Chile 85-90; Dir.-Gen., Dept. of Cent. & S. Am. Aff., MOFA 90-94; Rep., TECO in Mexico 94-98; *Add.* Apartado No. 5285, Panama 5, Repub. of Panama.

LAN, SHUN-TE 藍順德
Dir., Nat. Inst. for Compilation & Transl. 97-; Dir. & Exec. Sec.-Gen., Educ. Res. Coun. 98-; *b.* Twn. Nov. 16, '50; *m.* Ou, Yu-shaung; 1 *s.*, 1 *d.; educ.* BA, PA, NCHU 79; MA, Inst. of Educ., NTNU 86; Tchr., Yuanshulin Elementary Sch. 70-75, Tacheng Elementary Sch. 75-76; Staff Mem., Educ. Bu., Taoyuan County Govt. 76-79; Sect. Chief, Educ. Bu., Keelung City Govt. 79-84; Head of subdiv., Educ. Bu., TCG 84-84; Sec., MOE 84-85, Dep. Dir., Dept. of Elemen-

tary & Jr. High Educ. 85-91; Insp., MOE 91-92, Dir., Dept. of Gen. Aff. 92-94, Dir., Dept. of Elementary & Jr. High Educ. 94-97. *Publ.: The Contents of Civil Educ.; Add.* 247 Chou Shan Rd., Taipei 106.

LAN, SUNG-CHIAO 藍松喬
Lawyer; Exec. Dir., Nat. Bar Assn. of the ROC 98-; *b.* Twn. Aug. 30, '35; *m.* Chang, Chih-mei; 2 *s.; educ.* LL.B., Soochow U.; Chmn., Taoyuan County Chungli Elementary Sch. Parents' Assn. 76-78; Pres., Twn. Prov. Chungli Jr. High Sch. Alumni Assn. 91-96; Exec. Dir., Taoyuan Bar Assn. 96-98; Gov., Dist. 3490, Rotary Intl. 91-92; Chmn., Coun. of Past Govs. in Twn. Rotary Intl. 94-95; *Add.* 2nd Fl., 94 Chung Cheng Rd., Chungli, Taoyuan County 320.

LAO, KAN 勞榦
Mem., Acad. Sinica 58-; Prof. Emeritus, UCLA 74-; *b.* Shensi Jan. 13, '07; *m.* Chou, Yen-pu; 3 *s.*, 1 *d.; educ.* BA, Nat. Peking U.; Res., Acad. Sinica & Harvard U. 32-62 & 53-55; Lectr., Nat. Peking U. 36-37; Prof., NCU 46-48, NTU 49-61, & UCLA 62-74. *Publ.: Studies in Wooden Ships of the Han Dynasty from Edzin Gol; Hist. of the Han Dynasty; Hist. of the Six Dynasties; An Anthology of the Articles in Acad. Works; Cheng-lu Shih-kao, A Collection of Poems; A New Explanation of the Han & Chin Wooden Ships; On the Problems of Cul. & Hist. in Ancient Ch.; Add.* 777 Valley Boulevard #88, Alhambra, CA 91801, USA.

LAU, LAWRENCE J. 劉遵義
Mem., Acad. Sinica; Kwoh-ting Li Prof. of Econ. Dev.; Prof. of Econ. & Dir., Cent. for Econ. Policy Res., Stanford U.; Bd. Mem., Chiang Ching-kuo Found. for Intl. Scholarly Exchange; Mem., Gov.'s Coun. Econ. Policy Adv., CA 93-; *b.* Kweichow Dec. 12, '44; *m.* Jablonski, Tamara; 1 *s.; educ.* BS, Stanford U. 64; MA & Ph.D., UC-Berkly. 66-69; Acting Asst. Prof. of Econ., Stanford U. 66-67, Asst. Prof. 67-73, Assc. Prof. 73-76. *Publ.: Farmer Educ. & Farm Efficiency; Models of Dev.—A Comparative Study of Econ. Growth in S. Korea & Twn.;* & over 140 articles & papers; *Add.* Dept. of Econ., Stanford U., Stanford, CA 94305-6072, USA.

LEAN, ERIC G.H. 林耕華
Mem., Acad. Sinica 98-; Gen. Dir., Opto-Elect. & Systems Lab. (OES) 94-; *b.* Fukien Jan. 11, '38; *m.* Lean, Alice Tien-li; 2 *d.; educ.* BSEE, NCKU 59; MSEE, U. of Washington 63; DSEE, Stanford U. 67; Mgr., Acoustic Phys., IBM 69-70, Optical Solid-State Tech. 71-79, & Printing Tech. 80-85, Sr. Staff Mem., Res. Tech. Planning 85-87, Dept. Mgr. Storage Tech. 87-92; Dep. Gen. Dir., OES 92-

94. *Publ.:* 27 theses & 3 articles; *Add.* Bldg. 78, 195-8 Chung Hsin Rd., Sect. 4, Chutung, Hsinchu County 310.

LEE, A-CHING 李阿青
Chmn., Twn. Shiseido Co. Ltd. 91-; Chmn., Manufacturers Assc. of Daily Hygienic Chem. Products of Twn. 93-; *b.* Twn. Aug. 6, '24; *m.* Lee, Huang-tsu; 2 *s.*, 2 *d.; educ.* Hon. Dr. of Chem. Engr., U. of Texas at Austin 93; *Add.* 5th Fl., 37 Pao Ching Rd., Taipei 100.

LEE, AN
(See LEE, ANG 李安)

LEE, ANG 李安
Film Dir. 91-; *b.* Twn. Oct. 23, '54; *m.* Lin, Jane Huey-chai; 2 *s.; educ.* Diploma, Nat. Twn. Acad. of Arts 76; BFA, U. of Illinois 80; M. of Fine Arts, New York U. 84. *Films: Pushing Hands; Wedding Banquet; Eat Drink Man Woman; Sense & Sensibility; The Ice Storm; Ride with the Devil; Add.* 2nd Fl., 526 W. 25th St., New York, NY 10001, USA.

LEE, CHE-LANG
(See LEE, JANE-LONG 李哲朗)

LEE, CHENG-CHIA
(See LEE, CHEN-CHIA 李成家)

LEE, CHEN-CHIA 李成家
Mem., NA; Mem., CC, KMT; Chmn., Maywufa Co. Ltd., Twn. Prov. Ind. Assn., ROC Fed. of Nonprofit Assn.; Comr., Ind. Dev. Adv. Coun., Supervisory Cttee. of Nat. Health Ins.; *b.* Twn. Mar. 12, '48; *m.* Tsai, Yu-yun; 2 *d.; educ.* BA, Pharmacy, Kaohsiung Med. Coll. 71; Grad. Sch. of Business Admin., NCCU 81-84; MBA, John F. Kennedy U. 86; Sales Rep., Bristol-Myers (Twn.) Co. Ltd. 73-74; Dist. Mgr. 74-76; Chmn., Nat. Assn. of Small and Medium Ent., Ch. Youth Career Dev. Assn., Taipei Dept. Stores Assn. *Publ.: No End for Career Dev.; Opportunities; Add.* 5th Fl., 167 Fu Hsing N. Rd., Taipei 105.

LEE, CHEN-HSIUNG 李辰雄
Amb. to the Repub. of the Gambia 97-; *b.* Twn. Nov. 25, '44; *m.* Lee, Grace; 1 *s.*, 1 *d.; educ.* LL.B., NTU. 67; MS, Northrop U., USA 86; Staff Mem., Dept. of Asia Pacific Aff., MOFA 72-74; 3rd & 2nd Sec., Emb. in Ivory Coast 74-79; Sect. Chief, Dept. of Info., MOFA 80-83; 1st Sec., TECO in Los Angeles 83-86, Dep. Dir., Seattle 87-90; Dep. Dir., Dept. of African Aff., MOFA 90-92; Rep., Sp. Del. of the ROC to Angola 92-97. *Publ.: An Observation from Seattle* (2 Vol.), & many other articles; *Add.* P.O. Box 916, Banjul, Repub. of the Gambia.

LEE, CHEN-LIN
(See LEE, CHENG-LIN 李槙林)

LEE, CHEN-YUAN 李鎮源
Mem., Acad. Sinica 70-; Prof. Emeritus, Pharmacological Inst., NTU 86-; Hon. Mem., Am. Soc. Pharmacology & Experimental Therapeutics 77-; Hon. Mem., Japanese Pharmacol Soc. 87-; *b.* Twn. Dec. 4, '15; *m.* Lee, Shu-yue; 1 *s.*, 4 *d.; educ.* MD & Dr. Med. Sc., Taihoku Imperial U.; Res. Fel., U. of Penn. 52-53, & U. of Oxford 58-59; Asst. Prof., Faculty of Med., Taihoku Imperial U. 44-45; Assc. Prof., Coll. of Med., NTU 45-49, Prof. 49-86 & Dean 72-78; Counsl., Acad. Sinica 69-96; Pres., Ch. Pharmacol Soc. 81-88; Pres., Intl. Soc. Toxinology 85-88; Pres., Ch. Toxicol Soc. 87-93; Pres., Med. Profs. Alliance in Twn. 92-98; Chmn., Twn. Independence Party 96-98. *Publ.: Discovered Bungarotoxins* 63; *Snake Venom* (ed.) 79; & over 150 original papers; *Add.* 2 Lane 32, Shao Hsing S. St., Taipei 100.

LEE, CHENG-LIN 李槙林
Chmn., VAC 99-2000; *b.* Shantung Oct. 25, '33; *m.* Hsu, Mei-fen; 1 *s.*, 1 *d.; educ.* Army Acad. 54; Federal Def. Cmd. U., Germany 69; War Coll., Armed Forces U., ROC 73; Div. Cmdr., Army 79-81; Asst. Dep. Chief, Gen. Staff for Op., MND 81-83; CG, Army Infantry Training Cmd., & Cmdt., Army Infantry Sch. 83-85; Cmdt., Army CGSC, Armed Forces U. 85-87; Dep. Chief, Gen. Staff for Op., MND 87-90; CG, Kinmen Def. Cmd. 90-92; Strategic Adv. & Dep. C-in-C, Army 92-93; C-in-C, Army 93-96; Cmdt., Armed Forces U. 96-99; *Add.* 222 Chung Hsiao E. Rd., Sect. 5, Taipei 110.

LEE, CHENG-TAO
(See LEE, TSUNG-DAO 李政道)

LEE, CHER-JEAN 李雪津
Dep. Dir.-Gen., GIO 2000-; *b.* Taipei July 27, '54; *m.* Wang, Kung; 1 *d.; educ.* BA, French, Fu Jen Catholic U. 76; MS, Computer Sc., Boston U. 83; Sp. & Sect. Chief, RDEC 84-86, Resr. 86-88, Dep. Dir., Dept. of Data Processing 88-90, Dir. 90-2000; *Add.* 2 Tientsin St., Taipei 100.

LEE, CHI-CHU
(See LEE, JIH-CHU 李紀珠)

LEE CHIAO 李喬
Writer 82-; Ed.-in-Chief, *Twn. Lit.* 94-; *b.* Twn. June 15, '34; *m.* Lee Hsiao, Ying-chiao; 1 *s.*, 3 *d.; educ.* Hsinchu Normal Sch. 54; Tchr., elementary & high schs., agr. & voc. schs. 54-82; Ed.-in-Chief, *Twn. Lit.* 83-84. *Publ.:*

Informer; Cold Night Trilogy; Love Without Regret; The Dark Side of Twn.; Dilemma & Transition of Twn. Movements; Add. 261-10 Lin 16, Yuchuan, Yuchuan Village, Kungkuan, Miaoli County 363.

LEE, CHIEN-CHUAN
(See LEE, JEN-CHYUAN 李健全)

LEE, CHIN-LUNG
(See LEE, JIN-LONG 李金龍)

LEE, CHIN-YUN 李慶雲
Prof. Emeritus, Coll. of Med., NTU 98-; Coordinator, Adv. Cttee. of Immunization Prog., DOH 87-; *b.* Twn. Jan. 24, '28; *m.* Chang, Ming-tseng; 1 *s.,* 3 *d.; educ.* MB, NTU 53; M. of Preventive Med., Sch. of Med., U. of Washington 64; Dr. of Med. Sc., So-Do Med. Coll., S. Korea 64; Resident, Pediatrics, NTU Hosp. 53-58; Instr., Coll. of Med., NTU 61-65, Assc. Prof. 65-72, Prof. 72-98, Chmn. 86-93. *Publ.:* 175 sc. papers; *Add.* 8th Fl., 28 Roosevelt Rd., Sect. 1, Taipei 100.

LEE, CHIN-YUNG 李進勇
Mayor, Keelung City 97-; *b.* Twn. Aug. 1, '51; *m.* Huang, Jui-chen; 2 *s.,* 1 *d.; educ.* LL.B., NCHU 75; LL.M., NTU 81; Judge, Hualien, Ilan & Taichung Dist. Courts 89-85; Lawyer, Civil Law 85-92; Dir., Keelung City Cttee., DPP 92-94; Mem., Legis. Yuan 92-97, Convener, Trans. & Jud. Cttee. 96-97, Convener, Procedures Cttee. 96, Chief Exec., DPP Caucus 97; Exec. Mem. & V. Chmn., Chengyi Faction, DPP 94-97; Founder, Oceanic City Cul. & Educ. Found. 96, Bd. Chmn. 96-98; *Add.* 1 Yi I Rd., Keelung 202.

LEE, CHING-HUA 李慶華
Former Convener, NP 99-2000; Mem., Educ. Cttee., Legis. Yuan 97-; *b.* Chekiang Dec. 3, '48; *m.* Lee Chow, Shau-chin; 1 *s.,* 1 *d.; educ.* Ph.D. in Hist., New York U. 84; Co-founder, NP; Convener, NP Caucus, Legis. Yuan, Mem., Nat. Def. Cttee. 94; *Add.* Rm. 802, 8th Fl., 371 Chi Nan Rd., Sect. 1, Taipei 100.

LEE, CHING-PING 李慶平
Pres., BCC 98-; *b.* Kwangtung July 14, '46; *m.* Wu, Delhi; 1 *s.,* 1 *d.; educ.* LL.B., Dip. Dept., NCCU 69, LL.M. 73; Fel., Prog. for Sr. Mgrs. in the Govt., John F. Kennedy Sch. of Govt., Harvard U.; Dir., Cul. Div., TECRO, USA 86-92; Dep. Sec.-Gen., SEF 92-98; *Add.* 53 Jen Ai Rd., Sect. 3, Taipei 106.

LEE, CHING-YUN
(See LEE, CHIN-YUN 李慶雲)

LEE, CHUNG-RU 李宗儒
Rep., TECO in Greece 98-; *b.* Hunan Dec. 21, '45; *m.* Chen, Chia-chun; 1 *s.,* 3 *d.; educ.* LL.B., Dip., NCCU 66; LL.M., Pol. Sc., NTU 69; Staff Mem., Dept. of Intl. Org., MOFA 69-72; 3rd Sec., Emb. in Gambia 72-75; Consul., Consl. Gen. in Johannesburg, S. Africa 75-77; Sect. Chief, Dept. of European Aff., MOFA 77-81; Dir., Public Aff. Div., Free Ch. Cent. in London 81-88; Dep. Dir., Dept. of Intl. Org., MOFA 88-91; Rep., TECO in Australia 91-94; Dir., Dept. of European Aff., MOFA 94-95; Amb. to Gambia 95-97; Dir.-Gen., TECO in Los Angeles 97-98. *Publ.: US Open Door Policy & Ch.; Add.* 57 Marathonodromon Avenue, 154 52 Psychico, Athens, Greece.

LEE, DAVID TAWEI 李大維
Dep. Min. of For. Aff. 98-; Assc. in Res., Fairbank Cent., Harvard U. 93-; *b.* Twn. Oct. 15, '49; *m.* Chih, Lin; 1 *s.,* 1 *d.; educ.* BPS, NTU 73; MA & Ph.D., For. Aff., U. of Virginia 82; Mng. Ed., Asia & the World Forum 76-77; Staff Consultant, TECRO, USA 82-88; Prin. Asst. to the Min. of For. Aff. 88-89; Adjunct Assc. Prof., Intl. Pol., Grad. Sch., NTNU 88-93; Dep. Dir., Dept. of Intl. Info. Services, GIO 89-90; Dep. Dir., Dept. of N. Am. Aff., MOFA 90-93; Dir., TECO in Boston 93-96; Dir., Dept. of N. Am. Aff., MOFA 96; Dep. Dir.-Gen., GIO 96-97, Dir.-Gen. 97-98. *Publ.: Legis. Process of the Twn. Rel. Act* 89; *Cong. vs. Pres.: A Case Study of the Twn. Rel. Act; The Making of the Twn. Rel. Act (20 Yrs. in Retrospect);* & many articles on Sino-Am. Rel. & Am. Nat. Inst.; *Add.* 2 Kaitakelan Boulevard, Taipei 100.

LEE, HSING 李行
Pres., Dir. Guild of Twn., ROC 90-; Pres., Twn. Film Cul. Co. 96-; *b.* Shanghai May 20, '30; *m.* Lee Wang, Wei-jean; 1 *s.,* 1 *d.; educ.* Dept. of Educ., Twn. Prov. Normal Coll.; Tchr. & Tng. Sect. Chief, Affiliated High Sch. of Prov. Normal Coll. 52-54; Corr., *Independent Evening Post* 55-57; Film Dir. 58-90; Chmn., Taipei Golden Horse Film Festival Exec. Cttee. 90-94; Award for Best Film, Golden Horse Film Festival; Award for Best Dir., Golden Horse Film Festival. *Films: Beautiful Duckling; Life in a Small Alley* 63; *4 Lovers* 64; *The Monument of Virtue* 65; *The Rd.* 67; *Execution in Autumn* 71; *My People My Country* 75; *He Never Gives Up* 78; *The Story of a Small Town; Good Morning Taipei* 79; *Ch., My Native Land* 80; *The Heroic Pioneers* 86; *Add.* 2nd Fl., 3 Alley 35, Lane 300, Jen Ai Rd., Sect. 4, Taipei 106.

LEE, HSUEH-CHIN
(See LEE, CHER-JEAN 李雪津)

LEE, HUAN 李煥
Sr. Adv. to the Pres. 90-; Mem., CAC, KMT 99-; *b.* Hankow Sept. 24, '17; *m.* Pan, Hsiang-ning; *2 s., 2 d.; educ.* LL.B., NCCU 44; Ed.M., Columbia U. 56; Hon. Ph.D., Dankuk U., S. Korea 78; Hon. LL.D., Sung Kyun Kwan U., S. Korea 81; Dir., *Shenyang Daily News* 46-48; Sec.-Gen., Dep. Dir., & Dir., Ch. Youth Corps 52-77; Prof., NCCU 62-79; Chmn., NYC 67-72; Chmn., Twn. Prov. Cttee., KMT 68-72, Dir.-Gen., Dept. of Org. Aff., CC 72-78, Dir., Sun Yat-sen Inst. on Policy Res. & Dev. 76-78; Prof., NTNU 78-79; Pres., Nat. Sun Yat-sen U. 79-84; Min. of Educ. 84-87; Sec.-Gen., CC, KMT 87-89; Premier 89-90; Mem., CSC, KMT 88-99. *Publ.: Guidance of Youth; Dr. Sun Yat-sen & Youth: Essays on Educ.; Pres. Chiang Kai-shek & Youth; An Indepth Study of Multiparty Politics; Half a Century by His Side; Add.* 23 Lane 44, Ssu Wei Rd., Taipei 106.

LEE, JANE-LONG 李哲朗
Chmn. & concur. Pub., *The Commons Daily* 96-; Pres., Nanchen Gas Co. 97-; *b.* Twn. Sept. 7, '40; *m.* Huang, Ping-chun; *2 s.; educ.* B. of Econ., U. of Waseda, Japan 64; Gen. Mgr., *The Commons Daily* 70-77, Pres. 74-95, V. Chmn. 95-96; *Add.* 180 Min Chuan 2nd Rd., Kaohsiung 806.

LEE, JEN-CHYUAN 李健全
V. Chmn., COA 97-; Chmn., Ovs. Fisheries Dev. Coun. of ROC 97-; Adjunct Assc. Prof., NTU 82-; *b.* Twn. June 5, '45; *m.* Lin, Kue-mei; *2 s., 1 d.; educ.* BS, NTNU 67; MS, Grad. Sch. of Zoology, NTU 72; Ph.D., Dept. of Fisheries & Allied Aquacul., Auburn U. 79; Jr. Sp., JCRR 73-80; Sr. Sp., CAPD 80-84; Dep. Dir. & Dir., Fisheries Dept., COA 84-90 & 90-96, Sec.-Gen. 96-97; *Add.* 37 Nan Hai Rd., Taipei 100.

LEE, JIH-CHU 李紀珠
Chmn., NYC 98-2000; Prof., Econ., NCCU 86-; *b.* Twn. Apr. 22, '60; *educ.* BA, Econ., NCCU 82; Ph.D., Econ., NTU 86; Visiting Scholar, Dept. of Econ., Stanford U. & Harvard U.; Sr. Examiner, Exam. Yuan 86-96. *Publ.:* "The Determinants of Intl. Banking Investment: the Case of US," *Jour. of Mng. Sc.,* Ch. Mng. Assn. 93, "The Optimal Adjusting Rule for an Adjustable Currency Basket System" 92, "Financial Cooperation & Competition Among Twn., Hong Kong, & Mainland Ch.," & over 50 acad. papers & publs.; *Add.* 14th Fl., 5 Hsuchow Rd., Taipei 100.

LEE, JIN-LONG 李金龍
Dep. Auditor-Gen., Nat. Audit Off., Control Yuan 94-; *b.* Twn. July 16, '42; *m.* Tsai, Ho; *1 s., 2 d.; educ.* B., Com.,

Tamkang U.; Sect. Chief, Nat. Audit Off. 74-78, Dir., Hualien County Audit Off. 78-80, Pingtung County Audit Off. 83-85, Taipei County Audit Off. 86-86, Taipei Mun. Audit Dept. 87-88, Comr., 2nd Bu. & 5th Bu. 90-91 & 91-94; *Add.* 1 Hangchow N. Rd., Taipei 100.

LEE, JO-I 李若一
Admin. V. Min. of Civil Service, Exam. Yuan 94-; *b.* Twn. Oct. 25, '42; *m.* Wu, Mei-chin; *1 s., 2 d.; educ.* Prov. Tainan Normal Sch. 61; LL.B., Ch. Cul. U. 68, MPS 71; Sect. Chief, CPA 74-76, Dir., Pers. Dept. 76-78, Sr. Sp. 78-81, Dep. Dir. 81-83; Dep. Dir., Pers. Dept., TPG 83-84; Exec. Sec., CPA 84, Dir. 84-89; Dir., Pers. Dept., TCG 89-94; *Add.* Min. of Civil Service, 1 Shih Yuan Rd., Wenshan, Taipei 116.

LEE, KAO-CHAO 李高朝
V. Chmn., CEPD 95-; *b.* Twn. May 17, '38 ; *m.* Liang, Chiu-mei; *2 s., 1 d.; educ.* MS, Agr. Econ., NTU 64; M., Econ., Vanderbilt U., USA 73; Sp., Econ. Planning Coun., Exec. Yuan 69-74, Sr. Sp. 74-83; Dep. Dir., Econ. Res. Dept., CEPD 83-84, Dir. 84-95. *Publ.: On the Leakage of Repercussion Effects* 70; *Short- & Mid-term Resources Utilization Model of Twn.* 80; *The Impact of Changes in Energy Supply & Prices on Twn. Econ.* 81; *Add.* 3 Pao Ching Rd., Taipei 100.

LEE, KUANG-HSIUNG
(See LEE, KWANG-SHIANG 李光雄)

LEE, KUO-HSIUNG 李國雄
Mem., Acad. Sinica 96-; Dir., Natural Products Lab., U. of N. Carolina at Chapel Hill 83-, Kenan Prof., Medicinal Chem. 92-, Chmn. 98-; Adjunct Prof., Kaohsiung Med. Coll. 77-; *b.* Twn. Jan. 4, '40; *m.* Chen, Lan-huei; *1 s., 1 d.; educ.* Ph.D., U. of Minnesota 68; Postdr., UCLA 68-70; Asst. Prof., U. of N. Carolina 70-74, Assc. Prof. 74-77, Prof. 77-91; Elected Fel., Acad. of Pharmaceutical Sc. 78; Fel., Am. Assn. of Pharmaceutical Sc. 86; Fel., Am. Assn. for Advancement of Sc. 94; *Add.* Sch. of Pharmacy, CB# 7360, Beard Hall, U. of N. Carolina, Chapel Hill, NC 27599-7360, USA.

LEE, KWANG-SHIANG 李光雄
Mem. (ministerial rank), Exam. Yuan 96-; *b.* Twn. Aug. 1, '45; *m.* Lu, Ai-jane; *1 s.; educ.* BA, Pol., NTU 67, MPS 71; M.Lit. in Soc. Psychology, U. of Glasgow, UK 74; Dir., Pers. Off., Exam. Yuan 74-80, Sr. Compiler 80-82; Sr. Sec. to the V. Premier 82-84; Dep. Dir., Pers. Dept., TPG 84-87, Dir. 87-93; Dep. Dir.-Gen., CPA 93-94; Pol. V. Min. of Exam. 94-96. *Publ.: The Legis. Process of US Cong.: A*

Case Study of the Civil Rights Act; A Comparative Study of the Attitudes of Scottish & Twn. Students; The Exam. & Pers. Systems of the ROC Since 1912; Compilation on Personnel Admin.; Add. 1 Shih Yuan Rd., Wenshan, Taipei 116.

LEE, LIN-SHAN 李琳山
Prof., Dept. of EE & Dept. of Computer Sc. & Info. Engr., NTU 82-; *b.* Twn. Sept. 23, '52; *m.* Mei, Chia-ling; 1 *c.; educ.* BSEE, NTU 74; MS, Stanford U. 75, Ph.D. 77; Tech. Consultant, Edutel Comms. & Dev. Inc., USA 77-79; Assc. Prof., Dept. of EE, NTU 79-82, Head, Dept. of Computer Sc. & Info. Engr. 82-87; Dir., Inst. of Info. Sc., Acad. Sinica 91-97. *Publ.:* About 220 tech. papers (60 on intl. jour. & 130 in intl. conf.); *Add.* 3rd Fl., 7 Lane 58, Wen Chou St., Taipei 106.

LEE, MING-LIANG 李明亮
Dir.-Gen., DOH 2000-; *b.* Twn. June 26, '36; *m.* Liau, Ya-hwei; 3 *d.; educ.* MD, NTU 62; Ph.D., Molecular Biology & Biochem., U. of Miami 69; Helen Hay Whitney Fel., MRC, U. of Cambridge, Eng. 69-72; Pediatric Residency, Med. Cent., Duke U., Durham 65; Visiting Prof., NTU 71-72; Asst. Prof., Sch. of Med., U. of Miami 72-76; Chief Fel. in Med. Genetics, Johns Hopkins Hosp., Baltimore 76-77; Assc. Prof., Tenuar Prof., & Chief, Div. of Med. Genetics, Dept. of Pediatrics, Robert Wood Johnson Med. Sch., U. of Med. & Dentistry, New Brunswick, New Jersey 77-92; Pres., Tzu Chi Coll. of Med. & Humanities 94-2000; *Add.* 100 Aikuo E. Rd., Taipei 100.

LEE, NENG-CHI 李能棋
(See LEE CHIAO 李喬)

LEE, SHEN-I 李伸一
Mem., Control Yuan 93-; *b.* Twn. Aug. 14, '42; *educ.* LL.B., NTU; LL.D., Ch. Cul. U.; Passed the Sr. Civil Service Exam. for Lawyers; Passed the Sr. Civil Service Exam. for Pers. Admin.; Lawyer 73; Bd. Chmn., ROC Consumers' Found.; Pres., Shihlin Br., Rotary Club; Mem., Fair Trade Com. *Publ.: Laws on Consumers' Life; Consumers' Protection Org. & Legis. in the Philosophy of Soc. Well-being; Commentary on Consumer Protection Law; Add.* 2 Chung Hsiao E. Rd., Sect. 1, Taipei 100.

LEE, SI-CHEN 李嗣涔
Prof., NTU 86-, Dean of Acad. Aff. 96-; *b.* Twn. Aug. 13, '52; *m.* Cheng, May-ling; 1 *s.,* 1 *d.; educ.* BE, NTU 74; MS, Stanford U. 77, Ph.D. 81; Resr., Energy Conversion Devices Inc. 80-82; Assc. Prof., NTU 82-86, Chmn., Dept. of EE 89-92; Counsl. to the Min., MND 93-94. *Publ.: Phys. of*

Semiconductor Devices; & over 200 jour. and conf. papers; *Add.* 5th Fl., 5 Alley 1, Lane 40, Chou Shan Rd., Taipei 106.

LEE, SZU-TSEN
(See LEE, SI-CHEN 李嗣涔)

LEE, TA-WEI
(See LEE, DAVID TAWEI 李大維)

LEE, TE-WU 李德武
V. Chmn., VAC 98-; *b.* Honan Oct. 11, '36; *m.* Tong, Gwo-guey; 2 *s.,* 2 *d.; educ.* LL.B., Soochow U. 59; Sect. Chief & Sr. Sp., NYC 66-81; Dir., MOTC 81-87, Counsl. 87-93; Dir., 7th Dept., Exec. Yuan 93-97, Adv. 97-98; *Add.* 222 Chung Hsiao E. Rd., Sect. 5, Taipei 110.

LEE, TENG-HUI 李登輝
Pres., ROC 88-2000; Chmn., KMT 88-2000; *b.* Twn. Jan. 15, '23; *m.* Tseng, Wen-fui; 2 *d.; educ.* Kyoto Imperial U. 45; BS, NTU 49; MA, Iowa State U. 53; Ph.D. in Agr. Econ., Cornell U. 68; Asst. Prof., NTU 49-55, Assc. Prof. 56-58; Res. Fel., Twn. Cooperative Bk. 53; Sp. & Econ. Analyst, Dept. of Agr. & Forestry, TPG 54-57; Sp., JCRR 57-61, Sr. Sp. & Consultant 61-70; Chief, Rural Econ. Div., JCRR 70-72; Prof., NCCU 58-78; Min. without Portfolio 72-78; Mayor, Taipei City 78-81; Gov., TPG 81-84; V. Pres., ROC 84-88. *Publ.: Agr. Dev. & Its Contributions to Econ. Growth in Twn.; An Analytical Review of Agr. Dev. in Twn.; Intersectoral Capital Flows in the Econ. Dev. of Twn., 1895-1960; Initial Conditions of Agr. & Dev. Policy; Process & Pattern of Growth in Agr. Production of Twn.; Agr. Diversification & Dev.; On the Problems of Agr. Price Policy & Price Level; Add.* 11 Chung Shan S. Rd., Taipei 100.

LEE, TENG-MU
(See LEE, THOMAS D.M. 李登木)

LEE, THOMAS D.M. 李登木
Former Dep. Mayor, Kaohsiung City 98-2000; *b.* Twn. Sept. 18, '36; *m.* Pan, Margaret G.J.; 3 *s.,* 2 *d.; educ.* BA, Fine Arts, NTNU 61; Hon. Ph.D., Mng. & Policy, S.Ea. U., USA; Dean of Studies, Kaohsiung Mun. Chienchen Jr. High Sch. 65-70; Chmn., Star Co. Ltd. 70-79, Kaohsiung Jr. Chamber 74, Stars Construction Co. Ltd. 76-99, Rotary Club of Kaohsiung W. Dist. 79-80, Lee's Hotel 86-99, Twn. Kaohsiung Chamber of Com. 87-93, Royal Lees Hotel 93-99; *Add.* 2 Ssu Wei 3rd Rd., Lingya, Kaohsiung 802.

LEE, TSU-TIAN 李祖添
Prof., EE & Dean, Off. of Res. & Dev., Nat. Twn. U. of Sc. & Tech. 98-; Adv., MOE 99-; Dir., Automatic Control

Prog., Dept. of Engr. & Applied Sc., NSC 98-; *b.* Taipei Feb. 1, '49; *m.* Lue, Fay Suzanne; 2 *s.; educ.* BS, NCTU 70; MSEE, U. of Oklahoma 73; Ph.D., U. of Oklahoma 75; Assc. Prof., Prof., & Chmn., Dept. of Control Engr., NCTU 75-86; Visiting Prof., EE, U. of Kentucky 86-87, Full Prof. 87-90; Prof. & Chmn., EE, Nat. Twn. U. of Sc. & Tech. 90-98. *Publ.:* Over 160 papers in automatic control, robotics, fuzzy systems, & neural networks in prof. jour.; *Add.* 43 Keelung Rd., Sect. 4, Taipei 106.

LEE, TSU-TIEN
(See LEE, TSU-TIAN 李祖添)

LEE, TSUNG-DAO 李政道
Mem., Acad. Sinica 57-; Enrico Fermi Prof. of Phys., Columbia U. 64-, U. Prof. 84-; *b.* Shanghai Nov. 25, '26; *m.* Chin, Jeannette; 1 *s.*, 1 *d.; educ.* Nat. Chekiang U. 43-44; Nat. S.We. Assc. U. 45-46; Ph.D., U. of Chicago 50; D.Sc., Princeton U. 58; LL.D., Ch. U. of Hong Kong 69; D.Sc., City Coll., CUNY 78; Dip. di Perfezionamento in Phys., Scuola Normale Superiore, Pisa, Italy 82; D.Sc., Bard Coll. & Peking U. 84 & 85; Res. Assc., Astronomy, U. of Chicago 50; Res. Assc. & Lectr. of Phys., U. of Calif. 50-51; Mem., Inst. of Advanced Study, Princeton U. 51-53; Asst. Prof., Phys., Columbia U. 53-55, Assc. Prof. 55-56, Prof. 56-60, Adjunct Prof. 60-62; Loeb Lectr., Harvard U. 57 & 64; Guggenheim Fel. 66; Mem., Am. Acad. of Arts & Sc., Am. Philosophical Soc., Acad. Nazionaledej Lincei, Rome; *Add.* Dept. of Phys., Columbia U., New York, NY 10027, USA.

LEE, TZUNG-JU
(See LEE, CHUNG-RU 李宗儒)

LEE, WANG-TAI 李旺臺
Dep. Sec.-Gen, DPP 98-; *b.* Twn. Mar. 14, '48; *m.* Lee, Jin-ju; 1 *s.*, 1 *d.; educ.* BA, Nat. Kaohsiung Normal U. 76; Ed.-in-Chief, *Twn. Times* 90-93, & *The Common Daily* 93-97; Dep. Ed.-in-Chief, *Liberty Times* 97-98; Dir., Dept. of Cul. & Info., DPP 98-99. *Publ.: The Assays about New Twn.* 91; *The Hist. of the Opposition Movement in Twn.* 92; *Add.* 8th Fl., 30 Pei Ping E. Rd., Taipei 100.

LEE, WEN-HUA
(See LEE, WEN-HWA 李文華)

LEE, WEN-HWA 李文華
Mem., Acad. Sinica 94-; Dir., Inst. of Biotech., Chair & Prof., Dept. of Molecular Med., U. of Texas Health Sc. Cent., San Antonio, 91-; *b.* Twn. June 1, '50; *m.* Lee, Eva; 1 *s.*, 1 *d.; educ.* BS, Biology, NTNU 72; MS, Biochem.,

NTU 77; Ph.D., Molecular Biology, UC-Berkly. 81. *Publ.:* Co-author of "Human Retinoblastoma Susceptibility Gene: Cloning, Identification & Sequence," *Sc.* (235; 1987), "The Retinoblastoma Gene Product Regulates Progression Through the G1 Phase of the Cell Cycle," *Cell* (67; 1991); "Mice Deficient for RB Are Nonviable & Show Defects in Neurogenesis & Hematopoiesis," *Nature* (359; 1992); *Add.* 15355 Lambda Drive, San Antonio, Texas 78245-3207, USA.

LEE, YEOU-CHI 李友吉
Mem., Control Yuan 99-; Standing Mem., Ch. Fed. of Labor 75-; *b.* Oct. 19, '39; *educ.* Grad., Nat. Twn. Acad. of Arts 71; Mem., NA 73-81; Chmn., Twn. Prov. Tobacco & Wine Ind. Unions 72-76; Mem., Home & Border Aff. Cttee., Legis. Yuan 94-98; *Add.* 2 Chung Hsiao E. Rd., Sect. 1, Taipei 100.

LEE, YING-MING 李英明
Chmn., Ch. Shipbldg. Corp. 94-; *b.* Peking Dec. 25, '34; *m.* Feng, Shu-chuan; 1 *s.*, 1 *d.; educ.* Ch. Naval Acad. 59; Naval Inst. Sch. 62; War Coll., CGSC 84; Mng. Dir., 2nd & 4th Naval Shipyards, ROCN 85-88, Logistics Off. 88-90, Dep. C/S, Navy GHQ 90-94, Cmdr., Navy Logistics Cmd. 93-94; *Add.* 3 Chung Kang Rd., Hsiaokang, Kaohsiung 812.

LEE, YU-CHI
(See LEE, YEOU-CHI 李友吉)

LEE, YU-LIN
(See LEE, YUH-LIN 李玉麟)

LEE, YUAN-CHUAN 李遠川
Mem., Acad. Sinica 94-; Prof., Johns Hopkins U. 65-; *b.* Twn. Mar. 30, '32; *m.* Reiko Takasaka; 1 *s.; educ.* Ph.D., Biochem., U. of Iowa. *Publ.:* Over 200 articles in prof. jour.; *Add.* Johns Hopkins U., 3400 N. Charles St., Baltimore, MD 21218, USA.

LEE, YUAN-CHUAN 李源泉
Dir.-Gen., Dept. of Soc. Aff., CC, KMT 99-; *b.* Twn. May 20, '44; *m.* Chang, Mei-tsu; 1 *s.*, 2 *d.; educ.* BS, Hydraulic Engr., NCKU 67; MS, Agr. Engr., NTU 70; Ph.D., Agr. Sect., Ch. Cul. U. 88; Assc. Mng. Sp., Head of Working Station, Mng. Sp., Chief of Regional Off., & Chmn., Tainan Irrigation Assn. 74-93; Mem., CC, KMT 88-97; Chmn., Twn. Joint Irrigation Assn. 90-93; Mem., Legis. Yuan 93-96; Consultant, Exec. Yuan 96; V. Chmn., Public Construction Com., Exec. Yuan 96-98; V. Chmn., COA 98-99; *Add.* 3rd Fl., 11 Chung Shan S. Rd., Taipei 100.

LEE, YUAN-CHE
(See LEE, YUAN-TSEH 李遠哲)

LEE, YUAN-TSEH 李遠哲
Pres., Acad. Sinica 94-, Mem. 80-; *b.* Twn. Nov. 29, '36; *m.* Wu, Bernice; 2 *s.*, 1 *d.; educ.* BS, NTU 59; MS, NTHU 61; Ph.D., UC-Berkly. 65, Postdr. Fel. 65-67; Res. Fel., Harvard U. 67-68; Asst. Prof., U. of Chicago 68-71, Assc. Prof. 71-72, Prof. 73-74; Fel., Am. Phys. Soc.; Mem., Nat. Acad. of Sc., USA, Am. Acad. Arts & Sc., & Am. Chem. Soc.; Prof. of Chem., UC-Berkly. 74-94; Nobel Prize in Chem. 86; Nat. Medal of Sc., White House, USA 86; Peter Debye Award for Phys. Chem., ACS 86; Faraday Medal 92; Nat. Policy Adv. to the Pres. 91-95. *Publ.:* Numerous articles on chem. phys. in prof. jour.; *Add.* Acad. Sinica, Nankang, Taipei 115.

LEE, YUH-LIN 李玉麟
Dep. Dir.-Gen., DGBAS 96-; *b.* Twn. Sept. 9, '44; *m.* Huang, Shu-chuan; 1 *s.*, 1 *d.; educ.* BA in Acct., NCCU 67; Staff Mem., 2nd Bu., DGBAS 71-73, Insp. 73-74, Sect. Chief 74-79, Sr. Sp. 79-81, Dep. Dir., 2nd Bu., DGBAS 81-86; Dir., Acct. Dept., MOEA 86-89; Dir., 2nd Bu., DGBAS 89-93, & Dept. of Budget, Acct. & Statistics, TCG 93-96; *Add.* 1 Chung Hsiao E. Rd., Sect. 1, Taipei 100.

LEE, YUNG-SAN 李庸三
Chmn., Intl. Cml. Bk. of Ch. 98-, & Bankers Assn. of Taipei 97-; *b.* Twn. Dec. 7, '38; *m.* Tzeng, S.C.; 3 *d.; educ.* BA, NTU 61; MA, U. of Wisconsin 68, Ph.D. 70; Asst., Inst. of Econ., Acad. Sinica 62-66, Asst. Res. Fel. 66-70, Assc. Res. Fel. 70-73, Res. Fel. 73-90, Dep. Dir. 85-87, Dir. 88-90; Assc. Prof., NTU 70-73, Prof. 73-94; Visiting Scholar, Harvard U. 76-77; Dir., Econ. Res. Dept., CBC 77-85; Sup., City Bk. of Taipei 78-90; Consultant, CEPD 88-91; Pres., Chiao Tung Bk. 90-94; Chmn., Farmers Bk. of Ch. 94-98. *Publ.: Expectation in the Consumption Function: Permanent Income Hypothesis Revisited* 70; *Econometric Methods* 73; *Analysis of Changes in Prices in Twn.* 74; *Comparative Analysis of Interest Receipts & Payments by Major Econ. Sectors in Twn. 1965-85* 87; *Add.* 100 Chi Lin Rd., Taipei 104.

LENG, JO-SHUI
(See LENG, ROCK JO-SHUI 冷若水)

LENG, ROCK JO-SHUI 冷若水
Rep., Taipei Rep. Off. in Hungary 96-; *b.* Chungking Oct. 10, '39; *m.* Sha, Chi-yen; 1 *s.*, 1 *d.; educ.* BA, NCCU 61; MA, Am. U., Washington, D.C. 73; MPA, Harvard U. 88; Reporter & Corr., CNA 64-81, Dep. Ed.-in-Chief & Ed.-in-Chief 83-

86, Chief, Washington Bu. 86-92; V. Chmn., Policy Planning Bd., MOFA 92-94, Spokesman 94-96. *Publ.: Press and Politics in the USA; 18 years in Washington, D.C.; Add.* 1088 Budapest, Rakoczi ut 1-3/III Em., Hungary.

LEU, HSI-MUH 呂溪木
Mem., Control Yuan 99-; Bd. Mem., Ch. Math. Soc. 62-; Bd. Chmn., Ch. Educ. Soc. 97-; *b.* Twn. Nov. 6, '40; *m.* Tseng, Yue-mei; 3 *d.; educ.* BS in Math., NTNU 63; Ph.D. in Math., Washington State U. 72; Bd. Chmn., Ch. Sc. Educ. Soc. 80-91; Rep., Intl. Cong. of Math. Educ. 75-93; Teaching Asst. & Tchr. 63-68; Asst. Prof., Washington State U. 72-73; Visiting Assc. Prof., NTNU 73-75, Assc. Prof. & concur. Chmn. 75-78; Dir., Sc. Div., NScC 85-87; Dir., Sc. Div., TECO in Los Angeles 87-90; Dean of Acad. Aff., NTNU 90-93, Pres. 93-99; Bd. Chmn., Ch. Tchr. Educ. Soc. 95-97. *Publ.: Morita Contexts & Rings of Quotients* 72; "On Semi-Simple Rings of Quotients" & "Rings of Quotients of R & eRe.," *Ch. Jour. of Math.* 74 & 76; "Idempotent Kernel Factors & Quotient Rings," *Bulletin of Inst. of Math., Acad. Sinica* 77; etc.; *Add.* 2 Chung Hsiao E. Rd., Sect. 1, Taipei 100.

LI, CHENG-CHANG 李成章
Pres., NCHU 97-; *b.* Twn. Oct. 2, '36; *m.* Hung, Su-chung; 1 *s.*, 1 *d.; educ.* BS, NCHU 60; MS, Nat. Philippines U. 65; Ph.D., U. of Calif.-Davis 75; Head, Dept. of Agronomy, NCHU 85-90, Dean, Coll. of Agr. 90-96. *Publ.: Glossary of Genetics* (in Ch.) 84; *Rice Genetics & Breeding* (in Eng.) 91; & over 140 res. papers on crop genetics & breeding & crop physiology; *Add.* 250 Kuo Kuang Rd., Taichung 402.

LI, CHIEN-CHUNG
(See LI, JOHN CHIEN-CHUNG 李建中)

LI, CHING-CHUN 李景均
Mem., Acad. Sinica 62-; Prof. of Biometry & Human Genetics, U. of Pittsburgh; *b.* Tientsin Oct. 27, '12; *m.* Lem, Clara; 1 *s.*, 1 *d.; educ.* BS, U. of Nanking; Ph.D., Cornell U.; Prof. of Agronomy, U. of Nanking 43-46; Chmn., Dept. of Agronomy, Nat. Peking U. 46-50; Pres., Am. Soc. of Human Genetics 60. *Publ.: Population Genetics; No. from Experiments; Human Genetics; Introduction to Experimental Statistics; Path Analysis; Analysis of Unbalanced Data; Add.* 1360 Terrace Drive, Pittsburgh, PA 15228-1637, USA.

LI, CHUNG-KUEI
(See LI, JEANNE TCHONG-KOEI 李鍾桂)

LI, HUI-LIN 李惠林

Mem., Acad. Sinica 64-; Prof. Emeritus, U. of Penn.; *b.* Kiangsu July 15, '11; *m.* Hsu, Chih-ying; 2 *d.; educ.* BS, Soochow U.; MS, Yenching U.; Ph.D., Harvard U.; Instr., Soochow U. 32-40; Tech. Asst., Arnold Arboretum 41-42; Res. Assc., Acad. of Natural Sc. of Philadelphia 42-46; Head & Prof., Dept. of Botany, NTU 47-50; Prof. of Botany, U. of Penn. 63-79; Dir., Morris Arboretum 70-75. *Publ.: Woody Flora of Twn.; Add.* 201 W. Evergreen Avenue, Philadelphia, PA 19118, USA.

LI, I-YUAN
(See LI, YIH-YUAN 李亦園)

LI, JEANNE TCHONG-KOEI 李鍾桂

Pres., Ch. Youth Corps 87-, & Cul. Promotion Assn. 82-; Pres., Ch. Basketball Alliance 95-; Chmn., Fed. for Asia Cul. Promotion 90-; Mem., CC, KMT 69-; Prof., NCCU & NTU 65-; Res. Fel., Inst. of Intl. Rel., NCCU 69-; *b.* Kiangsu July 7, '38; *m.* Shih, Chi-yang; *educ.* BA, NCCU; LL.D., U. of Paris; Chmn., Dept. of Dip., NCCU 70-72; Dir., Bu. of Intl. Cul. & Educ. Rel., MOE 72-77; Pres., Pacific Cul. Found. 77-87; Dep. Dir.-Gen., Dept. of Youth Aff., CC, KMT 79-87, Dir.-Gen., Dept. of Women's Aff. 88-93; Dep. Sec.-Gen., CC, KMT 93-95, Mem., CSC 93-94. *Publ.: The Evolution of the Anglo-French Dip. Rel. Between the 2 World Wars; A Study of the European Problems; World Aff. in the Past & Future; Sino-Am. Rel. & Our Nation's Prospect; Nat. Sec. & Human Rights; Add.* 219 Sungkiang Rd., Taipei 104.

LI, JOHN CHIEN-CHUNG 李建中

V. Chmn., Public Construction Com., Exec. Yuan 95-; Prof., NCU 84-; *b.* Shanghai Nov. 21, '47; *m.* Shen, Hsiao-ling; 1 *s.,* 1 *d.; educ.* BS, NCKU 71; MS, Michigan State U. 75, Ph.D. 79; Asst. Prof., Dept. of Civil Engr., Wayne State U. 79-80; Assc. Prof., Dept. of Civil Engr., NCU 80-84; Dir., Off. of Planning & Res., Ret-Ser Engr. Agency 85-88; Chmn., Civil Engr. Dept., NCU 88-91; Dep. Exec. Sec., Public Construction Supervisory Bd., Exec. Yuan 91-95. *Publ.:* Over 100 tech. papers; *Add.* 9th Fl., 4 Chung Hsiao W. Rd., Sect. 1, Taipei 100.

LI, KUO-TING
(See LI, KWOH-TING 李國鼎)

LI, KWOH-TING 李國鼎

Sr. Adv. to the Pres.; Mem., NScC, & CAC, KMT; Hon. Bd. Chmn., Chiang Ching-kuo Found. for Intl. Scholarly Exchange 95-; *b.* Nanking Jan. 28, '10; *m.* Sung, Pearl; 1 *s.;*

educ. BS, NCU, Nanking; Cambridge U.; Hon. Ph.D., Econ., Sung Kyun Kwan U., S. Korea 78; D.Sc., NCU 83 & U. of Maryland 89; Ph.D., Engr., NCTU 89; Ph.D., Chung Yuan Christian U. 90; LL.D., Boston U. 90; Hon. Fel., Emmanuel Coll., Cambridge U. 91; LL.D., Ch. U. of Hong Kong 91; Hon. D.Lit., New York State U. at Stony Brook 95; Hon. Dr. of Engr., NTHU 97, & NTU 98; Pres. & Prof., Nat. Wuhan U. 37-40; Twn. Shipbldg. Corp. 48-53; Mem., Ind. Dev. Com., Econ. Stabilization Bd. 53-58; Sec.-Gen., CUSA 58-63; V. Chmn., CIECD 63-73; Min. of Econ. Aff. 65-69; Min. of Finance 69-76; Gov., Intl. Bk. for Recon. & Dev., Intl. Dev. Assn. 69-76; Min. without Portfolio 76-88; Bd. Chmn., Chiang Ching-kuo Found. for Intl. Scholarly Exchange 89-95. *Publ.: Symposium on Nuclear Phys.; British Ind.; Japanese Shipbldg. Ind.; The Econ. Transformation of Twn.; The Growth of Private Ind. in Free Ch.; The Experience of Dynamic Econ. Growth on Twn.; The Evolution of Policy Behind Twn.'s Dev. Success; Vision & Devotion* 87; *Witnessing Econ. & Soc. Dev. on Twn., ROC; Experience & Belief* 91; etc.; *Add.* 3 Lane 2, Tai An St., Taipei 100.

LI, LIEN-CHUN
(See LI, RIEN-CHUN 李連春)

LI, RIEN-CHUN 李連春

Nat. Policy Adv. to the Pres. 76-; *b.* Twn. Jan. 10, '04; *m.* Wang, Pao-yu; 2 *s.,* 2 *d.; educ.* Grad., Cml. Sch., Kobe, Japan; Comr. & concur. Dir., Food Bu., TPG, & Bd. Chmn., Cooperative Bk. of Twn. 46-70; Min. without Portfolio 70-76; *Add.* 8 Hsi Ning S. Rd., Taipei 108.

LI, TING-I
(See LI, TINGYE 厲鼎毅)

LI, TINGYE 厲鼎毅

Mem., Acad. Sinica 94-; Independent Consultant 99-; *b.* Nanking July 7, '31; *m.* Wu, Edith Hsiu-hwei; 2 *d.; educ.* BSEE, U. of Witwatersrand, S. Africa 53; MSEE, N.We. U. 55, Ph.D. 58; Hon. Engr. Dr., NCTU 91; Mem. of Tech. Staff, AT&T Bell Labs. 57-67, Head, Lightwave Systems Res. Dept. 67-96; Mem., Nat. Acad. of Engr. 80; Div. Mgr., AT&T Labs. 96-98. *Publ.:* Over 100 papers in the areas of antennas, microwaves, lasers, optical comms.; 15 patents in the above areas; 2 bk. on lightwave comms.; *Add.* 563 Locust Place, Boulder, CO 80304, USA.

LI, TZU-LIANG
(See LAI, TZE-LEUNG 黎子良)

LI, YA-CHING 李雅景

Magis., Chiayi County 93-; *b.* Twn. July 23, '49; *m.* Chen, Hsiu-tuan; 3 *s.; educ.* Grad., Tatung Com. Coll. 70; Mem., Chiayi CoCoun. 73-85, & TPA 85-93; *Add.* 1 Shiang Ho 1st Rd., E. Sect., Shiangho Hsien Tsun, Taipao, Chiayi County 612.

LI, YIH-YUAN 李亦園

Mem., Acad. Sinica; Pres., Chiang Ching-kuo Found. for Intl. Scholarly Exchange 89-; Yu Kuo-hua Chair Prof. of Anthropology, NTHU; *b.* Fukien Aug. 20, '31; *m.* Liu, Shih-shun; 3 *c.; educ.* BA, NTU; MA, Anthropology, Harvard U.; Prof., NTU 63-84; Assc. Dir., Inst. of Ethnology, Acad. Sinica 69-71, Dir. 71-77; Fulbright Visiting Prof., U. of Pittsburgh 80-81; Dean, Coll. of Humanities & Soc. Sc., NTHU 84-90; Fel., Royal Anthropological Soc.; Nat. Cul. Award 98. *Publ.: Belief & Cul.; Cul. & Behavior; Anthropology & Modern Soc.; Soc. & Cul. of the Twn. Aborigines; The Nat. Character of the Ch.; The Images of Cul.; Essays on Religion & Myth; Albums from the Field: An Anthropologist's Journey;* etc.; *Add.* 4 Alley 3, Lane 4, Yen Chiu Yuan Rd., Sect. 2, Nankang, Taipei 115.

LI, YU-HSI
(See NI, YUE-SI 黎玉璽)

LI, YUAN-TSU
(See LI, YUAN-ZU 李元簇)

LI, YUAN-ZU 李元簇

Sr. Adv. to the Pres. 96-; V. Chmn., KMT 93-; *b.* Hunan Sept. 24, '23; *m.* Hsu, Man-yung; 2 *s.; educ.* LL.B., NCCU; LL.D., Bonn U.; Hon. DPS, Sung Kyun Kwan U., S. Korea; Hon. LL.D., Hanyang U., S. Korea; Dir., Legal Dept., MND 69-72; Chmn., Legal Com., Exec. Yuan 72-73; Dean, Grad. Sch. of Law, NCCU 70-73, Pres. 73-77; Min. of Educ. 77-78; Dir.-Gen., Ch. Youth Corps 77-78; Min. of Justice 78-84; Nat. Policy Adv. to the Pres. 84-89; Sec.-Gen. to the Pres. 88-90; V. Pres., ROC 90-96. *Publ.: Inwieweit Sind die Auslaendischen Strafrechte im Inlande Anwendbar? Add.* c/o Off. of the Pres., Taipei 100.

LIANG, CHENG-CHIN
(See LIANG, PATRICK C.J. 梁成金)

LIANG, PATRICK C.J. 梁成金

Chmn., Chiao Tung Bk. 98-; *b.* Twn. Mar. 16, '39; *m.* Liang, Nancy; 1 *s.,* 1 *d.; educ.* BBA & MBA, NCCU; Pres., Cent. Depository Ins. Corp. 85-88; Dir.-Gen., Banking Dept., CBC;

V. Chmn., CEPD 92-95; Dep. Gov., CBC 95-98; Chmn., Farmers Bk. of Ch. 98; *Add.* 91 Heng Yang Rd., Taipei 100.

LIANG, TUNG-TSAI
(See WAY, E. LEONG 梁棟材)

LIAO, CHENG-CHING 廖正井

Chmn., Taipei Bk. 97-; *b.* Twn. Jan. 8, '45; *m.* Yang, Chi-chin; 1 *d.; educ.* BA, Dept. of Public Finance, Feng Chia U. 73; MA, Public Finance, NCCU 76; Passed the Civil Service Sp. Exam. A 86; Staff Mem., CBC 73-74; Auditor & Sp., MOF 74-77; Sect. Chief & Sp., Twn. Tobacco & Wine Monopoly Bu. 77-83; Sect. Chief, MOI 84-86; Adjunct Assc. Prof., Ming Chuan U. & Feng Chia U. 84; Sr. Off., MOI 86-87; Counsl. 87-88; Counsl., TCG 88-90, Dir., Finance Bu. 90-94; Acting Chmn., Taipei Bk. 94; Sec.-Gen., TCG 94-97; *Add.* 50 Chung Shan N. Rd., Sect. 2, Taipei 104.

LIAO, CHIEN-NAN
(See LIAO, JIANN-NAN 廖健男)

LIAO, HSIU-PING
(See LIAO, SHIOU-PING 廖修平)

LIAO, HUI-YING 廖輝英

Writer 88-; *b.* Twn. Apr. 2, '48; *m.* Yang, Po-nan; 1 *s.,* 1 *d.; educ.* BA, NTU 70; Ed., Kuo Hua Advertising Co. 70-74; Ed., Women's World Mag. 74-76; Kai-mei Housing Co. 76-78; Ogilvy & Mather (Twn.) Co. Ltd. 78-80; Lun Lin Bldg. Co. 80-82. *Publ.: Blind Spot; Migratory Birds in the City; The Shadow of the Moon; Add.* 3rd Fl., 19 Lane 63, Tun Hua S. Rd., Sect. 2, Taipei 106.

LIAO, I-CHIU 廖一久

Mem., Acad. Sinica 92-; Dir.-Gen., Twn. Fisheries Res. Inst. 87-; Prof., Zoology, NTU 74-; Mem., 3rd World Acad. of Sc. 90-; *b.* Twn. Nov. 4, '36; *m.* Chao, Nai-hsien; 2 *s.; educ.* BS, Zoology, NTU 60; M. of Agr., U. of Tokyo 64, Ph.D. 68; Res. Fel., Rockefeller Found. Prog. 68-69; Assc. Prof., Dept. of Zoology & Inst. of Oceanology, NTU 68-74; Dir., Tungkang Marine Lab., Twn. Fisheries Res. Inst 71-87; Tech. Adv., Milkfish Project, US Agency for Intl Dev. 84-90; Bd. Mem., Asian Fisheries Soc. 84-92; Chmn. Asian Fisheries Soc., Twn. Chapter 85-98. *Publ.: Generation Cycle of Grey Mullet, Mugil Cephalus in Captivity; &* 327 papers; *Add.* 199 Ho I Rd., Keelung 202.

LIAO, JIANN-NAN 廖健男

Mem., Control Yuan 99-; *b.* Twn. Aug. 16, '44; *m.* Lee, Su-chi; 1 *s.,* 2 *d.; educ.* LL.B., NTU 67, LL.M. 72; LL.M., U of Washington 90; Partner, Ming-Dir Law Off. 78-80, Century Law Off. 80-86, First Law Off. 86-87, & Baker & McKenzie Law Off.87-92; Dir., Candor Law Off. 92-99. *Publ.:* Many papers on legal issues; *Add.* 2 Chung Hsiao E. Rd., Sect. 1, Taipei 100.

LIAO, KUANG-SHENG
(See LIAO, TONY K.S. 廖光生)

LIAO, SHENG-HSIUNG 廖勝雄
Dir.-Gen., 1st Bu., Off. of the Pres. 99-; Pres., Ch. Assn. of Admin. Dev. 91-; *b.* Twn. Sept. 7, '43; *m.* Fu, Meng-ching; 1 *s.,* 1 *d.; educ.* BA, Tunghai U. 65; MA, NTU 68; Ph.D., Florida State U. 78; Prof. of Pol. Sc., Tunghai U. 83-88; Visiting Prof., U. of Massachusetts 85-86; Dep. Sec.-Gen., TPG 88-93, Acting Sec.-Gen. 93; Dean of Student Aff., Tunghai U. 94-97. *Publ.: The Mukden Incident 1931 & the League of Nations* 69; *The Bill of Rights in the Stalin Const.* 73; *The Quest for Constitutionalism in Late Ching Ch.* 79; *The Elite & Pol. Dev.* 80; *3rd Parties & Gen. Election* 84; *The Sources of Productivity: HRD* 88; *Circuitousness of Const. Dev.* 94; *Add.* 122 Chungking S. Rd., Sect. 1, Taipei 100.

LIAO, SHIOU-PING 廖修平
Artist; Mem., Soc. of Am. Graphic Artists; Adjudicator, Intl. Biennial Prints Exhibition of Twn. & Nat. Twn. Fine Arts Exhibition; *b.* Twn. Sept. 2, '36; *m.* Wu, Shur-jen; 2 *c.; educ.* BA, NTNU 59; MA, Tokyo U. of Educ. 64; Res. at L'école des Beau-Arts, Paris 65-68; Continued Printmaking Work at Pratt Graphics Cent., New York; Assc. Prof., NTNU; Adjunct Prof., Coll. of Ch. Cul. & Nat. Twn. Acad. of Arts 73-76; Lectured at Ch. U. of Hong Kong 74, Japan Aichi Art U. 78, & Tsukuba U.; Adjunct Prof. of Art, Ston Hall U. 79-92; Nat. Lit. & Art Lifetime Achievement Award 98; *Exhibitions:* Taipei Fine Arts Museum 89; Tainan Museum of Art 92; Shanghai Museum of Art 93; Howard Salon, Art Galleries Fair 94; Virant Gallery, Tokyo 97; Cite Internationale des Arts, Paris 98; Taipei Art Fair Intl. 99; Marche Bonsecours, Montreal, Canada 2000; Hong Kong Art Cent., Hong Kong 2000. *Publ.: The Art of Printmaking; Appreciation of Modern Printmaking; Printmaking Techniques; Add.* 160 Jen Ai Rd., Sect. 3, Taipei 106.

LIAO, SHU-TSUNG
(See LIAO, SHUTSUNG 廖述宗)

LIAO, SHUTSUNG 廖述宗
Mem., Acad. Sinica 94-; Prof., Dept. of Biochem. & Molecular Biology, Ben May Inst., U. of Chicago, Cttee. on Dev. Biology, Cttee. on Cancer Biology, Cancer Res. Cent. 72-; Mem., N. Am. Twn. Prof. Assn. (NATPA) 80-, & Am. Acad. of Art and Sc. 97-; *b.* Twn. Jan. 1, '31; *m.* Kuo, Shuching; 4 *d.; educ.* BS, NTU 53, MS 56; Ph.D., U. of Chicago 61; Asst. Prof., U. of Chicago 64-69, Assc. Prof. 69-71; Pres., NATPA 80-81. *Publ.:* Over 200 articles in prof. jour. in the fields of molecular action of steroid hormones, androgen & other nuclear receptors, gene mutations in hereditary abnormalities, carcinogenesis & chemotherapy of cancers; *Add.* U. of Chicago, 5841 S. Maryland Avenue, MC 6027, Chicago IL 60637, USA.

LIAO, TA-SHENG 廖大昇
V. Chmn., ROC Small & Medium Ent. Assn. 98-; Gen. Mgr., Ching Tai Resins Chem. Co. Ltd. 81-; Standing Bd. Mem., Twn. Glue Painting Assn. 94-; *b.* Twn. Sept. 13, '39; *m.* Tsay, jen-shii; 2 *d.; educ.* Grad., Taichung Normal Sch. 58; Tech. Art Prog., NTNU 69; Elementary Sch. Tchr. 58-68; Jr. High Sch. Tchr. 68-78; Gen. Mgr., Fushou Dept. Store 78-79; Sales Mgr., Minyin Co. Ltd. 79-81. *Publ.: Liao Ta sheng Glue Paintings I & II; Let's Improve Together* (prose) 91-92; *Add.* 50 Kung II Rd., Yu Shih Ind. Zone, Tachia, Taichung County 412.

LIAO, TONY K.S. 廖光生
Sr. Adv., NSC 96-; Adjunct Prof., Coll. of Law, NTU 96-; *b.* Twn. May 14, '41; *m.* Liao, Kuanya; 1 *d.; educ.* BA, NTU 63; DPS, U. of Michigan 74; Chmn., Dept. of Gov. & PA, Ch. U. of Hong Kong 74-95, Dep. Dir., Cent. of Contemporary Asian Studies 84-89; Legis. 93-95. *Publ.: The New Intl. Order in E. Asia; Pol. of Econ. Cooperation in the Asia-Pacific Region; Antiforeignism & Modernization in Ch.; Econ. & Public Aff. in Hong Kong; Modernization & Dip. of Ch.; Add.* 122 Chungking S. Rd., Sect. 1, Taipei 100.

LIAO, YUNG-LAI 廖永來
Magis., Taichung County 97-; *b.* Twn. Aug. 1, '56; *m.* Lin, Ju-chiung; *educ.* Grad., Prov. Tchrs. Jr. Coll. of Taichung 76; Mem., Legis. Yuan 93-96, & CSC, DPP 96-97; *Add.* Taichung County Govt., 36 Yang Ming Rd., Fengyuan, Taichung County 420.

LIAU, MARIETTA 高青雲
Sec.-Gen., CCNAA, Hqs. for TECRO in the US 99-; *b.* Taipei Feb. 16, '49; *m.* Liau, Hermann; 1 *s.,* 1 *d.; educ.* BA, Fu Jen Catholic U.; Tourism Bu., MOTC 72-78; Staff Mem., MOFA 78-82; Sp. Asst. & Sr. Asst., TECRO 82-89; Sect. Chief & Asst. Dir.-Gen., MOFA 89-92; Dir.-Gen.,

TECO in Hamburg, Germany 92-96; Dir.-Gen., TECO in Atlanta 96-99; *Add.* 133 Po Ai Rd., Taipei 100.

LIEN, CHAN 連戰
V. Pres., ROC 96-2000; Acting Chmn., KMT 2000-; *b.* Sian Aug. 27, '36; *m.* Fang, Yui; 2 *s.,* 2 *d.; educ.* BPS, NTU 57; MA, Intl. Law & Dip., U. of Chicago 61, DPS 65; Asst. Prof., Dept. of Pol. Sc., U. of Wisconsin 66-67 & U. of Connecticut 67-68; Visiting Prof., Dept. of Pol. Sc., NTU 68-69, Prof. & Chmn., Dept. of Pol. Sc. & concur. Dir., Grad. Inst. of Pol. Sc. 69-75; Amb. to El Salvador 75-76; Dir.-Gen., Dept. of Youth Aff., CC, KMT 76-78, Dep. Sec.-Gen. 78; Chmn., NYC 78-81; Min. of Comms. 81-87; Mem., CSC, KMT 84-93; V. Premier, ROC 87-88; Min. of For. Aff. 88-90; Gov., TPG 90-93; Premier, ROC 93-97; V. Chmn., KMT 93-2000. *Publ.: The Found. of Dem.; Twn. in Ch.'s External Rel.; The We. Pol. Thought; Add.* 11 Chung Shan S. Rd., Taipei 100.

LIN, BIH-JAW 林碧炤
Dep. Sec.-Gen., Off. of the Pres. 99-2000; *b.* Twn. Jan. 20, '49; *m.* Lin, Lien; 2 *s.; educ.* LL.B., NCCU 70; MA, U. of Manchester, UK 74; Ph.D., U. of Wales, UK 81; Asst. Resr., Inst. of Intl. Rel. (IIR), NCCU 77-80, Assc. Resr. & Sect. Chief of Intl. Cooperation 81-84; Assc. Prof. & Dean, Grad. Sch. of Law & Dip., NCCU 84-87, Prof. & Dean 88-90, Dir., IIR 90-94. *Publ.: Intl. Rel. & For. Policy; Add.* c/o, Off. of the Pres., 122 Chungking S. Rd., Sect. 1, Taipei 100.

LIN, CHANG-SHOU 林長壽
Mem., Acad. Sinica 98-; Prof., Math., Nat. Chung Cheng U. 90-; *b.* Twn. Apr. 17, '51; *m.* Chou, Ya-jung; 1 *s.,* 1 *d.; educ.* BS, Math, NTU; MS & D.Sc., Math, New York U.; Prof., Math, NTU 87-90; Dir. & Prof., Inst. of Math, Nat. Chung Cheng U. 90-92; *Add.* 160 Sanhsing Tsun, Minhsiung Hsiang, Chiayi County 621.

LIN, CHENG-CHIH
(See LIN, HELEN CHEN-CHI 林澄枝)

LIN, CHENG-HONG 林政弘
V. Chmn., Nat. Coun. on Phys. Fitness & Sports, Exec. Yuan 98-; *b.* Twn. Jan. 20, '41; *m.* Chiu, Chiu-yueh; 1 *s.,* 1 *d.; educ.* BS, NCCU 64; Dir., Dept. of Pers., MOE 86-94; Sec.-Gen., NTU 94-98. *Publ.: The Op. & Mng. of Museums in the ROC; Add.* 10th Fl., 80 Chien Kuo N. Rd., Sect. 1, Taipei 104.

LIN, CHENG-HUNG
(See LIN, CHENG-HONG 林政弘)

LIN, CHI-CHENG
(See LIN, KI-TSENG 林基正)

LIN, CHI-YANG 林淇瀁
Author; Lectr., Providence U. 96-; *b.* Twn. May 7, '55; *m.* Lin, Li-chen; 2 *d.; educ.* BA, Ch. Cul. U. 77, MA 94; Dir. & concur. Ed., *Independence Evening News* 82-87, Ed.-in-Chief 87-89; Ed.-in-Chief, *Independence Morning News* 89-94. *Publ.: Four Seasons; Song of the Land; Pray for Twn.;* etc.; *Add.* 15-10 Lane 36, Shui Yuan Rd., Keelung 205.

LIN, CHIA-CHENG 林嘉誠
Dir.-Gen., RDEC 2000-; Prof., Dept. of Sociology, Soochow U.; *b.* Twn. Aug. 27, '52; *m.* Chen, Ling-hua; 1 *c.; educ.* Ph.D., Dept. of Pol. Sc., NTU; Chmn., Res., Dev., & Evaluation Com., TCG 94-98; Dep. Mayor, Taipei City 97-98; *Add.* 1 Chung Hsiao E. Rd., Sect. 1, Taipei 100.

LIN, CHIANG-TSAI 林將財
Mem., Control Yuan 99-; *b.* Twn. Nov. 4, '34; *m.* Chen, Chun-ju; 1 *d.; educ.* B., Engr., NCKU; Capt., Div. of City Planning & Survey, TCG 73-77, Dir. 77-82; Dep. Comr., Dept. of Recon., TPG 82-93, Dir., Bu. of Housing & Urban Dev. 93-96, Comr., Dept. of Recon. 96-99; *Add.* 2 Chung Hsiao E. Rd., Sect. 1, Taipei 100.

LIN, CHIEN-CHANG 林見昌
Pres., Nat. Huwei Inst. of Tech. 99-; *b.* Twn. July 6, '41; *m.* Wu Yuan-kuei; 1 *s.,* 2 *d.; educ.* BS, NCHU 65; MS, Georgia Inst. of Tech., USA 69, Ph.D. 73; Assc. Prof., Dept. of Applied Math, NCHU 73-76, Prof. 76-99, Chmn. 79-85; Dir., Computer Cent., NCHU 80-84, Dean, Coll. of Sc. 88-94; *Add.* 64 Wen Hua Rd., Huwei, Yunlin County 632.

LIN, CHIN-CHING 林金莖
Chmn., Assn. of E. Asian Rel. 96-; Chmn., Sino-Japanese Found. for Cul. & Educ.; *b.* Twn. July 18, '23; *m.* Lin Wu, Ai-kuei; 4 *s.,* 1 *d.; educ.* LL.B., NTU 50; LL.D., Waseda U., Japan 62; Ph.D., Asia U., Japan 88; Passed the Sr. Civil Service Exam. for Lawyers, Admin., & Dip.; Sec., MOJ 50-51; Sect. Chief, TPG 51-58; Sp., Dept. of E. Asian & Pacific Aff., MOFA 58-59; 3rd Sec., Emb. in Japan 59-62; Consul, Osaka, Japan 62-67; Sect. Chief, Dept. of E. Asian & Pacific Aff., MOFA 67-71; Pol. Counsl., Emb. in Japan 71-73; Dep. Rep., Tokyo Off., AEAR 73-89; Mem., CEPD & Adv., MOFA 90-93; Rep., TECROJ 93-96. *Publ.: Criminal Anthropology on Criminal Law; Aboriginal Admin. in Twn. Prov.; Election System in New Zealand; UN Peace Forces; Rel. between the ROC & Japan After World War*

II; *Sino-Japanese Rel. & Intl. Law; On the Const. of Japan;* *Add.* 4th Fl., 7 Roosevelt Rd., Sect. 1, Taipei 100.

LIN, CHIOU-SHAN 林秋山
Mem., Control Yuan 93-; Prof., Ch. Cul. U. 65-; *b.* Twn. Jan. 28, '36; *m.* Liao, Pi-ring; 2 *d.; educ.* LL.B., NCCU 59; MA, Kyung Hee U., Korea 63, Ph.D. 73; Dep. Dir., GIO 66-67; Sr. Sp., Dept. of Cul. Aff., MOE 67-73; Mem., NA 87-93. *Publ.: Gen. Introduction to Korea* (6 Vol.); *Biography of Pres. Park Chong-hee* 77; *Dev. of the Korean Press System of Self-restraint* 68; *New Discourse of Korean Hist.* (transl.); *System of the Korean Const.* (transl.); *Modern Hist. of Korea* (transl.); *Comprehensive Theses on Korea* (6 Vol.); *Add.* 2 Chung Hsiao E. Rd., Sect. 1, Taipei 100.

LIN, CHIU-SHAN
(See LIN, CHIOU-SHAN 林秋山)

LIN, CHIU-JUNG
(See LIN, CHU-YUNG 林秋榮)

LIN, CHONG-PIN 林中斌
V. Chmn., MAC 96-; *b.* Yunnan May 7, '42; *m.* Chang, Chia-pei; *educ.* BA, Geol., NTU 65; MA, Geol., Bowling Green State U., USA 69; MBA, UCLA 75; Ph.D., Govt., Georgetown U. 86; Sr. Geologist/Financial Analyst, Johns-Manville Corp. 76-78; Res. Asst. to US Amb. Jeane Kirkpatrick 86-87; Sun Yat-sen Prof. of Ch. Studies, Georgetown U. 90-92.; Resident Scholar & Assc. Dir., Asian Studies Prog., Am. Ent. Inst., USA 87-95; Adjunct Prof., Govt. Dept., Georgetown U. 88-94; Prof., Nat. Sun Yat-sen U. 95-96. *Publ.: PRC Tomorrow; Ch.'s Nuclear Weapons Strategy: Tradition Within Evolution* 88; "The Role of the PLA in the Process of Reunification: Exploring the Possibilities," *PLA Year Bk.* 93; "The Coming Ch. Earthquake," *Intl. Econ.* 92; "Beijing & Taipei," *Ch. Quarterly* 93; "Red Fist: Ch.'s Army in Transition," *Intl. Def. Review* 95; "The Mil. Balance in the Twn. Straits," *Ch. Quarterly* 96; *Add.* 16th Fl., 2-2 Chi Nan Rd., Sect. 1, Taipei 100.

LIN, CHU-LIANG 林鉅鋃
Mem., Control Yuan 99-; *b.* Twn. Mar. 28, '47; *m.* Lee, Yueh-ying; 2 *s.; educ.* LL.M., NCU 74; Staff, 1st Dept., Exec. Yuan 72-74, Dept. Chief, Sp. & Sec., Laws & Regln. Cttee. 75-88, Counsl. & Dir., 1st Dept. 88-95, Chmn., Laws & Regln. Cttee. 95-97; Admin. V. Min. of Justice 97-98. *Publ.: Res. on Indirect Crimes; Add.* 2 Chung Hsiao E. Rd., Sect. 1, Taipei 100.

LIN, CHU-YUNG 林秋榮
Mem., Acad. Sinica 98-; Prof., Dept. of Botany, NTU 76; *b.* Twn. Aug. 25, '28; *m.* Yang, Peng-chen; 1 *s.,* 2 *d.; educ.* BS, NTU 51; Ph.D., U. of Oklahoma 63; Visiting Assc. Prof., NTU 66-67, Visiting Prof. 67-68, Prof. 68-69; Resr., U. of Georgia, USA 69-75; Chmn., Dept. of Botany, NTU 76-82, Dean, Coll. of Sc. 90-93. *Publ.: Expression of a Gene Encoding a 16.9 kDa Heat-shock Protein; Add.* 6th Fl., 5-1 Alley 15, Lane 96, Ho Ping E. Rd., Sect. 2, Taipei 106.

LIN, CHUAN 林全
Dir.-Gen., DGBAS 2000-; *b.* Kiangsu Dec. 13, '51; *educ.* B., Econ., Fu Jen Catholic U. 74; MS, Public Finance, NCCU 78; Ph.D., Econ., U. of Illinois 84; Assc. Res. Fel., Chung-Hua, Inst. of Econ. Res. 84-89; Adv., Tax Reform Cttee., MOF 87-89; Assc. Prof., Dept. of Public Finance, NCCU 89-90, Prof. 90-95 & 98-2000; Adjunct Prof., Dept. of Econ. & Grad. Inst. of Building & Planning, NTU 92-95; Gen. Dir., Bu. of Finance, TCG 95-98. *Publ.:* 15 papers in periodicals, 4 conf. papers, & 26 res. papers; *Add.* 1 Chung Hsiao E. Rd., Sect. 1, Taipei 100.

LIN, CHUAN-HUAI 林傳槐
Pres., Ta Hwa Inst. of Tech., Prof. 85-; *b.* Twn. May 22, '10; *m.* Peng, chin; 2 *s.,* 1 *d.; educ.* Eng., NTNU 58, BA, Public Tng., NTNU 78; MA, Public Educ., U. of Missouri 85; Tchr., Twn. Prov. Hsinchu Tchrs. Coll.-affiliated Elementary Sch. 52-58, Hsinchu County Kuanghua Jr. High Sch. 60-79; Lectr., Ta Hwa Ind. Coll. 79-81, Assc. Prof. 81-85; *Add.* 1 Ta Hua Rd., Chiunglin Hsiang, Hsinchu County 307.

LIN, CHUN-I
(See LIN, JUN-YI 林俊義)

LIN, CHUNG
(See LIN, FRANK C. 林鍾)

LIN, CHUNG-HSIUNG
(See LIN, JONG-SHONG 林鐘雄)

LIN, CHUNG-PIN
(See LIN, CHONG-PIN 林中斌)

LIN, CHUNG-SEN
(See LIN, JOIN-SANE 林中森)

LIN, CHUNG-SHENG 林中生
Pres., Chung Shan Med. & Dental Coll. 98-; *b.* Twn. Apr. 20, '47; *m.* Hsu, Su-mei; 2 *s.,* 1 *d.; educ.* MD, Chung Shan

Med. & Dental Coll. 71, & Tokyo Med. Coll. 89; Dean, Sch. of Med., Chung Shan Med. & Dental Coll. 88-89; Supt., Taichung Rehabilitation Hosp. 89-94; Dean, Acad. Aff., Chung Shan Med. & Dental Coll. 94-95, Chief, Med. Res. Inst. 95-98, V. Supt. 96-98. *Publ.:* More than 20 articles; *Add.* 110 Chien Kuo N. Rd., Sect. 1, Taichung 402.

LIN, DAVID S.M. 林世明
Pres., Ming-hsin Inst. of Tech. 97-, Prof. 92-; *b.* Chekiang Sept. 23, '43; *m.* Lu, Chia-yu; 2 *d.; educ.* BA, NCCU 66; MA, Ch. Cul. U. 71; MA, Ea. New Mexico U. 76; Doctoral Prog., State U. of New York 78; Tachu Middle Sch. 66-71; Lectr. & Assc. Prof., Ming-hsin Jr. Coll. 71-79 & 79-92. *Publ.: A Study on the Mutual Protection Movement by Provinces in S.E. Ch. During the Boxer Uprising; A Study on Regional Groups in Ching Dynasty; Add.* 4th Fl., 7 Lane 237, Fu Ho Rd., Yungho, Taipei County 234.

LIN, FANG-MEI 林芳玫
Chairperson, NYC 2000-; *b.* Taipei Dec. 1, '61; *m.* Hung, Wan-sheng; *educ.* Ph.D., Sociology, U. of Penn.; Assc. Prof., Dept. of Jour., NCCU 92-96, Prof. 96-2000; *Add.* 14th Fl., 5 Hsuchow Rd., Taipei 100.

LIN, FENG-CHENG
(See LIN, FONG-CHENG 林豐正)

LIN, FONG-CHENG 林豐正
Sec.-Gen., KMT 2000-; *b.* Twn. Mar. 20, '40; *m.* Hwang, Hsieu; 1 *s.,* 2 *d.; educ.* LL.B., NCHU 63; Chief Exec., Taoyuan County Cttee., Ch. Youth Corps 73; Dir., Dept. of Civil Aff., Taipei County Govt. 73-74, & Dept. of Soc. Aff. 74-76; Chief Sec., Taipei County Govt. 76-78, Dir., Dept. of Soc. Aff. 78-80; Chmn., Tainan County Cttee., KMT 80-81; Magis., Taipei County 81-89; Comr., Dept. of Civil Aff., TPG 90-92; Chmn., Twn. Prov. Cttee., KMT 92-93; Sec.-Gen., TPG 93-94, Pol. Lt. Gov. 94-96; Min. of the Int. 96-97; Min. without Portfolio 97-98; Min. of Trans. & Comms. 98-2000; *Add.* 11 Chung Shan S. Rd., Taipei 104.

LIN, FRANK C. 林鍾
Rep., TECO in New Zealand 94-; *b.* Fukien Jan. 8, '35; *m.* Tai, Hong-hwa; 1 *s.,* 2 *d.; educ.* BPS, NTU 55; 1st Sec., Emb. in the Dominican Repub. 75-77; Consul, Consl. at Bananguilla in Colombia 77-80; Dep. Exec. Sec.-Gen., Com. of Intl. Tech. Cooperation, MOFA 80-81, Dep. Dir., Dept. of E. Asian & Pacific Aff. 81-83; Consul-Gen., Emb. at Seoul 83-86, Min. 88-91; Min., Emb. at Riyadh 86-88; Dir., Dept. of Pers. & Govt. Ethics, MOFA 91-94; *Add.* 21st Fl., 105 The Terrace, Wellington, New Zealand.

LIN, HELEN CHEN-CHI 林澄枝
Chmn., CCA 96-2000; *b.* Twn. Feb. 17, '39; *m.* Shieh, Mung-shiung; 4 *d.; educ.* Grad., Home Econ. Dept., Shih Chien U. 61; Grad. Study at Tchrs.' Coll., Columbia U. 69; Pres., Shih Chien U. 78-83; Mem., NA 92-97; Dir.-Gen., Dept. of Women's Aff., CC, KMT 93-96; *Add.* 60 Hsin Sheng S. Rd., Sect. 2, Taipei 106.

LIN, HSI-SHAN 林錫山
Sec.-Gen., Legis. Yuan 99-, Mem. 90-; *b.* Twn. Mar. 17, '62; *m.* Liu, Hsin-wei; 1 *s.; educ.* MA candidate, Architectural & Urban Planning, Ch. Cul. U.; Dir., Job Placement Office, Chungchou Jr. Coll. of Tech. 89; Dir., Changhua Br., Service Cent. for Reserved Soldiers, KMT 88-94, Bd. Mem., Changhua Br., Public Service Cent. 89-94; *Add.* 1 Chung Shan S. Rd., Taipei 100.

LIN, HSIANG-NENG
(See LIN, SHIANG-NUNG 林享能)

LIN, HSIEN-HUI
(See LIN, SHEAN-HUEI 林顯輝)

LIN, HSIEN-LANG
(See LIN, SAMUEL H.L. 林賢郎)

LIN, HSIN-I 林信義
Min. of Econ. Aff. 2000-; *b.* Twn. Dec. 2, '46; *m.* Lin Yeh, Mei-yin; 3 *c.; educ.* B., Mech. Engr., NCKU 70; Engr., Engr. Div., Ch. Motor Corp. 72, Dep. Mgr. 74-76, Dep Mgr., Marketing Div. 76-79, Yangmei Plant Mgr. 80-82 V. Pres. 82-87, Exec. V. Pres. 87-90, Pres. 91-96; Chmn. Auto motive Res. & Testing Cent., Sino Diamond Motors Ltd., & Newa Ins. Co., Ltd.; *Add.* 15 Foochow St., Taipei 100.

LIN, HUAI-MIN
(See LIN, HWAI-MIN 林懷民)

LIN, HWAI-MIN 林懷民
Choreographer; Writer; Founder & Artistic Dir., Cloud Gate Dance Theatre 73-; *b.* Twn. Feb. 19, '47; *educ.* BJ, NCCU 68; M. of Fine Arts, U. of Iowa 72; Resident Artist, Danc Dept., UCLA & Am. Dance Festival 78; Fulbright Schola Performance Study, New York U.; Producer, Taipei Festi val of Intl. Dance Acad. 86; Founding Chmn. & Assc. Prof Dance Dept., Nat. Inst. of the Arts 83-88. *Publ.: Cicada 69 On Dance* 81; *Passing by Brushing the Shoulders* 85; *Add* 5th Fl., 19 Lane 231, Fu Hsing N. Rd., Taipei 105.

LIN, I-FU
(See LIN, YI-FU 林義夫)

LIN, I-HSIUNG 林義雄

Chmn., DPP 98-; *b.* Twn. Aug. 24, '41; *m.* Fang, Su-min; 1 *d.; educ.* LL.B., NTU 64; MPA, John F. Kennedy Sch. of Gov., Harvard U. 96; Attorney-at-Law 67-79; Mem., TPA 77-80; Pres., Tse-Lin Cul. & Educ. Found. 91-98; *Add.* 10th Fl., 30 Pei Ping E. Rd., Taipei 100.

LIN, JOIN-SANE 林中森

Admin. V. Min. of the Int. 99-; *b.* Twn. Dec. 17, '44; *m.* Chu, Sheue-ying; 1 *s.,* 1 *d.; educ.* LL.D., NCCU 86; Sp., MOI 74-77; Chief, Dept. of Land Aff., TCG 77-81, Sp. 81-83, Sr. Sp. 83; Dep. Dir., Dept. of Land Aff., Kaohsiung City Govt. 83-84, Dir. 85-90, Sec.-Gen. 90-94; Dep. Mayor, Kaohsiung City 94-98. *Publ.: Study of the Compensation for Expropriation; Study of the Land Value Issues in Taipei; Study of Twn.'s Idle Farm Land; The Econ. Model for Urban Land's Utilization; A Study on the Impact of Urban Land Consolidation on Urban Utilization—An Empirical Analysis of Kaohsiung Sp. Mun.; Add.* 9th Fl., 5 Hsuchow Rd., Taipei 100.

LIN, JONG-SHONG 林鐘雄

Chmn., E. Sun Bk. 92-; *b.* Twn. Mar. 24, '38; *m.* Lee, Hui-mei; 1 *s.,* 1 *d.; educ.* BA, NTU 60, MA 64; Sp., CIECD 64-71; Assc. Prof., Econ. Dept., NCCU 71-76, Prof. 76-81; Prof., Finance Dept. NTU 81-92. *Publ.: Money & Banking* 69; *Study of Quantity Theory of Money* 67; *Econ.* 84; *Hist. of Econ. Thought* 86; *Econ. Hist. of Europe* 87; *Post-War Econ. Dev. of Twn.* 89; *Essays on Econ. Hist. of Twn.* 95; *Add.* 77 Wu Chang St., Sect. 1, Taipei 100.

LIN, JUN-YI 林俊義

Admin., EPA 2000; *b.* Twn. July 23, '38; *educ.* Grad., Tamkang Coll.; BA, For. Lang. Dept., NTU 60-63; Stud-ied, Inst. of For. Lang., NTNU; BA, Biology, Goshen Coll., USA 65-67; M. & Ph.D., Biology, Indiana U.; Dir., Bu. of Environmental Protection, TCG 95-97; Prof., Biology, Tunghai U. 97-2000. *Publ.:* "Coll. Reform—From Crisis to Liveliness, a Dialogue Between Lee Yuan-tseh & Lin Jun-yi," *Rebirth of Coll. Educ.* (Ho, Te-feng ed.) 90; "Professionalization & Twn. Sc. Dev.," *Sc.-Tech Dev. & Nativism* (Lin Ho ed.) Nat. Policy Res. Cent. 92; "A Di-emma of Acad. Freedom & Coll. Automony—A Circuitious Hist. of Twn. Dem.," *A Collection in Memory of the 30th Anniversary of Lei Chen Case* 92; *The Lizard of Twn.* (with H.Y. Cheng) 90; *Ecological Impacts of Adapt-ng Non-indigenous Animals—On Avifauna* 90; *50 Simple Ways to Save the Earth for Twn. (Ch.)* 90; "Note on Clutch Size of *Japalura brevipes* (Reptilia, Agamidae) from Twn.," *Acta Zoological Taiwanica* & "Note on the Reproduction of the Skink, *Sphenomorphus taiwanensis,* from Twn.,"

Twn. Mus. (with W.H. Chou) 92; "The Male Reproductive Cycle of the Toad, *Bufo bankorensis,* in Twn.," *Zoological Studies* (with W.S. Huang & J. Y-L Yu) 96; "Geographical Variations of *Rana sauteri* (Anura: Ranidae) in Twn., With Description of New Species," *Zoological Studies* (with W.H. Chou; forthcoming); "Male Reproductive Cycle of the Toad, *Bufo bankorensis,* in Twn.," *Zoological Sc.,* Japan (forthcoming); *Add.* 41 Chung Hua Rd., Sect. 1, Taipei 108.

LIN, JUNG-HSING 林榮星

Spkr., Ilan CoCoun. 94-; *b.* Twn. June 29, '40; *m.* Fan, Shu-jung; 4 *s.,* 2 *d.; educ.* Grad., Ilan County Toucheng High Sch.; Bd. Chmn., Lita Minerals 75-86; Mem., Ilan CoCoun. 82-94, Dep. Spkr. 86-94; Gen. Mgr., Tung-i Iron & Steel Co. Ltd. 87-94; Bd. Chmn., Mei-chou Concrete Ind. Co. Ltd. 92-94; *Add.* 98 Wei Shui Rd., Ilan 260.

LIN, JUNG-TAI

(See LIN, RUNGTAI 林榮泰)

LIN, JUNG-YAO

(See LIN, JUNG-YAW 林榮耀)

LIN, JUNG-YAW 林榮耀

Mem., Acad. Sinica 96-; Prof., NTU 72-; *b.* Taipei May 27, '34; 2 *s.,* 2 *d.; educ.* BS, NTU 57, MS, 60; Ph.D., UC-Berkly. 67; Instr., NTU 60-67, Assc. Prof. 67-72, Dir., Inst. of Biochem. Coll. of Med. 85-91; Pres., Ch. Biochem. Assn. 76-77, & Pharmaceutical Assn. of the ROC 88-92; Dir., Div. of Life Sc., NScC 85-90. *Publ.:* 121 papers; *Add.* 1 Jen Ai Rd., Sect. 1, Taipei 100.

LIN, KAI-FAN 林鎧藩

Dir., Finance Aff. Cttee., KMT 93-2000; *b.* Fukien Jan. 21, '23; *m.* Tseng, Yu-chin; 1 *s.,* 3 *d.; educ.* B., NCCU 48; Sect. Chief & Sr. Sp., Dept. of Budget, Acct. & Statistics, TPG 48-67, Dir. 74-83; Chief Sec., Dept. of Budget, Acct. & Statistics, TCG 67-69, Dir. 71-74; Insp., DGBAS 69-71, Dep. Dir.-Gen. 83-86; Chmn., Cent. Deposit Ins. Corp. 86-92; Chmn., Twn. Telecom. Network Service Co. 92-93; *Add.* 11 Chung Shan S. Rd., Taipei 104.

LIN, KENG-HUA

(See LEAN, ERIC G.H. 林耕華)

LIN, KI-TSENG 林基正

V. Min. of For. Aff. 2000-; *b.* Twn. June 5, '36; *m.* Yin, Su-mey; 2 *s.,* 1 *d.; educ.* LL.B., NTU 59; Sp. Asst., Taipei Post Off. 58-61; Sec., Info. Dept., MOFA 61-64; 3rd Sec., Emb. in Dominican Repub. 64-66; Sect. Chief, Treaty Dept.,

MOFA 66-71; Sec., Ch. Del. to UN Conf. of Treaties, Vienna, Austria 69; Mem., Ch. Del. for Negotiation on Bilateral Treaties 67-71; 1st Sec., Emb. in Spain 71-74, & Emb. in Portugal 74-77; Dep. Dir., Dept. of Cent. & S. Am. Aff., MOFA 77-80; Sr. Adv., Oficina Cml. del Lejano Oriente, Bogotá, Colombia 80-81; Dir., Oficina Cml. de Twn., ROC in Caracas, Venezuela 81-90; Dir., Dept. of Consl. Aff., MOFA 90-91; Amb. to Nicaragua 91-97; Rep., TECO in Spain 97-2000; *Add.* 2 Kaitakelan Boulevard, Taipei 100.

LIN, KUANG-HUA
(See LIN, KWANG-HUA 林光華)

LIN, KUO-HSIEN 林國賢
Chmn., Cttee. on the Discipline of Public Functionaries, Jud. Yuan 99-; Prof. of Laws, NCHU 93-, & Dr. Sun Yat-sen Inst., Ch. Cul. U. 92-; *b.* Twn. Feb. 6, '36; *m.* Lu, Hsueh-hua; 3 *s.,* 1 *d.; educ.* LL.B., NTU 60; LL.M., Ch. Cul. U. 71, J.S.D. 81; Justice, Supreme Court 82-84; Comr., Criminal Dept., Jud. Yuan 85-90; Pres., Shihlin Dist. Court 90-93; Dep. Sec.-Gen., Jud. Yuan 93-94; Lectr., Judges & Prosecutors Tng. Inst.; Mem., Sr.- & Jr.-Grade Civil Service Exam. Bd., Min. of Exam., Exam. Yuan; Grand Justice, Jud. Yuan 94-97, Sec.-Gen. 97-99. *Publ.: The Five-Power Const. & the Current Const.; The Self-Appeal System of Criminal Procedure; Add.* 124 Chungking S. Rd., Sect. 1, Taipei 100.

LIN, KWANG-HUA 林光華
Magis., Hsinchu County 97-; *b.* Twn. Oct. 25, '45; *educ.* Grad., NTNU; Founding Mem., DPP, Mem., CAC; Convener, Trans. & Comms. Cttee., Legis. Yuan, Mem., Jud. Cttee. 94-97; *Add.* 10 Kuang Ming 6th Rd., Chupei, Hsinchu County 302.

LIN, LIANG 林良
Writer, Prose & C.'s Lit.; Pres. & concur. Pub., *Mandarin Daily News* 93-; *b.* Fukien Oct. 10, '24; *m.* Jeng, Shiou-jy; 3 *d.; educ.* Sp. Course, Ch. Lang., NTNU 52; BA, Eng. Lang. & Lit., Tamkang U. 70; Ed., *Mandarin Daily News* 48-63, Chief Ed., Pub. Dept. 64-71, Mgr. 72-93. *Publ.: Little Sun; The Art of Simple Lang.; 16 Letters from My Father;* & over 200 bk. for c.; *Add.* 19 Lane 15, Chungking S. Rd., Sect. 3, Taipei 100.

LIN, MARK 林明儒
Pres., Twn. Steel Union Co. Ltd. 96-; Gen. Mgr., Feng Hsin Iron & Steel Co. Ltd. 91-; Bd. Mem., Even Transit Intl. Co. Ltd. 98-, Feng I Hsin Investment Co. Ltd. 99-; Sup., Sino-prosperity Co. Ltd. 97-; *b.* Twn. June 1, '47; *m.* Chang, Hsu-wen; 2 *s.,*

2 *d. Publ.: Personnel Op. Manual; Financial Op. Manual; Purchasing/Warehousing Op. Manual; Business Op. Manual; Add.* 36 Hsien Kung N. 1st Rd., Changhua Coastal Ind. Park, Shenkang Hsiang, Changhua County 509.

LIN, MENG-KUEI 林孟貴
Nat. Policy Adv. to the Pres. 99-; *b.* Twn. Oct. 30, '43; *educ.* MPA, San Francisco State U.; Mem., Control Yuan 93-99; *Add.* c/o Off. of the Pres., 122 Chungking S. Rd., Sect. 1, Taipei 100.

LIN, MING-JU
(See LIN, MARK 林明儒)

LIN, MING-TE
(See LIN, MING-TEH 林明德)

LIN, MING-TEH 林明德
Chief Justice, Supreme Court, Jud. Yuan 97-; Pres., Judges Assn. of the ROC; *b.* Taipei Nov. 18, '31; *m.* Lin Chien, Tuang-li; 2 *s.,* 3 *d.; educ.* LL.B., NTU; Prosecutor, Judge, Chief Judge, dist. courts & high courts 56-71; Chief Prosecutor, Yunlin Dist. Court 71-72, & Keelung Dist. Court 72-78; Mem., Cttee. on the Discipline of Public Functionaries, Jud. Yuan 79-80, Dep. Sec.-Gen. 89-90; Pres., Taipei Dist. Court 90-93, & Taichung Br., Twn. High Court 93-95; Pres., Admin. Court, Jud. Yuan 95-97. *Publ.: A Review of Court Decisions on the ROC's Current Jud. Practice Relevant to Mainland Residents; A Report on Japan's Appellant Criminal Procedures & the Precise Procedural Rule System; Add.* 6 Changsha St., Sect. 1, Taipei 100.

LIN, NAN 林南
Prof. of Sociology & Dir., Asia-Pacific Studies Inst., Duke U., USA 90-; *b.* Chungking Aug. 21, '38; *m.* Pan, Alice P.; 2 *s.; educ.* BA, Tunghai U. 60; MA, Syracuse U. 63; Ph.D., Michigan State U. 66; Asst. Prof., Johns Hopkins U. 66; Assc. Prof., State U. of New York at Albany 71-76, Prof. 76-90. *Publ.: Study of Hunan Comm.* 73; *Found. of Soc. Res.* 76; *Soc. Network & Soc. Studies* 82; *Soc. Support, Life Events & Depression* 86; *Soc. Capital: A Theory of Soc. Studies & Action* 2000; *Add.* Dept. of Sociology, Box 90088, Duke U., Durham, NC 27708-0088, USA.

LIN, NENG-PAI 林能白
Min. without Portfolio & concur. Chmn., Public Construction Com., Exec. Yuan 2000-; Prof., Dept. & Grad. Inst. of Business Admin., NTU 94-; *b.* Twn. June 1, '53; *m.* Hung, Su-chen; 2 *d.; educ.* BCE, NTU 75; Ph.D., Mng., Ohio State U. 89; Assc. Prof., Dept. & Grad. Inst. of Busines

Admin., NTU 89-94, Chairperson 95-98, Dean, Coll. of Mng. 99-2000. *Publ.* Co-author, "Investigating the Relationship Between Service Providers' Personality & Customers' Perceptions of Service Quality Across Gender," *Total Quality Mng.* (forthcoming); "The Effects of Environmental Factors on the Design of Master Production Scheduling Systems," *Jour. of Op. Mng.* 94; SQ-NEED: "An Instrument Measuring Service Quality from the Theory of Needs," presented at the 5th Intl. Conf. of the DSI, Greece 99; "The Effects of Server's Personality on Service Quality," presented at INFORMS Intl. Conf., Israel 98; & about 30 other theses published in acad. jour. or presented at acad. conf., & 39 project reports; *Add.* 9th Fl., 4 Chung Hsiao W. Rd., Sect. 1, Taipei 100.

LIN, PI-CHAO
(See LIN, BIH-JAW 林碧炤)

LIN, PO-JUNG 林博容
Pres., Lin Bo Rong Architects & Engrs. Assc.; Assc. Prof., Tainan Women's Coll. of Arts & Tech. & Kung Shan Inst. of Tech.; *b.* Taipei July 6, '47; *m.* Su, Chin-chao; 2 *s.,* 1 *d.; educ.* B. & M. of Architecture, NCKU; Lectr. & Assc. Prof., NCKU. *Publ.: An Analysis of the Construction Labor Force from an Ind. Perspective; Portfolio: Identified Picture—Clean Architecture; Add.* 196-17 Chung Hua Rd., Yungkang, Tainan County 710.

LIN, PO-JUNG
(See LIN, PO-RUNG 林柏榕)

LIN, PO-RUNG 林柏榕
Spkr., Twn. Prov. Consultative Coun. 99-; *b.* Twn. Nov. 18, '36; *m.* Guo, Yueh-ching; 1 *s.,* 2 *d.; educ.* BA, For. Lang., NTU 60; Advanced Studies, Harvard U. 75; Prin., Lizen High Sch. 71-81; Mayor, Taichung City 81-85; Adv. & Exec. Sec. for Sister State Rel., TPG 85-86; Pres., Twn. Chapter, Life Philosophy Res. Soc.; Sec.-Gen., Twn. Cttee., Ch. Inst. in Am.; Pres., Taichung Life Line Assn.; Chmn., Intl. Life Line Assn., World Fed.; Bd. Chmn., Lizen High Sch.; Mayor, Taichung City 89-96; Mem., TPA 98, Spkr. 99. *Publ.: The Thought of Soc. Conservatism in the Poetry of Robert Foster; A Common Gardener; The Prospects of the Rel. Between the ROC & USA & the Rel. Between the ROC & PROC; Add.* 99 Min Chuan Rd., Taichung 403.

LIN, RUNGTAI 林榮泰
Pres. & Prof., Mingchi Inst. of Tech. 96-; *b.* Twn. Feb. 26, '53; *m.* Lee, Sandy; 1 *s.; educ.* Diploma, Ind. Design, Mingchi Inst. of Tech. 73; BS, Ind. Mng., Nat. Twn. U. of

Sc. & Tech. 82; MS, Engr. Design, Tufts U. 88, Ph.D. 92; Lectr., Dept. of Ind. Design, Mingchi Inst. of Tech. 83-90, Assc. Prof. 91-96, Chmn. 94-96; Chmn., Dept. of Ind. Design, Chang Gung U. 94-96. *Publ.:* 15 articles published in prof. jour.; *Add.* 84 Kung Chuan Rd., Taishan Hsiang, Taipei County 243.

LIN, SAMUEL H.L. 林賢郎
Bd. Chmn., Certified Public Accts. (CPA) Assn. 98-; Sr. Partner, KPMG CPA 73-; Bd. Mem., Wu Tsun-hsien Found. 81-; *b.* Twn. Mar. 4, '41; *m.* Tseng, Cathy; 1 *s.,* 1 *d.; educ.* BBA, NTU; Insp., MOF 69-71; Bd. Mem., Twn. Prov. CPA Assn. 80-83; Standing Bd. Mem., Taipei City CPA Assn. 89-98; Bd. Mem., Nat. Fed. of CPA Assn. of the ROC 94-97; *Add.* 12th Fl., 367 Fu Hsing N. Rd., Taipei 105.

LIN, SHEAN-HUEI 林顯輝
Pres., Nat. Pingtung Tchrs. Coll. 99-, Prof. 83-; *b.* Kaohsiung Mar. 1, '50; *m.* Wang, Pao-hsu; 1 *s.,* 1 *d.; educ.* MS, Earth Sc., Ch. Cul. U. 77; MA, Sc. Educ., N.E. Missouri State U. 79; Ph.D., Sc. Educ., U. of Iowa 89; Assc. Prof. & Dean of Gen. Aff., Twn. Prov. Pingtung Tchrs. Coll. 82-83, Dean of Acad. Aff. 83-87; Dean of Student Aff., Nat. Pingtung Tchrs. Coll. 91-92, Dean of Acad. Aff. 92-96, V. Pres. 96-99. *Publ.: Over 30 papers published in prof. journals & seminars; Add.* 4-18 Min Sheng Rd., Pingtung 900.

LIN, SHENG-HSIEN 林聖賢
Mem., Acad. Sinica 84-, Dir. & Sp. Disting. Res. Fel., Inst. of Atomic & Molecular Sc. 93-; Adjunct Prof., Arizona State U. 95-, Regent's Prof. 88-; Hon. Prof., Nanking U. 88-; Adjunct Prof., Shantung U. 90-; Prof., Dept. of Chem., NTU 94-; Hon. Prof., Xiamen U. 97-; *b.* Twn. Sept. 17, '37; *m.* Lin Pi, Hsiu-ping; 2 *s.; educ.* BS & MS, NTU; Ph.D., U. of Utah; Postdoctoral Fel., Columbia U. 64-65; Asst. Prof., Arizona State U. 65-68, Assc. Prof. 68-72, Prof. 72-95, Alfred P. Sloan Fel. 67-71; John Simon Guggenheim Fel. 71-73; Visiting Prof., Cambridge U. 72-73, Tech. U. of Munich 79-80 & 87, & Louis Pasteur U. 86. *Publ.:* 16 bk. & 352 papers; *Add.* 1915E Calle De Caballos, Tempe, AZ 85284, USA.

LIN, SHIANG-NUNG 林享能
Chmn., COA 99-2000; Chmn., Twn. Meat Dev. Found.; *b.* Twn. Dec. 20, '36; *m.* Huang, Kuei-mei; 1 *s.,* 2 *d.; educ.* LL.B., NCCU 60; MA, Ch. Cul. U. 65; Sect. Chief, MOFA 72-75, Dep. Dir., Dept. of Cent. & S. Am. Aff. 75; Dir., Cml. Off. of Twn. in Venezuela 75-81, & Cml. Off. of Taipei in Chile 81-84; Coordinator to Parliament, MOFA 88-89;

Chmn., Cttee. of Intl. Tech. Cooperation 89-97, & Ovs. Fisheries Dev. Coun., ROC 93-97; V. Chmn., COA 89-99. *Publ.: Peaceful Strategy of J.F. Kennedy; Analysis of CBI Initiative; Legal Basis of the High Seas Driftnet Fishing in the N. Pacific Ocean between CCNAA & AIT; Wildlife Conservation on Twn.; Add.* 37 Nan Hai Rd., Taipei 100.

LIN, SHIH-CHI
(See LIN, SHU-CHI 林時機)

LIN, SHIH-MING
(See LIN, DAVID S.M. 林世明)

LIN, SHOU-HUI 林壽惠
Pres., Nat. Taipei Coll. of Nursing (NTCN) 94-; Chief Exec. NTCN Hosp. 95-; Standing Mem., Nurses' Assn. of ROC, & Nat. Union Nurses' Assn., ROC; Mem., Adv. Nursing Coun., DOH; *b.* Twn. June 1, '44; *educ.* Grad., Twn. Prov. Jr. Coll. of Nursing 65; BS, Nursing Sc., Syracuse U. 77; MS, Nursing Sc., Boston U. 80; D.Sc., Nursing Sc., Rush U., Chicago 91; Dean of Studies, NTCN 82-87; Dean, NTCN Hosp. 90-91. *Publ.:* Numerous articles published in prof. jour.; *Add.* 365 Ming Te Rd., Peitou, Taipei 112.

LIN, SHOU-HUNG 林壽宏
Pres., Chung Hwa Inst. of Tech. 95-; V. Dir., Tainan Br., Ch. Youth Corps 95-; *b.* Twn. Nov. 24, '40; 1 *s.,* 2 *d.; educ.* BA, NCKU 63; Ed.M., Cheyney U. of Pennsylvania 92; Tchr. & Dean of Students, Tainan City Jr. High Sch. 64-72; Lectr. & Dean of Students, So. Twn. U. of Tech. 72-83, V. Pres. & Dir. of Night Div. 83-87, Prof. & Dir. of Night Div. 87-91, Prof. & Bd. Sec. 91-95; 89 Wen Hua 1st St., Jen Te Hsiang, Tainan County 717.

LIN, SHU-CHI 林時機
Mem., Control Yuan 99-; Lawyer 74-; *b.* Twn. Aug. 2, '39; *m.* Ding, Yu-wei; 2 *s.,* 1 *d.; educ.* LL.B., NTU 67, LL.M. 69; Instr. & Assc. Prof., Fu Jen Catholic U. 69-94; Mem., Legis. Yuan 87-90; Pub., *Ch. Daily News* 95-98; *Add.* 2 Chung Hsiao E. Rd., Sect. 1, Taipei 100.

LIN, SHUI-CHI
(See LIN, SUI-CHI 林水吉)

LIN, SUI-CHI 林水吉
Rep., Taipei Econ. & Trade Off. in Indonesia 99-; *b.* Twn. Mar. 21, '38; *m.* Lin, Su-man; 2 *s.,* 1 *d.; educ.* LL.B., NCCU 60, LL.M., Dip. 64; 3rd & 2nd Sec., Emb. in Vietnam 65-70; 1st Sec., Emb. in S. Korea 71-72; Sect. Chief,

Dept. of E. Asian & Pacific Aff., MOFA 73-75; Consul, Consl. in Pago Pago, Am. Samoa 75-78; Dep. Dir., Dept. of Info, MOFA 79-81; Adv., TECRO, USA 82; Dir.-Gen., TECO in Boston 83-90; Dir., Dept. of E. Asian & Pacific Aff., MOFA 90-92; Rep., TECO in Vietnam 93-98; Sec.-Gen., MOFA 98-99; *Add.* Gedung Artha Graha Lt. 17, Jl. Jend. Sudirman Kav. 52-53, Jakarta 12190, Indonesia.

LIN, TA-HSIUNG 林達雄
Dep. Admin., EPA 93-; *b.* Twn. Oct. 23, '44; *m.* Lu, Hsiu-chen; 2 *s.; educ.* BS, Dept. of Soil & Water Conservation, NCHU; Div. Chief, Bu. of Environmental Protection, DOH 82-85, Dep. Dir. 85-87; Dir., Bu. of Water Quality Protection, EPA 87-89, Bu. of Air Quality Protection & Noise Control 89-92, Bu. of Performance Evaluation & Dispute Settlement 92-93; *Add.* 41 Chung Hua Rd., Sect. 1, Taipei 100.

LIN, TING-SHENG 林挺生
Sr. Adv. to the Pres. 91-; Chmn., Presidium, CAC, KMT; Prof. & Pres., Tatung U.; Chmn., Tatung Co.; Mem., Intl. Adv. Bd., Am. U., Washington, D.C.; Gov., Asian Inst. of Mng., Manila; Bd. Mem., Assc. Harvard Business Sch., USA; Mem., Faculty Exchange Promotion Cttee. between Tatung U. & U. of Glasgow, UK; *b.* Twn. Nov. 15, '19; *educ.* BS, Chem., NTU 42; Hon. D.Sc., Chungang U., S. Korea 73; Hon. LL.D., Pepperdine U., USA 78; Hon. DE, Inha U., S. Korea 78; Hon. D.Sc., U. of Glasgow, UK 91; Hon. Dr., Engr., Worcester Polytechnic Inst., USA 98; Mem., Legis. Yuan; Mng. Dir., Ch. Nat. Fed. of Ind.; Chmn., Twn. Assn. of Mach. Ind., Twn. Elec. Appliance Manufacturers' Assn., & Taipei Mun. Cttee. of Ch. Youth Anti-Communists & Nat. Salvation Corp.; Mem., CSC, & Chmn., Taipei Mun. Cttee., KMT; Chmn., Chung-hsin Elec. & Mach. Mfg. Corp.; Pres., Ch. Chem. Soc. 62, & Ch. Inst. of Engrs. 67; Spkr., Taipei CCoun. 69-81; Mem., ROC Del. to the UN 71; Chmn., Ch. Nat. Fed. of Ind. 75-81; Leader, Econ. Goodwill Mission of the ROC for Celebrating the Bicentennial of the Founding of the USA 76; *Add.* 22 Chung Shan N. Rd., Sect. 3, Taipei 104.

LIN, TSAI-MEI 林彩梅
Pres., Ch. Cul. U. 93-, Prof., Intl. Business Mng. 86-; *b.* Twn. Nov. 12, '36; *educ.* Dr., Business Admin., Kinki U., Japan; Dir., Dept. of Ind. Mng., Intl. Trade, Cooperative Econ., Mng. Sc., Tamkang U. 77-86; Pres., Assn. of Intl. Business Studies 85-89; Chmn., Grad. Sch. of Business Admin., Ch. Cul. U. 86-87 & 90, Dean of Acad. Aff. 88-93, Dean of Business Coll. 86-93, & Acting Pres. 93. *Publ.:* 4 bk. & 48 articles; *Add.* 55 Hua Kang Rd., Yangmingshan, Taipei 111.

LIN, TSUN-HSIEN 林尊賢

Rep., Taipei Mission in Korea 94-; *b.* Twn. July 20, '30; *m.* Lin, Lucy Hsiu-chu; 2 *s.,* 1 *d.; educ.* BA, NTU 53; MA, NCCU 55; 2nd Sec., Emb. in Australia 59-64; 1st Sec., Emb. in Japan 66-72; Dep. Dir., Protocol Dept., MOFA 72-75; Rep., Trade Mission to Fiji 75-80; Dir., Dept. of E. Asian & Pacific Aff., MOFA 80-83; Dir., TECO in Atlanta 83-89; Dep. Rep., TECRO, USA 89-92; Amb. to Grenada, Dominica, St. Lucia, St. Kitts & Nevis, & St. Vincent & Grenadines 92-93; *Add.* 6th Fl., Kwanghwamoon Bldg., 211 Sejong-Ro Chongro-Ku, Seoul, Korea 110-050.

LIN, TSUNG-SUNG 林宗嵩

Pres., Jin-wen Inst. of Tech. 90-; Sec.-Gen., Nat. Educ. Assn. of ROC 97-; Chmn., Ch. Aeronautical Meteorological Assn. 96-; *b.* Taipei Oct. 23, '52; *m.* Chang, Hsiu-ying; 1 *s.,* 1 *d.; educ.* Ph.D., Earth Sc., Ch. Cul. U. 86; Pres., Jin-wen High Sch. 81-83; Pres., Jin-wen Ind. & Cml. Voc. Sch. 83-88; Coordinator, Bu. of Planning & Dev., Jin-wen Coll. of Business & Tech. 88-90. *Publ.: A Theory on Regional Air Quality and Meteorological Monitoring Network Facilities* (dissertation) 86; *A Simulation Study of Ozone Deterioration in No. Twn.* 97; & 18 articles published in acad. jour.; *Add.* 99 An Chung Rd., Hsintien, Taipei County 231.

LIN, TSUNG-YUNG

(See LIN, TZONG-YEONG 林宗勇)

LIN, TUNG-YEN 林同棪

Mem., Acad. Sinica 72-, & Nat. Acad. of Engr., Washington, D.C.; Bd. Chmn., Lin Tung Yen Ch. Consulting Engr. 53-; *b.* Fukien Nov. 14, '11; *m.* Kao, Margaret Shun-chun; 1 *s.,* 1 *d.; educ.* BS, Tangshan Coll. & NCTU; MS, UC-Berkly.; LL.D., Ch. U. of Hong Kong & Golden Gate U., San Francisco; NCTU; Tongji U., Shanghai; Hon. Bd. Chmn., T.Y. Lin Intl. Consulting Engr. 53-92; Prof. of Civil Engr., U. of Calif., Chmn., Div. of Structural Engr., & Dir., Structural Engr. Lab. 46-76. *Publ.:* Design of Prestressed Concrete Structures; Design of Steel Structure, Structural Concepts & Systems; *Add.* 315 Bay St., San Francisco, CA 94133, USA.

LIN, TZONG-YEONG 林宗勇

Chmn., Sec. & Futures Com., MOF 98-; *b.* Twn. Nov. 16, '51; *m.* Chao, Ling-mei; 2 *s.; educ.* LL.B., NCHU 74; LL.M., NTU 77; Mem., Tax Data Cent., MOF 80-82, Insp., Dept. of Monetary Aff. 82-83, Dep. Chief, Acting Chief, Sec.-Gen., & V. Chmn., Sec. & Exchange Com. 83-94; V. Chmn. & Pres., Fubon Sec. Corp. 94-98; Chmn., Grand Cathay Sec. Corp. 98; *Add.* 85 Hsin Sheng S. Rd., Sect. 1, Taipei 100.

LIN, WEN-JUI 林文睿

Dir., Twn. Br., Nat. Cent. Lib. 92-; *b.* Twn. May 24, '49; *m.* Liu, Mei-feng; 3 *s.; educ.* LL.B., NCHU 82; M., NTU 89; Sect. Chief, MOE 84-87; Sect. Chief, CPA 97-92, Sr. Sp. 92. *Publ.: The Study of U. Lib.; Personnel System in the Twn. Area; Add.* 1 Hsin Sheng S. Rd., Sect. 1, Taipei 100.

LIN, WEN-LI 林文禮

Strategy Adv. to the Pres. 96-; Mem., CC, KMT 94-; *b.* Szechwan Aug. 5, '30; *m.* Fan, Ying-ping; 2 *s.,* 2 *d.; educ.* Ch. Air Force Preparatory Sch. 48; Ch. Air Force Acad. 51; Cmd. & Staff Coll., Air Force U., US Air Force, USA 66; War Coll., Armed Forces U. 79; C-in-C, ROCAF 89-92; Personal C/S to the Pres. 92-93; Dir.-Gen., Aero Ind. Dev. Cent. 93-96; *Add.* 8th Fl., 3 Lane 31, Wo Lung St., Taipei 106.

LIN, WEN-SHAN 林文山

Dir., 3rd Dept., Exec. Yuan & concur. Counsl. 93-; *b.* Twn. Aug. 6, '46; *m.* Hung, Tsui-pin; 2 *s.; educ.* MPA, NCCU 73; Staff Mem., Exec. Yuan 82-88, Admin. Sec. 88-93. *Publ.: Planning-Programming-Budgeting System; Add.* 1 Chung Hsiao E. Rd., Sect. 1, Taipei 100.

LIN, YANG-KANG 林洋港

Candidate, 1996 Election for ROC Pres.; *b.* Twn. June 10, '27; *m.* Chen, Ho; 1 *s.,* 3 *d.; educ.* BS, NTU; Sec., TPG 64-67; Chmn., Yunlin County Cttee., KMT 64-67; Magis., Nantou County 67-72 & concur. Chmn., Nantou County Cttee., KMT 68-70; Chmn., Nantou County Br., Ch. Youth Corps 67-72; Comr., Dept. of Recon., TPG 72-76; Mayor, Taipei City, & Mem., CC, KMT 76-78; Gov., TPG 78-81; Mem., CSC, KMT 78-93; Min. of the Int. 81-84; V. Premier, ROC 84-87; Pres., Jud. Yuan 87-94; Sr. Adv. to the Pres. 94-96; *Add.* 4th Fl., 65 Kuang Fu S. Rd., Taipei 105.

LIN, YI-FU 林義夫

Admin. V. Min. of Econ. Aff. 97-; V. Chmn., CETRA; *b.* Taipei Nov. 15, '42; *m.* Lin, Mei-shiow; 3 *d.; educ.* BA, NCCU; Asst. Cml. Attaché, Emb. in the Philippines 73-75; Cml. Attaché, Econ. Div., Taipei Econ. & Trade Off. in Thailand 75-82; Sect. Chief, 3rd Dept., Bd. of For. Trade, MOEA 82-83, Dep. Dir. & Dir., 2nd Dept. 83-85 & 86-88; Dir., Far E. Trade Service Inc., Toronto 88-90; Dep. Dir.-Gen., Bd. of For. Trade, MOEA 90-95, Dir.-Gen. 95-97; *Add.* 15 Foochow St., Taipei 100.

LIN, YU-SAN 林玉山

Artist, Ch. Painting; Prof. of Arts, NTNU; *b.* Twn. Apr. 1, '07; *m.* Huang, Hui; 2 *s.,* 5 *d.; educ.* Kawabata Painting Sch., Tokyo; Painting Exhibition 70, 86 & 91. *Publ.:*

Painting Collections of Lin Yu-san (4 Vol.); *Add.* 5 Alley 1, Lane 199, Chin Hua St., Taipei 106.

LIN, YU-SHAN
(See LIN, YU-SAN 林玉山)

LIN, YU-SHENG 林毓生
Mem., Acad. Sinica 94-, Adjunct Fel., Inst. of Hist. & Philology 83-; Prof., Dept. of Hist., U. of Wisconsin-Madison 81-; Hon. Prof., Ch. Cul. Coll. (Peking) & Inst. of Ch. Cul. (Shanghai) 88-; *b.* Shenyang Aug. 7, '34; *m.* Sung, Tsu-gein; 1 *s.,* 1 *d.; educ.* BA, Hist. Dept., NTU 58; Ph.D., U. of Chicago 70; Postdr. Studies, E. Asian Cent., Harvard U. 69-70; Lectr., Yale U. 62; Visiting Asst. Prof., Hist. Dept., U. of Virginia 66-67; Acting Asst. Prof., U. of Oregon 68; Asst. Prof., Dept. of Hist. & Dept. of E. Asian Lang. & Lit., U. of Wisconsin-Madison 70-75, Assc. Prof. 75-81; Sr. Res. Fel., Inst. of E. Asian Philosophies, Singapore 88-90. *Publ.: The Crisis of Ch. Consciousness: Radical Anti-Traditionalism in the May Fourth Era* 79; *Thought & Personalities* 83; *Pol. Order & Pluralistic Soc.* 89; *From the Perspective of Civil Soc.* 2000; & 21 articles; *Add.* Dept. of Hist., 3211 Humanities Bldg., U. of Wisconsin-Madison, 455 N. Park St., Madison, WI 53706, USA.

LIN, YUNG-MOU 林永謀
Grand Justice, Jud. Yuan 94-; *b.* Twn. Nov. 2, '38; *m.* Wang, Shu-hui; 2 *s.,* 1 *d.; educ.* LL.B., NTU 61; Judge, Chiayi Dist. Court 63-65; Prosecutor, Taichung Dist. Court 65-71; Judge, Pingtung Dist. Court 71-73, Taichung Br., Twn. High Court 73-78, & Twn. High Court 78-81; Justice, Supreme Court 81-94. *Publ.:* 40 articles on criminal law; *Add.* 124 Chungking S. Rd., Sect. 1, Taipei 100.

LING, RONG-SAN 林榮三
Sr. Adv. to the Pres. 97-; *b.* Twn. May 27, '39; *m.* Chang, Su-o; 4 *c.; educ.* Grad., Kai Nan Com. & Tech. High Sch.; Pres., Lang Bong Bldg. Ltd. 65-80; Mem., Legis. Yuan 75-79; Mem., Control Yuan 80-91, V. Pres. 92-93; Nat. Policy Adv. to the Pres. 93-96; *Add.* 18th Fl., 109 Min Sheng E. Rd., Sect. 3, Taipei 105.

LIOU, CHING-TIEN 劉清田
Pres., Nat. Twn. U. of Sc. & Tech. 90-; *b.* Twn. Mar. 13, '44; *m.* Lin, Liang-ching; *educ.* BS, NCKU 66; MS, Purdue U. 71, Ph.D. 72, & Postdr. Resr. 72-73; Prof. & Chmn., NCTU 73-78; Prof., Chmn., & Dean of Acad. Aff., Nat. Twn. Inst. of Tech. 78-90; Chief Sec., MOE 87-90. *Publ.:* 200 papers & tech. reports; *Add.* 43 Keelung Rd., Sect. 4, Taipei 106.

LIU, AN-CHI 劉安之
Pres., Feng Chia U. 98-, Prof., Dept. of Info. Engr. 89-; *b.* Twn. Apr. 26, '51; *m.* Lee, Wei-shiuan; 1 *s.,* 1 *d.; educ.* BSEE, NCTU 73, MSEE 77; Ph.D., U. of Illinois at Chicago 81; Asst. Prof., N. Dakota State U. 81-82; Chief Software Engr., Gemini Computers Inc. 82-83; Asst. Prof., Dept. of Elec. & Computer Engr., Illinois Inst. of Tech. 83-89; Visiting Assc. Prof., NScC 89-92; Chmn., Dept. of Info. Engr., Feng Chia U. 89-94, Dir., Grad. Sch. of Info. Engr. 91-95, Dean, Coll. of Engr. 94-98, V. Pres. 98; *Add.* 100 Wen Hua Rd., Taichung 407.

LIU, BOR-NAN 劉伯男
Pres., Yung Ta Inst. of Tech. & Com. 95-; *b.* Twn. Oct. 10, '39; *m.* Chen, Yuan-jen; 1 *s.,* 2 *d.; educ.* B., NCKU; Tchr., Private Ping Rong Voc. High Sch. 63-65, Pingtung County Chaochou Jr. High Sch. 65-67; Dir., Registration Off., Yung Ta Jr. Tech. Coll. 67-78, Lectr. 67-73, Assc. Prof. 73-81, Prof. 81-95, Dean of Studies 78-95. *Publ.: A Study of the SB Distribution Choice & Its Solutions; Add.* 316 Chung Shan Rd., Linluo Hsiang, Pingtung County 909.

LIU, CHAN-AO
(See LIU, CHAN-NAO 劉占鰲)

LIU, CHAN-NAO 劉占鰲
Mem., Acad. Sinica; Prof., Med. Sch., U. of Penn.; *b.* Hopei Mar. 17, '10; *m.* Chao, Chung-yu; 1 *s.,* 1 *d.; educ.* BS, Nat. Peking Normal U.; Ph.D., U. of Penn. *Publ.:* Papers on the regeneration & sprouting of the cent. nervous system following injury; *Add.* 109 Grasmere Rd., Bala Cynwyd, PA 19004, USA.

LIU, CHAO-HAN 劉兆漢
Mem., Acad. Sinica 98-; Pres., NCU 90-; *b.* Hunan Jan. 3, '39; *m.* Mong, Tsuei-chu; 1 *s.,* 1 *d.; educ.* Ph.D., Brown U. 65; Res. Assc., U. of Illinois 65-66, Asst. Prof. 66-70, Assc. Prof. 70-74, Prof. 74-90; Visiting Scientist, Max Plank Inst. for Aeronomy, Germany 74 & 77; Chair Prof., Dept. of EE, NTU 81, & NCU 89-90; Sc. Sec., Sc. Coun. on Solar-terrestrial Phys. 81-94; Chmn., coun. of Sc. Cttee. on Solar-Terrestrial Phys., Intl. Coun. of Sc. Union (ICSU) 94-99. *Publ.: A Model for Spaced Antenna Observational Mode for MST Radars; Spatial Interferometer Measurements with the Chungli VHF Radars; Add.* NCU, Chungli, Taoyuan County 320.

LIU, CHAO-HSUAN
(See LIU, CHAO-SHIUAN 劉兆玄)

LIU, CHAO-SHIUAN 劉兆玄

V. Premier, ROC 97-2000; Chmn., Consumers Protection Com. 97-; Prof., NTHU 75-; *b.* Szechwan May 10, '43; *m.* Chien, Ming-sai; 1 *s.*, 2 *d.; educ.* BS, NTU; Ph.D., U. of Toronto; Assc. Prof., NTHU 71-75; Dir., Div. of Planning & Evaluation, NScC 79-82; Dean, Coll. of Sc., NTHU 82-84; V. Chmn., NScC 84-87; Pres., NTHU 87-93; Min. of Trans. & Comms., & concur. Min. of State 93-96; Chmn., NScC 96-98. *Publ.:* 60 papers on inorganic & organometallic chem.; *Add.* 1 Chung Hsiao E. Rd., Sect. 1, Taipei 100.

LIU, CHEN 劉眞

Sr. Adv. to the Pres. 97-; Pres., Dr. Sun Yat-sen Cul. Found. 91-; V. Pres., Nat. Cul. Assn. 95-; Dir., Steering Cttee. of Humanistic & Soc. Sc. Educ., MOE 87-; Dir., Dictionary Compilation Cttee., Nat. Inst. for Compilation & Transl. 91-; Pres., Inst. of Ch. Lang. & Lit. 81-; Chmn., Presidium, CAC, KMT 93-; *b.* Anhwei Oct. 17, '13; *m.* Shih, Yu-ching; 2 *s.*, 1 *d.; educ.* Grad., Anhwei U.; Studied at Tokyo Normal Coll. & U. of Penn.; Prof., Nat. Hopei Normal Coll. 41-44; Mem., Legis. Yuan 48-53; Pres., Twn. Prov. Normal U. 49-51 & NTNU 55-57; Comr., Dept. of Educ., TPG 57-63; Dir., Grad. Sch. of Educ., NCCU 63-73; Mem., Nat. Dev. Planning Group & concur. Dir., Cul. Group, NSC 57-91; Standing Mem., Coun. of Acad. Review & Evaluation, MOE 61-89; Nat. Policy Adv. to the Pres. 91-97. *Publ.: Educ. Admin.; Res. on European & Am. Educ.; Religion & Educ.; The Future of Ch. Cul.; Educ. & Dedication;* etc.; *Add.* 11 Foochow St., Taipei 100.

LIU, CHI-HSIEN

(See LIU, CHI-SHIEN 劉繼先)

LIU, CHI-SHIEN 劉繼先

Pub., *Ch. Daily News* 99-; *b.* Peking Dec. 8, '45; *m.* Guo, Sheau-ling; 2 *s.; educ.* World Coll. of Jour. & Com.; Reporter & Dep. Chief of Reporters, *Ch. Daily News* 67-80, Dep. Chief & Chief of Corr. 81-88, Dep. Ed.-in-Chief, Air Transport Dept. 88-93, Ed.-in-Chief 93-94, V. Pub. 95-99; *Add.* 57 Hsi Hua St., Tainan 704.

LIU, CHIN-PIAO

(See LIU, KING 劉金標)

LIU, CHING-TIEN

(See LIOU, CHING-TIEN 劉清田)

LIU, CHIUNG-LANG

(See LIU, CHUNG-LAUNG 劉炯朗)

LIU, CHUNG-LAUNG 劉炯朗

Pres., NTHU 98-, Prof., Dept. of Computer Sc. 98-; *b.* Kwangtung Oct. 25, '34; *m.* Cheng, Yun-shi; 1 *d.; educ.* BS, EE, NCKU 56; MS, EE, MIT, Ph.D. 62; Asst. Assc. Prof., EE, MIT 62-72; Visiting Assc. Prof., Harvard U. 70-71; Prof., Computer Sc., U. of Illinois at Urbana-Champaign 72-98, Assc. Provost 95-98; Convener, External Adv. Cttee., Inst. of Info. Sc., Acad. Sinica 91-98. *Publ.: Introduction to Combinatorial Math.* 68; *Topics in Combinatorial Math.* 72; *Elements of Discrete Math.* 77 & 85; *Linear Systems Analysis* 75; *Fault Covering Problems in Reconfigurable VLSI Systems* 92; *Add.* Pres.'s Off., NTHU, 101 Kung Fu Rd., Sect. 2, Hsinchu 300.

LIU, FENG-HSUEH

(See LIU, FENG-SHUEH 劉鳳學)

LIU, FENG-SHUEH 劉鳳學

Artistic Dir., Neo-Classic Dance Co. 76-; *b.* Nunkiang June 19, '25; *m.* Chi, Pei-lin; *educ.* Ed.B., Nat. Changpai Tchrs. Coll. 49; Ph.D., Laban Cent. for Movement & Dance, U. of Goldsmith's Coll., London 87; Studied at Tokyo U. of Educ. 66-67, & Volkwang Hochschule, Essen, Germany 71-72; Teaching Asst., Nat. Changpai Tchrs. Coll. 49-50; Twn. Prov. Taichung Tchrs. Coll. 50-53; Lectr., Assc. Prof. & Prof., NTNU 54-85; Prof. & Dir., Dance Dept., Nat. Twn. Acad. of Arts 85-88; Dir., Mng. & Planning Coun., Nat. Theater & Concert Hall 88-90; Dance Works: Nilpotent; other 106 pieces. *Publ.: Educ. Dance; Introduction of Dance; Study of Ethic Dance—Mankind Dance; Add.* 2nd Fl., 25 Alley 4, Lane 118, Ho Ping E. Rd., Sect. 2, Taipei 106.

LIU, FRANK RONG-HO 劉融和

Dir.-Gen., TECO in Seattle 98-; *b.* Twn. July 18, '48; *m.* Liu, Judy; 1 *s.*, 1 *d.; educ.* LL.B., Soochow U.; Grad. Studies, PA, Cape Town U.; Staff, Dept. of N. Am. Aff., MOFA 79-81; V. Consul, Consl.-Gen. of the ROC, Cape Town, Rep. of S. Africa 82-85, Consul 85-89; Sect. Chief & Dir., Dept. of Consl. Aff., MOFA 90-95, Dep. Dir.-Gen., Bu. of Consl. Aff. 95-98; *Add.* 24th Fl., Westin Bldg., 2001 Sixth Ave., Seattle, Washington 98121, USA.

LIU, HALE S.C. 劉三錡

Dep. Dir.-Gen., DGBAS 96-; *b.* Twn. July 16, '47; *m.* Chang, Pao-chin; 1 *s.*, 1 *d.; educ.* BS, Acct., Soochow U. 75; Sect. Chief, Budget Bu., DGBAS 83-87, Sr. Ed. 87-89, Sr. Sp. 89-90, Dep. Dir. 90; Chief Comptroller, MOE 90-96; *Add.* 1 Chung Hsiao E. Rd., Sect. 1, Taipei 100.

LIU, HO-CHIEN 劉和謙
Strategy Adv. to the Pres. 95-; *b.* Anhwei Sept. 28, '26; *m.* Ku, Wei-ping; 2 *c.; educ.* Ch. Naval Acad. 47; Naval CGSC 58; Armed Forces U. 72; Amphibious Warfare Course, USN 53, P.G. Sch. 61, Naval War Coll. 69; Sea Duties & Staff Assignments 47-70; Dep. Cmdr., Destroyer & Patrol Squadron, Cmdr., Service Squadron 70-72, Chief, Bu. of Op., & Dep. C/S, ROCN Hqs. 70-75; Dep. Chief, Gen. Staff for Planning, MND 75-78; Cmdr., Fleet Cmd., ROCN 78-80, Dep. C-in-C 80-83, C-in-C 83-88; Dir., Joint Op. Tng. Dept., MND 88-89; Strategy Adv. to the Pres. 89-92; Chief of the Gen. Staff, MND 92-95; *Add.* P.O. Box 90011, Taipei.

LIU, HSIANG-CHUAN 劉湘川
Pres., Nat. Taichung Tchrs. Coll. 94-; *b.* Szechwan Apr. 6, '41; *m.* Pan, Fei; 1 *s.,* 1 *d.; educ.* BS, Math., NTNU 66; MS, Experimental Statistics, NTU 82, D.Sc. 87; Tchr., Taichung Tchrs. Coll. 66-70, Taichung 1st High Sch. 70-73; Lectr., Assc. Prof., & Prof., Prov. Tchrs. Jr. Coll. of Taichung 73-94; Prof., Dept. of Math. & Sc., Nat. Taichung Tchrs. Coll. 87-94, Chmn. 87-90, Acting Dean of Acad. Aff. 90-91, Dean 91-93, Dean & concur. Acting Pres. 93-94. *Publ.: Optical Feasible High Degree Polynomial STEIN-RULE Estimators for Gaussian Linear Models; A Study on Ridge Regression Analysis & Selecting of Variables; A Study on Magic Squares; Add.* 140 Min Sheng Rd., Taichung 403.

LIU, HSIANG-HUNG
(See LIU, SHIANG-HORNG 劉祥宏)

LIU, HSIEN-TA
(See LIU, SHAN-DA 劉顯達)

LIU, HSIN-SUN 劉興善
Mem. (ministerial rank), Exam. Yuan 96-; Prof., NCCU 78-; *b.* Twn. May 6, '49; *m.* Wong, May; 2 *d.; educ.* LL.B. NTU 71; M.C.L., U. of Virginia 75, S.J.D. 77; Mem., Legis. Yuan 84-93; *Add.* 3rd Fl., 9 Alley 32, Chia Hsing St., Taipei 110.

LIU, HSING-SHAN
(See LIU, HSIN-SUN 劉興善)

LIU, JUI-SHENG
(See LIU, MICHAEL R.S. 劉瑞生)

LIU, JUNG-HO
(See LIU, FRANK RONG-HO 劉融和)

LIU, KING 劉金標
Chmn., Giant Mfg. Co. 72-, & Giant Sales Co. 81-; Standing Bd. Mem., Twn. Trans. Vehicle Mfrs.' Assn. 84-; Chmn., Twn. Bicycle Exporters' Assn. 92-; *b.* Twn. July 2, '34; *m.* Wang, Liu-hsia; 1 *s.,* 3 *d.; educ.* Grad., Taichung Jr. Coll. of Ind.; *Add.* 19 Shun Fan Rd., Tachia, Taichung County 437.

LIU, KUANG-CHING
(See LIU, KWANG-CHING 劉廣京)

LIU, KUO-SUNG 劉國松
Artist, Modern Ch. Ink Painting; Prof. & Dean, Grad. Sch. of Plastic Art, Nat. Tainan Coll. of the Arts 96-; *b.* Shantung Apr. 26, '32; *m.* Lee, Mo-hua; 1 *s.,* 2 *d.; educ.* BA, Fine Arts Dept., NTNU 56; Lectr., Assc. Prof., & Prof., Architecture Dept., Chung Yuan Christian U. 60-71; Visiting Prof., Stout State U. of Wisconsin 69-70; Visiting Prof., Iowa U. 75-76; Dir., Art Dept., Ch. U. of Hong Kong 71-92; Prof., Fine Arts Dept., Tunghai U. 92-96. *Publ.: Whither Ch. Modern Painting* 65; *Copying, Drawing, Creating* 66; *Calligraphy and Painting Sketches of Pu Shih-yu* 76; *Add.* 13th Fl.-1, 1-28 Hsi Ping S. Alley, Hsi Tun Rd., Sect. 3, Taichung 407.

LIU, KWANG-CHING 劉廣京
Mem., Acad. Sinica 76-; Prof. of Hist., U. of Calif., Davis 65-; *b.* Peking Nov. 14, '21; *m.* Warren, Edith; 1 *s.,* 1 *d.; educ.* BA, Harvard U. 45, MA 47, Ph.D. 55; Teaching Fel., Regional Studies, Harvard U. 47-48; Ch. Translator, UN Secretariat 48-56; Res. Fel. in Ch. Econ. Studies, Harvard U. 55-57, Instr. in Hist. 57-60, Res. Fel. in E. Asian Studies 60-62; Visiting Assc. Prof. of Hist., Yale U. 62-63; Assc. Prof. of Hist., U. of Calif., Davis 63-65; Visiting Prof. of Hist., Harvard U. 68-69; Visiting Chair Prof., NTU 93 & 94-95. *Publ.: Orthodoxy in Late Imperial Ch.* 90; *Statecraft & the Rise of Ent.* 90; *Am. & Ch.: A Hist. Essay & a Bibliography* 63; *Anglo-Am. Steamship Rivalry in Ch., 1862-1874* 62; Co-ed., *The Cambridge Hist. of Ch.* (Vol. 11, Late Ch'ing, 1800-1911) 80; *Add.* Dept. of Hist., U. of Calif., Davis, CA 95616, USA.

LIU, MICHAEL R.S. 劉瑞生
Pres., Nat. Ilan Inst. of Tech. 97-; *b.* Hupei May 5, '44; *m.* Wei, Shih-tai; 2 *s.; educ.* Ph.D., Veterinary Med., NTU 84; Dean of Students Aff., NTU 89-93, Chmn., Veterinary Med. 90-91; Mem., Legis. Yuan 93-96. *Publ.:* Over 20 articles on veterinary med.; *Add.* 1 Shen Nung Rd., Ilan 260.

LIU, PING-HUA
(See LIU, PING-HWA 劉炳華)

LIU, PING-HWA 劉炳華
Dep. Sec.-Gen., NSC 97-; *b.* Twn. Oct. 6, '55; *m.* Cheng, Hsueh-fong; *2 s., 1 d.; educ.* LL.B., NTU 76; MPA, U. of So. Calif. 83; Ed.D., US Intl. U. 89; Assc. Prof., Sze Hai Inst. of Tech. & Com. 89-93, & Tamkang U. 89-95; Mem., Legis. Yuan 93-96; Dir., Congressional Liasion Off., Off. of the Pres. 96-97; *Add.* 122 Chungking S. Rd., Sect. 1, Taipei 100.

LIU, PO-LUN 劉伯倫
Rep., TECO in Australia 98-; *b.* Kiangsu Oct. 24, '35; *m.* Chang, Ka-chen; *1 s., 3 d.; educ.* LL.B., NTU 59; Georgetown U. 64-65; LL.D., U. of Pangasinan, Philippines; H.D. (honoris causa), Angeles U., Philippines; 3rd & 2nd Sec., Emb. in USA; 1st Sec. & Consul-Gen., Thailand 71-75; Dep. Dir., Dept. of Consular Aff., MOFA 75-76, Dep. Dir., Dept. of African Aff. 76-77; Rep. to the Netherlands 78-80; Dir.-Gen., TECO in Chicago 82-86; Dir., Dept. of N. American Aff., MOFA 86-89; Amb. to Grenada, Dominica, St. Christopher & Nevis, St. Lucia, & St. Vincent & the Grenadines 89-92; Rep., TECO in the Philippines 92-95; Dir.-Gen., For. Service Inst. 95-97. *Publ.: On the Regime of Continental Shelf; Add.* Unit 8, Tourism House, 40 Blackall St., Barton, Canberra ACT 2600, Australia.

LIU, PO-NAN
(See LIU, BOR-NAN 劉伯男)

LIU, SAN-CHI
(See LIU, HALE S.C. 劉三錡)

LIU, SHAN-DA 劉顯達
Pres., Nat. Pingtung U. of Sc. & Tech. 93-; *b.* Twn. Oct. 10, '47; *m.* Chen, Hsiang-yin; *2 s.; educ.* BS, Dept. of Plant Pathology, NCHU 70, MS 73; Ph.D., Plant Pathology, Colorado State U. 79; Assc. Prof. & Sec., Nat. Pingtung Inst. of Agr. 79-84, Prof. 83-93, Dean of Acad. Aff. 83-85, Head, Dept. of Plant Protection 84-90, Dir., Tech. Cooperation Dept. 91-93; Chmn., Ch. Plant Pathology Soc. 94-96. *Publ.:* "Integrated Control of Chrysanthemum Stem Rot," *Plant Protection Bulletin* (Co-author) 90, "Biolological Control of Adzuki-bean Root Rot Diseases Caused by Rhizoctonia solani" 91; & over 40 res. papers; *Add.* 1 Hseuh Fu Rd., Neipu, Pingtung County 912.

LIU, SHIANG-HORNG 劉祥宏
Architect; Pres., Liu & Assc. 72-; *b.* Twn. Mar. 19, '45; *m.* Hsu, Hsin-yin; *1 s., 1 d.; educ.* Grad., Civil Engr., Nat. Taipei Inst. of Tech.; *Add.* 6th Fl., 216 Tun Hua S. Rd., Sect. 2, Taipei 106.

LIU, SHOU-CHENG 劉守成
Magis., Ilan County 97-; Chmn., Ilan Cul. & Educ. Found. 97-; *b.* Twn. Mar. 20, '51; *m.* Tien, Chiu-ching; *1 s., 1 d.; educ.* BA, NCCU 78; MA, Fu Jen Catholic U. 80; Mem., TPA 89-97. *Publ.: Res. on Spiritual Concept of Lyle; The Introduction of Eng. Philosophy-Berkly.; Transcend the Summit; Add.* 451 Ho Ping Rd., Ilan 260.

LIU, SHUEI-SHEN 劉水深
Pres., Da Yeh U. 90-; *b.* Twn. Feb. 15, '42; *m.* Huang, Hsiu-mei; *1 s., 2 d.; educ.* BS, NCKU 67; MBA, NCCU 70; Ph.D., N.We. U. 75; Lectr., NCCU 70-71, Assc. Prof. 74-79, Prof. 79-89, Dean 79-86; Dean, NCKU 89-90. *Publ.: Op. Mng.-A Systematic Approach; Product Mng.; Add.* 112 Shan Chiao Rd., Tatsun Hsiang, Changhua County 515.

LIU, SHUI-SHEN
(See LIU, SHUEI-SHEN 劉水深)

LIU, TA-JEN 劉達人
Chmn., CCNAA, TECRO Hqs. 94-; *b.* Shanghai Dec. 24, '19; *m.* Liu, Eve Y.F.; *2 s.; educ.* BA, NCU; MA, New York U.; Ph.D., Santo Tomas U., Philippines; Counsl., Emb. in Italy 66-67; Counsl. & Consul-Gen., Emb. in the Philippines 67-69; Dir., Dept. of Gen. Aff., MOFA 69-72; Amb. to Lesotho 72-80; Dir., Inf. Dept., MOFA 80-83; Dir.-Gen., TECO in Los Angeles 83-88; Rep., TECO in the Philippines 88-92, & TECO in Greece 92-94. *Publ.: Australia & Ch.; Ryukyu Islands; A Hist. of Sino-Am. Official Rel., 1840-1990; US-Ch. Rel., 1784-1992; Add.* CCNAA, 133 Po Ai Rd., Taipei 100.

LIU, TAI-PING 劉太平
Mem., Acad. Sinica; Prof., Math., Stanford U. 90-; *b.* Twn. Nov. 18, '45; *m.* Liu, Leslie Y.; *2 s.; educ.* BS, NTU 68; MS, Oregon State U. 70; Ph.D., U. of Michigan 73; Asst. Prof., U. of Maryland 73-78, Prof. 78-88; Prof., New York U. 88-90. *Publ.:* Math. papers on shock wave theory & nonlinear PDE; *Add.* Dept. of Math., Stanford U., Stanford, CA 94305, USA.

LIU, TAI-YING 劉泰英
Chmn. & Chief Exec. Off., Ch. Dev. Ind. Bk. 92-; Pres., Twn. Res. Inst. 93-; Consultant, CEPD & MOEA; *b.* Twn. May 14, '36; *m.* Hung Yen, Anna; *2 s.; educ.* BA, NTU 55-59; MA, U. of Rochester, New York 65-67; Ph.D., Cornell U. 67-71; Sp., CEPD 62-65; Dir., 3rd Div., Tax Reform Com. 68-70; Dep. Dir.-Gen., Dept. of Customs, MOF 72-76; Dean of Business Sch., Tamkang U. 80-83; Sec.-Gen., Ch. Mem. Cttee. of PBEC in Taipei 84-91; Sec.-Gen. & Mem., Ind. Dev. Adv. Coun., MOEA 85-93; Dep. Dir.,

Twn. Inst. of Econ. Res. 76-82, Dir 82-89, Pres. 89-93; Chmn., Business Mng. Cttee., KMT 93-2000;. *Publ.: Econ. Problems Should Be Solved by Econ. Measures; Principles of Econ.; Trade Relationship between Twn., ROC & Japan—An Interregional Input-Output Analysis; Add.* 15th Fl., 125 Nanking E. Rd., Sect. 5, Taipei 105.

LIU, TIEH-CHENG 劉鐵錚
Grand Justice, Jud. Yuan; *b.* Chungking Sept. 8, '38; *m.* Chiu, Helen S.I.; 1 *s.,* 1 *d.; educ.* LL.B., NCCU; MCL, So. Methodist U., USA; J.D., U. of Utah; Assc. Prof., NCCU 71-74, Prof. 74-85, Dir., Dept. of Law 77-83, Dean, Grad. Sch. of Law 81-85. *Publ.: Selected Essays on the Conflict of Laws; Add.* 124 Chungking S. Rd., Sect. 1, Taipei 100.

LIU, TSUI-JUNG 劉翠溶
Mem., Acad. Sinica 96-, Res. Fel. 79-, Dir., Inst. of Twn. Hist., Preparatory Off. 98-; Prof., NTU 80-; *b.* Twn. Dec. 5, '41; *educ.* BA, NTU 63, MA 66; MA, Harvard U. 70, Ph.D. 74; Assc. Res. Fel., Acad. Sinica 74-78; Postdoctoral Fel., U. of Penn. 76-77; Adjunct Prof., NTNU 79-80; Fulbright Fel., Prof. in Georgetown U. 84; Visiting Prof., UCLA 89. *Publ.: Lineage Population & Socio-Econ. Changes in the Ming-Ch'ing Periods 92;* & many articles on Ch. econ. hist. & hist. demography; *Add.* Inst. of Twn. Hist., Preparatory Off., Acad. Sinica, Taipei 115.

LIU, TSUN-I
(See LAU, LAWRENCE J. 劉遵義)

LIU, VICTOR W. 劉維琪
Pres., Nat. Sun Yat-sen U. 96-; *b.* Greece Nov. 17, '52; *m.* Fang, Grace F.; 1 *s.,* 1 *d.; educ.* BBA, NCKU 74; MBA, N.We. U. 78, Ph.D. 82; Assc. Prof., Prof., Dept. Head, & Dir., Nat. Sun Yat-sen U. 82-90, Dean of Mng. Sch. 90-91; Dir., Dept. of Higher Educ., MOE 91-93; Pres., Cent. Investment Holding Co. Ltd. 93-96. *Publ.: Public Utility Pricing with Asymmetric Info.; The Determination of the Dev. Priority of Sc. & Tech.; Case Studies in Financial Mng.;* & many papers on finance & managerial acct.; *Add.* Nat. Sun Yat-sen U., 70 Lien Hai Rd., Kaohsiung 804.

LIU, WAN-HANG
(See LIU, WANN-HONG 劉萬航)

LIU, WANN-HONG 劉萬航
V. Chmn., CCA 85-; *b.* Chungking June 1, '39; *m.* Tung, Chia-li; 3 *c.; educ.* BA, NCHU; M. of Fine Arts, So. Illinois U.; Assc. Res. Fel., Nat. Palace Museum 71-75, Res. Fel. 75-81, Res. Fel. & concur. Curator of Conservation Dept.

81-85. *Publ.: Res. on the Mfr. of Bronze Art Objects (Casting Tech.); A Study on the Ind. Mfr. of Jewelry; Casting Reproductions of Ch. Bronze Vessels by the Lost-Wax Process; A Study of Mfr. of Nonferrous Metal Art Objects by Forging & Raising Method; Add.* 102 Ai Kuo E. Rd., Taipei 100.

LIU, WEI-CHI
(See LIU, VICTOR W. 劉維琪)

LIU, YUAN-CHUN
(See LIU, YUAN-TSUN 劉源俊)

LIU, YUAN-TSUN 劉源俊
Pres., Soochow U. 96-, Prof. 76-; *b.* Yunnan Feb. 5, '45; *m.* Fu, B.L.; 1 *s.,* 1 *d.; educ.* BS, NTU 66; Ph.D. in Phys., Columbia U. 72; Assc. Prof., Phys. Dept., Soochow U. 72-76, Dept. Head 74-83, Dean, Sch. of Sc. 77-83 & 87-88, Dean of Acad. Aff. 83-87; V. Pres., Coll. Entrance Exam. Cent. 90-93. *Publ.: Effective Energy Forumlation for the Random Impurity System, Annals of Phys. 73; Collected Articles on Educ.; Collected Articles on Sc.; Add.* Pres.'s Off., Soochow U., Shihlin, Taipei 111.

LO, BENJAMIN J.Y. 羅致遠
Dep. Rep., TECRO in USA 98-; *b.* Hupei Mar. 23, '40; *m.* wang, Yun-tsun; 1 *s.,* 1 *d.; educ.* BA, Dip., NCCU, MA, Intl. Law & Dip.; MA, Intl. Rel., U. of Santo Tomas, Philippines; Staff Mem., Dept. of Intl. Org., MOFA 64-66; 3rd & 2nd Sec., Emb. in the Philippines 66-70; Dir., ROC Off. in Hong Kong 70-74; Dir. Attaché, Dept. of Inf. & Cul. Aff., MOFA 74-76, Sect. Chief 76-78; Dir., Secretariat, Taipei Econ. & Trade Off. in Thailand 78-88; Dep. Rep., Taipei Econ. & Trade Off. in Indonesia 88-91; Dir., Dept. of W. Asian Aff., MOFA 91-94; *Add.* 4201 Wisconsin Avenue, N.W., Washington, D.C. 20016, USA.

LO, CHENG-TIEN 羅成典
Dep. Sec.-Gen., Legis. Yuan 92-; *b.* Twn. Nov. 4, '40; *m.* Lu, Shu; 2 *s.,* 3 *d.; educ.* LL.B., NCCU 65, LL.M. 69; Sp., Organic Laws Cttee., Legis. Yuan 70-87, Sec. 75-90 & Chief Sec., Secretariat 90-92. *Publ.: Res. on Urban Population of Twn. & the Utilization of Urban Land; Tech. on Legislation; The Standard Laws for Cent. Regln.; Add.* 1st Fl., 11 Alley 19, Lane 160, Min Chuan E. Rd., Sect. 3, Taipei 105.

LO, CHI-TANG
(See LO, JAMES C.T. 羅際棠)

LO, CHIH-YUAN
(See LO, BENJAMIN J.Y. 羅致遠)

LO, HAO
(See LOH, HORACE H. 羅浩)

LO, JAMES C.T. 羅際棠
Chmn., Bk. of Twn. 95-; *b.* Twn. Apr. 20, '30; *m.* Cheng, Kin-lan; 3 *d.; educ.* BA, Econ., NTU; Studied at Washington State U.; Clerk & Sect. Chief, Hua Nan Cml. Bk. 54-67, Asst. V. Pres. 67-71, V. Pres. 71-73, Sr. V. Pres. & Gen. Mgr. 73-80, Exec. V. Pres. 80-85; Pres., Taipei City Bk. 85-88 & Hua Nan Cml. Bk. 88-91; Chmn., Twn. Cooperative Bk. 91-94; Chmn., Hua Nan Cml. Bk. 94-95; *Add.* 120 Chungking S. Rd., Sect. 1, Taipei 100.

LO, KWOK-YUNG 魯國鏞
Mem., Acad. Sinica 98-, Disting. Res. Fel. & Dir., Inst. of Astronomy & Astrophys. 97-; Prof. of Astronomy, U. of Illinois at Urbana-Champaign 86-; Adjunct Prof., NTU 98-; *b.* Nanking Oct. 19, '47; *m.* Chen, Helen Brokwan; 2 *s.; educ.* BS, MIT 69, Ph.D. 74; Asst. Res. Astronomer, Radio Astronomy Lab, UC-Berkly. 78; Sr. Res. Fel. in Radio Astronomy, Caltech 78-80, Asst. Prof. 80-86; Chmn., Astronomy Dept., U. of Illinois 95-97. *Publ.:* Numerous papers on astronomy; *Add.* 128 Yen Chiu Yuan Rd., Sect. 2, Taipei 115.

LO, PEN-LI 羅本立
Strategy Adv. to the Pres. 98-; Gen., ROC Army; *b.* Anhwei Feb. 11, '27; *m.* Chang, Tzu-hsia; 2 *s.,* 1 *d.; educ.* Mil. Acad. 49; Advanced Class, Infantry Sch. 59; Army CGSC 64; War Coll., Armed Forces U. 79; Div. Cmdr. 74-77; Corps Cmdr. 79-80; Dean, Army CGSC, Armed Forces U. 80-83; Field Army Cmdr. 83-86; Pres., Armed Forces U. 87-89; C-in-C, CSF 89-93; V. Chief of the Gen. Staff & Exec. Off., MND 93-95; Chief of the Gen. Staff, MND 95-98; *Add.* P.O. Box 90011, Taipei.

LO, PING-CHANG
(See LOH, PING-CHEUNG 羅平章)

LO, TUNG-BIN 羅銅壁
Mem., Acad. Sinica 86-; Pres., Coll. Entrance Exam. Cent. 93-; *b.* Twn. Feb. 15, '27; *m.* Wu, Su-shia; 3 *s.; educ.* BS, NTU; D.Sc., Tohoku Imprial U.; Assc. Fel., UC-Berkly. 59-61; Visiting Prof., U. of Calif., San Francisco 68-69; Dir., Grad. Inst. of Biochem. Sc., NTU 72-78, & Inst. of Biochem., Acad. Sinica 72-80; Dean, Coll. of Sc., NTU 78-84, Dean of Acad. Aff. 84-90; Prof. of Biochem., NTU 64-95; V. Pres., Acad. Sinica 93-96. *Publ.:* 110 sc. papers on snake venom & pituitary hormone; *Add.* 237 Chou Shan Rd., Taipei 106.

LO, TUNG-PI
(See LO, TUNG-BIN 羅銅壁)

LOH, HORACE H. 羅浩
Mem., Acad. Sinica 86-; Frederick & Alice Stark Prof. & Chmn., Dept. of Pharmacology, U. of Minnesota; Prof., Med. Cent., U. of Calif.; *b.* Kwangtung May 28, '37; *m.* Loh, Dana; 1 *s.,* 1 *d.; educ.* BS, NTU 58; Ph.D., U. of Iowa 65. *Publ.:* About 350 res. papers on pharmacology; *Add.* Dept. of Pharmacology, 3-249 Millard, U. of Minnesota, 435 Delaware St., S.E., Minneapolis, MN 55455, USA.

LOH, I-CHENG 陸以正
Amb.-at-Large 98-; *b.* Kiangsu Aug. 29, '24; *m.* Yeh, Jane; 2 *s.,* 1 *d.; educ.* BA, NCU; MS, Columbia U.; With UN Forces in S. Korea 51-53; City Ed., *Ch. News* 53-54; Asst. Mng. Ed., *Ch. Daily News* 55-56; Dir., Dept. of Intl. Info. Services, GIO 56-63; Min. & Counsl. for Info., Emb in USA & concur. Dir., Ch. Info. Service, New York 63-78; Pres. & Dir., Inst. of Ch. Cul., Vienna, Austria 79-81; Amb. to Guatemala 81-90; Amb. to S. Africa 90-97; *Add.* 11th Fl., 206 Chung Hsiao E. Rd., Sect. 4, Taipei 106.

LOH, JEN-KONG 陸潤康
Chmn. & Chief Exec. Off., Dah An Cml. Bk. 91-2000; Chmn., Rule of Law Dev. Found. 94-; Mem., CC, KMT 93-; *b.* Kiangsu June 19, '27; *m.* Lin, De-yun; 2 *s.; educ.* LL.B., Soochow U. 56; MCL, So. Methodist U., USA 59; Comr., Nat. Tax Admin. of Taipei, MOF 74-78, Dir.-Gen., Dept. of Customs 78-80; Pres., CTC 80-81; Pol. V. Min. of Finance 81-84; Min. of Finance 84-85; Mng. Dir., CBC 84-85; Mem., CEPD 84-85; Mng. Partner, Alliance Intl. Law Off. 87-91. *Publ.: The Const. of the USA; Credit & Sec. in the ROC* 74 (in Eng.); *Add.* 3rd Fl., 117 Min Sheng E. Rd., Sect. 3, Taipei 105.

LOH, PING-CHEUNG 羅平章
Sec.-Gen., Intl. Cooperation & Dev. Fund 96-; *b.* Kiangsu Apr. 18, '37; *m.* Cheng, Ming-jean; 1 *d.; educ.* LL.B., NTU 59; MCL, Columbia U. 61; LL.M., Yale U. 63; Worked for World Bk. 64-96, Country Dir., Latin Am. region; *Add.* 12-15th Fl., 9 Lane 62, Tienmu W. Rd., Shihlin, Taipei 111.

LU, ALEXANDER YA-LI 呂亞力
Prof., Pol. Sc., NTU 77-; Mem., CEIC; *b.* Chekiang Sept. 18, '35; *m.* Tso, Ding-wen Cindy; 2 *s.; educ.* BA, NTU 57; MA, Indiana U. 63, Ph.D. 71; Asst. Prof., Pol. Sc., Berry Coll., Georgia 67-71; Assc. Prof., NTU 71-76; Prof. & Dir., Inst. of Pol. Sc., Nat. Sun Yat-sen U. 93-95. *Publ.: An Introduction to Pol. Sc.; Pol. Sc. Methodology; Pol. Dev. &*

Dem.; Pol. Opposition in Twn.; The Future Dem. Dev. in the ROC; Pol. Modernization in the ROC; Pol. Dev. in the ROC; Pol. Dev. in the ROC; Add. 2nd Fl., 11 Lanc 60, Chou Shan Rd., Taipei 106.

LU, BENJAMIN C. 魯肇忠
Nat. Policy Adv. to the Pres. 97-; *b.* Anhwei Dec. 5, '34; *m.* Wey, J.H.; 1 *s.,* 2 *d.; educ.* BA, Econ., NTU 58; Resr., Inst. of Econ. Dev. & Planning, UN 66-67; Auditor, For. Exchange & Trade Com. 64-66; Consultant, Econ. Com. for Far E. & Asia, UN 67-69; Dep. Dir. & Dir., Bd. of For. Trade, MOEA 69-77, Dep. Dir.-Gen. 78-82; Dir., Econ. Div., TECRO, USA 82-88; Dir., Majestic Trading Co. & concur. Dir., Far E. Trade Service in Belgium 88-91; Rep., TECO in Belgium 91-94; Rep., TECRO in USA 94-96; Nat. Policy Adv. to the Pres. 96; Bd. Mem., TECRO 97; *Add.* c/o Off. of the Pres., Taipei 100.

LU, CHAO-CHUNG
(See LU, BENJAMIN C. 魯肇忠)

LU, HSI-MU
(See LEU, HSI-MUH 呂溪木)

LU, HSIU-LIEN
(See LU, HSIU-LIEN ANNETTE 呂秀蓮)

LU, HSIU-LIEN ANNETTE 呂秀蓮
V. Pres., ROC 2000-; *b.* Twn. June 7, '44; *educ.* LL.B., NTU 67; MCL, U. of Illinois 71; LL.M., Harvard U. 78; Sect. Chief, Exec. Yuan 71-74; Founder, Pioneer Press & Women's Resource Cent. 76-77; Asst. Pub., *Formosa Mag.* 79; Jailed for Kaohsiung Incident 79-85; Founder, Clean Election Coalition 89; Founder, Coalition for Dem. 90; Founder, Alliance for Election Reform & Nat. Org. for Women in Twn. 91; Founder, Twn. Intl. Alliance to press for Twn.'s entry into the UN 93; Mem., Legis. Yuan 93-96, Convener, For. Aff. Cttee. 94; Chmn., Global Summit of Women 94; Chmn., Feminist Summit for Global Peace 95; Nat. Policy Adv. to the Pres. 96-97; Magis., Taoyuan County 97-2000. *Publ.: Searching for Another Window* 74; *New Feminism* 74; *Twn.: Past, Present, Future* 78; *Counting the Footsteps of the Pioneer* 76; *Helping Them to the Sunlight* 76; *New Feminism: Where to Go?* 77; *These Three Women* 85; *Between Male & Female* 85; *I Love Twn.* 88; *Retrying the Formosa Case* 91; *Empathy* 98; *Add.* c/o Off. of the Pres., Taipei 100.

LU, I-CHENG
(See LOH, I-CHENG 陸以正)

LU, JUN-KANG
(See LOH, JEN-KONG 陸潤康)

LU, KUO-YUNG
(See LO, KWOK-YUNG 魯國鏞)

LU, P.W. 陸炳文
Dir., 7th Dept. & concur. Counsl., Exec. Yuan 97-; *b.* Fukien Feb. 5, '43; *m.* Shih, Ying; 1 *s.,* 2 *d.; educ.* Ed.B., NTNU 65; Dir., Dept. of Secretariat, Bu. of Engr. Service (BES) 87-90, Dep. Gen. Mgr. & concur. Spokesman 90-92; Adv. & concur. Gen. Coordinator with the Legis. Yuan, MOEA 92-93; Pres., BESTPR Co. Ltd. 93-97. *Publ.: PR & Crisis Mng.; Top Gun in Crisis Mng.; The Comm. Master; Add.* 1 Chung Hsiao E. Rd., Sect. 1, Taipei 100.

LU, PING-WEN
(See LU, P.W. 陸炳文)

LU, YA-LI
(See LU, ALEXANDER YA-LI 呂亞力)

MA, AN-LAN 馬安瀾
Nat. Policy Adv. to the Pres.; *b.* Liaoning Apr. 27, '16; *m.* Wu, Fu-yin; 2 *s.,* 1 *d.; educ.* 10th Class, Mil. Acad.; 18th Class, Army War Coll.; 1st Class, Joint Op. Sch.; Sp., 1st Class, CGSC, US Army; 8th Class, Armed Forces Staff Coll.; Cmdr., 10th Infantry Div., ROC Army 56-59; Cmdr., 2nd Corps, & Dep. CG, Kinmen Def. Cmd. 60-65; Cmdr., 2nd Field Army, ROC Army 65-69; CG, Kinmen Def. Cmd. 69-72; Dep. C-in-C, ROC Army 72-75, C-in-C 75-78; Exec. V. Chief of the Gen. Staff, MND 78-81; Personal C/S to the Pres.; *Add.* c/o Off. of the Pres., Taipei 100.

MA, CHANG-SHENG 馬長生
Gen. Mgr., Twn. Broadcasting Co. Ltd. 78-; Pres., Nat. Joint Assn. of Private Radio Stations of the ROC 92-; *b.* Anhwei Jan. 21, '50; *m.* Kao, Yu; 2 *s.,* 1 *d.; educ.* BS, Agr., NCHU 71; MS, U. of Wisconsin 77; *Add.* 11th Fl., 17 Chungking S. Rd., Sect. 3, Taipei 100.

MA, CHI-CHUANG 馬紀壯
Sr. Adv. to the Pres. 90-; Chmn., AEAR 91-; *b.* Hopei Oct. 14, '12; *m.* Li, Liang-pi; 2 *d.; educ.* Ch. Naval Acad.; Studied in USA; Nat. War Coll.; Served successively as Squadron Cmdr., C/S, ROCN, C-in-C 52-54; Asst. CG, MND 54-55; V. Min. of Nat. Def. 55-59; C-in-C, CSF 59; Exec. V. Chief of the Gen. Staff, MND 59-65; V. Min. of Nat. Def. 65-72; Dep. Chmn., Nat. Gen. Mobilization Cttee., NSC 67-72; Amb. to Thailand 72-75; Chmn., Ch.

Steel Corp. 75-78; Sec.-Gen., Exec. Yuan 78; Sec.-Gen. to the Pres. 78-84; Min. without Portfolio 84-86; Rep., Tokyo Off., AEAR 86-90; *Add.* 2 Lane 1, Tai An St., Taipei 100.

MA, CHIA-CHEN 馬家珍
Chmn., Ch. Muslim Assn. 96-; *b.* Anhwei May 1, '29; *m.* Ma Liu, Chu-hsien; 1 *s.*, 2 *d.; educ.* LL.B., Fu Hsing Kang Coll. 53; Grad., Armed Forces U.; Chief, Welfare Admin., MND 84-85; Dir., Pol. Dept., GHQ, Army 85-88; Dep. Dir., Gen. Pol. Dept., MND 88; Dep. Sec.-Gen., VAC 88-92; Pres., Shih-Tao Natural Gas Co. Ltd. 92-96; *Add.* 62 Hsin Sheng S. Rd., Sect. 2, Taipei 106.

MA, SHU-LI
(See MAII, SOO-LAY 馬樹禮)

MA, SHUI-LONG 馬水龍
Prof., Dept. of Music, Nat. Inst. of the Arts 95-; Composer; Chmn., ROC Nat. Cttee., Asian Composers' League; Chmn., ROC Composers' Assn.; Mem., Sc. & Tech. Adv. Off., MOE, Coun. of Acad. Reviewal & Evaluation; Trustee, Nat. Fund for Lit. & Art; Music Mem. & Trustee, CCA, USA 88-; *b.* Twn. July 17, '39; 2 *s.; educ.* Grad., Music Dept., Nat. Twn. Acad. of the Arts 64; Diploma, Regensburg Kirchenmusik Hochschule 75; Scholar, Fulbright Found., Columbia U., & U. of Penn. 86-87; Prof., Dept. of Music, Soochow U. 75-81; Prof. & Chmn., Music Dept., Nat. Twn. Acad. of the Arts 81-82; Prof. & Chmn., Dept. of Music, Nat. Inst. of the Arts 82-87, Dean of Acad. Aff. 87-91; Sec.-Gen., Asian Composers' League 84-86; Pres., Nat. Inst. of the Arts 91-94; Scholar & Resr., CCPD Found., USA 94-95. *Publ.: Counterpoint Theory; 12-Tone Composition Study; From the Ballet Liao Tien-ting to a Discussion of the Creation of Dance Music;* & over 40 works of orchestra, chamber, vocal, & solo; etc.; *Add.* 5th Fl., 11 Lane 20, Ta Chih St., Taipei 104.

MA, SHUI-LUNG
(See MA, SHUI-LONG 馬水龍)

MA, SUN 馬遜
Pres., Huafan U. 95-; Pres., ROC Phi Tau Phi Scholastic Hon. Soc. 99-; *b.* Hunan June 7, '47; *educ.* BS, NTU 70; Diplom Chemiker, RWTH, Aachen, Germany 77, Dr. rer. Nat. 80; Asst., RWTH, Aachen 77-80; Assc. Prof., NCKU 80-86, Prof. 86-95; Dir., Tainan Regional Inst. Cent. 88-93. *Publ.:* 50 papers; *Add.* 1 Hua Fan Rd., Shihting Hsiang, Taipei County 223.

MA, YING-JEOU 馬英九
Mayor, Taipei City 98-; Mem. CSC, KMT 99-, Mem., CC 93-; *b.* Hunan July 13, '50; *m.* Chou, Christine Mei-ching; 2 *d.; educ.* LL.B., NTU 72; LL.M., New York U. 76; S.J.D., Harvard U. Law Sch. 81; Consultant, Law Off., First Nat. Bk. of Boston, USA 80-81; Assc., Cole & Deitz Law Off., New York 81; Res. Consultant, U. of Maryland Law Sch. 81; Dep. Dir., 1st Bu., Off. of the Pres. 81-88; Dep. Sec.-Gen., CC, KMT 84-88; Sr. Sec., Off. of the Pres. 88; Chmn., RDEC 88-91; V. Chmn., MAC 91-93, Mem. 88; Min. of Justice, & concur. Min. of State 93-96; Min. without Portfolio 96-97; Assc. Prof., NCCU 97-98. *Publ.: Legal Problems of Seabed Boundary Delimitation in the E. Ch. Sea; 2 Maj. Legal Issues Relating to the Intl. Status of the ROC; Taipei-Beijing Rel. & E. Asian Stability: Implications for Europe; The ROC (Twn.)'s Entry into the WTO: Progress, Problems & Prospects;* etc.; *Add.* 1 Shih Fu Rd., Taipei 110.

MAH, SOO-LAY 馬樹禮
Sr. Adv. to the Pres. 90-; Chmn., Presidium of CAC, KMT 88-, Ch. Reunification Alliance 88-, & Coun. for the Promotion of Nat. Unification & Recon. of the ROC 98-; *b.* Kiangsu Aug. 3, '09; *m.* Wu, Wei-lin; *educ.* Meiji U. 30; BS, U. of Santo Tomas, Philippines 38; Hon. LL.D., Meiji U. 82; Hon. LHD, U. of Santo Tomas 88; Ed., *Minkuo Daily News,* Singapore 31-33, & *New Ch. Herald,* Manila 36-38; Ed.-in-Chief & Dir., *Front Daily News,* Anhwei-Kiangsi-Fukien-Shanghai 38-49; Mem., Legis. Yuan 48-89; Dir. & Ed.-in-Chief, *Ch. Cml. Daily News,* Jakarta 53-59; Adv. to Ch. Mission to 24th, 25th, & 26th UNGA 69-71; Chief, 3rd Dep., CC, KMT 62-72, Mem. 63-88; Prof., Nat. War Coll. 65-70; Rep., Tokyo Off., AEAR 72-85; Bd. Chmn., BCC 72-85; Sec.-Gen., CC, KMT 85-87, Convener, Sup. Panel for Mainland Op. 88-89; Chmn., CTV 87-90, & AEAR 90-91. *Publ.: Hist. of Indonesia's Independence; Indonesia in Turmoil; Twelve Years as the ROC Rep. in Japan; Dasar 2 Anti Komunis by Pres. Chiang Kai-shek* (Indonesian Transl.); *Add.* 11th Fl., 7 Lane 26, Yat Sen Rd., Taipei 110.

MAI, CHAO-CHENG 麥朝成
Mem., Acad. Sinica 94-; Pres., Chung-Hua Inst. for Econ. Res. 96-; Res. Fel., Sun Yat-sen Inst., Acad. Sinica 79-; Prof., NTU 80-; *b.* Twn. Feb. 26, '43; *m.* Lin, Su-chen; 1 *d.; educ.* BA, NTU 66, MA, NTU 70; MA, U. of Rochester 73; Ph.D., Texas A&M U. 76; Assc. Prof., NCCU 76-79; Assc. Prof., NTU 77-80; Prof., NCCU 79-81; Visiting Scholar, Harvard U. 81-82; Dir., Sun Yat-sen Inst., Acad. Sinica 87-93; Fulbright Visiting Scholar & Visiting Prof. of Alabama State U. 90-91. *Publ.:* 130 papers; *Add.* 75 Chang Hsing St., Taipei 106.

MAI, CHUN-FU 麥春福

Nat. Policy Adv. to the Pres. 96-; *b.* Twn. Feb. 9, '24; *m.* Lu, Su-o; 2 *s.,* 5 *d.; educ.* BA, Kinki U., Japan; V. Spkr., 7th, 8th, 9th Taipei CoCoun.; Chmn., Tamsui 1st Credit Cooperative Bk. 54-80; Chmn., Credit Cooperative Bk. Union of the ROC 85-90; Comr., TPG 90-94; Sr. Adv. to the Premier 94-96; *Add.* 70 Po Ai St., Tamsui, Taipei County 251.

MAO, CHI-KUO 毛治國

Admin. V. Min. of Trans. & Comms. 93-2000; Cttee. Mem., Nat. Info. Infrastructure Project, Exec. Yuan 94-; Comr., Investment Com., MOEA 93-; Bd. Mem., Yangming Marine Trans. Corp. 93-; Bd. Dir., Chung Hwa Telecomm. Corp. 95-; Chmn., ROC Computer Soc. 99-; *b.* Chekiang Oct. 4, '48; *m.* Chien, Yin-yin; 1 *s.,* 1 *d.; educ.* BCE, NCKU 71; MS, Asian Inst. of Tech., Bangkok 75; Ph.D., MIT 82; Prof. & Dept. Head, Mng. Sc. Dept., NCTU 82-87; Sec.-Gen., MOTC 87-88, Dir.-Gen., Tourism Bu. 89-91, & Provisional Engr. Off. of High Speed Rail 91-93; Dir.-Gen., Civil Aeronautics Admin. 94; Bd. Chmn., Ch. Inst. of Trans. 93-97. *Publ.:* 101 jour. articles, reports, conf. papers, & essays; *Add.* Rm. 403, 2 Changsha St., Sect. 1, Taipei 100.

MAO, CHIH-KUO
(See MAO, CHI-KUO 毛治國)

MAO, HO-KWANG 毛河光

Mem., Acad. Sinica 94-; Geophysicist, Geophys. Lab., Carnegie Inst. of Washington (CIW) 72-; Mem., Nat. Acad. of Sc., USA; For. Mem., Ch. Acad. of Sc. (Ch. mainland); *b.* Shanghai June 18, '41; *m.* Mao Liu, Agnes; 3 *c.; educ.* BS, NTU 63; MS & D.Sc., U. of Rochester, New York 66 & 68; Assc. Resr., U. of Rochester 67-68; Postdr. Fel. & Assc. Resr., Geophys. Lab., CIW 68-70 & 70-72. *Publ.:* 380 papers on high pressure, phys., chem., & geol. in jour. & symposia; *Add.* 11322 Edenderry Drive, Fair Fox, VA 22030, USA.

MAO, KAO-WEN 毛高文

Amb. to Costa Rica 96-; Mem., CC, KMT 93-; *b.* Chekiang Feb. 9, '36; *m.* King, May-ling; 1 *d.; educ.* BS, NTU; MS, UC-Berkly.; Ph.D., Carnegie-Mellon U., USA; Res. Engr., Electrochem. Dept., Gen. Motors Res. Labs., USA 64-65; Project Engr., Chem. Engr. Dept., Carnegie-Mellon U. 65-69; Sr. Res. Engr., Electrochem. Dept., Gen. Motors Res. Labs. 69-74; Prof. & Dir., Inst. of Ind. Chem., NTHU 72-73; Prof. & Dean, Coll. of Engr. 74-78; Ed.-in-Chief, *Jour. of the Ch. Inst. of Engr.* 78-82; Pres., Ch. Inst. of Ind. Engr. 81, Nat. Twn. Inst. of Tech. 78-81, & NTHU 81-87; Min. of Educ. 87-93; V. Pres., Exam. Yuan 93-96. *Publ.:* More than 20 papers on chem. engr. & electrochem.; *Add.* Apartado 907-1000, San Jose, Costa Rica.

MEI, CHIANG-CHUNG 梅強中

Mem., Acad. Sinica 94-; E.K. Turner Prof., Civil & Environmental Engr., MIT 93-; Prof. Mech. Engr., 99-; *b.* Ch. Apr. 4, '35; *m.* Schmitt, Caroline; 1 *d.; educ.* B., Engr., NTU 55; M., Engr., Stanford U. 57; Ph.D., Calif. Inst. of Tech. 63, Postdr. Res. 63-65; Asst. Prof., MIT 65-68, Assc. Prof. 68-74, Prof. 74-93; Guggenheim Fel. 72-73; Visiting Scholar, Cambridge U., UK; Visiting Prof., U. of Adelaide (Australia), U. of Tronheim (Norway), U. of Joseph Fourier (France), & NTU; Mem., US Nat. Acad. of Engr. 86. *Publ.:* "Applied Dynamics of Ocean Surface Waves," *World Sc.; Math. Analysis in Engr.*; *Add.* 1-353, Dept. of Civil Environment Engr., MIT, Cambridge, MA 02139, USA.

MEI, TSU-LIN 梅祖麟

Mem., Acad. Sinica 94-; Hu Shih Prof. of Ch. Lit. & Philology, Dept. of Asian Studies, Cornell U. 94-; *b.* Peking Feb. 14, '33; *m.* Yip, Teresa; 1 *s.,* 2 *d.; educ.* BA, Oberlin Coll. 54; MA, Harvard U. 55; Ph.D., Yale U. 62; Instr., Philosophy, Yale U. 62-64; Asst. Prof., Ch., Harvard U. 64-69, Assc. Prof. 69-71; Assc. Prof., Ch. Lit., Cornell U. 71-79, Prof. 79-94, Chmn., Dept. of Asian Studies 72-77, Dir., Ch.-Japan Prog. 77-80, Prof., Ch. Lit. & Philosophy 70-94; Disting. Visisting Prof., Inst. of Linguistic Res., Ch. Acad. of So. Sc. 89. *Publ.:* Over 50 articles in *Harvard Jour. of Asian Studies, Bulletin of the Inst. of Hist. & Philology* & other jour.; *Add.* Dept. of Asian Studies, Rockefeller Hall, Cornell U., Ithaca, NY 14853-2502, USA.

MIAO, FENG-CHIANG
(See MIAU, MATTHEW F.C. 苗豐強)

MIAU, MATTHEW F.C. 苗豐強

Pres., Synnex Intl. 99-, Mitac Intl. Corp. 98-; *m.* Hsu, Anchen; 2 *s.; educ.* BEE, UC-Berkly. 70; MBA, Santa Clara U., USA 76; Engr., Elect. Arrays Inc., Calif., USA 70-71; Engr. & Marketing Mgr., Intel Corp. 71-76; *Add.* 1 Yen Fa 2nd Rd., Sc.-based Ind. Park, Hsinchu 300.

MOU, TSUNG-TSAN
(See MU, PAUL TZUNG-TSANN 牟宗燦)

MU, PAUL TZUNG-TSANN 牟宗燦

Pres., Nat. Dong Hwa U. 94-; *b.* Shantung Oct. 13, '39; *m.* Mu, Corrina H.; 1 *s.,* 1 *d.; educ.* BA, Econ., NTU 60; MS, Econ., U. of Nevada 65; Ph.D., Econ., U. of Calif., Davis 70; Asst. Prof., Econ., Calif. State U., Los Angeles 69-72,

Prof. 77-91, Assc. V. Pres., Acad. Aff. 86-88; Visiting Prof., Nat. Sun Yat-sen U. 80-81; Mem., Legis. Yuan 86-91; Dir., Preparatory Off., Nat. Dong Hwa U. 91-94. *Publ.: Income Taxes, Econ. Growth, & Quality-of-Life Mng.* 95; *Aboriginal Migration to Urban Environments—A Socioecon. Case Study of Twn.*, Published by the Pacific Econ. Corp. Coun. 97; *Add.* Nat. Dong Hwa U., 1 Ta Hsueh Rd., Sect. 2, Chihhsueh Village, Shoufeng, Hualien 974.

NI, TUAN-CHIU 倪搏九

Nat. Policy Adv. to the Pres. 91-; Dep. Sec.-Gen., Ch. Reunification Alliance 82-; *b.* Shantung Aug. 7, '16; *m.* Chou, Shang-hsien; 4 *s.*, 1 *d.; educ.* LL.B., NCCU 46; Resr., Inst. of Rev. Implementation 50, Workshop on Joint War Aff. Op. by the Party, Govt. & Armed Forces 54, & Workshop on Pol. War Aff. 67; Sec. & Sect. Chief, MTAC 46-48; Sec. & Dir., Legis. Yuan 48-67; Mem., Nat. Dev. Planning Group, NSC 67-73; Adv. & Dep. Sec.-Gen., Const. Res. Cttee., NA 73-91; Adv., World Freedom & Dem. League 68-97. *Publ.: Gen. Ho Yin-chin's Hist. Chronicle; Biography of Gen. Ho Yin-chin; Conceptual Theory on Accomplice; The Collected Poetry & Lyric Verse of Ni Tuan-chiu; Add.* 9th Fl., 306 Shih Tung Rd., Shihlin, Taipei 111.

NI, WEN-YA

(See NIEH, WEN-YA 倪文亞)

NI, YUE-SI 黎玉璽

Strategy Adv. to the Pres. 78-; *b.* Szechwan May 28, '14; *m.* Ha, Chun-chi; 1 *s.; educ.* Ch. Naval Acad.; Mil. Staff Coll.; Naval Tng. at Miami; Nat. Def. Coll.; Cmdg. Off., PCE 46-47; Chief, Op. Dept., GHQ, Navy 47-48; Cmdg. Off., DE-21 48-49; Cmdr., 2nd Squadron 49-50; C/S, GHQ, ROCN 50-52, Dep. C-in-C & concur. Fleet Cmdr. 52-59, C-in-C 59-65; V. Chief of the Gen. Staff, MND 65, Chief of the Gen. Staff 65-67; Personal C/S to the Pres. 67-70; Amb. to Turkey 70-71; Personal C/S to the Pres. 73-78; Pres., ROC Amateur Athletic Fed. 73-82. *Publ.: On Adm. Lord Nelson* (transl.); *Add.* 62 Chin Shan S. Rd., Sect. 1, Taipei 100.

NIEH, WEN-YA 倪文亞

Sr. Adv. to the Pres. 89-; Chmn., CAC, KMT 93-; *b.* Chekiang Mar. 2, '05; *m.* Kuo, Shirley W.Y.; 2 *s.*, 3 *d.; educ.* MA, Columbia U.; Hon. LL.D., Hanyang U., S. Korea; Mem., Const. NA; Min. of Youth; Chmn., Twn. Prov. Cttee., KMT; Mem., CC, KMT 41; Prof. & Head, Dept. of Educ., Great Ch. U., & Nat. Ch. U.; Chmn., APPU Coun.; V. Pres. & Pres., Legis. Yuan 61-72 & 72-89; Mem., CSC, KMT 47-93; *Add.* Apt. 1, 11th Fl., 289 Tun Hua S. Rd., Sect. 1, Taipei 106.

NING, CHI-KUN 甯紀坤

Rep. to Fiji 93-; *b.* Honan July 17, '31; *m.* Chen, Yung-fan; 2 *s.; educ.* LL.B., NCHU 59; Chief, Public Rel. Sect., Exec. Yuan 60-63; Sec., MOFA 64-66; 1st Sec., Emb. in the Holy See 66-69, & Permanent Mission of the ROC to the UN 69-71; Consul, Consl. Gen., New York 72-77; Dep. Dir. & Dir., Dept. of Gen. Aff., MOFA 77-81; Rep. to Fiji 81-86; Amb. to Solomon Islands 86-90; Dir.-Gen., 1st Bu., & Keeper of Nat. Seal, Off. of the Pres. 90-93; *Add.* Trade Mission of the ROC, G.P.O. Box 53, Suva, Repub. of Fiji.

NIOU, EMERSON 牛銘實

Assc. Prof., Pol. Sc., Duke U., 88-; *b.* Twn. July 28, '58; *m.* Lin, Pao-Hwa; 3 *d.; educ.* BA, Pol., NTU; Ph.D., U. of Texas at Austin; Asst. Prof., State U. of New York at Stony Brook 87-90. *Publ.:* Published many scholarly articles in *Am. Pol. Sc. Review, Am. Jour. of Pol. Sc.*; etc.; *Add.* Dept. of Pol. Sc., Duke U., Durham, NC 27708-0204, USA.

NIU, MING-SHIH

(See NIOU, EMERSON 牛銘實)

OU, CHIN-DER 歐晉德

Pol. Dep. Mayor, Taipei City 98-; *b.* Fukien Nov. 19, '44; *m.* Huang, Mai-chi; 2 *s.; educ.* BCE, NCKU 66, MCE, 68; Ph.D., Case We. Reserve U. 72; Res. Asst., Case We. Reserve U. 69-73; Assc. Engr., Ch. Engr. Consultants Inc. 73-76; Sr. Engr. & Mgr., Moh & Assc. Inc. 76-79; V. Pres. & Resident Mgr., Moh & Assc. Private Ltd., Singapore 79-82; Sr. V. Pres., Moh & Assc. Intl. 82-87; Chief Engr., Ret-Ser Engr. Agency, VAC 87-89; Dir., Taipei-Ilan Expressway Project Off. 89-90; Dir.-Gen., Twn. Area Nat. Expressway Engr. Bu., MOTC 90-95; Chmn., Public Construction Com., Exec. Yuan 96-98. *Publ.:* 73 Geotech. related publ. in intl. & domestic jour.; *Add.* 1 Shih Fu Rd., Taipei 110.

OU, CHIN-TE

(See OU, CHIN-DER 歐晉德)

OU, FRANCISCO H.L. 歐鴻鍊

Rep. TECO in Spain 99-; *b.* Twn. Jan. 5, '40; *m.* Liu, Chih-yuan; 2 *s.*, 2 *d.; educ.* LL.B., Dept. of Dip., NCCU 62; 3rd & 2nd Sec., Emb. in Lima 67-71; Sect. Chief, Dept. of Cent. & S. Am. Aff., MOFA 71-73, Dep. Dir. 73-75; Dir., Ch. Com. Off., Chile 75-81, & Dept. of Cent. & S. Am. Aff., MOFA 81-84; Amb. to Nicaragua 84-85; Rep., Ch. Cml. Off. in Argentina 86-90; Amb. to Guatemala 90-96; V. Min. of For. Aff. 96-99; *Add.* Apartado 36016, 28080 Madrid, Spain.

OU, HAO-NIEN
(See AU, HO-NIEN 歐豪年)

OU, HSI-CHI 歐錫祺
Pres., Nat. Kaohsiung Marine Jr. Coll. 90-; Pres. Nat. Kaohsiung Inst. of Marine Tech. 97-; *b.* Twn. Mar. 1, '34; *m.* Lin, Kuei-hua; 2 *s.,* 1 *d.; educ.* Grad., Twn. Prov. Marine Jr. Coll. 56; BS, Twn. Prov. Ocean Coll. 70; MS, Fishery Tech., U. of Nagassaki, Japan 74; Ph.D., Agr., U. of Tokyo 80; Asst. Lectr., Nat. Kaohsiung Marine Jr. Coll. 58-63, Lectr. 63-64, Assc. Prof. & Head, Fishery Dept. 64-78; Prof., Nat. Twn. Ocean Coll. 80-88; Prof., Twn. Prov. Ocean Coll., Nat. Twn. Ocean U. 89-90; Pres., Nat. Kaohsiung Inst. of Marine Tech. 90. *Publ.: Fish Population Estimation & Length Composition Through Pulse Enumeration— An Experimental Echo Survey in Lake Yunoko, Nikko;* & more than 50 papers; *Add.* 142 Hai Chuan Rd., Nantzu, Kaohsiung 811.

OU, HUNG-LIEN
(See OU, FRANCISCO H.L. 歐鴻鍊)

OU, YU-CHAN 歐育誠
Dep. Dir.-Gen., CPA 94-; *b.* Twn. Nov. 26, '39 *m.* Wu, Shu-nu; 1 *s.,* 1 *d.; educ.* LL.B., Ch. Cul. U. 74; Studied, Grad. Sch. of Senshu U., Japan 80; Sp., CPA 70-71, Sect. Chief 71-77, Comr. 77-79, Dep. Dir. 79-84, Dir. 84-90, Chief Sec. 90-94. *Publ.: Problems & Mng. of Small & Medium-sized Ent.; The Japanese Pers. System of Civil Servants*; *Add.* 10th Fl., 2-2 Chi Nan Rd., Sect. 1, Taipei 116.

OU, YU-CHENG
(See OU, YU-CHAN 歐育誠)

OU, YUNG-SHENG 歐用生
Pres., Nat. Taipei Tchrs.' Coll. 95-, Prof. 80-; *b.* Twn. Aug. 27, '43; *m.* Chuang, Hsiu-chin; 1 *s.,* 1 *d.; educ.* Grad., Twn. Prov. Tainan Tchrs.' Sch. 62; Ed.B., NTNU 69; Ed.M., U. of Tokyo 79; Ed.D., NTNU 88; Tchr., Elementary Sch. 62-65, Secondary Sch. 69-71; Teaching Asst. 71-72; Instr. 79-80; Assc. Prof. 80-84; Dean of Acad. Aff., Jr. Tchrs.' Coll. & Tchrs.' Coll. 84-86 & 87-91; Dir., Sp. Educ. Cent. 86-87; Dir., Twn. Prov. Inst. for Elementary Sch. Tchrs'. Educ. 91-93. *Publ.: Methodologies in Curriculum Res.; Qualitative Res.; Educ. Innovation in an Open Soc.; Tchrs.' In-Service Educ. & Prof. Dev.; Tchrs.' Prof. Growth & Learning; Educ. Dev. in a New Era; Cultivating Tchrs. in a New Era; Reforming Curriculum in the New Century: Cross-*

Strait Views; Sch. in the New Century; Add. 134 Ho Ping E. Rd., Sect. 2, Taipei 106.

OU-YANG, CHAO-HO 歐陽兆和
Mem., Acad. Sinica 84-; Prof. Emeritus, NTU 89-; Mem. Emeritus, Sc. Coun., MOE 91-; *b.* Twn. May 27, '19; *m.* Hong, Shiu-hong; 1 *s.,* 3 *d.; educ.* MD, Taihoku Imperial U.; MD, Kyoto U.; Teaching Asst., NTU 47-53, Instr. 53-56, Assc. Prof. 56-61, Prof. 61-89; Chmn., Dept. of Pharmacology, Pharmacological Inst., NTU 72-78; Ed. Bd., *Toxicon* 82; Mem., Sc. Coun., MOE 88-91. *Publ.:* About 70 papers concerning snake venoms, blood coagulation & platelet aggregation; *Add.* 54 Alley 2, Lane 65, Chung Shan N. Rd., Sect. 2, Taipei 104.

OU-YANG, JUI-HSIUNG 歐陽瑞雄
Rep., Taipei Rep. Off. in Singapore 97-; *b.* Twn. Nov. 23, '40; *m.* Tang, Pee-yin; 2 *s.; educ.* BA, NCCU; MA, NTU; Staff Mem., MOFA 68-70; Sec., Trade Mission of the ROC to Singapore 70-79; Dir., Dept. of For. Aff., TPG 79-81; Dir., Protocol Dept., MOFA 82-83; Dep. Dir.-Gen., TECO, Los Angeles 84-86; Dir.-Gen., TECO, Kanasa City, Missouri 86-90; Dir.-Gen., TECO, Houston, Texas 90-91; Spokesman, MOFA, & concur. Dir., Info. & Cul. Dept. 91-94; Dir.-Gen., TECO, Los Angeles 94-97. *Publ.: Studies on ASEAN; Add.* 460 Alexandra Rd., #23-00, PSA Bldg., Singapore 119963.

PAI, HSIU-HSIUNG
(See BAI, HSIU-HSIUNG 白秀雄)

PAN, CHEN-CHIU
(See PAN, CHEN-CHEW 潘振球)

PAN, CHEN-CHEW 潘振球
Pres., Acad. Historica 95-2000; *b.* Kiangsu June 2, '18; *m.* Chu, Chu-i; 3 *s.,* 1 *d.; educ.* Nat. Tchrs.' Coll.; Postgrad. Studies, NCCU; Nat. War Coll.; LL.D., Konkuk U., S. Korea; Dean of Trainees, Kiangsu Prov. Civil Service Tng. Cent. 46-48; Prin., Youth Middle Sch., Hangchow 48-49, Twn. Prov. Taichung 2nd Middle Sch. 49-50, & Twn. Prov. Taipei Chengkung Middle Sch. 50-56; Dir., Twn. Prov. Tng. Corps 56-64; Prof., Inst. of Ch. Cul. 62-63; Comr. Dept. of Educ., TPG 64-72; Chmn., NYC 72-78, & Twn. Prov. Cttee., KMT 78-79; Dir.-Gen., Ch. Youth Corps 79-87; Dir., Org. Aff. Dept., CC, KMT 87-88; Nat. Policy Adv. to the Pres. 88-95. *Publ.: The Educ. Thought of Mencius; Add.* 5th Fl.-3, 43 Hsin Yi Rd., Sect. 3, Taipei 106.

PAN, HUANG-LUNG
(See PAN, HWANG-LONG 潘皇龍)

PAN, HWANG-LONG 潘皇龍

Composer; Music Educator; Dir., Res. & Dev. Cent., Cent. for the Study of Art & Tech., Nat. Inst. of the Arts 98-, Prof. 91-; Exec. Dir., Asian Composer's League, ROC Nat. Cttee. 82-; Jury, Music Adv. Cttee., Nat. Theater & Nat. Concert Hall 90-; Mem., Adv. Cttee., Nat. Cul. Cent.; *b.* Twn. Sept. 9, '45; *m.* Lin, Yu-ching; 2 *s.; educ.* BA, NTNU 71; Diploma, Musikhochschule und Musikakademie in Zürich 76; Staatliche Hochschule für Musik und Theater in Hannover, Germany 76-78; Hochschule der Künste Berlin 78-80; Berlin Philharmonic Orchestra 82; Assc. Prof., Nat. Inst. of the Arts 82-91; Mem., Music Cttee., CCA 87-91; Founding Pres., Twn. Chapter, Intl. Soc. for Contemporary Music 89-93; Del., Intl. Rostrum of Composers (IRC)/ UNESCO 91-96. *Publ.: Focus of Modern Music; Let's Appreciate Modern Music; Add.* 7th Fl., 230 Ta An Rd., Sect. 1, Taipei, 106.

PANG, PAI-HSIEN 彭百顯

Magis., Nantou County 97-; Assc. Prof., Dept. of Econ., NCHU 83-; Pres., New Soc. Found. 93-; *b.* Twn. June 14, '49; *m.* Wu, Wen-wan; 1 *s.,* 1 *d.; educ.* MA, Econ., Ch. Cul. U. 76; Sr. Sp., Twn. Cooperative Bk. 74-90; Resr., Financial Group, MOF 82-88; Dir., Dept. of Banking, Ch. Cul. U. 82-83; Mem., Legis. Yuan 90-96. *Publ.: The Analysis of Money Supply in Twn.* 77; *Economist of Love-spreading: K.E. Boulding* 82; *Effect of Financial Service Adjustment Toward Financial Dev. in Twn.* 83; *Never Doubt the Govt.'s Capacity of Spending* 91; *Showing Love to the Land: The Way Toward Twn.'s Modernization* (10 Vol.) 92; *Creating the New Century* (12 Vol.) 95; *Achieving Efficient Govt.* 94; *Heart of Twn.: Nantou Econ.* 97; *Add.* 660 Chung Hsing Rd., Nantou County.

PAO, I-HSING
(See PAO, YIH-HSING 鮑亦興)

PAO, PING 鮑彲

Pres., Wen Tzao Ursuline Coll. of Modern Lang. 92-; *b.* Kiangsu July 18, '39; *m.* Shih, Mo Ching; 3 *s.; educ.* BA, Twn. Prov. Normal U. 59-63; Studied, U. of Cambridge, UK 95; Tchr., Keelung's Tung Hsin Elementary Sch. 57-59; Tchr., Twn. Prov. Feng Shan Sr. High Sch. 63-67; Lectr. & Assc. Prof., Wen Tzao Ursuline Jr. Coll. 67-92. *Publ.: A Study of Demonstrative Pronouns in the Analects of Confucius; A Comparison to Su T'ung-po's Reflection on the Poem of T'ao Yuan-ming; Add.* 900 Min Tzu 1st Rd., Kaohsiung 807.

PAO, TE-MING
(See PAO, TEH-MING 包德明)

PAO, TEH-MING 包德明

Nat. Policy Adv. to the Pres. 96-; Founder & Pres. Emeritus, Ming Chuan U. 99-; V. Chmn., People to People Intl., USA 92-; Pres., People to People Assn., ROC 98-; Chmn., Found. for Intl. Educ. & Mng. Sc. 88-; *b.* Szechwan July 22, '13; *m.* Lee, Ying-chao; 3 *s.,* 1 *d., educ.* LL.B., Nat. Peking U. 35; Hon. Ph.D., Wesleyan Women's Coll. 80; V. Chmn., Coun. of Sr. Adv., Intl. Assn. of U. Pres., NGO, UN; Chmn., Asian Women Football Confed.; Mem., Bd. of Dir., CDN; Mem., NA 46-49; Asst. Mgr., CTC 56-68; *Add.* 250 Chung Shan N. Rd., Sect. 5, Taipei 111.

PAO, YIH-HSING 鮑亦興

Mem., Acad. Sinica 86-; Mem., US Nat. Acad. of Engr. 85-; Prof. Emeritus, NTU 98-; Joseph C. Ford Prof. of Theoretical & Applied Mech., Cornell U. 84-; *b.* Nanking Jan. 19, '30; *m.* Shih, Amelia K.T.; 3 *c.; educ.* BCE, NTU 52; MS, Rensselaer Polytech. Inst. 55; Ph.D., Columbia U. 59; Hon. Dr., NCTU 95; Asst. Prof., Cornell U. 58, Prof. 68, Chmn., Dept. of Theoretical & Applied Mech. 74-80; Dir., Inst. of Applied Mech., NTU 84-86, 89-94, Prof. 89-98. *Publ.: Diffraction of Elastic Waves & Dynamics Stress Concentration* (with C.C. Mow) 72; & more than 100 papers published in sc. & engr. jour.; *Add.* Inst. of Applied Mech., NTU, Taipei 106.

PENG, HUAI-NAN
(See PERNG, FAI-NAN 彭淮南)

PENG, MING-TSUNG 彭明聰

Mem., Acad. Sinica 78-; Prof. Emeritus, NTU 88-; Bd. Chmn., Ch. Fund of Family C., Twn. 97-; Bd. Mem., Childhood Burn Found., ROC & Kaohsiung Med. Coll.; *b.* Twn. Nov. 28, '17; *m.* Yuan, Sen-chin; 3 *s.,* 1 *d.; educ.* B., Med., Taihoku Imperial U. 41, Ph.D. 45; Prof. of Physiology, Coll. of Med., NTU 48-88, Dean of Acad. Aff. 61-72, Chmn., Dept. of Physiology 72-78, Dean, Coll. of Med. 78-83; Dir., McKay Sch. of Nursing 88-93; Res. Fel., Coll. of Phys. & Surgeons, Columbia U. 56-57, & Neuroendocrinology Group, Oxford U. 63-64; Guest Resr., NIH, USA 89. *Publ.:* "Changes in Hormone Uptake & Receptors in the Hypothalamus during Aging," in *Neuroendocrinology of Aging* (J. Meites, ed.); "Rejuvenation of Sexual Behavior of Aging Rats with Neurotransmitters," *Interdisciplinary Topics in Gerontology* (Vol. 24; A.V. Everitt, J.R. Walton); *Add.* 4th Fl.-B, 1 Lane 91, Jen Ai Rd., Sect. 2, Taipei 100.

PENG, PAI-HSIEN
(See PANG, PAI-HSIEN 彭百顯)

PENG WANG, CHIA-KANG
(See WHANG-PENG, JACQUELINE 彭汪嘉康)

PERNG, FAI-NAN 彭淮南
Gov., CBC 98-; *b.* Twn. Jan. 2, '39; *m.* Lai, Yang-chu; 2 *s.; educ.* BA, Econ., NCHU 62; MS, Econ., U. of Minnesota 71; Dir., Econ. Res. Dept., CBC 86-89, Gen. Mgr., For. Exchange Dept. 89-94, Dep. Gov. 94-95; Chmn., CTC 95-97; Chmn., Intl. Cml. Bk. of Ch. 97-98. *Publ.: Possible Methods to the Liberalization of For. Exchange Control; Money Supply & For. Exchange; Balance of Payment & For. Exchange; Add.* 2 Roosevelt Rd., Sect. 1, Taipei 100.

PIAN CHAO, RULAN 卞趙如蘭
Mem., Acad. Sinica 90-; Prof. Emerita, Harvard U. 92-; Hon. Prof., Cent. Ch. U. of Tech., Wuhan, Ch. 90-; Hon. Res. Fel., Shanghai Conservatory of Music, Ch. 91-; Hon. Prof., Cent. S. U. of Tech., Changsha, Ch. 91-; Hon. Res. Fel., Res. Inst. of Music, Ch. Acad. of Arts, Peking, Ch. 97-; *b.* USA Apr. 20, '22; *m.* Pian, Theodore Hsueh-huang; 1 *d.; educ.* BA & MA, We. Music Hist. & Theory, Radcliffe Coll., Ph.D., Musicology & Far Ea. Lang.; Teaching Asst., Harvard U. 47-58, Instr. 59-61, Lectr. 61-74; Visiting Prof., Ch. U. of Hong Kong 75, 78-79, 82, & 94, NTHU 90, & NCU 92; Faculty Mem., Cttee. on Degrees in Folklore & Mythology, Harvard U. 76, Full Prof., Dept. of E. Asian Lang. & Civilizations, & Dept. of Music 74-92; Hon. Prof., S.W. Chiaotung U., Chengtu, Ch. 94; Hon. Permanent Pres. of the Conf. on Ch. Oral & Performing Lit. 95. *Publ.: A Syllabus for the Mandarin Primer; Sung Dynasty Musical Sources & Their Interpretation; Complete Musical Works of Yuen Ren Chao; Found. Work in Pronunciation of Mandarin Ch.*; & 30 articles; *Add.* 14 Brattle Circle, Cambridge, MA 02138, USA.

PIEN CHAO, JU-LAN
(See PIAN CHAO, RULAN 卞趙如蘭)

PING, HSIN-TAO
(See PING, SHIN-TAO 平鑫濤)

PING, SHIN-TAO 平鑫濤
Pres., Crown Cul. Corp. 54-; *b.* Kiangsu June 26, '27; *m.* Chen, Che; 1 *s.,* 2 *d.; educ.* B., U. of Ta Tung, Shanghai 49; Ed.-in-Chief, *United Daily News. Publ.: Under the Sky; Add.* 50 Lane 120, Tun Hua N. Rd., Taipei 105.

RAU, CHYI-MING 饒奇明
Admin. V. Min. of Exam., Exam. Yuan 94-; *b.* Twn. Mar. 10, '38; *m.* Chiu, Min-chen; 2 *s.,* 2 *d.; educ.* B., Lit., NTNU 61; Studied, Pittsburgh State U. 85; Grad., Grad. Sch. of Law, Civil Servants' Cent., NCCU 91; Elementary & Secondary Sch. Tchr. 56-66; Dir., Dept. of Gen. Aff., Min. of Exam. 87-89 & Dept. of Sp. Exam. 89-93, Chief Sec. 93-94; *Add.* 1 Shih Yuan Rd., Wenshan, Taipei 116.

SA, CHIH-TANG
(See SAH, CHIH-TANG 薩支唐)

SAH, CHIH-TANG 薩支唐
Mem., Acad. Sinica 98-; Robert C. Pittman Eminent Scholar, U. of Florida 88-, Grad. Res. Prof. 88-, Chief Scientist, Coll. of Engr. 88-; *b.* Peking Nov. 10, '32; *m.* Linda Chang; 1 *s.,* 1 *d.; educ.* BSEE, U. of Illinois at Urbana-Champaign 53, BS, Engr. Phys. 53; MSEE, Stanford U. 54, DSEE 56; Head, Phys. Dept., Fairchild Semiconductor Corp. 59-62; Prof., EE & Phys., U. of Illinois 61-88. *Publ.:* 3 texts & 260 jour. articles; *Add.* U. of Florida, Elect. & Computer Engr., 211 Benton Hall, P.O. Box 116200, Gainesville, FL 32611-6200, USA.

SCHIVE, CHI 薛琦
V. Chmn., CEPD 93-; Adjunct Prof. of Econ., NTU 88-; *b.* Chungking June 28, '47; *m.* Ho, Jane Bih-yih; 2 *s.; educ.* BA, Econ., NTU 69, MA, Econ. 72; MA, Econ., Case We. Reserve U., USA 74, Ph.D., Econ. 78; Lectr., NTU 76-77, Assc. Prof. 78-83, Prof. 83-85; Prof. & Dir., Grad. Inst. of Ind. Econ., NCU 85-88, Dean, Coll. of Mng. 85-87; Consultant Mem., CEPD 88-93; Visiting Prof., Free U., Berlin 90; Dir., Dept. of Econ., NTU 90-93; Representing Ch. Taipei as V. Chair of the APEC Econ. Cttee. 95-98. *Publ.: For. Factor—The Multinat. Corp.'s Contribution to the Econ. Modernization of the ROC; Twn.'s Econ. Role in E. Asia*; & many other articles; *Add.* 3 Pao Ching Rd., Taipei 100.

SHAM, LU-JEU 沈呂九
Mem., Acad. Sinica 98-; Prof., Phys., U. of Calif., San Diego 75-, Chmn., Phys. Dept.; Asst. Ed., *Phys. Letters A* 92-; *b.* Ch. Apr. 28, '38; *m.* Georgina Bien; 1 *s.,* 1 *d.; educ.* Studied, Coll. of Tech., Portsmouth, Eng. 55-57; BS, U. of London (Imperial Coll.), Eng. 60; Ph.D., U. of Cambridge 63; Asst. Res. Physicist, U. of Calif., San Diego 63-66, Assc. Prof. 68-74; Asst. Prof., U. of Calif., Irvine 66-67; Reader, U. of London (Queen Mary Coll.) 67-68; Res. Physicist, IBM Res. Cent., Yorktown Heights, NY 74-75; Guggenheim Fel. 83; Bernd T. Matthias Scholar, Los Alamos Nat. Lab. 91; Dean, Div. of Natural Sc., U. of Calif., San Diego 85-89, Dir., Inst. of pure Sc. & Applied Phys. Sc. 91-95, Chmn., Dept. of Phys. 95-98; Visiting Miller Professorship, UC-Berkly. 98; Election to the US

Nat. Acad. of Sc. 98. *Publ.*: 186 articles in Sc. jour.; *Add.* Dept. of Phys. 0319, U. of Calif., San Diego, 9500 Gilman Drive, La Jolla, CA 92093-0319, USA.

SHAN, KUO-HSI 單國璽
Bishop, Kaohsiung Diocese 91-; Pres., Ch. Regional Bishops Conf. 87-; Mem., Cent. Cttee., Fed. of Asian Bishops Conf. 87-, Mem., Pontifical Coun. for Soc. Comms. 90-; *b.* Hopei Dec. 2, '23; *educ.* MA, Berchmans Coll. 51; M.Th., Bellarmino Theological Coll. 56; Ph.D., Gregorian U., Rome 61; Rector, Jesuit Manresa Seminary 64-70; Rector & Prin., St. Ignatius High Sch. 70-76; Pres., Kuangchi Prog. Service 76-80; Bishop, Hualien Diocese 79-91; Pres., FABC Off. for Soc. Comm. 85-91; Bd. Dir., Fu Jen Catholic U. 91-94; Elevated Cardinal 98; Dir. of Board of Dir., Fu Jen Catholic U. 99. *Publ.: Dedication & Leadership; How to Be a Leader; Elevated Cardinal* 98; *Add.* 125 Ssu Wei 3rd Rd., Kaohsiung 802.

SHAO, CHING-MING
(See SHAO, TIM 邵慶明)

SHAO, TIM 邵慶明
Exec. Dir., World Vision Twn. 98-; Coun. Mem., Soc. Welfare Coun. of the Exc. Yuan; Convener, Twn. Ovs. Aid & Dev. Alliance; *b.* Twn. Mar. 14, '42; *m.* Shao, Helen; *educ.* BA, For. Lang., Soochow U. 60; M., Soc. Work, U. of N. Carolina; Cert. of Merit in Community Dev., Soc. & Rehabilitation Service, Dept. of Health, Educ. & Welfare, Washington, D.C. 71-72; Cert., Pol. & Admin. Dev. Course, Duke U. 72; Tng. Workshop on Child Protective Services, the Am. Humane Assn., C.'s Div., Denver 74; Protective Services for the Elderly, U. of N. Carolina 75; Dist. Coordinator, S. Carolina Dept. of Soc. Services 73-75; Sr. Soc. Worker (Geraldton & Perth), Dept. for Community Services, W. A. 75-84; Nat. Dir. (Sidney), Australian Coun. of Churches 85-89; Soc. Worker Class 2, Dept. of Soc. Sec. 89-90; Soc. Worker-in-Charge (Nowra), Shoalhaven Dist. Memorial Hosp. 90-92; Prin. Soc. Worker, Disability Services Com., We. Australia 92-97; *Add.* 5th Fl., 30 Chung Shan N. Rd., Sect. 3, Taipei 104.

SHAO, YU-MING
(See SHAW, YU-MING 邵玉銘)

SHAW, YU-MING 邵玉銘
Dep. Sec.-Gen., KMT 99-; Prof., Dept. of Dip., NCCU, 91-; Res. Fel., NUC 95-; Bd. Mem., Cul. Found. of the United Daily News Group 92-; *b.* Harbin Nov. 3, '38; *m.* Lu, Shiow-jyu; 1 *s.*, 1 *d.; educ.* LL.B., NCCU 61; MA, Fletcher Sch. of Law & Dip., Tufts U., USA 67; Ph.D., U. of Chicago 75; Hon. Dr., Franklin Coll., USA 91; Asst. Prof. of Hist., Newberry Coll., S. Carolina 67-68 & 72-73; Res. Assc., Cent. for Far Ea. Studies, U. of Chicago 76-77; Visiting Sp., Acad. Sinica 79-81; Reviewer, Panelist & Evaluator, Nat. Endowment for the Humanities, USA 79-82; Assc. Prof., Dept. of Hist., U. of Notre Dame, Indiana 73-81, Tenured Assc. Prof. 81-82; Dir., Asia & World Inst. 83-84; Dean, Grad. Inst. of Intl. Law & Dip., NCCU 84, Dir., Inst. of Intl. Rel. 84-87; Dir.-Gen., GIO & Govt. Spokesman 87-91; Adjunct Prof., Grad. Inst. of Intl. Law & Dip., NCCU 83-91; Thornton D. Hooper Fel. in Intl. Aff., For. Policy Res. Inst., USA 92-93; Dir., Inst. of Intl. Rel., NCCU 94-99. *Publ.: Ch. & Christianity; Problems in 20th Century Ch. Christianity; 20th Century Sino-Am. Rel.; From the Open Door Policy to the US Dip. Rupture with the ROC; Hist. & Pol. in Modern Ch.; Discourses on Nat. Issues by Ch. Intellectuals; Intl. Pol. & Ch.'s Future; Beyond the Econ. Miracle: Reflections on the Dev. Experience of the ROC on Twn.; Lit., Pol., & Intellectuals; Amidst Great Change: Reflections of a Public Servant; An Am. Missionary in Ch.: John Leighton Stuart & Ch.-Am. Rel.; Add.* 10th Fl., 11 Chung Shan S. Rd., Taipei 100.

SHEA, JIA-DONG 許嘉棟
Min. of Finance 2000-; Res. Fel., Inst. of Econ., Acad. Sinica 82-; Prof., NTU 83-; Bd. Dir., Chung-Hua Inst. for Econ. Res. 93-; *b.* Twn. Oct. 9, '48; *m.* Kuo, Ruey-huey; 2 *s.*, 1 *d.; educ.* BA, NTU 70, MA 74; Ph.D., Econ., Stanford U. 78; Dir., Acad. Sinica 91-96; V. Pres., Ch. Econ. Assn. 95-96; Pres., Twn. Econ. Assn. 98; Dep. Gov., CBC 96-2000. *Publ.: Ch. Taipei—The Origins of the Econ. "Miracle"* (Dessus, Sebastien, Jia-dong Shea, & Mau-shan Shi) 95; *Add.* 2 Ai Kuo W. Rd., Taipei 100.

SHEN, CHIH-HUI
(See SHEN, CHICH-HWEI 沈智慧)

SHEN, CHICH-HWEI 沈智慧
Pres., M. Radio 94-; Mem., Legis. Yuan 94-; *b.* Twn. Sept. 16, '57; *educ.* BJ, Ch. Cul. U. 81; Reporter, *The Commons Daily* 82-83; Convener, Financial & Econ. Sect., *Twn. Times* 83-87; Reporter, *Ch. Times* 87-90; *Add.* Rm. 429, 5th Fl.-9, 4 Tsingtao E. Rd., Taipei 100.

SHEN, CHING-PENG 沈景鵬
Chmn., RSEA Engr. Corp. 98-; *b.* Shantung June 3, '41; *m.* Chang, Ching-yi; 1 *s.*, 1 *d.; educ.* BS, Prov. Maritime Coll. 66; MS, Civil Engr., U. of Texas at Austin 77; Jr. Engr., Keelung Harbor Bu. 65-69; Jr. Engr. & Assc. Engr.,

Taichung Harbor Bu. 69-77, Sect. Chief, Design Sect. 77-80, Dep. Dir., Harbor Construction Div. 80, Dir. 80-82; Chief, Design Sector, Ret-Ser Engr. Agency, VAC 82-84, Dir., Hydraulic & Harbor Construction Div. 85-86, & Civil Construction Div. 86, V. Pres. 87-98, Pres. 98; *Add.* 207 Sungkiang Rd., Taipei 104.

SHEN, CHING-SUNG
(See, SHEN, VINCENT 沈清松)

SHEN, HSUEH-YUNG 申學庸
Prof., Dept. of Music, Ch. Cul. U. & Nat. Twn. Acad. of Arts; Hon. Dir., Asia Opera Co. 86-; Bd. Dir., Nat. Music Coun. of Ch. 88-; Mem., Preparatory Cttee. for Ch. Public TV 91-; *b.* Szechwan Oct. 5, '29; *m.* Quo, James C.; 1 *s.,* 1 *d.; educ.* Grad., Szechwan Prov. Acad. of Arts; Isabella Rosati Musicale, Italy; Tokyo U. of Arts; Aspen Festival & Music Sch., USA; Chmn., Music Dept., Nat. Twn. Acad. of Arts 57-63, & Ch. Cul. U. 63-69; Dir., 3rd Dept., CCPD 81-84, Mem. 88-93, Chmn. 93-94; Mem., CSC, KMT 93-94; *Add.* 6th Fl., 28-5 Lane 200, Kuang Fu S. Rd., Taipei 105.

SHEN, KUO-HSIUNG 沈國雄
Amb. Extraordinary Plenipotentiary to Belize 98-; *b.* Twn. Nov. 23, '37; *m.* Chien, Hui-mei; 1 *s.,* 1 *d.; educ.* LLB, Coll. of Law & Com., NCHU; Dir.-Gen., Fukuoka Off., Japan, 90-93; Dir.-Gen., Dept. of Intl. Org., MOFA, 93-98; Mem., AEC, Exec. Yuan 93-98; Mem., Ch. Taipei Olympic Cttee. 93-98; Ch. Taipei Sr. Official to APEC 93-98; *Add.* P.O. Box 1020, Belize City, Belize (Cent. Am.).

SHEN, LU-HSUN
(See SHEN, LYUSHUN 沈呂巡)

SHEN, LU-CHIU
(SEE SHAM, LU-JEU 沈呂九)

SHEN, LYUSHUN 沈呂巡
Dep. Rep., TECRO in USA, 99-; *b.* Twn. Nov. 12, '49; *m.* Shen, Christine C.; 1 *d.; educ.* LL.B, NCHU 72; MA, U. of Pennsylvania, USA 79, Ph.D. 81; Res. Assc., U. of Maryland, USA 81-82; Exec. Ed., *Ch. Yearbk. of Intl. Law & Aff.* 81-82; Staff Consultant, CCNAA, Off. in USA 82-88; Chief, 1st Sect., & concur. Sr. Sp., Dept. of N. Am. Aff., MOFA 88-90; Assc. Prof., Ch. Cul. U. 89-90; Dir.-Gen., CCNAA, Off. in Kansas City 91-93; Div. Dir., Secretariat & Public Aff. (consecutively), TECRO in USA, 93-96; Counselor & Dir.-Gen., Dept. of N. Am. Aff. MOFA 96-99. *Publ.: The ROC's Perspective on the US Omnibus Trade & Competitiveness Act of 1988; The Issue of US Arms*

Sales & Peking's Policy Toward Twn.; Is Peking's Claim Over Twn. Internationally Recognized?; Peking's Policy Toward Twn. in the 1970s: A Study from the Strategic Perspective; Add. 4201 Wisconsin Avenue, N.E., Washington, D.C. 20016, USA.

SHEN, SHAN-FU 沈申甫
Mem., Acad. Sinica 72-, & Nat. Acad. of Engr., USA; Corr. Mem., Intl. Acad. of Astronautics; John Edson Sweet Prof. Emeritus of Engr., Cornell U. 92-; *b.* Shanghai Aug. 31, '21; *m.* Tung, Ming-ming; 1 *s.,* 1 *d.; educ.* BS, Aeronautical Engr., NCU 41; D.Sc., Aeronautical Engr., MIT 49; Res. Asst., Ch. Air Force Inst. of Aeronautical Res. 41-45; Res. Assc., Dept. of Math., MIT 48-50; Asst. Prof. & Prof., Dept. of Aeronautical Engr., U. of Maryland 50-61; Prof., Grad. Sch. of Aeronautical Engr., Cornell U. 61-78, John Edson Sweet Prof. of Engr. 78-92; *Add.* Sibley Sch. of Mech. & Aerospace Engr., Cornell U., Upson & Grumman Halls, Ithaca, NY 14853-7501, USA.

SHEN, SHEN-FU
(See SHEN, SHAN-FU 沈申甫)

SHEN, VINCENT 沈清松
Prof., Philosophy Dept., NCCU 80-; Pres., Intl. Soc. for Ch. Philosophy 97-; Mem., Coun. for Cul. Planning & Dev. 96-; *b.* Twn. July 10, '49; *m.* Liu, Johanna; 1 *s.; educ.* MA, Fu Jen Catholic U. 75; Diplome Spéciàl, Institut de Pays en Voie de Dévelopment, Université Catholique de Louvain, Belgium (U.C.L.) 77; Licence en Philosophie, U.C.L. 78; Ph.D., U.C.L. 80; Chmn., Philosophy Dept., NCCU 86-92; Bd. Dir., Nat. Found. for Cul. & Arts 95-98; European Chair for Ch. Studies, IIAS, Leiden U. 88-89; Verbiest Chair, U.C.L. 85-86; Visiting Prof., Vienna U. 93 & 96. *Publ.: Essays on Philosophy E. & W.* 83; *Disenchantment of the World* 98; *After Phys.* 87; *Rebirth of Tradition* 92; *Confucianism, Taoism & Constructive Realism* 94; *Add.* 4th Fl., 31-1 Chih Nan Rd., Sect. 3, Wenshan, Taipei 116.

SHEN, Y.R. 沈元壤
Mem., Acad. Sinica 96-; Chancellor's Prof. of Phys., U. of Calif.; Prof., Phys. Dept., UC-Berkly. 70-; Elected Mem., Nat. Acad. Sc., Am. Acad. Arts & Sc., & Ch. Acad. of Sc.; *b.* Shanghai Mar. 25, '35; *m.* Shen, Hsiao-lin; 1 *s.,* 2 *d.; educ.* BS, NTU 56; MS, Stanford U. 59; Ph.D., Harvard U. 63, Postdr. Resr. 63-64; Sloan Fel. 66-68; Asst. Prof., UC-Berkly. 64-67, Assc. Prof. 67-70; Visiting Prof., Harvard U. 72, & U. de Paris, Orsay, France 73; Guggenheim Fel. 72-73; Visiting Sr. Scholar, Max-Plank-Inst. in Quantenoptik, Germany 84 & 88; Visiting Prof., Tech. U.

of Wien, Austria 90. *Publ.: The Principles of Nonlinear Optics*; & more than 300 papers in periodicals & mags.; *Add.* Phys. Dept., UC-Berkly., Berkeley, CA 94720, USA.

SHENG YEN 聖嚴

Chmn., Dharma Drum Mountain Cul. & Educ. Found. 92-, Dharma Drum Mountain Buddhist Found. 97-; Founder, Dharma Drum Retreat Cent., New York, USA 97-; Pres. & Prof., Chung-Hwa Inst. of Buddhist Studies, Taipei 85-; Pres., Chan Meditation Cent., Inst. of Chung-Hwa Buddhist Cul., New York 80-; Abbot, Nung-Chan Temple 79-; Pres., Ch. Buddhist Cul. Inst. 78-; *b.* Kiangsu Dec. 4, '30; *educ.* MA, Rissho U., Tokyo 71, D.Lit. 75; Prof., Ch. Cul. U. 78-87, & Soochow U. 86-88; Coordinator & Sup., 1st, 2nd, & 3rd Chung-Hwa Intl. Conf. on Buddhism 90, 92, & 96; 3rd ROC Soc. Movement Ho-Feng Award (Outsdg. Leader of Soc. Movement) 93; 1st Ch. Outsdg. Person Award 96; 1st Nat. Civic Award, Twn. 98. *Publ.:* 100 bk. (Ch., Japanese, & Eng.) & 13 res. papers; *Add.* 89 Lane 65, Ta Yeh Rd., Peitou, Taipei 112.

SHEN, YUAN-JANG

(See SHEN, Y.R. 沈元壤)

SHEU, KE-SHENG 許柯生

V. Chmn., MAC 97-2000; *b.* Kiangsi Apr. 15, '33; *m.* Chang, Chung-ching; *educ.* BA, NTU 57; MA, U. of Hawaii 68; Dir., 1st & 4th Dept., Bd. of For. Trade (BOFT), MOEA 69-74; Trade Rep. in London & Brussels 75-87; Dir., Econ. Div., TECRO, USA 87-89; Dir.-Gen., BOFT 89-93; Admin. V. Min. of Econ. Aff. 93-97; *Add.* 16th Fl., 2-2 Chi Nan Rd., Sect. 1, Taipei.

SHI, HWEI-YOW 許惠祐

V. Chmn. & concur. Sec.-Gen., SEF 98-; *b.* Twn. Nov. 2, '52; *m.* Chang, Chong-wen; 1 *s.*, 1 *d.; educ.* LL.B., NCCU 75, LL.M. 80, LL.D. 87; Judge, Tainan Dist. Court 81-84, Shihlin Br., Taipei Dist. Court 84-90, & Taipei Dist. Court 90-91; Dep. Sec.-Gen., SEF 93-96; V. Chmn., MAC 96-97; Dir.-Gen., Dept. of Secretariat, KMT 97-98. *Publ.: A Study on Travel Contracts; The Use of Computers in Trials; Add.* 17th Fl., 156 Min Sheng E. Rd., Sect. 3, Taipei 105.

SHI, W.L. 許文龍

Nat. Policy Adv. to the Pres. 96-; Chmn., Chi Mei Corp. 59-, Chi Mei Cul. Found. 77-, Chi Mei Found. Hosp. 87-; Chi Mei Elect. Corp. 97-; Chi Mei Optoelect. Corp. 97-; Pro Arch Tech. Inc. 99-; *b.* Twn. Feb. 25, '28; *m.* Liao, Hsiu-lan; 1 *s.*, 2 *d.; educ.* Tainan Voc. High Sch. 48; Exec.

Dir., Chi Lin Plastics Co. Ltd. 65-74; Founder & Exec. Dir., Poly Chem. Co. Ltd. 68-85, & Jen Te Ind. Co. Ltd. 68-90; *Add.* 59-1 Sanchia Village, Jente, Tainan County 717.

SHIEH, LUNG-SHENG 謝隆盛

Nat. Policy Adv. to the Pres. 99-; Mem., CSC, & CC, KMT 93-; *b.* Twn. Apr. 24, '41; *m.* Wu, Hsueh-hui; 1 *s.*, 3 *d.; educ.* B., Tatung Inst. of Tech.; 19th Class, Sun Yat-sen Inst. on Policy Res. & Dev.; Mem., Taipei CoCoun.; Bd. Chmn., Szehai Inst. of Tech. & Com.; Mem., Disciplinary Cttee., KMT Caucus, NA; Dep. Dir.-Gen., Dept. of Org. Aff., CC, KMT; Chmn., Presidium, NA; Dir.-Gen., Dept. of Party-Govt. Coordination, NA, & Party Whip, KMT Caucus; V. Spkr., NA 96-99; *Add.* 6 Alley 7, Lane 763, Chung Shan N. Rd., Sect. 6, Taipei 111.

SHIEH, MUNG-SHIUNG 謝孟雄

Pres., Shih Chien U. 99-; Prof., Taipei Med. Coll. 83-; Pres., Ch. Community Dev. Assn. 77-; *b.* Kwangtung Oct. 12, '34; *m.* Lin, Cheng-chih; 4 *d.; educ.* MD, Kaohsiung Med. Coll. 60; MD, Grad. Sch. of Med., U. of Penn. 66; Pres., Shih Chien Coll. 72-78, Taipei Med. Coll. 78-83, Shih Chien U. 83-93, Ch. Nutrition Soc. 74-83, & Ch. Home Econ. Assn. 87 91; Mcm., Bd. of Exam., Min. of Exam., Exam. Yuan 81-93; Mem., Control Yuan 93-99. *Publ: A Res. on Abnormal Bleeding in the Uterus; Diseases of Middle-aged Women & Their Prevention; An Overall Res. on the Population Plan—An Ecological Approach; Marriage & Health; Pregnancy & Nursing; The Sunshine of Shih Chien; Soc. Work & Med. Care; Photography of Shieh Mung-shiung 90; Photography Album of Swan Lake 96; Add.* 70 Ta Chih St., Taipei 104.

SHIEH, SAMUEL C. 謝森中

Nat. Policy Adv. to the Pres. 94-; Adv., CBC 94-; Chmn., Exec. Bd., Ind. Bk. of Twn; V. Chmn., SEF 97-; Chmn., Bd. of Trustees, Chung-Hua Inst. of Econ. Res. 96-; *b.* Kwangtung Nov. 13, '19; *m.* Shieh, Alice Yen-hee; 2 *s.*, 2 *d.; educ.* BA, NCU 43, MA 45; Ph.D., U. of Minnesota 57; Hon. LL.D., U. of the Philippines 93; Prof., NTU 50-60; Sr. Sp., Chief Economist, & Sec.-Gen., JCRR 51-65; Dir., Projects Dept., Asian Dev. Bk. 67-81; V. Chmn., CEPD 81-83; Chmn., Chiao Tung Bk. 83-89; Gov., CBC 89-94. *Publ.: The Rice & Sugarcane Competition in Cent. Twn.: The Application of Linear Programming Technique to Crop Competition Study; Linear Programming as a Modern Technique in Ind. Mng. & Econ. Res.; An Analytical Review of Agr. Dev. in Twn.—An Input-Output & Productivity Approach; Environmental, Technological, & Inst. Factors in the Growth of Rice Production—Philippines, Thailand,*

& Twn.; Gov. Samuel C. Shieh's Selected Addresses & Messages (4 Vol.); *Add.* 101 Sung Jen Rd., Taipei 110.

SHIEH, SHINN-LIANG 謝信良
Dir.-Gen., Cent. Weather Bu. 94-; *b.* Twn. Jan. 1, '44; *m.* Tseng, Li-hua; 1 *s.,* 1 *d.; educ.* BS, Meteorology, NTU 68; MS, Atmospheric Sc., U. of Washington 75; Forecaster, Twn. Prov. Weather Bu. 69-70; Chief, Forecast Sect., Cent. Weather Bu. 71-73, Dep. Dir. 76-81, Dir. 82-89; Sec.-Gen., Cent. Weather Bu. 90-91, Dep. Dir.-Gen. 91-94; *Add.* 64 Kung Yuan Rd., Taipei 100.

SHIEH, TUNG-MIN 謝東閔
Sr. Adv. to the Pres. 85-; *b.* Twn. Jan. 25, '07; *m.* Pan, Ying-ching (deceased); 4 *s.,* 1 *d.; educ.* Grad., Nat. Sun Yat-sen U.; Magis., Kaohsiung County; Dep. Dir., Dept. of Civil Aff., V. Comr. of Educ., Comr., & Sec.-Gen., TPG; Pres., Twn. Prov. Tchrs.' Coll.; Chmn., Cooperative Bk. of Twn.; Bd. Chmn., *Hsin Sheng Daily News*; Pres., Shih Chien Coll.; Dep. Dir., Ch. Youth Corps; Spkr., TPA; Gov., TPG 72-78; V. Pres., ROC 78-84; Mem., CSC, KMT. *Publ.: Econ. Geog.; Japanese Grammar Readings; Add.* 70 Ta Chih St., Taipei 104.

SHIH, CHANG-JU 石璋如
Mem., Acad. Sinica 78-; *b.* Honan Oct. 4, '05; *m.* Yuan, Shin; 1 *s.,* 1 *d; educ.* BA, Honan U. 32; Assc., Inst. of Hist. & Philology, Acad. Sinica 34-49, Assc. Res. Fel. 49-78, Ed. 47-49, Resr. 49, Dir., 3rd Bu. 79-83; Adjunct Prof., Coll. of Lib. Arts NTU 52-59. *Publ.: Yin-Hsu Architectural Remains; Hsiao-Tun, Architectural Remains; Hsiao-Tun, Burials of the Nr. Sect.; Hsiao-Tun, Burials of the Middle Sect.; Hsiao-Tun, Burials of the So. Sect.; Hsiao-Tun, Burials Above & Underneath the B-area Founds.; Hsiao-Tun, Burials at the C-area; Hsiao-Tun, Pit Provenience of the Oracle Bones; Hsiao-Tun, Pit Provenience of the Oracle Bones Illustrations; Hsiao-Tun, Pit Provenience of the Oracle Bones II; Ta-Ma-Lin; Hou-Chia-Chuang IX; Mo-Kao-Ku-Hsing; Add.* Inst. of Hist. & Philology, Acad. Sinica, Nankang, Taipei 115.

SHIH, CHEN-JUNG
(See SHIH, STAN 施振榮)

SHIH, CHI-YANG 施啓揚
Sr. Adv. to the Pres. 99-; *b.* Twn. May 5, '35; *m.* Li, Jeanne Tchong-koei; *educ.* LL.B., NTU 58, LL.M. 62; LL.D., Heidelberg U., Germany 67; Assc. Prof., Dept. of Law, NTU 67-71, Adjunct Prof. 71-87; Res. Asst., Inst. of Intl. Rel., NCCU 67-69, Res. Fel. 69-71; Dep. Dir., 5th Dept., CC, KMT 69-72, & Dept. of Youth Aff. 72-76; Pol. V. Min. of Educ. 76-80; Pol. V. Min. of Justice 80-84; Min. of

Justice 84-88; V. Premier, ROC 88-93; Sec.-Gen., NSC 93-94; Mem., CC & CSC, KMT 84-94; Pres., Jud. Yuan 94-99. *Publ.: The W. German Federal Const. Court; Add.* Off. of the Pres., Taipei 100.

SHIH, CHIA-MING 施嘉明
Mem. (ministerial rank), Exam. Yuan 90-; *b.* Twn. Mar. 10, '33; *m.* Wang, Fang-shue; 3 *d.; educ.* LL.B., TPLCC 59; LL.M., NCCU 62; Dep. Dir., Dept. of Recon., TPG 77-78, & Dept. of Civil Aff. 78-79; Counsl. & Dept. Dir., Exec. Yuan 79-86; Admin. V. Min. of Exam., Exam. Yuan 86-89; Pol. V. Min. of Exam. 90. *Publ.: Local Coun. of Japan; An Outline of Japanese Hist.; Civil Servant Readings* 96; *Shih Chia-ming on Local Self-governance* 98; *Add.* 3rd Fl., 1 Alley 15, Lane 31, Shao Hsing N. St., Taipei 100.

SHIH, CHIN-HSIN 施慶星
Bd. Chmn., ROC I-Kuan-Tao Assn. 96-; Pres., Tien Yuan Chem. Co. Ltd. 74-; Pres., Chiar Yuan Ent. Co. Ltd. 88-; *b.* Kaohsiung Sept. 8, '33; 4 *s.; educ.* Grad., Kaohsiung 2nd Mun. Jr. High Sch.; *Add.* 6th Fl., 62 Nanking E. Rd., Sect. 2, Taipei 104.

SHIH, CHIN-TAI
(See SHIH, CHINTAY 史欽泰)

SHIH, CHING-HSING
(See SHIH, CHIN-HSIN 施慶星)

SHIH, CHINTAY 史欽泰
Pres., Ind. Tech. Res. Inst. 94-; *b.* Twn. Oct. 15, '46; *m.* Chen, Fung-yong; 1 *d.; educ.* BSEE, NTU 68; DSEE, Princeton U. 75; MS, Mng., Stanford U. 85; Engr. Mgr., Plant Mgr., & Dep. Dir.-Gen., Elect. Res. & Service Org. 76-84, V. Pres. & Dir.-Gen. 84-89; Exec. V. Pres., Ind. Tech. Res. Inst. 89-94; *Add.* 195 Chung Hsin Rd., Sect. 4, Chutung, Hsinchu 300.

SHIH, KE-MIN
(See SHIH, KERMIN 施克敏)

SHIH, KERMIN 施克敏
Rep., TECO in Norway 97-; *b.* Twn. Aug. 15, '36; *m.* Teresa S.H.; 1 *s.,* 1 *d.; educ.* B., NTNU 59; M., Am. U. 71; Reporter, *Ch. Daily News* 59-63, *United Daily News* 63-68, Washington Corr., 68-76; Washington Bu. Chief, *United Daily News* group 76-93, Ed. Writer, *The World Jour.,* USA; Dep. Dir., Cul. Aff. Dept., KMT 93-94, Counsl., Off. of Pres.; Pres., CNA 94-97. *Publ.: To Observe Taipei from Washington;* papers & articles on USA-Twn.-Ch. Rel.; *Add.* Riddervolds Gate 3, 0258 Oslo, Norway.

SHIH, MING-TE
(See SHIH, MING-TEH 施明德)

SHIH, MING-TEH 施明德
Former Chmn., DPP 93-96; Mem., Legis. Yuan 93-; Convener, Cttee. for Rebuilding New Twn. 92-; *b.* Kaohsiung Jan. 15, '41; 2 *d.; educ.* B., Artillery Sch. 61; Jailed 68-77; Reporter, *Twn. Times* 78; Sec.-Gen., Tangwai (outside the then KMT Party) Cent. Backing Cttee. for the 1978 Elections 78; Gen. Mgr., *Formosa Mag. of Twn. Dem. Movement* 79; Jailed 80-90; Chmn., Twn. Assn. for Human Rights 90-91; Res., Pol. Dept. & Human Resources Cent., San Diego State U. 91; Mem., CC, DPP 91-93; Convener, DPP Caucus, Legis. Yuan 93. *Publ.: Spring in the Prison; Shih Ming-teh's Pol. Will;* etc.; *Add.* Rm. 601, 10 Tsingtao E. Rd., Taipei 100.

SHIH, STAN 施振榮
Nat. Policy Adv. to the Pres. 96-; Chmn. & Chief Exec. Off., The Acer Group; *b.* Twn. Dec. 18, '44; *m.* Yeh, Carolyn; 2 *s.,* 1 *d.; educ.* MSEE, NCTU, Hon. DSEE; Unitron Ind. Corp. 71-72; Qualitron Ind. Corp. 72-76. *Publ.:* Over 100 articles on mng., marketing, res. & dev., & ent. cul.; *Add.* 21st Fl., 88 Hsin Tai 5th Rd., Sect. 1, Hsichih, Taipei County 221.

SHIH, WEN-SEN
(See SZE, VINCENT 施文森)

SHU, SHIEN-SIU 徐賢修
Mem., Acad. Sinica 80-; Prof. Emeritus, Purdue U. *b.* Chekiang Sept. 12, '12; *m.* Hsia, Irene; 2 *s.,* 2 *d.; educ.* BS, NTHU 35; Ph.D., Applied Math., Brown U. 47; Hon. Ph.D., Purdue U. 93; Lectr., NTHU 35-43; Mem., Inst. for Advanced Study, Princeton U. 47-48; Res. Assc., MIT 48; Asst. & Assc. Prof. of Math., Illinois Inst. of Tech. 48-55; Prof. of Engr. Sc., Purdue U. 55-63; Prof., Illinois Inst. of Tech. 63-68; Prof. of Aeronautic, Astronautic & Engr. Sc., Purdue U. 68-70; Consultant, Cook Elec. Lab., RCA, Gen. Elec., Boeing Airplane Co., Mid-W. Applied Sc. Corp., & Argonne Nat. Lab.; Pres., NTHU 70-75; Chmn., NScC 73-81; Bd. Chmn., Ind. Tech. Res. Inst. 78-89. *Publ.: Fourier Transformer; Group Theory; Non-Linear Differential Equation: Aerodynamics; Add.* 110 Colony Rd., W. Lafayette, IN 47906-1209, USA.

SIEW, VINCENT C. 蕭萬長
Premier, ROC 97-2000; Mem., CC & CSC, KMT 88- & 93-; *b.* Twn. Jan. 3, '39; *m.* Chu, Susan; 3 *d.; educ.* MA, Intl. Law of Dip., NCCU; Eisenhower Exchange Fel. 85; V. Consul, Kuala Lumpur, Malaysia 66-69, Consul 69-72; Sect. Chief, MOFA 72; Dep. Dir. & Dir., 4th Dept., Bd. of For. Trade, MOEA 72-77, Dep. Dir.-Gen. 77-82, Dir.-Gen. 82-88; V. Chmn., CEPD 88-89; Dir.-Gen., Dept. of Org. Aff., CC, KMT 89-90; Min. of Econ. Aff. 90-93; Chmn., CEPD 93-94; Chmn., MAC 94-95; Mem., Legis. Yuan 96-97. *Publ.: Res. on Improvement of the For. Trade Structure; Add.* Exec. Yuan, 1 Chung Hsiao E. Rd., Sect. 1, Taipei 100.

SOONG, CHANG-CHIH 宋長志
Strategy Adv. to the Pres. 91-; Mem., CC & CSC, KMT 93-; *b.* Liaoning June 10, '16; *m.* Fang, Cheng-ying; 3 *s.,* 1 *d.; educ.* Ch. Naval Acad. 37; Royal Naval Coll., Greenwich, UK; 4th Class, Nat. War Coll.; 1st Class, Armed Forces U.; Hon. Ph.D., Konkuk U., S. Korea 82; Hon. LL.D., S.Ea. U., USA 85; Cmdg. Off. on Bd. Various Combat Ships & Rating Tng. Sch. 49-52; Cmdr., Landing Ship Squadron 54-55; Supt., Ch. Naval Acad. 55-62; Cmdt., 1st Naval Dist. 62-65; C/S, ROCN GHQ 65-67, Dep. C-in-C 67-70, C-in-C 70-76; Chief of the Gen. Staff, MND 76-81; Min. of Nat. Def. 81-86; Strategy Adv. to the Pres. 86-87; Amb. to Panama 87-91; *Add.* 538 Pei An Rd., Taipei 104.

SOONG, JAMES C.Y. 宋楚瑜
Chmn., People First Party 2000-; Independent Candidate, 2000 Election for ROC Pres. (10th term); Res. Fel., Inst. of Intl. Rel., NCCU 74-; *b.* Hunan Mar. 16, '42; *m.* Chen, Viola; 1 *s.,* 1 *d.; educ.* LL.B., NCCU 64; MA, UC-Berkly. 67; M.A.L.S., Catholic U. of Am. 71; Ph.D., Georgetown U. 74; Eisenhower Fel. 82; Hon. Ph.D., Catholic U. 95; Hon. Ph.D., U. of S. Australia 95; Sec., Exec. Yuan 74-77; Assc. Prof., NTU 75-78, & NTNU 75-80; Dep. Dir.-Gen., GIO 77-79, Dir.-Gen. & Govt. Spokesman 79-84; Personal Sec. to the Pres. 78-81 & 84-89; Mem., CC, KMT 81-99, & CSC 88-99; Dir.-Gen., Dept. of Cul. Aff., CC, KMT 84-87; Mng. Dir., CTV 84-93, & TTV 84-93; Dep. Sec.-Gen., CC, KMT 87-89, Sec.-Gen. 89-93; Gov., Twn. Prov. 93-98. *Publ.: A Manual for Acad. Writers; How to Write Acad. Papers; Pol. & Public Opinion in the USA; Keep Free Ch. Free; Add.* P.O. Box 43-99, Taipei.

SOONG, MAYLING 宋美齡
(Madame Chiang, Kai-shek)
Pres. & Founder, Nat. Women's League of the ROC; Chmn., Bd. of Trustees, Fu Jen Catholic U.; Bd. Chmn. & Founder, Hua Hsing C.'s Home, Hua Hsing High School, & Chen Hsing Rehabilitation Med. Cent.; Dir.-Gen., Women's Assn., KMT; Hon. Pres., Taipei Intl. Women's Club, Nurses' Assn. of Ch., Girl Scouts Assn. of Ch., & Ch.

Women's Relief Assn. of New York; Hon. Chmn., Am. Bu. for Med. Aid to Ch.; Mem., Bd. of Govs., Nat. Palace Museum, Catherine Lorillard Wolfe Art Club, & Tau Zeta Episilon; Hon. Mem., Phi Beta Kappa, Eta Chapter, Phi Delta Gamma, & New York Zoological Soc.; *b.* Kwangtung Feb. 12, 1898; *m.* Chiang, Kai-shek (deceased); *educ.* LHD, Bryant Coll., Providence, Rhode Island; Hobart & William Smith Coll., Geneva, New York; John B. Stetson U., Deland, Florida; Nebraska Wesleyan U., Lincoln, Nebraska; Piedmont Coll., Demorest, Georgia; LL.D., Goucher Coll., Baltimore, Maryland; Hahnemann Med. Coll., Philadelphia; Loyola U., Los Angeles; Russell Sage Coll., Troy, New York; Rutgers U., New Brunswick, New Jersey; U. of Hawaii; U. of Michigan, Ann Arbor; Wellesley Coll., Wellesley, Massachusetts; Wesleyan Coll., Macon, Georgia; LL.D. Honoris Causa, Boston U. Sesquicentennial; 1st Ch. Woman Appointed Mem., C. Labor Com.; inaugurated Moral Endeavor Assn.; established Schs. in Nanking for C. of Rev. Martyrs; Mem., Legis. Yuan; 1st Sec.-Gen. & Mem., Ch. Com. on Aeronautical Aff.; Dir.-Gen., New Life Movement; Chmn., Women's Adv. Coun.; frequently made inspection tours with the Pres. to all areas of free Ch.; Chmn. & Founder, Nat. Assn. for Refugee C., Nat. Ch. Women's Assn. for War Relief; Hon. Pres., Cttee. for Promotion of Welfare of the Blind; Hon. Chmn., British United Aid to Ch. Fund, Soc. for the Friends of the Wounded; Can. Red Cross Ch. Cttee.; Bd. Mem., India Famine Relief Cttee.; Patroness, Intl. Red Cross Com.; Life Mem., San Francisco Press Club & Assn. of Countrywomen of the World; Hon. Mem., Bill of Rights Commemorative Soc. & Filipino Guerrillas of Bataan Assn.; Chmn., CAC, KMT. *Publ.: Madame Chiang Kai-shek Messages in War & Peace 30-40; Sian: A Coup d'Etat 37; Ch. in Peace & War 39; Ch. Shall Rise Again 40; This is our Ch. 40; We Ch. Women 42; Am. Tour Speeches 42-43; Madame Chiang Kai-shek, Selected Speeches 58-59, 65-66; 10 Eventful Years, Encyclopedia Britannica 46; Albums of Reproductions of Paintings 52, 62; The Sure Victory 55: Speech Delivered to the Am. U. Club, Taipei 55; Speech Delivered at Shriners' Annual Ceremonial Banquet 57; Religious Writings 63; Album of Bamboo Paintings 72; Anti-Practiced Moral Cowardice & Anti-Marginal Thinking 72; Album of Landscape Paintings 73; Album of Floral Paintings 74; 3 Unobscured Vistas-Tout Court 74; Gems of Truth Versus Brummagems 74; We Do Beschrei It 75; Maj. Gen. Claire Lee Chennault in Memoriam 75; Conversations with Mikhail Borodin 76; Messages to the Graduating Classes of Fu Jen Catholic U. 77-89; Christian Businessmen's Cttee. Intl. 3rd Asian CBMCI Convention 78; In Commemoration of the 50th Anniversary of Fu Jen Catholic U. 79; Madame Chiang*

Reminds Liao Cheng-chih of Communist Atrocities 82; Pledge of Resurgam 86; Sursum Corda 86; And Shall It Be See Ye To It? 86; An Introduction to Gen. Albert C. Wedemeyer's Book "On War & Peace" 87; Madame Chiang Kai-shek's Comments on Gen. Albert C. Wedemeyer's Bk. "On War & Peace" 87; Add. to the 13th Nat. Cong. of the KMT of Ch. 88; Boston U. Convocation Add. 89; A Salute to D-Day (June 6, 1944) on Pres. Eisenhower's Birthday Centenary 90; 50th Anniversary of AVG in Ch. 91; Message to Am. Volunteer Group in Ch. 91.

SU, CHEN-CHANG
(See SU, TSENG-CHANG 蘇貞昌)

SU, CHEN-PING 蘇振平
Auditor-Gen., Nat. Audit Off., Control Yuan 89-2000; *b.* Twn. Oct. 28, '27; *m.* Huang, Su-mei; 2 *s.,* 1 *d.; educ.* Grad., NTU; Resr., Syracuse U.; Auditor, Sect. Chief, & Dir., Nat. Audit Off., Control Yuan 53-78, Dep. Auditor-Gen. 78-89; *Add.* 1 Hangchow N. Rd., Taipei 100.

SU, CHI 蘇起
Chmn., MAC 99-2000; Prof., Dept. of Dip., NCCU 90-; *b.* Twn. Oct. 1, '49; *m.* Chen, Grace; 1 *s.,* 1 *d.; educ.* BA, Dip., NCCU 71; MA, Johns Hopkins U. 75; MPS, Columbia U. 80, DPS 84; Assc. Prof., Dept. of Dip., NCCU 84-89, Sec., Off. of the Pres. 89-90; Dep. Dir., Dept. of Mainland Aff., CC, KMT 92-93; Sec.-Gen., Ch. Pol. Sc. Assn. 90-91; Dep. Dir., Inst. of Intl. Rel., NCCU 90-93; Comr., RDEC 90-94; V. Chmn., MAC 93-96; Govt. Spokesman & Dir.-Gen., GIO 96-97; Min. without Portfolio 97, Nat. Policy Adv. to the Pres.; Dep. Sec.-Gen., Off. of the Pres. 97-99. *Publ.: The Normalization of Sino-Soviet Rel.;* more than 20 papers & commentaries; *Add.* 16th Fl., 2-2 Chi Nan Rd., Sect. 1, Taipei 100.

SU, CHIA-CHUAN
(See SU, JIA-CHYUARN 蘇嘉全)

SU, CHING-SEN
(See SU, CHING-SHEN 蘇青森)

SU, CHING-SHEN 蘇青森
Sr. V. Chmn., AEC 95-; *b.* Kwangtung Oct. 10, '30; *m.* Lee, Kuei-chen; 1 *s.,* 2 *d.; educ.* BS, Naval Coll. of Tech. 54; MS, NTHU 63; Ph.D., Renselaer Polytechnic Inst. 66; Sr. Res. Assc., Marshall Space Flight Cent. 73-74; Dir., NScC 76-86; Assc. Prof. & Prof., NTHU 67-95, Dean 88-95. *Publ.: Vacuum Tech.* 78; & 100 papers; *Add.* 67 Lane 144, Keelung Rd., Sect. 4, Taipei 106.

SU, CHUN-HSIUNG
(See SU, J.H. 蘇俊雄)

SU, J.H. 蘇俊雄
Grand Justice, Jud. Yuan 94-; *b.* Twn. Aug. 12, '35; *m.* Su, Millie; 1 *s.,* 1 *d.; educ.* LL.B., NTU 58, LL.M. 62; LL.D., Universität Freiburg, Germany 66; Asst., Inst. for Intl. Criminal Law, Freiburg, W. Germany 62-67; Res. Fel., U. of Kîln 67-70; Assc. Prof., NTU 70-74, Prof. 74-94; Sr. Fel., Cul. Learning Inst., E.-W. Cent., U. of Hawaii 75-76; Mem., TPA 77-81; Comr., TPG 84-90; Mem., NA 91-94. *Publ.: Theory of Contract & Its Applications; Regierung und Verwaltung der Volkspublik Ch.; Theses on Const. Law; Method of Case Study on Criminal Law; Theory on Rule of Law; German Party Law; Criminal Law Gen. Part; Add.* 10th Fl., 54 Sungkiang Rd., Taipei 104.

SU, JIA-CHYUARN 蘇嘉全
Magis., Pingtung County 97-; *b.* Twn. Oct. 22, '56; *m.* Hung, Heng-chu; 2 *d.; educ.* B., Nat. Twn. Ocean U.; Mem., NA 86-93; Mem., Legis. Yuan 93-97; *Add.* 527 Tzu Yu Rd., Pingtung 900.

SU, KUN-HSIUNG 蘇崑雄
Spkr., Penghu CoCoun. 98-; *b.* Twn. Apr. 7, '56; *m.* Hwang, Shii-noan; 1 *s.,* 2 *d.; educ.* Grad., Prov. Makung Sr. High Sch. 74; Coun., 12th & 13th Sess. of Penghu CoCoun. 90-98; *Add.* 76 Chung Cheng Rd., Makung, Penghu County 880.

SU, TSENG-CHANG 蘇貞昌
Magis., Taipei County 97-; *b.* Twn. July 28, '47; *m.* Chan, Hsiu-ling; 3 *d.; educ.* LL.B., NTU; Mem., TPA; Co-founder, DPP 86; Mem., CC, DPP, Sec.-Gen., CEC; Dir. & Sec.-Gen., Ch. Comparative Jurisprudence Soc.; V. Pres., ROC Gen. Chamber of Intl. Jr. Chamber; Pres., Taipei Intl. Jr. Chamber; Magis., Pingtung County 89-93; Mem., Legis. Yuan 96-97; *Add.* 32 Fu Chung Rd., Panchiao, Taipei County 220.

SU, YAN-KUIN 蘇炎坤
Dir., Div. of Engr. & Applied Sc., NScC 98-; Prof., NCKU 83-; Adjunct Prof., New York State U. 91-; Dir., ROC Vacuum Sc. Soc. 94-; *b.* Twn. Aug. 23, '48; *m.* Wang, Shiu-chi; 1 *s.,* 2 *d.; educ.* BA, NCKU 71, MA 73, Ph.D. 79; Chmn., Dept. of EE, NCKU 90-94, Assc. Dean 93-95; Visiting Prof., Stuttgart U., Germany 93-93. *Publ.:* 170 papers published in intl. jour. & conf.; *Add.* 36 Lane 201, Tung Ning Rd., Tainan 701.

SU, YANN-HUEI 蘇燕輝
Chmn., Ho Yu Investment Co. 81-, Kuo Zui Motors Ltd. 88-, & Ho Tai Motor Co. Ltd. 92-; *b.* Twn. Nov. 1, '27; *m.* Wang, Ching-yun; 1 *s.,* 3 *d.; educ.* Changhua Tech. Sch. 43; Gen. Mgr., Ho Tai Motor Co. Ltd. 59-77, V. Chmn. 78-92; Chmn., Ch. Gravure Ind. Inc. 67-87, & Ho Tai Dev. Co. Ltd. 71-77; V. Chmn., Kuo Zui Motors Ltd. 84-88; *Add.* 14th Fl., 121 Sungkiang Rd., Taipei 104.

SU, YEN-HUI
(See SU, YANN-HUEI 蘇燕輝)

SU, YEN-KUN
(See SU, YAN-KUIN 蘇炎坤)

SUN, CHIH-PING
(See SUN, TSE-PING 孫治平)

SUN, I-HSUAN
(See SUN, I-SHUAN 孫義宣)

SUN, I-SHUAN 孫義宣
Chmn., Banking Inst. of the ROC; Exec. Dir., Bd. of Govs., CBC; Bd. Mem., Intl. Cml. Bk. of Ch.; *b.* Chekiang June 26, '20; *m.* Wang, Jeanne; 1 *s.,* 3 *d.; educ.* BS, Econ., St. John's U., Shanghai 42; Ph.D., Econ., U. of Wisconsin 53; Alt. Exec. Dir., Intl. Monetary Fund, Washington, D.C. 60-65; Dep. Gov., CBC, & concur. Gen. Mgr., For. Exchange Dept. 66-71; Pres., CTC 71-77 & Chiao Tung Bk. 77-80; Chmn., Bankers Assn. of the ROC 79-89, Export-Import Bk. of the ROC 80-86, & Bk. of Twn. 86-90. *Publ.: Salt Taxation in Ch.; Trade Policies & Econ. Dev. in Twn.; Add.* 4th Fl., 3 Nan Hai Rd., Taipei 100.

SUN, JACK T. 孫道存
Pres. & Exec. Dir., Pacific Elec. Wire & Cable Co. Ltd. 86-; Chmn., Twn. Aerospace Corp. 94-, & Pacific Cellular Corp. 97-; Exec. Sup., Walsin Lihwa Corp. 99-; V. Chmn., Pacific Construction Co. Ltd. 92-; Hon. Chmn., Coun. for Ind. & Com. Dev. 96-; Chmn., Twn. Elec. Wire & Cable Ind. Assn. 99-; Chmn., Twn. Aerospace Ind. Assn. 97-; Exec. Dir., Ch. Nat. Fed. of Ind. 97-; *b.* Hopei Aug. 27, '50; 3 *s.,* 3 *d., educ.* Grad., Tamkang U.; Exec. Dir., Walsin Lihwa Corp. 72-99; Chmn., Twn. Elec. Wire & Cable Ind. Assn. 96-99; Dir., Ch.Nat. Fed. of Ind. 91-97; Chmn., Coun. for Ind. & Com. Dev. 94-96; *Add.* 4th Fl., 285 Chung Hsiao E. Rd., Sect. 4, Taipei 106.

SUN, MING-HSIEN
(See SUN, PAUL MING-HSIEN 孫明賢)

SUN, PAUL MING-HSIEN 孫明賢
Nat. Policy Adv. to the Pres. 96-, Adv., COA, Chmn., Twn. Grains & Feeds Dev. Found.; Mem., CAC 97-; *b.* Twn. June 8, '37; *m.* Shen, Chia-huei; 1 *s.,* 2 *d.; educ.* BS, NTU 60; MS, U. of Minnesota 66; Ph.D., Purdue U. 71; Hon. Ph.D., Purdue U. 96; Tchr., Tainan Mun. Nanning Jr. High Sch. 61-62; Tech., Tainan Dist. Agr. Improvement Station 62-67; Asst. Sp., Sr. Sp., & Chief, Plant Ind. Div., JCRR 67-79; Adjunct Assc. Prof., & Prof., NCHU 72; Adjunct Assc. Prof. & Prof., NTU 73-80; Sr. Sp. & concur. Chief, Plant Ind. Div., COA 79-80; Dep. & Acting Dir.-Gen., Asian Vegetable Res. & Dev. Cent. 80-88; Comr., TPG 81-82, & Dept. of Agr. & Forestry 88-92; Chmn., COA 92-96; Mem., CC, KMT 93-; *Add.* 3rd Fl., 7 Roosevelt Rd., Sect. 1, Taipei 100.

SUN, SEN-YEN 孫森焱
Grand Justice, Jud. Yuan 94-; *b.* Twn. Nov. 6, '33; *m.* Huang, Lu-hsing; 1 *s.,* 2 *d.; educ.* LL.B., NTU 56; Prosecutor, Taipei Dist. Court 61-63; Judge, Keelung Dist. Court 63-70, Twn. High Court 70-79; Justice, Supreme Court 79-94, Div. Chief Justice 90-94. *Publ.: On Civil Law;* & several essays on laws & regln.; *Add.* 4th Fl., 124 Chungking S. Rd., Sect. 1, Taipei 100.

SUN, TA-CHUAN 孫大川
V. Chmn., Coun. of Aboriginal Aff., Exec. Yuan (CAA) 96-, & concur. Dir.-Gen., Legal Cttee. & Dir., Cent. Off. 99-; Lectr., Philosphy, Soochow U. 88-; Chief Exec., *Shanhai Wenhua* Mag. 96-; Standing Mem., Soc. of Community Mng., ROC 96-; Bd. Mem., Aboriginal Music Cul. & Educ. Found. 96-, & Soc. of Aboriginal Educ., ROC 98-; Mem., Archives Cttee. of Taiepi City 98-; Dir. of the Bd., Ch. Motor Corp.'s Aboriginal Cul. & Educ. Found. 99-; *b.* Twn. (Puyuma) Dec. 18, '53; *educ.* BA, Ch. Lit., NTU 76; MA, Philosophy, Fu Jen Catholic U. 83; MA, Ch. Studies, U. of Leuven, Beligium 88, Ph.D. Candidade 89; Sec.-Gen., Twn. Aboriginal Cul. Dev. Assn. 93-96; Ed.-in-Chief, *Shanhai Wenhua* Mag. 93-96. *Publ.: A Drink after a Long Long Time* 91; *Beauty of Myth: The Fantasy World of the Twn. Aborigines; Add.* 17th Fl., 4 Chung Hsiao W. Rd., Sect. 1, Taipei 100.

SUN, TA-MING
(See SUN, TOM 孫大明)

SUN, TAO-TSUN
(See SUN, JACK T. 孫道存)

SUN, TAO-YU
(SUN, TONG T.Y. 孫韜玉)

SUN, TONG T.Y. 孫韜玉
Dep. Min. of Nat. Def. 99-2000; *b.* Shantung Dec. 6, '43; *m.* Liu, Sen-mei; 1 *s.,* 1 *d.; educ.* Ch. Mil. Acad. 68; Advanced Course, Armor Sch. 74; Army CGSC 79; Ed.M., Wayne State U., USA 82; War Coll., Armed Forces U. 87; Platoon Leader 69-70; Cmdr. of co. & bn. 73-74 & 77-78, tank battle group 84-86, separated armor brig. 88-89; Dep. C/S for Intelligence, Army GHQ 89-92; Mil. Attaché in USA 92-95; Dir., Procurement Bu., MND 95-99; *Add.* 122 Chungking S. Rd., Sect. 1, Taipei 100.

SUN, TSE-PING 孫治平
Nat. Policy Adv. to the Pres.; Mem., Com. of the Grand Alliance for Ch.'s Reunification under the Three Principles of the People; *b.* Kwangtung, Nov. 15, '13; *m.* Chang, May; 1 *s.; educ.* BA, UC-Berkly. 39; MA, New York U. 40; *Add.* Rm. A, 4th Fl., 261 Nanking E. Rd., Sect. 3, Taipei 105.

SUN, YUN-HSUAN
(See SUN, YUN-SUAN 孫運璿)

SUN, YUN-SUAN 孫運璿
Sr. Adv. to the Pres. 84-; *b.* Shantung Nov. 11, '13; *m.* Yu, Hui-hsuan; 2 *s.,* 2 *d.; educ.* BEE, Harbin Polytechnic Inst. 34; Engr. Tng. in Tennessee Valley Authority 43-45; Hon. Ph.D., Asian Inst. of Tech., Thailand 86; Engr., Nat. Resources Com. 37-40; Supt., Tienshui Elec. Power Plant 40-43; Head Engr., Elec. & Mech. Dept., Twn. Power Co. 46-50, Chief Engr. 50-53, V. Pres. & concur. Chief Engr. 53-62, Pres. 62-64; CEO & Gen. Mgr., Electricity Corp. of Nigeria 64-67; Min. of Comms. 67-69; Min. of Econ. Aff. 69-78; Premier, ROC 78-84; *Add.* 7th Fl., 106 Ho Ping E. Rd., Sect. 2, Taipei 106.

SUNG, CHANG-CHIH
(See SOONG, CHANG-CHIH 宋長志)

SUNG, CHU-YU
(See SOONG, JAMES C.Y. 宋楚瑜)

SUNG, JUEI-LOW 宋瑞樓
Mem., Acad. Sinica 82-, Intl. Soc. for the Study of the Liver 67-; Prof. Emeritus, Coll. of Med., NTU 87-; Hon. Pres., Digestive Endoscopy Soc. of Twn. 92-, Gastroenterology Soc. of Twn., ROC 94-; Pres. Emeritus, Sun Yat-sen Cancer Center, Koo Found. 98-; *b.* Twn. Aug. 6, '17; *m.* Wu, Fang-ing; 1 *s.,* 3 *d.; educ.* MB, Taihoku Imperial U.; MD, Kyushu U.; Prof., Dept. of Internal Med., NTU 55-87, Chmn., Dept. of Clinical Pathology 55-58, Dir., Sch. of Med. Tech. 56-58, Chmn., Dept. of Internal Med. 71-77, &

Inst. of Clinical Med. 78-83; Dir., Clinical Res. Cent., NTU Hosp. 82-89; Pres., Gastroenterological Soc. of the ROC 71-91; Rep. of the ROC, Chapter of the Intl. Soc. for Diseases of the Esophagus 81-85; Chmn., Hepatitis Control Cttee., DOH 83-96; Pres., Formosan Med. Assn. for the Study of the Liver 90-91; V. Pres., World Org. of Digestive Endoscopy 90-94; Dir., Sun Yat-Sen Cancer Cent., Koo Found. 90-98. *Publ.: Lab. Exam. of Hepato-Biliary Disease; Hepatitis B Virus Infection & Its Sequelae in Twn.; Control of Hepatitis B in Twn.; Hepatocellular Carcinoma: Early Detection & Treatment; Prevention of Hepatocellular Carcinoma; Add.* 17th Fl., 63 Jen Ai Rd., Sect. 2, Taipei 100.

SUNG, JUI-LOU
(See SUNG, JUEI-LOW 宋瑞樓)

SUNG, KUO-HSIEN 松國賢
(See ISQAQAVUT, YOHANI 尤哈尼・伊斯卡卡夫特)

SUNG, MEI-LING
(See SOONG, MAYLING 宋美齡)

SZE, VINCENT 施文森
Grand Justice, Jud. Yuan 94-; *b*. Chekiang Mar. 11, '33; *m*. Sze, Celestina; 2 *s.; educ.* LL.B., NTU 58; MS, Oregon U. 62; Jur.D., Willamette U., USA 65; Visiting Scholar, Harvard U. 70; Assc. Prof. of Law, NCCU 67-70, Prof. 71-94, Chmn., Dept. of Law 69-72, Dean, Grad. Sch. of Ins. 85-92, Chmn., Dept. of Ins. 90-92. *Publ.: Law of Negotiable Instruments; Law of Ins.; Essays on Ins. Law; Analytical Study of Ins. Cases; Add.* P.O. Box 1-191, Taipei.

TAI, JUI-MING
(See TAI, RAYMOND R.M. 戴瑞明)

TAI, RAYMOND R.M. 戴瑞明
Amb. Extraordinary & Plenipotentiary of the ROC to the Holy See 96-; Mem., CAC, KMT 97-; *b*. Chekiang July 21, '34; *m*. Lu, Teresa S.N.; 1 *d.; educ.* BA, For. Lang. & Lit., NTU 65; MA, Am. Studies, U. of Hawaii 68; Sch. of Intl. Aff., Columbia U. 68; Georgetown Leadership Seminar, Sch. of For. Aff., Georgetown U. 84; Sp., Dept. of N. Am. Aff., MOFA 68-70; Instr., Dept. of For. Lang. & Lit., NTU 69-71; 3rd Sec., Del. to the UN 71; 3rd Sec., Emb. in the USA 72-75, 2nd Sec. 75; Adv., Del. to Intl. Telecom. Satellite Org. 72-75; Dir., Dept. of Ovs. Prog., GIO 75-79, Sec.-Gen. 79-80, Dep. Dir.-Gen. 80-87; Prof., Dept. of Jour., Ch. Cul. U. 86-87; Dir.-Gen., Dept. of Cul. Aff., CC, KMT 87-

89; Sec. to the Pres. 89-90; Adv. & V. Chmn., Res. & Planning Bd., MOFA 90; Rep., Taipei Rep. Off. in the UK 90-93; Dep. Sec.-Gen., Off. of the Pres. 93-96; Spokesman, Off. of the Pres. 93-96; Res. Fel. & Convener, Res. Cttee., NUC 93-96, Exec. Sec., Secretariat 93-96; Mem., CC, KMT 93-97. *Publ.: A Study of Am. Public Opinions & Ch. Policy 76; Ovs. Images of the ROC 82; Add.* The Emb. of the ROC to the Holy See, Presso la Santa Sede, Piazza Delle Muse 7, 00197 Roma, Italia.

TAI, SEN-HSIUNG 戴森雄
Chief Mem., Civil Law Cttee., Twn. Bar Assn. 96-; Assc. Prof., Fuji U. 98-; Mng. Partner, Tali Attorney-at-Law 80-; *b*. Twn. Mar. 20, '38; *m*. Tai, Chien Hhu-yun; 2 *s.*, 2 *d.; educ.* Grad., Law Dept., NTU 61; MA, Law Dept., NTU 70; Prosecutor, Tainan Dist. Court 65-66; Prosecutor, Taichung Dist. Court 66; Judge, Kaohsiung Dist. Court 66-71; Judge, Taipei Dist. Court 71-74; Presiding Judge, Taichung Dist. Court 74-75; Presiding Judge, Taoyuan Dist. Court 75-79; Judge, Tainan Br., Twn. Supreme Court 79-80; Exec. Dir., Taipei Bar Assn. 90-93, Dir. 93-96; Chief Mem., Legal Res. Cttee., Taipei Bar Assn. 94-96. *Publ.: Knowledge of Civil Law; Civil Law & Life; Civil Law Practice; Compilations of the Abstracts of the Precedents of Civil Law; Austin's Theory on Law & Ethics; Abandonment between Husband & Wife; Add.* 7th Fl., 18 Chao Chou St. Taipei 100.

TAN, CHIEN-KUO
(See TARN, JIANN-QUO 譚建國)

TANG, FEI 唐飛
Premier, ROC 2000-; *b*. Kiangsu Mar. 15, '32; *m*. Chang, Ming-tsan; 1 *s.*, 2 *d.; educ.* Grad., Air Force Preparatory Sch. 50; Ch. Air Force Acad. 52; Air Force Squadron Off. Course 63; Air Cmd. & Staff Coll., Armed Forces U. 71, & War Coll. 79; Pilot 53-60; Op. Off. 60-61; Flight Leader 61-65; Squadron Cmdr. 68-72; Asst. Air AttachÇ, Emb. in the USA 72-75; Chief, Op. Sect., 3rd Wing 75-76; Group Cmdr. 76-78; Military Attaché, Emb. in S. Africa 79-83; Wing Cmdr. 83-84; Dep. Chief-of-Staff/Planning, GHQ, ROCAF 84-85; Supt., Air Force Acad. 85-86; Dir., Pol. Warfare Dept., GHQ, ROCAF 86-89; CG, Combat Air Cmd. 89; V. C-in-C, ROCAF 89-91; Insp.-Gen., MND 91-92; C-in-C, ROCAF 92-95; V. Chief of the Gen. Staff (Exec.), MND 95-98; Chief of the Gen. Staff, MND 98-99; Gen., ROCAF (Retired); Min. of Nat. Def. 99-2000; *Add.* Exec. Yuan, 1 Chung Hsiao E. Rd., Sect. 1, Taipei 100.

TANG, YAO-MING
(See TANG, YIAU-MING 湯耀明)

TANG, YIAU-MING 湯耀明
Chief of the Gen. Staff, MND 99-; *b.* Twn. Nov. 29, '38; *m.* Liu, Hsiu; 2 *s.,* 1 *d.; educ.* BS, Ch. Mil. Acad. 62; Army CGSC, Armed Forces U. 74, War CGSC 87; Div. Cmdr., ROC Army 84-86, Corps Cmdr. 88-90, Dep. Field Army Cmdr. 90-93, Field Army Cmdr. 93-95, Dep. C-in-C 95-96; C-in-C, ROC Army 96-99; *Add.* Gen. Staff Hqs., MND, Taipei 100.

TAO, CHIN-SHENG
(See TAO, JING-SHEN 陶晉生)

TAO, JING-SHEN 陶晉生
Mem., Acad. Sinica 90-; Prof., E. Asian Studies, U. of Arizona 76; *b.* Hupei '33; *m.* Pao, Chia-lin; 3 *d.; educ.* BA & MA, NTU; Ph.D., Indiana U. 67; Assc. Prof. & Prof., Hist. Dept., NTU; Assc. Res. Fel. & Res. Fel., Acad. Sinica 73; Chmn., Dept. of Oriental Studies, U. of Arizona 87-88; Chair Prof., Ch. U. of Hong Kong 88-90. *Publ.: The Jurchen in 12th-Century Ch.; Two Sons of Heaven; Add.* Dept. of E. Asian Studies, U. of Arizona, Tucson, AZ 85721, USA.

TAO, PAI-CHUAN 陶百川
Nat. Policy Adv. to the Pres. 77-; Mem., NUC 90-; *b.* Chekiang Jan. 19, '03; *m.* Chang, Shu-chun; 4 *s.,* 1 *d.; educ.* LL.B., Shanghai Law Coll.; Res. Fel., Harvard U.; Mem., Nat. Pol. Coun.; Mng. Dir., CDN; Mem., Control Yuan. *Publ.: Searching for Truth in the USSR; The Three Principles of the People & Communism; The Cold War & Ch.'s Situation; Comparative Parliamentary Control of Admin.; The Complete Works of Tao Pai-chuan* (33 Vol.); etc.; *Add.* 57 6th St., Cent. Villa, Hsintien, Taipei County 231.

TARN, JIANN-QUO 譚建國
Prof., Dept. of Civil Engr., NCKU 68-; *b.* Kwangtung July 25, '46; *m.* Tarn Yang, Lih-jean; 3 d; *educ.* BS & MS, NCKU 68 & 71; Ph.D., Duke U., USA 76, Res. Asst. 71-75; Assc. Prof., NCKU 65-68, Chmn. 74-79. *Publ.: Hybrid FEM for Multilayer Laminated Composites; Shakedown of Unidirectional Composites; A Differential Scheme for Multiphase Composites; Asymptotic Theory of Laminated Plates & Shells; Add.* 2 Ta Hsueh Rd., Tainan 701.

TCHEN, HIONG-FEI 陳雄飛
Nat. Policy to Pres. 99-; Sr. Adv., MOFA 84-; *b.* Shanghai Feb. 27, '11; 3 *s.*; Docteur en droit, Université l'Aurore, Shanghai 30; Docteur en droit, Paris U. 41; Sp., Sect. Chief, Treaty Dept. MOFA 43-49; Counsl., Min. Chargé d'Affaires, Ch. Emb. Paris 49-63; Amb. & Sp. Envoy to the newly independent French-speaking countries of Africa 60-63; Head or Mem. of Del. to the Gen. Ass., Admin. Coun.,

Exec. Cttee. Meetings of UN, UNESCO, ITU, UPU, WMO, IMCO, etc. & other IGO or NGO 50-63; Amb. to Belgium & concur. Min. & Amb. to Luxemburg 63-71; Mem., Friendship Sp. Mission to Costa Rica, Guatemala, Brazil; Mem., Sp. Mission to Paraguay for the Inauguration of the Pres. Mandate 73; Admin. V. Min. of For. Aff. 71-73; Amb. to Uruguay 73-81; Chmn., Europe-Asia Trade Org. 85-88; Dir., Bophuthatswana Trade & Tourism Cent. in the ROC 92-94. *Publ.: Esquisse d'une histoire du droit constitutionnel chinois* 30; *La "Family Provision" en droit successoral comparé* 41; *Add.* 3rd Fl.-2, 84 Fu Hsing S. Rd., Sect. 2, Taipei 106.

TCHEN, YU-CHIOU 陳郁秀
Chairperson, CCA 2000-; Chairperson, Egret Cul. Found. 93-; Mem., Art Educ. Cttee., MOE, Consultative Cttee. of Sp. Educ., & the ad hoc cttee. for selecting visiting artists to the CitÇ Internationale des Arts, France 97-; Mem., Prof. Consultative Cttee., Preparatory Off. of Folk Music Cent., CCA; Adv., Exec. Cttee. of Taipei Arts Festival, TCG; Chairperson, Consultative Cttee., Nat. Concert Hall's Orchestra, Nat. Chiang Kai-shek Cul. Cent.; *b.* Taipei Apr. 22, '49; *m.* Lu, Hsiu-yi (deceased); 1 *s.,* 2 *d.; educ.* Grad., Conservatoire Superieur de Paris with "Peix de Piano" & "Prix de Masque de Chamber," France 75; Assc. Prof., Dept. of Music, NTNU 76, Prof. 92, Dept. Head & Grad. Inst. Dir. of Music 94-97, & Dean of Coll. of Fine & Applied Arts 97-2000; Visiting Prof., U. of Wisconsin 83; Chairperson, the ROC Musical Educ. Soc. 95. *Publ.: Res. on the Complete Piano Works of Maurice Ravel* 84; *The Music Exhibition of Twn.* 96; *The Centennial Twn.—The Thesis Collection* 97; *The Centennial Music Twn.* 98; *Life in Red Shoes—Ancestral Grace Treasured by Mr. Kuo Ju-yuan* 99; *Chang Fu-Hsing—The First Contemporary Musician of Twn.* 2000; *Add.* CCA, 102, Ai Kuo E. Rd., Taipei 100.

TENG, CHANG-LI
(See TENG, LEE C. 鄧昌黎)

TENG, CHARLES S.S. 鄧申生
Dir.-Gen., TECO in New York 98-; *b.* Shanghai Oct. 17 '40; 2 *s.; educ.* BA, NCCU 64; Dip. Trainee, Australia Nat. U. 72; Asst. Ed., CNA 67-70; Staff, Dept. of N. Am Aff., MOFA 72-74; V. Consul, Consl. in Portland, USA 74-76; 3rd Sec., Emb. in the USA 76-79; Sr. Asst., CCNAA Washington, D.C. 79-82; Dep. Dir., Dept. of N. Am. Aff. MOFA & concur. Sect. Chief, 1st Sect. 82-86; Dep. Dir. Gen., CCNAA, New York 86-89; Dir., Secretariat CCNAA, Washington, D.C. 89-93; Rep., TECO, Austria

93-96; Dep. Rep., TECRO, Washington, D.C. 96-98; *Add.* 885 2nd Avenue., 47th Fl., New York, NY 10017.

TENG, LEE C. 鄧昌黎

Mem., Acad. Sinica 66-; Fel., Am. Phys. Soc.; Mem., Bd. of Dir., Synchrotron Radiation Res. Cent., ROC 83-; Hon. Chmn., Fu Jen Alumni Assn. 84-; Adjunct Prof. of Phys., U. of Wisconsin 91-; Head, Accelerator Phys., Advanced Photon Source Project, Argonne Nat. Lab., USA 89-; *b.* Peking Sept. 5, '26; *m.* Huang, Nancy Lai-shen; 1 *s.; educ.* BS, Peiping Fu Jen Catholic U. 46; MS, U. of Chicago 48, Ph.D. 51; Lectr., U. of Minnesota 51-52, Asst. Prof. 52-53; Asst. Prof., Wichita State U. 53-54, Assc. Prof. 54-55; Asst. Physicist, Argonne Nat. Lab. 55-56, Assc. Physicist 56-61, Sr. Physicist 61-67; Visiting Prof., NTHU 59; Head of Theoretical Group, Particle Accelerator Div., Argonne Nat. Lab. 56-62, Div. Dir. 62-67; Professorial Lectr., U. of Chicago 63-69; Dir., US-Korea "Sister Lab." Arrangements (AEC-AID Prog.) 64-67 & US-Ch. "Sister Lab." Arrangements (AEC-AID Prog.) 64-70; Head, Accelerator Theory Sect., Fermi Nat. Accelerator Lab. 67-72, Assc. Dir., Accelerator Div. 72-76, Head, Advanced Projects Dept., Accelerator Phys. Dept. 80-87, Lab. Dir.'s Off. for Sp. Projects 87-89; Chmn., US Nat. Accelerator Conf. 77; Dir., Synchrotron Radiation Res. Cent. Project Off., ROC 83-85; Argonne Fel. 85-87. *Publ.:* About 400 tech. papers on high energy phys. & particle accelerator phys.; *Add.* 400 E. 8th St., Hinsdale, IL 60521, USA.

TENG, P.Y. 鄧備殷

Amb., Emb. of ROC, Solomon Islands 98-; Non Resident Amb. to Repub. of Nauru & Tuvalu 99-; *b.* Ch. Jan. 9, '43; *m.* Gi, Yann-erl; 1 *s.,* 1 *d.; educ.* BA, NCCU 65, MA 69; Jr. Clerk, MOFA 72-73; Sec., Dir., & Rep., MOFA Off. in Hong Kong 73-90; Dep. Dir., Bu. of Consl. Aff., MOFA 91-92, Dir., Dept. of E. Asian & Pacific Aff. 92-95; Rep., Taipei Econ. & Cul. Cent. in New Delhi 95-98; *Add.* Emb. of ROC, P.O. Box 586, Honiara, Solomon Islands.

TENG, PEI-YIN
(See TENG, P.Y. 鄧備殷)

TENG, SHEN-SHENG
(See TENG, CHARLES S.S. 鄧申生)

TENG, TA-LIANG 鄧大量

Mem., Acad. Sinica 90-; Prof. of Geophys., U. of So. Calif. 76-; *b.* Kwangsi July 3, '37; *m.* Lee, Evelyn May; 1 *s.,* 1 *d.; educ.* BS, Geol., NTU 59; Ph.D., Geophys. & Applied Math., Calif. Inst. of Tech. 66; Res. Fel., Seismological Lab., Calif. Inst. of Tech. 66-67; Asst. Prof., U. of So. Calif. 67-70, Assc. Prof. of Geophys. 70-76; Visiting Prof., NTU 72-73; Visiting Res. Assc., Seismological Lab., Calif. Inst. of Tech. 74-75. *Publ.:* About 100 sc. publ.; *Add.* 1474 Rose Villa St., Pasadena, CA 91106, USA.

TENG, TZU-LIN 鄧祖琳

V. Chief of Gen. Staff, MND 99-; *b.* Ch., Oct. 8, '42; *m.* Chen, Hsiu-lan; 2 *d.; educ.* Army Acad. 66; Army Cmd. & Staff Coll., Armed Forces U. 76, War Coll. 81, & Mil. Sc. Inst. 84; Cmdt., Armed Forces Preparatory Sch. 88-90; CG, Airborne & Sp. Forces Cmd. 90-92; Cmdt., Pol. Warfare Coll. 92-96; CG, 6th Field Army 96-98; Dep. C-in-C, ROC Army 98-99; *Add.* 1st Fl., 17 Lane 17, Kuang Fu S. Rd., Taipei 105.

TIAO, CHIN-HUAN
(See TIAO, GEORGE C. 刁錦寰)

TIAO, GEORGE C. 刁錦寰

Mem., Acad. Sinica 76-; W. Allen Wallis Prof. of Statistics, Grad. Sch. of Business, U. of Chicago 82-; *b.* London Nov. 8, '33; *m.* Chu, Pao-hsing; 4 *c.; educ.* BS, Econ., NTU 55; MBA, New York U. 58; Ph.D., U. of Wisconsin 62; Asst. Prof., U. of Wisconsin 62-65, Assc. Prof. 66-68, Prof. 68-81, Chmn., Dept. of Statistics 73-75; Visiting Chair Prof., NTU 75-76; Visiting Ford Found. Prof. of Statistics 80-81; Bascom Prof. of Statistics & Business, U. of Wisconsin 81-82. *Publ.: Bayesian Inference in Statistical Analysis; Directions in Time Series; The Collected Works of G.E.P. Box;* & 100 articles; *Add.* Grad. Sch. of Business, U. of Chicago, 1101 E. 58th St., Chicago, IL 60637, USA.

TIEN, CHANG-LIN 田長霖

Mem., Acad. Sinica 88-; NEC Disting. Prof. of Engr., UC-Berkly. 97-, Faculty Mem. 90-; Chmn., Chief Exec.'s Com. on Innovation & Tech., H.K.; Coun., Nat. Acad. of Engr., USA; *b.* Hupei July 24, '35; *m.* Liu, Di-hwa; 3 *c.; educ.* BS, NTU 55; MS, Mech. Engr., U. of Louisville 57; MA & Ph.D., Princeton U. 59; Faculty Mem., Mech. Engr., UC-Berkly. 59-88, Prof. of Mech. Engr. 68-88, Chair, Thermal Systems Div. 69-71, & Dept. of Mech. Engr. 74-81, V. Chancellor-Res. 83-85; Consultant & Bd. Mem. of numerous ind., govt., & educ. org. 83-85; A. Martin Berlin Chair Prof. of Mech. Engr., UC-Berkly. 87-88 & 90-97, Chancellor 90-97; Exec. V. Chancellor & UCI Disting. Prof., U. of Calif., Irvine 88-90. *Publ.:* 1 bk., 12 ed. Vol., 25 review & monograph articles, & over 300 referred res. papers in heat transfer, thermal radiation, & other related energy & environmental subjects; *Add.* Dept. of Mech. Engr., UC-Berkly., Berkeley, CA 94720-1740, USA.

TIEN, HUNG-MAO 田弘茂
Min. of For. Aff. 2000-; Bd. Mem., Evergreen Found. 91-; *b.* Twn. Nov. 7, '38; *m.* Kuo, Amy M.H.; 1 *s.,* 1 *d.; educ.* BA, Tunghai U. 61; MA, U. of Wisconsin 66, Ph.D. 69; Chmn., Wisconsin Ch. Coun., USA 79-81, & Assn. for Asian Studies Cttee. on Twn. Studies 85-88; Visiting Scholar, Hoover Inst., Stanford U. 83 & 86; Mem., Ch. Coun. & the Contemporary Aff. Cttee., Asia Soc. 83-90; Adv., Columbia U. Twn. Studies Project 89-90; Adv. Bd. Mem., Ch. Times Cul. & Educ. Found. 87-90; Sr. Fel., U. of Wisconsin Law Sch. 90-93; Mem., Wisconsin Equal Rights Coun. 89-91; Dep. Convener, ROC Nat. Dev. Conf. 96; Nat. Policy Adv. to the Pres. 96-2000; Adv. to the Premier 98-2000; Prof. of Pol. Sc., U. of Wisconsin 68-2000; Pres. & Chmn. of the Bd., Inst. for Nat. Policy Res. 91-2000; Res. Fel., NUC 92-2000; Trustee, Found. for Intl. Cooperation & Dev., Exec. Yuan 96-2000; Mem., NUC 97-2000. *Publ.: Democratization in Twn., Implications for Ch.; Ch. Under Jiang Zemin; Sec. Environment in the Asia-Pacific Region: Many Problems Few Bldg. Blocks; Consolidating the Third Wave Democracies, Themes & Perspectives; Twn.'s Electoral Pol. & Dem. Transition; The Great Transition, Soc. & Pol. Changes in the ROC; Mainland Ch., Twn., & US Policy; Govt. & Pol. in KMT Ch. 1927-37; Add.* 2 Kaitakelan Boulevard, Taipei 100.

TIEN, PING-KENG
(See TIEN, PING-KING 田炳耕)

TIEN, PING-KING 田炳耕
Mem., Acad. Sinica 88-; Fel. Emeritus & Sr. Staff-Consultant, Photonics Res, Bell Labs./Lucent Tech. USA; Mem., Nat. Acad. of Sc., Nat. Acad. of Engr., USA, & 3rd World Acad. of Sc.; *b.* Chekiang Aug. 2, '19; *m.* Tien, Nancy N.Y.; 2 *d.; educ.* BEE, NCU 42; MEE, Stanford U. 48, DSEE 51; Mem., Tech. Staff, AT&T Bell Labs. 52-59, Head, Elect. Res. 59-66, Electron-Phys. Res. 66-74, Dept. of Microelect. Res. 80-84, & Dept. of High Speed Elect. Res. 84-90; Dir., Intl. Summer Sch. of Phys., Hong Kong 82; Hon. Prof., Shanghai Jiao Tong U. 83; Ed.-in-Chief, *Intl. Jour. of High Speed Elect. & Systems* 90-98. *Publ.:* More than 50 articles in microwave tech. & electron dynamics, parametric amplifier, acoustic & acousto-elec. effect, wave phenomena, superconductivity, optics & lasers, integrated optics, high speed elect.; *Add.* Bell Labs. Lucent Tech., HO-4F-307, 101 Crawfords Corner Rd., Holmdel, NJ 07733, USA.

TIEN, WEI-HSIN 田維新
Mem. (ministerial rank), Exam. Yuan 90-; Prof., Grad. Inst. of For. Lang. & Lit., NTU; *b.* Shensi Aug. 16, '34; *m.* Lin, Su-o; 2 *s.; educ.* Ph.D., Michigan State U.; Asst., NTNU 64-66, Instr. 66-72, Assc. Prof. 72-78; Prof., NCU 78-87, Prof. & Dept. Chmn. 79-85, Prof. & Coll. Dean 82-86; Res. Fel., Acad. Sinica 87-90. *Publ.: Mailer's Search for a Hero; A Study of Faulkner's Trilogy; Ideological Encounters; Add.* 14th Fl.-3, 9 Lane 22, Hsien Yen Rd., Wenshan, Taipei 116.

TING, CHAO-CHUNG
(See TING, SAMUEL CHAO-CHUNG 丁肇中)

TING, MAO-SHIH
(See DING, MOU-SHIH 丁懋時)

TING, MAO-SUNG
(See DING, MOW-SUNG 丁懋松)

TING, PANG-HSIN 丁邦新
Mem., Acad. Sinica 86-; Dean of the Sch. of Humanities & Soc. Sc., Hong Kong U. of Sc. & Tech.; *b.* Kiangsu Oct. 15, '36; *m.* Chen, Chi; 3 *c.; educ.* BA & MA, Ch. Linguistics, NTU; Ph.D., Asian Lang. & Lit., U. of Washington; Assc. Res. Fel., Acad. Sinica 70-75; Assc. Prof., NTU 72-75, Prof. 75-89; Chmn., Linguistics Sect., Inst. of Hist. & Philology, Acad. Sinica 73-81, Assc. Dir. 81-85, Dir. 85-89; Prof. of Ch. Linguistics, UC-Berkly. 89-94, Agassiz Prof. of Ch. Linguistics 94-98. *Publ.: The Origin of Twn. Lang.; Ch. Phonology of the Wei-Chin Period; The Tan Chou Tsun-Hua Dialect; Add.* Rm. 3361, Acad. Bldg., Inst. of Humanities & Soc. Sc., Hong Kong U. of Tech., Clear Water Bay, Kowloon, Hong Kong.

TING, SAMUEL CHAO-CHUNG 丁肇中
Mem., Acad. Sinica 75-; Prof. of Phys., MIT 69-; Prof., Thomas Dudey Cabot Inst. 77-; *b.* Ch. Jan. 27, '36; *m.* Marks, Susan Carol; 1 *s.,* 2 *d.; educ.* BS, U. of Michigan 59, MS 60, Ph.D. 62, Hon. D.Sc. 78; Hon. D.Sc., Ch. U. of Hong Kong 87, U. of Bologna, Italy 88; Fel., European Org. Nuclear Res., Geneva 63; Instr. of Phys., Columbia U. 64, Asst. Prof. 65-67; Group Leader, Deutsches Elektronen-Synchrotron, Hamburg, W. Germany 66; Assc. Prof., Phys., MIT 67-68; Prog. Consultant, Div. Particles & Fields, Am. Phys. Soc. 70; Fel., Am. Acad. Arts & Sc. 75; Mem., Pakistani Acad. Sc.; Assc. Ed., *Nuclear Phys. Bulletin* 70; Ed. Bd., *Nuclear Instruments & Methods; Add.* CERN, Geneva 23, Switzerland; Dept. of Phys., MIT, 51 Vassar St., Cambridge, MA 02139, USA.

TING, YUAN-CHIN 丁原進
Dir.-Gen., Nat. Police Admin. (NPA), MOI 97-; *b.* Shantung Feb. 5, '39; *m.* Gung, Pei-ling; 1 *s.,* 2 *d.; educ.* LL.B., Cent.

Police U.; Dir., Educ. Div., NPA 89-92; Dir., Police Dept., Tainan County 92-93; Sec.-Gen., NPA 93-96, Dep. Dir.-Gen. 96; Dir., Taipei City Police Hqs. 96-97; *Add.* 7 Chung Hsiao E. Rd., Sect. 1, Taipei 100.

TONG, SHEN-NAN 童勝男
Comr., TPG 98-; *b.* Twn. Feb. 10, '44; *m.* Chiang, Wen-chiao; 2 *s.; educ.* Ph.D., Polymer Inst., U. of Akron, USA 82; Dept. Dir., Union Ind. Res. Lab., Ind. Tech. Res. Inst. 73-82; Visiting Scientist, Case We. Reserve U., USA 78; V. Pres. Ch. Carbon Fiber Ind. Corp. 83-85; Dip. Dir.-Gen., Union Chem. Lab., Ind. Tech. Res. Inst. 85-89; Mayor, Hsinchu City 89-97. *Publ.:* 21 patents & 80 articles; *Add.* 9 Lane 182, Lin Sen Rd., Hsinchu 300.

TOU, CHOU-SENG 杜筑生
Amb. to Senegal 96-; *b.* Kweichow Mar. 30, '42; *m.* Chiu, Maria Da-rouin; 2 *s.; educ.* LL.B., NTU; Docteur en droit, U. of Paris; Fel., Cent. for Intl. Aff., Harvard U. 88-89; Adjunct Assc. Prof., Soochow U. 76-79; Sect. Chief, MOFA 77-81; Dep. Dir.-Gen., TECO, Belgium 81-85; Sr. Sp., Dept. of European Aff., MOFA 85-86, Dep. Dir., Dept. of Treaty & Legal Aff. 86-89; Dir.-Gen., TECO, Greece 89-91, CCNAA Off. in Chicago 91-93, Dept. of Protocol, MOFA 93-94, Dept. of N. Am. Aff. 94-96; Adjunct Prof., Tamkang U. *Publ.: La Personnalité Juridique Internationale d'Organes Subsidiaires des Nation-unies* 75; *The External Rel. of the European Communities* 87; *The Impact of the Single European Act on the Rel. Between the EC & E. Asia* 89; *Add.* 30 Avenue Nelson Mandela, B.P. 4164, Dakar, Senegal.

TOU, JULIUS T. 竇祖烈
Mem., Acad. Sinica 72-; Grad. Res. Prof.; Dir., Cent. for Info. Res.; *b.* Shanghai Aug. 15, '26; *m.* Lisa; 3 *s.,* 1 *d.; educ.* BS, NCTU; MS, Harvard U.; Ph.D., Yale U.; Project Engr., Philco Corp. 52-54; Asst. Prof., U. of Penn. 54-57; Assc. Prof., Purdue U. 57-61; Prof., N.We. U., USA 61-64; Dir., Battelle Inst. 64-67; Adjunct Prof., Ohio State U. 64-67. *Publ.: Digital Control Systems* 59; *Optimum Control Systems* 63; *Modern Control Theory* 64; *Computer & Info. Sc. I & II* 63 & 66; *Software Engr.* 69; *Info. Systems* 72; *Pattern Recognition Principles* 74; *Computer-based Automation* 82; *Highly Redundant Sensing in Robotic Systems* 89; *Add.* Cent. for Info. Res., Coll. of Engr., U. of Florida, 314 CSE Bldg., Gainesville, FL 32611, USA.

TOU, TSU-LIE
(See TOU, JULIUS T. 竇祖烈)

TSAI, ANTONIO T.S. 蔡德三
Amb. to Nicaragua 99-; *b.* Twn. Nov. 16, '39; *m.* Chen, Hsiu-chuan; 2 *s.,* 1 *d.; educ.* Grad., NCU; Res., U. of Chile; Ch. Emb. in Guatemala 72-75; Dep. Dir., Consl. Agency in Guayaquil 75-78; Sect. Chief, MOFA 79-82; Counsl., Ch. Emb. in Panamá 82-85; Rep., Far E. Cml. d Consl. Off. La Paz, Bolivia 90-95; Rep., Cml. Off. Quito, Ecuador 98-99; *Add.* Apartado Postal 4653, Managua 5, Nicaragua.

TSAI, BIH-HWANG 蔡璧煌
Dir.-Gen., Inst. on Policy Res. & Dev., KMT 97-2000; Prof., NTNU 85-; *b.* Twn. Sept. 29, '45; *m.* Lee, Mei-li; 2 *s.; educ.* Ed.B., NTNU 72; MA, NCCU 77; Ph.D., Stanford U. 85; Sect. Chief, Dept. of Educ., TPG 71-72; Instr., Tung Nan Jr. Coll. of Tech. 78-79, Dep. Sec.-Gen., Nat. Educ. Assn.; Dir.-Gen., Dept. of Cul. Aff., CC, KMT 96-97; Mem., Legis. Yuan 90-93, 96-99. *Publ.: Sch. & Students' Pol. Socialization; Classroom Climate & Pol. Socialization; Add.* 290 Mucha Rd., Sect. 1, Taipei 116.

TSAI, CHAO-YANG
(See TSAY, JAW-YANG 蔡兆陽)

TSAI, CHENG-WEN 蔡政文
Mem. (ministerial rank), Exam. Yuan 99-; Prof., Pol. Sc., NTU 78-; Mem., RDEC 88-; Mem., CEC, KMT 95-; *b.* Taipei May 23, '40; *m.* Pien, Yun-li; 2 *s.; educ.* BA, NTU 58-62; Licencié en Sc. Politiques et Sociales, U. Catholique de Louvain, Belgium 64-67; Ph.D., Katholike U., Belgium 67-73; Chmn., Dept. & Grad. Inst. of Pol. Sc., NTU 85-91; Dep. Dir.-Gen., Dept. of Org., CC, KMT 91-92; Min. without Portfolio 96-97; Nat. Policy Adv. to the Pres. 97-99; *Add.* 1 Chung Hsiao E. Rd., Sect. 1, Taipei 100.

TSAI, CHING-YEN
(See TSAY, CHING-YEN 蔡清彥)

TSAI, HSIEN-LIU
(See TSAI, SHIANN-LIOW 蔡憲六)

TSAI, HSUN-HSIUNG
(See TSAI, HSUNG-HSIUNG 蔡勳雄)

TSAI, HSUNG-HSIUNG 蔡勳雄
Admin., EPA 96-2000; Coun. Mem., CEPD 96-; Mem., NScC & AEC 96-; Mem., Bd. Dir., Ch. Inst. of Regional Sc. 84-; *b.* Twn. June 23, '41; *m.* Wang, Shu-yung; 1 *s.,* 1 *d.; educ.* LL.B., NTU 64; MA, Urban Planning, MIT 74; Ph.D., Princeton U. 79; Sr. Sp., CEPD 79-80, Dep. Dir., Dept. of Urban & Housing Dev. 80-83, Dir. 83-92; Pres.,

Ch. Inst. of Urban Planning 81-82; Com. Mem., City Planning Com., MOI 83-92; Prcs., Ch. Inst. of Regional Sc. 86-87; Dep. Exec. Sec., Environmental Protection Cttee., Exec. Yuan 86-88, Exec. Sec. 88-90; Com. Mem., RDEC 92-96; V. Chmn., CEPD 92-96. *Publ.:* Many articles published in *Ind. of Free Ch.; Add.* 10th Fl., 41 Chung Hua Rd., Sect. 1, Taipei 100.

TSAI, ING-WEN 蔡英文
Chmn., MAC 2000-; Adv. on intl. econ. org., MOEA 92-; Mem., Intl. Trade Com. 93-; Prof. of Law, Grad. Inst. of Intl. Trade, NCCU 93-; *b.* Taipei Aug. 31, '56; *educ.* LL.B. NTU 78; LL.M., Cornell U. 80; Ph.D., Lodon Sch. of Econ. & Pol. Sc., U. of London 84; Assc. Prof., Law Sch., NCCU 84-90, Prof., Grad. Law Sch. 90-91; Prof., Grad. Law Sch., Soochow U. 91-93;Mem., Fair Trade Com. 95-98; Convener, Drafting/Res. Group on Hong Kong/Macau Relations Act 94-95; Mem., Adv. Cttee. of the MAC 94-98 & Adv. Cttee. of the Copyright Com. of MOI 97-99; Sr. Adv., NSC 99-2000. *Publ.: The Accession of the ROC to the Gen. Agreement on Tariffs & Trade* 81; "Principles of Intl. Trade Law—Their Application & Changes in a Transitional World Econ.," *NCCU Law Review* 83; "Patterns if Current Intl. Trade Disputes & Sectoralization of Trade Laws," *NTU Law Review* 84; "Safeguarding Domestic Markets in Intl. Trade—Article 19 of the GATT, VERs & MFA" 85 & "State Intervention & Intl. Trade Law—Law of Subsidies," *NCCU Law Review* 85; *The Implication of EC Competition & Trade Policies for Twn.—the Legal Perspective* 92; *The Role of the GATT in the World Econ. & An Accessment of the ROC Accession* 88; *Add.* 15th-18th Fl., 2-2 Chi Nan Rd., Sect. 2, Taipei 100.

TSAI, JEN-CHIEN 蔡仁堅
Mayor, Hsinchu City 97-; Dir., Dept. of Publicity, DPP; *b.* Twn. Oct. 27, '52; *educ.* B., Pharmacology, Taipei Med. Coll.; M., PA, John F. Kennedy Sch. of Govt., Harvard U.; Mem., Hsinchu CCoun.; Mem., NA 92-97; Mem., Civil Service Protection & Training Com., Exam. Yuan; *Add.* 120 Chung Cheng Rd., Hsinchu 300.

TSAI, JUEI-HSIUNG 蔡瑞熊
Pres., Kaohsiung Med. Coll. (KMC) 91-, Prof. of Internal Med. 73-; Phys. in Internal Med., Chung Ho Memorial Hosp. attached to KMC 70-; *b.* Twn. Dec. 26, '35; *m.* Chang, Fown-tzu; 2 *d.; educ.* MD, KMC 60; DMS, Tokyo U. 69; Res. Fel., Pharmacology Div., Nat. Inst. of Radiological Sc., Japan 69; Visiting Fel., Cellular & Molecular Res. Lab., Cardiac Unit, Massachusetts Gen. Hosp., Med. Sch., Harvard U. 90-91; Resident, KMC Hosp. 61-64; Assc.

Prof. of Internal Med., KMC 69-73, Dean of Student Aff. 72-73; Dir., Dept. of Internal Med., Chung Ho Memorial Hosp. 73-80 & 83-87, Dir., Dept. of Nuclear Med. 80-84; Visiting Prof. of Med., U. of Arkansas for Med. Sc. 82; V. Supt., Chung Ho Memorial Hosp. 85-90. *Publ.:* 155 original acad. reports & 372 abstract articles; *Add.* 100 Shih Chuan 1st Rd., Kaohsiung 807.

TSAI, JUI-HSIUNG
(See TSAI, JUEI-HSIUNG 蔡瑞熊)

TSAI, LIANG-WEN 蔡良文
Dep. Sec.-Gen., Exam. Yuan 96-; Assc. Prof., Ch. Cul. U.; *b.* Twn. Dec. 2, '54; *m.* Tseng, Hsiu-chu; 2 *s.,* 1 *d.; educ.* Grad., Hsinchu Tchr. Coll. 75; LL.B., Ch. Cul. U. 83; LL.M., NTU 86; LL.D., NCCU 96; Sr. Sp., Min. of Exam. 89-91, Dep. Dir. 91, Sr. Sec. 91-92; Counsl., Exam. Yuan 92-94, Dir., Secretariat 94-96. *Publ.: A Study of the Exam. & Selection System of the Civil Servants in the US; The Dev. of the Power of Exam. of the Five-Power Const. of the ROC; Pers. Admin.; Admin. Neutrality & Pol. Dev.; Add.* 1 Shih Yuan Rd., Taipei 116.

TSAI, M.H. 蔡茂興
Bd. Chmn., Chang Hwa Bk. Ltd. 95-; *b.* Twn. Nov. 9, '39; *m.* Chang, Ming-chao; 2 *s.; educ.* B., Cooperative Econ., NCHU 62; Clerk, Twn. Cooperative Bk. 63-70; Sect. Chief, Monetary Aff. Dept., MOF 70-75; Div. Chief, Dept. of Finance, TPG 75-78; Exec. V. Pres., Twn. Dev. & Trust Corp. 78-80; Pres., Twn. Life Ins. Co. Ltd. 80-87, Medium Business Bk. of Twn. 87-91, Hua Nan Cml. Bk. 91-94, & Bk. of Twn. 94-95. *Publ.: Preferential Tariff & Dev. Countries; Tax Problems of Cooperative Org. in Various Nations; Add.* 57 Chung Shan N. Rd., Sect. 2, Taipei 104.

TSAI, MAO-HSING
(See TSAI, M.H. 蔡茂興)

TSAI, NAN-HAI
(See CHUA, NAM-HAI 蔡南海)

TSAI, MIN-CHUNG 蔡敏忠
Prof., Grad. Inst. of Phys. Educ., Ch. Cul. U. 93-; Adv., ROC Sports Fed. 93-; *b.* Honan Sept. 16, '23; *m.* Hung Chow-pao; 1 *d.; educ.* Ed.B., NTNU 52; MS, Phys. Educ. Indiana U., USA 62, MS, Health & Safety, 63; Ph.D., Phys. Educ., U. of Minnesota 71; Prof., NTNU, & Dir., Phys. Educ. & Sports Dept., MOE 73-82; Admin. Off., Cul. & Soc. Cent., Asian & Pacific Coun. 82-85; Dir., Preparatory Off., Nat. Coll. of Phys. Educ. & Sport 85-86, Pres. 86-90. *Publ.: Res*

Methods in Phys. Educ. 80; *Handbk. for Jr. High Sch. Phys. Educ. Tchrs.* 82; *Survey of Manpower of Phys. Educ. & Sports of the ROC, MOE* 76; *One Wall Handball* (Transl. from Eng.) 65; *Add.* 55 Hua Kang Rd., Taipei 111.

TSAI, MING-LIANG 蔡明亮
Film Dir.; *b.* Ch. Oct. 27, '57; *educ.* BA, Ch. Cul. U.; Golden Bell Award for Best Dir. 92 & 93; Bronze Prize for Best Film, Tokyo Film Festival 93; Award for Best Film, Turin Intl. Festival of Young Cinema 93; Golden Lion Award, Venice Film Festival 94; Award for Best Film, Taipei Film Festival 94; Golden Horse Award for Best Dir. & Best Feature Film 94; Award for Best Dir., Nantes Film Festival 94; Award for Best Film, Singapore Film Festival 95; Silver Bear Award, Berlin Film Festival 95; Fipresci Award, Cannes Film Festival 98. *Theatrical Works: Instant Bean Sauce Noodle* 81; *A Sealed Door in the Dark* 82; *A Wardrobe in the Rm.* 83; *Apt. Romance* 94; *TV Productions: Endless Love* 89; *Far Away* 90; *Li Hsiang's Love Line, Give Me a Home, & The Kid* 91; *Films: Rebels of the Neon God* 92; *Vive L'amour* 94; *My New Friends* 96; *The River* 97; *The Hole* 98; *Add.* 10th Fl., 37 Kuang Fu N. Rd., Taipei 105.

TSAI, PI-HUANG
(See TSAI, BIH-HWANG 蔡璧煌)

TSAI, SHIANN-LIOW 蔡憲六
Mem. (ministerial rank), Exam. Yuan 96-; *b.* Twn. Aug. 31, '39; *m.* Lee, Shiou-chih; 1 *s.,* 1 *d.; educ.* MPS, NCCU 66; Staff Mem., Ch. Youth Corps 66-69; Sup., Twn. Prov. Cttee., KMT 69, Sec., Kaohsiung Mun. Cttee. 69-73, Chmn., Taitung County Cttee. 73-74; V. Comr., Dept. of Soc. Aff., TPG 79-87, Dep. Sec.-Gen. 87, Comr., Dept. of Labor Aff. 88-91; V. Chmn., CLA 91-95; Pres., Twn. Film Cul. Co. 95-96. *Publ.: Theory & Practice of Job Evaluation; Mng. of Salaries in Ent.; Add.* 1 Shih Yuan Rd., Wenshan, Taipei 116.

TSAI, HSIEN-LIU
(See TSAI, SHIANN-LIOW 蔡憲六)

TSAI, TE-SAN
(See TSAI, ANTONIO T.S. 蔡德三)

TSAI, TSO-YUNG
(See CHAI, CHOK-YUNG 蔡作雍)

TSAI, TUNG-JUNG
(See CHAI, TRONG R. 蔡同榮)

TSAI, WAN-TSAI 蔡萬才
Chmn., Fubon Group; Adv., Exec. Yuan & CC, KMT; Bd. Chmn., Assn. of Friends of Police, ROC; *b.* Taipei Aug. 5, '29; *m.* Yang, Shiang-shun; 2 *s.,* 2 *d.; educ.* LL.B., NTU; Mem. & Convener, Legis. Yuan; Chmn., ROC Amateur Athletic Fed., & Taipei Chamber of Com.; *Add.* 2nd-4th Fl., 169 Jen Ai Rd., Sect. 4, Taipei 106.

TSAI, WEN-CHING
(See TSAI, WEN-JING 蔡文景)

TSAI, WEN-HSIANG 蔡文祥
Prof. & Dean of Acad. Aff., NCTU 84-; Chmn., Ch. Assn. of Image Processing & Pattern Recognition 98-; Ed.-in-Chief, *Jour. of Info. Sc. & Engr* 97-; *b.* Twn. May 10, '51; *m.* Kuo, Chih-hua; 1 *s.,* 1 *d.; educ.* BEE, NTU 73; MS, Brown U., USA 77; Ph.D., EE, Purdue U. 79; Head, Dept. of Computer & Info. Sc., NCTU 84-88; Ed., *Pattern Recognition* 88-97; Coordinator, Info. Sc. Sect., NScC 93-95; Dean of Gen. Aff., NCTU 95-97. *Publ.:* 90 acad. jour. papers; 120 conf. papers; 67 tech. reports; & 4 patents; *Add.* Dept. of Computer & Info. Sc., NCTU, Hsinchu 300.

TSAI, WEN-JING 蔡文景
Spkr., Hualien CoCoun. 94-, Mem. 82-; *b.* Twn. June 8, '46; 1 *s.,* 3 *d.; educ.* Grad., Sr. High Sch.; Dep. Spkr., Hualien CoCoun. 90-94; *Add.* 23 Fu Chien Rd., Hualien 970.

TSAI, WEN-PIN 蔡文斌
Mem. (ministerial rank), Exam. Yuan 96-; Mem., NA 92-; Nat. Pres., ROC Jaycees 87-; Convener, DPP caucus, NA 93-; *b.* Twn. Mar. 29, '53; *m.* Chen, Mei-hui; 1 *s.,* 1 *d.; educ.* BA, NTU 75; Lawyer 77-96; Mem., Presidium, NA 93-94. *Publ.: Practice Rules of Parliamentary Procedure; See You Tomorrow, Mr. Pres. (Notes of the NA); Notes of the Exam. Yuan; Add.* 1 Shih Yuan Rd., Wenshan, Taipei 116.

TSAI, YING-WEN
(See TSAI, ING-WEN 蔡英文)

TSAO, AN-PANG
(See TSO, PAUL O.P. 曹安邦)

TSAO, HSING-CHENG
(See TSAO, ROBERT H.C. 曹興誠)

TSAO, ROBERT H.C. 曹興誠
Nat. Policy Adv. to the Pres. 96-; Chmn., United Microelect. Corp. (UMC) 91-, Unipac Microelect. Corp. 89-, World Wiser Elect. Inc. 89-; V. Chmn., TECO Info. System Co.

Ltd. 95-; Standing Bd. Mem., Ch. Nat. Fed. of Ind. (CNFI); *b.* Shantung Feb. 24, '47; *educ.* BS, NTU 69; MS, NCTU 72; Dep. Dir., Elect. Res. Service Org. 79-81; V. Pres., UMC 80, & Pres. 82-91; Chmn., Assn. of Allied Ind. in Sc.-based Ind. Park 87-93; Chmn., Intellectual Property Protection Cttee., CNFI 91-94; *Add.* 3 Lin Hsin 2nd Rd., Sc.-based Ind. Park, Hsinchu 300.

TSAO, WEN-SHENG 曹文生

Dir.-Gen., Pol. Warfare Dept., MND; *b.* Hunan Feb. 17, '43; *m.* Chang, Hsiu-chuan; 1 *d.; educ.* 35th Class, Mil. Acad.; Studied in USA; Regular Class, Army CGSC 81, War Coll., Armed Forces U. 86; Cmdr., co., bn., & div.; Chief Aide-de-Camp to the Pres.; C-in-C, ROC Mil. Police; Dep. C-in-C, ROC Army; *Add.* P.O. Box 90012, Taipei 10012.

TSAY, CHING-YEN 蔡清彦

Min. without Portfolio 2000-; Adjunct Prof., NTU; *b.* Twn. Sept. 29, '44; *m.* Wu, Su-hwa; 1 *s.,* 1 *d.; educ.* BS, NTU 67; Ph.D., U. of Utah 72; Postdr. Fel., Nat. Cent. for Atmospheric Res., USA 72-73; Res. Fel., Harvard U. 73-74; Assc. Prof., NTU 74-78, Prof., 78-89, Chmn., Dept. of Atmospheric Sc. 82-88; Dir.-Gen., Cent. Weather Bu., MOTC 89-94; Dir.-Gen., Civil Aeronautics Admin., MOTC 95-96; V. Chmn., NScC 96-2000. *Publ.:* More than 50 papers in domestic & intl. jour.; *Add.* 19th Fl., 106 Ho Ping E. Rd., Sect. 2, Taipei 106.

TSAY, JAW-YANG 蔡兆陽

Min. without Portfolio 98-2000, & concur. Chmn., Public Construction Com., Exec. Yuan 99-2000; *b.* Twn. Jan. 2, '41; *m.* Wei, Shu-hui; 1 *s.; educ.* BE, NCKU 63; Studied, Hygienic Engr., Calif. State U. 73; Resr., MIT 93; Sect. Chief, TPG 74-76; Acting Dir., TCG 76-78; Dep. Dir.-Gen., Construction Dept., TPG 79-81, Dir.-Gen., 81-88; Dir.-Gen., MOI 88-91; Admin. V. Min. of Trans. & Comms. 94-96, Min. 96-98; *Add.* 9th Fl., 4 Chung Hsiao W. Rd., Sect. 1, Taipei 100.

TSENG, CHIANG-YUAN 曾江源

Dir., Nat. Dr. Sun Yat-sen Memorial Hall 97-; *b.* Twn. June 18, '34; *m.* Lai, Hwei-mei; 1 *s.,* 2 *d.; educ.* Taichung Tchrs.' Coll. 54; Educ. Inst., NTNU 69; BA, Tamkang Arts Coll. 75; Nat. Yokohama U. 82; Prin., Hsi Ling Elementary Sch. 68-69; Sp., Dept. of Tech. & Voc. Educ., MOE 74, Sect. Chief 74-83, Sr. Sp. 83-88, Dep. Dir. 88-89, Educ. Sup., & Chmn., Ovs. Ch. Educ. Cttee. 89-97; *Add.* 505 Jen Ai Rd., Sect. 4, Taipei 110.

TSENG, CHIH-LANG

(See TZENG, OVID J.L. 曾志朗)

TSENG, CHING-YUAN 曾慶源

Dir.-Gen., TECO in San Francisco 98-; *b.* Peking Aug. 7, '48; *m.* Chang, Shu-ying; 2 *d.; educ.* BA, Ch. Cul. Coll. 70; MA, NCCU 74; MA, Intl. Rel., Columbia U. 85, Cert. of the W. Averell Harriman Inst. for Advanced Study of the Soviet Union 87; V. Consul, Consl.-Gen. in New York City 77-79; Sect. Chief in charge of USSR desk, MOFA 82-84; Dep. Dir.-Gen., CCNAA in Chicago 89-93; Dep. Dir., Dept. of W. Asian Aff., MOFA 93-96; Dep. Rep., Rep. Off. in Moscow 96-98. *Publ.: On the Rel. Between the E. European Countries & the PRC; Add.* 555 Montgomery St., Suite 501, San Francisco, CA 94111, USA.

TSENG, HUA-SUNG 曾華松

Grand Justice, Jud. Yuan 94-; *b.* Twn. June 7, '36; *m.* Liang, Shu-yun; 2 *s.,* 1 *d.; educ.* LL.B., Twn. Prov. Law & Com. Coll. 59; Attorney-at-Law 61; Judge, Dist. Court 63-64, Prosecutor 64-71; Judge, Dist. Court 71-72, Twn. High Court 72-79; Justice, Admin. Court 79-85, Divisional Chief Justice 85-94. *Publ.: Admin. Litigation on Taxation; Admin. Litigation on Trademark Law; Admin. Court's Judgments on Re-measurement of Land Chart; Comparative Study of ROC & PRC Admin. Trial; Add.* 4th Fl., 124 Chungking S. Rd., Sect. 1, Taipei 100.

TSENG, IKE 曾鼎煌

Bd. Chmn., Merida Ind. Co. Ltd. 72-; Exec. Dir., Long Bon Construction Co. Ltd. 88-, & Chief Construction Corp. 89-; Bd. Mem., United Epitaxy Co. Ltd. 93-; *b.* Twn. Dec. 14, '32; *m.* Lin, Hsiu-feng; 1 *s.,* 1 *d.; educ.* High Sch. Grad.; V. Pres., Far E. Mach. Co. Ltd. 52-57; Bd. Chmn., Far Great Plastic Ind. Co. Ltd. 57-72; Pres., Merida Ind. Co. Ltd. 72-74; *Add.* 116 Mei Kang Rd., Meikang Village, Tatsun, Changhua County 515.

TSENG, JAMES T.T. 曾宗廷

Nat. Policy Adv. to the Pres. 96-; Counsl., Exec. Yuan 93-; Attorney-at-Law 59-; *b.* Twn. Oct. 31, '33; *m.* Tsai, Shirley; 2 *s.,* 1 *d.; educ.* LL.B., NTU 57; Mem., Tainan CoCoun. 64-72; Pres., Rotary Club of Taipei S. 82-83; Pres., Nat. Bar Assn. 92-93; *Add.* 15th Fl., 168 Tun Hua N. Rd., Taipei 105.

TSENG, TANG-KUANG 曾騰光

Pres., Chaoyang U. of Tech. 94-; *b.* Twn. Mar. 9, '38; *m.* Chen, Hsiu-ling; 1 *s.; educ.* BA, Sociology, Tunghai U. 67; Ed.M., Oklahoma City U. 87; Ed.D., Drake U., USA 91; Sect. Chief, Soc. Youth Services, Tainan City Cttee., Ch. Youth Corps 69-71, Sec.-Gen., Chiayi County Cttee. 71-74, V. Sect. Chief, Soc. Youth Services, Taipei Hqs. 75-78, Dir. 78-91; Adjunct Lectr., Ch. Cul. U. 88-89; Adjunct

Assc. Prof., NCCU 91-92; Assc. Prof. & concur. Dean of Student Aff., Tunghai U. 92-94. *Publ.: A Study of the Effect of a Counseling Tng. Prog. on Job Satisfaction of Volunteer Counsl.; A Study of the Perception of Characteristics of Voluntary Work & Willingness to Participate in Voluntary Work Among Coll. Students; A Study of the Sup. & Mng. of Volunteers; Add.* 168 Chi Feng E. Rd., Wufeng, Taichung County 413.

TSENG, TENG-KUANG
(See TSENG, TANG-KUANG 曾騰光)

TSENG, TING-HUANG
(See TSENG, IKE 曾鼎煌)

TSENG, TSUNG-TING
(See TSENG, JAMES T.T. 曾宗廷)

TSENG, YUNG-FU 曾勇夫
Pol. V. Min. of Justice 99-; *b.* Twn. Jan. 12, '43; *m.* Ou, Nuan; 3 *d.; educ.* LL.B., NTU 66; Pers. Off., Dept. of Finance, TPG 70-73; Judge, Chiayi Dist. Court; Public Prosecutor, & Div. Chief Public Prosecutor, Public Prosecutor's Off., Taichung Dist. Court 73-77; Public Prosecutor, Public Prosecutor's Off., Twn. Superior Court 77-84; Prosecutor-Gen., Public Prosecutor's Off., Kinmen, & Taitung, & Yunlin, & Chiayi, & Tainan Dist. Court, & Hsiamen Br., Fukien Superior Court 84-96; Div. Chief Public Prosecutor, Twn. Supreme Court; Sec.-Gen., MOJ; Prosecutor-Gen., Public Prosecutor's Off., Taipei Dist. Court 96-99; *Add.* 130 Chungking S. Rd., Sect. 1, Taipei 100.

TSO, CHI-KUO
(See TSO, PAUL J.K. 左紀國)

TSO, PAUL J.K. 左紀國
Rep., TECO in Malaysia 97-; *b.* Nanking Oct. 21, '32; *m.* Ma, Regina; 2 *s.; educ.* LL.B., NTU 55; LL.M., New York U. 59; Sp. & Sect. Chief, MOFA 62-68; 2nd Sec., Ch. Permanent Mission to the UN 68-71; 1st. Sec., Emb. in the USA 72-76; Consul, Portland, Oregon, USA 76-77; Consul-Gen., Boston 77-79; Sec.-Gen., CCNAA 79-81, Dir.-Gen.; TECO in Honolulu 81-89; Dir., Treaty & Legal Aff. Dept., MOFA 89-91; Sec.-Gen., CCNAA 91-94; Rep., TECO, Norway 94-97. *Publ.: Mem. of the Intl. Community; Add.* 9.01 Level 9, Amoda Bldg., 22 Jalan Imbi, 55100 Kuala Lumpur, Malaysia.

TSO, PAUL O.P. 曹安邦
Mem., Acad. Sinica 72-, & European Acad. of Arts, Sc. & Humanities 80-; Prof. of Biophys., Dept. of Biochem., Sch. of Hygiene & Public Health, Johns Hopkins U.; *b.* Hong Kong July 17, '29; *m.* Wong, Muriel M.Y.; 1 *s.,* 2 *d.; educ.* BS, Lingnan U. 49; MS, Michigan State U. 51; Ph.D., Calif. Inst. of Tech. 55; Res. Fel., Biology Div., Calif. Inst. of Tech. 55-61, Sr. Res. Fel. 61-62; Co-organizer (with Prof. James Bonner) of the 1st World Conf. on Histone Biology & Chem. 63; Assc. Prof., Biophys. Chem., Dept. of Radiological Sc., Johns Hopkins U. 62-67, Prof. 67-73; 1st Dir., Inst. of Molecular Biology (IMB), & concur. Chmn., IMB Adv. Cttee., Acad. Sinica 82-94; Co-organizer (with Dr. J. Dipaolo) of World Symposium on Model Studies in Chem. Carcinogenesis 72; Organizer of Intl. Symposium on Molecular Biology of Mannalian Genetic Apparatus 75; Co-organizer (with Prof. B. Pullman & Dr. E.L. Schneider) of Jerusalem Symposium on Carcino-Genesis-Fundam. Mech. & Environmental Effects 80; Organizer, Symposium on Establishment of a Bioassay System for Risk Assessment in Energy Tech. 82; Organizer, 4th Gen. Meeting of European Expert Cttee. on Biophys., UNESCO 82; Co-organizer (with Prof. C. Nicolini), 4th Course of Intl. Sch. Pure & Applied Biostructure, NATO Adv. Study Inst. 83; Co-organizer (with Prof. B. Pullman & Dr. E.L. Schneider), Jerusalem Symposium on Interrelation Among Differentiation, Cancer, & Aging 85; Organizer, Intl. Conf. on Nucleic Acid Med. Applications, Mexico 93. *Publ.:* Over 350 sc. papers, 13 bk., & 40 reviews; *Add.* Cell Works Inc., TEC Bldg. 1, 5202 Westland Boulevard, Baltimore, MD 21227-2349, USA.

TSONG, TIEN T. 鄭天佐
Disting. Res. Fel. 92-; Mem. Acad. Sinica 92-; *b.* Twn. Sept. 6, '34; *m.* Tsong, Miaw F.; 3 *d.; educ.* BS, Phys., NTNU 60; MS, Phys., Penn. State U. 64, Ph.D. 66; Postdr. Resr., Phys. Dept., Penn. State U. 67-69, Asst. Prof. 69-71, Assc. Prof. 71-75, Prof. 75-90, Disting. Prof. 90-93; Dir., Inst. of Phys., Acad. Sinica 90-99. *Publ.: Field Ion Microscopy, Principles & Applications; Field Ion Microscopy, Field Ionization & Field Evaporation; Atom-Probe Field Ion Microscopy*; & over 300 articles; *Add.* Inst. of Phys., Acad. Sinica, Taipei 115.

TSOU, CHIEN 鄒堅
Nat. Policy Adv. to the Pres. 90-; *b.* Fukien Aug. 16, '21; *m.* Pei, Linda Hsiang-yuen; 2 *s.,* 2 *d.; educ.* Ch. Naval Acad.; Royal Naval Coll., Greenwich, UK; Royal Naval Submarine Sch., UK; War CGSC, Armed Forces U.; Capt., Destroyer-14 59-60; Aide-de-Camp to the Pres. 60-64; Cmdg. Off., Naval Post Grad. Sch. 64-65; Naval AttachÇ, Emb. in the USA 65-69; Cmdr., Destroyer Squadron 69-71, Surface Force 62, & Taskforce 71-72; Chief Aide-de-Camp to the Pres. 72-75; Dep. C-in-C, ROCN 75-76, C-in-C 76-83;

Dep. Chief of the Gen. Staff, MND 83-86; Amb. to S. Korea 86-90; *Add.* 26 Lane 378, Chung Shan N. Rd., Sect. 5, Taipei 111.

TSOU, CHIH-CHUANG
(See CHOW, GREGORY CHI-CHONG 鄒至莊)

TSUANG, MING T. 莊明哲
Mem., Acad. Sinica 96-; Mem., Inst. of Med., Nat. Acad. of Sc. USA 94-; Stanley Cobb Prof. & Head, Harvard Dept. of Psychiatry at Massachusetts Mental Health Cent., & Dir., Harvard Inst. of Psychiatric Epidemiology & Genetics 93-; Fel., Royal Coll. of Psychiatrists 92-; Prof., Harvard 85-; *b.* Twn. Nov. 16, '31; *m.* Tsuang, Snow H.; 1 *s.,* 2 *d.; educ.* MD, Coll. of Med., NTU 57; Ph.D., Psychiatry, U. of London 65, D.Sc., Psychiatric Epidemiology & Genetics, Faculty of Sc. 81; Prof., U. of Iowa 75-82; Prof. & V. Chmn., Brown U. 82-85. *Publ.:* 243 reviews papers, 61 chapters, & 14 bk.; *Add.* Supt.'s Off., Mass. Mental Health Cent., 74 Fenwood Rd., Boston, MA 02115, USA.

TSUI, CHI
(See TSUI, DANIEL C. 崔琦)

TSUI, DANIEL C. 崔琦
Mem., Acad. Sinica 92-; Arthur LeGrand Doty Prof. of Elec. Engr., Princeton U. 82-; Fel., Am. Phys. Soc., & Am. Assn. for the Advancement of Sc.; *b.* Honan '39; *educ.* Ph.D., Phys., U. of Chicago 67; Res. Assc., U. of Chicago 67-68; Mem. of Tech. Staff, Bell Labs. 68-82; Buckley Prize for Condensed Matter Phys. 84; Benjamin Franklin Medal in Phys., & Nobel Prize in Phys. 98. *Publ.: Quantum Hall Effect from Finite Frequency Studies* (with L.W. Engel & Y.P. Li) 96; & many other articles; *Add.* Dept. of Elec. Engr., Princeton U., P.O. Box 5263, Princeton, NJ 08544, USA.

TSUI, LAP-CHEE 徐立之
Mem., Acad. Sinica 92-; Fel., Royal Soc. of Can. & Royal Soc. of London; Geneticist-in-Chief, Hosp. for Sick C., Toronto 96-; U. Prof., U. of Toronto 94-; Scientist & Sr. Scientist, Res. Inst., Hosp. for Sick C. 83-; H.E. Sellers Chair in Cystic Fibrosis 89-; *b.* Shanghai Dec. 21, '50; *m.* Tsui, Lan-fong; 2 *s.; educ.* B.Sc., Ch. U. of Hong Kong 72, M., Philosphy 74; Ph.D., U. of Pittsburgh 79; Resr., Biology Div., Oak Ridge Nat. Lab. 79-80, & Dept. of Genetics, Hosp. for Sick C. 81. *Publ.:* Over 240 sc. papers in peer-reviewed jour. & over 50 review articles on human genetics, cystic fibrosis, chromosome 7 mapping & lens dev.; *Add.* Dept. of Genetics, Hosp. for Sick C., 555 University Avenue, Toronto, Ontario M5G 1X8, Can.

TU, CHENG-SHENG 杜正勝
Dir., Nat. Palace Museum 2000-; Mem., Acad. Sinica 92-; *b.* Twn. June 10, '44; *m.* Chen, Fang-mei; 1 *s.,* 1 *d.; educ.* Grad., Hist. Dept., NTU 70; MA, NTU 74; Resr., London Sch. of Hist. & Pol. Sc. 74-76; Lectr., Soochow U. 76-79, Asst. Prof. 79; Asst. Resr., Acad. Sinica 80-84, Resr. 84, Dir., Inst., Hist. & Philology 84-2000 & 96-2000; Ed.-in-Chief, *New Hist. & Mainland Mag. Publ.: City-States of the Chou Dynasty; Registrating the Common People: The Making of the Traditional Ch. Pol. & Soc. Structure; State & Soc. in Ancient Ch.; The Rebirth of Hist.; The Classic & the Actual in Soc.; Add.* 221 Chih Shan Rd., Sect. 2, Waishuanghsi, Shihlin, Taipei 111.

TU, CHI-KWANG 屠繼光
Amb. to Tuvalu, & Nauru; *b.* Chekiang Apr. 20, '32; *m.* Tu Tsen, Huey-Hsien; 1 *s.; educ.* LL.B., NCCU 58; LL.M., Sydney U., Australia 86; Sr. Off., MOFA 64-66; 3rd Sec., Emb. in Australia 66-70, 2nd Sec., 70-73; Sect. Chief, MOFA 73-76; Consul, Consl. Gen. in New York 76-85; Sr. Sp. & Sect. Chief, MOFA 85-86, Dep. Dir. 86-89; Rep., TECO, New Zealand 89-94; Dir., MOFA 94-96; Amb. of the ROC in Kingdom of Tonga 96-98; *Add.* P.O. Box 294, Repub. of Nauru, Cent. Pacific.

TU, CHIN-JUNG 杜金榮
Strategy Adv. to the Pres. 97-; *b.* Chekiang Nov. 21, '32; *m.* Chen, Yu-hui; 2 *s.; educ.* BA, Mil. Acad. 55; War CGSC, Armed Forces U. 75; Div. Cmdr.; Dep. Army Cmdr., Army Logistics Cmd.; Dir., Dept. of Inspection, MND, Dep. Chief of the Gen. Staff, Dir.-Gen., Gen. Pol. Warfare Dept. 94-97; *Add.* 22 Lane 98, An Chu St., Taipei 106.

TU, CHIUNG-FENG
(See DUO, JEONG-FEONG 杜炯烽)

TU, CHU-SHENG
(See TOU CHOU-SENG 杜筑生)

TU, SHAN-LIANG 杜善良
Sec.-Gen., Control Yuan 99-; *b.* Kaohsiung Aug. 28, '40; *m.* Chang, Kuei-ying; 2 *s.,* 1 *d.; educ.* LL.B., NCCU 65, MPA 69; Sect. Chief, RDEC 72-78, Sr. Resr. & concur. Sect. Chief 76-78; Sr. Sp., CEPD 78-81, Dep. Dir. 81-87, Dir. 87-95; Counsl. & Dir., 1st Dept., Exec. Yuan 95-98; Adv. to Exec. Yuan & Exec. Sec., Off. in S. Twn., Exec. Yuan. *Publ.: Evaluation of Econ. Dev. Plans; Problems of Public Construction Projects & Countermeasures; Add.* 2 Chung Hsiao E. Rd., Sect. 1, Taipei 100.

TU, TE-CHI
(See TU, TEH-CHI 涂德錡)

TU, TEH-CHI 涂德錡
Dep. Sec.-Gen., CC, KMT 93-2000; *b.* Twn. Nov. 28, '34; *m.* Lin, Chun-lan; 2 *s.,* 1 *d.; educ.* Grad., Twn. Prov. Tainan Normal Sch. 53; Res., Grad. Sch. of PA, Tunghai U.; Primary Sch. Tchr. 53-60; Asst. Sec., Chiayi County Govt. 60-62; Chief Admin., Chiayi City Off. 62-64; Sup., Chiayi County Govt. 64-68; Clerk, Twn. Prov. Cttee., KMT 68-70, Sec., Yunlin County Cttee. 70-71, Chmn., Taitung & Changhua County Cttee. 71-76, Chmn., Twn. Prov. Cttee. 76-77; Magis., Chiayi County 77-85; Comr., TPG 86-90; V. Chmn., Twn. Prov. Cttee., KMT 90-92; Comr., Dept. of Civil Aff., TPG 92-93; Acting Gov., TPG 93; Chmn., Twn. Prov. Cttee., KMT 93-94, Dir.-Gen., Dept. of Org. Aff., KMT 94-95; Min. without Portfolio 95-97; Nat. Policy Adv. to the Pres. 97-98. *Publ.: A Trip to the US; I Love My Home; Add.* 359 Yung An St., Chiayi 600.

TUNG, HSIANG-FEI 董翔飛
Grand Justice, Jud. Yuan 94-; Adjunct Prof., NCHU 94-; *b.* Kiangsu July 21, '33; *m.* Shen, Jung; 2 *s.,* 1 *d.; educ.* LL.B., NCHU 58; LL.M., NCCU 69; Visiting Scholar, Calif. State U., Sonoma 86; Dep. Dir., Dept. of Civil Aff., MOI 69-79; Dep. Sec.-Gen., CEIC 72-78; Assc. Prof., NCHU 79-83, Prof. 83-95, Chmn., Dept. of PA 80-93, Sec.-Gen. 93-94; Mem., NA 92-94; Adjunct Prof., NCCU, NTNU, Tunghai U. & Soochow U. *Publ.: A Theory of Local Self-Govt.; The Const. & Govt. of the ROC; Add.* 9th Fl.-3, 226 Fu Hsing N. Rd., Taipei 105.

TUNG, SHENG-NAN
(See TONG, SHEN-NAN 童勝男)

TZEN, WEN-HUA 鄭文華
Rep., Taipei Rep. Off. in the UK 97-; *b.* Twn. May 30, '36; *m.* Chang, Mei-yu; 2 *d.; educ.* BA, NTU 58; MA, U. of Hawaii 63; Staff Mem., MOFA 63-66; V. Consul, Consl., Cebu 66-68; Sect. Chief, Dept. of African Aff., MOFA 68-73; 1st Sec., Emb. in Swaziland 73-78; Rep. to New Zealand 78-84; Dep. Dir., Dept. of African Aff., MOFA 84-86, Dir., Dept. of E. Asian & Pacific Aff. 86-87; Rep., Taipei Econ. & Trade Off. in Indonesia 87-91; Dep. Rep., CCNAA, Off. in Washington, D.C. 91-94; Dep. Sec.-Gen., NSC 94-96; Admin. V. Min. of For. Aff. 96-97; *Add.* 50 Grosvenor Gardens, London SW1W OEB, UK.

TZENG, OVID J.L. 曾志朗
Min. of Educ. 2000-; Mem., Acad. Sinica 94-; Dean, the Coll. of Soc. Sc., NCKU 92-, Dir., Cognitive Sc. Cent. 90-; Visiting Scientist, Salk Inst. for Biological Sc., La Jolla 83-; *b.* Twn. Sept. 8, '44; *m.* Hung, Daisy Lan; 1 *s.; educ.* BA, NCCU 66, MA 69; Ph.D., Penn. State U. 73; Visiting Assc. Prof., UC-Berkly. 78-79, the Haskins Lab., Yale U. 80-81; Visiting Prof., NTU 84-85; Prof., U. of Calif., Riverside 80-94; V. Pres. Nat. Yang-ming U. 97-99, Pres., 99-2000. *Publ.:* Co-author of "Cross-Linguistic Studies of Aphasia: A Ch. Perspective," *Handbk. of Ch. Psychology;* "The Classifier Problem in Ch. Aphasia," *Brain & Lang.;* "Lateralization of Reading: Neurolinguistic Studies on Writing Systems," *Oxford Intl. Encyclopedia of Linguistics; Add.* 5 Chung Shan S. Rd., Taipei 104.

WAN, CHI-CHAO 萬其超
Sec.-Gen., K.T. Li Found. 92-; Prof., Dept. of Chem. Engr., NTHU 80-; *b.* Nanking July 12, '47; *m.* Pai, I-min; 2 *d.; educ.* BS, NTU 69; MS, Columbia U. 72, D.Sc. 74; *Add.* P.O. Box 7-936, Taipei 106.

WANG, ADRIAN M.T. 王曼肇
V. Chmn., AEC 93-; *b.* Ch. June 6, '47; *m.* Wu, Mei-luen; 1 *s.,* 1 *d.; educ.* BS, Phys., Tamkang U. 73; MS, Phys., Florida Inst. of Tech. 75; Ph.D., Phys., U. of Alabama 82; Asst. Prof., Judson Coll., USA 81-82, & U. of Alabama 82-84; Assc. Prof., Nat. Yang Ming Med. Coll. 85-90, & Nat. Def. Med. Cent. 86-90; Consultant, Veterans Gen. Hosp. 85-90; Dir., AEC 90-92; *Add.* 67 Lane 144, Keelung Rd., Sect. 4, Taipei 106.

WANG, BILL 江萬里
Pres., CNA 97-; *b.* Chungking Nov. 20, '45; *m.* Wang, Eileen; 2 *s.; educ.* BA, NCCU 68; MA, Cent. Michigan U. 75; MPA, Harvard U. 90; Reporter, CNA 69-77, Corr. 77-82, Dir., For. News Dept. 84-87; V. Pres. & Mng. Ed., *Ch. News* 87-89; V. Pres., CNA 90-92, Chief, Washington Bu. 92-97; *Add.* 209 Sungking Rd., Taipei 104.

WANG, C.C. 王正中
Mem., Acad. Sinica 92-; Prof., U. of Calif., San Francisco 81-; *b.* Peking Feb. 10, '36; *m.* Lee, Alice; 1 *s.,* 1 *d.; educ.* BS, NTU 58; Ph.D., Biochem., UC-Berkly. 66; Postdr. Fel., Columbia U. 66-67, Princeton U. 67-69; Sr. Investigator, Merck & Co. Inc. 69-81; Dir., Inst. of Molecular Biology, Acad. Sinica 91-94. *Publ.:* 150 peer-reviewed papers, 40 bk. chapters, 130 abstracts, & 8 patents; *Add.* 22 Miraloma Drive, San Francisco, CA 94127, USA.

WANG, CHAO-CHEN 王兆振
Mem., Acad. Sinica 68-; *b.* Chiangsu Oct. 20, '14; 1 *d.; educ.* BEE, NCTU, Shanghai 36; MS, Harvard U. 38, D.Sc. 40; Res. Engr., Westinghouse Elec., USA 41-45; Res. Engr.

& Chief Scientist, Sperry Gyroscope Corp., USA 47-73; Fel., Inst. of Elec. & EE 57; Fel., Am. Assn. for the Advancement of Sc. 61; Victor Emanuel Disting. Prof., Cornell U. 60-61; Visiting Prof., NCTU 60-68; Pres., Ind. Tech. Res. Inst. 73-77; *Add.* 12 Chestnut Ridge Rd., Holmdel, NJ 07733, USA.

WANG, CHAO-MAO 王朝茂
Pres., Fortune Inst. of Tech. 96-; Chmn., Bd. of Kao-shih Found. 91-; *b.* Kaohsiung Apr. 18, '38; *m.* Shue, Shi-lin; 2 *s.; educ.* Studied at Tainan Normal Sch. 57; BA, Tamkang Coll. of Arts & Sc. 64; M., Nat. Kaohsiung Normal U. 84, Ed.D. 94; Elementary Sch. Tchr., 54-57; Jr. & Sr. High Sch. Tchr. 65-79; High Sch. Prin. 79-96; Lectr. & Assc. Prof. 91-96; Pres. of Jr. Coll. 96-99. *Publ.: The Study of EMR Students' Adaptive Behaviors & Achievement Motivation; The Study of Tchrs.' Irrational Belief & Their Implication Factors; Educ. of Elementary Sch. in Japan & Korea; Belief's Inventory of Tchrs.; The Study of Hermeneutics; Secondary Edu.; Add.* 14 Lane 164, Nen Chiang St., Sanming, Kaohsiung 807.

WANG, CHEN-KU 王振鵠
Mem., CCA 86-; Ed., *Jour. of Lib. & Info. Sc.* 75-; Adjunct Prof., NTU 64-; *b.* Hopei July 18, '24; *m.* Wang, Shuo-fen; 2 *s.,* 1 *d.; educ.* MA, George Peabody Coll., Vanderbilt U.; Hon. LL.D., Ohio U. 88; Prof., & Lib. 60-77; Dir., Dept. of Soc. Educ., NTNU 72-77; Dir., Nat. Cent. Lib. 77-89; Dir., Cent. for Ch. Studies 81-89. *Publ.: Selection & Acquisition of Lib. Materials; Librarianship in the USA; Collected Essays on Lib. Sc.; Add.* 6th Fl., 28 Alley 6, Lane 118, Ho Ping E. Rd., Sect. 2, Taipei 106.

WANG, CHENG-CHUNG
(See WANG, C.C. 王正中)

WANG, CHIA-YI 王甲乙
Nat. Policy Adv. to the Pres. 97-; *b.* Twn. Oct. 29, '26; *m.* Lin, Tung-hsin; 2 *s.,* 2 *d.; educ.* Judges & Prosecutors Tng. Inst.; Hon. LL.D., New Coll. of Calif. 85; Judge, Dist. Court & Twn. High Court 56-65; Chief Prosecutor, Dist. Court 65-67; Presiding Judge, Twn. High Court 67-72; Justice & concur. Chief of the Supreme Court 72-76; Pol. V. Min. of Justice 76-80; Pres. Admin. Court 80-87; Sec.-Gen., Jud. Yuan 87-93; Chief Justice, Supreme Court 93-96; Exec. Dir., Judges' Assn., ROC 96-97. *Publ.: Revised Civil Procedure; A Study of Civil Procedure; Add.* 10 Alley 1, Lane 24, Jen Ai Rd., Sect. 3, Taipei 106.

WANG, CHIEN-HSUAN
(See WANG, CHIEN-SHIEN 王建煊)

WANG, CHIEN-SHIEN 王建煊
NP Candidate, 1998 Election for Taipei City Mayor; Chmn., Ch. Mng. Assn. 90-; *b.* Anhwei Aug. 7, '38; *m.* Su, Fa-jau; *educ.* BA, NCKU 61; MA, NCCU 65; Intl. Taxation Prog., Harvard U. 71; Sr. Sp., Taxation & Tariff Com., MOF 71-73, Dir., 1st Div., Dept. of Taxation 73-76; Dir., 4th Dept., Exec. Yuan 76-80; Dir.-Gen., Dept. of Customs Admin., MOF 80-82, Public Finance Tng. Inst. 82-84; Admin. V. Min. of Econ. Aff. 84-89; Pol. V. Min. of Econ. Aff. 89-90; Min. of Finance 90-92; Convener, NP 94-98; Mem., Legis. Yuan 93-98. *Publ.: A Study of the Depreciation Systems for Business; Income Tax; A Study of the Income Tax; Tax Acct.; Taxation Law; Add.* 4th Fl., 65 Kuang Fu S. Rd., Taipei 110.

WANG, CHI-KUNG 王紀鯤
Prof., Architecture, Tamkang U. 86-; Architect, 77-; *b.* Nanking Nov. 13, '36; *m.* Pai, Ling; 1 *s.,* 1 *d.; educ.* B., Civil Engr., NCKU 62; M. Arch., Cranbrook Acad. of Art 71; Res., Urban Planning, Washington U.; Assc. Prof., Fengchia U.; Designer, H.E. Hwang Architect & Assc.; Chief Designer, Haigo Architect & Assc. 85-86; Head, Dept. of Architecture & concur. Dir., Grad. Sch. of Architecture, Tamkang U. 86-92. *Publ.: Res. of the Jury System of the Educ. of Architecture 99; The Subcul. of Design Studio in the Educ. of Architecture 98; Types of Architect Practice & Responsibilities 97; Add.* 3th Fl., 101 Aikuo E. Rd., Taipei 106.

WANG, CHIH-KANG 王志剛
Min. of Econ. Aff. 96-2000; Mem., CSC, KMT 99-; Prof., Sch. of Business, NTU 78-; *b.* Hopei Sept. 7, '42; *m.* Sung, Ye-li; 1 *s.,* 1 *d.; educ.* Ph.D., Texas A&M U.; Lectr., Business Coll., Texas A&M U. 77-78; Chmn., Dept. of Intl. Trade, NTU 85-87; Exec. Sec., Investment Com., MOEA 88-89; Dir.-Gen., Dept. of Com. 89-90; Admin. V. Min. of Econ. Aff. 90-92; Chmn., Fair Trade Com., Exec. Yuan 92-96. *Publ.: Theory of Marketing; Introduction to Business Admin.; Marketing;* etc.; *Add.* 15 Foochow St., Taipei 100.

WANG, CHIN-FENG 王慶豐
Magis., Hualien County 93-; *b.* Twn. May 7, '33; *m.* Huang, Yi-yi; 2 *s.,* 2 *d.; educ.* Grad., Hualien Sr. High Sch.; Studied in Japan & USA; Mem., Hualien CoCoun. 61-86, Spkr. 71-86; Bd. Chmn., Medium Business Bk. of Twn. 86-90; Mem., TPA 90-93; *Add.* 17 Fu Chien Rd., Hualien 970.

WANG, CHIN-PING
(See WANG, JIN-PYNG 王金平)

WANG, CHING-FENG
(See WANG, CHIN-FENG 王慶豐)

WANG, CHO
(See WANG, JAMES C. 王倬)

WANG, CHUN 王郡
Dir.-Gen., Coast Guard Admin., Exec. Yuan 2000-; *b*. Twn. Aug. 13, '36; *m*. Lin, Su-o; 2 *s.*, 1*d.; educ*. Grad., 31st Regular Class, Cent. Police Coll., MOI 64; Dir., Taitung County's Police Dept., Nat. Police Admin. of MOI 89-91, Dep. Comr. & Comr., Criminal Investigation Bu. 91-92 & 94-95, Cmdt., 7th Peace Preservation Police Corps 92-94; Dir., Kaohsiung Police Hqs., Kaohsiung City Govt. 95-97; Dep. Dir.-Gen., Nat. Police Admin., MOI 97-2000; *Add*. 296 Hsing Lung Rd., Sect. 3, Wenshan, Taipei 116.

WANG, CHUNG-YU 王鍾渝
Chmn. of the Bd., Ch. Steel Corp. 93-; Mng. Dir., Bk. of Kaohsiung 97-; Dir. of the Exec. Cttee., Intl. Iron & Steel Inst. 93-; *b*. Kiangsu Apr. 1, '45; *m*. Wang, Dai Li-sa; 1 *s.*, 1 *d.; educ*. BS, Chung Yuan Christian U. 68; Gen. Mgr., Marketing Dept., Ch. Steel Corp. 82-84, Asst. V. Pres., Cml. Div. 84-86; CEO, Com. of Nat. Corp., MOEA 91-92; Pres., Ch. Steel Corp. 92-93; *Add*. 1 Chung Kang Rd., Lin Hai Ind. Dist., Hsiaokang, Kaohsiung 812.

WANG, CORA L.S. 王力行
Pub. & Ed.-in-Chief, *Global Views Monthly* 86-, & *Commonwealth Mag.* 82-; *b*. Chungking Oct. 16, '45; *m*. Chang, Tsuan-sheng; 2 *s.; educ*. BA, NCCU 67; Mng. Ed., *Women's Mag.* 72-78; Dir., *Ch. Times* (Hong Kong Off.) 78-80; Dep. Ed.-in-Chief, *Ch. Times Mag.* 80-81; Dep. Ed.-in-Chief, *Commonwealth Mag.* 81-86. *Publ.: Meeting the Influential; With a Clear Conscience; Dedication: In Search of Vision; Add*. 2nd Fl., 1 Lane 93, Sungkiang Rd., Taipei 104.

WANG, FEI
(See WANG, STEVEN F. 王飛)

WANG, HO-HSIUNG 王和雄
Grand Justice, Jud. Yuan 94-; *b*. Twn. Sept. 2, '41; *m*. Lin, Yueh-ling; 1 *s.*, 2 *d.; educ*. LL.D., NCCU 92; Judge, Taipei Dist. Court 71-80, Prosecutor 80-81; Prosecutor, Twn. High Court 81-82, Kinmen Dist. Court 82-83, Twn. High Court 83-87, & Supreme Court 87-88; Adv., MOJ 88-89; Prosecutor, Kinmen Br., Fukien High Court 90-93; Sec.-Gen., MOJ 93-94. *Publ.*: 30 articles on the sc. of law; *Add*. 124 Chungking S. Rd., Sect. 1, Taipei 100.

WANG, HSIAO-LAN
(See WANG, SHAW-LAN 王效蘭)

WANG, JAMES C. 王倬
Mem., Acad. Sinica 82-; Mallinckrodt Prof. in Biochem. & Molecular Biology, Harvard U. 88-; Mem., US Nat. Acad. of Sc. 86-; Fel., Am. Acad. of Arts & Sc. 84-; Mem., Ed. Bd., *Quarterly Reviews of Biophys.* 88-; *b*. Ch. Nov. 18, '36; *educ*. BS, NTU 59; MA, U. of S. Dakota 61; Ph.D., U. of Missouri 64; Asst. Instr., NTU 59-60; Res. Fel., Calif. Inst. of Tech. 64-66; Asst. Prof., Assc. Prof., & Prof. of Chem., UC-Berkly. 66-77; Mem., NIH Biophys. & Biophys. Chem. Study Sect. 72-76; Mem., Ed. Bd., *Jour. of Molecular Biology* 75-78; Prof. of Biochem. & Molecular Biology, Harvard U. 77-88; Mem., Nat. Sc. Found. Adv. Cttee. for Physiology, Cellular & Molecular Biology 80-82; Mem., Ed. Cttee., *Annual Review of Biochem.* 80-85, & Ed. Bd., *Nuclei Acids Res.* 81-85; Chmn., Dept. of Biochem. & Molecular Biology, Harvard U. 83-85; Dir., Inst. of Molecular Biology, Acad. Sinica 86-87; Mem., NIH Molecular Biology Study Sect. 87-90, Chmn. 90-91; *Add*. Fairchild Bldg., 7 Divinity Avenue, Cambridge, MA 02138, USA.

WANG, JIN-PYNG 王金平
Pres., Legis. Yuan 99-, Mem. 75-; Mem., CSC, KMT 99-; *b*. Twn. Mar. 17, '41; *m*. Chen, Tsai-lien; 1 *s.*, 2 *d.; educ*. BS, NTNU 65; Convener, Finance Cttee., Legis. Yuan; V. Chmn., Policy Cttee., CC, KMT, Chmn., Finance Cttee.; Dir., Dept. of Party-Govt. Coordination of the Legis. Yuan, & concur. Sec.-Gen., KMT Caucus; Mem., CSC, KMT; Pres., Sino-Japanese Interparliamentary Amity Assn.; V. Pres., Legis. Yuan 93-99; *Add*. 1 Chung Shan S. Rd., Taipei 100.

WANG, JUI-HSIN 王瑞駪
Mem., Acad. Sinica 66-; Einstein Prof. of Sc., State U. of New York, Buffalo 72-; *b*. Peking Mar. 16, '21; *m*. Yang, Yen-chan (deceased); 2 *d.; educ*. BS, Nat. S.W. Assc. U. 45; Ph.D., Washington U. 49; Postdr. Fel., Washington U. 49-51; Res. Fel., Yale U. 51-53, Instr., Dept. of Chem. 53-55, Asst. Prof. 55-58, Assc. Prof. 58-60, Prof. 60-62; Eugene Higgins Prof. of Chem. 62-64; Eugene Higgins Prof. of Chem. & Molecular Biophys. 64-72; Guggenheim Fel., Cambridge U. 60-61, & Yale U. 71-72; Mem., Am. Chem. Soc., Chem. Soc. (London), Am. Soc. of Biochem., Biophys. Soc., Am. Phys. Soc., Materials Res. Soc., Am. Soc. of Photobiology, & Electrochem. Soc., Sigma Xi; Fel., Am. Assn. for the Advancement of Sc. & Am. Acad. of Arts & Sc. *Publ.:* Numerous articles published in prof. jour. & chapters in several monographs; *Add*. Nat. Sc. Complex, State U. of New York at Buffalo, Buffalo, NY 14260-3000, USA.

WANG, KANG-PEI 王亢沛
Pres., Tunghai U. 95-; *b.* Fukien Dec. 10, '38; *m.* Wang Chen, Chi-hsiang; 1 *s.,* 1 *d.; educ.* BS, Tunghai U. 59; Ph.D., Temple U. 68; Prof., NTU 70-95; Pres., Ch. Phys. Soc. 77-78, 81-82 & 84-85; Visiting Prof., Cornell U. 85-86; Chmn., Dept. of Phys., NTU 91-93. *Publ.:* 34 papers; *Add.* 181 Taichung Kang Rd., Sect. 3, Taichung 407.

WANG, KUANG-TSAN
(See WANG, KUNG-TSUNG 王光燦)

WANG, KUN 汪錕
Nat. Policy Adv. to the Pres. 96-; Chmn., Joint Credit Info. Cent. 96-; Mem., CAC, KMT 97-; *b.* Kansu Jan. 9, '23; *m.* Lu, Ming-che; 1 *s.,* 2 *d.; educ.* LL.B., Econ., NCCU 48; Res. Fel., Michigan State U. 59; Nat. War Coll. 70; Sun Yat-sen Inst. on Policy Res. & Dev. 77; Statistician, Bu. of Statistics, DGBAS 48-50, Insp., Bu. of Budget 50-57, Sect. Chief, 1st Bu. 57-64, Sec. & Sr. Sp. 64-70, Dir. 70-78, Dep. Dir.-Gen. 78-90; Bd. Chmn., Intl. Trade Bldg. Corp., Taipei World Trade Cent. 90-93; Dir.-Gen., DGBAS 93-96; *Add.* 10th Fl., 2 Chungking S. Rd., Sect. 1, Taipei 100.

WANG, KUNG-TSUNG 王光燦
Disting. Res. Fel., Inst. of Biochem., Acad. Sinica 72-; Prof., Dept. of Chem., NTU 68-; *b.* Twn. Oct. 19, '29; *m.* Yang, Mei-nien; 3 *s.,* 1 *d.; educ.* BS, Chem., NTU 52; D.Sc., Tohoku U., Japan 62; Teaching Asst., Dept. of Chem., NTU 54-58, Instr. 58-64; Assc. Res. Fel., Dept. of Chem., Stanford U. 62-64; Assc. Prof., Dept. of Chem., NTU 64-68; Visiting Scientist, Hormone Res. Lab., U. of Calif., San Francisco 69-71; Res. Fel. & Dir., Inst. of Biochem., Acad. Sinica 80-86. *Publ.:* 220 papers; *Add.* 7 Lane 58, Wenchow St., Taipei 106.

WANG, LI-HSING
(See WANG, CORA L.S. 王力行)

WANG, MAN-CHAO
(See WANG, ADRIAN M.T. 王曼肇)

WANG, MAO-LING
(See WANG, MAW-LING 王茂齡)

WANG, MAW-LING 王茂齡
Prof., Dept. of Chem. Engr., & Dean, Acad. Aff., Nat. Chung Cheng U. 97-; *b.* Twn. Aug. 21, '45; *m.* Lee, You-nan; 2 *s.; educ.* BS, NCKU 67, MS 69; Ph.D., Clarkson U., USA 74; Postdr. Res., Cornell U. 74-75; Assc. Prof., NTHU 76-79; Visiting Scholar, UC-Berkly. 79-80; Prof., Dept. of

Chem. Engr., NTHU 79-97, & Chmn. 85-88. *Publ.:* 190 articles in domestic & for. sc. jour.; *Add.* Dept. of Chem. Engr., Nat. Chung Cheng U., Chiayi County 621.

WANG, MING-HSIEN
(See WANG, MING-SHEAN 王銘顯)

WANG, MING-SHEAN 王銘顯
Pres., Nat. Twn. Coll. of Arts 98-, & Prof. 93-; *b.* Twn. July 31, '42; *m.* Masako Tomotoshi; 3 *s.; educ.* BA, Tsukuba U., Japan 67; MA in Environment Design, Meiji U. 70; Lectr., Assc. Prof., Mingchi Inst. of Tech., Japan 70-76; Assc. Prof., Prof., Dir., Ind. Arts Dept. & Dean of Gen. Aff., Nat. Twn. Acad. of Arts 76-93; Visiting Prof., Tsukuba U., Japan 86-87; Prof. & Dir., Ind. Arts Dept., Nat. Twn. Coll. of Arts 93-98. *Publ.: Design Application in Traffic Sign* 86; *An Outline of Ind. Arts* 87; *Add.* 59 Ta Kuan Rd., Sect. 1, Panchiao, Taipei County 220.

WANG, NAI-CHANG 王乃昌
Pres., Far E. Coll. 99-; *b.* Shantung Feb. 1, '24; *m.* Sun, Chia-li, 1 *s.,* 3 *d.; educ.* LL.B., U. of Chinan 47; M., Kinki U., Japan 74; Hon. Dr., Lincoln U., USA 77; Tchr. 47-65; Supt. 65-67; Prof. 68-73; Pres. 73-99; *Add.* 49 Chung Hua Rd., Hsinshih, Tainan County 744.

WANG, NAI-HUNG
(See WANG, NAI-PHON 王乃弘)

WANG, NAI-PHON 王乃弘
Pres., Hungkuang Inst. of Tech. 97-; Bd. Mem., Ch. Med. Coll. 87-; Bd. Mem., ROC Hosp. Assn. 92-; Pres., Taichung Med. Assn. 93-; *b.* Twn. Sept. 7, '41; *m.* Liu, M.Y.; 3 *d.; educ.* MB, Taipei Med. Coll. 66; M., Ch. Med. Coll.; MD, Japan U.; Assc. Prof., New Jersey Med. Coll. 81-87; Pres., Kuang Ten Gen. Hosp. 87-97; *Add.* 34 Chung Chi Rd., Shalu, Taichung County 433.

WANG, NENG-JANG 王能章
Dir.-Gen., Ovs. Aff. Dept., KMT 96-; *b.* Twn. Nov. 17, '43; *m.* Liu, Yu-mei; 1 *s.,* 2 *d.; educ.* LL.B., NCCU 67; MA & Ph.D., U. of Madrid 73; Prof., Fu Jen Catholic U., Tunghai U., & Nat. Twn. Ocean U. 73-81; Adv., Ch. Youth Corps 75-76; Chmn., Keelung City Cttee., KMT 76-78, Twn. Prov. Cttee. 78-79, & Pingtung County Cttee. 79-81; Corr. in Latin Am. 81-86; Adv., A.S.P.E.C.T., & Pres., Ch. Cul. Cent., Paris 86-93; Comr., OCAC 91-93, V. Min. OCAC 93-96. *Publ.: Comparative Governmental Systems; The Policy & Admin. of Ovs. Ch. Aff.; Add.* 6th Fl., 11 Chung Shan S. Rd., Taipei 100.

WANG, PI-LI
(See WANG, PI-LY 王必立)

WANG, PI-LY 王必立
Pub., *Econ. Daily News,* Ch. Econ. News Service, *United Evening News;* CEO, United Daily News Group; *b.* Szechwan May 2, '45; 1 *s.; educ.* Grad., Cml. Coll., Waseda U., Japan; Res. at Wright State U., USA; Japan & US Corr., *Econ. Daily News* 72-73, Asst. to Pub. 73-74, V. Pres. 74-77; *Add.* 555 Chung Hsiao E. Rd., Sect. 4, Taipei 110.

WANG, SAN-CHUNG 王三重
V. Chmn., CLA 94-; *b.* Twn. May 10, '39; *m.* Liang, Feng-yi; 3 *s.,* 1 *d.; educ.* LL.B., NTU 63; Pers. Off., Employment Service Dept., Bu. of Soc. Aff., TCG 70; Sp., Secretariat, TPG 70-74, Sect. Chief, Laws & Regln. Cttee. 74-79, Sec.-Gen. 79-85; Chmn., Laws & Regln. Cttee., Kaohsiung City Govt. 85-87; V. Comr., Dept. of Soc. Aff., TPG 87-89, Dep. Sec.-Gen. 89-93; Chmn., Sup. Com. of Labor Ins. for Twn.-Fukien Area 93-94; *Add.* 15th Fl., 132 Min Sheng E. Rd., Sect. 3, Taipei 105.

WANG, SHAW-LAN 王效蘭
Pub., *Min Sheng Daily* & *United Daily News; b.* Chekiang July 7, '41; 1 *s.,* 1 *d.; educ.* Grad., World Coll. of Jour.; Université de Fribourg, Institut de Langue Française, Switzerland; Hon. Dr., Fu Jen Catholic U.; Reporter, *United Daily News* 64-78; *Add.* 555 Chung Hsiao E. Rd., Sect. 4, Taipei 110.

WANG, SHENG 王昇
Nat. Policy Adv. to the Pres. 92-; Pres., Acad. Found. for the Promotion of Ch. Modernization; *b.* Kiangsi Oct. 28, '17; *m.* Hsiung, Hui-ying; 4 *s.,* 1 *d.; educ.* Grad., 16th Class, Ch. Mil. Acad.; 1st Class, Res. Dept., Cent. Pol. Cadre Coll.; 3rd Combined Combat Class, Sun Yat-sen Inst. on Policy Res. & Dev., KMT; 4th Class, Inst. of Nat. Def. Res.; Hon. LL.D., Dankok U., S. Korea; Chief, Mil. Sect., Govt., Kan Hsiang County 41-45; Prefect, Chia Hsing Youth High Sch., MND 45-46, Insp. (Col.), Bu. of Preparatory Cadres 47-48, Cmdr. (Maj. Gen.), Pol. GP 49, Dir. (Maj. Gen.), Gen. Pol. Warfare Dept. 50-51; Asst. Cmdt. (Maj. Gen.), Pol. Staff Coll. 52-54, Cmdt. (Maj. Gen.) 54-60; Exec. Dep. Dir. (Lt. Gen.), Gen. Pol. Warfare Dept., MND 60-74, Dir. (Gen.) 74-83; Amb. to Paraguay 83-91. *Publ.: The Theory & Practice of Enlightenment; The Theory & Practice of Pol. Warfare; Dr. Sun Yat-sen's Thoughts; A Study of San-Min-Chu-I; A Tour of Am.: Outlook on Vietnam; A Comparative Study of San-Min-Chu-I & Other Isms; Leader & Nat.: A Study of the Strategy Behind Russia's Invasion of Ch.; Life & Thoughts of Pres. Chiang Kai-shek; Duties of the Intellectuals; Impressions of a Visit to the US; Add.* 5th Fl., 5 Lane 31, Wo Lung St., Taipei 106.

WANG, SHIH-YUAN
(See WANG, WILLIAM S.Y. 王士元)

WANG, SHU-CHING 王述親
Nat. Policy Adv. to the Pres. 98-; *b.* Anhwei. Nov. 23, '26; *m.* Yu, Huai-ling; 1 *s.,* 1 *d.; educ.* BBA, Feng Chia U.; Passed Sr. Civil Service Exam.; Sec., Changhua County Cttee., KMT 64-68; Chmn., Yunlin County, Tainan City, Hsinchu County & Taoyuan County Cttees., KMT 68-81; Comr., TPG 81-83; Sec.-Gen., Voc. Cttee., KMT 83-84; Sec.-Gen., & concur. V. Chmn., Twn. Prov. Cttee., KMT 84-85; Dep. Dir., Dept. of Org. Aff., CC, KMT 85-89; Chmn., Taipei Mun. Cttee., KMT 89-92; Dir.-Gen., Dept. of Org. Aff., KMT 92-93; Mem., NA 92-96; Pres., BCC 93-98; *Add.* c/o Off. of the Pres., Taipei 100.

WANG, STEVEN F. 王飛
Rep., Oficina Economica y Cul. de Taipei en Chile 90-; *b.* Kirin July 7, '38; *m.* Ta, Mary; 2 *c.; educ.* LL.B., NCCU; Princeton-in-Asia Fel., Woodrow Wilson Sch. of Public & Intl. Aff., Princeton U.; Chargé d'Affaires, Ch. Legation, Portugal 65-69; Dir., Cent. of Sun Yat-sen, Spain 73-77; Dir., Dept. of Intl. Aff., MOFA 78-82, & Dept. of European Aff. 82-85; Amb. to Swaziland 85-87; Pol. V. Min. of For. Aff. 87-89; Amb. to S. Africa 89-90; *Add.* Burgos 345, Las Condes, Santiago, Chile.

WANG, SUNG-MAO 王松茂
Exec. Sec., STAG 92-; Mem., Adv. Coun., RDEC; *b.* Twn. Nov. 3, '23; *m.* Hsu, Liu-yu; 2 *s.,* 1 *d.; educ.* BS, NTNU 51; Ph.D., Chem., Duquesne U., USA 65; Asst. to Instr., NTNU 51-61; Res. Assc., Duquesne U. 65-66; Assc. Prof. & Prof., NTHU 66-82, Dir., Inst. of Chem. 66-76, Dean of Acad. Aff. 76-82; Dir. of Planning Div. & V. Chmn., NScC 82-84; Prof., NTHU 84-87; V. Chmn., NScC 87-92. *Publ.:* 50 papers on chem., including NMR Studies of Metal Complexation, Solvent Extraction Chem., Hemocyanin & Model Compounds in Jour.: *Am. Chem. Soc., Nuclear & Inorganic Chem., Inorganic Chem. Acta,* & etc.; *Add.* 4th Fl., 7 Alley 20, Lane 96, Ho Ping E. Rd., Sect. 2, Taipei 106.

WANG, TO-NIEN 王多年
Nat. Policy Adv. to the Pres.; *b.* Antung Oct. 20, '13; 1 *s.,* 1 *d.; educ.* 10th Class, Ch. Mil. Acad.; 18th Class, Ch. Army U.; 2nd Class, Nat. Def. Coll.; US Army CGSC; Cmdr., Kinmen Def. Cmd. 61-65; Dep. C-in-C, ROC Army 65-72;

Dep. C/S, MND 72-75; C-in-C, CSF 75-78; Cmdt., Armed Forces U. 78-83; *Add.* 14 Alley 11, Lane 16, Wen Chang St., Taipei 111.

WANG, TSO-JUNG
(See WANG, TSO-YUNG 王作榮)

WANG, TSO-YUNG 王作榮
Sr. Adv. to the Pres. 99-; *b.* Hupei Jan. 6, '19; *m.* Fang, Hsin-hsiang (deceased); 2 *s.*, 1 *d.; educ.* BA, NCU 43; MA, U. of Washington 49, & Vanderbilt U., Nashville 58; Counsl. & Dir., Econ. Res. Cent., CUSA 59-63; Dir., 3rd Div., CIECD 63-65, Adv. 65-66; Chief, Ind. Studies Sect., ECAFE, UN 67-70; Prof. of Econ., NTU 53-88; Mem. (ministerial rank), Exam. Yuan 84-90; Ed.-Writer, *Ch. Times* & *Cml. Times* 64-90; Min. of Exam. 90-96; Pres., Control Yuan 96-99. *Publ.: Essays on Twn.'s Econ. Dev.; Essays on Twn.'s Econ. & Financial Problems; Twn.'s Econ. Miracle; Add.* 6th Fl., 22 Lane 116, Kuang Fu S. Rd., Taipei 106.

WANG, WAN-LI
(See WANG, BILL 汪萬里)

WANG, WEN-HSIEH
(See WANG, WEN-SHIEH 王文燮)

WANG, WEN-SHIEH 王文燮
Strategy Adv. to the Pres. 99-; *b.* Sept. 28, '32; *m.* Wang, Wen-hwa; 2 *s.*, 1 *d.; educ.* Cavalry Class, Ch. Mil. Acad. 54; Army CGSC, Armed Forces U. 66, War Coll. 73; Cmdr. (Maj. Gen.), 193rd Div., ROC Army 76-78, Dep. C/S (Maj. Gen.) for Op., GHQ 80-82, Cmdr., 69th Corps 82-83 (Lt.-Gen.), Cmdr., 43rd Corps (Lt.-Gen.), & concur. Cmdr., Penghu Def. Cmd. 83-84, C/S, GHQ (Lt.-Gen.) 84-87, Cmdr., 8th Army (Lt.-Gen.) 87-89; Dep. C-in-C, GHQ, CSF (Lt.-Gen.) 89-92; Dir., Inspection Dept., MND (Gen.) 92-93; C-in-C, GHQ, CSF (Gen.) 93-96; V. Min., MND 96-99; *Add.* 2nd Fl., 17 Lane 32, Kuang Fu S. Rd., Taipei 105.

WANG, WEN-YUAN
(See WONG, WILLIAM W. 王文淵)

WANG, WILLIAM S.Y. 王士元
Mem., Acad. Sinica 92-; Prof., Linguistics, Grad. Sch., UC-Berkly. 66-; Chair Prof. of Lang. Engr., City U. of Hong Kong; *b.* Shanghai Aug. 14, '33; 2 *s.*, 2 *d.; educ.* Ph.D., U. of Michigan 60; Prof. of Linguistics, UC-Berkly. 65-94; Fellowship from A.C.L.S., Fulbright Prog., Cent.

for Advanced Studies, at Stanford 69, at Bellagio, Italy 83. *Publ.: Explorations in Lang.; Add.* Dept. of Elect. Engr., City U. of Hong Kong, Tat Chee Avenue, Kowloon, Hong Kong.

WANG, YOU-THENG 王又曾
Chmn., Ch. Bk.; Mem., CSC, KMT 94-; Chmn., Gen. Chamber of Com. of the ROC; V. Chmn., Ch. Business Coun. of the ICC in Taipei; Hon. Chmn., Ch. Rebar Co. Ltd., Chia Hsin Food & Synthetic Fiber Co. Ltd., Union Ins. Co. Ltd., & Omni Bk. N.A., USA; *b.* Hunan Mar. 5, '27; *m.* Ching, She-ying; 6 *s.*, 2 *d.; educ.* Hunan Prov. Coll. of Com.; Hon. Dr., St. John's U., USA; *Add.* 8th Fl., 219 Chung Hsiao E. Rd., Sect. 4, Taipei 106.

WANG, YU-CHEN
(See WANG, YU-CHENG 王玉珍)

WANG, YU-CHENG 王玉珍
Pres., Hua Eng Wire & Cable Co. Ltd.; Pub., *Twn. Times; b.* Twn. Oct. 26, '43; *m.* Wu, Li-yen; 4 *c.; educ.* Grad., World Coll. of Jour.; Pub., *Twn. Times* 82-88; *Add.* 170 Chung Cheng 4th Rd., Chienchin Kaohsiung 801.

WANG, YU-TSENG
(See WANG, YOU-THENG 王又曾)

WANG, YU-YUN 王玉雲
Nat. Policy Adv. to the Pres. 88-; Sr. Adv., Twn. Fertilizer Co. Ltd. 88-; *b.* Kaohsiung Mar. 22, '25; *m.* Lee, Su-mei; 4 *s.*, 4 *d.; educ.* Grad., Sauno Jr. Coll., Japan; Mem., Kaohsiung CCoun. 58-68, Dep. Spkr. 61-64, Spkr. 64-68; V. Chmn., Kaohsiung Mun. Cttee., KMT 68-73; Mayor, Kaohsiung City 73-81; Bd. Chmn., Twn. Fertilizer Co. Ltd., & concur. V. Chmn., Com. of Nat. Corp., MOEA 81-88; *Add.* 55 Chi Nan Rd., Sect. 2, Taipei 100.

WANG, YUNG-CHING 王永慶
Bd. Chmn., Formosa Plastics Corp., Nan Ya Plastics Corp., Formosa Chem. & Fibre Corp., & Cyma Plywood & Lumber Co. Ltd.; Chmn., Ming-chi Inst. of Tech., Chang Gung Memorial Hosp., & Chang Gung U.; *b.* Twn. Jan. 18, '17; *m.* Wang, Yueh-lan; 2 *s.*, 8 *d.; Add.* 201 Tun Hua N. Rd., Taipei 105.

WAY, E. LEONG 梁棟材
Mem., Acad. Sinica 80-; Prof. Emeritus, U. of Calif., San Francisco 87-; *b.* Ch. July 10, '16; *m.* Li, Madeline; 1 *s.*, 1 *d.; educ.* BS, MS & Ph.D., UC-Berkly. & U. of Calif., San Francisco; Pharmaceutical Chemist, Merck & Co., USA 42-43; Instr., George Washington U. 43-46, Asst. Prof. 46-48; Asst. Prof., U. of Calif., San Francisco 49-52, Assc.

Prof. 52-57, Prof. 57-87, V. Chmn. 57-67, Acting Chmn. 66-67, Chmn. 73-78; Tsumura Prof., Neuropsychopharmacology, Gunma U., Japan 89-90; Sr. Staff Fel., Nat. Inst. on Drug Abuse 90-91. *Publ.: New Concepts in Pain; Fundamentals of Drug Metabolism & Drug Disposition; The Biologic Disposition of Morphine & Its Surrogates; Endogenous & Exogenous Opiate Agonists & Antagonists;* sc. reviews & 400 original articles on drug metabolism, analgetics, dev. pharmacology, drug tolerance, dependence & Ch. materia medica; *Add.* Dept. of Pharmacology, U. of Calif., San Francisco, CA 94143-0450, USA.

WEA, CHI-LIN 魏啓林
Sec.-Gen., Exec. Yuan 2000-; Dir.-Gen., CPA 97-; Prof., Grad. Inst. of Business Admin., NTU 93-; *b.* Twn. Dec. 23, '47; 1 *s.; educ.* BBA, NCHU 70; M., Mng. Sc., Imperial Coll., U. of London, UK 77; Dr. of Human Sc., U. of Paris, France 81; Assc. Res. Fel., Intl. Div., Chung Hua Inst. for Econ. Res. 82-85; Assc. Prof. & Dir., Dept. of Intl. Trade, Tamkang U. 85-87; Assc. Prof. & Prof., Dept. of Intl. Trade, NTU 87-90, Prof. & Dir. 90-92, Prof. & Dir., Dept. & Grad. Inst. of Intl. Business 92 93; Mem., Bd. of Dir., SEF 93-96; Sec.-Gen., Interparty Caucus for the Promotion of Financial & Econ. Legislation, Legis. Yuan 96-97; Chmn., RDEC 99-2000, *Add.* Exec. Yuan, 1 Chung Hsiao E. Rd., Sect. 1, Taipei 100.

WEI, CHI-LIN
(See WEA, CHI-LIN 魏啓林)

WEI, CHIEN-KUANG
(See WEI, JAMES 韋潛光)

WEI, DUAN 韋端
Dir.-Gen., DGBAS 96-2000; *b.* Kwangsi Feb. 12, '49; *m.* Cheng, Su-ming; 2 *d.; educ.* BS, NTHU 71; MS, U. of S. Carolina 75, Ph.D. 77; Prof., Nat. Sun Yat-Sen U. 80-83; Dir., Dept. of Statistics, VAC 81-84; Dep. Dir., 3rd Bu., DGBAS 84-86, Dir. 86-92; Dir., Dept. of Budget, Acct. & Statistics, TCG 92-93; Dep. Dir.-Gen., DGBAS 93-96. *Publ.: Laws of Large No. of Tight Random Elements in Normed Linear Spaces; Nat. Sec., Nat. Def. & Econ. Dev.; Practical World Almanac; Practical Soc. Indicator; On the Structure of Public Expenditure; Add.* 1 Chung Hsiao E. Rd., Sect. 1, Taipei 100.

WEI, HAI-MING 魏海敏
Ch. Opera Actress 79-; Dir., Ch. Opera Assn. of the ROC 90-; Chmn., Taipei Ch. Opera Soc. 90-; *b.* Taipei Nov. 13, '57; *m.* Wong, Kwok-yue; 1 *s.,* 1 *d.; educ.* Grad., Hai-kuang Ch. Opera Sch. 78; Nat. Twn. Acad. of Arts 86;

Performed in *The Kingdom of Desire* (a Ch. adoption of *Macbeth*), *War & Eternity* (a Ch. adoption of *Hamlet*) with the Contemporary Legend Theatre; *Add.* 3rd Fl., 203 Sung Jen Rd., Taipei 110.

WEI, JAMES 韋潛光
Mem., Acad. Sinica 82-; Dean, Sch. of Engr. & Applied Sc., Princeton U. 91-; Pres., Am. Inst. of Chem. Engr. 88-; *b.* Shanghai Dec. 7, '30; *m.* Fang, Virginia; 4 *c.; educ.* NCTU, Shanghai; BS, Georgia Inst. of Tech. 52; D.Sc., MIT 55; Engr., Mobil Oil Co. 55-70; Prof., U. of Delaware 71-77; Prof. & Head, Dept. of Chem. Engr., MIT 78-91; V. Pres., Am. Inst. of Chem. Engr. 87-88. *Publ.: Structure of Chem. Process Ind.; Add.* Engr. Quadrangle, Princeton U., Olden Avenue, Princeton, NJ 08544-5263, USA.

WEI, TUAN
(See WEI, DUAN 韋端)

WEI, YUNG 魏鏞
Mem., CC, KMT 93-; Prof., NCTU 90-; Bd. Chmn. & Pres. of Policy Res. Inst., Vanguard Found. 91-; Mem., IISS, London 81-; *b.* Hupei May 5, '37; *m.* Sun, Serena Ning; 2 *d.; educ.* LL.B., NCCU 59; MA, U. of Oregon 63, Ph.D. 67; Instr. & Asst. Prof., Dept. of Pol. Sc., U. of Nevada 66-68; Asst. Prof., Dept. of Pol. Sc., Memphis State U. 68-69, Assc. Prof. 69-74, Prof. 74-76; NSF Visiting Scholar, Survey Res. Cent., U. of Michigan 69; Visiting Assc. Prof., NCCU 70-71; Nat. Fel., Hoover Inst., Stanford U. 74-75; Dep. Dir., Inst. of Intl. Rel., NCCU 75-76; Visiting Scholar, Brookings Inst. 77; Chmn., RDEC 76-88; Chancellor, Sun Yat-sen Inst. on Policy Res. & Dev. 88-90; Mem., Legis. Yuan 92-95. *Publ.: The Nature & Methods of the Soc. Sc.; Twn.: A Modernizing Ch. Soc.; Pol. Dev. in the ROC on Twn.; Analysis & Projections; A Methodological Critique of Current Studies on Ch. Pol. Cul.; Policy Planning: Theories & Practice; Sc., Elite, & Modernization; Striving for a Future of Growth, Equality, & Sec.; Add.* 4th Fl., 15 Chi Nan Rd., Sect. 1, Taipei 100.

WEN, SHING-CHUN 溫興春
Nat. Policy Adv. to the Pres. 96-; Prin., Mei Ho Jr. Coll. of Nursing & Admin., Pingtung 90-; *b.* Twn. Nov. 16, '26; *m.* Wen Chung, Den-mei; 1 *s.; educ.* BE, NTNU 51; Prin., Pingtung's Chung Cheng, Kaohsiung's Fenghsi, & Pingtung's Ming Cheng & Chih Cheng Jr. High Sch. 66-70, 70-74, 75-82, & 82-84; Prin., Pingtung's Chaochow Sr. High Sch. 84-85, Yunlin's Peikang Agr. & Ind. Voc. High Sch. 85-87; Mem., Legis. Yuan 87-90; *Add.* 88 Min Hsueh Rd., Pingtung 900.

WENG, CHENG-I 翁政義
Pres., NCKU 97-, Prof. 80-; Chmn., Aviation Safety Coun. 98-; *b.* Twn. Apr. 9, '44; *m.* Chen, Pi-yuen; 1 *s.,* 1 *d.; educ.* BS, NCKU 66; MS & Ph.D., U. of Rochester, USA; Res. Assc., U. of Rochester 72-73; Assc. Prof., NCKU 73-77; Prof. & Head, Dept. of Mech. Engr., NCTU 77-80, & NCKU 80-86; Prof. & Dir., Tjing Ling Mfg. Cent. 86-88; Chmn., Twn. Mach. Mfg. Co. 88-89; Dean of Acad. Aff., NCKU 89-94; Bd. Mem., Twn. Mach. Mfg. Co. 85-96. *Publ.:* Over 100 acad. jour. & conf. papers; *Add.* 1 Ta Hsueh Rd., Tainan 701.

WENG, CHI-HUI
(See WONG, CHI-HUEY 翁啓惠)

WENG, YUEH-SHENG 翁岳生
Pres., Jud. Yuan 99-; Prof., NTU 70-; *b.* Twn. July 1, '32; *m.* Chuan, Shu-chen; 3 *d.; educ.* LL.B., NTU; D.J., Heidelberg U., W. Germany; Assc. Prof., NTU 66-70; Comr., Legal Com., Exec. Yuan 71-72, & RDEC 72; Visiting Prof., Sch. of Law, U. of Washington 91; Grand Justice, Jud. Yuan 72-99. *Publ.: Die Stellung der Justiz im Verfassungsrecht der Republik Ch.; Admin. Law & Rule of Law; Admin. Law & Jud. in a State under the Principle of the Rule of Law; Add.* 19 Alley 9, Lane 143, Chun Kung Rd., Taipei 116.

WHANG-PENG, JACQUELINE 彭汪嘉康
Mem., Acad. Sinica 84-, Adv. Cttee., Lab. of Biomed. Sc. 85-; Chief, Cytogenetic Oncology Sect., Med. Br., NCI, NIH, Med. Off. & Sr. Staff 68-; Med. Dir., Public Health Service 76-; *b.* Kiangsu Sept. 19, '32; *m.* Peng, George Pih-hsi; 2 *s.,* 2 *d.; educ.* MD, Coll. of Med., NTU 56; Intern, Resident & Chief Resident in Surgery, New UK Hosp., Boston 57-60; Visiting Fel., Sc. in Med. Br., NCI 60-68; Resident in Med., George Washington U. Hosp., Washington, D.C. 79. *Publ.:* Over 200 articles; *Add.* 201 Shih Pai Rd., Sect. 2, Taipei 112.

WONG, CHI-HUEY 翁啓惠
Mem., Acad. Sinica 94-; Ernest W. Hahn Prof. of Chem., Dept. of Chem., Scripps Res. Inst., USA 89-; Elected Fel., Am. Acad. of Arts & Sc. 96-; Head, Frontier Res. Prog. on Glycotechnology, Riken, Japan 91-; *b.* Twn. Aug. 3, '48; *m.* Wong, Yieng-li; 1 *s.,* 1 *d.; educ.* BS, NTU 70, MS 77; Ph.D., MIT 82; Postdr. Fel., Harvard U. 83; Asst. Prof., Texas A&M U. 83-86, Assc. Prof. 86-87, Prof. 87-89. *Publ.:* Over 300 essays on bio-organic chem., enzyme chem., & biotech.; *Add.* The Scripps Res. Inst., 10550 N. Torrey Pines Rd., La Jolla, CA 92037, USA.

WONG, WILLIAM W. 王文淵
Chmn., Formosa Taffeta Co. Ltd. 98-; Pres., Formosa Chem. & Fibre Corp. 97-; *b.* Twn. May 20, '47; *m.* Wong, Mei-ling; 2 *d.; educ.* M., Ind. Engr., U. of Houston; *Add.* 201 Tun Hua N. Rd., Taipei 105.

WOO, SAVIO LAU-YUEN 胡流源
Mem., Acad. Sinica 96-; V. Chmn. & Dir., Musculoskel-etal Res. Cent., U. of Pittsburgh 90-, Prof. of Mech. Engr. 90-, A.B. Ferguson Prof. of Orthopaedic Surgery 93-, Prof. Civil & Environmental Engr. 94-, Prof. of Rehabilitation Sc. & Tech., 94-, Prof., Bioengr. 98-; Visiting Prof., Biomech. Engr., Stanford U. 2000-; *b.* Shanghai June 3, '42; *m.* Woo, Patricia; 1 *s.,* 1 *d.; educ.* BS, Chico State Coll., USA, MS, U. of Washington, Ph.D. & D.Sc., Calif. State U.; Asst. Res. Bioengr., U. of Pittsburgh 70-74, Assc. Res. Bioengr. & Lectr. 74-75, Assc. Prof. 75-80, Prof. of Surgery & Bioengr. 80-90; Prof. of Orthopaedic Surgery. *Publ.:* Over 200 published acad. papers & numerous acad. chapters & monographs; *Add.* 3471 5th Avenue, Suite 1000, Pittsburgh, PA 15213, USA.

WU, AH-MING 吳阿明
Pub., *Liberty Times* 99-; *b.* Twn. Jan. 22, '24; *m.* Lee, Yu-yeh; 2 *s.,* 1 *d.; educ.* Grad., Keelung Cml. Acad.; Mem., Taipei CCoun. 54-68; Bd. Chmn., Twn. Gen. Trade Union 63-72; Mem., Taipei Provisional CCoun. 68-70; Pres. & Pub., *Liberty Times* 91-96; *Add.* 11th Fl., 137 Nanking E. Rd., Sect. 2, Taipei 104.

WU, AN-CHIA 吳安家
V. Chmn., MAC 97-; Res. Fel., Inst. of Intl. Rel. (IIR), NCCU 85-; *b.* Twn. Oct. 21, '43; *m.* Kao, Yun-hua; 2d.; *educ.* BA, Fu Jen Catholic U. 58; MA, E. Asian Studies, NCCU 73; MA, St. John's U., USA 78; Ph.D., E. Asian Studies, NCCU 87; Convener, Mainland Res. Group, IIR 89-94, Dep. Dir. 94-97. *Publ.: Cross Twn. Strait Rel.: Ret-rospect & Prospect; The Pol. Dev. in Mainland Ch.; Mainland Ch. in 40 Years: A Retrospect & Prospect; Change & Continuity of CCP's Ideology; Add.* 16th Fl., 2-2 Chi Nan Rd., Sect. 1, Taipei 100.

WU, ANDREW J.S. 吳仁修
Amb. to Guatemala 97-; *b.* Twn. Apr. 2, '37; *m.* Chen, Fu-mei; 2 *s.; educ.* LL.B., NCCU 60; MA, Pol. Sc., U. Pedre Henriquez Urena, Dominican Repub. 84; Sr. Mem., Proto-col Dept., MOFA 63-66; 3rd & 2nd Sec., Emb. in Guate-mala 66-71; 2nd & 1st Sec., Emb. in Venezuela 71-74; 1st Sec., Emb. in Panama 74-76; Sect. Chief & Sr. Sp., MOFA 76-79; Counsl., Emb. in Dominican Repub. 79-87; Dep

Dir.-Gen., MOFA 87-90; Rep., TECO in Venezuela 90-96. *Publ.: Const. Law of the ROC; Add.* Apartado Postal 1646, Guatemala City, Guatemala.

WU, CHARLES C.L. 吳中立
V. Chmn., CCA 97-2000; Adjunct Prof., Coll. of Public Health, NTU 88-; *b.* Hopei Feb. 25, '50; *m.* Chou, Yung-yung; 2 *s.; educ.* BA, Econ., NTU 71; MA, Econ., State U. of New York (SUNY) at Albany 80, Ph.D., Econ. 82; Passed Civil Service Sp. Exam. A 88; Teaching Asst., Dept. of Econ., NTU 73-74; Adjunct Instr., Inter-U. Prog. for Ch. Lang. Studies, Stanford Cent. in Taipei 73-74, Admin. Off. 74-76; Grad. Res. Asst., Dept. of Econ., SUNY, Albany 76-78, Grad. Teaching Asst. 78-81; Grad. Student Intern, Dept. of Soc. Services, New York 79; Adjunct Lectr., Dept. of Econ., SUNY, Albany 81-82; Adjunct Instr., Dept. of Business Admin. & Econ., N. Adams State Coll., Massachusetts 82; Adjunct Assc. Prof., Inst. of Business Admin., Chung Yuan Christian U. 83-87, & Inst. of Public Health, Coll. of Med., NTU 83-88; Adjunct Assc. Resr., Inst. of Intl. Rel., NCCU 85; Assc. Resr., Inst. of Econ., Acad. Sinica 82-88, Resr. 88-89; Dir., Dept. of Domestic Info. Services, GIO 89-92 ; Dep. Dir.-Gen., GIO 92-97. *Publ.: An Econometric Analysis of the Demand for Higher Educ. in the US, 1947-1978; Demand for Health—Past & Present;* & many other articles; *Add.* CCA, 1st-4th Fl., 102 Ai Kuo E. Rd., Taipei 100.

WU, CHENG-WEN 吳成文
Mem., Acad. Sinica 84-; Pres. & Disting. Investigator, Nat. Health Res. Inst. 96-; Disting. Res. Fel., Inst. of Biomed. Sc., Acad. Sinica 92-; Fel., Am. Inst. of Chemists 86-; *b.* Taipei June 19, '38; *m.* Chen, Felicia Y.H.; 2 *s.,* 1 *d.; educ.* MD, NTU 64; Ph.D., Biochem., Case We. Reserve U., USA 69; Postdr. Assc., Cornell U. 69-71; Sp. Fel., Yale U. 71-72; Asst. to Full Prof., Albert Einstein Coll. of Med. 72-79; Visiting Prof., Pasteur Inst., France 79-80; Prof. of Pharmacological Sc., State U. of New York, Stony Brook 80-90; Sp. Med. Res. Chair, NScC 88-92; Dir., Inst. of Biomed. Sc. 88-95. *Publ.:* Over 160 articles on biology & med.; *Add.* 128 Yen Chiu Yuan Rd., Sect. 2, Taipei 115.

WU, CHIA-LIN 吳嘉璘
Chmn. & CEO, Infopro Group Inc. 84-; *b.* Twn. July 23, '54; *m.* Wu Hsueh, Lin-hui; 1 *s.,* 3 *d.; educ.* B., Dept. of Forestry, NTU; M., Mng. Sc., Tamkang U.; Marketing Planner, Twn. Xerox Corp. 77-78; Reporter, *Cml. Times* 78-81, Dep. Chief Reporter 81-84; Mem., Private Sector Adv. Cttee., NII Promotion Taskforce, Exec. Yuan 98-; Bd. Dir., CNA 99-; *Add.* 8th Fl., 131 Nanking E. Rd., Sect. 3, Taipei 104.

WU, CHIEN-KUO
(See WU, JIANN-KUO 吳建國)

WU, CHIN-TSAN
(See WU, KING-CHAN 吳金贊)

WU, CHING
(See WU, JIN 吳京)

WU, CHING-CHI
(See WU, CHING-JI 吳清基)

WU, CHING-CHI
(See WU, JING-JYI 吳靜吉)

WU, CHING-JI 吳清基
Admin. V. Min. of Educ. 99-; *b.* Twn. June 15, '51; *m.* Liu, Shu-mei; 1 *s.,* 2 *d.; educ.* Ed.D., NTNU 85; Dir., Twn. Prov. Inst. of Primary Sch. 87-90; Dir.-Gen., Dept. of Secondary Educ., MOE 90-94; Prof., Dept. of Educ., NTNU 90-99; Dir.-Gen., Dept. of Technological & Voc. Educ., MOE 94-97; Dir., 6th Dept., Exec. Yuan 97-99. *Publ.: Theories & Practices of Decision-making of Educ. Admin.; Theories of Decision-making by H.A. Simon & Educ. Admin.; Educ. & Admin.; Tchr. & Training; Betterness of Educ.; Transformation & Dev. of Voc. Educ.;* & etc.; *Add.* 5 Chung Shan S. Rd., Taipei 100.

WU, CHING-KUO 吳經國
Mem., Intl. Olympic Cttee.; Exec. Mem., Ch. Taipei Olympic Cttee.; Chmn., Olympia Found.; Pres., C.K. Wu & Assc. Intl. Architect & Engr.; *b.* Ch. Oct. 18, '46; *m.* Hsin, Liu; 2 *d.; educ.* BS, Tunghai U.; M.Arch., Liverpool U., UK; Architect, Milton Keynes Dev. Corp., UK 75-79; Tech. Adv., Ch. Engr. Consultants Inc. 80-82; Mem., Ch. Taipei Olympic Cttee. 83-85, V. Pres. 86-90. *Publ.: The Olympic Movement & World Peace; Add.* 8th Fl., 20 Chu Lun St., Taipei 104.

WU, CHING-SHAN 吳清山
Pres., Taipei Mun. Tchrs. Coll. 99-; *b.* Twn. Aug. 20, '56; *m.* Kuo, Shiow-lan; 1 *s.,* 3 *d.; educ.* BA, Nat. Kaohsiung Normal U. 68; MA & Ph.D., Educ., NCCU 72 & 78; Assc. Prof. & Sec.-Gen., Taipei Mun. Tchrs. Coll. 87-89, Assc. Prof. & Chair, Dept. of Elementary Educ. 89-92, Prof. & Dir., Grad. Inst. of Elementary Educ. 92-98. *Publ.: Sch. Admin.; Sch. Effectiveness; Educ. Org. & Admin. in USA; Educ. Reform & Dev.; Educ. Improvement; Elementary Educ.; Add.* 1 Ai Kuo W. Rd., Taipei 100.

WU, CHING-TANG 吳慶堂
Govt. Rep. in Ecuador 99-; *b.* Twn. May 5, '40; *m.* Chen, Elena H.T.; 1 *d.; educ.* LL.B., NCCU 63; Studied at Grad. Sch. of Dip., NCCU 65, & Grad. Sch. of Business Admin., Evansville U., USA 70; Ph.D., Lincoln U., USA 82; Asst., MOFA 64-67; 3rd Sec., Emb. in Dominican Repub. 67-70; Sp. & Sect. Chief, MOFA 71-73; 2nd Sec., Emb. in Paraguay 73-76; Dir., Dept. of For. Aff., TPG 76-79, & US Liason Cent. of the Gen. Chamber of Com. 79-82; Dir., Dept. of Gen. Aff., MOI, & concur. Dep. Sec.-Gen., CElC 82-84; Counsl., Exec. Yuan 84; Dep. Dir.-Gen., Bd. of For. Trade, MOEA 84-90, Dir.-Gen., Dept. of Com. 90-92; Rep., TECO, Poland 92-97; Amb. to Nicaragua 97-99. *Publ.: The Role of US Chamber of Com. in Am. Pol. & Business; Add.* P.O. BOX 17-17-1788, Quito, Ecuador, S. Am.

WU, CHUNG-LI
(See WU, CHARLES C.L. 吳中立)

WU, DELON 吳德朗
Pres., Chang Gung U. 99-; *m.* Twn. Sept. 17, '41; *m.* Hung, Iou-jih; 1 *s.; educ.* MD, NTU 66; Intern & Resident in Med., Cook County Hosp., Illinois 67-69; Resident in Med. & Fel. in Cardiology, U. of Illinois 69-73; Asst. & Assc. Prof., U. of Illinois 73-78; V. Supt., Chang Gung Memorial Hosp. 78-82; Prof., U. of So. Calif. 82-84; Chancellor, Chang Gung Coll. of Med. & Tech. 84-97; V. Pres., Chang Gung U. 97-99. *Publ.:* More than 150 original sc. papers on cardiology; *Add.* 5 Fu Hsing St., Kueishan, Taoyuan County 333.

WU, DEN-YIH 吳敦義
Nat. Policy Adv. to the Pres. 98-; Mem., CC, KMT 88-, & CSC 93-; *b.* Twn. Jan. 30, '48; *m.* Tsai, Lihng-yir; 3 *s.,* 1 *d.; educ.* BA, NTU 70; Ed.-Writer & Jour., *Ch. Times* 71-73; Mem., Taipei CCoun. 73-81; Magis., Nantou County 81-89; Chmn., Taipei Mun. Cttee., KMT 89-90; Former Mayor, Kaohsiung City 90-98. *Publ.: The Voice Beneath the Grassroots; Add.* 11th Fl.-2, 150 Ho Ping W. Rd. Sect. 1, Taipei 100.

WU, ERIC T. 吳東昇
Pres., Twn. Korea Cul. & Econ. Exchange Assn. 2000-; Sec.-Gen., Asian-Pacific Cul. Cent., APPU 97-; Chmn. of the Bd., Twn. Sec. Co. Ltd.; Mem., NA; *b.* Twn. July 14, '53; *m.* Wu, Anne; 2 *s.; educ.* LL.B., NTU 75; LL.M. & S.J.D., Harvard Law Sch. 78 & 90; MBA, Harvard Business Sch. 80; Assc. Prof., Soochow U.; V. Chmn., Taishin Intl. Bk.; Mem., Legis. Yuan 93-96. *Publ.: Twn. Rel. Act: The Birth of a New Soc.; Groundwork for Our Future: 3 Years in the Nat. Legis.; Add.* 14th Fl., 123 Nanking E. Rd., Sect. 2, Taipei 104.

WU, FENG-SHAN 吳豐山
Chmn., Public TV Service Found. 98-; *b.* Twn. Jan. 24, '45; *m.* Wu Tsai, Suesy; 2 *s.,* 1 *d.; educ.* BA, NCU 69, MS, Jour. 71; Mem., NA 72-93; Pub., The Independence Newspaper Group 93-98. *Publ.: Twn. 1999; Add.* 100 Lane 75, Kang Ning Rd., Sect. 3, Taipei 114.

WU, GENG 吳庚
Grand Justice, Jud. Yuan; Prof. of Law & Pol. Sc., NTU; *b.* Hainan Jan. 28, '40; *m.* Liu, S.L.; 1 *s.,* 1 *d.; educ.* LL.B. & MPS, NTU; DPS, Public Law, U. of Vienna; Prosecutor, dist. courts 68-73; Assc. Prof., NTU 77-81, Chmn., Dept. & Grad. Sch. of Pol. Sc. 84-85; Mem., Laws & Regln. Cttee., Exec. Yuan 79-85. *Publ.: Die Staatslehre des Han Fei; Pol. Neo-Romanticism; On Governmental Contacts; Admin. Law: Theory & Practice; Add.* 5th Fl., 101 Chaochow St., Taipei 106.

WU, HSIA-HSIUNG 吳夏雄
Bd. Chmn., Twn. Architects Assn. 92-; Dir., Wu Hsia-hsiung Architect & Assn. 87-; *b.* Twn. June 16, '44; *m.* Cheng, Yu-chen; 1 *s.,* 1 *d.; educ.* BA, Ch. Cul. U. 69; Sp., Construction & Planning Admin., MOI 70-74; Sect. Chief, Tainan County Govt. 74-76; Chmn., Nat. Union of Architect Assn. ROC 95; Sec., Lion Clubs Intl. Dist. 300D1 96; Chmn., Intl. Ch. Architecture Assn. 98; *Add.* 6th Fl., 83 Ho Ping St., Chiali, Tainan County 722.

WU, HSIN-HSING 吳新興
Dep. Sec.-Gen., SEF 98-; Prof., Grad. Inst. of Pol. Econ., NCKU 91-; *b.* Kaohsiung Dec. 26, '53; *m.* Chow, Ding-yi; 2 *s.,* 1 *d.; educ.* BA, Soochow U. 82; MA, New Mexico State U. 84; Ph.D., U. of Melbourne 90; Mem., Adv. Cttee., MAC 93-98; Mem., Res. Cttee., NUC 96-98; Dir., Grad. Inst. of Pol. Econ., NCKU 96-98. *Publ.: Bridging the Strait: Twn., Ch. & the Prospects for Reunification* 94; *Integration Theory & the Two Chs. Rel.* 95; *Add.* 17th Fl., 156 Min Sheng E. Rd., Sect. 3, Taipei 105.

WU, HSUAN-SAN
(See WU, SHIUAN-SHAN 吳炫三)

WU, HUA-PENG 吳化鵬
Nat. Policy Adv. to the Pres. 93-; *b.* Mongolia Nov. 21, '25; *educ.* LL.B., NCCU; LL.M., U. of Oregon; Res. Fel., U. of Washington; 12th Class, Sun Yat-sen Inst. on Policy Res. & Dev., KMT; Rep., Mongolian Off. to the Nat. Govt. 46; Comr., MTAC 47-86; Mem., NA 47-89, Planning Bd., MOC 52, Planning Bd., Exec. Yuan 53-58; Mem., CC, KMT 53-59; Educ. Sp., MOE 61-67; Adv., CAC, KMT 62-

93; Mem., Const. Res. Coun. 68; Cul. Attaché & Counsl., Emb. in the USA 68-75; Rep., MTAC in Europe & USA 83-86; Chmn., MTAC 86-93; Comr., MAC 92-93; Chmn., Mongolian & Tibetan Found.; *Add.* 4th Fl., 3 Lane 8, Ching Tien St., Taipei 106.

WU, HUNG-HSIEN 吳鴻顯
Sec.-Gen., Exam. Yuan 99-; Mem., CC, KMT 93-; *b.* Twn. Sept. 16, '40; *m.* Hsu, Chi-wen; 4 *d.; educ.* LL.B., NCU; LL.M., Meiji U.; Passed Sr. Civil Service Exam. 73; Studied at the Judges & Prosecutors Tng. Inst., MOJ; Adjunct Assc. Prof., Ch. Cul. U.; Dep. Dir.-Gen., Twn. Prov. Mining Inspection Cttee.; Sec.-Gen., Kaohsiung CCoun.; Dep. Dir.-Gen., Dept. of Org. Aff., CC, KMT; Chmn., Kaohsiung Mun. Cttee., KMT 93-96; Sec.-Gen., Control Yuan 96-99; *Add.* 1 Shih Yuan Rd., Taipei 116.

WU, JEN-HSIU
(See WU, ANDREW J.S. 吳仁修)

WU, JIANN-KUO 吳建國
Pres., Nat. Twn. Ocean U., 97-, Dean of Acad. Aff. 93-; *b.* Taipei, July 15, '50; *m.* Wu Kuo, Li-hwa; 1 *s.,* 2 *d.; educ.* Grad., Taipei Inst. of Tech. 71; MS, S. Dakota Sch. of Mines 81; Ph.D., U. of Nebraska 84; Engr., Sup., Twn. Metal & Mining Corp. 73-80; Assc. Prof. & Prof., Tatung Inst. of Tech. 85-89; Convener, Preparatory Cttee. of the Materials Engr. Inst., Nat. Twn. Ocean U. 92-93; Acting Pres. 96-97. *Publ.:* Over 200 jour. & conf. papers on materials Sc. & electrochem.; *Add.* Nat. Twn. Ocean U., Keelung, Taiwan 202.

WU, JIN 吳京
Mem., Acad. Sinica 86-; Prof. of Hydraulic & Ocean Engr. & Chair of Outstanding Scholarship, NCKU 94-; Mem., Nat. Acad. of Engr. 95-; Emeritus H. Fletcher Brown Prof. 97-; Adv., Tainan Hydraulics Lab., NCKU 77-; *b.* Nanking Apr. 9, '34; *m.* Chang, Tze-chen; 3 *s.; educ.* BS, Civil Engr., NCKU 56; MS, Mech. & Hydraulics, U. of Iowa 61, Ph.D. 64; Civil Engr., ROCN Hqs. 56-58; Tchr., Prov. Taitung Sr. High Sch. 58-59; Res. Asst., Inst. of Hydraulic Res., U. of Iowa 59-60, Res. Assc. 60-63; Head, Fluid Motions Div. 66-72, & Div. of Geophys. Fluid Dynamics 72-74; Visiting Lectr., Von Karman Inst. for Fluid Dynamics, Belgium 70; Coordinator, Phys. Oceanography Prog., Grad. Coll. of Marine Studies, U. of Delaware 74-75 & 79-80; Assc. Prof., Marine Studies & Civil Engr., U. of Delaware 74-75, Prof. 75-80; Dir., Air-Sea Interaction Lab., USA 79-97; Expert-Consultant, Naval Res. Lab., USA 80; Prof., H. Fletcher Brown Chair, U. of Delaware 80-97; Hon. Res. Consultant, NScC 83; Visiting Prof., U. of Calif.

85; Mem., Hydrodynamics Adv. Com., Dept. of Def., USA 85; Nat. Invitation Chair, Inst. of Oceanography, NTU 86, & Coll. of Engr., NCKU 87; Adv. Cttee. Mem., Res. Inst. for Applied Mech., NTU 88; Mem.-Consultant, Intl. Adv. Panel, Nat. Acad. of Sc. 88; Ocean Sc. Educator, Off. of Naval Res., USA 91-97; Pres., NCKU 94-96; Pres., Ch. Soc. of Marine Sc. & Tech. 95-97; Min. of Educ. 96-98. *Publ.:* 200 papers in intl. jour.; *Add.* Dept. of Hydraulic & Ocean Engr., NCKU, 1 Ta Hsueh Rd., Tainan 701.

WU, JING-JYI 吳靜吉
Nat. Policy Adv. to the Pres. 96-; Mem., CCA 93-; Adv., MAC 98-; Exec. Dir., Found. for Scholarly Exchange 77-; Adjunct Prof., NCCU 77-; *b.* Twn. May 3, '39; *educ.* BA, NCCU 62; Ph.D., Educ. Psychology, U. of Minnesota 67; Res. Asst., U. of Minnesota 65-67; Lectr., Queen's Coll., New York 67-68; Asst. Prof., Yeshiva U., New York 68-73; Artistic Dir., Asian-Am. Repertory Theater, La Ma Ma, ETC, New York 69-72; Adjunct Assc. Prof., City Coll. of New York 71-72; Visiting Prof., Dept. of Psychology, NCCU 72-77; Artistic Dir., Lanling Theater Workshop 79-94; Bd. Dir., SEF 90-93; Bd. Chmn., Ch. C.'s Fund 91-94. *Publ.: In Search of Self-identity; Shyness, Loneliness & Love; Initial Experiment of Lanling Theater Workshop; Psychology; Educ. Psychology; Psychology & Life; Psychology & Living; Four Great Dreams of Youth; Add.* 2nd Fl., 1-A Chuanchow St., Taipei 100.

WU, JUI
(See WU, RAY 吳瑞)

WU, JUI-PEI
(See WU, RUEY-BEEI 吳瑞北)

WU, JUNG-I
(See WU, RONG-I 吳榮義)

WU, KENG
(See WU, GENG 吳庚)

WU, KING-CHAN 吳金贊
Nat. Pol. Adv. to the Pres. 98-; Mem., CC, KMT 93-; *b.* Fukien Dec. 8, '36; *m.* Tang, Ching-ming; 4 *c.; educ.* Ph.D., Agr., Ch. Cul. U. 80; Dir., Forestry Aff. Off., Kinmen 64-71; Mem., Legis. Yuan 71-85; Gov., Fukien Prov. 86-98. *Publ.: What Am I Doing in Legis. Yuan; Devoting to My Native Place for 14 Years; Add.* c/o Off. of the Pres., Taipei 100.

WU, LI-PING
(See WU, LISA 吳麗萍)

WU, LISA 吳麗萍
Mng. Dir., Nong Nong Intercult. Group 84-; Bd. Dir., Singapore Lianhe Pub. Private Ltd. 93-; Mng. Dir., Asia Century Pub. Private Ltd. (Twn. Br.) 97-; Pub., *Nong Nong Mag.* 84-; Mng. Dir., *Mom Baby Mag.* 87-; Bd. Dir., *Citta Bella Mag.* (Singapore) 93-, (Malaysia) 97-; Pub., *Living Mag.* 97-; *b.* Twn. Dec. 23, '50; *m.* Shen, I-hui; 1 *s.; educ.* Grad., Pingtung Normal Sch. 69, Ming Chuan Coll. 76; BS, Mng., Baker U. (Kansas) 92; Mng. Dir., *Cosmopolitan* (Twn. Version) 89-92; Pub., *Disney/Parents Mag.* 92-93. *Publ.: A Successful Hit of a Working Woman; How to Possess the New World As a Modern Woman in the New Age; Add.* 7th Fl., 531-1 Chung Cheng Rd., Hsintien, Taipei County 231.

WU, MAO-HSIUNG 吳茂雄
Nat. Policy Adv. to the Pres. 99-; Mem., NA 91-; Counsl., Control Yuan 99-; *b.* Twn. July 7, '38; *m.* Ko, Hsing-tzu; 2 *s.; educ.* LL.B., Soochow U.; Attorney 74-; Bd. Mem. & Dep. Sec.-Gen., Twn. Bar Assn. 91-95; Lectr., Ch. Cul. U.; Assc. Prof., Takming Jr. Coll. of Com.; Lectr., Nat. Taipei U. of Tech. *Publ: Study of the Prescription of Rent, Tax, & Loan; Exercise & Protection of Rights; Law & Daily Life; Add.* 2th Fl., 192 Chung Hua Rd., Sect. 1, Taichung 400.

WU, MING-YEN 吳明彥
Rep. to Repub. of Finland 99-; *b.* Twn. Oct. 3, '39; *m.* Wu Lin, Mei-shiue; 3 *d.; educ.* LL.B., NCU 62; Staff, MOFA 64-67; 2nd Sec., ROC Emb. in New Zealand 67-73; Sect. Chief, MOFA 73-75; Div. Chief, ROC Rep. Off. in Thailand 75-78; 1st Sec., ROC Emb. in Korea 78-84; Dep. Dir.-Gen., Dept. of Consl. Aff., MOFA 84-87; ROC Rep. in Sweden 87-90; ROC Rep. in Fiji 90-93; Dir.-Gen., Off. of Records & Data Processing, MOFA 93-96; Amb. to Commonwealth of the Bahamas 96-97; Counsl. MOFA 97-98; Chief of Secretariat, NSC 98-99; *Add.* Taipei Econ. & Cul. Off., World Trade Cent., P.O. Box 800, FIN-00101 Helsinki, Finland.

WU, POH-HSIUNG 吳伯雄
Sr. Adv. to the Pres. 97-; Mem., CC, KMT 76-, & CSC 86-; Pres., Brotherhood Cul. & Educ. Found.; *b.* Twn. June 19, '39; *m.* Dai, Mei-yu; 2 *s.,* 1 *d.; educ.* BS, NCKU 62; Sun Yat-sen Inst. on Policy Res. & Dev.; 2nd Class, Construction Policy Res., Nat. Construction Inst.; Tchr., Twn. Prov. Chungli Cml. High Sch. 63-65; Mem., TPA 68-72; Assc. Prof., Nan Ya Jr. Coll. of Tech. 71-73; Magis., Taoyuan County 73-76; Dir., Inst. of Ind. Tng. for Workmen, & Friends of Labor Assn., & concur. Dir.-Gen., Twn. Tobacco & Wine Monopoly Bu. 76-80; Chmn., ROC Amateur Boxing Assn. 81-82; Dir.-Gen., Secretariat, CC, KMT 82-84; Min. of the Int. 84-88; Chmn., CEC, KMT; Mayor, Taipei City 88-90; Min. without Portfolio 90-91 & 94; Min. of the Int., Mem. & Chmn. of the CEIC, & Mem. of the PPRC 91-94; Sec.-Gen., Off. of the Pres. 94-96; Sec.-Gen., KMT 96-97; *Add.* c/o Off. of the Pres., Taipei 100.

WU, RAY 吳瑞
Mem., Acad. Sinica 82-; Prof. of Biochem., Molecular & Cell Biology, Cornell U. 66-; *b.* Peking Aug. 14, '28; *m.* Chan, Christina; 1 *s.,* 1 *d.; educ.* BS, U. of Alabama 50; Ph.D., U. of Penn. 55; Asst. Instr., Biochem. Dept., U. of Penn. 51-55; Postdr. Fel., Dept. of Biochem., Public Health Res. Inst., New York 55-57, Asst. 57-58, Assc. 58-61, Assc. Mem. 61-66; Sr. Visiting Investigator, Stanford U. 65-66; Assc. Prof., Cornell U. 66-72; Sr. Visiting Scholar, MRC Lab. of Molecular Biology, Cambridge, UK 71; Visiting Assc. Prof., MIT 72; Chmn., Sect. of Biochem., Molecular & Cell Biology, Cornell U. 76-78. *Publ.:* Over 320 res. papers & 9 ed. bk.; *Add.* 111 Christopher Circle, Ithaca, NY 14850, USA.

WU, RONG-I 吳榮義
Dir., Twn. Inst. of Econ. Res. 97-; Dir.-Gen., Ch. Taipei Pacific Econ. Cooperation Cttee. 93-; Sec.-Gen., Ind. Dev. Adv. Coun., MOEA 93-; Prof., Inst. of Econ., NCHU 84-; Mem., Com. on Nat. Income Statistics, DGBAS 80-, & Adv. Cttee., CEPD 77-; *b.* Twn. Dec. 15, '39; *m.* Lin, Hui-mei; 1 *s.,* 1 *d.; educ.* BS, Econ., NTU 62, MS 66; MS, Econ., U. Catholique de Louvain, Belgium 70, D.Sc. 71; Assc. Prof., Prof., Acting Chmn. & Chmn., Dept. of Econ., NCHU 75-79, Prof. & Dir., Inst. of Econ. 79-84; Sr. Res. Fel. & Dir., 1st Div., Twn. Inst. of Econ. Res. 85-92, V. Pres. 91-92, Pres. 93-96; Dep. Dir.-Gen., Pacific Econ. Cooperation Cttee., Ch. Taipei 91-92; Dir.-Gen., Ch. Mem. Cttee., Pacific Basin Econ. Coun. 91-92; Comr., Fair Trade Com., Exec. Yuan 92-93; Sec.-Gen., Control Yuan 96-97. *Publ.: The Strategy of Econ. Dev.: A Case Study of Twn.; Some Aspects of Export Trade & Econ. Dev. in Post-War Twn.;* & many articles published in prof. jour.; *Add.* 7th Fl., 16-8 Te Hui St., Taipei 104.

WU, RUEY-BEEI 吳瑞北
Dir., Nat. Cent. for High-performance Computing 98-; Prof., NTU 90-; *b.* Twn. Oct. 27, '57; *educ.* BA, EE, NTU 79, Ph.D. 85; Teaching Asst., Instr., Assc. Prof., Dept of EE, NTU 82-90; Postdr., IBM/GTD, E. Fishkill, New York 86-87; Consultant, ITRI/ERSO, Hsinchu 88-89; Visiitng Prof., Dept. of EE, UCLA 94-95; Assc. Chmn., Dept. of EE, NTU 95-97. *Publ.:* Over 80 papers in intl. jour. & conf., & 4 patents; *Add.* Rm. 340, Dept. of EE, NTU, 1 Roosevelt Rd., Sect. 4, Taipei 106.

WU, SHIH-WEN 伍世文
Min. of Nat. Def. 2000-; *b.* Kwangtung July 24, '34; *m.* Chang, Wei-hsien; 2 *d.; educ.* B., Naval Acad. 55; Naval Cmd. & Staff Coll. 70; US Naval Coll. 88; Cmdr., Landing Ship Squadron 84-85; Amphibious Training Cmd. 85; Dir., Weaponry Dept., Navy GHQ 85-86, Chief, Bu. of Pers., 86-88; Cmdr., Fleet Training Cmd. 88-90; Supt., Naval Acad. 90-92; Dep. C-in-C, Navy 92-93; V. Chief of the Gen. Staff, MND 93-97; C-in-C, ROC Navy 97-99; V. Min. of Nat. Def. 99-2000; *Add.* 2nd Fl., 164 Po Ai Rd., Taipei 100.

WU, SHIUAN-SHAN 吳炫三
Painter; *b.* Twn. Nov. 14, '42; *m.* Lee, Shou-ching; 1 *s.,* 1 *d.; educ.* BA, NTNU; MA, Madrid U., Spain; Modern arts res. in New York 73-76; Primitive painting res. in Africa 79-80, 83-84. *Publ.: Adventure in Africa, Challenge Among the Africans*; & many art exhibitions held in ROC, Japan, US, Spain, Paris, & Brazil; *Add.* Wu Shiuan-shan Studio, B1, 10 Lane 7, Alley 113, Ming Sheng E. Rd., Sect. 3, Taipei 105.

WU, SHUN-WEN
(See YEN, VIVIAN W. 吳舜文)

WU, TA-CHUN
(See WU, TAI-TSUN 吳大峻)

WU, TAI-CHENG 吳泰成
Mem. (ministerial rank), Exam. Yuan 96-; *b.* Twn. Nov. 28, '45; 2 *s.; educ.* LL.B., NCHU 69; LL.M., NCCU 79; Staff, Sp., Sect. Chief, Authorized Rank Insp., & Certified Public Acct. 71-83; Sec.-Gen., Pers. Dept., TCG 83-85; Dir., Off. of Res. & Control, Min. of Civil Service 85-87, & Laws & Regln. Dept. 87-90; Sec.-Gen., Min. of Civil Service, Exam. Yuan 90-93, Admin. V. Min. of Civil Service 93-94, Pol. V. Min. of Civil Service 94-96. *Publ.: A Study of the Position Classification System in the ROC; Add.* 1 Shih Yuan Rd., Taipei 116.

WU, TAI-TSUN 吳大峻
Mem., Acad. Sinica 80-; Prof., Harvard U.; *b.* Shanghai Dec. 1, '33; *m.* Yu, Sau-lan; *educ.* BS, U. of Minnesota 53; MS, Harvard U. 54, Ph.D. 56; Putnam Scholar 53; Heineman Prize, Am. Inst. of Phys. 99; Jr. Fel., Soc. of Fel., Harvard U. 56-59, Asst. Prof. 59-63, Assc. Prof. 63-66; Mem., Inst. for Advanced Studies, Princeton U. 58-59, 60-61, & 62-63; Visiting Prof., Rockefeller U., USA 66-67; Sc. Assc., Deutsches Elektronen-Synchrotron, Hamburg, W. Germany 70-71 & 82-83; Kramers Prof., U. Utrecht, the Netherlands 77-78; Sc. Assc., CERN, Geneva, Switzer-land 77-78. *Publ.: Scattering & Diffraction of Waves* (with Ronold W.P. King); *The Two-Dimensional Ising Model* (with Barry M. McCoy); *Antennas in Matter: Fundamentals, Theory, & Applications* (with Ronold W.P. King, Glenn S. Smith, & Margaret Owens); *Expanding Protons: Scattering at High Energies* (with Hung Cheng); *The Ubiquitous Photon: Helicity Method for QED & QCD* (with Raymond Gastmans); *Lateral Electromagnetic Waves: Theory & Applications to Comms., Geophysical Exploration, & Remote Sensing* (with Ronold W.P. King & Margaret Owens); *Add.* Gordan Mckay Lab., Harvard U., 9 Oxford St., Cambridge, MA 02138, USA.

WU, TE-LANG
(See WU, DELON 吳德朗)

WU, THEODORE YAO-TSU 吳耀祖
Mem., Acad. Sinica 84-; Prof. of Engr. Sc., Calif. Inst. of Tech. 61-; Mem., Nat. Acad. of Engr., USA 82-; *b.* Kiangsu Mar. 20, '24; *m.* Shih, Chin-hua; 1 *s.,* 1 *d.; educ.* BS, NCTU, Shanghai 46; MS, Iowa State Coll. 48; Ph.D., Calif. Inst. of Tech. 52; Res. Fel., Asst. Prof. & Assc. Prof., Calif. Inst. of Tech. 52-61. *Publ.:* Over 100 res. articles in prof. jour.; *Add.* Calif. Inst. of Tech., Pasadena, CA 91125, USA.

WU, TIEH-HSIUNG 吳鐵雄
Pres., Nat. Tainan Tchrs.' Coll. 92-; *b.* Twn. Sept. 28, '39; *m.* Tsai, Lily; 2 *s.; educ.* Grad., Twn. Prov. Tainan Jr. Tchrs.' Coll. 58; BA, NTNU 66; MA, U. of Rochester, USA 72; Ph.D., State U. of New York, Buffalo 79; Teaching Asst., Dept. of Psychology, Chung Yuan Christian U.; Res. Assc., Dept. of Behavioral Sc., State U. of New York, Buffalo 77-79; Assc. Prof., Dept. of Educ., Nat. Kaohsiung Tchrs. Coll. 79-80; Prof., Dept. of Educ. Psychology, NTNU 80-85, Dir., Computing Cent. 80-86, Chmn. & Prof., Dept. of Info. & Computer Educ. 85-91, Prof. 91-92. *Publ.: CAI in Twn.: State & Problems; A Long-term Effect for Promoting Computer Educ. in the ROC; Add.* 33 Shu Lin St., Sect. 2, Tainan 700.

WU, TONG-LIANG 吳東亮
Chmn., Taishin Intl. Bk. 92-; Chmn., Shin Kong Synthetic Fibers Corp. 97-; *b.* Taipei Apr. 11, '50; *m.* Peng, Hsueh-fen; 2 *s.; educ.* B., Chem., Fu Jen Catholic U. 72; MBA, UCLA 75; Hon. Ph.D., Com., St. John's U., USA 95; Pres., Shin Kong Synthetic Fibers Corp. 78-97; *Add.* 8th Fl., 123 Nanking E. Rd., Sect. 2, Taipei 104.

WU, TUN-I
(See WU, DEN-YIH 吳敦義)

WU, TUNG-LIANG
(See WU, TONG-LIANG 吳東亮)

WU, TUNG-MING 吳東明
Dep. Sec.-Gen., NSC 95-2000; *b.* Kiangsi July 5, '37; *m.* Tan, Ching-ho; 1 *d.; educ.* BS, Ch. Mil. Acad. 60; Basic Off. Corps, US Army Infantry Sch. 61; MS, Purdue U. 67; Advance Off. Corps, ROC Army Infantry Sch. 69; Ph.D., Purdue U. 73; Army CGSC, Armed Forces U. 76, War CGSC 83; Div. Cmdr., Infantry Div. 81-83; Dir., Services Coordination Div. CCNAA 83-84; Chief Aide-de-Camp to the Pres. 84-88; Dep. Dir., Investigaiton Bu., MOJ 88-89, Dir. 89-95; *Add.* 122 Chungking S. Rd., Sect. 1, Taipei 100.

WU, TUNG-SHENG
(See WU, ERIC T. 吳東昇)

WU, TZU-DAN 吳子丹
V. Min. of For. Aff. 98-; *b.* Ch. July 28, '37; *m.* Ma, L.M.; 2 *s.; educ.* LL.B., NCCU 59, LL.M. 65; Staff, MOFA 63-66; 3rd & 2nd Sec., Emb. in Japan 66-71; Sect. Chief & Exec. Asst. to Min. of For. Aff. 71-76; Counsl., Emb. in S. Africa 76-78; Dep. Consul-Gen., Consl. Gen. in New York 78-79; Dep. Dir.-Gen., CCNAA, New York 79-85, Dir.-Gen., Kansas City 85-86, & Chicago 86-88; Dir.-Gen., Dept. of Intl. Orgs., MOFA 88-93; Dir.-Gen., CCNAA, New York 93-94; Dir.-Gen., TECO, New York 94-98. *Publ.: The Legal Status of Outer Space; Add.* 2 Kaitakelan Boulevard, Taipei 100.

WU, TZU-TAN
(See WU, TZU-DAN 吳子丹)

WU, WAN-LAN 吳挽瀾
Min. of Exam. 99-; *b.* Kiangsi July 13, '33; *m.* Yueh, Jiun-shen; 4 *d.; educ.* LL.B., NCHU 58; MPA, U. of Manila 73; Sec.-Gen., Chiayi County Govt. 68-72; Dir., Dept. of Soc. Work, Ch. Youth Corps 73-78; Sec.-Gen., Twn. Prov. Cttee., KMT 78-81; Dep. Dir., Dept. of Org., CC 81-83; Chmn., Kaohsiung Mun. Cttee. 83-87; V. Pres., Hqs., Ch. Youth Corps 87-94; Dir.-Gen., Dept. of Soc. Aff., CC, KMT 94-95; Chmn., Twn. Prov. Cttee. 95-96; Chmn., Exec. Yuan 96-97; Sec.-Gen., Exam. Yuan 97-99. *Publ.: Admin. Org. & Mng.; The Study of Modern PA; Natural Environment, Mental Environment, & Significant Environment; Add.* 1 Shih Yuan Rd., Taipei 116.

WU, YAO-TSU
(See WU, THEODORE YAO-TSU 吳耀祖)

WU, YI-HSIUNG
(See WU, YI-SHIUNG 吳義雄)

WU, YI-SHIUNG 吳義雄
Dep. Admin., EPA 96-; *b.* Twn. Oct. 7, '42; *m.* Cheng, Mei-hsiang; 3 *s.; educ.* BA, Acct. Dept., NCKU 72; Studied on Civic Aff., PA Grad. Sch., NCCU 91; Dep. Dir., Dept. of Environmental Protection, TCG 87-90, Dep. Dir., Dept. of Soc. Aff. 90-91; Dir., Dept. of Environmental Protection 91-94; Sec.-Gen. 94; Adv. to the Premier 94-96; *Add.* 41 Chung Hua Rd., Sect. 1, Taipei 100.

YANG, C.C. 楊振忠
Mem., Acad. Sinica 90-; Disting. Chair Prof., NTHU 94-; *b.* Taipei July 15, '27; *m.* Lin, Yeh-hsiang; 2 *s.*, 3 *d.; educ.* Grad., Med. Coll., NTU 50; DMS, Tokyo Ji-Kei U. 56; Res. Assc., U. of Wisconsin-Madison 61-62; Assc. Prof., Kaohsiung Med. Coll. 56-58, Prof. 58-73; Nat. Res. Chair Prof., NScC 64-67; Pres., Kaohsiung Med. Coll. 67-73; Dep. Dir., Ch. Youth Corps 73-78; Dir., Inst. of Molecular Biology, NTHU 73-85, Prof., Inst. of Life Sc. 73-94; Pres., Ch. Biochem. Soc. 79-81; Coun. Mem., Intl. Soc. on Toxinology 88-91; Ed. Bd., *Toxicon* Mag.; Mem., Acad. Review Cttee., MOE; Mem., Consultative Cttee., NScC; Standing Mem., Gen. Consultative Cttee., Acad. Sinica. *Publ.:* Over 150 res. articles on biochem. & immunochem. of snake venom proteins published in intl. jour.; *Add.* 5th Fl., 61 W. Compound, NTHU, Hsinchu 300.

YANG, CHAO-HSIANG
(See YUNG, CHAUR-SHIN 楊朝祥)

YANG, CHEN-CHUNG
(See YANG, C.C. 楊振忠)

YANG, CHEN-NING 楊振寧
Mem., Acad. Sinica 58-; Einstein Prof., State U. of New York, Stony Brook 66-; *b.* Anhwei Sept. 22, '22; *m.* Tu, Chih-li; 3 *c.; educ.* BS, Nat. S.we. Assc. U. 42; Ph.D., U. of Chicago 48; Instr., U. of Chicago 48-49; Mem., Inst. for Advanced Studies 49-55, Prof. 56-66; Nobel Prize in Phys. 57; *Add.* Dept. of Phys., State U. of New York, Stony Brook, NY 11794, USA.

YANG, CHIH-LIANG
(See YAUNG, CHIH-LIANG 楊志良)

YANG, CHUAN-KUANG
(See YANG, CHUAN-KWANG 楊傳廣)

YANG, CHUAN-KWANG 楊傳廣

Tng. Dir., ROC Amateur Athletic Fed.; *b*. Twn. July 10, '33; *m*. Jue, Daisy; 2 *c.; educ*. Grad., Dept. of Phys. Educ., UCLA; Silver Medal Winner in the decathlon, Rome Olympics 60; Coach 64-77; Mem., Legis. Yuan 72-75; *Add*. P.O. Box 7855-39, Tsoying, Kaohsiung 813.

YANG, CHUNG-TAO 楊忠道

Mem., Acad. Sinica 68-; Prof. Emeritus, U. of Penn. 91-; *b*. Chekiang May 4, '23; *m*. Kang, Agnes Ying-fong; 1 *s.,* 2 *d.; educ*. BS, Nat. Chekiang U. 46; Ph.D., Tulane U., USA 52; Asst., Nat. Chekiang U. 46-48, & Acad. Sinica 48-49; Asst. Mem., Acad. Sinica & concur. Lectr., NTU 49-50; Res. Assc., U. of Illinois 52-54; Mem., Inst. for Advanced Studied, Princeton U. 54-56; Asst. Prof., U. of Penn. 56-58, Assc. Prof. 58-61, *&* Prof. 61-91, Chmn., Dept. of Math. 78-83; Assc. Dir., Nankai Inst. of Math. 90-95. *Publ.:* Over 40 acad. articles published in various math. jour.; *Add*. 311 Hidden River Rd., Narberth, PA 19072, USA.

YANG, HENRY T.Y. 楊祖佑

Mem., Acad. Sinica 92-; Chancellor, U. of Calif. at Santa Barbara 94-; Mem., US Nat. Acad. of Engr. 91-; Dir., Allied Signal Bd. 96-; *b*. Chungking Nov. 29, '40; *m*. Yang, Dilling; 2 *d.; educ*. BS, NTU 62; MS, W. Virginia U. 64; Ph.D., Cornell U. 68; Hon. Dr., Purdue U. 96; Head, Sch. of Aeronautics & Astronautics, Purdue U. 79-84, Dean, Sch. of Engr. 84-94, Neil Armstrong Disting. Prof. 88-94; Mem., Def. Sc. Bd. 89-91. *Publ.:* One bk. & 150 jour. papers; *Add*. U. of Calif., Santa Barbara, CA 93106-2030, USA.

YANG, HSIANG-FA

(See YANG, SHANG-FA 楊祥發)

YANG, HUEY-ING 楊慧英

Grand Justice, Jud. Yuan 94-; *b*. Twn. July 14, '34; *m*. Hsu, Hsiang-neng; 1 *s.,* 1 *d.; educ*. LL.B., NTU 57; Judge, Hsinchu Dist. Court 61-62, Taichung Dist. Court 62-64; Procurator & Judge, Taichung Dist. Court 64-71; Chief Judge, Taipei Dist. Court 71-72; Judge, Twn. High Court 72-79; Justice, Admin. Court 79-80; Judge, Supreme Court 90-92, Presiding Justice 92-94; *Add*. 4th Fl., 124 Chungking S. Rd., Sect. 1, Taipei 100.

YANG, HUI-YING

(See YANG, HUEY-ING 楊慧英)

YANG, JEN-SHOU 楊仁壽

Dep. Sec.-Gen., Jud. Yuan 95-; Adjunct Assc. Prof., Grad. Inst. of Law, Soochow U. 91-; Chair, Judges & Prosecutors

Tng. Inst. 81-; *b*. Twn. Feb. 17, '42; *m*. Cheng, Tzu-mei; 1 *s.,* 1 *d.; educ*. LL.B., NTU 64; LL.M., Ch. Cul. U. 72; Prosecutors & judges, dist. courts 67-79; Judge, high courts 79-84; Justice, Supreme Court 84-85; Dept. Chief, Jud. Yuan 85-90; Pres., Taoyuan Dist. Court 90-92, Panchiao Dist. Court 92-93, Kaohsiung Dist. Court 93-95, Taipei Dist. Court 95-96, Twn. High Court (Kaohsiung Br.) 96-97; Twn. High Court 97-99. *Publ.: Navigation Laws* (2 Vol.); *On Maritime Law; Bills of Lading; The Hamburg Rules; Commentaries on Court Decisions of Maritime Law Cases; Methodology in Construction on Law; Methodology in Legal Sc.; Add*. 7th Fl.-3, 56 Ho Ping W. Rd. Sect. 1, Taipei 100.

YANG, KUO-SHIH 楊國賜

Pol. V. Min. of Educ. 99-; *b*. Twn. Sept. 26, '39; *m*. Yang Ho, Fu-mei; 2 *s.,* 1 *d.; educ*. Ed.D., NTNU 77; Res. at London U.; Prof., Dept. of Soc. Educ., NTNU 78-88, Dir. 85-88, Dean, Grad. Sch. of Soc. Educ. 84-88; Dir., Dept. of Soc. Educ., MOE 88-92, Sec.-Gen. 92-93, Dir., Dept. of Higher Educ. 93-95; Admin. V. Min. of Educ. 95-99. *Publ.: The Ideas of Soc. Educ.; Progressivism & Educ. Philosophy; The Thought of Contemporary Educ.; Comparative Educ. Methodology; Modernization & Educ. Innovation; Add*. 5 Chung Shan S. Rd., Taipei 100.

YANG, KUO-SZU

(See YANG, KUO-SHIH 楊國賜)

YANG, MING-HSING

(See YOUNG, MING-SHING 楊明興)

YANG, NIEN-CHU C. 楊念祖

Mem., Acad. Sinica 82-; Gustavus F. & Ann M. Swift Disting. Service Prof., Dept. of Chem., U. of Chicago 92-; *b*. Shanghai May 1, '28; *m*. Hwang, Ding-djung; 2 *s.,* 1 *d.; educ*. BS, St. John's U. 48; Ph.D., U. of Chicago 52; Res. Assc., MIT 52-55; Res. Fel., Harvard U. 55-56; Asst. Prof., U. of Chicago 56-61, Assc. Prof. 61-63, Prof. 63-92. *Publ.:* Over 150 articles published in sc. jour.; *Add*. 5729 S. Blackstone Avenue, Chicago, IL 60637, USA.

YANG, NIEN-TSU

(See YANG, NIEN-CHU C. 楊念祖)

YANG, PAO-FA 楊寶發

Pol. V. Min. of the Int. 93-2000; Mem., CC, KMT 93-; *b*. Twn. Oct. 29, '30; *m*. Wu, Su-chu; 2 *s.,* 1 *d.; educ*. LL.B., NTU 53; Sect. Chief, Dept. of Civil Aff., TPG 54-61; Insp. & Sr. Sp., MOI 61-66; Chmn., Miaoli County Cttee., KMT

66-70, & Nantou County Cttee. 70-72; Dir., Dept. of Civil Aff., TCG 72-77; Magis., Tainan County 77-85; Mng. Dir., Bk. of Land 87-90; Comr., TPG, & concur. Chmn., EPC 90-93. *Publ.: Outline Map of Twn. Prov.; Nat. Rev. & Twn.; Add.* 9th Fl., 5 Hsuchow Rd., Taipei 100.

YANG, HSIANG-FA
(See YANG, SHANG-FA 楊祥發)

YANG, SHANG-FA 楊祥發
Disting. Res. Fel. & V. Pres., Acad. Sinica 96-, Mem. 92-; Mem., Nat. Acad. of Sc., USA 90-; Prof., U. of Calif., Davis 74- & Hong Kong U. of Sc. & Tech. 94-; Fel., Guggenheim Found. 82-; *b.* Twn. Nov. 10, '32; *m.* Yang, Eleanor; 2 *s.; educ.* BS, NTU 56, MS 58; Ph.D., Utah State U. 62; Postdr. Resr., U. of Calif., Davis 62-63, New York U. 63-64, & U. of Calif., San Diego 64-65; Visiting Prof., U. of Konstanz, Germany 74, NTU 83, & Cambridge U., UK 83. *Publ.:* Over 200 papers on plant biochem. & molecular biology; *Add.* Mann Lab., U. of Calif., Davis, CA 95616, USA.

YANG, SHENG-TSUNG 楊勝宗
Dir.-Gen., TECO in Chicago 97-; *b.* Twn. Sept. 6, '44; *m.* Yang Chen, Esther; 1 *d.; educ.* LL.B., NTU 67, MA, Pol. Sc. 72; MSFS, Georgetown U. 82; Staff Mem., MOFA 70-73; V. Consul, Consl. in Guam 73-79; Sp. Asst., Dep. Dir., Secretariat, CCNAA, Washington, D.C. 84-91; Dep. Dir.-Gen. & Dir.-Gen., Dept. of Treaty & Legal Aff., MOFA 92-97; *Add.* Two Prudnetial Plaza, 57th & 58th Fl., 180 N. Stetson Avenue, Chicago, IL 60601, USA.

YANG, SHIH-CHIEN 楊世緘
Min. without Portfolio 96-2000; *b.* Shanghai Oct. 5, '44; *educ.* BEE, NTU; MEE & Ph.D., N.we. U., USA; Res. Engr., Chung Shan Inst. of Sc. & Tech. 73-78; Sr. Engr., Sectoral Planning Dept., CEPD 78-80, Dep. Dir. 80-83; Dir., Planning & Evaluation Div., NScC 83-84; Dep. Dir.-Gen., Sc.-based Ind. Park Admin. 84-86; Dir.-Gen., Ind. Dev. Bu., MOEA 86-92; Pol. V. Min. of Econ. Aff. 93-96; *Add.* 1 Chung Hsiao E. Rd., Sect. 1, Taipei 100.

YANG, SU-YUAN
(See YANG, SUH-YUAN 楊肅元)

YANG, SUH-YUAN 楊肅元
Nat. Policy Adv. to the Pres. 99-; *b.* Jan. 25, '39; *educ.* Tchrs. Sp. Prog., Kinmen Sr. High Sch.; Chmn., Assn. of Com., Kinmen 84-90; Mem., NA 92-99; *Add.* 21-3 Min Tsu Rd., Chincheng, Kinmen County 893.

YANG, TE-CHIH 楊德智
Chmn., VAC 2000-; *b.* Twn. Dec. 25, '41; *m.* Chen, Wei-jeng; 3 *d.; educ.* BS, Ch. Mil. Acad. 64; Armor Off. Advanced Course, Armor Sch., Ch. Army 69; Army CGSC, Armed Forces U. 78; War Coll., Armed Forces U. 82; Armored Cavalry Troop Cmd. 70-71; Tank Bn. Cmd. 74-76; Instr., Armor Sch. 76-77; Instr., Army CGSC, Armed Forces U. 79-81; Tank Group Cmd. 82-84; Separate Armored Brigade Cmd. 85-87; Mechanized Div. Cmd. 87-89; Dep. C/S, Intelligence, Gen. Hqs., Army 89; Cmdg. Gen. & Cmdt., Armor Training Cmd. & Armor Sch., Army 89-91; Supt., Ch. Mil. Acad. 91-93; Cmd., Logistics Cmd., Army 93-95; Dep. Chief of Gen. Staff, Logistics, MND 95-96, V. Chief of Gen. Staff 96-98; C-in-C, CSF 98-2000; *Add.* 222 Chung Hsiao E. Rd., Sect. 5, Taipei 110.

YANG, TING-YUN 楊亭雲
Nat. Policy Adv. to the Pres. 99-; Mem., CSC, KMT 99-; *b.* Hupei Dec. 27, '28; *m.* Fang, Chih-shun; 2 *s.,* 1 *d.; educ.* Pol. Warfare Coll. 55; War CGSC, Armed Forces U. 79; Dean, Polwar Cadre Tng. Cent., MND 76-77; Dir., Pol. Warfare Dept., 10th Field, Army 77-79, Pol. Warfare Dept., Mil. Police Cmd. 79-81, & Pol. Warfare Dept., Twn. Garrison Cmd. 81-84; Dep. Dir.-Gen., Gen. Pol. Warfare Dept., MND 84-87; Dep. C-in-C, Twn. Garrison Cmd. 87-88; Dep. Dir.-Gen., Gen. Pol. Warfare Dept., MND 88-90, Dir.-Gen. 90-94; Chmn., VAC 94-99; *Add.* c/o Off. of the Pres., Taipei 100.

YANG, TOU-HSIUNG 楊頭雄
Chmn., Vedan Ent. Corp. 88-; Dir., Chung Shing Cml. Bk. 92-; *b.* Twn. Dec. 1, '42; *m.* Lin, Pi-chu; 5 *s.; educ.* Grad., Tamsui Oxford Coll.; Pres., Vedan Ent. Corp. 79-88; Mng. Dir., Bioind. Dev. Assn. 89-92; Twn. MSG's Assn. 88-94; Chmn., Taichung County Task Cttee., Ch. Youth Corps. 92-96; Bd. Dir., Ch. Nat. Fed. of Ind. 91-97; *Add.* 65 Hsing An Rd., Shalu, Taichung 433.

YANG, TSU-YU
(See YANG, HERNY T.Y. 楊祖祐)

YANG, YEONG-BIN 楊永斌
Dean, Coll. of Engr., NTU 99-; Prof. of Civil Engr., NTU 88-; Pres., Ch. Soc. of Structural Engr. 98-; *b.* Fukien Aug. 22, '54; *m.* Huang, Ru-wong; 1 *s.,* 2 *d.; educ.* BS, NTU 76, MS 80; Ph.D., Cornell U. 84; Assc. Prof., Dept. of Civil Engr., NTU 84-88, Chmn. 95-98. *Publ.:* 4 bk., 87 jour. papers, 90 conf. papers & 65 reports; *Add.* c/o Dept. of Civil Engr., NTU, 1 Roosevelt Rd., Sect. 4, Taipei 106.

YANG, YUNG-PIN
(See YANG, YEONG-BIN 楊永斌)

YAO, ENG-CHI 饒穎奇
V. Pres., Legis. Yuan 99-; Dir., Coun. of Soc. Service, ROC Chapter 93-; Mem., Legis. Yuan 81-; Pres., Twn. Soc. Aff. Coun. 87-; *b.* Twn. Nov. 5, '34; *m.* Kao, Shu-duan; *3 d.; educ.* BA, NCHU 63; Studied, Sun Yat-sen Inst. on Policy Res. & Dev.; Sr. Sp., TCG; Instr., NCHU; Dep. Sec.-Gen., CC, KMT 92-93, Exec. Sec., Policy Coordination Cttee. 96-99, Dir., Dept. of Party-Govt. Coordination of the Legis. Yuan 93-99. *Publ.: Theory & Practice of Soc. Work; Welfare for the Elderly; Services for the Elderly; Hakka—One of the Main Ethnic Groups of the Han People; Add.* 1 Chung Shan S. Rd., Taipei 100.

YAU, SHING-TUNG 丘成桐
Mem., Acad. Sinica 84-; Prof. of Math., Harvard U. 87-; *b.* Kwangtung Apr. 4, '49; *m.* Kuo, Yu-yun; *2 s.; educ.* Ph.D., UC-Berkly. 71; D.Sc., Ch. U. of Hong Kong; Prof., Stanford U. 74-79, Inst. for Advanced Studies, Princeton U. 79-84, & U. of Calif., San Diego 84-87; For. Mem., Ch. Acad. of Sc. 94; MacArthur Fel. 85; Nat. Medal of Sc., USA 97; *Add.* Dept. of Math., Harvard U., 1 Oxford St., Cambridge, MA 02138, USA.

YAUNG, CHIH-LIANG 楊志良
Dep. Min., DOH 99-; Prof., Sch. of Pub. Health, NTU 90-; Chmn., Health Care Cost Arbitration Cttee., Nat. Health Ins. (NHI) Prog. 98-; Chmn., NHI Sup. Cttee. 99-; *b.* Twn. Mar. 12, '46; *m.* Lee, Chao-ho; *1 d.; educ.* MB, NTNU 68; MPH, NTU 72; Ph.D., Population Planning, U. of Michigan 79; Jr. Sp., Twn. Prov. Inst. of Family Planning 68-69; Teaching Asst., Sch. of Pub. Health, NTU 72-74, Instr. 74-80, Assc. Prof. 80-90, Chmn. 84-87; Chief Adv., Taskforce for NHI Plan, CEPD 88-90; Dir., Info. Dept., NTU Hosp. 92-96; Cttee. Mem., NHI Dispute Review Cttee. 94; Prof. & Dir., Inst. of Health Care Org. Admin., NTU 96-99; *Add.* 14th Fl., 100 Ai Kuo E. Rd., Taipei 100.

YEE, CHIEN-CHIU 易勁秋
Nat. Policy Adv. to the Pres.; Mem., CAC, KMT; *b.* Szechwan Jan. 17, '18; *m.* Lin, Chih-jung; *2 s., 1 d.; educ.* LL.B., NCCU; Cent. Pol. Cadre Sch.; Nat. Def. Coll.; Dir., Pers. Admin. Bu., MND 59-66; Chief, Cadre Mng., CC, KMT 66-72, Chmn., Taipei Mun. Cttee. 72-79; Bd. Chmn., CTS 79-92; Mem., CC, KMT; *Add.* P.O. Box 20-15, Hsintien, Taipei County 231.

YEH, ALBERT T.H. 葉天行
Rep., TECO, Luxembourg 96-; *b.* Chekiang Jan. 10, '34; *m.* Sun, Pu-fei; *1 d.; educ.* BS, Econ., NTU 56; M., Jour., NCCU 58; Passed Sr. Civil Service Exam. 57, & Sp. Exam.

A 68; Staff Mem., GIO 58-62; Asst. Press Sp., Emb. in Thailand 63-69; Sr. Sp., GIO 69-71; Liaison Off. in Mid-E. Area 71-76; Dir., Press Div., ROC Rep. Off. in Thailand 76-77; Dep. Dir., Intl. Info. Services Dept., GIO 77-79, Dir., Publ. Aff. Dept. 79-80, & Intl. Info. Services Dept. 80-84; Dep. Dir.-Gen. & concur. Dir. of Press Div., Taipei Wirtschafts- und Kulturbüro, Bonn 84-91; Dep. Dir.-Gen., GIO 91-96. *Publ.:* "A Study of the Econ. News in Twn.'s Newspapers," *Jour. Semiannually,* Vol. 2, No. 4; *Add.* TECO, 50 Route d'Esch, Luxembourg-Ville, L-1470 Grand-Duche de Luxembourg.

YEH, CHANG-TUNG 葉昌桐
Strategy Adv. to the Pres. 94-; *b.* Fukien Aug. 2, '29; *m.* Chao, Jung; *1 s., 2 d.; educ.* Ch. Naval Acad. 49; US Naval Post Grad. Sch. 61; US Naval War Coll. 67; Destroyer Cmdr. 69-70; Dep. Dir., 3rd Bu., Off. of the Pres. 73-75; Cmdr., Destroyer Squadron 75-76; Dep. C/S, GHQ, ROCN 76-77; Dep. Chief of the Gen. Staff Planning, MND 77-82, V. Chief of the Gen. Staff 82-88; C-in-C, GHQ, ROCN 88-92; Pres., Armed Forces U. 92-94; *Add.* 3rd Fl., 3 Lane 31, Wo Lung St., Taipei 106.

YEH, CHAO-HSIANG 葉肇祥
Chmn., Kaohsiung Mun. Cttee., KMT 99-; *b.* Fukien Aug. 12, '34; *m.* Lin, Hsiu-hsing; *3 s.; educ.* Studied, 2nd term, Pol. Staff. Sch. 54; Passed with hon., Sp. Exam. B 66; Studied, 17th term, Inst. of Policy Res. & Dev., KMT 83; Dir., Keelung Investigation Station KMT's cttees. in MOJ 68-70, Chief, Kaohsiung Investigation Station 82-85; Chmn., Chiayi City, Tainan County & Taichung City 88-94; V. Chmn., KMT's Kaohsiung Mun. Cttee. 94-99; *Add.* 463 Chien Kuo 1st Rd., Kaohsiung 807.

YEH, CHIN-FENG
(See YEH, CHIN-FONG 葉金鳳)

YEH, CHIN-FONG 葉金鳳
Min. of Justice 99-2000; Mem., Standing Cttee., Twn. Prov. Br., Soc. for Strategic Studies, ROC 91-; Mem., CC, KMT 88-; *b.* Twn. June 22, '43; *m.* Lin, Yao-tung; *educ.* LL.B., NCHU 65; Judge & Presiding Judge, Taichung & Yunlin dist. courts 69-81; Mem., NA 81-93; Adjunct Prof., Nat. Chin Yi Inst. of Tech. 84-92; Chmn., Presidium, 81-92; Judge, Taichung Br., Twn. High Court, & Supreme Court 81-86; Sr. Sp., Jud. Yuan 86-87; Justice, Supreme Court 87-88; V. Chmn., MAC 92-96; Chmn., ROC Hqs. of Zonta Intl. 91-95; Min. without Portfolio 96-97; Mem., CAC, KMT 97; Min. of Int. 97-98; Dep. Sec.-Gen., KMT 98-99. *Publ.: Discussing the Rotation System of Judge & Dist.*

Attorney; *A Study of Petition & Petition Laws; Reinforcing the Claim of Violent & Econ. Crime in Order to Maintain the Soc. Order; Implementation of Const. & the Soc. Status of the Women; Women & Pol. Dev.; A Discussion of Contemporary Const. Reform; Scrutinizing the Controversy of Revising & Drafting the Const.;* etc.; *Add.* 130 Chungking S. Rd., Sect. 1, Taipei 100.

YEH, CHU-LAN 葉菊蘭

Min. of Trans. & Comms. & concur. Min. of State 2000-; Pres., Chen-Nan-Zon Memorial Found. 89-; *b.* Twn. Feb. 13, '49; *m.* Chen, Nan-zon (deceased); 1 *d.; educ.* LL.B., Fu Jen Catholic U. 71; Tchr., Miaoli Yu-min Ind. & Com. High Sch. 71-73; Dir., Business Dept., United Advertising Co., Ltd. 73-89; Convener, Int. Aff. Cttee., 1st Sess., Legis. Yuan 93, Mem. 90-2000; *Add.* 2 Changsha St., Sect. 1, Taipei 100.

YEH, HSIEN-CHING

(See YEH, SHIAN-CHING 葉憲清)

YEH, KOU-I 葉國一

Bd. Chmn., Inventec Group 75-, Inventec Elect. (M) SDN BHD 89-, Besta Elect. Co. Ltd. 89-, & Inventec Elect. (Shanghai) Co. Ltd. 91-; *b.* Taipei Apr. 21, '41; *m.* Wang, Fu-tai; 2 *s.; educ.* Hon. Dr., Chongju U., Korea; Dir., Twn. Elec. Appliance Mfrs.' Assn.; Dir., Elec. & Elect. Products Dev. Assn. of the ROC; V. Chmn., Sino-Japanese Found. for Educ. & Cul., & Japanese Studies Assn. of the ROC; Dir., Sino-Korean Cul. Found., & Ch. Found. for Mentally Retarded; V. Chmn., Great Cooperation Soc. Intl., Taipei Br.; V. Pres., Taipei Investors' Assn. in Malaysia; *Add.* 66 Hou Kang St., Shihlin Dist., Taipei 111.

YEH, NENG-CHE 葉能哲

Pres., Aletheia U. 99-; *b.* Taipei Sept. 14, '34; *m.* Yeh Lin, Tzu-huei; 5 *s.,* 3 *d.; educ.* B., Tamkang Coll. of Arts & Sc. 63; M., NTHU 65; Ph.D., Kyushu U. 69; M., Twn. Theological Coll.; Prof., Dept. of Math., Tamkang Coll. of Arts & Sc. 69-71, Dean, Grad. Sch. of Math. 70-71; Prof., Grad. Sch. of Math., NTHU 69-75; Pres., Tamsui Oxford Coll. 71-94; Pres., Tamsui Oxford U. Coll. 94-99. *Publ.:* 14 bk. & 8 theses on statistics & math.; *Add.* 32 Chen Li St., Tamsui, Taipei County 251.

YEH, SHIAN-CHING 葉憲清

Pres., Nat. Coll. of Phys. Educ. & Sports 99-; *b.* Twn. Oct. 30, '36; *m.* Chen, Chin-chu, 1 *s.,* 3 *d.; educ.* BS of Phys. Educ., NTNU 63; Studied, Tsukupa U., Japan 85; Dir., Dept. of Phys. Educ., Nat. Kaohsiung Tchrs.' Coll. 74-82;

Dir., Tso Ying Sports Training Cent., Ch. Phys. Educ. Promotion Assn. 82-84; Dean of Student Aff., Nat. Coll. of Phys. Educ. & Sports 86-90, Dean of Acad. Aff. 90-96, Chmn., Dept. of Sports Training Sc. 91-93. *Publ.:* 11 bk., 72 papers on periodicals, 17 conf. papers, & 5 res. papers; *Add.* 3th Fl., 46 Lane 416, Chung Shan Rd., Sect. 2, Panchiao, Taipei County 220.

YEH, SHIH-TAO 葉石濤

Writer; *b.* Twn. Nov. 1, '25; *m.* Chen, Yueh-te; 2 *s.; educ.* Grad., Tainan Normal Coll. 66; Tchr., Tainan City's Li-jen & Yung-fu elementary sch. 44-48 & 49-51, Chiayi City's Kuo-lu Elementary Sch. 55-57, Tainan County's Wen-hsien Elementary Sch. 57-65, Ilan County's Kuang-hsing Elementary Sch. 66-67, & Kaohsiung County's Chia-wei Elementary Sch. 67-91. *Publ.: Essays of Native Twn. Writers; Toward Twn. Lit.; A Little Twn. Man "A Tao"; The Red Shoes; Girl Friend;* etc.; *Add.* 196 Sheng Li Rd., Tsoying, Kaohsiung County 813.

YEH, SHU 葉曙

Mem., Acad. Sinica 66-; Part-time Prof., NTU 78-, Prof. Emeritus; *b.* Hupei Mar. 16, '08; *m.* Hsu, Siu-lien; 1 *s.,* 1 *d.; educ.* MB, Chiba Med. Coll., Japan 34, MD 38; Pathologist, Juntendo Hosp., Tokyo 39-43; Prof., Shanghai S.E. Med. Coll. 42-46, & NTU 46-78; Prof., Pathology, NTU, Dir., Grad. Inst. of Pathology. *Publ.: Skin Cancer in Chronic Arsenicism; Cancer in Twn.; Add.* 2729 Peawood Court, San Jose, CA 95132, USA.

YEH, TIEN-HSING

(See YEH, ALBERT T.H. 葉天行)

YEN, BING-FAN 顏秉璠

Amb. to Repub. of El Salvador 96-; *b.* Kiangsu June 5, '35; *m.* Liu, Rosa Hsiao-mei; 1 *d.; educ.* BA, NTNU; Madrid C.U., Spain; 3rd Sec., Emb. in Italy & Spain 70 & 70-72; Sec., Sun Yat-sen Cent., Spain 72-77; Dir., Quayaquil Br., Ch. Cml. Off., Ecuador 77-82; Dep. Dir., Dept. of Cent. & S. Am. Aff., MOFA 82-84; Rep., TECO, Brazil 84-94; Dir.-Gen., Dept. of Cent. & S. Am. Aff., MOFA 94-96; *Add.* Apartado Postal (06)956, San Salvador, El Salvador, C.A.

YEN, CHEN-HSING 閻振興

Sr. Adv. to the Pres. 94-; Prof. Emeritus, NTU 81-; Mem., Acad. Sinica 82-; *b.* Honan July 10, '12; *m.* Yen, Sou-lien; 2 *s.,* 1 *d.; educ.* BS, NTHU; MS & Ph.D., U. of Iowa; Engr., Yunnan-Burma Highway Bu. 41; Prof., Nat. S.we. Assc. U. 41-46; Chief Engr., Yellow River Engr. Bu. 46-47; Dean, Coll. of Engr., Honan U. 47-48; Dir., Engr. Dept., GHQ,

Ch. Navy 48-49; Chief Engr., Kaohsiung Harbor Bu. 49-57; Dean, Coll. of Engr., NTU 53-55; Comr. of Educ., TPG 62-63; Pres., NCKU 57-65; Min. of Educ. 65-69; Pres., Ch. Inst. of Engr. 66-67; Chmn., NYC 66-70, & AEC 66-72; Pres., NTHU 69-70, Chung Shan Inst. of Sc. & Tech. 69-75, & NTU 70-81; Chmn., AEC 81-90; Nat. Policy Adv. to the Pres. 90-94. *Publ.: The Tractive Force on Pebbles by Flowing Water; Determination of the Best Proportion of Canal Bends; Soil Consolidation & Settlement; Soil Compaction & Its Application; Gap-Closure Work of Yellow River at Hue-Yuan-Kou; The Educ. Thought of Confucius; The Planning & Implementation of 9-Year Free Educ.; Add.* 3 Lane 11, Ching Tien St., Taipei 106.

YEN, CHIN-LIEN 顏清連
Prof. of Civil Engr., NTU 77-; *b.* Twn. Sept. 7, '37; *m.* Yen Lin, Agnes Feng; 2 *d.; educ.* BS, NTU 60; MS, Queen's U., Can. 64; Ph.D., U. of Iowa 67; Asst. Prof. of Engr., U. of Puerto Rica, USA 66-67; Asst. Prof., Assc. Prof., & Prof., Howard U. 68-77; Chmn., Dept. of Civil Engr. 79-83; Sc. & Tech. Adv., MOE 85-87; Dean, Coll. of Engr., NTU 90-93; Miller Visiting Prof., U. of Illinois 94. *Publ.:* More than 70 papers & 40 tech. reports on hydraulics; *Add.* c/o Dept. of Civil Engr., NTU, 1 Roosevelt Rd., Sect. 4, Taipei 106.

YEN, CHING-CHANG 顏慶章
Pol. V. Min. of Finance 96-; *b.* Twn. Apr. 7, '48; *m.* Lo, Yueh-ching; 1 *s.,* 1 *d.; educ.* LL.B., NTU 70, LL.M. 74; MS, Comparative Law, U. of Michigan 81; Sec.-Gen., Medium Business Bk. of Twn. 78-79; Sr. Sp., MOF 81-83; Exec. Sec., Legal Com., MOF 83-85, & Taxation & Tariff Com. 85-92; Dep. Dir.-Gen., 1st Bu., Off. of the Pres. 92-93; Dir.-Gen., 1st Bu. & Keeper of Nat. Seals, Off. of the Pres. 93-96; Eisenhower Exchange Fel. 95. *Publ.: The Anti-Dumping Act & Customs Policy; Legal Problems of Sino-Am. Trade Negotiations; Unveil "GATT": Order & Trend of World Trade; Laws & Regln. of Intl. Econ. Rel.; Add.* 2 Ai Kuo W. Rd., Taipei 100.

YEN, CHING-LIEN
(See YEN, CHIN-LIEN 顏清連)

YEN, CHUNG-CHENG 顏忠誠
Gov., Fukien Prov. 98-; *b.* Fukien Sep. 26, '38; *m.* Yen Cheng, Chin-pao; 1 *s.,* 2 *d.; educ.* BS, Ch. Mil. Acad. 62; Army CGSC, Armed Forces U. 72, War CGSC 76, 84; Sun Yat-sen Inst. on Policy Res. & Dev., KMT 81; Cmdr., 319th Div. 86-88, 32nd Corps 88-89, Hualien & Taitung Def. Cmd. 89-91, Matsu Def. Cmd. 91-92; Chief of the Gen. Staff, GHQ, ROC Army 92-93; Cmdr., Kinmen Def.

Cmd. 93-96; Dep. C-in-C, GHQ, ROC Army 96-98; *Add.* 34 Ming Chuan Rd., Chincheng, Kinmen County 893.

YEN, KAI-TAI
(See YEN, KENNETH K.T. 嚴凱泰)

YEN, KAN-LIN 嚴甘霖
Bd. Chmn., Ch. Elec. Mfg. Corp. 88-; Pres., Wellin Investment Co. Ltd., Ta-Te Construction Co. Ltd., TOA Elevam Corp., & Hwa Chih Glass Co. Ltd.; Dir., Twn. Elec. & Elect. Mfg. Assn.; Sup., Mineral Assn., ROC; Mng. Dir., Miner Hosp. of Twn.; *b.* Twn. Nov. 16, '37; *m.* Chen, Hsiu-hsia; 1 *d.; educ.* BS, Chem. Engr., NTU; Studied, U. of Michigan; *Add.* 9 Chung Hsiao E. Rd. Sect. 2, Taipei 100.

YEN, KENNETH K.T. 嚴凱泰
CEO, Yulon Group; Dir., Ch. Motor Co. Ltd.; V. Chmn. & concur. Pres., Yulon Motor Co. Ltd.; Chmn., Nissan Twn. Ltd., Diamond Hosiery & Thread Co. Ltd., Yu Ki Ind. Co. Ltd., Yue Sheng Ind. Co. Ltd., Uni-Calsonic Corp., Ch. Ogihara Corp., Kian Shen Metal Works Co. Ltd., ROC-Spicer Ltd., ROC-Keeper Ind. Ltd.; V. Chmn., Tai Yuen Textile Co. Ltd., Sino Diamond Motors Corp., Carnival Ind. Ltd., Twn. Acceptance Corp., Newa Ins. Co. Ltd., Century Semi Conductor Inc.; *b.* Taipei May 23, '65; *m.* Chen, Li-lien; *educ.* Ridder Coll., USA; Chief Exec. V. Pres., Yulon Motor Co. Ltd. 89-99; *Add.* 19th Fl., 2 Tun Hua S. Rd., Sect. 2, Taipei 106.

YEN, PING-FAN
(See YEN, BING-FANG 顏秉璠)

YEN, VIVIAN W. 吳舜文
Bd. Chmn., Tai Yuen Textile Co. Ltd., Yulon Motor Co. Ltd., & Ch. Motor Co. Ltd.; Chmn., Automobile Safety Assn., ROC 81-; *b.* Kiangsu Nov. 5, '12; *m.* Yen, Tjing-ling (deceased); 1 *s.; educ.* B., St. John's U., USA; M., Columbia U.; Hon. Dr., St. John's U., & John F. Kennedy Coll.; Mem., Cttee. of Higher Exam. of the ROC 61-66; Prof., Soochow U. 57-76; Chmn., Nat. Shippers' Coun. Assn. 73-79, & Twn. Trans. Vehicle Mfg. Assn. 81-87; *Add.* 16th Fl., 2 Tun Hua S. Rd., Sect. 2, Taipei 106.

YIN, SHIH-HAO
(See YIN, SHIU-HAU 尹士豪)

YIN, SHIU-HAU 尹士豪
Mem., Control Yuan 99-; *b.* Anhwei Mar. 10, '38; *m.* Teng, Loah-sheng; 2 *s.; educ.* BS, Mech. Engr., NTU 64; MS, Mech. & Aerospace Engr., Montana State U. 69, Ph.D. 72;

Hon. D.Sc., Cleveland State U. 91; Assc. Prof. & Head, Mech. Engr. Dept., Chung Yuan Christian U. 72-80; Prof., NTU 75-81; Prof. & Dean, Coll. of Engr., Chung Yuan Christian U. 75-82, Pres. 82-91; Dir.-Gen., Dept. of Youth Aff., CC, KMT 91-93; Chmn., NYC 93-96; Bd. Chmn., Tang Eng Iron Works Co. Ltd. 96-99; *Add.* 2 Chung Hsiao E. Rd., Sect. 1, Taipei 100.

YIN, TSUNG-WEN 殷宗文
Sec.-Gen., NSC 99-2000; *b.* Kiangsu June 2, '32; *m.* Chen, Hsueh-mei; 2 *s.; educ.* 25th Class, Mil. Acad. 54; 3rd Class, Elite Offs.' Course 64; Cmd. & Staff U. of Germany 70; War Coll., Armed Forces U. 76; Platoon Leader, Com. Cmdr., Bn. Cmdr., Brig., Div. Cmdr., Army Cmdr. 54-83; Asst. Dept. Chief of the Gen. Staff, J-3, MND 83-85; C/S, Army Corps 85-87; Cmdr., Penghu Def. Cmd. 87-89; Dir., Mil. Intelligence Bu., MND 89-93; Dep. Dir.-Gen., Nat. Sec. Bu. 93, Dir. 93-99; *Add.* 122 Chungking S. Rd., Sect. 1, Taipei 100.

YIN, YUN-PENG
(See YING, DIANE 殷允芃)

YING, DIANE 殷允芃
Pub. & Ed.-in-Chief, *Common Health Mag.* 98-; Pub. & Ed., *Common Wealth Mag.* 81-; Comr., NUC 90-, Nat. Cul. Assn.; *b.* Sian May 13, '41; *educ.* BA, Eng. Lit., NCKU; MS, Jour., U. of Iowa; Staff Reporter, *Philadelphia Inquirer* 68-70; Twn. Corr., *United Press Intl.* 73-76, *Asian Wall St. Jour.* 77-81, & *New York Times* 77-79; Lectr., NCCU 70-87. *Publ.: The Brilliance of the Ch. & Others; The Rising Generation; The Decision-makers; People of the Pacific Century; Waiting for Heroes; One Who Lights the Lamp; Respect Heaven & Love People; Add.* 4th Fl., 87 Sungkiang Rd., Taipei 104.

YOUNG, MING-SHING 楊明興
Pres., Nat. Chin-Yi Inst. of Tech. 99-; Prof. of EE, NCKU 91-; Summoner of Med. Engr., NScC 98-; *b.* Twn. Sep. 20, '52; *m.* Chuang, Hsiu-yuan; 1 *s.;* 1 *d.; educ.* BSEE, NCKU 75, MS 77, & Ph.D. 83; Chief Sec., Engr. Coll., NCKU 87-93, Chmn., Dept. of EE 93-96; Dir., Engr. & Tech. Promotion Cent., NScC 96-97; Pres., Nat. Chin-Yi Jr. Coll. of Tech. 96-99. *Publ.:* 10 papers in domestic jour., 21 papers in intl. jour., 35 domestic conf. papers, & 38 intl. conf. papers; *Add.* Nat. Chin-Yi Inst. of Tech., 35 Lane 215 Chung Shan Rd., Sect. 1, Taiping, Taichung County 411.

YU, ALBERT 余建新
Pub., *Ch. Times* 85-; *b.* Taipei May 31, '52; *m.* Cheng, Sophia; 2 *c.; educ.* Grad., San Francisco U.; Chief, San Francisco Off., *Ch. Times* (US Edition) 77-78, Dep. Gen. Mgr. 78-82, Gen. Mgr. 82-84; *Add.* 132 Ta Li St., Taipei 108.

YU, CHENG
(See YU, CHEN S. 俞政)

YU, CHEN S. 俞政
Chmn., Fubon Cml. Bk. 99-; *b.* Kiangsu Feb. 10, '30; *m.* Yu Hu, Doris; 1 *d.; educ.* BS, U. of Wisconsin; Exec. V. Pres., Export-Import Bk. of ROC 79-80, Chiao Tung Bk. 80; Dir., Dept. of Sec., CBC 80-81, Gen. Mgr., Dept. of For. Exchange 81-85; Dep. Gov. of CBC 85-94; Chmn., Chiao Tung Bk. 94-98; *Add.* 25th Fl., 169 Jen Ai Rd., Sect. 4, Taipei 106.

YU, CHENG-HSIEN 余政憲
Magis., Kaohsiung County 93-; *b.* Twn. Sept. 8, '59; *m.* Cheng, Kuei-lien; 1 *s.,* 2 *d.; educ.* BA, Feng Chia U.; Staff, Supt.'s Off., Chang Gung Memorial Hosp. (Kaohsiung) 84-86; Mem., Legis. Yuan 87-93; *Add.* 132 Kuang Fu Rd., Sect. 2, Fengshan, Kaohsiung County 830.

YU, CHIEN-HSIN
(See YU, ALBERT 余建新)

YU, HSI-KUN
(See YU, SHYI-KUN 游錫堃)

YU, KUO-HUA
(See YU, KUO-HWA 俞國華)

YU, KUO-HWA 俞國華
Sr. Adv. to the Pres. 89-; V. Chmn., KMT 97-; *b.* Chekiang Jan. 10, '14; *m.* Toong, Me-tsung; 2 *s.; educ.* NTHU 34; Grad. Sch., Harvard U. 44-46; London Sch. of Econ., UK 46-47; Hon. Dr. of Com., St. John's U., USA 73; Sec. to the Pres., NMC 36-44; Alt. Exec. Dir., Intl. Bk. for Recon. & Dev. 47-50, & Intl. Monetary Fund 51-55; Pres., CTC 55-61; Mng. Dir., Ch. Dev. Corp. 59-67; Bd. Chmn., Bk. of Ch. 61-67, & Ch. Ins. Co. 61-67; Alt. Gov., Intl. Bk. for Recon. & Dev. 64-67; Min. of Finance 67-69; Gov., Intl. Bk. for Recon. & Dev. for the ROC 67-69, & CBC 69-84; Min. without Portfolio 69-84; Gov., Intl. Monetary Fund for the ROC 69-80, & Asian Dev. Bk. for the ROC 69-84; Chmn., CEPD 77-84; Premier 84-89; *Add.* c/o Off. of the Pres., Taipei 100.

YU, KUANG-CHUNG
(See YU, KWANG-CHUNG 余光中)

YU, KUANG-HUA
(See YU, KUANG-HWA 余光華)

YU, KUANG-HWA 余光華
Chmn., Twn. Salt Ind. Corp. 94-; *b.* Hupei May 20, '40; *m.* Lu, Li-kang; 1 *s.,* 2 *d.; educ.* BS, Mining & Metallurgy Engr., NCKU 64; V. Gen. Mgr., Twn. Aluminium Corp. 65-85; Dir., Prof. Tng. Cent., MOEA 85-89; Pres., Twn. Salt Works 89-94. *Publ.: Factor of the Influence on Electrolytic Pot-line; Application of Computer in Operating the Electrolytic Cell; Study on Saving Energy of Anode Block; Add.* 297 Chien Kang Rd., Sect. 1, Tainan 702.

YU, KWANG-CHUNG 余光中
Chair Prof., Inst. of For. Lang. & Lit., Nat. Sun Yat-Sen U. 91-; *b.* Nanking Sept. 9, '28; *m.* Fan, Wo-chun; 4 *d.; educ.* BA, NTU; MA, Iowa State U. ; Lectr., NTNU 58-66; Assc. Prof., W. Michigan U. 65-66, & NTNU 66-70; Chmn., Dept. of W. Lang. & Lit., NCCU 72-74; Prof., Ch. U. of Hong Kong 74-85; Dean, Coll. of Lib. Arts, Nat. Sun Yat-Sen U. 85-91; Sun Yat-sen Chair Prof.; Pres., Taipei Ch. Cent., PEN Intl.; Hon. Fel., Hong Kong Transl. Soc. *Publ.: White Jade Bitter Gourd; The Untrammeled Traveler; Assns. of the Lotus; Selected Poetry of Yu Kwang-chung; Memory is Where the Railway Reaches; Calling for Ferry; Dream & Geog.; The Night Watchman; From Hsu Hsia-ke to van Gogh; The Pomegranate; Prefaces in Order; Ch. Versions of Oscar Wilde's: The Importance of Being Earnest; Lady Windermere's Fan; & An Ideal Husband; Add.* 70 Lien Hai Rd., Kaohsiung 804.

YU, SHYI-KUN 游錫堃
V. Premier, ROC 2000-; Mem., Cent. Exec. Cttee., DPP; Prof., Nat. Fine Arts Acad.; Chmn., Lanyang Cul. & Educ. Found. 90-; *b.* Twn. Apr. 25, '48; *m.* Yang, Pao-yu; 2 *s.; educ.* Grad., Chih Lee Coll. of Business 75; BA, Pol., Tunghai U. 85; Farmer 62-70; Mem., TPA 81-89; Sec.-Gen., Tangwai (outside the KMT Party) Cent. Backing Cttee. for the '83 Elections; Founder, *Kavalan Jour.,* Pres. 86-88; Convener, Tangwai's Nat. Backing Cttee. for the '86 Elections; Mem., CSC, DPP 87-90; Founder, Youngsun Cul. & Educ. Found. 90; Magis., Ilan County 89-97; Chmn., Taipei MRT 98-99; Sec.-Gen., CC, DPP 99-2000. *Publ.: The Resignation of Tangwai Assemblymen 85; The Rd. to Dem., The Love for Native Land 89; Add.* Exec. Yuan, 1 Chung Hsiao E. Rd., Sect. 1, Taipei 100.

YU, TSUNG-HSIEN
(See YU, TZONG-SHIAN 于宗先)

YU, TZONG-SHIAN 于宗先
Mem., Acad. Sinica 88-; Dir., Ch. Inst. of Econ. & Business 97-; *b.* Shantung Sept. 10, '30; *m.* Chao, Hsiu-ying; 3 *d.;* *educ.* BS, Econ., NTU 56; MS, Jour., NCCU 59; Ph.D., Econ., Indiana U. 66; Assc. Res. Fel., Inst. of Econ., Acad. Sinica 66-70, Res. Fel. 71-91, Dep. Dir. 72-76, Dir. 76-82; Assc. Prof. of Econ., NTU 66-70, Prof. 71-91; V. Pres., Chunghua Inst. for Econ. Res. 81-90, Pres. 90-96; Pres., Ch. Econ. Assn. 86-88. *Publ.: Econ. Forecasting; The Contemporary For. Trade of the ROC; Breakthrough in Econ. Thinking; Response to Econ. Challenges; Complications of Econ. Dev.; Twn.'s Econ. in Transition; The Bubble Econ. in Twn.; The Story of Twn.: Econ.; Bottlenecks & Breakthrough of Twn. Econ. Dev.; Twn.'s Inflation; Prediction for Aggregate Supply & Demand; Ed.,* 30 vol. of econ. studies, 145 articles on econ.; *Add.* 75 Chang Hsing St., Taipei 106.

YU, YING-SHIH 余英時
Mem., Acad. Sinica 74-; Michael Henry Strater U. Prof., Princeton U.; *b.* Tientsin Jan. 22, '30; *m.* Chen, Monica Shu-ping; 2 *d.; educ.* BA, New Asia Coll., Ch. U. of Hong Kong 52; Ph.D., Harvard U. 62; Hon. LL.D., Ch. U. of Hong Kong 74; Hon. Dr., Hong Kong U. 84; Instr., Harvard U. 62; Asst. Prof., U. of Michigan 62-66; Assc. Prof. & Prof. of Ch. Hist., Harvard U. 66-77; Pres., New Asia Coll., & concur. Pro-V. Chancellor, Ch. U. of Hong Kong 73-75; Charles Seymour Prof. of Hist., Yale U. 77-87; Prof., Princeton U.; Hu Shih Lecture Prof. 91-92. *Publ.: Trade & Expansion in Han Ch.; Fang I-chih: His Last Years & His Death; Tai Chen & Chang Hsueh-cheng; A Study in Mid-Ch'ing Intellectual Hist.; Hist. Studies on the Ch. Intelligentsia; Add.* 4588 Prov. Line Rd., Princeton, NJ 08540, USA.

YU-CHEN, YUEH-YING 余陳月瑛
Nat. Policy Adv. to the Pres.; Founder & Chmn., Kao Yuan Jr. Coll. of Tech. & Com.; *b.* Twn. Sept. 20, '25; *m.* Yu, Jui-yen; 2 *s.,* 4 *d.; educ.* Grad., Kinki U., Japan; Grad., Yu In U., USA; Mem., TPA; Mem., Legis. Yuan 84-85; Magis., Kaohsiung County 85-93; Mem., Deliberation Cttee. of Educ. Reform, Exec. Yuan; *Add.* 1 Yu Liao Rd., Tungling, Chiaotou, Kaohsiung 825.

YUAN, CHIA-LIU
(See YUAN, LUKE CHIA-LIU 袁家騮)

YUAN, CHIEN-SHENG
(See YUAN, JASON C. 袁健生)

YUAN, DANIEL TA-NIEN 阮大年
Pres., Nat. Taichung Tech. Inst. 99-; Mem., CC, KMT 88-; *b.* Kiangsu May 25, '40; *m.* Wang, Shao-fan; 1 *s.,* 3 *d.; educ.* BS, Chem. Engr., Tunghai U.; MS, Chem., N. Texas State U.; Ph.D., Materials Sc., U. of So. Calif. ; Prof.,

Chung Yuan Christian Coll. of Sc. & Engr. 74-75, Pres. 75-80; Pres., Chung Yuan Christian U. 80-82; Excc. Sec., Sc. & Tech. Adv. Group, Exec. Yuan 82-84; Pol. V. Min. of Educ. 84-87; Pres., NCTU 87-92; Pres., Tunghai U. 92-99. *Publ.: Eureka; Stabilized Zirconia as an Oxygen Pump; Sodium Activity in Liquid Sodium-Tin Alloys; An Electro-Chem. O2 & S2 Vapor Gauge; Add.* 129 San Min Rd., Sect. 3, Taichung 404.

YUAN, I-CHIN 袁貽瑾
Mem., Acad. Sinica 48-; *b.* Hupei Oct. 30, 1899; *m.* Chen, Be-yuan; 2 *s.,* 1 *d.; educ.* MD, Peking Union Med. Coll. 27; Dr.PH & D.Sc., Johns Hopkins U. 30 & 31; Delta Omega 30; Prof. of Public Health & Dept. Head, Peking Union Med. Coll. 37-42; Dir., Inst. of Epidemiology, & Nat. Inst. of Health 46-48; Dep. Min. of Health 48; Dep. Dir., Tuberculosis Res. Off., WHO 49-52; WHO Med. Dir. & concur. Chief Med. Adv. to UNICEF at the UN Hqs. 53-59; Visiting Prof. of Public Health, Coll. of Med., NTU 60-63; Visiting Scholar, E.-W. Cent., U. of Hawaii 63-64; Dir.-Gen., Acad. Sinica 64-68; Mem., Sino-Am. Sc. Cttee. 64-68. *Publ.:* Articles on public health, including biostatistics, epidemiology, demography, tuberculosis, nutrition, family planning; & etc.; *Add.* 2441 Webb Avenue, Apt. 15C, Bronx, New York, NY 10468, USA.

YUAN, JASON C. 袁健生
Dir.-Gen., TECO in Los Angeles 98-; *b.* Kweichow Feb. 1, '42; *m.* Yuan, Margaret; 1 *s.,* 1 *d.; educ.* B., Ch. Naval Acad. 63; MBA, S.ea. U., Washington, D.C. 77; Asst. Naval Attaché, Emb. in the USA 74-79 & Acting Naval Attaché 79; Sr. Staff, Public Aff. Div., CCNAA 79-80, Dep. Dir. 80-86, Dir. 86-91; Dir.-Gen., Dept. of N. Am. Aff., MOFA 91-94; Rep., TECO, Can. 94-96; Amb. to the Repub. of Panama 96-98; *Add.* 3731 Wilshire Blvd., Suite 700, Los Angeles, CA 90010, USA.

YUAN, LUKE CHIA-LIU 袁家騮
Mem., Acad. Sinica 59-; Bd. Chmn., Synchrotron Radiation Res. Cent., ROC 83-; Chief Coordinator, Feasibility Study of Prototype of a Superconducting Microsphere Camera for Energy Determination of a Charged Partical by Transition Radiation (ROC & France); Hon. Prof., Ch. U. of Sc. & Tech. (Hefei), Nankai U. (Tientsin), Honan U. (Kaifeng), S.we. U. (Nanking), Chengzhou U (Honan); Mem., New York Acad. of Sc.; Hon. Mem., Honan Acad. of Sc.; Mem., Ch. Academy of Sc., ROC; Fel., Am. Phys. Soc.; Mem., Sigma Xi; *b.* Honan Apr. 5, '12; *m.* Wu, Chien-hsiung; 1 *s.; educ.* BS, Yenching U. 32, MS 34; Ph.D., Calif. Inst. of Tech. 40; Hon. D.Sc., Nanjing U. PROC 94; Intl. House Fel., U. of Calif. 36-37; Grad. Asst., Calif. Inst. of Tech. 37-40, Res. Fel. 40-42; Res. Physicist, RCA Lab. 42-46; Res. Assc., Princeton U. 46-49; Assc. Physicist, Physicist, & Sr. Physicist, Brookhaven Nat. Lab. 49-82; Guggenheim Fel. 58; Visiting Prof., Centre d'Etudes Nucléaires de Saclay, France, & CERN, Geneva, Switzerland 72-76; Visiting Prof., European Org. Nuclear Res. 72-78; Bd. Dir., Adelphi U. Energy Res. Cent. 78-87; Visiting Prof., Inst. for High Energy Phys., Serpukhov, USSR 79, & U. of Paris 82; Upton Consultant 82-87. *Publ.: Nature of Matter; Interaction of Particle Phys. Res. in Sc. & Tech.; Sc. Papers & Methods of Experimental Nuclear Phys.; Add.* 15 Claremont Avenue, #73, New York, NY 10027, USA.

YUAN, TA-NIEN
(See YUAN, DANIEL TA-NIEN 阮大年)

YUNG, CHAUR-SHIN 楊朝祥
Min. of Educ. 99-2000; *b.* Twn. Nov. 5, '47; *m.* Gou, Jen-huey; 1 *s.,* 1 *d.; educ.* BA, NTNU 70; MA, U. of Minnesota 75; Ph.D., Penn. State U. 78; Asst. Prof., Voc. Tchr. Educ., U. of Arkansas 78-80; Assc. Prof., Ind. Educ., NTNU 80-82, Prof. & Dept. Head, Ind. Arts Educ. 82-86; Dir.-Gen., Dept. of Tech. & Voc. Educ., MOE 86-89; Admin. V. Min. of Educ. 89-94; Pol. V. Min. of Educ. 94-97; Chmn., RDEC 97-99. *Publ.: Career Guidance—Lifelong Process; Terminology of Voc. & Tech. Educ.; The Found. of Voc. Tech. Educ.; Job-seeking Skills; Add.* 7th Fl., 2-2 Chi Nan Rd., Sect. 1, Taipei 100.

Who's Who in the ROC II

Sample II

[1] **CHAI, TRONG R.** 蔡同榮
[2] Mem., Legis. Yuan 93-; [3] *b.* June 13, '35; [4] *educ.*
LL.B., NTU 58; DPS, U. of So. Calif. 69; [5] *Pol. Affi.*
DPP; [6] *Const.* Chiayi County; [7] Founding Pres., World
United Formosans for Independence 70-71 & Formosan
Assn. for Public Aff. 82-83; Mem., CSC, DPP; Pub., *Par-
liamentary Biweekly,* Legis. Yuan; [8] *Add.* 7th Fl.-7, 7
Tsingtao E. Rd., Taipei 100.

Item

[1] Name	[5] Political affiliation
[2] Occupation	[6] Constituency
[3] Vital statistics	[7] Political experience
[4] Education	[8] Address

Members of the Fourth Legislative Yuan
(February 1, 1999—January 31, 2002)

CHAI, TRONG R. 蔡同榮
Mem., Legis. Yuan 93-; *b.* June 13, '35; *educ.* LL.B., NTU
58; DPS, U. of So. Calif. 69; *Pol. Affi.* DPP; *Const.* Chiayi
County; Founding Pres., World United Formosans for Independence 70-71 & Formosan Assn. for Public Aff. 82-
83; Mem., CSC, DPP; Pub., *Parliamentary Biweekly,* Legis.
Yuan; *Add.* 7th Fl.-7, 7 Tsingtao E. Rd., Taipei 100.

CHANG, CHING-FANG 張清芳
Mem., Legis. Yuan 99-; *b.* Nov. 23, '52; *educ.* LL.B.,
Soochow U.; *Pol. Affi.* DPP; *Const.* Taipei County; Mem.,
TPA; *Add.* Rm. 808, 3-1 Chi Nan Rd., Sect. 1, Taipei 100.

CHANG, CHUAN-TIEN 張川田
Mem., Legis. Yuan 99-; *b.* Aug. 15, '45; *educ.* BPS, Tunghai
U. 73; *Pol. Affi.* DPP; *Const.* Ilan County; Mem., CAC,

DPP 90-92; Mem., NA 92-99; *Add.* Rm. 511, 3-1 Chi Nan
Rd., Sect. 1, Taipei 100.

CHANG, CHUN-HUNG 張俊宏
Mem., Legis. Yuan 95-; *b.* May 17, '38; *educ.* BPS & MPS,
NTU; *Pol. Affi.* DPP; *Const.* Nat.; Mem., TPA 77-79; Jailed
for Kaohsiung Incident 79-87; Sec.-Gen., DPP 88-91;
Mem., CSC, DPP 92-; Mem., NA (Nat.) 92; Mem., Legis.
Yuan (Taipei) 93-95; Mem., For. & Ovs. Ch. Aff. Cttee., Legis.
Yuan 94; *Add.* 6th Fl., 16 Pei Ping E. Rd., Taipei 100.

CHANG, FU-HSIN 張福興
Mem., Legis. Yuan 99-; *b.* July 21, '42; *educ.* LL.M., Kinki
U., Japan, Studied, Dr. Prog.; *Pol. Affi.* KMT; *Const.*
Hualien County; Mem., NA; Mem., CC, KMT; Mem., TPA
94-98; *Add.* Rm. 3406, 1 Tsingtao E. Rd., Taipei 100.

CHANG, FU-HSING
(See CHANG, FU-HSIN 張福興)

CHANG, HSIU-CHEN 張秀珍
Mem., Legis. Yuan 99-; *b.* Aug. 1, '51; *educ.* Grad., Ming Chuan U.; *Pol. Affi.* DPP; *Const.* Ovs. Nat.; Mem., NA 96-99; *Add.* Rm. 2123, 3-1 Chi Nan Rd., Sect. 1, Taipei 100.

CHANG, HSU-CHENG
(See CHANG, PARRIS H. 張旭成)

CHANG, HSUEH-SHUN 張學舜
Mem., Legis. Yuan 99-; *b.* Mar. 14, '60; *educ.* B., Shih Hsin U.; *Pol. Affi.* DPP; *Const.* Hsinchu County; Mem., TPA; *Add.* Rm. 201, 3-1 Chi Nan Rd., Sect. 1, Taipei 100.

CHANG, JEN-HSIANG 章仁香
Mem., Legis. Yuan 96-; *b.* June 27, '53; *educ.* MA, Ch. Cul. U.; *Pol. Affi.* KMT; *Const.* Lowland Aborigines; Lectr., Ch. Cul. U.; Mem., Home & Border Aff. Cttee., Legis. Yuan 96, & Budget Cttee. 97; *Add.* Rm. 515, 3-1 Chi Nan Rd., Sect. 1, Taipei 100.

CHANG, MING-HSIUNG 張明雄
Mem., Legis. Yuan 99-; *b.* Dec. 2, '44; *educ.* Grad., Yuanlin Sr. Agr. Sch.; *Pol. Affi.* KMT; *Const.* Nantou County; Mem., 10th Nantou CoCoun.; Magis., Chushan Urban Township, Nantou County; Mem., TPA; *Add.* Rm. 313, 3-1 Chi Nan Rd., Sect. 1, Taipei 100.

CHANG, PARRIS H. 張旭成
Mem., Legis. Yuan 93-; *b.* Dec. 30, '36; *educ.* MPS, U. of Washington 63; Ph.D., Columbia U. 69; *Pol. Affi.* DPP; *Const.* Ovs. Nat.; Prof. Emeritus, Pol. Sc., Penn. State U. 97-; Dir., Twn. DPP Mission in the USA; Pres., Steering Cttee., Unrepresented Nations & Peoples Org. 93-, & Twn. Inst. for Pol. Econ. & Strategic Studies 94-; Convener, For. & Ovs. Ch. Aff. Cttee., Legis. Yuan 93; *Add.* 7th Fl., 3-2 Tsingtao E. Rd., Taipei 100.

CHANG, SHIH-LIANG 張世良
Mem., Legis. Yuan 99-; *b.* July 7, '42; *educ.* MBA, John F. Kennedy U.; *Pol. Affi.* NP; *Const.* Nat.; Mem., Legis. Yuan (2 terms); Convener, Budget Cttee., Econ. Aff. Cttee., & For. Aff. Cttee., Legis. Yuan; *Add.* Rm. 3210, 1 Tsingtao E. Rd., Taipei 100.

CHANG TSAI, MEI 張蔡美
Mem., Legis. Yuan 99-; *b.* Feb. 4, '27; *educ.* MBA, Seattle Pacific U., USA; *Pol. Affi.* KMT; *Const.* Hsinchu City;

Mem., Hsinchu CCoun., Hsinchu CoCoun., & TPA; *Add.* Rm. 916, 3-1 Chi Nan Rd., Sect. 1, Taipei 100.

CHANG, WEN-YI 張文儀
Mem., Legis. Yuan 93-; *b.* Nov. 15, '48; *educ.* Ching Shui Sr. High Sch.; *Pol. Affi.* KMT; *Const.* Taichung County; Mem., NA 92-93; Convener, Finance Cttee., Legis. Yuan 94; *Add.* Rm. 609, 3-1 Chi Nan Rd., Sect. 1, Taipei 100.

CHAO, ERH-CHUNG 曹爾忠
Mem., Legis. Yuan 93-; *b.* Aug. 24, '54; *educ.* LL.M., Cent. Police Coll.; *Pol. Affi.* KMT; *Const.* Lienchiang County; Dir., Lienchiang County Police Station 90-92; Convener, Organic Laws Cttee., Legis. Yuan 94, Mem., Nat. Def. Cttee. 97; *Add.* Rm. 610, 3-1 Chi Nan Rd., Sect. 1, Taipei 100.

CHAO, YUNG-CHING
(See JAO, EUGENE YUNG-CHING 趙永清)

CHEN, CHAO-JUNG 陳朝容
Mem., Legis. Yuan 93-; *b.* Feb. 25, '56; *educ.* Grad., Nat. Taichung Inst. of Com. 90; *Pol. Affi.* KMT; *Const.* Changhua County; Mem., Changhua CoCoun. 86-93; Mem., Econ. Cttee., Legis. Yuan 96, Trans. & Comms. Cttee. 96-97, & Nat. Def. Cttee. 97; *Add.* Rm. 409, 3-1 Chi Nan Rd., Sect. 1, Taipei 100.

CHEN, CHAO-MING 陳超明
Mem., Legis. Yuan 99-; *b.* Dec. 17, '51; *educ.* B., PA, NCCU; *Pol. Affi.* Independent; *Const.* Miaoli County; Mem., TPA; *Add.* Rm. 2121, 3-1 Chi Nan Rd., Sect. 1, Taipei 100.

CHEN, CHAO-NAN
(See CHEN, ZAU-NAN 陳昭南)

CHEN, CHEN-HSIUNG 陳振雄
Mem., Legis. Yuan 99-; *b.* Jan. 6, '44; *educ.* Grad., Nat. Taichung Inst. of Com.; *Pol. Affi.* KMT; *Const.* Changhua County; Mem., Changhua CoCoun., & TPA; *Add.* Rm. 3510, 10 Tsingtao E. Rd., Taipei 100.

CHEN, CHEN-SHENG 陳振盛
Mem., Legis. Yuan 99-; *b.* Jan. 25, '50; *educ.* MA, Ch. Cul. U.; MPA, Tunghai U.; *Pol. Affi.* Independent; *Const.* Nantou County; Staff, Nantou County Govt.; Sec., Translator, Sect. Chief, Sp., Counsl., TPG; Counsl., Off. of the Pres.; Lectr., Shih Hsin U., Nat. Open U., Chaoyang U. of Tech.; *Add.* Rm. 3503, 10 Tsingtao E. Rd., Taipei 100.

CHEN, CHI-MAI 陳其邁
Mem., Legis. Yuan 96-; *b.* Dec. 23, '64; *educ.* MPH, NTU; *Pol. Affi.* DPP; *Const.* Kaohsiung City; Mem., Trans. & Comms. Cttee., Legis. Yuan; *Add.* Rm. 815, 3-1 Chi Nan Rd., Sect. 1, Taipei 100.

CHEN, CHIEH-JU 陳傑儒
Mem., Legis. Yuan 93-; *b.* Nov. 25, '37; *educ.* BA, NCKU; *Pol. Affi.* KMT; *Const.* Nat.; Mem., 7th & 8th Taichung CoCoun.; Mem., Taichung County Cttee., KMT, & Twn. Prov. Cttee.; Sec.-Gen., KMT Caucus, Legis. Yuan 93-96, Mem., Econ. Cttee.; *Add.* Rm. 601, 3-1 Chi Nan Rd., Sect. 1, Taipei 100.

CHEN, CHIEN-CHIH 陳健治
Mem., Legis. Yuan 99-; *b.* Jan. 25, '44; *educ.* M., N.E. Missouri State U.; *Pol. Affi.* KMT; *Const.* Nat.; Mem., Dep. Spkr., Spkr., Taipei CCoun.; *Add.* Rm. 2132, 3-1 Chi Nan Rd., Sect. 1, Taipei 100.

CHEN, CHIN-JUN 陳景峻
Mem., Legis. Yuan 99-; *b.* June 15, '56; *educ.* Res., Pol. Sc., NTU; B., Ch. Cul. U.; *Pol. Affi.* DPP; *Const.* Taipei County; Mayor, Sanchung City, Taipei County; *Add.* Rm. 803, 3-1 Chi Nan Rd., Sect. 1, Taipei 100.

CHEN, CHIN-TING 陳進丁
Mem., Legis. Yuan 99-; *b.* Sept. 26, '46; *educ.* Grad., Army Trans. Acad.; *Pol. Affi.* Independent; *Const.* Changhua County; Mem., NA; Chmn., Changhua Trans. Assn.; *Add.* Rm. 203, 3-1 Chi Nan Rd., Sect. 1, Taipei 100.

CHEN, CHING-CHUN
(See CHEN, CHIN-JUN 陳景峻)

CHEN, CHING-PAO 陳清寶
Mem., Legis. Yuan 93-; *b.* Dec. 9, '55; *educ.* BA, Nat. Twn. Ocean U.; *Pol. Affi.* KMT; *Const.* Kinmen County; Mem., Trans. & Comms. Cttee., Legis. Yuan 94, & Budget Cttee. 97; Convener, Expenditure Inspection Cttee., Legis. Yuan, Disciplinary Cttee., Nat. Def. Cttee., & Rules Cttee.; *Add.* Rm. 805, 3-1 Chi Nan Rd., Sect. 1, Taipei 100.

CHEN, CHIUNG-TSAN
(See CHEN, GENE-TZN 陳瓊讚)

CHEN, CHUNG-HSIN
(See CHEN, CHUNG-SHIN 陳忠信)

CHEN, CHUNG-SHIN 陳忠信
Mem., Legis. Yuan 99-; *b.* April 15, '49; *educ.* BS, Tunghai U.; *Pol. Affi.* DPP; *Const.* Nat.; Dep. Sec.-Gen., DPP; *Add.* Rm. 210, 3-1 Chi Nan Rd., Sect. 1, Taipei 100.

CHEN, GENE-TZN 陳瓊讚
Mem., Legis. Yuan 96-; Dir.-Gen., Dept. of Org. Aff., KMT 97-; *b.* July 1, '41; *educ.* LL.B., NTU; *Pol. Affi.* KMT; *Const.* Nat.; Tchr.; Mem., NA; Prosecutor, Kaohsiung Dist. Court, & Taipei Dist. Court; Lawyer; Mem., Finance Cttee., Legis. Yuan, 96-; *Add.* Rm. 307, 3-1 Chi Nan Rd., Sect. 1, Taipei 100.

CHEN, HORNG-CHI 陳鴻基
Mem., Legis. Yuan 96-; *b.* Sept. 30, '49; *educ.* BA, Nihon U., Japan; *Pol. Affi.* KMT; *Const.* Taipei City; Mem., NA; Dep. Dir., Dept. of Party-Govt. Coordination of the Legis. Yuan, KMT; Mem., Home & Border Aff. Cttee., Legis. Yuan 96-; *Add.* 2nd Fl., 5-1 Chen Chiang St., Taipei 100.

CHEN, HSUEH-SHENG
(See CHEN, SHEI-SAINT 陳學聖)

CHEN, HUNG-CHANG 陳宏昌
Mem., Legis. Yuan 94-; *b.* Mar. 2, '56; *educ.* M., Far Ea. U., Philippines; *Pol. Affi.* KMT; *Const.* Taipei County; Chmn., Taipei County Folk Athletics Cttee.; *Add.* Rm. 903, 3-1 Chi Nan Rd., Sect. 1, Taipei 100.

CHEN, HUNG-CHI
(See CHEN, HORNG-CHI 陳鴻基)

CHEN, JUNG-SHENG
(See CHEN, RONG-SHEN 陳榮盛)

CHEN, KEN-TE 陳根德
Mem., Legis. Yuan 99-; *b.* Jan. 18, '56; *educ.* Grad., Nat. Taoyuan Inst. of Agr.; *Pol. Affi.* KMT; *Const.* Taoyuan County; Spkr., Taoyuan CoCoun.; *Add.* Rm. 503, 3-1 Chi Nan Rd., Sect. 1, Taipei 100.

CHEN, MING-WEN 陳明文
Mem., Legis. Yuan 99-; *b.* May 13, '54; *educ.* B., Tunghai U.; *Pol. Affi.* KMT; *Const.* Chiayi County; Mem., Chiayi CoCoun.; Spkr., 10th Chiayi CoCoun.; Mem., TPA 86-98; *Add.* Rm. 3101, 1 Tsingtao E. Rd., Taipei 100.

CHEN, RONG-SHEN 陳榮盛
Mem., Legis. Yuan 99-; *b.* May 4, '46; *educ.* MBA, Seattle Pacific U., USA; *Pol. Affi.* KMT; *Const.* Tainan City; Mem.,

TPA 94-98; *Add.* Rm. 2113, 3-1 Chi Nan Rd., Sect. 1, Taipei 100.

CHEN, SHEI-SAINT 陳學聖
Mem., Legis. Yuan 99-; *b.* Sept. 28, '57; *educ.* M., Metro. State U., USA; *Pol. Affi.* KMT; *Const.* Taipei City; Mem., Taipei CCoun. 91-98; *Add.* Rm. 810, 3-1 Chi Nan Rd., Sect. 1, Taipei 100.

CHEN, SHENG-HUNG 陳勝宏
Mem., Legis. Yuan 99-; *b.* June 5, '44; *educ.* B., Feng Chia U.; *Pol. Affi.* DPP; *Const.* Nat.; Mem., 3rd, 4th, 5th, 6th, 7th term, Taipei CCoun. *Add.* Rm. 212, 3-1 Chi Nan Rd., Sect. 1, Taipei 100.

CHEN, ZAU-NAN 陳昭南
Mem., Legis. Yuan 99-; *b.* Dec. 11, '42; *educ.* Grad., Hochschule für Musik und Darstellende Kunst Wien, Austria; *Pol. Affi.* DPP; *Const.* Nat.; Mem., Legis. Yuan 93-96; *Add.* Rm. 816, 3-1 Chi Nan Rd., Sect. 1, Taipei 100.

CHENG, CHAO-MING
(See, CHENG, TSAO-MIN 鄭朝明)

CHENG, CHIN-LING 鄭金玲
Mem., Legis. Yuan 99-; *b.* Aug. 6, '46; *educ.* B., Takushoku U., Japan; *Pol. Affi.* KMT; *Const.* Taoyuan County; Mem., Taoyuan CoCoun., & TPA; *Add.* Rm. 3108, 1 Tsingtao E. Rd., Taipei 100.

CHENG, FENG-SHIH 鄭逢時
Mem., Legis. Yuan 93-; *b.* Dec. 27, '41; *educ.* Grad., Supplementary Open Jr. Coll. for PA, NCCU; MPA, Tunghai U.; *Pol. Affi.* KMT; *Const.* Nat.; Mem., Taipei CoCoun. 68-73, NA 73-79, & TPA 81-93; Dep. Dir., Twn. Prov. Cttee., KMT 89-93; Dir.-Gen., Dept. of Intra- & Inter-Party Rel., CC, KMT 93; Mem., Trans. & Comms. Cttee., Legis. Yuan 94, & Educ. Cttee. 97; *Add.* 4th Fl., 3-2 Tsingtao E. Rd., Taipei 100.

CHENG, LONG-SHUI 鄭龍水
Mem., Legis. Yuan 96-; *b.* Dec. 7, '59; *educ.* BA, Tamkang U.; *Pol. Affi.* NP; *Const.* Nat.; Founder, Pub. & Ed.-in-Chief, *Echo*; Mem., Educ. Cttee., Legis. Yuan 96; *Add.* 3-1 Chi Nan Rd., Sect. 1, Taipei 100.

CHENG, PAO-CHING 鄭寶清
Mem., Legis. Yuan 96-; *b.* Jan. 10, '55; *educ.* MPA, NCHU; *Pol. Affi.* DPP; *Const.* Taoyuan County; Mem., NA, & Convener; Dir., Secretariat, CC, DPP, Chmn., Taoyuan County Cttee., Pres., Nat. Soc. of Cttee. Chmn.; Mem.,

Educ. Cttee., Legis. Yuan 96, & Trans. & Comms. Cttee. 97; *Add.* Rm. 602, 3-1 Chi Nan Rd., Sect. 1, Taipei 100.

CHENG, TSAO-MIN 鄭朝明
Mem., Legis. Yuan 96-; *b.* Mar. 9, '52; *educ.* MBA, Mercer U., USA; *Pol. Affi.* DPP; *Const.* Pingtung County; Exec. Dir., 1st Pingtung Cttee., DPP; Mem., 10th Pingtung CoCoun.; Dep. Spkr., 11th Pingtung CoCoun.; Mem., Budget Cttee., Legis. Yuan 96, & Organic Laws Cttee. 97; *Add.* Rm. 1009, 3-1 Chi Nan Rd., Sect. 1, Taipei 100.

CHENG, YUNG-CHIN 鄭永金
Mem., Legis. Yuan 96-; *b.* Oct. 8, '49; *educ.* Grad., Tahua Ind. Coll.; *Pol. Affi.* KMT; *Const.* Hsinchu County; Dep. Spkr., Hsinchu CoCoun., & Spkr.; Convener, Trans. & Comms. Cttee., Legis. Yuan 96; *Add.* Rm. 1005, 10th Fl., 3-1 Chi Nan Rd., Sect. 1, Taipei 100.

CHIANG, CHI-WEN
(See CHIANG, YI-WEN 江綺雯)

CHIANG, YI-WEN 江綺雯
Mem., Legis. Yuan 99-; *b.* Mar. 20, '49; *educ.* Ed.D., Drake U., USA 90; *Pol. Affi.* KMT; *Const.* Kaohsiung City; Prof., Wen Tzao Coll. of Modern Lang.; Prof., Sch. of Adult Educ., Nat. Kaohsiung Normal U.; Mem., NA 92-96; *Add.* Rm. 207, 3-1 Chi Nan Rd., Sect. 1, Taipei 100.

CHIEN, HSI-CHIEH 簡錫堦
Mem., Legis. Yuan 96-; *b.* Mar. 15, '47; *educ.* BA, Tamsui Oxford U. Coll.; *Pol. Affi.* DPP; *Const.* Nat.; Mem., CC, DPP 86-87; Sec.-Gen., Twn. Labor Front 90-95; Adv., Twn. Labor Union of Comms. Ind., & Twn. Labor Union of Petroleum Ind.; Convener, Jud. Cttee., Legis. Yuan 96, & Home & Border Aff. Cttee. 96; Pres., Quality Life Cul. & Educ. Found.; *Add.* Rm. 312, 3-1 Chi Nan Rd., Sect. 1, Taipei 100.

CHIN, HUI-CHU 秦慧珠
Mem., Legis. Yuan 99-; *b.* Mar. 27, '55; *educ.* MA, Fu Jen Catholic U.; Ph.D. Candidate, Ch. Cul. U.; *Pol. Affi.* KMT; *Const.* Taipei City; Mem., Taipei CCoun.; Mem., CC, KMT; *Add.* Rm. 3203, 1 Tsingtao E. Rd., Taipei 100.

CHIN TSENG, CHEN-LI
(See CHIN TSENG, JEAN-LIE 靳曾珍麗)

CHIN TSENG, JEAN-LIE 靳曾珍麗
Mem., Legis. Yuan 96-; *b.* Aug. 29, '33; *educ.* MS, Nursing, U. of Dubuque, Iowa, USA; *Pol. Affi.* KMT; *Const.* Nat.; Mem., Nat. Def. Cttee., Legis. Yuan 99; Pres., Nurses' AIDS Pre-

vention Found., & The Nat. Union of Nurses' Assn., ROC; *Add.* Rm. 405, 3-1 Chi Nan Rd., Sect. 1, Taipei 100.

CHIU, CHING-CHUN 邱鏡淳
Mem., Legis. Yuan 99-; *b.* Dec. 8, '49; *educ.* M., St. Thomas Aquinas Coll., USA; *Pol. Affi.* KMT; *Const.* Hsinchu County; Mem., TPA; *Add.* Rm. 3207, 1 Tsingtao E. Rd., Taipei 100.

CHIU, CHUANG-LIANG 邱創良
Mem., Legis. Yuan 99-; *b.* Sept. 10, '55; *educ.* Grad., Yu Ta Jr. Coll. of Com.; Res., Grad. Prog., Tamkang U.; *Pol. Affi.* Independent; *Const.* Taoyuan County; Dep. Spkr., Taoyuan CoCoun.; Mem., TPA; *Add.* Rm. 3505, 10 Tsingtao E. Rd., Taipei 100.

CHIU, CHUI-CHEN 邱垂貞
Mem., Legis. Yuan 93-; *b.* Oct. 13, '51; *educ.* Grad., Ch. Jr. Coll. of Marine Tech.; *Pol. Affi.* DPP; *Const.* Taoyuan County; Jailed for Kaohsiung Incident 79-85; Chmn., Taoyuan County Cttee., DPP 88-91, Dir., Dept. of Soc. Movement 91-92; Convener, Econ. Cttee., Legis. Yuan 94-; *Add.* Rm. 913, 3-1 Chi Nan Rd., Sect. 1, Taipei 100.

CHIU, TAI-SAN 邱太三
Mem., Legis. Yuan 99-; *b.* Aug. 30, '56; *educ.* LL.B., Dept. of Law, NTU 79; *Pol. Affi.* DPP; *Const.* Taichung County; Prosecutor; Lawyer; Mem., NA; *Add.* Rm. 2128, 3-1 Chi Nan Rd., Sect. 1, Taipei 100.

CHO, JUNG-TAI 卓榮泰
Mem., Legis. Yuan 99-; *b.* Jan. 22, '59; *educ.* B., Dept. of Law, NCHU; *Pol. Affi.* DPP; *Const.* Taipei City; Mem., Taipei CCoun. 91-98; *Add.* Rm. 3111, 1 Tsingtao E. Rd., Taipei 100.

CHOU, CHENG-CHIH 周正之
Mem., Legis. Yuan 99-; *b.* July 30, '40; *educ.* MBA, United States Intl. U.; *Pol. Affi.* KMT; *Const.* Nat.; Cmdr., Army Logistic Cmd.; V. Cmdr., Coast Guard Cmd.; *Add.* Rm. 2127, 3-1 Chi Nan Rd., Sect. 1, Taipei 100.

CHOU, CHING-YU 周清玉
Mem., Legis. Yuan 99-; *b.* June 12, '44; *educ.* B., NTU; Studied, U. of San Francisco; *Pol. Affi.* DPP; *Const.* Nat.; Mem., NA; Magis., Changhua County; Mem., TPA; *Add.* Rm. 410, 3-1 Chi Nan Rd., Sect. 1, Taipei 100.

CHOU, DAVID P.L. 周伯倫
Mem., Legis. Yuan 93-; *b.* Nov. 13, '54; *educ.* LL.B., Soochow U. 82; *Pol. Affi.* DPP; *Const.* Taipei County; Exec. Mem., 1st, 2nd, 3rd, & 6th CC, DPP, & Mem., CSC; Mem., Taipei CCoun. 87-92; Exec. Dir., DPP Caucus, Taipei CCoun.; Mem., Educ. Cttee., Legis. Yuan 94, & Organic Laws Cttee. 97; Exec. Dir., DPP Caucus, 6th Sess., 2nd & 3rd Legis. Yuan; *Add.* Rm. 513, 3-1 Chi Nan Rd., Sect. 1, Taipei 100.

CHOU, HSI-WEI 周錫瑋
Mem., Legis. Yuan 99-; *b.* Mar. 11, '58; *educ.* MBA, U. of So. Calif, MA, PA; *Pol. Affi.* Independent; *Const.* Taipei County; Mem., TPA; *Add.* Rm. 3410, 1 Tsingtao E. Rd., Taipei 100.

CHOU, HUEI-YING 周慧瑛
Mem., Legis. Yuan 99-; *b.* Jan. 20, '55; *educ.* BA, Tunghai U.; *Pol. Affi.* DPP; *Const.* Taipei County; Mem., TPA; Mem., CAC, DPP; *Add.* Rm. 3301, 1 Tsingtao E. Rd., Taipei 100.

CHOU, PO-LUN
(See CHOU, DAVID P.L. 周伯倫)

CHOU, WU-LIU 周五六
Mem., Legis. Yuan 99-; *b.* Aug. 8, '50; *educ.* Grad., Tseng Wen Sr. Agr. & Ind. Sch.; *Pol. Affi.* KMT; *Const.* Tainan County; Mem., Dep. Spkr., & Spkr., Tainan CoCoun.; *Add.* Rm. 2117, 3-1 Chi Nan Rd., Sect. 1, Taipei 100.

CHOU, YA-SHU 周雅淑
Mem., Legis. Yuan 99-; *b.* Aug. 12, '66; *educ.* LL.B., NTU; *Pol. Affi.* DPP; *Const.* Taipei County; Mem., Taipei CoCoun.; Magis., Hsichih Urban Township, Taipei County; Adv., Taipei County Govt.; *Add.* Rm. 309, 1 Tsingtao E. Rd., Taipei 100.

CHU, FENG-CHIH
(See CHU, HELEN FONG-CHI 朱鳳芝)

CHU, HELEN FONG-CHI 朱鳳芝
Mem., Legis. Yuan 93-; *b.* June 27, '48; *educ.* BS, NCKU 74; MBA, Northrop U., USA 86; *Pol. Affi.* KMT; *Const.* Taoyuan County; Mem., Taoyuan CoCoun.; Convener, Nat. Def. Cttee., Legis. Yuan, & Organic Laws Cttee. 94; Dep. Dir.-Gen., Dept. of Party-Govt. Coordination of the Legis. Yuan, KMT, & Dep. Sec.-in-Chief.; Mem., Nat. Def. Cttee., Legis. Yuan 97; *Add.* Rm. 2109, 3-1 Chi Nan Rd., Sect. 1, Taipei 100.

CHU, HSING-YU 朱星羽
Mem., Legis. Yuan 93-; *b.* Dec. 22, '56; *educ.* Grad., Dept. of Ind. Mng., Chenghsiu Jr. Coll. of Tech. & Com.; *Pol. Affi.* DPP; *Const.* Kaohsiung City; Mem., Kaohsiung

CCoun. 75-93; Mem., CSC, DPP; Mem., Finance Cttee., Legis. Yuan 94; *Add.* Rm. 1106, 11th Fl., 3-1 Chi Nan Rd., Sect. 1, Taipei 100.

CHU, HUI-LIANG 朱惠良
Mem., Legis. Yuan 96-; *b.* Dec. 16, '50; *educ.* Ph.D., Princeton U.; *Pol. Affi.* Independent; *Const.* Taipei City; Assc. Prof., NTU; Mem., Educ. Cttee., Legis. Yuan 96; Independent Candidate, 2000 Election for ROC V. Pres.; *Add.* Rm. 406, 3-1 Chi Nan Rd., Sect. 1, Taipei 100.

CHU, LI-LUAN 朱立倫
Mem., Legis. Yuan 99-; *b.* June 7, '61; *educ.* Ph.D., Acct., New York U.; *Pol. Affi.* KMT; *Const.* Taoyuan County; Prof., NTU; *Add.* Rm. 1116, 11th Fl., 3-1 Chi Nan Rd., Sect. 1, Taipei 100.

CHU, LI-LUN
(See CHU, LI-LUAN 朱立倫)

CHUNG, CHIN-CHIANG
(See CHUNG, CHIN-KIANG 鍾金江)

CHUNG, CHIN-KIANG 鍾金江
Mem., Legis. Yuan 99-; *b.* Oct. 26, '46; *educ.* BA, Ch. Cul. U.; Studied, Boston U.; *Pol. Affi.* DPP; *Const.* Ovs. Nat.; Mem., CC, Formosan Assn. for Public Aff.; *Add.* Rm. 2103, 3-1 Chi Nan Rd., Sect. 1, Taipei 100.

CHUNG, LI-TE 鍾利德
Mem., Legis. Yuan 96-; *b.* June 15 '42; *educ.* BA, NCHU; *Pol. Affi.* KMT; *Const.* Hualien County; Dir., Bu. of Civil Aff., Hualien County Govt., & Planning Dept.; Dep. Dir., Secretariat, KMT Caucus, Legis. Yuan; *Add.* Rm. 2118, 3-1 Chi Nan Rd., Sect. 1, Taipei 100.

CHUNG, SHAO-HO 鍾紹和
Mem., Legis. Yuan 99-; *b.* Jan. 11, '56; *educ.* B., Ch. Cul. U.; Studied, Res. Class in PA, Nat. Sun Yat-sen U.; *Pol. Affi.* KMT; *Const.* Kaohsiung County; Mem., TPA; Mem., CC, KMT; *Add.* Rm. 3107, 1 Tsingtao E. Rd., Taipei 100.

FAN, HSUN-LU
(See FAN, SUN-LU 范巽綠)

FAN, SUN-LU 范巽綠
Mem., Legis. Yuan 96-; *b.* Oct. 3, '52; *educ.* MA, Tamkang U.; *Pol. Affi.* DPP; *Const.* Nat.; Dir., Secretariat, CC, DPP, & Mem., 1st-3rd CAC; Convener, Educ. Cttee., Legis. Yuan 96; *Add.* Rm. 1109, 3-1 Chi Nan Rd., Sect. 1, Taipei 100.

FAN, YANG-SHENG 范揚盛
Mem., Legis. Yuan 99-; *b.* Oct. 21, '37; *educ.* M., Waseda U., Japan; *Pol. Affi.* KMT; *Const.* Ovs. Nat.; Mem., NA 92-96; Mem., OCAC; *Add.* Rm. 2131, 3-1 Chi Nan Rd., Sect. 1, Taipei 100.

FANG, YI-LIANG 方醫良
Mem., Legis. Yuan 99-; *b.* Mar. 5, '37; *educ.* Nan Ying Sr. Voc. Sch.; Studied, Sun Yat-sen Inst. on Policy Res. & Dev.; Finished Courses of PA, NCHU; *Pol. Affi.* KMT; *Const.* Tainan County; Mem., 9th & 10th Tainan CoCoun.; Mem., TPA 86-98; *Add.* Rm. 2129, 3-1 Chi Nan Rd., Sect. 1, Taipei 100.

FENG, HU-HSIANG
(See FUNG, HU-HSIANG 馮滬祥)

FENG, TING-KUO 馮定國
Mem., Legis. Yuan 96-; *b.* Sept. 24, '50; *educ.* Ph.D., U. of Denver; *Pol. Affi.* NP; *Const.* Taichung County; Mem., CC, KMT; Mem., 5th Taipei CCoun.; Mem., Presidium, NA; Mem., Budget Cttee., Legis. Yuan 96, & Home & Border Aff. Cttee. 97, Convener, internal Aff. Cttee.; *Add.* Rm. 906, 3-1 Chi Nan Rd., Sect. 1, Taipei 100.

FUNG, HU-HSIANG 馮滬祥
Mem., Legis. Yuan 99-; *b.* May 8, '48; *educ.* Ph.D., Boston U.; *Pol. Affi.* NP; *Const.* Taipei City; Sec. to the Pres. 79-86; Adv., Exec. Yuan 91-92; Prof., NCU; Sec.-Gen., Alliance for Dem. Reform; Mem., NA; NP Candidate, 2000 Election for ROC V. Pres.; *Add.* Rm. 2122, 3-1 Chi Nan Rd., Sect. 1, Taipei 100.

HAN, DANIEL K.Y. 韓國瑜
Mem., Legis. Yuan 93-; *b.* June 17, '57; *educ.* BA, Soochow U.; LL.M., NCCU; *Pol. Affi.* KMT; *Const.* Taipei County; Outsdg. Coll. Students' Rep. of the ROC 84 & 86; Pres., Mainland Aff. Inst.'s Promotional Cent., Ch. Cul. U. 88; Lectr., Nat. Hualien Tchrs.' Coll. 88-89, & The World U. of Jour. & Comms. 88-89; Resr., Mainland News Cent., *Ch. Times* 89-90; Mem., Taipei CoCoun. 90-92; Chmn., Taipei County Assn. of Hakka Filiation; Chmn., Assn. for the Dev. of Small & Medium-sized Ent., Taipei County; Mem., Nat. Def. Cttee., Legis. Yuan 96; *Add.* Rm. 2118, 3-1 Chi Nan Rd., Sect. 1, Taipei 100.

HAN, KUO-YU
(See HAN, DANIEL K.Y. 韓國瑜)

HAO, LUNG-PIN
(See HAU, LUN-PIN 郝龍斌)

HAU, LUN-PIN 郝龍斌
Mem., Legis. Yuan 96-; *b.* Aug. 22, '52; *educ.* Ph.D., U. of Massachusetts; *Pol. Affi.* NP; *Const.* Taipei City; Project Adv., ROC Red Cross; Convener, Educ. Cttee., Legis. Yuan 96, Convener & Dep. Convener, NP Caucus, Mem., Budget Cttee. 97; *Add.* Rm. 603, 3-1 Chi Nan Rd., Sect. 1, Taipei 100.

HER, JYH-HUEI 何智輝
Mem., Legis. Yuan 99-; *b.* Apr. 17, '50; *educ.* B., Nat. Twn. Inst. of Tech.; *Pol. Affi.* KMT; *Const.* Miaoli County; Magis., Miaoli County; Dep. Spkr., Miaoli CoCoun.; Mem., Legis. Yuan; *Add.* 6th Fl., 5 Chen Chiang St., Taipei 100.

HO, CHIA-JUNG 何嘉榮
Mem., Legis. Yuan 99-; *b.* Dec. 24, '45; *educ.* LL.M., NCCU; *Pol. Affi.* DPP; *Const.* Chiayi County; Magis., Chiayi County; Mem., 7th CEC, DPP; *Add.* Rm. 401, 3-1 Chi Nan Rd., Sect. 1, Taipei 100.

HO, CHIH-HUI
(See HER, JYH-HUEI 何智輝)

HONG, CHI-CHANG 洪奇昌
Mem., Legis. Yuan 89-; *b.* Aug. 23, '51; *educ.* MPH, NTU; M., Health Sc., U. of Toronto, Can.; *Pol. Affi.* DPP; *Const.* Taipei City.; Mem., NA 86-89; Convener, Econ. Cttee., Legis. Yuan, & Mem., For. & Ovs. Ch. Aff. Cttee.; *Add.* Rm. 905, 3-1 Chi Nan Rd., Sect. 1, Taipei 100.

HONG, YUH-CHIN 洪玉欽
Mem., Legis. Yuan 93-; *b.* July 11, '43; *educ.* LL.B., Soochow U. 67; LL.M., Ch. Cul. U., LL.D. 79; *Pol. Affi.* KMT; *Const.* Tainan County; Dep. Sec.-Gen., Cent. Policy Cttee., KMT 88-89, Dir.-Gen., Dept. of Intra- & Inter-Party Rel., Dir.-Gen., Dept. of Party-Govt. Coordination of the Legis. Yuan 92-93, & Dep. Sec.-Gen., CC 94-96; Mem., Econ. Cttee., Legis. Yuan 94, & For. & Ovs. Ch. Aff. Cttee. 95 & 96; *Add.* Rm. 1002, 10th Fl., 3-1 Chi Nan Rd., Sect. 1, Taipei 100.

HOU, HUI-HSIEN 侯惠仙
Mem., Legis. Yuan 99-; *b.* Aug. 29, '58; *educ.* Grad., Touliu Sr. Voc. Sch.; Studied, Calif. State U.; *Pol. Affi.* KMT; *Const.* Yunlin County; Mem., 12th & 13th Yunlin CoCoun.; Mem., TPA 94-98; *Add.* Rm. 202, 3-1 Chi Nan Rd., Sect. 1, Taipei 100.

HSIAO, CHIN-LAN 蕭金蘭
Mem., Legis. Yuan 93-; *b.* Aug. 26, '48; *educ.* B., Dept. of Acct., NCCU 70; *Pol. Affi.* KMT; *Const.* Kaohsiung County; Mem., CC, KMT; Mem., Kaohsiung CoCoun.; Convener, Budget Cttee., Legis. Yuan, & Organic Laws Cttee.; Exec. Mem., KMT Caucus, Legis. Yuan; Mem., Finance Cttee., Legis. Yuan 94, & Budget Cttee. 97; Convener, Sanitation, Environmental, & Soc. Welfare Cttee. 99; *Add.* Rm. 1007, 3-1 Chi Nan Rd., Sect. 1, Taipei 100.

HSIAO, YUAN-YU 蕭苑瑜
Mem., Legis. Yuan 99-; *b.* Oct. 12, '73; *educ.* B., Calif. State U.; *Pol. Affi.* KMT; *Const.* Chiayi County; Sp. Asst. to Chiayi CCoun. Spkr.; *Add.* Rm. 306, 3-1 Chi Nan Rd., Sect. 1, Taipei 100.

HSIEH, C.T. 謝啓大
Mem., Legis. Yuan 93-; *b.* Feb. 10, '49; *educ.* LL.M., NTU 84; *Pol. Affi.* NP; *Const.* Hsinchu City; Judge, Hualien Br., Twn. High Court, Hsinchu Dist. Court, & Ilan Dist. Court; Convener, Organic Laws Cttee., Legis. Yuan 96, Mem., Jud. Cttee. 97; *Add.* Rm. 407, 3-1 Chi Nan Rd., Sect. 1, Taipei 100.

HSIEH, CHANG-CHIEH 謝章捷
Mem., Legis. Yuan 99-; *b.* Sept. 24, '58; *educ.* Grad., Nat. Taichung Inst. of Com.; *Pol. Affi.* KMT; *Const.* Changhua County; Mem., Changhua CoCoun.; *Add.* Rm. 710, 3-1 Chi Nan Rd., Sect. 1, Taipei 100.

HSIEH, CHI-TA
(See HSIEH, C.T. 謝啓大)

HSIEH, YEN-HSIN 謝言信
Mem., Legis. Yuan 99-; *b.* Dec. 13, '29; *educ.* B., Kinki U., Japan; *Pol. Affi.* KMT; *Const.* Changhua County; Mem., Changhua CoCoun.; Mem., TPA; *Add.* Rm. 2105, 3-1 Chi Nan Rd., Sect. 1, Taipei 100.

HSU, CHENG-KUN
(See HSU, ROBERT 徐成焜)

HSU, CHIH-MING 徐志明
Mem., Legis. Yuan 99-; *b.* Mar. 26, '57; *educ.* High Sch. Grad.; *Pol. Affi.* DPP; *Const.* Kaohsiung County; Magis., Taliao Rural Township, Kaohsiung County; Mem., 12th Kaohsiung CoCoun.; *Add.* 1 Tsingtao E. Rd., Taipei 100.

HSU, CHING-YUAN 徐慶元
Mem., Legis. Yuan 99-; *b.* Feb. 13, '57; *educ.* BBA, NCKU; *Pol. Affi.* Dem. Alliance; *Const.* Taitung County; Mem., Taitung CoCoun., Dep. Spkr.; Mem., TPA; *Add.* Rm. 3206, 1 Tsingtao E. Rd., Taipei 100.

HSU, CHUNG-HSIUNG
(See SHYU, JONG-SHYONG 徐中雄)

HSU CHUNG, PI-HSIA 許鍾碧霞
Mem., Legis. Yuan 99-; *b.* Mar. 20, '48; *educ.* Ed.B., NCCU; *Pol. Affi.* DPP; *Const.* Taoyuan County; Tchr., Jr. High Sch.; *Add.* Rm. 211, 3-1 Chi Nan Rd., Sect. 1, Taipei 100.

HSU, DEN-KOUN 許登宮
Mem., Legis. Yuan 99-; *b.* Dec. 22, '40; *educ.* Minhsiung Elementary Sch.; *Pol. Affi.* KMT; *Const.* Chiayi County; Mem., TPA 94-98; *Add.* Rm. 3411, 1 Tsingtao E. Rd., Taipei 100.

HSU, JUNG-SHU 許榮淑
Mem., Legis. Yuan 99-; *b.* Dec. 27, '39; *educ.* B., NTNU; *Pol. Affi.* DPP; *Const.* Nat.; Mem., Legis. Yuan; Mem., Presidium, NA; Mem., CSC, DPP, Adv., CEC; *Add.* Rm. 3116, 1 Tsingtao E. Rd., Taipei 100.

HSU, ROBERT 徐成焜
Mem., Legis. Yuan 93-; *b.* Jan. 4, '47; *educ.* BPS, NTU; *Pol. Affi.* Dem. Alliance; *Const.* Miaoli County; Convener, Econ. Cttee., Legis. Yuan 94, Mem. 95 & 97; Chmn., New Policy Assn., Legis. Yuan; Dep. Sec.-in-Chief, Dept. of Party-Govt. Coordination of the Legis. Yuan, KMT; *Add.* Rm. 801, 3-1 Chi Nan Rd., Sect. 1, Taipei 100.

HSU, SHAO-PING 徐少萍
Mem., Legis. Yuan 96-; *b.* May 16, '41; *educ.* LL.B., Soochow U.; *Pol. Affi.* KMT; *Const.* Keelung City; Mem., For. & Ovs. Ch. Aff. Cttee., Legis. Yuan 96; Convener, Trans. & Comms. Cttee, Legis. Yuan; *Add.* Rm. 505, 5th Fl., 3-1 Chi Nan Rd., Sect. 1, Taipei 100.

HSU, SHU-PAO 許舒博
Mem., Legis. Yuan 96-; *b.* July 10, '63; *educ.* BA, Luven U., Belgium; *Pol. Affi.* KMT; *Const.* Yunlin County; Convener, Econ. Cttee., Legis. Yuan 96, Mem. 97; Mem., CC, KMT; *Add.* Rm. 711, 7th Fl., 3-1 Chi Nan Rd., Sect. 1, Taipei 100.

HSU, SU-YEH 許素葉
Mem., Legis. Yuan 99-; *b.* Dec. 16, '33; *educ.* Grad., Kaohsiung Girls' Sr. High Sch.; *Pol. Affi.* KMT; *Const.* Nat.; Mem., Penghu CoCoun., Spkr.; Mem., TPA; Mem., CAC, KMT; Adv., CC, KMT; *Add.* Rm. 411, 3-1 Chi Nan Rd., Sect. 1, Taipei 100.

HSU, TAIN-TSAIR 許添財
Mem., Legis. Yuan 93-; *b.* Jan. 23, '51; *educ.* M., Econ., Ch. Cul. U. 76; *Pol. Affi.* Independent; *Const.* Tainan City; Mem., World United Formosans for Independence, & N. Am.'s Twn. Prof. Assn.; Convener, Budget Review Cttee., Legis. Yuan, Mem., Rules Cttee., & Finance Cttee.; *Add.* Rm. 1016, 10th Fl., 3-1 Chi Nan Rd., Sect. 1, Taipei 100.

HSU, TENG-KUNG
(See HSU, DEN-KOUN 許登宮)

HSU, TIEN-TSAI
(See HSU, TAIN-TSAIR 許添財)

HUANG, CHAO-SHUN 黃昭順
Mem., Legis. Yuan 93-; *b.* Aug. 22, '53; *educ.* B., Pharmacology, Kaohsiung Med. Coll.; *Pol. Affi.* KMT; *Const.* Kaohsiung City; Mem., Kaohsiung CCoun. 81-92; Mem., Trans. & Comms. Cttee., Legis. Yuan 94, & Jud. Cttee. 97; *Add.* Rm. 1113, 3-1 Chi Nan Rd., Sect. 1, Taipei 100.

HUANG, ERH-HSUAN 黃爾璇
Mem., Legis. Yuan 93-; *b.* Mar. 5, '36; *educ.* MPA, NCCU, DPS; *Pol. Affi.* DPP; *Const.* Nat.; Sec.-Gen., DPP 86-88; Mem., CEC, & CAC, DPP; Mem., Home & Border Aff. Cttee., Legis. Yuan 94, Econ. Cttee. 96, & Nat. Def. Cttee. 97; Convener, DPP Caucus, Legis. Yuan; *Add.* Rm. 705, 3-1 Chi Nan Rd., Sect. 1, Taipei 100.

HUANG, HSIEN-CHOU
(See HUANG, SHAN-JOU 黃顯洲)

HUANG, HSIU-MENG 黃秀孟
Mem., Legis. Yuan 96-; *b.* Oct. 2, '44; *educ.* B., NTNU; Finished Courses, Grad. Inst. of Educ., Nat. Kaohsiung Normal U.; *Pol. Affi.* KMT; *Const.* Tainan County; Mem., TPA 82-94; Mem., CC, KMT; *Add.* Rm. 302, 3-1 Chi Nan Rd., Sect. 1, Taipei 100.

HUANG, MIN-HUI 黃敏惠
Mem., Legis. Yuan 99-; *b.* Jan. 20, '59; *educ.* BA, NTNU; *Pol. Affi.* KMT; *Const.* Chiayi City; Mem., NA, Dep. Dir., KMT Secretariat; *Add.* Rm. 3112, Tsingtao 1st Kuan, 1 Tsingtao E. Rd., Taipei 100.

HUANG, MING-HO 黃明和
Mem., Legis. Yuan 99-; *b.* Mar. 1, '40; *educ.* MD, NTU; M., Pub. Health, Johns Hopkins U.; Ph.D., Japan; *Pol. Affi.* Independent; *Const.* Changhua County; Mem., Legis. Yuan 87-93; Dir., Hsiu Chuan Memorial Hosp.; *Add.* 2-1 Fl., 4 Tsingtao E. Rd., Taipei 100.

HUANG, MU-TIEN
(See HWANG, MUB-TIEN 黃木添)

HUANG, SHAN-JOU 黃顯洲
Mem., Legis. Yuan 99-; *b.* Feb. 28, '59; *educ.* BS, NTU; MS, Illinois Inst. of Tech. 86; *Pol. Affi.* KMT; *Const.* Taichung City; Mem., NA 92-96; *Add.* Rm. 2107, 3-1 Chi Nan Rd., Sect. 1, Taipei 100.

HUANG, YI-CHIAO 黃義交
Mem., Legis. Yuan 99-; *b.* Mar. 12, '53; *educ.* B., Tamkang U.; MA, Ch. Cul. U.; *Pol. Affi.* Independent; *Const.* Taichung City; Dir., Dept. of Info., Spokesman, TPG; *Add.* Rm. 2119, 3-1 Chi Nan Rd., Sect. 1, Taipei 100.

HUNG, CHAO-NAN 洪昭男
Mem., Legis. Yuan 81-; *b.* Aug. 24, '43; *educ.* BA, Soochow U.; MA, U. of Arkansas; *Pol. Affi.* KMT; *Const.* Nat.; Consul, Consl. Gen., San Francisco 68-80; Dep. Dir.-Gen., Dept. of Ovs. Aff., CC, KMT 93-94, Dep. Dir., Cent. Policy Cttee.; Mem., Trans. & Comms. Cttee., Legis. Yuan 94, & Organic Laws Cttee. 97; *Add.* Rm. 3208, 1 Tsingtao E. Rd., Taipei 100.

HUNG, CHI-CHANG
(See HONG, CHI-CHANG 洪奇昌)

HUNG, HSING-JUNG 洪性榮
Mem., Legis. Yuan 93-; *b.* May 13, '40; *educ.* B., Nat. Changhua U. of Educ.; *Pol. Affi.* KMT; *Const.* Changhua County; Mem., Changhua CoCoun.; Mem., 7th & 8th TPA; Adv., TPG; Mem., Finance Cttee., Legis. Yuan 94, & Organic Laws Cttee. 97; *Add.* Rm. 812, 3-1 Chi Nan Rd., Sect. 1, Taipei 100.

HUNG, HSIU-CHU 洪秀柱
Mem., Legis. Yuan 93-; *b.* Apr. 7, '48; *educ.* LL.B., Ch. Cul. U. 70; Ed.M., N.E. Missouri State U. 91; *Pol. Affi.* KMT; *Const.* Nat.; Dir., Dept. of Women's Aff., Taipei County Cttee., KMT 80-86, Sup., Twn. Prov. Cttee. 86-90; Dep. Sec.-Gen., KMT Caucus, Legis. Yuan 93-94; Dep. Dir., Cent. Policy Cttee. of the Legis. Yuan, KMT 93-94; Mem., Educ. Cttee., Legis. Yuan 94; Dep. Dir., Dept. of Youth Aff., CC, KMT 94; *Add.* Rm. 305, 3rd Fl., 3-1 Tsingtao E. Rd., Sect. 1, Taipei 100.

HUNG, TU 洪讀
Mem., Legis. Yuan 99-; *b.* Mar. 13, '36; *educ.* B., Dept. of Dip., NCCU 63, M., 67; *Pol. Affi.* KMT; *Const.* Ovs. Nat.; Mem., NA; Mem., CC, KMT; *Add.* Rm. 3512, 10 Tsingtao E. Rd., Taipei 100.

HUNG, YU-CHIN
(See HONG, YUH-CHIN 洪玉欽)

HWANG, MUB-TIEN 黃木添
Mem., Legis. Yuan 99-; *b.* Nov. 10, '36; *educ.* M., N.E. Missouri State U.; *Pol. Affi.* KMT; *Const.* Taoyuan County; Mem., TPA, Dep. Dir., KMT Caucus; *Add.* Rm. 3307, Tsingtao 1st Kuan, 1 Tsingtao E. Rd., Taipei 100.

JAO, EUGENE YUNG-CHING 趙永清
Mem., Legis. Yuan 93-; *b.* Nov. 9, '57; *educ.* BPS, NCCU; MPS, New York U.; *Pol. Affi.* KMT; *Const.* Taipei County; Founding Mem., New Policy Assn., Legis. Yuan, Convener, Home & Border Aff. Cttee. 94; *Add.* Rm. 509, 5th Fl., 3-1 Chi Nan Rd., Sect. 1, Taipei 100.

JAO, YING-CHI
(See YAO, ENG-CHI 饒穎奇)

KAO, YANG-SHENG 高揚昇
Mem., Legis. Yuan 96-; *b.* July 11, '52; *educ.* B., Fu Jen Catholic U.; *Pol. Affi.* KMT; *Const.* Highland Aborigines; *Add.* Rm. 1008, 10th Fl., 3-1 Chi Nan Rd., Sect. 1, Taipei 100.

KAO, YU-JEN 高育仁
Mem., Legis. Yuan 93-; *b.* Aug. 30, '34; *educ.* LL.B., NTU 56; Hon. LL.D., St. John's U., USA 90; *Pol. Affi.* KMT; *Const.* Nat.; Magis., Tainan County 73-76; Admin. V. Min. of the Int. 76-78; Dir., Secretariat, CC, KMT 78-79; Comr., Dept. of Civil Aff., TPG 79-81; Spkr., TPA 81-89; Chmn., the 21st Century Found., Ch. Assn. for Human Rights, UN Assn. of ROC; Mem., Trans. & Comms. Cttee., Legis. Yuan 94, & Finance Cttee. 97; *Add.* 10th Fl., 380 Keelung Rd., Sect. 1, Taipei 110.

KER, CHIEN-MING 柯建銘
Mem., Legis. Yuan 93-; *b.* Sept. 8, '51; *educ.* Grad., Chung Shan Med. & Dental Coll.; *Pol. Affi.* DPP; *Const.* Hsinchu City; Convener, Arbitrary Cttee., Hsinchu City Br., DPP 86-93; Dep. Dir., DPP Caucus, Legis. Yuan 93-94, Mem., Econ. Cttee. 94; *Add.* 3rd Fl., 3 Tsingtao E. Rd., Taipei 100.

KO, CHIEN-MING
(See KER, CHIEN-MING 柯建銘)

KUANG, WO-NUAN 關沃暖
Mem., Legis. Yuan 99-; *b.* Mar. 27, '45; *educ.* BCE, NCKU; *Pol. Affi.* KMT; *Const.* Ovs. Nat.; *Add.* Rm. 3302, 1 Tsingtao E. Rd., Taipei 100.

KUO, JUNG-CHEN 郭榮振
Mem., Legis. Yuan 99-; *b.* June 7, '50; *educ.* Grad., Chih Yung Coll. of Com.; *Pol. Affi.* KMT; *Const.* Taichung County; Mem., TPA; *Add.* Rm. 3509, 10 Tsingtao E. Rd, Taipei 100.

KUO, SU-CHUN 郭素春
Mem., Legis. Yuan 99-; *b.* Dec. 11, '55; *educ.* MBA, NCHU; *Pol. Affi.* KMT; *Const.* Taipei County; Gen. Mgr., Business Admin. Corp.; Mem., NA; *Add.* 9th Fl., 346 Chang Chun Rd., Taipei 104.

KUO, TING-TSAI 郭廷才
Mem., Legis. Yuan 93-; *b.* Sept. 28, '36; *educ.* Grad., Dept. of Business Mng., Calif. Multiversity U., USA; *Pol. Affi.* KMT; *Const.* Pingtung County; Magis., Tungkang Urban Township, Pingtung County 68-78; Mem., Pingtung CoCoun. 78-92, & Spkr. 82-92; Mem., Finance Cttee., Legis. Yuan 94; *Add.* Rm. 1108, 3-1 Chi Nan Rd., Sect. 1, Taipei 100.

LAI, CHING-LIN 賴勁麟
Mem., Legis. Yuan 99-; *b.* Jan. 27, '62; *educ.* BPS, NTU; *Pol. Affi.* DPP; *Const.* Taipei County; Dir.-Gen., Twn. Labor Movement Assn.; Mem., NA; *Add.* Rm. 508, 3-1 Chi Nan Rd., Sect. 1, Taipei 100.

LAI, CHING-TE
(See LAI, WILLIAM C.D. 賴清德)

LAI, SHIH-PAO
(See LAI, SHYH-BAO 賴士葆)

LAI, SHYH-BAO 賴士葆
Mem., Legis. Yuan 99-; *b.* June 20, '51; *educ.* Ph.D., U. of So. Calif.; *Pol. Affi.* NP; *Const.* Taipei City; Mem., NA; Prof., NCCU; *Add.* Rm. 3201, 1 Tsingtao E. Rd., Taipei 100.

LAI, WILLIAM C.T. 賴清德
Mem., Legis. Yuan 99-; *b.* Oct. 6, '59; *educ.* MD, NCKU; *Pol. Affi.* DPP; *Const.* Tainan City; Physician, NCKU Hosp.; Mem., NA; *Add.* Rm. 907, 3-1 Chi Nan Rd., Sect. 1, Taipei 100.

LEE, CHENG-CHONG 李正宗
Mem., Legis. Yuan 99-; *b.* Oct. 10, '48; *educ.* Grad., World Coll. of Jour. & Comms. 77; *Pol. Affi.* KMT; *Const.* Nat.; Pres., Ch. Fed. of Labor; Mem., NUC, & NA; *Add.* 11th Fl., 201-18 Tun Hua N. Rd., Taipei 105.

LEE, CHENG-TZUNG
(See LEE, CHENG-CHONG 李正宗)

LEE, CHIA-CHIN 李嘉進
Mem., Legis. Yuan 99-; *b.* Mar. 6, '57; *educ.* M., Econ., Nat. Tsukuba U., Japan; *Pol. Affi.* KMT; *Const.* Taipei County; Sect. Chief, MOE; Lectr., Soochow U. *Add.* Rm. 2110, 3-1 Chi Nan Rd., Sect. 1, Taipei 100.

LEE, CHING-AN 李慶安
Mem., Legis. Yuan 99-; *b.* Jan. 17, '59; *educ.* BA, Dept. of Jour., NCCU; *Pol. Affi.* KMT; *Const.* Taipei City; Mem., Taipei CCoun.; Mem., CC, KMT; Anchorwoman, Ch. TV System; *Add.* Rm. 3209, 1 Tsingtao E. Rd., Taipei 100.

LEE, CHING-HSIUNG 李慶雄
Mem., Legis. Yuan 99-; *b.* Aug. 13, '38; *educ.* LL.B., NTU, LL.M.; *Pol. Affi.* Twn. Independence Party; *Const.* Kaohsiung City; Convener, Organic Laws Cttee., Legis. Yuan 90, Jud. Cttee., Mem., DPP Caucus 91; Lawyer; *Add.* Rm. 2125, 3-1 Chi Nan Rd., Sect. 1, Taipei 100.

LEE, CHING-HUA 李慶華
Mem., Legis. Yuan 93-; *b.* Dec. 3, '48; *educ.* Ph.D., Hist., New York U. 84; *Pol. Affi.* NP; *Const.* Taipei County; Cofounder, NP; Convener, NP Caucus, Legis. Yuan; Mem., Nat. Def. Cttee., Legis. Yuan 94, & Educ. Cttee. 97-98; *Add.* Rm. 802, 3-1 Chi Nan Rd., Sect. 1, Taipei 100.

LEE, CHU-FENG
(See LEE, JUH-FENG 李炷烽)

LEE, CHUN-I
(See LEE, CHUN-YEE 李俊毅)

LEE, CHUN-YEE 李俊毅
Mem., Legis. Yuan 96-; *b.* Mar. 20, '59; *educ.* MCE, NCCU; *Pol. Affi.* DPP; *Const.* Tainan County; Sp., CEC, DPP, Exec. Dir., Tainan County Cttee. 92; Election campaign mgr. for Chen Ding-nan, Chen Tan-sun, Peng Ming-min, & Hsieh Chang-ting; Mem., Organic Laws Cttee., Legis. Yuan 96, & Home & Border Aff. Cttee. 97-98; *Add.* Rm. 208, 3-1 Chi Nan Rd., Sect. 1, Taipei 100.

LEE, HSIEN-JEN
(See LEE, SHANGREN 李先仁)

LEE, HSIEN-JUNG
(See LEE, SEN-ZONG 李顯榮)

LEE, JUH-FENG 李炷烽
Mem., Legis. Yuan 99-; *b.* May 6, '53; *educ.* Ed.B., NTNU; Finished Courses, Grad. Inst. of Educ., NTU; *Pol. Affi.* NP;

Const. Nat.; Sec., Kinmen County Govt.; Tchr., Kinmen Agr. Sr. High Sch.; Mem., NA; *Add.* Rm. 2120, 3-1 Chi Nan Rd., Sect. 1, Taipei 100.

LEE, SEN-ZONG 李顯榮
Mem., Legis. Yuan 93-; *b.* July 23, '47; *educ.* M., Public Engr., U. of San Francisco; *Pol. Affi.* KMT; *Const.* Taipei County; Mem., Taipei CoCoun. 81-89; Convener, Home & Border Aff. Cttee., Legis. Yuan 93-94, & Trans. & Comms. Cttee. 94; Mem., Trans. & Comms. Cttee., Legis. Yuan 94-98; *Add.* Rm. 1015, 3-1 Chi Nan Rd., Sect. 1, Taipei 100.

LEE, SHANG-REN 李先仁
Mem., Legis. Yuan 99-; *b.* Nov. 6, '63; *educ.* BS, Naval Architecture, NTU 86; MS, Ind. Engr., Stanford U. 90, & Statistics 92; *Pol. Affi.* KMT; *Const.* Taipei County; Drafter of Nat. Standards, Nat. Bu. of Standards, MOEA 92-99; Tech. Promotion Adv., Tech. Res. Lab. 92-99; Dep. Party Whip, KMT Caucus, NA 96-99; Chmn., Const. Res. Cttee., KMT; *Add.* Rm. 510, 3-1 Chi Nan Rd., Sect. 1, Taipei 100.

LEE, YING-YUAN 李應元
Mem., Legis. Yuan 96-; *b.* Mar. 16, '53; *educ.* Ph.D., Health Econ., U. of N. Carolina at Chapel Hill, USA; *Pol. Affi.* DPP; *Const.* Taipei County; Standing Mem., Gen. Sec., & V. Chmn., World United for Formosa Independence; Gen. Dir., "One Ch.-One Twn." Action Union; Exec. Dir., Civilian Const. Formulation Movement; *Add.* Rm. 1013, 3-1 Chi Nan Rd., Sect. 1, Taipei 100.

LI, CHUANG-CHIAO 李全教
Mem., Legis. Yuan 99-; *b.* Feb. 25, '60; *educ.* MEE, USA; Studied, Dr. Prog., U. of Illinois; *Pol. Affi.* KMT; *Const.* Nat.; *Add.* Rm. 707, 3-1 Chi Nan Rd., Sect. 1, Taipei 100.

LI, M.K. 李鳴皋
Mem., Legis. Yuan 93-; *b.* Nov. 22, '32; *educ.* Grad., Naval Cmd. & Staff Coll., Armed Forces U. 70, & Naval War Coll. 80; *Pol. Affi.* KMT; *Const.* Nat.; Fleet Cmdt.; Rear Adm.; V. Adm., Logistic; C-in-C, Admiralty; *Add.* Rm. 1112, 3-1 Chi Nan Rd., Sect. 1, Taipei 100.

LI, MING-KAO
(See LI, M.K. 李鳴皋)

LI, WEN-CHUNG 李文忠
Mem., Legis. Yuan 99-; *b.* June 20, '58; *educ.* Studied, Pol. Sc., NTU; *Pol. Affi.* DPP; *Const.* Taipei County; Mem., Labor Educ. Cttee., Taipei County Govt., & NA; *Add.* Rm. 901, 3-1 Chi Nan Rd., Sect. 1, Taipei 100.

LIANG, MU-YANG 梁牧養
Mem., Legis. Yuan 99-; *b.* Apr. 27, '51; *educ.* Res., Nat. Tsukuba U., Japan; *Pol. Affi.* DPP; *Const.* Kaohsiung City; Nat. Party Rep., DPP, Mem., CAC; *Add.* Rm. 3403, 1 Tsingtao E. Rd., Taipei 100.

LIAO, FENG-TE
(See LIAO, FUNG-TE 廖風德)

LIAO, FU-PEN
(See LIAO, HWU-PENG 廖福本)

LIAO, FUNG-TE 廖風德
Mem., Legis. Yuan 99-; *b.* April 17, '51; *educ.* Ph.D., NCCU; *Pol. Affi.* KMT; *Const.* Nat.; Dir., Secretariat, V. Pres.'s Off.; *Add.* Rm. 2116, 3-1 Chi Nan Rd., Sect. 1, Taipei 100.

LIAO, HSUEH-KUANG 廖學廣
Mem., Legis. Yuan 96-; *b.* Jan. 23, '54; *educ.* LL.B., NTU; MA, San Diego State U.; *Pol. Affi.* Independent; *Const.* Taipei County; Mem., 10th & 11th term, Taipei CoCoun.; Magis., 11th & 12th term, Hsichih Urban Township, Taipei County; *Add.* Rm. 205, 3-1 Chi Nan Rd., Sect. 1, Taipei 100.

LIAO, HWU-PENG 廖福本
Mem., Legis. Yuan 84-; *b.* June 1, '38; *educ.* B., NTU; M., Ch. Cul. U.; *Pol. Affi.* KMT; *Const.* Yunlin County; Chmn., Hualien County Cttee., KMT 77-79; Sect. Chief, Dept. of Civil Aff., TPG 79-81; Dep. Party Whip, KMT Caucus, Legis. Yuan; Dep. Dir.-Gen., Dept. of Ovs. Aff., CC, KMT; Dir.-Gen., Dept. of Party-Govt. Coordination of the Legis. Yuan, KMT 94; *Add.* Rm. 703, 3-1 Chi Nan Rd., Sect. 1, Taipei 100.

LIAO, WAN-JU 廖婉汝
Mem., Legis. Yuan 99-; *b.* Jan. 27, '60; *educ.* B., NTNU 83; *Pol. Affi.* KMT; *Const.* Pingtung County; Mem., NA, Dep. Dir., KMT Caucus; Prin., Pingtung Private Ming Der Sr. High Sch. 93-99; *Add.* Rm. 3102, 1 Tsingtao E. Rd, Taipei 100.

LIN, CHENG-ERH 林正二
Mem., Legis. Yuan 99-; *b.* Jan. 2, '52; *educ.* Ed.M., NTNU; *Pol. Affi.* KMT; *Const.* Lowland Aborigines; Mem., NA, Dep. Dir., KMT Caucus; Mem., TPA 94-98; Tchr., & Prin., Jr. High Sch.; *Add.* Rm. 608, 3-1 Chi Nan Rd., Sect. 1, Taipei 100.

LIN, CHENG-TSE
(See LIN, JUNQ-TZER 林政則)

LIN, CHIEN-JUNG 林建榮

Mem., Legis. Yuan 94-; *b.* Jan. 18, '46; *educ.* Ed.M., NTNU; *Pol. Affi.* KMT; *Const.* Ilan County; Mayor, 9th, 11th, & 12th term, Ilan City; Convener, Trans. & Comms. Cttee., Legis. Yuan; *Add.* Rm. 1011, 10th Fl., 3-1 Chi Nan Rd., Sect. 1, Taipei 100.

LIN, CHIH-CHIA 林志嘉

Mem., Legis. Yuan 99-; *b.* Mar. 31, '58; *educ.* BS, Chem., Fu Jen Catholic U. 81; MS, Chem., Tennesse State U. 87; *Pol. Affi.* Dem. Alliance; *Const.* Taipei County; Convener, Home & Border Aff. Cttee., Legis. Yuan 91-92 & 94-97, Dep. Dir., KMT Caucus 92-93; *Add.* Rm. 2111, 3-1 Chi Nan Rd., Sect. 1, Taipei 100.

LIN, CHIN-CHUN 林進春

Mem., Legis. Yuan 99-; *b.* Aug. 26, '47; *educ.* Grad., Sr. High Sch.; *Pol. Affi.* KMT; *Const.* Changhua County; Mem., Changhua CoCoun.; Mem., 9th & 10th term, TPA, Dir., KMT Caucus; *Add.* Rm. 3205, 1 Tsingtao E. Rd., Taipei 100.

LIN, CHO-SHUI 林濁水

Mem., Legis. Yuan 93-; *b.* Mar. 25, '47; *educ.* B., NCCU; *Pol. Affi.* DPP; *Const.* Taipei City; Mem., CAC, DPP; Convener, Organic Laws Cttee., Legis. Yuan 94; Chief Ed. Writer, *New Tide Mag.*, & *Dem. Progressive Jour.*; *Add.* Rm. 215, 2nd Fl., 3-1 Chi Nan Rd., Sect. 1, Taipei 100.

LIN, CHUNG-CHENG 林忠正

Mem., Legis. Yuan 96-; *b.* Jan. 9, '54; *educ.* BA, Econ., Tunghai U.; MA, NTU; Ph.D. Econ., U. of Hawaii, Cert., Population Studies; *Pol. Affi.* DPP; *Const.* Nat.; Sp. Asst. to the Chmn., DPP, Dir., Dept. of Ch. Aff., & Dep. Sec.-Gen., CEC; Res. Fel., Sun Yat-sen Inst. for Soc. Sc. & Philosophy, Acad. Sinica; Prof., Econ., NTU; Prof. & concur. Dir., Dept. of Econ., NCU; *Add.* Rm. 1006, 10th Fl., 3-1 Chi Nan Rd., Sect. 1, Taipei 100.

LIN, CHUNG-MO 林重謨

Mem., Legis. Yuan 99-; *b.* Apr. 2, '47; *educ.* BS, Chung Yuan Christian U.; *Pol. Affi.* DPP; *Const.* Taipei City; Sec.-Gen., Assn. of Public Calamity Prevention; Mem., NA; *Add.* Rm. 412, 3-1 Chi Nan Rd., Sect. 1, Taipei 100.

LIN, CHUNG-TE 林春德

Mem., Legis. Yuan 99-; *b.* July 5, '47; *educ.* BSE, NTNU; *Pol. Affi.* KMT; *Const.* Highland Aborigines; Magis., Jenai Rural Township, Nantou County; Mem., TPA 90-98; *Add.* Rm. 713, 3-1 Chi Nan Rd., Sect. 1, Taipei 100.

LIN, FENG-SHI 林豐喜

Mem., Legis. Yuan 96-; *b.* Dec. 12, '50; *educ.* Fuchun Elementary Sch., Taichung County; *Pol. Affi.* DPP; *Const.* Taichung County; Chmn., Twn. Farmers Alliance; Exec. Mem., CC, DPP; Mem., Taichung CoCoun.; Mem., Budget Cttee., Legis. Yuan 96; *Add.* Rm. 209, 2nd Fl., 3-1 Chi Nan Rd., Sect. 1, Taipei 100.

LIN, HONG-CHUNG 林宏宗

Mem., Legis. Yuan 96-; *b.* Oct. 26, '41; *educ.* Grad., Kaohsiung Ind. High Sch.; *Pol. Affi.* KMT; *Const.* Kaohsiung City; *Add.* Rm. 615, 3-1 Chi Nan Rd., Sect. 1, Taipei 100.

LIN, HUNG-TZUNG

(See LIN, HONG-CHUNG 林宏宗)

LIN, JUI-TU 林瑞圖

Mem., Legis. Yuan 99-; *b.* June 10, '56; *educ.* B., Tamkang U.; *Pol. Affi.* Independent; *Const.* Taipei City; Mem., Taipei CCoun. 91-98; *Add.* Rm. 3507, 10 Tsingtao E. Rd., Taipei 100.

LIN, JUNQ-TZER 林政則

Mem., Legis. Yuan 96-; *b.* Feb. 5, '44; *educ.* MS, Nat. U., USA; *Pol. Affi.* KMT; *Const.* Hsinchu City; Mem., Hsinchu CCoun.; Mem., NA; *Add.* Rm. 216, 3-1 Chi Nan Rd., Sect. 1, Taipei 100.

LIN, KUO-HUA 林國華

Mem., Legis. Yuan 99-; *b.* Sept. 19, '35; *educ.* BCE, NTU; *Pol. Affi.* DPP; *Const.* Yunlin County; Mem., 1st CEC, DPP; *Add.* Rm. 3407, 1 Tsingtao E. Rd., Taipei 100.

LIN, KUO-LUNG 林國龍

Mem., Legis. Yuan 90-; *b.* Dec. 8, '44; *educ.* Grad., Nat. Taitung Tchrs. Coll. 64, & Nat. Pingtung Tchrs. Coll. 77; *Pol. Affi.* KMT; *Const.* Nat.; Magis., Linpien Rural Township, Pingtung County 78-81; Mem., Pingtung CoCoun. & TPA 82-85 & 86-89; Convener, Econ. Cttee., Legis. Yuan 94; *Add.* Rm. 606, 3-1 Chi Nan Rd., Sect. 1, Taipei 100.

LIN, MING-I 林明義

Mem., Legis. Yuan 93-; *b.* June 1, '54; *educ.* Grad., Chianan Sr. Voc. Sch. for Home Econ. & Com. 80; *Pol. Affi.* KMT; *Const.* Yunlin County; Mem., Yunlin CoCoun. 85-92; *Add.* Rm. 2126, 3-1 Chi Nan Rd., Sect. 1, Taipei 100.

LIN, NAN-SHENG 林南生

Mem., Legis. Yuan 99-; *b.* Jan. 28, '52; *educ.* Grad., Intl. Jr. Coll. of Com.; MBA, USA; *Pol. Affi.* KMT; *Const.* Tainan City; Dep. Spkr., Tainan CCoun.; Mem., TPA 94-98; *Add.* 1st Fl., 4-11 Tsingtao E. Rd., Taipei 100.

LIN, PING-KUN 林炳坤
Mem., Legis. Yuan 96-; *b.* Aug. 15, '48; *educ.* BA, NTU; *Pol. Affi.* KMT; *Const.* Penghu County; Chmn., Police's Friends Assn.; *Add.* Rm. 403, 3-1 Chi Nan Rd., Sect. 1, Taipei 100.

LIN, TSENG-NAN 林宗南
Mem., Legis. Yuan 99-; *b.* June 26, '42; *educ.* M., Meiji U., Japan; *Pol. Affi.* DPP; *Const.* Nantou County; Magis., Tsaotun Urban Township, Nantou County; Mem., CEC, DPP; Mem., TPA 86-98; *Add.* Rm. 712, 3-1 Chi Nan Rd., Sect. 1, Taipei 100.

LIN, TSUNG-NAN
(See LIN, TSENG-NAN 林宗南)

LIN, WEN-LAN 林文郎
Mem., Legis. Yuan 96-; *b.* Mar. 12, '45; *educ.* Grad., Taipei Cml. High Sch.; *Pol. Affi.* DPP; *Const.* Nat.; Mem., Taipei CCoun.; Mem., For. & Ovs. Ch. Aff. Cttee., Legis. Yuan 96; Mem., CSC, DPP; *Add.* Rm. 811, 3-1 Chi Nan Rd., Sect. 1, Taipei 100.

LIN, YAO-HSING
(See LIN, YAW-SHING 林耀興)

LIN, YAW-SHING 林耀興
Mem., Legis. Yuan 96-; *b.* Oct. 17, '59; *educ.* Ph.D., Nat. Ssiga Med. U., Japan; *Pol. Affi.* KMT; *Const.* Taichung County; *Add.* Rm. 502, 3-1, Chi Nan Rd., Sect. 1, Taipei 100.

LIN, YEN-SAN 林源山
Mem., Legis. Yuan 93-; *b.* Dec. 2, '40; *educ.* BBA, U. of Lincoln, San Francisco; *Pol. Affi.* KMT; *Const.* Kaohsiung County; Mem., TPA 81-93; Adv., TPG 85-89; Mem., Kaohsiung CoCoun. 88-92; *Add.* Rm. 3501, 10 Tsingtao E. Rd., Taipei 100.

LIN, YI-SHIH 林益世
Mem., Legis. Yuan 99-; *b.* Aug. 19, '68; *educ.* MB, Taipei Med. Coll.; *Pol. Affi.* KMT; *Const.* Kaohsiung County; *Add.* Rm. 3211, Tsingtao E. Rd., Taipei 100.

LIN, YUAN-SHAN
(See LIN, YEN-SAN 林源山)

LIU, CHENG-HUNG 劉政鴻
Mem., Legis. Yuan 99-; *b.* Nov. 12, '47; *educ.* Grad., Twn Prov. Chunan Sr. High Sch.; *Pol. Affi.* KMT; *Const.* Miaoli County; Mem., Miaoli CoCoun.; Mem., Legis. Yuan 91-94; Bd. Mem., Farmers' Assn., Miaoli County; Dep. Sec.-Gen., Cent. Policy Cttee., KMT; *Add.* 2nd Fl., 4-4 Tsingtao E. Rd., Taipei 100.

LIU, CHUAN-CHUNG 劉銓忠
Mem., Legis. Yuan 99-; *b.* Apr. 5, '42; *educ.* Sr. Voc. Sch. Grad.; *Pol. Affi.* KMT; *Const.* Taichung County; Mem., Taichung CoCoun.; Mem., TPA; *Add.* Rm. 3401, 1 Tsingtao E. Rd., Taipei 100.

LIU, CHUN-HSIUNG 劉俊雄
Mem., Legis. Yuan 99-; *b.* Jan. 4, '51; *educ.* Finished Courses of Business Admin., Nat. Sun Yat-sen U.; *Pol. Affi.* DPP; *Const.* Nat.; Dir.-Gen., Kaohsiung City Br., DPP, Mem., Nat. Cong.; *Add.* Rm. 3305, 1 Tsingtao E. Rd., Taipei 100.

LIU, HSIEN-TUNG
(See LIU, SEN-TONG 劉憲同)

LIU, KUANG-HUA 劉光華
Mem., Legis. Yuan 93-; *b.* Sept. 19, '43; *educ.* LL.D., NCCU 81; *Pol. Affi.* KMT; *Const.* Nat.; Convener, Jud. Cttee., Legis. Yuan; Assc. Prof., NCCU, Tamkang U., Ch. Cul. U., & Tunghai U.; *Add.* Rm. 507, 3-1 Chi Nan Rd., Sect. 1, Taipei 100.

LIU, PING-WEI 劉炳偉
Mem., Legis. Yuan 99-; *b.* Nov. 30, '52; *educ.* Grad., Hsingwu Jr. Coll. of Com.; *Pol. Affi.* KMT; *Const.* Taipei County; Mem. 7th & 8th term, TPA, Dep. Spkr., 9th term, Spkr., 10th term; *Add.* Rm. 3402, 1 Tsingtao E. Rd., Taipei 100.

LIU, SEN-TONG 劉憲同
Mem., Legis. Yuan 99-; *b.* Mar. 24, '52; *educ.* B., Feng Chia U.; MBA, Regis U., USA; *Pol. Affi.* KMT; *Const.* Kaohsiung City; Mem., NA; Pres., Sym Wang Iron Steel Co. Ltd. & Airstar Ent. Co. Ltd.; Chmn., Presidium, NA; Mem., CC, KMT; *Add.* Rm. 3405, 1 Tsingtao E. Rd., Taipei 100.

LIU, SHENG-LIANG 劉盛良
Mem., Legis. Yuan 96-; *b.* Mar. 18, '39; *educ.* BCoS, Tatung Inst. of Tech.; *Pol. Affi.* KMT; *Const.* Taipei County; Mem., 9th, 10th, & 11th term, Taipei CoCoun.; Chmn., Veterans Assn., Taipei County; Mem., Legis. Yuan 90-93; Convener, Nat. Def. Cttee., Legis. Yuan 96, & Budget Review Cttee.; *Add.* Rm. 3306, 1 Tsingtao E. Rd., Taipei 100.

LIU, SUNG-FAN
(See LIU, SUNG-PAN 劉松藩)

LIU, SUNG-PAN 劉松藩
Mem., Legis. Yuan 73-; *b.* Dec. 3, '31; *educ.* Grad., Twn. Prov. Taichung Inst. of Com., & Kinki U., Japan; *Pol. Affi.* Independent; *Const.* Taichung County; Dep. Sec.-Gen., Policy Coordination Cttee., KMT 88-89, Dir., Secretariat, CC 89-90, Mem., CSC 93-99; V. Pres., Legis. Yuan 90-92, Pres. 92-99; *Add.* 12th Fl., 3-1 Chi Nan Rd., Sect. 1, Taipei 100.

LIU, WEN-HSIUNG 劉文雄
Mem., Legis. Yuan 99-; *b.* Sept. 18, '54; *educ.* B., Land Admin., NCCU; *Pol. Affi.* Independent; *Const.* Keelung City; Mem., TPA; *Add.* 1 Chung Shan S. Rd., Taipei 100.

LO, FU-CHU 羅福助
Mem., Legis. Yuan 96-; *b.* July 2, '43; *educ.* Hon. Dr., Sociology, USA; Hon. Dr., Business Mng., UK; *Pol. Affi.* Independent; *Const.* Taipei County; Mem., Trans. & Comms. Cttee., Legis. Yuan 96, Convener 97-98, & Jud. Cttee.; *Add.* 1 Chung Shan S. Rd., Taipei 100.

LO, MING-TSAI 羅明才
Mem., Legis. Yuan 99-; *b.* Jan. 15, '67; *educ.* MBA, USA; *Pol. Affi.* KMT; *Const.* Taipei County; Mem., NA; Mem., CC, KMT; *Add.* Rm. 605, 3-1 Chi Nan Rd., Sect. 1, Taipei 100.

LU, HSIN-MIN
(See LU, SHIN-MING 呂新民)

LU, HSIU-YEN
(See LU, SHIOW-YEN 盧秀燕)

LU, SHIN-MING 呂新民
Mem., Legis. Yuan 99-; *b.* Nov. 30, '41; *educ.* B., NTNU; *Pol. Affi.* KMT; *Const.* Taoyuan County; Magis., Pate Rural Township, Taoyuan County; Mem., Legis. Yuan 91-94; *Add.* Rm. 3105, Tsingtao E. Rd., Taipei 100.

LU, SHIOW-YEN 盧秀燕
Mem., Legis. Yuan 99-; *b.* Aug. 31, '61; *educ.* B., Land Admin., NCCU; *Pol. Affi.* KMT; *Const.* Taichung City; Mem., TPA; Reporter & City Ed., CTS; *Add.* Rm. 3106, 1 Tsingtao E. Rd., Taipei 100.

LU, YI-FENG 盧逸峰
Mem., Legis. Yuan 99-; *b.* Nov. 25, '62; *educ.* Grad., Fushin Inst. of Tech.; *Pol. Affi.* KMT; *Const.* Ilan County; Mem., TPA & Dep. Dir., KMT Caucus; *Add.* Rm. 3109, 1 Tsingtao E. Rd., Taipei 100.

MU, MING-CHU 穆閩珠
Mem., Legis. Yuan 99-; *b.* Aug. 15, '49; *educ.* Ed.M., Oregon State U. 79, Ph.D. 83; *Pol. Affi.* KMT; *Const.* Taipei City; V. Chmn., Assn. of Ovs. Students 88; Chmn., ROC Sports Assn. for the Disabled 89; Mem., NA 91-94, & Presidium; *Add.* Rm. 1001, 3-1 Chi Nan Rd., Taipei 100.

PAN, TINA WEI-KANG 潘維剛
Mem., Legis. Yuan 93-; *b.* Mar. 31, '57; *educ.* Grad., Dept. of Acct. & Statistics, Ming Chuan Coll. 89; Diploma, Grad. Sch. of PA, NCCU 91; *Pol. Affi.* KMT; *Const.* Taipei City; Mem., Taipei CCoun. 81-93; Mem., CC, KMT 88-; Mem., Organic Laws Cttee., Legis. Yuan 94; Pres., Modern Women Found.; *Add.* 2nd Fl., 5 Tsingtao E. Rd., Taipei 100.

PAN, WEI-KANG
(See PAN, TINA WEI-KANG 潘維剛)

PAYEN-TALU 巴燕達魯
Mem., Legis. Yuan 96-; *b.* Dec. 16, '51; *educ.* Jr. High Sch. Grad.; *Pol. Affi.* DPP; *Const.* Hsinchu County; *Add.* Rm. 709, 7th Fl., 3-1 Chi Nan Rd., Sect. 1, Taipei 100.

PENG, SHAO-CHIN 彭紹瑾
Mem., Legis. Yuan 96-; *b.* Feb. 28, '57; *educ.* LL.D., Munich U., Germany; *Pol. Affi.* DPP; *Const.* Taoyuan County; Lawyer; Assc. Prof., Soochow U., Ming Chuan U.; Mem., Jud. Cttee., Legis. Yuan 96, & Home & Border Aff. Ctte.; *Add.* Rm. 908, 3-1 Chi Nan Rd., Sect. 1, Taipei 100.

SHEN, CHIH-HUI 沈智慧
Mem., Legis. Yuan 93-; *b.* Sept. 16, '57; *educ.* BJ, Ch. Cul. U. 81; *Pol. Affi.* KMT; *Const.* Taichung City; Convener, Trans. & Comms. Cttee., Legis. Yuan 94, Dep. Dir., KMT Caucus; Corr., *Ch. Times, Twn. Times, Min Chung Daily News*; *Add.* Rm. 0715, 3-1 Chi Nan Rd., Sect. 1, Taipei 100.

SHEN, FU-HSIUNG 沈富雄
Mem., Legis. Yuan 93-; *b.* Aug. 23, '39; *educ.* MD, NTU 65; Ph.D., San Francisco Med. Cent. U. 69; Postdr. Fel., U. of Washington 72; *Pol. Affi.* DPP; *Const.* Taipei City; Mem., CC, Formosan Assn. for Public Aff., Washington, D.C. 82; Exec. Mem., Assn. for Plebiscite in Twn., & Twn. Found. for Intl. Rel.; *Add.* Rm. 1102, 11th Fl., 3-1 Chi Nan Rd., Sect. 1, Taipei 100.

SHIH, MING-TEH 施明德
Mem., Legis. Yuan 93-; *b.* Jan. 15, '41; *educ.* Army Artillery Coll. 61; *Pol. Affi.* DPP; *Const.* Tainan City; Jailed 62-77 & 80-90; Pres., Twn. Human Rights Promotion Assn.

90-91; Guest Prof., Dept. of Pol. Sc., San Diego State U. 91; Mem., CSC, DPP 91-93; Chmn., DPP 93-96; Convener, DPP Caucus, Legis. Yuan 93, Mem., For. & Ovs. Ch. Aff. Cttee. 98; *Add.* Rm. 607, 3-1 Chi Nan Rd., Sect. 1, Taipei 100.

SHYU, JONG-SHYONG 徐中雄

Mem., Legis. Yuan 93-; *b.* Oct. 17, '57; *educ.* BPS, Soochow U. 81; M., U. of Nr. Colorado 84, Ph.D. 87; *Pol. Affi.* KMT; *Const.* Taichung County; Convener, Home & Border Aff. Cttee., Legis. Yuan; Asst. Resr., Tng. Inst. for High Sch. Tchrs., TPG, Sp., Dept. of Soc. Aff.; *Add.* Rm. 2101, 3-1 Chi Nan Rd., Sect. 1, Taipei 100.

SONG, SHIUN-GUANG 宋煦光

Mem., Legis. Yuan 99-; *b.* Oct. 29, '53; *educ.* B., NCCU; *Pol. Affi.* KMT; *Const.* Tainan County; Mem., NA 92-96 & Presidium; *Add.* Rm. 708, 3-1 Chi Nan Rd., Sect. 1, Taipei 100.

SU, HUAN-CHIH
(See SU, HUAN-DJI 蘇煥智)

SU, HUAN-DJI 蘇煥智

Mem., Legis. Yuan 93-; *b.* July 20, '56; *educ.* LL.B., NTU; LL.M., Fu Jen Catholic U.; *Pol. Affi.* DPP; *Const.* Tainan County; V. Pres., Twn. Assn. for Human Rights; Convener, Jud. Cttee., Legis. Yuan 94, Exec. Mem., DPP Caucus; Lectr., NTHU; *Add.* Rm. 702, 3-1 Chi Nan Rd., Sect. 1, Taipei 100.

SUNG, HSU-KUANG
(See SONG, SHIUN-GUANG 宋煦光)

TAI, CHEN-YAO 戴振耀

Mem., Legis. Yuan 99-; *b.* April 2, '48; *educ.* Grad., Kangshan Sr. High Sch.; Studied, Human Resources Dev. Cent., U. of San Diego; *Pol. Affi.* DPP; *Const.* Nat.; Jailed for Kaohsiung Incident 78-81; V. Pres., Twn. Assn. for Farmers' Rights; Mem., Legis. Yuan 90-96, Dep. Convener, DPP Caucus; *Add.* Rm. 3502, 10 Tsingtao E. Rd., Taipei 100.

TANG, CHIN-CHUAN 湯金全

Mem., Legis. Yuan 99-; *b.* Dec. 15, '46; *educ.* LL.M., NTU; *Pol. Affi.* DPP; *Const.* Kaohsiung City; Prosecutor, Chiayi & Kaohsiung Public Prosecutors' Off.; Judge, Chiayi Dist. Court; Lawyer; Mem., Kaohsiung CCoun.; Mem., CAC, DPP; *Add.* Rm. 3117, 1 Tsingtao E. Rd., Taipei 100.

TANG, PI-O 唐碧娥

Mem., Legis. Yuan 99-; *b.* May 3, '49; *educ.* BA, Nat. Utsunomiya U., Japan; *Pol. Affi.* DPP; *Const.* Tainan City; Bd. Mem., Japan Br., Formosan Assn. for Public Aff. 88-90; Mem., NA 92-98; *Add.* Rm. 3202, 1 Tsingtao E. Rd., Taipei 100.

TING, SHOU-CHUNG 丁守中

Mem., Legis. Yuan 90-; *b.* Sept. 1, '54; *educ.* BS, NTU 76; M., Fletcher Sch. of Law & Dip., Harvard U. 82, Ph.D., Intl. Pol. 85; *Pol. Affi.* KMT; *Const.* Taipei City; Dep. Dir., Asia & World Inst. 85-87; Convener, Nat. Def. Cttee., Legis. Yuan 91-92; Chmn., Bridge Across the Straits Found. 91-96; Mem., Nat. Def. Cttee., Legis. Yuan 94; Dir.-Gen., Dept. of Youth Aff., CC, KMT 95-97; *Add.* Rm. 912, 3-1 Chi Nan Rd., Sect. 1, Taipei 100.

TSAI, CHIA-FU 蔡家福

Mem., Legis. Yuan 99-; *b.* May 4, '56; *educ.* Grad., Yu Ta Jr. Coll. of Com.; *Pol. Affi.* KMT; *Const.* Taipei County; Mayor, Hsinchuang City, Taipei County; *Add.* Rm. 611, 3-1 Chi Nan Rd., Sect. 1, Taipei 100.

TSAI, CHUNG-HAN
(See TSAY, CHUNG-HAN 蔡中涵)

TSAI, HAO 蔡豪

Mem., Legis. Yuan 99-; *b.* Aug. 1, '58; *educ.* Grad., Ch. Mil. Acad.; *Pol. Affi.* Independent; *Const.* Pingtung County; *Add.* 22nd Fl., 88 Chung Hsiao E. Rd., Sect. 2, Taipei 100.

TSAI, HUANG-LANG 蔡煌瑯

Mem., Legis. Yuan 96-; *b.* July 5, '60; *educ.* Studied, PA Class, NCCU; *Pol. Affi.* DPP; *Const.* Nantou County; Mem., Nantou CoCoun.; Dir., Nantou County Br., DPP; Mem., Educ. Cttee., Legis. Yuan 96; *Add.* Rm. 402, 3-1 Chi Nan Rd., Sect. 1, Taipei 100.

TSAI, KUEI-TSUNG
(See WALIS-PELIN 瓦歷斯・貝林)

TSAI, LING-LAN 蔡鈴蘭

Mem., Legis. Yuan 99-; *b.* May 13, '42; *educ.* Grad., Nat. Taichung Inst. of Com.; Hon. Ph.D., Union U., USA; *Pol. Affi.* KMT; *Const.* Nat.; Bd. Chmn., 11th Credit Co-operative Assn. of Taichung; Gov., Soroptimist Intl. of Twn. Region; Bd. Chmn., Twn. Prov. Women's Assn., ROC; *Add.* Rm. 613, 3-1 Chi Nan Rd., Sect. 1, Taipei 100.

TSAI, MICHAEL M. 蔡明憲

Mem., Legis. Yuan 96-; *b.* Aug. 9, '41; *educ.* MBA, U. of Wisconsin 72; J.D., Calif. We. Sch. of Law 89; *Pol. Affi.*

DPP; *Const.* Taichung City; Mem., NA; Mem., Jud. Cttee., Legis. Yuan 96, DPP Caucus 96-97, Home & Border Aff. Cttee. 97, Nat. Def. Cttee. 98 & 99; & Budget Review Cttee. 99; Attorney-at-Law; *Add.* Rm. 1010, 3-1 Chi Nan Rd., Sect. 1, Taipei 100.

TSAI, MING-HSIEN
(See TSAI, MICHAEL M. 蔡明憲)

TSAI, TUNG-JUNG
(See CHAI, TRONG R. 蔡同榮)

TSAO, CHI-HUNG 曹啓鴻
Mem., Legis. Yuan 99-; *b.* Mar. 1, '48; *educ.* BA, Ch. Cul. U.; Finished Courses, Grad. Inst. of Educ., Nat. Kaohsiung Normal U.; *Pol. Affi.* DPP; *Const.* Pingtung County; Mem., NA, & TPA 94-98; *Add.* Rm. 3409, 1 Tsingtao E. Rd., Taipei 100.

TSAO, ERH-CHUNG
(See CHAO, ERH-CHUNG 曹爾忠)

TSAY, CHUNG-HAN 蔡中涵
Mem., Legis. Yuan 87-; *b.* Sept. 25, '43; *educ.* Ph.D., Sociology, Tokyo U., Japan; *Pol. Affi.* Independent; *Const.* Lowland Aborigines; Mem., Budget Cttee., Legis. Yuan 94; *Add.* Rm. 1110, 11th Fl., Chi Nan Rd., Sect. 1, Taipei 100.

TSENG, ALLEN 曾振農
Mem., Legis. Yuan 93-; *b.* Feb. 25, '51; *educ.* Grad., Shenchou Supplementary Sr. High Sch.; *Pol. Affi.* KMT; *Const.* Nat.; Dep. Dir.-Gen., Dept. of Party-Govt. Coordination of the Legis. Yuan, KMT; Convener, Trans. & Comms. Cttee., Legis. Yuan; Mem., CC, KMT; *Add.* Rm. 1012, 10th Fl., Chi Nan Rd., Sect. 1, Taipei 100.

TSENG, CHEN-NUNG
(See TSENG, ALLEN 曾振農)

TSENG, HUA-TE 曾華德
Mem., Legis. Yuan 99-; *b.* May 15, '53; *educ.* Grad., Pingtung Tchrs.' Coll.; *Pol. Affi.* KMT; *Const.* Highland Aborigines; Magis., Laiyi Rural Township, Pingtung County; Mem., 9th & 10th term, TPA, & KMT Caucus; Adv., Taitung County Govt.; *Add.* Rm. 2112, 3-1 Chi Nan Rd., Sect. 1, Taipei 100.

TSENG TSAI, MEI-TSUO 曾蔡美佐
Mem., Legis. Yuan 99-; *b.* May 18, '45; *educ.* Grad., Tzung Sheng Sr. Voc. Sch.; Studied, Sun Yat-sen Inst. on Policy Res. & Dev.; *Pol. Affi.* KMT; *Const.* Yunlin County; Mem.,

10th & 11th Yunlin CoCoun.; Mem., TPA 90-98; *Add.* Rm. 3115, 1 Tsingtao E. Rd., Taipei 100.

TSENG, YUNG-CHUAN 曾永權
Mem., Legis. Yuan 93-; *b.* Nov. 1, '47; *educ.* M., Ind. Mng., Northrop U., USA; *Pol. Affi.* KMT; *Const.* Pingtung County; Mem., NA; Dep. Sec.-Gen., Ch. Taipei Olympic Cttee.; Adv., Directorate Gen. of Customs, MOF; Convener, Trans. & Comms. Cttee., Legis. Yuan 94, & Budget Review Cttee., Dir., KMT Caucus; *Add.* 9th Fl., 910 Chi Nan Rd., Sect. 1, Taipei 100.

WALIS-PELIN 瓦歷斯・貝林
Mem., Legis. Yuan 93-; *b.* Aug. 8, '52; *educ.* B.Th., Fu Jen Catholic U., BA, Philosophy 75; *Pol. Affi.* Independent; *Const.* Highland Aborigines; Mem., Nantou CoCoun. 86-90; Mem., Educ. Cttee., Legis. Yuan 94; *Add.* Rm. 512, 3-1 Chi Nan Rd., Sect. 1, Taipei 100.

WANG, CHAO-CHUAN 王兆釧
Mem., Legis. Yuan 99-; *b.* Nov. 9, '46; *educ.* B., Civil Engr., NTU; *Pol. Affi.* DPP; *Const.* Taipei County; Mem., NA; Mem, 8th & 10th term, TPA; *Add.* Rm. 301, 3-1 Chi Nan Rd., Sect. 1, Taipei 100.

WANG, CHIN-PING
(See WANG, JIN-PYNG 王金平)

WANG, HSING-NAN 王幸男
Mem., Legis. Yuan 99-; *b.* June 27, '41; *educ.* Grad., Hsin Feng Sr. High Sch.; *Pol. Affi.* DPP; *Const.* Tainan County; Jailed 76-90; Confidential Sec. to Tainan County Magis. Chen Tan-sun 94-98; *Add.* Rm. 1101, 3-1 Chi Nan Rd., Sect. 1, Taipei 100.

WANG, HSUEH-FUNG 王雪峰
Mem., Legis. Yuan 96-; *b.* Aug. 26, '64; *educ.* LL.M., Cornell U.; *Pol. Affi.* DPP; *Const.* Taipei City; Acting Dir., Dept. of So. Movement, CC, DPP; Mem., NA, & Jud. Cttee., Legis. Yuan 96; *Add.* Rm. 311R, 3-1 Chi Nan Rd., Sect. 1, Taipei 100.

WANG, JIN-PYNG 王金平
Pres., Legis. Yuan 99-, Mem. 75-; *b.* Mar. 17, '41; *educ.* BS, NTNU 65; *Pol. Affi.* KMT; *Const.* Kaohsiung County; Mem., Organic Laws Cttee., Legis. Yuan, For. Aff. Cttee., Home & Border Aff. Cttee., Econ. Aff. Cttee., & Finance Cttee.; Mem., CSC, KMT, Dir.-Gen., Dept. of Party-Govt. Coordination of the Legis. Yuan, CC; Sec.-Gen., KMT Caucus, Legis. Yuan; V. Pres., Legis. Yuan 93-99; *Add.* 1 Chung Shan S. Rd., Taipei 100.

WANG, LING-LIN 王令麟

Mem., Legis. Yuan 96-; *b.* Feb. 23, '55; *educ.* Grad., Tamsui Oxford U. Coll.; *Pol. Affi.* KMT; *Const.* Nat.; Chmn., Taipei Chamber of Com.; Chmn., ROC Business Arbitrary Assn.; Mem., Legis. Yuan 90-93; Dir., KMT Caucus, Legis. Yuan; *Add.* 9th Fl., 42 Kuan Chien Rd., Taipei 100.

WANG, SHIH-HSUN 王世勛

Mem., Legis. Yuan 99-; *b.* Jan. 15, '50; *educ.* Grad., Nat. Taichung Inst. of Com.; *Pol. Affi.* DPP; *Const.* Taichung City; Mem., 11th & 12th term, Taichung CCoun., & 10th term, TPA; *Add.* Rm. 309, 3-1 Chi Nan Rd., Sect. 1, Taipei 100.

WANG, TEIN-GING 王天競

Mem., Legis. Yuan 90-; *b.* July 23, '47; *educ.* B., Ch. Cul. U.; M., Roosevelt U.; *Pol. Affi.* KMT; *Const.* Kaohsiung City; Convener, Nat. Def. Cttee., Legis. Yuan 92-94, & Jud. Cttee.; Mem., Bd. of Trustees, Assn. of Free Ch. in the USA; Sec.-Gen., Kaohsiung Mun. Cttee., KMT, & Dept. of Ovs. Aff.; *Add.* Rm. 706, 3-1 Chi Nan Rd., Sect. 1, Taipei 100.

WANG, TIEN-CHING
(See WANG, TEIN-GING 王天競)

WANG, TO 王拓

Mem., Legis. Yuan 96-; *b.* Jan. 9, '44; *educ.* MA, NCCU; *Pol. Affi.* DPP; *Const.* Keelung City; Dir., Dept. of Org., CEC, DPP; Mem., NA; *Add.* Rm. 310, 3-1 Chi Nan Rd., Sect. 1, Taipei 100.

WANG, YU-TING 王昱婷

Mem., Legis. Yuan 99-; *b.* Oct. 3, '73; *educ.* LL.B., Fu Jen Catholic U.; *Pol. Affi.* KMT; *Const.* Tainan City; *Add.* Rm. 2102, 3-1 Chi Nan Rd., Sect. 1, Taipei 100.

WENG, CHIN-CHU
(See WONG, CHIN-CHU 翁金珠)

WENG, CHUNG-CHUN
(See WONG, CHUNG-CHUN 翁重鈞)

WONG, CHIN-CHU 翁金珠

Mem., Legis. Yuan 93-; *b.* Jan. 31, '47; *educ.* B., NTNU 77; *Pol. Affi.* DPP; *Const.* Changhua County; Chmn., Extraordinary Presidium, NA 87-93, & New Tide Movement 93-94; Convener, Educ. Cttee., Legis. Yuan 94,; *Add.* Rm. 1103, 3-1 Chi Nan Rd., Sect. 1, Taipei 100.

WONG, CHUNG-CHUN 翁重鈞

Mem., Legis. Yuan 90-; *b.* May 31, '55; *educ.* BA, Ch. Cul. U. 77, MBA 97; *Pol. Affi.* KMT; *Const.* Nat.; Mem., Chiayi

CoCoun. 82-89; Convener, Econ. Cttee., Finance Cttee., Trans. & Comms. Cttee., Nat. Def. Cttee., & Budget Review Cttee., Legis. Yuan 90-99; Bd. Mem., Chung Hsing Bills Finance Corp. 95-; Mem., CC, KMT; *Add.* Rm. 315, 3-1 Chi Nan Rd., Sect. 1, Taipei 100.

WU, CHING-CHIH 吳清池

Mem., Legis. Yuan 99-; *b.* May 20, '49; *educ.* Studied, Law Prog., NCCU; Sr. Voc. Sch. Grad.; *Pol. Affi.* KMT; *Const.* Taipei County; Mem., Taipei CoCoun.; Magis., Panchiao City, Taipei County; *Add.* Rm. 2130, 3-1 Chi Nan Rd., Sect. 1, Taipei 100.

WU, KO-CHING
(See WU, LUKE K.C. 吳克清)

WU, KUANG-HSUN 吳光訓

Mem., Legis. Yuan 99-; *b.* June 17, '50; *educ.* Grad., Yungtah Jr. Coll. of Tech. & Com.; *Pol. Affi.* KMT; *Const.* Kaohsiung County; Mem., NA 92-99; *Add.* Rm. 3506, 10 Tsingtao E. Rd., Taipei 100.

WU, LUKE K.C. 吳克清

Mem., Legis. Yuan 99-; *b.* Apr. 29, '54; *educ.* BA, Tamkang U. 77; *Pol. Affi.* KMT; *Const.* Taoyuan County; Pres., Chuan Shuai Ent. Co. Ltd.; Mem., NA, & Legis. Yuan 91-94; *Add.* 6th Fl., 5 Tsingtao E. Rd., Taipei 100.

WU, TSE-YUAN 伍澤元

Mem., Legis. Yuan 99-; *b.* Aug. 17, '45; *educ.* Dr., Ch. Cul. U.; *Pol. Affi.* Independent; *Const.* Kaohsiung County; Magis., Pingtung County; Dep. Sec.-Gen., TPG; *Add.* 1 Chung Shan S. Rd., Taipei 100.

YANG, CHI-HSIUNG 楊吉雄

Mem., Legis. Yuan 93-; *b.* July 8, '43; *educ.* Sr. High Sch. Grad.; *Pol. Affi.* KMT; *Const.* Nat.; Mem., Presidium, NA 86-91; Convener, Budget Cttee., Legis. Yuan 94; *Add.* 1 Chung Shan S. Rd., Taipei 100.

YANG, CHIU-HSING 楊秋興

Mem., Legis. Yuan 99-; *b.* May. 15, '56; *educ.* MCE, NTU; *Pol. Affi.* DPP; *Const.* Kaohsiung County; Mem., Educ. Cttee., TPA; *Add.* Rm. 616, 3-1 Chi Nan Rd., Sect. 1, Taipei 100.

YANG, CHIUNG-YING 楊瓊瓔

Mem., Legis. Yuan 99-; *b.* Oct. 19, '64; *educ.* B., Sociology, Tunghai U.; *Pol. Affi.* KMT; *Const.* Taichung County; Mem., TPA; Mem., CC, KMT; *Add.* Rm. 416, 3-1 Chi Nan Rd., Sect. 1, Taipei 100.

YANG, JEN-FU 楊仁福
Mem., Legis. Yuan 99-; *b.* Feb. 16, '42; *educ.* BPS, NTU; *Pol. Affi.* KMT; *Const.* Lowland Aborigines; Mem., TPA 86-98; *Add.* Rm. 2108, 3-1 Chi Nan Rd., Sect. 1, Taipei 100.

YANG, TSUO-CHOU
(See YANG, TZOU-CHOW 楊作洲)

YANG, TZUO-CHOW 楊作洲
Mem., Legis. Yuan 99-; *b.* Mar. 15, '29; *educ.* M., Meiji U., Japan; Ph.D., USA; *Pol. Affi.* KMT; *Const.* Ovs. Nat.; *Add.* Rm. 3511, Tsingtao 2nd Kuan, 10 Tsingtao E. Rd., Taipei 100.

YANG, WEN-HSIN 楊文欣
Mem., Legis. Yuan 99-; *b.* July 17, '62; *educ.* Grad., Tung Nan Jr. Coll. of Tech.; *Pol. Affi.* KMT; *Const.* Taichung County; Mem., 9th term, TPA, Dep. Spkr. 10th term; *Add.* Rm. 701, 3-1 Chi Nan Rd., Sect. 1, Taipei 100.

YAO, ENG-CHI 饒穎奇
V. Pres., Legis. Yuan 99-, Mem. 81-; *b.* Nov. 5, '34; *educ.* B., NCHU 63; *Pol. Affi.* KMT; *Const.* Nat.; Sec.-Gen., KMT Caucus, Legis. Yuan; Mem., Organic Laws Cttee., Legis. Yuan 94, & For. & Ovs. Ch. Aff. Cttee. 97-99; Exec. Sec., Policy Coordination Cttee., KMT, Dir., KMT Caucus, Mem, CSC, KMT; *Add.* 12th Fl. (Dep. Spkr. Off.), 3-1 Chi Nan Rd., Sect. 1, Taipei 100.

YAO, YING-CHI
(See YAO, ENG-CHI 饒穎奇)

YEH, HSIEN-HSIU 葉憲修
Mem., Legis. Yuan 99-; *b.* June 1, '48; *educ.* Grad., Shen Chou Sr. High Sch.; *Pol. Affi.* Dem. Alliance; *Const.* Taipei County; Mem., Legis. Yuan 91-94, Convener, Educ. Cttee.; Convener, Dem. Alliance; *Add.* Rm. 506, 3-1 Chi Nan Rd., Sect. 1, Taipei 100.

YEH, YI-CHIN
(See YEH, YI-JIN 葉宜津)

YEH, YI-JIN 葉宜津
Mem., Legis. Yuan 99-; *b.* Aug. 21, '60; *educ.* M., U. of Bridgeport, USA; Grad., Hochschule für Musik und Darstellende Kunst Wien, Austria; *Pol. Affi.* DPP; *Const.* Tainan County; Mem., TPA 94-98; *Add.* Rm. 501, 3-1 Chi Nan Rd., Sect. 1, Taipei 100.

YEN, CHING-FU 顏錦福
Mem., Legis. Yuan 93-; *b.* Mar. 2, '37; *educ.* BS, NTNU; *Pol. Affi.* DPP; *Const.* Nat.; Mem., 5th & 6th Taipei CCoun.; Chmn., Taipei Cttee., DPP, Mem., CEC & CSC; Cofounder, DPP; Mem., Trans. & Comms. Cttee., Legis. Yuan 94; *Add.* Rm. 7, 11th Fl., 3-1 Chi Nan Rd., Sect. 1, Taipei 100.

YING, CHIH-HUNG
(See YING, LEVI C. 營志宏)

YING, LEVI C. 營志宏
Mem., Legis. Yuan 99-; *b.* July 4, '49; *educ.* J.D., Whittier Coll. Law Sch., USA; *Pol. Affi.* NP; *Const.* Ovs. Nat.; Pres., Friends of NP Assn., Los Angeles; Mem., NA; Attorney-at-Law, USA; *Add.* Rm. 1001, 3-1 Chi Nan Rd., Sect. 1, Taipei 100.

YIU, HUAI-YIN 游淮銀
Mem., Legis. Yuan 93-; *b.* Apr. 26, '42; *educ.* MBA, U. of San Francisco 83; Hon. LL.D., St. John's U., USA 94; *Pol. Affi.* KMT; *Const.* Nat.; Mem., Budget Cttee., Legis. Yuan 94, Convener, Finance Cttee., Dep. Sec.-Gen., KMT Caucus; *Add.* Rm. 612, 6th Fl., 3-1 Chi Nan Rd., Sect. 1, Taipei 100.

YU, CHENG-TAO
(See YU, JAN-DAW 余政道)

YU, HUAI-YIN
(See YIU, HUAI-YIN 游淮銀)

YU, JAN-DAW 余政道
Mem., Legis. Yuan 99-; *b.* Sept. 27, '63; *educ.* LL.M., U. of So. Calif.; *Pol. Affi.* DPP; *Const.* Kaohsiung County; Mem., TPA; *Add.* Rm. 308, 3-1 Chi Nan Rd., Sect. 1, Taipei 100.

YU, YUEH-HSIA 游月霞
Mem., Legis. Yuan 99-; *b.* Feb. 6, '60; *educ.* Grad., Nat. Taichung Inst. of Com., & Nat. Open U.; *Pol. Affi.* KMT; *Const.* Changhua County; Mem., 9th & 10th term, TPA; *Add.* Rm. 206, 3-1 Chi Nan Rd., Sect. 1, Taipei 100.

Appendices

 Treasuring the earth's resources is the common responsibility of all inhabitants of the global village.

Chronology: January 1911 - December 1999

1911

Oct. 10 — A revolt against the Manchu (Ch'ing) dynasty erupts in Wuch'ang and is followed by revolutionary activities throughout China.

1912

Jan. 1 — The Republic of China is founded, with Dr. Sun Yat-sen as the first provisional president.

28 — A provisional senate is established in Nanking.

Feb. 12 — Henry Pu Yi abdicates as emperor, ending the rule of the Manchu dynasty.

13 — Dr. Sun tenders his resignation to the provisional senate.

15 — Yuan Shih-kai is elected provisional president by the provisional senate.

Mar. 11 — A provisional constitution is promulgated.

Apr. 2 — The provisional senate resolves to move the seat of the government to Peking.

Aug. 25 — The Tung-meng Hui (Society of the Common Cause) is reorganized as the Kuomintang (Nationalist Party).

1913

Apr. 6 — The provisional senate is dissolved.

8 — The Republic's first congress is organized.

May 2 — The United States recognizes the Republic of China.

July 12 — Li Lieh-chun of the Kuomintang starts the second revolution against Yuan's dictatorial rule.

Oct. 6 — Yuan forces the congress to elect him president.

10 — Yuan formally assumes the presidency.

1914

May 1 — Yuan annuls the provisional constitution.

June 23 — The Kuomintang is reorganized as the Chung-hua Ke-ming Tang (Chinese Revolutionary Party) in Tokyo. Dr. Sun is elected director-general.

Aug. 6 — Yuan declares China's neutrality in World War I.

1915

Jan. 18 — Japan presents the notorious 21 Demands to the Peking government.

May 15 — Yuan signs the "*Sino-Japanese Agreement*" (the 21 Demands).

Dec. 12 — Yuan proclaims himself emperor.

25 — Tsai O, Tang Chi-yao, and Li Lieh-chun revolt against Yuan in Yunnan Province.

1916

June 6 — Yuan dies, and the republican form of government is restored.

7 — Li Yuan-hung becomes president of the Peking government.

1917

July 12 — An attempted coup d'état by Chang Hsun to restore the Manchu dynasty fails.

Aug. 14 — The Peking government declares war on Germany and Austro-Hungary.

25 — Dr. Sun forms a military government in Canton.

Sept. 1 — The congress elects Dr. Sun Yat-sen as grand marshal of the Army and Navy of the Chinese Military Government.

1918

Sept. 4 — The "Militarists' Parliament" in the north elects Hsu Shih-chang president.

Nov. 23 — The Ministry of Education adopts the National Phonetic Symbols.

1919

Apr. 30 — The Paris Peace Conference allows Japan to take over Germany's prewar rights in Shantung Province.

May 4 — More than 3,000 students demonstrate in Peking against the Paris Peace Conference decision.

June 28 — China refuses to sign the *Versailles Treaty* on grounds that German rights in Shantung were given to Japan.

Oct. 10 — The Chung-hua Ke-ming Tang (Chinese Revolutionary Party) is reorganized as the Chung-kuo Kuo-min Tang (abbreviated as Kuomintang, or Nationalist Party).

1920
June 29 — China joins the League of Nations.

1921
May 5 — Dr. Sun Yat-sen assumes the presidency of the newly formed southern government in Canton.

1922
Feb. 4 — China signs an agreement with Japan in Washington to settle the Shantung dispute.
June 2 — Hsu Shih-chang resigns as president of the Peking government.
11 — Li Yuan-hung resumes the presidency in Peking.
16 — Chen Chiung-ming revolts against Dr. Sun.
Aug. 15 — Dr. Sun issues a manifesto urging the unification of China by peaceful means.

1923
Jan. 26 — Dr. Sun and Adolf Joffe, representative of the Soviet Communist Party, issue a joint statement declaring that neither the communist social order nor the Soviet system is suitable for China.

1924
Jan. 20 — The first National Congress of the Kuomintang in Canton adopts a policy of cooperation with the Soviet Union and the Chinese Communist Party.
May 3 — Chiang Kai-shek is appointed superintendent of the Whampoa Military Academy.
Nov. 10 — Dr. Sun, in a manifesto, calls for the early convocation of a national people's convention and the abolition of unequal treaties.
24 — Tuan Chi-jui becomes provisional chief executive in Peking.

1925
Mar. 12 — Dr. Sun dies in Peking at the age of 59.
July 1 — The national government is established in Canton.
Nov. 3 — The Kuomintang proposes disciplinary measures to restrict communist activities.

1926
Apr. 9 — Tuan Chi-jui resigns as provisional chief executive.
June 5 — Chiang Kai-shek becomes commander-in-chief of the National Revolutionary Forces.
27 — Chiang Kai-shek launches the Northern Expedition from Canton.

1927
Apr. 12 — The Kuomintang starts a "purification" movement by expelling communist members.
18 — The national government is established in Nanking by the Kuomintang.
Aug. 1 — The Chinese communists stage the Nanch'ang Uprising against the national government.
13 — Commander-in-chief of the National Revolutionary Forces, Chiang Kai-shek, resigns in order to unify the Nanking and Hankow factions of the Kuomintang.

1928
May 3 — Japanese troops attack the Northern Expeditionary Forces in Tsinan, touching off the May 3 (Tsinan) Incident.
June 4 — Chang Tso-lin is killed on a train by a bomb explosion. His son, Chang Hsueh-liang, succeeds him as ruler of Manchuria.
29 — Peking is renamed Peiping.
Oct. 8 — Chiang Kai-shek is elected chairman of the national government of the Republic of China.

Dec. 5 — The Legislative Yuan is formally established.

29 — Chang Hsueh-liang pledges allegiance to the national government, which leads to the unification of China.

1929

May 20 — Japanese troops withdraw from Tsinan.

July 23 — The national government severs diplomatic relations with the Soviet Union.

Dec. 30 — The Ministry of Foreign Affairs proclaims the nullification of consular jurisdiction in China to rid China of foreign privileges.

1930

Jan. 6 — The Examination Yuan is formally established.

July 13 — Rebels set up a government in Peking under the leadership of Wang Ching-wei.

1931

Feb. 16 — The Control Yuan is formally established.

May 5 — The National People's Convention is held in Nanking under the chairmanship of Chiang Kai-shek.

June 1 — The Provisional Constitution for the Period of Political Tutelage is promulgated.

July 4 — Korean immigrants occupy Wanpaoshan in Kirin Province at the instigation of Japanese militarists.

Sept. 18 — Japanese troops occupy Shenyang (Mukden) in a surprise attack. Important cities in Liaoning and Kirin provinces fall to the Japanese.

Oct. 24 — The Council of the League of Nations adopts a resolution urging Japan to withdraw its troops from Northeast China by November 16.

26 — Japan turns down the League's resolution.

27 — Nanking and Canton representatives meet in Shanghai for peace negotiations.

Nov. 18 — Ma Chan-shan puts up a stiff fight against the Japanese in Heilungkiang.

Dec. 15 — Chiang Kai-shek retires in the interest of party unity.

28 — The national government is reorganized, with Lin Sen as chairman.

1932

Jan. 3 — The Chinese communists set up a Soviet regime in Kan Hsien in Kiangsi.

8 — US Secretary of State Henry Stimson declares that the United States will not recognize any treaty that violates the Open Door Policy.

28 — Japanese naval forces attack Shanghai. The 19th Army Corps puts up stiff resistance.

Feb. 6 — The National Military Council is established.

19 — The United States refuses to recognize Japanese puppet state of "Manchukuo" (State of Manchuria).

Mar. 14 — The League of Nations' Lytton Commission arrives in China to investigate the Shenyang (Mukden) Incident.

18 — Chiang Kai-shek becomes chairman of the National Military Council.

May 5 — China and Japan sign an armistice in Shanghai.

June 28 — Chiang Kai-shek arrives in Hankow from Lushan to direct the campaign against the Chinese communists.

Dec. 12 — China resumes diplomatic relations with the Soviet Union.

1933

Feb. 14 — The League of Nations refuses to recognize "Manchukuo."

Apr. 18 — Fighting spreads in North China. Several strategic passes along the Great Wall fall to the Japanese.

May 31 — The *Sino-Japanese Tangku Armistice Agreement* is signed, ending hostilities in North China.

Nov. 20 — Leaders of the 19th Army Corps form a "People's government" in Fukien.

1934

Feb. 19 — Chiang Kai-shek launches the "New Life Movement" in Nanch'ang.

Mar. 1 — Henry Pu Yi is enthroned as "Emperor of Manchukuo" in Ch'angch'un by the Japanese militarists.

Oct.   10 — The main forces of the Chinese communist troops flee their bases in Kiangsi to
the northwest, launching the "Long
March."

21 — Government troops capture Juichin, the
communist capital in Kiangsi.

1935
Oct.   2 — Chiang Kai-shek is appointed commander-
in-chief of the Northwestern Communist-
Suppression Army and Chang Hsueh-
liang, deputy commander-in-chief, with
headquarters in Sian.

Nov.   4 — The national government proclaims the
nationalization of all silver, making notes
issued by the Central Bank of China and
the Bank of Communications legal tender.

1936
May   5 — The government promulgates the May 5
Draft Constitution.

Dec.   12 — Chang Hsueh-liang's troops mutiny in
Sian and hold Chiang Kai-shek and other
ranking government officials hostage.

22 — Madame Chiang, accompanied by W.H.
Donald and T.V. Soong (Sung Tzu-wen),
fly to Sian.

25 — Chang Hsueh-liang accompanies Generalissimo Chiang Kai-shek and Madame
Chiang to Loyang, en route to Nanking.

1937
July   7 — Japanese troops near Lukouchiao (Marco
Polo Bridge), southwest of Peking, attack Wanping city at night, formally starting the war between China and Japan.

17 — In a speech at Kuling, Chiang Kai-shek
lays down four conditions for settlement
of the Lukouchiao Incident.

Aug   21 — China and the Soviet Union sign a non-
aggression treaty in Nanking.

Sept.   28 — The League of Nations adopts a resolution
denouncing Japan's aggression in China.

Oct.   6 — The US State Department condemns Japan's invasion of China.

7 — The League of Nations adopts a resolution pledging moral support for China.

30 — The national government decides to move
the capital from Nanking to Chungking.

Nov.   3 — China presents her case at The Nine-
Power Conference in Brussels.

Dec.   13 — Japanese troops occupy Nanking. During the following two months, the aggressors rape and kill some 300,000
defenseless Chinese.

1938
Mar.   28 — The Ministry of Foreign Affairs issues a
statement denouncing the "Reform Government of China," a puppet regime set
up by the Japanese in Nanking.

Apr.   1 — The Emergency National Congress of
the Kuomintang in Wuch'ang elects
Chiang Kai-shek as its director-general
and decides to organize a People's Political Council and a San-min-chu-i Youth
Corps.

July   6 — The first session of the People's Political
Council opens in Hankow and adopts a
program of armed resistance and national
reconstruction.

7 — Chinese troops win a victory in T'ai-
erhchuang.

9 — The San-min-chu-i Youth Corps is established with Chiang Kai-shek as head.

Oct.   25 — Chinese troops evacuate Wuch'ang and
Hankow.

Dec.   22 — The Japanese prime minister, Prince
Konoye, lays down three points as guiding principles for the settlement of the
Sino-Japanese conflict and the establishment of the "New Order in East Asia."

26 — Chiang Kai-shek reiterates China's determination to carry on the war of resistance against Japan and charges that
Konoye's statement clearly reveals Japan's intention to conquer China.

1939
Jan.   28 — The fifth plenary session of the Fifth
Central Committee of the Kuomintang
decides to create a Supreme National
Defense Council with Chiang Kai-shek
as chairman.

Nov.   20 — Chairman Chiang Kai-shek is appointed

to the concurrent post of president of the Executive Yuan.

1940

Mar. 29 — Wang Ching-wei establishes a puppet regime in Nanking which is recognized by Japan on November 19.

30 — The Ministry of Foreign Affairs declares the Nanking puppet organization illegal.

Sept. 6 — Chungking is proclaimed provisional capital of China.

1941

Jan. 4 — The Communist New Fourth Army revolts against the national government.

14 — The revolt of the New Fourth Communist Army is suppressed.

Apr. 14 — Condemning the *Soviet-Japanese Neutrality Pact*, Foreign Minister Wang Chung-hui declares that Outer Mongolia and the northeastern provinces are Chinese territory and that the Soviet-Japanese statement is not binding on China.

17 — US President Roosevelt approves the first military aid program of US$45 million for China.

Sept. 30 — Chinese troops win the second battle of Ch'angsha.

Dec. 9 — China formally declares war on Japan.

1942

Jan. 2 — Chinese Expeditionary Forces enter Burma.

— Generalissimo Chiang assumes office as supreme commander of the China Theater of War.

15 — Chinese troops win the third battle of Changsha.

Mar. 4 — General Joseph Stilwell arrives in Chungking to assume duties as chief of staff of the China Theater of War and also to take command of all American armed forces in China, Burma, and India.

Apr. 19 — Chinese Expeditionary Forces capture Yenangyuang, rescuing more than 7,000 British and Burmese troops from Japanese encirclement.

June 2 — Foreign Minister T.V. Soong and US Secretary of State Cordell Hull sign the *Sino-American Lend-Lease Agreement* in Washington.

Oct. 10 — The US and UK governments announce their intention to relinquish extraterritoriality and related rights in China.

1943

Jan. 11 — China signs the new *Sino-American Treaty* in Washington and the new *Sino-British Treaty* in Chungking.

Oct. 10 — Chiang Kai-shek is sworn in as chairman of the national government.

Nov. 23 — Chiang Kai-shek, US President Franklin D. Roosevelt, and UK Prime Minister Winston Churchill confer in Cairo.

Dec. 3 — The Joint Declaration of the Cairo Conference is issued simultaneously in Chungking, Washington, and London.

1944

June 16 — Chinese Expeditionary Forces capture Kaimaing in northern Burma.

18 — US Vice President Henry Wallace visits China.

25 — Chinese Expeditionary Forces capture Magaung in northern Burma.

Sept. 29 — The Chinese-American-British phase of the Dumbarton Oaks Conference begins.

Oct. 9 — China, the US, the UK, and the USSR promulgate the draft for the *Charter of the United Nations*.

29 — US General Albert C. Wedemeyer is appointed chief of staff of the China Theater of War.

1945

Feb. 4 — The US, UK, and the USSR hold a conference in Yalta. A secret agreement, among other conclusions, is reached on Feb. 11 by the three that the USSR shall enter the war against Japan on condition that its former rights (in China) plundered by Japan in 1904 shall be restored.

Mar.　5 — China, the US, the UK, and the USSR issue joint invitations to the United Nations Conference in San Francisco on April 25.

June　26 — Representatives of 50 nations, including China, sign the UN Charter in San Francisco.

July　26 — Chiang Kai-shek, US President Truman, and UK Prime Minister Churchill issue a joint ultimatum, calling for Japan's unconditional surrender.

Aug.　9 — Soviet troops enter Manchuria.

11 — The Chinese communist headquarters in Yenan order communist troops to launch an all-out revolt against the government.

14 — Japan surrenders.
— The *Sino-Soviet Treaty of Friendship and Alliance* is signed in Moscow.
— Chiang Kai-shek invites Mao Tse-tung to come to Chungking for a conference.

15 — The Legislative Yuan unanimously approves the *Charter of the United Nations*.

23 — Soviet troops occupy Manchuria.

Sept.　2 — Japan's surrender is signed on the USS Missouri, with General Hsu Yung-chang signing for China.

9 — General Ho Ying-chin receives the formal surrender of Japanese forces in China from General Okamura in Nanking.

Oct.　25 — Taiwan is formally retroceded to China after 50 years of Japanese occupation.

Dec.　20 — Soviet troops move an estimated US$2 billion worth of machinery from Manchuria to the Soviet Union.

22 — General George C. Marshall arrives in Chungking as US President Truman's special envoy.

28 — The Big Three Foreign Ministers' Conference in Moscow announces agreements on a commission and allied council for Japan, the ultimate establishment of a free Korea, and the withdrawal of Soviet and US troops from China.

1946
Jan.　7 — Government and communist representatives hold their first truce meeting with General Marshall as mediator.

10 — The government issues a cease-fire order.
— The Political Consultative Conference opens.

13 — The UN Security Council is created, with China as one of the five permanent members.

Feb.　11 — US Secretary of State James Byrnes makes public the *Yalta Secret Agreement*.

20 — The Ministry of Foreign Affairs declares the *Yalta Secret Agreement* not binding on China.

22 — More than 20,000 students demonstrate against the *Yalta Secret Agreement* and call for the Soviet Union to withdraw its forces from China.

Mar.　5 — The Ministry of Foreign Affairs announces that China has rejected the Soviet claim to all Japanese military enterprises in Manchuria.

13 — Government forces enter Mukden following the evacuation of Soviet troops.

Apr.　17 — Communist troops enter Ch'angch'un.

26 — Communist troops take over Harbin and Tsitsihar as the Soviet forces evacuate.

May　5 — The national government moves back to Nanking.

23 — Government troops recapture Ch'angch'un.

June　6 — Chiang Kai-shek accepts General Marshall's proposal to issue a second cease-fire order during the 15-day armistice.

July　3 — The Supreme National Defense Council votes to convene the National Assembly on November 12, 1946.

Aug.　17 — Yenan issues a second mobilization order instructing all communist forces to launch full-scale war against the government.

Sept.　3 — Chiang Kai-shek agrees to create a committee of five headed by US Ambassador J. Leighton Stuart to pave the way for a coalition government.

Oct.　16 — Chiang Kai-shek presents the communists with eight conditions for a nationwide cease-fire.

18 — The communists reject the government's latest peace offer.

Nov.　4 — China and the United States sign a five-year *Treaty of Friendship, Commerce, and Navigation*.

8 — Chiang Kai-shek issues a third cease-fire.

15 — The National Assembly officially opens. Chiang Kai-shek announces termination of Kuomintang tutelage.

Dec.　25 — The National Assembly completes drafting the new Constitution.

1947

Jan.　1 — The government promulgates the Constitution.

29 — The US State Department announces abandonment of efforts to mediate between the national government and the communists.

Feb.　28 — Rioting breaks out in Taipei, following an incident between police and a peddler who violated the tobacco monopoly.

Mar.　19 — Government troops capture Yenan.

May　26 — The third plenary session of the Fourth People's Political Council adopts a resolution to invite communist members to attend.

June　25 — The Ministry of Foreign Affairs reveals repeated Soviet Union attempts to block Chinese troops from entering Dairen and Port Arthur.

July　22 — General Albert C. Wedemeyer, US President Truman's special representative, arrives in Nanking.

Nov.　21 — The first general elections in China are held.

Dec.　25 — The government adopts the Constitution.

1948

Mar.　29 — China's first National Assembly under the Constitution opens with 1,629 delegates attending.

Apr.　18 — The first National Assembly approves, by a two-thirds majority, temporary provisions granting emergency powers to the president during the period of the anti-communist campaign.

19 — The first National Assembly elects Chiang Kai-shek as China's first president under the new Constitution by 2,430 out of 2,704 votes.

21 — Government troops evacuate Yenan.

May　20 — President Chiang Kai-shek and Vice President Li Tsung-jen are sworn in.

1949

Jan.　5 — General Chen Cheng is sworn in as governor of Taiwan.

15 — Tientsin falls.

21 — President Chiang announces his retirement from the presidency and leaves for Hangchow. Vice President Li Tsung-jen is empowered to exercise presidential powers temporarily.

Apr.　5 — The national government begins talks with the Chinese communists.

12 — The Farm Rental Reduction Program goes into effect in Taiwan.

21 — The communists resume their all-out offensive and cross the Yangtze River.

23 — Government forces evacuate Nanking.

May　15 — Government forces evacuate Hankow and Wuch'ang.

27 — Shanghai is evacuated.

June　15 — Taiwan adopts a new currency.

July　10 — At the invitation of Philippine President Elpidio Quirino, President Chiang flies to Baguio to discuss formation of a Far Eastern anti-communist alliance.

Aug.　6 — At the invitation of Korean President Syngman Rhee, President Chiang flies to Chinhae, Korea, to discuss formation of a Pacific alliance.

15 — The Southeast China Governor's Office is established in Taipei, with General Chen Cheng as governor.

Sept.　27 — China files a complaint with the UN General Assembly against the Soviet Union's aid to the Chinese communists and violation of the *Sino-Soviet Treaty* of 1945 and the *UN Charter*.

Oct.　1 — The communists set up a regime in Peking with Mao Tse-tung as "chairman," which is recognized by the Soviet Union the next day.

3 — The ROC severs diplomatic relations with the USSR.

— The US State Department reaffirms US recognition of the national government as the only legal government of China.

13 — Government troops evacuate Canton.

25 — Government troops win a victory at Kinmen (Quemoy) against a communist attack.

Dec. 7 — The government moves its seat to Taipei.

10 — President Chiang flies from Chengtu to Taipei.

15 — The Executive Yuan names Wu Kuo-chen governor of Taiwan.

1950

Jan. 6 — The Republic of China severs diplomatic relations with Britain following Britain's recognition of the communist regime.

11 — The UN Security Council rejects a Soviet proposal for the immediate expulsion of the ROC delegation.

28 — The Ministry of Foreign Affairs declares that the Republic of China will not be bound by any agreement signed between the Chinese communist regime and the Soviet Union.

Mar. 1 — President Chiang Kai-shek resumes office in Taipei.

7 — President Chiang nominates General Chen Cheng as president of the Executive Yuan (premier).

Apr. 5 — The Executive Yuan grants Taiwan authority to carry out self-government by popular election in counties and cities within two months.

June 27 — US President Truman orders the US Seventh Fleet to prevent a communist attack on Taiwan and asks the ROC government to cease air and sea operations against the mainland.

July 2 — A popular election for a Hualien county council is held, marking the beginning of self-government in Taiwan.

31 — General Douglas MacArthur arrives in Taipei to confer with President Chiang.

Aug. 10 — Karl L. Rankin arrives in Taipei as chargé d'affaires of the US embassy.

16 — Taiwan, formerly consisting of eight counties and nine cities, is redivided into 16 counties and five cities.

Nov. 1 — The Chinese communists announce aid to the Korean communists in the fight against UN forces in Korea.

30 — The UN Security Council orders the Chinese communist forces to leave Korea.

1951

Feb. 1 — The UN General Assembly condemns the Chinese communists as aggressors in Korea.

May 1 — US Major General William C. Chase arrives in Taipei as the first chief of the Military Assistance Advisory Group (MAAG) in Taiwan.

18 — The UN General Assembly approves a global embargo on shipments of arms and war material to the Chinese and North Korean communists.

25 — The Legislative Yuan adopts the *37.5 Percent Farm Rental Reduction Act.*

30 — The government announces plans to sell arable public land to tenant farmers on easy payment terms.

Dec. 11 — The Taiwan Provincial Assembly is established.

1952

Feb. 1 — The UN General Assembly finds the Soviet Union guilty of violation of the 1945 *Sino-Soviet Treaty of Friendship and Alliance.*

Apr. 28 — The *Treaty of Peace between the Republic of China and Japan* is signed in Taipei.

Oct. 22 — The first worldwide Overseas Chinese Conference opens in Taipei.

31 — The China Youth Corps is organized.

1953

Jan. 10 — The Legislative Yuan adopts the *Land-to-the-Tiller Act.*

25 — President Chiang announces abrogation of the *Sino-Soviet Treaty of Friendship*

and *Alliance* of 1945 and its related documents.

Apr. 2 — Karl L. Rankin becomes the American ambassador to the ROC.

12 — The Legislative Yuan passes a bill submitted by President Chiang, extending the term of office for legislators another year, i.e., to May 7, 1954.

July 17 — Guerrillas on Kinmen conduct a successful raid against the communist-held Tungshan Island off the southern coast of Fukien.

Sept. 27 — President Chiang recommends an extension of the term of office of the delegates to the first National Assembly, elected in 1947, until the second National Assembly can be elected.

Nov. 24 — The government protests to the United States against the proposed American transfer of the Amami Oshima Islands to Japan.

27 — Korean President Syngman Rhee arrives in Taipei.

1954

Jan. 23 — More than 14,000 Chinese communist POW's in Korea, who refused to return to the Chinese mainland, arrive in Taiwan.

Mar. 11 — The second session of the first National Assembly approves indefinite extension of the *Temporary Provisions Effective During the Period of Communist Rebellion*.

22 — Chiang Kai-shek is reelected president for a second six-year term.

24 — Chen Cheng is elected vice president.

May 20 — President Chiang nominates O.K. Yu to be president of the Executive Yuan (premier).

June 4 — President Chiang appoints Yen Chia-kan governor of Taiwan.

Dec. 3 — The *Sino-American Mutual Defense Treaty* is signed in Washington.

1955

Jan. 26 — The US House of Representatives approves a resolution authorizing President Eisenhower to employ American armed forces to defend Taiwan, the Pescadores, and "related positions and territories."

Feb. 7 — Government troops begin to evacuate the Tachen Islands.

Mar. 3 — Foreign Minister George K.C. Yeh and US Secretary of State John Foster Dulles exchange instruments of ratification of the *Sino-American Mutual Defense Treaty* in Taipei.

1956

Jan. 12 — The Taiwan Provincial Government promulgates the *Rules for the Enforcement of the Statute on Urban Land Reform*.

May 28 — Foreign Minister George K.C. Yeh informs Philippine Ambassador Narciso Ramos that the ROC has full sovereignty over the Nansha Islands.

July 7 — Ground is broken for the construction of the East-West Cross-Island Highway.

1957

Apr. 21 — Taiwan voters go to the polls for the third time to elect county magistrates, city mayors, and provincial assemblymen.

May 3 — The Council of Grand Justices of the Judicial Yuan rules that the nation's three top representative organs—the Legislative Yuan, the Control Yuan, and the National Assembly—shall collectively represent the Chinese parliament in all international parliamentary organizations.

Aug. 8 — General Chow Chih-jou is appointed governor of Taiwan, succeeding C.K. Yen.

Sept. 26 — The first council meeting of the Asian Peoples' Anti-Communist League opens in Taipei.

Oct. 20 — President Chiang is reelected Tsungtsai (director-general) of the Kuomintang.

1958

May 14 — Mohammed Reza Pahlevi, the Shah of Iran, arrives in Taipei for a five-day state visit.

Aug. 1 — An insurance program covering 180,000 government employees is put into effect.

23 — The Battle of the Taiwan strait begins with the Chinese communists firing on the Kinmen Islands.

Oct. 23 — President Chiang and US Secretary of State John Foster Dulles issue a joint communiqué reaffirming solidarity between the two countries and stating that Quemoy and the Matsu Islands are "closely related" to the defense of Taiwan and the Pescadores under present conditions.

1959

Mar. 6 — The Faith (36,000 tons), the first tanker built in the ROC, is launched at Keelung.

9 — King Hussein of Jordan arrives in Taipei for an eight-day state visit.

13 — Some 300,000 Tibetans revolt against the communists.

July 21 — The Legislative Yuan revises the *Conscription Law*, stipulating that 19-year-old men are to be drafted for two years' service in the army or three years in the navy or air force.

Aug. 15 — The ROC Army receives Nike-Hercules ground-to-air guided missiles from the United States under a military aid program.

Sept. 1 — The *Law on Compensation for Wrongful Detentions and Convictions*, designed to compensate people in cases of miscarriages of justice, goes into effect.

1960

Feb. 2 — The Council of Grand Justices of the Judicial Yuan announces that the total membership of the National Assembly, under the present period of national emergency, shall be 1,576.

23 — The ROC establishes diplomatic relations with Cameroon.

Mar. 11 — The third session of the first National Assembly adopts an amendment to the *Temporary Provisions Effective During the Period of Communist Rebellion.*

19 — The third session of the first National Assembly decides to set up a committee to study the exercise of initiative and referendum by the National Assembly.

22 — Chiang Kai-shek is reelected to a third

term as president, and Chen Cheng, to a second term as vice president.

May 2 — Philippine President and Mrs. Carlos Garcia arrive in Taipei for a six-day state visit.

9 — The East-West Cross-Island Highway is opened to traffic.

June 18 — US President Eisenhower arrives in Taipei for a state visit.

19 — President Chiang and US President Eisenhower issue a joint communiqué pledging that their governments will continue to stand solidly behind the *Sino-US Mutual Defense Treaty* against the Chinese communists in this area.

— The Chinese communists hit Kinmen, and the ROC artillery units retaliated.

Aug. 15 — The Council of Grand Justices of the Judicial Yuan rules that, courts of all levels shall be placed under the jurisdiction of the Judicial Yuan.

— The ROC recognizes the Congo (Brazzaville) Republic.

25 — The ROC Olympic Team in the opening procession of the Olympic Games in Rome protests the International Olympic Committee's ruling compelling ROC athletes to compete under the name of "Taiwan" instead of the "Republic of China."

Sept. 6 — Yang Chuan-kuang, the ROC's decathlon champion, wins the ROC's first Olympic silver medal.

1961

May 14 — US Vice President and Mrs. Lyndon B. Johnson visit the ROC.

Oct. 7 — Two defecting Chinese communist pilots, Shao Hsi-yen and Kao Yu-tsung, arrive in Taipei from South Korea.

27 — The 16th UN General Assembly votes for the admission of Outer Mongolia. The Republic of China abstains.

Dec. 1 — The first nuclear reactor in the ROC, installed by Chinese scientists at the National Tsinghua University campus in Hsinchu, is put into operation.

18 — The ROC establishes diplomatic ties with Upper Volta.

1962

Mar. 14 — Foreign Minister Shen Chang-huan declares that the ROC does not recognize Japan's so-called "residual sovereignty" over the Ryukyu Islands.

Apr. 3 — President and Mme. Philbert Tsiranana of the Malagasy Republic arrive for a six-day state visit.

Oct. 30 — The ROC rejects the McMahon Line as the boundary between China and India.

Nov. 22 — General Huang Chieh is appointed governor of Taiwan, succeeding General Chow Chih-jou.

Dec. 28 — The Ministry of Foreign Affairs declares border agreements signed between the Peking regime and Outer Mongolia and Pakistan illegal and not binding on the ROC.

1963

June 5 — King Bhumibol Adulyadej and Queen Sirikit of Thailand arrive in the ROC for a state visit.

Aug. 4 — The Ministry of Foreign Affairs declares that the ROC does not recognize the border treaty signed between the Peking regime and Afghanistan.

23 — Ambassador to the United States Tsiang Ting-fu signs the nuclear test ban treaty on behalf of the ROC.

Sept. 1 — The Council for International Economic Cooperation and Development is inaugurated to replace the Council for US Aid.

Oct. 6 — Dahomey President and Mme. Hubert Maga arrive for a six-day state visit.

Nov. 16 — The new premier, Yen Chia-kan, assumes office.

1964

Feb. 12 — Japanese Premier Shigeru Yoshida arrives in the ROC to confer with President Chiang Kai-shek.

June 14 — The NT$3,200 million multipurpose Shihmen Dam is dedicated.

Oct. 27 — The ROC and Korea sign a treaty of amity in Seoul.

1965

Apr. 9 — The ROC and the United States conclude in Taipei an accord to establish a Sino-American fund for economic and social development in Taiwan.

May 14 — Thomas Wen-yi Liao returns from Tokyo after renouncing his "Taiwan Independence movement."

25 — The ROC and the United States sign in Taipei an inventory of atomic equipment and materials to be reported to the International Atomic Energy Agency.

July 1 — The United States phases out economic aid to the ROC.

31 — The ROC and the United States sign an agreement in Taipei on the status of US forces in China.

Nov. 11 — Malagasy President Tsiranana arrives for a four-day visit.

23 — US warships return to the ROC 102 cases of rare books that were sent to the United States for safekeeping during World War II.

1966

Jan. 1 — US Vice President Hubert H. Humphrey arrives in the ROC to confer with Chinese leaders.

Feb. 15 — Korean President Park Chung Hee arrives for a four-day state visit.

Mar. 21 — The National Assembly elects President Chiang Kai-shek to a fourth term as president of the Republic.

22 — The National Assembly elects Premier Yen Chia-kan the third vice president of the Republic.

26 — The Ministry of Foreign Affairs announces the ROC's opposition to US recognition of Outer Mongolia.

July 3 — US Secretary of State Dean Rusk arrives in Taipei to confer with Chinese leaders.

6 — The Legislative Yuan approves the *Sino-Haitian Treaty of Amity* signed in Port-au-Prince on Feb. 15, 1966.

1967

Feb.　1 — The National Security Council is established by President Chiang Kai-shek with Vice Premier Huang Shao-ku as secretary-general and Ku Shu-tung as his deputy.

Apr.　4 — Australian Prime Minister Harold E. Holt arrives for a three-day visit.

July　1 — Taipei becomes a special municipality, with Kao Yu-shu as its mayor.

　　　28 — The Chinese Cultural Renaissance Movement is officially organized, with President Chiang Kai-shek as its head.

Aug.　3 — The Executive Yuan decides to extend the period of compulsory education from six to nine years beginning in 1968.

　　　4 — Malawi President Dr. H. Kamuzu Banda arrives for an eight-day state visit.

Sept.　25 — The first conference of the World Anti-Communist League opens in Taipei, with more than 200 leaders from 72 nations and areas attending.

Nov.　24 — The Chinese Economic Development Research Institute is inaugurated in Taipei.

1968

Aug.　24 — Taichung's Golden Dragons baseball team wins the 23rd Little League World Championship.

　　　25 — Lesotho Premier Leabua Jonathan arrives in the ROC for an official visit.

Oct.　23 — Nigerian President Hamani Diori arrives in the ROC for an official visit.

Dec.　17 — The Chinese National Committee of the International Press Institute is established in Taipei.

　　　20 — The nation chooses 26 new members to the National Assembly and the Legislative Yuan.

1969

May　26 — Sierra Leone Premier Siaka P. Stevens arrives in Taipei to confer with ROC leaders.

1970

July　12 — ROC athlete Chi Cheng breaks the women's 200-meter record in West Germany, with a time of 22.44 seconds.

1971

Aug.　14 — Ground for the construction of the North-South Freeway is broken near Linkou.

Oct.　25 — The Republic of China withdraws from the United Nations.

1972

Mar.　21 — President Chiang Kai-shek is reelected to a fifth six-year term.

May　26 — Former Vice Premier Chiang Ching-kuo becomes premier after approval by the Legislative Yuan.

Aug.　20 — The ROC Mei Ho baseball team wins the Senior League world title.

　　　27 — The Taipei Little League baseball team wins the world title.

Sept.　29 — The Republic of China severs diplomatic relations with Japan.

Oct.　16 — President Dawda Kairba Jawara of Gambia arrives for an eight-day visit.

Nov.　12 — The Republic of China wins the World Cup Golf Championship in Melbourne.

Dec.　23 — An election of additional members to the National Assembly, Legislative Yuan, the Taiwan Provincial Assembly, and of new mayors and county magistrates is held in Taiwan, Kinmen, and Matsu.

1973

Jan.　22 — H.R.H. Prince Tuipelehake, C.B.E., prime minister of the Kingdom of Tonga, arrives for a one-week visit.

Oct.　30 — Tsengwen Dam and Reservoir, the largest in Taiwan, are completed.

Dec.　25 — Construction of the Suao-Hualien railroad is launched.

1974

Jan.　26 — Premier Chiang Ching-kuo announces an across-the-board price adjustment to help stabilize the economy.

Apr.　20 — The ROC announces the termination of Taiwan-Japan flights by China Airlines and Japan Airlines.

May 14 — Chen Te-nien, director of the Taiwan Railway Administration, and Peter Godwin, representing Lazard Brothers Co., sign an agreement under which a British consortium will loan £575 million to TRA's railway electrification project.

July 29 — The Sanchung-Chungli section of the North-South Freeway is opened to traffic.

Oct. 30 — The first F5E Freedom jet fighter made in the Republic of China rolls off the assembly line.

1975

Feb. 17 — The China Steel Corp., the Continental Illinois National Bank, and the Trust Company of Chicago sign a US$200 million loan contract to help finance construction of a steel mill in Kaohsiung.

Mar. 21 — Chinese officials stationed in Phnom Penh return to Taipei.

Apr. 5 — President Chiang Kai-shek passes away.

6 — Yen Chia-kan, vice president of the Republic of China since 1966, takes the oath of office as the nation's second constitutional president.

26 — The Embassy of the Republic of China in Saigon suspends operations.

28 — Premier Chiang Ching-kuo is elected chairman of the Central Committee of the ruling Kuomintang.

June 9 — The Republic of China terminates diplomatic relations with the Republic of the Philippines.

July 1 — The ROC terminates diplomatic relations with Thailand.

9 — The Republic of China and Japan sign a private aviation agreement that restores the Taiwan-Japan services of China Airlines and a Japanese airline.

26 — The newly built southern portion of the Suao-Hualien railroad is opened to traffic.

Aug. 29 — A nova in the Cugnus constellation is discovered by the Taipei observatory.

Oct. 21 — The second naphtha cracking plant of the Chinese Petroleum Corp. begins production.

1976

Mar. 26 — Dr. Lin Yu-tang, 81, one of the best known Chinese writers in English, dies in Hong Kong.

July 17 — The ROC team withdraws from the Montreal Games to protest competing under the name of "Taiwan."

Aug. 21 — Prince Maphevu Harry Dlamini, prime minister of the Kingdom of Swaziland, accompanied by Madame Dlamini and a party of eight, arrives for a seven-day visit.

Oct. 31 — Taichung Port in west central Taiwan is formally opened.

1977

Mar. 26 — The Chinese research vessel Hai Kung returns to Keelung after a 115-day exploratory expedition to the Antarctic.

May 18 — China Airlines' new Boeing 747SP begins nonstop service between Taipei and the US West Coast.

June 3 — The 445,000-ton tanker Burmah Endeavour, built by the China Shipbuilding Corp. for US Gatx Oswego, is launched at Kaohsiung. It is the world's third largest vessel.

July 9 — President Yen Chia-kan leaves for a three-day state visit to Saudi Arabia, at the invitation of King Khaled Bib Abdul Aziz Al-Saud.

Sept. 19 — King Taufa'ahau Tupou IV and Queen Halaevalu Mata'aho of the Kingdom of Tonga arrive for a week's state visit at the invitation of President and Madame Yen Chia-kan.

Oct. 17 — Akira Nishiyama, former Japanese ambassador to South Korea, arrives to assume his duties as director of the Japan Interchange Association's Taipei office.

1978

Mar. 21 — Premier Chiang Ching-kuo is elected by the National Assembly as president for the sixth constitutional presidential term of the Republic of China.

30 — The first generator of Taiwan's first

nuclear power plant begins its full capacity operation of 636,000 kilowatts.

May 26 — The Legislative Yuan endorses President Chiang's appointment of Sun Yun-suan, former minister of economic affairs, as the new premier.

June 20 — The Republic of China is listed the 25th largest trading country in the world by the International Monetary Fund.

Oct. 31 — The Taiwan Area Freeway, with a total length of 377 km, is opened to traffic.

Dec. 8 — The Legislative Yuan passes the revised *Foreign Exchange Management Regulations* under which the New Taiwan dollar is no longer pegged to the US dollar.

16 — President Chiang Ching-kuo strongly condemns the US decision to sever diplomatic relations with the Republic of China in favor of the Peking regime.

1979
Mar. 1 — The US embassy in Taipei formally closes, to be succeeded by the American Institute in Taiwan.

— The Washington Office of the Coordination Council for North American Affairs of the Republic of China opens.

Apr. 10 — US President Jimmy Carter signs legislation permitting continued commercial and cultural relations between the US government and the ROC following the break in diplomatic ties.

July 1 — The electrification of Taiwan's 1,153-km-long west coast trunk line railway between Keelung and Kaohsiung is completed.

— Kaohsiung becomes a special municipality under the direct jurisdiction of the Executive Yuan.

Sept. 6 — The Cabinet announces the extension of the ROC's territorial waters to 12 nautical miles, and the establishment of a 200-mile economic zone.

Nov. 16 — The Republic of China and the United States conclude 40 days of talks on the revision of their air transportation agreement. Under the memorandum issued by

the two parties, the ROC will open civil air services to four new US stops: Guam, Seattle, New York, and Dallas-Fort Worth.

1980
Jan. 3 — The US government informs the ROC government that it will resume arms sales to the ROC after a one-year suspension.

Dec. 27 — Twenty-two supplementary members are elected to the Control Yuan from among 54 candidates by members of the Taiwan Provincial Assembly, the Taipei City Council, and the Kaohsiung City Council.

1981
Apr. 2 — President Chiang Ching-kuo is reelected chairman of the Kuomintang by acclamation at the 12th National Congress in Taipei.

May 4 — The first European Trade Fair in the Republic of China is held at the Taipei World Trade Center with some 293 companies from 13 Western European countries participating.

1982
May 12 — The Council for Agricultural Planning and Development (CAPD) reveals the second phase of the land reform program.

20 — The Cabinet approves the draft of a *Genetic Health Law* to legalize abortion and prevent couples with known genetic diseases from having children.

June 20 — The Directorate General of Telecommunications (DGT) opens the first public data switching service in the ROC.

Oct. 16 — Aleksandr I. Solzhenitsyn, 1970 Nobel Literature Prize winner, arrives in Taiwan from Tokyo at the invitation of Wu San-lien of the Literary Foundation of the ROC.

1983
Jan. 14 — The Legislative Yuan passes a revision of the *Trademark Law* to impose prison terms for infringement of trademarks.

Feb. 16 — The Dutch airline Martinair inaugurates flight service to Taiwan, marking the opening of air service between the Netherlands and the Republic of China.

Apr. 12 — China Airlines inaugurates regular flight service to Amsterdam as the first step toward establishing a world-girdling commercial air service.

June 7 — The Legislative Yuan passes the *Firearms Control Law*, placing the manufacture, possession, and use of firearms and other weapons under stricter control.

July 12 — A groundbreaking ceremony is held to mark the start of Taipei's underground railway project.

Oct. 31 — Taipei's 809-meter long Kuantu Bridge, the first multi-arch steel bridge in East Asia, is opened to traffic.

1984

Jan. 12 — The Cabinet approves a plan to build a synchrotron research center within five years.

Mar. 1 — The Republic of China's first domestically developed jet trainer AT-3 rolls off the assembly line. The twin-seat trainer, fitted with two Garrett TFE 731-2-2L engines, each with a thrust of 1,590 kg, was developed by the Aeronautical Institute of Science and Technology.

21 — President Chiang Ching-kuo is reelected for a second six-year term.

May 20 — President Chiang Ching-kuo nominates Yu Kuo-hwa, chairman of the Council for Economic Planning and Development and governor of the Central Bank of China, as the new premier.

June 29 — The Legislative Yuan approves the long-awaited and controversial *Genetic Health Law*.

July 20 — The Legislative Yuan passes the *Labor Standards Law*.

Aug. 1 — ROC athlete Tsai Wen-yee wins a bronze medal in the weightlifting events of the 1984 Olympic Games.

Sept. 20 — The ROC Council of Agriculture is formally established.

Oct. 12 — The ROC-Australia Trade Association and the Chinese-New Zealand Business Council are formally inaugurated in Taipei.

1985

Jan. 8 — The Hong Kong Affairs Task Force under the Executive Yuan decides to simplify exit and entry application procedures, relax controls on foreign exchange, and adopt incentive measures to encourage large enterprises and monetary institutions in Hong Kong to move to Taiwan.

Apr. 16 — The first test tube baby in the Republic of China is born at Veterans General Hospital in Taipei.

22 — The Industrial Technology Research Institute successfully develops an amorphous-silicon solar battery of high commercial value.

July 9 — The last part of a transoceanic telecommunication cable system, which will link Taiwan, Hong Kong, and Singapore, is hauled ashore in Toucheng, Ilan.

19 — The Ministry of National Defense announces that a domestically developed surface-to-air missile named "Sky Bow" made a successful debut in a test firing.

Sept. 29 — ROC decathlon athletes Ku Chin-shui and Li Fu-en win a gold and silver medal respectively in the sixth Asian Track and Field Championships in Jakarta, Indonesia.

1986

Apr. 23 — National Taiwan University Hospital separates a pair of 14-day-old Siamese twins, saving one of the baby girls' life and setting a world record for separating the youngest Siamese twins.

24 — ROC Minister of Foreign Affairs Chu Fu-sung and Paraguayan Foreign Minister Carlos Augusto Saldivar sign an extradition treaty in Taipei on behalf of their respective governments.

May 18 — The Ministry of National Defense announces that an air-to-air "Sky Sword"

653

missile has been successfully tested by shooting down a Hawk missile.

Aug. 3 — Construction of the Synchronous Radiation Research Center is started at the Hsinchu Science-Based Industrial Park.

Sept. 25 — The Republic of China, after withdrawing 13 years ago, is readmitted to the Olympic Council of Asia (OCA).

Oct. 6 — The Ministry of Economic Affairs decides to invest NT$1.2 billion in developing anti-pollution technology over the next three years.

15 — Lee Yuan-tseh, a member of the Academia Sinica, wins the 1986 Nobel Prize in chemistry.

Nov. 6 — The Democratic Progressive Party (DPP) holds its first Representative Assembly and releases a draft of its charter and platform.

1987

June 23 — The Legislative Yuan passes the *National Security Law during the Period of National Mobilization for Suppression of the Communist Rebellion*. After the law becomes effective, the *Emergency Decree* in Taiwan and the Pescadores (Penghu) will be lifted.

July 15 — The *Emergency Decree* is lifted in the Taiwan area, the *National Security Law* is promulgated, and foreign exchange controls are relaxed.

Aug. 1 — The Council of Labor Affairs is formally established under the Executive Yuan.

Nov. 2 — The ROC Red Cross Society begins accepting applications from local residents wishing to visit relatives in mainland China.

10 — ROC-US talks on intellectual property rights begin in Taipei.

1988

Jan. 1 — Registrations for new newspapers are opened, and restrictions on the number of pages per issue are relaxed.

11 — The Legislative Yuan passes the *Law on Assembly and Parades during the Period*

of National Mobilization for Suppression of the Communist Rebellion, which outlines three fundamental principles and specifies areas that will be off-limits to demonstrators.

13 — President Chiang Ching-kuo passes away of heart failure and hemorrhage at 3:50 p.m.

— Vice President Lee Teng-hui is sworn in as president of the Republic of China to complete the late President Chiang's second six-year term, which runs from 1984 to 1990.

Mar. 3 — The Council for Economic Planning and Development approves the establishment of an US$11 billion International Economic Cooperation and Development Fund to assist developing countries.

24 — The Government Information Office and the Ministry of National Defense reiterate that the ROC has never engaged in the development of nuclear weapons. This is confirmed by the US government.

Apr. 18 — The ROC Red Cross Society begins forwarding mail from Taiwan residents to mainland China.

28 — An ROC delegation attends the annual convention of the Asian Development Bank (ADB) in Manila.

July 8 — Acting Chairman Lee Teng-hui is elected chairman of the Kuomintang at the ruling party's 13th National Congress.

28 — The Executive Yuan approves regulations governing the import of publications, films, and radio and television programs from communist-controlled areas.

Aug. 18 — The Mainland Affairs Task Force is established under the Executive Yuan.

30 — ROC-US talks on finance and banking open in Washington. The ROC negotiators agree to open the Taiwan market to credit card companies and to expand credit for foreign banks.

Sept. 5 — The Executive Yuan announces that the long-range Hsiung Feng II missile has been successfully developed and will soon be added to the ROC arsenal.

Oct. 25 — A comprehensive farmer health insurance is initiated.

Nov. 3 — The Mainland Affairs Task Force revises regulations to allow mainland compatriots to visit sick relatives or attend their funerals in Taiwan.

17 — The Executive Yuan approves the private installation of small satellite dish antennas, which will allow viewers to tune into the KU-band and receive television programming from Japan's NHK station.

Dec. 1 — The Executive Yuan announces guidelines governing unofficial participation in international academic conferences and cultural and athletic activities held on the mainland, as well as regulations governing visits to Taiwan by overseas mainland scholars and students.

1989

Jan. 10 — The ROC and the Commonwealth of the Bahamas establish diplomatic relations.

20 — The Legislative Yuan passes the *Law on Civic Organizations*.

26 — The Legislative Yuan passes the *Law on the Voluntary Retirement of Senior Parliamentarians*.

Mar. 6 — President and Madam Lee Teng-hui arrive in Singapore for a four-day visit.

27 — The Central Bank of China announces the cancellation of limits on the daily fluctuation of the NT dollar against the US greenback, to be effective April 3.

Apr. 7 — The Chinese Taipei Olympic Committee announces that ROC athletic teams and organizations will participate in international sports events held on the mainland under the name "Chinese Taipei."

17 — The Mainland Affairs Task Force passes the proposal to allow teachers and staff of public schools to travel to the Chinese mainland for family visits. On the 18th, the council decides to permit newsgathering and filmmaking on the mainland.

30 — Finance Minister Shirley Kuo leads an ROC delegation to the 22nd annual Asian Development Bank meeting in Peking.

May 28 — Ching Kuo, the first ROC-developed and manufactured indigenous defense fighter, successfully completes its first test flight.

31 — One million students participate in a Hand in Hand, Heart to Heart rally in support of the mainland democracy movement.

June 1 — Lee Huan is sworn in as premier of the ROC.

4 — President Lee Teng-hui issues a statement condemning the Tienanmen Massacre.

10 — Direct telephone links are opened between the two sides of the Taiwan Straits.

19 — The Hong Kong and Macau Affairs Task Force announces the government's plan to simplify procedures for the relocation of Hong Kong and Macao compatriots in Taiwan and to provide assistance for their emigration to a third country.

July 11 — The Legislative Yuan approves a partial revision of the *Banking Law* which completely abolishes interest rate controls and deregulates entry into the banking system. The law goes into effect on July 19.

20 — The ROC establishes formal diplomatic ties with Grenada.

Aug. 1 — A foreign currency call loan market is established in Taipei, designed to make the metropolis an international financial center.

Sept. 4 — Guatemalan President Marco Vincicio Cerezo Arevalo and President Lee Teng-hui sign a joint communiqué in Taipei calling for closer bilateral relations.

15 — Prime Minister Mary Eugenia Charles of the Commonwealth of Dominica arrives in Taipei for a six-day visit.

25 — The Sky-bow Weapons System, developed and manufactured by the ROC, is added to the nation's military defense system.

26 — The Executive Yuan permits pro-democracy supporters from the mainland to settle in Taiwan.

Oct. 2 — The ROC and Liberia re-establish diplomatic relations. Peking severs formal
ties with Liberia in protest.

12 — The ROC and Belize announce the establishment of diplomatic relations.

— King Mswati III of Swaziland arrives for
a five-day visit.

Dec. 2 — Elections for the Legislative Yuan, Taiwan
Provincial Assembly, Taipei and Kaohsiung
city councils, county magistrates, and provincial-level city mayors are held.

1990

Jan. 14 — President Lee Teng-hui and President Pros-
per Avril of Haiti sign a joint communiqué
calling for stronger bilateral cooperation.

16 — Low-ranking government employees are
permitted to visit relatives across the
Straits, and native Taiwanese who moved
to the mainland before 1949 are allowed
to visit relatives in Taiwan.

Feb. 13 — The Mainland Affairs Task Force permits Taiwan's performing artists to stage
commercial performances on the mainland and to participate in activities sponsored by the Chinese communists.

26 — President Lee Teng-hui and El Salvadoran
President Alfredo Felix Cristiani Burkard
sign a joint communiqué for closer bilateral cooperation.

Mar. 1 — The Executive Yuan approves direct trade
between the ROC and the Soviet Union
and Albania.

17 — Thousands of university students stage a
sit-down protest at the Chiang Kai-shek
Memorial Hall Plaza to express opposition to the National Assembly's attempt
to expand its authority.

21 — Lee Teng-hui is elected the eighth-term
president of the ROC.

22 — Li Yuan-zu is elected vice president of
the ROC.

27 — The eighth plenum of the National Assembly approves a motion to force members who failed to attend the plenary
session to retire by the end of July 1990.

Apr. 5 — The ROC reestablishes diplomatic relations with the Kingdom of Lesotho.

Peking severs ties with Lesotho two
days later.

8 — Economics Minister Chen Li-an and
Singaporean Minister of Trade and Industries, Lee Hsien Loong, preside over
the first ministerial-level conference between the two countries on economic
cooperation.

30 — Elected officials of all levels are permitted to make private visits to the mainland
during recesses. Veterans who were
stranded on the mainland after the national government moved to Taiwan in
1949 are allowed to apply for resettle-
ment in Taiwan.

May 16 — The KMT Central Standing Committee
accepts the resignation of Premier Lee
Huan and his Cabinet ministers.

20 — Lee Teng-hui and Li Yuan-zu are inaugurated as president and vice president of
the ROC.

— President Lee Teng-hui announces a special amnesty, which includes the pardon-
ing of dissidents Hsu Hsin-liang and Shih
Ming-teh.

26 — The ROC establishes diplomatic relations with Guinea Bissau.

29 — Premier nominee Hau Pei-tsun is approved by the Legislative Yuan, and is
immediately appointed premier by President Lee Teng-hui.

June 17 — President Andres Rodriguez of Paraguay
arrives in Taipei to sign a joint communiqué calling for closer bilateral relations with the ROC.

21 — The Council of Grand Justices announces
that senior parliamentarians should terminate their responsibilities by December 31, 1991.

25 — Reporters from the mainland are permitted to visit Taiwan for newsgathering
purposes, and government employees from
Taiwan are allowed to visit sick relatives
or attend funerals on the mainland.

July 4 — The National Affairs Conference concludes in Taipei, after six days of discussions on parliamentary reforms, the

central and local government systems, the Constitution, and mainland policy.

22 — The ROC severs diplomatic relations with Saudi Arabia, after the latter switches formal recognition to communist China.

Aug. 10 — The ROC government declares its support of a United Nations call for world sanctions against Iraq over its invasion of Kuwait.

31 — Premier Hau Pei-tsun advises the Legislative Yuan that ROC relations with the mainland will operate under the concept of "one country, two areas."

Sept. 1 — Premier Hau Pei-tsun announces the objectives of the Six-Year National Development Plan, which includes public construction projects affecting economics, culture, education, and medicine.

17 — A team of 200 athletes and coaches flies to the Chinese mainland for the ROC's first attendance of the Asian Games in 20 years.

19 — The Red Cross societies of the ROC and the mainland reach agreement on procedures for the repatriation of illegal mainland entrants to Taiwan.

Oct. 7 — The National Unification Council is established under the Office of the President to help plan the policy framework for national unification, and to integrate various opinions about the issue at all levels of society.

11 — The Ministry of the Interior reiterates that the Tiaoyutai island group belongs to the ROC. The chain of eight uninhabited islets, located in the East China Sea, also is claimed by Japan and communist China.

18 — The Mainland Affairs Council is established under the Executive Yuan to formulate and implement mainland policy.

27 — Moscow City Mayor Gavriil H. Popov arrives for a formal visit to the ROC to discuss the strengthening of ROC-Soviet trade relations.

Nov. 1 — President Lee Teng-hui receives an

Outstanding International Alumnus Citation from Cornell University.

15 — The Ministry of Foreign Affairs announces the ROC-Canadian agreement to exchange aviation rights and establish Taipei economic and cultural offices in major Canadian cities.

20 — The first ROC-USSR fishery cooperation conference is held in Tokyo for discussions on technological exchanges and expansion of fishing zones.

21 — The Straits Exchange Foundation, a private intermediary organization financially supported by the government, is established to handle technical affairs arising from people-to-people contacts between Taiwan and the mainland.

1991

Jan. 6 — A memorandum is signed between the ROC and Saudi Arabia for the mutual establishment of representative offices in their capital cities.

7 — French Minister of Industry and Territorial Development Roger Fauroux participates in the seventh ROC-France Economic Cooperation Conference in Taipei

31 — The Executive Yuan approves a budget of about US$303 billion for the Six-Year National Development Plan.

Mar. 14 — The Executive Yuan passes the *Guidelines for National Unification*, which are now the highest directives governing ROC mainland policy. Its long-term goal is to establish a democratic, free, and equitably prosperous China.

Apr. 22 — The second extraordinary session of the First National Assembly passes, at its sixth plenary meeting, the *Additional Articles of the Constitution of the ROC* and approves the abolishment of the *Temporary Provisions Effective During the Period of Communist Rebellion*.

30 — President Lee Teng-hui declares the termination of the Period of National Mobilization for Suppression of the Communist Rebellion, effective on May 1. He abolishes the *Temporary Provisions* and

promulgates the *Additional Articles of the Constitution*, also effective on May 1.

May   9 — Visa application restrictions for USSR nationals are relaxed, and visa applications for purposes other than business are permitted.

     24 — The Legislative Yuan approves the abolishment of the *Statutes for the Purging of Communist Agents*.

June   26 — Approval is given to 15 of the 19 applications to set up private commercial banks.

     27 — Government Spokesman Shaw Yu-ming announces that mainland journalists will no longer have to renounce their membership in the Chinese Communist Party when applying to visit Taiwan.

July   4 — The ROC and Czechoslovakia agree to exchange representative offices.

     8 — The ROC and the Central African Republic resume diplomatic relations.

Aug.   5 — President Lee Teng-hui receives Fijian Prime Minister Ratu Sir Kamisese Mara; an ROC-Fiji technological cooperation agreement is signed on August 6.

     12 — Two mainland journalists arrive in Taipei, marking the first-ever visit by the mainland Chinese press.

     18 — Vice President Li Yuan-zu leaves for a state visit to Costa Rica, Nicaragua, and Honduras, and to attend the 23rd Plenary Meeting of the World League for Freedom and Democracy at San José, Costa Rica.

Sept.   25 — The Mainland Affairs Council announces the establishment of a task force to combat crime across the Taiwan Straits.

Oct.   11 — Direct air service begins between Australia and the ROC.

Nov.   6 — The ROC and Latvia sign memoranda for economic cooperation and the exchange of trade offices.

     13 — The ROC joins the Asia-Pacific Economic Cooperation (APEC) along with Hong Kong and mainland China.

     15 — South African President Frederik Willem de Klerk signs a joint communiqué with President Lee Teng-hui for closer relations between the two countries.

Dec.   21 — The ruling Kuomintang wins 71 percent of the vote and 254 of the 325 seats in the election for the Second National Assembly.

     22 — Dissident mainland Chinese astrophysicist Fang Li-chih visits Taipei.

     31 — All senior delegates to the First National Assembly, Control Yuan, and Legislative Yuan retire from office.

1992

Jan.   20 — The French Secretary of State for Foreign Trade Jean-Noël Jeanneney visits Taipei to discuss participation in the Six-Year National Development Plan and further economic cooperation between the ROC and France.

     27 — The Fair Trade Commission is established under the Executive Yuan.

     29 — The ROC and Latvia announce the establishment of relations at the consulate-general level.

Feb.   4 — The *Fair Trade Law* goes into effect.

     18 — A delegation from the US President's Export Council arrives to promote ROC-US trade.

     28 — The ROC and the Philippines sign an official investment guarantee agreement to protect investments by Taiwan businessmen.

Mar.   7 — Nicaraguan President Violeta Barrios de Chamorro and President Lee Teng-hui sign a joint communiqué in Taipei for stronger bilateral relations.

     23 — The first-ever meeting convenes in Peking between the SEF and the mainland's Association for Relations Across the Taiwan Straits, to discuss issues related to document verification and indirect registered mail services.

     27 — The ROC and Bulgaria agree to establish direct air links between Taipei and Sofia.

Apr.   17 — Legislative proceedings are completed for the *National Employment Act*, which will serve as the basis for the employment of foreign nationals in the ROC.

     19 — Minister of Foreign Trade Yvonne C.M.T.

van Rooy of the Netherlands visits Taipei to seek stronger bilateral relations.

29 — Bolivian Vice President Luis Ossio Sanjines officiates the inauguration of the Bolivian Commercial and Financial Representative Office in Taipei.

May 10 — Swedish Minister of Transport and Communications, Mats Odell, visits Taipei to discuss closer cooperation and future exchanges with the ROC.

11 — President Andre Kolingba of the Central African Republic visits Taipei.

17 — Wu Ta-you, president of Academia Sinica, attends academic conferences in Peking and Tientsin.

30 — The *Additional Articles* 11 through 18 of the Constitution go into effect.

31 — The Mainland Affairs Council allows Chinese mainlanders to come to Taiwan and care for their old or sick relatives.

June 10 — A revised *Copyright Law* goes into effect, providing explicit legal protection for intellectual property rights and imposing heavier penalties for infringement of copyright.

14 — Ronald Freeman, Vice President of the European Bank for Reconstruction and Development, visits the ROC to discuss Sino-European trade and financial relations.

19 — The ROC resumes diplomatic relations with Niger.

— The Legislative Yuan approves the *Law on Foreign Futures Contracts*, which will take effect in January 1993.

July 3 — The Legislative Yuan passes a revision of the *Law on Civic Organizations*, which calls for a Political Party Review Committee be formed under the Ministry of the Interior.

7 — The Legislative Yuan passes a revision of the *National Security Law*, which would reduce the number of black-listed persona non grata from 282 to five.

9 — The Argentine Trade and Cultural Office is opened in Taipei after a 20-year break in diplomatic relations.

16 — The Legislative Yuan passes the *Statute Governing Relations Between People of the Taiwan Area and the Mainland Area.*

19 — The ROC's five-year lease of three Knox class frigates from the United States is approved by US President George Bush.

23 — Former French Premier Michel Rocard visits the ROC to strengthen friendship between the two countries.

Aug. 1 — The National Unification Council defines "one China" as "one country and two areas separately ruled by two political entities."

— Taiwan Garrison General Headquarters, the ROC's highest security institution in the Taiwan area, is disbanded; and the Coastal Patrol General Headquarters is established under the Ministry of National Defense.

18 — The Department of Anti-Corruption is established under the Ministry of Justice.

23 — The ROC severs diplomatic relations with South Korea.

25 — Niger's Prime Minister Amadou Cheiffou arrives in Taipei to advance mutual understanding between the two countries.

30 — Former British Prime Minister Margaret Thatcher expresses support for the ROC's entry into the GATT during her visit to Taipei.

Sept. 2 — President Lee Teng-hui and Guatemalan President Jorge Antonio Serrano sign a joint communiqué calling for closer bilateral cooperation in Taipei.

— Canadian International Trade Minister Michael Wilson visits Taipei to boost ROC-Canada trade ties; he is the first ministerial official to visit the ROC since bilateral ties were severed in 1970.

— The Bureau of Entry and Exit announces that members of the Chinese People's Political Consultative Conference in mainland China may apply to visit Taiwan for cultural and academic exchanges.

6 — Direct air service between the ROC and

Vietnam resumes for the second time in 13 months.

13 — Latvian Prime Minister Ivars Godmanis visits Taipei to seek mutually beneficial cooperation; an ROC-Latvia investment guarantee agreement is signed on September 17.

21 — The US Department of Defense decides to sell 12 SH-2F light airborne multipurpose system helicopters to the ROC.

22 — Political Vice Foreign Minister John Chang and Oleg Lobov, Chairman of the Export Council to the Russian President Boris Yeltsin, sign two diplomatic memoranda and a document of state protocol pledging the promotion of trade, tourism, investment, cultural, and scientific and technological exchanges.

24 — Foreign Minister Fredrick Chien and his Vanuatu counterpart Serge Vohor sign a joint communiqué pledging reciprocal recognition.

29 — The ROC is granted observer status in the GATT, which also resolves to accept the ROC's application into GATT under the name, the "Separate Customs Territory of Taiwan, Penghu, Kinmen and Matsu".

Oct. 11 — President Lee Teng-hui and Panamanian President Guillermo Endara sign a joint communiqué to expand bilateral cooperation.

12 — Premier Hau Pei-tsun receives Austrian Minister for Economic Affairs Wolfgang Schüssel.

22 — Belgian Foreign Trade Minister Robert Urbain visits Taipei to relay a message of welcome to Taiwan businessmen intending to invest in Belgium and pledges support for the ROC's bid to join GATT.

27 — Australian Tourism and Resources Minister Alan Griffiths visits Taipei to promote closer bilateral trade relations. Mr. Griffiths is the first Australian Minister visiting Taipei since 1972.

Nov. 3 — Indonesian Minister of Research and Technology Bacharuddin Habibie leads a 30-member delegation to Taiwan.

4 — Vice Minister of Economic Affairs Chiang Pin-kung heads an observer delegation to the Geneva meeting of GATT Council of Representatives after the ROC's absence of 21 years.

7 — After more than three decades of military administration, Quemoy (Kinmen) and Matsu revert to civilian rule as the *Statute Governing the Security and Guidance of the Kinmen, Matsu, Tungsha, and Nansha Areas* goes into effect.

9 — Saint Lucia's Prime Minister John George Melvin Compton visits Taipei.

10 — The Nigerian Trade Office is set up in Taipei to promote economic relations with the ROC.

12 — ROC and US defense representatives sign a letter of offer and acceptance for the ROC's purchase of 150 F-16A and F-16B jet fighters from the United States.

18 — German Vice Chancellor Jürgen Möllemann and Economics Minister Vincent C. Siew reach an agreement on the establishment of direct air links and channels of communication on trade between the ROC and Germany.

19 — The Council of Agriculture bans all import, export, and trade of rhino-horn products.

30 — United States Trade Representative Carla A. Hills visits Taipei.

Dec. 19 — The Kuomintang wins 53.02 percent and the Democratic Progressive Party 31.03 percent of the popular vote in the election for the Second Legislative Yuan.

1993
Jan. 14 — The Legislative Yuan approves a US$12.47 billion budget for the purchase of 150 F-16 jet fighters from the United States and 60 Mirage 2000-5s from France.

15 — ROC and Philippine officials sign an agreement in Manila, setting the guidelines for transforming the former US naval facility at Subic Bay into an industrial complex.

Feb. 22 — Taiwan-made film *The Wedding Banquet* wins a Golden Bear Award for Best Picture at the 43rd annual Berlin International Film Festival.

26 — Two China mainland basketball teams arrive in Taiwan to play exhibition matches against local teams; this marks the first time in four decades that athletes from Taiwan and the mainland will compete in Taiwan.

27 — Taiwan Provincial Governor Lien Chan succeeds Hau Pei-tsun as premier of the ROC following his confirmation by the Legislative Yuan.

Mar. 21 — Republic of Nauru President Bernard Dowiyogo visits Taipei.

26 — In an interview with the US Cable News Network, President Lee Teng-hui stresses the ROC's willingness to form a regional collective security system with Asia-Pacific countries.

29 — Direct air service between the ROC and the United Kingdom begins.

— New Zealand's Minister of Customs and Associate Minister of Tourism, Murray McCully leads a nine-member delegation to Taipei. Mr. McCully is the first New Zealand's Minister visiting Taipei since 1972.

Apr. 22 — The Legislative Yuan ratifies the 1989 ROC-US copyright agreement and passes amendments to the *Copyright Law*, which go into effect on April 26.

— Tonga's Prime Minister Vaea and Madame Vaea visit the ROC.

29 — Representatives of the Straits Exchange Foundation and its mainland counterpart, the Association for Relations Across the Taiwan Straits, sign three agreements and a joint accord at a historic meeting in Singapore; the agreements and accord go into effect on May 29.

May 1 — The Taipei Economic and Trade Office in Tel Aviv begins operation.

7 — The first ROC-made PFG-2 missile frigate, the Cheng-kung, goes into service.

8 — A 186-member team from the ROC participates in the first East Asian Games in Shanghai.

13 — Former US Secretary of Defense Dick Cheney visits Taipei.

15 — Tuvalu's Prime Minister Bikenibeu Paeniu and Madame Paeniu visit the ROC.

June 11 — President Lee Teng-hui receives former Philippine President Corazon Aquino.

21 — An ROC-US agreement for technical cooperation in the field of environmental protection is signed in Washington, D.C.

29 — President Lee Teng-hui receives former US Vice President Dan Quayle.

30 — The Executive Yuan approves an Economic Stimulus Package to accelerate industrial upgrading and to develop Taiwan into an Asia-Pacific Regional Operations Center.

July 2 — The *Public Functionary Assets Disclosure Law* goes into effect.

8 — The ROC and Nicaragua sign a joint communiqué pledging bilateral cooperation.

10 — Vietnam's Economic and Cultural Office in Taipei opens.

12 — The Taipei-Moscow Economic and Cultural Coordination Commission begins operation in Moscow.

Aug. 10 — The New KMT Alliance breaks with the ruling Kuomintang and forms the New Party.

11 — The *Cable Television Law* goes into effect.

16 — The 14th National Congress of the KMT opens. President Lee Teng-hui is re-elected chairman of the KMT; while Vice President Li Yuan-zu, former Premier Hau Pei-tsun, Judicial Yuan President Lin Yang-kang, and Premier Lien Chan are elected vice chairmen on August 18.

17 — The ROC and Australia sign two memoranda on the protection of industrial property rights and on investment promotion and technical cooperation.

Sept. 2 — The Executive Yuan passes an administrative reform package to eradicate corruption and inefficiency in the government.

23 — The ROC and Belgium sign three

investment cooperation agreements to boost economic and technological ties.

Oct. 26 — The ROC and Mexico sign a pact to promote investment and technology transfer.

Nov. 19 — Vincent C. Siew, chairman of the Council for Economic Planning and Development, represents President Lee Teng-hui at the APEC leaders economic conference in Seattle.

25 — South Korea opens its Korean Mission in Taipei to replace the embassy closed after South Korea and the ROC broke off diplomatic relations.

30 — The ROC signs an investment promotion and protection pact with Argentina to strengthen economic ties with South America.

Dec. 9 — The Government Information Office lifts the ban on radio stations and approves the applications of 13 broadcasting companies for operation licenses.

15 — The Legislative Yuan approves a revision of the *University Law*, which gives more autonomy to colleges and allows students to participate in meetings related to school affairs.

1994

Jan. 11 — The *Consumer Protection Law* goes into effect; manufacturers are held responsible for harming consumers even when negligence or intent to do harm are not found to be factors.

12 — The ROC and Lesotho sever diplomatic relations.

15 — Lee Yuan-tseh succeeds Wu Ta-you as president of Academia Sinica.

Feb. 9 — President Lee leaves for the Philippines, Indonesia, and Thailand on an eight-day visit.

Mar. 2 — The ROC and Belize sign a joint communiqué pledging bilateral cooperation.

23 — The Legislative Yuan increases the annual number of permanent residency permits for mainland spouses from 300 to 600.

25 — The SEF and the ARATS hold talks in Peking on fishery disputes and the repatriation of illegal entrants and hijackers.

28 — The ROC and the Central African Republic sign a joint communiqué pledging further cooperation.

Apr. 12 — The Mainland Affairs Council decides to suspend all cultural and educational exchanges with the mainland before the Chinese communists provide reasonable and satisfactory explanations of the Qiandao Lake tragedy on Mar. 31 in which 24 Taiwan tourists are killed.

May 2 — The ROC and Grenada sign a joint communiqué pledging bilateral cooperation.

4 — President Lee Teng-hui leaves for Nicaragua, Costa Rica, South Africa, and Swaziland on a 13-day official visit.

June 6 — Premier Lien Chan pays the first visit of a high-ranking ROC official to Mexico in 23 years after the two severed diplomatic ties.

29 — The Peruvian Trade Office opens in Taipei.

July 7 — The Legislative Yuan passes the *Self-governance Law for Provinces and Counties*, explicitly stipulating that provincial governors be chosen by direct election. The *Self-governance Law for Special Municipalities* is passed the next day.

13 — Seven foreign ministers and representatives from Central American countries come to Taiwan to participate in the Third Mixed Commission Conference of Central American Nations, and sign a joint declaration with the ROC supporting the ROC's bid for UN participation.

30 — The SEF and the ARATS start talks in Taipei. This is the first high-level dialogue between the two organizations since the Qiandao Lake incident on Mar. 31, 1994.

Aug. 8 — The SEF and the ARATS sign and make public a joint press release confirming the results of the second round of Chiao-Tang talks.

9 — The US government announces trade sanctions against the ROC under the Pelly Amendment, placing a ban on imports of

Taiwan wildlife products effective from August 19, 1994.

Sept.   7 — US Assistant Secretary of State Winston Lord formally notifies the ROC representative in Washington, Ding Mou-shih, of the result from the Clinton administration's policy discussions about Taiwan: The US agrees to the ROC representative office changing its name to the Taipei Economic and Cultural Representative Office in the United States, and to ROC officials visiting all US government offices except the White House and the Department of State on official business.

19 — On behalf of their respective governments, the ROC representative in Washington, Ding Mou-shih, and the chairman of the American Institute in Taiwan, Natale Bellocchi, sign a *Trade and Investment Framework Agreement*.

22 — The chairman of the UN General Committee drops the proposal on the ROC's UN membership from the agenda after a 90-minute debate in which seven nations support the ROC and 20 oppose the proposal.

Oct.   27 — The Legislative Yuan passes revisions to the *Wildlife Conservation Law*, greatly toughening penalties against violators and stipulating that the breeding in captivity of endangered animals must cease within three years.

Dec.   3 — The first popular elections for the governor of Taiwan Province and mayors of Taipei and Kaohsiung municipalities are held. James C.Y. Soong is elected governor of Taiwan. Chen Shui-bian and Wu Den-yih win the mayor seats of Taipei and Kaohsiung, respectively.

4 — US Secretary of Transportation Federico Pena visits the ROC, becoming the first US cabinet member to carry out the new US policy governing high-ranking official visits to Taipei.

12 — The Lien cabinet is re-organized and new cabinet members are sworn in on December 15.

29 — The first squadron of Ching-kuo indigenous defense fighters is officially commissioned, upgrading the combat ability of the ROC Air Force and demonstrating initial results of research and development.

1995

Jan.   5 — The Executive Yuan Council approves the plan for developing Taiwan into an Asia-Pacific Regional Operations Center.

30 — Mainland Chinese President Jiang Zemin offers an eight-point proposal, urging Taiwan to hold talks with the mainland to officially end the hostile standoff between the two sides.

Feb.   28 — President Lee expresses an apology to families of the victims of the Feb. 28, 1947 Incident at the Taipei New Park, where a monument commemorating the tragedy was built with government sponsorship.

Mar.   1 — The National Health Insurance program is formally inaugurated.

6 — A Coordination and Service Office for the Asia-Pacific Regional Operations Center (also known as the APROC Window) is established in the Council for Economic Planning and Development to ensure that the Asia-Pacific Regional Operations Center plan is faithfully implemented.

20 — Sheu Yuan-dong replaces Liang Kuo-shu as governor of the Central Bank of China.

23 — *Regulations Governing the Management and Compensation for Victims of the Feb. 28, 1947 Incident* passes the Legislative Yuan. According to the regulations, a foundation will be established to manage affairs concerned, and Feb. 28 will be designated a national commemoration day.

— The two-day convention of secretaries-general of the Olympic Council of Asia member nations opens in Kaohsiung. Following international practice, the convention hoists the flags of all OCA members—including the five-star flag of mainland China.

Apr. 1 — President Lee starts his four-day visit to the United Arab Emirates and Jordan.

8 — At the meeting of the National Unification Council, President Lee offers a six-point proposal for Taiwan-mainland relations.

19 — Malawi President Bakili Muluzi pays a state visit to Taipei.

May 19 — The Legislative Yuan approves the temporary statute on welfare payments for elderly farmers, granting them a monthly stipend of NT$3,000.

22 — The ROC and Papua New Guinea sign a joint communiqué in Taipei and establish mutual recognition in order to improve cooperation on the basis of reciprocal benefits.

June 7 — President Lee arrives in the United States for a reunion at his alma mater, Cornell University.

15 — Premier Lien Chan launches a six-day visit to three European countries: Austria, Hungary, and Czechoslovakia. He is the highest ROC official to visit Europe since the ROC government moved to Taipei in 1949.

30 — The US government officially announces cancellation of the sanctions against Taiwan issued under the Pelly Amendment.

July 1 — The ROC resumes full diplomatic relations with Gambia after a 21-year hiatus.

19 — The Legislature approves the *Presidential and Vice Presidential Election and Recall Law*, setting ground rules for the March 23, 1996, popular election of the ROC president and vice president.

21 — The Chinese mainland begins eight days of firing surface-to-surface missiles into the East China Sea about 140 kilometers north of Taiwan.

26 — The US Congress honors Madame Chiang Kai-shek at a Capitol Hill reception in recognition of her contribution to Allied efforts during World War II.

Aug. 15 — The Chinese mainland begins eleven days of firing tactical guided missiles and live

artillery shells into the sea 136 kilometers north of Taiwan.

17 — Control Yuan President Chen Li-an announces his candidacy for president and, on the following day, renounces his 42-year KMT membership.

19 — The Foreign Ministry issues a position paper entitled "Why the UN Resolution No. 2758 Adopted in 1971 Should Be Reexamined Today." The paper stressed that UN Resolution 2758, which excluded the ROC from the UN system and its activities, is obsolete and unjust and ought to be reexamined.

22 — The KMT convenes its 14th National Congress and Lee Teng-hui, party chairman, announces he will seek the party's presidential nomination. Lin Yang-kang, a KMT vice chairman, declares his intention not to seek the nomination but to run as an independent.

24 — President Juan Carlos Wasmosy of Paraguay leads a delegation to Taipei for a 4-day visit.

31 — The KMT nominates incumbent President Lee as its presidential candidate; the next day President Lee names Premier Lien as his running mate.

Sept. 7 — The ROC and Singapore initial an agreement to cooperate on a project to launch a telecommunications satellite.

17 — An exhibition of 71 landscape paintings from the collection of the Louvre in Paris opens at the National Palace Museum in Taipei. The exhibition runs through Jan. 15.

21 — Economics Minister Chiang Pin-kung leads a delegation to the 19th Joint Conference of ROC-USA and USA-ROC Economic Councils in Anchorage, Alaska.

25 — The DPP nominates Peng Ming-min, a former political science professor and a long-time dissident in exile, as its presidential candidate after a 15-week primary; Peng later names Legislator Frank Hsieh as his running mate.

— Rodrigo Oreamuno, vice president of

Costa Rica, arrives in Taipei for a weeklong visit.

27 — Jeffrey Koo, chairman of the Chinese National Association of Industry and Commerce, leads a delegation to the Pacific Economic Cooperation Council meeting in Peking.

Oct. 3 — Manuel Saturnino da Costa, prime minister of Guinea-Bissau, arrives in Taipei for a six-day visit.

17 — The ROC and Macau establish a five-year renewable air pact allowing Eva Airways, Transasia Airways, and Air Macau to fly routes between Taiwan and Macau.

21 — Independent presidential candidate Chen Li-an names Wang Ching-feng, a Control Yuan member, as his running mate.

Nov. 15 — Independent presidential hopeful Lin Yang-kang names former Premier Hau Pei-tsun as his running mate.

17 — Koo Chen-fu, a senior adviser to the ROC president, arrives in Osaka, Japan, to attend the Asia-Pacific Economic Cooperation forum summit in place of President Lee.

21 — The ROC and Australia sign a memorandum of understanding to permit temporary duty-free entry of certain goods as a means of increasing two-way trade.

25 — The ROC and Poland, to boost economic ties, initial an agreement to avoid double taxation and prevent tax evasion by investors.

Dec. 2 — The Republic of China elects 164 lawmakers to the Third Legislative Yuan.

1996

Jan. 3 — The ROC and the Republic of Senegal resume full diplomatic relations, increasing to 31 the number of nations with which the ROC maintains such relations.

11 — Vice President Li Yuan-zu leaves for the Republic of Guatemala to attend the inaugural ceremony of President Alvaro Enrique Arzu Irigoyen, traveling via Los Angeles, USA.

16 — The Legislature passes three telecommunications laws—the *Telecommunications*

Act, the *Organizational Statute of the Directorate General of Telecommunications, Ministry of Transportation and Communications*, and the *Statute of Chunghwa Telecom Co., Ltd.* These laws relieve the DGT of the function of providing telecommunications services, making it a regulatory agency only; open the telecommunications sector to private and foreign investment; and strengthen controls on transmission frequencies.

23 — An ROC Ministry of Education ad hoc committee decides that 452 works of art from the National Palace Museum in Taipei will be allowed to go on a 13-month exhibition trip to the United States. This is one of the largest bodies of national treasures ever to tour overseas.

Feb. 12 — Faced with threatening military maneuvers undertaken by Peking, the Executive Yuan sets up a temporary policy-making task force to closely follow developments and coordinate the actions of various agencies to respond to the situation.

Mar. 8 — The Chinese mainland begins eight days of test-firing surface-to-surface missiles in waters close to major ports in northeastern and southwestern Taiwan.

12 — The Chinese mainland commences nine days of naval and air military exercises in an area of the Taiwan Straits only 53 kilometers from Kinmen and 70 kilometers from the Penghu Islands.

18 — The Chinese mainland begins eight days of war games involving ground, air, and naval forces in an area of sea 85 kilometers northwest of Taiwan proper.

23 — Four pairs of candidates compete in the first-ever direct election of the ROC president and vice president. The Lee-Lien ticket wins, garnering 54 percent of the vote. At the same time, 334 members of the Third National Assembly are also elected.

28 — After eight years of construction, the Mucha Line of the Taipei Mass Rapid

Transit Systems officially commences operations.

Apr. 29 — On the third anniversary of the Koo-Wang talks, Koo Chen-fu, chairman of the ROC's Straits Exchange Foundation, appeals to the Chinese mainland not to postpone the second Koo-Wang talks so that both sides can resume their pursuit of reunification.

28 — The Ministry of Economic Affairs announces that starting July 1, 1996, imports of another 1,609 categories of industrial commodities will be allowed from the Chinese mainland, marking the ROC government's largest-scale relaxation of restrictions on mainland imports.

May 20 — Lee Teng-hui and Lien Chan are sworn in as ROC president and vice president, respectively.

In his inaugural address, President Lee emphasizes that it is neither necessary nor possible to adopt a so-called "Taiwan independence" line. He expresses his hope that the two sides will counter animosity with peace and forgiveness and turn to the important task of ending the enmity across the Straits. President Lee also indicates his willingness to make a "journey of peace" to the Chinese mainland. He says that in order to bring forth a new era of communication and cooperation between the two sides, he is willing to meet and directly exchange opinions with the top mainland leadership.

June 5 — President Lee Teng-hui appoints Vice President Lien Chan to serve concurrently as ROC premier. A cabinet reshuffle is passed three days later.

7 — At his first press conference as Vice President/Premier, Lien Chan indicates that the ROC has not ruled out the possibility of the two sides exchanging visits by high-ranking officials. He also emphasizes the need to reopen channels for cross-strait talks.

28 — The ROC exchanges economic and trade representative office with the Republic of Belarus. Belarus is the second (Russia being the first) member of the Commonwealth of Independent States to establish such a level of relations with the ROC.

30 — South African Foreign Minister Alfred Nzo arrives for a three-day visit. On July 2, South African President Nelson Mandela, speaking in South Africa, states that before the Chinese "domestic problem" is solved, he will not establish diplomatic ties with the Chinese mainland at the cost of relations with the Republic of China.

July 4 — The National Assembly convenes and subsequently elects Fredrick Chien speaker and Shieh Lung-sheng deputy speaker.

11 — Paraguayan President Juan Carlos Wasmosy visits the ROC.

15 — Honduran President Carlos Roberto Reina arrives in Taipei for a five-day visit.

18 — The European Parliament passes a resolution supporting ROC efforts to be represented in international organizations.

24 — The Foreign Ministry protests Japan's decision to include the Tiaoyutai Islets in its 200-nautical-mile exclusive economic zone.

30 — Chen Jing wins a silver medal in women's table tennis singles at the Olympics in Atlanta.

Aug. 12 — Vice President and Premier Lien Chan departs for the Dominican Republic to attend the Aug. 16 inauguration of President Leonel Fernandez.

19 — Vice President and Premier Lien Chan visits Ukraine.

— Niger switches diplomatic ties from Taipei to Peking.

24 — The ROC wins the 1996 Little League World Series in the US city of Williamsport, Pennsylvania.

28 — El Salvador President Armando Calderon Sol visits the ROC.

Sep. 11 — The US removes the ROC from a wildlife conservation watchlist in recognition of its progress in protecting endangered species.

12 — The ROC states a four-point position
in the Tiaoyutai Islets dispute with
Japan: the ROC's absolute sovereignty,
a rational attitude, no cooperation with
Peking, and the protection of Taiwan's
fishing rights.

24 — The US House of Representatives endorses
a July 18 European Parliament resolution
supporting ROC efforts to participate in
the international community.

Oct. 31 — Former Polish President Lech Walesa
visits the ROC.

Nov. 20 — Gambian President Yahya Jammeh visits the ROC.

27 — South Africa says it will switch full
diplomatic recognition from Taipei to
Peking on Jan. 1, 1998.

Dec. 2 — Foreign Minister John Chang departs
for South Africa.

6 — The Legislature revises the *Labor Standards Law* so that employees in nearly all
industries will be covered by the end of
1998.

10 — The Cabinet-level Council of Aboriginal Affairs is established.

— The Taiwan Independence Party (TAIP),
a DPP splinter group, is established.

19 — The ceiling on foreign institutional investments in the stock market is raised from
US$400 million to US$600 million.

23 — The five-day National Development
Conference begins. Discussion focuses
on three major topics: enhancing constitutional system of government and
multiparty politics; economic development; and cross-strait relations.

31 — Taiwan Provincial Governor James
Soong submits his resignation to Premier Lien Chan.

1997

Jan. 7 — Vice President and Premier Lien Chan
departs for Nicaragua to attend the Jan.

10 inauguration of President Arnoldo
Aleman.

14 — Vice President and Premier Lien Chan
meets with Pope John Paul II and shares
with him views on world peace and
humanitarian pursuits.

16 — Vice President and Premier Lien Chan
pays an academic visit to Ireland.

Feb. 23 — The Legislative Yuan passes the
amendment to the fourth article of the
*February 28 Incident Disposition and
Compensation Act*, stipulating that
February 28, also named "Peace Me-
morial Day," be a national holiday.

Mar. 1 — Taipei and Kaohsiung cities officially
launch a system that prohibits physicians
from directly dispensing medicines.

17 — Madame Chiang Kai-shek celebrates her
centennial birthday.

— Former Chairman of the US Joint
Chiefs of Staff General Colin L. Powell
visits the ROC.

22 — Tibetan spiritual leader Dalai Lama
pays a six-day visit to the ROC.

Apr. 2 — US House of Representatives Speaker
Newt Gingrich meets with President
Lee Teng-hui during his four-hour visit
to the ROC, praising Taiwan's political progress and economic achievement. The *Statute Governing Relations with Hong Kong and Macau* is
promulgated by President Lee Teng-
hui and will go partially into effect on
July 1 of this year for Hong Kong, and
1999 for Macau.

May 5 — The second session of the Third National Assembly begins to amend the
Constitution. The focus of the session
is to streamline the local government;
reform the election process for the
president and members of the National
Assembly; and clarify the president's
relations with the Executive Yuan and
the Legislature.

6 — The ROC establishes formal diplomatic relations with the Democratic
Republic of Sao Tome and Principe in
western Africa.

15 — The Cabinet is partially reshuffled, with new heads being selected for the Ministry of the Interior, Council of Labor Affairs, Council of Agriculture, and Government Information Office.

18 — The Ministry of Foreign Affairs announces ROC's decision to immediately terminate its diplomatic ties with the Bahamas.

31 — The Legislative Yuan passes the third reading of the *Public Television Bill*, which will enable the public television station to begin broadcasting in 1998.

June 14 — Vice President and Premier Lien Chan announces that the government will establish a Ministry of Culture.

21 — Koo Chen-fu, chairman of the Straits Exchange Foundation, is invited by mainland's Association for Relations Across the Taiwan Straits to attend the ceremony marking the transfer of Hong Kong's sovereignty to the Chinese mainland on June 30.

July 1 — The Mainland Affairs Council sets up the Hong Kong Affairs Bureau to handle ties between Taipei and Hong Kong after Hong Kong is reverted to the Chinese mainland.

27 — The Ministry of Foreign Affairs announces the closure of the Taipei Economic and Cultural Representative Office in Phnom Penh, Cambodia.

Aug. 1 — The Council of Grand Justice rules that legislators who engage in violence during legislative sessions will no longer be immune from arrest and prosecution.

6 — Nicaragua President Arnoldo Alemán Lacayo arrives in Taipei for a five-day visit.

10 — The ROC and Costa Rica sign a media cooperation agreement.

12 — The Republic of Chad resumes official ties with the ROC after a 25-year hiatus.

21 — Vice President and Premier Lien Chan heads the cabinet and tenders resignation to the president. Legislator Vincent C. Siew will succeed him to be the new premier of the ROC.

26 — President Lee Teng-hui is re-elected chairman of the ruling Kuomintang with 93 percent of the votes cast by over 2,000 party representatives of KMT's 15th National Congress.

28 — KMT's 15th Central Committee elects 17 members to the enlarged Central Standing Committee, along with 16 appointed by the chairman, immediately following conclusion of National Congress.

Sep. 1 — The ROC swears in a new cabinet with Vincent C. Siew as the premier. At a press conference after his inauguration, Premier Siew vows to improve law and order, further develop the economy, raise people's quality of life, and normalize cross-strait relations.

4 — President Lee Teng-hui leaves for Latin America via the US to attend the World Congress on the Panama Canal in Panama City, where he will meet with heads of state of ROC allies including Panama, Nicaragua and Honduras.

19 — The ROC's *Tobacco Hazard Control and Prevention Law* goes into effect.

Oct. 3 — Swaziland King Mswati III visits the ROC through Oct. 5. During his trip to Taipei, the King and the ROC President Lee Teng-hui will sign a joint communiqué to further strengthen bilateral relations.

5 — Vice President Lien Chan embarks on a 12-day visit to Iceland and Austria to strengthen ROC's substantive ties with the two nations.

9 — Taiwan film "Such a Life" wins the Best Picture Award at the 42nd Asia-Pacific Film Festival.

15 — Steven Chu, member of the ROC Academia Sinica, wins the 1997 Nobel Prize for physics.

26 — Chad President Idriss Deby visits the ROC through Oct. 30.

Nov. 5 — Liberian President Charles Ghankay Taylor, accompanied by his wife and a 43-member delegation, arrives in Taipei for a 7-day state visit.

22 — The ROC signs a letter of intent with Hungary on cooperation in customs affairs.

25 — Koo Chen-fu, chairman of the Straits Exchange Foundation, represents President Lee Teng-hui to attend the APEC summit in Vancouver.

26 — Stricter regulations on firearms go into effect as part of the ROC government's efforts to strengthen and stabilize social order.

29 — In the election for county magistrates and city mayors, the ruling KMT takes eight seats out of the 23 seats at stake. The Democratic Progressive Party doubles its number of seats from six of the last election to 12. The remaining three seats go to the hands of independents.

Dec. 2 — The *Asian Wall Street Journal*, the first multinational newspaper to set up a printing site in Taipei, launches printing operations.

31 — The ROC severs its official ties with South Africa, thereby putting an end to diplomatic relations between the two nations established in 1976.

1998

Jan. 1 — Vice President Lien Chan and his wife start a four-day private visit to Singapore. Discussions over financial turmoil in the Asia-Pacific with high-ranking officials of the host nation stand high on his agenda.

12 — Premier Vincent C. Siew arrives in Manila for an unofficial visit.

20 — Premier Vincent C. Siew arrives in Jakarta, where he is scheduled to meet with Indonesian President Suharto to discuss over the possibility of establishing a financial cooperative mechanism in the Asia-Pacific region.

21 — Bishop Shan Kuo-hsi of the Catholic diocese in Kaohsiung is formally appointed one of only three cardinals representing the world's Chinese communities by Pope John Paul II.

24 — The Republic of China elects local-level county and city councilmen, and rural and urban township chiefs. The ruling KMT wins a landslide victory.

29 — The ROC suspends relations with the Central African Republic.

Feb. 5 — A partial reshuffling of the cabinet results in eight position assignments including interior and education ministers.

11 — Malaysian Deputy Prime Minister Anwar Ibrahim pays a visit to the ROC as part of his government's drive to seek cooperative measures to stabilize the region's troubled financial sector.

14 — Foreign Minister Jason C. Hu launches a 12-day visit to ROC allies in Africa including Senegal, Gambia, Liberia, Burkina Faso, Chad and Sao Tome and Principe to cement ties with these nations.

24 — Jordan University confers an honorary doctorate upon Vice President Lien Chan. During his trip to Jordan, Lien also meets with top officials of the host nation to strengthen bilateral cooperative relations.

Mar. 4 — On his way back to Taiwan from a trip to Jordan, Bahrain and the United Arab Emirates, Vice President Lien Chan arrives in Kuala Lumpur for a four-day private visit. Lien is scheduled to meet with Malaysian Prime Minister Mahathir Mohamad and his deputy Anwar Ibrahim to discuss possible cooperative measures for tackling the current financial troubles in Asia.

Apr. 3 — The Ministry of Foreign Affairs announces that President Lee Teng-hui has been nominated for the 1998 Nobel Peace Prize. It is the second time in three years that President Lee has been nominated for the honor.

21 — Haitian President René Garcia Preval arrives in Taipei for a four-day state visit. He and President Lee will sign a communiqué to strengthen bilateral friendship and cooperation.

22 — A delegation sent by the Straits Exchange Foundation with its deputy secretary-

general, Jan Jyh-horng, at the head arrives in Peking. Jan is scheduled to meet with his ARATS counterpart and set agendas for the second round of Koo-Wang Talks slated to be held in autumn. The visit marks the restoration of cross-strait consultation and negotiation, which were unilaterally broken off by Peking since 1995 following ROC President Lee Teng-hui's journey to the US to visit his alma mater, Cornell University in June of the same year.

24 — The ROC signs a memorandum of understanding on customs cooperation with the Slovak Republic.

— The ROC announces the severance of diplomatic ties with Guinea-Bissau of western Africa.

25 — Premier Vincent C. Siew starts his three-day visit to Kuala Lumpur to meet with high-ranking officials of the host nation. How to further bolster bilateral ties and deal with the Asian financial turmoil stand as the centerpiece of the meeting.

— The president of the Central Bank of China, Perng Fai-nan, leads a delegation to attend the 31st board director meeting of the Asian Development Bank in Geneva.

May 5 — Vice President Lien Chan, sent by President Lee as a special envoy, leaves for Costa Rica to attend the inauguration of President-elect Miguel Angel Rodríguez slated for May 8. Also included in his itinerary is a three-day visit to Grenada and meetings with heads of state of other Caribbean nations, which maintain diplomatic ties with the ROC.

11 — The ROC armed forces conduct their annual routine joint military exercise in the eastern Taiwan counties of Hualien and Taitung. The drill, code-named "Han Kuang No. 14" will serve as a review of the military's combat readiness and ability to ensure national security.

22 — ROC President Lee Teng-hui and Nauru President Kinza Clodumar sign a joint

communiqué to reinforce bilateral cooperation. The head of the Republic of Nauru and his entourage pay a four-day visit to the ROC.

31 — Gyorgy Ujlaky, Hungary's newly appointed representative to the ROC, arrives in Taipei to set up a trade office in Taipei to promote bilateral exchanges. Following the Czech Republic and Poland, Hungary will become the third central European country to open a trade office in Taiwan.

June 1 — Premier Vincent C. Siew presides over the opening ceremony of the newly established Southern Taiwan Service Center in Kaohsiung City. The center aims to guarantee efficient service and decisive problem-solving for residents of the southern part of Taiwan.

15 — Democratic Republic of Sao Tome and Principe President Miguel A.C.L. Trovoada and his wife arrive in Taipei for a five-day state visit.

July 2 — Premier Vincent Siew embarks on a 9-day Pacific trip to consolidate bilateral relation with ROC diplomatic partners in the region.

21 — The opening of the Taiwan International Mercantile Exchange is a milestone for Taiwan's financial sector.

Oct. 9 — The Legislative Yuan passes the statute to streamline the Taiwan Provincial Government, making the TPG a nonautonomous body under the central government.

13 — Daniel C. Tsui, member of the ROC's Academia Sinica, wins the 1997 Nobel Prize for physics.

14 — Straits Exchange Foundation Chairman Koo Chen-fu arrives in Shanghai to meet with his ARATS counterpart Wang Daohan. During his trip, Mr. Koo states that the conciliatory spirit of agreements signed between the two sides in Singapore five years ago will be restored.

Nov. 2 — The ROC severs diplomatic ties with Kingdom of Tonga.

3 — President Lee Teng-hui meets with former German Chancellor Helmut Schmidt to exchange views on world economic development.

9 — US Secretary of Energy Bill Richardson arrives in Taiwan to attend the 22nd annual USA-ROC Economic Council.

16 — P. K. Chiang, chairman of the Council for Economic Planning and Development, heads for Malaysia to attend the APEC annual conference on behalf of President Lee Teng-hui.

20 — The ROC and the Marshall Islands sign a joint communiqué to formalize diplomatic relations, as the Marshall islands becomes the ROC's 27th diplomatic ally.

Dec. 5 — Vice President Lien Chan leads a humanitarian delegation of government officials and representatives from charity and religious organizations on an 11-day visit to hurricane-stricken allies including Nicaragua, Honduras, El Salvador, and Guatemala.

— In the election for the Fourth Legislative Yuan the ruling KMT secures 123 of the 225 seats and the DPP garners 70 seats while the rest goes to the NP and other minority parties. The KMT also triumphs in elections for Taipei mayor and councilmen of Taipei and Kaohsiung cities, but it loses the mayoral election in Kaohsiung City.

21 — Operations begin to streamline the provincial government, a vital part of the efficiency-oriented master plan to restructure the government in Taiwan.

1999

Jan. 9 — Premier Vincent Siew heads for the Dominican Republic, Haiti, and Belize to consolidate relations in the Caribbean.

12 — The Legislative Yuan unanimously abolishes the Publication Law.

26 — The ROC launches ROCSAT-1, its first wholly-owned and operated satellite, into orbit from Cape Canaveral, Florida, USA,

marking the ROC's entry into the era of advanced space technology.

27 — The ROC and the Republic of Macedonia sign a joint communiqué to establish formal relations. Macedonia thus becomes ROC's second diplomatic ally in Europe, after the Holy See.

Feb. 5 — President Imata Kabua of the Marshall Islands arrives in Taipei for a one-week visit.

Mar. 5 — Foreign Minister Jason Hu signs a memorandum with his Macedonian counterpart, Aleksandar Dimitrov, in Skopje to promote bilateral economic cooperation.

7 — The President of the Assembly of Macedonia, Savo Klimovski, arrives in Taipei for a six-day reciprocal visit.

17 — The Atomic Energy Council issues a permit for Taiwan Power Company to construct the ROC's fourth nuclear power plant.

22 — Costa Rican President Miguel Angel Rodriguez arrives in Taipei for a six-day visit.

29 — Former US President Jimmy Carter visits Taiwan at the invitation of a private think tank in Taipei.

Apr. 28 — The Embassy of the Republic of Macedonia commences operation with Verka Modanu as Macedonia's first resident envoy to the ROC.

30 — Foreign Minister Jason C. Hu arrives in the Marshall Islands for a three-day official visit to strengthen bilateral ties in such areas as tourism, fisheries, and investment.

May 27 — Premier Vincent Siew heads to the Central Caribbean to attend the inauguration of El Salvador President Francisco Flores. During his visit there, the premier meets with the Presidents of Nicaragua and Panama.

June 4 — The Legislative Yuan passes the third reading of the Cigarette and Wine Management Law, revoking the decades-old monopoly tax system.

6 — Macedonian President Ljubco Georgievski, head of a 59-member delegation, arrives Taipei for a six-day official visit. During his visit to the ROC, he signs agreements on economic cooperation, investment guarantees, and prevention of the double taxation of investors to strengthen relations with the ROC government.

7 — In an international press conference, President Lee Teng-hui announces that the ROC will provide US$300 million Balkans aid package to ease the plight of Kosovo war refugees.

16 — The Legislature passes the third reading of the amendments to the public lottery act, ensuring the right of lottery issuance by the central government.

23 — The ROC signs a press cooperation agreement with Panama.

24 — The Domestic Violence Prevention Law goes into effect.

July   9 — In an interview with the German Broadcasting company Deutsche Welle, President Lee Teng-hui first announces the concept that Taiwan and the Chinese mainland have a "special state-to-state relationship."

— To enhance bilateral economic and trade ties, the ROC and Thailand sign pacts on aviation exchanges and avoidance of double taxation.

20 — President Lee Teng-hui further elaborates his recent remarks of the "special state-to-state relationship" between the two sides of the Taiwan Strait by saying that he did not put forth the statement to seek Taiwan independence but simply to reiterate the fact that both sides are separately governed.

Aug.   1 — Premier Vincent Siew, head of an 80-member delegation, departs for the Republic of Macedonia to enhance bilateral relations. During his visit to the ROC's new diplomatic ally in south Europe, the premier officiates at the groundbreaking ceremony for the Taiwan-funded export processing zone near Macedonia's capital city of Skopje.

30 — Premier Vincent Siew departs for Panama to attend the Sept. 1 inauguration of Panamanian President-elect Mireya Moscoso.

Sep.   4 — The Third National Assembly passes a constitutional amendment which extends the current terms of the deputies from May 2000 to June 2002, and includes the appointment of all deputies on the basis of party proportional representation in the fourth Assembly.

7 — The second ROC-Central American summit is held in Taipei. During the summit, President Lee signs a joint communiqué with the leaders of seven Central American allies.

9 — P. K. Chiang, chairman of the Council for Economic Planning and Development, participates in the APEC leadership summit in Auckland as an envoy of President Lee Teng-hui.

21 — Taiwan is hit by its deadliest earthquake in more than 60 years. The 7.3 magnitude quake claims more than 2,000 lives and injures over 8,000.

25 — President Lee issues an emergency decree to cut through red tape and expedite reconstruction work in the wake of Taiwan's devastating earthquake. The decree, which supersedes certain existing laws, is effective for six months.

Oct.   1 — The Civil Aeronautics Administration announces the indefinite suspension of direct flights between Taipei and Manila after a breakdown in negotiations on weekly passenger quotas.

20 — The ROC government extends its congratulations to Indonesia's President-elect Abdurrahman Wahid.

26 — The Taipei-based China External Trade Development Council opens a branch office in Bombay, India. The new office will play an extensive role in promoting the ROC's trade with India.

Nov. 6 — Independent candidate Chang Jung-wei wins the by-election for county magistrate in Yunlin County, beating rivals from the ruling Kuomintang and the main opposition Democratic Progressive Party.

7 — "Darkness and Light," a film by Taiwan director Chang Tso-chi, is awarded the prize for best picture at the 12th Tokyo International Film Festival.

13 — Tokyo Governor Shintaro Ishihara arrives in Taiwan for a three-day visit at the invitation of President Lee Teng-hui. Ishihara has been the highest-profile Japanese official to visit Taiwan since the two countries cut diplomatic relations in 1972.

14 — Michael Campbell of New Zealand wins the 1999 Johnnie Walker Classic, held at the Ta Shee Golf and Country Club in northern Taiwan.

17 — The decision-making Central Standing Committee of the ruling Kuomintang approves a disciplinary committee proposal to oust independent presidential candidate James Soong from the KMT.

20 — President Lee greets visiting Nauru President Rene Harris and his wife in Taipei.

26 — Rene Liu of Taiwan wins the best actress award at the 1999 Asia-Pacific Film Festival, held in Bangkok, for her performance in "The Personals."

Dec. 1 — President Lee presides over a welcoming ceremony for Malawi President Bakili Muluzi in Taipei.

— The ROC Ministry of Finance launches the National Welfare Lottery.

10 — Chen Shui-bian, presidential candidate of the main opposition Democratic Progressive Party, announces Taoyuan County Magistrate Annette Lu as his running mate for the March 2000 election.

16 — The ROC is named a permanent observer of the Central American Parliament Speakers Forum at the ninth meeting of the CAPSF in Panama.

20 — ROC President Lee Teng-hui receives U.S. Congresswoman Nancy Pelosi in Taipei.

28 — The ROC renames its representative office in Macau the Taipei Economic and Cultural Center.

30 — The ROC establishes formal diplomatic relations with Palau.

Appendix II

The Constitution of the Republic of China and the Additional Articles

(Adopted by the National Assembly on December 25, 1946, promulgated by the national government on January 1, 1947, and effective from December 25, 1947)

The National Assembly of the Republic of China, by virtue of the mandate received from the whole body of citizens, in accordance with the teachings bequeathed by Dr. Sun Yat-sen in founding the Republic of China, and in order to consolidate the authority of the State, safeguard the rights of the people, ensure social tranquillity, and promote the welfare of the people, do hereby establish this Constitution, to be promulgated throughout the country for faithful and perpetual observance by all.

Chapter I. General Provisions

Article 1. The Republic of China, founded on the Three Principles of the People, shall be a democratic republic of the people, to be governed by the people and for the people.

Article 2. The sovereignty of the Republic of China shall reside in the whole body of citizens.

Article 3. Persons possessing the nationality of the Republic of China shall be citizens of the Republic of China.

Article 4. The territory of the Republic of China according to its existing national boundaries shall not be altered except by resolution of the National Assembly.

Article 5. There shall be equality among the various racial groups in the Republic of China.

Article 6. The national flag of the Republic of China shall be of red ground with a blue sky and a white sun in the upper left corner.

Chapter II. Rights and Duties of the People

Article 7. All citizens of the Republic of China, irrespective of sex, religion, race, class, or party affiliation, shall be equal before the law.

Article 8. Personal freedom shall be guaranteed to the people. Except in case of *flagrante delicto* as provided by law, no person shall be arrested or detained otherwise than by a judicial or a police organ in accordance with the procedure prescribed by law. No person shall be tried or punished otherwise than by a law court in accordance with the procedure prescribed by law. Any arrest, detention, trial, or punishment which is not in accordance with the procedure prescribed by law may be resisted.

When a person is arrested or detained on suspicion of having committed a crime, the organ making the arrest or detention shall in writing inform the said person, and his designated relative or friend, of the grounds for his arrest or detention, and shall, within 24 hours, turn him over to a competent court for trial. The said person, or any other person, may petition the competent court that a writ be served within 24 hours on the organ making the arrest for the surrender of the said person for trial.

The court shall not reject the petition mentioned in the preceding paragraph, nor shall it order the organ concerned to make an investigation and report first. The organ concerned shall not refuse to execute, or delay in executing, the writ of the court for the surrender of the said person for trial.

When a person is unlawfully arrested or detained by any organ, he or any other person may petition the court for an investigation. The court shall not reject such a petition, and shall, within 24 hours, investigate the action of the organ concerned and deal with the matter in accordance with law.

Article 9. Except those in active military service, no person shall be subject to trial by a military tribunal.

Article 10. The people shall have freedom of residence and of change of residence.

Article 11. The people shall have freedom of speech, teaching, writing and publication.

Article 12. The people shall have freedom of privacy of correspondence.

Article 13. The people shall have freedom of religious belief.

Article 14. The people shall have freedom of assembly and association.

Article 15. The right of existence, the right of work, and the right of property shall be guaranteed to the people.

Article 16. The people shall have the right of presenting petitions, lodging complaints, or instituting legal proceedings.

Article 17. The people shall have the right of election, recall, initiative and referendum.

Article 18. The people shall have the right of taking public examinations and of holding public offices.

Article 19. The people shall have the duty of paying taxes in accordance with law.

Article 20. The people shall have the duty of performing military service in accordance with law.

Article 21. The people shall have the right and the duty of receiving citizens' education.

Article 22. All other freedoms and rights of the people that are not detrimental to social order or public welfare shall be guaranteed under the Constitution.

Article 23. All the freedoms and rights enumerated in the preceding Article shall not be restricted by law except by such as may be necessary to prevent infringement upon the freedoms of other persons, to avert an imminent crisis, to maintain social order or to advance public welfare.

Article 24. Any public functionary who, in violation of law, infringes upon the freedom or right of any person shall, in addition to being subject to disciplinary measures in accordance with law, be held responsible under criminal and civil laws. The injured person may, in accordance with law, claim compensation from the State for damage sustained.

Chapter III. The National Assembly

Article 25. The National Assembly shall, in accordance with the provisions of this Constitution, exercise political powers on behalf of the whole body of citizens.

Article 26. The National Assembly shall be composed of the following delegates:

1. One delegate shall be elected from each hsien, municipality, or area of equivalent status. In case its population exceeds 500,000, one additional delegate shall be elected for each additional 500,000. Areas equivalent to hsien or municipalities shall be prescribed by law;

2. Delegates to represent Mongolia shall be elected on the basis of four for each league and one for each special banner;

3. The number of delegates to be elected from Tibet shall be prescribed by law;

4. The number of delegates to be elected by various racial groups in frontier regions shall be prescribed by law;

5. The number of delegates to be elected by Chinese citizens residing abroad shall be prescribed by law;

6. The number of delegates to be elected by occupational groups shall be prescribed by law; and

7. The number of delegates to be elected by women's organizations shall be prescribed by law.

Article 27. The function of the National Assembly shall be as follows:

1. To elect the President and the Vice President;

2. To recall the President and the Vice President;

3. To amend the Constitution; and

4. To vote on proposed Constitutional amendments submitted by the Legislative Yuan by way of referendum.

With respect to the rights of initiative and referendum, except as is provided in Items 3 and 4 of the preceding paragraph, the National Assembly shall make regulations pertaining thereto and put them into effect, after the above-mentioned two political rights shall have been exercised in one-half of the hsien and municipalities of the whole country.

Article 28. Delegates to the National Assembly shall be elected every six years.

The term of office of the delegates to each National Assembly shall terminate on the day on which the next National Assembly convenes.

No incumbent government official shall, in the electoral area where he holds office, be elected delegate to the National Assembly.

Article 29. The National Assembly shall be convoked by the President to meet 90 days prior to the date of expiration of each presidential term.

Article 30. An extraordinary session of the National Assembly shall be convoked in any of the following circumstances:

1. When, in accordance with the provisions of Article 49 of this Constitution, a new President and a new Vice President are to be elected;

2. When, by resolution of the Control Yuan, an impeachment of the President or the Vice President is instituted;

3. When, by resolution of the Legislative Yuan, an amendment to the Constitution is proposed; and

4. When a meeting is requested by not less than two-fifths of the delegates to the National Assembly.

When an extraordinary session is to be convoked in accordance with Item 1 or Item 2 of the preceding paragraph, the President of the Legislative Yuan shall issue the notice of convocation; when it is to be convoked in accordance with Item 3 or Item 4, it shall be convoked by the President of the Republic.

Article 31. The National Assembly shall meet at the seat of the Central Government.

Article 32. No delegate to the National Assembly shall be held responsible outside the Assembly for opinions expressed or votes cast at meetings of the Assembly.

Article 33. While the Assembly is in session, no delegate to the National Assembly shall, except in case of *flagrante delicto,* be arrested or detained without the permission of the National Assembly.

Article 34. The organization of the National Assembly, the election and recall of delegates to the National Assembly, and the procedure whereby the National Assembly is to carry out its functions, shall be prescribed by law.

Chapter IV. The President

Article 35. The President shall be the head of the State and shall represent the Republic of China in foreign relations.

Article 36. The President shall have supreme command of the land, sea and air forces of the whole country.

Article 37. The President shall, in accordance with law, promulgate laws and issue mandates with the counter-signature of the President of the Executive Yuan or with the counter-signatures of both the President of Executive Yuan and the Ministers or Chairmen of Commissions concerned.

Article 38. The President shall, in accordance with the provisions of this Constitution, exercise the powers of concluding treaties, declaring war and making peace.

Article 39. The President may, in accordance with law, declare martial law with the approval of, or subject to confirmation by, the Legislative Yuan. When the Legislative Yuan deems it necessary, it may by resolution request the President to terminate martial law.

Article 40. The President shall, in accordance with law, exercise the power of granting amnesties, pardons, remission of sentences and restitution of civil rights.

Article 41. The President shall, in accordance with law, appoint and remove civil and military officials.

Article 42. The President may, in accordance with law, confer honors and decorations.

Article 43. In case of a natural calamity, an epidemic, or a national financial or economic crisis that calls for emergency measures, the President, during the recess of the Legislative Yuan, may, by resolution of the Executive Yuan Council, and in accordance with the *Law on Emergency Decrees*, issue emergency decrees, proclaiming such measures as may be necessary to cope with the situation. Such decrees shall, within one month after issuance, be presented to the Legislative Yuan for confirmation; in case the Legislative Yuan withholds confirmation, the said decrees shall forthwith cease to be valid.

Article 44. In case of disputes between two or more Yuan other than those concerning which there are relevant provisions in this Constitution, the President may call a meeting of the Presidents of the Yuan concerned for consultation with a view to reaching a solution.

Article 45. Any citizen of the Republic of China who has attained the age of 40 years may be elected President or Vice President.

Article 46. The election of the President and the Vice President shall be prescribed by law.

Article 47. The President and the Vice President shall serve a term of six years. They may be re-elected for a second term.

Article 48. The President shall, at the time of assuming office, take the following oath:

"I do solemnly and sincerely swear before the people of the whole country that I will observe the Constitution, faithfully perform my duties, promote the welfare of the people, safeguard the security of the State, and will in no way betray the people's trust. Should I break my oath, I shall be willing to submit myself to severe punishment by the State. This is my solemn oath."

Article 49. In case the office of the President should become vacant, the Vice President shall succeed until the expiration of the original presidential term. In case the office of both the President and the Vice President should become vacant, the President of the Executive Yuan shall act for the President; and, in accordance with the provisions of Article 30 of this Constitution, an extraordinary session of the National Assembly shall be convoked for the election of a new President and a new Vice President, who shall hold office until the completion of the term left unfinished by the preceding President. In case the President should be unable to attend to office due to any cause, the Vice President shall act for the President. In case both the President and Vice President should be unable to attend to office, the President of the Executive Yuan shall act for the President.

Article 50. The President shall be relieved of his functions on the day on which his term of office expires. If by that time the succeeding President has not yet been elected, or if the President-elect and the Vice-President-elect have not yet assumed office, the President of the Executive Yuan shall act for the President.

Article 51. The period during which the President of the Executive Yuan may act for the President shall not exceed three months.

Article 52. The President shall not, without having been recalled, or having been relieved of his functions, be liable to criminal prosecution unless he is charged with having committed an act of rebellion or treason.

Chapter V. Administration

Article 53. The Executive Yuan shall be the highest administrative organ of the State.

Article 54. The Executive Yuan shall have a President, a Vice President, a certain number of Ministers and Chairmen of Commissions, and a certain number of Ministers without Portfolio.

Article 55. The President of the Executive Yuan shall be nominated and, with the consent of the Legislative Yuan, appointed by the President of the Republic.

If, during the recess of the Legislative Yuan, the President of the Executive Yuan should resign or if his office should become vacant, his functions shall be exercised by the Vice President of the Yuan, acting on his behalf, but the President of the Republic shall, within 40 days, request a meeting of the Legislative Yuan to confirm his nominee for the vacancy. Pending such confirmation, the Vice President of the Executive Yuan shall temporarily exercise the functions of the President of the said Yuan.

Article 56. The Vice President of the Executive Yuan, Ministers and Chairmen of Commissions, and Ministers without Portfolio shall be appointed by the President of the Republic upon the recommendation of the President of the Executive Yuan.

Article 57. The Executive Yuan shall be responsible to the Legislative Yuan in accordance with the following provisions:

1. The Executive Yuan has the duty to present to the Legislative Yuan a statement of its administrative policies and a report on its administration. While the Legislative Yuan is in session, Members of the Legislative Yuan shall have the right to question the President and the Ministers and Chairmen of Commissions of the Executive Yuan.

2. If the Legislative Yuan does not concur in any important policy of the Executive Yuan, it may, by resolution, request the Executive Yuan to alter such a policy. With respect to such resolution, the Executive Yuan may, with the approval of the President of the Republic, request the Legislative Yuan for reconsideration. If, after reconsideration, two-thirds of the Members of the Legislative Yuan present at the meeting uphold the original resolution, the President of the Executive Yuan shall either abide by the same or resign from office.

3. If the Executive Yuan deems a resolution on a statutory, budgetary, or treaty bill passed by the Legislative Yuan difficult of execution, it may, with the approval of the President of the Republic and within ten days after its transmission to the Executive Yuan, request the Legislative Yuan to reconsider the said resolution. If after reconsideration, two-thirds of the Members of the Legislative Yuan present at the meeting uphold the original resolution, the President of the Executive Yuan shall either abide by the same or resign from office.

Article 58. The Executive Yuan shall have an Executive Yuan Council, to be composed of its President, Vice President, various Ministers and Chairmen of Commissions, and Ministers without Portfolio, with its President as Chairman.

Statutory or budgetary bills or bills concerning martial law, amnesty, declaration of war, conclusion of peace or treaties, and other important affairs, all of which are to be submitted to the Legislative Yuan, as well as matters that are of common concern to the various Ministries and Commissions, shall be presented by the President and various Ministers and Chairmen of Commissions of the Executive Yuan to the Executive Yuan Council for decision.

Article 59. The Executive Yuan shall, three months before the beginning of each fiscal year, present to the Legislative Yuan the budgetary bill for the following fiscal year.

Article 60. The Executive Yuan shall, within four months after the end of each fiscal year, present final accounts of revenues and expenditures to the Control Yuan.

Article 61. The organization of the Executive Yuan shall be prescribed by law.

Chapter VI. Legislation

Article 62. The Legislative Yuan shall be the highest legislative organ of the State, to be constituted of members elected by the people. It shall exercise legislative power on behalf of the people.

Article 63. The Legislative Yuan shall have the power to decide by resolution upon statutory or budgetary bills or bills concerning martial law, amnesty, declaration of war, conclusion of peace or treaties, and other important affairs of the State.

Article 64. Members of the Legislative Yuan shall be elected in accordance with the following provisions:

1. Those to be elected from the provinces and by the municipalities under the direct jurisdiction of the Executive Yuan shall be five for each province or municipality with a population of not more than 3,000,000, one additional member shall be elected for each additional 1,000,000 in a province or municipality whose population is over 3,000,000;

2. Those to be elected from Mongolian Leagues and Banners;

3. Those to be elected from Tibet;

4. Those to be elected by various racial groups in frontier regions;

5. Those to be elected by Chinese citizens residing abroad; and

6. Those to be elected by occupational groups.

The election of Members of the Legislative Yuan and the number of those to be elected in accordance with Items 2 to 6 of the preceding paragraph shall be prescribed by law. The number of women to be elected under the various items enumerated in the first paragraph shall be prescribed by law.

Article 65. Members of the Legislative Yuan shall serve a term of three years, and shall be re-eligible. The election of Members of the Legislative Yuan shall be completed within three months prior to the expiration of each term.

Article 66. The Legislative Yuan shall have a President and a Vice President, who shall be elected by and from among its Members.

Article 67. The Legislative Yuan may set up various committees.

Such committees may invite government officials and private persons concerned to be present at their meetings to answer questions.

Article 68. The Legislative Yuan shall hold two sessions each year, and shall convene of its own accord. The first session shall last from February to the end of May, and the second session from September ber to the end of December. Whenever necessary, a session may be prolonged.

Article 69. In any of the following circumstances, the Legislative Yuan may hold an extraordinary session:

1. At the request of the President of the Republic;

2. Upon the request of not less than one-fourth of its Members.

Article 70. The Legislative Yuan shall not make proposals for an increase in the expenditures in the budgetary bill presented by the Executive Yuan.

Article 71. At the meetings of the Legislative Yuan, the Presidents of the various Yuan concerned and the various Ministers and Chairmen of Commissions concerned may be present to give their views.

Article 72. Statutory bills passed by the Legislative Yuan shall be transmitted to the President of the Republic and to the Executive Yuan. The President shall, within ten days after receipt thereof, promulgate them; or he may deal with them in accordance with the provisions of Article 57 of this Constitution.

Article 73. No Member of the Legislative Yuan shall be held responsible outside the Yuan for opinions expressed or votes cast in the Yuan.

Article 74. No Member of the Legislative Yuan shall, except in case of *flagrante delicto,* be arrested or detained without the permission of the Legislative Yuan.

Article 75. No Member of the Legislative Yuan shall concurrently hold a government post.

Article 76. The organization of the Legislative Yuan shall be prescribed by law.

Chapter VII. Judiciary

Article 77. The Judicial Yuan shall be the highest judicial organ of the State and shall have charge of civil, criminal, and administrative cases, and over cases concerning disciplinary measures against public functionaries.

Article 78. The Judicial Yuan shall interpret the Constitution and shall have the power to unify the interpretation of laws and orders.

Article 79. The Judicial Yuan shall have a President and a Vice President, who shall be nominated and, with the consent of the Control Yuan, appointed by the President of the Republic.

The Judicial Yuan shall have a certain number of Grand Justices to take charge of matters specified in Article 78 of this Constitution, who shall be nominated and, with the consent of the Control Yuan, appointed by the President of the Republic.

Article 80. Judges shall be above partisanship and shall, in accordance with law, hold trials independently, free from any interference.

Article 81. Judges shall hold office for life. No judge shall be removed from office unless he has been found guilty of a criminal offense or subjected to disciplinary measure, or declared to be under interdiction. No judge shall, except in accordance with law, be suspended or transferred or have his salary reduced.

Article 82. The organization of the Judicial Yuan and of the law courts of various grades shall be prescribed by law.

Chapter VIII. Examination

Article 83. The Examination Yuan shall be the highest examination organ of the State and shall have charge of matters relating to examination, employment, registration, service rating, scale of salaries, promotion and transfer, security of tenure, commendation, pecuniary aid in case of death, retirement and old age pension.

Article 84. The Examination Yuan shall have a President and a Vice President and a certain number of Members, all of whom shall be nominated and, with the consent of the Control Yuan, appointed by the President of the Republic.

Article 85. In the selection of public functionaries, a system of open competitive examination shall be put into operation, and examinations shall be held in different areas, with prescribed numbers of persons to be selected according to various provinces and areas. No person shall be appointed to a public office unless he is qualified through examination.

Article 86. The following qualifications shall be determined and registered through examination by the Examination Yuan in accordance with law:

1. Qualification for appointment as public functionaries; and

2. Qualification for practice in specialized professions or as technicians.

Article 87. The Examination Yuan may, with respect to matters under its charge, present statutory bills to the Legislative Yuan.

Article 88. Members of the Examination Yuan shall be above partisanship and shall independently exercise their functions in accordance with law.

Article 89. The organization of the Examination Yuan shall be prescribed by law.

Chapter IX. Control

Article 90. The Control Yuan shall be the highest control organ of the State and shall exercise the powers of consent, impeachment, censure and auditing.

Article 91. The Control Yuan shall be composed of Members who shall be elected by Provincial and Municipal Councils, the local Councils of Mongolia and Tibet, and Chinese citizens residing abroad. Their numbers shall be determined in accordance with the following provisions:

1. Five Members from each province;

2. Two Members from each municipality under the direct jurisdiction of the Executive Yuan;

3. Eight Members from Mongolian Leagues and Banners;

4. Eight Members from Tibet; and

5. Eight Members from Chinese citizens residing abroad.

Article 92. The Control Yuan shall have a President and a Vice President, who shall be elected by and from among its Members.

Article 93. Members of the Control Yuan shall serve a term of six years and shall be re-eligible.

Article 94. When the Control Yuan exercises the power of consent in accordance with this Constitution, it shall do so by resolution of a majority of the Members present at the meeting.

Article 95. The Control Yuan may, in the exercise of its powers of control, request the Executive Yuan and its Ministries and Commissions to submit to it for perusal the original orders issued by them and all other relevant documents.

Article 96. The Control Yuan may, taking into account the work of the Executive Yuan and its various Ministries and Commissions, set up a certain number of committees to investigate their activities with a view to ascertaining whether or not they are guilty of violation of law or neglect of duty.

Article 97. The Control Yuan may, on the basis of the investigations and resolutions of its committees, propose corrective measures and forward them to the Executive Yuan and the Ministries and Commissions concerned, directing their attention to effecting improvements.

When the Control Yuan deems a public functionary in the Central Government or in a local government guilty of neglect of duty or violation of law, it may propose corrective measures or institute an impeachment. If it involves a criminal offense, the case shall be turned over to a law court.

Article 98. Impeachment by the Control Yuan of a public functionary in the Central Government or in a local government shall be instituted upon the proposal of one or more than one Member of the Control Yuan and the decision, after due consideration, by a committee composed of not less than nine Members.

Article 99. In case of impeachment by the Control Yuan of the personnel of the Judicial Yuan or of the Examination Yuan for neglect of duty or violation of law, the provisions of Articles 95, 97 and 98 of this Constitution shall be applicable.

Article 100. Impeachment by the Control Yuan of the President or the Vice President of the Republic shall be instituted upon the proposal of not less than one-fourth of the whole body of Members of the Control Yuan, and the resolution, after due consideration, by the majority of the whole body of Members of the Control Yuan, and the same shall be presented to the National Assembly.

Article 101. No Member of the Control Yuan shall be held responsible outside the Yuan for opinions expressed or votes cast in the Yuan.

Article 102. No Member of the Control Yuan shall, except in case of *flagrante delicto,* be arrested or detained without the permission of the Control Yuan.

Article 103. No Member of the Control Yuan shall concurrently hold a public office or engage in any profession.

Article 104. In the Control Yuan, there shall be an Auditor General who shall be nominated and, with the consent of the Legislative Yuan, appointed by the President of the Republic.

Article 105. The Auditor General shall, within three months after presentation by the Executive Yuan of the final accounts of revenues and expenditures, complete the auditing thereof in accordance with law, and submit an auditing report to the Legislative Yuan.

Article 106. The organization of the Control Yuan shall be prescribed by law.

Chapter X. Powers of the Central and Local Governments

Article 107. In the following matters, the Central Government shall have the power of legislation and administration:

1. Foreign affairs;
2. National defense and military affairs concerning national defense;
3. Nationality law and criminal, civil and commercial law;
4. Judicial system;
5. Aviation, national highways, state-owned railways, navigation, postal and telegraph service;
6. Central Government finance and national revenues;
7. Demarcation of national, provincial and hsien revenues;
8. State-operated economic enterprises;
9. Currency system and state banks;
10. Weights and measures;
11. Foreign trade policies;
12. Financial and economic matters affecting foreigners or foreign countries; and
13. Other matters relating to the Central Government as provided by this Constitution.

Article 108. In the following matters, the Central Government shall have the power of legislation and administration, but the Central Government may delegate the power of administration to the provincial and hsien governments:

1. General principles of provincial and hsien self-government;
2. Division of administrative areas;
3. Forestry, industry, mining and commerce;
4. Educational system;
5. Banking and exchange system;
6. Shipping and deep-sea fishery;
7. Public utilities;
8. Cooperative enterprises;
9. Water and land communication and transportation covering two or more provinces;
10. Water conservancy, waterways, agriculture and pastoral enterprises covering two or more provinces;
11. Registration, employment, supervision, and security of tenure of officials in Central and local governments;
12. Land legislation;
13. Labor legislation and other social legislation;
14. Eminent domain;
15. Census-taking and compilation of population statistics for the whole country;
16. Immigration and land reclamation;
17. Police system;
18. Public health;
19. Relief, pecuniary aid in case of death and aid in case of unemployment; and
20. Preservation of ancient books and articles and sites of cultural value.

With respect to the various items enumerated in the preceding paragraph, the provinces may enact separate rules and regulations, provided these are not in conflict with national laws.

Article 109. In the following matters, the provinces shall have the power of legislation and administration, but the provinces may delegate the power of administration to the hsien;

1. Provincial education, public health, industries and communications;

2. Management and disposal of provincial property;

3. Administration of municipalities under provincial jurisdiction;

4. Province-operated enterprises;

5. Provincial cooperative enterprises;

6. Provincial agriculture, forestry, water conservancy, fishery, animal husbandry and public works;

7. Provincial finance and revenues;

8. Provincial debts;

9. Provincial banks;

10. Provincial police administration;

11. Provincial charitable and public welfare works; and

12. Other matters delegated to the provinces in accordance with national laws.

Except as otherwise provided by law, any of the matters enumerated in the various items of the preceding paragraph, in so far as it covers two or more provinces, may be undertaken jointly by the provinces concerned.

When any province, in undertaking matters listed in any of the items of the first paragraph, finds its funds insufficient, it may, by resolution of the Legislative Yuan, obtain subsidies from the National Treasury.

Article 110. In the following matters, the hsien shall have the power of legislation and administration:

1. Hsien education, public health, industries and communications;

2. Management and disposal of hsien property;

3. Hsien-operated enterprises;

4. Hsien cooperative enterprises;

5. Hsien agriculture and forestry, water conservancy, fishery, animal husbandry and public works;

6. Hsien finance and revenues;

7. Hsien debts;

8. Hsien banks;

9. Administration of hsien police and defense;

10. Hsien charitable and public welfare works; and

11. Other matters delegated to the hsien in accordance with national laws and provincial Self-Government Regulations.

Except as otherwise provided by law, any of the matters enumerated in the various items of the preceding paragraph, in so far as it covers two or more hsien, may be undertaken jointly by the hsien concerned.

Article 111. Any matter not enumerated in Articles 107, 108, 109 and 110 shall fall within the jurisdiction of the Central Government, if it is national in nature; of the province, if it is provincial in nature; and of the hsien, if it concerns the hsien. In case of dispute, it shall be settled by the Legislative Yuan.

Chapter XI. System of Local Government
Section 1. The Province

Article 112. A province may convoke a provincial assembly to enact, in accordance with the General Principles of Provincial and Hsien Self-Government, regulations, provided the said regulations are not in conflict with the Constitution.

The organization of the provincial assembly and the election of the delegates shall be prescribed by law.

Article 113. The Provincial Self-Government Regulations shall include the following provisions:

1. In the province, there shall be a provincial council. Members of the provincial council shall be elected by the people of the province.

2. In the province, there shall be a provincial government with a provincial governor who shall be elected by the people of the province.

3. Relationship between the province and the hsien.

The legislative power of the province shall be exercised by the Provincial Council.

Article 114. The Provincial Self-Government Regulations shall, after enactment, be forthwith submitted to the Judicial Yuan. The Judicial Yuan, if it deems any part thereof unconstitutional, shall declare null and void the articles repugnant to the Constitution.

Article 115. If, during the enforcement of the Provincial Self-Government Regulations, there should arise any serious obstacle in the application of any of the articles contained therein, the Judicial Yuan shall first summon the various parties concerned to present their views; and thereupon the Presidents of the Executive Yuan, Legislative Yuan, Judicial Yuan, Examination Yuan and

Control Yuan shall form a Committee, with the President of the Judicial Yuan as Chairman, to propose a formula for solution.

Article 116. Provincial rules and regulations that are in conflict with national laws shall be null and void.

Article 117. When doubt arises as to whether or not there is a conflict between provincial rules or regulations and national laws, interpretation thereon shall be made by the Judicial Yuan.

Article 118. The self-government of municipalities under the direct jurisdiction of the Executive Yuan shall be prescribed by law.

Article 119. The local self-government system of the Mongolian Leagues and Banners shall be prescribed by law.

Article 120. The self-government system of Tibet shall be safeguarded.

Section 2. The Hsien

Article 121. The hsien shall enforce hsien self-government.

Article 122. A hsien may convoke a hsien assembly to enact, in accordance with the General Principles of Provincial and Hsien Self-Government, hsien self-government regulations, provided the said regulations are not in conflict with the Constitution or with provincial self-government regulations.

Article 123. The people of the hsien shall, in accordance with law, exercise the rights of initiative and referendum in matters within the sphere of hsien self-government, and shall, in accordance with law, exercise the rights of election and recall of the magistrate and other hsien self-government officials.

Article 124. In the hsien, there shall be a hsien council. Members of the hsien council shall be elected by the people of the hsien.

The legislative power of the hsien shall be exercised by the hsien council.

Article 125. Hsien rules and regulations that are in conflict with national laws, or with provincial rules and regulations, shall be null and void.

Article 126. In the hsien, there shall be a hsien government with a hsien magistrate who shall be elected by the people of the hsien.

Article 127. The hsien magistrate shall have charge of hsien self-government and shall administer matters delegated to the hsien by the central or provincial government.

Article 128. The provisions governing the hsien shall apply *mutatis mutandis* to the municipality.

Chapter XII. Election, Recall, Initiative and Referendum

Article 129. The various kinds of elections prescribed in this Constitution, except as otherwise provided by this Constitution, shall be by universal, equal, and direct suffrage and by secret ballot.

Article 130. Any citizen of the Republic of China who has attained the age of 20 years shall have the right of election in accordance with law. Except as otherwise provided by this Constitution or by law, any citizen who has attained the age of 23 years shall have the right of being elected in accordance with law.

Article 131. All candidates in the various kinds of elections prescribed in this Constitution shall openly campaign for their election.

Article 132. Intimidation or inducement shall be strictly forbidden in elections. Suits arising in connection with elections shall be tried by the courts.

Article 133. A person elected may, in accordance with law, be recalled by his constituency.

Article 134. In the various kinds of elections, the number of women to be elected shall be fixed, and measures pertaining thereto shall be prescribed by law.

Article 135. The number of delegates to the National Assembly and the manner of their election from people in interior areas, who have their own conditions of living and habits, shall be prescribed by law.

Article 136. The exercise of the rights of initiative and referendum shall be prescribed by law.

Chapter XIII. Fundamental National Policies

Section 1. National Defense

Article 137. The national defense of the Republic of China shall have as its objective the safeguarding of national security and the preservation of world peace.

The organization of national defense shall be prescribed by law.

Article 138. The land, sea and air forces of the whole country shall be above personal, regional, or party affiliations, shall be loyal to the state, and shall protect the people.

Article 139. No political party and no individual shall make use of armed forces as an instrument in a struggle for political powers.

Article 140. No military man in active service may concurrently hold a civil office.

Section 2. Foreign Policy

Article 141. The foreign policy of the Republic of China shall, in a spirit of independence and initiative and on the basis of the principles of equality and reciprocity, cultivate good-neighborliness with other nations, and respect treaties and the Charter of the United Nations, in order to protect the rights and interests of Chinese citizens residing abroad, promote international cooperation, advance international justice and ensure world peace.

Section 3. National Economy

Article 142. National economy shall be based on the Principle of the People's Livelihood and shall seek to effect equalization of land ownership and restriction of private capital in order to attain a well-balanced sufficiency in national wealth and people's livelihood.

Article 143. All land within the territory of the Republic of China shall belong to the whole body of citizens. Private ownership of land, acquired by the people in accordance with law, shall be protected and restricted by law. Privately-owned land shall be liable to taxation according to its value, and the Government may buy such land according to its value.

Mineral deposits which are embedded in the land, and natural power which may, for economic purposes, be utilized for the public benefit shall belong to the State, regardless of the fact that private individuals may have acquired ownership over such land.

If the value of a piece of land has increased, not through the exertion of labor or the employment of capital, the State shall levy thereon an increment tax, the proceeds of which shall be enjoyed by the people in common.

In the distribution and readjustment of land, the State shall in principle assist self-farming land-owners and persons who make use of the land by themselves, and shall also regulate their appropriate areas of operation.

Article 144. Public utilities and other enterprises of a monopolistic nature shall, in principle, be under public operation. In cases permitted by law, they may be operated by private citizens.

Article 145. With respect to private wealth and privately-operated enterprises, the State shall restrict them by law if they are deemed detrimental to a balanced development of national wealth and people's livelihood.

Cooperative enterprises shall receive encouragement and assistance from the State.

Private citizens' productive enterprises and foreign trade shall receive encouragement, guidance and protection from the State.

Article 146. The State shall, by the use of scientific techniques, develop water conservancy, increase the productivity of land, improve agricultural conditions, plan for the utilization of land, develop agricultural resources and hasten the industrialization of agriculture.

Article 147. The Central Government, in order to attain a balanced economic development among the provinces, shall give appropriate aid to poor or unproductive provinces.

The provinces, in order to attain a balanced economic development among the hsien, shall give appropriate aid to poor or unproductive hsien.

Article 148. Within the territory of the Republic of China, all goods shall be permitted to move freely from place to place.

Article 149. Financial institutions shall, in accordance with law, be subject to State control.

Article 150. The State shall extensively establish financial institutions for the common people, with a view to relieving unemployment .

Article 151. With respect to Chinese citizens residing abroad, the State shall foster and protect the development of their economic enterprises.

Section 4. Social Security

Article 152. The State shall provide suitable opportunity for work to people who are able to work.

Article 153. The State, in order to improve the livelihood of laborers and farmers and to improve their productive skill, shall enact laws and carry out policies for their protection.

Women and children engaged in labor shall, according to their age and physical condition, be accorded special protection.

Article 154. Capital and labor shall, in accordance with the principle of harmony and cooperation, promote productive enterprises. Conciliation and arbitration of disputes between capital and labor shall be prescribed by law.

Article 155. The State, in order to promote social welfare, shall establish a social insurance system. To the aged and the infirm who are unable to earn a living, and to victims of unusual calamities, the State shall give appropriate assistance and relief.

Article 156. The State, in order to consolidate the foundation of national existence and development, shall protect motherhood and carry out the policy of promoting the welfare of women and children.

Article 157. The State, in order to improve national health, shall establish extensive services for sanitation and health protection, and a system of public medical service.

Section 5. Education and Culture

Article 158. Education and culture shall aim at the development among the citizens of the national spirit, the spirit of self-government, national morality, good physique, scientific knowledge, and the ability to earn a living.

Article 159. All citizens shall have equal opportunity to receive an education.

Article 160. All children of school age from six to 12 years shall receive free primary education. Those from poor families shall be supplied with books by the Government.

All citizens above school age who have not received primary education shall receive supplementary education free of charge and shall also be supplied with books by the Government.

Article 161. The national, provincial, and local governments shall extensively establish scholarships to assist students of good scholastic standing and exemplary conduct who lack the means to continue their school education.

Article 162. All public and private educational and cultural institutions in the country shall, in accordance with law, be subject to State supervision.

Article 163. The State shall pay due attention to the balanced development of education in different regions, and shall promote social education in order to raise the cultural standard of the citizens in general. Grants from the National Treasury shall be made to frontier regions and economically poor areas to help them meet their educational and cultural expenses. The Central Government may either itself undertake the more important educational and cultural enterprises in such regions or give them financial assistance.

Article 164. Expenditures of educational programs, scientific studies and cultural services shall not be, in respect of the Central Government, less than 15 percent of the total national budget; in respect of each province, less than 25 percent of the total provincial budgets; and in respect of each municipality or hsien, less than 35 percent of the total municipal or hsien budget. Educational and cultural foundations established in accordance with law shall, together with their property, be protected.

Article 165. The State shall safeguard the livelihood of those who work in the fields of education, sciences and arts, and shall, in accordance with the development of national economy, increase their remuneration from time to time.

Article 166. The State shall encourage scientific discoveries and inventions, and shall protect ancient sites and articles of historical, cultural or artistic value.

Article 167. The State shall give encouragement or subsidies to the following enterprises or individuals:

1. Educational enterprises in the country which have been operated with good record by private individuals;

2. Educational enterprises which have been operated with good record by Chinese citizens residing abroad;

3. Persons who have made discoveries or inventions in the fields of learning and technology; and

4. Persons who have rendered long and meritorious services in the field of education.

Section 6. Frontier Regions

Article 168. The State shall accord to the various racial groups in the frontier regions legal protection of their status and shall give them special assistance in their local self-government undertakings.

Article 169. The State shall, in a positive manner, undertake and foster the development of education, culture, communications, water conservancy, public health, and other economic and social enterprises of the various racial groups in the frontier regions. With respect to the utilization of land, the State shall, after taking into account the climatic conditions, the nature of the soil and the life and habits of the people, adopt measures to protect the land and to assist in its development.

Chapter XIV. Enforcement and Amendment of the Constitution

Article 170. The term "law," as used in this Constitution, shall denote any legislative bill that shall have been passed by the Legislative Yuan and promulgated by the President of the Republic.

Article 171. Laws that are in conflict with the Constitution shall be null and void.

When doubt arises as to whether or not a law is in conflict with the Constitution, interpretation thereon shall be made by the Judicial Yuan.

Article 172. Ordinances that are in conflict with the Constitution or with laws shall be null and void.

Article 173. The Constitution shall be interpreted by the Judicial Yuan.

Article 174. Amendments to the Constitution shall be made in accordance with one of the following procedures:

1. Upon the proposal of one-fifth of the total number of the delegates to the National Assembly and by a resolution of three-fourths of the delegates present at a meeting having a quorum of two-thirds of the entire Assembly, the Constitution may be amended.

2. Upon the proposal of one-fourth of the Members of the Legislative Yuan and by a resolution of three-fourths of the Members present at a meeting having a quorum of three-fourths of the Members of the Yuan, an amendment may be drawn up and submitted to the National Assembly by way of referendum. Such a proposed amendment to the Constitution shall be publicly published half a year before the National Assembly convenes.

Article 175. Whenever necessary, enforcement procedures in regard to any matters prescribed in this Constitution shall be separately provided by law.

The preparatory procedures for the enforcement of this Constitution shall be decided upon by the same National Assembly which shall have adopted this Constitution.

The Additional Articles of the Constitution of the Republic of China

Adopted by the second extraordinary session of the First National Assembly on April 22, 1991, and promulgated by the president on May 1, 1991

Adopted by the extraordinary session of the Second National Assembly on May 27, 1992, and promulgated by the president on May 28, 1992

Adopted by the fourth extraordinary session of the Second National Assembly on July 28, 1994, and promulgated by the president on August 1, 1994

Adopted by the second session of the Third National Assembly on July 18, 1997, and promulgated by the president on July 21, 1997

Revised by the fourth session of the Third National Assembly on September 3, 1999, and promulgated by the president on September 15, 1999

The Council of Grand Justices, in its Constitutional Interpretation No. 499 on March 24, 2000, announced that the Additional Articles of the Constitution approved on September 15, 2000, were void, effective immediately. The revised Additional Articles promulgated on July 21, 1997 would remain in effect.

The revision of the Additional Articles of the Constitution of the Republic of China was approved by the fifth session of the Third National Assembly on April 24, 2000, and promulgated by the president on April 25, 2000.

To meet the requisites of the nation prior to national unification, the following articles of the ROC Constitution are added or amended to the ROC Constitution in accordance with Article 27, Paragraph 1, Item 3; and Article 174, Item 1:

Article 1. Three hundred delegates shall be elected by proportional representation to the National Assembly within three months of the expiration of a six-month period following the public announcement of a proposal by the Legislative Yuan to amend the Constitution or alter the national territory, or within three months of a petition initiated by the Legislative Yuan for the impeachment of the president or the vice president. The restrictions of Articles 26, 28, and 135 of the Constitution shall not apply. The election of the delegates by proportional representation shall be regulated by law.

The powers of the National Assembly shall be as follows, and the provisions of Article 4; Article 27, Paragraph 1, Item 1 through 3; Article 27, Paragraph 2; and Article 174, Item 1 shall not apply:

1. To vote, in accordance with Article 27, Paragraph 1, Item 4 and Article 174, Item 2 of the Constitution, on Legislative Yuan proposals to amend the Constitution;

2. To vote, in accordance with Article 4, Paragraph 5 of the Additional Articles, on Legislative Yuan proposals to alter the national territory; and

3. To deliberate, in accordance with Article 2, Paragraph 10 of the Additional Articles, a petition for the impeachment of the president or the vice president initiated by the Legislative Yuan.

Delegates to the National Assembly shall convene of their own accord within ten days after the election results have been confirmed and shall remain in session for no more than one month. The provisions of Articles 29 and 30 of the Constitution shall not apply.

The term of office of the delegates to the National Assembly shall terminate on the last day of the convention, and the provisions of Article 28 of the Constitution shall cease to apply. The term of office of the delegates to the Third National Assembly shall terminate on May 19, 2000. The Organic Law of the National Assembly shall be revised accordingly within two years of the adjustment of the powers and responsibilities of the National Assembly.

Article 2. The president and the vice president shall be directly elected by the entire populace of the free area of the Republic of China. This shall be effective from the election for the ninth-term president and vice president in 1996. The presidential and the vice presidential candidates shall register jointly and be listed as a pair on the ballot. The pair that receives the highest number of votes shall be elected. Citizens of the free area of the Republic of China residing abroad may return to the ROC to exercise their electoral rights and this shall be stipulated by law.

Presidential orders to appoint or remove from office the president of the Executive Yuan or personnel appointed with the confirmation of the Legislative Yuan in accordance with the Constitution, and to dissolve the Legislative Yuan, shall not require the countersignature of the president of the Executive Yuan. The provisions of Article 37 of the Constitution shall not apply.

The president may, by resolution of the Executive Yuan Council, issue emergency decrees and take all necessary measures to avert imminent danger affecting the security of the State or of the people or to cope with any serious financial or economic crisis, the restrictions in Article 43 of the Constitution notwithstanding. However, such decrees shall, within ten days of issuance, be presented to the Legislative Yuan for ratification. Should the Legislative Yuan withhold ratification, the said emergency decrees shall forthwith cease to be valid.

To determine major policies for national security, the president may establish a national security council and a subsidiary national security bureau. The organization of the said organs shall be stipulated by law.

The president may, within ten days following passage by the Legislative Yuan of a no-confidence vote against the president of the Executive Yuan, declare the dissolution of the Legislative Yuan after consulting with its president. However, the president shall not dissolve the Legislative Yuan while martial law or an emergency decree is in effect. Following the dissolution of the Legislative Yuan, an election for legislators shall be held within 60 days. The new Legislative Yuan shall convene of its own accord within ten days after the results of the said election have been confirmed, and the term of the said Legislative Yuan shall be reckoned from that date.

The terms of office for both the president and the vice president shall be four years. The president and the vice president may only be re-elected to serve one consecutive term; and the provisions of Article 47 of the Constitution shall not apply.

Should the office of the vice president become vacant, the president shall nominate a candidate(s) within three months, and the Legislative Yuan shall elect a new vice president, who shall serve the remainder of the original term until its expiration.

Should the offices of both the president and the vice president become vacant, the president of the Executive Yuan shall exercise the official powers of the president and the vice president. A new president and a new vice president shall be elected in accordance with Paragraph 1 of this article and shall serve out each respective original term until its expiration. The pertinent provisions of Article 49 of the Constitution shall not apply.

Recall of the president or the vice president shall be initiated upon the proposal of one-fourth of all members of the Legislative Yuan, and also passed by two-thirds of all the members. The final recall must be passed by more than one-half of the valid ballots in a vote in which more than one-half of the electorate in the free area of the Republic of China takes part.

Should a motion to impeach the president or the vice president initiated and submitted to the National Assembly by the Legislative Yuan be passed by a two-thirds majority of all delegates to the National Assembly, the party impeached shall forthwith be dismissed from office.

Article 3. The president of the Executive Yuan shall be appointed by the president. Should the president of the Executive Yuan resign or the office become vacant, the vice president of the Executive Yuan shall temporarily act as the president of the Executive Yuan pending a new appointment by the president. The provisions of Article 55 of the Constitution shall cease to apply.

The Executive Yuan shall be responsible to the Legislative Yuan in accordance with the following provisions; the provisions of Article 57 of the Constitution shall cease to apply:

1. The Executive Yuan has the duty to present to the Legislative Yuan a statement on its administrative policies and a report on its administration. While the Legislative Yuan is in session, its members shall have the right to interpellate the president of the Executive Yuan and the heads of ministries and other organizations under the Executive Yuan.

2. Should the Executive Yuan deem a statutory, budgetary, or treaty bill passed by the Legislative Yuan difficult to execute, the Executive Yuan may, with the approval of the president of the Republic and within ten days of the bill's submission to the Executive Yuan, request the Legislative Yuan to reconsider the bill. The Legislative Yuan shall reach a resolution on the returned bill within 15 days after it is received. Should the Legislative Yuan be in recess, it shall convene of its own accord within seven days and reach a resolution within 15 days after the session begins. Should the Legislative Yuan not reach a resolution within the said period of time, the original bill shall become invalid. Should more than one-half of the total number of Legislative Yuan members uphold the original bill, the president of the Executive Yuan shall immediately accept the said bill.

3. With the signatures of more than one-third of the total number of Legislative Yuan members, the Legislative Yuan may propose a no-confidence vote against the president of the Executive Yuan. Seventy-two hours after the no-confidence motion is made, an open-ballot vote shall be taken within 48 hours. Should more than one-half of the total number of Legislative Yuan members approve the motion, the president of the Executive Yuan shall tender his resignation within ten days, and at the same time may request that the president dissolve the Legislative Yuan. Should the no-confidence motion fail, the Legislative Yuan may not initiate another no-confidence motion against the same president of the Executive Yuan within one year.

The powers, procedures of establishment, and total number of personnel of national organizations shall be subject to standards set forth by law.

The structure, system, and number of personnel of each organization shall be determined according to the policies or operations of each organization and in accordance with the law as referred to in the preceding paragraph.

Article 4. Beginning with the Fourth Legislative Yuan, the Legislative Yuan shall have 225 members, who shall be elected in accordance with the following provisions, the restrictions in Article 64 of the Constitution notwithstanding:

1. One hundred and sixty-eight members shall be elected from the Special Municipalities, counties, and cities in the free area. At least one member shall be elected from each county and city.

2. Four members each shall be elected from among the lowland and highland aborigines in the free area.

3. Eight members shall be elected from among the Chinese citizens who reside abroad.

4. Forty-one members shall be elected from the nationwide constituency.

Members for the seats set forth in Item 3 and Item 4 of the preceding paragraph shall be elected according to a formula for proportional representation among political parties. Where the number of seats for each Special Municipality, county, and city as set forth in Item 1, and for each political party as set forth in Item 3 and Item 4, is not fewer than five and not more than ten, one seat shall be reserved for a female member. Where the number exceeds ten, one seat out of each additional ten shall be reserved for a female member.

When the Legislative Yuan convenes each year, it may hear a report on the state of the nation by the president.

Following the dissolution of the Legislative Yuan by the president and prior to the inauguration of its new members, the Legislative Yuan shall be regarded as in recess.

The territory of the Republic of China, defined by its existing national boundaries, shall not be altered unless initiated upon the proposal of one-fourth of all members of the Legislative Yuan, passed by three-fourths of the members of the Legislative Yuan present at a meeting requiring a quorum of three-fourths of all the members, and approved by three-fourths of the delegates to the National Assembly present at a meeting requiring a quorum of two-thirds of all the delegates.

Should the president issue an emergency decree after dissolving the Legislative Yuan, the Legislative Yuan shall convene of its own accord within three days to vote on the ratification of the decree within seven days after the session begins. However, should the emergency decree be issued after the election of new members of the Legislative Yuan, the new members shall vote on the ratification of the decree after their inauguration. Should the Legislative Yuan withhold ratification, the emergency decree shall forthwith be void.

Impeachment of the president or the vice president by the Legislative Yuan shall be initiated upon the proposal of more than one-half of all members of the Legislative Yuan and passed by more than two-thirds of all the members of the Legislative Yuan, whereupon it shall be submitted to the National Assembly. The provisions of Article 90 and Article 100 of the Constitution and Article 7, Paragraph 1 of the Additional Articles of the Constitution shall not apply.

No member of the Legislative Yuan may be arrested or detained without the permission of the Legislative Yuan, when that body is in session, except in case of flagrante delicto. The provisions of Article 74 of the Constitution shall cease to apply.

Article 5. The Judicial Yuan shall have 15 grand justices. The 15 grand justices, including a president and a vice president of the Judicial Yuan to be selected from amongst them, shall be nominated and, with the consent of the Legislative Yuan, appointed by the president of the Republic. This shall take effect from the year 2003, and the provisions of Article 79 of the Constitution shall not apply. The provisions of Article 81 of the Constitution and pertinent regulations on the lifetime holding of office and payment of salary do not apply to grand justices who did not transfer from the post of a judge.

Each grand justice of the Judicial Yuan shall serve a term of eight years, independent of the order of appointment to office, and shall not serve a consecutive term. The grand justices serving as president and vice president of the Judicial Yuan shall not enjoy the guarantee of an eight-year term.

Among the grand justices nominated by the president in the year 2003, eight members, including the president and the vice president of the Judicial Yuan, shall serve for four years. The remaining grand justices shall serve for eight years. The provisions of the preceding paragraph regarding term of office shall not apply.

The grand justices of the Judicial Yuan shall, in addition to discharging their duties in accordance with Article 78 of the Constitution, also form a Constitutional Court to adjudicate matters relating to the dissolution of unconstitutional political parties.

A political party shall be considered unconstitutional if its goals or activities endanger the existence of the Republic of China or the nation's free and democratic constitutional order.

The proposed budget submitted annually by the Judicial Yuan may not be eliminated or reduced by the Executive Yuan; however, the Executive Yuan may indicate its opinions on the budget and include it in the central government's proposed budgetary bill for submission to the Legislative Yuan for deliberation.

Article 6. The Examination Yuan shall be the highest examination body of the State, and shall be responsible for the following matters; and the provisions of Article 83 of the Constitution shall not apply:

1. Holding of examinations;

2. Matters relating to the qualification screening, security of tenure, pecuniary aid in case of death, and retirement of civil servants; and

3. Legal matters relating to the employment, discharge, performance evaluation, scale of salaries, promotion, transfer, commendation and award of civil servants.

The Examination Yuan shall have a president, a vice president, and several members, all of whom shall be nominated and, with the consent of the Legislative Yuan, appointed by the president of the Republic; and the provisions of Article 84 of the Constitution shall not apply.

The provisions of Article 85 of the Constitution concerning the holding of examinations in different areas, with prescribed numbers of persons to be selected according to various provinces and areas, shall cease to apply.

Article 7. The Control Yuan shall be the highest control body of the State and shall exercise the powers of impeachment, censure and audit; and the pertinent provisions of Article 90 and Article 94 of the Constitution concerning the exercise of the power of consent shall not apply.

The Control Yuan shall have 29 members, including a president and a vice president, all of whom shall serve a term of six years. All members shall be nominated and, with the consent of the Legislative Yuan, appointed by the president of the Republic. The provisions of Article 91 through Article 93 of the Constitution shall cease to apply.

Impeachment proceedings by the Control Yuan against a public functionary in the central government, or local governments, or against personnel of the Judicial Yuan or the Examination Yuan, shall be initiated by two or more members of the Control Yuan, and be investigated and voted upon by a committee of not less than nine of its members, the restrictions in Article 98 of the Constitution notwithstanding.

In the case of impeachment by the Control Yuan of Control Yuan personnel for dereliction of duty or violation of the law, the provisions of Article 95 and Article 97, Paragraph 2 of the Constitution, as well as the preceding paragraph, shall apply.

Members of the Control Yuan shall be beyond party affiliation and independently exercise their powers and discharge their responsibilities in accordance with the law.

The provisions of Article 101 and Article 102 of the Constitution shall cease to apply.

Article 8. The remuneration or pay of the members of the Legislative Yuan shall be regulated by law. Except for general annual adjustments, individual regulations on increase of remuneration or pay shall take effect starting with the subsequent Legislative Yuan. Expenses for the convention of the delegates to the National Assembly shall be regulated by law.

Article 9. The system of self-government in the provinces and counties shall include the following provisions, which shall be established by the enactment of appropriate laws, the restrictions in Article 108, Paragraph 1, Item 1; Article 109; Article 112 through Article 115; and Article 122 of the Constitution notwithstanding:

1. A province shall have a provincial government of nine members, one of whom shall be the provincial governor. All members shall be nominated by the president of the Executive Yuan and appointed by the president of the Republic.

2. A province shall have a provincial advisory council made up of a number of members, who shall be nominated by the president of the Executive Yuan and appointed by the president of the Republic.

3. A county shall have a county council, members of which shall be elected by the people of the said county.

4. The legislative powers vested in a county shall be exercised by the county council of the said county.

5. A county shall have a county government headed by a county magistrate who shall be elected by the people of the said county.

6. The relationship between the central government and the provincial and county governments.

7. A province shall execute the orders of the Executive Yuan and supervise matters governed by the counties.

The modifications of the functions, operations, and organization of the Taiwan Provincial Government may be specified by law.

Article 10. The State shall encourage the development of and investment in science and technology, facilitate industrial upgrading, promote modernization of agriculture and fishery, emphasize exploitation and utilization of water resources, and strengthen international economic cooperation.

Environmental and ecological protection shall be given equal consideration with economic and technological development.

The State shall assist and protect the survival and development of private small and medium-sized enterprises.

The State shall manage government-run financial organizations, in accordance with the principles of business administration. The management, personnel, proposed budgets, final budgets, and audits of the said organizations may be specified by law.

The State shall promote universal health insurance and promote the research and development of both modern and traditional medicines.

The State shall protect the dignity of women, safeguard their personal safety, eliminate sexual discrimination, and further substantive gender equality.

The State shall guarantee insurance, medical care, obstacle-free environments, education and training, vocational guidance, and support and assistance in everyday life for physically and mentally handicapped persons, and shall also assist them to attain independence and to develop.

The State shall emphasize social relief and assistance, welfare services, employment for citizens, social insurance, medical and health care, and other social welfare services. Priority shall be given to funding social relief and assistance, and employment for citizens.

The State shall respect military servicemen for their contributions to society, and guarantee studies, employment, medical care, and livelihood for retired servicemen.

Priority shall be given to funding education, science, and culture, and in particular funding for compulsory education, the restrictions in Article 164 of the Constitution notwithstanding.

The State affirms cultural pluralism and shall actively preserve and foster the development of aboriginal languages and cultures.

The State shall, in accordance with the will of the ethnic groups, safeguard the status and political participation of the aborigines. The State shall also guarantee and provide assistance and encouragement for aboriginal education, culture, transportation, water conservation, health and medical care, economic activity, land, and social welfare, measures for which shall be established by law. The same protection and assistance shall be given to the people of the Penghu, Kinmen, and Matsu areas.

The State shall accord to nationals of the Republic of China residing overseas protection of their rights of political participation.

Article 11. Rights and obligations between the people of the Chinese mainland area and those of the free area, and the disposition of other related affairs may be specified by law.

ROC Government Directory

The following information on the new government to be installed on May 20 was announced as of May 4, 2000. Current information is available on line at: *http://www.gio.gov.tw/info/chief/index_e.htm*

Office of the President 總統府

122 Chungking South Road, Section 1, Taipei
Phone: (02) 2311-3731
Fax: (02) 2314-0746 (The First Bureau)
 (02) 2311-5877 (Protocol Section)
 (02) 2331-1604 (Spokesman's Office)
Website: http://www.oop.gov.tw
E-mail: public@www.oop.gov.tw
President: CHEN, Shui-bian 陳水扁
Vice President: LU, Hsiu-lien Annette 呂秀蓮
Secretary-General: CHANG, Chun-hsiung 張俊雄

Academia Sinica 中央研究院
128 Yen Chiu Yuan Road, Section 2, Taipei
Phone: (02) 2782-2120
Fax: (02) 2785-3847
Website: http://www.sinica.edu.tw
E-mail: service@sinica.edu.tw
President: LEE, Yuan-tseh 李遠哲

Academia Historica 國史館
406 Pei Yi Road, Section 2, Hsintien
Taipei County
Phone: (02) 2217-4540
Fax: (02) 2217-0415
Website: http://www.drnh.gov.tw
E-mail: 513b@sun1.drnh.gov.tw
President: CHANG, Yen-hsien 張炎憲

National Security Council 國家安全會議
122 Chungking South Road, Section 1, Taipei
Phone: (02) 2361-6132
Fax: (02) 2361-1214
Chairman: CHEN, Shui-bian 陳水扁
Secretary-General: CHUANG, Ming-yao 莊銘耀

National Unification Council 國家統一委員會
122 Chungking South Road, Section 1, Taipei
Phone: (02) 2311-9807
Fax: (02) 2314-1814
Chairman: CHEN, Shui-bian 陳水扁

National Assembly 國民大會

53 Chung Hua Road, Section 1, Taipei
Phone: (02) 2331-1312
Fax: (02) 2314-2056
Website: http://www.nasm.gov.tw

Executive Yuan 行政院

1 Chung Hsiao East Road, Section 1, Taipei
Phone: (02) 2356-1500
Fax: (02) 2394-8727
Website: http://www.ey.gov.tw
E-mail: eyemail@eyemail.gio.gov.tw
Premier: TANG, Fei 唐飛
Vice Premier: YU, Shyi-kun 游錫堃
Secretary-General: WEA, Chi-lin 魏啓林

Ministers without portfolio 政務委員
HUANG, Jong-tsun 黃榮村
CHEN, Chin-huang 陳錦煌
CHANG, Yu-huei 張有惠
TSAY, Chin-yen 蔡清彥
HU, Ching-piao 胡錦標

Ministry of the Interior 內政部
5 Hsuchow Road, Taipei
Phone: (02) 2356-5000
Fax: (02) 2356-6201
Website: http://www.moi.gov.tw
E-mail: service@mail.moi.gov.tw
Minister: CHANG, Po-ya 張博雅

Ministry of Foreign Affairs 外交部
2 Kaitagelan Boulevard, Taipei
Phone: (02) 2348-2999
Fax: (02) 2348-2118
Website: http://www.mofa.gov.tw
E-mail: eyes@mofa.gov.tw
Minister: TIEN, Hung-mao 田弘茂

Ministry of National Defense 國防部

2nd Floor, 164 Po Ai Road, Taipei
Phone: (02) 2311-6117
Fax: (02) 2314-4221
Website: http://www.mnd.gov.tw
E-mail: mnd@mnd.gov.tw
Minister: WU, Shih-wen 伍世文
Chief of the General Staff: TANG, Yiau-min 湯曜明

Ministry of Finance 財政部

2 Ai Kuo West Road, Taipei
Phone: (02) 2322-8000
Fax: (02) 2396-5829
Website: http://www.mof.gov.tw
E-mail: mof@mail.mof.gov.tw
Minister: SHEA, Jia-dong 許嘉棟

Ministry of Education 教育部

5 Chung Shan South Road, Taipei
Phone: (02) 2356-6051
Fax: (02) 2397-6949
Website: http://www.moe.gov.tw
E-mail: moemail@moe98b.gov.tw
Minister: TZENG, Ovid J.L. 曾志朗

Ministry of Justice 法務部

130 Chungking South Road, Section 1, Taipei
Phone: (02) 2314-6871
Fax: (02) 2389-6274
Website: http://www.moj.gov.tw
E-mail: hotline@www.moj.gov.tw
Minister: CHEN, Ding-nan 陳定南

Ministry of Economic Affairs 經濟部

15 Foochow Street, Taipei
Phone: (02) 2321-2200
Fax: (02) 2391-9398
Website: http://www.moea.gov.tw
E-mail: service@moea.gov.tw
Minister: LIN, Hsin-i 林信義

Ministry of Transportation and Communications 交通部

2 Changsha Street, Section 1, Taipei
Phone: (02) 2349-2900
Fax: (02) 2311-8587
Website: http://www.motc.gov.tw
E-mail: motceyes@motc.gov.tw
Minister: YEH, Chu-lan 葉菊蘭

Mongolian & Tibetan Affairs Commission 蒙藏委員會

4th Floor, 5 Hsuchow Road, Taipei
Phone: (02) 2356-6428
Fax: (02) 2356-6419
Website: http://www.mtac.gov.tw
E-mail: mtacservice@mtac.gov.tw
Chairman: HSU, Cheng-kuang 徐正光

Overseas Chinese Affairs Commission 僑務委員會

15th-17th Floor, 5 Hsuchow Road, Taipei
Phone: (02) 3343-2600
Fax: (02) 2356-6323
Website: http://www.ocac.gov.tw
E-mail: ocacinfo@mail.ocac.gov.tw
Minister: CHANG, Fu-mei 張富美

The Central Bank of China 中央銀行

2 Roosevelt Road, Section 1, Taipei
Phone: (02) 2393-6161
Fax: (02) 2357-1974
Website: http://www.cbc.gov.tw
E-mail: adminrol@mail.cbc.gov.tw
Governor: PERNG, Fai-nan 彭淮南

Directorate General of Budget, Accounting and Statistics, Executive Yuan 行政院主計處

1 Chung Hsiao East Road, Section 1, Taipei
Phone: (02) 2356-1500
Fax: (02) 2397-0196
Website: http://www.dgbasey.gov.tw
E-mail: dgbas@emc.dgbas.gov.tw
Director-General: LIN, Chuan 林全

Government Information Office, Executive Yuan 行政院新聞局

2 Tientsin Street, Taipei
Phone: (02) 2322-8888
Fax: (02) 2356-8733
Website: http://www.gio.gov.tw

E-mail: service@mail.gio.gov.tw
Director-General: CHUNG, Chin 鍾琴

Central Personnel Administration,
Executive Yuan 行政院人事行政局
9th-11th Floor, 2-2 Chi Nan Road, Section 2, Taipei
Phone: (02) 2397-9298
Fax: (02) 2397-5565
Website: http://www.cpa.gov.tw
E-mail: chief@cpa.gov.tw
Director-General: CHU, Wu-hsien 朱武獻

Department of Health, Executive Yuan
行政院衛生署
100 Ai Kuo East Road, Taipei
Phone: (02) 2321-0151
Fax: (02) 2322-3877
Website: http://www.doh.gov.tw
E-mail: dohes@dohr6.doh.gov.tw
Director-General: LEE, Ming-liang 李明亮

Environmental Protection Administration,
Executive Yuan 行政院環境保護署
41 Chung Hua Road, Section 1, Taipei
Phone: (02) 2311-7722
Fax: (02) 2311-6071
Website: http://www.epa.gov.tw
E-mail: www@sun.epa.gov.tw
Administrator: LIN, Jun-yi 林俊義

Council for Economic Planning and Development,
Executive Yuan 行政院經濟建設委員會
3 Pao Ching Road, Taipei
Phone: (02) 2316-5300
Fax: (02) 2370-0415
Website: http://www.cepd.gov.tw
E-mail: cepdey@sun.cepd.gov.tw
Chairman: CHEN, Po-chih 陳博志

Veterans Affairs Commission, Executive Yuan
行政院國軍退除役官兵輔導委員會
222 Chung Hsiao East Road, Section 5, Taipei
Phone: (02) 2725-5700
Fax: (02) 2723-7610
Website: http://www.vac.gov.tw
E-mail: eyes@mail.vac.gov.tw
Chairman: YANG, Te-chih 楊德智

National Youth Commission, Executive Yuan
行政院青年輔導委員會
14th Floor, 5 Hsuchow Road, Taipei
Phone: (02) 2356-6232
Fax: (02) 2356-6307
Website: http://www.nyc.gov.tw
E-mail: nyc@nyc.gov.tw
Chairperson: LIN, Fang-mei 林芳玫

National Palace Museum 國立故宮博物院
221 Chih Shan Road, Section 2, Wai-shuang-hsi
Shihlin, Taipei
Phone: (02) 2881-2021
Fax: (02) 2882-1440
Website: http://www.npm.gov.tw
E-mail: service@npm.gov.tw
Director: TU, Cheng-sheng 杜正勝

Atomic Energy Council, Executive Yuan
行政院原子能委員會
67 Lane 144, Keelung Road, Section 4, Taipei
Phone: (02) 2363-4180
Fax: (02) 2367-6200
Website: http://www.aec.gov.tw
E-mail: public@aec.gov.tw
Chairman: HSIA, Der-yu 夏德鈺

National Science Council, Executive Yuan
行政院國家科學委員會
17th-22nd Floor, 106 Ho Ping East Road, Section 2
Taipei
Phone: (02) 2737-7586
Fax: (02) 2737-7668
Website: http://www.nsc.gov.tw
E-mail: nsc@nsc.gov.tw
Chairman: CHEN, Tan-sun 陳唐山

Research, Development and Evaluation
Commission, Executive Yuan
行政院研究發展考核委員會
6th-8th Floor, 2-2 Chi Nan Road, Section 2, Taipei
Phone: (02) 2341-9066
Fax: (02) 2396-9444
Website: http://rdec.gov.tw
E-mail: rdec@rdec.gov.tw
Chairman: LIN, Chia-cheng 林嘉誠

Council of Agriculture, Executive Yuan
行政院農業委員會
37 Nan Hai Road, Taipei
Phone: (02) 2381-2991
Fax: (02) 2331-0341
Website: http://www.coa.gov.tw
E-mail: agri@coa.gov.tw
Chairman: CHEN, Hsi-huang 陳希煌

Council for Cultural Affairs, Executive Yuan
行政院文化建設委員會
102 Ai Kuo East Road, Taipei
Phone: (02) 2343-4000
Fax: (02) 2322-2937
Website: http://www.cca.gov.tw
E-mail: wwwadm@www.cca.gov.tw
Chairperson: TCHEN, Yu-chiou 陳郁秀

Council of Labor Affairs, Executive Yuan
行政院勞工委員會
5th-15th Floor, 132 Min Sheng East Road, Section 3
Taipei
Phone: (02) 8770-1866
Fax: (02) 2514-9240
Website: http://cla.gov.tw
E-mail: cla@mail.cla.gov.tw
Chairperson: CHEN, Chu 陳菊

Mainland Affairs Council, Executive Yuan
行政院大陸委員會
15th-18th Floor, 2-2 Chi Nan Road, Section 2
Taipei
Phone: (02) 2397-5589
Fax: (02) 2397-5300
Website: http://www.mac.gov.tw
E-mail: macst@mac.gov.tw
Chairperson: TSAI, Ing-wen 蔡英文

Fair Trade Commission, Executive Yuan
行政院公平交易委員會
12th-14th Floor, 2-2 Chi Nan Road, Section 2
Taipei
Phone: (02) 2351-7588
Fax: (02) 2397-4997
Website: http://www.ftc.gov.tw
E-mail: ftcse@ftc.gov.tw
Chairperson: CHAO, Yang-ching 趙揚清

Council of Aboriginal Affairs, Executive Yuan 行政院原住民委員會
16th-17th Floor, 4 Chung Hsiao West Road
Section 1, Taipei
Phone: (02) 2388-2122
Fax: (02) 2389-1967
Website:http://www.apc.gov.tw
Chairman: ISQAQAVUT, Yohani 尤哈尼‧伊斯卡卡夫特

Public Construction Commission, Executive Yuan 行政院公共工程委員會
9th Floor, 4 Chung Hsiao West Road, Section 1
Taipei
Phone: (02) 2361-8661
Fax: (02) 2331-5808
Website: http://www.pcc.gov.tw
E-mail: secr@mail.pcc.gov.tw
Chairman: LIN, Neng-pai 林能白

Consumers Protection Commission, Executive Yuan 行政院消費者保護委員會
1 Chung Hsiao East Road, Section 1, Taipei
Phone: (02) 2321-4700
Fax: (02) 2321-4538
Website: http://www.cpc.gov.tw
E-mail: tcpc@ms1.hinet.net
Chairman: YU, Shyi-kun 游錫堃

Central Election Commission
中央選舉委員會
5 Hsuchow Road, Taipei
Phone: (02) 2356-5484
Fax: (02) 2397-6900
Website: http://www.cec.gov.tw
E-mail: post@cec.gov.tw
Chairman: HUANG, Shih-cheng 黃石城

National Council on Physical Fitness and Sports, Executive Yuan 行政院體育委員會
20 Chulun Street, Taipei
Phone: (02) 2509-2310
Fax: (02) 2509-1444
Website: http://www.ncpfs.gov.tw
E-mail: public@nscey.gov.tw
Chairman: HSU, I-hsiung 許義雄

Coast Guard Administration 海岸巡防署
296 Hsing Lung Road, Section 3, Taipei
Phone: (02) 2239-9201
Fax: (02) 2239-9258
Director General: WANG, Chun 王郡

Legislative Yuan 立法院

1 Chung Shan South Road, Taipei
Phone: (02) 2358-5858
Fax: (02) 2358-5255
Website: http://www.ly.gov.tw
President: WANG, Chin-ping 王金平
Vice President: YAO, Eng-chi 饒穎奇
Secretary General. LIN, Hsi-shan 林錫山

Judicial Yuan 司法院

124 Chungking South Road, Section 1, Taipei
Phone: (02) 2361-8577
Fax: (02) 2371-5583
Website: http://www.judicial.gov.tw
E-mail: judical@judical.gov.tw
President: WENG, Yueh-sheng 翁岳生
Vice President: CHENG, Chung-mo 城仲模
Secretary-General: YANG, Jen-shou 楊仁壽

Supreme Court 最高法院
6 Changsha Street, Section 1, Taipei
Phone: (02) 2314-1160
Fax: (02) 2311-4246
President: LIN, Ming-teh 林明德

Administrative Court 行政法院
1 Lane 126, Chungking South Road
Section 1, Taipei
Phone: (02) 2311-3691
Fax: (02) 2311-1791
President: JONG, Yaw-tarng 鍾曜唐

Commission on the Disciplinary Sanctions of Functionaries 公務員懲戒委員會
3rd Floor, 124 Chungking South Road
Section 1, Taipei
Phone: (02) 2331-7908

Fax: (02) 2331-1934
Chief Commissioner: LIN, Kuo-hsien 林國賢

Examination Yuan 考試院

1 Shih Yuan Road, Taipei
Phone: (02) 2236-3081
Fax: (02) 2236-5240
Website: http://www.exam.gov.tw
E-mail: exam@exam.gov.tw

Ministry of Examination 考選部
1 Shih Yuan Road, Taipei
Phone: (02) 2236-3081
Fax: (02) 2236-9592
Website: http://www.moex.gov.tw
E-mail: boss@mis.moex.gov.tw

Ministry of Civil Service 銓敘部
1 Shih Yuan Road, Taipei
Phone: (02) 2236-3081
Fax: (02) 2236-9207
Website: http://www.mocs.gov.tw
E-mail: mop@mocs.gov.tw

Civil Service Protection and Training Commission 公務人員保障暨培訓委員會
136 Roosevelt Road, Section 6, Taipei
website: http://www.csptc.gov.tw
Phone: (02) 2935-9500
Fax: (02) 2935-9521

Supervisory Board of the Civil Servants Pension Fund 公務人員退休撫卹基金監理委員會
5th Floor, 1 Nan Hai Road, Taipei
Phone: (02) 2322-4222
Fax: (02) 2321-9406
Website: http://www.fund.gov.tw

Control Yuan 監察院

2 Chung Hsiao East Road, Section 1, Taipei
Phone: (02) 2341-3183
Fax: (02) 2356-6570
Website: http://www.cy.gov.tw

E-mail: *pdoc@ms.cy.gov.tw*
President: CHIEN, Fredrick F. 錢復
Vice President: CHEN, Meng-ling 陳孟鈴
Secretary-General: TU, Shan-liang 杜善良

National Audit Office 審計部
1 Hangchow North Road, Taipei
Phone: (02) 2397-1366
Fax: (02) 2397-7889
Website: http://www.audit.gov.tw
Auditor-General: SU, Chen-ping 蘇振平

Taipei City Government
臺北市政府

1 Shih Fu Road, Taipei
Phone: (02) 2720-8889
Fax: (02) 2727-8809
Website: http://www.taipei.gov.tw
E-mail: mayor@mail.tcg.gov.tw
Mayor: MA, Ying-jeou 馬英九

Secretariat 秘書處
1 Shih Fu Road, Taipei
Phone: (02) 2720-8889
Fax: (02) 2759-8997

Bureau of Civil Affairs 民政局
1 Shih Fu Road, Taipei
Phone: (02) 2720-8889
Fax: (02) 2759-8799

Bureau of Finance 財政局
1 Shih Fu Road, Taipei
Phone: (02) 2720-8889
Fax: (02) 2720-6022

Bureau of Education 教育局
1 Shih Fu Road, Taipei
Phone: (02) 2720-8889
Fax: (02) 2759-3380

Bureau of Reconstruction 建設局
1 Shih Fu Road, Taipei
Phone: (02) 2720-8889
Fax: (02) 2720-5698

Bureau of Public Works 工務局
1 Shih Fu Road, Taipei
Phone: (02) 2720-8889
Fax: (02) 2725-6801

Bureau of Transportation 交通局
1 Shih Fu Road, Taipei
Phone: (02) 2720-8889
Fax: (02) 2729-1814

Bureau of Social Affairs 社會局
1 Shih Fu Road, Taipei
Phone: (02) 2720-8889
Fax: (02) 2720-6552

Bureau of Labor Affairs 勞工局
1 Shih Fu Road, Taipei
Phone: (02) 2720-8889
Fax: (02) 2720-6651

Taipei City Police Headquarters 警察局
96 Yen Ping South Road, Taipei
Phone: (02) 2331-3561
Fax: (02) 2331-8898

Bureau of Health 衛生局
1 Shih Fu Road, Taipei
Phone: (02) 2720-8889
Fax: (02) 2759-3002

Bureau of Environmental Protection 環境保護局
1 Shih Fu Road, Taipei
Phone: (02) 2720-8889
Fax: (02) 2759-7986

Bureau of Urban Development 都市發展局
1 Shih Fu Road, Taipei
Phone: (02) 2720-8889
Fax: (02) 2759-3321

Taipei Fire Department 消防局
1 Sung Jen Road, Taipei
Phone: (02) 2729-7668
Fax: (02) 2758-4642

Bureau of Cultural Affairs 文化局
1 Shih Fu Road, Taipei

Phone: (02) 2345-1556
Fax: (02) 2725-3496

Department of Land Administration 地政處
1 Shih Fu Road, Taipei
Phone: (02) 2720-8889
Fax: (02) 2720-1802

Department of Public Housing 國民住宅處
9th Floor, 8 Roosevelt Road, Section 4, Taipei
Phone: (02) 2321-1828
Fax: (02) 2357-2864

Department of Information 新聞處
1 Shih Fu Road, Taipei
Phone: (02) 2720-8889
Fax: (02) 2720-7975

Department of Military Service 兵役處
9th Floor, 92 Roosevelt Road, Section 4, Taipei
Phone: (02) 2365-4361
Fax: (02) 2367-3072

Department of Budget, Accounting and Statistics
主計處
1 Shih Fu Road, Taipei
Phone: (02) 2720-8889
Fax: (02) 2759-5109

Department of Personnel 人事處
1 Shih Fu Road, Taipei
Phone: (02) 2720-8889
Fax: (02) 2720-9111

Government Ethics Department 政風處
1 Shih Fu Road, Taipei
Phone: (02) 2720-8889
Fax: (02) 2759-5690

**Research, Development and Evaluation
Commission** 研究發展考核委員會
1 Shih Fu Road, Taipei
Phone: (02) 2720-8889
Fax: (02) 2759-3593

Commission of Administrative Appeals
訴願審議委員會
1 Shih Fu Road, Taipei

Phone: (02) 2720-8889
Fax: (02) 2759-3266

Rules and Regulations Commission 法規委員會
1 Shih Fu Road, Taipei
Phone: (02) 2720-8889
Fax: (02) 2759-6695

Council of Aboriginal Affairs
原住民事務委員會
1 Shih Fu Road, Taipei
Phone: (02) 2720-8889
Fax: (02) 2720-5996

Urban Planning Commission 都市計畫委員會
1 Shih Fu Road, Taipei
Phone: (02) 2720-8889
Fax: (02) 2759-3013

Department of Rapid Transit Systems
捷運工程局
7 Lane 48, Chung Shan North Road, Section 2
Taipei
Phone: (02) 2521-5550
Fax: (02) 2521-7639

Taipei Feitsui Reservoir Administration
台北翡翠水庫管理局
43 Hsin Wu Road, Section 3, Hsintien, Taipei County
Phone: (02) 2666-7811
Fax: (02) 2666-7264

Taipei Water Department 臺北自來水事業處
131 Chang Hsing Street, Taipei
Phone: (02) 2735-2140
Fax: (02) 2732-3432

Taipei Bank 台北銀行
50 Chung Shan North Road, Section 2, Taipei
Phone: (02) 2542-5656
Fax: (02) 2542-4396

Civic Worker Training Center
公務人員訓練中心
20 Lane 21, Wan Mei Street, Section 2, Taipei
Phone: (02) 2932-0212
Fax: (02) 2931-3299

Taipei Rapid Transit Co.
臺北大衆捷運股份有限公司
7 Lane 48, Chung Shan North Road, Section 2
Taipei
Phone: (02) 2536-3001
Fax: (02) 2511-5003

Kaohsiung City Government

高雄市政府

2 Ssu Wei Third Road, Kaohsiung
Phone: (07) 336-8333
Fax: (07) 333-7633
Website: http://www.kcg.gov.tw
E-mail: mayor@mail.kcg.gov.tw
Mayor: HSIEH, Frank 謝長廷

Secretariat 秘書處
2 Ssu Wei Third Road, Kaohsiung
Phone: (07) 332-3377
Fax: (07) 335-3132

Bureau of Civil Affairs 民政局
2 Ssu Wei Third Road, Kaohsiung
Phone: (07) 335-6111
Fax: (07) 331-5944

Bureau of Finance 財政局
2 Ssu Wei Third Road, Kaohsiung
Phone: (07) 334-7866
Fax: (07) 334-7866

Bureau of Education 教育局
2 Ssu Wei Third Road, Kaohsiung
Phone: (07) 334-0022
Fax: (07) 334-0022

Bureau of Reconstruction 建設局
2 Ssu Wei Third Road, Kaohsiung
Phone: (07) 336-6252
Fax: (07) 713-1739

Bureau of Public Works 工務局
2 Ssu Wei Third Road, Kaohsiung
Phone: (07) 333-5386
Fax: (07) 331-5426

Bureau of Social Affairs 社會局
2 Ssu Wei Third Road, Kaohsiung
Phone: (07) 337-3365
Fax: (07) 331-5490

Bureau of Labor Affairs 勞工局
6 Chen Chung Road, Chien Chen District, Kaohsiung
Phone: (07) 811-9799
Fax: (07) 812-4783

Police Headquarters 警察局
260 Chung Cheng Fourth Road, Kaohsiung
Phone: (07) 261-3355
Fax: (07) 241-0973

Fire Department 消防局
3 Chung Cheng 3rd Road, Kaohsiung
Phone: (07) 227-1125
Fax: (07) 227-1058

Health Department 衛生局
261 Chung Cheng Fourth Road, Kaohsiung
Phone: (07) 261-8387
Fax: (07) 281-4327

Department of Environmental Protection
環境保護局
2 Ssu Wei Third Road, Kaohsiung
Phone: (07) 337-3395
Fax: (07) 331-6164

Bureau of Rapid Transit Systems 捷運工程局
2 Ssu Wei Third Road, Kaohsiung
Phone: (07) 331-4546
Fax: (07) 331-4366

Department of Land Administration 地政處
2 Ssu Wei Third Road, Kaohsiung
Phone: (07) 337-3445
Fax: (07) 331-4105

Department of Public Housing 國民住宅處
2 Ssu Wei Third Road, Kaohsiung
Phone: (07) 337-3515
Fax: (07) 331-5080

Department of Information 新聞處
2 Ssu Wei Third Road, Kaohsiung
Phone: (07) 331-4990
Fax: (07) 331-5017

Department of Conscription 兵役處
2 Ssu Wei Third Road, Kaohsiung
Phone: (07) 331-6502
Fax: (07) 331-6506

Department of Budget, Accounting and Statistics
主計處
2 Ssu Wei Third Road, Kaohsiung
Phone: (07) 334-1766
Fax: (07) 331-4803

Department of Personnel 人事處
2 Ssu Wei Third Road, Kaohsiung
Phone: (07) 337-3640
Fax: (07) 331-5652

Department of Government Ethics 政風處
2 Ssu Wei Third Road, Kaohsiung
Phone: (07) 330-6816
Fax: (07) 331-3655

Human Resource Development Institute
公務人力資源發展中心
801 Chung Te Road, Kaohsiung
Phone: (07) 342-2170
Fax: (07) 342-2124

Research, Development and Evaluation Commission 研究發展考核委員會
2 Ssu Wei Third Road, Kaohsiung
Phone: (07) 337-3700
Fax: (07) 331-8191

Rules and Regulations Commission 法規委員會
2 Ssu Wei Third Road, Kaohsiung
Phone: (07) 337-3690
Fax: (07) 330-8971

Commission for Examining Petitions and Appeals 訴願審議委員會
2 Ssu Wei Third Road, Kaohsiung
Phone: (07) 337-3690
Fax: (07) 330-8971

Commission of Aboriginal Affairs
原住民事務委員會
2 Ssu Wei Third Road, Kaohsiung
Phone: (07) 337-3205
Fax: (07) 334-0804

Urban Planning Committee 都市計畫委員會
2 Ssu Wei Third Road, Kaohsiung
Phone: (07) 337-3260
Fax: (07) 336-3937

Bank of Kaohsiung 高雄銀行
21 Wu Fu Third Road, Kaohsiung
Phone: (07) 348-0536
Fax: (07) 348-0524

Appendix IV
Directory of ROC Representatives Abroad

ROC Embassies and Consulates

Asia

Embassy of the Republic of China
Majuro, Republic of Marshall Inslands
P.O. Box 1229, Majuro
Marshall Islands, MH 96960
Phone: (+692) 625-4051
Fax: (+674) 625-4056
E-mail: eoroc@ntamar.com

Embassy of the Republic of China
Yaren, Republic of Nauru
P.O. Box 294
Republic of Nauru, Central Pacific
Phone: (+674) 555-4399
Fax: (+674) 555-4594
E-mail: rocnauru@cenpac.net.nr

Embassy of the Republic of China
Honiara, Solomon Islands
Panatina Plaza 1st FL., Honiara
Solomon Islands
Mailing Address:
P.O. Box 586, Honiara
Solomon Islands
Phone: (+677) 38-050
Fax: (+677) 38-060
E-mail: embroc@welkam.solomon.com.sb

Emabssy of the Republic of China
Funafuti, Tuvalu
P.O. Box 130, Funafuti, Tuvalu
Phone: (+688) 29-278
Fax: (+688) 20-277

Africa

Ambassade de la République de Chine
Ouagadougou, Burkina Faso
01 B.P. 5563, Ouagadougou 01
Burkina Faso

Phone: (+226) 316-195
Fax: (+226) 316-197
E-mail: ambachine@fasonet.bf

Embassy of the Republic of China
N'Djamena, Republic of Chad
Mailing Address:
B.P. 1150, N'Djamena
Republic of Chad
Phone: (+235) 524-405
Fax: (+235) 524-402
E-mail: ambchine@intnet.td

Embassy of the Republic of China
Banjul, Republic of The Gambia
26, Radio Gambia Road
South Kanifing
Mailing Address:
P.O. Box 916, Banjul, The Gambia, West Africa
Phone: (+220) 374-046
Fax: (+220) 374-055
E-mail: rocemb@qanet.gm

Embassy of the Republic of China
Monrovia, Republic of Liberia
Tubman Blvd. Congo Town Monrovia, Libera
Mailing Address:
P.O. Box 5970, Monrovia, Liberia (West Africa)
Phone: (+231) 228-024
Fax: (+231) 228-025
E-mail: chineseemb.monrovia@libnet.net

Embassy of the Republic of China
Lilongwe, Republic of Malawi
Area 40, Plot No. 9
Capital City, Lilongwe, Malawi
Mailing Address:
P.O. Box 30221
Capital City, Lilongwe 3, Malawi
Phone: (+265) 783-611
Fax: (+265) 784-812
E-mail: rocemml@malawi.net

Embaixada da República da China
Sao Tome, República Democrática de
Sao Tome e Principe
Avenida 12 de Julho Sao Tome
República Democrática de
Sao Tome e Principe
Mailing Address:
Caixa Postal 839
República Democrática de Sao Tome e Principe
Phone: (+239-12) 23-529
Fax: (+239-12) 21-376
E-mail: rocstp@sol.stome.telepac.net

Ambassade de la République de Chine
en République du Senegal
30, Avenue Nelson Mandela
Dakar, Senegal
Mailing Address:
B.P. 4164, Dakar
République du Senegal
Phone: (+221) 8219-819
Fax: (+221) 8219-821
E-mail: embchine@sonatel.senet.net

Embassy of the Republic of China
Mbabane, Kingdom of Swaziland
Warner Street, Mbabane
Kingdom of Swaziland
Mailing Address:
P.O. Box 56, Mbabane
Kingdom of Swaziland
Phone: (+268) 404-4740
Fax: (+268) 404-6688
E-mail: chineseembassy@iafrica.sz

Europe

Embassy of the Republic of China
Vatican City, Holy See
Ambasciata Della Republica di Cina
Presso la Santa Sede
Piazza Delle Muse, 7
00197 Roma, Italia
Phone: (+39) 06808-3166
Fax: (+39) 06808-5679
E-mail: embroc@pelagus.it

Embassy of the Republic of China
Skopje, Rebuplic of Macedonia
Salvador Aljende 73, 91000 Skopje
Repbulic of Macedonia
Phone: (+389-91) 176-675
Fax: (+389-91) 133-554
E-mail: embroc@unet.com.mk

Central and South America

Embassy of the Republic of China
Belize City, Belize
3rd Floor, James Blade Building
Corner Huston/Eyre Street
Belize City, Belize
P.O. Box 1020, Belize City
Belize , C.A.
Phone: (+501) 278-744
Fax: (+501) 231-890
E-mail: embroc@btl.net

Embassy of the Republic of China
San José, Republic of Costa Rica
300 mts. al norte y 150 al este de la lglesia
Santa Teresita, Barrio Escalante
San José, Costa Rica, C.A.
Mailing Address:
Apartado 676-2010 Zapote, Costa Rica
Phone: (+506) 224-8180
Fax: (+506) 253-8333
E-mail: embajroc@sol.racsa.co.cr

Embassy of the Republic of China
Roseau, Commonwealth of Dominica
Check Hall/Massacre
Commonwealth of Dominica
Mailing Address:
P.O. Box 56, Roseau
Commonwealth of Dominica
West Indies
Phone: (+1-767) 449-1202
Fax: (+1-767) 449-2085
E-mail: rocemb@cwdom.dm

Embassy of the Republic of China
Santo Domingo, Dominican Republic
Edificio Palic-Primer Piso

No. 952 Ave. Abraham Lincoln, Esq. José
Amado Soler, Santo Domingo
República Dominicana
Mailing Address :
Apartado Postal 4797, Santo Domingo
República Dominicana
Phone: (+1-809) 562-5555
Fax: (+1-809) 563-4139
E-mail: e.china@codetel.net.do

Embassy of the Republic of China
San Salvador, Republic of El Salvador
Paseo General Escaloón No. 5333
Condominio Penthouse
7 Piso Colonia Escalón
San Salvador
República de El Salvador, C.A.
Mailing Address:
Apartado Postal (06) 956, San Salvador
El Salvador, C.A.
Phone: (+503) 263-1275
Fax: (+503) 263-1329
E-mail: sinoemb@es.com.sv

Embassy of the Republic of China
St. George's, Grenada
Archibald Avenue, St. George's
Grenada, West Indies
Mailing Address:
P.O. Box 36, St. George's
Grenada
West Indies
Phone: (+1-473) 440-3054
Fax: (+1-473) 440-4177
E-mail: rocemgnd@caribsurf.com

Embassy of the Republic of China
Guatemala City, Republic of Guatemala
4a. Avenida "A" 13-25
Zona 9, Guatemala City, Guatemala, C.A.
Mailing Address:
Apartado Postal 1646, Guatemala City
Guatemala, C.A.
Phone: (+502) 339-0711
Fax: (+502) 332-2668
E-mail: echina@intelnet.net.gt

Embassy of the Republic of China
Port-au-Prince, Republic of Haiti
10 Place Boyer, Petion-Ville, Haiti
Mailing Address:
P.O. Box 655, Port-au-Prince, Haiti
Phone: (+509) 257-5568
Fax: (+509) 257-9594

Embassy of the Republic of China
Tegucigalpa, Republic of Honduras
Colonia Lomas del Guijarro
Calle Eucaliptos No. 3750
Tegucigalpa, M.D.C., Honduras, C. A.
Mailing Address:
Apartado Postal 3433
Tegucigalpa, M.D.C., Honduras, C.A.
Phone: (+504) 231-1484
Fax: (+504) 232-7645
E-mail: embchina@david.intertel.hn

Consulate-General of the Republic of China
San Pedro Sula, Republic of Honduras
12 Ave. B, 11 y 12 Calle B
Col. Trejo, San Pedro Sula
Honduras
Mailing Address:
Apartado Postal 4298, San Pedro Sula
Republic of Honduras, C.A.
Phone: (+504) 556-8490
Fax: (+504) 556-5802
E-mail: consulchina@globalnet.hn

Embajada de la República de China
Managua, República de Nicaragua
Planes de Altamira, Lotes #19 y 20
Frente de la Cancha de Tenis, Managua 5
Nicaragua
Mailing Address:
Apartado Postal 4653, Managua 5
Nicaragua
Phone: (+505) 270-6054
Fax: (+505) 267-4025
E-mail: embchina@ibw.com.ni

Embassy of the Republic of China
Panama City, Republic of Panama
Edificio Torre Hong Bank

10 Piso, Ave. Samuel Lewis, Panama
Republic of Panama
Mailing Address:
Apartado 4285, Panama 5
Republic of Panama
Phone: (+507) 223-3424
Fax: (+507) 263-5534
E-mail: embchina@pan.gbm.net

**Consulate-General of the Republic of China
Colon, Republic of Panama**
Apartado 540, Calle 8
Ave. Roosevelt, Casa #10-084
Colón, Republic of Panama
Mailing Address:
Apartado No. 540, Colón
Republic of Panama
Phone: (+507) 441-3403
Fax: (+507) 441-3784
E-mail: congencn@sinfo.net

**Embassy of the Republic of China
Asunción, Republic of Paraguay**
Avenida Mcal. López 1133, Asunción, Paraguay
Mailing Address:
Casilla de Correos 503, Asunción, Paraguay
Phone: (+595-21) 213-362
Fax: (+595-21) 212-373
E-mail: emroc@highway.com.py

**Consulate-General of the Republic of China
Eastern City, Republic of Paraguay**
No. 1349 Avda. Mcal. Estigarribia
(Ave. Lago de la Republica), Ciudad del Este
Paraguay
Mailing Address:
Casilla Postal No. 131
Ciudad del Este, Paraguay
Phone: (+595-61) 500-329
Fax: (+595-61) 510-931
E-mail: cogechcde@fnn.net

**Embassy of the Republic of China
Basseterre, Saint Christopher and Nevis**
Taylor's Range, Basseterre
Saint Kitts, West Indies

Mailing Address:
P.O. Box 119, Basseterre
Saint Kitts, West Indies
Phone: (+1-869) 465-2421
Fax: (+1-869) 465-7921
E-mail: rocemb@caribsurf.com

**Embassy of the Republic of China
Kingstown, Saint Vincent and the Grenadines**
Murray's Road
Saint Vincent and the Grenadines
Mailing Address:
P.O. Box 878
Saint Vincent and the Grenadines, West Indies
Phone: (+1-784) 456-2431
Fax: (+1-784) 456-2913
E-mail: rocemsvg@caribsurf.com

ROC Representative Offices

Asia

**Taipei Economic and Cultural Office
in Brunei Darussalam**
No. 5, Simpang 1006
Jalan Tutong, B.S. Begawan
Brunei Darussalam
Mailing Address:
P.O. Box 2172, B.S. Begawan, BS8674
Brunei Darussalam
Phone: (+673-2) 652-113
Fax: (+673-2) 651-406
E-mail: twnrocbr@pso.brunet.bn

**Chung Hwa Travel Service
Hong Kong**
40th Floor, Lippo Tower, Lippo Centre
No. 89, Queensway, Hong Kong
Mailing Address:
G.P.O. Box 13485, Hong Kong
Phone: (+852) 2525-8315
Fax: (+852) 2810-0591
E-mail: rochkg@netvigator.com

**Taipei Economic and Cultural Center
in New Delhi**
3A Palam Marg, Vasant Vihar, New Delhi

India
Phone: (+91-11) 614-6881
Fax: (+91-11) 614-6880
E-mail: tecc@giasdl01.vsnl.net.in

**Taipei Economic and Trade Office
Jakarta, Indonesia**
7th Floor, Wisma Dharmala, Sakti
J1. Jend Sudirman No. 32, Jakarta 10220
Indonesia
Mailing Address:
P.O. Box 2922, Jakarta Pusat
Indonesia
Phone: (+62-21) 570-3047
Fax: (+62-21) 570-4052
E-mail: teto@uninet.net.id

**Taipei Economic and Cultural Representative
Office in Japan**
20-2, Shiroganedai 5-chome
Minato-Ku, Tokyo 108-0071
Japan
Phone: (+81-3) 3280-7811
Fax: (+81-3) 3280-7934
E-mail: teco-tky@www.roc-taiwan.or.jp

**Taipei Economic and Cultural Representative
Office in Japan, Yokohama Branch**
2nd Floor, Asahiseime Yokohama Building
No. 60, Nihonohdori, Nakaku, Yokohama
Japan
Phone: (+81-45) 641-7736
Fax: (+81-45) 641-6870
E-mail: teco-ykh@ma.kcom.ne.jp

**Taipei Economic and Cultural Office
in Osaka**
4th Floor, No. 4-8, Nichie Building
Dosabori, 1-chome, Nishi-Ku, Osaka
Japan
Phone: (+81-6) 443-8481
Fax: (+81-6) 443-8577
E-mail: teco-osa@ma.kcom.ne.jp

**Taipei Economic and Cultural Office in Osaka,
Fukuoka Branch**
12-42, Sakura-zaka, 3-chome, Chuo-ku

Fukuoka, Japan
Phone: (+81-92) 734-2810
Fax: (+81-92) 734-8219
E-mail: teco-fkk@ma.kcom.ne.jp

Taipei Mission in Korea
6th Floor, Kwanghwamoon Building
211 Sejong-ro, Chongro-Ku
Seoul, Korea 110-050
Phone: (+82-2) 399-2767
Fax: (+82-2) 730-1296
E-mail: tmik@taeback.kornet.nm.kr

Taipei Trade and Tourism Office, Macau
Edificio Comercial Central
15 Andar, Avenida Infante D. Henrique No. 60-64
Macau
Mailing Address:
P.O. Box 3072, Macau
Phone: (+853) 306-282
Fax: (+853) 306-153
E-mail: tpe@macau.ctm.net

**Taipei Economic and Cultural Office
in Malaysia**
9.01 Level 9, Amoda Building
22 Jalan Imbi, 55100 Kuala Lumpur
Malaysia
Phone: (+60-3) 242-5549
Fax: (+60-3) 242-3906
E-mail: teco@po.jaring.my

**Taipei Economic and Cultural Office
in the Philippines**
28th Floor, Pacific Star Building
Sen. Gil J. Puyat Avenue
Corner Makati Avenue
Makati, Metro Manila
Philippines
Mailing Address:
P.O. Box 1097
Makati Central Post Office
1250 Makati, Metro Manila
Philippines
Phone: (+63-2) 892-1381
Fax: (+63-2) 811-5165
E-mail: tecoph@usinc.net

**Taipei Representative Office
in Singapore**
460 Alexandra Road
#23-00, PSA Building
Singapore 119963
Mailing Address:
PSA Building Post Office, P.O. Box 381
Singapore 911143
Phone: (+65) 278-6511
Fax: (+65) 271-9107
E-mail: tperep@pacific.net.sg

**Taipei Economic and Trade Office
in Thailand**
10th Floor, Kian Gwan Building (1)
140 Witthayu Road, Bangkok
Thailand
Phone: (+66-2) 251-9393
Fax: (+66-2) 254-9276
E-mail: teto@infonews.co.th

**Taipei Economic and Cultural Office
Hanoi, Vietnam**
5th Floor, HITC, Km 8, Highway 32
Cau Giay, Hanoi, Vietnam
Mailing Address:
GPO Box 104, Hanoi, Vietnam
Phone: (+844) 833-5501
Fax: (+884) 833-5508
E-mail: tecohn@netnam.org.vn

**Taipei Economic and Cultural Office
Ho Chi Minh City, Vietnam**
117B Nguyen Dinh Chinh
Quan Phu Nhuan, TPHCM, Vietnam
Phone: (+848) 845-8651
Fax: (+848) 845-8649
E-mail: tecocon@hcm.fpt.vn

Oceania

Taipei Economic and Cultural Office, Australia
Unit 8, Tourism House, 40 Blackall Street
Barton, Canberra, ACT 2600, Australia
Phone: (+61-2) 6273-3344
Fax: (+61-2) 6273-3228
E-mail: oftpecbr@dynamite.com.au

**Taipei Economic and Cultural Office
Melbourne, Australia**
Level 38, 120 Collins Street
Melbourne, VIC 3000, Australia
Phone: (+61-3) 9650-8611
Fax: (+61-3) 9650-8711
E-mail: tecom@sprint.com.au

**Taipei Economic and Cultural Office
Sydney, Australia**
Suite 1902, Level 19, M.L.C. Center, King Street
Sydney, N.S.W. 2000, Australia
Phone: (+61-2) 9223-3207
Fax: (+61-2) 9223-0086
E-mail: syteco@magna.com.au

**Trade Mission of the Republic of China
Suva, Republic of Fiji**
6th Floor, Pacific House, Butt Streets, Suva
Republic of Fiji
Mailing Address:
G.P.O. Box 53, Suva
Republic of Fiji
Phone: (+679) 315-922
Fax: (+679) 301-890
E-mail: tmroc@is.com.fj

**Taipei Economic and Cultural Office
New Zealand**
21st Floor, 105 The Terrace, Wellington
New Zealand
Mailing Address:
P.O. Box 10250, The Terrace, Wellington
New Zealand
Phone: (+64-4) 473-6474
Fax: (+64-4) 499-1458
E-mail: tecowlg@actrix.gen.nz

**Taipei Economic and Cultural Office
Auckland, New Zealand**
11th Floor, Norwich Union House
Cnr. Queen and Durham Streets
Auckland, New Zealand
Mailing Address:
C.P.O. Box 4018, Auckland
New Zealand

Phone: (+649) 303-3903
Fax: (+649) 302-3399
E-mail: tecoakl@pcnet.co.nz

Trade Mission of the Republic of China (on Taiwan)
Port Moresby, Papua New Guinea
6th Floor, Defense Haus, Hunter Street
Port Moresby, Papua New Guinea
Mailing Address:
P.O. Box 334, Port Moresby, Papua New Guinea
Phone: (+675) 321-2922
Fax: (+675) 321-3510
E-mail: taiwantramis@datec.com.pg

West Asia

Trade Mission of the Republic of China
Manama, State of Bahrain
Flat 1, Abulfatih Building, Bldg.172
Block 319, Road 1906
Manama Town 319, Al Hoora Area
State of Bahrain
Mailing Address:
P.O. Box 5806, Manama
State of Bahrain
Phone: (+973) 292-578
Fax: (+973) 293-852
E-mail: tmorocb1@batelco.com.bh

Taipei Economic and Cultural Office in
Tel-Aviv, Israel
270 Hayarkon Street, Tel-Aviv 63504, Israel
Mailing Address:
P.O. Box 6115, Tel-Aviv 61060, Israel
Phone: (+972-3) 544-0250
Fax: (+972-3) 544-0249
E-mail: tpeeco@inter.net.il

Commercial Office of the Republic of China
(Taiwan), Jordan
Mailing Address:
P.O. Box 2023, Amman 11181, Jordan
Phone: (+962-6) 593-1530
Fax: (+962-6) 593-2607
E-mail: kanda186@go.com.jo

Taipei Commercial Representative Office
in the State of Kuwait
House No. 18, Block 6, Street No. 111
Al-Jabriah, State of Kuwait
Mailing Address:
P.O. Box 732-32008
Hawalli, Kuwait
Phone: (+965) 533-9988
Fax: (+965) 533-3497
E-mail: tseng@qualitynet.net

Taipei Economic and Cultural Office
Muscat, Oman
Mailing Address:
P.O. Box 1536 Ruwi
Postal Code 112, Muscat
The Sultanate of Oman
Phone: (+968) 605-695
Fax: (+968) 605-402
E-mail: taipei@omantel.net.om

Taipei Economic and Cultural Representative
Office in the Kingdom of Saudi Arabia
Diplomatic Quarter, Riyadh, Saudi Arabia
Mailing Address:
P.O. Box 94393, Riyadh 11693, Saudi Arabia
Phone: (+966-1) 488-1900
Fax: (+966-1) 488-1716
E-mail: tecroksa@shabakah.net.sa

Taipei Economic and Cultural Representative
Office in the Kingdom of Saudi Arabia,
Jeddah Office
Mailing Address:
P.O. Box 1114, Jeddah 21431, Saudi Arabia
Phone: (+966-2) 660-2264
Fax: (+966-2) 667-5843
E-mail: tecro@naseej.com.sa

Taipei Economic and Cultural Mission
in Ankara, Turkey
Resit Galip Cad. No. 97
Gaziosmanpasa, Ankara, Turkey
Phone: (+90-312) 436-7255
Fax: (+90-312) 437-6013
E-mail: chnkeng@domi.net.tr

Commercial Office of the Republic of China
to Dubai, United Arab Emirates
Al Nakheel Building
Office No. 109, Plot No. 273
at Al Hamriyah, Dubai, U. A. E.
Mailing Address:
P.O. Box 3059, Dubai, U. A. E.
Phone: (+971-4) 358-177
Fax: (+971-4) 358-180
E-mail: corocdxb@emirates.net.ae

Africa

**Delegation Especial da República da China
Luanda, República de Angola**
Rua Comandante Stona
No. 85/87, Alvalade, Luanda
República de Angola
Mailing Address:
Caixa Postal 6051, Luanda
República de Angola
Phone: (+244-2) 398-127
Fax: (+244-2) 322-299
E-mail: ago@netangola.com

**Délégation Spéciale de la République de Chine
Antananarivo, République de Madagascar**
Villa Bakory VIII,
Lot Pres VR61 B Ambohidraserika
Ambohimiandra-Antananarivo
Madagascar
Mailing Address:
B.P. 3117, Antananarivo 101, Madagascar
Phone: (+261-20) 223-4838
Fax: (+261-20) 222-8971
E-mail: sdroc@bow.dts.mg

**Trade Mission of the Republic of China
Port Louis, Mauritius**
Rm. 706, St. James Court, Rue St. Denis
Port Louis, Mauritius
Mailing Address:
P.O. Box 695, Bell Village, Port Louis
Mauritius
Phone: (+230) 212-8534
Fax: (+230) 212-4587
E-mail: tmroc@bow.intnet.mu

**The Trade Mission of the ROC (TAIWAN)
Lagos, Federal Republic of Nigeria**
292E, Ajose Adeogun Street
Victoria Island Annex, Lagos, Nigeria
Mailing Address:
P.O. Box 80035, Victoria Island, Lagos
Nigeria
Phone: (+234-1) 261-6350
Fax: (+234-1) 261-8194
E-mail: roctm@alpha.linkserve.com

**Taipei Liaison Office in the Republic of
South Africa**
1147 Schoeman Street, Haifield, Pretoria 0083
Republic of South Africa
Mailing Address:
P.O. Box 649, Pretoria 0001
Republic of South Africa
Phone: (+27-12) 436-071
Fax: (+27-12) 435-816
E-mail: embroc@icon.co.za

Taipei Liaison Office in Cape Town
1004, 10th Floor, Main Tower
Standard Bank Center, Foreshore, Cape Town
Republic of South Africa
Mailing Address:
P.O. Box 1122, Cape Town 8000
Republic of South Africa
Phone: (+27-21) 418-1188
Fax: (+27-21) 253-022
E-mail: taiwan@iafrica.com

Taipei Liaison Office in Johannesburg
10th Floor, Safren House, 19 Ameshoff Street
Braamfontein, Johannesburg 2001
Republic of South Africa
Phone: (+27-11) 403-3281
Fax: (+27-11) 403-1679
E-mail: roccon@icon.co.za

Europe

**Taipei Economic and Cultural Office
Institute of Chinese Culture
Vienna, Austria**
Praterstr. 31/15 OG, A-1020 Wien, Austria

Phone: (+43-1) 212-4720
Fax: (+43-1) 212-4703
E-mail: tecovie@atnet.at

**Taipei Economic and Trade Mission
in Minsk, Belarus**
Mailing Address:
P.O. Box 149
220030 Minsk
Republic of Belarus
Phone: (+375-17) 223-9289
Fax: (+375-17) 210-5676
E-mail: taiwanmsq@europe.com

**Taipei Representative Office
in Belgium**
Avenue des Arts 41, 1040 Bruxelles
Belgium
Phone: (+32-2) 511-0687
Fax: (+32-2) 511-1789
E-mail: roc.bxl@pophost.eunet.be

**Taipei Economic and Cultural Office
Prague, Czech Republic**
Revolucní 13, 7P, 110 00, Praha I
Czech Republic
Phone: (+42-2) 2480-3257
Fax: (+42-2) 2480-3277
E-mail: tecoprag@mbox.vol.cz

**Taipei Representative Office
in Denmark**
Amaliegade 3, 2F
1256 Copenhagen K
Denmark
Phone: (+45) 3393-5152
Fax: (+45) 3393-2235
E-mail: trodnk@teliamail.dk

**Taipei Economic and Cultural Office
Helsinki, Finland**
Aleksanterinkatu 17, 4th Floor
00100, Helsinki, Finland
Phone: (+358-9) 6969-2420
Fax: (+358-9) 6969-2421
E-mail: taipei.economic@wtc.fi

**Bureau de Représentation de Taipei
en France**
78 rue de l'Université, 75007 Paris
France
Phone: (+33-1) 4439-8820
Fax: (+33-1) 4439-8871
E-mail: taipiao.brtf@magic.fr

**Taipeh Vertretung in der Bundesrepublik
Deutschland, Büro Berlin**
Markgrafen Strasse 35, 10117 Berlin
Federal Republic of Germany
Phone: (+49-30) 2036-1120
Fax: (+49-30) 2036-1101
E-mail: taipeiwk@t-online.de

**Taipeh Vertretung in der Bundesrepublik
Deutschland, Büro Hamburg**
Mittelweg 144, 20148 Hamburg
Federal Republic of Germany
Phone: (+49-40) 447-788
Fax: (+49-40) 447-187
E-mail: 106266.1666@compuserve.com

**Taipeh Vertretung in der Bundesrepublik
Deutschland, Büro München**
Tengstrasse 38/2. Stock
80796 München
Federal Republic of Germany
Phone: (+49-89) 271-6061
Fax: (+49-89) 273-1121
E-mail: 106224.1257@compuserve.com

**Taipei Economic and Cultural Office
Athens, Greece**
57 Marathonodromon Avenue
154 52 Psychico, Athens
Greece
Phone: (+30-1) 677-6750
Fax: (+30-1) 677-6708
E-mail: 777teco@otenet.gr

**Taipei Representative Office
Budapest, Hungary**
Rakóczi út 1-3/III em., 1088 Budapest
Hungary
Phone: (+36-1) 266-2884

Fax: (+36-1) 266-4003
E-mail: taipeiro@mail.elender.hu

**Taipei Representative Office
in Ireland**
8, Lower Hatch Street
Dublin 2, Ireland
Phone: (+353-1) 678-5413
Fax: (+353-1) 676-1686
E-mail: tpeire@indigo.ie

**Ufficio Di Rappresentanza di Taipei
in Italia**
Via Panama 22 PI, Int. 3
00198 Roma, Italia
Phone: (+39-6) 884-1362
Fax: (+39-6) 884-5772
E-mail: c.hsieh@flashnet.it

Taipei Mission in the Republic of Latvia
Room 602, World Trade Center
2 Elizabets Street, LV-1340, Riga
Latvia
Phone: (+371) 732-1166
Fax: (+371) 783-0125
E-mail: tmil@mail.bkc.lv

**Taipei Economic and Cultural Office
Luxembourg**
50, route d'Esch, Luxembourg-Ville,
L-1470 Grand-Duché de Luxembourg
Phone: (+352) 444-772/4
Fax: (+352) 250-485

**Taipei Representative Office
in the Netherlands**
Javastraat 46-48
2585 AR, The Hague
The Netherlands
Phone: (+31-70) 346-9438
Fax: (+31-70) 360-3836
E-mail: tperep@wxs.nl

**Taipei Economic and Cultural Office
Oslo, Norway**
P.O. Box 2643 Solli
Riddervolds gate 3, 0203 Oslo

Norway
Phone: (+47) 2255-5471
Fax: (+47) 2256-2531
E-mail: twteco@online.no

**Taipei Economic and Cultural Office in
Warsaw, Poland**
4th Floor, Koszykowa Street 54
00-675 Warszawa, Poland
Mailing Address:
P.O. Box 51, ul. Senatorska 40
Urzad Pocztowo-Telekomunikacyjny
Warszawa 84, Poland
Phone: (+48-22) 630-8438
Fax: (+48-22) 630-8431
E-mail: taiwan@polbox.pl

**Centro Economico e Cultural de Taipei
Lisbon, Portugal**
Rua Castilho N 14 6, 1250 Lisbon, Portugal
Phone: (+351-1) 315-1279
Fax: (+351-1) 315-1288
E-mail: tecc.lisboa@ip.pt

**Representative Office in Moscow for
the Taipei-Moscow Economic and Cultural
Coordination Commission**
3rd Floor, 24/2 Tverskaya Street, Korpus 1
Gate 4, Moscow 103050
Russian Federation
Phone: (+7-095) 956-3786
Fax: (+7-095) 956-3625
E-mail: anhwei@aha.ru

**Oficina Económica y Cultural de Taipei
Madrid, España**
C/Rosario Pino 14-16
18 Dcha., 28020 Madrid, Spain
Mailing Address:
Apartado 36016, 28080 Madrid, Spain
Phone: (+34) 91571-4729
Fax: (+34) 91570-9285
E-mail: ofitaipei@mad.servicom.es

Taipei Mission in Sweden
Wenner-Gren Center, 18tr., Sveavägen 166
S-113 46 Stockholm, Sweden

Phone: (+46-8) 728-8513
Fax: (+46-8) 315-748
E-mail: taipei.mission@tmis.se

**Délégation Culturelle et Economique de
Taïpei, Berne, Suisse**
Monbijoustrasse 30, 3011 Berne, Suisse
Phone: (+41-31) 382-2927
Fax: (+41-31) 382-1523 ·
E-mail: taipei.delegation@spectraweb.ch

**Délégation Culturelle et Economique de
Taïpei, Bureau de Geneve**
56 Rue de Moillebeau
1209 Geneve, Suisse
Phone: (+41-22) 919-7070
Fax: (+41-22) 919-7077
E-mail: tpe-gva@iprolink.ch

Taipei Representative Office in the UK
50 Grosvenor Gardens, London SW1W OEB
United Kingdom
Phone: (+44-171) 396-9152
Fax: (+44-171) 396-9145
E-mail: tro@netcomuk.co.uk

**Taipei Representative Office in the UK
Edinburgh Office**
1 Melville Street
Edinburgh EH3 7PE
United Kingdom
Phone: (+44-131) 220-6886
Fax: (+44-131) 226-6884
E-mail: troed@dial.pipex.com

North America

Taipei Economic and Cultural Office, Canada
Suite 1960, World Exchange Plaza
45 O'Connor Street, Ottawa, Ontario K1P 1A4
Canada
Phone: (+1-613) 231-5080
Fax: (+1-613) 231-7112
E-mail: teco@magi.com

Taipei Economic and Cultural Office, Toronto
151 Yonge Street, Suite 1202, Toronto

Ontario M5C 2W7, Canada
Phone: (+1-416) 369-9030
Fax: (+1-416) 369-0548
E-mail: tecotron@pathcom.com

**Taipei Economic and Cultural Office,
Vancouver**
2008, Cathedral Place, 925 West Georgia Street
Vancouver, B.C. V6C 3L2, Canada
Phone: (+1-604) 689-4111
Fax: (+1-604) 689-0101
E-mail: tecovan@uniserve.com

**Taipei Economic and Cultural Representative
Office in the United States**
4201 Wisconsin Avenue, NW
Washington, DC 20016-2137, U.S.A.
Phone: (+1-202) 895-1800 (20 lines)
Fax: (+1-202) 363-0999
E-mail: tecrotcd@erols.com

Taipei Economic and Cultural Office in Atlanta
Suite 1290, Two Midtown Plaza
1349 West Peachtree Street, NE
Atlanta, Georgia 30309, U.S.A.
Phone: (+1-404) 872-0123
Fax: (+1-404) 873-3474
E-mail: tecoatl@mindspring.com

Taipei Economic and Cultural Office in Boston
99 Summer Street, Suite 801
Boston, MA 02110, U.S.A.
Mailing Address:
P.O. Box 120529, Boston, MA 02110
U.S.A.
Phone: (+1-617) 737-2050
Fax: (+1-617) 737-1684
E-mail: teco@epartner.com

**Taipei Economic and Cultural Office
in Chicago**
Two Prudential Plaza, 57th & 58th Floor
180 N. Stetson Avenue, Chicago, Illinois 60601
U.S.A.
Phone: (+1-312) 616-0100
Fax: (+1-312) 616-1490
E-mail: tecochg@allways.net

Taipei Economic and Cultural Office in Guam
Suite 505, Bank of Guam Building
111 Chalan Santo Papa Road
Hagatna, Guam 96932, U.S.A.
Mailing Address:
P.O. Box 3416, Hagatna, Guam 96932, U.S.A.
Phone: (+671) 472-5865
Fax: (+671) 472-5869
E-mail: tecogm@ite.net

Taipei Economic and Cultural Office in Honolulu
2746 Pali Highway
Honolulu, Hawaii 96817
U.S.A.
Phone: (+1-808) 595-6347
Fax: (+1-808) 595-6542
E-mail: tecohnl@aloha.net

Taipei Economic and Cultural Office in Houston
11 Greenway Plaza, Suite 2006
Houston, Texas 77046, U.S.A.
Phone: (+1-713) 626-7445
Fax: (+1-713) 626-1202
E-mail: tecohou@sprynet.com

Taipei Economic and Cultural Office in Kansas City, Missouri
3100 Broadway, Suite 800
Kansas City, MO 64111, U.S.A.
Mailing Address:
P.O. Box 413617
Kansas City, MO 64141
U.S.A.
Phone: (+1-816) 531-1298
Fax: (+1-816) 531-3066
E-mail: kcteco@primenet.com

Taipei Economic and Cultural Office in Los Angeles
3731 Wilshire Boulevard, Suite 700
Los Angeles, CA 90010, U.S.A.
Phone: (+1-213) 389-1215
Fax: (+1-213) 389-1676
E-mail: lateco2@pacbell.net

Taipei Economic and Cultural Office in Miami
2333 Ponce de Leon Boulevard, Suite 610
Coral Gables, Florida 33134, U.S.A.
Phone: (+1-305) 443-8917
Fax: (+1-305) 444-4796
E-mail: tecomia@icanect.net

Taipei Economic and Cultural Office in New York
885 Second Avenue, 47th Floor
New York, NY 10017, U.S.A.
Phone: (+1-212) 317-7300
Fax: (+1-212) 754-1549
E-mail: tecony@abcst.com

Taipei Economic and Cultural Office in San Francisco
555 Montgomery Street, Suite 501
San Francisco, CA 94111, U.S.A.
Phone: (+1-415) 362-7680
Fax: (+1-415) 362-5382
E-mail: tecosf@amer.net

Taipei Economic and Cultural Office in Seattle
Westin Building, Suite 2410
2001 Sixth Avenue, Seattle, WA 98121, U.S.A.
Phone: (+1-206) 441-4586
Fax: (+1-206) 441-4320
E-mail: teco@aa.net

Central and South America

Oficina Comercial y Cultural de Taipei en la República Argentina
Av. de Mayo 654, piso 4, 1084 Capital Federal
Buenos Aires, Argentina
Mailing Address:
Casilla de Correos No. 196
1041 Capital Federal, Buenos Aires, Argentina
Phone: (+54-1) 334-0653
Fax: (+54-1) 334-5581
E-mail: taipei@impsatl.com.ar

Oficina Comercial-Consular de la República de China, La Paz, Bolivia
Calacoto, Calle 12, No. 7978, La Paz

República de Bolivia
Mailing Address:
Casilla No. 13680, La Paz
Bolivia
Phone: (+591-2) 797-307
Fax: (+591-2) 797-303
E-mail: oconstwn@caoba.entelnet.bo

**Escritório Econômico e Cultural de Taipei
Brasil**
SNIS QI 09, Conjunto 16, Casa 23
CEP 71625-160, Brasilia, DF
Brasil
Phone: (+55-61) 364-0221
Fax: (+55-61) 364-0234
E-mail: eect@brnet.com.br

**Escritório Econômico e Cultural de Taipei
Rio de Janeiro, Brasil**
Rua Voluntârios da Pátria
45 Sala 405 CEP, 22270-000
Rio de Janeiro-RJ
Brasil
Mailing Address:
P.O. Box 9200, Rua Sao Clemente 24 Loja B
CEP 22260-000-Rio de Janeiro-RJ, Brasil
Phone: (+55-21) 286-0039
Fax: (+55-21) 537-1031
E-mail: taipeirj@prolink.com.br

**Escritório Econômico e Cultural de Taipei
São Paulo, Brasil**
Av. Paulista, 2073-Ed. Horsa II
Conj. 1203 e 1204-12 Andar
01311-940-São Paulo, SP
Brasil
Phone: (+55-11) 285-6194
Fax: (+55-11) 287-9057
E-mail: mofasp@intercall.com.br

**Oficina Económica y Cultural de Taipei
Santiago, República de Chile**
Burgos 345, Las Condes, Santiago, Chile
Mailing Address:
Casilla 175-Santiago 34, Santiago
Chile

Phone: (+56-2) 228-2919, 228-3185
Fax: (+56-2) 206-3635
E-mail: rocoect@netline.cl

**Oficina Comercial de Taipei
Bogotá, D.E., República de Colombia**
Carrera 7, No. 79-75, Of. 501
Santafe de Bogotá D.C., Colombia, S.A.
Mailing Address:
Apartado Aéreo No. 51620 (Chapinero)
Santafe de Bogotá, D.C., Colombia, S.A.
Phone: (+57-1) 235-4713
Fax: (+57-1) 314-5237
E-mail: oftaipei@impsat.net.co

**Oficina Comercial de la República de China
Quito, Ecuador**
Av. República de El Salvador 733 y
Portugal, 2do. Piso, Quito, Ecuador
Mailing Address:
Casilla P.O. Box 7-17-1788, Quito
Ecuador
Phone: (+593-2) 242-829
Fax: (+593-2) 461-883
E-mail: keting@uio.satnet.net

**Oficina Económica y Cultural de Taipei en
México**
Paseo de la Reforma 1945
Col. Lomas de Chapultepec
CP 11000, México D.F.
México
Phone: (+525) 596-1412
Fax: (+525) 251-0960
E-mail: tpeecomex@compuserve.com.mx

**Oficina Económica y Cultural de Taipei
Lima, República del Perú**
Av. Benavides No. 1780
Miraflores, Lima 18
Perú
Mailing Address:
Casilla: 18-1052, Lima 18, Perú
Phone: (+51-1) 242-1817
Fax: (+51-1) 447-9576
E-mail: oftaipe@amauta.rcp.net.pe

Oficina Económica de Taipei
República Oriental del Uruguay
Echevarriarza 3478, Montevideo
Uruguay
Mailing Address:
Casilla de Correo No. 16042
Distrito 6 C.P. 11600, Montevideo, Uruguay
Phone: (+598-2) 622-0801
Fax: (+598-2) 628-0263
E-mail: oetroc@adinet.com.uy

Oficina Económica y Cultural de Taipei
Caracas, República de Venezuela
Avenida Francisco de Miranda
Torre Delta, Piso 4, Altamira, Caracas, Venezuela
Mailing Address:
Apartado 68717, Altamira 1062-A, Caracas
Venezuela
Phone: (+58-2) 265-2184
Fax: (+58-2) 264-1163
E-mail: oect@ccs.internet.ve

Appendix V
Directory of Foreign Embassies and Representatives in the ROC

Foreign Embassies in the ROC

Embassy of Beliez
11th Floor, 9 Lane 62, Tienmou West Road
Tienmou, Taipei 111
Phone: (+886-2)
Fax: (+886-2)

Embassy of Burkina Faso
6th Floor, 9-1 Lane 62, Tienmou West Road
Tienmou, Taipei 111
Phone: (+886-2) 2873-3096
Fax: (+886-2) 2873-3071

Embassy of the Republic of Chad
8th Floor, 9-1 Lane 62, Tienmou West Road
Tienmou, Taipie 111
Phone: (+886-2) 2874-2943
Fax: (+886-2) 2874-2971

Embassy of the Republic of Costa Rica
5th Floor, 9-1 Lane 62, Tienmou West Road
Tienmou, Taipei 111
Phone: (+886-2) 2875-2964
Fax: (+886-2) 2875-3151

Embassy of the Dominican Republic
6th Floor, 9 Lane 62, Tienmou West Road
Tienmou, Taipei 111
Phone: (+886-2) 2875-1357
Fax: (+886-2) 2875-2661

Embassy of the Republic of El Salvador
15 Lane 34, Ku Kung Road
Taipei 111
Phone: (+886-2) 2881-7995
Fax: (+886-2) 2881-9887

Embassy of the Republic of the Gambia
9th Floor, 9-1 Lane 62, Tienmou West Road
Tienmou, Taipei 111
Phone:(+886-2) 2875-3911
Fax:(+886-2) 2875-2775

Embassy of the Republic of Guatemala
2nd Floor, 334 Shihpai Road, Section 2
Taipei 112
Phone: (+886-2) 2785-6952
Fax: (+886-2) 2784-0699

Embassy of the Republic of Haiti
8th Floor, 9-1 Lane 62, Tienmou West Road
Tienmou, Taipei 111
Phone: (+886-2) 2876-6718
Fax: (+886-2) 2876-6719

Embassy of the Holy See (Apostolic Nunciature)
87 Ai Kuo East Road, Taipei 106
Phone: (+886-2) 2321-6847
Fax: (+886-2) 2391-1926

Embassy of the Republic of Honduras
9th Floor, 9 Lane 62, Tienmou West Road
Tienmou, Taipei 111
Phone: (+886-2) 2875-5507
Fax: (+886-2) 2875-5726

Embassy of the Republic of Liberia
11th Floor, 9-1 Lane 62, Tienmou West Road
Tienmou, Taipei 111
Phone: (+886-2) 2875-1212
Fax: (+886-2) 2875-1313

Embassy of the Republic of Macedonia
5th Floor, 9 Lane 62, Tienmou West Road
Tienmou, Taipei 111
Phone: (+886-2) 2876-0189
Fax: (+886-2) 2872-9254

Embassy of the Republic of Marshall Islands
4th Floor, 9-1 Lane 62, Tienmou West Road
Tienmou, Taipei 111
Phone: (+886-2) 2873-4884
Fax: (+886-2) 2875-4914

Embassy of the Republic of Nicaragua
3rd Floor, 9 Lane 62, Tienmou West Road

Teinmou, Taipei 111
Phone: (+886-2) 2784-9034
Fax: (+886-2) 2784-9080

Embassy of the Republic of Panama
6th Floor, 111 Sungkiang Road, Taipei 104
Phone: (+886-2) 2509-9189
Fax: (+886-2) 2509-9801

Embassy of the Republic of Paraguay
7th Floor, 9-1 Lane 62, Tienmou West Road
Tienmou, Taipei 111
Phone: (+886-2) 2873-6310
Fax: (+886-2) 2873-6312

Embassy of the Republic of Senegal
10th Floor, 9-1 Lane 62, Tienmou West Road
Tienmou, Taipei 111
Phone: (+886-2) 2876-6519
Fax: (+886-2) 2873-4909

Embassy of Kingdom of Swaziland
10th Floor, 9 Lane 62, Tienmou West Road
Tienmou, Taipei 111
Phone: (+886-2)
Fax: (+886-2)

Foreign Representatives in the ROC

American Institute in Taiwan, Taipei Office
7 Lane 134, Hsin Yi Road, Section 3, Taipei 104
Phone: (+886-2) 2709-2000
Fax: (+886-2) 2702-7675

American Institute in Taiwan, Kaohsiung Office
3rd Floor, 2 Chung Cheng Third Road
Kaohsiung 800
Phone: (+886-7) 224-0154
Fax: (+886-7) 223-8237

Argentina Trade and Cultural Office
Room 1003, 333 Keelung Road, Section 1
Taipei 110

Phone: (+886-2) 2757-6556
Fax: (+886-2) 2757-6445

Australian Commerce and Industry Office
Room 2608, 333 Keelung Road, Section 1
Taipei 110
Phone: (+886-2) 2720-2833
Fax: (+886-2) 2757-6074

Austrian Trade Delegation
Suite 608, Bank Tower, 205 Tun Hua North Road
Taipei 105
Phone: (+886-2) 2715-5220
Fax: (+886-2) 2717-3242

Austrian Tourism Delegation
5th Floor, 164 Fu Hsing North Road, Taipei 104
Phone: (+886-2) 2712-8598
Fax: (+886-2) 2514-9980

Belgian Trade Association, Taipei
Suite 901, World Wide House
131 Min Sheng East Road, Section 3, Taipei 105
Phone: (+886-2) 2715-1215
Fax: (+886-2) 2712-6258

Bolivian Commercial and Financial Representation
Room 7E-13, 5 Hsin Yi Road, Section 5
Taipei 110
Phone: (+886-2) 2723-8721
Fax: (+886-2) 2723-8764

Brazil Business Center
5th Floor, 197 Chung Shan North Road
Section 6, Tienmou, Taipei 111
Phone: (+886-2) 2835-7388
Fax: (+886-2) 2835-7121

British Trade and Cultural Office
9th Floor, 99 Jen Ai Road, Section 2 , Taipei 100
Phone: (+886-2) 2322-4242
Fax: (+886-2) 2393-1985

Canadian Trade Office in Taipei
13th Floor, 365 Fu Hsin North Road, Taipei 105

Phone: (+886-2) 2547-9500
Fax: (+886-2) 2712-7244

Chilean Trade Office, Taipei
Room 7B-07, 5 Hsin Yi Road, Section 5
Taipei 110
Phone: (+886-2) 2723-0329
Fax: (+886-2) 2723-0318

Colombian Trade Office
Room 1005, 333 Keelung Road, Section 1
Taipei 110
Phone: (+886-2) 2757-6055
Fax: (+886-2) 2757-6304

Czech Economic and Cultural Office
8th Floor-3, 51 Keelung Road, Section 2
Taipei 110
Phone: (+886-2) 2738-9768
Fax: (+886-2) 2733-3944

Danish Trade Organizations, Taipei Office
Room 1207, 12th Floor, 205 Tun Hua North Road
Taipei 105
Phone: (+886-2) 2718-2101
Fax: (+886-2) 2718-2141

Fiji Trade and Tourism Representative Office in ROC
Room 3212, 333 Keelung Road, Section 1
Taipei 110
Phone: (+886-2) 2757-9596
Fax: (+886-2) 2757-9597

Finland Trade Center
Room 7E-04, 5 Hsin Yi Road, Section 5
Taipei 110
Phone: (+886-2) 2722-0764
Fax: (+886-2) 2725-1517

French Institute in Taipei
Room 1003, 10th Floor, 205 Tun Hua North Road
Taipei 105
Phone: (+886-2) 2545-6061
Fax: (+886-2) 2718-4571

German Cultural Centre
11th Floor, 24 Hsin Hai Road, Section 1
Taipei 100
Phone: (+886-2) 2365-7294
Fax: (+886-2) 2368-7542

German Trade Office, Taipei
4th Floor, 4 Min Sheng East Road, Section 3
Taipei 104
Phone: (+886-2) 2501-6188
Fax: (+886-2) 2501-6139

Office of Representative A.H. Hellenic Organization for the Promotion of Exports (Greece)
6th Floor-2, 125 Roosevelt Road, Section 3
Taipei 106
Phone: (+886-2) 2363-5597
Fax: (+886-2) 2362-6140

Hungarian Trade Office
2nd Floor, 3 Chung Cheng Road, Section 2
Taipei 111
Phone: (+886-2) 2834-3701
Fax: (+886-2) 2837-7151

India-Taipei Association
Room 2010, 333 Keelung Road, Section 1, Taipei 110
Phone: (+886-2) 2757-6112
Fax: (+886-2) 2757-6117

Indonesian Economic and Trade Office to Taipei
16th Floor, 49 Min Sheng East Road, Section 3
Taipei 104
Phone: (+886-2) 2516-9050
Fax: (+886-2) 2516-9056

The Institute for Trade and Investment of Ireland
Room 7B-09, 5 Hsin Yi Road, Section 5
Taipei 110
Phone: (+886-2) 2725-1691
Fax: (+886-2) 2725-1653

Israel Economic and Cultural Office
Room 2408, 333 Keelung Road, Section 1

Taipei 110
Phone: (+886-2) 2757-9692
Fax: (+886-2) 2757-7247

**Italian Economic, Trade and Cultural
Promotion Office**
Room 1808, 333 Keelung Road, Section 1
Taipei 110
Phone: (+886-2) 2345-0320
Fax: (+886-2) 2757-6260

Interchange Association (Japan), Taipei Office
10th Floor, 245 Tun Hua South Road, Section 1
Taipei 106
Phone: (+886-2) 2741-2116
Fax: (+886-2) 2731-1757

**Interchange Association (Japan),
Kaohsiung Office**
4th Floor, 174 San To First Road, Kaohsiung 802
Phone: (+886-7) 771-4008
Fax: (+886-7) 771-2734

The Jordanian Commercial Office
1st Floor, 110 Chung Cheng Road, Section 2
Taipei 111
Phone: (+886-2) 2871-7712
Fax: (+886-2) 2872-1176

Korean Mission in Taipei
Room 1506, 333 Keelung Road, Section 1
Taipei 110
Phone: (+886-2) 2758-8320
Fax: (+886-2) 2757-7006

**Malaysian Friendship and Trade Centre
Taipei**
8th Floor, 102 Tun Hua North Road, Taipei 105
Phone: (+886-2) 2713-2626
Fax: (+886-2) 2514-9864

Manila Economic and Cultural Office
4th Floor, 107 Chung Hsiao East Road, Section 4
Taipei 106
Phone: (+886-2) 2778-6511
Fax: (+886-2) 2778-4969

**Manila Economic and Cultural Office
Extension Office in Kaohsiung**
2nd Floor, 146 Ssu Wei Second Road
Kaohsiung 802
Phone: (+886-7) 331-7752
Fax: (+886-7) 331-7806

**Manila Economic and Cultural Office
Extension Office in Taichung**
2nd Floor, 476 Chung Cheng Road, Taichung 403
Phone: (+882-4) 205-1306
Fax: (+882-4) 205-1317

Mexican Trade Services
Room 2905, 333 Keelung Road, Section 1
Taipei 110
Phone: (+886-2) 2757-6526
Fax: (+886-2) 2757-6180

**Moscow-Taipei Economic and
Cultural Coordination Commission in Taipei**
10th Floor, 2 Hsin Yi Road, Section 5
Taipei 110
Phone: (+886-2) 8780-3011
Fax: (+886-2) 8780-2511

Netherlands Trade and Investment Office
Room B, 5th Floor, 133 Min Sheng East Road
Section 3, Taipei 104
Phone: (+886-2) 2713-5760
Fax: (+886-2) 2713-0194

New Zealand Commerce and Industry Office
Room 2501, 333 Keelung Road, Section 1
Taipei 110
Phone: (+886-2) 2757-6725
Fax: (+886-2) 2757-6973

Nigeria Trade Office in Taiwan, R.O.C.
Room 1706, 333 Keelung Road, Section 1
Taipei 110
Phone: (+886-2) 2757-6987
Fax: (+886-2) 2757-7111

Norwegian Trade Council
8th Floor, 101 Nanking East Road, Section 2
Taipei 104

Phone: (+886-2) 2543-5484
Fax: (+886-2) 2581-1878

The Sultanate of Oman Commercial Office, Taipei
Room 7G-05, 5 Hsin Yi Road, Section 5
Taipei 110
Phone: (+886-2) 2722-0684
Fax: (+886-2) 2722-0645

Commercial Office of Peru in Taipei
Room 2411, 333 Keelung Road, Section 1
Taipei 110
Phone: (+886-2) 2757-7017
Fax: (+886-2) 2757-6480

Saudi Arabian Trade Office
6 Lane 105, Yang Te Boulevard, Section 3
Taipei 111
Phone: (+886-2) 2862-6831
Fax: (+886-2) 2862-6830

Singapore Trade Office in Taipei
9th Floor, 85 Jen Ai Road, Section 4, Taipei 106
Phone: (+886-2) 2772-1940
Fax: (+886-2) 2772-1943

Liaison Office of the Republic of South Africa
13th Floor, 205 Tun Hua North Road, Taipei 105
Phone: (+886-2) 2715-3250
Fax: (+886-2) 2712-5109

Spanish Chamber of Commerce
10th Floor-2, 76 Tun Hua South Road, Section 2
Taipei 106
Phone: (+886-2) 2325-6234
Fax: (+886-2) 2754-2572

Exportradet Taipei, Swedish Trade Council
Room 812, 333 Keelung Road, Section 1
Taipei 110
Phone: (+886-2) 2757-6573
Fax: (+886-2) 2757-6723

Trade Office of Swiss Industries
Room 3101, 333 Keelung Road, Section 1

Taipei 110
Phone: (+886-2) 2720-1001
Fax: (+886-2) 2757-6984

Thailand Trade and Economic Office
7th Floor, 150 Fu Hsing North Road
Taipei 104
Phone: (+886-2) 2712-1882
Fax: (+886-2) 2713-0042

Turkish Trade Office in Taipei
Room 1905, 333 Keelung Road, Section 1
Taipei 110
Phone: (+886-2) 2757-7318
Fax: (+886-2) 2757-9432

Vietnam Economic and Cultural Office in Taipei
3rd Floor, 65 Sungkiang Road, Taipei 104
Phone: (+886-2) 2516-6626
Fax: (+886-2) 2504-1761

Warsaw Trade Office
Room 3111, 333 Keelung Road, Section 1
Taipei 110
Phone: (+886-2) 2757-6325
Fax: (+886-2) 2757-6086

U.S. State Trade Offices in the ROC
Located in the Taipei World Trade Center
5 Hsin Yi Road, Section 5, Taipei

State of Arizona, Asian-Pacific Trade Office
Room 7D17/18
Phone: (+886-2) 2725-1l34
Fax: (+886-2) 2725-1146

State of California, Taipei Trade Office
Room 7C04
Phone: (+886-2) 2758-6223
Fax: (+886-2) 2723-9973

State of Florida, Taipei/Pacific Rim office
Room 7E01
Phone: (+886-2) 2758-5181
Fax: (+886-2) 2723-5892

State of Hawaii, U.S.A. Office in Taipei
Room 7G07
Phone: (+886-2) 2723-0017
Fax: (+886-2) 2723-0229

State of Idaho-Asia Trade Office
Room 7D15
Phone: (+886-2) 2725-2922
Fax: (+886-2) 2725-1248

Indiana Department of Commerce,
Taipei Office
Room 7D16
Phone: (+886-2) 2725-2060
Fax: (+886-2) 2725-2062

State of Louisiana, Taipei Office
Room 7D13
Phone: (+886-2) 2723-1921
Fax: (+886-2) 2723-1862

Missouri International Business
Office in Taipei
Room 7D09
Phone: (+886-2) 2725-1622
Fax: (+886-2) 2723-2731

Montana Department of Commerce
Taipei Office
Room 7D21
Phone: (+886-2) 2723-1762
Fax: (+886-2) 2723-1763

Oregon Department of Commerce Taipei Office
Room 7C14
Phone: (+886-2) 2723-2310
Fax: (+886-2) 2723-2312

City of Carrollton, Texas Asian-Pacific Trade
Office
Room 7C06
Phone: (+886-2) 2345-4111
Fax: (+886-2) 2345-7208

Utah Department of Commerce Taipei Offfice
Room 7A18

Phone: (+886-2) 2725-2522
Fax: (+886-2) 2725-2459

West Virginia Taiwan Office
Room 7D12
Phone: (+886-2) 2722-6047
Fax: (+886-2) 2722-6049

Washington State Trade Development
Office in Taipei
Room 7G01
Phone: (+886-2) 2725-2499
Fax: (+886-2) 2723-2545

Located elsewhere:

State of Alaska, USA, Trade Office in Taiwan
4th Floor, 135 Pa Te Road, Section 4, Taipei
Phone: (+886-2) 2764-6538
Fax: (+886-2) 2747-0267

Government of the District of Columbia
Taipei Representative Office
12th Floor, 3 Min Sheng East Road, Section 3
Taipei
Phone: (+886-2) 2503-6811
Fax: (+886-2) 2509-7915

Massachusetts Taiwan P.R. Representative
Office
3rd Floor, 150 Tun Hua Nroth Road, Taipei
Phone: (+886-2) 2546-6086
Fax: (+886-2) 2546-6087

State of Oklahoma Marketing Office
7th Floor, 11 Jen Ai Road, Section 2, Taipei
Phone: (+886-2) 2357-8016
Fax: (+886-2) 2395-5542

Commercial Representative of Vermont in
Taiwan
Kiangling Building, 9th Floor-1, 108-1 Ming Chuan
Road
Tsintien City, Taipei County
Phone: (+886-2) 2218-7869
Fax: (+886-2) 2218-2995

Appendix VI
Weights and Measures in Use in the ROC

The metric system is the official system of weights and measures in the ROC, and it is used for nearly all purposes. Certain things, however, continue to be measured according to various other systems. Real estate property, for example, is usually measured in p'ing (tsubo), or the size of a six-by-six-foot tatami mat, a remnant from Taiwan's period of Japanese occupation. There are measures for gold, Chinese herbal medicine, and other specialized commodities (the market system). The following tables give equivalents in the diverse systems in use in Taiwan: the market system, the metric system, and the English system.

Length

Taiwan System	Market System	Metric System	English System
1 ts'un 寸 (inch)	0.90909 ts'un	3.0303 cm	1.193 in.
1 ch'ih 尺 (foot) (=10 ts'un)	0.90909 ch'ih	0.30303 m	0.99419 ft.
1.1 ts'un	1 ts'un (inch) (=10 fen 分)	3.3333 cm	1.3123 in.
1.1 ch'ih	1 ch'ih (=10 ts'un)	0.33333 m	1.0936 ft.
11 ch'ih	1 chang 丈 (=10 ch'ih)	3.3333 m	3.6453 yd.
1,650 ch'ih	1 li 里 (=150 chang)	0.5 km	0.3107 mi.

Area

Taiwan System	Market System	Metric System	English System
1 p'ing 坪 (tsubo)	0.00496 mu	3.30579 sq. m	35.5896 sq. ft.
1 mu 畝 (=30 p'ing)	0.14876 mu	0.99174 are	0.02451 acre
1 chia 甲 (=2,934 p'ing)	14.5488 mu	96.9917 ares	2.39672 acres
—	1 sq. ch'ih 尺 (=100 sq. ts'un 寸)	0.1111 sq. m	1.196 sq. ft.
3.361 p'ing	1 sq. chang 丈 (=100 sq. ch'ih)	11.1111 sq. m	13.28888 sq. yd.
25.7753 chia	1 sq. li 里 (=22,500 sq. chang)	25 hectares	61.776 acres
20.1666 p'ing	1 fen 分 (=6 sq. chang)	66.6666 sq. m	79.7328 sq. yd.
6.72222 mu	1 mu (=10 fen)	6.66667 ares	0.16441 acre
6.8736 chia	1 ch'ing 頃 (=100 mu)	6.66667 hectares	16.441 acres

Weights

Taiwan System	Market System	Metric System	English System
1 ch'ien 錢	0.75 ch'ien	3.75 g	0.12056 oz.
1 liang 兩 (tael) (=10 ch'ien)	0.75 liang	37.5 g	1.2056 oz.
1 chin 斤 (catty) (=16 liang)	1.2 chin	0.6 kg	1.3228 lb.
1 tan 石 (picul) (=100 chin)	1.2 tan	60 kg	132.277 lb.
1.3333 ch'ien	1 ch'ien	5 g	0.1764 oz.
1.3333 liang	1 liang (tael) (=10 ch'ien)	50 g	1.7637 oz.
0.8333 chin	1 chin (catty) (=10 liang)	0.5 kg	1.1023 lb.
0.8333 tan	1 tan (picul) (=100 chin)	50 kg	110.231 lb.

Appendix VII
National and Popular Holidays

Founding Day of the Republic of China *
中華民國開國紀念日
January 1

The ROC president presides over a ceremony commemorating the January 1, 1912, founding of the Republic, which is attended by the presidents of each of the five Yuan (branches) of the central government, heads of the ministries, and other high-level officials.

Government offices are closed.

Farmer's Day 農民節
February 4

The start of spring 立春 has been traditionally marked by Farmer's Day, honoring the most important activity in traditional Chinese agrarian society. It falls at the beginning of one of the 24 seasonal periods of the year, on either February 4 or 5.

Chinese New Year 春節 *
February 5, 2000 (1st day, 1st moon)

Chinese New Year, also known as the Spring Festival, is the biggest festival celebrated in Taiwan. Chinese New Year's Day falls on the second new moon of the lunar calendar after the winter solstice. Thus, the first day of the lunar new year falls between January 21 and February 19 on the Gregorian calendar.

According to the Chinese lunar calendar, an ordinary year contains 12 lunar months of 29 or 30 days. A leap year occurs once every three years, when a 13th intercalary month is added to reestablish agreement with the solar year. The Chinese lunar calendar follows a 60-year cycle.

Festivities begin on the eighth day of the last lunar month of the old year and continue until the 15th day of the first month of the new year. On the eighth day of the last moon, commonly known as *la-pa* 臘八, people eat hot sweet congee, believed to bring good luck during the New Year season.

Families clean out their homes and offer sacrifices to the earth god on the 16th day of the last moon, commonly known as *wei-ya* 尾牙. Employers hold banquets for their employees to show their appreciation.

Offerings are made to propitiate the God of the Hearth 灶神 on the 24th day of the last moon. According to legend, the deity returns to heaven on this day to report to the Jade Emperor 玉皇大帝 the doings and misdoings of every member of the household he guards.

The climax of the festivities is on New Year's Eve 除夕, when every member of the family returns home to partake in a sumptuous family dinner, the last meal of the year, which includes fish and dumplings and other foods with symbolic meaning. Children receive *hung-pao* 紅包, or money placed in red envelopes, as the new year is ushered in with firecrackers.

On New Year's Day, ceremonial candles are lit and incense and sacrificial paper money burned. Endless strings of firecrackers are exploded and spring couplets are pasted on doors or at either side of the doorways to scare away the legendary *nien* 年 monster and evil spirits. People visit temples to pay respects to the gods before calling on their friends and relatives.

On the second day of the New Year 初二, firecrackers sound again as sacrifices are offered to the gods. Married daughters return to visit their parents' homes.

People usually stay at home on the third day, which is believed to be a time for bad luck. According to legend, field mice hold their weddings on this day. Some families place rice outdoors for the occasion.

On the fourth day, the deities, including the God of the Hearth, are welcomed back to earth with sacrificial offerings and firecrackers.

Most people return to work on the fifth day, when businessmen make offerings to the God of Wealth 財神.

On the seventh day, families light seven candles and prepare dinners of seven dishes to mark the anniversary of the creation of man.

The eighth day marks the resumption of normal schedules for those not yet back at work, usually factory workers.

The birthday of the Jade Emperor, the supreme Taoist deity and ruler of heaven, is celebrated on the ninth day.

The New Year season draws to a close with the Lantern Festival (see below) on the 15th day of the first lunar month.

Government offices are closed for five days starting on New Year's Eve.

Lantern Festival 元宵節
February 19, 2000 (15th day, lst moon)

Most temples are illuminated by colorful lanterns of all shapes and sizes in the evening. Riddle-solving contests are held at temples, parks, and public places, with members of the public invited to find answers to clues written in couplets. Glutinous rice dumplings called *yuan-hsiao* 元宵 are eaten.

Tourism Day 觀光節
February 19, 2000 (15th day, lst moon)

Tourism Day coincides with the Lantern Festival, the last day of Tourism Week, which begins on the ninth day of the first lunar month. Since the inception of Tourism Week in 1978, the Tourism Bureau has organized a series of events for visitors to Taiwan, including folk arts presentations and folk dance performances.

Peace Memorial Day 和平紀念日*
February 28

In remembrance of those lost in the unrest and aftermath of the February 28 Incident of 1947, and in hopes of healing the wounds and closing the divisions left by the episode, February 28 is observed as a national memorial day. In 1997, Peace Memorial Day was elevated to the status of a national holiday after the Legislative Yuan amended the *February 28 Incident Disposition and Compensation Act* 二二八事件處理及補償條例 on February 25 and the president promulgated the revised legislation on the same day.

Earth God's Birthday 土地公誕辰
March 7, 2000 (2nd day, 2nd moon)

The birthday of the Earth God 土地公 is celebrated with great pomp, and temples are packed with worshippers from early morning till noon. Followers also make simpler offerings to the deity at temples and in front of their homes or stores on the first and 15th day of each lunar month. Every community and home is believed to be guarded by its own Earth God. According to legend, the Earth God was a tax collector who won popular acclaim for his kindness, and was deified after his death.

Women's Day 婦女節
March 8

Women's Day has been observed in the ROC since 1924, following the introduction of the women's movement from the West.

This holiday is currently celebrated in conjunction with Children's Day on April 4.

Arbor Day 植樹節
March 12

Trees are planted by school children in remembrance of Dr. Sun Yat-sen's encouragement of afforestation. The ROC government designated the day of Dr. Sun's passing as Arbor Day four years after his death in 1925.

Kuan Yin's Birthday 觀音誕辰
March 24, 2000 (19th day, 2nd moon)

Kuan Yin's birthday is celebrated with offerings of fruit and vegetables. A patron goddess of both Taoists and Buddhists, she is worshipped by seafarers, farmers, travellers, merchants, and women hoping for offspring.

Youth Day 青年節
March 29

Youth Day was initially observed on May 4 in commemoration of student participation in the May Fourth Movement 五四運動 in 1919. It was changed to March 29 in 1943 in remembrance of the young revolutionary fighters' role in the tenth uprising against the Manchus in Canton in 1912.

Women's/Children's Day 婦幼節*
April 3

Activities are held at schools and by educational institutions to mark what used to be known as Children's Day 兒童節, which has been observed since 1932.

Children have the day off from school.

Tomb-Sweeping Day 清明節*
Passing of President Chiang Kai-shek
蔣公逝世紀念日
April 4

Family graves are swept, and meats, fruits, and wine are arranged before the tombs. Services for President Chiang Kai-shek, who passed away on April 5, 1975, are held on this day.

Government offices are closed.

God of Medicine's Birthday 保生大帝誕辰
April 19, 2000 (15th day, 3rd moon)

Performing groups, including stilt walkers and musical bands, draw crowds to one of the most elaborate processions in Taiwan, held in Hsuehchia 學甲, Tainan County 台南縣, in honor of the tenth century healer, Wu Pen 吳本. Wu was later immortalized as the Great Emperor Pao Sheng 保生大帝.

Matsu's Birthday 媽祖誕辰
April 27, 2000 (23rd day, 3rd moon)

The birthday of Matsu, the goddess of the sea and patron saint of Chinese fishermen, is celebrated islandwide on this day. According to one version of the legend, Matsu saved her father, brother and a number of fishermen from drowning while she physically remained at home; in a different version of the legend, however, she failed to save another brother. She is believed to have ascended to heaven at the age of 28.

Labor Day 勞動節
May 1

Following the inception of Labor Day by an international alliance in 1889, five years after an "eight-hour movement" was initiated by American workers for better treatment, Chinese workers in Canton began to observe the occasion in 1920. Labor Day was not celebrated nationwide, however, until after the conclusion of the Northern Expedition in 1928.

Workers have the day off.

Literary Day 文藝節
May 4

Awards for outstanding literary achievements are presented on this day. Literary Day has been observed since 1968 in commemoration of the role played by university students in the May Fourth Movement, and their call for democracy, scientific development, and the promotion of literature.

Buddha's Birthday 佛誕日
May 11, 2000 (8th day, 4th moon)

Believers attend ceremonies at Buddhist shrines and chant sutras in celebration of the birthday of Siddhartha Gautama, founder of the religion. Images of the Buddha are bathed on this day.

Mother's Day 母親節
May 14, 2000

Awards are presented to model mothers by municipal governments and women's organizations on the second Sunday of May.

Opium Suppression Movement Day 禁煙節
June 3

This day has been observed since 1930 in commemoration of the burning of imported opium in 1839 during the Opium War against the British.

Dragon Boat Festival 端午節 / 詩人節 *
June 6, 2000 (5th day, 5th moon)

Dragon boat races are held and glutinous rice dumplings wrapped in bamboo leaves are eaten in remembrance of Chu Yuan 屈原, a famous scholar-statesman of the Warring States Period. Chu drowned himself after failing to convince the king of Chu 楚王 to guard the kingdom against the enemy.

Government offices are closed.

Kuan Kung's Birthday 關公誕辰
June 14, 2000 (13th day, 5th moon)

Sacrificial offerings are made to Kuan Kung, the god of war and righteousness. Kuan Kung was a mighty warrior during the period of the Three Kingdoms.

Cheng Huang's Birthday 城隍誕辰
June 14, 2000 (13th day, 5th moon)

The largest procession honoring Cheng Huang, the city god, takes place at Taipei's Cheng Huang Temple 城隍廟. The deity is believed to protect the city from danger and guard it from enemies. According to legend, Cheng Huang was a river ghost whose harmlessness so impressed the ruler of Hades that he was later elevated to the status of city god.

Chi Hsi Festival 七夕
August 6, 2000 (7th day, 7th moon)

On this Chinese version of Valentine's Day, lovers visit the Lovers' Temple 情人廟 in Peitou 北投, Taipei, where the Cowherd 牛郎 and Weaving Maid 織女 are enshrined. Legend has it that the Weaving Maid abandoned her work at the spinning wheel after she fell in love with the Cowherd. The Mother Goddess of Heaven 王母娘娘 was so angry that she separated the couple and allowed them to meet only once a year, on the seventh day of the seventh moon, when magpies come together to form a bridge over the Milky Way, which divides the two.

Father's Day 父親節
August 8

This day was designated Father's Day in 1945. The Chinese characters for "eight" 八 (eighth day of the eighth month of the solar year) and "father" 爸 are both pronounced *pa*.

Ghost Festival 中元節
August 14, 2000 (15th day, 7th moon)

On the first day of the seventh moon, the gates of Hades are opened and the spirits are allowed a month of feasting and revelry in the land of the living. The climax is reached on the Ghost Festival, the 15th day of Ghost Month 鬼月, when great sacrificial feasts are set out in temples and in front of homes to appease wandering souls. Paper money is burned and lanterns floated on lakes and streams to deliver the dead.

Ami Initiation Festival 阿美族成年禮
End of August or beginning of September

The initiation ceremony of Ami boys at the age of 17 is preceded by performances of tribal dancers dressed in red and black. The festival is celebrated by the Ami tribes in Hualien.

Armed Forces Day 軍人節
September 3

Armed Forces Day was first observed in 1955 in memory of the contributions of military servicemen during the eight-year Sino-Japanese War, which ended with the Japanese surrender on September 3, 1945.

Servicemen are given leave in accordance with Ministry of National Defense directives.

Mid-Autumn Festival 中秋節 *
September 12, 2000 (15th day, 8th moon)

Families reunite in the evening to eat moon cakes 月餅 and gaze at the full moon. Legend has it that Chang O 嫦娥 was swept to the moon after swallowing a pill of immortality. She later came to be known as the moon goddess.

Government offices are closed.

Teachers' Day 教師節
Confucius' Birthday 孔子誕辰紀念日
September 28

Teachers' Day is observed on the birthday anniversary of Confucius, the great sage and teacher who has had far-reaching influence on Chinese philosophy and culture. Ceremonies are held at all Confucian temples, the largest one being at Taipei's Confucian Temple 台北孔廟, where a special dance in honor of the great teacher is performed each year. Awards are presented by the government to distinguished teachers.

Double Ninth Festival 九九重陽節
October 6, 2000 (9th day, 9th moon)

Also known as the Chung Yang Festival 重陽節, this day has been set aside to honor senior citizens since 1966. Senior Citizens' Week is observed from the ninth to the 15th day of the ninth lunar month. According to legend, on the ninth day of the ninth lunar month, Matsu 媽祖, goddess of the sea, decided to climb a mountain overlooking the sea in search of her father, who was drowning while out fishing. Senior Citizens' Day is observed on this day in remembrance of Matsu's filial piety.

Double Tenth National Day 雙十節 / 國慶日 *
October 10

The Double Tenth National Day is observed in commemoration of the Wuchang Uprising 武昌起義 on October 10, 1911, which led to the establishment of the ROC on January 1, 1912. The president gives a public address in front of the Presidential Office Building, followed by a parade of armed forces academies, representatives of different professions, folk dancers, and dragon dancers. A massive fireworks display lights up the sky over the Tamsui River 淡水河 in the evening.

Government offices are closed.

Overseas Chinese Day 華僑節
October 21

The ROC government shows its appreciation for the support and contributions of overseas Chinese on this day.

Taiwan's Retrocession Day 光復節
October 25

This day marks the restoration of Taiwan to Chinese rule in 1945 after half a century of Japanese occupation.

Chiang Kai-shek's Birthday 蔣公誕辰紀念日
October 31

Memorial services are held islandwide and government leaders pay their respects to late President Chiang Kai-shek at his temporary resting place on Tzuhu 慈湖.

Saisiat Festival 賽夏節
November 10, 2000 (15th day, 10th moon)

The five-day *Pas-taai* Festival 矮靈祭 of the Saisiat tribe is celebrated with aborigines dancing to the ringing of bells, and an exhibition of huge "dance hats" carried by teams of men. These ceremonies in Nanchuang 南庄, Miaoli County 苗栗縣 are held once every two years to seek the forgiveness of a long-gone tribe of pygmies who were double-crossed by the Saisiats more than 500 years ago.

Dr. Sun Yat-sen's Birthday 國父誕辰紀念日 *
November 12

Respects are paid to the Founding Father of the nation at the Sun Yat-sen Memorial Hall 國父紀念館 on this day. Doctors' Day 醫師節 and Cultural Renaissance Day 中華文化復興節 are also observed on this day.

Government offices are closed.

Winter Festival 冬至節
December 21, 2000

Glutinous rice dumplings are eaten to mark the beginning of the winter season. The Winter Festival falls on or around the winter solstice (December 21, 22, or 23) every year. The festival's lunar calendar date varies from year to year.

Constitution Day 行憲紀念日*
December 25

The *Constitution of the ROC* was promulgated on January 1, 1947, and went into effect on December 25 of the same year.

* *Denotes a national holiday and government offices are closed.*

Appendix VIII

A Comparison of Various Chinese Romanization Systems

The Mandarin Phonetic Symbols (MPS) are used in ROC schools to teach children how to read Chinese (see Chapter 4, Language). Accordingly, MPS is the most widely known and used system in Taiwan for rendering the Mandarin 國語 pronunciation of Chinese characters into phonetic form. It is, however, much less well known in the West.

Wade-Giles is the Romanization system generally employed in the ROC today and has traditionally been the most frequently used system in Western scholarship. A drawback of this system is the use of apostrophes (') to indicate aspirated consonant sounds. Thus what English speakers hear as a *d-* is written *t-*, and what they know as *t-* is written *t'-*. The original idea was to indicate that Mandarin has no voiced/unvoiced consonant distinctions (like the English *d/t* contrast), but rather differentiates between aspirated and unaspirated consonant initials. While linguistically sound as a transcription system for the Mandarin language of its era, it is confusing for speakers of English. To make things worse, the apostrophes are often left out of some publications due to aesthetic or other concerns, leaving no way to distinguish aspirated from unaspirated consonant sounds.

Another problem is that, while tones can be indicated in the Wade-Giles system with numeral superscripts (e.g. *jen²*), they are usually omitted out of convenience. The umlaut in the front rounded vowel sound (*ü*) also tends to be left out due to difficulties in typesetting. With these omissions, it becomes impossible to know the exact pronunciation of any given word without checking the original Chinese. These disadvantages aside, the system does give a general idea of how to pronounce a word.

The Yale system is a relatively consistent and efficient one that is fairly easy for native speakers of American English to master. Its use, however, has never spread beyond a small number of Chinese language teaching texts.

The Pinyin system is the one adopted by the Chinese communists in mainland China, and by the Western news media. It corresponds closely to the MPS system. Its main potential drawback is its use of "leftover" letters like c, q, and x to represent Mandarin sounds that lack a handy equivalent in the Latin alphabet. These letters often confound those uninitiated in the Pinyin system, news broadcasters in particular. The Yale and Pinyin systems both add marks over the main vowel of a syllable to indicate tone. But again, the marks are often omitted as an expedient.

The Gwoyeu Romatzyh (GR) system was the ROC's official (since 1932) system of Romanizing Chinese, but was little known and seldom used. It had the unique feature of incorporating the tone of a word into its Romanized spelling, which was admittedly a convenience in typesetting.

The rules for "spelling" the tones, however, were highly complicated; they varied according to the phonetic composition of the syllable in question. The difficulties in popularizing this system were obvious.

In order to find a solution to such problems, the Ministry of Education held a meeting in January, 1984. A resolution was reached that the Gwoyeu Romatzyh should be revised and a working committee should be established. After extensive and intensive study and comparison of all existing transcription systems for Mandarin, the committee proposed a revised system which was officially called Mandarin Phonetic Symbols II (MPS II).

On May 10, 1984 the Ministry of Education announced that MPS II would be subject to trial use for a period of one year. On January 28, 1986, upon the completion of all relevant revisions after the trial use period, the Ministry of Education formally announced the final official version of MPS II.

In April 1997, the Taipei City Government adopted Tongyong Pinyin as the official Romanization system for street and place names in the Taipei area. The reasons behind the decision were that the new system can be used to Romanize not only Mandarin but also local languages in Taiwan, such as Southern Fukienese and Hakka, and that it is compatible with Hanyu Pinyin.

The following comparison table of Romanization systems is intended to clear up some of the confusion caused by the simultaneous use of the different systems. It is also a convenient reference when reading Chinese with the aid of the Mandarin Phonetic Symbols.

A hyphen after a symbol or symbols (e.g. *p-*) means it is used as an initial; a hyphen before a symbol or symbols (e.g. *-ung*) signals a syllabic final. For the MPS symbols ㄣ and ㄥ, the vowel *e* is given in parentheses. This is to be transcribed into the other systems only when no other vowel is indicated in the MPS spelling. Multiple spellings for certain sounds in the Wade-Giles system indicate equally correct alternatives unless otherwise noted.

Ultimately, none of the systems has proven better than the others; each has its strengths and shortcomings. Romanization system preferences seem to be strongly tied to which system one learns first and is most accustomed to.

MPS	**Wade-Giles**	**Yale**	**Hanyu Pinyin**	**MPS II**	**Tongyong Pinyin**
ㄅ	p-	b-	b-	b	b-
ㄆ	p'-	p-	p-	p-	p-
ㄇ	m-	m-	m-	m-	m-
ㄈ	f-	f-	f-	f-	f-
ㄉ	t-	d-	d-	d-	d-
ㄊ	t'-	t-	t-	t-	t-
ㄋ	n-	n-	n-	n-	n-
ㄌ	l-	l-	l-	l-	l-
ㄍ	k-	g-	g-	g-	g-
ㄎ	k'-	k-	k-	k-	k-
ㄏ	h-	h-	h-	h-	h-
ㄐ	ch-	j-	j-	j(i)-	z(i)-
ㄑ	ch'-	ch-	q-	ch(i)-	c(i)-
ㄒ	hs-	sh-	x-	sh(i)-	s(i)-
ㄓ	chih, ch-	jr, j-	zhi, zh-	jr, j-	zhii, zh-
ㄔ	ch'ih, ch'-	chr, ch-	chi, ch-	chr, ch-	chii, ch-
ㄕ	shih, sh-	shr, sh-	shi, sh-	shr, sh-	shii, sh-
ㄖ	jih, j-	r	ri, r-	r, r-	rii, r-
ㄗ	tzu, ts-	dz	zi, z-	tz, tz-	zii, z-

MPS	Wade-Giles	Yale	Hanyu Pinyin	MPS II	Tongyong Pinyin
ㄘ	tz'u, ts'-	ts	ci, c-	tsz, ts-	cii, c-
ㄙ	szu, ssu s-	sz	si s-	sz, s-	sii, s-
ㄚ	a	a	a	a	a
ㄛ	-o	-o	-o	-o	-o
ㄜ	-o, -e	-e	-e	-e	-er
ㄝ	-(i)eh	-(y)e	-(i)e	-(i)e	-e
ㄞ	ai	ai	ai	ai	ai
ㄟ	-ei	-ei	-ei	-ei	-ei
ㄠ	ao	au	ao	au	ao
ㄡ	ou	ou	ou	ou	ou
ㄢ	an	an	an	an	an
ㄣ	(e)n	(e)n	(e)n	en	(e)n
ㄤ	ang	ang	ang	ang	ang
ㄥ	-(e)ng	-(e)ng	-(e)ng	-(e)ng	-(e)ng
ㄦ	(e)rh	(e)r	(e)r	er	err
ㄧ	i, (y)i	yi, -i	yi, -i	yi, -i	yi, -i
ㄨ	wu, -u	wu, -u	wu, -u	wu, -u	wu, -u
ㄩ	yü, -ü	yu	yu, -u, -ü*	yu, -iu	yu
ㄧㄚ	ya, -ia	ya	ya, -ia	ya, -ia	ya, -ia
ㄧㄝ	yeh, -ieh	ye	ye, -ie	ye, -ie	ye, -ie

MPS	Wade-Giles	Yale	Hanyu Pinyin	MPS II	Tongyong Pinyin
一ㄞ	yai	yai	yai	yai	yai
一ㄠ	yao, -iao	yau	yao, -iao	yau, -iau	yao, -iao
一ㄡ	yu, -iu	you	you, -iu	you, -iou	you -i(o)u
一ㄢ	yen, -ien	yan	yan, -ian	yan, -ian	yan, -ian
一ㄣ	yin, -in	yin, -in	yin, -in	yin, -in	yin, -in
一ㄤ	yang, -iang	yang	yang -iang	yang, -iang	yang, -iang
一ㄥ	ying, -ing	ying, -ing	ying, -ing	ying, -ing	ying, -ing
ㄨㄚ	wa, -ua	wa	wa, -ua	wa, -ua	wa, -ua
ㄨㄛ	wo, -o, -uo**	wo,	wo, -uo	wo, -uo	wo, -uo
ㄨㄞ	wai, -uai	wai	wai, -uai	wai, -uai	wai, -uai
ㄨㄟ	wei, -ui, -uei***	wei	wei, -ui	wei, -uei	wei, -u(e)i
ㄨㄢ	wan, -uan	wan	wan, -uan	wan, -uan	wan, -uan
ㄨㄣ	wen, -un	wen, -wun	wen, -un	wen, -uen	wun -un

MPS	Wade-Giles	Yale	Hanyu Pinyin	MPS II	Tongyong Pinyin
ㄨㄤ	wang, -uang	wang	wang, -uang	wang, -uang	wang, -uang
ㄨㄥ	weng, -ung	weng, -ung	weng, -ong	weng, -ung	wong, -ong
ㄩㄝ	yüeh, -üeh	ywe,	yue, -ue -üe*	yue, -iue	yue,
ㄩㄢ	yüan, -üan	ywan	yuan, -uan	yuan, -iuan	yuan,
ㄩㄣ	yün, -ün	yun	yun, -un	yun, -iun	yun,
ㄩㄥ	yung, -iung	yung	yong, -iong	yung, -iung	yong,

---

*   *Used after l- and n-.*
**   *Used with the initials k-, k'-, h-, n-, l-, and sh-.*
*** *Used with the initials k- and k'-.*

The tone marks for the MPS and Tongyong Pinyin systems are: first tone, no mark; second tone, ´; third tone, ˇ; fourth tone, ˋ; and neutral tone, ˙. The Yale, Hanyu Pinyin and MPS II systems use the same tone marks, but add a first tone mark, ¯.

Index